# Fundamentals of Human Sexuality

# Fundamentals of Human Sexuality

## Fifth Edition

### Herant Katchadourian
*Stanford University*

HOLT, RINEHART AND WINSTON, INC.

Fort Worth   Chicago   San Francisco
Philadelphia   Montreal   Toronto
London   Sydney   Tokyo

*For Stina, Nina, and Kai*

| | |
|---|---|
| Acquisitions Editor | Susan Arellano |
| Developmental Editor | Jane Knetzger |
| Senior Project Manager | Paula Cousin |
| Design Supervisor | Judy Allan |
| Production Manager | Annette Mayeski |
| Text Designer | Edward A. Butler |

Cover photo by Jack Deutsch.
Author photo by Chuck Painter, News and Publications, Stanford University.

**Library of Congress Cataloging-in-Publication Data**

Katchadourian, Herant A.
    Fundamentals of human sexuality / Herant A. Katchadourian.—5th
ed.
        p. cm.
    Bibliography: p.
    Includes index.
    ISBN 0-03-014068-4:
    1. Sex.    I.    Title.
    HQ31.K36    1989
    612'.6—dc19                                                                88-28440
                                                                                      CIP

ISBN 0-03-014068-4

Printed in the United States of America
9 0 1 2    015    9 8 7 6 5 4 3 2

Holt, Rinehart and Winston, Inc.
The Dryden Press
Saunders College Publishing

# Preface

When the first edition of this text was published in 1972, modern courses in human sexuality were only beginning to appear on college campuses. Since then, the field and the text have grown together and contributed to each other's further development. There are now over a dozen college texts to choose from, but none are equal to the fifth edition of *Fundamentals* in longevity of service to the field.

A successful textbook must retain its recognized strengths and distinctiveness while being innovative and responsive to the changing needs of the times. This is what we have tried to accomplish over the years. This edition remains true to its basic purposes: to provide students with a broad, interdisciplinary perspective on the biological, psychological, and sociocultural aspects of human sexuality; to expose students to the research and scholarship that constitute the underpinnings of knowledge in the field; to encourage students to reflect on what they read and to apply what they learn to their personal lives. To that end, the book informs, instructs, and challenges students; it does not preach or editorialize.

While retaining its strengths, the fifth edition has been revised extensively in substance, style, and format. Some of these changes have been necessitated by new developments in the field and new problems, such as AIDS, requiring greater attention. Other changes have been in response to the thoughtful comments and criticisms of four sets of reviewers representing a broad spectrum of disciplines and teaching experiences in the field. As a result, we have shifted the level of emphasis in a number of areas; we have made the level of presentation more accessible to a broader range of students; and we have been responsive to the needs of instructors in a greater variety of institutions, while retaining the intellectual vigor and integrity of the text. Equally important changes have been made in the figures and photographs illustrating the text.

The text attempts to be comprehensive without being exhaustive in coverage. Many important aspects of sex are dealt with, but the main emphasis is on topics likely to be of concern to the majority of readers.

## ORGANIZATION OF THE TEXT

The fifth edition retains the basic format of the text with some important changes. Earlier editions dealt with the biological, behavioral, and cultural aspects of sexuality in three parts; the current edition subsumes chapters into six parts. After the introductory chapter, Parts 1 through 6 discuss, in order, sexual structures and functions, sexual reproduction, sexual development, varieties of sexual experience, sex and human relationships, and sex and society.

This approach draws from the disciplinary strengths in the contributory fields to sexuality and allows students to focus on one major topic at a time. However, there is a consistent effort to provide an integrative, multidisciplinary perspective throughout the book. The biological, psychological, and social aspects of various issues and their interrelationships are highlighted. Evolutionary, cross-cultural and historical dimensions are brought to bear, whenever applicable, to provide breadth as well as depth to the understanding of students.

## NEW FEATURES

Virtually all of the chapters in this edition have been rewritten. The changes from the previous edition thus amount to more than an ordinary revision.

1. *Updating.* There are over 1,000 new references added to the text. Fast-moving areas like AIDS research have been monitored well into the production schedule of the book to provide readers with the most up-to-date information possible. The text now provides an extensive coverage of AIDS and other sexually transmitted diseases. In addition to the biomedical and the psychosocial aspects of these problems, special care has been taken to provide students with the necessary information and guidance to help them make safe and sensible sexual decisions. The same is true for contraception and other topics with a bearing on sexual health.

In a comprehensive effort to place greater emphasis on the relational aspects of sex, we have drawn from the recently expanded research literature on love. There is likewise a good deal more emphasis on the relationship of gender and various aspects of sexual behavior. Marriage and its alternatives receive focused attention. The more negative aspects of sexuality—exploitation and aggression—are likewise confronted with objectivity and the sense of urgency they require.

The updating of the chapter on sex and society has mainly focused on the law and its important recent developments. Yet at the same time, issues like sexual morality have been rethought to provide students with as current a perspective as possible.

2. *New Chapters.* Sexual development was covered in a single chapter in previous editions. In the fifth edition, it has been expanded to three chapters: The first deals with sexual development in childhood; the second with adolescence and adulthood; and the third with gender and sexuality—an area of increasing attention and importance.

The second major expansion is in the area of sex and human relationships (Part 5). One chapter has been expanded to four, dealing respectively with sexual intimacy and love, marriage and its alternatives, sexual exploitation, and sexual aggression.

In addition, the material in Chapter 8 (sexual behavior) was eliminated in part and the rest redistributed. Chapters 17 and 18, which dealt respectively with sexuality in the ancient world and sexuality in Western culture, were compressed into a single chapter in the fifth edition (Chapter 20) dealing with sexuality in historical perspective. The chapter on sex and society was likewise revised and recast as sexuality in cultural perspective (Chapter 21). These changes were made to better accommodate the needs of instructors by making the text organization more consistent with their class syllabus.

3. *Illustrations.* Some of the most important changes in the fifth edition pertain to the illustrations. We now have a uniform style for figures and charts, all of which have been redrawn. While retaining the best of the fine art reproductions, we have significantly increased the number of photographs. The purpose of these illustrations is to add substance to the text, not to decorate it. The inclusion of a four-color insert showing embryonal development through a set of extraordinary photographs is another important new feature. The addition of a second color has likewise provided an important new aspect to the appearance and instructional purposes of the text.

4. *Instructional Aids.* The effectiveness of a text depends first on its content, then on its manner of presentation. If there is no substance to a book, no amount of "pedagogical" gimmickry will make it worthwhile. However, if the material presented does not engage the reader's attention, it will do little good.

We continue to use boxes to highlight special topics and to present literary excerpts. Key terms in the text are italicized. At the end of each chapter there is a set of review questions and thought questions. Suggested readings provide a list of accessible sources for further study. A detailed glossary (with pronunciation guide) defines important terms. More than 1,500 references provide documentation of sources and direct the student to additional sources of information.

5. *Ancillary materials.* The text is accompanied by an instructor's manual, test bank, computerized test bank, and study guide.

## ACKNOWLEDGMENTS

Numerous colleagues and reviewers have contributed greatly to the text's success through the successive editions. Space limitations do not permit the reiteration of acknowledgments from previous editions, but that does not diminish my appreciation for their help.

In the preparation of the fifth edition, Julian Davidson was particularly helpful with the updating of materials on physiology and hormones; Sylvia Cerel Bowen on contraception and sexually transmitted diseases; Sherrie Matteo, with respect to the sexual-development and gender-related issues; and Rutledge Martin, with the chapter on sex and the law.

A special word of thanks is owed to the successive groups of reviewers who provided invaluable advice and criticisms at various phases of working. They are: John M. Allen, The University of Michigan; Wayne Anderson, University of Missouri, Columbia; Ann Auleb, San Francisco State University; Elaine Baker, Marshall University; Janice Baldwin, University of California, Santa Barbara; M. Betsy Bergen, Kansas State University; Ruth Blanche, Montclair State College; Stephen W. Bordi, West Valley College; James E. Cherry, Charles Stewart Mott Community College; Dennis M. Dailey, The University of Kansas; Ronald S. Daniel, California State Polytechnic University, Pomona; Wayne Daugherty, San Diego State University; William A. Fisher, The University of Western Ontario; Susan Fleischer, Queens College; Suzanne G. Fray-

ser, University of Denver; Grace Galliano, Kennesaw College; Frederick P. Gault, Western Michigan University; Brian A. Gladue, North Dakota State University; Barbara Gordon-Lickey, University of Oregon; John T. Haig, Philadelphia College of Textiles and Science; Sandra Hamilton, University of Oregon; Donald E. Herrlein, Northeastern State University; Ray W. Johnson, North Texas State University; Ethel Kamien, University of Lowell; Sander M. Latts, University of Minnesota; Ronald S. Mazer, University of Southern Maine; Roger N. Moss, California State University, Northridge; Daniel P. Murphy, Creighton University; Andrea Parrot, Cornell University; Sara Taubin, Drexel University; Richard M. Tolman, University of Illinois, Chicago; Marlene Tufts, Clackamas Community College; Charles Weichert, San Antonio College; Donald Whitmore, The University of Texas, Arlington; Edward W. Wickersham, Pennsylvania State University; Midge Wilson, DePaul University.

The production of a book is almost as arduous a task as its writing. Laurie Burmeister went through the rigors of typing and preparing the manuscript for publication with her competent, tireless, and cheerful dedication. Jane Knetzger, developmental editor, played a central role throughout the process. Paula Cousin, senior project manager, masterfully guided the complex task of preparing the book for production. I also wish to thank Susan Driscoll, publisher of the Behavioral and Social Sciences; Susan Arellano, acquisitions editor; Kristin Zimet, copy editor; Annette Mayeski, production manager; Judy Allan, design supervisor; Lisa Bossio, who wrote the glossary; Elsa Peterson and Marion Geisinger, who assisted with the photo program.

The members of my family, to whom this book is dedicated, and in particular, my wife, Stina, relieved me of many burdens to make this task easier. To her, and to our children, Nina and Kai, I express my affectionate gratitude.

# About the Author

Herant Katchadourian, M.D., is Professor of Psychiatry and Behavioral Sciences, Professor of Human Biology, and Professor of Education (by courtesy) at Stanford University, where he has also served as Vice Provost and Dean of Undergraduate Studies. He received his undergraduate and medical degrees (with Distinction) from the American University of Beirut and his specialty training in psychiatry at the University of Rochester, New York.

In addition to this text (which has been translated into French, Spanish, Portuguese, and Chinese), Dr. Katchadourian is the author of *Human Sexuality: Sense and Nonsense, The Biology of Adolescence,* and *Fifty: Midlife in Perspective.* He is the co-author of *Careerism and Intellectualism Among College Students* and the editor of *Human Sexuality: A Comparative and Developmental Perspective.* His other publications are in the areas of cross-cultural psychiatry and the life cycle.

In 1968, Dr. Katchadourian initiated one of the first college courses in human sexuality at a major American university. Since then, well over 12,000 students have taken his course. He has been selected Outstanding Professor and Class Day speaker six times by Stanford seniors. He received the Richard W. Lyman Award of the Stanford Alumni Association in 1984. He is a member of the Alpha Omega Alpha medical honor society.

# CREDITS

The author is indebted to the following for photographs and permission to reproduce them. Copyright for each photograph belongs to the photographer or agency credited, unless specified otherwise.

*Part Opening Photos:* **1,** Leonardo *Human proportions according to Vitruvius,* Alinari/Art Resource; **2,** Michelangelo *Mother and child,* Galleria Buonarroti, Alinari/Art Resource; **3,** Picasso *Girl before a mirror,* Museum of Modern Art, New York/Art Resource; **4,** Bosch *Garden of earthly delights,* Prado, Madrid, Marburg/Art Resource; **5,** Rodin *The kiss,* Musee Rodin, Paris, Giraudon/Art Resource; **6,** Brueghel *Dance of the peasants,* Uffizi, Florence, Marburg/Art Resource. **P. 7,** The Granger Collection; **10,** British Museum, reproduced by courtesy of the Trustees; **11,** Giraudon/Art Resource; **12,** (top) The Granger Collection, (bottom) The Bettmann Archive; **13,** The Bettmann Archive; **14,** The Bettmann Archive; **15,** Sophia Smith Collection, Northampton, Massachusetts, reprinted by permission from *Margaret Sanger: An Autobiography* (New York: Norton, 1938); **16,** Stanford University Archive; **17,** by permission of the Kinsey Institute for Research in Sex, Gender, and Reproduction; **44,** National Archaeological Museum, Athens/Joel Gordon; **60,** courtesy Dr. Julian Davidson; **88,** (left and right) from Tanner, J. M. (1962) *Growth at Adolescence,* 2nd edition (Oxford: Blackwell); **89,** from Tanner, J. M. (1962) *Growth at Adolescence,* 2nd edition (Oxford: Blackwell); **99,** (left and right) from Williams, Blizzard and Migeon (1965) *The Diagnosis and Treatment of Endocrine Disorders in Childhood and Adolescence;* **100,** (left and right) from Money, J. (1968) *Sex Errors of the Body* (Baltimore: John Hopkins); **108,** from *Bilder Lexicon;* **125,** from Dodson and Hill (1962) *Synopsis of Genitourinary Disease,* 7th edition (St. Louis: Mosby), 201; **126,** courtesy of The Centers for Disease Control; **130,** (top left) courtesy of the Centers of Disease Control, (center left) Dr. John Wilson/Photo Researchers; **131,** courtesy Candy Tedeschi, R.N.C.; **167,** Suzanne Arms Wimberley; **171,** (left) Mariette Pathy Allen/Peter Arnold Inc., (right) Suzanne Szasz/Photo Researchers; **172,** Erika Stone; **174,** Suzanne Arms Wimberley; **194,** Joel Gordon; **196,** Joel Gordon; **197,** Joel Gordon; **224,** Erika Stone; **225,** Hella Hammid/Photo Researchers; **226,** Copyright © 1969 by Grove Press, a division of Wheatland Corporation, reprinted by permission; **230,** Harlow Primate Laboratory, University of Wisconsin; **231,** Harlow Primate Laboratory, University of Wisconsin; **238,** Andrew Bailey; **250,** Erika Stone; **257,** Barbara Alper/Stock Boston; **265,** Erika Stone/Photo Researchers; **269,** UPI/Bettmann Newsphotos; **276,** Jeffry Myers/Stock Boston; **285,** UPI/Bettmann Newsphotos; **288,** (left) Frances M. Cox/Stock Boston, (right) Michael Weisbrot and Family; **289,** (top) Bob Daemmrich/The Image Works, (bottom) Jean-Claude Lejeune/Stock Boston; **293,** courtesy Dr. Donald Laub; **296,** (left and right) Dr. Steve Dain; **297,** (left and right) courtesy Dr. Donald Laub; **318,** Museum of Fine Arts, Boston; **320** (top) Museum of Fine Arts, Boston, (bottom) Harlow Primate Laboratory, University of Wisconsin; **324,** Jill Palmer; **328,** Comfort, A. (1967) *The Anxiety Makers,* copyright © by Books & Broadcasts Ltd. Reprinted by permission of Dell Publishing, a division of Bantam, Doubleday, Dell Publishing Group, Inc.; **335,** Joel Gordon; **336,** Tomas D. W. Friedmann/Photo Researchers; **337,** Jack Deutsch; **341,** SIPA/Art Resource; **343,** Harlow Primate Laboratory, University of Wisconsin; **344,** Collection Royal Museum of Central Africa, Tervuren, Belgium; **364,** Gerard Koskovich, Gay & Lesbian Alliance at Stanford; **369,** (top) Petit Palais, Paris/J. E. Bulloz, (bottom) Museum of Fine Arts, Boston; **374,** Joel Gordon; **375,** Ronald L. C. Kienhuis; **387,** Jan Lukas/Photo Researchers; **392,** Museo de Arte de Ponce, Puerto Rico; **395,** Anati (1961) *Camonica Valley,* 128; **396,** courtesy of the National Gallery, London; **397,** Phototeque; **398,** (top) Chester Higgins, Jr./Photo Researchers, (bottom) Phototeque; **400,** (top) 18th century anon., (bottom) *Bilder Lexicon;* **402,** (left) etching from Caylus, *Therese Philosophe,* (right) 18th century illustration for *Fanny Hill* by J. Cleland; **417,** Abraham Menashe/Photo Researchers; **444,** (left) Kal Muller/Woodfin Camp, (right) The Bettmann Archive; **449,** (left) Phototeque © Paramount, (right) George Holz/The Image Works, **450,** (left) Dan Chidester/The Image Works; (right) Robert Alexander/Photo Researchers; **453,** (left and right) The Metropolitan Museum of Art, New York (Harris Brisbane Dick Fund); **467,** Alinari/Art Resource; **475,** Kenneth Garrett/Woodfin Camp; **476,** courtesy Dr. Herant A. Katchadourian; **485,** Michael Weisbrot & Family; **502,** Bill Bachman/Photo Researchers; **509,** Michael Weisbrot & Family; **510,** Marvin E. Newman/Woodfin Camp; **511,** Joel Gordon; **512,** Stephen Shames/Visions; **519,** (left) Joel Gordon, (right) © 1972 Mitchell Bros. Film Group, San Francisco; **526,** Mark Antman/The Image Works; **531,** Innervisions; **535,** Bronzino, *Guidobaldo della Rovere,* Palazzo Pitti, Florence, SEF/Art Resource; **536,** From Wickler, W. (1972) *The Sexual Code,* 54; **543,** The Art Institute of Chicago; **544,** Janus Films/The Museum of Modern Art Film Stills Archive; **556,** Suzanne Arms Wimberley; **561,** Franz Masereel, "Sex Murder" (book illustration, Ginzberg *L'Enfer,* 185); **567,** Department of Library Services, American Museum of Natural History (neg. no. K15872); **573,** Museum of Fine Arts, Boston; **575,** Scala/Art Resource; **577,** The J. Paul Getty Museum; **579,** Museum of Fine Arts, Boston; **584,** From Andersen, I. (1977) *The Witch on the Wall* (London: Allen and Unwin/Copenhagen: Rosenkilde & Bagger); **591,** Jian Chen/Art Resource; **595,** National Museums and Galleries on Merseyside, Walker Art Gallery; **598,** Philadelphia Museum of Art; **605,** Bonnie Freer/Photo Researchers; **608,** etching by F. Hogenbergh, 1578, *Bilder Lexicon;* **610,** Jim Andersen/Woodfin Camp; **620,** Scala/Art Resource; **631,** Mark Antman/The Image Works; **632,** Wide World Photos; **657,** Gustave Dore, "Jesus and the Woman Taken in Adultery," illustration for *The Bible Gallery;* **659,** Fine Arts Museums of San Francisco, Mildred Anna Williams Collection; **665,** Gustave Dore, "The Lustful," illustration for Dante's *Divine Comedy;* **666,** Gustave Dore, "Devils and Seducers," illustration for Dante's *Divine Comedy;* **670,** Courtesy John La Plante; **671,** Chuck Painte/Stanford University News Service.

**22,** From Kinsey et al., 1948, p. 220; 1953, p. 548. Courtesy of the Institute for Sex Research; **36** and **37,** (bottom) Based on F.H. Netter, *Reproductive system.* Summit, N.J.: Ciba, 1965, p. 92; **48,** From K.L. Moore, *The Developing human,* 3d ed. Philadelphia: Saunders, 1982, p. 16; **61,** (left) From Masters and Johnson, *Human sexual response.* Boston: Little, Brown, 1966, p. 5; **61,** (right) From Masters and Johnson, *Human sexual response.* Boston: Little, Brown, 1966, p. 5; **65,** Based on Masters and Johnson, *Human sexual response.* Boston: Little, Brown, 1966; **66,** Based on Masters and Johnson, *Human sexual response.* Boston: Little, Brown, 1966; **72,** From Bohlen, Held, and Sanderson, *Archives of sexual behavior,* 9:6, 1980 and *11*:5, 1982; **77,** (left) Based on VanArsdalen, Malloy, and Wein, *Monographs in urology,* 1983, p. 140; **77,** (right) Based on Kedia and Markland; **86,** From J.M. Tanner, "Sequence and tempo in somatic changes in puberty." In Grumbach et al., *Control of onset of puberty.* New York: Wiley, 1974; **90,** From F.H. Netter, *Reproductive system.* Summit, N.J.: Ciba, 1953; **122,** Based on *Sexually transmitted disease statistical letter,* 1982, CDC, p. 5; **125,** Based on *Sexually transmitted disease statistical letter,* 1982, CDC, p. 4; **129,** From S.C. Bowen, Ed., *Sexually transmitted diseases and society.* Stanford: Stanford University Press, 1988; **153,** Based on K.L. Moore, *The developing human,* 3d ed. Philadelphia: Saunders, 1982, p. 15; **154,** From B.M. Patten, *Human embryology,* 3d ed. New York: McGraw-Hill, 1968, p. 145; **163,** From S.H. Cherry, *For women of all ages.* New York: Macmillan, 1979, p. 186; **169,** From Pritchard and McDonald, *Williams Obstetrics,* 16th ed. New York: Appleton-Century-Crofts, 1980; **188,** Based on Ory et al., *Making choices.* New York: Alan Guttmacher Institute, 1963, p. 11; **204,** From Hatcher et al., *Contraceptive technology, 1986–1987.* New York: Irvington, 1986, p. 243; **212,** From Shapiro, *The birth control book.* New York: St. Martin's, 1975, p. 165; **187,** From C.R. Austin and R.V. Short, *Reproduction in mammals,* vol. 5. New York: Cambridge, 1986, p. 194; **226,** From Kinsey et al., *Sexual behavior in the human male,* 1948, p. 162. Courtesy of the Institute for Sex Research; **227,** From Kinsey et al., *Sexual behavior in the human female,* 1953, p. 129. Courtesy of the Institute for Sex Research; **240,** Based on N.E. Campbell, *Biology.* Menlo Park, CA: Benjamin/Cummings, p. 1094; **256,** From Beach, *Reproductive behavior,* Montagna and Sadler, Eds. New York: Plenum, 1974; **259,** From A.M. Vener, C.S. Stewart, and D.L. Hager, "The sexual behavior of adolescents in middle America." *Journal of Marriage and the Family, 34,* November 1972, pp. 696–705; **291,** From Money and Ehrhardt, *Man and woman, boy and girl.* Baltimore, MD: Johns Hopkins University Press, 1972, p. 3; **325,** From Kinsey et al., *Sexual behavior in the human male,* 1948, p. 502; and from Kinsey et al.,

# Brief Contents

Preface    v

Chapter 1 Learning about Sexuality    2

PART 1    SEXUAL STRUCTURE AND FUNCTION    28
Chapter 2 Sexual Anatomy    30
Chapter 3 Sexual Physiology    55
Chapter 4 Sex Hormones    81
Chapter 5 Sexual Health and Illness    112

PART 2    SEXUAL REPRODUCTION    146
Chapter 6 Pregnancy and Childbirth    148
Chapter 7 Contraception and Abortion    184

PART 3    SEXUAL DEVELOPMENT    218
Chapter 8 Sexual Development in Childhood    220
Chapter 9 Sexuality in Adolescence and Adulthood    252
Chapter 10 Gender and Sexuality    280

PART 4    VARIETIES OF SEXUAL EXPERIENCE    306
Chapter 11 Solitary Sexual Behavior    308
Chapter 12 Sexplay and Coitus    333
Chapter 13 Homosexuality and Bisexuality    361
Chapter 14 Paraphilias    384
Chapter 15 Sexual Dysfunction and Therapy    411

PART 5    SEX AND HUMAN RELATIONSHIPS    440
Chapter 16 Sexual Intimacy and Love    442
Chapter 17 Marriage and Its Alternatives    473
Chapter 18 Sexual Exploitation    505
Chapter 19 Sexual Aggression    533

PART 6    SEX AND SOCIETY    564
Chapter 20 Sexuality in Historical Perspective    566
Chapter 21 Sexuality in Cultural Perspective    600
Chapter 22 Sex and the Law    626
Chapter 23 Sex and Morality    652

Glossary    675
References    687
Subject Index    721
Name Index    740

# Detailed Contents

Chapter 1   Learning about Sexuality   2
  THE STUDY OF HUMAN SEXUALITY   3
    *Biological Perspectives*   3
    *Psychosocial Perspectives*   5
    *Humanistic Perspectives*   7
  THE FIELD OF SEX RESEARCH   11
    *History of Sexology*   11
    *The Field Today*   17
  METHODS OF SEX RESEARCH   19
    *Basic Considerations*   19
    *Clinical Research*   22
    *The Research Interview*   23
    *Questionnaires*   23
  *Direct Observation and Experimentation*   25


PART 1   SEXUAL STRUCTURE AND FUNCTION   28

Chapter 2   Sexual Anatomy   30
  THE REPRODUCTIVE SYSTEM   31
    FEMALE SEX ORGANS   32
    *External Sex Organs*   32
    *Internal Sex Organs*   36
      *Breasts*   40
    MALE SEX ORGANS   41
    *External Sex Organs*   41
    *Internal Sex Organs*   45
  HOW GERM CELLS DEVELOP   46
    *Development of Sperm*   47
    *Development of the Ovum*   47
  HOW THE REPRODUCTIVE SYSTEM DEVELOPS   50
    *Differentiation of the Gonads*   51
    *Differentiation of the Genital Ducts*   51
    *Differentiation of the External Genitals*   52

Chapter 3   Sexual Physiology   55
  SEXUAL AROUSAL   56
    *Physical Stimulation*   56
    *Psychological Stimulation*   58
  SEXUAL RESPONSE   58
    *Response Patterns*   61

*Physiological Mechanisms*    63
*Excitement and Plateau Phases*    63
*Orgasm*    69
*Resolution Phase and Aftereffects*    75
CONTROL OF SEXUAL FUNCTIONS    75
*Spinal Control*    76
*Brain Control*    78

Chapter 4    Sex Hormones    81
HORMONAL SYSTEMS AND SEXUAL FUNCTIONS    82
*Gonadal Hormones*    82
*Pituitary Hormones*    84
*Hypothalamic Hormones*    84
*Control Systems*    84
PUBERTY    86
*Somatic Changes*    86
*Reproductive Maturation*    87
*Neuroendocrine Control*    89
THE MENSTRUAL CYCLE    91
*Menarche*    91
*Phases of the Menstrual Cycle*    92
*Menstrual Discomfort*    95
ATYPICAL SEXUAL DEVELOPMENT    98
*Chromosome Disorders*    100
*Hormone Disorders*    101
*Tissue Disorders*    101
HORMONES AND SEXUAL BEHAVIOR    102
*Mammalian Behavior*    102
*Human Behavior*    106

Chapter 5    Sexual Health and Illness    112
MAINTAINING SEXUAL HEALTH    113
*Keeping Clean*    113
*Toxic Shock Syndrome*    113
*Sex during Menstruation*    114
COMMON AILMENTS OF THE REPRODUCTIVE SYSTEM    114
*Genitourinary Infections*    114
*Cancer*    116
SEXUALLY TRANSMITTED DISEASES    120
*Prevalence*    120
*Types of STDs*    120
BACTERIAL STDs    121
*Gonorrhea*    121
*Chlamydia*    123

*Pelvic Inflammatory Disease*    123
*Syphilis*    124
*Other STDs Caused by Bacteria*    127
STDs CAUSED BY MISCELLANEOUS ORGANISMS    127
*Enteric Organisms*    127
*Parasitic Infections*    128
VIRAL STDs    128
*Genital Herpes*    128
*Genital Warts*    131
*Hepatitis*    132
AIDS AND THE HUMAN IMMUNODEFICIENCY VIRUS    132
*The Virus and the Immune System*    134
*Transmission of AIDS*    134
*Symptoms*    137
*Testing*    139
*Counseling*    139
*Treatment*    140
*Cost of AIDS*    141
*Prevention*    141


PART 2    SEXUAL REPRODUCTION    146


Chapter 6    Pregnancy and Childbirth    148
CONCEPTION    149
*The Journey of the Sperm*    150
*The Migration of the Egg*    150
*Fertilization and Implantation*    151
PREGNANCY    152
*The First Trimester*    152
*The Second Trimester*    157
*The Third Trimester*    159
*Psychological Aspects*    160
*Sexual Interest and Activity*    160
*The Father's Experience*    161
CHILDBIRTH    163
*Labor*    164
*Methods of Childbirth*    164
*Early Parent-Child Interaction*    173
THE POSTPARTUM PERIOD    173
*Physiological Changes*    173
*Emotional Reactions*    174
*Nursing*    174
*Ovulation and Menstruation*    175
*Sex in the Postpartum Period*    175

PRENATAL CARE    176
*Nutrition and Exercise*    176
*Smoking, Alcohol, and Drugs*    176
COMPLICATIONS OF PREGNANCY    177
*Difficulties in Carrying to Term*    177
*Birth Defects*    178
INFERTILITY    179
*Causes*    179
*Psychological Impact*    179
*Treatment*    181

Chapter 7    Contraception and Abortion    184
PATTERNS OF CONTRACEPTIVE USE    185
*Reasons for Using Contraceptives*    185
*Prevalence of Contraceptive Use*    187
*Reasons for* Not *Using Contraceptives*    189
*Taking Responsibility*    191
CONTRACEPTIVE METHODS    192
*Abstinence*    192
*Hormonal Methods*    192
*The Intrauterine Device*    196
*Barrier Methods*    198
*Spermicides*    201
*Fertility Awareness Techniques*    203
*Prolonged Nursing*    205
*Withdrawal*    205
*Sterilization*    206
*Future Birth Control*    209
ABORTION    211
*Methods of Abortion*    212
*Psychological Aspects of Abortion*    214

PART 3    SEXUAL DEVELOPMENT    218

Chapter 8    Sexual Development in Childhood    220
THE STUDY OF CHILDHOOD SEXUALITY    221
INBORN RESPONSIVE CAPACITY    222
*Reflexive Responses*    223
*Sources of Arousal*    224
SEXUAL BEHAVIOR IN CHILDHOOD    224
*Autoerotic Play*    224
*Sociosexual Play*    225
*Sex between Siblings*    227

*How Should Parents React?*    227
SEXUAL SOCIALIZATION    228
*Primate Development*    228
*Early Attachment and Bonding*    231
*Maturation and Sexual Learning*    233
*The Role of the Family*    234
*The Role of School*    236
*The Role of the Media*    238
*Sex with Adults*    238
THEORIES OF SEXUAL BEHAVIOR AND DEVELOPMENT    239
*Instincts and Drives*    239
*Psychoanalytic Theories*    241
*Erikson's Approach*    245
*Cognitive Development Models*    245
*Theories of Conditioning*    246
*Social Learning Models*    247

Chapter 9    Sexuality in Adolescence and Adulthood    252
ADOLESCENT SEXUALITY    253
*Adaptation to Puberty*    253
*Sexual Behavior*    256
*Sexual Values*    261
*Consequences of Sexual Intercourse*    264
SEXUALITY IN YOUNG ADULTHOOD    268
*Sociosexual Aspects*    268
*Premarital Sex*    269
SEXUALITY IN MIDDLE ADULTHOOD    272
*Male Midlife Transition*    272
*Female Midlife Transition*    273
SEXUALITY IN LATE ADULTHOOD    275
*Changes in Sexual Response*    275
*Patterns of Sexual Behavior*    276

Chapter 10    Gender and Sexuality    280
THE COMPONENTS OF SEXUAL IDENTITY    281
*Gender Identity*    281
*Gender Role*    282
*Gender Stereotyping*    282
*Androgyny*    284
GENDER DIFFERENCES THROUGH THE LIFE-CYCLE    286
*Infancy*    287
*Childhood*    287
*Adolescence*    288
*Adulthood*    289

HOW GENDER IDENTITY DEVELOPS    290
*Interactional Models    290*
*Special Cases    291*
*Sex-Dimorphic Behavior    293*
GENDER DISORDERS    294
*Gender Identity Disorder of Childhood    294*
*Later Gender Identity Disorder    295*
*Transsexualism    295*
GENDER AND SEXUAL BEHAVIOR    297
*Sexual Drive and Behavior    297*
*Response to Erotica    298*
*Orgasmic Capacity    299*
*Relational Aspects    300*
*Explaining the Differences    301*


PART 4    VARIETIES OF SEXUAL EXPERIENCE    306


Chapter 11    Solitary Sexual Behavior    308
EROTIC FANTASY    309
*The Nature of Erotic Fantasies    310*
*Fantasy and Sexual Behavior    313*
*Gender Differences    316*
*Theoretical Perspectives    317*
SEXUAL DREAMS    317
*The Neurophysiology of Dreaming    319*
*Nocturnal Orgasms    319*
MASTURBATION    320
*Methods of Masturbation    322*
*Prevalence of Masturbation    325*
*Functions of Masturbation    327*
*Masturbation, Health, and Society    327*


Chapter 12    Sexplay and Coitus    333
VARIETIES OF SEXPLAY    334
*Kissing    334*
*Touching and Caressing    335*
*Oral-Genital Stimulation    338*
*Other Means of Sexplay    341*
*Length of Sexplay    341*
COITUS    342
*Intromission    342*
*Coital Postures    343*
*Coital Movements    347*
*Orgasmic Control    348*
*Variant Forms of Reaching Orgasm    351*

*The Aftermath*    352
ENHANCING COITAL PLEASURE    352
   *Physical Factors*    354
   *Time and Place*    354
   *Erotic Aids and Practices*    355
   *Psychological Factors*    356

Chapter 13    Homosexuality and Bisexuality    361
THE CONCEPT OF HOMOSEXUALITY    362
   *The Problem of Definition*    362
   *The Problem of Identification*    364
   *The Problem of Bias*    365
HOMOSEXUAL BEHAVIOR    367
   *Prevalence*    367
   *Sexual Practices*    367
   *Active and Passive Roles*    370
HOMOSEXUALITY AS A WAY OF LIFE    370
   *The Homosexual Subculture*    370
   *Homosexual Relationships*    371
   *Meeting Places*    374
THE DEVELOPMENT OF SEXUAL ORIENTATION    376
   *Biological Determinants*    376
   *Psychosocial Determinants*    378
SOCIAL PERSPECTIVES ON HOMOSEXUALITY    381
   *Social Judgments*    381
   *Medical Judgments*    381

Chapter 14    Paraphilias    384
THE CONCEPT OF PARAPHILIAS    385
*Historical and Current Conceptions*    385
   *Basic Features*    386
PARAPHILIAC BEHAVIORS    387
   *Pedophilia*    387
   *Incest*    391
   *Zoophilia*    394
   *Fetishism*    395
   *Transvestism*    397
   *Necrophilia*    399
   *Voyeurism*    399
   *Exhibitionism*    400
   *Obscene Calls*    401
   *Sadomasochism (S-M)*    401
   *Other Paraphilias*    405
   *Sexual Addiction*    405
CAUSES AND TREATMENTS    406

*The Development of Paraphilias*   407
*The Treatment of Paraphilias*   408

**Chapter 15   Sexual Dysfunction and Therapy**   411
TYPES OF SEXUAL DYSFUNCTION   412
*Definitions*   412
*Prevalence*   413
SEXUAL DESIRE DISORDERS   413
*Hypoactive Sexual Desire Disorder*   414
*Sexual Aversion*   415
*Hyperactive Sexual Desire*   415
SEXUAL AROUSAL DISORDERS   415
*Male Erectile Disorder*   415
*Female Sexual Arousal Disorder*   416
ORGASM DISORDERS   418
*Inhibited Female Orgasm*   418
*Premature Ejaculation*   418
*Inhibited Male Orgasm*   419
SEXUAL PAIN DISORDERS   419
*Dyspareunia*   419
*Vaginismus*   420
CAUSES OF SEXUAL DYSFUNCTION   420
*Organic Causes*   420
*Organic or Psychogenic?*   423
*Psychogenic Causes*   424
TREATMENTS   427
*Sex Therapy*   427
*Psychotherapy and Behavior Therapy*   432
*Group Therapy*   434
*Self-Help*   434
*Treatment with Drugs*   434
*Physical Treatment Methods*   436
*Surgical Methods*   437
*Prevention of Sexual Dysfunction*   438

PART 5   SEX AND HUMAN RELATIONSHIPS   440

**Chapter 16   Sexual Intimacy and Love**   442
SEXUAL ATTRACTION   443
*Physical Aspects*   443
*Psychological Determinants*   445
*Social Factors*   447
*Gender Differences*   447
SEXUAL INTIMACY   449
*Patterns of Sexual Interaction*   450

*Building and Sustaining Intimacy*    454
*Problems in Intimacy and Commitment*    457
EROTIC LOVE    461
*Varieties of Love*    462
*Falling in Love*    464
*Companionate Love*    467
*The Relationship of Sex and Love*    467

**Chapter 17    Marriage and Its Alternatives    473**
MARRIAGE    474
*Demographic Changes*    477
*Changes in Family Patterns*    479
*Mate Selection*    480
ALTERNATIVE COMMITMENTS    484
*Cohabitation*    484
*Gay Couples*    486
*Other Alternatives*    487
BEING SINGLE    487
*The Never Married*    488
*The Divorced*    489
*The Widowed*    491
SEXUAL ACTIVITY AND SATISFACTION    492
*Marital Sex*    492
*Extramarital Sex*    494
*Cohabiting Couples*    500
*Nonmarital Sex*    501
*Celibacy*    503

**Chapter 18    Sexual Exploitation    505**
THE VALUATION OF SEX    506
*The Sexual Value of the Person*    506
*The Value of Emotional Commitment*    507
*Fair Exchange*    507
*Gender Considerations*    508
PROSTITUTION    509
*Types of Prostitutes*    509
*Prevalence*    512
*Psychosexual Aspects*    513
*Consequences*    516
PORNOGRAPHY    517
*The Problem of Definition*    517
*The Problem of Consequences*    521
*The Problem of Censorship*    527
SEX AND ADVERTISING    528
*Advertising to Sell Sex*    528

*Sex to Sell Advertising*    529
*Effects of Sex in Advertising*    530

Chapter 19    Sexual Aggression    533
AGGRESSIVE ELEMENTS IN SEX    534
*Dominance*    534
*Hostility*    536
*Coercion*    537
SEXUAL HARASSMENT    537
*Determinants*    538
*Contexts*    539
*Handling Sexual Harassment*    542
RAPE    543
*The Nature of Rape*    543
*The Setting*    545
*Prevalence*    546
*Varieties of Rape*    547
*The Rape Victim*    551
*The Rapist*    557

PART 6    SEX AND SOCIETY    564

Chapter 20    Sexuality in Historical Perspective    566
SEXUALITY AND THE ORIGINS OF CULTURE    567
THE JUDAIC TRADITION    568
*Sexuality in Biblical Times*    568
*Judaic Attitudes to Sexuality*    569
GREECE AND ROME    572
*Eros in Greece*    572
*Sexuality in Rome*    577
THE RISE OF CHRISTIANITY    579
*The Influence of Judaism*    579
*The Influence of Stoicism*    580
*The Apocalyptic Expectation*    580
*The Patristic Age*    581
THE MIDDLE AGES    582
*The Early Middle Ages*    582
*The Late Middle Ages*    585
THE RENAISSANCE AND THE REFORMATION    587
*Renaissance Sexuality*    587
THE ENLIGHTENMENT    590
*Manners and Morals*    590
*Erotic Art and Literature*    591
*Life in the American Colonies*    592

THE NINETEENTH CENTURY    593
*Victorian Sexual Ideology*    593
*Erotic Art and Literature*    594
*Sexual Behavior*    595
THE MODERNIZATION OF SEX    597

Chapter 21    Sexuality in Cultural Perspective    600
THE SEXUAL REVOLUTION    601
CAUSES OF THE SEXUAL REVOLUTION    601
*Political Events*    601
*Economic Factors*    602
*The Separation of Sex and Reproduction*    603
*The Resurgence of Feminism*    603
MANIFESTATIONS OF THE SEXUAL REVOLUTION    604
*The Rise of the Counterculture*    604
*The Liberation of Female Sexuality*    606
*Gay Liberation*    607
*Public Sexual Expression*    610
*Sex and Marriage*    611
*Is the Sexual Revolution Over?*    612
*The Conservative Reaction*    613
*The Balance Sheet*    614
SOCIAL REGULATION OF SEXUALITY    614
*Socialization*    615
*Social Norms and Sanctions*    615
*Sources of Social Control*    616
*Social Judgments*    617
*Justifications for Social Control*    618
*Sex and Social Status*    620
CROSS-CULTURAL PATTERNS OF SOCIAL CONTROL    622
*Sexual Diversity and Unity*    622
*Repressiveness and Permissiveness*    623

Chapter 22    Sex and the Law    626
LAWS ON MARRIAGE AND PROCREATION    627
*Marriage Law*    627
*Laws on Reproduction*    629
AIDS AND THE LAW    634
*Mandatory Testing*    634
*Quarantine*    635
*Legal Liability*    636
LAWS ON ADULT CONSENSUAL BEHAVIOR    636
*Heterosexual Behaviors*    636
*Homosexual Behaviors*    637

SEXUAL OFFENSES AGAINST PERSONS    641
*Rape*    641
*Marital Rape*    642
*Sexual Offenses against the Young*    643
*Public Nuisance Offenses*    644
LAWS ON COMMERCIAL EXPLOITATION OF SEX    645
*Prostitution*    645
*Pornography*    647

Chapter 23    Sex and Morality    652
THE BASES OF SEXUAL ETHICS    653
*Secular Bases*    653
*Religious Bases*    654
THE CONSERVATIVE MORAL PERSPECTIVE    654
*The Case for Conservative Morality*    656
*The Case against Conservative Morality*    658
THE LIBERAL MORAL PERSPECTIVE    662
*The Case for Liberal Morality*    665
*The Case against Liberal Morality*    671
ENVOI    673
Glossary    675
References    687
Subject Index    721
Name Index    740

# Boxed Features

The Mosher Survey    16
Sex Surveys    24
Female Circumcision    34
Defloration    35
Size of the Vagina    37
Male Circumcision    43
Size of the Penis    44
The Masters and Johnson Study of Sexual
   Response    59
New Technology in Sex Research    60
The Grafenberg Spot and Female
   Ejaculation    67
Varieties of Female Orgasm    70
Ejaculatory Control    73
Menstrual Taboos    91
Behavior and PMS    97
Precocious Puberty    99
Pheromones    103
Eunuchs    108
How to do a Breast Self-Exam    117
How to Examine Your Testicles    119
AIDS Blood Testing    140
Estimating a Sex Partner's Risk for AIDS    144
Boy or Girl    151
Theories of Embryonal Development    155
Amniocentesis and Chorionic Villi Testing    158
Childbearing and Age    180
Early Contraception    186
Population Control    187
Orgasm in Infancy    223
Childhood Sexuality in Other Cultures    229
Nature Versus Nurture    242
The Changing Body    254
Premarital Sex in Other Cultures    263
Effects of Adolescent Childbearing    266
Poems on Aging and Sexuality    277
Language and Gender Stereotypes    283
Critical Period of Gender Differentiation    292
Some Erotic Fantasies of College Men    311
Some Erotic Fantasies of College Women    312
Masturbation in Cross-Cultural Perspective    321
Masturbatory Insanity    328
Masturbation in Literature    330
Cunnilingus: Current Attitudes    339

Fellatio: Current Attitudes    340
Coitus Reservatus    350
Sex Manuals    353
Aphrodisiacs    357
Same-Sex Encounters Among Animals    366
Homosexuality in Other Cultures    368
Two Poems by C. P. Carafy    374
Father-Daughter Incest    394
The Literature of Sadomasochism    403
Sex and the Handicapped    417
Psychosexual Treatment of a Sexually
   Dysfunctional Couple    428
Treatment Outcomes of Sex Therapy    433
Getting Help for Sexual Dysfunction    435
Sexual Jealousy    460
A Love Affair    468
Addicted Love    470
Keeping Love Alive    471
I am Not a Significant Other    484
Old Knots Just Get Stronger    494
Swinging    497
The Hustler    513
Pornotopia    514
Pornography or Erotica: Student Views    520
Attorney General's Commission on Pornography
   (1986): Some Conclusions    523
Sexual Coercion in College    549
Men as Rape Victims    552
Preventing Rape    554
Jewish Marriage    570
Erotic Themes in Greek Mythology    576
Erotic Art and Literature in the
   Renaissance    589
Civilization and Its Discontents    621
The Nature and Use of Sex Laws    628
Issues in Abortion    633
Punishments for Sexual Misconduct    638
Excerpts from *Humanae Vitae,* Encyclical Letter
   of Pope Paul VI    655
What's Wrong, What's Right—The Popular
   View    663
The Humanistic Perspective on Marital
   Fidelity    664
Eroticism in Eastern Religions    670

# Fundamentals of Human Sexuality

# Learning About Sexuality

CHAPTER

# 1

*Sex isn't the best thing in the world, or the worst thing in the world—but there's nothing else quite like it.*

W.C. FIELDS

OUTLINE

THE STUDY OF HUMAN
  SEXUALITY
Biological Perspectives
  Medicine
  Biology
Psychosocial Perspectives
  Psychology
  Sociology
  Anthropology
Humanistic Perspectives
  Art
  Literature
  Film
  History
  Philosophy and Religion
THE FIELD OF SEX RESEARCH
History of Sexology
  Origins
  Establishment
  Revival

The Field Today
  Sex Research
  Sex Education
  Sex Therapy
METHODS OF SEX RESEARCH
Basic Considerations
  Purpose and Perspective
  The Problem of Bias
  The Choice of Variables
  Ethical Considerations
  Sampling
  Use of Statistics
Clinical Research
The Research Interview
Questionnaires
Direct Observation and
  Experimentation

Sex is the source of human life and central to life from birth to death. Whether or not we actively engage in it, sexuality is part of our everyday thoughts and feelings; it is rooted in our dreams and longings, fears and frustrations.

Sex dominates the lives of some people; for others it plays a lesser role, either by choice or by circumstance. For most of us sexual interests wax and wane, depending on a host of internal needs and external circumstances. At each phase of life sexuality unfolds in distinctive ways.

At the biological level, the primary function of sex is reproduction—having children. Biology provides the machinery for sexual functions and behavior. Its components range from genes to genitals. Sexual functions are regulated by your nerves and hormones and sustained by the circulatory, muscular, and other systems of your body.

At the psychological level, sex consists of a variety of behaviors and relationships aimed at erotic pleasure, affection, and other needs.

At the societal level, sex pervades numerous facets of life. It makes your culture unique, flavoring its art, its history, its laws, and its values.

In addition sexuality has many indirect roles in your life. It is a big part of your gender identity (masculinity, femininity) and of what people expect of you in various social roles. Sex can express dominance or hostility. It contributes to your self-esteem and social status, and in many other ways shapes your life from infancy to old age.

As we explore all these facets of sexuality, bear in mind what they may mean to you personally. Our primary focus will be on sexual behavior—erotic thoughts, feelings, and actions. Why do you behave sexually? How do you behave sexually? How should you behave sexually?

In this chapter we will begin by examining how investigators in various fields, especially in sex research, go about answering these questions. In the rest of the book we will discuss the answers that they have come up with, and challenge you to find answers of your own.

## THE STUDY OF HUMAN SEXUALITY

Sexuality is so pervasive in human life that virtually all fields of study could be related to it. Because it is everybody's business, the study of sex has ended up being nobody's business, until recently.

The general store of sexual information gathered over the centures is vast; the catalog of the Library of Congress has over 500 subject headings listed under "sex." This information has mainly been a by-product of many fields of study—biological, psychological, and humanistic. Geneticists studying sex chromosomes, anthropologists charting lineages, and art historians analyzing erotic symbolism may be said to be part of the general field of sexuality.

The specific study of sexuality as a specialized field, or *sex research*, is by comparison modest in scope and brief in history. It is like a tiny statue standing on the broad pedestal formed by the other approaches; but what it lacks in size, it makes up for in focus.

### Biological Perspectives

The biomedical sciences have helped us understand the structure, functions, and diseases of the sexual organs. There are also important linkages to the study of sexual behavior, both through specialties like psychiatry, and through comparisons of animal sexual behavior, carried out by biologists and primatologists.

Medicine  Attempts to study sexual structures and functions go back to the ancient medical traditions of Egypt and the classical world of Greece and Rome. More scientific approaches began in the Renaissance (Chapter 20), as exemplified by the anatomical sketches of Leonardo da Vinci (Figure 1.1). With the rise of medical specialties during the 18th and 19th centuries, a number of fields took on a special interest in sexual functions. For instance, anatomists study genital structures; embryologists, development before birth; physiologists,

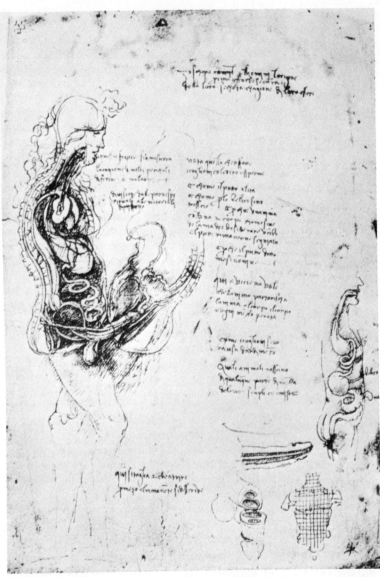

Figure 1.1   Leonardo da Vinci: Figures in coitus and anatomical sketches.

sexual functions; and geneticists, the hereditary mechanisms underlying sexual development and behavior. In the clinical fields, endocrinologists study hormones and their disturbances; urologists deal with diseases of the urinary tract, which in the male involves the genital organs as well; obstetricians and gynecologists specialize in childbirth and female reproductive disorders; dermatologists have a particular interest in sexually transmitted diseases, which often show up as sores on the skin. Specialists in epidemiology and public health are concerned with the patterns of transmission and prevention of sexually transmitted diseases. The medical study of sexual behavior and the treatment of disturbed sexual functions and behavior are the domain of psychiatry as well as psychology.

Biology    Biologists have been primarily concerned with the study of plants and animals, but their work also helps us understand human sexual functions and behavior (Hinde, 1974). First, the study of animals leads to the development of methods that can be adapted to humans; most medical experiments and treatment trials are first worked out with animals. Because animal patterns of behavior are simpler, they can be more readily described and analyzed; the insights gained can then be used for the study of human social behavior.

Second, animals can be used in experiments where ethical considerations exclude the use of humans. For instance, the effects of separating monkey infants from their mothers have led to important findings about sexual development. Similarly, the administration of sex hormones to pregnant animals has shown how the reproductive system develops and how hormones affect gender identity. Such experiments could not conceivably be carried out with human mothers and infants.

Third, the study of animal behavior can generate principles and rules of behavior whose applicability to humans can be tested. For example, the discovery of the "contact comfort" infant monkeys obtain by clinging to their mother has led to a better appreciation of the importance of early nurturance for human babies. The study of social associations between male and female primates has likewise suggested ways of understanding human sexual relationships (Symons, 1979).

There are, however, important limitations in applicability of animal studies to human sexuality. There is nothing we learn from the study of animals that can be automatically extended to people: what applies to humans must be demonstrated among humans. Superficial comparisons with humans and use of animal behavior as a metaphor are likely to lead to false conclusions. Sexual behavior that seems the same among even closely related species may serve different purposes; likewise, the same basic sexual purpose may be attained by different behaviors.

The basic organizing principle in biology is the theory of *evolution*, the work of Charles Robert Darwin (1809–1882). Evolution helps explain the emergence not only of physical forms but also of behavior. Biology shows us sexual evolution from the actions of simplest organisms to the awesome complexity of human behavior.

Over the past several decades new fields within biology have focused directly on behavior. Ethology studies social behavior in animals. Sociobiology studies human behavior using evolutionary principles (Wilson, 1975; 1978). To explain sexuality, it draws on many sources: studies of the social behavior of animals, especially *primates* (monkeys and apes); the study of the fossils of early humans (*hominids*); cross-cultural data gathered by anthropologists; and current studies of human behavior. The purpose of this approach is to see how the biological and social aspects of human interactions have been connected from the beginning (LeBoeuf, 1978; Symons, 1979.)

The study of animal sexuality is not the exclusive domain of biologists. Experimental psychologists do much of their research with animals as well. Similarly, many primatologists are trained in anthropology. Even some sociologists now follow a biosocial orientation. The biological perspective on sexuality is therefore not a narrow enterprise. It is a multidisciplinary approach to the study of sexuality across the entire spectrum of living things.

## Psychosocial Perspectives

Approaches to the study of sexuality should be complementary rather than competitive. However, because of historical reasons, differences in ideas and methods, disciplinary self-interest, and politics, this ideal has yet to be achieved. Even though there is wide recognition that mind and body interact in sexual behavior, scientists continue to quarrel over their relative importance.

For most behavioral scientists, the role of biology in sexual behavior is similar to its role in the acquisition of language. A healthy set of vocal cords allow the articulation of human sounds, and the brain has the capacity to learn languages. But whether or not you learn to speak a given language is a function of whether or not you are taught that language, or live in a certain culture. By the same reasoning, you are born with sex organs and the capacity to behave sexually, but your sexual behaviors and orientation are acquired through social circumstances.

Psychology   Sexual behavior includes the sexual interactions between people as well as the more private worlds of erotic fantasies and dreams. Psychologists are concerned with the scientific study of all observable sexual behavior. Developmental psychologists focus on the emergence of sexuality as a child grows up. Social psychologists study the relationship between belief systems (such as attitudes) and behavior. Personality psychologists are concerned with the interactions among personality traits, situational factors, and behavior.

Although experimental psychologists heavily rely on animals in their work and physiological psychologists deal with the physical side of mental processes, their approaches are different from those of biologists. Whereas evolution is the key biological concept, *learning* is the cornerstone of psychological theories and practice.

Psychologists have made major contributions to the study of sex differences (Maccoby and Jacklin, 1974), but until recently, they have shown much less interest in sexual behavior. The development of children has been observed and documented in exquisite detail, but even massive volumes on child psychology barely touch the subject of sex. Until recently it was only an exceptional investigator who addressed these issues (Sears et al., 1957).

During the more recent past, there has been an upsurge of interest in sexuality within psychology, both with respect to sexual behavior, and to related topics like gender identity, and sex roles. Of all the specialists in the fields of sex research and sex education, psychologists now constitute the largest group (Polyson et al., 1986). New methods of sex therapy over the past two decades largely depend on behavior modification techniques developed by psychologists (Caird and Wincze, 1977).

Sociology   Sociologists used to be preoccupied with sex-related institutions like the family, but not with sexual behavior. The most famous sociological study of sex was conceived and carried out by Alfred C. Kinsey, who was not a sociologist but a biologist, even though his methods and interpretations were distinctly sociological. Currently there are many sociologists working in the field of human sexuality.

Sociology has enriched the study of sexuality in a number of important areas. Sociologists remain the foremost experts on marriage and the family in our society, which are the primary institutions for the expression and regulation of sex. Also, the survey, which is the most often-used procedure to gather behavioral data about sex, is a sociological technique.

The concept of roles, which has been extensively studied by sociologists, has direct applications to the issue of sex roles. Your sexual behaviors can be seen as determined by roles more or less defined for you by society. In other words, the sociological approach provides the larger social framework within which to understand individual sexual behavior (Kando, 1978; Henslin and Sagarin, 1978). The interests of sociologists may also overlap with those of anthropologists (Reiss, 1986).

Anthropology   Given the critical role that culture plays in shaping human sexual behavior, the comparative study of sexuality across cultures is indispensable.

Sex is a biological given, but it is only through socialization that it assumes form and meaning (Davenport, 1977). All cultures shape sexual behavior, but no two cultures do it exactly the same way. Because no single society represents the human race as a whole, no serious understanding of sexuality is possible in just one social context. The only way to know the human family is to know something about its many members (Ford and Beach, 1951).

Cultural anthropologists have traditionally studied societies markedly different from our own (Figure 1.2). Referred to by various labels ("primitive," "tribal," "preliterate," and so on), these societies have usually been relatively small, homogenous, technologically less advanced, and changing at a slower pace, and thus easier to study (Davenport, 1977).

Studies of different cultures have yielded a vast amount of material that attests to the variety and richness of human sexual behavior, customs, and symbols (Gregersen, 1983; Ford and Beach, 1951; Murdock, 1949). But the anthropological approach to sexuality has limitations. Much of sexual behavior occurs in private, out of direct observation. The anthropologist must rely on reports of such behavior, which are liable to distortion due to the fear of disclosure or to exaggeration. Talking about sex is itself a form of sexual behavior, so people of conservative views or in sexually repressive settings are reluctant to reveal their sexual lives to outsiders. Therefore, reports on such societies tend to portray their sexual values as more restrictive than may be the case. Similarly, sexually liberal societies are likely to appear more liberal than they are in reality.

Assessing the gains and shortcomings of anthropological studies of sex, Davenport (1977) sums it up:

> While some favorite assumptions and dated theories can now be shown to be either misconceptions or ethnocentric generalizations from our own culture, virtually no non-obvious and significant theoretical generalizations can yet be made. We are just beginning to sense the extent and limits of cultural variations. We do not know how and why these variations occur (pp. 1–2).

### Humanistic Perspectives

Sexuality goes beyond the biomedical and the psychosexual perspectives. A rich tradition of literary, artistic, philosophical, and historical exploration of sexual themes gives us deep insights into human sexuality.

Figure 1.2    People of the Watutsi tribe in Africa, photographed in the 1930s. Because of their exotic origins such figures could be publicly shown which helped liberalize sexual attitudes.

The behavioral sciences themselves owe their origins to the intellectual movement known as *humanism,* which flourished during the Renaissance (Kagan et al., 1987). Humanism held forth the possibility of human improvement through education and study. Based on this ideal, the spirit of rational inquiry into human intentions and actions gradually developed over the centuries into the systematic disciplines of the social sciences and by extension into the study of sexuality as a distinct field of inquiry.

The humanities currently include literature, art, music, philosophy, religion, and history. The contributions of these fields are the earliest and broadest attempts to make sense of sex and other human experience.

Art    Erotic art provides the oldest record of human sexual activity. Sexual respresentations in naturalistic or symbolic form are among the earliest surviving artifacts of human culture (Field, 1975).

In its earliest forms, art was not meant to represent reality but to *be* reality (Eitner, 1975). When Paleolithic people fashioned statues of pregnant women or painted bisons pierced by arrows on cave walls, they were generating a new reality and enacting a ritual through which they hoped to increase fecundity and the food supply. The magical and religious use of sexual symbolism—with the genital organs in stylized form (see figures in Box 23.4)—has persisted through the ages, often in subtle and obscure forms.

Art is also a pictorial record of sexual behavior. Depictions of the nude body and scenes of sexual interaction provide us with accounts of times past, slices of life gone forever. When we look at Greek vase paintings that depict sexual scenes, we learn volumes about who these people were.

Equally important is the artist's interpretive analysis of human sexual emotions and actions. Looking at Picasso's erotic drawings that depict the interactions of the artist with the model, we learn little about sexual anatomy or coital postures. Instead the genius of the artist captures the mood of the act.

The purpose of erotic art is also to please the eye, to titillate, to arouse the viewer. Erotic imagery is among the most popular and powerful sources of sexual arousal, ranging from the priceless nudes gracing the walls of museums to the pornographic trash displayed in sex shops. Every society has to come to terms with erotic art. What a society does with it reveals a great deal about the society's sexual values and culture (Eitner, 1975; Webb, 1975).

Literature    Literary approaches to sex, like art, have served the purposes of description, analysis, and erotic arousal. The writer's approach to sexuality is closer to that of the clinician than that of the behavioral scientist. The emphasis is on individuals rather than groups, on keen observation and intuition rather than the systematic gathering and analysis of data. D. H. Lawrence's Lady Chatterly and James Joyce's Leopold Bloom may not be representative of either women or men; they may not even be realistic portrayals of a single woman or man; yet the writer captures in a single imaginary character a universal element, the essence of some aspect of sex, which no survey could ever hope to distill.

Western erotic literature, like art, has mainly served secular purposes. It has taken many forms, with varying degrees of social acceptability. Much literature dwells on the exploration of love, understating the sexual element. Flagrantly erotic works have been labeled *pornography* (Chapter 18).

The tendency of great writers to treat sexual themes subtly rather than flagrantly may be only in part due to the fear of social censure; erotic themes often carry a more powerful charge if some things are left to the imagination of the reader. Most erotic literature, at least of the more explicit variety, has been written by men and for men. Women are prominent as subjects but exist to fulfill male desires (Purdy, 1975a).

Though much of erotic literature dwells on heterosexual intercourse, other varieties of sexual experience have also been explored. If we were to expand our purview to include works on love, jealousy, infidelity, and other topics that have a bearing on sex, we would have to take on the bulk of the literature of the world since ancient times.[1]

Film    Compared with art and literature, the cinema is a newcomer to the erotic scene, but what it lacks in age it makes up for in presence. Over the past several decades, people have been exposed to films and television to a far greater extent than to art and literature. Furthermore, romance and sex have been among the main staples of their scripts.

The cinema, like theater, is a true art form, which has produced memorable explorations of erotic themes (Purdy, 1975b). Television, by contrast, remains largely awash in soap operas. Although the cinematic depiction of sexual scenes and the exploration of controversial subjects have become commonplace, there is still a substantial, though fuzzy, distinction between films produced for general consumption and the pornographic film ("blue film").

Blue movies go back to the very origins of the film industry. Long an underground activity, the making of pornographic films mushroomed in the 1960s with the liberalization of censorship laws. Still, the value of pornographic films for the exploration of sexuality has been minimal, despite their explicitness and the fact that sex is their sole purpose.

Pornographic films may be dreary, but there is an intrinsic force in sexual acts that will assert itself no matter how ineptly presented. At least the unadorned depictions of genital organs and sexual activities probably serve an educational function.

Films are also used now in sex research, education, and therapy. Educational films depicting coitus, masturbation, and homosexual interactions began to be developed in the 1970s. Whether used in classrooms or in therapy, these films are helpful, but they also suf-

fer from some of the same limitations as commercially made pornographic movies.

History    Historians have produced a stupendous amount of writing, but little of it has dealt with sexual behavior. That little has focused on the lives of people with power and social privilege. We know next to nothing about the sexual behaviors of the great mass of ordinary men and women in the past.

There was no sex survey before the modern era, so our understanding of sexual behavior in the past depends mainly on historical records. Historians also play a crucial role in elucidating the broader social context within which sexual relationships unfolded and in showing us the thread of continuity running through civilization.

Bias is unavoidable in historical research. Historians, like everyone else, have beliefs and prejudices that color their perceptions, often without their being aware of it. Such bias has been plentiful in sexual matters. Deliberate distortion has also compromised the historical record, especially with socially problematic sexual behaviors like homosexuality (Boswell, 1980).

Another major source of bias is the almost exclusively male perspective in history. Although female characters are present in great profusion, they are seen through the eyes of men, as in erotic art and literature. This picture has been changing over the past two decades or so, as the historical record has begun to be cautiously reconstructed. Historians are now much more concerned with the "private side" of history. Family history and women's history are new fields.[2]

Philosophy and Religion    All human inquiry and knowledge was originally the domain of philosophy. Among the ancient Greeks, philosophers often focused on love and sex, and

---

[1]For a brief overview of the erotic in literature, see Purdy (1975a), which also provides a selected bibliography. Legman (1963) and Atkins (1973, 1978) give more extensive coverage. Marcus (1966) has an excellent discussion of the nature of pornographic literature.

[2]Freedman (1982; 1988). For a review of surveys of historical literature on sexuality, see Burnham (1972). Examples of the more specialized treatment of sexual topics by historians are Degler (1974); Boswell (1980); Robinson (1976); Foucault (1978). In a more popular vein, sex throughout history is presented by Tannahill (1980).

their ideas have shaped sexual concepts and values in Western culture (Chapter 20). For instance, the duality in Plato's philosophy between the pleasures of the body and the higher aspirations of reason has persisted in the Christian conflict between the sexual demands of the flesh and the loftier yearnings of the spirit (Edman, 1956).

Religion has played an even more critical role in determining how people think about sex and behave sexually. Christianity has been the dominant force in the Western world in influencing the ethical dimension of sexual behavior (Chapter 23). Once closely connected to religion and now more independent of it is the law, which is the primary means in secular societies of regulating sexual behavior (Chapter 22).

*Creation myths* of ancient cultures have fascinating sexual themes. As in art, we see sexual expression serving the most profound human impulses to make sense of our life. The Judaic account of creation with which we are most familiar is exceptional in its asexuality: God formed man from the "dust of the ground" and breathed life into his nostrils; He then took one of his ribs and fashioned his female companion (Gen. 2:7, 21–23). In contrast, con-

sider the Egyptian creation myths. The sun god Atum-Re created the first couple, Shu and Tefnut, by ejaculating into his hand, transferring the semen into his mouth, and spitting it out again. A drop of semen fell into the waters and formed the first solid land. Shu became the god of air, and Tefnut his sister, the goddess of moisture. They mated incestuously and gave birth to Geb, the earth god, and Nut the sky goddess. Geb and Nut were united in continuous coitus until wrenched apart by their father, who raised Nut to become the starry vault of heaven, out of reach of Geb's phallus, which continued to thrust skyward vainly trying to reach his sister-wife (Figure 1.3). Bereft of her consort, Nut was impregnated each night by swallowing the disk of the sun, which was reborn each morning from between her legs (Field, 1975).

The study of Hinduism and other Eastern religions provides especially rich opportunities for exploring erotic themes in religious traditions, doctrines, and architecture (Figure 1.4), an issue we return to in Chapter 23.[3]

[3]For a discussion of erotic themes in ancient Egyptian mythology see Manniche (1987). Parrinder (1980) addresses sex in the world's religions; Larue (1983), sexual themes in the Bible.

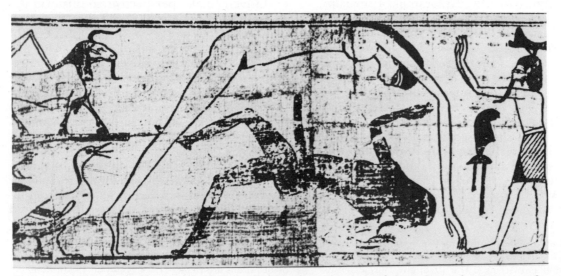

Figure 1.3   The Egyptian earth-god, Geb, and his sister the sky-god, Nut. From the Papyrus of Taneniu, 1102–952 B.C.

Figure 1.4    Temple reliefs, sixteenth century A.D. Kandariya Mahadevo temple, Khajuraho, India.

## THE FIELD OF SEX RESEARCH

The field of sex research or *sexology* focuses only on sex, unlike the disciplines we have discussed so far. Despite significant progress over the past two decades, sexology today is still an "ill understood, ill-defined academic and therapeutic enterprise" (Haeberle, 1983a). It lacks both a distinctive research method of its own and a firm theoretical foundation (Haeberle, 1984). Moreover, its future is uncertain. Should sex become more clearly the concern of every relevant field, from biology to theology; or should there be a specialized discipline that concerns itself with various aspects of sexuality? These questions are hotly debated (Reiss, 1982; Moser, 1983).

People usually associate sex research with the post-World War II period, especially the sexual revolution of the 1960s; yet there was significant sex research long before that. The history of sexology goes back at least 200 years.

### History of Sexology

The term "sexology," though currently out of favor, is the only term that covers sex research, education, and therapy. No single term is an adequate substitute. The history of this enterprise can be divided into three phases: origins, establishment, and revival (Haeberle, 1982, 1983b; Hoenig, 1977).

*Origins*    The present-day study of sexuality can be traced to the broader concerns of Enlightenment figures like Jean Jacques Rousseau (1712–1778), who addressed themselves to problems of sexual relationships and their proper place in society. At this point the study of sexuality was merely part of larger intellectual inquiries into human nature and behavior.

*Establishment*    Attention began to focus on sexual behavior in central Europe in the 19th century. Physicians, mostly psychiatrists, tried to extend the benefits of scientific study to the area of sexuality. The concept of sexual problems as sickness had been expounded in France, but it was in Germany, in the second half of the 19th century, that the foundations of sexology were laid. These physicians' interest in sex was a natural extension of their concern with the human body, and they had the social standing and credibility to stand the heat of criticism (of which there was a great deal), for trespassing into this area.

Two early figures were especially influential. The first was *Richard von Krafft-Ebing*, a German neuropsychiatrist who systematized case studies of sexual aberrations in his *Psychopathia sexualis*, first published in 1886 and revised through 12 editions (Figure 1.5) (Krafft-Ebing, 1978). In the tradition of clinical psychiatry, Krafft-Ebing used the *case history*, the account of a patient's illness, as his investigative tool. Because his primary interests were forensic medicine (medicine as applied to law) and psychopathology (the study of mental illness), he chose mostly extreme cases.

The theoretical basis of much of what Krafft-Ebing had to say has turned out to be wrong. However, by drawing together, for the first time, materials on sexual behavior in a systematic and reasoned manner, he prepared the ground for the foundations of sexology. Even though Krafft-Ebing was a highly respected figure, he came under considerable criticism. He justified dealing with forbidden sexual topics by declaring that "the sacred ministry of the physician, while obliging him to see everything, also permits him to say everything" (Krafft-Ebing, 1978).

*Sigmund Freud* also started his career as a physician, and his interest in sex was at first incidental to his more basic concern with personality development and psychopathology (Figure 1.6). Sexuality came to dominate his theories as the driving force behind human motivation. The two important concepts we owe to Freud are the unconscious and infantile sexuality.[4] Freud did not discover (or invent) either of these concepts (Whyte, 1960). He articulated them with such persuasiveness,

Figure 1.6   Sigmund Freud (1856–1939).

though, that they became highly influential in the modern Western world.

Freud had some dealings with the early sexologists but never quite joined their budding movement (Sulloway, 1979). Nonetheless, his work has had a far greater impact in making sexuality a subject to be reckoned with than anyone else's. Freud was wrong in a lot of ways. Some of his views have become objectionable, and their validity is by no means firmly established (Chapter 8). However, his theories provide a comprehensive and internally consistent account of sexual development and behavior.

The centrality of sex in the work of psychoanalytic theorists varies widely. Some of Freud's major disciples, like Carl Jung and

Figure 1.5   Richard von Krafft-Ebing (1840–1902).

[4]Freud's first major analysis of the unconscious is in the *Interpretation of dreams* published in 1900. Five years later appeared his *Three essays on the theory of sexuality*, in which the theory of infantile sexuality was first formulated. For Freud's complete works, see *The standard edition of the complete psychological works of Sigmund Freud*, edited by J. Strachey (Freud, 1957–1964). There are many biographies of Freud; an excellent one is by Gay (1988).

Alfred Adler, thought he put too much emphasis on sexuality. Others, like Wilheim Reich, thought Freud did not do full justice to it.

*Wilhelm Reich* (1897–1957) was a Viennese physician who rose to prominence in the early psychoanalytic movement. Reich was also a Marxist who became increasingly dissatisfied with Freud's neglect of social and political issues. Reich thought Marx's concept of alienation should be extended to include sexuality, because the way of life imposed by the capitalist system crippled the free and healthy expression of sexuality (Reich, 1969). Furthermore, all neuroses and character problems resulted from the damming up of sexual energy.

To rectify the neglect of political thinking in psychoanalysis and the neglect of sexuality in Marxism, Reich in 1929 organized the Socialist Society for Sexual Advice and Sexual Research. It proved an unworkable match; Reich was expelled both from the Communist and the psychoanalytic camps. In his later years (when he lived in the United States) Reich developed outlandish ideas about trapping "biological energy" in his "orgone box," and his work was discredited. Subsequently, he has been heralded as a champion of sexual and political freedom by radicals in the New Left (Robinson, 1976).

The establishment of sexology as a distinct discipline was mainly brought about by three other German physicians: Iwan Bloch, Albert Moll, and Magnus Hirschfeld. Through the leadership of these men and several other collaborators the field of sexuality was established at the turn of the century and thrived for a few decades until its suppression by the rise of Nazism (Haeberle, 1981).

*Iwan Bloch* (1872–1922) was a dermatologist with a special interest in the venereal diseases and a broadly educated man with an impressive fund of knowledge in the social sciences and humanities. Though he remained committed to the theories of sexual degeneracy that were espoused by the medical profession of his day, Bloch broke through the narrow confines of biology and introduced the perspectives of the social sciences (especially anthropology) into the study of sexuality. To reflect this multidisciplinary approach, in 1906 he coined the term *Sexualwissenschaft*—the "science of sex" or sexology.

*Albert Moll* (1862–1939) was a neuropsychiatrist. Though he lacked Bloch's erudition, Moll made up for it with his organizational skills. In 1913 he founded the International Society for Sex Research as well as the Society for Experimental Psychology. Moll was a man with great respect for institutions and social acceptability, traits that often brought him into conflict with the more radical Hirschfeld. His early contributions include monographs on homosexuality and the libido. His ideas on infantile sexuality (which may have influenced Freud) were given expression in his 1909 volume on the sexual life of the child.

*Magnus Hirschfeld* (1868–1935) was the most versatile and leading figure of early sexology (Figure 1.7). Aspiring first to be a writer, Hirschfeld switched to medicine. Starting as a general practitioner, he developed an early interest in sexual matters and became a full-time specialist in sex research and treatment, as well as an activist, organizer, and crusader for sexual freedom.

Figure 1.7   Magnus Hirschfeld (1868–1935).

Hirschfeld's primary interest was in homosexuality. A homosexual himself, he often took up the defense of other homosexuals in courts of law and tirelessly pursued the goal of reforming sex laws aimed at homosexuals.

Hirschfeld was just as enterprising as a researcher. In 1903, he surveyed 3000 university students and then almost twice as many metal workers, in an attempt to ascertain the prevalence of homosexuality (his response rates were better than many modern studies) (Lesser, 1967). In addition to a number of shorter works, Hirschfeld wrote a massive compendium of what was known about homosexuality in a series edited by Iwan Bloch. He coined the term "transvestism" and wrote the first systematic account of what we now call transsexualism. In 1928, he published his culminating work—a five-volume presentation of the field of sexology (Hoenig, 1977).

Hirschfeld's vision of sexology was an elaboration of Bloch's multifaceted view. In 1908 he used Bloch's term for sexology in the title of the first journal of sexology, (*Zeitschrift für Sexualwissenschaft*), which he edited. Along with Bloch, he was among the founders of the first sexological society. In 1919, Hirschfeld realized his greatest ambition with the founding of the world's first Institute for Sexology. Housed in an elegant building in Berlin, the Institute conducted research, provided clinical services (including premarital guidance), and gave medical-legal aid. It also served as a training center and housed a library with 20,000 volumes, 35,000 photographs, collections of art, and some 40,000 biographical case materials (Haeberle, 1982).

All of this and other promising developments (including sexological programs in two major universities) were stifled when the Nazis came to power. All three pioneers were Jewish, hence marked for persecution. Hirschfeld's ethnicity, homosexuality, and political radicalism proved to be a calamitous combination; his Institute was ransacked by a mob and its contents publicly burned in 1933—three months after Hitler came to power. (Hirschfeld was in France at the time, where he remained.)

The demise of sexology in Germany appears to have inhibited potential developments elsewhere. *Auguste Forel* (1848–1931) in Switzerland and *Henry Havelock Ellis* (1858–1939) in England (Figure 1.8) were contemporaries of the German sexologists with close ties to them. In their respective countries, they were unable to make as much progress to organize sexology.

Ellis, nonetheless, exerted a great deal of influence on the sexual attitudes of the English-speaking world. He did no original research, but gathered a vast amount of sexual materials in his *Studies in the Psychology of Sex*, which he wrote and periodically revised between 1896 and 1928 (Ellis, 1942). It made his scholarly reputation, but he was subjected early on to great deal of social disapproval.

Ellis and his wife Edith were both active in the women's movement. They also had an unconventional marriage, which was emotion-

Figure 1.8    Havelock Ellis (1858–1939).

Figure 1.9    Margaret Sanger (1883–1966).

ally close but precluded sex (each carried on affairs with other women, with mutual consent). He did not attain full sexual fulfillment until his later years. Ellis' personal experiences and difficulties with the Victorian morality of the time made him a persistent advocate of tolerance for sexual diversity. Because of his open and positive views of sex, Brecher (1969) has called him the "first of the Yea-Sayers."[5]

Largely absent from this cast of characters are women. The social climate of the Victorian era would have not tolerated their involvement in this field. Women who braved such criticism were usually social reformers who devoted their efforts to issues like birth control, which most directly affected women's lives. Examples are the work of *Marie Stokes* (1880–1958) in England and of *Margaret Sanger* (1883–1966) (Figure 1.9) in the United States.

[5]For Ellis' biography, see Grosskurth (1980); for his autobiography, Ellis (1939). Ellis' role in the modernization of sex is discussed in Robinson (1976).

It is also possible that sex research undertaken by women has gone unnoticed. For example, in 1973, Carl Degler discovered in the Stanford archives an elaborate survey conducted by *Clelia Duel Mosher* (1863–1940). Carried out between 1892 and 1920, it was a questionnaire study of the sexual attitudes of 45 women. The findings of this work have helped place Victorian female sexuality in a new light (Box 1.1) (Mahood and Wenburg, 1980).

Revival    Although the events in Germany of the 1930s were a serious setback, various people continued to study sexuality. In the United States, by the start of World War II, a number of behavioral investigations had been carried out as well as numerous clinical studies. (For a review of this work, see Kinsey et al., 1948). The full resurgence of these efforts, which marked the beginning of the modern field of sex research, did not start until Kinsey's work in the 1940s.

*Alfred C. Kinsey* (1894–1956) was a zoologist at Indiana University. He turned to the systematic study of human sexual behavior, prompted by the need to find answers to the questions his students put to him in a course on marriage, in which he had been prevailed upon to participate. From these early beginnings, Kinsey and his collaborators (Wardell B. Pomeroy, Clyde E. Martin, and Paul H. Gebhard) collected over 16,000 sex histories from people in all walks of life across the United States—a feat unprecedented and unequalled. Kinsey alone collected 7000 such histories—an average of two a day for ten years. He died, however, long before he could fulfill his goal of interviewing 100,000 individuals (Figure 1.10).[6]

The Kinsey studies on the sexual behavior of the male and the female, despite the passage of almost four decades, remain the most comprehensive and systematic source of informa-

[6]Kinsey left no autobiography. There are many brief accounts of his career: see Brecher (1969). Detailed biographies have been published by Christenson (1971) and Pomeroy (1972). Also see Robinson (1976).

# Box 1.1

## THE MOSHER SURVEY

In 1973 Carl Degler discovered in the Stanford University archives a questionnaire survey of the sexual attitudes of 45 American women, 70 percent of them born before 1870. These handwritten documents, never published at the time, constitute the first known sex survey ever conducted and a unique source on female sexuality in the 19th century.

The survey was the work of Clelia Duel Mosher, whose own life is an interesting study in Victorian womanhood (see the figure). Mosher was born in Albany, New York, in 1863 into a family of physicians—her father and four of her uncles were doctors. She began her survey when still an undergraduate at the University of Wisconsin in 1892 and did not conclude it until 1920; during this period she had obtained a masters degree from Stanford and an M.D. degree from Johns Hopkins. She spent most of her professional life at Stanford as a physician in the health service and professor of hygiene. Degler describes her life in Mahood and Wenburg (1980).

The women surveyed by Mosher were not representative of the general population but well-educated, middle-class wives of professional men. Their responses reveal a remarkable degree of sexual candor and contradict the stereotype of sexually inhibited Victorian womanhood.

The majority (35 out of 45) of Mosher's respondents felt the desire for coitus, independent of their husband's interest in sex; only nine said they never or rarely felt it. Mosher must have assumed that women regularly experience orgasm, because she asked not whether the woman experienced orgasm but whether she "always" reached orgasm during coitus: 35 percent said they "always" or "usually" did so; another 40 percent experienced orgasm "sometimes" or "not always." If the women born before 1875 are considered separately, the incidence of orgasm (at least once) is 82 percent—quite similar to the women in the Kinsey sample born between 1900 and 1920.

The comments these women made on sex are equally revealing. Sexual intercourse "makes more normal people"; "even if there are no children, men love their wives more if they continue this relationship, and the highest devotion is based upon it, a beautiful thing, and I am glad nature gave it to us"; "the desire of both husband and wife for this expression of their union seems to me the first and highest reason for intercourse. The desire for offspring is a secondary, incidental, although entirely worthy motive, but could never make intercourse right unless the mutual desire were also present" (quoted in Degler, 1980, p. 264).

On the other hand, these women also had a number of sexual anxieties. Fear of pregnancy colored their views, because contraceptives were not reliable. Despite their being well-educated, many said they knew nothing about sex before marriage. Of the 45 women, 25 reported having coitus once a week or less; 10 had it once or twice a week, and 9 more frequently. However, only 8 out of 37 respondents said they wanted intercourse weekly or more—so over half the women engaged in sex more frequently than they would have liked. In balance, though, the positive views of these Victorian women are the most impressive findings of the Mosher survey. (You can read about the whole survey in Mahood and Wenburg, 1980.)

Dr. Clelia Duel Mosher (1863–1940).

Figure 1.10    Alfred C. Kinsey (1894–1956).

tion on human sexual behavior. A number of studies have glibly compared themselves to Kinsey's work but come nowhere near it in scope and thoroughness.

The Institute for Sex Research founded by Kinsey (renamed the Kinsey Institute for Research in Sex, Gender, and Reproduction) has pursued other extensive investigations of sexual behavior, including studies of sex offenders and homosexuality. The Institute library also performs an outstanding archival and educational function with its collection of books, journals, films, and extensive pictorial materials and artifacts of relevance to sexuality.

Kinsey's work received such extensive public notice that in addition to describing the patterns of sexual behavior, it well may have changed them. The sex survey became a common tool as other investigators, sexual entrepreneurs, and journalists kept probing and prodding people to reveal their sexual lives. Popular books dealing with sex became a sub-

stantial industry, with modest contributions to our sexual knowledge.

The next threshold crossed in sex research was laboratory investigation of human sexual physiology. Kinsey had anticipated the need for direct observation of sexual activity, but the move from interviewing to observing did not take place until the 1960s with the studies of *William Masters* (a gynecologist) and his research associate, *Virginia Johnson* (Masters and Johnson, 1966).

Working with 694 volunteer men and women, aged 18 to 89, these investigators observed, monitored, and filmed the responses of the body during 10,000 orgasms attained through masturbation or coitus. Their findings established at least a preliminary understanding of the physiology of sex, a matter long neglected by experts in physiology and sexology. Their subsequent work with the treatment of sexual dysfunction established the modern field of sex therapy (Brecher, 1969; Robinson, 1976).

### The Field Today

The field of human sexuality today has three major components: research, education, and therapy.

Sex Research    Most research in sexuality is undertaken in universities. Biomedical scientists continue to explore the biological aspects of sex, but the majority of investigators of sexual behavior are behavioral scientists, many of them psychologists.

In some ways the field of human sexuality remains marginal compared to other disciplines. The quality of sex research, though rapidly improving, is still largely substandard compared to better established fields like psychology or biology. Its practitioners include both highly trained professionals and people with meager credentials. Reputations are all too often made through best-selling books rather than solid research or scholarly accomplishments.

There are two primary journals devoted to sex research: *Archives of Sexual Behavior* and

*Journal of Sex Research.* Over a dozen more specialized journals and newsletters also furnish useful information—for instance, the SIECUS *Report.* Furthermore, important research on sexuality is just as likely to be reported in the scholarly publications of other fields.

Sex Education   In various ways, educators have provided instruction in sexuality at the college level since the start of the century. Pioneers like Prince A. Morrow were primarily concerned with the prevention of venereal diseases. In the period following the Second World War, courses in marriage and the family became popular, but it was not until the 1960s that human sexuality courses like the one you are taking made their appearance.[7]

Although there are no comprehensive data on the number and nature of human sexuality courses in college, a 1986 survey of 225 institutions found that 41 percent had one or more courses in this area, and 44 percent of them were taught in the psychology department (Polyson et al., 1986). These figures are similar to a survey conducted over a decade earlier (Sheppard, 1974), which suggests that after expansion in the early 1970s, the teaching of sexuality in college has remained stable.

Human sexuality courses have proven highly popular with students; they are generally perceived by the faculty as academically marginal. Except for a few fledgling attempts to develop graduate-level programs, this area remains a neglected field in higher education. Most established academics who work in this area have their primary appointments in some other department.

Sex education for adolescents and children has been fraught with more controversy. Who should provide sexual instruction to youngsters, in what form, and for what purposes continue to be vexing problems (Chapter 8). There have been important developments in sex education over the past several decades. Yet there is still reason to be concerned with the level of adequacy of programs, which often operate with limited funding, self-taught instructors who have to work under a cloud of potential social disapproval, and so on.

The threat of AIDS now represents an unprecedented challenge, as well as opportunity, for sex education at all levels. Never before has there been as much public willingness to expose children to explicit sexual topics in school. How society will eventually deal with this issue remains to be seen.

The organization that has been most prominent (and most actively attacked) in efforts to promote sex education is *SIECUS* (Sex Information and Education Council of the United States) cofounded in 1960 and led by *Mary Steichen Calderone.* A wide concept of sexuality underlies the organization's philosophy:

> The SIECUS concept of *sexuality* refers to the totality of being a person. It includes all of those aspects of the human being that relate specifically to being boy or girl, woman or man, and is an entity subject to life-long dynamic change. Sexuality reflects our human character, not solely our genital nature. As a function of the total personality it is concerned with the biological, psychological, sociological, spiritual, and cultural variables of life which, by their effects on personality development and interpersonal relations, can in turn affect social structure (Brown, 1981, p. 252).

The standard argument against sex education has been that it intrudes upon the sexual innocence of children and fuels the flames of adolescent sexuality; thus, the argument goes, while attempting to inform, sex education encourages sexual experimentation with all its dire consequences. The advocates of sex education claim that it helps prevent sexually transmitted diseases, unwanted pregnancy, and crippling attitudes toward sexuality: by providing the right information and instilling the right attitudes, it leads to more fulfilling sexual lives.

---

[7]For an overview of sex education in the United States, see Kirkendall (1981). How human sexuality came to be taught in one major university is described in Katchadourian (1981). Also see McCary (1975), Anderson (1975), and Sarrel and Coplin (1971).

Sex Therapy    Most people with sexual dysfunctions like impotence and failure to reach orgasm have been treated by medical practitioners, clinical psychologists, and other counselors. Now a new field of sex therapy has emerged over the past two decades, with its own methods (Chapter 15). It is unclear whether this *new sex therapy* will evolve into a full-fledged specialty or be absorbed into the mainstream of established disciplines.

Despite its shortcomings, the field of sexuality is now poised to expand and occupy its rightful place as a subject worthy of study and instruction. After centuries of neglect and oppression, this vital topic deserves to be treated with the same honesty, rigor, and integrity that have been brought to bear on other aspects of human life.

## METHODS OF SEX RESEARCH

We have to approach a topic as complex as sexual behavior with a variety of research methods. Each method has its advantages and shortcomings, but a number of basic considerations apply to all of them. Let us address these issues first, before we turn to the specifics of each method.

### Basic Considerations

Problems of methodology are common in any field of behavioral research but especially pressing in sex research because of the novelty of the field, the peculiarities of the subject matter, and social prejudices. Still, sexual scientists have become increasingly sophisticated as the field of sexuality has opened up to more and better qualified investigators during the past decade (Jayne, 1986).

Purpose and Perspective    Every study must have a definite focus; a haphazard collection of data is of little value. There are so many facets and wrinkles to even the simplest sexual act that unless investigators set out with a clear idea of what they are investigating, they are likely to get lost.

The point is not to prove a preconceived idea. Instead, the starting point is a *hypothesis*, a tentative assertion that is subject to verification, restatement, or negation. The use of hypotheses helps to focus the investigation and to understand its outcome—to decide if the idea tested was right or wrong. There are innumerable studies that report that so many men do this and so many women do that. Although all carefully gathered data are interesting, it is hard to know what to make of such findings, which stand by themselves.

The Problem of Bias    Sex researchers, like other investigators, are members of a profession, heirs to intellectual traditions, and human beings with personal needs and aspirations. They have their own sexual values (to which they are entitled) and their prejudices (which they try to keep out of their work). Some may be either unaware of their biases or bent on furthering them through their work.

In these respects, sex researchers are not basically different from other behavioral scientists, except that there may be more axes to grind in this field than in others. A healthy skepticism (but not cynicism) is a good starting point in evaluating any piece of sex research.

The Choice of Variables    Investigators cannot look at every aspect of every issue they choose to study; they have to be selective. As a result, the kinds of questions they ask and how they ask them determine in part what answers they get. For example, if we want to know how often men and women desire sex, we might ask a random sample of volunteers to complete a questionnaire about the number of orgasms they had for the past month. After the proper statistical analyses, we find that men report more orgasms than women and we conclude that men desire sex more frequently than women. Now, is the number of orgasms per week a *valid* measure of sexual desire? If we want to know how often men and women desire sex, shouldn't we also ask them about the number of times they initiated sexual activity, regardless of the outcome? Or about the number of times their partners initiated sex, but they themselves declined? What about the number of sexual thoughts and fantasies they experienced, alone or with their partners? All of these factors are important components of sexual desire, though only some include orgasm. The number of orgasms people have may be an important aspect of their sexual lives but not an adequate measure of sexual desire.

A second problem is the *reliability* of the test instruments used. Whereas validity of a test or a variable ensures that it measures what it is supposed to measure, reliability is the consistency with which it measures it. To be reliable, the questions must elicit more or less the same answers when put to the subjects repeatedly. When we ask people to recall their sexual activities in the past, we might be concerned about the accuracy of recall and whether we would obtain the same pattern of results if we repeated the study at a later time.

Another potential pitfall is to assume that a given variable, such as orgasm, represents the same experience for men and women or people of different ages.

In addition to the problems we already mentioned in using orgasm as a measure of sexual desire, other psychosocial and situational factors could affect the number of orgasms women and men report. For example, suppose our volunteers are primarily heterosexual and prefer the "man-on-top" position for sexual intercourse. Because it may take longer for most women to achieve orgasm in this position, the man may often reach orgasm first. Unless the couple has the time and inclination to continue their lovemaking to bring the woman to orgasm, the sexual act may end there. Moreover, ideas about female and male sex roles may make it more difficult for women than for men to ask their partners to do what is necessary to bring them to orgasm. Similar considerations apply when we try to determine whether men and women respond more readily to a given set of erotic stimuli. The criteria for erotic stimuli have usually been set by men; the responses of women to such stimuli therefore may not be comparable to those of men.

**Ethical Considerations**    Investigators have generally been conscious of their responsibility not to harm their subjects. Currently more formal and stringent regulations are imposed by institutions and governmental agencies to ensure that human subjects are protected from harm. (Animal research is also regulated, but there is a far greater latitude in what can be done with animals.)

Protection from harm has several components. The study must not expose its subjects to pain, harm, or serious distress. We would not, for example, give pregnant women testosterone to study its androgenizing effects on the fetus. Nor would we expose children to sexual experiences with adults to see how that would affect their sexual development.

The issue of confidentiality is particularly important in research of sexual behavior. Kinsey and his collaborators devised an elaborate coding system that protected the identity of thousands of subjects. Clinical records are likewise considered privileged information. The revelation of the sexual details of a person's life could lead to scandal, social ostracism, marital strife, professional jeopardy, and legal action.

Even if the research is carefully designed to avoid harm, its consequences for subjects cannot be entirely predicted. For this reason it is essential that every participant give *informed consent* after being fully informed about what the experience will entail. To further protect them, subjects are debriefed after the experiment is over. The investigator clarifies the true nature of the study (if there was deception involved) and helps overcome whatever disturbing thoughts or feelings the subject may have as a result of the experience.

The use of deception raises its own special problems. There are experiments that are based on the subjects not knowing the true nature of the situations they are put in. With groups that are unlikely to admit outsiders, some investigators gain entry by pretending to be persons of similar sexual interest. For example, one anthropologist and his wife associated themselves with "swingers" to study group sex. They managed to stay sexually uninvolved through various excuses ("It's my wife's period") while sustaining the false assumption that they were active swingers themselves (Bartell, 1971).

Though such investigators do not intend to harm their subjects, the stealth with which such work is conducted and the absence of both informed consent and of debriefing raise questions about their propriety as research endeavors. The counterargument is that without such methods, certain areas of sexuality would be impossible to explore. Besides, our society permits their use by the police and investigative journalists.

Sampling   A basic aim of all behavioral research is to discover common patterns. We want to be able to make generalizations—statements that apply not to a few individuals but to entire populations. For instance, we would want to know how college students behave not only in one institution but everywhere; and how a particular sexual activity varies with age, marital status, socioeconomic class, or some other variable.

Information about the sexual behavior of a few individuals is not enough, but studying entire populations is usually not feasible. As a result, investigators must select a *sample*, a subset of the population they are interested in. If this sample is representative, or typical of the larger population, then the findings from the sample can be generalized to the rest of the population.

There are many methods of sampling. A common method is *random sampling*, in which every member of the population has an equal likelihood to be selected by chance. Thus, to find out how often the members of a freshman class masturbate, the question is asked to a subgroup of freshmen who have been selected by lot (the proper size of the sample for a given purpose is determined by a number of statistical considerations).

Random samples are not always adequate. In the above example, there may be too few women, blacks, or Catholics in the freshman class chosen randomly; if we expect these variables to make a significant difference, then we cannot rely on chance alone to yield appropriate ratios of freshmen from the three subgroups. We could better achieve such representation by relying on a *stratified sample,* in which members from each subgroup are randomly selected and certain to be present in appropriate proportions within the overall sample.

Virtually all general studies of sexual behavior suffer from serious *sampling bias.* The nature of such bias varies with the type of study and often is due to the unwillingness of chosen subjects to participate. Thus, even if the sample is chosen randomly, low response rate can make it into a *self-selected sample,* which is probably less representative. Other forms of sampling bias are specific to particular types of studies. For example, in studies of gay men, samples of younger men are likely to be unrepresentative of the total population (Harry, 1986); or in studies of the psychophysiology of sexual response, volunteers are likely to be sexually less inhibited than most others (Morokoff, 1986).

Studies based on questionnaire responses and face-to-face interviews have their own biases (Catania et al., 1986). Because people with conservative sexual values, and presumably more restrictive sexual patterns, are less likely to participate in a sexual survey or volunteer to be subjects in a sexual study, most studies convey an overly liberal picture. On the other hand, socially problematic or unconventional behaviors tend to be underreported to the extent that subjects refuse to reveal them.

No general study of sexual behavior has yet been conducted whose findings could be extended to large segments of the population, let alone the country as a whole. Nonetheless, it is possible to extract some valid findings from flawed and biased samples. Beware, though, of studies that claim to measure prevalence, such as the proportion of people engaged in a given sexual behavior, within the overall population (Brecher and Brecher, 1986).

Use of Statistics   Investigators gather, organize, and interpret information through statistics, which are mathematical techniques to analyze quantitative data. Statistics are a powerful tool in helping us to understand sexual behavior, but they can be abused by conveying a false sense of accuracy. They can be especially misleading when the sample on which they are based is highly selective. Thus, in a study where only 5 percent of the people contacted respond, even if 90 percent say yes to a question, you still do not know what 95 percent of the whole sample would say.

Given the wide variation in sexual behavior, it is especially important that we have a general basis for comparison. The fact that a person has one orgasm per day, month, or year means little if we do not know how the larger group to which the person belongs behaves sexually as a whole. By the same token, statistics help us realize that the concept of sexual behavior is an abstraction: in reality, many different groups and individuals within them behave in many different ways; there is not one but many patterns of sexual behavior. Even when careful study has uncovered the patterns of behavior in a given group, this information cannot be automatically applied to all its members.

*Averages* tell us about clusters of people, not individual human beings. To understand a person you must study that person. For instance, Figure 1.11 shows the average (mean)

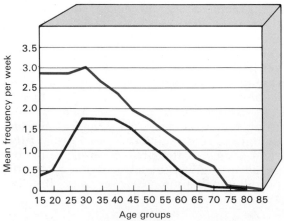

Figure 1.11    Average frequency of orgasm for males and females by age.

number of orgasms per week (from any source) for the male and female subjects in the Kinsey surveys. Individuals in that study had frequencies well above and below the average. Therefore it helps to know the range of *variance* for the group. Studies of individuals and of groups are meant to complement each other, not substitute for each other.

Statistical measures are not always necessary. The study of a single case may be highly revealing. Writers and artists do not work with representative samples; yet they can attain profound insights into human sexual behavior. Statistics are but one tool, and they should be neither uncritically accepted nor blindly rejected.

### Clinical Research

Investigations that study patients or clients under care are referred to as *clinical research* (from Greek for "bedside"). Traditionally this work has been the domain of physicians, but more recently clinical psychologists, social workers, marriage and family counselors have joined the clinical field with their own special perspectives.

Clinical research may consist of a single *case study,* or it may be based on a series of cases. The research component in clinical work may be part of the broader treatment procedure or conducted separately. The tradition of single case study continues, but clinical research in sexuality is now more typically conducted on larger groups of patients, with more emphasis on control groups and the quantitative analysis of data.

The strength of the clinical approach is threefold. First, clinical investigators tend to be well-trained professionals. Any enterprising journalist is at liberty to conduct a magazine survey, but to be permitted to treat patients and clients, formal training and certification are required. Second, clinical research has a higher likelihood of focusing on significant issues. People seek treatment because they are hurting; hence clinicians deal with people with real problems and are less likely to fiddle with contrived issues. Third, the clinical setting allows deeper investigations. Even short-term psychological therapy usually entails a greater intensity of contact than the typical research interview or questionnaire.

The shortcomings of the clinical approach are the flip side of its advantages. The fact that clinicians see their research subjects personally and over extended periods of time means that they can only deal with a limited number of such subjects (though cases from many sources may be pooled together). These subjects are self-selected and therefore unlikely to be representative of the general population. Furthermore, the case studies that get published often involve dramatic and atypical situations.

These shortcomings are compounded by the fact that subjects of clinical research are in distress and therefore may behave in special ways. The clinical context is not neutral nor geared for dispassionate inquiry. The primary purpose of the encounter is treatment; both investigator and subject have a personal stake in the process that may well interfere with the objectivity with which issues should be studied. Therapists may only want to hear what fits with their theoretical bias, and patients may oblige by saying what the therapists want to hear.

Finally, even clinicians who are well-trained as therapists, they often have substantially less training in experimental methodology and statistics. They may draw conclusions about normal sexual behavior from case histories that would not hold up under more carefully controlled empirical investigations.

In sum, the clinical approach provides the deepest information on the smallest number of people with regard to real-life concerns, but considerations of pathology and cure are most likely to color the behaviors being observed.

The Research Interview
The research interview has much in common with taking a case history, the story of a patient's illness. In taking a *sex history*, the investigator inquires into various aspects of sexual behavior or focuses on a particular type of activity.

In the *structured interview*, a predetermined set of issues is explored and the same questions are put to all subjects. In the *open-ended interview*, subjects are encouraged to reveal their sex life spontaneously with minimal guidance or prodding. The former approach yields more systematic and uniform data; the latter results in more spontaneous and free revelations. The two methods are complementary.

Unlike clinical research, which deals with patients, the research interview method uses a broad, randomly chosen group of subjects. This advantage, however, is often not realized because only some of the subjects selected agree to participate, which results in a self-selected sample. What these people say may not be representative of people who choose not to take part in the interview.

Another drawback is the relatively superficial contact between interviewer and subject. Particularly in a sensitive area like sexual behavior, a person may not reveal intimate details to a virtual stranger who, unlike the clinician, is not there to help. If we add failings of memory and the tendency to conceal or exaggerate sexual experiences, then what we can learn from research interviews becomes further compromised.

Still, in the hands of a skillful researcher like Kinsey, the research interview can produce a wealth of information over a matter of hours. Box 1.2 discusses the best-known surveys. Because of its scope and historical importance, we consider the Kinsey studies in greatest detail. Though other studies have used the interview method, none has come close to the Kinsey effort in magnitude. Typically, interviews are conducted to supplement a larger questionnaire study. For example, in the Hunt survey, subjects were interviewed in addition to the 2000 questionnaire respondents. In other cases, interviews have provided a convenient device to obtain titillating vignettes, to dress up the drab data obtained by other means.

Questionnaires
The questionnaire is an extension of the structured interview. The subject responds to a set of written questions instead of voicing answers

# Box 1.2

## SEX SURVEYS

The studies of sexual behavior by Alfred Kinsey and his associates were the most ambitious effort at sex research based on interviews. After four decades they remain unsurpassed in their scope, sophistication, and social impact.

Kinsey and his associates undertook extensive training as interviewers. They relied on a standard set of questions to obtain comparable answers and the hundreds of questions they put to their subjects included numerous cross-checks (such as comparing answers given by husbands and wives) to ensure the reliability of the responses. They also memorized their codes so that the answers were recorded directly in code, allowing greater accuracy and confidentiality.

Between 1938 and 1950 these researchers interviewed more than 16,000 persons. The samples used as the bases of the reports consisted of 5940 female and 5300 male residents of the United States.

Kinsey was aware that it would be difficult to get a random sample of the population to participate in his study; many were likely to refuse, leaving an unrepresentative group. Instead he selected a wide variety of groups (such as churches, prisons, colleges) and then tried to persuade everyone within these groups to be interviewed. In one-quarter of the groups, he managed to obtain 100 percent samples—a sex history was obtained for every member. The groups were drawn from many sectors of society.

The 11,240 people whose histories were analyzed included a wide variety of ages, marital status, educational levels, occupations, geographical locations, religious denominations, and so on. All these groups were represented in sufficient numbers to permit comparison, so the Kinsey sample was *stratified*. It was not *representative*, because each group in the sample population was not proportionate to the size of that group in the population at large. Lower educational levels and rural groups were underrepresented. Some groups were not represented at all: for example, all of the subjects whose histories were used were white; Kinsey collected histories from blacks, but not enough to permit statistical analysis. Three-quarters of the women subjects had been to college. Many of the lower-class males were ex-convicts. Most subjects were representative of the white, urban, Protestant, college-educated population of the northeastern United States. Kinsey was aware of these sampling problems and made no claims to the contrary. He called it a study of sexual behavior within certain groups of the human species, not a study of the sexual behavior of all cultures and of all races (Kinsey et al., 1948; 1953).

In the early 1970s, the Playboy Foundation sponsored a national sex survey that was carried out by an independent market survey and behavioral research organization. The sample consisted of 2026 adults randomly chosen from the phone directories of 24 cities in the United States. Its 982 males and 1044 females paralleled closely the United States population of persons 18 years old and over. However, not everyone is listed in a phone directory; therefore the sample cannot be said to be representative, especially in light of the fact that 80 percent of those contacted refused to participate.

The data were gathered by means of an extensive self-administered questionnaire. An additional sample of 100 men and 100 women were selected for more intensive investigation through interviews by Morton Hunt and Bernice Kohn, both professional writers. Hunt wrote the report, so we refer to it as the Hunt survey (Hunt, 1974). Though hardly in the same class as the Kinsey survey, the Hunt survey is useful as a point of comparison with the Kinsey results two decades earlier.

In the late 1970s a questionnaire study of female sexuality by Shere Hite attracted wide public notice (Hite, 1976). Its respondents were reached mainly through women's groups and recruited through magazines and newsletters. After all was said and done, only 3000 persons responded out of the 100,000 who had received questionnaires—a response rate of 3 percent. A similar study was done with 8000 men (with a response rate of 6 percent) (Hite, 1981). A third volume on women and love was based on a sample of about 4500 women, out of 100,000 contacted—a response rate of 4.5 percent (Hite, 1987).

The Hite reports have been criticized for being

based on unrepresentative samples, the author's polemical style, and political agenda. Yet the personal experiences of Hite's subjects make compelling reading. At some level, what they say must resonate with the thoughts and feelings of countless others, hence the popularity of her books. (For critiques of Hite's latest book, see Wallis, 1987).

The ultimate in the mass gathering of questionnaire data is the magazine survey. A magazine prints the questionnaire in an issue and invites its readership to respond. Those who respond constitute the study sample. Given the large readership of some magazines, even a 1 percent response may yield thousands of responses. The results cannot be generalized even to the readership of magazines, which itself is hardly representative of the population at large. Sex surveys of this sort have been conducted by *Psychology Today* (Athanasiou et al., 1970), *Redbook* (Tavris and Sadd, 1977), *Ladies Home Journal* (Schultz, 1980), *Cosmopolitan* (Wolfe, 1981), and *Playboy* (Peterson et al., 1983). Within its limitations, such information can be of interest. Numerous other sex surveys have been carried out with more limited populations and objectives. College students are the most common subjects of such studies.

---

to an interviewer. Just as it takes skill and training to be a good interviewer, the construction of an effective questionnaire is a difficult task that requires special expertise.

The main strengths of the questionnaire method are in the large numbers of subjects that it can easily reach, the consistency with which it presents its questions, and the opportunity it provides for comparing large numbers of responses to the same questions. It took heroic effort for the Kinsey group to interview some 16,000 subjects; far less skillful investigators with much less effort have gotten responses from ten times as many respondents.

On the other hand, the questionnaire method suffers from poor response rates. Whether people respond more truthfully to a person or to a questionnaire is hard to settle. It is possible that under the cloak of anonymity, respondents are more truthful in response to a questionnaire; but the presence of an interviewer enhances the chances that the subject understands the questions and responds seriously. The interviewer can also probe a particular area, asking more questions and pursuing leads.

Questionnaires are more objective tools than case studies, but they are by no means free of bias. The way that the questions are phrased may affect the answers. Apart from such "loading," subjects are likely to respond, just as they do in other contexts, in the direction of social desirability; that is, they give the answers that they think are compatible with dominant social values or the expectations of the investigator.

The questionnaire approach thus is the opposite extreme from the case study—it provides more superficial information for larger numbers of people over a shorter period of time. Many questionnaire studies have been conducted over the past two decades. We describe some of the best-known ones in Box 1.2.

The examples of research we have cited so far have all been general studies of sexual behavior. These same methods have also been used to focus on specific forms of behavior (such as premarital sex) or special facets of a given behavior (such as the interpersonal aspects of homosexual interactions). We shall often refer to such specialized research.

### Direct Observation and Experimentation

In the study of sexual behavior, direct observation, participant observation, and experimentation have had limited scope so far. Among the reasons are the requirements of privacy that shroud sexual experience in most cultures. The most significant and thorough application of direct observation in sex research has been so far in laboratory studies, such as those conducted by Masters and Johnson. However, in this work the primary focus was on the physiological aspects of sexual function.

There is a long tradition of participant observation in anthropology, but little of it has been applied to studying sexual behavior. It is easier, of course for an anthropologist to witness a marriage ceremony than to be present when the sexual union is consummated. Therefore anthropologists frequently derive inferences from informants' self-reports and from various observations rather than eyewitness accounts of sexual behavior.

Experimentation is even more ticklish in sex research because it entails the most active intrusion on the part of the researcher. Direct observations may involve no more than simply watching what people would be doing anyway, such as engaging in coitus; but in an experimental setup, the subjects would be induced to perform certain acts in prescribed ways to fulfill the experimenter's purposes. The increasingly stringent standards and controls that have been instituted in recent years to ensure the safety of experimental subjects are difficult to satisfy in sexual experiments. Nevertheless, a number of such approaches has been used. One example is the exposure of subjects to sexually arousing materials while special instruments monitor physiological responses.

More typically, investigators rely on the effects of so-called "natural experiments." For example, they cannot give a pregnant woman hormones, but they can study a woman already exposed to hormones to find out the effects on her child's development (Chapter 10).

You will read about research of all kinds in this book. Remember as we go the pros and cons, the benefits and pitfalls of each method we have been describing. Some studies contradict each other or give small pieces of a greater puzzle. You will find yourself sometimes confronted with several choices or alternative explanations. That is one of the reasons why sexuality is an exciting field. There is plenty of room for you to interpret, to judge, and to draw your own conclusions.

## REVIEW QUESTIONS

1. What are the main features of the biological, psychosocial, and humanistic perspectives in the study of human sexuality?

2. What are the contributions of the pioneers in the field of sex research?

3. What are the relative strengths and weaknesses of the questionnaire and interview methods of studying sexual behavior?

4. In what ways do the biases of researchers and subjects interfere with studies in sexual behavior?

5. What are the strengths and weaknesses of the clinical approach to the study of sexual dysfunction, compared to other methods of investigation?

## THOUGHT QUESTIONS

1. Why has sex research been neglected for so long?

2. What positive and negative factors should a person take into consideration in deciding to become a sex researcher?

3. How could you study premarital sex at your college?

4. How would you combine the insights from biology, behavioral science, and the humanities to study masturbation?

5. In what kinds of sex research would you feel comfortable as a subject? Is studying sexual behavior an unethical intrusion into people's privates lives?

## SUGGESTED READINGS

Bullough, V. (Ed). (1979). *The frontiers of sex research.* Buffalo, N.Y.: Prometheus. A series of essays on various aspects of sex research.

Frayser, S. G., and Whitby, T. (1987). *Studies in human sexuality.* Littleton, Co.: Libraries Unlimited. An extensive annotated guide to books in the field of sexuality, covering most major topics. An excellent source.

*Journal of Sex Research* (1986). Vol. 22, no. 1. A series of articles on current methodological problems in sex research.

Robinson, P. (1976). *The modernization of sex.* New York: Harper & Row. A historical analysis and intellectual critique of the work of Havelock Ellis, Alfred Kinsey, and Masters and Johnson.

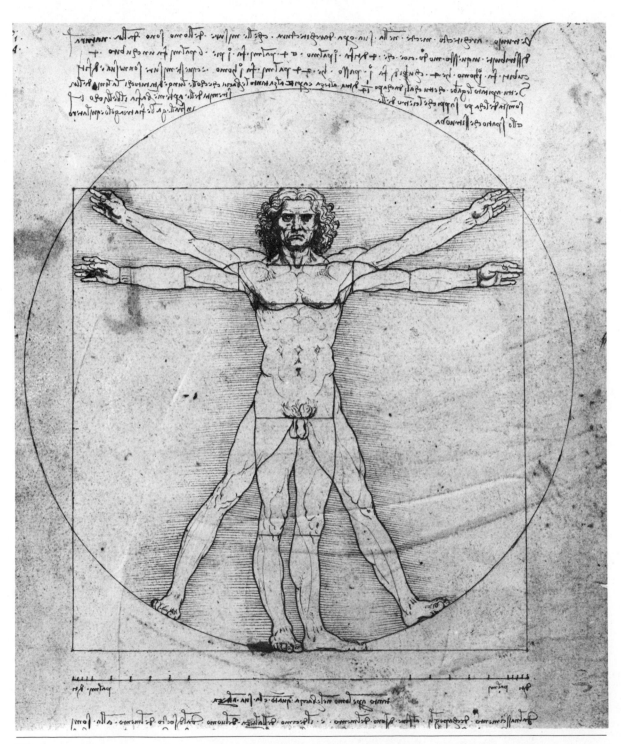

# PART 1

# Sexual Structure and Function

# Sexual Anatomy

CHAPTER

2

THE REPRODUCTIVE SYSTEM
  Sexual Reproduction
  The Basic Plan
FEMALE SEX ORGANS
External Sex Organs
  The Mons Pubis
  The Major Lips
  The Minor Lips
  The Clitoris
  The Urethral Opening
  The Vaginal Opening
Internal Sex organs
  The Ovaries
  The Fallopian Tubes
  The Uterus
  The Vagina
  Bulbourethral Glands
Breasts
MALE SEX ORGANS

External Sex Organs
  The Penis
  The Scrotum
Internal Sex Organs
  The Testes
  The Epididymis
  The Vas Deferens
  The Urethra
  Accessory Organs
HOW GERM CELLS DEVELOP
Development of Sperm
Development of the Ovum
HOW THE REPRODUCTIVE
  SYSTEM DEVELOPS
Differentiation of the Gonads
Differentiation of the Genital
  Ducts
Differentiation of the External
  Genitals

OUTLINE

*Praise be given to God, who has placed man's greatest pleasure in the natural parts of woman, and has destined the natural parts of man to afford the greatest enjoyment to woman.*

NEFZAWI,
*The Perfumed Garden*
(15th century)

In physical terms, sexual organs are no different than the organs of other bodily systems. They are all built to carry out a set of specialized functions. Vital organs like the heart and lungs keep us alive as individuals. Sexual organs let us survive as a species.

In this chapter we will focus on the anatomy of the reproductive system, with special attention to organs like the vagina and the penis, which play a key role in our sexual activities. Remember, though, that sexual behavior involves far more than the use of sex organs. Your whole body is part of your sexual being. So are your ideas and your feelings.

One day we may be able to think and talk about penises and vaginas as comfortably as we do about noses and mouths; but that day is not here yet. If you are approaching this chapter with mixed feelings, you are not alone.

Your attitudes toward your body were established in childhood, but you can change them as an adult. Traditionally, children in our society have been given little accurate information about their genitals, often not even a correct name. Currently, parents are more forthright, but explanations can still be confused and awkward.

We absorb a great many negative attitudes toward our sexual parts. We learn that they are somehow "dirty," maybe because of their closeness to the outlets of feces and urine. At the same time we learn how desirable it is to be "well-developed." Our society has a love-hate relationship towards sexual functions and behavior.

Since the 1960s sexual attitudes in Western societies have become more open, accepting, and informed. Nudity and genital exposure are now fairly commonplace in pictures, in films, and at some beaches. But some people worry that we are losing our modesty and blunting our sexual sensibility.

Traditionally, men have been fascinated and excited by female genitals, but simultaneously they have feared and deprecated them. Males often are ambivalent about their own genitals as well, both exaggerating their importance and worrying about their size,
shape, and capacity for performance. Female attitudes toward the genitals, their own or those of males, have had much less public expression, but women too have combined pride and pleasure with shame and confusion. Such attitudes have changed considerably in recent times.

It is not necessary to know detailed anatomy to have an active sex life, but some knowledge of anatomy is useful for other reasons.

First, by learning what your sex organs consist of and how they work, you can stop wondering and worrying.

Second, sexual activity can cause pregnancy and disease. To control the first and to avoid the second you need to know the parts of the body that are involved.

Finally, a responsible use of your sexuality requires that you accept your body and your partner's body. Beyond the practical benefits of learning about the "plumbing," a knowledge of anatomy is your foundation for a healthy acceptance of sexuality.

## THE REPRODUCTIVE SYSTEM

One of the basic functions of the sex organs is *reproduction,* the generation of offspring. Of course, not every single one of us can or should have children. Even if you want to become a parent someday, much of your sexual activity will have nothing to do with having children.

Nonetheless, the shape and structure of our sex organs can be best understood in terms of their reproductive functions. The reason is that the sex organs have evolved over millions of years to enhance their reproductive success. The type of organs that have been most successful in this respect are the ones that have survived.

Sexual Reproduction   Does all life depend on sex, then? No—sexual reproduction was not the original form nor is it the only method of generating offspring. *Asexual reproduction* is still the way that many simpler forms of life perpetuate themselves. An amoeba splits in two or the arm of a starfish breaks off and gives rise to a new organism without any sex. The offspring is identical to the parent, and there is no division into male and female forms (Campbell, 1987). Perhaps you have read about cloning. Scientists are trying to reproduce creatures from just one body cell. Cloning also would be asexual.

*Sexual reproduction* first evolved among marine organisms. It is the predominant form by which most species reproduce today. No one knows how and why the shift from asexual to sexual reproduction took place, but its evolutionary consequences have been enormous. Without it, complex organisms like ourselves could not have evolved (Raven and Johnson, 1986).

Sexual reproduction does not always mean "having sex." For example, female fish release a mass of mature *ova*, or eggs, into the water, and then male fish release *sperm* over the eggs. This *external fertilization* would not work for land animals, because eggs and sperm would dry up without seawater. Instead, land animals rely on *internal fertilization*. The male deposits sperm directly into the female's body to fertilize the egg. This act of *copulation*, or sexual intercourse, is the way reptiles, birds, and mammals (which include humans) reproduce.

The key feature of sexual reproduction is that two different cells—one from a male, the other from a female—combine. Because two different parents contribute genetic material, their offspring have tremendous diversity. Think of the differences among brothers and sisters you know. Such genetic diversity helps individuals to adapt and survive in many environments.

Becoming a human parent is a complex experience in psychological and social terms. In a plain biological sense, it is a process hundreds of millions of years old; we share it with a wide variety of other life forms.

The Basic Plan    Whether you are female or male, your reproductive system is built on the same basic plan to fulfill similar functions. The first is the production and transport of *germ cells* (*sperm* in the male; *ova* in the female). The

second is the production of *sex hormones,* which are secreted into the bloodstream (Chapter 4).

The reproductive system of both sexes centers in the *bony pelvis.* The main parts of each system and their relationship to the bony pelvis are shown in Figure 2.1. The male pelvis has a heavier bone structure; the female pelvis has a broader outlet to allow the passage of the baby during birth.

The bones of the pelvis consist of the *sacrum* (the triangular end of your backbone) and a pair of *hip bones* that are attached to the sacrum behind and to each other in front, at the *symphysis pubis.* The sexual organs are held in place by muscles that stretch across the opening of the pelvis and ligaments and sheets of connective tissue that attach them to the surrounding tissues and the pelvic bone. Although part of the same reproductive system, the organs that are located outside the body pelvis are referred to as the *external sex organs;* those inside the abdomen are the *internal sex organs.* The external sex organs are also called the *genitals.* They are the primary objects of sexual arousal and stimulation. If you are a woman, a mirror can help you to see your genitals more easily.

## FEMALE SEX ORGANS

### External Sex Organs
A woman's genitals are collectively called the *vulva* ("covering"). They include the *mons pubis,* the *major lips* and *minor lips,* the *clitoris,* and the *vaginal introitus* or opening (Williams and Warwick, 1980; Hollingshead and Rosse, 1985).[1]

The Mons Pubis    The mons pubis (or *mons veneris,* "mound of Venus") is the soft, rounded elevation of fatty tissue over the pubic symphysis. After it becomes covered with hair dur-

---

[1]The many colloquial names for the female genitals include: cunt, pussy, slit, box, quim, snatch, twat, beaver, and bearded clam. Ancient sex manuals like *The Perfumed Garden* have even more fanciful terms like: crusher, silent one, yearning one, glutton, bottomless restless, biter, sucker, wasp, hedgehog, starling, hot one, delicious one, and so on (Nefzawi, 1964 ed.). Such designations reveal a good deal about cultural attitudes toward female sexuality.

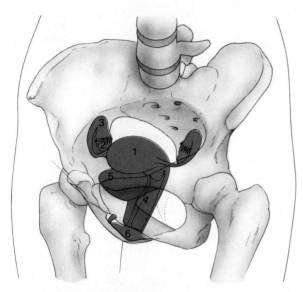

1. Uterus 2. Ovary 3. Fallopian tube
4. Vagina 5. Bladder 6. Labia

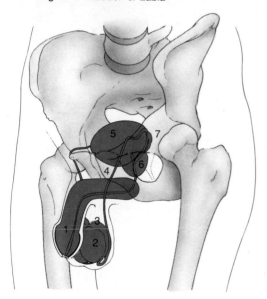

1. Penis 2. Testicle 3. Epididymis
4. Spermatic cord 5. Bladder 6. Prostate
7. Seminal vesicle

Figure 2.1    The reproductive system and the bony pelvis. (Top) Female organs: (1) uterus, (2) ovary, (3) fallopian tube, (4) vagina, (5) bladder, (6) labia majora and labia minora. (Bottom) Male organs: (1) penis, (2) testicle, (3) epididymis, (4) spermatic cord, (5) bladder, (6) prostate, (7) seminal vesicle.

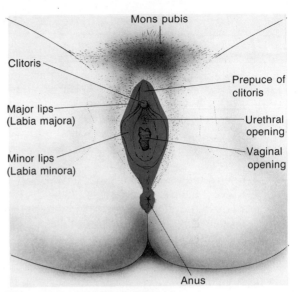

Figure 2.2    Female genitals.

ing puberty, the mons is the most visible part of the female genitals. It is quite responsive to sexual stimulation.

The Major Lips    The major lips or *labia majora* are two elongated folds of skin whose appearance varies a great deal: some are flat and hardly visible behind thick pubic hair; others bulge prominently. Ordinarily they are close together. The space between the major lips is the *pudendal cleft;* it becomes visible only when the lips are parted.

The outer surfaces of the major lips, covered with skin of a darker color, grow hair at puberty. Their inner surfaces are smooth and hairless. Within these folds of skin are bundles of smooth muscle fibers, nerves, and blood vessels.

The Minor Lips    The minor lips or *labia minora* are two lighter-colored hairless folds of skin between the major lips. Into the space between them open the vagina and urethra, as well as the ducts of Bartholin's glands (discussed below). The upper portions of the minor lips form a single fold of skin over the clitoris, which is called the *prepuce of the clitoris,* or the clitoral hood. The minor lips consist of spongy tissues, which become engorged (filled with blood) and swollen during sexual excitement.

# Box 2.1

## FEMALE CIRCUMCISION

The practice of female circumcision is far less known than its male counterpart, yet it has been widespread in some cultures and continues to be practiced, mainly on the African continent. Over 20 million African women are estimated to have undergone some version of this procedure (Remy, 1979).

As the counterpart of male circumcision (Box 2.4), the term "female circumcision" should be restricted to the removal of the prepuce of the clitoris, but it is usually extended to other procedures, such as the amputation of the clitoris (*clitoridectomy*) and *infibulation*, which involves cutting and sewing the edges of the major lips together, which blocks access to the vaginal area (except for a small opening to let out urine and menstrual blood). This closure makes coitus impossible; when the woman is deemed entitled to engage in intercourse, the orifice is enlarged by stretching it open.

Although the term "Pharaonic circumcision" is sometimes applied loosely to these procedures, there is no evidence that they were practiced by ancient Egyptians. It is not required in Judaism; only the Falashas, the black Jews of Ethiopia, observe it, presumably in imitation of neighboring groups (Gregersen, 1983).

These practices have been widely criticized. They interfere with female sexual responsiveness and health. The idea of sewing up the female genitals until the "rightful owner" can have access to them is a flagrant example of women being treated as property. Yet these procedures are defended by the societies that practice them on the grounds that cultures have the right to fashion their own rituals.*

The Western world has had its own version of female genital alterations. Early in the 19th century, "declitorization" was used both in Europe and the United States as a medical treatment for female masturbation, lesbianism, lack of sexual response ("frigidity"), and "excessive" sexual desire ("nymphomania").

*For more detailed accounts of these practices, see Gregersen (1983); Hayes (1975); Huelsman (1976); Paige (1978b); and Taba (1979).

---

They are also highly sensitive to erotic stimulation.

From front to back the minor lips surround the clitoris, the external urethral opening, and the vaginal opening. The anus, which is completely separate from the external genitals, lies farther back.

The Clitoris   The *clitoris* ("enclosed") consists of two masses of erectile spongy tissue (*corpora cavernosa*).[2] Most of it is covered by the upper folds of the minor lips, but its free, rounded tip, the *glans*, projects beyond it.

The clitoris becomes engorged with blood during sexual excitement. Richly endowed with nerves, it is highly sensitive, an important focus of sexual stimulation, which is its sole function. Given its importance for female sexual arousal, the clitoris has recently become the focus of research (Lowry and Lowry, 1976; Lowry, 1978). Some cultures subject it to ritual alteration (see Box 2.1).

The Urethral Opening   The external urethral opening or *meatus* ("passage") is the small, median slit of the female *urethra,* which conveys urine and is totally independent of the reproductive system. Among some women, however, there may be a discharge of fluid through the urethra during orgasm, which some people consider to be a female ejaculate (Chapter 3).

The Vaginal Opening   The vaginal introitus, or opening, is visible only when the inner lips are

[2]Colloquial terms for the clitoris include "clit," "button," and more fanciful terms like "little boy in the boat" (Rodgers, 1972).

parted. It is easy to tell from the urethral opening by its larger size and lower location. Its appearance depends to a large extent on the shape and condition of the *hymen*. This delicate membrane, which only exists in the human female, has no known physiological function, but its psychological and cultural significance as a "sign" of virginity has been enormous.

The hymen varies in shape and size and may surround the vaginal orifice, bridge it, or serve as a sievelike cover (Figure 2.3). Most girls' hymens will permit passage of a finger (or tampon), but cannot accommodate an erect penis without tearing. However, a flexible hymen will occasionally withstand intercourse. On the other hand, the hymen may be torn accidentally. These possibilities make the presence of the hymen unreliable evidence for virginity. In childbirth the hymen is torn further; only fragments remain attached to the vaginal opening. There is almost always some opening to the outside through the intact hymen. However, in rare instances the hymen is a tough fibrous tissue that has no opening (*imperforate hymen*). This condition is usually detected after a girl begins to menstruate and the products of successive menstrual periods accumulate, swelling the vagina and uterus. It is corrected by surgery, with no aftereffects.

Underneath the major and minor lips are several sets of muscles (especially the *pubococcygeus*) that are important to sexual function in women (Figure 2.4). They form a muscular ring around the lower end of the vagina. Such

## Box 2.2

### DEFLORATION

The hymen is an exclusively human body part. No other animals have it. Why and how the hymen evolved is not clear, but most societies seem to have made the most if it. The old custom of parading the blood-stained sheets on the wedding night as proof of the bride's chastity has been practiced in both Western and Eastern cultures, and persists in some societies. Egyptian peasants test for the virginity of the bride before the wedding night by the bridegroom wrapping a piece of cloth around his index finger and inserting it into the bride's vagina (Gregersen, 1983).

*Defloration* ("stripping of flowers") is the tearing of the hymen through intercourse. Where it has been thought to pose a magical threat, special men or women have been assigned to carry it out. In various cultures, horns, stone phalluses, or other implements have been used in ritual deflorations. Among the seminomadic Yungar of Australia, girls were deflowered a week before marriage by two old women. If a girl's hymen was discovered at this time not to be intact, she could be starved, tortured, mutilated, or even killed.

Mosaic law took proof of virginity seriously. To refute trumped-up charges that the bride was not a virgin, the parents had to show her stained garment. If convicted of falsely accusing the bride, the groom had to pay 100 pieces of silver to her father and lost the right ever to divorce her ("because he has given a bad name to a virgin of Israel"). If the accusation could not be refuted, the woman was stoned to death at the door of her father's house (Deuteronomy 22:1–21).

Actually, the hymen is not a reliable badge of virginity (or "maidenhead"). It can be ruptured by vigorous physical activity and masturbation, but sexual intercourse sometimes leaves it intact.

Under optimal circumstances, first coitus is an untraumatic event: in the heat of sexual excitement the woman feels minimal pain, and bleeding is generally slight. What sometimes makes the experience painful is the muscular tension that an anxious, unprepared, or unwilling woman experiences in response to clumsy and forcible attempts at penetration. In anticipation of such difficulties, some women with no premarital sexual experience used to have their hymens stretched or cut surgically before their wedding nights with the knowledge and consent of their grooms. By contrast, some women who have lost their hymen have had it "restored" through plastic surgery, a procedure that is reportedly popular in Japan.

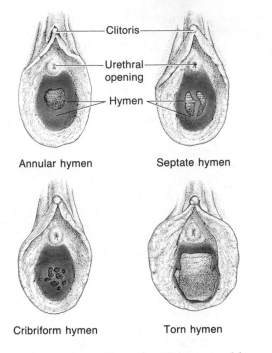

Annular hymen                Septate hymen

Cribriform hymen             Torn hymen

Figure 2.3  Types of hymens. (Top two and lower left) Intact hymens. (Lower right) The remnants of the hymen in a woman who has given birth.

muscular rings that constrict bodily orifices are known as *sphincters.* Women can voluntarily flex these muscles or involuntarily tense them, narrowing the vaginal opening. The level of control and tension can be of prime importance (Chapter 15).

Underneath the more superficial bulbo-cavernosus muscles are two elongated masses of erectile tissue called the *vestibular bulbs* (shown on the right in Figure 2.4). These structures, connected at their upper ends with the clitoris, become congested with blood during sexual arousal, increasing sexual responsiveness. Together with the vaginal sphincter, they determine the size, tightness, and "feel" of the vagina (Box 2.3).

### Internal Sex Organs

Let us turn to the internal sex organs of the female: the paired ovaries, the two uterine or fallopian tubes, the uterus, the vagina, and a pair of bulbourethral glands.

**The Ovaries**  The *ovaries* are the *gonads* or reproductive glands of the female. They produce *ova* ("eggs") and sex hormones (estrogens

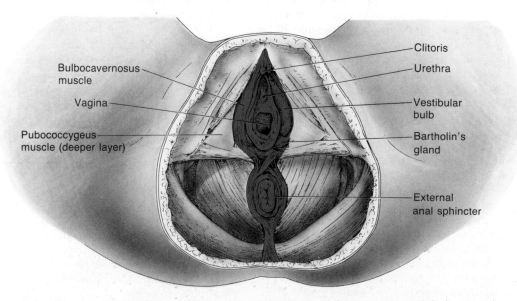

Figure 2.4  Muscles and structures in the vaginal area beneath the skin (above and facing page).

# Box 2.3

## SIZE OF THE VAGINA

The size of the vagina, like that of the penis, has been the object of much interest and speculation. Taoist sex manuals categorize vaginas into eight types, depending on their depth; they range from the Black Pearl (4 inches) to the Deep Chamber (6 inches), the Inner Door (7 inches), and the North Pole (8 inches) (Chang, 1977, p. 52). Popular notions differentiate between tight and relaxed vaginas, those that can actively "grasp" the penis and others that are passive. However, there has not been any formal research done to substantiate such notions.

Functionally it makes more sense to consider the vaginal entrance separately from the rest of its body. The vagina beyond it is a soft and stretchy organ; although it looks like a flat tube, it actually functions more like a balloon. Normally there is no such thing as a vagina that is permanently "too tight" or "too small." Properly stimulated, any normal adult vagina can accommodate the largest penis.

The claim that some vaginas are too large is more tenable. A vagina may not return to normal size after childbirth, and tears produced during the process can weaken the vaginal walls. Even in these instances, however, the vagina expands only to the extent that the penis requires. In short, most of the time there is no problem of "fit" between penis and vagina.

By contrast, the introitus is highly sensitive. The degree of congestion of the erectile tissues of the bulb of the vestibule and the level of tension of the vaginal sphincter make a great deal of difference in how relaxed or tight the vagina will feel to the woman and her partner. If these muscles tense up, they cause coital discomfort; if they are too lax, orgasm may not occur. To enhance her sexual experience, a woman can learn to relax or tighten her vaginal muscles and strengthen them with special exercises (Chapter 15).

There is a long-standing controversy as to whether the penis can be "trapped" inside the vagina (penis captivus). The theme is not limited to the Western world. Natives of the Marshall Islands in the Pacific believe that incestuous relations lead to vaginal spasm, which traps the penis. Other cultures have similar fears that penile entrapment will lead to the discovery of illicit relationships (Gregersen, 1983). Probably this notion is a misconception, arising from the observation of dogs. (The penis of the dog expands into a "knot" inside the vagina and cannot be withdrawn until loss of erection.) Occasional reports continue to refer to it in humans (Melody, 1977).

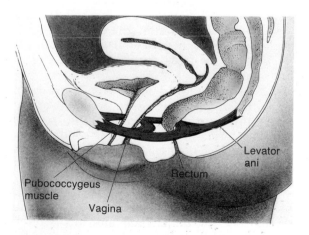

Pubococcygeus muscle

Vagina

Rectum

Levator ani

and progestins). They lie in the abdomen (Figures 2.5 and 2.6) on each side of the uterus, and are about an inch and a half long. The ovaries are held in place by folds and ligaments; these ligaments are solid cords, not to be confused with the fallopian tubes, which open into the uterine cavity.

The ovary has no tubes leading directly out of it. The ova leave the ovary by oozing out through its thin surface and becoming caught in the fringed end of the fallopian tube. Before puberty the ovary has a smooth, glistening surface; after the start of the ovarian cycle in puberty, its surface becomes increasingly scarred and pitted.

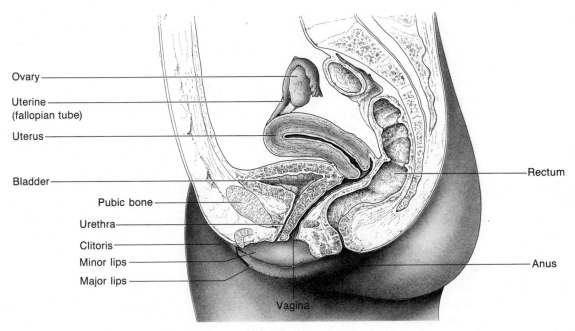

Ovary

Uterine
(fallopian tube)

Uterus

Bladder

Pubic bone

Urethra

Clitoris

Minor lips

Major lips

Vagina

Rectum

Anus

Figure 2.5    The female reproductive system (side view).

**The Fallopian Tubes**    The two *fallopian tubes* or oviducts are about four inches long. The tubes are named after the 16th-century Italian anatomist Gabriello Fallopio, who mistakenly thought they were "ventilators" for the uterus. In fact, the fallopian tubes connect the ovaries and the uterus. The ovarian end of the tube, called the *infundibulum* ("funnel"), is cone-shaped and fringed by irregular projections, the *fimbriae,* which cling to the ovary but are not attached to it (Figure 2.6). Leaving the ovarian surface, the ovum finds its way into the opening of the fallopian tube—a remarkable feat, considering that the ovum is about the size of the tip of a needle and the opening of the uterine tube is a slit about the size of a printed hyphen.

The lining of the fallopian tube is covered with tiny hairlike structures (*cilia*). The ovum, unlike the sperm, cannot move on its own; the sweeping of these cilia and the contractions of the tube push it along. If the ovum were the size of an orange, the cilia would be as small as eyelashes.

The ovum is usually fertilized in the outer third of the fallopian tube. Although the fallopian tubes are surgically not as accessible as the vas deferens of the male, they are still the most convenient sites for female sterilization (Chapter 7).

**The Uterus**    The *uterus* or womb is a hollow, muscular, pear-shaped organ in which the embryo (called a fetus after the eighth week) is sheltered and nourished until birth. It stretches as the fetus grows and shrinks again after childbirth.

The Greek word for uterus is *hystera,* a term that supplies the root for words like "hysterectomy" (surgical removal of the uterus) and "hysteria," a psychological condition in which the ancient Greeks supposed the uterus wandered through the body in search of a child (Veith, 1965).

The uterus is usually tilted forward or anteverted (Figure 2.5). Attempts at self-abortion or abortion by unqualified individuals often

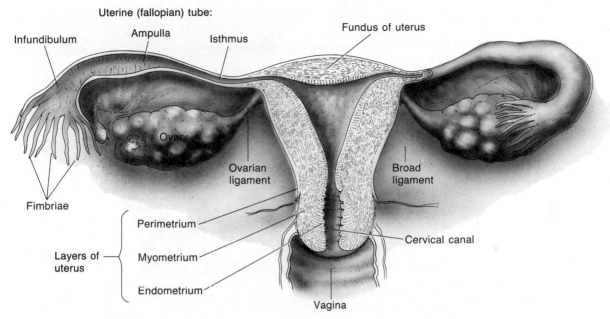

Figure 2.6    Internal female reproductive organs (front view).

end in disaster because of this tilt. When a probe or long needle is pushed blindly into the vagina, the instrument pierces the roof of the vagina, and instead of entering the uterus, penetrates the abdominal cavity, causing infection.

The uterus has several parts (Figure 2.6): the *fundus* ("bottom") is the rounded portion that lies above the openings of the uterine tubes; the *body*, is the main part; and the *cervix* ("neck") is the lower portion, which projects into the vagina. The opening of the *cervical canal* into the vagina is about the size of the lead in a pencil (Figure 2.5), but it stretches for childbirth.

The uterus has three layers. The inner mucosa or *endometrium* consists of numerous glands and a rich network of blood vessels. This is where the embryo develops. Its structure varies with the phases of the menstrual cycle (Chapter 4). The second layer, the *myometrium*, consists of smooth muscles. These muscles contract during childbirth, pushing the baby out. The third, the *perimetrium*, is the external cover.

**The Vagina**    The *vagina* ("sheath") is the female organ of copulation. Through it pass the menstrual discharge and the baby during birth. The vagina in its unstimulated state is a collapsed muscular tube, a potential, rather than permanent, space (Box 2.3). In anatomical illustrations it appears as a narrow cavity in the side views (Figure 2.5).

The inner lining of the vagina, called the *vaginal mucosa*, resembles the inside skin of the mouth. In contrast to the uterine endometrium, it contains no glands, but during sexual excitement the vaginal mucosa exudes a clear lubricating fluid (Chapter 3).

In adult women the vaginal walls have soft ridges and furrows (*rugae*). After women cease to menstruate during the menopause (Chapter 4), these become thinner and smoother. The vaginal walls are poorly supplied with nerves, so they are relatively insensitive. In gynecological examinations conducted for Kinsey, 98 percent of the women could feel a touch on the clitoris; in contrast, fewer than 14 percent could detect a touch in the vagina (Kinsey et al., 1953). However, the area surrounding the vaginal opening may be highly excitable. There also have been recent claims that the anterior wall of the vagina has an erotically sensitive zone (the *Grafenberg spot*). (See Box 3.2 in Chapter 3).

Underneath the vaginal mucosa is the *muscular layer* of the vaginal wall, which can stretch considerably during coitus and especially in childbirth.

Bulbourethral Glands    The *bulbourethral glands,* or *Bartholin's glands,* are two small structures located below the vestibular bulbs (Figure 2.4). Their ducts open on each side in the ridges between the edge of the hymen and the minor lips. These glands were formerly assumed to lubricate the vagina; now they are considered to play at most a minor role in this process.

Breasts

The *breasts* are not sex organs, but they have important reproductive and erotic significance. Characteristic of mammals, which suckle their young, they contain milk-producing organs called *mammary glands.* Among female primates, only women have large breasts even when not suckling. Within the breast, loosely packed fibrous and fatty tissues surround the mammary glands (Figure 2.7).

Although we generally associate breasts with females, males also have breasts, alike in structure but usually less developed. If a male is given female hormones, he will develop female-looking breasts (Chapter 10).

The *nipple* is the prominent tip of the breast, into which the milk ducts open. It has smooth muscle fibers, which make it erect in response to stimulation. The *areola* is the circular area around the nipple. The nipples, richly endowed with nerve fibers, are highly sensitive; they can play an important part in sexual arousal. Many (but not all) women, and only some men, find the stimulation of their nipples sexually arousing.

Nipples vary in size and may be pushed inward or *inverted.* These are usually harmless anatomical variations which do not usually interfere with breastfeeding.

The size and shape of the breasts varies

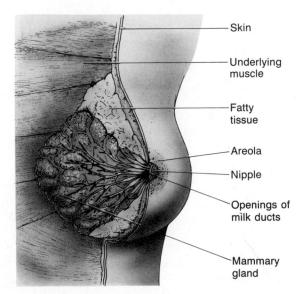

Figure 2.7    Internal structure of the breast.

widely among women and even in the same woman, with age, weight, and other factors (Figure 2.8). Small and large breasts go in and out of "fashion." Size and shape have no bearing on their capacity to produce milk or on their erotic responsiveness. In addition to personal preference, the sensitivity of the breast depends on the hormonal levels, which fluctuate with the menstrual cycle and in pregnancy.

The female breasts develop during puberty (Chapter 4, Figure 4.4). Sometimes one grows faster than the other, but eventually the two sides become approximately equal in size. With age, the breasts undergo other natural changes. As their supporting ligaments stretch, they tend to sag; following the menopause, they become smaller and less firm. Such changes, though physiologically normal, bother some women.

Exercises, creams, and similar methods that are claimed to augment breast size do not work. If a woman is truly unhappy, she can turn to plastic surgery. It can make breasts larger or smaller, and correct asymmetries (that occur naturally) and deformities (that

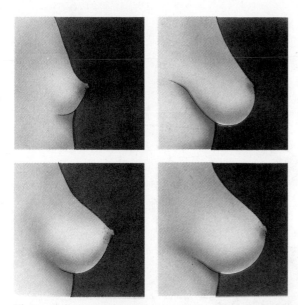

Figure 2.8    Normal variations in female breast size and shape.

may follow breast surgery). Breast enlargement with liquid silicone injections has led to numerous complications. A much safer approach now utilizes soft silicone implants; the materials introduced into the breast are in an inert sac and do not come into direct contact with breast tissue.

Can cosmetic surgery on healthy body parts be justified? It is a matter of personal choice. Some women feel happier following surgery; other women who have lost both breasts to cancer still consider themselves completely feminine, just as they are.

## MALE SEX ORGANS

### External Sex Organs

The external sex organs of the male are the *penis* and *scrotum*. You have probably heard many slang terms for them.[3]

**The Penis**    The *penis* ("tail") is the male organ for copulation and urination. It consists of three parallel cylinders of spongy tissue, through one of which runs the *urethra*, conveying both urine and semen (Figure 2.9).

The three cylinders of the penis are structurally similar. Two of them are called the cavernous bodies (*corpora cavernosa*), and the third, which contains the urethra, the spongy body (*corpus spongiosum*). Each cylinder is wrapped in a fibrous coat, but the cavernous bodies have an additional common covering that makes them appear to be a single structure for most of their length. In erection, the spongy body stands out as a distinct ridge on the underside of the penis.

As the terms "cavernous" and "spongy" suggest, the penis is a cluster of irregular spaces, like a dense sponge. These tissues are connected to a rich network of blood vessels. During sexual arousal they become engorged with blood. Pressing against their tough fibrous coat, they cause the penis to become erect and stiff.

The smooth, rounded head of the penis is known as the *glans* ("acorn"). The glans is formed entirely by the free end of the spongy body, which expands to shelter the tips of the cavernous bodies (Figure 2.10). Like the clitoris, the glans penis has particular erotic importance. It is richly endowed with nerves and highly sensitive. At its rim (*corona*), the glans slightly overhangs the neck of the penis, which forms the boundary between the body of the penis and the glans. At the tip of the glans is the longitudinal slit for the *urethral meatus* or opening.

The skin of the penis is hairless and unusually loose, which permits expansion during erection. Although the skin is fixed to the penis at its neck, some of it folds over and covers part of the glans (like the sleeve of an academic

---

[3]Modern colloquial terms for the penis include prick, poker, pecker, rod, tool, cock, dick, dong, joy stick, boner, and weenie (Haeberle, 1978, p. 491). Fifteenth-century descriptions were more exotic: housebreaker, ransacker, rummager, pigeon, shamefaced one, the indomitable, and swimmer (Nefzawi, *The Perfumed Garden,* 1964 ed., pp. 156–157). A dictionary of gay slang lists several pages of synonyms, many of them terms for food (salami); male names (Peter, Mickey, Mr. Wong); and weapons or tearing instruments (dagger, hammer, spear, gun) (Rodgers, 1972).

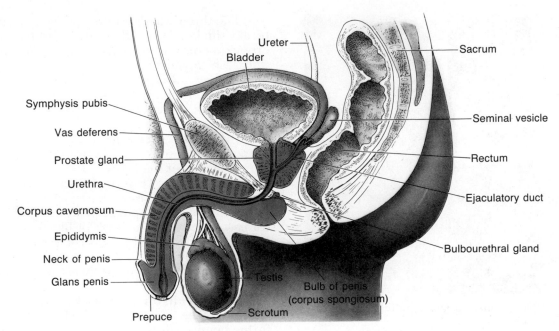

Figure 2.9   The male reproductive system (side view).

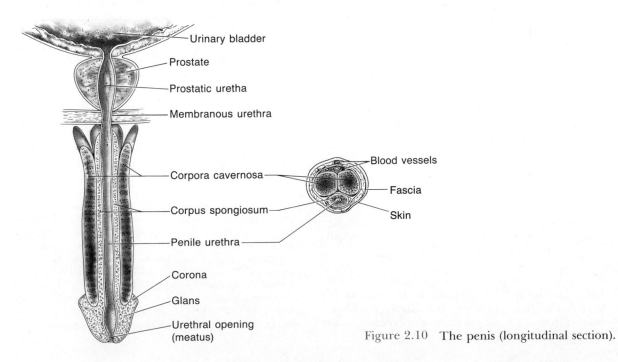

Figure 2.10   The penis (longitudinal section).

gown), forming the *prepuce,* or *foreskin.* Ordinarily the prepuce pulls back easily to expose the glans. *Circumcision* is the cutting away of the prepuce. In the circumcised penis the glans is always totally exposed (Box 2.4).

Small glands in the corona and the neck produce a soft yellowish substance called *smegma,* which has a distinctive smell. This local secretion accumulates under the prepuce. It has no known function and must not be con-

## Box 2.4

### MALE CIRCUMCISION

Circumcision, cutting off the penile prepuce or foreskin, has been practiced around the world as a religious ritual or a medical measure. About half of the males in the world are circumcised. In the circumcised male the glans and the neck of the penis are completely exposed (see figure).

Circumcision was performed in ancient Egypt as early as 2000 B.C. It long antedates the well-known practice among Jews and Moslems.* The Greek historian Herodotus, who traveled to Egypt in the 5th century B.C., wrote that Egyptians "circumcise for reasons of cleanliness," (quoted in Manniche, 1987, p. 8).

Circumcision is just one form of widespread attempts in many cultures to alter the shape of the genitals by cutting, piercing, slicing, or inserting objects. For example, the Burmese would insert tiny bronze bells under the penis; the Dayaks of Borneo would pierce the glans with a rod ("ampallang") with balls or brushes fixed to its end, to stimulate the vagina during coitus. Among Pacific islanders the foreskin is slit lengthwise (*superincision*). Other societies use *subincision* to slice the underside of the penis all the way to the urethra; as a result men have to squat like women when urinating (Gregersen, 1983).

Circumcision for medical purposes in the United States dates back to the 19th century. Its original justification was to help combat masturbation. After this rationale was discredited, its advocates endorsed the practice as hygienic, because circumcision prevents the accumulation of smegma under the prepuce. Further support for the practice came from reports that cancer of the penis ap-

The penis before and after circumcision.

peared to be less frequent among circumcised men, and cancer of the cervix to be less common among their spouses.

The validity of these associations has been called into question. Physicians are currently divided as to the necessity of circumcision in infancy. Although circumcision is not recommended by the American Academy of Pediatrics, nearly 1 million newborn boys (or 60 percent) undergo the procedure a year in the United States; by comparison, only 20 percent of Canadian infants are circumcised. The operation is performed without anesthesia.

Circumcision remains a medical necessity when the foreskin is so tight that it cannot be easily retracted over the glans (*phimosis*). This condition is rare and impossible to predict in infancy. It takes several years for the foreskin to become retractable among the majority of boys (Paige, 1978b).

It is often assumed that because of his fully exposed glans penis, the circumcised male is more rapidly aroused during coitus and more likely to ejaculate prematurely. Current research has failed to support this belief: there seems to be no difference between the excitability of the circumcised and uncircumcised penis (Masters and Johnson, 1966).

*The basis for the practice among Jews is set forth in Genesis 17:9–15. "You shall circumcise the flesh of your foreskin, and it shall be the sign of the covenant between us."

## Box 2.5

### SIZE OF THE PENIS

The average penis is three to four inches when flaccid and about twice as long when erect. Its diameter in the relaxed state is about 1 ¼ inches, with an increase of another ¼ inch in erection. Penises can, however, be considerably smaller or larger (Dickinson, 1949).

Variation in size and shape is the rule for all parts of the human body. Nevertheless, the size and shape of the penis are often the cause of special curiosity and concern. Representations of enormous penises can be found in numerous cultures, including some from remote antiquity (as in this Greek statuette of a satyr). These anatomical exaggerations may be caricatures or monuments to male vanity or symbols of fertility and power. Symbolic representations of the penis have often been used for religious and magical functions (Chapter 20).

The size and shape of the penis, contrary to popular belief, are not related to a man's body build, race, virility, or ability to give and receive sexual satisfaction. Furthermore, variations in size tend to be less in the erect state: the smaller the flaccid penis, the proportionately larger it tends to become when erect (Masters and Johnson, 1966). The penis does not grow larger through frequent use, pills, creams, or "exercise."

Many women do not care about the size of their sexual partner's penis, although this theme is popular in pornography (usually created by men). The size of the penis appears more important for enhancing sexual attractiveness for some gay men.

fused with semen, which comes out through the urethra.

Several popular ideas about the penis are myths. Size is not all-important (Box 2.5), as men often worry. The human penis (unlike that of the dog) has no bone, nor does it have voluntary muscles within it. The muscles that surround the base of the penis externally squirt out urine and semen, but they play no significant role in erection.

The Scrotum   The *scrotum* is a multilayered pouch. Its skin is darker than the rest of the

body, has many sweat glands, and at puberty becomes sparsely covered with hair. Underneath it there is a layer of loosely organized muscle fibers (*cremasteric muscle*) and fibrous tissue. These muscle fibers are not under voluntary control, but they contract in response to cold, sexual excitement, and other stimuli, making the scrotum appear compact and heavily wrinkled. When the inner side of the thigh is stimulated, the muscle contracts reflexively (the *cremasteric reflex*). Otherwise the scrotum hangs loose, and its surface is smooth.

The scrotal sac contains two separate compartments, each holding a single *testicle* and its *spermatic cord*. The spermatic cord contains the vas deferens, blood vessels, nerves, and muscle fibers. When these muscles contract, the spermatic cord shortens and pulls the testicle upward within the scrotal sac, an important feature in sexual arousal (Chapter 3).

### Internal Sex Organs
The internal sex organs of the male consist of a pair of testes or testicles, with their duct systems for the storage and transport of sperm: the paired epididymis, vas deferens, and ejaculatory ducts and the single urethra. The male also has paired seminal vesicles and bulbourethral glands and the single prostate gland.

The Testes    The *testes* are the gonads, or reproductive glands, of the male. *Testis* is derived from the root for "witness." In ancient times a man would place his hand on his genitals when taking an oath—hence our word "testify."

The two testicles are about the same size (about 2 inches long), although the left one usually hangs somewhat lower than the right (a fact noted by classical sculptors). They produce sperm and sex hormones (androgens). Each testicle is enclosed in a tight, whitish fibrous sheath that penetrates inside the testicle, subdividing it into conical lobes (Figure 2.11). Each lobe is packed with convoluted *seminiferous* ("sperm-bearing") *tubules*. These threadlike structures are the sites at which sperm are produced. Each seminiferous tubule is one to three feet long, and the combined length of the tubules of both testes extends over a quarter of a mile. This elaborate system of tubules allows for the production and storage of billions of sperm.

Sperm are produced within the seminiferous tubules; male sex hormone is produced in between them by *interstitial cells* (or *Leydig's cells*). The cells responsible for the two primary functions of the testes are entirely separate. Yet the hormones produced by Leydig's cells are essential for sperm to develop.

The testes contain a third type of cell called *Sertoli cells*, which are interspersed among the developing sperm cells within the seminiferous tubules. Their function in sperm

development will be discussed shortly. Sertoli cells also produce a hormone called *inhibin*, which we shall deal with in Chapter 4.

The Epididymis    The seminiferous tubules converge into an intricate maze of ducts which culminate in a single tube, the *epididymis*. The epididymis is a remarkably long tube (about 20 feet), that is so tortuous and convoluted that it appears as a C-shaped structure not much longer than the testis to whose surface it adheres (Figure 2.9). Its structure allows for the storage of large numbers of sperm.

The slow contraction of the seminiferous tubules moves sperm into the epididymis, where they mature and become able to move on their own with whiplash movements of their tails (Jensen, 1980).

The Vas Deferens    The *vas deferens* is the much shorter continuation of the epididymis. It travels upward in the scrotal sac before entering the abdominal cavity; its portion in the scrotal sac can be felt as a firm cord. The fact that the vas is surgically so accessible makes it the most convenient site for sterilizing men (Chapter 7).

The vas deferens joins the duct of the seminal vesicle to form the *ejaculatory duct* (Figure 2.9). This duct is a very short (less than one inch), straight tube, which runs its entire course within the prostate gland and opens into the urethra.

The Urethra    The *urethra* starts at the base of the urinary bladder, crosses the prostate gland, and then runs through the penis to its external opening (Figures 2.9 and 2.10). The two *ejaculatory ducts* and the multiple ducts of the prostate gland open into it (Figure 2.10). Here the various components of semen coming from the testes, seminal vesicles, and the prostate gland mix before ejaculation.

Semen and urine use the same urethral passage, but they are never mixed. Two urethral sphincters keep them apart: an *internal sphincter* (where the urethra enters the prostate), and an *external sphincter* (right below where the urethra exits from the prostate gland) (Figure 2.9). During urination, the internal sphincter and the external sphincter

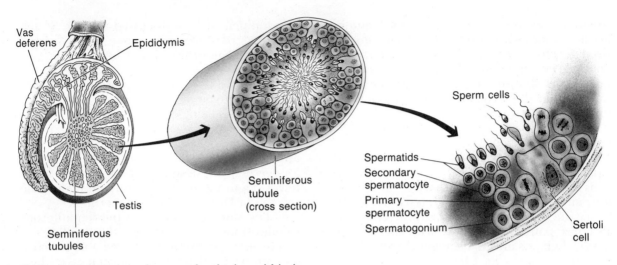

Figure 2.11   Testis and sperm developing within it.

(which is under voluntary control after infancy) relax, and the contraction of the bladder wall pushes urine out. During ejaculation, the internal sphincter remains closed, the external one open, allowing only semen to flow out of the penis.

Accessory Organs   Three other organs contribute to the production of semen. They are the prostate gland, two seminal vesicles, and two bulbourethral glands.

The *prostate* is about the size and shape of a chestnut. Its base is against the bottom of the bladder (Figure 2.10). It contains smooth muscle fibers and glandular tissue whose secretions contribute to the seminal fluid and its characteristic odor. *Prostaglandins,* hormones produced by the prostate (and many other tissues), have far-ranging effects on the functions of the body (Chapter 4).

The *seminal vesicles* are two sacs (Figure 2.9), each of which ends in a straight, narrow duct, which joins the tip of the vas deferens to form the ejaculatory duct. The seminal vesicles contribute much of the fluid in semen. Their secretions are rich in carbohydrates—especially fructose, which provides energy to sperm and enhances their mobility.

The *bulbourethral glands (Cowper's glands)* are two pea-sized structures attached to the urethra in the penis through their tiny ducts

(Figure 2.9). During sexual arousal these glands secrete a clear, sticky fluid that appears in droplets at the tip of the penis. Medieval theologians called it the "distillate of love." A Latin poet wrote the following epigram (quoted in Ellis, 1942):

> You see this organ . . . is humid
> This moisture is not dew nor drops of rain,
> It is the outcome of sweet memory
> Recalling thoughts of a complaisant maid.

There usually is not enough of this secretion to serve as a coital lubricant. However, as it is alkaline, it may help to neutralize the acidity of the urethra (which is harmful to sperm) before semen passes.

Although this secretion must not be confused with semen, it can contain stray sperm. For this reason if a condom is used for contraception, a man should put it on before he enters the vagina, no matter when he intends to ejaculate.

## HOW GERM CELLS DEVELOP

Now that you know the basics of male and female anatomies, we can return to their common purpose—producing the cells that make new life. How do these germ cells or *gametes*—the sperm and ova—develop? Their development (*gametogenesis*) follows the same basic principles in both sexes, although the sperm and egg are dissimilar cells, each with a specialized function (Moore, 1982; Sadler, 1985).

In the nucleus of every living cell are *chromosomes*. They carry *genes*, which transmit all hereditary characteristics. Gametogenesis relies on *mitosis*, or ordinary cell multiplication. In mitosis a cell divides into two cells with the same number of chromosomes. In addition, germ cells undergo a special kind of reduction division called *meiosis*, through which their number of chromosomes is halved.

All human cells (other than ova and sperm) have 46 chromosomes. Twenty-two pairs of autosomes are similar in both sexes; one pair of *sex chromosomes* is not. The cells of the female body have two X sex chromosomes; those of males one X and one Y sex chromosome. The genetic configuration (*genotype*) of female body cells is thus $44 + XX$; that of male body cells, $44 + XY$.[4]

The germ cells have half this number of chromosomes: ova have $22 + X$; sperm have either $22 + X$ or $22 + Y$ chromosomes. Therefore, when sperm and egg merge during fertilization, the normal number of chromosomes is recreated instead of doubled (Chapter 6).

## Development of Sperm

Sperm production (*spermatogenesis*) takes place within the seminiferous tubules, starting at puberty. Before then the tubules are solid cords with dormant germ cells. A cross-section of an adult's tubule shows germ cells in various stages of development (Figure 2.11). Sperm that are fully formed are released into the center of the tubule and transported to the epididymis, where they mature further. Spermatogenesis is in progress simultaneously in all

the tubules, so generations of sperm reach maturity in successive waves. The process takes approximately 64 days, and cycles follow each other uninterruptedly. The development of spermatozoa is guided by the Sertoli cells, which "nurse" them by providing physical support and nutrition (Kessel and Kardon, 1979).

Spermatogenesis has three phases (Figure 2.12). In the first phase, the earliest cell or *spermatogonium*, multiplies through mitosis. It is transformed into the *primary spermatocyte*, with the full 46 chromosomes. In the second phase, each primary spermatocyte undergoes meiosis (through two specialized divisions called the first and second meiotic divisions), giving rise to two *secondary spermatocytes*. In turn each splits into two *spermatids*. These four cells now have half the normal complement of chromosomes: two are $22 + X$; two are $22 + Y$. The third phase entails no further division. An extensive process of differentiation transforms spermatids into sperm.

Mature sperm have a head, middle piece, and a tail (Figure 2.13). The head contains the chromosomes; it is the only part kept in fertilization. The middle piece contains the part of the cell that produces energy. The tail moves the sperm with whiplash movements. Sperm are smaller than one-tenth of a millimeter, so they are not visible to the naked eye.

## Development of the Ovum

Unlike men, who produce billions of sperm during their lifetime, women are born with all the immature ova they will ever produce. These cells number some 2 million, of which about 40,000 survive to puberty; about 400 reach maturity during a woman's reproductive lifetime, and only a few ever get fertilized.

Figure 2.12 shows the maturation of the ovum (*oogenesis*). The development of the ovum begins before birth. The female infant is born with *primary oocytes*. The primary oocyte with its surrounding cells make up the *primary follicle*. Primary oocytes begin the first meiotic division before birth, but the process is suspended until puberty. After puberty, each month a cluster of follicles begins to mature.

---

[4]One of the two X chromosomes in female cells is inactive. It appears as a small dark area inside the nucleus, and is visible under a microscope. Called a *Barr body*, it provides a convenient way to verify that the person is a genetic female. It is sometimes used for that purpose with athletes (Arms and Camp, 1987).

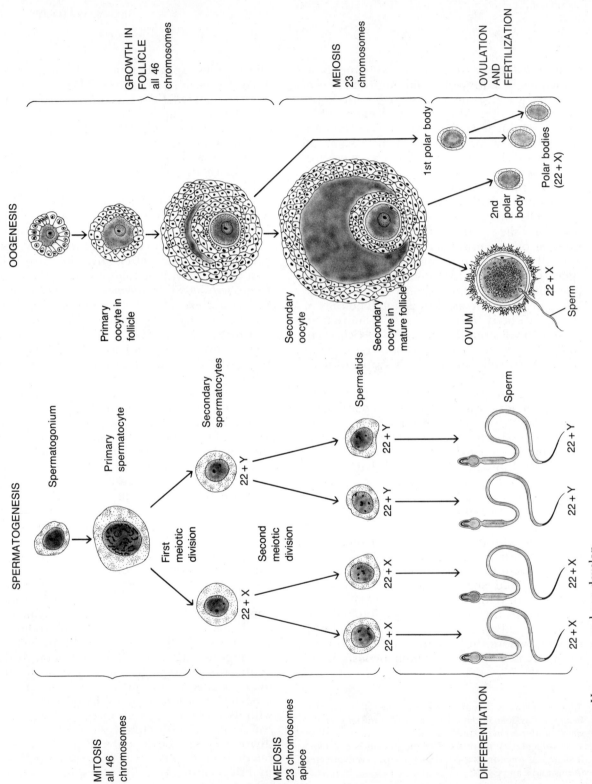

Figure 2.12    How sperm and egg develop.

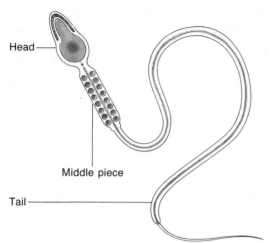

Figure 2.13   Human sperm. Component parts.

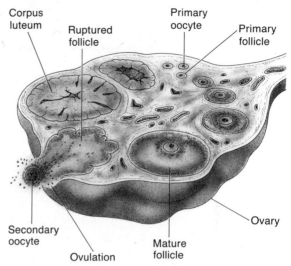

Figure 2.14   "Time-lapse" view inside of ovary. Each month one ovum matures. The follicle ruptures, becomes the corpus luteum, and then turns into scar tissue.

Usually one of them gets ahead and becomes progressively larger (while the others regress), until it is a mature follicle or *Graafian follicle* (Figure 2.14). This liquid-filled vesicle contains the ovum and *granulosa cells,* which surround it and line the follicle wall. (It is these granulosa cells that produce the female hormone estrogen). During ovulation (Chapter 4), the wall of the follicle breaks, freeing the ovum to enter the fallopian tube.

Shortly before ovulation, the primary oocyte completes the first meiotic division resulting in one *secondary oocyte* (with $22 + X$ chromosomes) and the *first polar body* (a small nonfunctional cell). At ovulation, the secondary oocyte begins the second meiotic division, but it does not complete it unless it is fertilized by a sperm. In that case cell division is completed and results in a *mature oocyte* (or ovum) and the *second polar body.* The first polar body meanwhile divides in two. Thus, the end result of oogenesis is one mature oocyte and three polar bodies which degenerate. This is unlike spermatogenesis, where four mature sperm develop from a simple primary spermatocyte.

To complete the story, let us now return to the follicle. After ovulation, the rest of the follicle is transformed into the *corpus luteum* ("yellow body"), a gland that takes over hormone production. At the end of the ovarian cycle, the corpus luteum turns into scar tissue.

The ovum is one of the largest cells in the body. Next to it the sperm looks minuscule (Figure 2.15). Nonetheless, the ovum is still scarcely visible to the naked eye. All the ova needed to repopulate the world would fill two

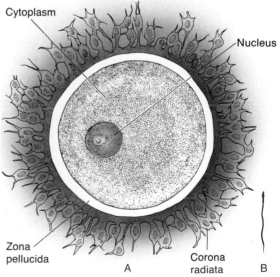

Figure 2.15   The human egg (A). A human sperm is in the lower right corner (B), for comparison.

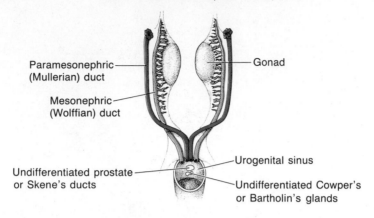

UNDIFFERENTIATED (5-6 WEEKS)

Paramesonephric (Mullerian) duct

Mesonephric (Wolffian) duct

Gonad

Undifferentiated prostate or Skene's ducts

Urogenital sinus

Undifferentiated Cowper's or Bartholin's glands

DIFFERENTIATED (10 WEEKS)

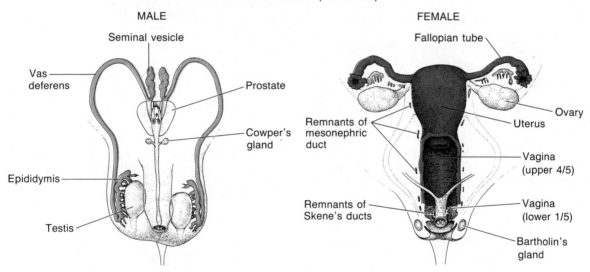

MALE

Seminal vesicle

Vas deferens

Prostate

Cowper's gland

Epididymis

Testis

FEMALE

Fallopian tube

Ovary

Uterus

Remnants of mesonephric duct

Vagina (upper 4/5)

Remnants of Skene's ducts

Vagina (lower 1/5)

Bartholin's gland

Figure 2.16   How internal sex organs develop male and female forms.

gallon jugs; all the sperm needed for the same purpose would fit into an aspirin tablet. The volume of DNA needed to produce the entire next generation of the world is less than one-tenth of an aspirin tablet (Stern, 1973).

The *nucleus* of the ovum, which contains the genetic material, is surrounded by a large amount of *cytoplasm*. This material is necessary for sustaining life after fertilization. (The sperm has a minimal amount of cytoplasm; to cover its long journey it must travel light). A clear area, the *zona pellucida*, forms a protective layer surrounded by follicular cells that remain attached to it after ovulation to form the *corona radiata* ("radiating crown").

## HOW THE REPRODUCTIVE SYSTEM DEVELOPS

We have seen how the male and female gametes develop. How does an embryo develop its male or female anatomy?[5]

The genital system of both sexes makes its appearance during the fifth to sixth week of intrauterine life, when the embryo is 5 to 12 millimeters long. At this stage any embryo—

[5]Discussion in this section is based on Sadler (1985); Gordon and Ruddle (1981); and Moore (1982). The modern understanding of the differentiations of the reproductive system was first envisioned by Alfred Jost (1953).

male or female—has a pair of undifferentiated *gonads,* two sets of *genital ducts,* and a *urogenital sinus*—a common opening to the outside for the genital ducts and the urinary tract (Figure 2.16). It also has the rudiments of external genitals (Figure 2.17).

At this time we cannot reliably tell the sex of the embryo even under a microscope; the gonads have not yet become either testes or ovaries, nor have the other structures differentiated. Of course, the sex of the child is already decided; genetic sex is determined at the moment of fertilization by the chromosomes of the sperm. If the fertilizing sperm carries a Y chromosome, the child will be male; otherwise it will be female (Chapter 6).

## Differentiation of the Gonads

How does the Y chromosome initiate the process of testicular development? It has been assumed that a testicular organizing substance, called the *X-Y antigen,* causes the undifferentiated gonad to develop into testes. Now it has been established that the factor that initiates male development is a single gene on the Y chromosome, called the *testes determining factor (TDF)* (Page et al., 1987). The testes determining gene acts as a biological "master switch," deciding whether or not other genes related to sexual development are turned on. "Maleness" is therefore determined by a minute piece of the Y chromosome.

It is in response to this initial "push" by the testes determining factor that gonadal cells organize into distinct strands (*testis cords*), the forerunners of the seminiferous tubules. By about the seventh week, if the organ is not recognizable as a developing testis, we presume that it will develop into an ovary. More definitive evidence of ovarian structure comes at about the tenth week, when the forerunners of the follicles become visible.

If the undifferentiated gonad is going to develop into a testis, further development occurs mainly in the inner or medullary portion of the gonad; if it is going to develop into an ovary, it is the peripheral or cortical portion of the gonad that develops, giving rise to the primitive germ cells which eventually become the ovarian follicles. Testosterone produced by the embryonal testis is necessary to promote the maturation of seminiferous tubules. The embryonal ovary also produces estrogenic hormones, but their role in the further development of ovaries is unclear.

## Differentiation of the Genital Ducts

In the undifferentiated stage, the embryo has *two* sets of ducts: the *paramesonephric* or *Mullerian* (the potential female) *ducts* and the *mesonephric,* or *Wolffian* (the potential male) *ducts* (Figure 2.16).

Just as the Y chromosome directs the undifferentiated gonad to become a testis, the embryonal testes determine the future of the genital ducts. They supply the male hormone *testosterone,* produced by Leydig cells, which promotes the further differentiation of the Wolffian system; and *Mullerian regression hormone,* produced by Sertoli cells, which inhibits the further development of the Mullerian ducts. As a result the Wolffian duct on each side eventually becomes the epididymus, vas deferens, and seminal vesicle, while the Mullerian ducts degenerate.

In the absence of these testicular hormones the Wolffian ducts degenerate, and the Mullerian ducts form the fallopian tubes, uterus, and the upper two-thirds of the vagina. (The lower third of the vagina, the bulbourethral glands, the urethra in both sexes, and the prostate gland are derived from the embryonal urinary system.)

The differentiation of the reproductive tract therefore depends first on the Y chromosome and then on testicular hormones. Without them both, the undifferentiated system will develop the female pattern. Regardless of genetic makeup, if the gonads are removed in animal experiments early in life, the reproductive tract will develop the female pattern.[6]

[6]Bernstein (1981). For further discussion of how chromosomes affect sex differentiation, see Gordon and Ruddle (1981) and Haseltine and Ohno (1981).

UNDIFFERENTIATED (5-6 WEEKS)

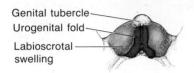

Genital tubercle
Urogenital fold
Labioscrotal
swelling

PARTIALLY DIFFERENTIATED (7 WEEKS)

MALE                           FEMALE

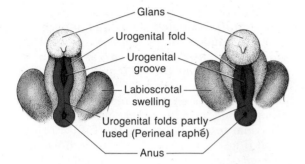

Glans
Urogenital fold
Urogenital
groove
Labioscrotal
swelling
Urogenital folds partly
fused (Perineal raphé)
Anus

FULLY DIFFERENTIATED (12 WEEKS)

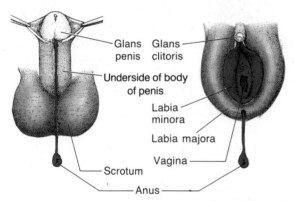

Glans    Glans
penis    clitoris
Underside of body
of penis
Labia
minora
Labia majora
Vagina
Scrotum
Anus

Figure 2.17   How the genitals develop male and female forms.

Both the testes and the ovaries develop in the abdominal cavity. There the ovaries remain until birth; subsequently they move down until they reach their adult positions in the pelvis.

In the male this early internal migration is followed by the further descent of the testes into the scrotal sac. In about 2 percent of male births, one or both of the testes fail to descend into the scrotum before birth. This condition is called *cryptorchidism*. In most of these boys the testes do descend by puberty. If not, hormonal or surgical intervention becomes necessary to move the undescended testicle into the scrotum, because the higher temperature of the abdominal cavity interferes with spermatogenesis, causing sterility. Undescended testes are also more likely to develop cancer.

The canal through which the testes move out of the abdominal cavity and into the scrotal sac normally closes during early infancy. Should this fail to occur, loops of intestine may find their way into it resulting in *congenital inguinal hernia*. This is different from the type of hernia ("rupture") which usually occurs in adult men as a result of weakening of abdominal muscles and severe exertion (such as when lifting a weight). Both types of hernias are easily treated by surgery.

## Differentiation of the External Genitals

Male and female genitals are also, at first, the same (Figure 2.17). Even after the gonads begin to be distinguishable by the second month of life, several more weeks are necessary for the more distinctive development of the external genitals. Not until four months are the genitals of the fetus unmistakably male or female.

The undifferentiated genitals have three main components: the *genital tubercle*, the *urogenital folds*, and the *labioscrotal swellings*. In the male, the genital tubercle grows into the glans penis; the urogenital folds elongate and fuse to form the body of the penis and urethra; and the fusion of labioscrotal swellings forms the scrotal sac. The genitals in the female undergo less marked changes in appearance: the genital tubercle becomes the clitoris; the urogenital folds, the labia minora; and the labioscrotal swellings, the labia majora.

The genitals, like the internal sex organs, differentiate under the influence of androgen. Its presence leads to the male pattern; its absence to the female pattern. However, whereas testosterone masculinizes the internal organs, one of its derivative hormones, called *dihydrotestosterone*, must transform the external ones.

(The significance of this point is discussed in Chapter 10.)

Because the reproductive systems of male and female develop from the same embryonal origins, each part has its developmental counterpart, or *homologue*, in the other sex. With the aid of figures 2.16 and 2.17, try to match the homologous pairs of organs in male and female. In principle it should be possible to identify the homologue to every part, even though the degenerated remnants of the Wolffian ducts in the female and the Mullerian ducts in the male are inconsequential structures. You can find a complete listing of all homologous pairs in Moore (1982, p. 216).

Seven homologous pairs of organs and parts are clearly functional in both sexes:

testis—ovary
Bartholin's gland—Cowper's gland

glans penis—glans of clitoris
corpora cavernosa of penis—corpora cavernosa of clitoris
corpus spongiosum of penis—bulb of the vestibule
underside of penis—labia minora
scrotum—labia majora.

The homologue of the prostate, the urethral and paraurethral glands, "Skene's glands," in the female, may be functional in some women, allowing them to "ejaculate" during orgasm, as we discuss in the next chapter.

The basic differences between the bodies of males and females are in the reproductive system. Yet the similarities underneath these differences suggest that men and women are after all more alike than our culture may lead us to believe.

## REVIEW QUESTIONS

1. List the organs of the female and male reproductive systems and identify their functions.
2. What are the major similarities and differences between the female and male sex organs?
3. Which organs in the reproductive systems of males and females produce fluids? What is the function of each?
4. List the successive cell stages in spermatogenesis and oogenesis.
5. Match the homologous organs and parts of the male and female reproductive systems.

## THOUGHT QUESTIONS

1. Should a woman with healthy breasts have surgery for cosmetic purposes?
2. Should female circumcision be prohibited by international law?
3. How do you explain the gigantic penises in the art of various cultures?
4. Why do you think the hymen evolved among humans?
5. What would you tell a young man who is concerned about the size of his penis?

## SUGGESTED FURTHER READINGS

Dickinson, R. L. (1949). *Atlas of human sex anatomy* (2nd ed.). Baltimore: Williams and Wilkins. A unique collection of sketches and measurements of the sex organs.

Kessel, R. G., and Kardon, R. H. (1979). *Tissues and organs: A text-atlas of scanning electron microscopy.* San Francisco: W. H. Freeman Photographs in Chapters 15 and 16 show genital tissues in extraordinary detail.

Moore, K. L. (1982) *The developing human* (3rd ed.). Philadelphia: Saunders. Sadler, T. W. (1985) *Medical embryology* (5th ed.). Baltimore: Williams and Wilkins. The embryonal development and differentiation of the genital system is succinctly described and well illustrated in both books.

Netter, F. H. (1965). *Reproductive system.* The Ciba Collection of Medical Illustrations, Vol. 2. Summit, N.J.: Ciba. Brief description of reproductive organs. Profusely illustrated with excellent color plates.

Nilsson, L. (1973). *Behold man.* Boston: Little, Brown. Superb color photographs of the reproductive organs.

# Sexual Physiology

## CHAPTER

3

*Whatever the poetry and romance of sex and whatever the social significance of human sexual behavior, sexual responses involve real and material changes in the physiological functioning of an animal.*

ALFRED C. KINSEY

## OUTLINE

SEXUAL AROUSAL
Physical Stimulation
   Touch
   Sights, Sounds, and Smells
Psychological Stimulation
SEXUAL RESPONSE
Response Patterns
Physiological Mechanisms
Excitement and Plateau Phases
   Male Sex Organs
   Female Sex Organs
   Other Reactions
Orgasm

Male Sex Organs
Female Sex Organs
Other Reactions
A Common Model
Resolution Phase and Aftereffects
   Reactions of Sex Organs
   Other Reactions
CONTROL OF SEXUAL
   FUNCTIONS
Spinal Control
   Erection and Ejaculation
   Reflexive Mechanisms in Women
   The Role of Neurotransmitters
Brain Control

A machine "turns on" at the flip of a switch. Does your sexual self "turn on" like a machine? The image of the body as a machine is a common metaphor, but it hardly does justice to the complexity of human sexuality. Many physiological processes underlie sexual activity. When discussing anatomy, we looked at *structure*. Physiology deals with *function*—the way your sexual parts and their control mechanisms operate.

Too often people make sharp distinctions between the *physiological* or bodily aspects of sex and its *psychological* or mental aspects. They speak as if mind and body were completely separate. Of course, that is not the case:

> Physiology and psychology relate to different levels of organization and not to different kinds of causal agents. At the physiological level we study the organization and interrelations of organs and organ systems; at the psychological level we concentrate upon functions of the total individual (Beach, 1947, p. 15).

As we explore the physical basis of sexuality, remember that we still need to deal with the psychological side. But psychology by itself cannot do justice to sexual experience. The two approaches must complement each other, not compete.

## SEXUAL AROUSAL

At the core of every sexual experience is the phenomenon of sexual arousal. Arousal is hard to define because it entails a variety of physiological and psychological states. Bancroft (1983) has proposed that sexual arousal has four basic components:

1. *Sexual drive*—the motivation to act sexually and the level of our sexual responsiveness or arousability.
2. *Central arousal*—the state of alertness in the brain when our attention is focused on the sensations of sexual stimulation (being "turned on").
3. *Genital responses*—the reactions of the sexual organs to erotic stimulation, such as erec-

tion of the penis and lubrication of the vagina.
4. *Peripheral arousal*—other bodily responses, such as increases in the heart rate and blood pressure.

The concept of sexual drive is intriguing but not easy to test. Later we shall discuss its connection with theories of sexual behavior (Chapter 8) and consider its possible linkage to sex hormones (Chapter 4). This chapter will deal with the process of sexual stimulation, the responses of the genital organs and the rest of the body to sexual arousal, and the control mechanisms that regulate these activities.

A useful approach to the study of sexual behavior is to view it as an interaction between a *stimulus* and its behavioral *response*. This model helps us to distinguish cause and effect more clearly.

Much of our sensory stimulation comes from the environment. Various sights, smells, and sounds strike us as sexy. In addition, there are internal triggers for sexual arousal. They include erotic thoughts and sexual fantasies (Chapter 11).

No matter what the erotic stimulus, the sexual response pattern of the body follows an orderly and predictable set of physiological changes: sexual arousal leads toward orgasm, followed by its aftermath. Although most sexual experiences stop short of orgasm, we shall discuss the whole sexual response cycle as our general model.

### Physical Stimulation

There are five basic sources or forms of sensation—sight, hearing, taste, smell, and touch—and all of them transmit messages that may be interpreted by the brain as erotic. There are no specialized sensory nerves for receiving sexual sensations.

Though vision and hearing are especially important in communicating verbal and non-verbal erotic messages, touch remains the most direct physical mode of erotic stimulation. It figures in almost all sexual arousal leading to orgasm. It is, in fact, the only type of stimulation to which the body can respond by *reflex*, independent of higher brain centers. Even if a man is unconscious or has a spinal cord injury that prevents any genital sensations from reaching the brain (but leaves sexual coordinating centers in the lower spinal cord intact), he may still have an erection when his genitals or inner thighs are caressed; similarly, a woman with a spinal cord injury may respond with vaginal lubrication.

Touch    The erotic component in being touched is part of the broader, more fundamental need for bodily contact that goes back to our infancy and to our primate heritage. A crucial component in infant care is touching, caressing, fondling, and cuddling by the adult caretakers. The problems that result from the deprivations of such contact have been well documented in studies of human infants in institutions (Spitz and Wolf, 1947) and other primates (Harlow, 1958). We discuss them in Chapter 8. Indeed, touch plays such a major part in primate life that the practice of grooming has been called the "social cement of primates" (Jolly, 1972, p. 153). Thus, the basis of sexual arousal may well be the more fundamental need for security and affection.

Touch sensations are received through special nerve endings in the skin and deeper tissues called *end organs.* They are distributed unevenly, so some parts (like the fingertips) are more sensitive than others (like the skin of the back).

The more richly endowed with nerves a part of the body is, the greater is its potential for stimulation. Some of the more sensitive areas of the body are especially susceptible to sexual arousal. These *erogenous zones* include the clitoris; the labia minora; the vaginal introitus; possibly parts of the front wall of the vagina; the glans penis, particularly the corona and the underside of the glans; the shaft of the penis; the area between the anus and the genitals; the anus itself; the buttocks; the inner surfaces of the thighs; the mouth, especially the lips; the ears, especially the lobes; and the breasts, especially the nipples.

Although it is true that these areas are more highly responsive to sexual stimulation, they are not the only ones: the neck, the palms and fingertips, the soles and toes, the abdomen, the groin, the center of the lower back, or any other part of the body may well be erotically sensitive for you (Goldstein, 1976). In unusual cases, some women have been reported to reach orgasm when their eyebrows are stroked or pressure is applied to their teeth (Kinsey et al., 1953, p. 50).

The concept of erogenous zones is very old. Explicit or implicit references to them are plentiful in ancient love manuals such as the *Kama Sutra* (Vatsyayana, 1966) and the *Ananga Ranga* (Malla, 1964). Some knowledge of erogenous zones has been rightly assumed to enhance effectiveness as a lover. However, people are profoundly affected by previous experience and the mood of the moment. No one can approach a sexual partner solely guided by an "erotic map" of the body and expect to elicit sexual arousal. For instance, even though the female nipple is generally highly responsive to erotic stimulation, not all women enjoy such stimulation at all times. The same holds true for the sensitive parts of the male, such as the glans penis.

Because individuals vary in what they find sexually arousing in general, or on a specific occasion, it is necessary that partners communicate their needs, likes, and dislikes to each other (Chapter 12).

Sights, Sounds, and Smells    What we see, hear, smell, and taste are also important sources of erotic stimulation. It is generally believed by most behavioral scientists that these means of sexual arousal, in contrast to touch, do not operate reflexively: we learn to experience certain sights, sounds, and smells as erotic and others as sexually neutral or offensive.

An alternative viewpoint suggests that although learning helps shape our arousal responses, nonetheless some responses to particular sexual cues are inborn. Just as animals react to certain "sexual triggers," humans presumably respond likewise to certain sexual cues, such as nudity, more or less universally (Morris, 1977). Cross-cultural and cross-species comparisons are offered in support of these views (Gregersen, 1983). Scientists who favor the view that arousal patterns are learned point to cultural diversity; those who favor biological models dwell on the similarities across cultures and between humans and animals (Symons, 1979).

The *sight* of the nude body in general and of the genital organs in particular is a nearly universal source of erotic excitement. Though there are great cross-cultural, individual, and gender differences (Chapter 10) in what sights are considered erotic, the importance of visual stimuli in sexual arousal can hardly be overestimated. Our preoccupation with physical attractiveness, cosmetics, and dress testifies to that. What most people consider "sexy" is largely, but by no means exclusively, a matter of physical appearance.

The effect of *sound* is less evident but quite significant. Tone and softness of voice help determine the erotic effect of what is said. The sighs, groans, and moans uttered during sex can in themselves be highly arousing to the participants (and to others within earshot). Similarly, certain types of music with pulsating rhythms or romantic qualities often serve as erotic stimuli, or set the mood for sex.

The importance of the sense of *smell* has declined in humans relative to other species. Among animals chemical substances called *pheromones* act as powerful erotic stimulants through the sense of smell. An intriguing possibility exists that humans too secrete pheromones (Box 4.4), but even without them, the use of scents and preoccupation with body odors in most cultures attests to the erotic importance of the sense of smell (Hopson, 1979).

We have dwelt so far on the positive effect of sensory stimulation in generating erotic arousal. Sights, sounds, and smells can exert an equally powerful inhibiting influence. Some people are more sensitive than others in this respect; for them even a minor unpleasant intrusion may act as a turn-off. For example, a person may look quite sexy but lose erotic appeal because of a slight bad odor. Effective sexual arousal thus is equally dependent on what signals we send and avoid sending.

## Psychological Stimulation

Despite all the power of physical stimulation, the key to human sexual arousal is psychological. Sexual arousal is, after all, an emotional state greatly influenced by other emotional states. Stimulation through the senses will normally result in sexual arousal if, and only if, it is accompanied by the appropriate emotional conditions. Affection and trust enhance, and anxiety and fear inhibit erotic response in most cases.

Given our highly developed central nervous systems, we can also react sexually to purely mental images—a dream, a wish, an idea. Sexual fantasy is the most common erotic stimulant (Chapter 11). Our responsiveness is not based solely on the external situation, but also on the store of memories from the past and thoughts projected into the future.

As human beings we share common developmental influences as well as a common biology. For example, we are all cared for as infants by adults who become the first and most significant influences in our lives. What was said earlier about erogenous zones is therefore applicable to the psychological realm as well. Just as most of us are likely to respond to gentle caressing on the inside of our thighs, we are also likely to respond positively to an expression of affectionate sexual interest. Still, as each of us is unique in our developmental histories, our sexual response will vary depending on the persons we deal with and the social circumstances under which we interact.

The issue of sexual stimulation is closely linked to other topics in this book. It relates to sexual attractiveness, or "sexiness," which we shall discuss in Chapter 16. The practical applications of how to generate sexual stimulation in a partner are discussed in Chapters 12 and 15. Gender differences in sexual arousal will be dealt with in Chapter 10.

## SEXUAL RESPONSE

How would you go about studying sexual response? We can examine changes in the sex organs, other bodily responses, or subjective reports of "how it feels."

# Box 3.1

## THE MASTERS AND JOHNSON STUDY OF SEXUAL RESPONSE

William Masters, a gynecologist and research director of the Reproductive Research Foundation in St. Louis, Missouri, published *The Human Sexual Response* with Virginia Johnson, his research associate, in 1966. Like the Kinsey reports, the book created a sensation among both professional circles and the general public. For the first time, it presented a detailed account of the reaction of the body during the sexual response cycle.

Masters and Johnson were primarily interested in investigating the physiology of orgasm in a laboratory setting. Their subjects were 694 normally functioning volunteers of both sexes between the ages of 18 and 89 years. The group included 176 married couples and 106 women and 36 men who were not married at the beginning of their participation in the project (though 98 in this group had been married before)—a total of 382 women and 312 men. Many were from a university community in St. Louis, Missouri, and the group was predominantly white.

Applicants were screened by detailed interviews and physical examinations, and all those considered to have physical abnormalities or to be emotionally unstable were eliminated. The subjects thus did not constitute a random sample of the general population, and in this sense they were not "average people." However, they were not specifically selected for their sexual attributes; the only requirement was that they be sexually responsive under laboratory conditions. In socioeconomic terms the group was, on the whole, better educated and more affluent than the general population, though there was some representation across social classes.

The research procedure was to observe, monitor, and sometimes film the responses of the body as a whole and the sex organs in particular to sexual stimulation and orgasm. Both masturbation and sexual intercourse were included in the experiment. In order to observe vaginal responses, a special camera was used; it was made of clear plastic, which permitted direct observation and filming of the inside of the vagina. All research subjects were told in advance about the exact nature of the procedures in which they would participate, and the unmarried subjects were assigned mainly to studies that did not involve coitus.

The laboratory in which the research took place was a plain, windowless room containing a bed and monitoring and recording equipment. The subjects were first left alone to engage in sex, and only when they felt comfortable in this setting were they asked to perform in the presence of the investigators and technicians monitoring the equipment (recording heart rates, blood pressures, brain waves, and so on). It was the type of setting in which hundreds of experiments of all kinds were conducted in medical centers all over the world. The only unique element was the specific physiological function under study.

During almost a decade (beginning in 1954) at least 10,000 orgasms were investigated. Because more of the subjects were women and because females were sexually more responsive than males under the circumstances, about three-quarters of these orgasms were experienced by women.

Although no one has yet attempted to replicate Masters and Johnson's study fully, the general validity of their physiological findings has been widely accepted.

In 1970 Masters and Johnson published a second volume, *Human Sexual Inadequacy*, which dealt with the treatment of sexual dysfunction (Chapter 15). Their work provided the basis of our modern methods of sex therapy.

---

The study of the physiology of sexual function was largely neglected until recently. In the fourth century B.C., Aristotle observed that the testes are lifted up within the scrotal sac during sexual excitement and that contractions of the anus accompany orgasm; more than 23 centuries passed before such observations were confirmed under laboratory conditions.

It is common knowledge that sexual

arousal leads to orgasm and is followed by sexual satiety. The pioneer sexologist Havelock Ellis characterized this process as a two-phase sequence, based on a male model: *tumescence* ("swelling") entailed the enlargement of the penis in erection and *detumescence* the return to its unstimulated state (Ellis, 1942). Nevertheless there were few systematic investigations of the physiology of orgasm until the research conducted by Masters and Johnson in the 1960s (Box 3.1). Since then, other studies have supplemented and sometimes amended their work (for instance, Bohlen et al., 1980; Bohlen, 1981) and new technologies have opened up opportunities for physiological research (Box 3.2).

## Box 3.2

### NEW TECHNOLOGY IN SEX RESEARCH

To monitor and measure the physiological changes during the sexual response cycle, a number of new instruments have been developed. The objective data obtained from their use supplements, in important ways, the subjective reports of men and women undergoing sexual arousal and orgasm. These instruments measure the two basic physiological processes that underlie the sexual response cycle—vasocongestion and increased muscular tension.

Genital vasocongestion in the male is assessed by measuring the degree of erection. A *penile strain gauge* consists of a flexible band that fits around the base of the penis and expands with the swelling penis. To study sexual arousal outside of the laboratory, the *Rigiscan monitor* collects data on penile rigidity and tumescence for up to three 10-hour sessions. The subject wears the battery-operated monitor strapped to his thigh with two loops attached to the tip and base of the penis (see the figure). This device easily records erections during sleep.

In the female, the *vaginal photoplethysmograph* accomplishes the same purpose by recording the color changes that result from vasocongestion. A transparent acrylic cylinder is placed within the vaginal opening (see the figure). The light within the cylinder illuminates the vaginal wall; the changes in color produced by the increased number of red blood cells are detected by the photoelectric cell. A more sophisticated device is a *bioimpedance*

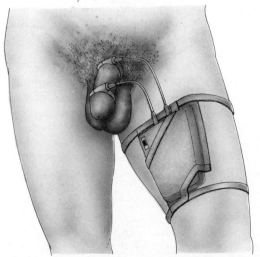 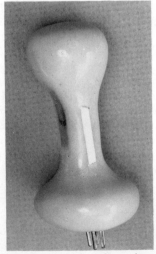

(Right) Vaginal probe monitors arousal two ways. A photoplethysmograph (note the photoelectric cell in the knob) measures vasocongestion, while a myograph (note the metal strip in the shaft) measures myotonia. (Left) The battery-operated Rigiscan monitor collects data on penile erection.

*analyzer,* which measures blood flow by changes in the electrical conductivity of a part of the body (Bradford, 1986).

Increases in muscular tension and the contractions of orgasm can be measured by a *perineometer.*

Placed in the vagina, this instrument will register changes in pressure. *Electronic perineometers* do this by detecting electrical activity when muscle fibers of the vagina and anus are activated (Ladas et al., 1982).

We shall be dealing throughout this chapter with typical patterns of human sexual response. Do not take them as standards of normality. Many variations are perfectly normal. No one else reacts exactly like you.

### Response Patterns

Sexual arousal and orgasm "feel" highly pleasurable, but it is difficult for us to be aware of their effects fully and objectively. Hence, these effects must be observed under laboratory conditions. Figures 3.1 and 3.2 summarize such observations by Masters and Johnson (1966). The sexual response pattern for males (Figure 3.1) and the three patterns for females (Figure 3.2) include the same four phases: *excitement, plateau, orgasm,* and *resolution.* These patterns show up no matter what type of stimulation produces them. The basic physiology of orgasm is the same, regardless of

whether it is brought about through masturbation, coitus, or some other activity.

The sexual responses of men and women are basically similar; yet there are also a number of differences. The first major difference is the greater variability of female response patterns. You probably noticed that although a single sequence characterizes the basic male pattern (Figure 3.1), three alternatives are shown for females (Figure 3.2). The second difference involves a *refractory period* in the male, but not the female, cycle. This obligatory rest period immediately follows orgasm and extends into the resolution phase. During this period, regardless of how intense the sexual stimulation, the male cannot achieve full erection and another orgasm; only after the refractory period has passed can he do so. The length of the refractory period seems to vary greatly among males and with the same person on different occasions. It may last anywhere

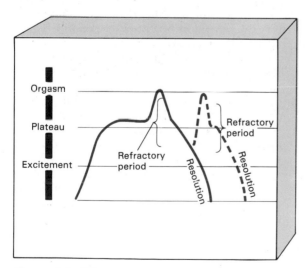

Figure 3.1   The male sexual response cycle.

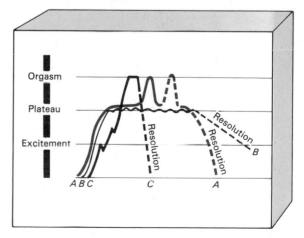

Figure 3.2   The female sexual response cycle.

from a few minutes to several hours. The interval usually gets longer with age and with successive orgasms during a sexual episode (Kolodny et al., 1979).

Arousability is a function not only of the refractory period but also of complex interactional factors. In many mammalian species, sexual response is strongest with new sexual partners, and the introduction of a new partner will revive sexual interest (Michael and Zumpe, 1978). This phenomenon (known as the "Coolidge effect") is usually stronger among males than females.[1] Whether or not a similar mechanism operates among humans has not been formally established, but a yearning for new or multiple sexual partners may be a manifestation of it (Chapter 16).

Females do not have refractory periods (Figure 3.2). Even in the pattern closest to that of the male (pattern A), soon after the first orgasm is over, the level of excitement can lead again to another climax. Women can therefore have "multiple orgasms," that is, consecutive orgasms in quick succession. Of course, not all women, all of the time, can or want to be multiorgasmic.

Male capacity for multiple orgasm is very limited, because of the refractory period. Among the subjects studied by Masters and Johnson (1966), only a few men seemed capable of repeated orgasm with ejaculation within minutes. Other evidence suggests that multiple orgasm is not rare if a man experiences orgasm without ejaculation (Robbins and

Jensen, 1976). We shall return to this issue shortly.

Apart from these differences, the basic physiological response patterns in the two sexes are the same. In males (Figure 3.1) and females (Figure 3.2, pattern A) excitement mounts in response to effective stimulation. If erotic stimulation is sustained, the level of excitement becomes stabilized at a high point, which is the plateau phase, until orgasm follows. This abrupt release is followed by a gradual dissipation of pent-up excitement during the resolution phase.

The lengths of these phases can vary greatly. In general the excitement and resolution phases are the longest. The plateau phase is usually relatively short, and orgasm usually is measured in a matter of seconds. The overall time for one complete response cycle may range from a few minutes to hours. Of course, not all episodes of arousal reach the point of orgasm. Among the Kinsey subjects, men reported reaching orgasm during sexual intercourse generally within four minutes, whereas it took women 10 to 20 minutes to do so. However, when women relied on self-stimulation, they could reach orgasm as fast as the men (Kinsey et al., 1948, 1953).

In alternative female patterns, the woman attains a high level of arousal during the plateau phase, but instead of an orgasmic peak, there is a period of protracted orgasmic release (pattern B in Figure 2.2). The term *status orgasmus* refers to this intensive orgasmic experience. A single prolonged orgasmic episode is superimposed on the plateau phase or a series of orgasms follow each other without discernible plateau-phase intervals (Masters and Johnson, 1966). Finally, pattern C shows a more abrupt orgasmic response, which bypasses the plateau phase and is followed by a quicker resolution of sexual tension.

What really goes on during the phases of the sexual response cycle? Numerous physiological changes occur in the genitals and in other parts of the body. We shall describe separately the changes for the male and female genital organs as well as other parts of the body common to both sexes.

---

[1]The term comes from a probably made-up story recounted by G. Bermant as follows: One day the President and Mrs. Coolidge were visiting a government farm. Soon after their arrival they were taken off on separate tours. When Mrs. Coolidge passed the chicken pens she paused to ask the man in charge if the rooster copulates more than once a day. "Dozens of times," was the reply. "Please tell that to the President," Mrs. Coolidge requested. When the President passed the pens and was told about the rooster, he asked "Same hen every time?" "Oh no, Mr. President, a different one each time." The President nodded slowly, then said, "Tell that to Mrs. Coolidge" (Symons, 1979, p. 211). The Coolidge effect is discussed in detail in Wilson (1982).

## Physiological Mechanisms

Two physiologic mechanisms explain how the body and its various organs respond to sexual stimulation: vasocongestion and myotonia (Masters and Johnson, 1966; deGroat and Booth, 1980; Jensen, 1980).

*Vasocongestion* is the filling of blood vessels and tissues with blood. When the flow of bood into a region exceeds the capacity of the veins to drain the blood away, it becomes *engorged*. Sexual excitement is accompanied by widespread vasocongestion in surface and deep tissues. Its most obvious manifestation is the erection of the penis. The physiology of erection has been the subject of considerable research, yet its precise mechanisms remain unclear (Benson et al., 1981; Newman and Northup, 1981; Krane and Siroky, 1981).

The primary cause of erection is increased arterial blood inflow and decreased venous outflow. When the penis is flaccid, the blood coming in through the arteries is drained through the deep veins within the penis, bypassing the spongy tissues of the penis. During sexual arousal, the increased blood inflow is shunted into the spongy tissue, causing the corpora cavernosa to expand (just as a garden hose becomes stiff when filled with water under pressure).

Women experience vasocongestion too: the clitoris enlarges, the labia swell, and the vagina moistens. We assume that similar physiological processes are at work, but new research may reveal different mechanisms (Levin, 1980). So far we know less about female than male sexual physiology (apart from reproduction). One reason is that much of the experimental work in this area has been done with animals. It is easy to see a male animal's erection, but hard to see a female's response. This same consideration applies to the exploration of nervous mechanisms, discussed in the next section.

*Myotonia* means increased muscular tension. Even when you are completely relaxed, your muscles maintain a certain degree of muscle tone. From this baseline, muscular tension increases during voluntary actions or involuntary contractions. During sexual activity increased myotonia is widespread. It affects both smooth (involuntary) and skeletal (voluntary) muscles. Myotonia culminates in orgasmic contractions, which involve muscles of both varieties. Although myotonia is present from the start of sexual excitement, it tends to lag behind vasocongestion and disappears shortly after orgasm.

## Excitement and Plateau Phases

Although described as separate phases by Masters and Johnson, excitement and plateau are a continuous process. The plateau phase is a time of sustained, intense excitement. Therefore, we will discuss them together.

In response to effective sexual stimulation, a sensation of heightened arousal develops. Thoughts and attention turn to the sexual activity at hand, and the person becomes progressively oblivious to other stimuli and events. Most people attempt to exert some control over the intensity and tempo of mounting sexual tensions. They may try to suppress it by diverting attention to other matters, or to enhance it by dwelling on its pleasurable aspects. If circumstances are favorable to fuller expression, these erotic stirrings are difficult to ignore. On the other hand, anxiety or distraction may easily dissipate sexual arousal during early stages.

Although excitement sometimes intensifies rapidly and relentlessly, it usually mounts more unevenly. In younger adults the progression is steeper, whereas in older people it tends to be more gradual. As the level of tension reaches the plateau phase, external distractions become less effective, and orgasm is more likely to occur. The prelude to orgasm is pleasurable in itself, and following a period of sustained excitement one may voluntarily forego the climax. Pelvic congestion unrelieved by orgasm can be a source of minor and transient discomfort for both sexes. Men experience localized heaviness and tension in the testes ("blue balls"), whereas women have a more diffuse sense of pelvic fullness with feelings of restlessness and irritability.

The behavioral and subjective manifestations of sexual excitement vary so widely that no one description can possibly encompass them all. With mild sexual excitement, few reactions may be visible to the casual observer; on the other hand, in intense excitement behavioral changes are dramatic. The person in the grip of intense sexual arousal appears tense from head to toe. The skin becomes flushed, salivation increases, the nostrils flare, the heart pounds, breathing grows heavy, and the person feels, looks, and acts quite differently than usual.

Sexual arousal may also have more personal effects: some stutterers speak more freely when sexually aroused; the gagging reflex may become less sensitive (which explains the ability of some people to take the penis deep into their mouths); persons afflicted with spastic paralysis coordinate their movements better; those suffering from hay fever may obtain temporary relief; bleeding from cuts decreases. The perception of pain is also blunted during sexual arousal (which may help people to withstand sadomasochistic practices).

Male Sex Organs    The penis undergoes striking changes during sexual excitement. Erection is the most obvious (Figure 3.3).

Erection is not an all-or-nothing phenomenon; there are many gradations between the totally flaccid penis and the maximally congested organ immediately before orgasm. As a penis becomes erect, it first increases to its full length and circumference, and then attains its maximum rigidity or hardness (Wein et al., 1981).

A certain degree of rigidity is necessary to enter the vagina. However, a less than fully erect penis can go in ("soft entry"). Especially among older men, it is not unusual for penetration to begin with only a partially erect penis; full rigidity follows during intercourse.

Erection can occur with remarkable rapidity: in younger males, less than ten seconds may be all the time required. Older men generally respond more slowly. During the plateau phase there is further engorgement, primarily in the corona of the glans, and its color deepens. Erection is now more stable, and the man

may temporarily turn his attention away from sexual activity without losing his erection.

The scrotum also contracts and thickens during sexual arousal. During the plateau phase there are no further scrotal changes. The changes undergone by the testes, though not as visible, are marked. First, during the excitement phase both testes are lifted up within the scrotum, mainly as a result of the shortening of the spermatic cords and the contraction of the scrotal sac. During the plateau phase this elevation progresses farther until the testes are actually pressed against the abdomen. For reasons that are unclear, full testicular elevation is a precondition for orgasm. The second major change is a marked increase in size (about 50 percent) because of vasocongestion.

The Cowper's glands show no evidence of activity during the excitement phase. During the plateau phase, drops of clear fluid produced by these glands appear at the tip of the penis; some men produce enough of it to wet the glans or even dribble freely; others produce very little fluid. The prostate gland enlarges during the plateau phase.

Female Sex Organs    The vagina responds like the penis to sexual stimulation. During the excitement phase the vagina shows lubrication, expansion of its inner end, and color change (Figure 3.4). Moistening of the vaginal walls is the first sign of sexual response in women; it may be present within 10 to 30 seconds. The amount of vaginal lubrication alone does not reflect the degree of sexual arousal; some women, though highly aroused, produce little fluid. The production of vaginal fluid gets less after the menopause. The resulting vaginal dryness may require lubricants, but it need not interfere with sexual enjoyment (Chapter 10).

Moistening by the clear, slippery, and mildly scented vaginal fluid is important for a woman's enjoyment of coitus. As the fluid is alkaline, it also helps neutralize the vaginal canal (which normally tends to be acidic) in preparation for the transit of semen.

The vaginal wall has no secretory glands, so it was assumed that the lubricant emanated

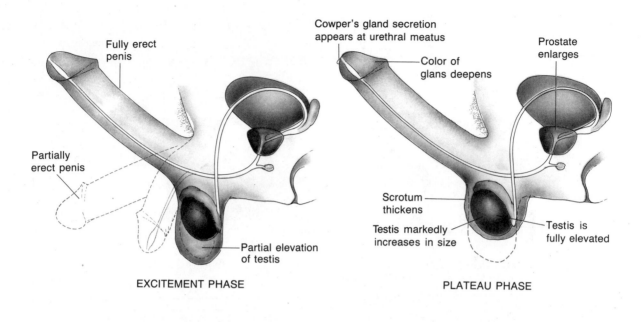

EXCITEMENT PHASE

Fully erect penis

Partially erect penis

Partial elevation of testis

PLATEAU PHASE

Cowper's gland secretion appears at urethral meatus

Color of glans deepens

Prostate enlarges

Scrotum thickens

Testis markedly increases in size

Testis is fully elevated

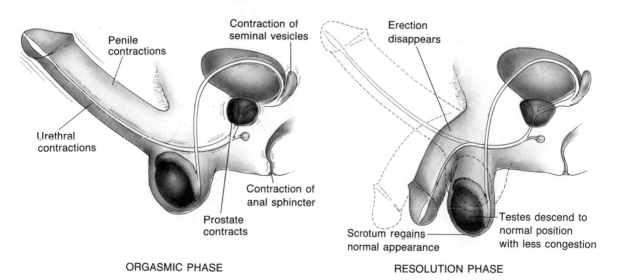

ORGASMIC PHASE

Penile contractions

Contraction of seminal vesicles

Urethral contractions

Contraction of anal sphincter

Prostate contracts

RESOLUTION PHASE

Erection disappears

Scrotum regains normal appearance

Testes descend to normal position with less congestion

Figure 3.3   Changes in male sex organs during the sexual response cycle.

from either the cervix, the Bartholin's glands, or both, until it was discovered by Masters and Johnson (1966) that this fluid comes out mainly from the vaginal walls. Although the vaginal lubricatory reaction is often compared to "sweating" of the skin, the analogy is not accurate. Sweat or perspiration is produced by sweat glands in the skin; the vaginal lubricant is not produced by glands. It seeps out of the congested blood vessels (capillaries) near the

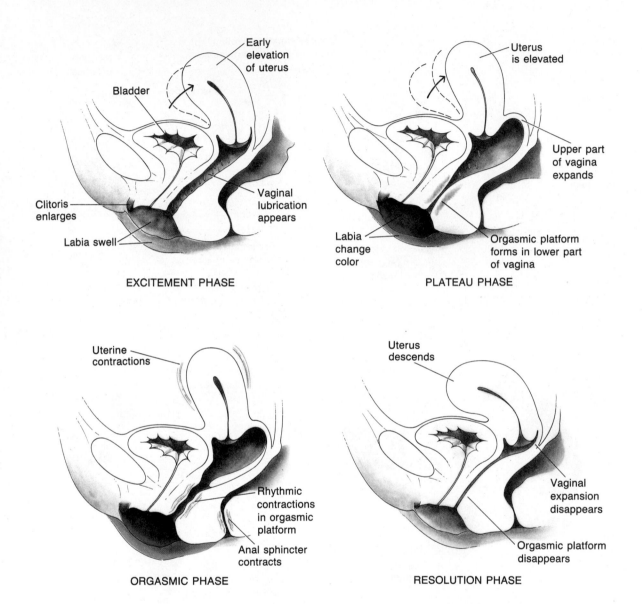

**EXCITEMENT PHASE**

Early elevation of uterus

Bladder

Clitoris enlarges

Labia swell

Vaginal lubrication appears

**PLATEAU PHASE**

Uterus is elevated

Upper part of vagina expands

Labia change color

Orgasmic platform forms in lower part of vagina

**ORGASMIC PHASE**

Uterine contractions

Rhythmic contractions in orgasmic platform

Anal sphincter contracts

**RESOLUTION PHASE**

Uterus descends

Vaginal expansion disappears

Orgasmic platform disappears

Figure 3.4    Changes in female sex organs during the sexual response cycle.

surface of the vaginal wall, and is known as a *transudate.*

The second major vaginal change during the excitement phase is the lengthening and expansion of the inner two-thirds of the vagina, known as "tenting," which creates the space where the ejaculate will be deposited. Finally, the vagina undergoes a color change. Its walls take on a darker hue reflecting the effects of progressive vasocongestion.

During the plateau phase the outer third of the vagina becomes swollen, forming the *or-*

*gasmic platform* and narrowing the vaginal opening. Meanwhile the tenting effect at the inner end attains full vaginal expansion. Vaginal lubrication tends to slow down, and if the plateau phase is unduly protracted, further production of vaginal fluid may cease altogether.

Recently, considerable interest has been elicited by reports that there exists an erotically sensitive area deep in the anterior (front) wall of the vagina that becomes swollen during sexual arousal. Named the *Grafenberg spot,* the exact physiology of this dime-sized region and its connection with "female ejaculation" are yet to be fully determined (Box 3.3).

The clitoris too becomes markedly con-

gested, late in the excitement phase. The clitoral glans may double its diameter. At the same time the minor labia swell. (At this point the penis has been erect for some time and the vagina is fully lubricated.)

During the plateau phase the clitoris is retracted under the clitoral hood, receding to half its unstimulated length (which may be misinterpreted by the sexual partner as indicating loss of sexual tension). When excitement abates, the clitoris reemerges from under the hood. During protracted plateau phases there may be several repetitions of this retraction–emergence sequence.

The labia of women who have not given birth (nulliparous labia) respond somewhat

# Box 3.3

## THE GRAFENBERG SPOT AND FEMALE EJACULATION

The question of whether or not women ejaculate has intrigued people for a long time. Until the 17th century, the vaginal lubricant fluid was assumed to be a female "ejaculate" analogous to male semen and therefore essential for conception. This misunderstanding was the basis of theological tolerance of female masturbation during coitus; if a woman could not reach orgasm during coitus it was permissible that she did so by manipulation; otherwise she would be unable to complement the male's semen with her own ejaculate to make conception possible. When the nature of human reproduction became better understood this notion was discarded, and women were declared incapable of ejaculation.

Still, the controversy lingered on. Reports kept appearing of women emitting fluid at orgasm, but there was much confusion about its composition. The suggested alternatives included urine, fluid from Bartholin's glands, vaginal lubricant expelled forcibly during orgasmic contractions, and fluid from the urethra.

In 1950, Ernest Grafenberg published an article in which he made two claims (Grafenberg, 1950). First, there exists an "erotic zone" on the front wall of the vagina along the course of the ur-

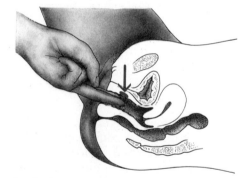

The Grafenberg Spot (G-spot).

ethra. This area becomes enlarged during sexual excitement and protrudes into the vaginal canal; following orgasm, it reverts to its nonstimulated state. Second, "large quantities of a clear transparent fluid" gush out of the urethra during orgasm, at least in the case of some women.

Grafenberg explained both phenomena by the hypothesis that there persisted in the female the homologue of the erectile tissues surrounding the male urethra (the corpus spongiosum) and the homologue of the prostate gland (known as "Skene's glands"). The existence of the first would explain the swelling of the anterior (front) vaginal wall. Similarly, the Skene's glands would function as a "female prostate," providing the fluid in female ejaculation (just as the ejaculatory fluid in the male is provided by the prostate). Grafenberg's hypothesis was plausible on the grounds of embryonal development, but he offered no anatomical evidence and little objective clinical data to support it.

Attention was refocused on this issue by Sevely and Bennett (1978). Based on a review of the literature, they concluded that women do ejaculate and that the fluid they emit is similar though not identical to prostatic fluid in the male. Perry and Whipple (1981) pursued further this line of research, and they named the "erotic zone" in the anterior vaginal wall the *Grafenberg spot* (G-spot). According to them and other researchers, the G-spot is located about two inches from the vagina's entrance (see the figure). When properly stimulated, it swells and leads to orgasm (often a whole series of them) in many women. During orgasm, many women emit a fluid through the urethra. These women are embarrassed because they believe they are losing urinary control; hence, to avoid it, they try to suppress their orgasms (Ladas et al., 1982).

What is the fluid these women emit? Some researchers have reported it to contain higher levels of acid phosphatase (an enzyme secreted by the prostate gland) and glucose (sugar), and lower levels of urea and creatinine (end products of protein metabolism excreted in urine) than contained in urine (Belzer, 1981). Acid phosphatase levels, though higher than in urine, have never been found as high as in the male ejaculate. Hence, in this view, women emit urethral fluid with some similarities to prostatic fluid in men (Addiego et al., 1981).

Attempts to validate these claims by other researchers have not generally been successful. In one study, the female "ejaculate" turned out to be urine (Goldberg et al., 1983). Even if a sensitive area exists in the anterior vaginal wall, no anatomical evidence has linked it to Skene's glands (Alzate and Hoch, 1986). Instead of just a discrete "spot," the entire anterior vaginal wall appears to be highly sensitive, and its stimulation likely to lead to orgasm (Hoch, 1986).

If further studies validate the existence of the G-spot and female ejaculation, it will help us understand female sexual physiology and treat problems. Meanwhile, the controversy may be causing undue anxiety if a woman believes that she is lacking sexually if she does not "ejaculate" or does not appear to be blessed with a G-spot.

---

differently from those of women who have (parous labia). Nulliparous major lips become flattened, thinner, and more widely parted during excitement, revealing the congested moist tissue within. Parous major lips are larger and, instead of flattening, become markedly engorged during arousal.

As the excitement phase progresses to the plateau level, the minor lips become severely engorged and double or even triple in size in both parous and nulliparous women. They also turn pink, or even bright red in light-complexioned women. In parous women the resulting color is a more intense red or a deeper wine color. This vivid coloration of the minor lips has been called the *sex skin*. Like full testicular elevation of the male, the presence of the sex skin in the sexually aroused woman

heralds impending orgasm.

Bartholin's glands secrete a few drops of fluid rather late in the excitement phase. The function of this fluid is not clear. It contributes little to vaginal lubrication.

The uterus responds to sexual stimulation by elevation from its tilted position, which pulls the cervix up and contributes to the tenting effect in the vagina. Full uterine elevation is achieved during the plateau phase and is maintained until resolution.

Other Reactions    Erection of the nipple is the first response of the female breast in the excitement phase. (A man's nipples too sometimes grow erect in the late excitement and plateau phases.) Engorgement of blood vessels is also responsible for the swelling of the woman's breasts. In the plateau phase the engorgement of the areolae is more marked. As a result, the erect nipples appear relatively smaller. The breast swells further during this phase, particularly if it has never been suckled. It may increase by as much as a fourth of its unstimulated size.

Sexual arousal results in definite skin reactions. The *sex flush* is more common and pronounced in women. It starts in the excitement phase as a rash-like redness of the skin in the center of the lower chest, which spreads to the breasts, the rest of the chest wall, and the neck. This sexual flush reaches its peak in the late plateau phase and is an important component of the excited, straining facial expression characteristic of the person about to experience orgasm. The appearance of tension is also conveyed by the musculature of the body in the platcau phase. The muscles of the feet, in particular, tense up, with rigid extension of the toes (carpopedal spasm).

The heart rate increases in the excitement phase, and by the plateau phase it reaches 100 to 160 beats a minute. (The normal resting heart rate is 60 to 80 beats a minute.) The blood pressure similarly increases. Changes in respiratory rate lag somewhat behind those in heart rate. Faster and deeper breathing becomes apparent only in the plateau phase.

These changes in cardiovascular function are comparable to levels reached in moderate physical effort, such as taking a brisk walk or going up a flight of stairs. The strain on the cardiovascular system is easily handled by most individuals. Nonetheless, a substantial proportion of men lose sexual interest, or develop problems with potency, following heart attacks. In most of these cases the problem is psychological; there is usually no medical reason why men and women with heart disease should not maintain an active sexual life, although it makes sense to check with the doctor (Kolodny et al., 1979).

## Orgasm

In physiological terms *orgasm* is the discharge of accumulated neuromuscular tension which results from sexual arousal. Subjectively, it is a high pitch of erotic tension, one of the most intense and profoundly satisfying human sensations; it lasts a fraction of a minute, yet it feels like an eternity. The term "orgasm" is derived from the Greek *orgasmos* ("to swell," "to be lustful"). Colloquial terms include "to climax," "to come," and "to spend."

The intensity of orgasmic experience varies somewhat with age, physical condition, and context, but it is usually felt by both men and women as an intensely pleasurable experience. Davidson (1980) characterizes it as a form of "altered state of consciousness."

In adult males the sensations of orgasm are linked to ejaculation, which occurs in two stages. First, there is a sense that ejaculation is imminent (or "coming") and unstoppable. Second, there is a distinct awareness of throbbing contractions at the base of the penis, followed by the sensation of fluid moving out under pressure.

Orgasm in the female starts with a feeling of momentary suspension or "stoppage." Sensations of tingling and tension in the clitoris then reach a peak and spread to the vagina and pelvis. This stage varies in intensity. It may also involve sensations of "falling," "opening up," or emitting fluid. (Some women compare it to mild labor contractions.) It is followed by a suffusion of warmth spreading from the pelvis through the rest of the body, culminating in throbbing sensations in the pelvis. One woman describes it as follows:

> There are a few faint sparks, coming up to orgasm, and then I suddenly realize that it is going to catch fire, and then I concentrate all my energies, both physical and mental, to quickly bring on the climax—which turns out to be a moment suspended in time, a hot rush, a sudden breathtaking dousing of all the nerves of my body in pleasure (Hite, 1976).

Due to the tell-tale evidence of ejaculation, a man can hardly miss identifying an orgasm, yet some women feel uncertain whether they have had one. Are all orgasms the same? No two sexual experiences of any kind are ever the same, but the male orgasmic experience seems to follow a more standard pattern than the female. Possibly women have different kinds of orgasms, based on different physiological mechanisms (Box 3.4). Other evidence suggests that the orgasmic experience in the two sexes is not that dissimilar. When brief descriptions of orgasm by men and women were submitted to a panel of psychologists, they were unable to identify the sex of the authors from the descriptions (Vance and Wagner, 1976).

**Male Sex Organs**    The characteristic rhythmic muscular contractions of orgasm begin in the prostate, seminal vesicles, and vas deferens, then extend to the penis (Figure 3.3), involving the entire length of the urethra, as well as the muscles covering the root of the penis. At first the contractions occur fairly regularly at intervals of approximately 0.8 second, but after the first several strong throbs they become weaker, irregular, and less frequent.

Studies subsequent to the work of Masters and Johnson have studied male orgasm as manifested in contractions of the anal sphinc-

# Box 3.4

## VARIETIES OF FEMALE ORGASM

Probably more has been written on the female orgasm than any other aspect of human sexuality (Levin, 1981). Until fairly recently, our ideas about the female orgasm were strongly influenced by psychoanalytic theory. According to Freud women experience two types of orgasm: clitoral and vaginal. *Clitoral orgasm* is attained exclusively through direct clitoral stimulation, usually by masturbation; *vaginal orgasm* results from vaginal stimulation, usually through coitus. This dual orgasm theory claims that in young girls the clitoris is the primary site of sexual excitement. With psychosexual maturity the sexual focus is said to shift from the clitoris to the vagina, so after puberty the vagina emerges as the dominant orgasmic zone (Chapter 8). That makes vaginal orgasm more "mature" than clitoral orgasm. With some variations, this model was reiterated by Freud's followers. Modern psychoanalysts, however, do not all adhere to this view (Salzman, 1968).

Kinsey and his associates (1953) doubted the validity of the Freudian concept of dual orgasm. Masters and Johnson (1966) reaffirmed these doubts and established that physiologically there is only one type of orgasm: orgasmic response to clitoral, vaginal, or any other form of stimulation is all the same (Masters and Johnson, 1966). Others further endorsed the single-type orgasm model. For instance, Sherfey (1973) favored it in her theory of the evolution of female sexuality. Furthermore, given the greater female capability for multiple or-

gasms, she hypothesized that females are endowed with an insatiable sexual drive, which has been socially suppressed so as not to interfere with maternal functions.

Investigators have nevertheless continued to distinguish different types of orgasm. Fisher (1973), based on his appraisal of psychological and physiological studies, has restated the distinction between clitoral and vaginal orgasm, while rejecting its psychoanalytic implications. Singer and Singer (1972), based on their physiological studies, have proposed three types of female orgasm. First is the *vulval orgasm*, characterized by involuntary rhythmic contractions of the vaginal entrance, which they consider to be the same as orgasms described by Masters and Johnson. Second, there is the *uterine orgasm*, which results from the repetitive displacement of the uterus and is dependent on coitus or a close substitute. The third type is the *blended orgasm*, combining elements of the other two.

As an extension of their work with the G-spot (Box 3.3), Ladas, Whipple, and Perry (1982) have suggested that a *continuum of orgasmic response* would integrate earlier orgasmic models with their own findings. At one end is the *clitoral orgasm* (the Singers' "vulval orgasm"); triggered by clitoral stimulation, it involves contractions of the circumvaginal muscles and is felt primarily at the orgasmic platform. At the other end is the *vaginal orgasm* (Singers' "uterine orgasm"); triggered by stimulation of the

G-spot, it involves contractions of the uterus and is hence experienced in the region of the pelvic organs. The vaginal orgasm is terminative—one is enough to attain sexual satiety. The clitoral orgasm is not and calls for repetition (Fisher, 1973; Bentler and Peeler, 1979).

This issue has also found its way into literature. In the *Golden Notebook,* the novelist Doris Lessing writes:

> A vaginal orgasm is emotion and nothing else, felt as emotion and expressed in sensations that are indistinguishable from emotion. The vaginal orgasm is a dissolving in a vague, dark, generalised sensation like being swirled in a warm whirlpool. There are several different sorts of clitoral orgasms, and they are more powerful (that is a male word) than the vagi-

nal orgasm. There can be a thousand thrills, sensations, etc., but there is only one real female orgasm and that is when a man, from the whole of his need and desire, takes a woman and wants all her response. Everything else is a substitute and a fake, and the most inexperienced woman feels this instinctively (Lessing, 1962, p. 186).

Whatever the experiential differences, it is best to avoid the notion that one form of female orgasm is "better" than another. Women were needlessly burdened in the past by the idea that clitoral orgasm was less "mature." Now they are made to feel they must have multiple orgasm and ejaculatory orgasm. Every woman should discover her own possibilities. No woman should have to "measure up" to anyone else's standards.

---

ter. Masters and Johnson reported that two to four anal contractions occurred during this period. Later Bohlen and his associates found an average of 17 anal contractions (Figure 3.5) (Bohlen et al., 1980). They occur over a period of 26 seconds, a close estimate of the length of male orgasm, although subject to considerable individual variation.

*Ejaculation* ("throwing out") entails the ejection of semen. It is the most obvious manifestation of orgasm in males following puberty, when the prostate and other glands produce seminal fluid. Before puberty, boys do not ejaculate, even though they can experience orgasm (Chapter 8).

Ejaculation has two distinct phases. During the first phase, called *seminal emission* (or *first-stage orgasm),* the smooth muscles of the prostate, seminal vesicles, and vas deferens contract, pouring their contents into the dilated urethral bulb. At this point the man feels ejaculatory pressure building up. In the second, or *expulsion phase* (*second-stage orgasm*), the semen is expelled by the vigorous contractions of the muscles surrounding the root of the penis, other muscles of the pelvic region, and the genital ducts. The inner sphincter of the urinary bladder simultaneously closes, preventing semen from flowing into the bladder.

The amount of fluid and the force with which it is ejaculated are popularly associated with strength of desire, potency, and so on, but these beliefs are difficult to substantiate. There does seem, however, to be a valid association between the emission phase and the onset of the refractory period. Some men are able to inhibit the emission of semen while they experience the orgasmic contractions—in other words, they have *nonejaculatory orgasms.* Such orgasms do not seem to be followed by a refractory period, so these men can have consecutive or multiple orgasms, like women. Only if emission of semen occurs with ejaculation does a refractory period follow. Ancient Chinese sex manuals have long extolled the virtues of nonejaculatory coitus (Box 3.5). The Indian practice of *Karezza* or *coitus reservatus* is a similar protracted coitus without ejaculation.

However, the matter is even more complicated. The fact that no ejaculate comes out of the penis does not necessarily mean that emission did not take place. In cases of *retrograde ejaculation,* the flow of semen is reversed, so that instead of flowing out of the urethra, it is emptied into the urinary bladder. The sensation of orgasm in this condition is unchanged, and a refractory period presumably follows normally. This condition occurs in

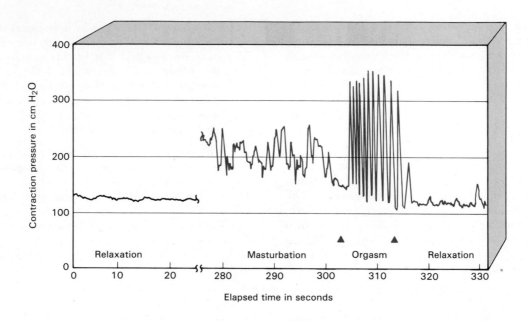

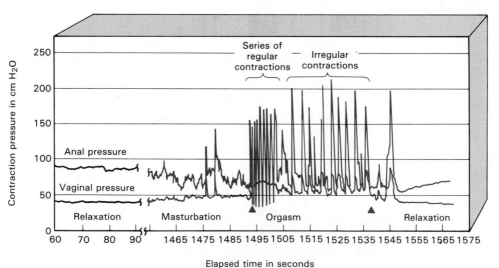

Figure 3.5    (Above) Computer-drawn plot of anal tension and contractions during male masturbation. (Below) Anal and vaginal pressures during female masturbation.

some illnesses and with the use of certain common tranquilizers and blood pressure drugs (Chapter 15).

Female Sex Organs    During female orgasm, the most visible effects occur in the orgasmic platform (Figure 3.4). This area contracts rhyth-

mically and with decreasing intensity (initially at approximately 0.8-second intervals). The more frequent and intense the contractions of the orgasmic platform, the more intense is the subjective experience of orgasm. At particularly high levels of excitement these rhythmic contractions are preceded by nonrhythmic

# Box 3.5

## EJACULATORY CONTROL

The aspect of male orgasm that has attracted the most attention is ejaculation. It is essential for fertilization and represents the peak of male orgasmic pleasure, but ejaculation can also be fraught with anxiety. For many a man, getting an erection is a bit like becoming airborne in a glider; he strives to remain aloft as long as he can, but he does not have full control. Once orgasm is triggered, he cannot stop it. If it occurs before he and his partner are satisfied, he feels he has failed to "perform." Ironically, his "performance anxiety" itself makes it more likely that he will fail to get an erection or he will ejaculate prematurely (Chapter 15).

An even deeper anxiety has plagued men since ancient times over the loss of semen. The ancient Greeks were mindful of its value: Hippocrates commented on its "precious" character; Pythagoras called it a "flower of the blood"; and Galen held that an ounce of semen was worth 40 ounces of blood, a notion that persisted into the Middle Ages. In the 12th century, the Talmudic scholar and physician Maimonides wrote:

> Effusion of semen represents the strength of the body and its life, and the light of the eyes. Whenever it [semen] is emitted to excess, the body becomes consumed, its strength terminates, and its life perishes. . . . He who immerses himself in sexual intercourse will be assailed by [premature] aging. His strength will wane, his eyes will weaken, and a bad odor will emit from his mouth and his armpits. . . . His teeth will fall out and many maladies other than these will afflict him. The wise physicians have stated that one in a thousand dies from other illnesses and the remaining [999 in the thousand] from excessive sexual intercourse.

The horror of wasting sperm dominated thinking through the 19th century (Chapter 20). Fantastic notions about "masturbatory insanity" and the ravages of "spermatorrhea" (nocturnal emission) were directly based on such theories of wasting from semen loss.

The notion of semen power is even more an-cient in Asia (Gregersen, 1983). Hindu ascetics practiced continence to enhance their physical and psychic powers. To the Chinese, semen embodied the essence of *yang*, the basic male element in nature (Chapter 10). As a vital essence, semen was not to be squandered. Rather than damning sexual intercourse, the Chinese devised a technique of engaging in protracted coitus without ejaculation, except at carefully controlled intervals. The point was not to avoid ejaculation, but to allow it at optimal intervals, depending on the age of the man, his state of health, the season of the year, and other factors.

This doctrine meant that a man extended his period of coital pleasure and provided his sexual partner with ample opportunity for her enjoyment. Because a woman supposedly did not ejaculate, there was no problem with her experiencing orgasm as often as she wished. Moreover, her vaginal secretions were a rich source of *yin*, the female element in nature. By extended exposure to vaginal secretions through prolonged coitus, a man absorbed the vital female elements; and by refraining from ejaculation, he conserved the male elements. As a result, he attained the ideal harmony of yin and yang, which led to good health and a long life. (Some modern applications of these ideas are discussed in Chang, 1977.)

In Taoist texts, these erotic wisdoms are often conveyed through dialogues between an emperor and his Tao of Loving advisors (usually women). In the following excerpts from *The Secrets of the Jade Chamber*, three advisors offer their views:

*TSAI NU:* It is generally supposed that a man derives great pleasure from ejaculation. But when he learns the Tao he will emit less and less; will not his pleasure also diminish?

*P'ENG TSU:* Far from it. After ejaculation a man is tired, his ears are buzzing, his eyes heavy and he longs for sleep. He is thirsty and his limbs inert and stiff. In ejaculation he experiences a brief second of sensation but long hours of weariness as a result. And that is certainly not a true pleasure. On the other hand, if a man reduces and regulates his ejaculation to an absolute minimum, his body will be strengthened, his mind at ease, and his vision and hearing improved. Although the man seems to have denied himself an ejaculatory sensation at times, his love for his woman will greatly increase. It is as if he could never have enough of her. And this is the true lasting pleasure, is it not? (Chang, 1977, p. 21)

*SU NU:*   When a man loves once without losing his semen, he will strengthen his body. If he loves twice without losing it, his hearing and his vision will be more acute. If thrice, all diseases may disappear. If four times, he will have peace of his soul. If five times his heart and blood circulation will be revitalized. If six times, his loins will become strong. If seven times, his skin may become smooth. If nine times, he will reach longevity. If ten times, he will be like an immortal. (Chang, 1977, p. 44)

---

(spastic) contractions of the orgasmic platform that last several seconds. Whether or not women ejaculate during orgasm is discussed in Box 3.3

Orgasmic contractions in the uterus start at the top (the fundus) and spread downward; although these contractions occur simultaneously with those of the orgasmic platform, they are less distinct and more irregular. It has often been assumed that the contractions of the uterus during coitus cause the semen to be sucked into its cavity. Such an effect was reported by Beck as early as 1874 (Levin, 1980). Masters and Johnson found no evidence to support this idea, but others claim to have done so (Fox and Fox, 1969).

Through new laboratory studies, we now have more precise measures of orgasm. One such approach is to simultaneously record anal and vaginal pressures (which reflect the activity of contracting muscles) during orgasm. As shown in Figure 3.5, pressures in both the anus and vagina erupt into regular and synchronized contractions with the onset of orgasm; in some but not all women, they are followed by irregular contractions to the end of the orgasm. The lengths of recorded orgasms range from 13 to 51 seconds; the period of signaled orgasms (that is, the interval between when the women say they started and stopped orgasm) ranges from about 7 to 107 seconds (Bohlen et al., 1982b). These investigators, unlike Masters and Johnson, found no correlation between the number of orgasmic contractions and level of satisfaction, perceived intensity, or sexual gratification.

Other Reactions   The breasts show no further changes during orgasm; but if a woman is nursing, milk may be ejected from her nipples. Temperature changes in the skin lead to feelings of pervasive warmth following orgasm; and there are popular references to sexual excitement as a "glow," "fever," or "fire." Superficial vasocongestion is the likely explanation of this sensation.

During orgasm, the heart rate reaches its peak, rising to 100 to 180 beats per minute. The respiratory rate may go up to 40 a minute (the normal rate is about 15 a minute, inhalation and exhalation counting as one). Breathing, however, becomes irregular; a person may momentarily hold the breath and then breathe rapidly (Fox and Fox, 1969). Some of the panting and grunts uttered during orgasm result from involuntary contractions of the muscles that force air through the respiratory passages. When the genital muscles contract, so do skeletal muscles in other parts of the body.

A Common Model   To integrate the patterns of male and female orgasm into a coherent scheme, Davidson (1980) has proposed a *bipolar hypothesis* of orgasm. He postulates that when sexual excitement passes a critical threshold, an orgasmic control area in the central nervous system triggers the orgasm. It sends neural impulses simultaneously in two directions: "upward" to higher brain areas in the cortex, producing an intense subjective experience, and "downward" to the genital-pelvic region, producing physiological reactions.

This model would apply to both sexes. It would link the psychological experience of orgasm with its physical aspects. It would explain why contractions without ejaculation in men and "vulval orgasm" in women would not induce a refractory period. On the other hand, a refractory period would follow ejaculation in the male and "uterine orgasm" in the female. Especially if the latter turns out to be accompanied by female ejaculation, then male and female orgasm would emerge as essentially identical.

### Resolution Phase and Aftereffects

Whereas the onset of orgasm is fairly distinct, its termination is less so. As the genital rhythmic throbs become progressively less intense and less frequent, neuromuscular tensions give way to a profound state of relaxation.

The manifestations of the postorgasmic phase are the opposite of those of the preorgasmic period. The entire musculature relaxes. The pounding heart and accelerated breathing revert to normal. Congested and swollen tissues and organs resume their usual color and size. As the body rests, the mind reverts to its ordinary state of consciousness.

The descent from the peak of orgasm may occur in one fell swoop or more gradually. Particularly at night, when the profound postcoital relaxation compounds natural weariness, some people tend to fall asleep. Others feel alert or even exhilarated.

It is not unusual to feel thirsty or hungry following orgasm. Smokers may crave a cigarette. There may be a need to urinate. Some people develop a headache, which is due to vasocongestion in the brain and may be treated with the appropriate drugs (Johns, 1986).

Regardless of the immediate postorgasmic response, a healthy person recovers fully from the aftereffects of orgasm in a short time. Pro-

tracted fatigue is often the result of activities that preceded or accompanied sex (drinking, drugs, lack of sleep), rather than of orgasm itself. When a person is in ill health, however, the experience itself may be quite taxing.

Reactions of Sex Organs   In the resolution phase the changes of the preceding stages are reversed (Figures 3.3 and 3.4). A man loses his erection in two stages: a rapid loss of tumescence, which reduces the organ to a semi-erect state, is followed by a more gradual decongestion, in which the penis returns to its unstimulated size.

After ejaculation, if the penis remains in the vagina it stays erect longer. If the man withdraws, is distracted, or attempts to urinate, detumescence is more rapid. (A man cannot urinate with a fully erect penis, because the internal urinary sphincter closes reflexively to prevent intermingling urine and semen.)

In the woman, the orgasmic platform subsides rapidly. The inner vaginal walls return much more slowly to their usual form. Lubrication may in rare instances continue into this phase, and such continuation indicates lingering or rekindled sexual tension. With sufficient stimulation, another orgasm may follow if the woman so desires.

Other Reactions   Changes in the rest of the body also are reversed following orgasm. In the resolution phase the areolae of the breasts appear less swollen, and the nipples regain their fully erect appearance ("false erection"). Gradually, breasts and nipples return to normal size. The sexual flush disappears. The heart and respiratory rates gradually return to normal. The musculature relaxes.

In 30 to 50 percent of individuals, there is a sweating reaction. Among men this response is less consistent and may involve only the feet and the palms.

## CONTROL OF SEXUAL FUNCTIONS

Underlying the patterns of sexual response are complicated mechanisms of control. Some of them are hormonal (Chapter 4). Others are neurophysiological and coordinated at two levels: in the spinal cord and in the brain (de-Groat, 1986).

## Spinal Control

Sexual functions are controlled at their most elemental level by *spinal reflexes*. An example of a reflex action is the way you kick when the tendon below your knee is tapped. Reflexes are involuntary in the sense that they are automatic. They do not require an "order" to act by the brain; yet, if you try, you can modify or inhibit them to some extent.

The knee-jerk reflex involves the *voluntary nervous system,* muscles that we can move at will. Other reflexes, including those involved in sexual functions, belong to the *autonomic nervous system.* This system operates involuntarily to control many of the internal functions of the body. Its activities are normally carried out without our being aware of them (Guyton, 1986).

The autonomic nervous system has two main subdivisions, both involved in sexual function: the *parasympathetic* and the *sympathetic* system. Stimulation of one or inhibition of the other has the same overall effect. One of the basic functions of autonomic nerves is to control the flow of blood by constricting or dilating arteries. In the case of genital blood vessels, parasympathetic stimulation causes arteries to dilate. Sympathetic stimulation makes them constrict.

Much of the research on the spinal control of sexual functions has been done with animals, and inferences have been drawn to humans. Male animals are easier to study (because of the ease with which erections and ejaculations can be monitored), so we know more about these male processes, which is what we shall describe first.

### Erection and Ejaculation

The reflex control centers of erection and ejaculation are located in the spinal cord. *Afferent* nerves bring in sensory impulses to these centers (such as sensations that arise by touching the genitals). These

centers are activated by these impulses and in turn send out "orders" through *efferent* nerves that bring about changes in the genital organs (such as causing vasocongestion of the penis). Although the spinal reflexes can function independently, they are in close communication with the brain center through messages that go up and down the spinal cord.

There are two *erection centers* in the spinal cord (Figure 3.6). The primary, or *parasympathetic,* center is located in the lowest, or sacral, portion of the spinal cord (between the segments S2 and S4). Into this center come the sensory impulses or sensations from the stimulation of the genitals or nearby erogenous zones. These nerve impulses travel to the spinal cord through the pudendal nerve. In response, the S2-S4 reflex center sends out impulses through efferent parasympathetic nerves which cause vasocongestion and erection of the penis.

A second erection center is located higher up, at the junction of the Thoracic and Lumbar segments of the spinal cord (T-11–L2). This center is part of the *sympathetic* system and receives impulses from the brain that have been generated by psychogenic stimulation such as through erotic sights or sounds, and erotic fantasies. Sympathetic nerves then carry efferent impulses to the genital organs which stimulate erection. The exact mechanism by which this occurs is not clear.

Through messages that go up and down the spinal cord, the brain is in constant communication with the spinal centers. Impulses reaching the brain from the spinal cord are interpreted as the subjective sensation of sexual arousal. Thus, the brain communicates its own state of arousal to the spinal cord, as well as being aroused by sensations from the spinal cord.

The same two locations in the spinal cord contain the *ejaculatory centers* (Figure 3.7). The *sympathetic* ejaculatory center is located in the T11–L2 segments. Sympathetic efferent nerves go out from this center to the smooth muscles of the prostate gland, seminal vesicle, and vas deferens. The contraction of these muscles results in seminal emission, or the first

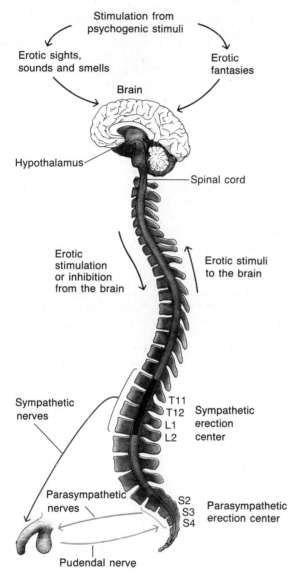

Figure 3.6    Spinal reflex for erection.

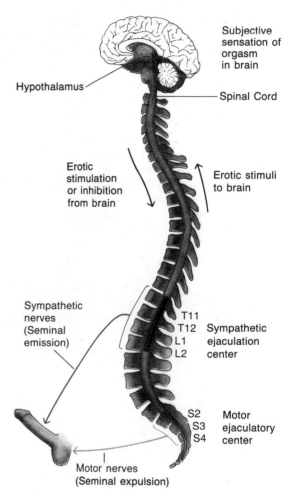

Figure 3.7    Spinal reflex for ejaculation.

phase of ejaculation. The second phase, or expulsion of semen, is triggered by the *voluntary* or *motor* (rather than the parasympathetic) center in the sacral segment of the spinal cord. These impulses go out through somatic efferent nerves to the muscles surrounding the base of the penis. Contractions of these muscles complete the ejaculation of semen (Jensen, 1980; Hart and Leedy, 1985).

Emission and ejaculation are thus closely integrated yet separate physiological processes. Ordinarily they occur together, but under some conditions one or the other may be experienced separately. Emission can take place without ejaculatory contractions; then semen simply seeps out of the urethra. Likewise, ejaculatory contractions can occur without semen being emitted (Tarabulcy, 1972; Bancroft, 1983).

The processes described so far are controlled by reflexes. They are independent of the brain, in the sense that they can occur without its assistance. For instance, a man whose spinal cord has been cut in an injury above the level of the reflex erection center may still be capable of erection. He will not feel the stimulation of his penis; for that matter, he may even be totally unconscious. His penis will respond "automatically."

Obviously, these reflex centers still can be influenced by the brain. Intricate networks link the brain to the reflex centers in the spinal cord. Daydreaming may trigger erection without physical stimulation; worries may inhibit erection despite persistent physical stimulation. Usually mind and body work together. Spurred by erotic thoughts, the man touches his genitals, or excited by a touch, he has erotic thoughts.

The instances in which erection seems to be nonsexual in origin involve tension of the pelvic muscles (as when lifting a heavy weight or straining during defecation). Irritation of the glans or a full bladder may have the same effect. Erections in infancy are explained on a reflex basis also. An additional gruesome example is erection experienced by men during execution by hanging.

Reflexive Mechanisms in Women    It is generally assumed that there are spinal centers in women that correspond to the erection and ejaculatory centers of men. The reflexive centers in the female spinal cord are less well identified in part because the manifestations of orgasm are difficult to ascertain among female experimental animals.

The effects of spinal cord injury on sexual function have been less well studied among women. Clinical experience shows women often lose the ability to reach orgasm because of diminished vasocongestion and vaginal lubrication (Kolodny et al., 1979). Nonetheless, the ability of women to engage in coitus in spite of spinal injuries is likely to be less limited than that of men. Women can engage in coitus without adequate vasocongestion (using artificial lubrication), whereas men cannot do so without an erection. Apart from coitus, both women and men can engage in other satisfying sexual interactions (Chapter 15).

The Role of Neurotransmitters    Some of the most exciting recent discoveries in neuroscience have involved the chemicals that transmit impulses in the brain and by peripheral nerves. Such *neurotransmitters* may help explain both how the genitals function and the brain processes underlying sexual motivation (Thompson, 1985).

Some neurotransmitters, such as *acetylcholine,* have long been known to transmit impulses from autonomic nerves to muscle cells. When muscles in the walls of arteries relax, the walls dilate and more blood flows; this mechanism underlies vasocongestion and erection.

More recently, other neurotransmitters have been discovered that may have an even more direct bearing on sexual functions. One unlikely-sounding substance is *vasoactive intestinal polypeptide (VIP).* First isolated in the gastrointestinal tract, VIP is also found in nerves of the genitourinary system, as well as in the vas deferens, prostate, and the cavernous bodies of the penis. It is hypothesized that VIP causes relaxation of cavernous smooth muscles, allowing increased blood flow; it may be important in starting and maintaining erection (Arsdalen et al., 1983; Goldstein, 1986). Other neurotransmitters may shed further light on many other aspects of sexual physiology. Our understanding of their role is just developing (Money, 1987).

### Brain Control

All sensory input must be interpreted in your brain before you feel any sensation. No thought, however trivial, and no emotion, however fleeting, can exist in an empty skull. Therefore all bodily experiences must be finally understood at the level of brain activity. Such understanding will not substitute for other ways of conceptualizing human experience, as in psychological or ethical terms, but neither can we ever dispense with understanding the physical basis.

There are many ways to investigate mechanisms in the brain. One is electrical stimulation. Erection, ejaculation, and copulatory behavior are elicited by stimulating certain areas in the brain. Related studies use an electroencephalograph to monitor the natural electrical activity of the brain during orgasm (Cohen et al., 1976).

The second method of study is destruction of brain centers. For instance, scientists have been able to eliminate male copulatory behavior in a variety of mammalian species by destroying the medial preoptic region of the brain. Similarly, they have eliminated sexual receptivity in female mammals by hypothalamic lesions. If stimulation of a brain area results in a sexual reaction such as erection, and destruction of the region eliminates it, then we can infer that the area is at least one link in the chain of brain mechanisms controlling that function. (Animal studies like these may be cruel, but they are often important for understanding physiological functions.)

A third and complementary approach is to identify brain areas that inhibit a given function. How we act is the outcome of the "push" to behave in a certain way and the "pull" restraining us. An activity appears or increases if scientists remove or destroy the parts of the brain that inhibit it. For example, removal of the temporal lobes in a monkey results in a striking increase in autoerotic, heterosexual, and homosexual behavior. These monkeys often show penile erections even when sitting quietly (the *Kluver-Bucy syndrome*). Similar reactions occur in humans whose temporal lobes on both sides have been removed for treatment purposes (Terzian and Dale-Ore, 1955).

The central core of the brain, the first part to evolve, controls the most basic life-sustaining activities. Of particular interest to sexuality in this region is the *hypothalamus*, which exerts a crucial influence on nerves and hormones (Chapter 4), and the *limbic system*.

The limbic system surrounds the upper portion of the central brain core, deep within the cerebral hemispheres (Figure 3.8). This portion of the brain probably provides the cen-

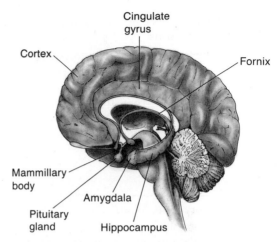

Figure 3.8    The limbic system.

tral nervous control of our sexual behavior. Because we know little of its workings, it has been called the "black box" of our sexuality (Bancroft, 1983). Included in this system are the hippocampus, the fornix, the amygdala, the mammillary bodies, and the cingulate gyrus. Closely interconnected with the hypothalamus, the limbic system is involved in many "instinctive" activities like feeding, attacking, fleeing from danger, and sex. Electrical stimulation of parts of the limbic system elicits penile erection, mounting, and grooming in male animals (MacLean, 1976). Certain regions of the limbic system are also involved in the experience of emotions and may be linked to feelings of sexual pleasure.

In the hypothalamus and related regions of the rat brain, areas have been identified whose electrical stimulation appears to be highly rewarding; they have been called *pleasure centers* (Olds, 1956). Similar centers may exist in the limbic system of the human brain (Heath, 1972).

At the moment, we cannot adequately explain the way sexual sensations feel by neurophysiological processes. No one yet has precisely localized sexual sensations in the human brain. Even if researchers found "sex centers," we still would need to understand how all the systems related to sexuality work together. As Beach (1976) explains,

> Instead of depending on one or more centers, sexual responsiveness and performance are served by a net of neural subsystems, including components from the cerebral cortex down to the sacral cord. Different subsystems act in concert, but tend to mediate different units or elements in the normally integrated patterns. (p. 216)

We are still a long way from understanding the physiological bases of the complex and subtle human sexual experience, but the rewards of such understanding will be enormous.

## REVIEW QUESTIONS

1. Which sensory systems are involved in sexual arousal?

2. Which two basic physiological processes underlie most signs of sexual arousal?

3. What are the stages and main genital manifestations of the sexual response cycle?

4. What are the other reactions of the body during the sexual response cycle?

5. What are the spinal reflexes involved in erection and orgasm?

## THOUGHT QUESTIONS

1. A perfume arouses you. Is your response due to psychological or physiological mechanisms?

2. How does ideology affect discussions of the varieties of female orgasm?

3. What studies would you conduct to settle the controversy about the G spot?

4. What would be the psychological and social consequences if it were to be established that discrete brain centers control sexual behavior?

5. What are the ethical arguments for and against doing laboratory studies of sexual physiology with humans?

## SUGGESTED READINGS

Masters, W. H., and Johnson, V. E. (1966). *Human sexual response*. Boston: Little, Brown. The original and still the standard source on sexual physiology.

Brecher, R., and Brecher, E. (1966). *An analysis of human sexual response*. A nontechnical and clear summary of the Masters and Johnson research on the sexual response cycle.

Davidson, J. M. (1980). "The psychobiology of sexual experience." In Davidson, J. M., and Davidson, R. (Eds.), *The psychobiology of consciousness*. New York: Plenum Press. A comprehensive and clear overview of the role of neuroendocrine factors in sexual experience.

Thompson, R. F. (1985). *The brain*. An excellent introduction to the neurosciences, including the neurophysiological mechanisms regulating sexual functions.

# Sex Hormones

## CHAPTER

# 4

*We must examine the powers of humors, and how they are related to one another.*

HIPPOCRATES (5th c. B.C.)

## OUTLINE

HORMONAL SYSTEMS AND
  SEXUAL FUNCTIONS
Gonadal Hormones
  Androgens
  Estrogens and Progestins
  Inhibin
Pituitary Hormones
Hypothalamic Hormones
Control Systems
PUBERTY
Somatic Changes
Reproductive Maturation
  Female Maturation
  Male Maturation
Neuroendocrine Control
THE MENSTRUAL CYCLE
Menarche
Phases of the Menstrual Cycle
  Preovulatory Phase
  Ovulation

Postovulatory Phase
Menstrual Phase
Menstrual Discomfort
  Dysmenorrhea
  Premenstrual Syndrome
ATYPICAL SEXUAL DEVELOPMENT
Chromosome Disorders
Hormone Disorders
Tissue Disorders
HORMONES AND SEXUAL
  BEHAVIOR
Mammalian Behavior
  Organization and Activation
  Sex Differences in the Brain
  Experimental Evidence
  Primate Behavior
Human Behavior
  Male Sexual Drive
  Female Sexual Drive

*Hormones* are chemical substances that are secreted directly into the bloodstream by ductless or *endocrine glands* and by specialized *neurosecretory cells*. Close to fifty hormones produced by some ten major endocrine sources are crucial to develop and sustain a vast range of vital physiological functions (Guyton, 1986). Sex and reproduction in particular simply could not exist without hormones.

The endocrine and the nervous systems, which are closely integrated, form a vast communication network within your body. The nervous system transmits electrical impulses through nerves; the endocrine system secretes hormones into the bloodstream to reach *target organs* and tissues whose development, sustenance, and functions it controls.

The concept of chemical control of bodily functions and temperaments can be traced to the ancient Greeks. They counted four *humors*—blood, mucous, yellow bile, and black bile—and ascribed a person's temperament to their balance in the body. Our modern science of endocrinology is young, though; the term *hormone* ("to excite") only goes back to the turn of this century (Crapo, 1985), and virtually everything we know about hormones, particularly their effects on sexual development and behavior, has been learned in the 20th century (Money, 1987).

## HORMONAL SYSTEMS AND SEXUAL FUNCTIONS

Many of the body's hormones have a bearing on sex and reproduction. We will deal here only with the hormones most specifically and directly linked to sexual functions. These hormones are produced by the *gonads* (testes and ovaries), the *adrenal cortex,* the *pituitary gland,* and the *hypothalamus* (Figure 4.1).[1]

### Gonadal Hormones

The hormones produced by the testes and ovaries are commonly referred to as *sex hormones*

[1] The general discussion of hormonal functions in this chapter is based on standard physiology and endocrinology texts, including West (1985), Greenspan and Forsham (1986), Guyton (1986), and Gilman et al. (1985).

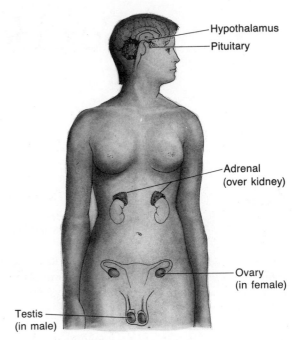

Figure 4.1    Endocrine glands that regulate sexual functions.

because of their gonadal origins and the crucial roles they play in sexual physiology. It is also common to refer to the hormones produced by the testis and by the ovary, respectively, as "male" and "female" sex hormones. Such designations can be misleading: sex hormones are also involved in functions other than sex; male and female hormones exist in both sexes (though in different concentrations). These hormones, as well as the related hormones produced by the cortex of the *adrenal glands* (located over the kidneys), belong to a family of chemical compounds called *steroids,* which have a common basic molecular structure (Gilman et al., 1985).

Androgens    *Androgen* is the generic name for a class of compounds of which *testosterone* is the most important (hence the two terms are often used synonymously). In the male, androgens are produced mainly by the testes, secreted by the interstitial Leydig's cells located between the seminiferous tubules (Chapter 2). Androgens are also produced in both sexes by the adrenal cortex, which is the main source of androgens in women, and in smaller quantities by the ovary (Murad and Haynes, 1985a).

Androgens are responsible for the sexual differentiation of the male reproductive system before birth (Chapter 2), the sexual maturation of males at puberty, and some of the secondary sexual characteristics of the female. They are also general *anabolic agents* that promote the building up of tissues. Testosterone is associated with the male sexual drive and possibly with aggressive behavior.

The effects of *castration* (removal of testes) in humans and animals have been known since antiquity. The ancient Egyptians and the Chinese castrated boys to produce *eunuchs.* Bulls are turned into tamer steers and stallions into geldings by castration.

Some of the earliest experiments in endocrinology were done in this area: in 1771 Hunter masculinized hens by transplanting testes from roosters. In 1849 Berthold showed that transplanting male gonads into castrated roosters prevented the typical effects of castration—the first formal experimental evidence for the existence of an endocrine gland. In the 1930s the testicular substance responsible for these effects was isolated and called testosterone (Gilman et al., 1985).

Estrogens and Progestins   The two principal classes of female sex hormones are *estrogens* and *progestins.* Though commonly referred to in the singular, there is no single hormone called "estrogen." Of the three main estrogens in humans, *estradiol* is the most potent. Similarly, *progesterone* is the most important of the progestins. However, in common usage, "estrogen" and "progesterone" have come to represent the two classes of female hormones.

Because the ovaries are not as accessible as the testes, their experimental removal (while keeping the animal alive) was not possible in former times. The fact that the ovaries control the female reproductive system with hormones was established only in 1900. Since the early 1920s an enormous amount of research has been undertaken with these substances, show-

ing their critical roles in reproduction and contraception (Murad and Haynes, 1985b).

Estrogens and progestins are secreted by the granulosa cells of the ovarian follicles (Chapter 2). Estrogens are produced while the follicles are maturing; progestins are produced after ovulation, when the follicle develops into the corpus luteum. During pregnancy the production of these hormones is taken over by the *placenta,* the organ through which the fetus is attached to the uterus and sustained until birth.

Estrogens do not seem to play a critical role in the differentiation of the female reproductive system before birth (Chapter 2), but they are responsible for most of the sexual maturational changes in girls at puberty. Estrogens and progestins regulate the menstrual cycle and are essential for reproduction. Estrogens are necessary for the implantation of the fertilized ovum and for sustaining the endometrium (the inner layer of the uterus) and the embryo. Progestins in turn provide optimal conditions for implantation and the initial growth of the fertilized ovum (Chapter 6). The relationship of these hormones to female sexual drive and behavior is unclear. Small amounts of estrogens are produced in the male by the testes and adrenal cortex but fulfill no known function.

In addition to the natural or *endogenous* forms of these hormones produced by the body, there are many *synthetic* products with the same properties. Estrogens and progestins can be taken orally or injected. They are the main constituents of birth control pills (Chapter 7). Estrogens are also readily absorbed through the skin and mucous membranes and are used, for instance, as creams in treating the vaginal dryness that affects some menopausal women (Chapter 9). Testosterone is much more effective when injected than taken orally. Unlike the female hormones, its medical uses are limited. Gonadal hormones are inactivated in the liver and their metabolic byproducts are excreted mainly in the urine.

Inhibin   The ovarian follicles and the Sertoli cells in the testes also produce a hormone called *inhibin,* which regulates the secretion of the pituitary hormone FSH, to be discussed shortly (Steinberger and Steinberger, 1976; DeJong and Sharpe, 1976). There is increasing evidence that the gonads produce other complex chemicals (polypeptides), which also affect gonadal action (Ying et al., 1986).

### Pituitary Hormones

The *pituitary gland* (or the *hypophysis*) is a small structure at the base of the brain (Figure 4.1). Its multiple hormonal functions have earned it titles like "the master gland" and "conductor of the endocrine orchestra"—quite a feat for a pea-sized organ that weighs in at less than 1 gram.

The pituitary actually consists of two main parts: the *anterior pituitary* (or adenohypophysis) and the *posterior pituitary* (or neurohypophysis). We are concerned here mainly with the anterior pituitary, which produces six hormones, two of which, known as *gonadotropins,* control gonadal functions. The two gonadotropins are the *follicle-stimulating hormone* (FSH) and the *luteinizing hormone* (LH). Though named after ovarian structures (because they were first discovered in females), these two hormones are identical in males and females. The anterior pituitary also produces *prolactin,* which stimulates milk production in lactating women (and may suppress sexual function in the male at abnormally high levels) (Bancroft, 1983). A posterior pituitary hormone, *oxytocin,* stimulates milk letdown and uterine contractions and may have a role in sexuality (Carmichael et al., 1987).

The placenta produces *human chorionic gonadotropin* (hCG) during pregnancy, which fulfills the same basic functions as the pituitary gonadotropins. (Its role in the detection of pregnancy is discussed in Chapter 6).

Unlike the steroid hormones, which are relatively simple chemicals, the gonadotropins are complex polypeptides (or proteins). The names of the gonadotropins are descriptive of their functions in the female: FSH stimulates the maturation of ovarian follicles and LH promotes the formation of the corpus luteum.

In the male, FSH is responsible for sustaining and regulating sperm production within the seminiferous tubules; LH stimulates the interstitial Leydig's cells to produce testosterone.

### Hypothalamic Hormones

The *hypothalamus* is a part of the brain closely linked to the pituitary. It functions both as a nervous center mediating various sexual functions (Chapter 3) and as an endocrine gland, sending its hormones to the pituitary. The hypothalamus itself is subject to complex influences from other parts of the brain.

Hypothalamic hormones control the levels of pituitary hormones by influencing not their production but their release; hence they are known as *releasing factors* (RF) or *releasing hormones* (RH). A single hormone, *gonadotropin-releasing hormone* (GnRH), controls the output of both FSH and LH by the anterior pituitary. How GnRH controls their release at different levels is not known.

Like pituitary hormones, the hypothalamic releasers are made up of complex molecules; yet they are relatively less complex. For example, GnRH is a chain of ten amino acids; LH has closer to 100.

### Control Systems

In one sense, the gonadal hormones do the footwork in influencing the target organs, the hypothalamus is in charge of the headquarters, and the pituitary hormones act as intermediaries. Hormones flow down from the hypothalamus to the anterior pituitary and on to the ovaries or testes. However, this flow is not one-way. The gonadal and pituitary hormones in turn travel upwards, influencing the output of the "higher" sources. Figure 4.2 diagrams this process for testosterone.

We call this kind of model a *cybernetic system* ("helmsman") whereby the components control each other (Hafez, 1980; Guyton, 1986). A basic mechanism in such models is *feedback.* A common example of feedback is a household thermostat: when the temperature in a room falls below the level at which the

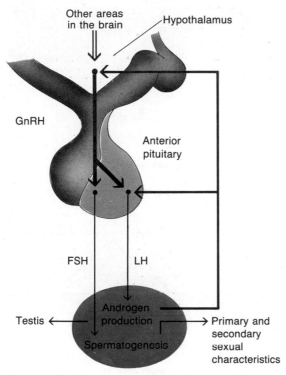

Figure 4.2    Hormonal control of gonadal function illustrated for the male.

links up the gonads with the hypothalamus-pituitary complex. With testosterone as the example, we see that GnRH from the hypothalamus prompts the pituitary to release LH, which in turn increases the production of testosterone by the testes; higher levels of testosterone in the bloodstream then inhibit GnRH production through "negative feedback." When the level of testosterone falls, the cycle repeats. The suppression of FSH by the testes is actually due also to inhibin (Brobeck, 1979; Ramasharma and Sairam, 1982). *Short feedback* similarly links the hypothalamus with the pituitary.

We could draw almost the same diagram for the female. The same hormones are involved at the hypothalamic and pituitary level. The ovary produces estrogens in response to FSH and progestins in response to LH stimulation; both ovarian hormones in turn travel upward to inhibit the production of GnRH, FSH, and LH. However, this model of hormonal regulation cannot be applied as neatly to females, because hormonal levels vary markedly and cyclically during the monthly cycle.

The target organs and tissues are outside of these feedback loops. They are acted upon by gonadal hormones, which regulate their development and functions. Sexual functions, and presumably sexual behavior as well, are thus dependent on appropriate levels of these hormones.

Different hormones are constantly circulating in the bloodstream. How do various tissues tell one hormone from another? The ability of a given hormone to influence a particular tissue depends on *receptors* either within the cell or on the cell membrane. Hormones are like suitcases on luggage carousels in airports—they go round and round until their owner recognizes them and picks them up.

In Chapter 2, we discussed the effects of sex hormones on the growth and differentiation of the reproductive system during embryonal development. Now we can turn to the maturational changes that these hormones bring about during puberty and to their effects on sexual behavior.

thermostat has been set, a sensing device turns on the furnace, which produces heat; when the room temperature goes above the set point, the furnace is turned off. In this way, room temperature and furnace mutually control each other so that the temperature remains at a predetermined level.

The concentration of hormones in the bloodstream is like the room temperature, and the endocrine gland is like the furnace. As the body uses up hormones, their concentration in the bloodstream falls below the physiological set point and more hormones are produced; as the hormone level goes up, its production is reduced. Later we shall look at the "thermostat" itself.

As Figure 4.2 shows, several feedback loops link the endocrine centers. *Long feedback*

## PUBERTY

During the second decade of life your body was transformed into that of an adult. *Puberty* ("growth of hair") refers to the biological aspects and *adolescence* to the psychosocial side of this process. Maturation of the reproductive system and the development of secondary sexual characteristics are the core events in puberty, yet the changes during this phase are so pervasive that almost all tissues in the body are affected (Tanner, 1984).

The primary changes of puberty are: acceleration and then slowing down of the growth of the skeleton (the adolescent growth spurt); changes in body composition as a result of skeletal and muscular growth: changes in the quantity and distribution of body fat; developments in the circulatory system and musculature that lead to greater strength and endurance; development of the reproductive organs and secondary sex characteristics (Marshall and Tanner, 1974).

These changes have two major biological outcomes with profound psychosocial repercussions. First, the child attains the body of an adult, including the capacity to beget or bear children. Second, most of the physical sex differences between male and female, or *sexual dimorphism*, become established.

### Somatic Changes

Puberty entails dramatic bodily, or somatic, changes. The first signs of puberty appear at about age 10 to 11 among girls and 11 to 12 among boys (Figure 4.3). There is, however, a wide range of normal timing. Boys and girls may normally enter puberty several years sooner or later than the average ages.

Some important changes of puberty are presented in Figures 4.4–4.7. Each of these developmental events has its own schedule and range of variability. Although the sequence of events shown in Figure 4.3 is generally consistent, it does not hold true in every case. For instance, the onset of menstruation is usually among the later events of puberty, but occasionally (and quite normally) it may be its first sign.

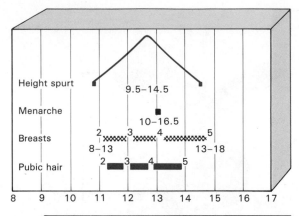

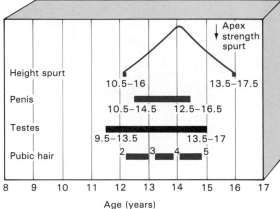

Figure 4.3   Timing of some events at puberty for an average Western girl (above) and boy (below). The normal range of ages for each event is given directly below it. Stages numbered 2–5 refer to the next three figures.

The pubescent *growth spurt* is among the most dramatic events in human development. Growth in height, or stature, is an ongoing process throughout childhood. By age ten boys have already attained 78 percent and girls 84 percent of their adult height. What makes the adolescent height spurt so striking is not the magnitude but the rate of growth. During the year of peak growth in height, a boy adds an average of three to five inches to his stature and a girl somewhat less (Tanner, 1984).

The weight gain during puberty follows a pattern similar to height gain, although it is less consistent. The factors that contribute to gain in weight are the increased size of the skeleton, muscles, and internal organs, and the greater amount of body fat. An important new sex difference is the amount and distribution of subcutaneous fat—the fat under the skin that contributes to shaping bodily contours. The average teenage girl enters adulthood with more subcutaneous fat than does the average teenage boy, especially in the region of the pelvis, the breasts, the upper back, and the backs of the upper arms. This fat accounts for the generally more rounded and softer contours of the female body.

There is a striking increase in the size and strength of the musculature at puberty in both sexes, but it is more pronounced for males. Among pubescent boys the increase in the number of muscle cells is fourteen-fold, among girls ten-fold. Similarly, among females maximum muscle cell size is reached by age 10 to 11, whereas in males, muscle cells continue to enlarge until the end of the third decade.

During puberty the body not only grows faster but undergoes marked changes in proportions. The various parts of the body grow at different rates. For example, legs accelerate in growth a year before the trunk, contributing to the stereotype of the gangling adolescent.

The face becomes distinctively adult as the profile becomes straighter, the nose and the jaw more prominent, and the lips fuller. These changes are more marked among males, whose facial appearance is further altered by the growth of facial hair and the recession of the hairline of the head.

Numerous internal changes accompany the external manifestations of puberty. The heart, like other muscles of the body, increases in size until its weight nearly doubles. Blood volume, hemoglobin, and the number of red blood cells are all increased. The same is true for lung size and respiratory capacity. All of these changes affect both sexes, but are more marked in the male.

The net effect of these and related physiological developments in puberty is to greatly increase the capacity of the adult for physical exertion. Greater exercise tolerance combined with superior strength permits individuals of both sexes to outperform vastly in physical effort their prepubescent selves.

Physical ability is both a function of biological endowment and the effect of exercise and training. There are no striking differences in the physical abilities of boys and girls before puberty. After puberty males have an advantage in overall muscular strength as well as in heart and lung functions. Nevertheless, the differences in physical ability we commonly observe between men and women are also to a significant extent the result of men typically using their bodies more strenuously in work and play. When women exercise to the same extent that men do, the difference in physical performance narrows considerably. This is true for ordinary activities as well as for peak performances by competitive athletes. For example, Olympic records in the 400-meter freestyle swimming events reveal that men were 16 percent faster than women in 1924, 11 percent faster in 1948, and only 7 percent faster in 1972. Both women and men have been improving their times throughout this period, but women have been improving faster. The female record in 1970 was faster than the male record in the mid-1950s (Wilmore, 1975, 1977).

### Reproductive Maturation

The maturation of the reproductive system in both sexes is the primary mark of puberty. It involves the accelerated growth of the internal sex organs and the genitals, which we call the *primary sexual characteristics*. It also involves the development of *secondary sexual characteristics*—the female breasts, male facial hair, pubic and axillary hair in both sexes, and voice changes (Savage and Evans, 1984).

Female Maturation    Breast development is usually the first visible sign of female puberty (Figure 4.4). It usually starts between the ages of 8 and 13 and is completed between 13 and 18. Sometimes the two breasts develop at different rates. This unevenness need not be a source of concern: the breast growing more slowly will eventually catch up, and the asymmetry is usually corrected by the end of adolescence.

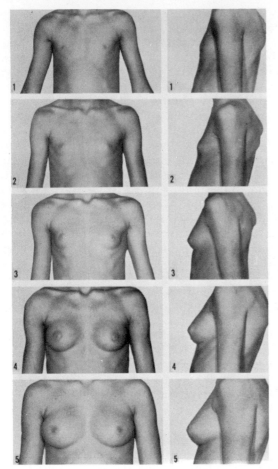

Figure 4.4  Stages of breast development in adolescent girls: (1) prepubertal flat appearance, like that of a child; (2) small, raised breast bud; (3) general enlargement and raising of breast and areola; (4) areola and papilla (nipple) form contour separate from that of breast; (5) adult breast with areola and breast in same contour.

Pubic hair usually appears next, attaining the adult pattern by about age 18. It precedes the growth of hair under the armpits (axillary hair) and on the legs by about one year. Both breast and pubic hair growth follow predictable patterns, which are useful for monitoring the rate of pubertal development (Figure 4.5).

The musculature of the uterus develops markedly during puberty. The vagina enlarges and its inner walls become thicker and more

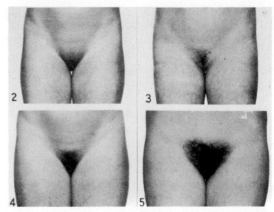

Figure 4.5  Stages of pubic hair development in adolescent girls: (1) prepubertal stage (not shown), with no true pubic hair; (2) sparse growth of downy hair, mainly at sides of labia; (3) pigmentation, coarsening, and curling with an increase in the amount of hair; (4) adult hair, but limited in area; (5) adult hair with horizontal upper border.

furrowed. The external genitals, including the clitoris, become enlarged and their erotic sensitivity heightened. The most fundamental change of all involves the ovaries, where the ovulatory cycle becomes activated, beginning the menstrual cycle, which we shall discuss later.

Male Maturation  The onset of puberty in males is marked by the enlargement of the testes, starting between the ages of 10 and 13 and continuing until the ages of 14 to 18. The development of pubic hair that occurs between 12 and 16 anticipates by two years or so the growth of hair on the face and the armpits. The first ejaculation usually occurs at about the age of 11 or 12, but mature sperm usually take a few more years to appear. Like girls, pubescent boys are usually not fully fertile, but that does not provide them with contraceptive security if they engage in sex.

The penis begins to grow markedly about a year after the onset of testicular and pubic hair development (Figure 4.6). Deepening of the voice, which results from the enlargement of the larynx, is a late event, but an important one for the adolescent boy's sense of masculinity. Girls experieince a similar change, but it is much less marked. Similarly, boys experience some breast enlargement, which may alarm them, but usually it is slight and eventually it disappears.

Another distressing event of puberty may be the appearance of acne, a transient skin condition that is more common among boys than girls and is related to the effects of androgen. Though usually no more than a minor cosmetic problem, acne can be severe enough to require medical treatment (Johnson, 1985).

As the reproductive system matures, pubescent boys begin to experience erections (nocturnal penile tumescence) and orgasm (nocturnal emission) in their sleep, and girls may manifest vaginal lubrication under similar conditions (Chapter 8).

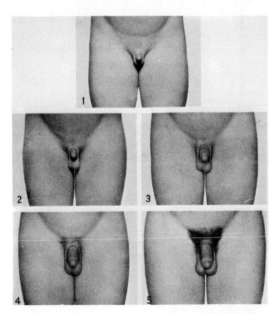

Figure 4.6  Stages of male genital development: (1) prepubertal stage, in which the size of the testes and penis is similar to that in early childhood; (2) testes become larger and scrotal skin reddens and coarsens; (3) continuation of stage 2, with lengthening of penis; (4) penis enlarges in general size, and scrotal skin becomes pigmented; (5) adult genitalia.

## Neuroendocrine Control

All these changes of puberty are triggered and regulated by nervous and hormonal mechanisms. Because they are closely integrated, we refer to them as neuroendocrine mechanisms. They involve the interaction of hormones from the hypothalamus, the anterior pituitary, the gonads, and the adrenal cortex. Their effects are illustrated in Figure 4.7.

Although the nature and actions of these hormones are now well known, the precise mechanism that initiates puberty remains unclear. The hypothalamic-pituitary-gonadal system can function before puberty. The pituitary, the gonads, and the target tissues, such as the breasts, can be stimulated to develop at any time if the person is given the appropriate hormones. The onset of puberty must be restrained by the brain, either at the hypothalamus or at some higher level (Guyton, 1986).

Before puberty, low levels of gonadal hormones are already circulating in the bloodstream. It is assumed that a hypothalamic center operates like a *gonadostat* (a term coined in analogy to a thermostat). This gonadostat is highly sensitive in childhood, so even the low levels of steroid hormones in circulation would keep it turned off through negative feedback and inhibit the production of GnRH. As the child matures, the hypothalamic gonadostat becomes less sensitive. It is no longer turned off by the low levels of circulating gonadal hormones. As a result, the hypothalamus produces more GnRH, prompting the pituitary to produce larger amounts of gonadotropin, which in turn increases gonadal hormonal output. Mounting levels of gonadal hormones finally reach a level that induces the tissues of the body to respond, and sets the physical changes of puberty in motion (Grumbach et al., 1974; Grumbach, 1980).

Other theories propose alternative processes. For instance, Frisch (1974) believes that puberty is triggered by reaching a critical body weight. Because children grow at somewhat different rates, they attain the critical weight level and enter puberty at different ages. Others ascribe the initiating function to the adrenal gland.

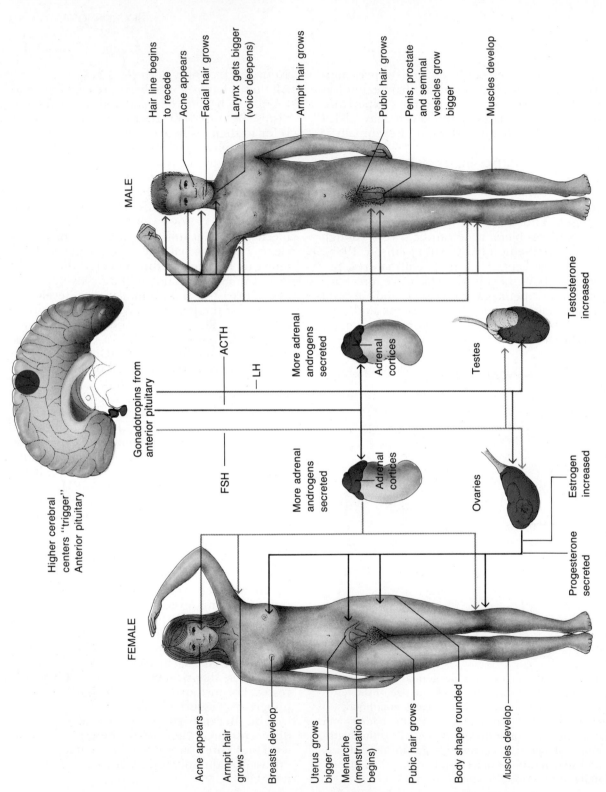

MALE

Hair line begins to recede
Acne appears
Facial hair grows
Larynx gets bigger (voice deepens)
Armpit hair grows
Pubic hair grows
Penis, prostate and seminal vesicles grow bigger
Muscles develop

Higher cerebral centers "trigger"
Anterior pituitary

Gonadotropins from anterior pituitary

ACTH
LH
More adrenal androgens secreted
Adrenal cortices
Testes
Testosterone increased

FSH
More adrenal androgens secreted
Adrenal cortices
Ovaries
Estrogen increased
Progesterone secreted

FEMALE

Acne appears
Armpit hair grows
Breasts develop
Uterus grows bigger
Menarche (menstruation begins)
Pubic hair grows
Body shape rounded
Muscles develop

Figure 4.7  Effects of sex hormones on development at puberty.

# Box 4.1

## MENSTRUAL TABOOS

In many societies over the centuries, menstruation has been regarded as rendering women ritually unclean. Menstrual blood, however, has not been the only "pollutant" among bodily fluids; semen too has been considered to render a person unclean. The origins of *menstrual taboos* are ancient. The Old Testament and the Koran are replete with regulations concerning the proper conduct of the menstruating woman. Not only are women considered impure during this period, but they are also deemed dangerous—more likely to harbor and transmit evil spirits (Delaney et al., 1988).

In cultures with such taboos, a menstruating woman was segregated from others, especially from people who were ill and women in labor. She was subjected to various restrictions in the home, such as having to sleep on the floor, avoid sexual relations, and refrain from all other physical contact with her husband, including touching his bed or preparing meals. In Judaism, seven days after the start of her period the woman would become clean again following a prescribed ritual bath called the *Mikvah* (Gregersen, 1983).

Among Native Americans of the southeastern United States, girls were secluded during their first menstruation, and from then on women either absented themselves from the household during their monthly period or were subjected to restrictive taboos. Among the monastic orders of India, nuns were relegated to secondary status; because they were periodically "polluted" they had to be barred from certain key rituals.

Even in societies with no specific menstrual taboos, sexual intercourse during menses has been often avoided or prohibited. In many instances this contact is presumed to harm the man: the Lepcha believed that if a man had sex with a menstruating woman he would get ill; Thonga men who had yielded to such temptation would tremble before battle or fail to fight; Mataco men would develop headaches (Ford and Beach, 1951).

The Roman historian Pliny, writing in 77 A.D., described the effects of exposure to menstrual blood:

> Contact with it turns new wine sour, crops touched by it become barren, grafts die, seeds in gardens are dried up, the fruit of trees falls off . . . the edge of steel and the gleam of ivory are dulled, hives of bees die, even bronze and iron are at once seized by rust, and a horrible smell fills the air, to taste it drives dogs mad and infects their bites with an incurable poison (Delaney, 1988).

We no longer believe in such effects, yet more subtle prejudices and fears of the menstrual "curse" still linger. There is no rational basis for any such concerns. Menstruation is a normal physiological function, and there is no reason why it should interfere with any activity. Women can swim, run, ride a bike, or engage in any other form of exercise they wish while having their period. Nor is menstruation, as such, incompatible with sexual enjoyment, although some couples prefer to refrain from sex at this time as a matter of personal preference and for health reasons (Chapter 5).

---

## THE MENSTRUAL CYCLE

The *menstrual cycle* is one of the key physiological functions of the female body. An ovarian cycle, or *estrus cycle,* is characteristic of all mammals, but *menstruation*, the periodic shedding of the uterine endometrium—"bleeding"—that accompanies the ovarian cycle, exists only in women, female apes, and some monkeys.

The significance of menstruation in women goes beyond physiology; it has important psychological and social ramifications (Box 4.1).

### Menarche

The onset of menstrual cycles in puberty is called *menarche;* the cessation of menstrual cycles in midlife is the *menopause*. Both are highly significant biological landmarks in a woman's life, with many psychological and social implications, which we shall discuss in Chapter 9.

The onset of menarche is determined by a variety of genetic and environmental factors. In the United States, menarche now occurs at the average age of 12.8 years, with a normal range of 9 to 18 years (Zacharias et al., 1976). Information from around the world shows considerable variation in this regard. For instance, among girls in Cuba the median age of menarche is 12.4 years, whereas among the Bundi tribes of New Guinea it is 18.8 years (Hiernaux, 1968).

Among industrialized societies the average age at menarche has gradually declined from 17 years in 1840 to the current levels, which stabilized a few decades ago. Teenage girls therefore now reach menarche at about the same ages that their mothers did.

The decline in the age of menarche, as well as cross-cultural differences, are generally attributed to environmental factors, such as better nutrition and improved health care. Nonetheless, the force of genetic factors is evident in family tendencies for the onset of menarche. For instance, randomly chosen girls reach menarche differing on the average by 19 months; for sisters who are not twins, the difference is 13 months; for nonidentical twins, it is 10 months; for identical twins, 2.8 months (Tanner, 1978).

Following menarche, it usually takes a few years before menstrual cycles become regularized (they become irregular again during the menopause before stopping altogether). During puberty, when the menstrual cycle is becoming established, ovulation tends to be inconsistent. *Anovulatory cycles* (cycles without ovulation) make it less likely that a teenager will get pregnant, but this relative adolescent sterility is highly unreliable as a birth control method. Millions of teenagers do get pregnant.

## Phases of the Menstrual Cycle

The length of the ovarian cycle is specific for each species. It is approximately 36 days in the chimpanzee, 20 days in the cow, 16 days in sheep, and 5 days in mice. Dogs and cats are seasonal breeders and usually ovulate only twice a year.

The average length of the human menstrual cycle is 28 days (hence its association with the lunar month and the derivation of "menstrual" from the Latin for "monthly"). Cycles that are shorter or longer by several days are also perfectly normal. Because the onset of menstrual bleeding is more abrupt than its gradual end, the time that bleeding starts is counted as day 1 of the menstrual cycle.

The menstrual cycle is a continuous process, one cycle following another. Once the cycles have become regularized, most women go through their menstrual periods on a fairly predictable rhythm. However, this rhythm is often influenced by physiological and psychological factors, so it is common for a woman's period to come a few days early or late.

The menstrual cycle is controlled by the hypothalamic, pituitary, and gonadal hormones. It involves the entire reproductive tract, especially the ovaries, uterus, and vagina. Though the menstrual cycle is one continuous process, we describe it in four phases: the *preovulatory phase*, *ovulation*, the *postovulatory phase*, and the *menstrual phase*.

Preovulatory Phase    The *preovulatory phase* starts as soon as menstrual bleeding from the previous cycle has ended. This period is also known as the *follicular phase*, because the ovarian follicles in the ovary develop at this time, and as the *proliferative phase*, because of the changes in the uterine lining.

As illustrated in Figure 4.8, while menstrual bleeding is in progress, the anterior pituitary increases its production of FSH. As a result, the production of estrogens from the ovaries begins to increase sharply. Higher levels of estrogen cause thickening of the endometrium with proliferation of its superficial blood vessels and uterine glands. The cervical glands produce a thick and cloudy mucous discharge, which gradually takes on a watery character. Simultaneously the lining of the vagina thickens, and its cells undergo characteristic changes. These changes are so distinctive

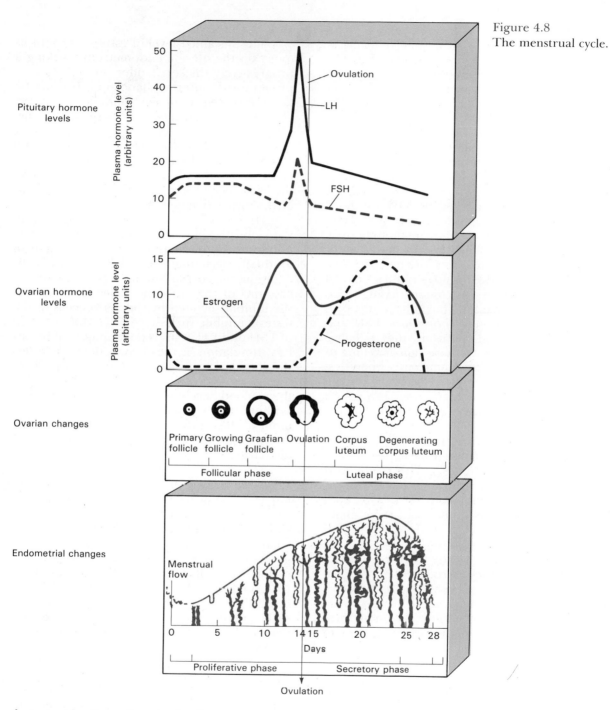

Figure 4.8
The menstrual cycle.

that examination of vaginal cells, cervical mucus, and the endometrial lining is used in tests of ovarian hormonal function.

Increasing levels of estrogen in the bloodstream gradually reduce the production of FSH through negative feedback. The production of LH and of progesterone remain low throughout the cycle's preovulatory phase.

Ovulation    The central event in the ovarian cycle is *ovulation,* which takes place at about the midpoint of a 28-day cycle. Ovulation always occurs approximately 14 days before the onset of menstruation, no matter low long the cycle. Differences in the length of menstrual cycles are due to the length of the preovulatory phase only.

Ovulation is triggered by an upsurge in LH secretion and to a lesser extent by a rise in FSH secretion. Both changes are thought to be caused by the rapid increase in the levels of estrogen, which act in a "positive feedback" relationship. Unlike the negative feedback model discussed earlier, in this case increasing levels of estrogen do not inhibit but enhance the production of the pituitary hormones. FSH and LH act synergistically (that is, they enhance each other's actions) to cause rapid swelling of the ovarian follicle. Simultaneously, there is a reduction in the secretion of estrogens, and an increase in the production of progesterone. All of these changes jointly trigger ovulation (Guyton, 1986).

Some women experience mild pain in midcycle during ovulation (called *Mittelschmerz,* German for "middle pain"). This symptom is most common in young women and consists of intermittent cramping pains on one or both sides of the lower abdomen that last for about a day.

Postovulatory Phase    As the discharged ovum starts on its journey through the fallopian tube, the menstrual cycle enters its *postovulatory phase.* Under the influence of high levels of LH and facilitated by the pituitary hormone prolactin, the corpus luteum is formed, leading to a sharp increase in the secretion of progestins. The production of estrogens, which had dropped sharply at the time of ovulation, now begins to climb again to a higher level. Because it is now the corpus luteum rather than the developing follicle that is the main source of hormones, the postovulatory phase is also known as the *luteal phase.*

The sustained level of estrogens continue to act on the uterine endometrium, making it progressively thicker. Under the influence of progestins the uterine glands now become active and secrete a nutrient fluid; hence *secretory phase* is another name for the postovulatory period. Secretions of cervical mucus gradually thicken and regain their cloudy and sticky consistency. Since the changes in cervical mucus are linked to the phases of the menstrual cycle, they are relied on in the "rhythm" method of birth control (Chapter 6).

High levels of estrogens and progestins in the bloodstream inhibit gonadotropin production by the anterior pituitary, which results in gradually declining levels of FSH and LH. In addition, the corpus luteum secretes moderate amounts of the hormone *inhibin* (the same as the inhibin secreted by the Sertoli cells of the testes); inhibin further reduces the secretion of FSH and LH. This reduction in turn means less stimulation of the corpus luteum and less production of estrogens and progestins. These hormones are being constantly used up, so their blood levels gradually decline as well. Without the sustenance provided by these hormones, the endometrial lining degenerates and sloughs off. This material is the menstrual discharge.

Menstrual Phase    Discharge of the uterine lining, which appears as vaginal bleeding, is called *menstruation.* It lasts four or five days, during which a woman loses 50 to 200 ml (about half a cup) of blood; however, the amount varies a good deal between individuals and in different cycles. Normally this blood loss is rapidly replenished, and there are no ill effects whatsoever. However, women who menstruate need sufficient iron in their diet, and some may need to supplement it with iron compounds to help the production of red blood cells.

As blood levels of estrogens and progestins go down during the menstrual phase, they stop inhibiting the anterior pituitary. As a result, FSH production rapidly picks up, heralding the start of the proliferative phase of the next cycle.

The foregoing description supposes that

the woman has not become pregnant. If she has, the cells of the developing placenta produce *chorionic gonadotropin,* which has the same effect as pituitary LH on the corpus luteum in maintaining high levels of hormone production. Under these conditions the uterine lining (which now holds the embryo) does not slough off, and the pregnant woman misses her period for the first time (Chapter 6).

A similar process explains how birth control pills function. The pill typically consists of some combination of synthetic estrogens and progestins. These hormones act the same way as their natural counterparts produced by the ovary. Taken on a daily basis, they maintain high blood levels of these hormones. The anterior pituitary has no way of telling if these hormones are coming from the ovary or the pharmacy. It suppresses production of gonadotropins through negative feedback, just as it does naturally in the postovulatory phase. Because the birth control pill suppresses the pituitary before ovulation, there is no LH surge, no ovulation, and no chance to become pregnant. When she stops taking the hormone pill at the end of each month, the endometrial lining sloughs off and menstruation follows. When she resumes taking the pill, another anovulatory cycle is repeated (Chapter 7).

## Menstrual Discomfort

The menstrual cycle is subject to a variety of disturbances beyond normal fluctuations in its timing, duration, and amount of flow. They include absence of menstruation (*amenorrhea*) and increased amount or duration of menstrual bleeding (*menorrhagia*). Also, for a significant number of women, menstruation entails some pain or discomfort. This discomfort is usually mild, but in a number of cases (usually among younger women) it is severe enough to necessitate bed rest.

Some of these conditions are clear-cut: they have specific causes and symptoms and interfere with normal reproductive functioning. Other conditions are more ambiguous. A case in point is the wide variety of sensations some women experience before or during the menstrual period. These women are not ill.

The process they are going through is physiologically normal; yet some of them feel acutely uncomfortable.

Many physical conditions can account for such menstrual disorders. So can emotional factors. Sometimes even an experience like going to college or going back home from college is enough to disrupt temporarily the menstrual rhythm. Following unprotected intercourse the fear of pregnancy may also cause delayed menstruation. The reason is that the hypothalamus takes part in the regulation of emotions and endocrine functions.

The symptoms of menstrual-cycle distress are categorized as premenstrual tension syndrome and dysmenorrhea (painful menstruation). Some 150 symptoms have been linked to the menstrual cycle (Moos, 1969). Premenstrual symptoms are manifested during the week preceding the menstrual flow; the symptoms of dysmenorrhea accompany menstruation itself. Though there may be some overlap in discomfort, these two conditions should be dealt with separately. Their manifestations, probable causes, and treatments differ.

Dysmenorrhea   Menstrual discomfort of varying severity affects half of all women in early adult life. Typically they have cramps in the lower abdomen, backache, and aches in the thighs. Less often, there may be nausea, vomiting, diarrhea, headache, and loss of appetite. When these symptoms become severe enough to interfere with work or school, and last two days or more, the woman can be said to suffer from *dysmenorrhea.*

If menstrual pain is due to pelvic disease, it is called *secondary* dysmenorrhea. Where there is no apparent illness causing it, then it is *primary* dysmenorrhea.

The menstrual cramps of primary dysmenorrhea come from spasms of the uterine muscles. Chemical substances called *prostaglandins* cause the spasms. In women they are normally released from the endometrial lining, shed during menstruation. Menstrual blood has four times the level of prostaglandins in ordinary uterine blood.

Prostaglandins were first isolated from

prostatic fluid (Chapter 2), but they are a family of compounds, widely distributed in various tissues of the body, with a broad range of actions. These actions include contraction of the smooth muscles of the uterus (hence their use in inducing labor); various effects on the gastrointestinal tract (causing diarrhea, cramps, nausea, and vomiting); dilation of blood vessels (causing hot flashes); and other changes in the endocrine and nervous systems of the body.

The time-honored, though not the best, remedy for dysmenorrhea is aspirin with bed rest and warm fluids. Aspiring is an *analgesic* (pain reliever). It also belongs to a class of compounds called *antiprostaglandins,* which can prevent as well as treat dysmenorrhea by inhibiting the synthesis and the actions of the prostaglandins. Other compounds are even more effective antiprostaglandins. For instance, among over-the-counter drugs ibuprofen (marketed as Advil, Nuprin, and other labels) is most effective, especially in its stronger form (Motrin), which must be prescribed. By contrast, pain killers such as acetominophen (Tylenol) do not have an antiprostaglandin action; so they are less useful for treating dysmenorrhea. Other substances like vitamin B6 may diminish the reaction to prostaglandins by relaxing the uterine muscles.

Women on the pill are also likely to get relief. Steroid hormones reduce the amount of endometrial sloughing and hence the level of prostaglandins released in the process. However, a woman should not put herself on the pill for this purpose only.

A similar caution applies to *menstrual extraction,* especially when practiced by self-help groups. This procedure is the same as the vacuum aspiration method of abortion (Chapter 7)—suctioning out the uterine contents. This so-called "five-minute period" may not be a safe procedure, particularly for women with a history of uterine infections, tumors, and a number of other conditions.

Premenstrual Syndrome    The symptoms of the *premenstrual syndrome* (PMS) are more varied and less distinct than those of dysmenorrhea.

No explanation of them has been widely accepted.

The symptoms of premenstrual tension appear two to ten days before the onset of menstrual flow and usually subside by the time the menses start. In some cases, these symptoms merge with dysmenorrhea, but either can occur alone.

The more common symptoms of premenstrual tension can be grouped in three categories. First are symptoms associated with *edema* (swelling): a bloated feeling in the abdomen, swelling of the fingers and legs, swelling and tenderness of the breasts, and weight gain. Second is headache. Third is emotional instability, including anxiety, irritability, outbursts of anger, depression, lethargy, insomnia, and cognitive changes such as difficulty concentrating and forgetfulness. More idiosyncratic reactions include changes in eating habits (such as a craving for sweets), excessive thirst, and shifts in sex drive (increase for some, decrease for others) (Rubinow, 1984). The implications of these changes are discussed in Box 4.2

There has been much confusion in the assessment of these symptoms and their causes. To begin with, it is unclear what proportion of women actually suffer from such symptoms: estimates range from 30 percent to 90 percent. Moreover, these symptoms tend to be highly subjective: though most women perceive them as unpleasant, other women experience bursts of energy and creative activity at this time. The symptoms of edema are ascribed to fluid retention, but recent studies have failed to document significant weight gain in the premenstrual period. The swelling must be explained by internal shifts of fluid from one part of the body to another. Finally, in studies where women with premenstrual tension believed that their mental or physical performance was impaired, tests and other objective measures have failed to substantiate these self-perceptions.

Does this mean that PMS is a myth? Do women imagine these symptoms? The experiences of countless women testify to the con-

# Box 4.2

## BEHAVIOR AND PMS

Some women claim that a variety of changes affect their thoughts, feelings, and actions in the premenstrual period. Cognitive changes include forgetfulness and difficulty in concentration; emotional changes include moodiness (especially depression and apathy) and instability (anxiety, irritability, anger) (Goldstein et al., 1983; Andersch et al., 1986). Long before PMS was acknowledged, it was observed that some women acted out of character about the time of their menstrual periods. Queen Victoria reportedly suffered from fierce tempers during her premenstrual period. "Even (Lord) Melbourne, a past master at dealing with women, had on one occasion quavered and feared to sit down as the fire blazed in the eyes of the eighteen-year-old queen" (quoted in Dalton, 1979, p. xiii).

Premenstrual distress is thought to be so overpowering that in some countries, such as France and England, it constitutes a mitigating circumstance in violent crimes. In 1981, a 33-year-old woman in Britain was found guilty of murdering her lover following a quarrel. The verdict: manslaughter due to diminished responsibility owing to the premenstrual syndrome. The woman was placed on three years' probation and released (Laws, 1983).

Do a significant proportion of women show significant behavioral changes at these periods? How should they be dealt with? At present, there are no convincing answers, but sharply divided opinions.

In Britain, Dalton (1969, 1979) has been among the chief proponents of the view that PMS is a clinical entity with distinct behavioral manifestations. She considers the four days before and the four days after the onset of menses (the *paramenstruum*) to be a particularly stressful time for women (Dalton, 1972). Statistics show higher rates of accidents, psychiatric admissions for acute illness, and attempted suicides during the paramenstruum. Similarly, this period has been associated with significantly higher rates of behaviors leading to imprisonment and absenteeism from work (Dalton,

1979). It follows from this perspective that the paramenstruum should be recognized as a time of higher risk and distress for women. Therefore, although it is part of a normal physiological process, serious attention should be paid to the anticipation of paramenstrual stress and the relief and management of its symptoms. Furthermore, it is argued that allowances must be made for the behaviors of women during these periods when their control of their actions is diminished.

The opposing view questions the very basis of the reported association of behavioral symptoms with the menstrual cycle (Rubinow et al., 1986; Ghadirian and Kamaraju, 1987). For one thing, the studies that relate abnormal behaviors to PMS are full of methodological pitfalls. They draw conclusions about hormonal effects without even measuring hormone levels. Systematic attempts to relate levels of estrogen and progestins to moods and daily activities have failed to show any correlation (Abplanalp et al., 1980). Although some women may well be adversely affected during the paramenstruum, their behavioral aberrations may have been highly exaggerated. There is no good evidence that the mental and physical capabilities of women are generally compromised during the paramenstruum. To make allowances or to recognize diminished responsibility for actions committed by women during this period casts an aura of unreliability on all women, and creates one more excuse to discriminate against them in various occupational and social settings (Reid, 1986).

To resolve this dilemma we need to rethink the concept of PMS and to reexamine its purported manifestations (Fausto-Sterling, 1985). Unless there is some agreement of what it is we are talking about, we can hardly make progress about its management. Meanwhile, women who experience genuine distress must not be burdened with guilt, and women who are undisturbed by PMS must not be assumed to be in distress.

trary. The symptoms can be considered so far to be the standard criterion for defining PMS (Abplanalp et al., 1980).

A variety of physiological causes have been proposed for premenstrual symptoms: the drop in *progesterone* level late in the post-ovulatory phase; *vitamin B-complex* deficiencies causing decreased liver metabolism, hence higher levels of estrogen; increased *aldosterone* (a steroid hormone secreted by the adrenal cortex); and abnormalities in *endorphin* production, causing estrogen-progesterone imbalances, and disturbances in the synthesis of neurotransmitters (Debrovner, 1983; Sondheimer, 1985).

Further evidence pointing to the physiological roots of the syndrome comes from the study of female baboons, who are reported to become less social during the premenstrual period and eat more (Hausfater and Skoblick, 1985).

The likelihood of experiencing menstrual distress also seems to be linked to psychological or cultural factors, such as religious background. Among college women, Catholics and Orthodox Jews tend to have a higher prevalence of menstrual distress (Paige, 1973). Negative attitudes toward menstruation and the expectation of menstrual discomfort may also create a self-fulfilling prophecy. For instance, in one study, women who were led to believe that their menstrual periods were due in a few days were more likely to experience premenstrual distress than other women who had been persuaded by the experimenter not to expect their period until quite a bit later (Ruble, 1977). Other attempts to establish a psychological origin for premenstrual tension have linked it to personality types and life circumstances (Kinch, 1979). Negative associations that society or an individual attaches to menstruation have received special attention. High levels of stress, such as family conflicts or even college exams, tend to accentuate premenstrual tension (Rubin et al., 1981).

Premenstrual tension may be helped by a low-salt diet during the week before the period, or by taking diuretics, both of which can counter fluid retention. Coffee, tea, cola drinks that contain caffeine, and sweets tend to worsen the condition. If symptoms of physical discomfort and headache are severe enough, analgesics may be helpful. One must be careful, however, not to substitute one problem for another by becoming dependent on drugs in dealing with the ordinary problems of menstrual distress.

There have also been claims of relief through the administration of progesterone and vitamin B-complex, to correct a deficiency that presumably causes the premenstrual symptoms (Freeman, 1985). On the other hand, these symptoms seem to be also relieved in a considerable proportion of cases by *placebos*, chemically inert substances which work because patients expect them to. Current treatments of PMS therefore emphasize stress reduction and emotional support. Finally, some women find that orgasm (through any means) relieves both premenstrual tension and menstrual cramps (Budoff, 1980; Holt and Weber, 1982).

## ATYPICAL SEXUAL DEVELOPMENT

We have been looking at normal sexual development, but a lot can be learned from abnormalities. A good deal of research on gender identity and gender-related behavior (Chapter 10) has been based on conditions caused by hormonal disturbances. Let us consider some representative examples.

Normally the reproductive system differentiates in the embryo (Chapter 2) and matures at puberty. Rarely, abnormalities in sexual differentiation occur at the level of the chromosomes, the hormones (hypothalamic, pituitary, or gonadal), or the target tissues.

The developmental variation may be unusual timing or faulty differentiation. When sexual development occurs unusually early, the result is *precocious puberty* (Box 4.3); if late, it leads to *delayed puberty*. Failure of puberty to occur altogether results in the inadequate development of sex organs; it is called *sexual infantilism*. New procedures now make the early diagnosis and treatment of these conditions more likely (Ortner et al., 1987).

# Box 4.3

## PRECOCIOUS PUBERTY

When puberty begins before age eight in girls and age ten in boys, it is considered precocious. Girls are twice as likely to have precocious puberty as boys. There are cases of menstruation beginning in the first year of life. The youngest known mother was a Peruvian girl who began menstruating at three years and gave birth (by Caesarean section) to a baby boy at the age of 5 years 7 months (see the figure) (Wilkins et al., 1965). Among precocious boys, penile development may begin at five months and spermatogenesis at five years (see figure). A seven-year-old boy was reported in the 19th century to have fathered a child (Reichlin, 1963).

In the majority of cases, especially in girls, precocious puberty does not reflect any underlying pathology; it is simply a natural variation in the body's timing mechanisms. However, in 20 percent of girls and in 60 percent of boys precocious puberty is caused by a serious underlying disease. For instance, tumors in the hypothalamic region of the brain, the gonads, or the adrenals can trigger the precocious production of gonadotropins or sex hormones, which in turn lead to the early sexual maturation of the body. These cases clearly show that puberty depends on the maturation of the hormonal system and not of the body tissues; the reproductive system is ready to mature at any time.

In some cases, a child may undergo incomplete precocious puberty, with early breast development or early growth of pubic hair, but no other changes. These cases are less likely to be related to an underlying illness. Precocious puberty is not accompanied by the heightened erotic and romantic interest typical of normal puberty. In other words, "erotic age" does not automatically match physical development (Money and Ehrhardt, 1972).

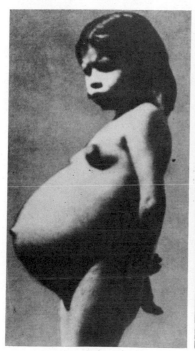 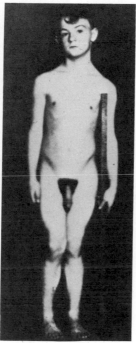

(Left) Linda Medina is the youngest known mother in the medical literature. She gave birth in 1939 at the age of 5 years 7 months. (Right) A five-year-old boy with unusual adrenal development has the height of an 11.5-year-old and precocious penile development.

Faulty sexual differentiation creates incongruous combinations of male and female structures. Individuals whose genitals are mismatched with the rest of their body have long been known since antiquity as *hermaphrodites* (a term derived from the Greek gods *Hermes* and *Aphrodite*).

The true hermaphrodite has both male and female gonads, or a mixture of ovarian and testicular tissue in the gonads. Though usually a genetic female (XX), such a person has external genitals that look predominantly male or female (Figure 4.9) or may combine features of both sexes, with one form predominating. Where the sex chromosomes are correctly matched with male or female gonads but mismatched with external genitals, the term *pseudohermaphrodite* is applied. A female pseudohermaphrodite will have female sex chromosomes (XX), ovaries, fallopian tubes, and uterus, but external genitals that appear to be male. A male pseudohermaphrodite will have male sex chromosomes (XY), testes, and other male structures, but female external genitals and even a feminine body build (Figure 4.10). There are many variants of these abnormalities and numerous causes (Imperato-McGinley, 1985).

## Chromosome Disorders

Instead of the normal complement of 46 chromosomes, including XX or XY chromosomes, some individuals are born with extra or miss-

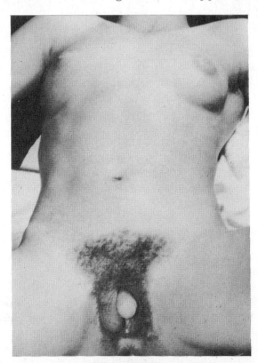

Figure 4.9   A true hermaphrodite, with one ovary and one testis. A genetic female who has always lived as a male.

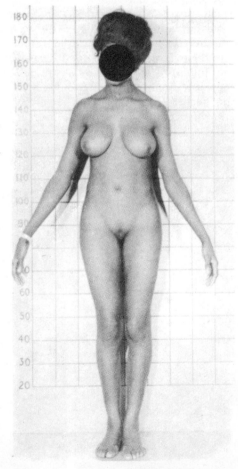

Figure 4.10   A male pseudohermaphrodite. A genetic male with the androgen insensitivity syndrome.

ing sex chromosomes. *Klinefelter's syndrome* results when a male has an extra X chromosome (XXY); *Turner's syndrome* results when a female is missing one X chromosome (XO) (Grumbach and Conte, 1985).

In Klinefelter's syndrome masculinization is incomplete, resulting in a small penis, small testes, low testosterone production, and therefore incomplete development of secondary sex traits. Some men show partial breast development at puberty. These men are infertile. Some have problems with social adaptation, perhaps because of their lower average intelligence (Federman, 1968), but others lead full lives.

Individuals with Turner's syndrome have a female body build, but ovaries are absent or rudimentary, incapable of producing ova or female hormones. Therefore, the XO female is infertile and does not undergo puberty unless treated with female sex hormones. These women are of short stature and may have congenital organ defects, and webbing between the fingers and toes or between the neck and shoulders. Despite incomplete development of the female organs, XO females usually have no gender problems during psychosexual development.

Another chromosomal abnormality with intriguing behavioral consequences is the presence of an extra Y chromosome in males (Hamerton, 1988). XYY individuals tend to be tall, have lower than average intelligence, and suffer from severe acne. The XYY syndrome has attained some notoriety because of its higher frequency among prisoners, implying greater aggressivity (Jacobs et al., 1965). Yet when a random sample of men outside of prison was examined, violence did not appear to be higher in XYY than in XY males. The validity of the association between an extra Y chromosome and antisocial sexual behavior is therefore doubtful (Witkin et al., 1976).

## Hormone Disorders

Disorders of differentiation due to chromosomes usually affect people by causing hormonal abnormalities. Such abnormalities can occur too even when sex chromosomes are normal. Hormones may be overactive or underactive at any level of the hypothalamic-pituitary-gonadal system of the embryo; or abnormal sexual differentiation may be caused by hormones produced or ingested by the mother during pregnancy.

In the female, hormones cause pseudohermaphroditism most commonly in *congenital adrenal hyperplasia* (CAH). This condition (also known as the *adrenogenital syndrome*) results from a genetic defect. Too much androgen is produced by the fetal adrenal cortex (Behrman and Vaughan, 1983). In a male child, this defect causes precocious puberty. The female infant is born with her external genitalia masculinized to various degrees. The clitoris may look like a penis, and the labial folds may be fused together, giving the appearance of a scrotum. The condition is treated by suppressing the excessive androgen production and surgically correcting the genitals within the first few weeks of life.

The same end result will occur in a perfectly normal female embryo if the pregnant mother produces abnormal amounts of androgen (for example, due to an androgen-producing tumor) or takes androgenic hormones. Some years ago pregnant women were given certain synthetic steroids to prevent miscarriage (before the masculinizing effects of these compounds were known), and they gave birth to female babies with masculinized genitals.

Male pseudohermaphroditism results if there is not enough androgen before birth, or if the hormones produced are not biologically active. In the absence of normal male hormone, genetically male embryos will develop female genitals.

## Tissue Disorders

Even where the hormonal system is quite normal, abnormalities will result if the bodily tissues do not respond normally to hormonal stimulation. Such a condition, known as *androgen insensitivity* or the *testicular feminization syndrome,* is the most common cause of male pseudohermaphroditism. In this case, a genetic male with androgen-producing normal testes will develop a female appearance with female genitals and breasts, because body tissues fail to respond to testosterone (Figure 4.10). The net effect is therefore the same as if no androgen were present. Because the body does respond to the Mullerian duct-inhibiting substance, no uterus or fallopian tubes develop. Genetically male infants with this syndrome look like normal baby girls. The condition is usually diagnosed at puberty when menarche fails to occur.

Unlike other forms of pseudohermaphroditism, which can be treated with surgery and hormones if detected early, people with complete testicular feminization must be reared as female. Although sex-change surgery and hormonal treatment could reverse the established female appearance (Chapter 10), these individuals have female gender identities (think of themselves as women) and do not desire such change.

Other rare conditions important for the study of gender development (such as transsexualism) are discussed in Chapter 10.

## HORMONES AND SEXUAL BEHAVIOR

How much of sexual behavior is controlled by hormones? Over the past half century a great deal of evidence has been gathered to demonstrate the role that hormones play in shaping and sustaining mammalian sexual behavior (Davidson et al., 1982). The extent to which this influence persists among humans is not yet fully established, but it seems certain that sex hormones are also significantly linked to some aspects of human sexual behavior.

### Mammalian Behavior

Our basic knowledge of the effects of steroid hormones on sexual behavior comes from research with rodents like the rat, and to a lesser extent with nonhuman primates such as chimpanzees, gorillas, and orangutans (Beach, 1971). These animals have predictable and gender-specific sexual behaviors that are mainly under the control of sex hormones.

The sexual behavior of the female animal is dependent on ovarian hormones and linked to the period of *estrus* ("frenzy") that coincides with ovulation, during which the animal is said to be "in heat." The removal of the ovaries stops sexual activity; the administration of ovarian hormones restores it. Female rodents are dependent on both estrogens and progesterone; dogs and cats require only estrogens for normal sexual function.

The estrous female arouses sexual interest in the male by physical changes in her genital region and the production of potent scent signals conveyed by pheromones (Box 4.4). Whereas hormones affect the individual producing them, pheromones influence the behavior of other animals of the same species.

The female animal's sexual interest is cyclical; the male is more or less ready to copulate anytime, provided there is a receptive female available. In effect, then, male sexual behavior is mainly controlled by female receptivity.

The male response is also dependent on an adequate level of testosterone. Castration of adult rats is followed by decline in sexual behavior; administration of testosterone restores the sexual behavior to its earlier levels (Goy and McEwen, 1980; Bermant and Davidson, 1974).

Equally important is the presence of testosterone during early life for adequate behavioral responses to testosterone during adulthood; reduced testosterone stimulation in infancy impairs sexual performance in adulthood. Based on animal research, the following model has been developed linking hormones to sexual behavior.

Organization and Activation    The influence of sex hormones on behavior occurs in two stages. The first stage is *organizational*. Hormones influence the development and differentiation of those portions of the brain that deal with sexual behavior. The second stage is *activational*. Hormones go on to initiate and maintain sexual behavior (Ehrhardt and Meyer-Bahlburg, 1981).

The organizational effects typically occur during a limited period of greater susceptibil-

# Box 4.4

## PHEROMONES

The term *pheromone* ("to transfer excitement") was coined in 1959 to describe chemical sex attractants in insects; its existence had been known since the 19th century. These substances are remarkably potent; the minute amount of pheromone in a single female gypsy moth is enough to sexually excite more than one billion males from as far as two miles away. In a number of insect species, the males in turn produce pheromones to induce the female to copulate. In the male cockroach this is an oily substance, the consumption of which induces the female cockroach to take the coital posture (Hopson, 1979).

There are numerous examples of the influence of pheromones in mammals' reproductive and social behavior: housing female mice together inhibits their ovarian cycles; exposure to a male or just his urine will revive the cycles; the odor of male mice will accelerate puberty of young female mice; the introduction of a male from a foreign colony will suppress the pregnancy of mice who have mated with their own males. When female rats live together (or just breathe the same air) they tend to ovulate and come into heat the same day (McClintock, 1983).

The menstrual cycles of women show a similar tendency to be influenced by the odors of other women. For example, the menstrual periods of women who live together in college dormitories, or other close quarters, often become synchronized, so they menstruate close to the same time (McClintock, 1971). In experiments on the effect of scents, when a "donor" woman wears cotton pads under her arms for a 24-hour period and other women are then exposed to her armpit odor, the menstrual periods of the recipient women shift to become closer to the periods of the donor (Russell et al., 1977).

There is also some correlation, if not a causal link, with the influence of male odors. In one study, women who seldom dated had longer cycles; those who dated more often had shorter and more regular cycles. Similarly, women who had slept with men once a week were more likely to have regular menstrual cycles and fewer fertility problems. Sexual activity is not the key factor in these studies (mastur-

bation makes no difference); it is the presence of the male, or to be more precise, his odor that makes the difference. Under-arm secretions from men mixed with alcohol and dabbed on the upper lip of women will also regularize their periods almost as effectively (Cutler et al., 1985).

What are the substances that exert such a curious influence? Some investigators have reported the presence of volatile fatty acids ("copulins") in vaginal secretions of rhesus monkeys in mid-cycle that stimulate male sexual interest, mounting, and ejaculation. Similar compounds have been identified in human vaginal secretions; they peak at mid-cycle, unless women are on the pill (Michael and Keverne, 1968; Michael et al., 1974, 1976; Bonsall and Michael, 1978). Other investigators have failed to confirm these findings. The role of such human "copulins" is unclear (Goldfoot et al., 1976).

People are apparently able to detect differences in vaginal odors (without being told the source) under experimental conditions; most men and women find them rather unpleasant, but less so for mid-cycle secretions (Doty et al., 1975). On the other hand, erotic literature is full of testimonials to the arousing smell of genital secretions; perhaps when sexually excited, people react to odors in quite different ways.

Vaginal secretions, moreover, need not be the primary source of erotic scent signals. Our body is studded with odor-producing glands, and despite our scrupulous efforts to eliminate and conceal them, they may still be part of the "silent language" of sex. One perfume company has marketed a fragrance that contains *alpha androstenol*, a synthetic chemical similar to a substance in human perspiration. This substance, when produced by boars, makes the sow in heat adopt the mating posture. However, there is no scientific evidence of its having any sexual effect on humans (Benton and Wastell, 1986). Even if human pheromones were to be identified—and they may well exist—it is unlikely that they would override all of the other characteristics that make people attractive to each other. Rather, pheromones would be one more element in this complex interaction.

ity, or *critical phase,* either before birth (the prenatal period) or around the time of birth (the perinatal period). Their influence tends to be long-term and permanent. By contrast, the activational effects of hormones are reversible, and not limited to a critical phase of development. The organizational effects of hormones are like the exposure of photographic film to light (which captures the image); the activational effect, like the effect of developing fluid on exposed film (which brings out the image) (Wilson, 1978). Through this double influence, hormones first develop portions of the brain that deal with sexual functions and then activate and maintain those functions.

This model suggests that the male and female brains are in some respects different. Just as the reproductive system becomes male or female before birth through the influence of sex hormones (Chapter 2), presumably the brain develops male or female structure, resulting in distinctive sexual behaviors. These differences are called *brain dimorphism.*

Sex Differences in the Brain    Evidence for sexual dimorphism in the mammal's brain comes from three areas. The first evidence is behavioral. Mammalian sexual behaviors are typically sex-specific. For instance, the sexually receptive female rat will arch its back (lordosis) while the male rat will mount and rhythmically thrust its pelvis during copulation. Because such behaviors are not acquired by learning, we infer that they reflect brain differences.

More direct evidence comes from physiological functions. In both sexes, the production of gonadal hormones is controlled by the same pituitary hormones (FSH and LH). The reason that the female produces gonadal hormones in a cyclical fashion and the male does not must reflect differences in brain function.

The third type of evidence is the demonstration of anatomical differences between the male and female mammalian brains (Gorski et al., 1978). In the male rat, the *medial preoptic area* of the hypothalamus is strikingly larger than in the female, a structural change that becomes apparent shortly after birth under the influence of testosterone (Raisman and Field,

1971; Goy and McEwen, 1980). The preoptic area is essential for the preovulatory release of LH that occurs in the female only; it is also important for both male and female sexual behavior (Lisk, 1967). Such a structural sex differnce in the brain is of considerable importance because it could cause differential sexual behaviors in the adult, even in the absence of immediate hormonal action (Thompson, 1985).

The significance of such animal findings for human sexual behavior remains to be demonstrated (Fausto-Sterling, 1985; Bleier, 1984). However, evidence is beginning to emerge that brain sex differences, such as the size of the medial preoptic area, may also exist in humans. Debate on the issue is lively.

Experimental Evidence    A good deal of evidence points to androgen as the key hormone in the sexual organization of the brain, as it is in the sexual differentiation of the reproductive system. How do we know? Let us follow a typical experiment.

First an adult male rat is castrated. He no longer reacts sexually. Treatment with estrogens and progestins has no effect in either restoring male activity (mounting) or instituting a female pattern of response (lordosis), but treatment with testosterone does restore normal male behavior. Next, a rat is castrated soon after birth. As an adult, he shows no sexual behavior. When given estrogen and progestins, he develops a female pattern of response (lordosis). Treatment with testosterone fails to set up a male pattern. Finally, the same experiment is repeated, but this time the rat is given an injection of testosterone right after being castrated in infancy. As an adult, his sexual responses are identical to that of the male rat castrated in adulthood: female hormones have no effect; testosterone restores normal male sexual function.

From this experiment two conclusions are clear. First, male sexual behavior is dependent on the presence of testosterone, both in infancy and in adulthood. Second, the presence of testosterone in infancy stamps the brain in the male pattern, following which female hormones have no effect. In the absence of testosterone in infancy, estrogen and progesterone induce female response in a genetic male.

Repeating the same experiment on a female rat, we get comparable results with a key difference. The adult female when castrated loses sexual function: estrogen and progesterone treatment restore normal female functions; testosterone has little or no effect. A female rat whose ovaries are removed in infancy behaves exactly like her castrated male counterpart: female hormones given in adulthood induce a female pattern of sexual behavior; testosterone has no effect. Finally—and this is the key point—a female rat whose ovaries are removed in infancy and who is given testosterone will also respond like her male counterpart. Estrogens and progestins then have no effect in adulthood; testosterone induces a male pattern of response. This female will mount another female and go through the ejaculatory motions, even though she cannot ejaculate (Daly and Wilson, 1978).

What determines the pattern of sexual response is clearly not genetic sex but sex hormones. The development of sexuality in both male and female mammals depends on the organizational effect of androgen or its absence in early life, complemented by the activational effects of male or female hormones in adulthood.

Many questions still need to be answered about these issues, and there are many complexities we have not dealt with here. For instance, androgens may not be the sole hormones with an organizational effect; progesterone may play a protective role against the effects of androgens on the brain; estrogens too, in low concentration, may exert an influence (MacLusky and Naftolin, 1981).

Further complicating the story, testosterone does not act directly on the brain cells. It must be first converted to estradiol in order to combine with the receptors on brain cells. Thus, ironically, it is the "female" hormone that is ultimately responsible for masculinizing the brain (Ehrhardt and Meyer-Bahlburg, 1981).

It would be misleading to think of hormones as a form of "sex fuel" that keeps the sexual drive going. The effects of hormones are highly influenced by the condition of the body on which they are acting. For example, age, conditions of rearing, sexual experience, nutrition, and the testing situation all influence how an animal will behave under the stimulation of sex hormones.

Primate Behavior   Sex hormones exert an important influence on the sexual behavior of nonhuman primates, but their role is not as definitive as in other mammals.

One way of assessing this role is to look at estrus, the key event that triggers the sexual activity of the female and the response of the male. Primates who evolved earlier, such as lemurs, show fairly distinct estrous cycles. In the more developed primates, however, such cycles tend to be influenced by social and environmental factors—in particular, the social structure of the species and the sexual drive of the male (Rowell, 1972).

For example, although the male gorilla lives with a group of females, he has a low sexual drive, and sexual activity in the group is sporadic, mainly initiated by the female. In this situation it is essential that sexual activity occur around ovulation to ensure reproduction. Indeed, female gorillas do show definite estrous patterns—behavior that invites copulation (Short, 1980).

The male orangutan is much more highly sexed. These apes are more isolated from each other, so a male will attempt to copulate with any female he encounters. In joint captivity this fact leads to a good deal of sexual activity, because the females cannot get away from the males. This setup makes it appear as if the females had no clear estrous period. However, if the males are caged separately with an opening to the females' cage that is too small for them but large enough for a female, then a clearer pattern emerges. Copulation is initiated by the female at the time of estrus but not otherwise (Nadler, 1977).

Chimpanzees live in small social groups. The female is sexually receptive almost anytime, but more so during her period of estrus, when her external genitals visibly swell. During this time the female mates actively with most of the males in the group, but because ovulation occurs toward the end of this period, this sexual activity usually does not lead to impregnation. Typically, the female will pair off with a single male at the end of this period, and conception is most likely to result from their temporary consortship (Tutin, 1980).

It is clear from these examples that in primates sexual interactions are influenced by hormones, but not in the lockstep fashion characteristic of rodents. Furthermore, as shown by chimpanzees, sex now serves needs that are not purely reproductive; the mating of the female prior to ovulation possibly fosters group cohesiveness by providing sexual access to all of the males, even though one of them is eventually selected by the female as consort. In other words, the stage appears to be set for the more complicated and socially influenced sexual interaction we encounter among humans.

Even at the level of primates, there is no longer a single answer to the question of whether or not hormones influence sexual behavior. They do and they do not, depending on what hormone we are looking at, which aspect of sexual behavior is involved, and under what circumstances it takes place. These considerations apply not only to different species and to differences in males and females, but even to the various aspects of sexual responsiveness. For instance, Beach (1976) distinguishes three aspects of female sexuality: *attractiveness* is some feature of the female that arouses the male's sexual interest; *receptivity* is the extent to which the female accepts the male's sexual advances; *proceptivity* is the extent to which the female takes the initiative in approaching the male (presumably a measure of the male's attractiveness). In the rhesus monkey female attractiveness is dependent on estrogens (which bring about swelling of the vulva and color changes during estrus); proceptivity depends on androgen; and receptivity seems to be less dependent on hormones (Bancroft, 1983).

## Human Behavior

The role of sex hormones in behavior is far more difficult to determine among humans than among other animals, for several reasons.

First, human sexual behavior is incomparably more complex than its animal counterpart. Cultural influences are so pervasive and infinitely varied that the subtlety and range of human sexual behavior is bewilderingly diverse (Gregersen, 1983). In studying the relationship of hormones to sexual behavior we have no simple measure like mounting or lordosis to go by.

Second, the key experiments conducted with animals cannot be replicated among humans. We are not about to castrate baby boys or give androgens to baby girls under experimentally controlled conditions to see what happens to their sexual development. Instead we must rely on studying conditions such as the androgenital syndrome.

Third, it may be argued that we have difficulty finding convincing evidence for the influence of hormones on human sexual behavior because there is no such influence to be found. Perhaps during the course of evolution, there has been a progressive "emancipation" of sexual behavior from hormonal control (Beach, 1947). Instead, social learning and individual experience have taken over as the forces that shape human sexual behavior.

The great role of social learning notwithstanding, there is now evidence that biological factors do influence human psychosexual differentiation. As we have seen, anatomical evidence is beginning to point to sex differences in the human brain, specifically in the medial preoptic area of the hypothalamus.

The cycles of gonadal hormone secretion in women, but not in men, presuppose differences in brain function, just as they do among other mammals. Furthermore, the surge in LH secretion in response to estrogen stimulation is just a female characteristic. Not only is this reaction present normally during the menstrual cycle, but it can be induced at other times with injections of estrogen. By contrast, men do not respond to estrogen injections with an increase in LH production. This difference too points to a difference in the brain (Gladue et al., 1984).

We need to ask more sophisticated questions than whether or not hormones have anything to do with sex. Hormones may have a significant impact on a particular facet of sexuality but not on another, under certain conditions but not others. In short, hormonal influences only make sense in the broader context of human experience, as one factor among many that predispose us to act. They are not some irresistible force that drive us into sexual activity willy-nilly. They encourage, but they do not compel us (Money, 1987).

Male Sexual Drive    Erotic desire is usually taken for granted as part of "human nature," but it is still a mystery. To what extent do biological factors—hormones in particular—generate and sustain sexual drive (Chapter 3)?

The most persuasive case for the effects of hormones on sexual drive is based on the role of androgens in the male. Let us first consider the effects of the lack of testosterone. It is now generally agreed that castration prevents normal sexual function in men (Box 4.5), but a lot of confusion has existed in this regard. Based on a review of the literature Kinsey concluded: "Human males who are castrated as adults are, in many but not in all cases, still capable of being aroused by tactile or psychogenic stimuli" (Kinsey et al., 1953, p. 744). Subsequent surveys also reported that some castrates remain responsive for years. These early studies were plagued with inconsistent methods and the failure to differentiate between changes in sexual desire and loss of erectile ability, or between response to various forms of sexual stimulation (Heim and Hursch, 1979; Heim, 1981). At present, there is "little doubt that after castration sexual behavior is . . . drastically reduced or completely suppressed in a high percentage of men" (Davidson et al., 1982). Although the decline in sexual drive usually follows castration quite rapidly (Davidson, 1980), the timing varies from one individual to another (Bancroft, 1983). Moreover, up to 63 percent (Sturup, 1979) of castrates may retain some degree of sexual

drive for years, although how effective it is remains unclear.

Further confirmation of the importance of androgen for male sexual drive comes from carefully controlled studies of *hypogonadal* men, who need hormone injections. If treatment stops, within a month there is a decline of sexual interest. Soon after they lose capacity for seminal emission, but not necessarily for orgasm (in other words, a man may be able to have an orgasm but without the ejaculation of semen). As a result of reduced sexual desire, sexual activity declines. All of these changes are reversed with one to two weeks of giving hormones again (Davidson et al., 1979; Skaakeback et al., 1981).

The relationship between androgens and the ability to have an erection is more complex. Hypogonadal men have impaired nocturnal penile tumescence (NPT) (Chapter 3), and treatment with androgen significantly improves their ability to have erections during sleep. These men seem unaffected in their ability to have erections in response to erotic films (Bancroft and Wu, 1983; Kwan et al., 1983). These findings suggest that some aspects of sexual arousal and erectile response are androgen-dependent, and other aspects are not (Bancroft, 1986a).

Drugs that have an *antiandrogenic* effect will interfere with sexual function, particularly sexual drive. Most notable are cyproterone and medroxyprogesterone, which are used in Europe and the United States, respectively, for the treatment of sexual offenders (Chapter 14).

Among normal males with no testosterone deficiency, levels of androgen do not relate significantly to sexual desire, excitement, or frequency of coitus (Persky, 1983). In other words, if a man has normal levels of androgen, giving him more androgen has no effect on his sexual behavior. As with a glass full of water, adding more water does not fill it up any further; the excess merely spills over.

This issue has an interesting corollary. Testosterone may increase aggression, which in turn may affect sexual activity. Ordinarily there are no discernible differences in testosterone levels between less and more aggressive

# Box 4.5

## EUNUCHS

Of the many causes of androgen insufficiency, the most dramatic is the removal of the testes by castration. Before puberty, castration results in inadequate genital development and the absence of the secondary sexual characteristics. The person, known as a *eunuch,* will have bypassed most of the changes of puberty (see figure). He will have a high-pitched voice, poor muscular development, underdeveloped genitals, no beard, no pubic or axillary hair, and female-type subcutaneous fat deposits with partially developed breasts. He will be of normal height or taller, because the long bones of the extremities continue to grow in the absence of androgen. Eunuchs have a low sexual drive though they are not necessarily impotent. Those castrated after puberty do not lose their secondary characteristics.

Castration has been practiced in many cultures for various reasons, most notably to provide "safe" guardians for women (*eunoukhos* means "guardian of the bed" in Greek). Best known in connection with Islamic and Chinese harems, the practice goes back to remote antiquity.

Some eunuchs wielded great power in Islamic and Chinese courts. With no family ties or offspring, their sole loyalty was to the ruler, and they often acted as members of his personal staff. At the peak of their influence, there were over 70,000 eunuchs in the service of the Ming dynasty. The eunuch system in China was not completely abolished until 1924, when the final 470 eunuchs were driven from the last emperor's palace (Mitamura, 1970).

In Europe as late as the turn of the 19th century, boys were castrated to maintain their soprano voices. These *castrati* sang in church choirs and performed female roles in opera, which excluded women. During our own century, castration has been used in Europe and the United States in efforts to modify sexual behaviors such as "chronic" masturbation, homosexuality, exhibitionism, and child molestation. Surgical castration is no longer

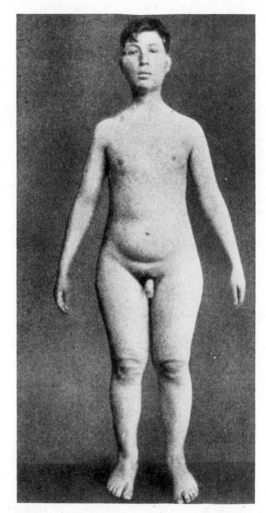

Twenty-two-year-old eunuch castrated before puberty.

practiced for punitive reasons or to alter behavior. But "chemical castration" through the use of antiandrogenic drugs is used occasionally in the treatment of sex offenders (Chapter 14).

men. It is possible, though, that for men already predisposed to violence, testosterone might facilitate it.

Female Sexual Drive    Unlike nonhuman primates and other mammals, women have no estrus. They are potentially sexually receptive at any time. Then is a woman's sexual drive completely free from hormonal influences? The question remains open. Studies in this regard have focused on the role of estrogens and progestins, as well as androgen.

The most obvious approach would be to look for fluctuations in sexual interest during the menstrual cycle, matching the clear and predictable shifts in hormone levels. Such attempts have led so far to inconclusive results (Persky, 1983).

Women have no estrus. Does that mean that they have no cyclic fluctuations whatsoever in the level of their sexual desire? Numerous studies have failed to answer that question with certainty. Several studies have shown an increase in the likelihood of intercourse at or shortly after ovulation at mid-cycle (Udry and Morris, 1968; Harvey, 1987). A similar pattern has been found based on self-ratings of sexual arousal among young women during various menstrual phases (McCance et al., 1952; Moos, 1969; James, 1971; Gold and Adams, 1978). However, many other studies have failed to support a mid-cycle peak of sexual interest (Bancroft, 1983).

These findings may be influenced by the fluctuations of sexual interest in the male partner. Whether or not a woman has coitus is not determined by her own level of interest alone but influenced by her partner. This problem may be less in lesbian relationships, where gender conflict, fear of pregnancy, and contraceptive usage are not an issue. In such couples, the significant peaks in sexual encounters and orgasm are found to be at mid-cycle (Matteo and Rissman, 1984).

Other studies show evidence of coitus to peak after menstruation with another peak at mid-cycle (McCance et al., 1952). The peak after menstruation may be compensating for the period of abstinence during menses.

Women who engage in coitus during their period do not show such a rebound reaction.

The mid-cycle peak, when it occurs, may be in response to increased levels of estrogen, or to higher levels of androgen, which are also present at this time. The decline in sexual activity during the postovulatory period is consistent with the higher levels of progestogens, which are known to inhibit libido.

Another approach is to look at women whose ovaries do not function, because of surgery or natural menopause. Traditionally, the menopause has supposedly meant not only the end of a woman's ability to bear children but a lessening of her sexual attractiveness and interest. These attitudes have recently changed markedly (Chapter 9). Nevertheless, several studies have shown that in a majority of women there is a definite decline in sexual interest and orgasmic response following the menopause (Hälström, 1973). A similar decline has been shown more generally for women between the ages of 45 and 55 (Pfeiffer, Verwoerdt, and Davis, 1972).

The fact that these changes correlate with the decline of ovarian hormones does not prove that they are caused by it. First, there appears to be a great deal of variation in how women respond to the menopause, both in the severity of symptoms (Chapter 9) and in sexual function. Some women experience a markedly negative change, others do not, and still others experience a positive enhancement of sexual interest and responsiveness in midlife (Masters and Johnson, 1970).

Second, the menopause brings about distinctive structural changes, with thinning of the vaginal tissues and reduction in the lubricatory response. If untreated, these changes may make intercourse painful for menopausal women. The loss of sexual interest may be a secondary effect of physical discomfort. Menopausal women must also still contend with the cultural prejudices with regard to the sexuality of older women, which cannot fail to influence their own self-perceptions. Finally, hormonal replacement therapy does not seem to have an effect on female sexual drive, although it distinctly improves vaginal dryness; this fact casts doubt on a direct relationship between the level of ovarian hormones and female sexual behavior (Bancroft, 1983).

For some reason, women who go through menopause before midlife because of surgical removal of the ovaries seem more likely to suffer sexually negative effects than those who become menopausal through normal aging, and they are more likely to respond to estrogen replacement (Dennerstein et al., 1980).

The behavioral effects of progestins are even less clear. Progesterone has been shown to inhibit sexual desire (Bancroft, 1980); yet young women who exhibit higher levels of sexual activity in the luteal phase of their cycle also have higher progestin levels than women who do not.

Studies of oral contraceptives have produced conflicting results about the effect of steroid hormones on female sex drive. When there is an impact, it seems that the birth control pill inhibits sexual desire. On the other hand, such a physiological effect can be more than counteracted by the freedom from fear of pregnancy, which promotes greater sexual interest and responsiveness. Furthermore, giving sex hormones to individuals who already have normal levels (such as women on birth control pills) is not a good test of whether or not hormones sustain the sexual drive. Recall that testosterone has no effect on men who have no hormonal deficiency.

Based on clinical studies, it has been suggested that androgens may be the hormones responsible for the female sexual drive. For example, removal of the adrenal glands (the main source of female androgen) reduces a woman's sexual desire, responsiveness, and ac-

tivity. However, such studies have involved women who were very ill and whose adrenals were surgically removed as part of their treatment; under such circumstances an objective assessment of sexual activity is hardly possible (Waxenburg et al., 1959). In other cases women receiving large doses of testosterone as part of the treatment for breast cancer have reported enhanced sex drive. Improvement here may be the result of the more general anabolic effects of testosterone on body tissue, or because androgen enlarges the clitoris, it may enhance its sensitivity as well (Gray and Gorzalka, 1980). Nonetheless, when, under controlled circumstances, androgens are given to menopausal women whose ovaries have been removed for medical reasons, there is an increase in the intensity of sexual desire and arousal, as well as in the frequency of sexual fantasies (Sherwin et al., 1985). Although the relationship of female sex drive to sex hormones remains unsettled, it is probable at least that arousal is in part dependent on the level of testosterone.

A great deal more needs to be learned about how hormones influence sexual behavior under ordinary circumstances, as well as in the laboratory. Nonetheless, we know gonadal hormones play an undisputable role in the sexual behavior of animals. We are sure they play a similar role in men; and although the issue is still controversial, we now question the nature and extent rather than the existence of such a role in women as well. More uncertain are the possible relationships between hormones and gender identity (Chapter 10), and the development of sexual orientation (Chapter 13), which we shall discuss separately.

## REVIEW QUESTIONS

1. Which hypothalamic, pituitary, and gonadal hormones are involved in sexual functions?

2. What changes happen to the body at puberty?

3. Give examples of disorders of sexual development in males and females caused by sex chromosomes, sex hormones, and tissue response.

4. Describe the changes during the menstrual cycle involving pituitary hormones, the ovary, ovarian hormones, and the uterine endometrium.

5. What are the symptoms of premenstrual syndrome and dysmenorrhea?

6. Compare and contrast the organizational and activational effects of hormones on sexual behavior.

## THOUGHT QUESTIONS

1. How can abnormal patterns of sexual development help you to understand sexual behavior?

2. Why are there menstrual taboos? Why do some modern women feel self-conscious about menstruation?

3. What would be the psychological and social consequences if an effective human pheromone were marketed?

4. Should PMS be a mitigating circumstance in crimes committed by women? Argue both ways.

## SUGGESTED READINGS

Crapo, L. (1985). *Hormones*. San Francisco: Freeman. An authoritative yet simply written introduction to hormones.

Delaney, J., Lufton, M. J., and Toth, E. (1988). *The Curse*. Urbana, Ill.: University of Chicago Press. A fascinating cultural history of various facets of menstruation.

Hopson, J. S. (1979). *Scent signals: The silent language of sex*. New York: Morrow. An informative and entertaining account of pheromones.

Katchadourian, H. (1977). *The biology of adolescence*. San Francisco: Freeman. Introductory-level text on aspects of puberty.

Kelley, K. (Ed.). (1987). *Females, males, and sexuality*. Albany: State University of New York Press. Chapter 2 provides an overview of hormones and sex-related behavior. Chapter 4 deals with the premenstrual syndrome.

# Sexual Health and Illness

*When I first realized that I had a sexually transmitted disease, I felt like a monster. I thought all my friends would be horrified if they knew I had such an affliction. . . . I wanted to crawl into a hole and die. . . ."*

ANONYMOUS
COLLEGE STUDENT
Miller, Rich, and Steinberg
(1987)

OUTLINE

MAINTAINING SEXUAL HEALTH
Keeping Clean
Toxic Shock Syndrome
Sex during Menstruation
COMMON AILMENTS OF THE
    REPRODUCTIVE SYSTEM
Genitourinary Infections
    Genital Discharge
    Vaginitis
    Candidiasis
    Cystitis
    Prostatitis
Cancer
    Cancer of the Breast
    Cancer of the Cervix
    Cancer of the Endometrium
    Cancer of the Prostate
    Cancer of the Testes
    Cancer of the Penis
SEXUALLY TRANSMITTED DISEASES
Prevalence
Types of STDs
BACTERIAL STDs
Gonorrhea
    Symptoms
    Treatment
Chlamydia
    Symptoms
    Treatment
Pelvic Inflammatory Disease
    Symptoms
    Treatment
Syphilis
    Primary Stage Syphilis
    Secondary Stage Syphilis
    Tertiary Stage Syphilis
    Congenital Syphilis
Other STDs Caused by Bacteria
STDs CAUSED BY MISCELLANEOUS
    ORGANISMS

Enteric Organisms
    Causative Agents
    Symptoms
Parasitic Infections
    Pubic Lice
    Scabies
VIRAL STDs
Genital Herpes
    Transmission
    Symptoms
    Treatment
Genital Warts
    Symptoms
    Treatment
Hepatitis
AIDS AND THE HUMAN
    IMMUNODEFICIENCY VIRUS
The Virus and the Immune System
Transmission of AIDS
    Anal Intercourse
    Shared Needles
    Heterosexual Intercourse
    Blood Transfusion
    Childbearing
    Accidental Infection
    How AIDS Is *Not* Transmitted
Symptoms
    Category 1
    Category 2
    Category 3
    Category 4
Testing
Counseling
Treatment
Cost of AIDS
Prevention
    Vaccines
    Safe Sex
    Risk-Taking Behavior
    The Joy of Sex

Sex is wonderful, but it can be dangerous. Currently, people are most worried about AIDS. It is the newest of many sexually transmitted diseases (STDs) people can get through sexual contact. Can it happen to you? Knowing the truth about these illnesses will keep your concerns realistic. It can keep you, your partner, and someday even your children healthy.

This chapter looks first at how to maintain a healthy reproductive system, then at ailments that system shares with the rest of the body, and finally at the STDs. In each case you can learn how to take care of yourself and when to go for help.

There are many facets to the STDs. Their clinical signs and symptoms, or patterns of transmission, are primarily medical concerns. But the STDs also have an important impact on how individuals behave sexually and relate to their sexual partners. By affecting large numbers of people, the STDs have serious economic and political consequences, and they raise difficult ethical and legal issues. This is a topic that we shall return to many times in subsequent chapters.

Diseases of sexual organs do not always interfere with sexual functions. A man may have herpes but no difficulty in having an erection; a woman may have gonorrhea but no problem reaching orgasm. In other circumstances, physical ailments interfere with sexual function, as do psychological and interpersonal problems. Disturbances in sexual performance or satisfaction are referred to as *sexual dysfunction;* we shall deal with them separately, in Chapter 15.

## MAINTAINING SEXUAL HEALTH

The human body is superbly designed, but it requires proper care and maintenance to work well. Prevention is the key to good health. That means knowing your own body, keeping fit, and getting medical attention through checkups, as well as at the first signs of illness.

### Keeping Clean

One key to sexual health for men and women is cleanliness. Apart from hygienic considerations, a clean and fresh body enhances sexual attractiveness. Cleanliness does not mean eliminating or covering up all natural odors. The natural scents of the body can be erotic; stale and offensive smells result from the action of skin bacteria and other microorganisms on accumulated body secretions.

Although the vagina is a self-cleansing organ, some women like to wash it by *douching* after menstruation or coitus. Douching is not necessary to keep clean. It may predispose a woman to yeast infections, because it disturbs the bacteria that normally live in the vagina.

For effective use of spermicides (foams, diaphram jelly, and so on) it is important *not* to douche for at least six hours after intercourse. Beyond that time a woman may douche to rinse off the residues of the contraceptive substances. Disposable douching kits are convenient, but they are a needless expense, and the chemicals may be irritating. A woman can instead buy a douche bag and use plain lukewarm tap water, or make it mildly acidic by adding two tablespoons of vinegar to one quart of water. Doctors recommend douching for certain infections, to convey the medication to the vagina.

### Toxic Shock Syndrome

To absorb the menstrual flow women use *tampons,* absorbent cylinders inserted into the vagina, or *sanitary napkins,* absorbent pads placed against the vaginal opening. Tampons come in various sizes and can be inserted into the vagina without damage to the hymen. It is preferable that the size of the tampon used on a given day be matched with the amount of menstrual flow expected. Small tampons will not be able to handle heavy flow; large ones will be insufficiently saturated by scanty flow to be taken out easily and may cause vaginal irritation.

A great deal of concern has been generated since 1980 by a newly recognized condition associated with tampon use, called *toxic shock syndrome (TSS).* It usually occurs in younger women during or immediately following menstruation. It is caused by toxins produced by certain bacteria *(Staphylococcus aureus)* that are normally present in many women but tend to multiply rapidly in and around absorbent tampons. A bacterial virus may be responsible for triggering these bacteria to produce their toxin.

The early symptoms of toxic shock are sudden high fever accompanied by sore throat, rash, vomiting, diarrhea, dizziness, and abdominal pain. The condition is very rare, occurring in less than 1 per 100,000 menstruating women (of whom there are 50 million in the United States), but it can be fatal; 88 deaths were ascribed to it between 1978 and mid-1982.

The more absorbent a tampon, the higher the risk of its causing toxic shock; the likelihood is 60 times higher for the most absorbent type (Berkeley et al., 1987). The particular brand of tampon *(Rely)* that was found to be most frequently associated with this condition has been taken off the market (Paige, 1978), but there has been no significant drop in the number of cases—still about 40 to 65 per month in the United States.

Though there are many other causes for the TSS-like symptoms, if a woman experiences them while wearing tampons, she should seek immediate medical care. To help reduce the risk, tampons should be changed at least every six hours, hands washed prior to insertion, sanitary napkins substituted at night, extremely absorbent types ("super" or "superplus") used only with heavy flow, and the use of superabsorbent tampons avoided by adolescents.

## Sex during Menstruation

Some women refrain from sexual intercourse while menstruating; others do not mind the presence of menstrual blood, which may be washed away before coitus or held back with a diaphragm. Until recently, personal rather than medical considerations determined these decisions. The situation has now changed; because certain health risks have become linked with having sexual intercourse while menstruating.

Intercourse during menstruation has been associated with increased risk of *pelvic inflammatory disease* (PID), infections of the uterus, and fallopian tubes. During menstruation, the cervix is more open, and the normal mucous plug is absent, while the free blood in the vagina and uterus provides a growth medium for bacteria (Hatcher et al., 1988). The risk of acquiring PID from a single act of intercourse is three to six times greater right around menstruation.

In a long-term mutually monogamous relationship, or if a condom is used, the risk of pelvic infection for the woman is negligible. However, menstrual blood is also a possible source of AIDS virus and hepatitis B virus, so a male who has intercourse with a menstruating woman may be taking a higher risk of exposing himself to these diseases. The risk is less if he uses a condom. Orgasm during menstruation through any means may relieve or sometimes increase menstrual cramping (Hatcher et al., 1988).

## COMMON AILMENTS OF THE REPRODUCTIVE SYSTEM

### Genitourinary Infections

The most serious infections of the genital and urinary tract are due to sexually transmitted diseases, which we discuss separately. A number of common, milder conditions should not be mistaken for them.

Genital Discharge   Normally, men should pass only urine and semen through the urethra; any other discharge, or the presence of blood in urine or semen, is abnormal and is probably due to infection.

Women, in addition to menstrual bleeding, secrete vaginal mucus during their monthly cycle (apart from vaginal fluid generated during sexual excitement). When vaginal discharge is excessive and contains pus cells it is called *leukorrhea* (Barclay, 1987). Almost every woman experiences leukorrhea at some time in her life. It is not a disease but a condition that can be caused by infections, chemicals, and physical changes. For example, irritating chemicals in douche preparations, foreign bodies such as contraceptive devices, and alterations in hormone balance (as during pregnancy or menopause) may cause it (Capraro et al., 1983). If excess discharge is associated with itching, pain, a bad odor, or an unusual color the woman should see her doctor to rule out a possible infection (Hatcher et al., 1988).

Vaginitis    Vaginitis is an inflammation of the vagina that causes itching, pain, discharge, and discomfort with intercourse (Eschenbach, 1986). Several organisms can cause vaginitis; only some of them are sexually transmitted. *Hemophilus vaginalis* is a frequent cause. Because it can often be found in the sexual partners of infected women, it is possible that the infection is sexually transmitted; but it is also found in people who have not had sexual intercourse.

A common vaginal infection is caused by a protozoan called *Trichomonas* ("Trich"). Close to one million women per year are seen by doctors for this condition. It is characterized by a smelly and foamy yellowish or greenish discharge that irritates the vulva, producing itching and burning. A man may harbor this organism in his urethra or prostate gland without symptoms, or he may have a slight urethral discharge. Because sexual partners usually infect each other, both partners are treated simultaneously with metronidazole (Flagyl) to prevent reinfection. Although usually sexually transmitted, trichomonas infections occasionally have been spread by genital contact with a wet bathing suit or washcloth. There are no known long-term consequences to men or women from this infection.

Candidiasis    Another common vaginal infection is *candidiasis* (or *moniliasis*). It is caused by a yeast-like fungus called *Candida albicans*. The thick white discharge it produces causes itching and discomfort, which may be severe. The organism is present in the vagina of a substantial number of women, but it produces problems only when it multiplies excessively.

Candidiasis is more commonly seen in women who are using oral contraceptives, diabetic, pregnant, or on prolonged antibiotic therapy. The condition responds to treatment with nystatin (Mycostatin) suppositories or cream, but is difficult to completely eradicate it.

Though much less common, the same infection occurs in about 15 percent of the male sexual partners of women with moniliasis. They usually have no symptoms, but there may be marked inflammation of the glans, especially under the foreskin. It is also treated with nystatin cream.

Cystitis    The closeness of the urethral opening to the vagina and anus predisposes women to urinary bladder infections *(cystitis)*. Sometimes bladder irritation is caused by frequent or vigorous coitus ("honeymoon cystitis").

Cystitis is most commonly found in young, sexually active women and in older men with an enlarged prostate. The cystitis of young women and older men is usually caused by bacterial infection irritating the bladder wall. Similar symptoms may be experienced by menopausal women whose bladders become irritated by pressure through thinned vaginal walls. Women who are sexually active are more likely to have urinary tract infection than those who are not (Leibovici et al., 1987).

The primary symptom of cystitis is frequent urination accompanied by pain and a burning sensation in the urethra. Although these symptoms may disappear spontaneously in a few days, it is advisable to receive proper treatment, because untreated infections may spread from the bladder to the kidneys, with more serious consequences.

Measures that help prevent cystitis are drinking lots of fluids, urinating after coitus, wearing cotton underpants, and maintaining good general hygiene. The use of condoms can also reduce the chances of infection (Hatcher et al., 1982).

Prostatitis    A common problem among men is inflammation of the prostate gland *(prostatitis)*, manifested by increased frequency and burning on urination, and painful ejaculation.

Sometimes there is no apparent bacterial cause. A curious association exists between prostatitis and irregular sexual activity—long periods of abstinence followed by bouts of intensive sex (hence, it is called the "sailor's disease") (Silber, 1981). However, in healthy young men prostatitis is usually (but not always) caused by one of the sexually transmitted diseases (Holmes et al., 1984).

## Cancer

The reproductive systems of both sexes, especially the female sex organs, are some of the most common sites for the development of cancer (Rutledge, 1986). The early detection of these cancers is of great importance in treating them. It is essential that everyone know enough about the early signs and symptoms to seek medical help promptly.

Cancer of the Breast    Cancers are malignant tumors which grow and spread in the body. Cancer of the breast is the most common form of cancer in women, accounting for 25 percent of all female cancers. In the United States about 5 percent of women develop breast cancer (100,000 new cases) a year; one out of ten women develops it in her lifetime. Though rare before age 25, it increases steadily in each decade thereafter. For women 40 to 44 years old it is the most common cause of death (Giuliano, 1987).

Women who are at higher risk include those over 50, those who have a family history of breast cancer, those who experience a late menopause, and those who have never had children. Men rarely develop breast cancer; only about 1 percent of breast cancers do occur in men.

The primary symptom of breast cancer is a painless mass in the breast; much less common are dimples on the breast surface or discharge from the nipple. The early cancerous lump will not show or make itself felt; so regular and systematic breast self-examination is of great importance. Examinations should be done by every woman, once a month, about a week after the end of the menses when the breasts are not likely to be tender. Detecting change requires having a sense of what the breast feels like normally. Doing it on a set day each month makes it easier to remember, and because breast tissues will be in a similar hormonal state, it is easier to feel changes (Box 5.1).

The most important factor that determines a woman's chance of surviving breast cancer is how early and how small the cancer is when detected and treated. Women who regularly examine their own breasts can detect a mass smaller and sooner than their physicians can at annual visits. Most breast masses, especially in younger women, are due to other causes, such as benign cysts, not cancer. A woman who feels a mass should not panic, but should seek prompt medical attention.

The basic treatment for breast cancer is either surgical removal of the lump, followed by radiation treatments, or the surgical removal of the breast (mastectomy). Though current surgical procedures cause as little disfigurement as possible, and breast reconstruction is possible through plastic surgery, women still worry that they will lose sexual attractiveness. Some women become so self-conscious following such surgery that they give up sex altogether if it involves nudity. They need reassurance that they are still sexually attractive. Counseling and support groups can help. Prosthetics can be worn to give the breast a normal contour.

Radiation treatments have the same success rate, without causing a dramatic change in body shape, but they do have side effects. The treatments can only be carried out successfully in patients who fit into certain guidelines, such as not being obese or having extremely large breasts. Radiation therapy requires almost daily visits to a specialist at a hospital with special equipment, for one or two months (Rubin, 1987).

Cancer of the breast can be rapidly fatal if it spreads to vital organs, but with early diagnosis and treatment the prognosis is much more favorable. About 65 percent of patients with cancer of the breast now remain alive for at least five years after the initial diagnosis.

# Box 5.1

---

## HOW TO DO A BREAST SELF-EXAM

1. *In the shower.* Examine your breasts during your bath or shower. Hands glide more easily over wet skin. Hold your fingers flat and move them gently over every part of each breast. Use the right hand to examine the left breast and the left hand for the right breast. Check for any lump, hard knot, or thickening.

2. *Before a mirror.* Inspect your breasts with arms at your sides. Next, raise your arms high overhead. Look for any changes in the contours of each breast: swelling, dimpling of skin, or changes in the nipple.

Then rest your palms on your hips and press down firmly to flex your chest muscles. Left and right breast may not exactly match—few women's breasts do. Again, look for changes and irregularities. Regular inspection will show what is normal for you and will give you confidence in your examination.

3. *Lying down.* To examine your right breast, put a pillow or folded towel under your right shoulder. Place your right hand behind your head; this distributes breast tissue more evenly on the chest. With the left hand, fingers flat, press gently in small circular motions around an imaginary clock face. Begin at outermost top of your right breast for 12 o'clock, the move to 1 o'clock, and so on around the circle back to 12. (A ridge of firm tissue in the lower curve of each breast is normal.) Then move 1 inch inward, toward the nipple, and repeat. Keep circling to examine very part of your breast, including the nipple—at least three more circles. Now slowly repeat the procedure on your left breast with a pillow under your left shoulder and left hand behind your head. Notice how your breast structure feels.

Finally, squeeze the nipple of each breast gently between the thumb and index finger. Any discharge, clear or bloody, should be reported to your doctor immediately. (From an American Cancer Society pamphlet. Used with permission.)

Breasts should be examined at the same point in the menstrual cycle each month—usually early in the cycle. In addition to the self-exam which all women over age 20 should do monthly, the following additional tests are important for early detection of breast cancer.

1. A doctor should examine the breasts every three years for women aged 20 to 40, and every year after 40.
2. A *mammogram* (breast X-ray) should be taken between the ages of 35 and 39 as a baseline for future comparisons.
3. Women with no symptoms should have the mammogram repeated every two years between age 40 and 49, and every year after 50.
4. Women of any age who have had breast cancer, have had a member of the family with breast cancer, or have other high-risk factors must set up with a physician a personal schedule of mammography (Brozan, 1987).

  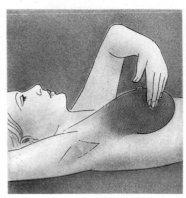 

Cancer of the Cervix    Cancer of the cervix is the second most common type of cancer in women, affecting about 2 out of 100 women (60,000 new cases a year). It is rare before age 20, but the incidence rises over the next several decades. The average age of women with cancer of the cervix is 45 (Hill, 1987).

The disease is more common in women who have had large numbers of sexual contacts and who have borne children. A study of 13,000 Canadian nuns failed to reveal a single case of cervical cancer. The disease is also rare among Jewish women, which suggests that perhaps circumcision in the sexual partner is somehow linked to preventing the disease. However, in India there is no difference in rates between Muslim and Hindu women, though the husbands of the former but not the latter are circumcised (Novak et al., 1970). Three factors are known to increase a woman's risk for cervical cancer: first sexual intercourse before age 20; three or more sexual partners in her lifetime; and a male partner with many sexual contacts (Richart, 1983).

A sexually transmitted virus, human papilloma virus, the same virus that causes genital warts (discussed later), has been associated with cervical cancer. Infection with this virus appears to cause, or at least to contribute to, the development of cervical cancer. The infected areas on the cervix may be invisible to the naked eye, but may be detected with tests.

Cancer of the cervix may cause no symptoms for five or ten years, but if it is detected early, treatment is highly successful. The well-known *Pap smear* test is the best means now available for identifying cancer of the cervix in these early stages. It should be done annually beginning at age 20 (or earlier if a woman is sexually active). The procedure is simple: the cervix is scraped lightly, picking up cells from the surface; the cells are transferred to a glass slide, which is then stained and examined for the presence of abnormal cells.

As cancer of the cervix begins to invade surrounding tissues, irregular vaginal bleeding or a chronic bloody vaginal discharge may develop. Treatment is less successful when the cancer has reached this stage. If treatment by surgery, radiation, or both is instituted before the cancer spreads beyond the cervix, the five-year survival rate is about 80 percent, but it drops precipitously as the disease reaches other organs in the pelvis. The overall five-year survival rate for invasive cancer of the cervix (including all stages of the disease) is about 58 percent.

Cancer of the Endometrium    Cancer of the lining of the uterus is less common than cancer of the cervix, affecting about 1 percent of women. It usually occurs in women over 35, most commonly those between 50 to 64. Many but not all cases are detected by the yearly Pap smear test, so women over 35 also should watch for any abnormal vaginal bleeding. The five-year survival rate for endometrial cancer is 77 percent (Lacey, 1987).

Cancer of the endometrium has been linked with estrogen replacement therapy, which we will discuss in connection with the menopause (Chapter 9). Birth control pills, on the contrary, seem to exert a protective influence (Chapter 6).

Cancer of the Prostate    In the male, the prostate is the organ that is the most frequent cause of disease in the reproductive system. It tends to grow larger in *benign hypertrophy* as men get older, obstructing the neck of the urethra and interfering with normal urination. As a result the man has to go to the bathroom frequently, getting up several times at night.

Cancer of the prostate is the most common cancer of male sex organs and the third most common cancer in men. About 5 percent of men will develop it (Walsh, 1985), but it is uncommon before age 60 and grows slowly. Those who have it are more likely to die of other causes, such as heart disease.

The initial symptoms of prostatic cancer are similar to those of benign enlargement of the prostate. Early in the course of the disease, sexual interest may increase because of frequent erections caused by local changes. Later on there is usually a loss of genital functioning.

A tentative diagnosis of cancer of the prostate can usually be made on the basis of a rectal examination (which involves feeling the surface of the gland with a finger inserted in the rectum), the history of symptoms, and laboratory tests. A prostate examination should therefore be part of an annual physical checkup for any man over 50. As with other cancers, the outcome is much more optimistic when it is diagnosed and treated early. The cause of prostatic cancer remains unknown, despite efforts to link it with hormones, infectious agents, sexual activity, or abstinence.

The treatment of prostatic enlargement and cancer often requires surgery. Such surgery may do damage to nerves in this region, resulting in loss of potency. This outcome is least likely (51 percent) if the prostatic tissues are removed through the urethra (Kolodny et al., 1979). Retrograde ejaculation is another possible complication (Chapter 3). Castration and estrogen therapy can cause regression of

the cancer, but it may also lead to sexual dysfunction (Chapter 15) (Walsh, 1985).

Cancer of the Testes    Unlike most other cancers, which strike later in life, cancer of the testes affects younger men. It is the most common cancer in males 29 to 35, yet it accounts for 0.7 percent of all cancers in males (Lipsett, 1985). Males who have undescended testes or whose testes descend after age six are at greater risk for developing testicular cancer (11–15 percent of these males will develop it).

If testicular cancer is detected early, it is curable; otherwise it can spread to other parts of the body and cause death. To check for early evidence of testicular cancer, a man should examine his testes periodically (Box 5.2). Treatment includes the removal of the affected testicle, which does not affect sexual activity or fertility. A synthetic implant is in-

## Box 5.2

### HOW TO EXAMINE YOUR TESTICLES

Because it is rare, much less attention is paid to early detection of cancer of the testicle than of the breast. However, the testes can be examined easily. Spending a few moments on them periodically may save your life.

The effectiveness of the testicular self-exam depends on several factors: doing it regularly, being thorough, and knowing what you are looking for. The best time is after a warm shower or bath, when the scrotal sac is relaxed. Examine one testicle at a time while you are seated or lying down. Hold the testicle between the fingers of one or both hands and roll it about, so that its surface passes under your fingertips. The point is to feel for small bumps, surface irregularities, or enlargement of the testicle itself. Do not be alarmed by the normal irregularities caused by the epididymis on the testicular surface. Get a good sense of how the testicular surface feels normally (it will take some practice). Do not become obsessed with the procedure, but whenever in doubt about a possible growth, consult a doctor promptly.

serted into the scrotum for cosmetic purposes. Some men need reassurance that lack of a testicle does not make them less masculine.

Cancer of the Penis    Cancer of the penis is rare in the United States, accounting for about 2 percent of all cancers in males. It almost never occurs among Jews, who undergo circumcision in infancy, and is also rare among Muslims, who get circumcised before puberty. In areas of the world where circumcision is not common, cancer of the penis is much more prevalent. For instance, it accounts for about 18 percent of all malignancies in Far Eastern countries. The usual explanation, though unconfirmed, is that circumcision prevents accumulation of potentially carcinogenic secretions (possibly harboring a virus) around the rim of the penis, which is the usual site of this tumor (Silber, 1981).

## SEXUALLY TRANSMITTED DISEASES

*Sexually transmitted diseases* (STDs) are infections caused by various microorganisms (bacteria, viruses, and protozoa) that are primarily acquired through sexual contact or during birth through an infected birth canal. They were formerly called, and still are popularly known as, *venereal diseases* (in reference to Venus, the Roman goddess of love).

### Prevalence
The STDs are one of the most serious public health problems. In the United States, over 10 million cases of STDs a year currently occur among the young adult population. Conservative estimates place the total cost of STDs to society at over $2 billion annually (Cates and Holmes, 1986). The spread of AIDS is likely to increase this cost greatly.

The prevalence of STDs has greatly increased in the recent past. Even rare sex-related diseases are on the rise (Leary, 1988). Younger people are particularly vulnerable; roughly two-thirds of all cases are in the 15 to 29 age group (Figures 5.1 and 5.2). It is estimated that half of the country's youth now

contracts a sexually transmitted disease by age 25; this figure does not mean that every other young person you know has or will get an STD; in some groups almost everyone, in others almost none will have it (Hatcher et al., 1988).

People who are poor, those who live in urban areas, and certain ethnic minorities have the highest reported rates of STDs for each age group (Cates and Holmes, 1986). Such figures are no ground for prejudice. Part of the reason their rates appear higher is because these people more frequently use public medical services, which probably report cases more frequently than do private doctors. The inner-city poor also have higher rates of many other diseases, including most other infectious diseases, because of unsanitary living conditions, overcrowding, and inadequate medical services.

It is important to realize that *anyone* can have a sexually communicable disease, irrespective of age, sex, marital status, education, affluence, social status, or sexual orientation. In one survey, people who called an STD hotline were 83 percent white, 88 percent heterosexual, and 26 percent married. One-third of them had bachelor's degrees and a quarter earned over $25,000 a year (Hoffman, 1981). Again, the figures are deceptive. These people are more likely to use such a service and hardly representative of the general population.

Blaming a group as "carriers" of sexually transmitted diseases provokes prejudice and damages efforts to identify, treat, and control STDs (Brandt, 1985). The social consequences of some diseases can be more harmful to the infected person than the disease itself.

### Types of STDs
Some two dozen microorganisms are transmitted sexually to cause a wide variety of clinical syndromes (clusters of signs or symptoms) or diseases. They include *bacteria, viruses, spirochetes, protozoa,* and *fungi* (Cates and Holmes, 1986). We shall only deal with the most common and important of the illnesses caused by these infectious agents.

A microorganism causes each illness but other conditions also affect the outcome—general health, level of immunity, the dose of the infecting organism, and so on. No one will ever develop gonorrhea, for instance, without the bacterium that causes it, but not everyone harboring the organism will develop symptoms of disease. Some people are only *carriers* of the organism, capable of infecting others although they themselves are free of symptoms. Whether a person succumbs to the illness is thus a function of the characteristics of both the *host* and the *parasite*. This model governs the way that all infectious diseases work.

There are various ways to classify STDs. For diagnosis, it is useful to categorize them by their symptoms. Some conditions primarily cause a urethral discharge (gonorrhea and chlamydia); others cause skin lesions (syphilis and herpes). The physician confronted with a patient who has a given symptom tries to sort out the underlying cause through *differential diagnosis*—a process of elimination and confirmation, using signs, symptoms, and clinical tests (Sparling, 1988).

A more fundamental method of classification, and more instructive for our purposes, is based on *etiology,* or causes. Even though herpes and hepatitis have different sets of symptoms and outcomes, they are both caused by viruses. Because viruses tend to behave similarly, we group them together. This approach provides a handle for research and treatment.

## BACTERIAL STDs

### Gonorrhea

Gonorrhea is an infection caused by the bacterium *Neisseria gonorrhoeae* (Hansfield, 1984). Ancient Chinese and Egyptian manuscripts refer to a contagious urethral discharge, which was probably gonorrhea. The Greek physician Galen (A.D. 130–201) is credited with coining the term *gonorrhea* from the words "seed" and "flow." This microorganism only infects humans and cannot survive for long outside the living conditions, temperature, and moisture provided by the human body.

Some 800,000 new cases of gonorrhea are reported each year in the United States, but the true incidence is estimated to be over 2 million cases a year. The rates of gonorrhea rose sharply in the 1960s and 1970s but declined somewhat in the 1980s. The rates are particularly high in 15 to 29-year-olds (Figure 5.1).

Gonorrhea is transmitted from one person to another during intimate contact with infected mucous membranes, including the membranes of the throat, genitals, or rectum. Women run a higher risk of infection following exposure than men. A woman has an approximately 50-percent chance of becoming infected with gonorrhea after one act of intercourse with an infected man; a man in the same situation runs a 25-percent chance of infection. This difference is presumably because the penis is exposed to the infectious female discharge only during coitus, whereas the infectious ejaculate is deposited deep in the vagina, where it remains after the withdrawal of the penis. Furthermore, post-coital urination can wash urethral bacteria out of the male; the vagina cleans itself much more slowly, so organisms have a greater opportunity to establish themselves. Nonetheless, post-coital urination may reduce female cystitis. Practices like post-coital washing and urination may be helpful but cannot be relied on to prevent gonorrhea (Stone et al., 1986). The use of condoms is much more effective.

Symptoms   In males, the primary symptom of gonorrhea ("clap") is a pus-filled yellow urethral discharge. The usual site of infection for men is the urethra, so this form of the disease is called *gonorrheal urethitis*. Most infected males show symptoms, but at least 10 percent do not; they are asymptomatic. A discharge from the tip of the penis usually appears within two to ten days after acquiring the infection. It is often accompanied by a burning sensation during urination and an itching feeling within the urethra. The inflammation may subside within two or three weeks without treatment, or it may persist in chronic form, in which case it may spread to the rest of the genital-urinary

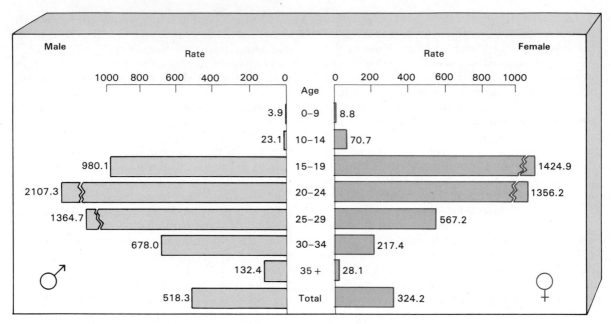

Figure 5.1     Gonorrhea: age-specific case rates (per 100,000 population) by sex, for the United States in 1982.

tract, involving the prostate glands, seminal vesicles, bladder, and rarely, kidneys. In some cases, the disease spreads to the joints, causing *gonorrheal arthritis* in both sexes.

The symptoms of gonorrhea in 50–80 percent of infected women are so mild or altogether absent that the woman does not realize that she is infected. This fact can lead to further complications for the woman herself, or she may act as a carrier of the disease, inadvertently spreading it to others. The primary site of infection in the woman is usually the cervix, causing *gonorrheal cervicitis.* The only early symptom may be a yellow vaginal discharge, which is difficult to distinguish from other common vaginal discharges. Untreated gonorrhea may spread up through the cervix into the uterine lining, the endometrium, and up to the fallopian tubes, causing *pelvic inflammatory disease,* which is described later.

The symptoms of nongenital gonorrhea are about the same in men as in women. *Pharyngeal gonorrhea,* an infection of the throat with gonorrhea, is transmitted most commonly during oral sex. Oral stimulation of the penis is more likely to be infectious than oral stimulation of the vulva, or kissing. The primary symptom of pharyngeal gonorrhea is a sore throat with or without fever and enlarged lymph nodes. In some cases there are no symptoms, although the person remains contagious.

*Rectal gonorrhea* is an infection of the rectum usually transmitted during anal intercourse. Less often, in women with gonorrheal cervitis, the infection sometimes spreads through the vaginal discharge to the rectum. The symptoms of rectal gonorrhea are itching associated with a rectal discharge. Many cases are mild or asymptomatic.

In earlier years a common cause of blindness in children was gonorrheal infection of the eyes (*gonococcal conjunctivitis*), acquired during passage through the mother's infected organs during birth. Instilling penicillin ointment or silver nitrate drops into the eyes of all newborn babies is now compulsory and has eradicated this disease.

It takes a laboratory test to diagnose gonorrhea. The symptoms and signs may suggest it, but it must be confirmed by identifying the causative organisms in the genital discharges or in the other infected sites. To detect asymptomatic infection, cervical or urethral specimens are taken even though there are no signs or symptoms. In men, a microscopic examination of the urethral discharge may establish the diagnosis. In women's cases, and in some men's cases, the organism must be cultured—grown in a nutrient medium—to confirm its presence. There is no routine blood test that can detect gonorrhea in either sex, which is one reason why identification of asymptomatic gonorrhea has been much less successful than identification of asymptomatic syphilis.

Treatment    The usual treatment of gonorrhea is with antibiotics, usually *penicillin*. However, some rare strains that are resistant to penicillin require other antibiotics. Vaccines against gonorrhea are currently being tested (Sparling, 1988).

## Chlamydia

*Chlamydia* is the common name for infections caused by *Chlamydia trachomatis,* bacteria that infect men, women, and babies (Stamm and Holmes, 1984).

Symptoms    The symptoms caused by chlamydia are similar to those of gonorrhea. In men, the primary infection caused by chlamydia is urethitis; it is commonly called *nongonoccal urethitis* because until recently the bacterium was difficult to identify in laboratory tests. The symptoms are painful urination, itching, and a mucoid discharge, which tends to be less profuse than that of gonorrhea. Some men have asymptomatic infections but carry the disease to others. Chlamydia does not spread to the rest of the genitourinary tract in men, nor does it cause arthritis in either sex.

In women the primary infection is cervicitis; it is called *mucopurulent cervicitis* because of a sticky yellow discharge from the cervix. Nonetheless, as with gonorrhea, the woman often cannot tell it from an ordinary vaginal discharge, and in up to 80 percent of cases she is not aware of being infected. Chlamydial infections in women can also rise through the cervix to the upper genital tract and cause pelvic inflammatory disease.

In newborns infected during passage through a mother's birth canal the sites of infection are the eyes and/or the lungs, causing *conjunctivitis* (which can lead to blindness if untreated) and *pneumonia*. The treatment given infants at birth to prevent gonorrhea does not protect against chlamydia, but most children with chlamydial conjunctivitis respond to treatment with antibiotics.

Other possible sites of infection in men and women include the pharynx and the eyes. The pharynx may be exposed during oral-genital intercourse, and the eyes contaminated through hand contact with infectious secretions.

The diagnosis of chlamydia is made by examining the likely sites of infection and noting a urethral or cervical discharge. Asymptomatic infections may be detected by growing the bacteria in culture, or by other laboratory tests that allow cheaper, more rapid diagnosis.

Treatment    The treatment of chlamydia in adults is with antibiotics, usually *tetracycline*. In infants, less potentially toxic antibiotics must be used.

## Pelvic Inflammatory Disease

*Pelvic inflammatory disease (PID)* is not a specific disease but an inflammation of the fallopian tubes (*salpingitis*) and/or of the lining of the uterus (*endometritis*) (McGee, 1984). The inflammation is usually due to infection with various bacteria, most often gonorrhea, or chlamydia that spread "upward" from the cervix to the uterus, fallopian tubes, and eventually the lower abdominal cavity itself.

Pelvic inflammatory disease is a widespread condition, afflicting an estimated one million women each year in the United States, causing some 300,000 of them to be hospitalized (Washington et al., 1984). Over $2.6 billion are spent annually to treat this condition. PID is largely responsible for the increase in infertility among women.

Sexual activity with multiple partners and a history of PID both increase a woman's risk of acquiring a new case of PID (Eschenbach, 1986). Adolescents, young women, and black women are most susceptible; nearly 70 percent of all cases occur in women who are younger than 25 (Westrom, 1980, 1985). Young and black women are at higher risk for contracting sexually transmitted diseases in general, which may explain in part why their rate of PID is higher. However, the increased risk of PID in adolescents is also attributable to biological factors such as cervical and immunological immaturity (Cates and Holmes, 1986; Washington et al., 1984).

The contraceptive intrauterine device (IUD) increases risk of pelvic inflammatory disease. Whether other methods of contraception increase or decrease the risk is more controversial (Lee et al., 1983). Most studies have shown oral contraceptives to reduce the risk of PID, but these studies have only looked at hospitalized cases; their validity for less acute forms of PID (which are more typically caused by chlamydia) is questionable. It has also been suggested that oral contraceptives actually facilitate the spread of chlamydial PID from the cervix to the uterus (Washington et al., 1984).

Symptoms   The symptoms of pelvic inflammatory disease may be minimal, or they may include pain and tenderness of the lower abdomen in the region of the uterus and the pelvis, chills, and fever. Gonococcal PID usually occurs in younger patients with a shorter period of pain before seeing a doctor (3 days) and higher fever; chlamydial PID is also associated with youth, but involves a longer period of pain before seeing a doctor (7-9 days), and less chance of high fever. Pelvic inflammatory disease caused by mixed bacterial infections are more common in older women, those with previous infections, and users of an IUD. It has a more acute and rapid onset, with fever and prostrating effect.

If PID becomes chronic, the symptoms of pelvic pain, pain during coitus, pelvic swelling, and tenderness may remain long after the original infection is gone. Furthermore, chronic PID will often lead to blockage of the fallopian tubes and sterility, as well as an increase in the chances of ectopic pregnancy (Chapter 6).

The diagnosis of PID is complicated by the difficulty in obtaining material from the endometrium and the fallopian tubes for a culture. However, a presumptive diagnosis is enough for a doctor to initiate treatment to relieve symptoms and to prevent sterility.

Treatment   The treatment of PID usually involves intravenous antibiotic therapy in a hospital. Treatment must begin as early as possible with more than one antibiotic, in order to provide a broad range of protection against the possible bacteria involved, even though they have not been identified.

Syphilis

Syphilis is caused by a *spirochete* (a corkscrew-shaped bacterium-like organism) called *treponema pallidum*. The term *syphilis* was introduced in 1530 by the Italian physician Girolamo Fracastoro, who wrote a poem in Latin about a shepherd boy named Syphilius (from the Greek for "crippled"), who was stricken with the disease as a punishment for having insulted Apollo (Rosenberg, 1965). It is generally believed that syphilis was brought into Europe from the New World by Columbus' crew. The first syphilis epidemic spread through Europe shortly after his return in 1493; Columbus himself died of advanced syphilis in 1508.

Syphilis is usually transmitted through intimate sexual contact, including kissing, but the spirochete can penetrate through all mucosal surfaces and through minor abrasions in the skin. Conceivably, syphilis could be transmitted through skin-to-skin contact of a nonsexual nature, but it is highly unlikely.

Syphilis (also called *lues*) is one of the most serious of the sexually transmitted diseases. Before the advent of antibiotics, syphilis epidemics posed an enormous public health threat. After the discovery of penicillin, the

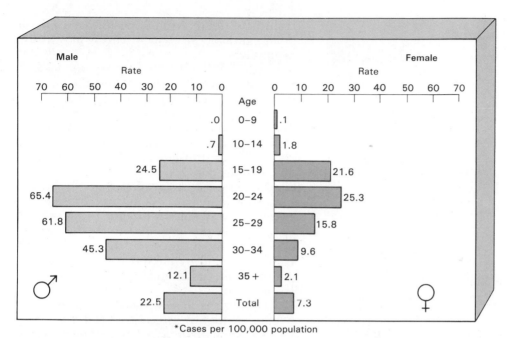

Figure 5.2 Primary and secondary syphilis: age-specific case rates (per 100,000 population) by sex, for the United States in 1982.

prevalence of syphilis went down to 4 cases per 100,000 population in 1957, but it then went up again to 12 cases per 100,000 during the years 1965–1983 (Sparling, 1988). Currently, about 85,000 new cases occur yearly (Leary, 1988). It is more prevalent among younger age groups (Figure 5.2), especially among males in poor neighborhoods.

The rates of syphilis among gay men have been especially high, but these rates are declining currently as they adopt safer sex practices to protect themselves against AIDS.

Primary Stage Syphilis   The clinical course or progression of untreated syphilis is divided into three stages. The first stage is marked by a skin lesion known as a *chancre* (pronounced "shank-er") at the site where the spirochete has entered the body (Figures 5.3 and 5.4). The chancre is a hard round ulcer with raised edges that is usually painless. In the male it most commonly appears on the penis, the scrotum, or in the pubic area. In the female it is usually on the external genitals, but it may be within

the vagina or on the cervix, so not readily visible. Chancres may also occur on the lips, the mouth, the rectum, the nipple, the hand, or

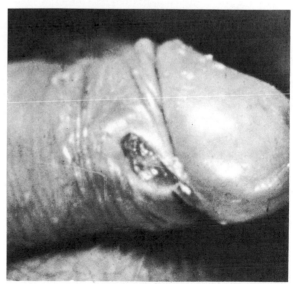

Figure 5.3   Chancre of the penis.

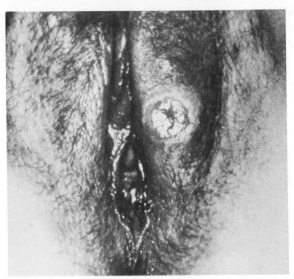

Figure 5.4    An unusually large chancre on the labia majora.

anywhere the organism has entered the body. The chancre appears about two to four weeks after infection, and if not treated usually disappears in several weeks, giving the false impression of recovery.

The syphilitic chancre must be differentiated from a similar genital ulcer called *chancroid* ("soft chancre"), which is caused by the bacterium *Hemophilus ducreyi*. Chancroid is also transmitted sexually, but in contrast to syphilis, the skin lesion has soft edges and is painful. The definitive diagnosis must be made, however, by identifying the organism through the microscope or by cultures. Treatment with sulfa drugs is effective. This infection is rare in Western countries but common in Asia and tropical regions.

Various blood tests (such as the *VDRL,* or *fluorescent treponemal antibody-absorption test*) screen for syphilis by identifying antibodies produced against the spirochete. As in all other laboratory tests, there may be false positive results in the absence of the disease or false negative results even when the person is infected. The definitive diagnosis is made by identifying the spirochete through a special technique called *dark field microscopy.* The treat-

ment of primary syphilis is with penicillin (or other antibiotics), which cures most cases promptly.

Secondary Stage Syphilis    When the primary stage is untreated, the secondary stage symptoms can appear anytime from several weeks to several months after the healing of the chancre. There is usually a generalized skin rash, which is transient and may or may not be accompanied by other symptoms, such as headache, fever, indigestion, sore throat, and muscle or joint pain. Many people do not associate these symptoms with the primary chancre as part of the same disease. At this stage of infection, the diagnosis is again made with blood tests and by attempts to isolate the organism from blood, genital secretions, or skin lesions.

During the first two stages of syphilis, the person is highly infectious. The spirochete may be shed in mucosal secretions (such as genital discharges and saliva), in blood, and in the skin lesions.

Following the secondary stage, there is a period called the *latency phase,* which may last from two years to many decades. During this period the person has no symptoms and is not infectious. However, spirochetes continue to cause internal damage—burrowing into blood vessels, bone, and the central nervous system.

Tertiary Stage Syphilis    Symptoms of the long-term infection constitute the third stage. Only about 50 percent of untreated cases actually reach the final or tertiary stage.

Tertiary syphilis may cause heart failure, ruptured blood vessels, loss of muscular control, disturbances in the sense of balance, blindness, deafness, and severe mental disturbances from brain damage. The cardiovascular system and the central nervous system are the main systems affected. Ultimately, the disease may be fatal, but treatment with penicillin even at the late stages may be beneficial, depending on the extent to which vital organs have already been damaged. Surgical or medical repair of the damage to the vital organs may also prevent or delay death. Because syphilis is usually treated early, few cases progress to this stage anymore.

Congenital Syphilis   Syphilis can be transmitted to the fetus through the placenta from the infected mother. Mandatory blood tests now identify untreated cases before the birth of a child. Nine out of ten pregnant women who have untreated syphilis will either miscarry, bear a stillborn child, or give birth to a living child with congenital syphilis. Congenital syphilis can cause a child to be mentally disturbed or retarded, to have facial and tooth malformations, or to have other birth defects. Treatment with penicillin during the first half of pregnancy prevents congenital syphilis (Murphy and Patamasucon, 1984).

### Other STDs Caused by Bacteria

There are a number of other STDs caused by bacteria or bacteria-like microorganisms. They are relatively uncommon (less than 1000 cases a year) in the United States, but more prevalent in tropical and subtropical areas (including part of the southern United States). One of them is *chancroid,* which we discussed in connection with syphilis. Two others require brief mention.

*Lymphogranuloma venereum (LGV)* is manifested by enlarged and painful lymph glands in the groin, accompanied by fever, chills, and headache. It responds well to sulfa drugs. *Granuloma inguinale* is characterized by ulcerated, painless, progressively spreading skin lesions, usually around the genitals. It responds well to antibiotics (Sparling, 1988).

## STDs CAUSED BY MISCELLANEOUS ORGANISMS

A number of STDs are caused by organisms that cut across various categories. But because of similarities in the way they are transmitted and the symptoms they cause they "fit" together.

### Enteric Organisms

Organisms that live in the intestines are called *enteric.* Enteric organisms cause STDs through anal sex or fecal-oral contamination.

The rectum is affected by some of the conditions that involve the urethra and the vagina. Gonorrhea is one. In addition, certain infections that are more specific to sexual activity involve the anus, such as anal intercourse and anal-oral contact, either directly or through contaminated fingers. As a result, a number of diseases are transmitted during sexual activity that also commonly spread through nonsexual means, such as through food or water contaminated with fecal matter.

Causative Agents   The most important enteric organisms involved in STDs are the bacteria that cause *shigella* and *salmonella* (Keusch, 1984); the *hepatitis* virus; and the protozoa that cause *amebiasis* and *giardiasis* (Guerrant and Ravd, 1984). Other organisms, like *E. coli* bacteria, normally occur in the rectum; they may cause local infections when transferred to the urethra or the prostate.

Until the AIDS epidemic, these conditions were seen more frequently in gay men, who are more likely to engage in anal sex. Given the hazards of AIDS, most gay men now avoid these risks or take precautions.

Heterosexual couples who engage in anal sexual activities are no less vulnerable. Men who have coitus following anal intercourse without carefully washing the penis in between, or wearing and changing condoms, risk infecting the vagina and their own urethra with fecal organisms. Transmission of such microorganisms can also occur indirectly when hands touch the anus or the fecally contaminated penis and then the mouth.

There are other reasons to worry about anal intercourse. The rectum is vulnerable to injury during anal intercourse or during the insertion of objects for anal masturbation. Because of the "pull" of the anal sphincter, objects that are inserted in the anus can be inadvertently drawn into the rectum. Repeated stretching of the anal sphincter may also lead to fecal incontinence (Rowan and Gillette, 1978).

Symptoms    The symptoms of these enteric infections frequently include diarrhea, nausea, possibly vomiting, and sometimes fever. As these organisms multiply, they irritate the lining of the bowel. These symptoms are different in cases that have been sexually transmitted. The symptoms of viral hepatitis will be described later, when we discuss virally caused STD. The long-term consequences of some of these enteric infections include weight loss, wasting, and possibly damage to the intestines, but usually they are self-limiting.

The diagnosis of these conditions may involve taking a stool specimen, blood tests, and other procedures. Treatment is usually with antibiotics.

### Parasitic Infections
The organisms we have discussed consist of single cells. Parasites are multicellular organisms and some of them may be transmitted by sexual or close contact and infest the skin, the pubic hair, or other external regions.

Pubic Lice    Pediculosis pubis ("crabs") is an infestation of pubic hair by crab lice (Phthirus pubis). They spread usually through sex but occasionally through infected bedding, towels, or clothing (Billstein, 1984). The primary symptom is intense itching. Cream, lotion, or shampoos with benzene hexachloride (Kwell) eliminate both adult lice, which are about the size of a pinhead, and their eggs, which cling to the pubic hair. To avoid reinfection, clothing or bedding that come in contact with the body must be decontaminated.

Scabies    Scabies is a contagious skin infection caused by the itch mite (Sarcoptes scabei). It causes intense itching and may cause a red rash. It can be transmitted by close personal contact, sexual contact, or infected clothing or bedding. Scabies is commonly found in the

genital areas, buttocks, and between the fingers.

The female itch mite burrows into the skin and lays eggs along the burrow. The larvae hatch within a few days. The body's reaction to these eggs and larvae is responsible for the itching, irritation, and redness that appear in small track patterns. The mites are more active at night, when they cause the most itching. The treatment is the same as for pubic lice (Orkin and Maibach, 1984).

### VIRAL STDs

Viruses are the smallest microorganisms. Despite their simplicity, they are highly specialized. They can only reproduce within the cells of a host—human, animal, plant, or bacterium. Some viruses are so well adapted that they live in human cells without causing harm; others cause ailments ranging from the common cold to fatal illnesses like rabies (Kilbourne, 1985). Among the STDs, they cause genital warts, genital herpes, hepatitis, and AIDS (which we shall discuss separately).

Once a person acquires the virus for an STD, it stays in the body. There may be occasional flare-ups of the condition. Even a person who stays asymptomatic continues to carry the virus and can pass it on under certain conditions.

The symptoms of viral infections usually subside by themselves, as in many cases of herpes, but they may become progressively more serious, as in many cases of AIDS. STDs caused by viruses are not cured by antibiotics. Other treatments may alleviate symptoms, but usually do not get rid of the infection. Because viruses mutate easily into different strains, it is difficult to develop effective vaccines against them.

### Genital Herpes
Genital herpes is a skin lesion with painful blisters caused by the herpes simplex virus, usually of the type II (HSV II) variety (Corey, 1984). Type I (HSV I) of the same virus usually

causes *oral herpes*—"cold sores" with lesions on the lips, mouth, or face. HSV I can also cause genital herpes and HSV II, oral herpes.

Although recognized for some time, genital herpes did not become highly prevalent in the United States until the 1960s. The number of cases seen by physicians increased almost ten-fold during the period from 1966 to 1984 (Figure 5.5). An estimated one in five adults in the United States (over 20 million persons) has had at least one episode of genital herpes. Each year another half million cases are added, making herpes a major focus of medical and public concern (Leary, 1988). A burst of attention in the popular media in the late 1970s generated much public fear and concern about this sexually transmitted disease.

Transmission of Herpes    Herpes is typically transmitted by contact with the infected areas of the sexual partner. Self-contamination is also possible if a person touches an infected lesion and then immediately touches another body surface or an eye. Genital herpes most often spreads through coitus, mouth-genital contact, or anal intercourse—any contact with the lesions or an infected site that is about to develop lesions. For this reason, all contact with an infected region must be avoided until the blisters have healed completely. When there are early signs of a recurrence—itching, burning, and tingling where the blisters are to appear—touching this region should also be avoided.

The chances of infection during an active period of disease are high. The risk of infection is much lower during asymptomatic periods (Judson, 1983), so herpes does not mean that a person will never again be reasonably safe as a sexual partner. Using condoms and spermicides and washing with soap and water after coitus further reduces the risk. However, when lesions are not restricted to the area covered, a condom cannot provide complete protection against transmission of the herpes virus (Stone et al., 1986; Del Rosario, 1987).

It is conceivable that herpes may also be transmitted through accidental contamination.

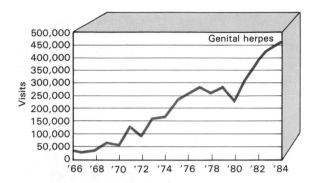

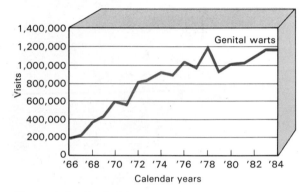

Figure 5.5    Genital herpes and genital warts: number of visits to private physician's offices in the United States, 1966–1984.

The virus has been shown to survive for short periods outside the body in warm mucosal secretions, which may contaminate a toilet seat or hot tub. However, there is no evidence of significant risk in practical terms.

Symptoms    At first the lesions of herpes are small, fluid-filled blisters surrounded by inflamed tissue. They usually appear 2 to 20 days after first exposure to the virus (Figure 5.6). Common sites of herpes infection in women include the inner surface of the vagina and the surface of the cervix, in addition to the external genital region. In men, the penis, pubic region, and scrotum are frequent sites of infection.

Herpes blisters cause painful burning and itching. When they break open the area may

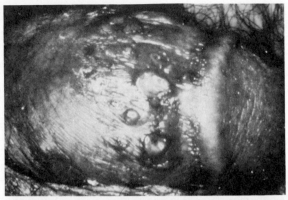

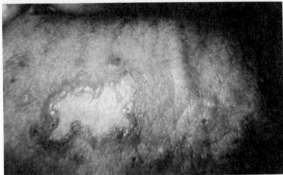

Figure 5.6    Herpes lesion on penis. Within hours or days, the blister-like eruptions (top) burst, leaving open sores (bottom).

become secondarily infected with bacteria, causing prolonged painful sores; otherwise, the blisters clear up spontaneously within a few weeks. Meanwhile, the virus moves along nerve fibers into nerve clusters, where the body's immune system cannot get to it. In the case of genital herpes, these nerve clusters are in the sacral spinal cord. In the case of oral herpes, they are in facial ganglia deep in the cheek. There is no way at present of getting rid of the virus.

An infected person may have no further symptoms or may have recurrences as frequently as twice a month or as rarely as once a decade. The chance of the recurrence of herpes appears to be linked to a number of triggers. These circumstances lower the body's

resistance, allowing the virus to cause symptoms again. Trauma, marked physical exertion, prolonged exposure to the sun, smoking, debilitating disease, menstruation, stress, and sexual activity itself (apart from reinfection) may all lead to recurrences of herpetic symptoms (Wickett, 1982). These triggers are also important in determining whether or not symptoms appear in the first place.

The long-term complications of herpes are rare but may be serious. Transferring the virus into the eyes after touching an infected area causes *herpes keratitis* and possible damage to the eye. Herpes on the lips may, in a small number of cases, lead to viral infection of the brain, or *viral encephalitis*. These complications are treated with the same drugs as other types of herpes.

Other long-term consequences of infection with the herpes virus may include an increased risk of cervical cancer. However, in most of the studies finding this risk, many of the patients were also infected with the human papilloma virus.

Occasionally a fetus may be infected before birth, and the virus may also be transmitted to babies during birth if the mother has an active lesion at the time of delivery. This condition affects about 100 to 200 babies per year in the United States. A pregnant woman who has an active outbreak at the time of delivery runs approximately a 50 percent risk that the newborn child will contract the disease. In babies infected with the disease, there is approximately a 50 percent risk of brain damage or other serious damage, and a high probability of death (Bowen, 1987; Hatcher et al., 1988). To avoid this danger, women with active lesions deliver by cesarian section. Persons with active oral lesions should not fondle or kiss an infant.

Treatment    The treatment of herpes so far can only limit the symptoms, decreasing the pain and shortening the duration of the blisters. There is no cure because no drug can eliminate the virus from nervous tissue. Although all sorts of remedies have been tried, the only proven benefits have been achieved with *acy-

*clovir,* which may be used as an ointment, taken orally, or in serious cases, administered intravenously. Acyclovir is thought to stop the herpes virus from multiplying. If used in the initial period the drug may alleviate the symptoms and shorten the duration of the attack. Washing with soap and water and the use of soothing agents also gives some relief. Personal hygiene is important during active symptoms, to avoid reinfection by touching the sores and then touching other parts of the body.

The oral tablets of acyclovir, known as *zovirax,* have been shown to reduce the length, severity, and frequency of outbreaks in people who take them before symptoms appear (Mertz, 1984). The long-term effect of taking this drug for many years is not known, so it should be taken only for six months to one year at a time, and not at all during pregnancy. Vaccines that could prevent acquiring the disease are actively being sought, but none are ready for marketing.

In comparison with other STDs, herpes is seldom a serious threat to health, yet emotional reactions to and fears of the disease may be severe. The stigma of having it may be more harmful than the disease itself. The threat of herpes infection was reportedly having widespread effects on patterns of sexual behavior among singles in the early 1980s, following strong media coverage (*Time,* 1981). Herpes has since been completely overshadowed by AIDS.

## Genital Warts

*Genital warts (Condylomata acuminata)* are commonly, though not always, transmitted by sexual contact. Though this fact has been known since the time of ancient Greece, it was only in the 1930s that their cause was identified as the *human papilloma virus,* of which there are over 50 varieties. The prevalence of genital warts has been rapidly rising (Figure 5.5). An estimated one million new cases appear each year. Ten percent of the adults in the United States are estimated to be infected with the papilloma virus (Schmeck, 1987).

The transmission of genital warts is similar to the transmission of syphilis: a mucosal membrane is exposed to virus particles shed by an infected person. People may not realize they are infected with the virus and may show no visible genital warts, though they are still infectious.

Symptoms     Warts are growths on the skin that appear within three to eight months after the infection. Genital warts in women most often appear on the vulva or inside the vagina or on the cervix (Figure 5.7). In some pregnant women, previously acquired warts grow rapidly, causing annoyance, itching, irritation, and unsightly masses several centimeters in size. In males, they are usually seen on the surface of the penis or around the anus. Warts may last only a few weeks or may become permanent.

Another kind of genital wart caused by the same virus is not visible to the naked eye. These "flat warts" usually occur on the cervix or on the penis. They may become apparent under a special microscope after they are exposed to vinegar, which whitens infected cells.

The long-term consequences of flat genital warts include predisposition to cervical cancer and (rarely in this country) cancer of the penis and anus (Gal et al., 1987). This type of infection may be recognized on a Pap smear in women. Usually men are not screened for

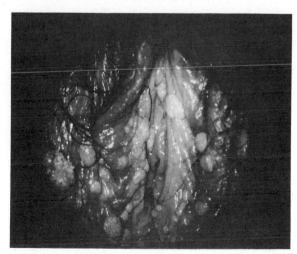

Figure 5.7     Genital warts on vulva.

it unless they are the partners of infected women.

The diagnosis of visible warts is usually based on their appearance. It may be confirmed by examining a small section, or biopsy, under the microscope to confirm the presence of abnormal "giant cells" (*koilocytes*), which indicate infection with the human papilloma virus (Oriel, 1984).

Treatment    Warts are treated by surgery, cauterization (burning), cryosurgery (freezing), or the application of various chemical compounds to kill the cells infected with the wart virus. Most forms of treatment require follow-up, especially the chemical forms, and all of them may be followed by a recurrence of warts in the same or adjacent areas.

## Hepatitis

*Hepatitis* is an inflammatory illness of the liver. When caused by the *hepatitis B virus* (HBV), it is usually acquired through sexual contact or blood transfusions (Lemon, 1984). In the United States, 5–20 percent of the general population has evidence of past hepatitis B infections, though not everyone has been ill with it. In developing countries and in homosexual male populations, previous hepatitis B infection may exceed 80 percent.

The symptoms of hepatitis B infection take two to six months to appear. They include skin rash, muscle and joint pain, profound fatigue, loss of appetite, nausea and vomiting, headache, fever, dark urine, jaundice, and liver enlargement and tenderness. Although this picture is similar to other forms of hepatitis, a patient with typical symptoms and history is considered to have hepatitis B. The definitive diagnosis is by special blood tests.

There is no specific treatment for hepatitis B, but supportive and systematic care can improve rate of recovery and comfort. There is a vaccine highly effective at preventing the infection. However, once a person has already become ill, vaccination does not help. Vaccination is urged for high-risk groups—medical personnel, partners of known carriers, and

people in the inner city, where the rates of HBV infection are high.

The potential complications of hepatitis B include persistence of the hepatitis in chronic form, cirrhosis of the liver, liver cancer, liver failure, and death. In rare cases, hepatitis may cause death within a few months. Some people with hepatitis remain, even after recovery, chronic carriers who may unknowingly transmit the virus to others through sexual contact or blood contact.

## AIDS AND THE HUMAN IMMUNODEFICIENCY VIRUS

In June 1981, the Centers for Disease Control (CDC) reported an unusual outbreak of a rare disease in Los Angeles. Five gay men had developed a pneumonia caused by *Pneumocystis carinii,* a protozoan infection usually seen in individuals whose immune system is seriously deficient (Gottlieb et al., 1981). The month after, CDC revealed that another rare disease, this time a skin cancer called *Kaposi's sarcoma,* also associated with compromised immune systems, had been diagnosed in 26 gay men over the previous two and a half years (Friedman-Kein et al., 1981).

From these isolated beginnings emerged a pattern of illness called the *Acquired Immunodeficiency Syndrome,* or *AIDS.* Along with a bewildering variety of related manifestations, AIDS has become the most formidable challenge to health that the world has faced during the past 50 years. Randy Shilts (1987) has reported how society reacted at first. It is a tale of initial neglect by the government (by the time President Reagan delivered his first speech about the epidemic, over 21,000 persons had already died of AIDS); scientists concealing crucial information from each other to garner credit; news media failing to focus on public policy issues; and gay leaders fearing that the truth about how AIDS is spread would compromise their hard-won liberties. Some find Shilts' critique to be unduly harsh (Reinhold, 1987). AIDS now receives high public attention, and the gay community is actively confronting the issues it raises.

The head of the World Health Organization has called it a "disaster of pandemic proportions" (Altman, 1986, p. 1), predicting that 100 million people will be infected by the AIDS virus by 1990, making it a global threat (Mahler, 1986). A National Academy of Sciences report predicts that by 1991, 270,000 people in the United States will have AIDS; 54,000 will die a year (more than deaths due to car accidents). Infection with the virus would have spread to 5 to 10 million people, of whom perhaps half will eventually die (Morgenthau and Hager, 1986).

The disease has so far been identified in over 120 countries. The largest number of reported cases is in the United States. By March 1988, a total of 56,212 cases had been reported in the United States since the disease was identified; over 31,400 had died of AIDS. Estimates of the number of people who carry the virus ranges from 1 million to 1.5 million Americans (*Morbidity and Mortality Weekly Report, 1988*).

AIDS is not a disease of homosexuals alone nor of the United States alone. Both in prevalence and in capacity to deal with it, central Africa (Zaire, Rwanda, and Burundi) is the most threatened by the epidemic; its annual incidence is 550 to 1000 new cases per million adults. The cost of caring for ten AIDS patients in the United States (about $450,000) is greater than the entire yearly budget of a large hospital in Zaire, where nearly 25 percent of all adults and children admitted test positive for the AIDS virus (Quinn et al., 1986). Most cases of AIDS in central Africa are in the heterosexual population and the prevalence of AIDS is about the same among men and women (Peterman and Curran, 1986). As we shall see, this is not the case in the United States, where over 90 percent of AIDS occurs among men.

How could such a devastating disease suddenly appear out of nowhere? The prevalence of the AIDS virus in central Africa suggests that the disease started on that continent, possibly in the African green monkey. Seventy percent of these animals are infected with the AIDS virus, although they do not suffer from its effects. It is suspected that during the past several decades the virus was transmitted to humans through monkey bites (this process has actually happened with another virus) (Essex, 1985).

It was at first assumed that the AIDS virus appeared in the United States sometime in the mid-1970s. It has now been established that a teenage boy (referred to as Robert R.) died in St. Louis in 1969 of what appears, in hindsight, to have been AIDS, suggesting that the virus had already entered the country in the 1960s. Robert was sexually active, and it is suspected that he was gay. The fatal illness that baffled his doctors fits well with the symptoms of AIDS, and frozen sections from his autopsy have tested positive for the AIDS virus (Kolata, 1987).

Epidemics are nothing new. They decimated the population of medieval Europe time and again. More recently, in 1918, 20 million people (including 500,000 in the United States) died of the Spanish flu. Syphilis epidemics also have raged in this century.

Will the story of AIDS match that of syphilis? Like syphilis, AIDS is sexually transmitted, has varied effects, is highly virulent, and evokes panic and prejudice (Brandt, 1987). However, AIDS is different in alarming ways. It is transmitted not only sexually but through blood transfusions and between intravenous drug users. The most serious consequences of syphilis come late in the disease, when people are older; AIDS kills mostly the young. Syphilis can be cured; AIDS cannot. Most importantly, AIDS is caused by a virus, which makes the discovery of treatments and vaccines much more difficult.

One of the reasons that the AIDS epidemic caught health workers by surprise was that it did not fit the classic picture of an epidemic illness. AIDS is not highly contagious. It is not transmitted through casual contact even over long periods of time. By all counts, it should be restricted to isolated pockets of the population.

What led to its rapid spread were the

changed social conditions in the 1970s. Extensive air travel exposed widely separated populations to each other. The dramatic rise in sexual permissiveness rapidly expanded the range of sexual contacts. The increase in intravenous drug use similarly set the stage for rapid infection (Kolata, 1987).

## The Virus and the Immune System

The pattern of AIDS transmission pointed early to a virus as the causative agent. By 1984—only a few years after the disease had become known—the AIDS virus was identified in France (Barre-Sinoussi et al., 1983) and in the United States (Gallo et al., 1984). It had taken several centuries for the causative agent of syphilis to be identified.

The AIDS virus was initially called LAV (*lymphadenopathy virus*) by some researchers, HTLV-3 (*Human T cell lymphotropic virus*) by others. It is now generally known as *HIV* or the *human immunodeficiency virus*. So far virtually all AIDS cases in the United States have been caused by the HIV-1 type of the virus. A second type, HIV-2, has been isolated in cases of AIDS in West Africa and may become established in the United States as well. It seems to spread the same way but may cause a less severe form of AIDS.

HIV belongs to a group of viruses called *retroviruses*. A retrovirus contains a small number of genes made of RNA (ribonucleic acid) instead of DNA. These viruses are able to replicate themselves inside other cells, using the machinery of the host cell to multiply in large numbers. The newly formed viruses trickle out of the cell, eventually destroying it, and they enter other cells and repeat the process.

Through this process, HIV destroys the cells that form the key link in the *immune system* of the body. To understand how this happens we need to know how the immune system works.

The immune system has several defensive lines. *Macrophages* ("big eater") provide the first line of defense. These large cells are like scavengers that enter the circulation and engulf cells that have already become infected. At the same time they sound the alarm by activating white blood cells, called *helper T cells*. These in turn initiate the immune response. They alert other T cells to destroy infected cells, thus cutting off multiplication of the virus, and induce *B cells* to produce *antibodies* that help destroy the virus in circulation (Raven, 1986).

The AIDS virus breaks this chain. Invading helper T cells, HIV stops them from signaling T cells and B cells to go into action; moreover, HIV turns the helper T cells into minifactories, producing more viruses and killing the cells in the process. The virus also multiplies in macrophages, disrupting their activities and infecting yet other cells (Kolata, 1988). The result is an unchecked spread of the virus and the collapse of the body's immune system, which leaves the person defenseless to other microorganisms, such as bacteria, fungi, and other viruses. It is the diseases caused by these "opportunistic" invaders that account for the symptoms of AIDS and eventual death (Mallis, 1985; Grierson, 1987).

Whether they are successful or not in combatting the invaders, the presence of antibodies against an organism is indirect but reliable evidence that the body has been infected with it. This fact is the basis of testing for the AIDS virus, which we will discuss later.

## Transmission of AIDS

Viruses are tiny organisms that, unlike bacteria, cannot be seen under an ordinary optical microscope. If an electron-microscope photograph of an AIDS virus were to be enlarged to look as big as a fingernail, a human hair, by comparison, would appear to be 25 feet wide (Lertola, 1986).

Unlike the viruses that cause the common cold, which are airborne, the AIDS virus can only be transmitted to another person through body fluids. Ten body fluids may contain the virus: blood, semen, vaginal secretions, menstrual blood, breast milk (not cow's milk), tears, saliva, urine, cerebrospinal fluid, and alveolar fluid (in the lungs). However, not all these fluids actually transmit the virus from one person to another. The few that can transmit it are not all equally likely to do so. There is no documented case of infection from saliva or tears. Only blood and semen effectively transmit the virus; vaginal fluid and breast milk are less likely to do so (Friedland and Klein, 1987).

How will someone exposed to AIDS catch it? It depends on two factors. First, to *which* of the body fluids has the person been exposed? Second, *where* did the infected fluid enter the body? For example, infected semen is more likely to lead to AIDS if deposited in the rectum than in the vagina or the mouth. These two variables determine how risky a certain sexual behavior is with an infected person.

Anal Intercourse   The most common sexual form of transmission of AIDS in the United States has so far been anal intercourse. Especially at risk is the person who receives infected semen in the rectum ("receptive" anal intercourse). In a study of over 2000 gay men who tested negative for the HIV, 11 percent of those who engaged in receptive anal intercourse had acquired the virus a year later; as against 0.5 percent who only engaged in the insertive role in anal intercourse. All of those who avoided anal intercourse altogether still tested negative at the end of the year (Kingsley et al., 1987).

Because anal intercourse is most common among gay men, they have been the most at risk. The spread of AIDS among gay men has also been facilitated by the tendency of some of them to have numerous sexual partners. In the early days of the AIDS epidemic, gay bathhouses (most of which have now closed down) served as an "amplification system." A concentrated group of infected people quickly infected many others, who in turn passed the infection to an ever expanding group (Shilts, 1987).

Shared Needles   The most common nonsexual form of transmission is the sharing of needles contaminated with blood containing the AIDS virus. Second only to gay and bisexual men, who account for about 70 percent of cases (78 percent of male cases), intravenous drug users account for about 17 percent of cases (15 percent of male and 53 percent of female cases). They are the most likely "bridge" for infection of the heterosexual population. These figures reflect the fact that there are many more gay men than IV drug users. However, in some cities IV drug users account for two-thirds of AIDS cases. Sharing needles is no less risky than anal intercourse.

Currently, as a result of greater awareness of AIDS, marked changes have occurred in the sexual behavior of gay men. The spread of the AIDS virus among gay and bisexual men has slowed dramatically in San Francisco and possibly in other urban areas with large homosexual populations (although half of the gay men in San Francisco are already infected) (Dowdle, 1987). However, AIDS continues to spread unabated among intravenous drug users, of whom there are 750,000 at risk (Des Jarlais, 1987). Unlike gay men, drug users are hard to reach, educate, and change. Attempts to make clean needles available to addicts have so far met with little headway; but arguments rage for and against it (Johnson and Joseph, 1987).

There has been a gradual concentration of cases in certain ethnic minorities that have higher prevalence of intravenous drug use and needle sharing; blacks and Hispanic people account for 17 percent of the adult population in the United States, but 39 percent of all AIDS cases. The Surgeon General reports that in the United States one in every four people with AIDS is black; nearly half of those under age 30 are either black or Hispanic; more than half of infants with AIDS are black, and one-quarter are Hispanic (*New York Times,* July 9, 1987). AIDS threatens to become one more massive problem for a segment of the population that is already heavily burdened.

Heterosexual Intercourse   Women and "straight" men also can catch AIDS. In the United States, 93 percent of adults with AIDS were male, 7 percent female—a total of 30,160 men against 2205 women—as of 1987 (Rubinstein, 1987). However, in central Africa the sex ratio is even.

The first studies showing AIDS among heterosexuals appeared in the early 1980s (Piot, 1984). These cases accounted for 1 percent of all AIDS cases in 1983, and 1.8 percent in 1987. Contrary to early fears, the disease did not appear to spread widely among the mainstream heterosexual population.

This reassuring picture was challenged by sex researchers Masters, Johnson, and Kolodny. Based on a study of 800 sexually active heterosexual adults, they found 6 percent of those with at least six sex partners during the preceding five years to be infected with HIV. From this and related findings, they concluded that the AIDS virus has established a beachhead in the heterosexual population and its spread would begin to escalate at an alarming pace (Masters et al., 1988).

The conclusions and recommendations of these investigators were widely criticized by public health experts and the media (Eckholm, 1988). Their findings were at odds with most other studies conducted by epidemiologists using much larger samples. For example, screening of 25 million blood donations and over 3 million military personnel and recruits had shown rates of infection to be a fraction of 1 percent; these rates had not changed over two years (Boffey, 1988).

Hearst and Hulley (1988) have presented more detailed and less alarming data about the chances of heterosexual transmission of AIDS. The risks vary tremendously based on circumstances. In the most dangerous case, engaging in coitus without a condom with a partner infected with HIV, there is a 1-in-500 risk of infection. With over 500 acts of intercourse with such a partner, the risk of infection goes up to 2 in 3. At the opposite extreme, engaging in coitus using a condom with a partner who has tested negative for the virus, the risk of infection is 1 in 5 billion. In between these extremes, one-time sex with someone who is not in a high-risk group but whose infectious status is untested carries a risk of 1 in 5 million (about the same as getting killed in a car accident

while driving for 10 miles). These estimates may prove to be overly optimistic.

Although using condoms and limiting the number of partners continue to be important considerations, it appears that who you have sex with is the more critical factor in who gets infected. This is consistent with the finding that in the United States nearly all of heterosexually transmitted infections (which account for 4 percent of all AIDS cases) have involved partners of drug users, bisexual men, or people from Africa or Haiti, where heterosexual spread is common. This population is largely concentrated among impoverished black and Hispanic communities in large cities. Until we know more about the heterosexual transmission of AIDS, guarded optimism combined with the exercise of caution provide the sensible approach.

The type of sexual activity among heterosexual couples also has a bearing on the risk of infection. Even in coitus, a woman is more likely to be infected by the man than the man by the woman: semen carries more virus and lingers in the vagina; the man is only exposed briefly to vaginal secretions, which carry less virus. (The same considerations make ejaculation in the mouth riskier than cunnilingus—oral stimulation of the vulva.) Anal intercourse carries a higher risk because of structural differences between the rectal and vaginal mucosa. The rectal wall will let the virus through more easily. Moreover, it is more likely to suffer slight tears during insertions of the penis (or a finger), allowing the virus to enter the bloodstream. The AIDS virus may also get attached to certain cells in the rectal mucosa and spread from this foothold.

Why is heterosexual coitus a far more common source of infection in central Africa than in the United States? One reason may be the high rates of other STDs that cause genital ulcers, such as chancroid and syphilis. Sores in the genital areas can be highly effective sites of viral shedding or attachment. Even in the United States, patients with genital ulcers seen at STD clinics are more likely to be infected with HIV than other patients, although the rate of such infection remains remarkably low (Quinn et al., 1988).

Blood Transfusion    Transmission through blood transfusions has received much public attention because it is a potential threat to large numbers of medical patients, including children. Since no one chooses to need blood, getting AIDS through transfusions seems more "unjust" than acquiring the disease through high-risk activities in which a person chooses to participate.

A total of 500 transfusion-related cases of AIDS have occurred in the United States since HIV was isolated; meanwhile, over the past decade, 30 million patients have received 100 million units of blood. *Hemophiliacs* (of whom there are 20,000 in the United States) require weekly infusions of blood-clotting factors, so they are at greater risk; 1 percent of all AIDS cases have occurred in patients with hemophilia and 6 percent of children with AIDS have been hemophiliacs (Klein and Alter, 1987). With more stringent screening of donors and testing of blood, the likelihood of getting AIDS from a blood transfusion is now no more than 1 in 100,000 (Lipson and Engleman, 1985). Some people choose to store a supply of their own blood before a planned operation, to be perfectly safe.

Childbearing    Some 750 children had developed AIDS by the end of 1987. A small proportion of these children were infected through blood transfusions; most of the rest (70 percent) had gotten the disease from their mothers before birth. The majority of these children are born to mothers who have been infected by IV drug users. Four out of five are black or Hispanic (Eckholm, 1986).

A woman infected with the AIDS virus who wants to get pregnant faces a serious dilemma. Pregnancy itself, with its alterations of the immune system, may increase the changes of an infected woman developing AIDS. There is also a 50 percent chance of transmitting the virus to the child (Hatcher et al., 1988). Breastfeeding the infant possibly exposes the child to further risk. Nonetheless, pregnant women are not at present routinely tested for AIDS; whether to do so is part of a larger issue of testing, which we shall address later (Ledger, 1987).

Accidental Infection    Unbroken healthy skin is an effective barrier to the entry of infectious organisms, unlike the mucous membranes that line body openings (like the mouth, nose, anus, vagina, and urethra), which are more permeable. Accidental infections with the AIDS virus therefore involve contact of infected fluid with mucous membranes or cuts in the skin.

Fourteen health workers, by 1988, have been reported to have been infected with the AIDS virus on the job. Eight of them had suffered accidental punctures with infected needles. Two had chapped hands and were not wearing gloves when exposed to infected blood. One was splashed with it in the face. Doctors, dentists, nurses, laboratory workers, and ambulance crews now wear gloves, masks, or goggles when they might be handling infected fluids. Special syringes and plastic lab containers also reduce the risk of accidental contamination (Pear, 1987).

How AIDS Is *Not* Transmitted    How safe is it to interact with individuals infected with the AIDS virus? The Surgeon General of the United States states that *you cannot get AIDS from casual contact,* such as shaking hands, hugging, social kissing, crying, coughing, or sneezing, or from swimming pools, hot tubs, or eating in restaurants (even if the cook or waiter has AIDS). You cannot get AIDS from toilet seats, doorknobs, telephones, office machinery, or household furniture—not even from shared bed linens, towels, cups, dishes, or eating utensils. Donating blood is absolutely safe. No child has ever gotten AIDS from another child in school. Dogs, cats, and other domestic animals are not a source of AIDS infection, nor are insects such as mosquitos (even though they can retain the virus in their bodies for a few days after ingesting infected blood) (Koop, 1986).

Symptoms

AIDS is not a simple disease. It is the most severe stage of infection with HIV. This virus makes the body vulnerable to many other infections, so there are many possible symptoms or illnesses that are associated with AIDS

(Groopman, 1988). The course of infection with HIV has been classified by the Centers for Disease Control into four categories.

Category 1   Category 1 forms the pyramid base, comprising people who have been infected with the virus and have developed antibodies against it. Most people in this group either have no symptoms or show a flu-like syndrome, with fever, fatigue, and muscular aches and pains. These symptoms, if present, usually occur about two to six weeks after infection. Antibodies usually begin to appear in the blood in two months, but they may take six months or even a year to reach detectable levels. During this period, the person does not yet have AIDS, and may never get it, but he or she is infectious, able to transmit the virus to another person. In the absence of antibodies, blood tests are negative, so these individuals are undetected, silent carriers.

Category 2   Persons in category 2 still have no significant clinical symptoms, although the infection has now taken hold. Laboratory tests show the presence of antibodies and may also show small reductions in the level of T-4 cells—evidence that the immune system is being undermined, though the person is not aware of it.

Category 3   Persons in category 3 are unmistakably ill. The lymph nodes of the body swell up and can be felt like little lumps in the armpits, groin, neck, and elsewhere in the body constituting the *lymphadenopathy syndrome (LAS)*. In addition, there may be persistent fever, night sweats, diarrhea, weight loss, fatigue, and uncommon infections such as yeast infections of the mouth (thrush) and of the vagina, or reactivation of the chicken-pox virus, causing a painful skin condition called shingles.

These symptoms were formerly referred to as ARC (AIDS-related complex). Typically, they are not life-threatening unless diarrhea and weight loss are severe. There is now a serious threat of progressing to category 4 diseases.

Category 4   Only conditions in category 4 are called AIDS. It ushers in one fatal disease or another, most commonly *Pneumocystis carinii pneumonia* or *Kaposi's sarcoma*. The symptoms of pneumonia are concentrated in the chest, including cough and shortness of breath. The external lesions of Kaposi's sarcoma consist of painless blue or brown nodules of varying size.

A large number of other *opportunistic infections* and other cancers may further complicate the picture, causing meningitis, tuberculosis, toxoplasmosis, and so on. Because the virus invades the nervous system, AIDS may actually present itself initially as a neurological or psychiatric illness (Price and Forejt, 1986).

The four categories form an "iceberg" (Figure 5.8). Categories 1 and 2, including the bulk of infected people, are "below the water"—they show no major clinical symptoms. Categories 3 and 4 have clear symptoms and constitute the visible part of the iceberg.

Most people are thought to ultimately progress from category 1 and 2 to category 3 and 4. As of 1987, 20–30 percent of people initially infected with the HIV virus had developed AIDS within five years. Similarly, about 30 percent of patients with LAS (category 3) go on to develop AIDS in five years (Kaplan et al., 1987). Current estimates suggest that at least 50 percent of all of those infected with the virus will go on to develop AIDS within ten years. Until more time has passed, it will be impossible to know what percentage of infected people develop AIDS over a lifetime.

Of patients diagnosed with AIDS (category 4), 50 percent die within 18 months of diagnosis; about 80 percent die within three years of diagnosis.

However, some people beat these odds. There are men infected with HIV who have developed no symptoms for almost ten years. A few patients have been known to live as long as six or more years with full-blown AIDS. It is as important to know why some people resist the disease as it is to know why others succumb

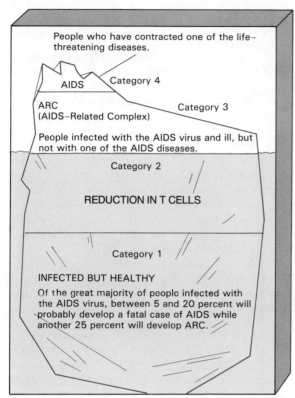

People who have contracted one of the life–threatening diseases.

AIDS

Category 4

ARC
(AIDS–Related Complex)

Category 3

People infected with the AIDS virus and ill, but not with one of the AIDS diseases.

Category 2

REDUCTION IN T CELLS

Category 1

INFECTED BUT HEALTHY

Of the great majority of people infected with the AIDS virus, between 5 and 20 percent will probably develop a fatal case of AIDS while another 25 percent will develop ARC.

Figure 5.8    AIDS "iceberg." (Not drawn to scale; otherwise, category 1 would be about 20 times as large as category 4.)

to it (Altman, 1987). The long-term prognosis of AIDS may change rapidly as we find out more and as new drugs become available for its treatment.

## Testing

How do we find out who carries the virus and who is ill with AIDS? The first question entails screening large groups of people; the second, diagnosing individuals.

A useful tool for both purposes is the *antibody test* (Box 5.3). As we discussed, the presence of antibodies in blood serum is indirect but reliable evidence of past exposure to the virus. Once the virus enters the body, it stays there indefinitely, so a *positive* test for antibodies also indicates current infection.

The antibody test is highly accurate, but it is not perfect. Antibodies to other, similar viruses can cause a *false positive* result. On the other hand, antibodies may not show up in an infected person, giving a *false negative* result; remember that it takes time for antibodies to develop. Even a true positive only reveals a potential for AIDS, if a person has no other symptoms. Tests cannot predict whether a virus carrier will develop AIDS in the future.

## Counseling

The results of a positive antibody test must be communicated with sensitivity. The person needs help to place the issue in perspective and come to terms with its emotional and practical consequences.

Most people respond to having any life-threatening illness predictably: anxiety and fear mingle with anger, despair, bewilderment, and a sense of helplessness. Persons with AIDS carry some additional burdens. Guilt and remorse may affect those who have acquired the disease through sexual activity. Anger may be directed at those who were the source of infection. The person may feel "unclean" and dangerous to others, or fear rejection. The knowledge that the virus is there for life and represents a threat to life is likely to have a major impact on facing and planning for the future. It will affect all significant human relationships, especially intimate and sexual ones.

In helping people cope with the knowledge that they carry the AIDS virus, two points are particularly important to get across. First, having a positive antibody test does not mean having AIDS. Although there is at least one chance in three of developing AIDS over the next six to eight years, it is not possible to tell who will develop it. A positive test for HIV is not a death sentence. It does carry certain serious implications; facing them, a person can live fully, and if necessary, prepare to die with dignity (Gonda and Ruarke, 1983).

Second, a positive test for HIV means that the person is potentially infectious to others by intimate sexual contact, by sharing needles, by childbearing, or by donating blood, semen, or

# Box 5.3

## AIDS BLOOD TESTING

Testing for infection with HIV is done on *serum*, the clear fluid of blood without cells. The first test, called *enzyme-linked immunosorbent assay (ELISA)*, is sensitive enough to detect almost all infected persons, but it also will give a large number of false positives in a low-risk population such as blood donors.

If the ELISA test is negative, the person is considered not to have been exposed to the AIDS virus, provided enough time has elapsed for antibodies to develop. If the test result is positive, the test is repeated twice on the same serum sample. If one of the two repeat tests is positive, then the ELISA test is considered positive; if both repeat tests are negative, the ELISA test is considered negative. In other words, for an individual to be reported as positive by ELISA at least two out of three tests on the same serum specimen should have been positive (Saah, 1987).

A confirmed positive by ELISA is followed by a more refined test called the *Western Blot,* to determine whether the antibodies present are specific to HIV antigens. Other refined tests are currently being developed or in limited use. For instance, the RIPA relies on radioisotopes; the IFA, on infected cells from tissue cultures; antigen detection tests use monoclonal antibodies. Technical problems and expense make the wider use of these tests impractical at this time.

If the Western Blot test is also positive, the person is considered to be infected with HIV. If it is negative, the person is probably not infected with HIV. Nevertheless, that person's blood should not be used for transfusions, and he or she must behave as if the test were positive for another six months. At that time if a repeat Western Blot test is negative, the individual can be considered not to carry the AIDS virus.

Double testing with ELISA and the Western Blot is expensive, it is only done if ELISA is repeatedly positive. Therefore the Western Blot test does not affect the false negative rate, but it does reduce the false positive rate. If the ELISA shows 0.25 percent of a low-risk group to test positive, the Western Blot will give positive results for only 0.1 percent, but they will be more specific to HIV and not some related virus (Saah, 1987).

Moreover, the significance of these tests depends on whether they are carried out in low-risk populations (such as blood donors, who are unlikely to have the virus) or high-risk populations (such as IV drug users, who are more likely to have the virus). In a high-risk population, where the prevalence of HIV infection may range from 30 percent to 70 percent, a positive ELISA is almost always confirmed by Western Blot, giving it a high prediction value. In a low-risk population, if 10 million people are tested by ELISA, 25,000 (0.25 percent) will be positive, whereas only 10,000 (0.1 percent) will be confirmed as positive by the Western Blot. This means 15,000 false positives by ELISA.

The use of ELISA for mass screening of low-risk populations will label many people as infected with HIV when in fact they are not. The social and psychological consequences of such a false verdict are considerable. Therefore, testing large segments of the population raises important social and political concerns.

---

body organs. No one should expose others to potential serious harm, at least not without their knowledge and consent. A carrier has an obligation to inform a sexual partner beforehand and take all possible precautions against infection through "safe sex" practices.[1]

[1]The Public Health Service offers information and counseling on these and other issues related to AIDS through hotlines (call 1-800-342-AIDS; 1-800-443-0366).

## Treatment

Despite intensive efforts, there is as yet no cure for AIDS or any way to eliminate the virus from the body. However, two types of drugs are being tested: antiviral agents to keep the virus from multiplying, and immune system stimulants to restore the damaged immune system.

The most promising drug so far is the antiviral agent *azidothymidine* (AZT). When given to ARC patients (category 3), AZT significantly reduces the chances of developing AIDS (Shilts, 1988). Given to patients suffering from *Pneumocystis carinii* pneumonia, it has shown a definite ability to lessen symptoms and prolong life. AZT interrupts the conversion of RNA to DNA by the virus, interfering with its multiplication. However useful it may prove to be, AZT is not a cure for AIDS.

Other antiviral agents under investigation are *ribavirin* and several other compounds. Immune system stimulants include *interleukin* and *interferon,* which also has antiviral properties. A combination of antiviral drugs and immune system stimulants may hold the most promise, especially if treatments start early, before the virus has caused severe damage.

## Cost of AIDS

Caring for people with AIDS is going to be costly—how costly remains to be seen. Here again, we should avoid inertia and panic.

Assuming that caring for each AIDS patient will cost no more than $50,000 a year, by 1991 AIDS is estimated to cost $10.9 billion—a substantial sum, yet only 1.4 percent of the nation's annual health budget (Morganthau et al., 1987). In this broader context, AIDS will be about as costly as cancer.

Directly or indirectly, everyone will pay for the treatment of AIDS patients. The money will have to come either from higher health insurance premiums or from Medicaid (the federal subsidy for the indigent) through higher taxes.

Private insurance companies fear that the cost of an unchecked AIDS epidemic will destroy their business. They are accused of "dumping" AIDS patients or rejecting their insurance claims; life insurers in turn claim that the illness preexisted at the time of enrollment and that some applicants have taken out policies after learning they carry the virus. Here again, although the sums are large, they are modest in the overall context of health care costs: less than 1 percent of the total payouts in the care of one major insurer. However, the total health insurance costs of AIDS is expected to reach $10 billion a year by 1991 (*New York Times,* July 13, 1987).

Even more serious is the fate of those left out of the U.S. health care system. An estimated 35 million people have no medical insurance. Faced with a catastrophic illness, they have to exhaust their personal assets before becoming eligible for public assistance. In addition to the personal cost, a substantial increase of AIDS cases in this population will place a tremendous strain on hospitals, especially on tax-supported big city hospitals. New hospitals will have to be established to care for AIDS victims or wider use will have to be made of alternative-care facilities such as hospices, nursing homes, and in-home care by visiting nurses. There are enormous problems to be faced with each of these alternatives. Unless there is a revamping of the existing health care system (such as by establishing a national health insurance) the care available to AIDS cases who are needy may be seriously hampered.

## Prevention

The ideal way to deal with a disease is to prevent it. The best way to accomplish that with infectious diseases is either to avoid exposure or to protect the body by bolstering its defenses. *Vaccines* protect by stimulating antibody production *before* the body is invaded by the microorganism, rather than merely in response to it.

Vaccines    Substances called *antigens,* which are akin to a disease-causing organism but harmless to the body, stimulate the body to produce antibodies that will provide immunity against the organism itself. For example, the vaccinia virus (from which the word "vaccine" derives) causes an infectious disease in cattle, called cowpox. Inoculated into humans, it causes the immune system to produce antibodies that protect it against smallpox. So successful has been this vaccine that smallpox has been virtually eliminated from the world.

Other viruses have proven difficult to vaccinate against; the viruses that cause the common cold are one example. There are so many variants and so many shifts in their properties that they are like a multiple moving target. The same is true for HIV. Therefore, although some vaccines are under trial, there is no way of telling if and when an effective and safe vaccine will be available (Scarpinato and Calabrese, 1987).

Safe Sex   Currently, avoiding high-risk activities and following safe sex practices remain the only safeguards against AIDS.

If you are not an intravenous drug user who shares needles, sexual contact is virtually the only way that you are likely to get infected with AIDS. You are *absolutely safe* from the threat of AIDS if you fulfill one of the three following conditions: you *abstain* from sex altogether; you engage in sex of any kind only with a partner with whom you have had a strictly *monogamous* relationship (no other sexual partners for either of you) since 1977 (when AIDS appeared in the United States); you engage in sex with a new partner with whom you establish a monogamous relationship, provided that neither of you is already infected with the AIDS virus. This condition means both of you test negative for AIDS antibodies and have not engaged in sex for a year with anyone who might carry the virus. You must fully trust yourself and your partner to know that; if in doubt, you and your partner must wait for a year and be tested again. During this interval, you may engage in the safer sex practices described below but avoid all genital contact or exposure to each other's body fluids. That means restricting yourself to hugging, caressing, "dry" kissing, and mutual masturbation that does not involve direct contact with semen or vaginal fluids (Kaplan, 1987).

These are stringent rules. Not everyone is willing to follow them. As we shall discuss below, what you do in any activity in life is in part a function of what level of risk you are willing to take. The only way to avoid an airplane crash is not to fly; the only truly safe sex with regard to AIDS is what is described above.

The term "safe sex" is now commonly used for sexual practices that more properly should be called "safer sex"—they provide considerable safety but fall short of being al-

together safe (Uline, 1987). Admittedly, there is a problem of semantics here. Vehicles and machinery approved as "safe" are not entirely safe either; they merely are expected to meet legal requirements. You will have to decide for yourself what "safety" should mean for you.

Once you move out of the truly safe sex category, the chances of exposure to AIDS are determined by what you do sexually, how often, and most importantly, with whom. *Safer sex practices* include vaginal and anal intercourse with condoms; oral-penile contact (fellatio or "sucking") that stops short of ejaculation or uses a condom; mouth-vaginal contact (cunnilingus) with a dental dam (a piece of stretched thin rubber), which prevents the mixing of saliva and vaginal secretions; and dry kissing. *Unsafe practices*, starting with the most risky, are anal intercourse without a condom (especially in the receptive role); vaginal intercourse without a condom; oral-anal stimulation ("rimming"); unprotected fellatio; and mouth-vaginal contact (Gong, 1987; Ulene, 1987).

Condoms have received a good deal of favorable publicity as safeguards against transmitting or acquiring AIDS. Laboratory tests have actually confirmed that the AIDS virus will not cross the walls of an intact latex condom (but may get through "natural" condoms made of animal intestines). The virus also cannot survive long periods of contact with the chemicals in spermicides. As a result, condoms certainly help reduce the chances of infection, but they are far from foolproof. Condoms could not be more effective in preventing AIDS than they are in preventing pregnancy. As we shall discuss (Chapter 7), condoms have a 2–10 percent failure rate. In other words, 10 percent of women who rely exclusively on their partner's using a condom will get pregnant every year. The failure rate of condoms with respect to HIV must be at least as high. Spermicides may increase the level of protection condoms provide, but it is unclear to what extent. The spermicide foam or cream must be placed in the vagina, not inside the condom, which would make it easier for the condom to slip off the penis during intercourse.

The most critical question is, with whom should you have sex? A few simple rules prevail. First, the greater the likelihood of your partner being infected, the greater the chance of your being infected. Intravenous drug users are hazardous partners for both sexes; bisexual men are far riskier partners than heterosexual men (all else being equal) for women. Men and women who have had some other STDs are more likely to have the AIDS virus. Even geographical location makes a difference in the probability of infection. Although no state or city is immune to AIDS, some areas have a higher incidence than others. In 1987, New York City and San Francisco each had over 1000 cases of AIDS per million population; Chicago had 96; much of the rest of the United States had 53. It is to be expected, therefore, that a sexually active person in a high-risk city is more likely to come in contact with the AIDS virus than someone in a low-risk city, even if the number of sexual partners they had were the same. (This risk applies only to those who are sexually active; simply living in New York or San Francisco does not carry a higher risk.) Box 5.4 summarizes the factors that determine a sex partner's risk for AIDS.

Second, the more partners you have and the more partners your partners have, the riskier the contact becomes (Goedert et al., 1987). Even after getting infected, repeated exposure to the virus seems to increase the chances of infection progressing to the development of symptoms. In a group of 1034 single men aged 25 to 34 in the San Francisco Bay area, 49 percent of the gay and bisexual men tested positive for the AIDS virus, but those with 50 or more partners were 71 per cent positive. None of the heterosexual men had evidence of infection (Winkelstein et al., 1987).

Prostitutes of either sex present a high-risk group because they have multiple partners and many are drug users; at least some female prostitutes are now more likely to insist that the customer use condoms, which makes them less of a hazard. Some studies have actually failed to implicate female prostitutes as a major source of transmission (Rabkin et al., 1987).

Much may depend on where the prostitute is from: 57 percent of prostitutes in Newark have tested AIDS positive, as against 1 percent in Atlanta or Colorado Springs and none in Las Vegas (Ulene, 1987).

Finally, how often you engage in an unsafe activity is of obvious significance. Even unprotected anal intercourse might not result in infection the first time, or even the tenth time, but the odds will catch up with you. The longer you persist in the behavior, the higher the risk of infection.

Risk-Taking Behavior    Driving motorcycles is much more dangerous than driving cars. Over a period of a year, 1 out of 1000 motorcycle users as against 1 out of 6000 drivers of cars will die in an accident (Hatcher et al., 1988). Similarly, various occupational and recreational activities differ widely in the level of risk they entail. How much chance we take, how often, and why defines the pattern of our risk-taking behavior. How dangerously we live can be a function of necessity (as in occupational hazards) or choice. Both are determined by complex psychological and social reasons.

Sexual behavior also entails a certain degree of risk. One in 50,000 women dies each year because of pelvic infections acquired through coitus. The risk of death in pregnancy is 1 in 10,000 per year (Chapter 6). Exposure to STDs, especially AIDS, greatly increases the risks in sexual activity.

It is up to every individual to make an informed choice about how much to risk in being sexually active in general and in a particular case. You must assume responsibility for protecting yourself, weighing the costs and the benefits. Consider, for instance, the use of condoms. Some people simply do not bother with them. Others consider the failure rate to be unacceptable, "when the price for failure is getting a disease that can kill you" (Ulene, 1987, p. 30). Abstinence from sex except under fully safe conditions is the only sensible choice for some, but too restrictive for others. At a minimum, you must take *calculated risks*, knowing the most likely consequences of your

# Box 5.4

## ESTIMATING A SEX PARTNER'S RISK FOR AIDS

| | No Risk | Low Risk | High Risk |
|---|---|---|---|
| Number of sexual partners | None, or one with mutual monogamy since 1977 | Few | Many |
| Sexual preference of partners | | Heterosexuals or homosexual females | Homosexual or bisexual males |
| Use of barrier contraceptives with others | | Always used condoms | Rarely or never used condoms |
| AIDS antibody test results | Negative and no sexual exposure for past six months | Negative and no sexual exposure for past three months | Positive or untested |
| Prior history of sexually transmitted disease | No | No | Yes |
| Use of drugs | No drug use by subject or partners | No IV drug use by subject or partners | Uses IV drugs, or sex partner uses them |
| Transfusions | None, or has been tested and found negative for AIDS antibodies | Transfused but not tested | Transfused many times or with large volume of blood; not tested |
| Places of residence | | Low-incidence area for AIDS | High-incidence area for AIDS |

From Art Ulene, *Safe Sex in a Dangerous World*. New York: Vintage Books, 1987, pp. 64–65.

actions and being as clear as possible about your motives.

The Joy of Sex    There are two unfortunate reactions to a condition like AIDS. One is to ignore and deny it, endangering yourself and others. The other is to allow it to stifle the joy of sexuality. With every sexual partner a potentially deadly source of infection, every sexual encounter a tangle of latex barriers, the game after a while seems no longer worth the candle.

There is much to be said for abstinence or playing it absolutely safe, but if you are willing to take calculated chances, as you do in other realms of your life, it should be possible to en-

gage in safer sexual activities without throwing caution to the winds. It will require the realization that there is far more to sexual intimacy than intercourse, or direct genital contact. By focusing on the erotic potential of the entire body—through physical closeness, caressing, hugging, and expressions of affection—our sexual interactions are enriched, even in situations that lead to intercourse (Chapter 12). "Outercourse" rather than intercourse, "dry" rather than "wet" sex, and sensuality rather than sexuality will have to provide the security needed in the age of AIDS.

Similarly, we need to learn to inquire about our sexual partner's past without becoming an inquisitor, to be alert to signs of illness without being clinical, to be romantic while remaining realistic.

Handling the STDs will call for massive education, radical changes in risk-taking behavior, and the exercise of self-restraint. The personal and social challenges of AIDS in particular are immense, and we shall return to them in subsequent chapters.

## REVIEW QUESTIONS

1. What cancers affect the female and male reproductive systems?

2. Which STDs cause an unusual vaginal discharge in women and a urethral discharge in men?

3. What STDs cause skin lesions in the genital area?

4. Rank the STDs by the threat they represent to personal health.

5. How is the AIDS virus transmitted?

6. What are the treatments for STDs?

## THOUGHT QUESTIONS

1. How would you respond to the charge that the STDs are a just punishment for immoral sexual behavior?

2. If you were a college president, would you let the health service test students for AIDS voluntarily? How about making the test mandatory? Explain.

3. As a public health official, how would you deal with the possibility that the STDs may be more prevalent among the gay male population in your city?

4. How should society deal with an individual who has AIDS yet continues to engage in behavior that is likely to transmit the virus to others?

## SUGGESTED READINGS

Holt, L. H., and Weber, M. (1982). *Woman care.* New York: Random House. Overview of issues related to women's health, written for a general audience.

Federation of Feminist Women's Health Centers. (1981). *A new view of a woman's body.* Illustrated guide to female health care.

Silber, S. S. (1981). *The male.* New York: Scribner's. Guide to male health care.

Rowan, R., and Gillette, P. J. (1978). *The gay health guide* (1978). Boston: Little, Brown. Useful guidance for health problems affecting gay men.

Bowen, S. C., and Yu, C. E., (1988). *Sexually transmitted diseases: A basic text.* An introductory level text for college students. A clear and reliable source.

Ulene, A. (1987) *Safe sex in a dangerous world.* A thoughtful and concise overview of AIDS and coping with its threat.

146

# PART 2

# Sexual Reproduction

Michelangelo. *Mother and child.*

# Pregnancy and Childbirth

## CHAPTER

# 6

*And God blessed them, and God said unto them, "Be fruitful and multiply."*

GENESIS 1:27–28

## OUTLINE

CONCEPTION
The Journey of the Sperm
The Migration of the Egg
Fertilization and Implantation
PREGNANCY
The First Trimester
    The Embryo Develops
    The Placenta Develops
    Signs and Symptoms
    Pregnancy Tests
    Expected Date of Delivery
The Second Trimester
    The Fetus Grows
    The Mother in the Second
        Trimester
The Third Trimester
    The Fetus Matures
    The Mother in the Third Trimester
Psychological Aspects
Sexual Interest and Activity
The Father's Experience
CHILDBIRTH
Labor

Methods of Childbirth
    Home Delivery
    Hospital Delivery
    Prepared Childbirth
Early Parent–Child Interaction
THE POSTPARTUM PERIOD
Physiological Changes
Emotional Reactions
Nursing
Ovulation and Menstruation
Sex in the Postpartum Period
PRENATAL CARE
Nutrition and Exercise
Smoking, Alcohol, and Drugs
COMPLICATIONS OF PREGNANCY
Difficulties in Carrying to Term
Birth Defects
INFERTILITY
Causes
Psychological Impact
Treatment

The desire to generate a new life runs deep in human nature. Having children is not for everyone, but for the human species as a whole no event is more critical. Though sex serves other purposes than reproduction, no other aspect of sexual relations carries more important biological, psychological, and social consequences. No decision requires more serious thought than becoming a parent and accepting responsibility for a new life.

You do not have to become a parent. Many individuals are voluntarily or involuntarily childless. The desire for parenthood and the fact of parenthood do not always match. On the one hand, about one in nine married couples in the United States is infertile. On the other hand, roughly half the pregnancies that do occur in the United States are unintended, and one-fourth are voluntarily aborted (Hatcher et al., 1988).

Motherhood entails much more than pregnancy, and there is more to fatherhood than impregnating a woman. Here we shall touch upon how it feels to become a parent. We shall discuss parenthood in more detail when we consider the development of sexuality in adulthood (Chapter 9). We shall also look at new trends in parenthood. Although most children are still born to couples who are married or in a stable relationship, a small but growing number of single women and men are choosing to raise children alone or sometimes within a gay relationship (Chapter 13).

No one knows when in human history the momentous discovery was made connecting coitus with reproduction. The association between the two is by no means obvious, and until fairly recent times it remained unknown to people in isolated cultures. For instance, Trobriand Islanders in the South Pacific thought a woman conceived when a spirit embryo entered her body through her vagina or head; the Kiwai of New Guinea ascribed pregnancy to something the woman ate (Ford and Beach, 1951). Myths persist even after people become aware of the true nature of reproduction. However, herding people as early as biblical times had already made the connection between the mating of their flock and the birth of baby animals in the spring.

There are many compelling reasons why people want children, apart from the enjoyment of engendering them. Some of these reasons are socioeconomic, others more personal and psychological. Traditionally, children have worked to help support the family, and the cycle of generations has depended on parents looking after their children and then the children looking after their parents. Also, children are a contribution parents make to the clan, ethnic group, and nation; parenthood makes them feel like full-fledged adult members of society. Though in modern industrialized societies children are much less of an insurance against the future, there is still considerable social pressure on young adults to become parents, both from their own parents and from society at large (Pohlman, 1969; Fawcett, 1970).

Powerful inner psychological forces also motivate us to have children. The notion of a "parental instinct," though hard to define and even harder to substantiate, aptly conveys the deep and elemental urge to have a baby, even when the rewards are uncertain or the costs prohibitive. To love and to be loved by a child, to share that love with others, and to feel the sheer enjoyment that children provide are not matched by many other human experiences.

Some pregnancies are motivated by the wrong reasons: to cement an uncertain or faltering marriage; to entrap another into a permanent relationship; to assert manhood or womanhood; to enhance self-esteem; to take a shortcut to adulthood; to fill idle time, and other manipulative and self-serving reasons.

## CONCEPTION

The fertilization of the egg by the sperm marks the beginning, or *conception*, of a new life.[1] For a fertile and sexually active woman trying to have a baby, it takes on the average six months

[1]The discussion of embryonal development is based on embryology texts, in particular Moore (1982) and Sadler (1985).

to get pregnant: a single act of intercourse at the time of ovulation has a 21 percent chance of resulting in pregnancy. Approximately 90 percent of women trying to get pregnant conceive within one year and another 5 percent within two years (Trussell and Vost, 1987; Hatcher et al, 1988). Some women get pregnant after the first act of coitus, others after more than a decade of trying.

## The Journey of the Sperm

Sperm cells develop within the seminiferous tubules (Chapter 2) and travel through the testicular duct system to the epididymis, where they attain full maturity. Then they move through the vas deferens to the ejaculatory duct. During emission (Chapter 3) sperm are mixed with the secretions of the seminal vesicles and the prostate gland, which nourish them and help them move.[2] This mixture, called *semen*, is ejaculated through the urethra. Up to this point, the movement of sperm has been assisted by the contractions of the male tubal system; now the sperm must move on their own (Plate 1, page 165).

The spermatic fluid in a normal ejaculation has a volume of 2 to 3 milliliters (approximately a teaspoonful), containing 300 million to 500 million sperm. Most of the fluid in the ejaculate comes from the seminal vesicles and the prostate (whose secretions are also responsible for its odor). Semen is whitish and semi-gelatinous, but it gets more watery after repeated ejaculations within a short time. It coagulates on exposure to air.

In the vagina the sperm begin to make their way into the uterus, leaving most of the fluid of the ejaculate behind. If the woman is lying on her back, more of the sperm will reach the cervix and enter the uterus. Keeping the penis for a while in the vagina following orgasm also helps the chances of impregnation. If the secretions of the cervix and vagina are

strongly acidic, sperm are destroyed quickly; even in a mildy acidic environment the movement of sperm ceases fairly quickly.

Sperm swim in fluid by lashing their tails, moving at a rate of one to two centimeters (less than one inch) an hour. The notion that orgasmic contractions suck in sperm through the cervix has not been substantiated. Actually, the sperm have to get by the plug of cervical mucus that blocks the entrance to the endometrium during most of the menstrual cycle. Passing through the uterus, they get into the fallopian tubes and complete the final two inches or so of their journey, assisted by contractions of the tubes and swimming against the current generated by the hairlike cilia that line them (which propel the ovum in the opposite direction).

The journey of the sperm ends several hours after ejaculation when they reach their usual fertilization site, at the lower third of the fallopian tube (Figure 6.1). Of the several hundred million sperm that start on this journey, only about 50 actually make contact with the egg, and then only one sperm eventually penetrates it.

## The Migration of the Egg

At the time of ovulation, the mature Graafian follicle protrudes from the surface of the ovary. It is filled with fluid under pressure, and its wall has become thin. The egg has become detached within the follicle and is floating freely in its fluid. At ovulation, the follicle wall breaks through the ovary's surface, and the ovum is carried in a stream of fluid into the fallopian tube by sweeping movements of the tube's fringed end. The follicle walls that remain behind develop into the corpus luteum.

Once the egg has entered the fallopian tube, it begins a leisurely journey toward the uterus, taking about three days to move three to five inches. The egg, in contrast to the sperm, has no means of self-propulsion. It is swept along by the current generated by the cilia lining the tube. If the egg is not fertilized, it will be expelled with the subsequent menstrual flow (Kaiser, 1986).

[2]Prostatic secretions are rich in *acid phosphatase*. Its presence in the vagina is used as presumptive evidence that coitus has occurred in legally contested cases (such as rape).

# Box 6.1

## BOY OR GIRL

The sex of the baby is determined at the time of fertilization by the type of sperm that fertilizes the egg: if the sperm carries an X chromosome, the child will be a girl; if it carries a Y chromosome, the child will be a boy.

If you could pick the sex of your child ahead of time, would you do it? Such attempts are as old as recorded history. Aristotle recommended having intercourse in a North wind if boys were desired, in a South wind if girls were desired. By the Middle Ages the formula had gotten more complicated: to ensure a son the man had to drink lion's blood, then have intercourse under a full moon (Wallis, 1984).

Recent attempts have been based on the fact that Y- and X-bearing sperm vary slightly in physical characteristics. The X-bearing sperm are heavier, and hardier in an acid environment.

One formula is to engage in intercourse two to three days before ovulation and then to abstain, if a girl is desired. (Supposedly, because X-bearing sperm are heavier, they will travel more slowly and get to the ovum at the right time.) To conceive a boy, the couple must limit intercourse to the time of ovulation. (The lighter Y-bearing sperm move faster.) This timetable is combined with an acid douche, shallow penetration, and no orgasm for the woman to conceive a girl, or an alkaline douche, deep penetration, and orgasm for the woman to conceive a boy (Shettles, 1972; Guerrero, 1975). This approach has now been largely discredited.

A more promising approach is to let semen drift down a solution in a glass column. In a sticky albumen solution, the Y-sperms make it faster to the bottom than the X-sperms; in gelatinous powder, the X-sperms get ahead. In either case, the concentration of sperm at the bottom can be used in artificial insemination to enhance the chances of sex selection. The proponents of this method claim a 77 percent success rate (Ericsson and Glass, 1982). Some investigators have been able to replicate these results; others have not.

Some couples go so far as to determine the sex of the fetus by amniocentesis (Box 6.3), and then abort it if it is the "wrong" sex. The practice is said to be more prevalent in certain third world countries that place a high premium on male infants.

A study of 5981 married women in the United States indicates that if sex selection could be successfully practiced, the long-term effect on the ratio of male to female births (currently 105 male to 100 female) would be negligible. However, there was a strong preference for their first child to be male, so the short-term effect would be a preponderance of male births, followed several years later by a preponderance of female births—provided that most couples have more than one child. When asked about the desirability of sex preselection, 47 percent of the women in the sample were opposed, 39 percent were in favor, and 14 percent were indifferent (Westoff and Rindfuss, 1974).

## Fertilization and Implantation

*Fertilization* is the fusion of sperm and ovum. The egg usually must be fertilized within 12 hours after ovulation; it ordinarily does not survive longer than 12 to 24 hours. Sperm also usually live for 24 hours, but some may remain capable of fertilizing the ovum for about three days. Frozen sperm are said to survive for up to ten years. (The use of such sperm for artificial insemination is discussed later.) For a woman to get pregnant, intercourse must usu-ally take place within a day before or after ovulation. Rhythm methods of contraception rely on avoiding this fertile period, but the exact timing of ovulation is not easy to determine (Chapter 7).

Sperm that reach the egg are held to its surface by minute projections (microvilli) from the follicular cells (corona radiata); this is why in electron microscope photographs, sperm appear over the egg surface (Plate 2, page 165). The fertilizing sperm must undergo critical changes before it can penetrate the ovum's protective layers. In this process of *capacitation* the sperm sheds the protein coating from its head, releasing enzymes that digest a path through to the ovum (the *acrosome reaction*). Normally, once a sperm has made its way into the ovum, no other sperm can get through. An immediate inhibitory reaction in the egg blocks the wall. Occasionally more than one sperm will penetrate the egg, but the result of such abnormal fertilization will abort sooner or later (Moore, 1982).

The head of the sperm that has successfully penetrated the ovum detaches from the rest of its body. The nucleus of the sperm and that of the egg merge, intermingling their sets of 23 chromosomes and restoring the full complement of 46 chromosomes typical of human cells. This new combination of genes from the parents determines the genetic makeup of the new organism, including its gender (Box 6.1).

The process of fertilization takes about 24 hours. The fertilized egg, which is called a *zygote*, now continues to move towards the uterus. After some 30 hours, the zygote divides into two cells; these two become four, the four become eight, and so on. Though there is no significant change in volume during these first few days, the zygote becomes a round mass of numerous cells called a *morula* ("mulberry") by the time it reaches the uterus in three days (Figure 6.1).

The cells of the morula arrange themselves around the outside of the sphere, leaving a fluid-filled cavity in the center. This structure, called a *blastocyst*, floats about in the uterine cavity. Sometime between the fifth and seventh days after ovulation it attaches itself to the uterine lining. This *implantation* is the real start of pregnancy. Though the normal site of implantation is in the uterus (usually in the back wall), occasionally it is outside it. Such a pregnancy leads to serious complications as we shall discuss further on.

Two ova that are fertilized simultaneously give rise to fraternal or *dizygotic twins*. When a single fertilized egg subdivides before implantation, identical or *monozygotic twins* develop.

Genetically, fraternal twins are like ordinary siblings. Identical twins have the same genetic makeup; they are always of the same sex and look alike. Twins occur in 1 out of 90 births; two out of three sets of twins are fraternal. Triplets occur about once in 5000 births; quadruplets, once in 500,000 births. Births of more than four children are extremely rare. The first quintuplets known to survive were the Dionne sisters, born in Canada on May 28, 1934.

## PREGNANCY

It is common practice to divide the nine months of pregnancy into three-month periods or *trimesters*.[3] During this period the growing organism is called an *embryo* (Greek, to "swell") for the first eight weeks and a *fetus* (Latin, "offspring") thereafter. The average length of pregnancy is 266 days. Some pregnancies are shorter or longer.[4] Babies born before the 36th week (252 days) are considered *premature*, but fetuses are *viable*, or able to survive, when they are 28 weeks and older.

### The First Trimester

The Embryo Develops    At the time the blastocyst is implanted, the uterine endometrium is at the peak of the secretory phase of the menstrual cycle (Chapter 4). The blastocyst burrows in as its enzymes digest the outer surface of the uterine lining, reaching the blood vessels and nutrients below. By the 10th to 12th day

---

[3]The discussion of pregnancy is based on obstetrical texts, including Pernoll and Benson (1987), Danforth and Scott (1986), and Pritchard et al., (1985).

[4]An authenticated upper limit of pregnancy is 349 days (Haynes, 1982). The possible length of pregnancy assumes legal importance in establishing the legitimacy of a child when the presumed father has been away for more than ten months. In the United States the longest pregnancy upheld by the courts as legitimate lasted 355 days.

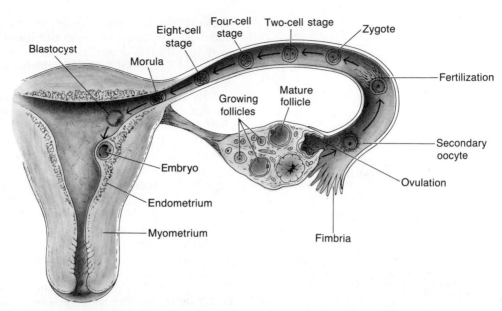

Figure 6.1    Diagram summarizing the ovarian cycle, fertilization, and implantation.

after ovulation, the blastocyst is firmly implanted in the uterine wall; but the woman does not yet know that she is pregnant, for her menstrual period, which she is going to miss, is not yet due for several more days.

This time is critical for the embryo's survival. The outer layer of the embryo, consisting of *trophoblast cells* (which will become part of the placenta), starts producing *chorionic gonadotropin*. This hormone stimulates the corpus luteum to maintain its output of estrogens and progestins. If the level of these hormones drops, the uterine lining will slough off and the embryo will be lost without the woman even realizing that she was pregnant (Yen, 1986).

In the early stages of development, a layer of cells forms across the center of the hollow blastocyst. From this *embryonic disk* will eventually grow all of the parts of the embryo. The surrounding cells will develop into the placenta and the fetal membranes. The membranes will form a sac filled with *amniotic fluid* ("bag of waters"), within which the fetus will float, cushioned and protected until birth.

The embryonic disk elongates into an oval shape by the end of the second week after fertilization. The embryo is still barely visible to the naked eye at this stage. Figure 6.2 shows the actual sizes of the embryo during the first seven weeks of life.

During the third week, the embryonic disk differentiates into its three distinctive layers: *endoderm, mesoderm,* and *ectoderm*. From the inner, endodermal layer will develop the internal organs; from the middle, mesodermal layer will arise muscles, skeleton, and blood; and from the outer, ectodermal layer, the brain and nerves, the skin, and other tissues.

The head end of the embryo develops faster than the rest of the body during these early stages. By the end of the third week the beginnings of eyes and ears are visible and the brain and other portions of the central nervous system are beginning to form (Plate 3, page 165). By the end of the first month, the embryo has a primitive heart and the beginnings of a digestive system. In the fifth week, precursors of arms and legs become visible; finger and toe forms appear between the sixth and eighth

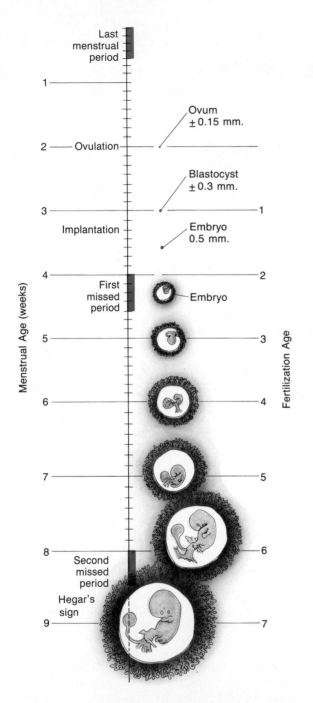

Menstrual Age (weeks)

Last menstrual period

1

Ovum ± 0.15 mm.

2 — Ovulation

Blastocyst ± 0.3 mm.

3

Implantation

Embryo 0.5 mm.

1

4

First missed period

Embryo

2

5

3

6

4

7

5

8

Second missed period

Hegar's sign

6

9

7

Fertilization Age

Figure 6.2    Actual sizes of embryos and their membranes during the first seven weeks of life.

weeks (Plate 4). Bones are beginning to ossify (harden with calcium), and the intestines are forming. By the seventh week the gonads are present, but cannot yet be clearly distinguished as male or female (Chapter 2).

By the end of eight weeks, when the embryonal period ends, the rudiments of all essential structures are present, and by four months the major organs are fairly well formed. The clearly defined external features now make the tiny fetus look human (Plate 5, page 166). From here on fetal development is mainly a matter of growth and differentiation. The way a simple cluster of cells develops into a complex organism has been a source of wonder, speculation, and study throughout history (Box 6.2).

The Placenta Develops    The embryo's lifeline to the mother is the *placenta*. The placenta develops from both fetal and maternal tissues, eventually growing to a sizable organ weighing about one pound (450 grams). It sustains the life of the fetus by conveying to it nutrients and oxygen and carrying away its waste products (Knuppel and Godlin, 1987). This transport takes place through the blood vessels of the *umbilical cord*, which connects the fetal circulatory system to the placenta (Plates 6 and 7, page 166). There nutrients and waste products are carried across and seep through the walls of an extensive capillary network. The fetal blood comes very close to the maternal blood without direct contact or intermingling.

The placental membrane that separates the maternal and fetal blood also allows the passage of hormones, electrolytes, and antibodies. It acts as a barrier to some but not all substances that may be harmful to the fetus. Most drugs pass the placental barrier. So do many infectious agents, which is how infants are born with congenital syphilis and AIDS (Chapter 5).

The placenta also functions as an endocrine gland, first producing chorionic gonadotropin to keep the corpus luteum active and then itself taking over the production of estrogens and progestins.

# Box 6.2

## THEORIES OF EMBRYONAL DEVELOPMENT

The discovery that coitus results in pregnancy, momentous as it was, did not resolve the mystery of how a complex being develops from formless elements. People speculated about this process until the modern science of embryology was able to elucidate its underlying mechanisms.

Aristotle believed that the human embryo originated from the union of semen and menstrual blood. This same notion has also been held in preliterate societies. For instance, the Venda tribe of East Africa believed that "red elements" like muscle and blood were derived from the mother's menses (which, they explained, ceased during pregnancy because the menstrual blood was being absorbed by the developing fetus); the "white elements"—like skin, bone, and nerves—developed from the father's semen (Meyer, 1939).

Following the invention of the microscope in the 17th century, sperm and ovum could be seen and their role in reproduction surmised, yet neither looked remotely "human." How could a child develop from them? Two schools of thought emerged to explain the mystery. The *ovists* claimed that a miniscule but fully formed baby was contained in the egg, and that the sperm functioned only to activate its growth. The *homunculists* held the opposite view, that the preformed baby resided inside the head of the sperm but did not begin to develop until it arrived in the fertile uterine environment. Looking through their crude early microscopes, some homunculists claimed to have actually seen a homunculus ("little man") inside the sperm (see the figure).

Ovists and homunculists were both *preformationists*—they presumed that a fully formed minia-

A homunculus as drawn by Niklaas Hartsoeker in 1694.

ture being simply grew bigger during development. This idea meant that all generations of humans, past and future, were stacked inside each other, like so many Russian dolls-within-dolls. Curiously, modern genetics provides some vindication for this fantastic notion: our genetic endowment is transmitted in a continuous line from one generation to another.

Preformationist theories died hard. Aristotle had considered the possibility of differentiation rather than simple growth. However, it was not until the 19th century that the theory of *epigenesis*, which embodies this doctrine, became established. In this theory, simple components develop into more complex parts in a continuous sequence of growth and differentiation (Arey, 1974).

Signs and Symptoms    How does a woman suspect she is pregnant? There are both objective signs and subjective symptoms (Taylor and Pernoll, 1987). Most common in early pregnancy are feelings of fatigue and drowsiness, but some women experience a sense of heightened energy and well-being. Physiological factors affect how a woman feels. The mood of the woman who knows she is pregnant also depends on circumstances. If the pregnancy is genuinely wanted, there is a sense of satisfaction and anticipation. If for any reason the pregnancy feels wrong, the experience may be colored by worry, anger, and depression.

The sign most commonly associated with pregnancy is a missed menstrual period. Although pregnancy usually stops menstruation, so can many other causes, including vigorous exercise, illness, and emotion. Women younger than 20 and older than 40 are more likely to skip a period. Conversely, the presence of a vaginal bloody discharge does not rule out pregnancy. About 20 percent of women have *spotting*, a short period of slight bleeding connected with implantation. Such bleeding is usually harmless but may also be an early sign of miscarriage. This bleeding may also be mistaken for a menstrual period.

Other physical signs of early pregnancy are swelling and tenderness of the breasts, frequent urination, irregular bowel movements, and increased vaginal secretion. A particularly bothersome symptom in many women during the first six to eight weeks of pregnancy is *morning sickness*. Queasy sensations upon awakening are accompanied by an aversion to food, or to the odors of certain foods. In some cases there is nausea, with or without vomiting. Some women experience these symptoms only in the evening. About one in four pregnant women experience no morning sickness, whereas in about one in 200 cases vomiting is so severe that the woman must be hospitalized. Treatment keeps this condition, known as *hyperemesis gravidarum*, from causing serious consequences, including malnutrition.

A doctor can find more objective evidence of early pregnancy. The vagina shows a purplish coloration (*Chadwick's sign*), as does the cervix. By the sixth week of pregnancy (a month after missing a period) a doctor can feel a soft and compressible area between the cervix and body of the uterus (*Hegar's sign*).

Occasionally, a woman develops some of the symptoms of pregnancy without being pregnant ("false pregnancy" or *pseudocyesis*). These women, who are usually intensely desirous of having a child, stop menstruating and develop symptoms of morning sickness, breast tenderness, a sense of fullness in the pelvis,

and the sensation of fetal movements in the abdomen (caused by contractions of the abdominal muscles). The absence of objective signs and negative pregnancy tests reveal the true condition.

Pregnancy Tests    The signs and symptoms above do not prove pregnancy. More definitive confirmation comes from laboratory tests for *human chorionic gonadotropin (hCG)* in blood or urine—a substance normally found only in pregnant women.

In earlier versions of these tests, urine or serum was injected into female mice or rabbits: the presence of hCG made the animals ovulate (or, injected into male frogs, made them ejaculate). At present, hCG is detected by immunologic tests that are simpler, less expensive, and 90–95 percent accurate.

The test consists of mixing a woman's blood or urine sample with specific chemicals; if hCG is present, even in small amounts, it can be detected within minutes. The test for hCG using urine is now the most common test for determining pregnancy. It can detect hCG as early as 7 to 12 days after conception. The blood test for hCG is used less frequently, in part because it is more expensive, but it can detect hCG within 6 to 8 days after fertilization.

The most sensitive test for hCG is *radioimmunoassay*, which is almost 100 percent accurate and can detect hCG within the first week of pregnancy. This method determines the concentration of substances in blood plasma through the use of radioactive antibodies.

Another version of the hCG test is available in pharmacies in the form of kits for home use. If used correctly, it can detect hCG in the urine of a pregnant woman as early as nine days after a missed period. Recent studies show that only in 3 percent of cases, home tests wrongly indicated pregnancy, but in 20 percent of tests giving negative results, the women were actually pregnant. When women with negative results performed a second test eight days later, test accuracy increased to 91 percent (McQuarrie and Flanagan, 1978).

All pregnancy tests can give *false negative* results when the woman is pregnant and *false positive* results when she is not. Absolute confirmation of pregnancy can be established only by one of three means: hearing the fetal heartbeat, seeing the fetal skeleton, or observing fetal movements. Until recent developments in technology, none of these signs of pregnancy could be verified until well into the second trimester; now they can be verified earlier.

Using a conventional stethoscope, a physician can hear the fetal heartbeat by the fifth month. (The fetal heart rate is 120 to 140 beats per minute, so it sounds different from the mother's heartbeat, which is usually 70 to 80 per minute.) A fetal *pulse detector* can detect the fetal heartbeat as early as 9 weeks, and quite reliably after 12 weeks.

Photographic evidence is obtained through *ultrasound*. Variations in the echo from an ultrasonic pulse reflect off the fetal skeleton. They are converted to a photographic image of the fetus in action. The image is far more distinct than a conventional X-ray; it is also much safer, because it does not involve radiation. The fetal heartbeat can also be seen on the ultrasound screen. Neither ultrasound nor X-ray is used routinely, but each can verify suspected complications, such as fetal head size larger than the pelvic opening, gross malformation, and multiple fetuses. Further information about the fetus can be obtained through newer techniques of *amniocentesis* and *chorionic villi sampling* (Box 6.3).

The mother begins to feel fetal movements in the abdomen usually by the end of the fourth month ("quickening"). They feel like the fluttering of a bird in the hand. The movements not only confirm pregnancy but indicate that the fetus is alive.

Expected Date of Delivery    Once pregnancy has been confirmed, the next question usually is, "When is the baby due?" The expected delivery date or *expected date of confinement (EDC)* can be calculated by the following formula: add one week to the first day of the last menstrual period, subtract three months, then add one year. For instance, if the last menstrual period began on January 8, 1988, adding one week (to January 15), subtracting three months (to October 15), and adding one year gives an expected delivery date of October 15, 1988. In fact, only about 4 percent of births occur on the day predicted by this formula; but 60 percent occur within five days of it.

## The Second Trimester

The Fetus Grows    Internal organ systems mature during the second trimester, and there is a substantial increase in size. By the end of the sixth month the fetus weighs about two pounds and is some 14 inches long. Among the changes during this period is the development of a temporary fine coat of soft hair (*lanugo*) on the body.

By the end of this period the facial and bodily features are well formed (Plates 8–12, pages 166–168). The fetus moves its arms and legs and alternates between periods of wakefulness and sleep. (Note in Plate 10 the fetus sucking its thumb.) Though the uterus is a sheltered environment, a loud noise or a rapid change in the position of the mother can disturb the tranquility of the womb and provoke a vigorous reaction. Changes in outside temperature are not perceived; the intrauterine temperature stays slightly above the temperature of the rest of the mother's body.

The Mother in the Second Trimester    For many women, the second trimester is the happiest time of pregnancy. The nausea, lethargy, and other troublesome symptoms of the earlier period have usually subsided, and the concerns about delivery are still in the future.

The pregnancy now feels secure, and the expanding abdomen and bustline (which may necessitate maternity clothes) make the pregnancy "public." The experience is also much more real because late in the fourth month the mother can feel the fetal movements more strongly. The "kicking" of the fetus becomes outwardly visible on the abdomen. The mother

# Box 6.3

## AMNIOCENTESIS AND CHORIONIC VILLI TESTING

Under certain circumstances it is important to know about the fetus as early as possible. For instance, if there is a likelihood of genetic abnormalities, because of family history or the age of the mother, an early determination gives the parents either reassurance or the option of aborting the fetus. In other cases, it may be possible to treat the problem while intrauterine development is still in progress.

*Amniocentesis* is the analysis of fetal cells floating in amniotic fluid in order to obtain genetic information about the fetus. First, ultrasound scans the womb for the position of the fetus. Next, a long needle is inserted through the abdominal wall into the uterus, and a small amount of amniotic fluid is drawn without harming the fetus (see the figure). Now fetal cells are recovered from the fluid and analyzed. The condition and number of the chromosomes in these cells (as well as the presence of XX or XY sex chromosomes, showing the sex of the child) can be determined accurately.

Amniocentesis is an accurate and relatively safe procedure for both mother and fetus. It is usually performed after the 14th week. Among the abnormalities that can be detected by amniocentesis are Down's syndrome (mongolism), neural tube closure defects (open spine), Tay-Sachs disease, cystic fibrosis, and Rh incompatibility. The analysis of amniotic fluid can reveal a wealth of information on such chromosomal, metabolic, and blood conditions. When abnormalities are diagnosed, parents can choose to have an abortion—although by the time the chromosome analysis is complete (the 20th week to 24th week of pregnancy), abortion is no longer a simple, risk-free operation (Chapter 7). Parents who choose to continue the pregnancy have time to prepare for the extra challenge.

Because a woman in her forties is 100 times more likely than a woman in her twenties to have ova with abnormal chromosomes, amniocentesis is recommended for women who become pregnant after the age of 35, and who have previously had a child with an abnormality that can be detected by analysis of fetal cells. It is also recommended for couples with family histories of certain hereditary problems. About 3 percent of newborns in the

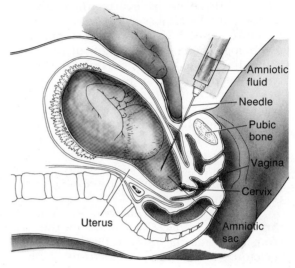

Amniocentesis.

United States suffer an obvious defect, so procedures like amniocentesis could be of wide benefit.

The newest test, *chorionic villi sampling (CVS)*, uses a small sample of tissue from the surface of the chorion, the outermost layer of the membranes enclosing the fetus. Though it may not be as accurate as amniocentesis or detect as many abnormalities, it can be done as early as the eighth week (but usually in the ninth to eleventh week) and the results are obtained in a few days (it takes two weeks for amniocentesis). This timing allows the mother to have a first trimester abortion with fewer complications. The risks with CVS are not significantly higher than in amniocentesis, but there is a 1–2 percent chance of causing a miscarriage. This risk is especially significant for women over 35, who may have more trouble conceiving again (Brozan, 1985).

Doctors can now draw fetal blood samples directly from the umbilical vessels. Using ultrasound to "view" the fetus, a thin needle is passed through the mother's abdomen into the umbilical cord. This allows for a greater range of abnormalities to be detected early and treated by drugs or transfusions (Kolata, 1988).

is now directly aware of the new life growing within her, and begins to relate to it. Other family members may do the same. Being more comfortable than earlier, and not yet as burdened as she will be later, more women are able to keep active during this time, at work, at home, or in sports and leisure; there is also heightened sexual interest.

Nevertheless, the second trimester has its own possible discomforts. Pressure from the expanding uterus may lead to indigestion and constipation. Varicose veins and hemorrhoids may appear or get worse. Fluid retention causes swelling of the feet and ankles (*edema*), and the woman may begin to gain excessive amounts of weight.

## The Third Trimester

**The Fetus Matures**  The last phase of development is mainly a period of further maturation. The fetus is becoming well enough formed to survive on its own; by the middle of the last trimester the prematurely born baby (six weeks early) has a 70–80 percent chance of survival.

Early in the trimester the fetus is in an upright or *breech* position. It keeps shifting around in its increasingly cramped quarters, and in 97 percent of cases assumes a *head-down* position by the time it reaches full term.

During the ninth month the fetus gains more than two pounds (0.9 kg), and essential organs like the lungs become ready for life in the outside world. At full term the average baby weighs 7.5 pounds (3.4 kg) and is 20 inches long (50.8 cm), but there is a great variation in birth weights, ranging usually from 5 to 9 pounds. (The largest baby known to have survived weighed 15.5 pounds at birth). Ninety-nine percent of full-term babies born alive in the United States now survive, a figure that could be improved even further if all expectant mothers and newborn babies received proper care.

**The Mother in the Third Trimester**  The relative comfort and tranquility of the second trimester gradually give way to the special discomforts of the third. Most of them have to do with the increased activity and size of the fetus, which displaces and presses upon maternal organs (Figure 6.3). What were occasional fetal movements now turn to periods of seemingly perpetual kicking, tossing, and turning, which may keep the mother awake at night.

The woman's weight, if not controlled up to this point, may become a problem. The optimal weight gain during pregnancy is 24 to 27 pounds (11 to 13 kg). The average infant at nine months weighs about 7.5 pounds (3.4 kg). The rest of the weight gain is accounted for as follows: the placenta, about 1 pound (0.4 kg); amniotic fluid, 2 pounds (0.9 kg); enlargement of the uterus, 2 pounds (0.9 kg); enlargement of the breasts, about 1.5 pounds (0.7 kg); and

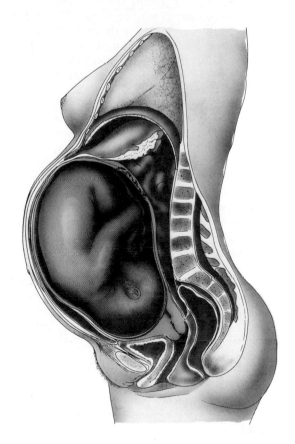

Figure 6.3   Full-term fetus.

the retained fluid and fat accumulated by the mother, the balance of 10 pounds (4.5 kg). Excessive weight gain is associated with a higher incidence of medical complications during pregnancy, such as strain on the heart and high blood pressure.

By the ninth month of pregnancy a woman is usually impatient. She speculates about the sex of the child and worries whether or not the baby is going to be all right. She may also feel some anxiety about the process of delivery. However, the properly prepared woman in good health also counts the days with pleasure and anticipation before she finally meets her baby face to face.

## Psychological Aspects

Almost any parent could tell you that pregnancy brings out strong feelings. There has been too little research on these vital aspects of pregnancy: the fluctuating emotional states, the formulation of new identities and roles for the mother and father, and the shifts in relationships (Hittelman and Simons, 1977).

Pregnancy and childbirth are among the most significant events of many women's lives. Childbearing has major consequences for a woman's health, intimate relationships, career, and sense of fulfillment. Few experiences have as profound an effect on women's lives as bearing children. Traditionally, having children has been expected of women in most societies, but modern women in the industrialized world exercise a great deal more choice. Whichever way a woman decides, her choice will affect her life.

It is hardly surprising that pregnancy and childbirth are emotionally rich and psychologically challenging experiences. How satisfying or distressing they will be depends to a large extent on the circumstances. To have a child with the right man, at the right time, is obviously a very different experience than when one or more key requirements are lacking. Some of the special problems of unwanted pregnancies will be discussed in connection with abortion (Chapter 7) and adolescent de-

velopment (Chapter 9). We shall focus here on pregnancies that occur under ordinary, if not always optimal, conditions.

The first set of psychological concerns has to do with the physical experience. As we have described, the female body undergoes a remarkable series of changes over a nine-month period, some of which entail considerable discomfort. This expecation and fear of the unknown cause anxiety: Will I get sick? Will I be able to keep active? Will childbirth be painful? Such questions naturally occur to many women. Closely related are concerns about the baby's health and safety: Will my child be normal? An expectant mother can hardly avoid wondering, especially if there is the slightest indication of something wrong.

Another set of questions, just as important, involves the relationship with the baby's father—typically the husband: Will our marriage change? Will we be able to afford this child? Will he still find me attractive? Some women worry that childbearing will make them less romantic, less sexy, more domestic and humdrum; other women expect the child to strengthen the marital bond, to deepen the commitment of the husband, or to complete the relationship.

Finally, women wonder about motherhood itself: Will I be a good mother? Will I know how to take care of a child? These considerations may stretch all the way to the child's adolescence. Questions about their own future tie in for working women: Will I be able to take off enough time after the baby's birth? Will I earn enough to provide for the baby? Will I be able to balance mothering with a career? How much responsibility will my husband assume?

## Sexual Interest and Activity

Pregnancy changes a woman in body and mind. No wonder it affects her sexual interest and behavior. There is much variation in its effect among women and in the different phases of pregnancy. In general, sex in pregnancy is quite safe for the mother and the fetus. Nonetheless, people often worry that it will affect the mother's well-being and the baby's safety.

Orgasm makes the uterus contract. It does have an effect on fetal heart rate, and mothers report an increase in fetal movements, but the significance of these effects is unclear (Chayen et al., 1986). Some cultures prohibit coitus during part or all of pregnancy; others permit sex all the way to the time of delivery (Ford and Beach, 1951). Due precaution or abstention are necessary in certain circumstances, such as when there is danger of miscarriage (Herbst, 1979). Otherwise, how a couple's sex life changes during pregnancy is usually a matter of personal choice.

Some studies show a steady decline in the frequency of coitus throughout the pregnancy (Pepe et al., 1987). Other studies reveal a different pattern. In the first trimester, women show a highly variable response. There may be a heightening of sexual feelings, no change, or a decline in sexual interest, often associated with morning sickness, fatigue, fear of disrupting the pregnancy, or high progesterone levels. In the second trimester, some 80 percent of women report an increase in sexual desire and responsiveness (Masters and Johnson, 1966; Tolor and DiGrazia, 1976). In the last trimester there is a consistent drop in the frequency of coitus linked with physical awkwardness and discomfort, a woman's feeling of being less attractive (a perception not always shared by the husband), and fear of hurting the baby (Calhoun et al., 1981).

There are two health concerns in this area: the chance that orgasm might cause miscarriage or premature labor, and the risk of infection. The risk from orgasm is realistic for women with a history of miscarriage or who are showing early signs of it (like vaginal bleeding). There seems to be no other correlation between experiencing orgasm and giving birth prematurely (Perkins, 1979). The risk of infection becomes a serious consideration if the membranes are ruptured or if the man is infected with a sexually transmitted disease (which may be asymptomatic).

Some of these problems related to sex during pregnancy are easily resolved. The woman-above position or rear entry coitus is less awkward in later months and less taxing on the woman. Use of condoms will help prevent infection, although it will not protect against herpes, which can be fatal for the baby. Noncoital sexual activities like masturbation or mouth-genital stimulation provide alternatives to coitus, but orgasm still can stimulate miscarriage. The practice of blowing air forcefully into the vagina (which some people do during cunnilingus) is dangerous in pregnancy, because it may introduce air bubbles into the woman's bloodstream, causing an air embolism that may be fatal (Sadock and Sadock, 1976).

Sex during pregnancy involves factors besides health. Just because a woman is pregnant, her sexual needs and those of her partner should not be ignored. Of the 79 husbands of pregnant women interviewed by Masters and Johnson (1966), 12 had turned to extramarital sex. Discovery of such an occurrence is likely to be particularly upsetting for a pregnant wife.

Sex is but one aspect of a couple's relationship significantly modified by pregnancy. In many other ways, a woman's pregnancy also affects the expectant father.

## The Father's Experience

The prospect of becoming a father is an enormously satisfying and joyful experience for many men. Much depends, of course, on the couple's relationship and the social and economic circumstances under which the pregnancy is taking place. To have a child in a loving and compatible relationship can be a tremendous satisfaction to a man, as it is to a woman, but an unwanted pregnancy in a tenuous or doomed relationship leaves the man feeling helpless. Some men distance themselves from the woman ("It's her problem"); others are racked by guilt and despair ("How could I have done this?") or anger ("How could she do this to me?").

Despite the difference in reactions, the prospect of fatherhood is likely to affect men in some common ways. This is particularly true when a man becomes a father for the first time, which is what we shall focus on here.

At a psychological level, a man may see parenthood as a confirmation of his manhood, just as a woman may see it as an affirmation of her womanhood. His capacity to impregnate is public evidence of his potency, but beyond that it confers on him, just as it does on a woman, an added measure of being *generative,* which is the quintessential mark of adulthood (Chapter 9). Hence, a man feels a deep pride and a strengthened self-esteem.

Having a child irrevocably changes a man's self-image, no less than it does that of a woman. His entire perspective on life is likely to be revised in the light of his expected responsibilities as a parent. All major life decisions must now take into account their impact on his children.

These positive reactions also have their negative counterparts. Most often, there is a mix of contradictory feelings. Expectant parenthood is never a wholly positive or wholly negative prospect.

Traditionally, marriage and parenthood have been supposed to provide a woman with security and fulfillment. For men they have supposedly meant getting "tied down." Friends joke that the man is giving up his carefree independence.

Currently, both men and women balance the anticipated joy of parenthood against the loss of freedom and social and financial responsibilities looming ahead. They both struggle with the same doubt: "Will I be a good parent?"

At the relational level, significant shifts take place. Some husbands identify with their pregnant wives so closely that they too suffer from morning sickness and other signs of early pregnancy. In one study, 23 percent of husbands in the United States showed such psychological manifestations (Lipkin and Lamb, 1982). In some preliterate societies, men actually went through "labor" in concert with their wives (*couvade*) in an effort to distract evil spirits away from the mother and baby (Davenport, 1977).

A man needs to adjust to the physical and psychological changes in the expectant mother. Those men who put great stock in the figure of their wife may be alarmed to see it change; other men are fascinated by these changes and even find them an added source of attraction.

Pregnancy makes a woman turn inward. She has a new being within her to relate to—a feeling that a man can never experience, hence never fully comprehend. Her preoccupation with the pregnancy and developing infant may draw her apart from the husband; yet other couples develop a greater intimacy than ever before. At this time a woman may also become closer to her mother or female friends, which is likely to make the man feel excluded.

The combination of the wife's physical changes, the novelty of the experience, and not knowing what to expect, makes the first trimester a particularly trying time for the man. The second trimester provides a breather—the woman feels better and the man is less anxious about her. The signs of pregnancy are now visible enough for him to be able to share more directly the mother's experience. For instance, by feeling the movements of the fetus through her abdomen, he too can now relate to this new "person" as yet unseen. At the doctor's office, he can hear his child's heart beating. He can begin to attend prenatal classes with his wife, and talk there with other "expectant fathers."

In the third trimester, the man confronts a new set of adjustments. As the time of birth approaches, the reality of what is happening becomes more tangible. The woman is no longer as physically active a companion as he is used to for housekeeping chores, work, play, or sex. More than ever before he must confront the question of whether by becoming a mother, she will be less of a wife, lover, companion, and friend. Jealousy and envy may begin to creep into his expectation of what life is going to be like. On the other hand, there is the exhilaration of meeting his child face-to-face and the expectation that the relationship will revert to what it was or even get better; but it will never be quite the same.

## CHILDBIRTH

In the past it was believed that babies struggled out of the uterus at birth. Actually the baby plays no active part in the birth process; it is passively propelled out of the birth canal. Most societies have devised various ways of assisting women in childbirth. In preliterate cultures, sitting, squatting, or kneeling postures for the mother were usually considered optimal. Women were also "helped" by being suspended, sat upon, tossed about in blankets (to shake the baby loose), and having smoke blown into their vagina.

Traditionally, women have been assisted in childbirth by other women, usually an experienced *midwife* (from "with wife"). In Europe, men were barred from attending women at childbirth until the 16th century: in 1552, a Hamburg physician called Wertt was burned at the stake for posing as a woman to attend a delivery. As late as the 18th century most physicians considered it beneath their dignity to care for pregnant women, and notions of modesty precluded their assisting at labor (Speert, 1986).

With the advent of modern obstetrics

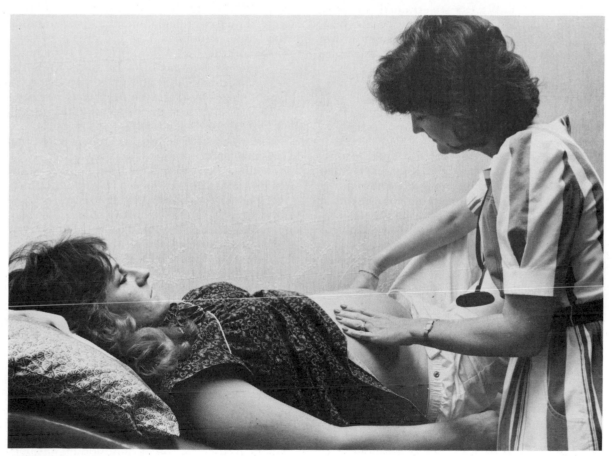

Figure 6.4    A midwife giving a prenatal checkup.

early in the 19th century, the delivery of children was taken over by physicians and became almost exclusively a medical practice in the industrialized world. Recently, objections have been raised to this practice on the grounds that the hospital setting turns childbirth into an impersonal, expensive, and needlessly medicalized procedure (Arms, 1975). As a result, a number of alternative methods of *natural childbirth* have been advocated. Some women now choose to deliver at home, or in *birthing centers* that combine medical facilities for any emergency with a home atmosphere. Meanwhile, hospitals have modified their routines to counter some of the criticisms.

Midwifery is making a comeback (Figure 6.4). Nurse-midwives are trained to assist throughout the pregnancy, delivery, and postnatal care, and to counsel about sexuality. Most of them work in cooperation with obstetricians.

## Labor

As the end of pregnancy nears, the expectant mother experiences sporadic contractions in her uterus—referred to as *false labor*. Three or four weeks before delivery the fetus "drops" to a lower position in the abdomen. The next major step is the softening and dilation of the cervix. Then, just before true labor begins, a small, slightly bloody discharge (*bloody show*) appears in the vagina, when the plug of mucus that blocked the cervix comes out. *Labor* follows this event usually within a few hours but sometimes after several days.

Labor consists of regular and rhythmic uterine contractions, which dilate the cervix and culminate in the delivery of the baby, the placenta, and the fetal membranes. It is the fetus rather than the mother who actually triggers labor (Daly and Wilson, 1978). A number of hormonal factors are known to be involved (Russell, 1987). The fetus' adrenal gland produces hormones that make the placenta and uterus increase the secretion of *prostaglandins*, which in turn stimulate the muscles of the uterus to contract. *Oxytocin*, a hormone produced by the mother's posterior pituitary gland, is also released in the late stages of labor; it stimulates the more powerful contractions required to expel the fetus. The effects of oxytocin depend on the presence of estrogen, and the uterus becomes much more responsive to the action of oxytocin late in pregnancy (Rall and Schleifer, 1985).

Labor is divided into three stages. The *first stage* is the longest, extending from the onset of regular contractions until the cervix is fully dilated to about 4 inches (10 centimeters) in diameter. This stage lasts about 15 hours in first pregnancies, and about eight hours in subsequent ones. (Deliveries after the first child are generally easier in all respects.) Uterine contractions begin at intervals as far apart as 15 to 20 minutes, occurring more frequently and with greater intensity and regularity over time. The fluid-filled amniotic sac surrounding the baby cushions it from the effects of these early contractions.

The *second stage* of labor starts when the cervix is fully dilated and ends with the delivery of the baby (Figure 6.5). It may last for a matter of minutes, or up to several hours in particularly difficult births. At some point during the first two stages, the fetal membranes rupture, and amniotic fluid gushes out. In 10 percent of the cases, premature rupture of the membranes initiates labor. In other instances the physician breaks the membranes deliberately to speed labor. After the baby is born and starts breathing, the umbilical cord is cut, severing the last physical link to the mother.

In the *third stage* of labor the placenta separates from the uterine wall and is discharged with the fetal membranes as the *afterbirth*. The uterus contracts markedly, and there is some bleeding, usually limited. The third stage of labor lasts about an hour. During this time the mother and baby are carefully examined for signs of trauma and other possible problems. If all is well, the parents can use this time to touch and bond with their child.

## Methods of Childbirth

Chances are that your grandmother was born at home. Your mother was probably born at the hospital, as were you. Where do you think

1

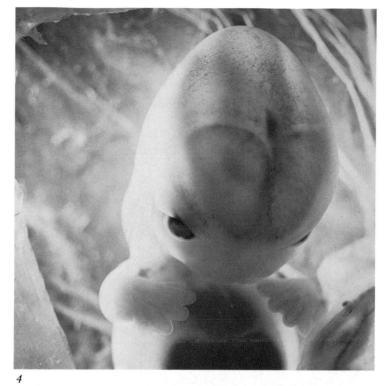

4

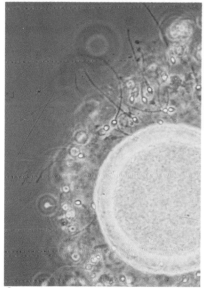

2

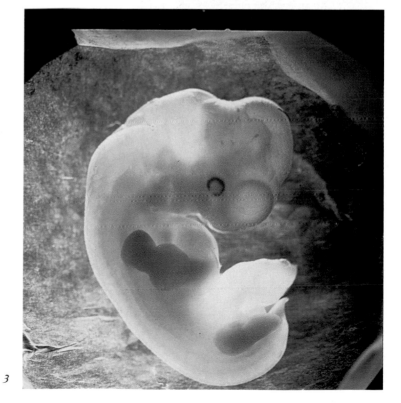

3

Plate 1   Traveling sperm
Plate 2   Egg and sperm
Plate 3   Embryo at six weeks
Plate 4   Embryo at six weeks

165

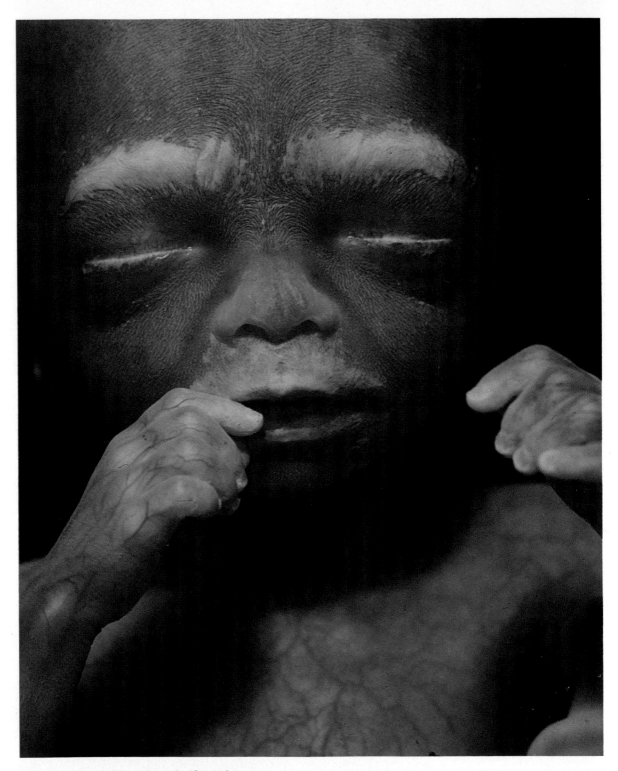

*Plate 12*   Fetus at five and one-half months

168

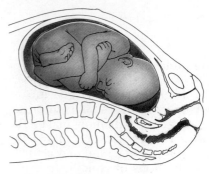

1. Head floats.

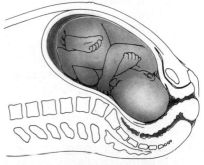

2. Head enters canal, neck bends down.

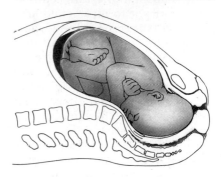

3. Baby descends and head turns.

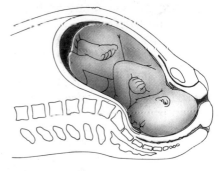

4. Neck begins to bend back.

Figure 6.5 The process of birth.

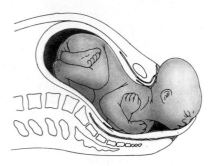

5. Neck bends back fully.

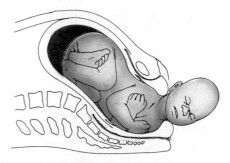

6. Head emerges, baby turns sideways.

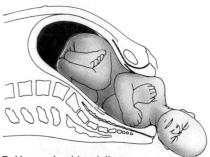

7. Upper shoulder delivers.

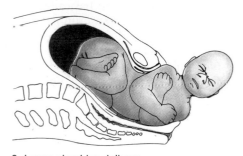

8. Lower shoulder delivers.

your child will be born? Most women in the United States today give birth in a hospital, but some women prefer to deliver at home, with a physician or a nurse-midwife attending.

Home Delivery    The advocates of home delivery argue that hospital settings, with their impersonal and forbidding atmosphere, place undue stress on the mother and turn what should be a natural and joyous family occasion into a costly surgical procedure. A safe choice exists between delivery in a hospital or at home only when the pregnancy has progressed normally and there are no anticipated complications. Childbirth can lead quickly to acute emergencies that endanger the life of mother and child, which can be best handled in a hospital. Only about half of the complications of delivery, such as a fetal head too large for the mother's pelvis, can be predicted before labor begins.

However, the majority of deliveries are quite normal, so many women, in fact, do have a choice. A couple considering home delivery should learn all the possible risks and the probable benefits. They should not let themselves be either pressured by convention or swayed by fads.

Hospital Delivery    The main advantage of a hospital delivery is the security it provides against unforeseen complications. It also relieves members of the family or friends of the responsibility of caring for the new mother and baby right away. A woman may also prefer the privacy of the hospital setting.

The experience of giving birth is basically the same wherever it takes place; yet a number of significant differences depend on the setting. In the hospital, the woman who is to give birth will be usually placed in a *labor room* where she is prepared for labor (having her pubic area shaved and/or cleansed, her bowels voided, and so on) and monitored; the actual birth takes place in the *delivery room* (which is like an operating room). Currently many hospitals allow labor and delivery to occur in the same *birthing room*, which is set up to convey a warm, soothing atmosphere.

While labor progresses, the baby's father, or a relative or friend, is encouraged to stay with the laboring mother. The comforting presence of a trusted companion makes the experience easier for the mother, allows the father or friend to share in it, and may actually reduce the complications of childbirth associated with stress and anxiety.

Hospital delivery usually involves procedures to forestall future problems. An IV needle is started, so no time will be lost if the woman winds up needing drugs, surgery, or glucose. Especially with first deliveries, an *episiotomy*—a cut in the perineum between vagina and anus—is made to avoid a jagged tear when the head passes. These precautions may well pay off, but sometimes prove needless.

Giving birth can entail considerable discomfort, even though it is a natural process and not an illness (Figure 6.6). After general anesthesia was introduced in the 19th century, physicians sought to use it to make childbirth painless. This practice was resisted for a while, because it seemed to be "unnatural" and nullified God's judgment on Eve ("I will greatly multiply your pain in childbearing; in pain you shall bring forth children"—Genesis 3:16). The practice only became popular after Queen Victoria delivered her eighth child under chloroform anesthesia in 1853.

General anesthesia is now used much less than in earlier decades. It entails considerable risk to the mother, slows down labor, and may interfere with the newborn's respiration. It also deprives the mother of assisting and witnessing the birth of the baby.

Hospitals sometimes give drugs routinely. A woman and her doctor should agree ahead of time on how to handle discomfort. A mild *analgesic* can lessen pain and anxiety; an *anesthetic* can block it. A *caudal* or *spinal block* is popular today. Temporarily the mother loses sensation and power to move below the waist. This method leaves her awake but unable to push. Some women prefer full awareness and participation. They ask the doctor to withhold all anesthesia.

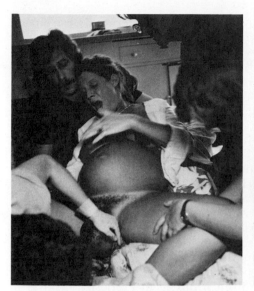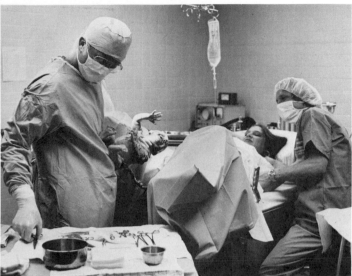

Figure 6.6   Giving birth at birthing center (left) and in a hospital (right).

Hospital deliveries can allow for the scheduled *induction of labor* through infusion of oxytocin when the mother is near the end of her term or is overdue. This procedure carries some risk but is necessary in select cases. The same is true for deliveries by *cesarean section*, a major surgical procedure in which the fetus is delivered by cutting through the abdominal wall into the uterus. (Although the procedure is named after Julius Caesar, it is highly unlikely he was in fact delivered in this fashion. The Roman practice was to remove the entire uterus to save the child if the mother was dying. Caesar's mother survived his birth.) The first authenticated cesarean delivery on a living patient was performed in 1610 (Speert, 1985). Almost one out of four births in the United States currently takes place through cesarean section (906,000 deliveries in 1986). This practice has quadrupled over the past two decades, and critics say it is overused (Schabecoff, 1987). Cesarian sections can increase the risk of complications for the mother and substantially increase the cost of having a baby. The mortality rate is higher than the rate of maternal deaths in vaginal deliveries. The fact

that a woman was delivered by surgery once does not preclude her giving birth vaginally on subsequent occasions.

However, in 12–16 percent of cases, there are compelling reasons for this procedure. Among its legitimate indications are discrepancies between the size of the baby's head and the mother's pelvis (making passage difficult or impossible); complications endangering the fetus (such as abnormal positioning or premature separation of the placenta); venereal disease in the birth canal (Chapter 5); and other conditions interfering with normal childbirth.

Prepared Childbirth    *Natural childbirth* is a set of attitudes and practices that seek to free the woman giving birth from unnecessary pain, anxiety, and medical intervention. To some, the term simply means giving birth at home, with the help of a midwife, without drugs and doctors. To others, it signifies one of several methods to facilitate birth through "natural" means rather than through the use of anesthesia, instrumentation, and so on.

The term "natural childbirth" was coined

by the English physician Grantly Dick-Read in 1932 in his book *Childbirth without Fear*. Dick-Read postulated that the pain of childbirth is primarily related to muscular tension brought on by fear. He sought to educate women about the birth process in order to break the cycle of fear, tension, and pain.

The *Lamaze* form of natural childbirth originated in Russia, but it was popularized by the French physician Bernard Lamaze in 1970. It entails teaching women how to relax their muscles, concentrate, and breathe properly during labor, coupled with various massage techniques (Lamaze, 1970). An expectant mother and her partner (usually the baby's father or a friend) attend prenatal classes for six to ten weeks before the date of birth. These classes are designed to inform prospective parents about each step of labor, to answer questions, and to dispel anxiety. The women learn a variety of exercises that increase muscle control (Figure 6.7). The tension of abdominal and perineal muscles is thought to make it harder for the baby to emerge. By learning to relax these muscles, women can allow the baby to pass through the birth canal more comfortably. By learning to contract them, they can help to push the baby out. Other techniques, such as massaging the abdomen or concentrating on visual targets, further distract attention from the contractions.

The woman's partner plays an important part. This "coach" not only provides comfort and encouragement but helps her to breathe properly and to relax, using all the techniques they have been taught together. Coaching is hard work—but the teamwork is rewarding. Fathers need not pace the corridors, nervous and useless, as used to be the case.

Another method of childbirth that has become popular in recent years was expounded by the French physician Frederick Leboyer in *Birth without Violence* (1975). This method is mainly concerned with protecting the infant from the trauma of childbirth. It is a slow, quiet method of delivery, often done in hos-

Figure 6.7   Couples attending a Lamaze childbirth class.

pitals. Everything is aimed at protecting the infant's delicate senses from shock. Birth takes place in a quiet and warm room where the lights are kept low, and unnecessary noises are avoided. Following birth, the baby is gently settled onto the mother's abdomen to adjust to its new environment for a few minutes while still attached by the umbilical cord. Only after breathing starts spontaneously is the cord cut and the baby gently lowered into a warm bath. (Leaving the cord uncut causes some of the baby's blood to drain into the placenta, which may weaken the baby.) This gentle entry into the world is a far cry from the usual image of the kicking and screaming infant, dangled by the feet and spanked to induce breathing. However, whether Leboyer's method results in more relaxed and healthy children in the long term remains to be substantiated (Nelson et al., 1980).

Natural childbirth approaches have already had an impact on hospital practices. Increasingly, hospitals have modified their regulations to allow husbands or partners to be present at delivery and to allow *rooming-in*—having newborn babies live in the same room with their mothers rather than in a separate nursery.

## Early Parent–Child Interaction

A related area of recent interest is the interaction between parent and infant soon after birth. Just as there are *critical periods* during which mother and offspring become *bonded* among animals, similar processes are assumed to operate among humans. Klaus and Kennell (1976) hypothesize that "the entire range of problems from mild maternal anxiety to child abuse may result largely from separation and other unusual circumstances which occur in the early newborn period."

To enhance early attachment, the newborn is shown to the parents right after birth and then placed next to the mother face-to-face to facilitate touching and eye contact. Sometimes the baby is put to the mother's breast right on the delivery table.

Cuddling, fondling, cooing, and other forms of tender and affectionate contact are encouraged from the start. The baby actively participates in this process by responding to its parents. In a few weeks, the *smiling response* further reinforces the parents' affectionate attention, encouraging more smiles (Scharfman, 1977). Such interactions help the child's psychological development. However, there is no convincing evidence that they work on the same bonding principles that operate among animals. We shall return to this topic in Chapter 8.

## THE POSTPARTUM PERIOD

The *postpartum period* (or the *puerperium*) is the period of six to eight weeks that follows delivery and ends with the resumption of ovulatory menstrual cycles. It is an important time for the mother, as well as the baby and the father, from physiological, psychological, and practical perspectives (Nory, 1987).

### Physiological Changes

We tend to take for granted the adaptation of the female body to the burden of pregnancy, losing sight of the tremendous changes it entails. In the postpartum period, tissues, organs, and physiological systems revert to their previous states—a considerable task.

After delivery, the uterus will shrink markedly (*involution*) and gradually regain its prepregnancy size; its weight drops from about two pounds to two ounces over a six-week period. The cervix, which is stretched and flabby after delivery, regains its tone and tightness within a week. For several weeks there is a uterine discharge, like menstrual flow, called *lochia*, which gradually turns from reddish-brown to yellowish-white.

The woman's body is meanwhile undergoing tremendous hormonal changes, as the high levels of progestin and estrogen that maintained the pregnancy decline. These hormonal changes affect not only the onset of milk production and uterine involution, but also the woman's emotional state.

## Emotional Reactions

The relief of having given birth and the pleasure of having the baby make the first few days after delivery an exhilarating time. A woman usually leaves the hospital two or three days after an uncomplicated delivery. The first week at home may be quite taxing to the new mother, who is trying to cope with the many needs of the baby (especially around-the-clock feedings). Fatigue may be a major complaint at this point, and a general feeling of "let-down" follows the earlier euphoria.

About two-thirds of women experience transient episodes of sadness and crying sometime during the first ten days after delivery, a phenomenon known as *postpartum depression* ("baby blues"). In one to two cases out of 1000 births, the disturbance is severe enough to lead to profound depression with hallucinations, and suicidal and infanticidal impulses, a condition that requires urgent psychiatric attention (Yalom et al., 1968).

These problems can seem puzzling, because they occur when the mother is expected to be especially happy over the arrival of the baby. However, in the emotional upheaval of the postpartum period, a woman may have considerable mixed feelings towards the infant and may fear that she could hurt it. Doubts about her competence as a mother, fatigue, feelings of being rejected or neglected by the father, and biochemical changes add to the upset (Simons, 1985). When the baby is unwanted, defective, or to be given up for adoption, additional concerns inevitably compound the depression. On the other hand, under more usual circumstances the woman needs only a little cheering up. The postpartum period then is a time of great joy and deep satisfaction, as both parents revel in the presence of the fledgling human being that they have brought into the world.

## Nursing

An infant animal sucking milk at the breast is *suckling*; a human infant is *nursing* or breastfeeding (Figure 6.8). Immediately following delivery the mother's breasts contain not milk

Figure 6.8    Breastfeeding.

but *colostrum*. This thin fluid has more protein, less fat, and as much sugar as normal milk. It is rich in antibodies that may help provide immunity to the infant.

Human milk production (*lactation*) begins two to three days after childbirth. Two pituitary hormones are involved: *prolactin* (from the anterior pituitary) stimulates the mammary glands to make milk, and oxytocin (from the posterior pituitary) causes the milk to flow from the breast to the nipple when the baby is nursed. After weaning, when a woman does not breastfeed, the breast is no longer stimulated by the nursing infant, and lactation ceases.

Nursing has been the universal method of feeding infants during most of human history and remains so in many parts of the world. Its decline elsewhere is mainly due to urbanization and industrialization. For mothers working outside the home, regular breastfeeding is not practical, unless the child is kept close by or the mother "pumps" out her milk for it. Mothers who work in the home have been influenced by trends or by manufacturers of milk substitutes to rely on alternative methods of feeding their babies. Women have been further discouraged from nursing by concerns that it might affect the shape of their breasts, although nursing has no permanent effect on breast size.

Breastfeeding is becoming popular again in the United States. It can be emotionally satisfying and pleasurable. It is not unusual for women to be sexually aroused, or in some cases to reach orgasm, while nursing. Some enjoy the experience; others react with anxiety and guilt. Commonly milk will ooze out of the nipples during orgasm, which may startle some people. The larger breasts of the lactating woman may be erotic to some men and disconcerting to others.

For the baby, the mother's milk is unquestionably superior to cow's milk or commercial formulas. Human milk contains the ideal mixture of nutrients and antibodies that protect the infant from certain infectious diseases; it is free of bacteria; it is always at the right temperature; and it costs nothing. On the other hand, breastfeeding is impractical for some women. Some are sick or absent; others do not produce sufficient milk. Drugs the mother must take are usually secreted in the milk. A few infants have a milk allergy. For such reasons a mother may decide not to nurse her infant, and she need not feel guilty about it.

## Ovulation and Menstruation

If a woman does not nurse her child, the menstrual cycle will usually resume within a few months after delivery, though in some cases it may take as long as 18 months. Lactation inhibits ovulation in women whose infants nurse around the clock, but it is not a reliable method of contraception, even though it has been widely used in many parts of the world (Chapter 7).

It should be realized that ovulation can occur before the first postpartum menstrual cycle; consequently, a woman can become pregnant without having had a menstrual period after the birth of her baby. The first few periods after pregnancy are usually somewhat irregular in length and flow, but they do become regularized in time. Also, women who have had painful periods may suffer less discomfort after they have had a child.

## Sex in the Postpartum Period

There is considerable variation in sexual activity after delivery. Fatigue, physical discomfort, sexual interest, and the obstetrician's advice play an important part in determining when a woman resumes sexual relations after childbirth. Women who nurse their babies reportedly have a higher sexual interest than those who do not.

Doctors used to advise women to refrain from intercourse "six weeks before, six weeks after." This rule does not hold any more (Easterling and Herbert, 1982). There is no medical reason why a healthy woman cannot have vaginal intercourse as soon as the episiotomy scars or other lacerations of the perineum have healed and the flow of lochia has ended, which usually takes about three weeks. The only medical risk at this time is the possibility of infection, but couples who use condoms or practice sexual activities other than vaginal intercourse need not be hampered by this concern.

The impact of the baby on a couple's relationship becomes even stronger after birth. Particularly with the first baby, the exclusive relationship of the couple must now make room for a third person, also an intimate part of the family, whose helplessness must take precedence over the personal needs of the adults. A child can boost the affection linking a couple and enhance their sexual attraction to each other. It can also be an intruder and a competitor for the affections, time, and energy of the parent. All these considerations can operate at once, making it necessary for a couple to go through a period of adjustment.

Eventually, most women recover their previous levels of sexual interest and orgasmic responsiveness, but it is also not uncommon to experience shifts in this regard. Some women reach orgasm more easily after becoming a mother. Others develop dysfunctions due to pain or the loss of tone in circumvaginal muscles (discussed in Chapter 15).

## PRENATAL CARE

As soon as she gets pregnant, a woman should have a doctor. Though pregnancy is a normal physiological process, not a disease, it is a period of increased medical risk. Before modern obstetrics, countless women died from complications of childbirth. Pregnancy nowadays carries minimal risk for most women who are under proper care.

In most cases, pregnancy should not seriously interfere with normal work, social activities, and sexual relations. Some adjustments may need to be made, but there is no reason why a healthy pregnant woman should be treated as if she were ill or handicapped. However, for the pregnancy to progress normally, appropriate *prenatal* ("before birth") *care* is necessary to safeguard the health of the mother and the baby (Taylor and Pernoll, 1987). Teenage mothers (below 15) and older mothers (over 35) are especially vulnerable to complications of pregnancy and need to be watched with particular care for signs of complications.

### Nutrition and Exercise

During pregnancy, a woman does not need to "eat for two," as conventional wisdom claims, but she does need about 200 calories above her normal daily intake (a grand total of 40,000 calories throughout pregnancy) (Moghissi, 1982). Her diet should be rich in proteins, supplemented by vitamins and minerals. Calcium, in particular, is necessary for the growth of the fetal skeleton, iron and niacin for the prevention of anemia.

Pregnancy is no time to indulge in dietary fads. Poor nutrition may endanger the moth-

er's health; it will also seriously compromise the development of the fetus, leading to premature or low-weight babies who are subject to higher death rates and more vulnerable to brain damage and mental retardation. The pregnant woman therefore walks a thin line with regard to food intake. On the one hand she must make sure she gets adequate nutrition; on the other she must watch for excessive weight gain, which carries its own penalties.

A similar situation exists with regard to physical activity. Ample exercise is as essential as adequate rest and sleep. Being pregnant is an added source of stress for the mother's body, and allowance must be made for it. The fatigue and lethargy that mark certain periods of pregnancy are adaptive reactions to induce the mother to rest more. How much to exert oneself is a matter of individual judgment. Some women are in better physical shape than others and can do more. Common sense would exclude hazardous sports, but activities like swimming and walking are beneficial to women with normal pregnancies. Running is a more controversial form of exercise; vigorous exertion may rob the uterus and fetus of oxygenated blood flow, and the repeated bouncing may also be harmful.

### Smoking, Alcohol, and Drugs

The fetus is vulnerable to all harmful substances that cross the placental barrier. Every chemical introduced into the mother's body must be considered with that risk in mind.

*Cigarette smoking* during pregnancy is harmful above and beyond the risks it ordinarily entails. Fetuses carried by women who smoke while pregnant have an increased risk of prematurity, lower birth weight, and death in the perinatal period (before and soon after birth) (Baird and Wilcox, 1985; Neiberg et al., 1985). Children born to mothers who are heavy smokers carry almost twice the risk of the children of nonsmokers of developing impulsive behavioral disturbances in childhood. They also are more likely to have lower IQs and poorer motor skills (Dunn et al., 1977). A woman who is a smoker but quits no later than mid-pregnancy does not risk similar effects to the fetus.

Heavy drinking by a pregnant woman can cause serious abnormalities in the child (*fetal alcohol syndrome*), including birth defects and mental retardation (Haynes, 1982). Even moderate drinking (one or two drinks a day) or a single "binge" may be enough to cause fetal damage.

The active ingredients in marijuana cross the placenta and have been shown to cause fetal damage in some animals (Harbison and Mantilla-Plata, 1972). Though the influence of smoking marijuana in pregnant women remains unclear, it would be safer to avoid its use during pregnancy and nursing.

The use of narcotics by the mother exposes the fetus to especially high risks, including addiction, which necessitates a gradual withdrawal after birth. Cocaine-addicted babies have recently increased in number in hospitals in the United States, with long-term consequences for growth and behavior.

In principle, *any* chemical substance or drug can be harmful to the fetus. Not only *teratogens* (substances that cause birth defects) like Thalidomide but commonly used items like aspirin and Valium pose risks. Similarly, some steroid hormones can have serious effects on fetal development that are manifested years later (Chapter 10). A pregnant woman should take as little medication as possible, and only with her doctor's approval.

## COMPLICATIONS OF PREGNANCY

Until the middle of the 19th century, *puerperal fever* or childbed fever caused the death of one woman in ten giving birth in hospitals. In 1847, after Ignaz Semmelweiss established the infectious origin of this illness, physicians began to disinfect their hands before delivery, and the mortality rate dropped dramatically. Currently, the maternal death rate in the United States is 9.4 maternal deaths per 100,000 births, or about one death in 10,000 births (as against 70 per 10,000 births in Bangladesh) (Thompson, 1986). Uncontrolled bleeding following delivery is currently the most common cause of maternal death in the United States.

### Difficulties in Carrying to Term

The most serious problem in the first trimester is *miscarriage* or *spontaneous abortion,* which accounts for the termination of 10–20 percent of pregnancies (three out of four occur before the sixth week). In about 60 percent of these cases a defect in the fetus is the probable cause (Scott, 1986). In the rest the miscarriage is due to some condition in the mother, such as illness, malnutrition, or trauma.

Another complication of pregnancy is *toxemia* (or *eclampsia*). The cause of toxemia is unknown; presumably a toxin produced by the body causes high blood pressure, headaches, protein in the urine, and the retention of fluids, causing swelling in feet, ankles, and other tissues. Toxemia is a condition that occurs only in pregnant women, usually in the last trimester, affecting some 6 percent of all pregnancies, but as high as 20 percent of women who are not under prenatal care (Mabie and Sibai, 1987).

As mentioned before, the blastocyst may become implanted in a site other than the uterus (97 percent in the fallopian tube), resulting in *ectopic pregnancy.* Its reported incidence varies from 1 in 80 to 1 in 200 of live births (25,000 to 30,000 cases a year in the United States (Droegemueller, 1986). It is usually caused when the progress of the blastocyst down the fallopian tube is blocked, often by pelvic inflammatory disease (Chapter 5). It is more common among older women. Though most ectopic pregnancies abort early, if they advance far enough the tube will rupture, with dangerous bleeding in the mother and death of the fetus.

During the third trimester, *premature birth* is the most serious concern (Pernoll, 1987). Because the date of conception is not always accurately estimated and because the age and weight of the fetus are highly correlated, prematurity used to be defined by weight rather than age. However, modern diagnostic methods, including ultrasound, allow doctors to determine the developmental level of the fetus and the expected birth date more accurately. Also, other reasons for babies weighing less than normal have been discovered, as important as prematurity. An infant who weighs less than 5 pounds 8 ounces (2.5 kg) at birth is considered to be of *low birth weight*. The mortality rate among premature or small infants is directly related to size: the smaller the infant, the poorer are its chances for survival.

The lower limit of a successful pregnancy is one that results in an infant's survival. Normally, fetuses are assumed to be *viable*—able to survive outside of the uterus—28 weeks after the last menstrual period of the mother. Fetuses typically weigh about 1000 grams at this stage. Both weight and length of gestation are important in determining viability. If delivered at the end of six months, the fetus may live for a few hours to a few days. With heroic efforts 5–10 percent of babies weighing no less than two pounds (900 grams) may live. A few infants born at less than 24 weeks of gestation have survived, as have a few others weighing less than 600 grams, but there is no reliable case of survival of any infant born at less than 24 weeks and weighing less than 600 grams (Tietze, 1983).

Fetuses can now be legally aborted up to 24 weeks. It is possible that some of them could survive with extraordinary efforts. The availability of a highly specialized neonatal intensive care unit is one of the critical determinants of whether or not a baby will be able to survive a premature birth. Continuing advances in medical technology will probably make it possible to sustain life for increasing numbers of such very prematurely-born infants, which further complicates the ongoing controversy on abortion (Chapters 7 and 22).

An estimated 7 percent of births in the United States are premature. Low birth weight may be associated with various maternal illnesses (such as high blood pressure, heart disease, and syphilis), heavy cigarette smoking, and multiple pregnancies; half the time the cause of prematurity or low birth weight is unknown.

Not all women are equally vulnerable to the complications of pregnancy. A woman's general health, her age, and the quality of prenatal care are all significant factors. Pregnancies before age 17 run a higher risk of toxemia, low birth weight, and infant mortality. These problems are often compounded by ignorance, negligence, and poor care.

Women who wish to become pregnant after age 35 face special problems. To start with, they are less likely to succeed, because of reduced fertility. If they do get pregnant, they run a higher risk of miscarriage and of having children with certain birth defects. However, with proper care many women who are in their thirties or even older are capable of bearing perfectly normal children.

## Birth Defects

The *infant mortality rate* is the number of infants who die within the first year of life; the current rate in the United States is 14.0 per 1000 live births. The *neonatal mortality rate* is the number of live-born infants who die within 28 days after birth, currently 9.8 per 1000.

A variety of maternal ailments harm the fetus, but developmental problems also arise independent of the mother. Abnormalities of structure or function present at birth are called *congenital malformations* or *birth defects*. They affect 3 percent of all live births. In 70 percent of cases there is no identifiable cause; about 20 percent are due to genetic factors inherited from the parents; 10 percent are due to chemicals (often drugs and alcohol used by the mother), radiation, infections, and other causes (Oakley, 1978).

One chromosomal disorder is *Down's syndrome*, which results when an egg has an extra chromosome in the nucleus (more likely in women over age 35). The condition results in severe mental retardation and defective internal organs. It affects one in 800 births, but the incidence rises sharply with maternal age to one in 300 births at age 35, and 1 in 40 births at age 45. For men older than 55, age is similarly linked to a higher incidence of this defect in the offspring.

Among infectious conditions, particularly damaging are certain viruses. German measles (*rubella*), for instance, if contracted during pregnancy in the first trimester causes serious defects in hearing, vision, and the heart, and mental retardation in up to 50 percent of cases.

Congenital disorders other than birth defects include sexually transmitted diseases, such as syphilis and AIDS, which the fetus contracts from the mother (Chapter 5). Another serious condition, whose symptoms become manifest soon after birth, is *Rh incompatibility*. The *Rh factor* is present (positive) or absent (negative) in human blood. When the mother is Rh-negative and the baby Rh-positive, the mother's body produces antibodies against the Rh factor. They destroy the red blood cells of the fetus, causing anemia, jaundice, and sometimes death. The development of Rh incompatibility can be prevented in Rh-negative pregnant women by medications that neutralize antibody formation. The condition is treated in the newborn by special transfusions (Durfee, 1987).

## INFERTILITY

In our preoccupation with new life, let us not lose sight of the opposite—the inability to reproduce. *Infertility* means failure of a woman to conceive or of a man to impregnate after trying for a period of time (usually one year). *Sterility* is permanent infertility (Marshall, 1987).

The world may have more people than it needs, but for an individual couple the failure to have children can be deeply frustrating. As we said earlier, about one in ten marriages in the United States are childless after attempts to conceive for a year or longer. Another one in ten couples would like to have more children than they do but cannot (Menning, 1977). The incidence of infertility among married women aged 20 to 24 (the most fertile age group) jumped 177 percent between 1965 and 1982 (Wallis, 1984). Much of this increase has been due to the increase in pelvic inflammatory disease (Chapter 5).

### Causes
The most important general factor that governs fertility is age. Men and women become fertile after puberty. Women cease to be fertile following the menopause, whereas the fertility of men is gradually reduced (but not completely lost) as they grow older. Even during the reproductively active years, age influences fertility (Box 6.4).

Infertility in a couple is due to the male partner in about 40 percent of cases and to the female partner in another 40 percent; in 20 percent both partners contribute to the problem. The most frequent cause of male infertility is a low sperm count; when the ejaculate contains fewer than 20 million sperm per milliliter, impregnation becomes highly unlikely. Additional causes are defects in a large proportion of sperm and blockage somewhere in the tubal system. These problems may be due to developmental abnormalities in the testes (including undescended testes), infections (including sexually transmitted diseases), exposure to radiation or chemicals, severe malnutrition, and general debilitating conditions. Steroid hormones will also inhibit spermatogenesis by suppressing gonadotropin production.

The most common causes of female infertility are the failure to ovulate and blockage of fallopian tubes. A large variety of causes may account for these problems, especially defects of reproductive organs, hormonal disorders, diseases of the ovary, severe malnutrition, chronic ailments, drug addiction, and scarring of the fallopian tubes by pelvic infections. The problem may even be psychosomatic—the anxiousness to get pregnant prevents it (Moghissi and Evans, 1982).

### Psychological Impact
The inability to have a child can be quite distressing, and the desire to become a parent may become almost an obsession. Traditionally, women have been thought to be especially desirous of having children as a fulfillment of their female "destiny."

Motherhood continues to be important for many women, but infertility also confronts many men with a difficult situation. In addition to the desire to continue their lineage, a man's fertility deeply involves his self-esteem,

# Box 6.4

## CHILDBEARING AND AGE

Only in humans, among our near relatives, does the end of female reproductive life precede the tidal wave of aging by many years. Evolutionary theory has it that the amount of energy put into begetting offspring is directly related to mortality; that is, life cycles seem genetically disposed to last about as long as it takes to reproduce. Thus, once monkeys and apes can no longer produce babies in the wild, they soon die. Not so for humans. Women come to an end of their reproductive capacity and they and their spouses live on for another 20, 30, or 40 years.

But consider the world in which we evolved— say, the world of 50,000 years ago. Life expectancy at birth was around 30 years, with the average skewed by high mortality in infancy. If you look now at life expectancy *after* childhood, in hunter-gatherer tribes that still exist much as they did in the Stone Age—the !Kung San, or Bushmen, of the Kalahari Desert in southern Africa, for instance— old age, as we understand it, is far from a sure thing. According to studies done by anthropologists Nancy Howell and Richard Lee, the average life expectancy, if you've made it to 15, is 55.

But interestingly, the average age at which a !Kung woman has her last child is about 39. The numbers may tell an evolutionary story: one that explains that humans are not so different from other animals after all. It's just that the human mother needs to stay around to care for her offspring, and humans have an extraordinarily long childhood. There needs to be enough energy to enable an animal to complete its reproductive cycle— to perpetuate itself. The last child, born, say, when the mother was 39, needs care to grow to an age at which its own reproduction could begin, at 16 or so, to ensure continuity of the lineage. The mother could then die at 55 with a certain, as it were, evolutionary peace of mind.

Such theories help explain why the human reproductive clock may have been *designed* to run out about when it does. They don't explain how the clockwork slows down. But new technology and research are beginning to provide that explanation.

. . . An analysis published last year in *Science* by Jane Menken and James Trussel of Princeton and Ulla Larsen of Lunds University in Sweden is among those that have confirmed declines in fertility with age: childlessness rose from around 5 percent in a group whose members married between ages 20 to 24, to around 9 percent in the 25–29 age group. For those marrying in the early 30s it was over 15 percent, in the late 30s, more than 25 percent. For marriages beginning between 40 and 44, it was over 60 percent.

The scarring of the ovary, though dramatic, is only one mechanism of reproductive aging. . . . New research also implicates the womb itself. The uterus, it turns out, loses its hospitality. The environment it creates for implantation and for the maintenance of pregnancy begins to be less suitable. It, too, depends on hormones that help prepare the uterine lining and enable the embryo to function. As the hormones decline, the uterus ages, loses half its weight from age 30 to 50, and begins to dry out. Collagen and elastin—two crucial proteins that make it durable and flexible, as they do skin and connective tissue throughout the body—decline markedly.

. . . Controversy continues about how to advise women. Certainly there is little risk in waiting until the early 30s to have a baby. In the late 30s the risk of involuntary childlessness becomes substantial, and in the early 40s great. Yet motherhood is possible for many women even until age 50 . . . And despite the generally unfavorable odds, there have been many successful in vitro attempts for individual women in their late 30s and early 40s.

Life holds risks, and the intelligent young woman can theoretically try to assess the loss she would feel if she ended up infertile, add in the likelihood of childlessness if she waits to a given age, and weigh the sum against the personal advantages of waiting.

Of course, real life is not that simple. Careers have a logic of their own. And, because most women are not willing to try this alone, the right man must come along. There is the possibility of adoption, though this itself is not emotionally painless. It can result in as much parental satisfaction as comes to biological parents.

How to guess the future? The medical frontier is continuously moving forward. Artificial insemination, in vitro, surrogacy—who knows what's next? Surely one can count on some future chemical magic that will enhance implantation and maintain pregnancy. Yet, neither that hope nor the consola-

tion of evolutionary understanding can erase the discomfort that arises from an arbitrarily waning force of life.

(By Melvin Konner, *New York Times Magazine*, Dec. 27, 1987, pp. 22–23).

---

self-image, and sense of adequacy. To be sterile makes him feel that he has a damaged body and is biologically defective (Schreiner-Engel, 1987).

Men who react most negatively to their infertility treat themselves initially as if they were their only child, getting involved in activities like body building, health foods, and "macho sexuality." They are unlikely to remain married or adopt a child. Other men, who have a more positive approach, get involved in child-rearing activities (like leading youth groups) and remain married. Nonetheless, they are less eager than their wives to adopt a child.

Infertility also affects a man's sexual life. He may feel less attractive sexually. With initial reactions of disappointment, anger, and grief, sexual interest goes down. Adjustment to infertility is helped by sharing the problem in support groups.[5]

## Treatment

Diagnosing infertility involves both the female and male. Once the problem has been pinpointed, it can often be corrected. Sometimes the woman takes a fertility drug like *clomiphene*, which induces the pituitary to produce LH and FSH, or, failing that, *human menopausal gonadotropin* (HMG), which acts directly on the ovary. In a high proportion of cases these drugs induce ovulation and make pregnancy possible. In fact, the ovaries are often overstimulated, resulting in multiple pregnancies. Also, microsurgery may succeed in opening blocked tubes.

Among couples who seek medical help for infertility, 40 percent subsequently conceive;

in another 40 percent the cause of infertility is found but cannot be cured; in the remaining 20 percent no cause is detected, yet pregnancy does not occur (Moghissi and Evans, 1986). Many couples who are not able to conceive will give up the idea of having children or will adopt a child, but some now go to greater lengths to conceive, by resorting to artificial insemination and surrogate mothers.

*Artificial insemination* is the placement of semen in the vagina by means other than sexual intercourse. When the source of the semen is the husband, this approach raises no unusual problems; it is simply a means of pooling sperm from several ejaculations (obtained through masturbation) to overcome a low sperm count. When the semen comes from a donor because the husband is sterile, then many concerns arise—psychological, social, and legal. There are no serious technical problems; 75 percent of women get pregnant if artificially inseminated with fresh donor sperm.

The donor is carefully selected for blood type, freedom from sexually transmitted diseases, physical appearance, general health, and genetic background. Though some couples select the donor personally, his identity is usually kept secret; he never sees the child, nor even knows if the artificial insemination worked.[6]

Artificial insemination can be done with fresh or frozen semen. Frozen sperm is safer, because it can be screened for the AIDS virus or other microorganisms before it is used, but it has a lower rate of success. Frozen sperm is kept in *sperm banks* as "fertility in-

---

[5]A national organization called Resolve provides support networks for infertile individuals. Further information may be obtained by calling (617) 643–2424.

[6]For women who "qualify" (by having high IQ, professional achievements, and good health), Germinal Choice in California will provide frozen sperm from Nobel laureates.

surance" by some men who are to undergo vasectomy (Chapter 7).

When it is the wife who is sterile, the male counterpart of artificial insemination is to have another woman get impregnated artificially with the semen of the husband. The *surrogate mother* carries the baby to birth and then relinquishes it to the couple, as stipulated by a contract. The comparison with artificial insemination is, however, not quite apt; for the surrogate mother to give up her child is a much more wrenching experience than for the sperm donor to suspect that he may be the biological father of a child somewhere. The legality of surrogate contracts has come under question (Chapter 22) and the practice raises a host of social concerns.

In 1978, a more astounding alternative became reality with the birth of Louise Brown, after a successful *in vitro fertilization (IVF)*. Over the next ten years, 1000 "test-tube babies" were born at the clinic where doctors Patrick Steptoe and Robert Edwards had developed the technique.

The procedure is to induce ovulation in the mother (who usually has defective fallopian tubes) through drug stimulation, which makes multiple eggs mature simultaneously. These mature ova are "harvested" about six at a time through a small incision in the follicles protruding from the ovarian surface. The eggs are extracted and fertilized with the father's sperm in an incubated laboratory dish containing appropriate nutrients. After the fertilized egg has reached the blastocyst stage, it is transferred to the mother's uterus, which has meanwhile been primed with hormones. From then on the embryo develops as in any ordinary pregnancy, making it possible for a woman to conceive who otherwise could not have done so.

Because the chances of success are not better than 20 percent several fertilized eggs are implanted at once. As a result, multiple pregnancies are common, including triplets, unless some of the embryos are selectively aborted. The cost of finally achieving pregnancy through IVF may run into the six figures.

Finally, in cases where a woman cannot ovulate, it is now possible for her to become pregnant by *embryo transfer*. In this method a donor woman is artificially impregnated with the sperm of the infertile woman's husband. The developing embryo is then flushed out of the donor's uterus and implanted in the infertile woman's uterus. Sometimes the embryo is frozen and implantation is attempted later. A number of normal babies have already been delivered by this method.

These technological developments and yet others to come are scientifically dazzling, but they have unleashed social, ethical, and legal problems of unprecedented complexity (Francoeur, 1985). Some see these procedures as a ray of hope for thousands of sterile women who wish to experience motherhood; for others they herald an Orwellian world of assembly-line produced humanity. For some, surrogate motherhood reduces women to commercial producers of infants and denigrates and exploits them. A counterview argues that a woman should have control over her body and use it for reproduction as she chooses, with the proper safeguards for all concerned. These issues are of great importance, and we shall reconsider them as part of our perspective on sex and society.

## REVIEW QUESTIONS

1. Trace the journey of the sperm from its origin in the testes till it fertilizes the egg; then list the stages the fertilized egg goes through until implanted in the uterus.

2. How do pregnancy tests work?

3. Describe the main features of a woman's physical and emotional experience of pregnancy through childbirth.

4. What does prenatal care entail?

5. What are the causes and remedies of infertility?

## THOUGHT QUESTIONS

1. How can you determine on physiological grounds when a developing organism is a "human being"?

2. To how long a period of maternity leave should a working woman be entitled at full pay? When should she use her leave time?

3. What should the role of the father be during a woman's pregnancy, at the time of birth, and in the postpartum period?

4. What type of artificial insemination would you prohibit, if any?

## SUGGESTED READINGS

Ashford, J. (1983). *The whole birth catalogue*. A broad survey of childbirth options. Trumansburg, N.Y.: Crossing Press.

Ingelman-Sandberg, A., Wirsen, C., and Nilsson, L. (1980). *A child is born* (2nd ed.). New York: Delacorte. Superb photographs of embryonal development with a concise and nontechnical text on pregnancy and childbirth.

Pritchard, J.A., MacDonald, P.C., and Gant, N.F. (1985). *Williams obstetrics* (17th ed.). New York: Appleton-Century-Crofts. A standard obstetrical text. Comprehensive and technical.

Witt, R.L., and Michael, J.M., (1982). *Mom, I'm Pregnant*. New York: Stein and Day. Clearly written book addressed to teenage girls who think they are, or are, pregnant.

# Contraception and Abortion

## CHAPTER

# 7

*Birth control affects nearly everybody—people either have used it, will use it or, at the very least, are against it.*

CARL DJERASSI,
*The Politics of Contraception*

## OUTLINE

PATTERNS OF CONTRACEPTIVE
   USE
Reasons for Using Contraceptives
Prevalence of Contraceptive Use
Reasons for *Not* Using
   Contraceptives
Taking Responsibility
CONTRACEPTIVE METHODS
Abstinence
Hormonal Methods
   Development of the Pill
   Types of Birth Control Pills
   Side Effects
   The Post-Coital Pill
The Intrauterine Device
Barrier Methods
   The Diaphragm
   The Cervical Cap
   The Contraceptive Sponge
   The Condom
Spermicides
Fertility Awareness Techniques
   The Calendar Method
   The Basal Body Temperature
      Method
   The Cervical Mucus Method

Prolonged Nursing
Withdrawal
Sterilization
   Male Sterilization
   Female Sterilization
Future Birth Control
   Male Methods
   Female Methods
ABORTION
Methods of Abortion
   Vacuum Aspiration
   Dilation and Curettage (D and C)
   Dilation and Evacuation (D and E)
   Saline Abortions
   Prostaglandin Abortions
   Pregnancy Reductions
   Experimental Methods
Psychological Aspects of Abortion
   Reactions to Unwanted Pregnancy
   Deciding among the Alternatives
   Reactions to Abortion

Will you have children, how many, and when? If you live in the United States, you probably take for granted your right and your ability to control that. Nevertheless, despite many cheap, effective contraceptive options, millions of women still have unwanted pregnancies. Worldwide, the availability and willingness to use effective contraception is one of the most critical issues. The growth of the world's population is potentially catastrophic.

There is nothing new about trying to have sex without pregnancy (Box 7.1). What is new today is that we have highly effective and reasonably safe ways to do it, and that we can offer them to large populations as a matter of public policy (Noonan, 1967; Djerassi, 1981).

*Contraception* ("against conception") and *birth control* (a term coined by Margaret Sanger in 1914) both mean attempts at avoiding reproduction or attaining *fertility control*. The spacing of children through birth control is called *family planning* (Tatum, 1987). Although the result is the same, there is a valid distinction between preventing pregnancy through contraception and terminating it through abortion, as there is between abortion and infanticide (killing a newborn or letting it die). Infanticide has been practiced in some cultures to survive harsh conditions (among Eskimos), to ease population pressure (in Polynesia), and to eliminate abnormal offspring or the issue of illicit relations (in ancient Greece). The ritual of first-born sacrifice has also been known since biblical times as a means of offering to the deity one's most precious possession (Genesis 22). Infanticide is no longer permitted in any contemporary society, although it is still practiced illegally.

This chapter looks at the biological and behavioral aspects of contraception and abortion. We will deal with the moral and legal aspects in Chapters 22 to 23.

## PATTERNS OF CONTRACEPTIVE USE

There are many reasons for not wanting children, or not wanting them at a particular time. Some reasons are personal: many couples wish to plan a family, others to avoid parenthood altogether. Apart from individual concerns, the bearing of children has many consequences at the national and global levels. Personal and societal interests do not always coincide, so we will discuss them separately.

### Reasons for Using Contraceptives

One major reason for avoiding parenthood is the couple's relationship. Although women occasionally choose to become single parents, most people wait till they are married, or have a stable relationship, before having children. Another is the general tendency to limit family size, especially among the middle classes. Unlike earlier times, when infant mortality rates were high, parents now can be fairly certain that their children will grow to maturity; there is no need to have many children to ensure that at least a few will survive to adulthood. In the industrialized world, fewer than 2 out of 100 babies die before the age of one; in the developing countries the infant mortality rate is 10 out of 100 babies (Camp and Spiedel, 1987).

Moreover, whereas in the past children were an added financial asset to the family through their labor, rearing children is now expensive. The estimated cost of raising one child to age 22, in a family of average income (excluding the cost of residential college education), is $215,000 in 1982 dollars (Ory et al., 1983). Therefore, not many parents can afford to have large families without straining their financial and personal resources. Other reasons for avoiding or postponing pregnancy include the health of the mother and career aspirations of both parents.

Childlessness used to mean the renunciation of sexual relationships or the inability to bear children. Sexually active individuals now have the choice not only to postpone childbearing but to avoid it altogether. Some people think the advantages of childlessness—in income, freedom, career, or health—outweigh the benefits of parenthood. To express the positive side of their choice, these couples are called *childfree* or said to follow a *childfree lifestyle* (Cooper et al., 1978).

# Box 7.1

## EARLY CONTRACEPTION

People have been attempting to prevent unwanted pregnancies for millenia.* With the exception of hormones, most of the contraceptive methods have their ancient precursors, which were based on the right ideas but were subject to the technological limitations of the time.

Probably the oldest and most common contraceptive practice has been withdrawal before ejaculation, attested to in the Old Testament (Gen. 8:8–11). The oldest known medical recipes to prevent conception are contained in the Egyptian Petri papyrus of 1850 B.C. Ancient Egyptians used vaginal pastes containing crocodile dung, honey, and sodium carbonate both as a barrier and a spermicidal agent. They also relied on vaginal douches containing mixtures of wine, garlic, and fennel.

In ancient Greece and Rome, there was much concern over contraception. People relied on absorbent materials, root and herb potions, devices to block off the uterus, and more permanent means of sterilization. Soranus, a Roman physician in the second century A.D., gives a clear account of the fertility control practices of the period, distinguishing between contraception and abortion-inducing agents (recommending reliance on the former). Through Islamic physicians, this classical knowledge passed on to medieval Europe and formed the basis of contraceptive practice up to the end of the 17th century.

Much of early contraception relied on barrier

*For a comprehensive history of contraception, see Himes (1970), Suitters (1967), and Draper (1976). Dawson et al. (1980) discuss fertility control in the United States before modern contraceptives were developed.

methods. Many materials were used in various cultures to provide obstacles to the passage of sperm (Cooper, 1928). Some Native American groups blocked the cervix with soft clay; the Japanese inserted paper; the French, balls of silk. Various types of sponge and cotton balls were also used, sometimes with medicated mineral oil or mild acid ointments to serve as spermicides. Pessaries made of gold, silver, or rubber have also been used in Europe to plug the cervix. They were inserted by a physician at the end of one menstrual period and removed at the onset of the next period. Intrauterine pessaries were extended into the uterus to decrease the likelihood of their slipping out of place.

Along with these rational, even if not very effective, methods, countless magical means have been resorted to, especially in preliterate societies, to avoid pregnancy (Ford and Beach, 1951; Gregersen, 1983). Among some North African tribes, for example, water that had been used for washing a dead person was secretly given to a woman to drink to make her infertile. In another group, a woman would eat bread into which had been ground a honeycomb containing a few dead bees. (The magical association between death and sterility was presumably the basis for these practices).

Other contraceptive attempts were more farfetched. Moroccan men would turn a special ring on a finger from one side to another following coitus. Papuan women of New Guinea who did not want a child tied a rope tightly around their waist during coitus. They also washed carefully following it, which probably helped a little and kept the two practices associated together.

---

Some couples arrive at the decision not to have children through a series of postponements; others decide early and enter marriage with that understanding (Veevers, 1974). The proportion of women who express their intention early to remain childless is quite small (about 6 percent). This group, especially its male members, has not yet been well studied.

It has been suggested that independence and achievement motivation among women make the choice of childlessness more likely. Such individuals must contend both with their own mixed feelings and with the pressures of our *pronatalist* society, which views parenthood as a normative part of adult life (Houseknecht, 1978).

# Box 7.2

## POPULATION CONTROL

The alarm over the dire consequences of population explosion was sounded by the English clergyman and economist Thomas R. Malthus (1766–1834). Malthus argued in *An Essay on the Principle of Population* (1798), that population grows exponentially by doubling, while the means of subsistence expands by simple increments. To avoid the inevitable prospects of famine and war that would result from this discrepancy, he advocated abstinence and late marriage. His successors shifted the emphasis to contraception, starting the *population control movement,* which attained great visibility in the 1960s (Ehrlich, 1968).

From human beginnings in prehistory, it took until 1830 for the population of the world to reach 1 billion. During the next century this figure doubled to 2 billion, and in our century it doubled again to 4 billion in less than half that time and has already grown to 5 billion (see the figure).

This measure of *doubling time* provides a dramatic picture of population growth and also shows it to be a highly regional pattern. For instance, the Third World is growing 2 percent per year and will double its population in 34 years, assuming its present rate of growth. Meanwhile the population of the more developed world (including the United States) is growing at 0.6 percent per year and will double in 122 years. At a further extreme, Pakistan, growing at 2.8 percent per year, will double its population in 25 years, whereas Italy will require 693 years to do the same at its current growth rate of 0.1 percent per year (Camp and Speidel, 1987).

When births equal deaths in a population, we have *zero population growth* (ZPG), which the advocates of population control call ideal. Not everyone shares this view. Some Third World countries (and ethnic groups within the United States) perceive population control as an attempt to curtail their growth and their power (some call it "genocide"). Some economists in the United States advocate the faster growth of the population so as to generate a wider base of tax revenue and enrich the populace in other ways (Julian, 1986).

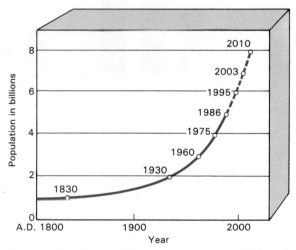

Increase in the world population since 1800 and projections until 2010.

---

A few people limit family size primarily out of concern for the world's expanding population. This matter is of great importance for social agencies and governments, particularly in developing countries with explosive rates of population growth (Box 7.2).

### Prevalence of Contraceptive Use

We can group contraceptive devices by their modes of action. There are hormonal methods (like the birth control pill); intrauterine devices (IUDs); barrier methods (condom, cervical cap, diaphragm, vaginal sponge); spermicides (foam, jelly, cream); withdrawal; and methods that rely on periodic abstinence. In addition, there are various agents that induce abortion (abortifacients) and permanent ways of achieving infertility through sterilization.

Which of these methods of birth control could you use? It depends on where you live in the world. For example, in Nigeria—the

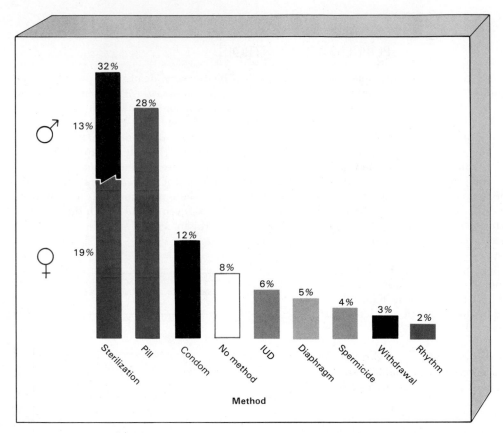

Figure 7.1    Percentage of women aged 15–44 and their partners using various contraceptive methods and no method (although not intending pregnancy) in the United States, 1982.

eighth most populous nation in the world— only 5.9 percent of all women have access to artificial birth control. About half the world population now has good to excellent access, 31 percent has fair access, and 19 percent have poor to very poor access. The level of industrial development generally correlates with availability of contraceptives, but not always. For instance, the USSR provides only fair access among developed countries; despite liberal laws on reproductive rights, contraceptives are difficult to obtain, and couples rely heavily on abortion (Population Crisis Committee, 1987). Relative costs and other factors (such as public education and dominant religion) are also different in other countries (Hatcher et al., 1988).

In the United States, because of free public birth control clinics and government funding for family planning services, everyone in most areas has access to safe, effective methods of birth control. As a result, the majority of the married female population aged 15 to 44 uses some contraceptive method. As shown in Figure 7.1, sterilization is the most common method in the United States, accounting for 19 percent of females and 13 percent of males. The Pill is next, with 28 percent, but it ranks as the single most frequently used device by women. It is also by far the most common method among the population aged 20 to 24 years, and to a lesser extent among those aged 15 to 19 and 25 to 29 years. Condoms and withdrawal are the only exclusively male methods; sterilization can be performed on either sex; the rest are all female methods.

At present, the main contraceptive responsibility clearly falls on women, burdening them with what many people think should be a shared concern. There are physiological reasons why it has been more feasible so far to develop female methods of contraception, especially hormonal methods (Djerassi, 1981). Technological breakthroughs and changes in social attitudes may alter this picture, but because it is only women who can get pregnant, contraception is likely to remain a matter of more concern to them.

Under ideal conditions, the only women who would get pregnant would be those who wished to do so. Instead, less than half (45 percent) of all pregnancies in the United States are intended; 40 percent occur before the woman wants them, or are mistimed (often involving unwed teenagers); and 15 percent are unwanted altogether. These figures do not mean that over half of all fertile women do not use contraceptives; rather, they reflect repeated nonuse by a smaller proportion. How many of these unplanned pregnancies result in unwanted children? Forty-six percent of unintended pregnancies are aborted, but 41 percent result in births (and 13 percent are miscarried). Some women are happy with an unplanned pregnancy after the fact, but others who do not get abortions are "stuck." Getting an abortion may not be an easy matter for them. Unfortunately, as with population problems on a global scale, these women are often the ones who can least afford the burden.

Especially serious is the situation for teenagers, who account for an estimated 1 million pregnancies a year—or one teenage pregnancy every 30 seconds. Of these teenagers, 30,000 are younger than 15 (Hatcher et al., 1988). Half of teenage women aged 15 to 19 report having engaged in premarital coitus. Of these women, 27 percent never use contraception and 62 percent get pregnant. For the sexually active teenage population as a whole (including contraception users and nonusers) the pregnancy rate is 16 percent per year, as against 11 percent for all women of childbearing age. Re-

cent trends show a somewhat greater use of contraception by young women. For instance, the percentage of those who used any method of contraception at first intercourse went up from 38 percent in 1976 to 49 percent in 1979 (Zelnik and Kantner, 1980). This change has been mainly due to an increased reliance on condoms and on the relatively ineffective method of withdrawal.

In addition to age, contraceptive use correlates with marital status, socioeconomic class, ethnicity, religious affiliation, and other factors (Ory et al., 1983). Younger, unmarried women rely more often on the Pill, less on IUDs, and a great deal on their partners using condoms or withdrawal. These trends are quite fluid, especially among well-educated younger women. For example, on one University of California campus, between 1974 and 1978, the percentage of women using contraceptives who were on the Pill fell from 89 percent to 63 percent and diaphragm usage went from 6 percent to 33 percent, while IUD use remained steady at 8 percent (Harvey, 1980).

### Reasons for *Not* Using Contraceptives

There are two populations that do not use contraceptives for obvious reasons: those who want to get pregnant and those who cannot get pregnant. In the latter group, some are sterile, and others do not engage in coitus. Apart from postmenopausal women, 15 percent of couples of childbearing age are involuntarily childless (Chapter 6). One out of five women aged 15 to 44 is not sexually active; half of teenage women aged 15 to 19 do not currently engage in coitus (Zelnik and Kantner, 1980).

Some 30 million women, or about 28 percent of the childbearing-age female population who are sexually active, do not use contraceptives (Hatcher et al., 1988). Close to 20 percent of them are teenagers; another 10 percent, women in their twenties (Forrest and Henshaw, 1983). It is with this group that we shall be concerned here.

Why is contraception not used? Religion is not the answer. The opposition of the Catholic church has attracted much public discussion

(Chapter 23), but a relatively small proportion of women shun contraception because of it. Among married Catholic women in the United States, two out of three now use a contraceptive device other than rhythm; among those married between 1970 and 1975, the proportion of Catholic couples using contraception was 90.5 percent (Westoff and Jones, 1977). These Catholics use various birth control methods to the same degree as non-Catholics, except for sterilization, which they use less frequently.

What stops people from using birth control is not conscience but ignorance, lack of access to contraceptives, and various psychological and social considerations. There is a great deal of sexual misinformation, particularly among teenagers, even sexually experienced ones. Many think they are "too young" to get pregnant. Although there is in fact a period of relative adolescent infertility before the ovarian cycle becomes well established, it does not offer contraceptive security (Chapter 4). Others assume that it takes repeated intercourse to lead to conception, or that if girls do not reach orgasm they will be protected (Evans et al., 1976). Some have the wrong idea about the safe period of the month; in one study of sexually active teenage girls, 70 percent of whom had taken sex education courses, only one-third knew correctly the period of highest risk (Zelnik, 1979). Some women think they must be sterile because coitus in the past did not result in pregnancy. Teenage boys, on their part, have a tendency to view contraception as a "woman's problem" and to assume that if she says nothing, she must be "safe." Some couples forego contraception for nothing more serious than because it is "too messy" or "too much trouble."

The element of guilt may also play a role. To use contraception clearly implies the intent to engage in sex. Some teenagers believe that it is not morally right to have sexual intercourse outside marriage or a committed love relationship. To be fitted with a contraceptive device or carry condoms on a date, then, proves an immoral intention. To "solve" this dilemma, they engage in sex without contraception and by implication without forethought. On the spur of the moment, the sexual indulgence feels less like a premeditated act.

Similar considerations apply to those who find the expectation of engaging in sex to be unromantic. They think sex should be spontaneous, sweeping the couple off their feet, with caution thrown to the winds. The man with a condom at the ready comes across in this perspective as "exploitative" and interested only in his sexual pleasure; the woman who is always ready is perceived as "promiscuous."

The unpredictable association between sex and pregnancy itself generates a false sense of security. In fact, there is only a 2–4 percent chance that any single act of coitus will lead to pregnancy, but the odds go up to 21 percent on the day of ovulation, and to 90 percent over the period of a year. The more often one has sex, and the more often one has sex in high risk times, the greater is the chance of getting pregnant; as in any gamble, the odds sooner or later catch up.

The willingness to take a chance is a universal human characteristic. We do it all the time, either "just this once" or regularly. Risk-taking behavior in sexual activity is no exception. The relative risks entailed in sexual intercourse and its reproductive consequences are listed in Table 7.1 along with several non-sexual behaviors for comparison.

Some people get pregnant even when it seems to others that they should not, because they want to. Among one group of sexually active teenagers, 7 percent said they wanted to get pregnant and another 9 percent said they would not mind if they did. Many more may have similar motivations without quite being conscious of it. Even under the most inauspicious circumstances, having a baby carries enormous psychological significance. It may represent a teenager's desperate chance to be someone, to have someone to love, and to receive a measure of affection and attention herself. For some young men, impregnating a woman is the ultimate sign of "machismo." Pregnancy is also a powerful tool to hold on to

**Table 7.1  Voluntary Risks**

| RISK | CHANCE OF DEATH IN A YEAR (U.S.) |
|---|---|
| Smoking | 1 in 200 |
| Motorcycling | 1 in 1000 |
| Automobile driving | 1 in 6000 |
| Power boating | 1 in 6000 |
| Rock climbing | 1 in 7500 |
| Playing football | 1 in 25,000 |
| Canoeing | 1 in 100,000 |
| Using tampons (toxic shock) | 1 in 350,000 |
| Having sexual intercourse (pelvic infection) | 1 in 50,000 |
| *Preventing Pregnancy* | |
| Oral contraception— nonsmoker | 1 in 63,000 |
| Oral contraception— smoker | 1 in 16,000 |
| Using IUDs | 1 in 100,000 |
| Using barrier methods | None |
| Using fertility awareness | None |
| Undergoing sterilization | |
| Laparoscopic tubal ligation | 1 in 20,000 |
| Hysterectomy | 1 in 1600 |
| Vasectomy | None |
| *Deciding about Pregnancy* | |
| Continuing pregnancy | 1 in 10,000 |
| Terminating pregnancy | |
| Illegal abortion | 1 in 3000 |
| Legal abortion | |
| Before 9 weeks | 1 in 400,000 |
| 9–12 weeks | 1 in 100,000 |
| 13–16 weeks | 1 in 25,000 |
| After 16 weeks | 1 in 10,000 |

From Hatcher et al., *Contraceptive Technology 1988–89.* New York: Irvington, 1988.

another, to force someone into marriage, to embarrass families, to punish others, and to assert oneself. Some teenagers reportedly get pregnant so as to be entitled to receive welfare payments, which then will allow them to leave home.

Additional obstacles to contraceptive usage are the practical problems of availability, cost, and access to contraceptive information and devices. Pharmacy shelves are full of condoms, but a person must still go to the counter to pay for them, which may be embarrassing, particularly for the young. Planned Parenthood clinics will give out advice and contraceptives, but clients first must be willing to accept their own sexual intentions in going to the clinic, which also may not be an easy matter. Where society makes it mandatory that teenagers' parents be notified of their receiving contraceptive help, you can imagine the reluctance to seek it.

Concern over the side effects of contraceptive agents is a final stumbling block. It may get so exaggerated that people fear to use them. However, the risks in contraception are minimal. Table 7.1 puts them in perspective.

### Taking Responsibility

We have looked at the reasons why people use and avoid contraception. How will you act in this respect?

The first step in making a decision is coming to terms with your sexuality both in general and in a particular relationship, on a specific occasion. The question is whether or not you will use birth control, not just in principle, but in the concrete context of a given sexual act. There are many cogent psychological and moral reasons to engage or not to engage in sex, but there are never any good reasons, only bad ones, for getting pregnant unless the circumstances are right. Effective contraception starts with that conviction.

Of equal importance is knowing your vulnerability. A woman needs to monitor her high-risk periods around the time of ovulation and be aware of those times in her life when she may use contraception less reliably. These times tend to cluster around periods of transition: the time of becoming fertile during adolescence, and infertile during the menopause; at the start of a new sexual relationship; early in marriage; and following childbirth or abortion. Women are more apt to forget contraception in periods of stress, such as during or following separation, divorce, breakups, and lovers' quarrels. Moving away from home, joining a new circle of friends, and experimenting with a different lifestyle are other situations where sexual activity may take place before you are consistent about contraception (Miller, 1973a). Under any circumstances, the responsibility is still yours.

## CONTRACEPTIVE METHODS

Whether you are a woman or a man, the ideal contraceptive would be socially acceptable, usable by either sex, fail-safe, free of side effects, aesthetically inoffensive, and readily and cheaply available. No such contraceptive now exists or is likely to in the foreseeable future (Djerassi, 1981).

What we have instead is a set of alternatives with a varying mix of assets and liabilities. Each method must be evaluated not just in the abstract, but with regard to the needs of a particular individual at a given time. No contraceptive method, other than abstinence from intercourse, is 100 percent foolproof in preventing pregnancy, but some methods in combination come close to it.

The only way to avoid pregnancy with absolute certainty is not to have sexual intercourse or to become sterilized. Those who are not willing to do either must be prepared to take certain contraceptive risks, just as they take risks every time they step into a car or cross the street. The sensible course is to take calculated risks—to know what benefits are likely at what probable cost.

The effectiveness of contraceptive methods is measured in terms of failure rates: the number of married (therefore regularly sexually active) women out of a hundred who get pregnant when a given method is used over a year. A further distinction is made between the best or the *lowest reported rates* of failure and the *typical failure rate,* or the failure rate of users who have not been given the extra training, selection, and attention subjects get in the research studies in which the lowest rates are established (Trussell and Kost, 1987). Human

error is responsible for the discrepancy between the two rates.

Table 7.2 (page 207) summarizes the first-year failure rates for all the methods to be discussed. For example, if a woman is using a diaphragm the typical failure rate is about 18 percent. This figure means 18 out of 100 sexually active "typical" women relying on the diaphragm are likely to get pregnant during their first year using it.

### Abstinence

To refrain from engaging in sexual intercourse by choice, or abstinence, is the most certain and safest method of avoiding pregnancy. If sexual intercourse only served reproductive needs, abstinence would be the most sensible contraceptive method. However, sexual relations serve other needs, and abstinence may prevent their fulfillment, although abstinence from coitus certainly does not preclude other forms of sexual expression or orgasm.

Abstinence remains an important means of avoiding pregnancy. Until the advent of effective contraception it was actually the only safe and certain way. In the 19th century, abstaining to limit family size was the key principle of the birth control movement. Recently there has been a resurgence of the idea. Teenagers are urged to "just say no" to avoid pregnancy and sexually transmitted diseases.

However desirable abstinence is in principle, it is not a reliable method for many people in practice. There are always going to be those who engage in coitus no matter what the consequences, especially the young. There will always be the temptation to make love "just this once." For these people other methods of contraception are more realistic.

Bear in mind that getting pregnant poses a considerably higher threat to health than using a contraceptive, particularly before age 15 (Chapter 6). No less serious is the daunting prospect of bringing an unwanted child into the world.

### Hormonal Methods

Hormones are the basic physiological way of dealing with birth control, because they turn off the reproductive process at its source. They are the most effective of all reversible contraceptive methods today. Properly used, the most effective hormonal methods provide over 99 percent protection. On the negative side, hormonal intervention intrudes the most on the body, and its side effects are the most serious. On the positive side, hormones have additional health benefits, which other methods do not.

Hormones can be taken as pills, by injection, and through other means like implantation under the skin. So far oral use has proven by far the most practical method.

Development of the Pill   Oral contraception became commercially available only in the early 1960s, but its use spread so rapidly and widely that it has come to be known simply as "the Pill."[1] Some 60 million women worldwide and 10 million in the United States now rely on the Pill, making it the most extensively used reversible contraceptive measure in the world. In the United States it accounts for 40 percent of contraceptive use by never-married women and 13 percent of married women (Hatcher et al., 1988). Pills are the most popular of all methods among younger women and teenagers; among women in this group who are sexually active, about half rely on it (Forrest and Henshaw, 1983).

The development of the Pill was a natural consequence of our modern understanding of the ovarian cycle. In the 1930s, it was established that progesterone inhibited ovulation and could prevent pregnancy. Simultaneously, the estrogens were chemically isolated and used to treat certain menstrual disorders. The first oral contraceptive chemical substance (*norethindrone*) was synthesized in 1951 at the Syntex laboratories in Mexico City, followed by wide-scale clinical trials in Puerto Rico in 1956. The first Pill (Enovid) became commercially available on the market in the 1960s.[2] Over the

next two decades, oral contraceptives were studied more extensively than any other drug, because they are used by millions of healthy women for a critically important reason (Djerassi, 1981).

Types of Birth Control Pills   The Pill has the major advantage of freeing the couple from having to take contraceptive measures just before, during, or right after sexual intercourse; sexual activity is not interrupted. Also, more than any other contraceptive device, the Pill puts a woman in full and effective charge of her own reproductive process.

Birth control pills contain various combinations of *synthetic steroids* that imitate estrogens and progestins. They inhibit the secretion of LH and FSH by the anterior pituitary, preventing ovulation (Chapter 4). They also influence the structure of the uterine endometrium, making implantation difficult, and cause thickening and increased acidity of the cervical mucus, making it a more effective barrier to sperm (Gilman et al., 1985).

Oral contraceptives come in several forms (Figure 7.2). One of the most common is the *combination Pill,* which consists mainly of progesterone and a small amount of estrogen. The combination Pill is taken once a day for 21 days. The woman then stops for seven days, during which withdrawal bleeding simulates the normal menstrual flow; then she resumes taking the Pill.

To help the user stay on schedule, manufacturers sometimes add seven inactive pills (or vitamin tablets) colored differently to be taken on the off days; thus the woman simply takes a pill of some variety every day. If she misses taking a birth control pill for a day, she takes two pills the next day; if two are missed, then both are added to the pill of the third day. If the Pill is missed for three days or more, the method may not be reliable for the rest of that cycle. Some other form of contraception must be used until the woman menstruates and then gets back on track by starting her next set of pills.

The combination Pill has been the most effective form of reversible contraception in

---

[1]It was Aldous Huxley who first referred to "the Pill" in *Brave New World Revisited* (1958).

[2]For a history of the Pill, see Pincus (1965). For an account of its development, see Djerassi (1981).

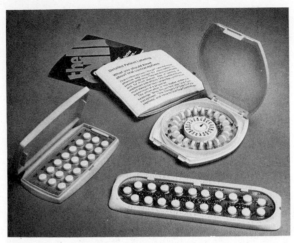

Figure 7.2    Various brands of oral contraceptives.

the United States. Under the best conditions no more than 1 in 1000 (0.1 percent) of sexually active women studied got pregnant over a year. Some studies have shown that women who used the method correctly had no pregnancies at all. However, the more typical failure rate is 3 percent.

Hormones change daily in the natural menstrual cycle. To imitate this sequence better, a *sequential pill* was developed that gave estrogen for 15 days followed by a combination of estrogen and progesterone for the next 5. Though these pills were effective, they had a higher risk of serious side effects and were withdrawn from the market. They were replaced with the safer *diphasic pill* and *triphasic pill*. These pills give lower daily doses in the early part of the cycle, reducing the total dose per cycle to less than most other pills supply.

The biphasic Pill provides a small amount of progestin and a higher level of estrogen for the first ten days, followed by a much higher level of progestin and the same level of estrogen for days 11 to 21. The triphasic formulation uses three combinations of progestins and estrogens in varying doses over successive phases of the cycle. These new formulations appear as effective as the more standard forms of the Pill (*Population Reports*, 1982). They have become the most widely prescribed oral contraceptives in the United States.

There have been many attempts to minimize the undesirable side effects of the Pill while retaining its effectiveness. Manufacturers have used progressively smaller doses of the hormones, especially estrogen, which is responsible for most of the side effects. As a result, the estrogen content of most Pills is now a fraction of the original quantity.

The *Minipill* contains only a small amount of progestin and no estrogen. It is taken every day, with no break for menstrual bleeding. Though it does have fewer side effects, it may lead to more irregular bleeding. The Minipill is also somewhat less effective in suppressing ovulation than the combination Pill. It has a lowest observed failure rate of 1 percent, compared with 0.1 percent for the combination Pill, but the same typical failure rate of 3 percent.

Side Effects    All drugs may cause undesirable side effects or secondary reactions. A wide variety of such side effects complicates the use of birth control pills. We shall restrict ourselves here to the more common and the more serious undesirable effects (Isung et al., 1979; Hatcher et al., 1988).

The most common possible minor side effect of the Pill is nausea. It is usually mild and generally disappears after a week or two of starting the Pill. Other symptoms may include breast tenderness, constipation, skin rashes (such as brown spots on the face), weight gain, vaginal discharge, and headaches; these effects may occur only during initial cycles, or each month. All of them are similar to the symptoms of early pregnancy, which are also caused by the increased levels of the natural estrogens and progestins.

The most serious risks posed by birth control pills relate to the cardiovascular system. There is increased chance of heart attack, stroke, hypertension, and formation of blood clots (Wahl et al., 1983). These clots (emboli) cause only local discomfort if lodged, for instance, in a leg vein, but if they travel to the brain, the heart, or the lungs, the result could be serious or fatal. Older women and smokers are particularly susceptible to these risks; for instance, women in their thirties who smoke and use the Pill are four times more likely to suffer a heart attack than nonsmokers.

What has caused the greatest public alarm is the fear that birth control pills may cause cancer of the uterus or the breast. Research has linked estrogen with uterine and breast cancer in several animal species; yet no such effect has been substantiated in women despite a great deal of research (Murad and Haynes, 1985). As time passes, it becomes less and less likely that any significant risk of cancer remains undetected (*Population Reports,* 1982).

Similarly, there is no evidence that birth control pills cause birth defects, unless they are taken by the mother when she is already pregnant (which is why a woman should only start taking the Pill right at the end of a menstrual period). Nor is there any evidence that oral contraceptives have a long-term effect on subsequent fertility, even though there may be a delay in returning to normal fertility levels for several months after they are discontinued. The use of the Pill has no effect on the onset of the menopause. Its influence on sexual interest follows no consistent pattern, because there are so many other factors (Chapter 4).

Some side effects are actually positive. The risks of getting cancer of the endometrium and cancer of the ovary are reduced by about 50 percent among users of the Pill. Women on the Pill are also protected to some extent from various other ailments, including some forms of pelvic inflammations, rheumatoid arthritis (the incidence of which the Pill reduces by half), anemia, ovarian cysts, menstrual irregularities, acne, and premenstrual tension (Droegemueller and Bressler, 1980, Altman, 1982; Hatcher et al., 1988). However, hormonal methods offer no protection against STDs, as condoms and spermicides do.

Nonetheless, a woman should think carefully and get medical advice before she decides to use the Pill. The risks should neither be minimized nor needlessly exaggerated. For many women who are young and who do not smoke, oral contraceptives are the best choice. For other women they are too risky: older women, smokers, and those suffering from cardiovascular disease, liver disease, diabetes, cancer of the breast, cancer of the reproductive organs, and some other conditions should avoid them.[3]

**The Post-Coital Pill**   A pill that works after coitus (*the morning-after pill*) has the great advantage of altering a woman's hormones only when coitus has taken place. It acts by interfering with implantation of the fertilized ovum, instead of preventing ovulation. Because the woman is not sure that she is pregnant (and she may not be), post-coital methods avoid the psychological turmoil of choosing abortion. To emphasize this fact, proponents call its effects *contragestion* instead of abortion. Opponents call it "chemical warfare" against the unborn (Murphy, 1986).

An early version of such a pill, not yet approved by the FDA for this purpose but legally available from physicians for other uses, contains a potent estrogen, *diethylstilbestrol* (DES), which prevents pregnancy if given to a woman twice a day for five days beginning within 72 hours (preferably within 24 hours) of unprotected intercourse. However, the estrogen content of the DES pill is 500 times the level of estrogen in ordinary birth control pills, so it causes severe nausea and vomiting. DES has also been linked with birth defects and increased risk of cancer in female children many years later if the drug is taken when the woman is already pregnant (Herbst, 1981). Hence, if the post-coital pill fails to interrupt the pregnancy, the risk to the offspring is an additional reason to consider abortion.

A more recent, safer, and less distressing version of the post-coital pill contains another form of estrogen (*ethinyl estradiol*), singly or in combination with a progestin (*norgestrel*). The first pill is taken as soon as possible after coitus, and a second dose in 12 hours (or sometime within 72 hours after coitus). Because the hormone content of these pills is not so high (only four times that of medium-dose oral contraceptives), nausea and vomiting are not as se-

---

[3]For a comprehensive list of contraindications to pill use, see Hatcher et al. (1988).

vere. Nevertheless, the dosage of estrogen in this newer form of post-coital pill is high enough to work (Yupze, 1982).

In a group of women exposed to single acts of unprotected coitus followed by the above regimen, only seven pregnancies occurred, instead of the 30 to 34 that would have been expected with no such intervention (*Population Reports*, 1982).

This post-coital pill is not yet available as a regular form of contraception. The number of times a person could safely use the method is probably limited, but studies are under way to explore broader uses.

French investigators have recently come up with a substance called *RU 486*. A single dose taken within ten days of a missed period has effectively prevented or interrupted pregnancy in 85 percent of cases without major side effects (Couzinet et al., 1986). RU 486 works by blocking progesterone receptors, canceling the progestins' essential role in sustaining pregnancy. As a result, the uterine lining sloughs off and the embryo is lost in a menstrual period.

RU 486 remains in the body for only 48 hours and does not impair fertility (Couzinet et al., 1986), but its long-term effects have not yet been fully studied, and the drug is not yet approved for use in this country. In many developing countries, where only one woman in five practices contraception, such a pill could stem the population growth (Sullivan, 1986). However, the newest (or most expensive) method developed in the West is not necessarily the best answer to the contraceptive needs of the developing world.

Most college health services and private physicians will prescribe post-coital contraceptives in cases of an "accident" or a rape, but federally funded clinics are not allowed to do so.

## The Intrauterine Device

The *intrauterine device (IUD)* is a plastic object about the size of a small paper clip, which is inserted in the uterus to provide contraceptive protection. The IUD goes back to the early 1930s, when Grafenberg in Germany and Ota in Japan experimented with metal rings, but its use became widespread only in the 1960s. Some 25 different forms of the IUD have been used in the past. At present there is only one type of IUD available in the United States (Figure 7.3). Lawsuits from women who developed pelvic inflammatory disease and became infertile caused pharmaceutical companies to withdraw the other products from the market (Hatcher et al., 1988). About 88,000 cases of infertility were probably related to IUD use, especially to the badly designed Dalkon Shield. Among women with tubal infertility, the percentage who had IUDs was over twice the percentage of those who had no IUDs (Daling et al., 1985).

The IUD is a close second to the Pill in effectiveness and prevalence of usage. Some 50 million women throughout the world rely on it, including 35 million in China, where one type of IUD is called the 'Flower of Canton" (Djerassi, 1981; Hatcher, 1988). It accounts for 5 percent of contraception by married women in the United States but less than 1 percent for those never married (Hatcher et al., 1988).

How the IUD works is unclear. The most widely accepted explanation is that it causes cellular and biochemical reactions in the uterine endometrium that interfere with implantation. Should implantation occur, it may also dislodge the blastocyst, in which case it would be more accurately viewed as inducing early abortion rather than providing contraception.

Early IUDs were made from various metals; the IUDs currently in use are made of a flexible plastic that can be squeezed into the inserter tube and then released in the uterus, where it returns to its usual "T" shape. A nylon thread or "tail" attached to the lower end of the IUD trails out of the cervix into the vagina, enabling the woman to check that the device is in place. Small amounts of barium are incorporated in the IUD to make it visible on X rays for a more definitive check. The IUD is taken out by special forceps.

The IUD has a lowest observed failure rate of 0.5 percent and a typical failure rate of 6 percent (including those who discontinue us-

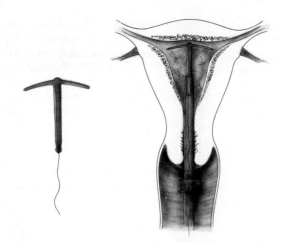

Figure 7.3 (Left) The Progestasert T, the only IUD currently in use in the United States. (Right) The IUD inserted into the uterus.

ing it without starting another method) (Hatcher, 1988). The failure rate tends to decline after the first year, because long-term users are women who tolerate it better. To improve effectiveness, IUDs rely on added chemical measures. Some available abroad have copper filament wrappings that slowly dissolve in the uterus. The Progestasert T releases progesterone at a slow rate. It does not inhibit ovulation, but it changes the lining of the uterus enough to interfere with implantation.

The Pill's effectiveness depends on the woman who takes it, but the responsibility to make the IUD work well rests with the health professional who inserts it. Proper placement greatly influences the effectiveness of the device. Once the IUD is in place, the woman need not do anything except occasionally check the thread to make sure the device is still in place. Unless there are complications, some IUDs can be left in place for up to four years, but the progesterone-releasing type must be replaced every year.

IUDs have also been experimented with as post-coital contraceptives. When inserted within five days of unprotected coitus, the copper-containing IUDs have been shown to prevent pregnancy. Further research should be done to confirm this finding and to look for complications (Yuzpe, 1979).

The IUD is just a mechanical device, not an ingested substance, so it does not cause systemic side effects. It does cause some local reactions that are undesirable. The two most common side effects are irregular bleeding and pelvic pain.[4] Mild bleeding or "spotting" may occur at various times in the menstrual cycle, and the menstrual periods of women with IUDs tend to be heavier than usual. Pelvic pain is caused by uterine cramps. It affects some 10–20 percent of users but tends to disappear after several months. In 10 percent of women, pain or bleeding are severe enough to necessitate removal of the IUD. Side effects are said to be less of a problem with IUDs containing progesterone. In 5–15 percent of users the IUD is expelled spontaneously (which is why women need to check the thread) (Sparks et al., 1981).

Less common, but more serious complications include perforation or piercing through the uterus, pelvic infection, and problems related to pregnancy (should it occur despite the IUD). The danger of uterine perforation is about 1 in 1000 insertions; it requires emergency surgery. IUD use among women with more than one sexual partner results in a five- to ten-fold increase in the risk of developing pelvic inflammatory disease (PID). The IUD tail acts as a conduit for bacteria from the vagina to the uterus, interfering with the protective mucus plug. Therefore, women with acute or recurrent pelvic infections are advised not to use IUDs.

Should a pregnancy occur while an IUD is in place there is a three-fold increase in the risk of spontaneous abortion, a ten-fold increase in the risk of ectopic pregnancy (5 percent of all IUD pregnancies are ectopic), and increased risk of infection during the pregnancy (Mishell, 1979; Droegemueller and Bressler, 1980). There is no danger that the IUD will cause cancer or birth defects.

[4]For a more detailed discussion of the side effects of IUDs, see Osser et al. (1980). Contraindications of IUD use are listed in full in Hatcher et al. (1988).

Despite the possibility of these complications, the IUD is an effective and fairly safe device. Generally it does not interfere with sexual activity. Some women experience pain during orgasm when the contractions of the uterus press on the IUD. Though most men do not even feel the string, a few complain that it irritates the penis.

## Barrier Methods

The principle of barrier methods of contraception is simple: they mechanically prevent sperm from reaching the ovum. Either the penis is covered with a *condom,* or the cervix is blocked by a receptacle—a *diaphragm, cervical cap,* or *contraceptive sponge*—filled with spermicide. Before the advent of the Pill and the IUD, barrier methods were the most reliable and most frequently used contraceptives. They remain in wide use today (Connell, 1979; Hatcher et al., 1988).

Barrier contraceptives are free from side effects and highly effective when used correctly with spermicides. Their main disadvantage is the likelihood of incorrect use; hence their higher typical failure rates, 18 percent for the diaphragm and 12 percent for the condom.

These devices may not be available when unexpectedly needed. Furthermore, some people dislike them for interrupting sexual activity and consider them unpleasant to use. It is possible to overcome these reactions. Couples may even learn to make placing a contraceptive part of lovemaking. For instance, putting on a condom can become part of the sex play preceding coitus.

The Diaphragm    Blocking the cervical opening for contraceptive purposes has been practiced for a long time (Box 7.1). The modern *diaphragm* was invented in 1882 in Germany. Like the modern condom, it was made possible by advances in the manufacture of rubber. Alone, the diaphragm is highly unreliable, so it is always used with a spermicidal cream or gel. It acts mainly by holding the spermicidal substance against the cervix. It is now used by

around 4 million women throughout the world. In the United States it accounts for about 4 percent of all methods among married women, and a somewhat lower proportion for those never married. It is most popular with women aged 20 to 34 and among those from higher socioeconomic backgrounds (Forrest and Henshaw, 1983). The diaphragm has a lowest observed failure rate of 2 percent but a typical failure rate of 18 percent.[5]

Diaphragms today consist of a thin rubber dome attached to a flexible, rubber-covered metal ring. They are inserted in the vagina in a way that will cover the cervix and prevent passage of sperm into the cervical canal (Figures 7.4 and 7.5). The inner surface of the diaphragm is coated with a layer of contraceptive jelly or cream before insertion; otherwise its effectiveness is greatly reduced. After it has been used, the diaphragm is washed, dried, and stored for reuse. Diaphragms wear out over time and must be replaced. *Disposable diaphragms* are under study but not approved for general use.

Diaphragms come in various sizes (most are around 3 inches in diameter) and must be individually fitted by a physician or another health professional. A woman must be refitted following pregnancy, major changes in body weight, and other circumstances that may alter the size and shape of her vaginal canal. Once they have been fitted and instructed, most women have no problem using the diaphragm, but because it involves the insertion of fingers into the vagina when putting it in and removing it, some women may feel uneasy about it.

The diaphragm must be inserted no earlier than six hours before intercourse in order for the spermicide to retain its effectiveness. If a woman has intercourse more than two hours after insertion of the diaphragm, she should leave it in place but add more spermicidal jelly or cream into the vagina. Similarly, more cream or jelly should be placed in the vagina (not the diaphragm) if intercourse is repeated. The diaphragm should be removed 6 to 8

---

[5]For the use of the diaphragm among college women see Hagen and Beach (1980).

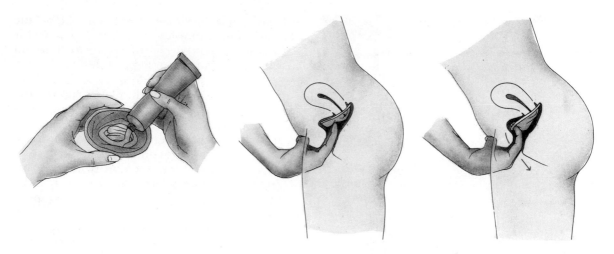

Figure 7.4    Diaphragm. (Left to right) Applying spermicide; checking placement; removing diaphragm.

hours after the last act of intercourse; though it can be left in place for as long as 12 hours. Keeping it in place for more than 12 hours is thought to increase the risk of toxic shock syndrome (Chapter 5).

Unless a woman knows in advance that she is going to have intercourse, she has to stop and insert the diaphragm in the midst of sexplay or risk pregnancy. This procedure is distracting to some, but others incorporate it into their foreplay, making a virtue of necessity. When the diaphragm has been properly inserted, neither partner is aware of its presence during intercourse. They also are likely to be unaware if the diaphragm becomes dislodged. This problem is more likely if it fits loosely, or if the woman moves vigorously during coitus.

The Cervical Cap    Though it works on the same general principle as the diaphragm, the *cervical cap* fits snugly around the cervical tip by suction. This suction may cause some "erosion" or damage of the mucosal surface of the cervix. It should be used only by women with normal Pap smears. As effective as the diaphragm, the cap must be individually fitted, used with spermicide, and may be kept in as long as 48 hours (as against 24 hours for the diaphragm).

One of the most popular forms of contraception in the 19th century, the cervical cap

was almost completely displaced by the newer methods. Although it remained in use in Europe, it was not approved by the Food and Drug Administration for use in the United States until 1988 (Figure 7.5).

The Contraceptive Sponge    A contraceptive device approved in 1983 by the Food and Drug Administration is the *vaginal sponge* (Figure 7.5). Made of polyurethane, the circular, highly absorbent sponge has a diameter of 2 inches and is permeated with a spermicide.

Inserted into the upper vagina, the sponge blocks the cervical opening and traps and kills sperm. The sponge stays effective for 24 hours (hence the trade name, Today), irrespective of the number of acts of coitus. Keeping it in place longer increases the risk of toxic shock syndrome (otherwise the risk is only 1 in 2 million uses).

The typical failure rate of the sponge is about 18 percent, comparable to that of the diaphragm. The sponge, for unclear reasons, is more effective in women who have never had a baby. So far, few side effects have been reported, mainly allergic reactions to the spermicide, vaginal dryness or irritation, and difficulty removing the sponge. There are anecdotal reports of cervical erosion and recent recommendations against using a sponge dur-

Figure 7.5 Barrier contraceptives and spermicides for women. From left to right: contraceptive jelly, cervical cap, diaphragm, vaginal contraceptive film, "female condom," contraceptive sponge. The vaginal contraceptive film, like the vaginal suppository, dissolves in the vagina, releasing spermicide. (It is being considered for approval by the FDA.)

ing menstruation.

The sponge does not require a prescription, does not need to be specially fitted, and is disposable. It appears to be most popular with women who have intercourse infrequently, who do not require contraceptive protection on a regular basis. Remember that its 18-percent failure rate refers to its use over a year of sexual activity; it does not mean that if 100 women use it for a single act of coitus, 18 will get pregnant.

The Condom    The *condom* is the only male contraceptive device in widespread use that is acceptably reliable (Figure 7.6). The rubber condom has been in use since the middle of the 19th century. Also known as *prophylactic,* or *rubber,* its earlier prototypes were made of linen. Casanova referred to the condom as "the English vestment which puts one's mind at rest" (Himes, 1970).

Manufacturers in the United States and Japan supply over a billion condoms a year worldwide to roughly 20 million men. Some 10 percent of couples in the United States rely on condoms for contraception. They are used by 21 percent of sexually active teenage men

(Forrest and Henshaw, 1983). The use of condoms is much more prevalent in Japan, where it is the preferred contraceptive method for three out of four married couples.

The modern condom is a cylindrical sheath usually made of thin latex rubber with a ring of harder rubber at the open end. Often a "nipple" at the closed end acts as a receptacle for the ejaculate; otherwise half an inch should be left loose at the end for that purpose. A *female condom* is being tested in Britain (Figure 7.5). Shaped like a large condom, it is introduced into the vagina first and then the penis is inserted into it.

Condoms are usually one uniform size, although "snug" versions are available that stretch to fit most penises.[6] Condoms are available in drugstores, campus stores, coin-operated dispensers in public restrooms, and by mail. They are sold rolled up in individual sealed packages. Explicit instructions are enclosed. Unopened condoms remain good for two years if stored away from heat. They should not come into contact with vaseline or other petroleum-based products. Spermicidal agents, K-Y jelly, and other water-soluble lubricants do not affect them. Fancier versions are made in different colors, with ribbed texture and lubrication for vaginal stimulation.

Condoms have a lowest reported failure rate of 4 percent used alone or 2 percent with spermicide. The addition of nonoxynal-9 enhances not only the contraceptive effect of condoms but also the protection they provide against AIDS (Chapter 5). Being manufactured to stringent specifications, they are unlikely to burst, especially if the vagina is adequately lubricated. Nonetheless, improper use results in a 12 percent typical failure rate.

The condom should be put on *before* the penis touches the female genitals. It is not safe to put it on just before ejaculation. There are two reasons: first, there is the slight risk that

[6]Barbara Seaman has suggested that just as women buy brassieres in different cup sizes, men should be able to buy condoms in different sizes—labeled "jumbo," "colossal," and "supercolossal," so that nobody has to ask for the "small" (quoted in Djerassi, 1981, p. 17).

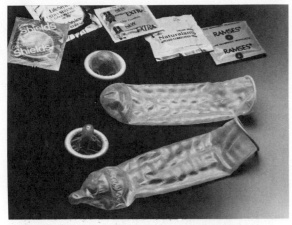

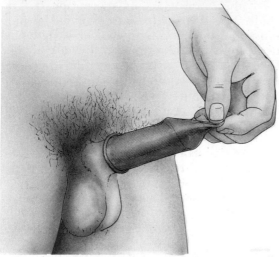

Figure 7.6 Condom rolled, unrolled, and applied. When putting on a condom without a reservoir end, leave a little space at the tip for semen.

stray sperm may be transmitted with the Cowper's gland secretions; second, the man may lose control and ejaculate before he intends to. However, a condom put on too early in foreplay may get damaged. To avoid leakage of semen, the penis should be withdrawn from the vagina before loss of erection, while holding on to the ring at the base of the penis. To engage in coitus again, the man should discard the used condom, wash or at least wipe his penis, and then put on a new condom. Unlike

the diaphragm, condoms are not reusable, even if they are washed and dried.

The condom is virtually free of side effects, though rarely a person may be allergic to the rubber or the lubricant. Women are generally not troubled by it, especially because it relieves them from the contraceptive burden, but some miss the sensation of ejaculation in the vagina. More often, men complain that it lessens their pleasure ("like taking a shower with a raincoat on"). To increase sensation, some condoms are made of animal intestines or of thinner rubber (Japanese condoms are much thinner than those made in the United States).

Men with potency problems find that the distraction of putting on the condom may make them lose their erections. By contrast, premature ejaculators sometimes find condoms helpful. In view of the protection it offers against certain sexually transmitted diseases (especially gonorrhea and AIDS), the condom is probably the single most useful contraceptive device for men and women engaging in sex with occasional partners. It can also render good service as extra protection or as a backup in more stable sexual relationships.

Public health campaigns aimed at the prevention of AIDS have greatly expanded awareness of ·condoms. For the first time in the United States, condoms are now advertised on television and in other media. The role of condoms against disease is discussed in Chapter 5.

## Spermicides

*Spermicides* are chemical agents that kill sperm. They also provide a physical obstacle to the passage of sperm into the cervix, so they can be considered a form of barrier contraception as well. Spermicides come in the form of *creams, jellies, foam, tablets, vaginal film,* and *suppositories.* The active chemical in all of them is usually *nonoxynol-9* (Figure 7.5).

All spermicides are placed directly in the vagina, but they vary in their effectiveness and their method of application (Figure 7.7). Tablets and vaginal suppositories must be in place for 10 minutes or so before they become effective. Foam works right away, but only for half an hour. Explicit instructions are enclosed with these products, which are available on open pharmacy shelves and require no prescription.

As a group, spermicides have a lowest observed failure rate of 3 percent, but improper usage results in a much higher typical failure rate of 21 percent. Aerosol foam is the most effective form of spermicide, followed by creams and jellies; tablets and suppositories are the least effective.

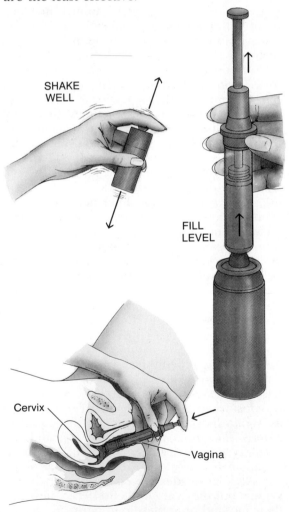

SHAKE WELL

FILL LEVEL

Cervix

Vagina

Figure 7.7    Inserting contraceptive foam with a plastic applicator. Foam must completely cover the cervical mouth.

There are no firmly established serious side effects of spermicidal substances. One controversial study linked them with a slightly higher rate of birth defects when women got pregnant while using them (2.2 percent for spermicide users against 1 percent for non-users). However, this association was later refuted (Hatcher et al., 1988). There was one controversial study with evidence of a slight increase in spontaneous abortions in spermicide users. Though these findings were never found in any other scientific study, it is safer for women to stop using spermicides as soon as they suspect they may be pregnant (Jick et al., 1981; Hatcher et al., 1988).

Other drawbacks of spermicide use include occasional complaints of genital burning sensations and of allergic reactions; potential users must first determine if they are allergic to it. Fastidious people may find them too messy. Others complain that vaginal foam makes intercourse feel "sloshy," and may make cunnilingus distasteful for the man, although some spermicides have no taste.

Nevertheless, spermicidal contraceptives have an important place, primarily in their use with barrier contraceptives. Only 4 percent of women who use contraceptives rely on spermicides exclusively; a larger number use them with a barrier method. Without cream or jelly, the diaphragm would not be safe enough to use; hence it is standard practice to combine the two. Although it has been less common to combine the use of foam with a condom, the combination would make them close to 100 percent effective and increase protection against sexually transmitted diseases as well. In cases where pregnancy must be avoided at all cost, spermicides may be combined with both diaphragm and condom used together, or some other combination. There is no reason to settle for just one method, especially when there is no risk of cumulative side effects.

Some women *douche*, or wash out the vagina, after coitus (Chapter 5). Douching is a spermicidal method of sorts, but it is so ineffective that it hardly deserves mention, no matter what fluid is used or how fast the woman rushes to use it.

## Fertility Awareness Techniques

All attempts at avoiding pregnancy are contraceptive practices, yet some people distinguish between methods that are "natural" and others that are not. The Catholic church, for instance, opposes all active or intrusive methods to avoid pregnancy as immoral. But it considers it morally permissible to take advantage of a woman's transient periods of infertility during the menstrual cycle to avoid conception. Aside from morality, fertility awareness techniques provide a method of birth control that needs no external devices, has no side effects, and costs nothing.

This approach, popularly known as the *rhythm method*, depends on *fertility awareness*. This knowledge can be used not only to avoid pregnancy but to increase the chances of bringing it about. It is simply a way of knowing when a woman is fertile and when she is not.

Currently, there are three ways of determining the "unsafe" periods when a woman is fertile. There are books that explain these methods in detail (Hatcher et al., 1988), but it is better to work with a trained counselor. The lowest reported failure rate is 2 percent, and the typical failure rate is 20 percent (Hatcher et al., 1988). Only 2 percent of sexually active women rely on fertility awareness methods, and most of them are older than 35 years (Forrest and Henshaw, 1983).

The Calendar Method    The original rhythm method is the least reliable one. Failure rates are estimated to be as high as 45 percent (Ross and Piotrow, 1974). The calendar method rests on the following three assumptions: in a regular 28-day cycle, ovulation occurs on day 14 (give or take two days); sperm remain viable for two to three days; and the ovum survives for 24 hours after ovulation.

Not all women have 28-day cycles, so the first task is to construct a personal *menstrual calendar* by noting the length of each menstrual cycle for eight months (counting the first day of bleeding in each cycle as day one). The earliest day on which the woman is likely to be fertile is calculated by subtracting 18 days from the length of her shortest cycle; the latest day

she is likely to be fertile is obtained by subtracting 11 days from the length of her longest cycle. For example, if a woman has regular 30-day cycles, ovulation will take place on day 17 or within two days earlier or later, which makes days 15 to 19 unsafe. Sperm deposited on the 13th or 14th day may live to day 15, making those days unsafe. The egg may still be alive on day 19 if ovulation took place on the 17th, so cross off day 20. This calculation means that the period from day 13 to day 20 is unsafe. As an extra measure of protection, three more days may be added at each end. To be even safer, the entire preovulatory period is excluded. If the couple also refrains from sex during the several days of menstruation (for other reasons) that still leaves from 7 to 11 days that are safe to engage in coitus. Including the period of menstruation, the safe period encompasses almost half of the month.

This system is logical but it does not work, because the menstrual cycle does not function like clockwork. Many physiological and psychological factors throw it off schedule. In an extreme case, a woman with a short cycle but a long period of bleeding may ovulate while she is still menstruating, so unprotected coitus even during menstruation is not entirely safe. To predict ovulation we have to look for better evidence than the calendar.

The Basal Body Temperature Method    This approach (also called the "sympto-thermal method") depends on the fact that ovulation is accompanied by a discernible rise in the *basal body temperature* (the lowest temperature during waking hours when the body is at rest). To pinpoint the temperature rise, hence the time of ovulation, a woman must take her temperature (by a special BBT thermometer) immediately upon awakening every morning, before she gets out of bed or does anything else. She records the temperatures on a chart. An increase of at least 0.4°F (0.2°C) over the temperature of the preceding five days, which is sustained for three days, indicates that ovulation has occurred. Sometimes the temperature drops before it begins to rise, which gives some forewarning (Figure 7.8). To avoid pregnancy,

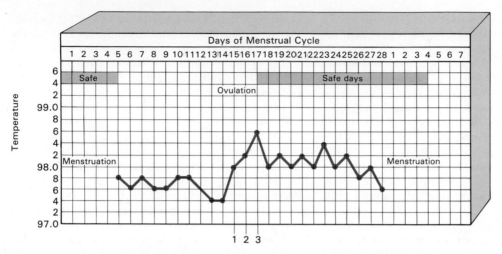

Figure 7.8    Basal body temperature variations during a sample menstrual cycle.

the woman abstains from sexual intercourse from the end of her menstrual period until three days after ovulation (the first day the temperature rose). To have coitus anytime before there is clear evidence for ovulation is risky.

This method is subject to considerable error. Many factors other than ovulation influence body temperature. Furthermore, in 20 percent of cycles, no temperature rise accompanies ovulation, so that entire month must be considered unsafe. If women scrupulously follow the method, success rates are sometimes reported to be extremely high (99.7 percent) (Doring, 1967, in Hatcher et al., 1988). Other researchers, however, regard this method as far less reliable (Bauman, 1981).

The Cervical Mucus Method    The third approach, also known as the *Billings method,* relies on changes in cervical mucus to predict ovulation. To use it, a woman must learn to identify changes in the amount and consistency of cervical mucus (Billings and Billings, 1974). For a few days before and shortly after menstruation, many women have "dry" periods, with no noticeable cervical discharge and a sensation of dryness in the vagina. These "dry" days are considered relatively safe for intercourse.

After the "dry" period following menstruation, the cervix produces a thick, sticky mucous discharge that may be white or cloudy. Gradually the mucus becomes more watery, slippery, and clear (looking like egg white). This *peak symptom* usually lasts for one or two days. Generally, a woman ovulates about 24 hours after the last peak symptom day. The mucus then changes back to being cloudy and sticky. Intercourse is not safe from the first day in which sticky mucus is present until four days after the last peak symptom day.

To help women make these determinations, an *ovutimer* has now been developed—a plastic device that is inserted into the vagina to measure the stickiness of cervical mucus. Another device, called the *Ovulation Predictor,* uses saliva to predict ovulation five days in advance. It has not yet been approved by the FDA as a contraceptive, although it is now available over-the-counter to enhance the chance of pregnancy.

A World Health Organization review in 1978 (before some of the new devices were available) concluded that even combinations of rhythm methods were relatively ineffective. However, it ascribed failures more to risk taking (by engaging in coitus during fertile periods) than to difficulties in interpreting BBT or cervical mucus changes. Ultimately, the effectiveness of any method must rest on personal style, will power, and motivation.

If a highly reliable and easy method of predicting ovulation far enough in advance became available, it would constitute an extraordinary advance in contraception. At least those who can restrain themselves for short periods of time would have a means of avoiding pregnancy that has no side effects and raises no moral objections.

## Prolonged Nursing

It has been long observed that nursing an infant seems to protect the mother from getting pregnant. In developing countries more pregnancies have been prevented by breastfeeding than by any other method; yet breastfeeding is widely regarded in the West as an unreliable form of contraception. How do we reconcile these conflicting observations?

Breastfeeding does inhibit ovulation and menstruation after childbirth, although the hormonal mechanisms underlying this effect are not fully understood. Sensory nerve endings at the nipple presumably send impulses to the brain, where they inhibit the hypothalamus from producing its releasing hormones. This depresses the secretion of LH from the pituitary, which in turn inhibits ovulation.

However, this mechanism only works if breastfeeding is done frequently and around the clock. Among certain nomadic tribes in the Kalahari desert in Africa, women on the average conceive at four-year intervals without relying on any other contraceptive. These mothers nurse their infants up to 60 times a day. The practice of giving the breast to the infant on demand remains common in many other developing countries. Even if there is no milk at a feeding, infants derive comfort from sucking, and frequent nipple stimulation keeps the mother's contraceptive mechanism active.

In recent years, breastfeeding has been rapidly losing its contraceptive function in the Third World, as it has in the West, because of the introduction of powdered milk and other food supplements that reduce the frequency of nursing. The Western practice of bottle feeding and the use of "pacifiers" in the form of rubber teats have compromised the suckling mechanism even when women do nurse their infants sporadically. However, this innate mechanism is by no means lost. A study of nursing women in Scotland has shown that if breastfeeding is carried out more than five times in 24 hours, including a night-time feed, ovulation can be inhibited for up to a year or more (Short, 1979).

Once menstruation returns, nursing exerts no further effect in preventing pregnancy. Even the absence of menstruation is not completely reliable, because 80 percent of breastfeeding women ovulate before their first period. All things considered, then, breastfeeding as currently practiced in the United States is not a reliable method of contraception (Hatcher et al., 1988).

## Withdrawal

Another ancient and widely used means of avoiding pregnancy is to interrupt coitus by withdrawing the penis before ejaculation—hence the term *coitus interruptus*. The biblical story of Onan is one of the earliest accounts of this practice (Chapter 23).

The major problem with coitus interruptus is that it requires a great deal of will power just at the moment when a man is most likely to throw caution to the winds. Nevertheless, this method costs nothing, requires no device, and has no physiological side effects—although some couples find it frustrating or otherwise unacceptable.

When withdrawal is the only contraceptive measure taken, the lowest observed failure rate is 7 percent, but the typical failure rate, 18 percent. Failures occur mainly because the male does not withdraw quickly enough or because some sperm seep out before ejaculation in prostatic and Cowper's gland secretions. Though withdrawal is not a method to count on, it may be, nonetheless, a useful last resort. The failure rate of withdrawal is admittedly bad, but that of not withdrawing is surely worse.

Since the unreliability of withdrawal has become well known, only 3 percent of women (which still amounts to close to a million women) continue to rely on male withdrawal for contraception. The practice is more popular among the young, where 5 percent of 15 to 19 year olds rely on it (Forrest and Henshaw, 1983).

## Sterilization

*Sterilization* is causing permanent (but sometimes reversible) infertility through surgery. It is the most effective method of contraception in both sexes and currently the most widely used method of birth control among married couples in the United States (Hatcher et al., 1988). Sterilization accounts for two-thirds of all methods used by Americans age 35 and older. The estimated number of couples who rely on it rose from 20 million in 1970 to 80 million in 1977; by 1975, one partner had been sterilized in a third of all married couples using contraception (Mishell, 1982). Well over 25 million people have so far undergone this procedure.

Until a few years ago women underwent sterilization in much larger numbers than men. More recently the proportion has been shifting towards a more equal distribution (Droegemeuller and Bressler, 1980). However, among blacks and Mexican-Americans, many more women than men continue to be sterilized.

Three out of four women now have all the children they want by age 30, but there are another 15 to 20 years during which they remain vulnerable to unwanted pregnancy. Sterilization provides such women a reliable, safe, and simple way to be free from contraceptive concerns once and for all.

Similar considerations apply to men when they reach a point where fatherhood is no more a likely or desirable prospect. This is why older men are more likely to choose this procedure. Vasectomy is not likely to be done for men younger than 24; it accounts for 17 percent of contraceptive choices for 25 to 29 year olds; and 23 percent for 40 to 44 year olds (Forrest and Henshaw, 1983).

The main disadvantage of sterilization is that it may preclude having any more children. The procedure cannot always be reversed successfully. If a person remarries after a divorce or death of the spouse and wants to start a new family, it may not be possible.

Male Sterilization    The operation typically used to sterilize the male is *vasectomy,* a procedure that can be done in a doctor's office in 15 minutes (Ackman et al., 1979; Samuel and Rose, 1980). Under local anesthesia a small incision is made on each side of the scrotum to reach the vas deferens (Figure 7.9). Each vas is then tied in two places; the segment between is removed or the ends are cauterized in order to prevent them from growing together again. Sperm continues to be produced, but it now accumulates in the testes and epididymis, breaks down, and is reabsorbed.

No changes in hormonal function follow vasectomy. The testes continue to secrete testosterone into the bloodstream in normal amounts. Erection and ejaculation remain intact. Because the contribution of the testes to semen accounts for less than 10 percent of its volume, most men cannot detect any change in their ejaculate. The only difference is that the semen is now free of sperm.

Sperm may still be found in the ejaculate two or three months later, due to their presence in the duct system beyond the site of the vasectomy. To avoid impregnation during the immediate postvasectomy period, the male tubal system can be flushed out at the time of the vasectomy, or some other contraceptive can be used for the next three months or until two successive ejaculations are sperm-free. From then on, the man is sterile as confirmed by the absence of sperm in his ejaculate on microscopic examination.

The rare cases of failure (Table 7.2) are due to unprotected coitus in the postvasectomy

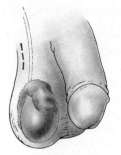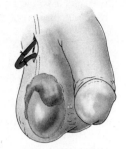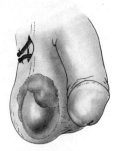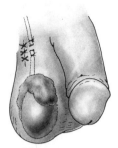

Figure 7.9    Vasectomy.

period before full sterility has been achieved. Very rarely the cut ends of the vas have reunited while the wound is still fresh; current techniques make this virtually impossible.

The main disadvantage of vasectomy, as we said above, is its permanency. Despite many advances in microsurgery that permit reuniting the vas (*vasovasostomy*), there is only a 50 percent chance that a vasectomized man can be made fertile again (depending on the sterilization and repair methods, the rates actually vary from 5 percent to 70 percent). About one in 500 vasectomized men seek vasovasostomies, usually following a new marriage.

**Table 7.2    First-Year Failure Rates for Contraceptives (Percentage of women who become pregnant)**

| METHOD | LOWEST REPORTED RATE | RATE FOR TYPICAL USERS |
|---|---|---|
| Tubal ligation | 0.3 | 0.4 |
| Vasectomy | 0.1 | 0.15 |
| Birth control pills | 0.1 | 3 |
| Minipills (progestin only) | 1 | 3 |
| IUD | 0.5 | 6 |
| Condoms | | |
|   Plain | 4 | 12 |
|   Spermicidal | 2 | — |
| Diaphragm with spermicide | 2 | 18 |
| Sponges | | |
|   No previous full-term pregnancy | 14 | 18 |
|   Previous full-term pregnancy | 28 | more than 28 |
| Cervical cap | 8 | 18 |
| Withdrawal | 7 | 18 |
| Fertility awareness | 2 | 20 |
| Spermicides | 3 | 21 |
| No method | — | 89 |

Adapted from: Trussell, J. and Kost, K. "Contraceptive Failure in the United States: A Critical Review of the Literature." *Studies in Family Planning* V18N5 Sept/Oct 1987, pp 237–283.

Before undergoing vasectomy, some men have a sample of their sperm frozen and deposited in a sperm bank, in case they want it for artificial insemination. This practice attracted considerable attention a decade ago, but enthusiasm for it has diminished. Although some pregnancies have been achieved with sperm that has been kept for several years, the success rate is much lower than with fresh sperm. Furthermore, the possibility that sperm will be damaged when stored over many years and will cause genetic defects in the offspring cannot be ruled out. Sperm banks, therefore, do not provide full fertility insurance for men who elect to undergo vasectomy (Ansbacher, 1978).

There are no serious side effects to vasectomy. The local discomfort after surgery is minimal and lasts only a few days with low risk of complications. One lingering concern is that *autoimmune reactions* may develop. The body may produce antibodies to the components of the sperm it reabsorbs (Shahani and Hattikudur, 1981). This reaction, in fact, is believed partly responsible for the lowered chance of fertility after vasovasostomy.

It has been found that vasectomized monkeys develop *atherosclerosis,* or fat deposits in the walls of blood vessels, which increases the risk of heart attacks. This effect has not been shown to hold for humans even over a decade (Clarkson and Alexander, 1980). We can never rule out the chance of finding new long-term effects, but that prospect becomes increasingly unlikely with the passage of time (Hussey, 1981).

On purely psychological grounds, vasectomy may interfere with sexual performance. A man may feel less virile, or sexually "damaged." Men who have problems with their erections to begin with or are likely to have their sense of masculinity seriously threatened may be better off avoiding this procedure. Resentment and conflict may also arise if a man feels pressured by his wife to have a vasectomy to relieve her of the burden of birth control, just as a woman would rightly feel resentful if pushed to such a choice. Despite these occasional concerns, the typical response to vasectomy is a sense of freedom and relief that leads to greater interest in sex.

Female Sterilization    Women who have their uterus removed (*hysterectomy*) or ovaries removed (*ovariectomy*) will become sterile, but these procedures are usually done for other reasons. The most common surgical procedure used for sterilizing women is *tubal ligation* (Tatum, 1987). Tying or severing the fallopian tubes prevents the meeting of eggs and sperm. The eggs that continue to be ovulated are simply reabsorbed by the body. The ovaries continue to supply their hormones into the bloodstream normally and the menstrual cycle is not interfered with, nor is sexual interest diminished.

Female sterilization used to be a major surgical procedure, but there are now effective and inexpensive procedures involving over one hundred techniques for cutting, closing, or tying the tubes (Figure 7.10). The current trend is to use outpatient procedures performed under local anesthesia. It is possible to approach the fallopian tubes through a small incision in the vagina (*culdoscopy*) or in the abdominal wall (sometimes the navel) and to perform the sterilization with the help of a *laparoscope* (a tube with a self-contained optical system that allows the physician to see inside the abdominal cavity).

Although these techniques are all called "ligation," the tubes are not just tied but cut and cauterized. Chemicals that solidify in the tubes and lasers that destroy a portion of the tubes are among new sterilization techniques under investigation.

Most methods currently used to sterilize women are virtually 100 percent effective (Table 7.2). Occasional failures in the past have been due to improper procedures. More often, the woman is already pregnant when the tubes are tied, but that fact is not known. Female sterilization, like its male counterpart, must be approached as a permanent procedure. The chances of becoming fertile again after reuniting the tubes is 10–50 percent, depending on the techniques used.

In the past, women have been generally

more willing than men to undergo sterilization. The fact that women will become sterile anyway at the menopause has been one factor facilitating their decision. More importantly, women have been more willing because it is they who usually carry the burden of contraception and the risk of pregnancy. However, female sterilization is a more difficult procedure, and a sense of shared responsibility has now made more men willing to undergo vasectomy.

There is some risk of complications with female sterilization as with any other surgical procedure, but serious consequences are rare. The fatality rate for female sterilization is approximately 1 in 20,000 cases; it is virtually nil for vasectomy (Hatcher et al., 1988). Adverse psychological reactions to sterilization are less common among women than men. Two percent of women who are sterilized regret the decision within a year (Forrest and Henshaw, 1983). More often women welcome the relief from the fear of pregnancy and freedom from the burden and side effects of contraceptives. Some women become sexually more interested and responsive as a result.

Despite the enormous expansion of contraceptive technology and use over the past two decades, we are still in the "horse and buggy days" of effective contraception, according to Alan Guttmacher, one of the pioneers in this field. The future prospects of contraception will depend on technological advances and on social attitudes influencing their use.

## Future Birth Control

Contraceptive research continues to be pursued actively, and the following are some of the more likely methods to come into use in the foreseeable future.

Male Methods    Currently, there are only two reliable male contraceptive methods: the condom and vasectomy. To improve condom use we need advances in attitude, not technology. To improve vasectomy, researchers are trying to increase reversibility.

A major breakthrough would be the development of a *male pill* that would interfere with spermatogenesis, or somehow neutralize the ability of sperm to fertilize. There are interesting leads in this area, as well as formidable problems. Such a pill has to suppress the

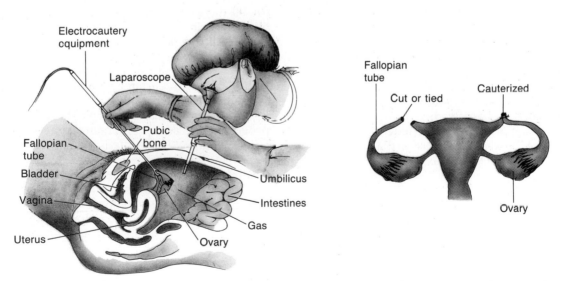

Figure 7.10    Tubal ligation with laparoscope. The abdominal cavity is slightly inflated with a harmless gas to gain easier access to the fallopian tubes.

normal process of spermatogenesis that is continuously in progress. It should do so without causing chromosomal mutations, damage to other cells, or loss of sexual drive or function.

Some drugs have shown promising results in reducing male fertility. *Danazol,* a synthetic hormone with a structure similar to the androgens, prevents the release of FSH and LH from the pituitary, thereby depressing sperm production. In preliminary studies, men who were given Danazol in conjunction with testosterone for six months at a time had their sperm counts drop to 0.5–5 percent of normal levels. These men did not suffer loss of sexual function, and they regained normal fertility within five months after the end of treatment.

It had been noted that men showed decreased fertility in certain parts of China where unrefined cottonseed oil is part of the daily diet. The substance in cottonseed oil that interferes with sperm production and mobility is *gossypol,* and thousands of Chinese men have been using it now for birth control, with apparent success. The Chinese claim the method is 99.8 percent effective. The men are reported to regain fertility readily after they stop taking gossypol (Kaufman et al., 1981; Hatcher et al., 1988).

Gossypol comes in tablet form, so it would be the closest thing to a "male pill" (though it is not a hormone). However, this method is not likely to be rapidly approved or adopted in the United States, because gossypol is known to have several toxic effects, including weakness, decrease in libido, change in appetite, nausea, and sometimes serious heart problems. Extensive testing would be needed to establish its safety. A "male pill" therefore appears to be many years away (Djerassi, 1981).

Female Methods    What about research in female contraception? Most of it is aimed at the improvement of existing methods that disrupt the hormonal cycle. The same hormones, estrogens and progestins, are put to use in intravaginal and intrauterine devices, and in longer-acting forms, to provide sustained protection against fertilization (Hatcher et al., 1988).

*Contraceptive vaginal rings* have been shown to be 98 percent effective in preventing ovulation. These rings have an inert core of plastic around which is a layer of steroid hormones. They are slighty smaller than a regular diaphragm and more easily inserted. They are placed in the vagina on the fifth day of the menstrual period and left in place for the next 21 days. Menstruation begins a few days after the ring is removed. Each ring can be used for up to six months. The estrogens and progestins in the rings are released slowly and absorbed through the vaginal wall into the woman's bloodstream. The hormones prevent ovulation, cause changes in the endometrium, and thicken the cervical mucus. There are few side effects, and the ring does not interfere with intercourse.

Instead of taking a pill every day, women in the future may take long-acting injections of hormones. One such preparation is already being used successfully in many parts of the world but has not yet been approved for contraceptive use in the United States (Hatcher et al., 1988). The preparation, marketed as Depo-Provera (or in tablet form, Provera), contains a synthetic form of progesterone (*medroxyprogesterone*), which prevents ovulation for 90 days. It is highly effective, but side effects include weight gain, loss of sex drive, menstrual irregularities, and an unpredictable (possibly irreversible) period of infertility following cessation of the shots. It has been linked with cancer in certain animals but not in women (Gilman et al., 1985).

Similarly, implants (Norplant) that release progesterone slowly are being tested in the United States. These plastic capsules are inserted under the skin of the arm through a small incision and can provide effective contraception for up to five years, but they may be removed at any time if pregnancy is desired or side effects arise. Norplant has already been approved in several European countries (Hatcher et al., 1988).

The IUD is also being tested for improvements. *Tailless IUDs,* for instance, may greatly reduce the risk of infection. Doctors would use ultrasound to check that the IUD stays in place. The progestin-releasing IUD, which now must be replaced on a yearly basis, may be refined to slowly release a powerful progestin like norgestral over six to ten years.

An *antipregnancy vaccine* would activate the immune system in the event of conception and terminate it. Antibodies are being developed that allow the female body to be immunized to its own hCG. Women with antibodies to hCG no longer respond to the gonadotropic signals to sustain the production of ovarian hormones (Chapter 4). As a result, the immunized woman menstruates and disrupts implantation. Such a vaccine thus induces early abortion rather than preventing conception. In principle, an antipregnancy vaccine would permanently sterilize a woman, but vaccines tend to "wear off" over time and may have to be readministered. The clinical testing of antipregnancy vaccines is now under way, but it would take a decade or more for a usable vaccine to be marketed (Ory et al., 1983).

Despite all of these developments women now in their early twenties are likely to reach the menopause before any major breakthroughs occur in male or female contraceptives. The birth control methods that will be available at the end of the century are most likely to be modifications of those we have today. Government regulatory controls mean that a scientific breakthrough today would take 12 to 15 years before becoming a practical device in general use. Meanwhile, 350,000 babies are born in the world every day, and only 200,000 persons die (Djerassi, 1981, p. 225).

## ABORTION

*Abortion* is the termination of an established pregnancy before the fetus can survive outside the uterus. Typically, a fetus is viable 28 weeks after the last menstrual period, when it typically weighs about 1000 grams (2.2 lbs.) (Chapter 6).

Abortions may be *spontaneous* or they may be *induced*—that is, brought about on purpose (Pritchard et al., 1985). Spontaneous abortions, also known as "miscarriages," typically

involve defective embryos. The reason there are so few babies with serious congenital abnormalities is that over 90 percent of fetuses with abnormalities do not survive to the end of the gestation period (Lauritsen, 1982; Scott, 1986). Either because of a genetic defect or some problem in the mother, about 15 percent of all pregnancies terminate in a miscarriage. These odds are not evenly distributed—some women are more likely to miscarry than others, and some do so repeatedly.

Induced abortions may be *therapeutic* or *elective*. A therapeutic abortion must be done for medical reasons; an elective one is done when other considerations lead to the decision not to have the child. Induced abortion may be legal or illegal, depending on local laws. The complex social, moral, and legal aspects of abortion are dealt with in Chapters 21 and 22.

Abortion laws were liberalized in the United States in the early 1970s. The number of abortions quickly doubled, from 744,600 in 1973 to 1,553,900 in 1980. An estimated 55 million abortions per year are reported worldwide (30 abortions per 100 pregnancies) (Tietze, 1983). In the United States, a quarter of all pregnancies, and about half of all unintended ones, were terminated in 1980 by elective abortion. This rate has remained steady during the 1980s.

The majority of abortions are performed on women under 25, many of them teenagers (Hatcher et al., 1988). About eight in ten abortions are obtained by unmarried women. Blacks are over twice as likely to have abortions as whites (Ory et al., 1983). Half of unmarried women and one-third of married women say they would consider getting an abortion in the case of unwanted pregnancy, but the proportion of women willing to do so is higher (66 percent) among those with no religious affiliation than among Catholics (33 percent), Protestants (42 percent), and Jews (64 percent) (Forrest and Henshaw, 1983).

Illegal abortions are dangerous. They led to 364 deaths a year during 1958–1962 in the United States. The death rate associated with abortions had declined dramatically by 1980 and has remained very low (Table 7.1). The higher risk of illegal abortions is due to the fact that they are usually carried out by unqualified people or under unhygienic circumstances. The instruments may be unclean, leading to infection. Improper techniques may cause excessive uterine bleeding or perforation of the uterus (Maltox, 1983). These risks are particularly high when women try to abort themselves with implements like knitting needles. That is why the wire coat hanger has come to symbolize the hazards of illegal abortions.

These trends have been repeated in the experience of other countries. For instance, abortion mortality rates declined 56 percent and 38 percent in Czechoslovakia and Hungary, respectively, after their abortion laws were liberalized in the mid-1950s. The opposite effect occurs when abortion laws become more restrictive: in Rumania in 1966, there was a seven-fold increase in deaths due to illegal abortion (Tietze, 1983).

## Methods of Abortion

The method used for abortion is usually determined by how far the pregnancy has advanced. During the first trimester, abortion is performed by removing, through the cervix, the embryo and its associated parts (the *concepsus*). Uterine evacuation is sometimes used as late as the 20th week, but during the second trimester, abortion is frequently performed by stimulating the uterus to expel its contents—in effect, inducing labor.

Although abortion does present certain risks, the overall death rate associated with legal abortions is low, especially during the first trimester (when the great majority of abortions are done). Maternal deaths in pregnancy are 1 in 10,000. In legal abortions performed before 9 weeks, the death rate is less than or equal to 1 in 400,000; after 16 weeks, 1 in 10,000 (Table 7.1). By contrast, 1 in 3000 women die during illegal abortions (Hatcher et al, 1988).

**Vacuum Aspiration**    Sucking out the contents of the pregnant uterus through *vacuum aspiration* or vacuum curettage is the preferred method for first trimester abortions because it

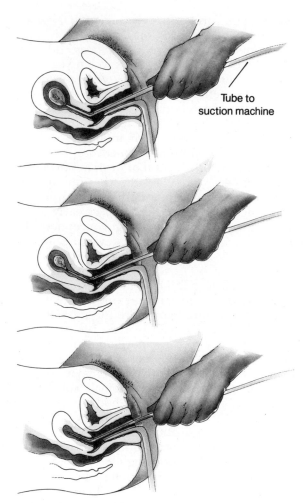

Tube to
suction machine

Figure 7.11    Abortion by vacuum aspiration. (Top to bottom) A suction curette is inserted through the cervical canal; uterine contents aspirated; uterus contracted after completion of evacuation.

can be performed on an outpatient basis, quickly, and at a relatively low cost. Up to eight weeks of pregnancy, little or no anesthesia may be needed, and less dilation of the cervix is required.

As shown in Figure 7.11, a *suction curette* is passed through the cervical opening into the uterus to scrape and to suck out its contents. Complications of vacuum aspiration are rare but may be serious. They include perforation of the uterus, hemorrhage, uterine infection, and cervical lacerations.

Women who do not wish to face having an abortion sometimes have a *menstrual extraction* if they have missed their period for more than two weeks. The technique is basically the same as vacuum aspiration, but it is done without a pregnancy test. There is no way of knowing whether the missed period was due to pregnancy or some other cause.

Dilation and Curettage (D and C)    Before the advent of vacuum aspiration in the 1960s, the most common method of abortion was *dilation* of the cervix *and curettage* (scraping) of the uterine lining. D and C is also employed for the diagnosis and treatment of a number of uterine disorders, so if a woman has undergone this procedure it does not necessarily mean she has had an abortion. The first step, cervical dilation, can be accomplished by passing a series of progressively larger metallic dilators through the cervical opening, but in recent years a less painful but slower method has become popular, using *laminaria sticks*. These sticks, made of compressed seaweed, or synthetic cellulose, are inserted into the cervix, where they absorb cervical secretions and expand to five times their dry size in about a day. When the cervix is enlarged sufficiently, a *curette* (a bluntly serrated metal instrument) is inserted to scrape off the uterine contents. The complications of D and C are the same as those of vacuum aspiration but occur more often, which is why D and C has now been largely superseded by vacuum aspiration.

Dilation and Evacuation (D and E)    After the 12th week of pregnancy, when the uterus is softer and its walls thinner, abortion becomes a somewhat more hazardous surgical procedure, and the rate of complications increases. One abortion technique that is often used between the 13th and 20th weeks of pregnancy is *dilation and evacuation*. D and E is similar to the two previous methods, but the fetus now being larger, it is not as easily removed. After adequate cervical dilation is achieved, suction, forceps, and curettage are used to remove the uterine contents.

Saline Abortions    During the second trimester, abortion is commonly induced by the injection of a concentrated salt (or urea) solution into the uterine cavity. Known as *saline abortion,* this is a technically more difficult procedure, especially in the fourth month when pregnancy is too far along to allow a safe, simple aspiration; but the uterus is not yet large enough to allow the physician easily to locate it through the abdominal wall.

Following the injection of saline solution into the uterine cavity, contractions usually begin within 12 to 24 hours, and about 80 percent of women deliver the fetus and placenta within 48 hours. Some physicians also administer oxytocin to stimulate more vigorous uterine contractions.

Uncommon but severe complications may occur with saline abortion. Most serious is *hypernatremia* ("salt poisoning") which can result in high-blood pressure, brain damage, and death. Other complications include uterine infection and hemorrhage. Delayed hemorrhage (days or weeks after the abortion) can occur if the fetus is aborted but part or all of the placenta remains behind.

Prostaglandin Abortions    Prostaglandins cause uterine contractions, so they can be used to induce abortion. They are usually injected directly into the uterus but can also be injected into the bloodstream or muscles. Laminaria sticks are sometimes used to dilate the cervix.

Complications with prostaglandin abortion include nausea, vomiting, and headache; at least 50 percent of women experience one or more of these side effects, which are temporary and rarely serious. Hemorrhage, infection, and uterine rupture (a danger with all types of second-trimester abortion) are infrequent with prostaglandin abortion. The likelihood of live births is higher with prostaglandin than with saline abortion, especially after the 20th week, which makes some physicians reluctant to perform abortions by this method so late.

Pregnancy Reductions    Women who take fertility pills or have multiple embryos implanted after in vitro fertilization (to ensure that at least one will survive) sometimes end up with multiple pregnancies. The number of fetuses may be as many as six or more, in which case there is virtually no chance of any of them surviving. Even if the chances of survival are better, as with quadruplets, a couple may not want to have more than one or two children. Under these circumstances, obstetricians are now aborting some of the fetuses at the woman's request. Usually only a pair of twins are left to grow to term. This still allows some reserve margin should one of the fetuses not make it; but in some cases women ask that only one fetus be spared (Kolata, 1988).

This procedure, known as *pregnancy reduction,* involves looking at the fetuses through ultrasound (Chapter 6) when they are about 1½ inches long. The doctor selects those that are most accessible and injects potassium chloride into the chest cavities of those that are to be eliminated. After the fetus dies, it is gradually absorbed by the mother's body.

The procedure is not without its risks. It may lead to bleeding, infection, or the induction of labor, which results in the miscarriage of all the fetuses. Moreover, the practice raises various ethical and social concerns, which we shall discuss in later chapters.

Experimental Methods    Some of the most promising advances in abortion include hormonal methods like the morning-after pill, and hormone blockers like RU 486, which we discussed earlier. Although often referred to as contraceptive devices, they are actually methods of abortion, because they disrupt the gestational process after fertilization.

If these newer methods become fully developed and widely available, a woman will be able to abort herself in the privacy of her home by simply taking a pill, or she will only need to take a pill before or after coitus to feel certain that she will not become or remain pregnant, without actually being aware of either event.

## Psychological Aspects of Abortion

The psychological reactions of women and their sexual partners who are faced with the prospect of abortion are likely to be complex and varied. Much depends on their perceptions of abortion in moral and psychological terms: for some, abortion is a matter of disrupting a physiological process whose continuation is not in their best interest; for others, it is a form of infanticide. Psychological issues in abortion are usually more significant for adolescents (Melton, 1986).

Reactions to Unwanted Pregnancy    The reality of an unwanted pregnancy and the prospect of abortion elicit strong feelings. A typical initial reaction is disbelief or denial, which may lead, especially among teenagers, to delays in confirming the pregnancy and coming to terms with it. A woman may also be shocked to discover that she is further along into the pregnancy than she assumed from her missed period (by which time she was already several weeks pregnant). In other cases, there is minimal conflict. The woman knows she does not want a baby, and whatever her previous attitude towards abortion, she gets rapidly mobilized to terminate the pregnancy.

The initial disbelief gives way to a cluster of negative feelings. Distress may be compounded by guilt and recrimination. There is anger and outrage, especially if seduction, deception, or pressure was used in the sexual interaction that led to the pregnancy. At the same time there may be a deep satisfaction in being pregnant and a reluctance to terminate it, however necessary or inevitable that may be.

The men involved in a pregnancy are also likely to react strongly. They are not immune to the same yearnings for parenthood, and their own anguish, anger, guilt, and helplessness often receive insufficient recognition. Because it is usually the woman who eventually determines what is to happen to the pregnancy, men also tend to feel helpless in these situations.

The most trying time is often between the discovery of the pregnancy and the decision to abort. Once there is the prospect of action, at least the burden of uncertainty is lifted. Sometimes, though, doubts persist and women continue to feel anxious and depressed.

Deciding among the Alternatives   No two cases of unwanted pregnancy are the same. A mature woman in a secure marriage who fully intended to have a child at some future date but got pregnant unexpectedly and the teenage girl who is not even sure who got her pregnant would be obviously facing the abortion decision from quite different perspectives.

A single woman who gets unintentionally pregnant faces four choices. Traditionally, the most desirable alternative has been marriage. If it would make good sense for the woman to marry the man at this time even if she were not pregnant by him, then marriage may be the answer. Otherwise, marriage under these circumstances may turn out to be only a short-term or face-saving solution, but a long-term liability. The prospect of an unhappy marriage or a divorce with a child in the picture deserves serious thought.

The next propect is single parenthood. Many more women decide on this alternative now than in the past, because society is more accepting and women are more independent. Raising a child on one's own is still not easy. The prospects of help from the man or other sources, the impact of single parenthood on a career and other related considerations must be taken into account. Teenage mothers frequently do not even finish high school, economically handicapping themselves and their children (Chapter 9).

The third alternative is to give up the child for adoption. This choice avoids both abortion, which may be unacceptable on moral or psychological grounds, and the need for dealing with the child. However, the decision to give up the child is not easy, either, and a woman may not be able to make up her mind until the baby is born. If there are no adoptive parents available, the child can live in a foster home. Before the baby can be placed for adoption, the father has the right to a legal hearing.

If these three alternatives are unavailable or undesirable, then the choice comes down to abortion—which is what four out of ten pregnant teenagers choose. The earlier the decision to abort is made, the better it is for health. For this reason it is important for women to monitor their menstrual cycles. A period that is late by a day or two means nothing, but if a woman loses track of when her period should have come, then she may not know soon enough when to become concerned and get a pregnancy test. Delay in getting confirmation of pregnancy is the major difference between women who receive first-trimester abortions and second-trimester abortions.

Though time is of the essence, a woman should not be rushed or pressured into an abortion decision. All women faced with this situation need information, support, and an opportunity for counseling. The discussions should review her moral values, life situation, aspirations for the future, feelings about her partner, and the conflicts she is experiencing in making a choice. In addition to traditional sources of guidance, such as physicians, organizations like Planned Parenthood provide such services in many communities.

Reactions to Abortion   You may have found it upsetting just to read about abortion methods. A woman's reaction to undergoing the procedure itself depends on the length of the pregnancy and the sensitivity with which she is treated. The later the abortion, the more upsetting it is likely to be. Women who have had children are startled to discover that induced uterine contractions feel just like labor pains, and these memories can be disturbing. Abortions that produce an alive fetus (that cannot survive) are particularly distressing.

Women do not take abortion lightly, but some suffer more than others. The loss of the fetus may feel like the death of a child, and the woman may grieve over it. Psychological burdens of guilt and regret may lead to depression. It is important to provide post-abortion counseling to women who need it.

These emotions are much influenced by

circumstances. Having an abortion is by no means a cause for ostracism in all groups (*Boston Women's Health Collective*, 1986). A woman's husband or lover, family, and friends can provide much emotional support. With help a woman can cope with the experience rather than being overwhelmed by it (Freeman, 1978).

The aftermath of an abortion is usually followed by a sense of relief. The mechanisms of denial and repression help to bury the experience in the past, yet painful doubts may also linger. Sooner or later these feelings begin to recede: by the end of several months, many of these women consider the matter resolved. In some cases women require more extensive counseling (David, 1978; Nadelson, 1978).

The law and large segments of professional and public opinion now endorse the right of each woman to make decisions regarding her own pregnancy. Because the fetus is part of the woman's body, it is argued that she ought to choose what can and cannot be done with it. This view may be unfair to the man, assuming he is known, is available, and cares about the outcome of the pregnancy; after all, he has feelings about the fetus, and society expects him to have a vital interest in the future of the child he has helped create. Does his fatherhood, with all its rights and responsibilities, start only after the moment of birth? On the other hand, to allow the father to decide would place an intolerable burden on the woman. Is she to bear a child that she does not want and then be primarily responsible for rearing that child as well?

There are no ready answers to these dilemmas, as we shall see when we discuss them in greater detail from society's perspective (Chapter 22). The need for abortion may never be eliminated entirely, but the effective use of contraception would certainly spare millions of people the experience of abortion and save them much grief.

## REVIEW QUESTIONS

1. Why do people use and refuse to use contraceptives?

2. List the various types of contraception, grouping them by their methods of action. Compare their effectiveness and their other advantages and disadvantages.

3. Prescribe a contraceptive plan for an unmarried and sexually active woman from the age of 15 to 50 years.

4. Prescribe a contraceptive plan for an unmarried and sexually active man from the age of 15 to 80.

5. Discuss the methods of abortion, with their positive and negative aspects.

## THOUGHT QUESTIONS

1. Respond to the argument that because pregnancy involves women's bodies, they should be responsible for contraception.

2. How would you choose between a contraceptive method that has a 0.1 percent failure rate but significant health risks, and another that has a 10 percent failure rate but no health risks?

3. As a physician, would you abort a woman because she would rather have a child of the opposite sex than that of the embryo she is carrying? As a legislator, would you pass a law prohibiting a physician from carrying out such an abortion?

4. What sort of program would you set up to help prevent teenage pregnancy?

5. What measures would you take to ensure that you do not cause or experience an unwanted pregnancy under any circumstances?

## SUGGESTED READINGS

Djerassi, C. (1981). *The politics of contraception*. New York: Norton. An authoritative, broad, and well-written account of the background, current status, and future of contraception.

Hatcher, R. A., et al. (1988). *Contraceptive technology 1988–89*. New York: Irvington. Detailed and clear descriptions of all contraceptive methods with instructions for their use.

Hatcher, R. A. (1982). *It's Your Choice*. New York: Irvington. Detailed instructions for choosing a contraceptive method and using it safely and effectively.

*Population Reports*. Baltimore: The Population Information Program of Johns Hopkins University.

*Population Council Fact Books*. New York: The Population Council. In-depth reports and review articles on ongoing research in contraceptive technology.

Denney, M. (1983). *A matter of choice: An essential guide to every aspect of abortion*. The biological, emotional, legal, social, religious, and political aspects of abortion are discussed clearly, candidly, and objectively.

Melton, G. B. (Ed.) (1986). *Adolescent Abortion*. Lincoln, Neb.: University of Nebraska Press. A collection of articles on the psychological, legal, and ethical aspects of adolescent abortion.

# PART 3

# Sexual Development

Pablo Picasso. *Girl before a mirror.*

# Sexual Development in Childhood

CHAPTER

# 8

*It is meaningless to speak of a
human child as if it were an
animal in the process of
domestication.*

ERIK ERIKSON

OUTLINE

THE STUDY OF CHILDHOOD
  SEXUALITY
INBORN RESPONSIVE CAPACITY
Reflexive Responses
Sources of Arousal
SEXUAL BEHAVIOR IN
  CHILDHOOD
Autoerotic Play
Sociosexual Play
Sex between Siblings
How Should Parents React?
SEXUAL SOCIALIZATION
Primate Development
  Maternal Love
  Infant–Mother Love
  Paternal Love
  Peer Love
  Heterosexual Love
Early Attachment and Bonding
Maturation and Sexual Learning
The Role of the Family
  Sex Education at Home
  Sexual Communication at Home
The Role of School
  What Children Want to Learn

What Children Should Be Taught
Socialization at School
The Role of the Media
Sex with Adults
THEORIES OF SEXUAL BEHAVIOR
  AND DEVELOPMENT
Instincts and Drives
  Animal Instincts
  Human Sexual Drive
Psychoanalytic Theories
  The Mental Apparatus
  Stages of Psychosexual
    Development
  Criticisms
Erikson's Approach
Cognitive Development Models
Theories of Conditioning
  Classical Conditioning
  Operant Conditioning
Social Learning Models
  The Role of Experience
  Scripts

Like the other important aspects of your life, your sexuality changes over time. We need to understand it in the perspective of a whole *life cycle*. What happens, and what does it mean, at every stage? We shall examine the development of sexual behavior in childhood in this chapter and follow it through adolescence and adulthood in the next.

Certain aspects of sexuality run as a common thread from childhood through old age. For instance, the physiological responses to sexual stimulation, like vasocongestion, are basically the same, no matter at what age they occur. Sex is pleasurable, and sexual experiences usually involve other people, no matter how old we are. Nonetheless, within such broad commonalities, the nature, significance, prevalence, and consequence of sexual experiences vary enormously. When a child, a teenager, and an adult masturbate they seem to be doing the same thing, but the purpose it serves is different for each of them. One of the aims of this chapter is to examine how sexual experiences vary during childhood itself.

A second aim is to see how the experiences hang together. How does each phase develop from the one before it? You do not go through random changes: you grow and mature.

There are major gaps in our knowledge, especially of childhood sexuality, and there is no definitive theory of psychosexual development. Meanwhile, the little we do know is worth learning about, and the theories we do have are a good beginning.

## THE STUDY OF CHILDHOOD SEXUALITY

It is only since the 17th century that childhood has come to be recognized as a discrete phase of life (Aries, 1962). Until then, children were thought to be miniature adults. It was to prevent their exploitation at work and to protect their welfare that social reformers increasingly sought to remove them from the adult world.

One of the consequences of this shift in the status of children was an exaggerated view of the differences between children and adults—and until the turn of the 20th century, adults included anyone past puberty. Our modern concept of adolescence, as a separate phase of life, is largely a 20th century idea.

A key distinction between immature and mature animals and humans is their capacity to reproduce. The fact that children cannot reproduce helped them seem different from adults; but because society equated reproduction with sexuality, children were viewed not only as incapable of reproducing but altogether asexual. Any evidence of sexuality in childhood was either denied or taken as a sign of abnormality.

Sigmund Freud is credited for rediscovering (some say "inventing") infantile and childhood sexuality at the turn of the century, but others were also taking a searching look at the sexual realities of children's lives (Chapter 1). For instance, sexologist Albert Moll wrote in 1912, "When we see a child lying with moist, widely opened eyes, and exhibiting all the other signs of sexual behavior as we are accustomed to observe in adults, we are justified in assuming that the child is experiencing a voluptuous sensation" (Moll, 1912).

Nonetheless, the recognition and grudging acceptance of childhood sexuality in the modern world was largely due to the influence of Freud's theories, in which childhood sexuality plays a central role. A critical problem with these theories is that they were based almost entirely on Freud's work with adult patients. Subsequently, many psychoanalysts have worked directly with children, but there is still no firm empirical base for Freud's views on psychosexual development in childhood.

Whereas psychoanalysts relied heavily on clinical work and speculation, early psychologists virtually avoided childhood sexuality altogether. Developmental psychologists like Arnold Gesell, who documented in systematic detail the developmental patterns of children, made no reference to sexual behavior (Gesell, 1940; Gesell and Ilg, 1946; Gesell et al., 1956). Most modern textbooks on child development still have little to say about preadolescent sexuality (Craig, 1987). Even when gender differences are the focus of specialized works, sexual behavior is likely to be left out (Maccoby and Jacklin, 1974).

Within the field of sexuality itself, much of the information on sexual behavior in childhood comes from surveys of adult subjects, such as the Kinsey and the Hunt reports. It, too, relies on the recollection of adults of their childhood experiences. The likelihood of these adults remembering and reporting what happened decades ago is probably even poorer than in clinical cases, where patients spend a great deal of time talking to a therapist rather than responding to a questionnaire or to an interviewer they do not know. The survey methods, however, do have the advantage of reaching a less self-selected (although not necessarily a representative) sample. Few direct investigations of children's sexuality have been attempted so far and will be referred to as we discuss various aspects of childhood sexuality.

There are several reasons why sexuality has not received its due attention in the painstaking research carried out by developmental psychologists, and continues to present serious obstacles to all researchers in the fields of sexuality. One reason is that sexual behavior in children tends to be infrequent and unpredictable. A psychologist watching children at play in a natural or an experimental setting is unlikely to observe any overt sexual activity and interaction. Even if children felt inclined to engage in sexual games, they would be unlikely to do so in public places. They learn early enough that such behavior would be frowned upon.

The primary method of studying adult sexuality is to ask people about their sexual activities (Chapter 1). This approach does not work as well with young children, who cannot easily conceptualize their subjective experiences and lack the vocabulary to describe them. They are likely to be inhibited from confiding in strangers. Children may also unwittingly misrepresent their experiences and occasionally confabulate events. Despite these pitfalls, it is still possible to obtain fairly reliable information from children's reports of sexual behavior, especially because they tend to make errors of omission rather than commission.

Because sexuality is a socially sensitive subject, many investigators shy away from it. They are particularly uncomfortable about sexual research with children. Despite the liberalization of sexual attitudes during the past several decades, there are still severe restraints on any type of intrusion into childrens' sexual lives. Unlike adult subjects, children cannot be expected to give informed consent. Respect for children's rights and concerns for their well-being impose strict and justifiable limits to the extent that we can learn directly about their sexuality (Chapter 22).

Despite these considerations, a substantial body of information concerning childhood sexuality has been gathered over the past several decades, and we shall examine it next.

## INBORN RESPONSIVE CAPACITY

The capacity for sexual arousal is present at birth; ultrasound studies suggest that reflex erections may even be present for several months before birth (Masters, 1980). Erections in childhood, long noticed by mothers and other caretakers of infants, have also been formally reported by investigators. In one study of nine baby boys aged 3 to 20 weeks, seven of them had erections from 5 to 40 times a day (Conn and Kanner, 1940). Vaginal lubrication, evidence for sexual arousal, has been similarly noted in baby girls (Langfeldt, 1981).

During erections, infants show more thumb-sucking and restless behavior, including stretching and stiffening their limbs, fretting, and crying; erections in two- and three-day-old males have been noted to be more common during periods of crying. Feeding, sucking, fullness of the bladder and bowels, urination, and defecation often seem to prompt erections (Halverson, 1940; Sears, Maccoby, and Levin, 1957). Infants experience erections during sleep even more commonly than adults (Karacan et al., 1968; Korner, 1969).

# Box 8.1

## ORGASM IN INFANCY

Orgasms can occur very early in life. This description is by a perceptive mother who watched her three-year-old daughter go through the experience:

Lying face down on the bed, with her knees drawn up, she started rhythmic pelvic thrusts, about one second or less apart. The thrusts were primarily pelvic, with the legs tensed in a fixed position. The forward components of the thrusts were in a smooth and perfect rhythm, which was unbroken except for momentary pauses during which the genitalia were readjusted against the doll on which they were pressed; the return from each thrust was convulsive, jerky. There were 44 thrusts in unbroken rhythm, a slight momentary pause, 87 thrusts followed by a slight momentary pause, then 10 thrusts, and then a cessation of all movement. There was marked concentration and intense breathing with abrupt jerks as orgasm approached. She was completely oblivious to everything during these later stages of the activity. Her eyes were glassy and fixed in a vacant stare. There was noticeable relief and relaxation after orgasm. A second series of reactions began two minutes later with series of 48, 18, and 57 thrusts, with slight momentary pauses between each series. With the mounting tensions, there were audible gasps, but immediately following the cessation of pelvic thrusts there was complete relaxation and only desultory movements thereafter.*

*From A. C. Kinsey, W. B. Pomeroy, C. E. Martin, and P. H. Gebhard, *Sexual behavior in the human female.* Philadelphia: Saunders, 1953, pp. 104–105.

Another case is reported by a pediatrician:

At about 7 months of age . . . the daughter of a physician . . . took great fancy to dolls. She would press her body against a large rag doll to which she was very attached and make rhythmic movements. The movements at first took place only in the evening at bedtime. At one year of age she and the doll became inseparable. She carried it about with her all day and from time to time would throw the doll on the floor, lie down on top of it, and rhythmically press her body against it "as in the sexual act," according to her parents. Attempts to distract her during these episodes caused screaming. She would cling to the doll until she "felt satisfied." The parents thought that she "completed an orgasm in her own way." By about 15 months of age the episodes had decreased in frequency and were of shorter duration and by 17 months the masturbation took place only at bedtime.

When heard from at 4½ years, she was to all appearances a normal child. Her mother described her as alert, bright, and vivacious. She practiced her habit occasionally, perhaps three or four times during the preceding two years. At present she is a medical student.†

†From H. Bakwin. Erotic feelings in infants and young children. *American Journal of Diseases of Children, 126* (July 1973): 52.

## Reflexive Responses

Given the contexts and the psychological immaturity of infants, it is assumed that such erections are reflexive. However, we know they are not erotically neutral (like a knee jerk), because some expression of pleasure accompanies them. Stimulation of the genital area of children of both sexes aged three to four months elicits smiles and cooing, frequently accompanied by erection in males (Martinson, 1980). Erections and vaginal lubrication start as reflexive reactions to genital stimulation, but they are soon endowed with pleasurable potential, or become eroticized, even though we do not know when and how.

Kinsey and others have reported orgasms among infant boys and girls (Kinsey et al., 1948, 1953; Bakwin, 1974), but we do not know what proportion of infants and children have such experiences or how often (Box 8.1). Although such activity may not be an everyday occurrence, more of it probably goes on than is observed by adults. Even when present, adults often ignore it or fail to recognize its sexual significance.

### Sources of Arousal

Sexual arousal in childhood and early adolescence is often part of a more generalized state of emotional excitement. A wide variety of sexual as well as nonsexual sources of stimulation have been reported to elicit erotic responses among boys (no comparable data are available for girls). Sexual sources of arousal may be mainly physical (such as friction with clothing) or emotional (exciting situations like watching fires, fights, accidents, or wild animals). The possibilities are extensive (Kinsey et al., 1948, pp. 164–165).

Such indiscriminate erotic reactions gradually give way to more selective responses. By the late teens sexual response is by and large limited to direct stimulation of the genitals or to clearly erotic cues.

### SEXUAL BEHAVIOR IN CHILDHOOD

Sexual behavior, like many other forms of childhood activity, takes the form of play. If the child plays alone, sex play is *autoerotic;* if with others, it is *sociosexual.* These terms are useful, but we should not ascribe adult meanings to them.

### Autoerotic Play

Self-exploration and self-manipulation are the most common forms of sex play in childhood (Figure 8.1). Such activity has been observed starting between 6 and 12 months (Spitz,

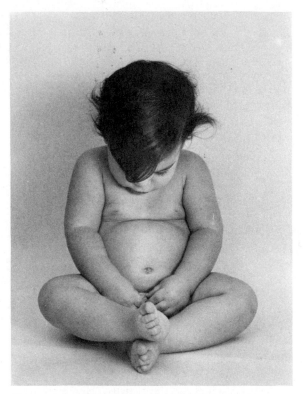

Figure 8.1   Self-exploration in childhood.

1949). In one study, mothers noted that over one-third of their one-year-olds played with their genitals (Newson and Newson, 1968).

Genital play starts somewhat earlier among boys (6 to 7 months) than girls (10 to 11 months) (Galenson and Rolphe, 1976). Masturbation has been noted among 61 percent of one-year-old infants in a residential treatment center, and 91 percent of infants from "superior home environments" (Spitz, 1949).

Such activity is thought to be discovered accidentally; as the infant explores his or her body in a random manner, contact with the genitals proves pleasurable, so it tends to be repeated. As the child grows older, self-exploration becomes more focused and its sexual intent more obvious (Kleeman, 1975).

Among the Kinsey subjects, an occasional individual could remember masturbating, sometimes to the point of orgasm, as early as at age 3. Autoerotic activities in infancy are more prevalent among boys. During the first year of life, males have been noted to engage in autoerotic activity about twice as frequently as females (Spitz, 1949). A higher prevalence for this activity among males has also been reported for ages 1 and 2 years (Kleeman, 1975) and 4 through 14 years (Gebhard and Elias, 1969).

Fondling the penis and manual stimulation of the clitoris are the most common autoerotic techniques (Spitz, 1949). Children also discover the erotic potential of thigh friction by rubbing against their beds, toys, and the like. Bakwin (1974) describes a young girl who would lie down on top of her rag doll and rhythmically press her body against it until she "felt satisfied" (Box 8.1).

Infantile masturbation may or may not lead to childhood masturbation. Most male children seem to relearn to masturbate from one another. In the Kinsey sample nearly all males reported having heard about the practice before trying it themselves, and quite a few had watched companions doing it. Fewer than one in three boys reported discovering this outlet by himself, and fewer than one in ten was led to it through homosexual contact.

By contrast, two out of three females in the Kinsey sample had learned to masturbate primarily through accidental discovery. Sometimes this discovery did not take place until adulthood. At other times it was not the act itself but awareness of its significance that came late; occasionally a woman would have masturbated for years before she realized that was what she was doing.

Though masturbation is now considered by most people to be a normal part of childhood, the practice is by no means universal. In samples of boys ranging from 4 to 14 years, only 38 percent report having masturbated, most often starting between the ages of 3 and 7 years (Elias and Gebhard, 1969).

## Sociosexual Play

The sexual activities of children include interactions with each other. By age two, children already respond to each other affectionately by touching, hugging, and kissing; such behavior may or may not be erotic. Where free expression of sexual activity is tolerated, such physical contact is simply extended to the genitals as well. Spiro (1956) describes such a situation among two-year-olds in a kibbutz.

A child of two to three years interacts with other children with sufficient intimacy to be able to introduce a sexual element into these associations. Most often, children investigate their playmates' genitals and exhibit their own (Figure 8.2). Such interest tends to be fairly cursory. Fondling the penis or sticking fingers into the vagina, for instance, is much less frequent than superficial exploration.

Children have popular games like "play-

Figure 8.2    Mutual exploration.

Figure 8.3    Boys masturbating.

ing house," or "papa and mama." Such play usually involves little more than lying on top of one another. Even when children occasionally undress, the activity does not proceed beyond mere genital apposition.

More adult types of sexual activity are more likely when one partner is older and more experienced; in these situations a child could be induced to engage in practically all forms of sexual activity, including mutual masturbation (Figure 8.3), oral-genital contact, and coitus (Gadpaille, 1975; Martinson, 1981). Children are also more likely to engage in such behavior if they have observed adults doing it. This is more likely to occur in families living in crowded conditions.

By age 5, youngsters have had their first sociosexual experiences in 10 percent of cases. In the Kinsey sample, prepubescent sex play among boys reached its peak at age 12, with 39 percent engaging in such activity (Figure 8.4). The peak period for girls was at age 9, but at a lower level of 14 percent. For most children, sex is a sporadic activity. One out of four boys in the Kinsey survey who engaged in sex play had done so during one year only, and some had participated in such play just

once before puberty. Only one in three boys had persisted in such play on and off over five or more years. These limitations applied even more strongly to prepubescent girls.

In both sexes, sexual activity did not increase with the approach of puberty. In fact, there was a slight but noticeable decline in sex play once the peak ages passed (Figures 8.4

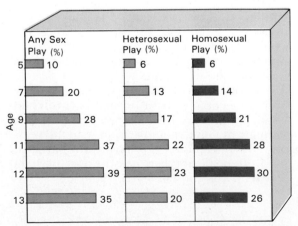

Figure 8.4    Percentages of prepubescent boys who engage in sociosexual play. (Kinsey et al., 1984)

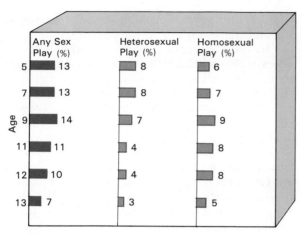

Figure 8.5    Percentages of prepubescent girls who engage in sociosexual play. (Kinsey et al., 1953)

and 8.5). This finding may seem to lend some support to the psychoanalytic concept of a *latency period,* when sexual interest and activity become temporarily suppressed at the end of childhood (discussed later). However, the latency period is supposed to start earlier (at about age 6 or so) than is the case in the Kinsey data. More recent research fails to substantiate such a decrease in sexual activity at any age. On the contrary, children become progressively more interested in sexual topics and behaviors from the ages of 5 to 15 (Goldman and Goldman, 1982). Evidence from nonhuman primates and some other human cultures also shows the sexual activity of the young to merge imperceptibly with adult behavior (Ford and Beach, 1951). When children appear to become more reticent about the public expression of sex at this period, they are probably becoming more sensitive to social restraints.

### Sex between Siblings

An important component in sociosexual play involves siblings. Children in a family engage in a good deal of affectionate expression and physical contact with each other that has no erotic intent. Given their natural curiosity about each other's bodies and their opportunities for privacy and close companionship,

they may also engage in sexual exploration and interaction. It is more likely to happen if they share a bedroom, especially if they sleep in the same bed.

In a literal sense, sexual interactions between siblings would be considered incestuous. However, we must be careful in attaching labels that are primarily meant to describe more adult forms of sexual behavior. The same consideration applies to the sexual activities of children with members of the same sex. Such behavior is "homosexual" in descriptive terms, but it does not represent an established sexual orientation. Most children with such experience do not become adult homosexuals.

In a study of college students, 15 percent of the women and 10 percent of the men reported some type of sexual experience involving a sibling; given the likelihood of forgetting or concealing such behavior, the true prevalence is probably higher (Finklehor, 1980).

Three-quarters of these sexual interactions were between brothers and sisters, and one-quarter between siblings of the same sex. In one out of four cases, the siblings were five years apart in age; in 73 percent at least one child was older than eight years. Looking at and touching each other's genitals were most common. Only some engaged in more overtly sexual activities, including 4 percent who attempted sexual intercourse. The period over which such interaction took place varied widely: one-third involved a single occurrence; 27 percent persisted over a year or more.

In about one-quarter of the cases enough coercion was used to make the child feel unhappy about the experience. Those who felt victimized were more often girls. More generally, positive and negative reactions were evenly divided. Few of the subjects had ever told anyone about these interactions.

### How Should Parents React?

Parents are likely to be perplexed—sometimes alarmed—on finding out about the sexual interaction of their children, and they usually feel at a loss as to how to deal with it. No general set of guidelines can help them. Each case is different, and must be dealt with in the context of each family's sexual values.

How adults respond to children's behavior may have a greater impact on the child than the sexual behavior itself. Parents must prevent unnecessary sexual stimulation and discourage coercive or exploitative behavior without stifling all sexual expression. The child should not be made to feel guilty for sexual curiosity. On the contrary, expression of such curiosity may provide an excellent opportunity to educate the child sexually.

Within the limitations of family space and resources, parents should use good judgment in setting up sleeping quarters for their children. It is best that children have their own beds and, if possible, their own bedrooms. Sharing a bathtub can be fun, as long as there is not much disparity in the age of the siblings and an adult supervises them. Children's privacy must be respected, but that does not mean they should be left alone to do as they please. There is some evidence that sexual interactions between siblings are more likely to occur in families with distant and inaccessible parents who at the same time create a sexually charged climate in the home through their own sexual activities (Smith and Israel, 1987).

Many children engage in some form of sexual behavior with siblings or peers. Some distinction should be made, however, between *deliberate* sexual interactions, which have an erotic intent, and simple *exploratory* interactions with no clear erotic intent, even though the participants may be incidentally sexually aroused. Exploratory behaviors are not likely to be problematic or even inappropriate.

If the more deliberate interaction involves nothing more than noncoercive looking and touching, children can be gently and matter-of-factly told, "We don't do that." Children usually accept that some behaviors—like driving or staying up late—are for grownups only. When there is coercion or intrusive sexual activity, most clinicians and counselors advise setting stricter limits. If a child appears markedly upset by the experience, psychological counseling may be necessary. The same is true

when a child persists in such behavior despite repeated parental intervention.

It could be argued that no childhood sexual expression should be discouraged. Just as sexual self-exploration now is widely accepted, why not leave children free to interact with each other sexually, as long as there is no coercion or upset? In fact, if sexual interactions in childhood are not harmful, why not actively encourage them and even teach them? Some cultures do just that (Box 8.2).

Our own culture has such diverse views as to what constitutes healthy and sexually acceptable sexual behavior that it is next to impossible to reach a consensus. For many parents, it is not easy to make these decisions, even for their own children. In the light of changing social attitudes, many people are uncertain about their own sexual values. Moreover, a child must be brought up not only to fit in with the family but also with society. Even if the parents are nudists, they would be reluctant to let the child run around naked in the street. These concerns are part of the broader task of sexual socialization, to which we shall turn next.

## SEXUAL SOCIALIZATION

Children become adults through two basic processes: biological development and socialization. In *socialization* children learn the behavioral norms of their society and acquire their own distinctive personalities, values, and beliefs.

Sexual development is only part of growing up in general, but for now we will focus on it alone. First we will take a look at sexual socialization among primates, our nearest evolutionary "cousins."

### Primate Development

It is tempting to think that animals like monkeys just "naturally" behave sexually when they attain biological maturity. Harry Harlow's classic experiments have shown otherwise. Infant

# Box 8.2

## CHILDHOOD SEXUALITY IN OTHER CULTURES

Cultures vary widely in their sexual permissiveness. Ford and Beach (1951) have categorized them as restrictive, semirestrictive, and permissive.

*Restrictive societies* vary in the severity of their control, but they all attempt to keep children from learning about sex and inhibit their spontaneous sexual activities. For instance, both the Apinaye (a primitive, peaceful, monogamous people in Brazil) and the Ashanti (a polygynous society in West Africa) expressly forbade children to masturbate from an early age. In New Guinea a Kwoma woman who saw a boy with an erection would strike his penis with a stick; these boys soon learned not to touch their penises even while urinating.

The secrecy that surrounds sex often extends to reproduction. In these societies children could not watch humans or even animals giving birth, and they got fictitious explanations of where babies come from. Special precautions were taken to keep children from surprising adults while they were engaged in coitus; children might even be placed in separate sleeping quarters at an early age.

Even in these restrictive societies the expression of sexuality in childhood could not be entirely checked. Children still engaged in sex play when they could, even though they may have done so in fear or shame.

Messenger (1971) has provided a detailed account of an unusually repressive island folk community in Ireland, which he calls Inis Beag:

> The seeds of repression are planted early in childhood by parents and kin through instruction supplemented by rewards and punishments, conscious imitation, and unconscious internalization. Although mothers bestow considerable affection and attention on their offspring, especially on their sons, physical love as manifested in intimate handling and kissing is rare in Inis Beag. Even breast-feeding is uncommon because of its sexual connotation, and verbal affection comes to re-

place contact affection by late infancy. Any form of direct or indirect sexual expression—such as masturbation, mutual exploration of bodies, use of either standard or slang words relating to sex, and often urination and defecation—is severely punished by word or deed. (p. 29)

Permissiveness towards sexual behavior during the developing years does not mean complete absence of rules. All societies have prohibitions on certain sexual activities in childhood and later. Compared to the cultures already discussed, however, *permissive societies* show remarkable laxity towards the sexual activity of youngsters.

Among various Pacific islanders and other permissive cultures, children of both sexes freely and openly engaged in autoerotic activities and sex play, including oral-genital contacts and imitative coitus. These children were either instructed in sex or allowed to observe adult sexual activity. In a few of these societies adults actually initiated children sexually. Siriono (polygynous nomads of Bolivia) and Hopi parents masturbated their youngsters. Mangaian women orally stimulated the penises of little boys.

In these permissive cultures sex play became progressively more sophisticated and gradually merged with adult forms of sexual activity. With the exception of incest, youngsters were generally free to gratify their growing and changing sexual needs. Sexual activity was actually encouraged early in life. The Chewa (polygynous advanced agriculturalists of central Africa) believed that children should be sexually active if they wished to ensure fertility in the future. The Lepcha (monogamous agriculturalists of the Himalayas) believed that sexual activity was necessary if girls were to grow up. At 11 or 12 years most girls were engaging in coitus, often with adult males. Trobriand boys of 10–12 years and girls of 6–8 years were initiated into coitus under adult tutelage.

monkeys require intimate interactions beyond the satisfaction of bodily needs to develop sexually. His work has a bearing on human sexual socialization.

Harlow has described five basic *love systems* among monkeys: maternal love, paternal love, infant–mother love, peer or age-mate love, and heterosexual love (Harlow et al., 1971).

Maternal Love    Maternal love begins when the mother monkey provides care and comfort, feeding, and protection to her clinging infant. At this stage, close contact between infant and mother is particularly important. Harlow raised newborn rhesus monkeys separated from their mothers. Each young monkey lived alone in a cage with two artificial "mothers" (Figure 8.6). One was a model built of wire with a milk bottle attached to it, which was the monkey's source of food. The other model was covered with soft terry-cloth but provided no milk. The monkey spent much more time clinging to the terry-cloth mother, because it provided what Harlow called *contact comfort*. Moreover, when frightened (as by a toy beating a drum) the monkey always took refuge with the cloth figure. The implications of this

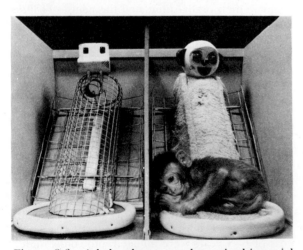

Figure 8.6    A baby rhesus monkey raised in social isolation clings to its terry-cloth mother for contact when frightened by a mechanical toy animal. A wire mesh "mother" with milk dispenser is on the left.

research for sexual function will be discussed below.

Infant–Mother Love    The reciprocal love of the infant for the mother is initially an "organic affection." Unlearned patterns prompt the infant to feed at the breast or seek contact comfort. As infants feel more secure, they tend to wander off, gradually becoming less dependent on the mother.

Paternal Love    The attachment of monkey fathers to infants seems to be less compelling, but monkey fathers care for and protect infants that they live with. Conversely, the infant's affectional tie to the father is less evident than is its attachment to the mother, although infants seek out adult males for comfort when no females are available.

Peer Love    Peer attachments among monkeys may be the most important of all affectional systems. The rudiments of love appear in early infancy and persist throughout childhood and adolescence. The primary vehicle for the development and expression of peer love is play. Through play earlier affectional systems are integrated and later ones are anticipated.

Heterosexual Love    Rooted in earlier love systems, heterosexual love emerges at puberty, matures during adolescence, and operates as the primary sociosexual affectional system for most adults.

The heterosexual love system develops through three subsystems: mechanical, hormonal, and romantic. The *mechanical subsystem* depends on the proper function of the sexual organs, physiological reflexes, and appropriate body postures and movements. Monkeys have a basic adult copulatory posture (see Figure 12.4). This posture arises out of earlier peer interactions. During infant play, monkeys establish dominance relationships through threat displays rather than fighting. In such confrontations, the female monkey usually yields by presenting her hindquarters to the more aggressive male, who may subsequently mount her (Figure 8.7). At this stage, there is

Figure 8.7    A basic presexual position in young monkeys.

no apparent sexual intent in the act of either animal. When monkeys reach puberty and are ready to copulate, this gender-linked behavior, which is already in place, leads to sexual intercourse.

The *hormonal subsystem* consists of the endocrine factors that change in puberty (Chapter 4). They are alike in humans and monkeys.

It may sound strange to refer to a *romantic subsystem* among monkeys. Nonetheless, sexual relationships among primates are not random. Expressions of special interest and attachments of varying permanence are easy to see (Chapter 16).

These heterosexual affectional subsystems vary in their vulnerability to disruption. Harlow raised some monkeys in total social isolation, without any contact with monkey or human. These socially deprived animals developed normal bodies at puberty, but the effects

of social isolation on sociosexual behavior was disastrous. These males would get visibly aroused in the presence of normal receptive females, but stood puzzled, not knowing what to do; or they groped aimlessly, acted clumsily, and sometimes assaulted the female. The impact of social isolation on females was somewhat less damaging. Although they mistrusted physical contact and would flee or attack males, they could be induced in time to endure at least partial sexual contact with normal males. When these females were artificially inseminated, they gave birth to normal infants but could not care for them. They ignored their infants or abused them by handling them roughly; in some cases, the mother chewed off the infant's toes and fingers, or bit it to death.

The effects of isolation on monkeys generally cannot be reversed by standard techniques of behavior modification. Far more successful has been the use of "therapist" monkeys. These normally reared monkeys, younger than their socially deprived "patients," are able to initiate social contact with them in a nonthreatening manner. Within six months of such interaction, the disturbed behavior of the socially deprived monkeys has given way to normal age-appropriate social and play behaviors (Suomi et al., 1972).

Monkeys clearly do not "automatically" learn how to copulate; first they need a long sequence of interactions with caretaker adults and peers. As Harlow has put it: "Sex secretions may create sex sensations, but it is social sensitivity that produces sensational sex" (Harlow et al., 1971, p. 86).

### Early Attachment and Bonding

The neonatal period that follows a human birth is of crucial importance for the baby's survival and psychological development (Chapter 6). It is during this time that the infant and mother experience *bonding*. Their strong early attachment forms the basis of the infant's subsequent relationships (Craig, 1987).

The capacity and the need to form such early attachments is deeply ingrained in us and may be part of our evolutionary heritage.

There are definite patterns of postpartum behavior among animals, involving licking and cradling of the newborn by the mother. It is through such early interactions that the offspring and the parent animal get to recognize and accept each other. Moreover, such attachment must occur during a specific *critical period,* or else the attachment will not take hold. For instance, for Harlow's rhesus monkeys the critical age seems to be between three and nine months; social deprivation during this period disrupts the development of social attachment.

A similar process binds the human infant to the mother, or some other primary caregiver: however, instead of fixed critical periods, there is more probably an optimal time or *sensitive period* for humans, when early attachments form most easily (Klaus and Kennell, 1976). Should bonding fail to occur during that optimal period it may still be possible to establish it later on, though it is apt to be more difficult. For instance, premature infants who are kept in incubators and miss the early neonatal contact with their mothers show some behavioral consequences, which tend to disappear by the end of the first year with proper care (Goldberg, 1979).

The early bond between mother and infant appears to form spontaneously. In the first encounter after the baby is born, the mother typically reaches out and touches her newborn's extremities with her fingertips and then cradles and massages the infant's belly with the palm of her hand. The baby in turn responds to the mother and moves to her gestures and voice. Attachment keeps growing as mother and infant snuggle, nuzzle, kiss, caress, coo, and engage in other affectionate behaviors. Normally, the infant establishes a secure attachment to the mother between the ages of six months and a year (Ainsworth et al., 1978).

The mother plays a key role in this interaction. If she is mentally or physically ill, incapacitated by alcohol or drugs, emotionally upset or resentful of the baby, the bonding process is disrupted and the infant will fail to thrive physically or psychologically. However, the infant in turn must respond. Infants who are unresponsive or seriously handicapped are more difficult to become attached to. The process has to be mutual: the baby prompts the mother to act in certain ways, and the mother's actions elicit further responses from the baby.

We have focused on the mother as the primary object of early attachment for the infant because she is most often the primary caregiver. It is not essential that the primary caregiver be the biological mother, or even female. Even when the mother plays the key role, the father, siblings, grandparents, and others close to the infant also engage in various forms of attachment behavior. In some cases one of them may be the primary caregiver.

What does this process have to do with sexuality? It is generally accepted that our capacity to engage in intimate relationships as adults is strongly influenced, if not irrevocably shaped, by patterns of early attachment.

It is difficult to demonstrate this linkage. No longitudinal study has yet specifically focused on this issue, and data from existing studies have proven inconclusive. For example, if we compare the relationship of the child with the mother to the child's subsequent relationships with peers in childhood and adolescence, or with the spouse in adulthood, we find some people to have done well and others poorly on all counts. In most cases, though, the quality of the early relationship does not seem to predict or correlate with the quality of subsequent ones (Skolnick, 1980). Such conclusions are far from definitive. These issues are so complex and our tools of exploring them are so elementary that investigators in the field are like the ancient astronomers gazing at the stars without telescopes.

Some observers have pointed out the apparent similarities between the parent-infant interactions and the behavior of couples in love. Parents, like lovers, are completely preoccupied with their love object; they idealize their baby, lavish on it their love and affection, rejoice in its presence, and are unhappy when separated from it for long. Conversely, the way lovers gaze at each other, seek each other's company, crave close physical contact, and use phrases of endearment (such as "baby") shows many similarities to early attachment behavior.

Liking and loving have certain basic elements that link intimate associations throughout the life span (Rubin, 1973).

Some parent-child interactions include apparent signs of sexual arousal. We referred earlier to the sexual stimulation some mothers experience when nursing their infants (Chapter 6), and to the erections some baby boys show while breastfeeding. Although in physiological terms they are clearly sexual responses, we cannot really call them sexual interactions: the mother is more likely responding to the hormonally induced muscular contractions of her uterus than to her baby as an erotic object; the infant's body is reacting reflexively to some sort of stimulation.

Some parents and children may harbor sexual feelings towards each other (and sometimes act on them). Whether or not we agree with Freud that such feelings are universal, an undercurrent of eroticism in any intimate and affectionate interaction cannot be ruled out.

Close and pleasurable physical contact between parents and children is a common experience. We need not view all such interactions as relentlessly sexual nor deny the subtle eroticism that may flavor them. Not only is such intimate interaction normal, but it is essential for the formation of early affectionate ties and subsequent emotional health. Like the isolated primate infants, human infants in institutions who are deprived of close human contact early in life have shown severe disruption of the developmental process (Spitz, 1947, 1949; Bowlby, 1969, 1973).

## Maturation and Sexual Learning

Beyond infancy, the twin forces of biology and socialization are still at work. Children's capacity to learn about sex is limited by their level of thinking—a function of the maturing brain. Piaget (1952, 1954) showed that children's thinking (their cognitive level) follows specific stages. By contrast, what they are taught and when is socially determined.

The way cognitive level shapes the sexual thinking of children is evident in a study of 838 children aged 7, 9, 11, 13, and 15 from

North America, England, Australia, and Sweden (Goldman and Goldman, 1982). For instance, in response to the question "How are babies made?" children in the earliest stages of cognitive development assume that babies preexist or are made somewhere ("Jesus makes them in a factory"). At the next level of reasoning, children's explanations vary mainly in how the baby is put into the mother's body. The idea of the baby somehow growing from a seed is commonly invoked ("The father waters it and it grows like a plant"). Some vague idea of sexual intercourse arises later on ("He lies on top. The fluid gets inside her"; "Father has things he pokes up with his cock, like tadpoles, and one gets up the mother's tube. It turns into a tiny baby"). Eventually children acquire a naturalistic understanding of the roles of sperm and egg ("When the man and woman have sex, the sperm from his penis goes into the vagina and fertilizes the egg.")

Bernstein and Cowan (1975) describe the stages of understanding in more detail. Stage 1 is the "geographical" notion that the body preexisted somewhere else, and stage 2 is the "manufacturing" idea that the parents somehow constructed the baby. Such conceptions predominate before age 4. By the time children get to be seven-year-olds, their thinking enters a third, transitional phase. They rely on more naturalistic processes of "manufacturing." In stage 4, the explanations become more physiological, with references to sperm and egg; but even by stage 5, when children are about 11 or 12, the embryo is envisaged as preformed, a tiny baby in the sperm or the egg. Conception and pregnancy are simply supposed to be the maturation of a preformed baby (an idea quite similar to theories of development two centuries ago, discussed in Box 6.3). After age 12, children usually give an adequate account based on physical causality; they describe the union of sperm and egg and the combination of their genetic contents at conception.

Cognitive development limits what a child can understand, but society limits what the child is allowed to learn. For this reason same-aged children from different countries show tremendous differences in sophistication of sexual thinking. Swedish children in the Goldman sample were generally the best informed sexually—hardly surprising, because Sweden is the only country in the study with compulsory courses in sex education for students aged 7 to 16 years. With proper instruction even seven-year-old children appear capable of understanding complex biological concepts. The fact that people find sexual intercourse pleasurable was acknowledged by most Swedish children by age 9 as against age 13 in the English-speaking countries. A similar discrepancy existed in the childrens' knowledge of contraception.

Within the schedule set by the maturing brain, socialization shapes the sexual knowledge, attitudes, and behaviors of children. The primary socializing agents in this respect are parents and teachers, although the public media and peers also play significant roles.

## The Role of the Family

Family and school usually play complementary roles. The family is crucial in the general socialization of the child, while the more formal tasks of academic instruction are left to teachers. When it comes to sex education, this collaborative arrangement does not seem to work. Controversy abounds instead around a number of key questions: *when* should children be taught about sex; *what* should they be taught; and by *whom*? The basic issue is whether sex education belongs in the home or in school.

Sex Education at Home    Everyone agrees that parents should teach their children about sex. In naming the genitals and their functions, and in answering the questions about where babies come from, the parents are clearly the most immediate sources of information. As children get older, parents may address other issues, such as sexual relationships, contraception, sexual values, and moral judgments. Such home-based instruction can keep pace with the evolving sexuality of children and adolescents all the way to adulthood.

People who say sex education belongs only at home often oppose the way schools tell teenagers about contraception, abortion, premarital sex, and homosexuality (Chapter 9). They fear that younger children exposed to sexual themes will be robbed of their childhood innocence, sexually stimulated too soon, and predisposed to engage in sexual activity on entering puberty. They claim that parents are more prudent, combining sexual information with moral values.

The central issue is not whether parents should play an active role in sexually educating their children—of course they should. The question is, do parents actually fulfill this role and how effectively do they do it?

Until recently, most studies showed that children received little explicit sexual instruction at home. A study of families with 3- to 11-year-old children, living in the Cleveland area, showed that the vast majority of children received little or no direct sexual information or advice from their parents. Fathers particularly were uninvolved in the sexual education of their children; both boys and girls directed their questions to the mothers (pregnancy and birth being the most talked-about topics). Furthermore, when parents responded to questions about sexuality, they usually dealt with them as one-time issues rather than as part of an ongoing dialogue (Roberts et al., 1978; Roberts, 1980).

The situation may now be changing. In the Goldman and Goldman study (1982) parents were the primary source of sexual information for children in the United States, Canada, and to a lesser extent, Australia (Table 8.1). By contrast, teachers were a more important source in Sweden and in England. Close to 90 percent of 11- to 13-year-old North American children said they would ask their parents about sex. In the majority of cases, the mother is the parent who is approached. Mothers are the primary source of sex information in 32 percent of cases, the father in 2 percent (both parents, 8 percent). More girls would turn to their mothers (93 percent) than boys would (about 25 percent). However, 7 percent of 9-year-old boys and 27 percent of

**Table 8.1  Sources of Sex Information in Childhood**

| SOURCES OF INFORMATION | PERCENTAGE NORTH AMERICA | SWEDEN |
|---|---|---|
| Parents | | |
| Mothers | 32 | 15 |
| Fathers | 2 | — |
| Both parents | 9 | 20 |
| Teachers and school lessons | 19 | 32 |
| Media (TV, films, books, encyclopedias, magazines) | 18 | 21 |
| Friends | 8 | 8 |
| Siblings (brothers, sisters, and other family) | 5 | 1 |
| Picked it up (on the street and playground) | 6 | 3 |
| Medical people (doctors, nurses, and others) | 1 | — |

Based on Ronald and Juliette Goldman, *Children's sexual thinking.* London: Routledge, 1982, p. 310.

11-year-old boys but virtually none of the girls would ask their father questions about sex.

Sexual Communication at Home    The prevailing view in our culture is that the best sexual teaching provokes no further questions and no sexual behavior. Few parents actively and openly instruct their children in sexual matters, but all parents cannot help communicating their own sexual attitudes and values.

Parents exercise three types of information control concerning sexual matters. First, through *unambiguous labeling*, parents point out and label certain behaviors as wrong but give no explanation why. A child may be simply told, "That's not nice," or "Good kids do not do that." Second, through *nonlabeling*, parents avoid sexual issues by distracting the child or by shifting the focus of conversation to a less sensitive area. A girl who asks how her mother got pregnant may be told that "Mommy and Daddy were in love," leaving the child no wiser. Third, through *mislabeling*, a sexual activity is condemned not for what it is but for some spurious reason; a boy may be told not to play with his penis so as not to "get germs" (Sears et al., 1957). Parents may also avoid labeling sex altogether or refer to genitals and sexual acts in ambiguous terms. These maneuvers all prevent understanding and compound ignorance with shame and anxiety.

Children will become aware of their sexuality whether parents like it or not. It is precisely because self-awareness of sexuality is unavoidable that appropriate communication about it is important. Knowing that sex is there, the child is puzzled, and made anxious if he or she is left in the dark.

The extraordinary range of colloquialisms, nicknames, and misnomers children use for the sexual organs and activities highlights this issue. Goldman and Goldman (1982) identified more than 60 pseudonyms children use for the penis, and more than 40 for the vagina. Some of these terms are associated with urination (such as "pee pee" and "wee wee" used for both sexes). Others are based on analogy (wiener, cucumber; hole, muffin). Names of people serve male and female respectively (Dick, Peter, Willy; Lilly, Mary, Virginia). Names of animals serve as well (cock, dicky bird, beaver, pussy), yet others are more fanciful (thingamebob; thingamejig). Even when children knew the correct term, they would not use it because it would be "rude," "dirty," or "naughty" to do so. At other times their attempts to use the correct terms led to comical distortions: fallopian tubes turned into "Phillipian tubes," contractions to "constructions," and condoms to "condemns." To have intercourse became "do intersections" (p. 209). In another context, "masturbate" ended up as "masturbath."

All of these examples use verbal communication. Equally important are the messages communicated to the child through nonverbal communication, such as facial expressions, gestures, and actions. When a parent reacts to a sexual question or situation by blushing, fidgeting, or freezing up, the child will pick up the negative message no matter what the parent answers (Kahn and Kline, 1980).

Why do parents still feel uncomfortable discussing sexual subjects? Even sophisticated parents may feel uncertain of their own sexual values. Some parents lack accurate information. Questions may bring back a parent's own unhappy childhood sexual experiences, or evidence of awakening sexuality in their teenage children may be disconcerting (Rosenfeld et al., 1982).

This situation is still widespread, but two recent changes may alter the picture: sexually more liberal parents and AIDS.

The men and women who were young adults during the sexual revolution have now matured to become parents themselves. It is possible that their more liberal sexual values will be reflected in greater openness with their children. Increasing numbers of parents now have the knowledge and confidence to give their children sensible guidance about reproduction. Some families even allow their children to be present at the birth of their siblings during home deliveries.

Sex education at home is easy at first. Very young children need to learn no more than the proper names of their genital organs—in the same manner that they are taught about other parts of their body. When children become curious about the differences between male and female bodies, they need simple, straightforward answers. If a five-year-old asks where babies come from, it may suffice to say "from the mommy's tummy" (or "uterus"). "How does the baby get there?" may be dealt with by a simple explanation of how Daddy puts the sperm that are in his penis in Mommy's vagina to join with her egg (Finch, 1982). As the questions get tougher, though, parents may have to seek information, guidance, and support.[1]

The threat of AIDS has greatly sensitized parents to the need for sex education, but it has also greatly complicated the task. It is one

thing to talk about where babies come from, and another to explain anal intercourse. Among respondents to a national poll, 48 percent of the mothers of 8-12 year olds said they had told their children about AIDS, about homosexuality (37 percent), and about sexual intercourse (34 percent). The percentages for fathers were considerably lower (Leo, 1986). Nonetheless, 69 percent of these parents said they were not doing as much as they should do to educate their children about sex (Leo, 1986a).

## The Role of School

Like the family, schools socialize children both directly and indirectly. Of North American children, 19.4 percent say they learned most about sex in school (Table 8.1). In Sweden, which has extensive programs in sex education, schools represent the primary source of sex instruction. However, in the United States schools have done little until recently to provide carefully thought-out sex education programs.

As early as 1970, a Gallup poll showed 71 percent of parents to be in favor of sex education in the schools (Breasted, 1970). In a national poll taken in 1986, 86 percent of respondents agreed sex education should be taught in school, and 83 percent wanted schools to teach children about AIDS.

Because of AIDS, a dramatic shift in favor of sex education in schools has come from Surgeon General C. Everett Koop, a person of conservative outlook, who declared, "There is no doubt that we need sex education in schools and that it must include information on heterosexual and homosexual relationships" (Leo, 1986a). What the Surgeon General had in mind was candid instruction "at the low-

[1]The Sex Information and Educational Council of the United States (1970) provides a book list for parents. Scanzoni (1982) provides guidance to Christian parents answering their children's sexual questions. For further discussion of the parents as sex educators, see Kelly (1981); Gilbert and Bailis (1980). Snyder and Gordon (1981) present an annotated bibliography.

est possible grade," which he identified as grade 3.

What Children Want to Learn    Children learn best what they are interested in knowing about a particular subject. The questions children ask about sex follow a fairly predictable pattern, depending on their level of development. Children in elementary school mainly inquire about reproduction: Where was I before I was born? How do babies start? Can a boy have a baby? They are also curious about menstruation: Do girls menstruate all their lives? Why don't boys menstruate?

In middle school or junior high school interest switches to dating: Is it good or bad? What do boys and girls look for in dates? Questions about menstruation become more specific. As they enter puberty, children wonder about bodily changes and sexual manifestations such as arousal, erection, and wet dreams (Schulz and Williams, 1968).

In the Goldman and Goldman (1982) sample, 97 percent of 11-year-old North American children said children should be taught about sex, and 87 percent agreed there "should be lessons about sex at school." However, only 23 percent said they would ask a teacher questions about sex, and the same proportion only was willing to ask their friends about sex.

What Children Should Be Taught    Even if we agree in principle that there should be sex education programs in schools, the questions of what to teach and when to teach it raise both pedagogic and political issues. In a national poll conducted in 1986, respondents were asked what should be taught to 12-year-olds in sex education courses. The danger of AIDS and sexually transmitted diseases topped the list of answers at 95 percent and 93 percent respectively. Birth control was not far below at 89 percent. Therefore, people seem to have a focused set of expectations from sex education. Other topics were considered somewhat less important: premarital sex (78 percent), how men and women have sexual intercourse (76 percent), homosexuality (76 percent), and

abortion (72 percent) were considered important topics (*Time*, November 24, 1986, p. 56). These percentages pertain to people who answered "Yes" to the question of whether these topics should be taught to 12-year-olds; the balance answered "No" or "Not sure." Hence, there is uncertainty as well as resistance to the teaching of such topics.

In addition to providing information, 70 percent of the respondents said that sex education programs should teach moral values (Leo, 1986). Morality for many people primarily entails self restraint and, hence, is part of the problem of keeping kids out of trouble.

Even where sex education programs do exist, sexuality often is the only subject where children are not taught in a progressive way, whereby what they learn at a given stage provides the foundation for subsequent learning. A haphazard approach, relying on one-time exposure to sexual issues, does not work. The third grade is considered to be an appropriate time for students to start a sex education program. They then can build on it gradually as is done with other subjects (Barron, 1987).

Instruction on reproductive processes is basic to any sex education program. But it must be supplemented with instruction about nonreproductive aspects of sex as well. The biology of sex likewise has to be combined with its emotional and social aspects. Sex education programs tend to be problem oriented. With prepubescent children, the teaching of self-protection skills to prevent child abuse is particularly important (Saslawsky and Wurtele, 1986), yet children should not be led to believe that sex, as such, is inevitably tinged with danger and harm. A more positive approach is needed that focuses on the joyful aspects of sex within a framework of love, commitment, and sense of humor (Gordon, 1986).

Socialization at School    Whether or not schools offer formal sex education courses, they still influence sexual socialization. A school sets dress codes, sets up male or female teachers and administrators as role models, limits courses to boys or girls, divides or unites athletic programs by gender, and allows or bans certain books. In addition, the school setting is an important arena for peer interaction. As children enter the school system, their peer contacts expand greatly. Coming in contact with children from diverse backgrounds, they are exposed to different sexual attitudes and sometimes experiences.

As children grow older, their interactions converge on three related areas: gender characteristics, romantic attachments, and sexual activity. Even though all three issues become more prominent among teenagers later in high school, the ground is prepared earlier as children begin to learn the "scripts" of how to behave as a boy or a girl, how to court and be courted, and what sexual activity to engage in, when, with whom, and under what conditions (Gagnon and Simon, 1973).

It is too bad that children should get so little direct and open adult guidance in forming one of the key facets of their personality. Instead, their sexual lives are submerged in a juvenile subculture, mostly out of reach of adult eyes and ears, with its rich repertory of "forbidden" riddles, songs, verses, and games suffused with sexual themes (Borneman, 1983).

Institutions other than schools play an important role in the sexual socialization of children. For instance, religious institutions with special youth programs and other groups influence sexual values and attitudes. More important, religious institutions shape the moral values of parents, which they transmit to their children. However, the unspoken values of a culture may be more powerful than any institution.

## The Role of the Media

Children nowadays grow up in a culture awash in sexual themes. The erotically charged ads, the soft-porn magazines on display in stores, found at home or shared with friends are full of sexual images of varying explicitness (Figure 8.8). As shown in Table 8.1, the public media constitute the primary source of sexual

Figure 8.8    In many locales, sexual literature is readily available and arouses children's curiosity.

learning for 17.6 percent of North American children.

The most pervasive social influence within the public media is television. Children spend more time watching TV than in any other leisure activity. The topics of programs, the advertisements, and the characters with whom children identify all add up to a persistent set of sexual and gender-linked messages (Himmelweit and Bell, 1980). Soap operas are full of sexual interactions and innuendos without portraying the realistic and problematic consequences. Cable television and an occasional X-rated videocassette left lying about the house confront the youngster with even more startling sexual images. As children grow older, popular music exerts increasing influence through the lyrics of songs and the public personalities and lifestyles of the performers (Chapter 18).

## Sex with Adults

In education, work, and play, adults not only teach children but show them how. In some cultures adults directly initiate children into sex. Mythological themes expressed in our art and literature have thinly veiled references to such interactions. Modern industrialized societies, however, forbid this form of socialization.

Direct and deliberate sexual interactions between adults and children are strictly illegal in the United States. They are viewed as exploitative and immoral. Children subjected to such experiences are considered to be victims of sexual abuse or child molestation (Chapter 14); adults who engage in such behaviors are punished as sex offenders by the law (Chapter 22) and treated as pedophiliacs by clinicians (Chapter 14).

Some people disagree with these social judgments and argue that affectionate sexual interactions with children which do not involve deception or coercion are not detrimental to the child and that children should have the freedom to engage in sex if they want to. There is no significant social support for these views. As a result, sexual interaction with adults is not part of the normative experience of childhood in American culture. Nevertheless, such interactions do occur, affecting perhaps as many as one in five boys and girls. This is why we shall discuss the issue of child sexual abuse at greater length in Chapter 14.

## THEORIES OF SEXUAL BEHAVIOR AND DEVELOPMENT

Once we go from how people behave to why—from facts to theory—sexuality is a real puzzle. No one theory of sexual behavior and development explains it all yet. Therefore, the theories we shall discuss are complementary, not competitive. But even at that, they fall short of providing a comprehensive and generally acceptable picture of sexual development or providing definitive answers to questions raised earlier in this chapter.

The reason we discuss theories of sexual development in this chapter is because most of them place their primary emphasis on childhood. But this is not to say that sexual development is completed by adolescence. On the contrary, sexual development is a lifelong process and what we discuss here is as applicable to subsequent chapters.

There are no behavioral theories just for sexuality; so we have to apply more general theories of human behavior. Understanding sexual behavior eventually depends on solving the basic riddle of human behavior in general.

Theories are useful only to the extent that they can be tested and verified by facts. If you want to prove a theory of sexual behavior you are in trouble: naturally occurring sexual behavior is generally concealed from observation, and sexual experimentation is socially unacceptable (Chapter 1). Theories of sexual behavior, therefore, tend to remain highly speculative.

Theories that pertain to sexuality are usually of two kinds: *motivational theories* attempt to explain why people behave sexually the way they do; and *developmental theories* (often called theories of psychosexual development) trace the maturational patterns of sexual behavior.

### Instincts and Drives

Before the theory of evolution, animals were seen as categorically different from humans. Without benefit of reason or soul, animal behavior was ascribed to *instincts* (from the Latin for "incite"). These biological forces were supposed to compel the organism to act in characteristic ways without the necessity of learning those behaviors. Animals copulated, reproduced, and looked after their offspring because that was part of their "animal nature"; they did not need to be taught how to perform any of these functions. The concept of instincts was extended to humans as well. By the turn of the century, this idea had caught on so firmly that psychologists like William McDougall sought to explain all human behavior through an ever-expanding list of instincts (McDougall, 1908).

By attempting to explain everything, instincts explained nothing; so the term gradually fell into disrepute among social scientists. The notion of a biological *predisposition*, or tendency, to act in certain ways persisted, but the term "instinct" was reserved for processes far more complex than previously understood.[2]

We still are not sure to what extent instinctual processes, as currently defined, apply to humans. Efforts to extend insights from animal to human sexual behavior continue. They include both naturalistic observations in the wild and experimental work in the laboratory.

Animal Instincts    The sexual behavior of animals is "involuntary." External stimuli—a courtship dance, a smell, a mating posture—set off predictable and relatively fixed behavior patterns. These patterns are inherited, complex, adaptive, and fairly stable under environmental changes. This fact gives animal sexual behavior a stereotyped, "automatic" quality—one fish or rat behaves pretty much like another. For example, the mating behavior of the stickleback progresses predictably: the male fish builds a nest and defends his territory against other males; he invites the egg-laden female to enter it (distinguishing her from males because the male has a red belly but the female does not); the female follows the male to the nest, where the pair go through set moves and countermoves; the sequence culminates with the male fertilizing the eggs laid by the female (Figure 8.9).

What makes a male stickleback's behavior so dependable? Why does he always behave the right way whenever he sees a red or white belly? Scientists believe it is neurophysiological mechanisms called *innate releasing mechanisms (IRM)* that guide such behaviors (Campbell, 1987). They call the cues that set these mechanisms off *cue stimuli* or *social releasers*. Does your sexual behavior get triggered this way? All the biological theories of human sexuality assume so.

Where did your innate patterns come

[2]Tinbergen (1951) has defined instinct as "a hierarchically organized nervous mechanism which is susceptible to certain priming, releasing, and directing impulses of internal as well as external origin, and which responds to these impulses by coordinated movements that contribute to the maintenance of the individual and species."

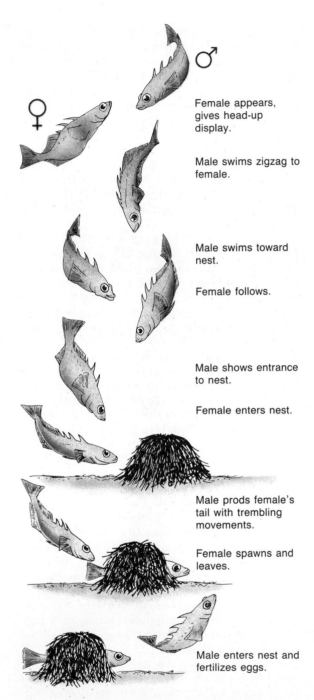

Female appears, gives head-up display.

Male swims zigzag to female.

Male swims toward nest.

Female follows.

Male shows entrance to nest.

Female enters nest.

Male prods female's tail with trembling movements.

Female spawns and leaves.

Male enters nest and fertilizes eggs.

Figure 8.9   The courtship and mating behavior of the three-spined stickleback.

from?[3] Did you inherit them by *nature*, or learn them after birth, by *nurture*? These labels force us to make a false choice. You got your looks partly from your genes, and partly from the way you grew up. The same is true of your behavior. Nonetheless, theorists have always argued over whether biology or culture is the more important. This *nature versus nurture* controversy (Box 8.3) is by no means resolved.

Human Sexual Drive   While biologists studied innate behaviors and psychoanalysts theorized on sexual instincts, psychologists by the 1920s came to favor the concept of drives. A *drive* is a state of psychological arousal in which some physiological need (such as hunger or the avoidance of pain) motivates behavior.

Drives are no less hypothetical than instincts; we can only guess they exist from certain behaviors. However, the concept of drives is more specific and it fits in with physiology.

Your body tends to maintain a constant internal environment—the same amount of sugar in the blood, the same temperature, and so on. This tendency is called *homeostasis* ("equal state").

When the body's balance is disturbed, you feel an urge to correct it. If your blood sugar drops, you feel an urge to eat. According to Clark L. Hull's *drive reduction theory*, formulated in the 1940s, the need to reduce body tension is the basic motive for behavior. In this homeostatic model, sexual arousal disturbs your inner calm. To reduce sexual tension you experience a drive towards orgasm (Hull, 1943).

Applied to sexual behavior, drive theory has several shortcomings. Unlike hunger or thirst, there is no evidence that sexual interest is generated by a physiological lack or imbalance, nor is sex essential to individual survival. However, sexual behavior does have a "driven" quality to it and is linked with specific physiological processes, so it remains convenient to refer to the *sex drive* as a motivating force (Beach, 1965; Davidson, 1977).

Another problem is that drive theory rests on the need to reduce tension. But tension reduction is clearly not a universal goal. On the contrary, there are many occasions when we seek tension through excitement; we go to great lengths to sexually arouse ourselves. Furthermore, we can be "pushed" into behavior by internal drives, but we can also be "pulled" by environmental incentives. For instance, if someone offers you your favorite food, you probably will eat it, even if you are not hungry. The same is true for sex.

In view of these considerations, *incentive theory* is a more satisfactory explanation of sexual behavior. The positive incentive in sex is the anticipated pleasure; you need not be sexually hungry to be aroused (although deprivation can enhance desire). A negative incentive would be the threat of pain or anxiety. If masturbation makes you feel guilty you will tend to shun it. The interplay of positive and negative incentives motivates us to behave in certain ways under given conditions.

Psychoanalytic Theories
The concept of sexual instinct is central in psychoanalytic theory. Freud viewed sex as a process both physical and mental, like hunger. He used the term *libido* ("lust") for the psychological aspects, the erotic longing.

Freud tried to explain the whole of human development in terms of libido. In his original *single-instinct* theory, sexual interest was the motive for all behavior. Later he shifted to a *dual instinct* concept. *eros* (the libido or "life instinct") coexisted with *thanatos* (aggression or the "death instinct").[4]

Freud's critics have attacked him for unduly stretching the meaning of sexuality. Some of his own followers, notably Carl Jung, deemphasized the erotic, equating sexuality with a

---

[3]For the various conflicting meanings of "innate" see Arms and Camp (1987); Symons (1979); Lehrman (1970).

[4]Freud's view on instincts are discussed in v. 14 (pages 111–140) and v. 18 (pages 3–64) of the *Complete Psychological Works of Sigmund Freud* (1953–1966).

# Box 8.3

## NATURE VERSUS NURTURE

Whether behavior is preordained by nature or acquired by nurture has preoccupied thoughtful observers since antiquity. In the 18th century there was a critical examination of these issues. Especially influential were the ideas of the English philosopher John Locke (1632–1704). Locke argued that our minds at birth are like blank tablets (*tabula rasa*); everything that defines us as individuals is learned (Russell, 1945).

In the middle of the 19th century, Darwin's theory of evolution by natural selection was a momentous challenge. Human beings were now seen as but one link in a long chain of organisms. Biological factors shaped by evolution determined the nature of individuals and societies. Darwin himself said little about these matters, but Francis Galton applied the concept of natural selection to all aspects of human character and history. It was Galton who in 1874 coined the phrase "nature and nurture" to separate "under two distinct heads the innumerable elements of which personality is compared. Nature is all that a man brings with him into the world; nurture is every influence from without that affects him after birth" (Freeman, 1983, pp. 3–50).

Galton had no doubt that nature was by far the more important determinative force. Under his influence, there developed a school of thought in biology that discounted the importance of cultural influences. The application of these principles led to the *eugenics* movement, aimed at "race improvement." These ideas and other excesses of *social Darwinism* were applied to justify colonialism, racism, and the dominance of the upper class in Victorian society.

Not all biologists adhered to these views. T. H. Huxley, for instance, insisted there were cultural processes in the "evolution of society," which was "a process essentially different from that which brought about the evolution of species, in the state of nature." However, by the early part of the 20th century, biological determinism had gained the upper hand.

The opposition to the extreme evolutionists was led by Franz Boas (1858–1942), the founder of anthropology in the United States, and his students: Alfred Kroeber, Robert Lowie, and later on Ruth Benedict and Margaret Mead, among others. The central issue for Boas was the ways in which cultures shaped and sometimes shackled the lives of individuals. He began his career at a time when evolutionary determinism reigned supreme not only in biology but in anthropology. E. B. Tyler represented the view that cultural phenomena were just as subordinate to the laws of evolution as natural phenomena: "Our thoughts, wills, and actions" accorded with "laws as definite as those that govern the motion of waves . . . and the growth of plants and animals." These laws were biologically determined. Against this view, Boas put forth his conviction that culture "is an expression of the achievements of the mind and shows the cumulative effects of the activities of many minds." These cultural activities entailed phenomena to which the laws of biology did not apply.

Discussions between these two intellectual camps proved increasingly futile as the evolutionists and eugenicists (now led by Charles Davenport in the United States) pressed their cause with fervor. In response, the proponents of cultural determinism undertook to go their separate way, declaring their complete independence: an "eternal chasm" (in the words of Kroeber) now separated cultural anthropology from biology. Subsequent conceptions of culture saw it as quite independent of evolutionary antecedents or origins. Culture was "not a link in any chain, not a step in any path, but a leap to another plane." The laws of biology and evolution had nothing to do with it.

The revolt of the anthropologists against biological determinism was reinforced by the work of other social scientists. In sociology, the doctrine of Emile Durkheim (1858–1917) that society is "a thing in itself," and in psychology the behaviorist theory of J. B. Watson (1878–1958) were highly compatible with cultural determinism. These developments, combined with discoveries in genetics and revulsion against Nazi eugenics in the 1930s, ensured the victory of cultural determinism.

The pendulum began to swing back over the past several decades as advances in genetics, the study of social behavior of animals by ethologists, and major fossil discoveries by paleontologists shed new light on human evolution. The application of evolutionary principles to understanding human behavior by sociobiologists is once again generating controversy.

general life force. By contrast, William Reich (1942) expanded the meaning of sexuality, eroticizing virtually the entire cosmos (Marcuse, 1955; Robinson, 1976).

Freud did not divest sex of its commonly understood meaning of pleasure through orgasm. Rather, he extended the term to other pleasurable experiences ordinarily considered to be nonsexual. In the same way he broadened the concept of "mental" from conscious experience alone to include the entire range of unconscious activity (Jones, 1957). Sexuality, in this broader sense, is the central theme of psychoanalytic theory, and infantile sexuality is the cornerstone of psychological development and mental health.

The Mental Apparatus    The key to Freud's conception of the mind is the *unconscious.* Freud neither discovered nor invented the concept of the unconscious (Whyte, 1960), but he did designate it as the pivotal point in mental functioning and the primary location of basic human motivations. Unconscious thoughts and feelings profoundly influence how we feel, what we think, and how we act, especially in sexual matters. To explain these processes, Freud proposed a model of the mind consisting of the id, the ego, and the superego—not parts of the brain, but categories of mental processes.

The *id* is the psychic side of biological instincts, and its contents are entirely unconscious. They come out only in veiled form, passing through the censorship of the ego. The id strives for expression through pleasure and immediate gratification regardless of practicality or social concerns.

The *ego* has a dual nature. Part of it (the *autonomous ego*) consists of mental processes like perception and memory. The ego also mediates between the demands of the id and the constraints of the superego. Through various *defense mechanisms* the ego blocks recognition of the raw demands of the id (such as by repression and denial), rechannels them (through sublimation and displacement), or distorts them (projection). The ego thus manages a working compromise between drive gratifica-

tion and social limitations. The ego is partly conscious, which accounts for self-awareness, but its defenses against the id are unconscious. (The most effective way of hiding something is to hide the very fact of doing so.)

The *superego* is popularly equated with the conscience. Part of its function is to maintain awareness of the social acceptability or morality of conduct. Another part is unconscious, for it too must work to block the id. Your superego embodies the value judgments of those who have helped to shape your life. It may be sensible and consistent or harsh and punitive. When the expectations of the superego are not met, we experience guilt and shame.

Stages of Psychosexual Development    Psychoanalysts assume that the newborn child is endowed with a sexual drive, or a certain libidinal "capital." Psychosexual development is the process by which this diffuse and shifting sexual energy is then "invested" in certain erogenous zones of the body (mouth, anus, genitals) at successive stages.[5]

The mouth is the first site of libidinal investment. During the *oral stage,* the mode of gratification is "taking in," or *incorporation.* Erotic gratification through the mouth persists through life. It is obtained through kissing, mouth-genital contact, and so on.

The zone invested with libido during the second stage of development is the anus. During the *anal stage,* the primary modes of gratification are *retention* and *elimination.* The conflict over toilet training (retaining or expelling the feces at will) leads to *ambivalence,* a love-hate relationship with the parents. From then on we neither exclusively love nor hate anyone. Anal erotism—sexual pleasure in anal functioning—now sets the stage for later activities such as anal intercourse.

The oral and anal stages generally extend through the first three years. As the genitals have not yet been invested with libido, these

[5]Freud's theory of infantile sexuality was first formulated in *Three essays on the theory of sexuality.* For a clear and comprehensive review of the psychoanalytic model of psychosexual development, see Meissner et al. (1975).

two stages are called the *pregenital phase* of psychosexual development. They are identical for both sexes.

Between the ages of 3 and 5, the zones invested with libido are the penis in the male and the clitoris in the female. During this *phallic stage,* behavior is dominated by *intrusion.* The main issue at this time is the development of the *Oedipus complex:* the child forms an erotic attachment to the parent of the opposite sex and hostility towards the same-sex parent. Because children also love the rival parent, they suffer guilt. A boy imagines that he will be punished by castration (by which Freud meant loss of the penis, not the testes). A girl's reaction to the discovery that boys have penises is to conclude that she has already been "castrated."

The Oedipal conflict is resolved by the child giving up the opposite-sex parent as an erotic object and identifying with the parent of the same sex. If so, the child becomes heterosexual. If the child identifies with the parent of the opposite sex and chooses the parent of the same sex, a homosexual orientation develops. In this view, every child has the potential of developing in either direction. To ensure that these unacceptable wishes will never become known, the entire conflict is buried in the unconscious. Oedipal wishes nevertheless continue to influence sexual behavior, and their derivatives occasionally seep into consciousness.

The resolution of the Oedipus complex signals the end of the phallic stage. During the next phase of development (*latency*), the sexual drive is relatively quiescent while intellectual growth and social maturation are given greater impetus. With adolescence, sexuality awakens. To the extent that past conflicts have been satisfactorily resolved, the person is free to initiate sexual interaction along adult lines, attaining *genital maturity.* The young man ceases to be preoccupied with his penis and reacts sexually with his whole self; the young woman incorporates the "inceptive" and "inclusive" modes into her psychosexual structure. The successful outcome of this period dissolves dependency on parents. The person is ready to establish a mature, nonincestuous, heterosexual relationship with another adult and pursue the aims of life, which Freud characterized as work and love.

Infantile sexuality is undifferentiated or *polymorphously perverse.* The child combines all sexual possibilities: heterosexual, homosexual, and paraphiliac (Chapter 14). Normally, these unbridled sexual wishes become repressed and transformed through sublimation into socially acceptable behaviors. A residue of these early wishes continues to break through in normal adult life in dreams, fantasies, and other symbolic forms, but by and large, early sexual thoughts and behaviors are thoroughly forgotten through the process of infantile amnesia.

Criticisms    Freud's concepts have enormously influenced Western concepts of sexuality (Chapter 1). His contributions towards a theory of human behavior are part of modern thought. The psychoanalytic model is still the most comprehensive and detailed account of how sexuality develops in childhood and is integrated in adult sexual functioning and personality. However, a number of serious criticisms have been directed towards this theory, as a whole (Sulloway, 1979; Mayer, 1985) and as it applies to women (Bettelheim, 1962; Horney, 1973; Lederer, 1968, 1976; Hayden, 1986). Overall criticisms include the lack of empirical data; the reliance on adult recollections of childhood, rather than on direct observations of children; the use of clinical material as the foundation for a theory of normal development; and the tendency to generalize across cultures without adequate supporting data from other cultures.

The criticisms of Freud's ideas concerning female sexuality mainly focus on his masculine bias. Despite the fact that Freud believed both women and men begin with a bisexual potential and are shaped by their culture to become primarily feminine or masculine, he used the male as his developmental model and extrapolated to women from it. As a result, the basic Freudian formulations "work" better when applied to males than females.

Psychoanalytic theory is currently in flux. It no longer dominates psychiatric thinking, and behavioral scientists are generally skeptical about it. Psychoanalytic concepts nonetheless continue to exert significant influence within intellectual circles. Moreover, the terminology and symbolism of psychoanalysis have become embedded in the thinking of our mainstream culture.

## Erikson's Approach

Building on psychoanalytic concepts, Erik Erikson (1963a) has developed a scheme of psychosocial development over the entire life span, rather than only the first few years of life. Erikson draws from psychoanalysis but uses observations of children from both clinical and nonclinical populations.

Erikson divides the life cycle—the entire life span from birth to death—into eight phases of psychosocial development. Each phase is defined by the primary accomplishment of a phase-specific task, even though the resolutions are generally prepared for in preceding phases and worked out further in subsequent ones.[6]

Erikson borrows from embryology the *epigenetic principle* "that anything that grows has a ground plan, and that out of this ground plan the parts arise, each part having its time of special ascendency, until all parts have arisen to form a functioning whole" (Erikson, 1968, p. 92). Viewed in this light, the child is not simply a miniature adult, and sexuality is a potential that will only develop if permitted and assisted.

Sexuality is an important factor in the task of *identity formation* (phase 5), the concept for which Erikson is best known. Biological features are the primary "givens," but they do not make us define ourselves as masculine or feminine. It is up to each of us to clarify and con-solidate our own sexual character as part of the larger task of identity formation. Cultures that provide clear and consistent models and guidelines facilitate this task for their members.

Despite the upsurge in sexual activity during adolescence, only after identity formation has been fairly well consolidated does true intimacy with the opposite sex (or with anyone else) become possible. Adolescent sexuality is often experimental and part of the search for identity; young people try to find themselves through each other.

The task of resolving the conflict of *intimacy versus isolation* belongs to young adulthood (phase 6). The young adult works out a compromise between these two polar opposites. Intimacy requires expressing, exposing, giving, and sharing oneself. Isolation ("distantiation") is also necessary. No matter how satisfying a relationship, certain distance helps people to keep each other in proper focus. When intimacy fails or is exploited, self-preservation requires severing destructive ties.

## Cognitive Development Models

Underlying all developmental theories is the concept of *maturation,* an innately governed pattern of growth that does not depend on particular environmental events, although environmental stimulation and support are essential for its unfolding. Developmental theories also postulate stages through which the individual progresses; closely related is the concept of critical periods, during which key events must take place.

Freud's theory of psychosexual development and Erikson's stages of psychosocial maturation are classic examples of this paradigm. Other theorists like Jean Piaget and Lawrence Kohlberg have proposed maturational theories based on stages of *cognitive development* or intellectual growth.

Piaget argues that mental development is characterized by qualitative changes. The child's mind gradually is able to shift from exclusive focus on the concrete realities of the here and now, to a conception of the world in

[6]Erikson's scheme of psychosocial development is briefly stated in Chapter 7 of *Childhood and Society* (1963a). It is more fully elaborated in *Identity and the life cycle* (1959), part 2, and *Identity: Youth and crisis* (1968), Chapter 3.

abstract and symbolic terms (Gleitman, 1983; Piaget 1952, 1972).

As the mind passes through successive stages of cognitive development, the child sees the world—including sexual relationships and moral rules—in new ways. Children, once they understand that gender is permanent and cannot change with the clothes they wear, are motivated to learn about and practice becoming a girl or a boy. Sex-specific behaviors and activities become rewarding, and children basically socialize themselves. Kohlberg thinks children go through three levels of development in moral judgment. In *level 1,* moral values are sustained to avoid punishment and to gain rewards. In *level 2,* moral values reside in fulfilling the proper duties in order to please others and avoid social disapproval (being a "good" boy or girl). In *level 3,* shared moral values are internalized. Duties are defined in terms of contractual agreements and commitments that must be fulfilled. Finally, conscience takes over to regulate behavior on the basis of moral principle (Kohlberg, 1969a, 1969b).

Every form of activity, including sexual behavior, depends on cognitive functions. How we perceive and interpret sexual stimuli, comprehend the methods and rules of sexual interaction, generate and manipulate sexual symbols all reflect cognitive processes. Not enough is known yet about their part in sexual development as such.

## Theories of Conditioning

Let us turn from theories of development to theories of motivation. Psychologists define learning as a relatively permanent change in behavior that occurs as a result of practice. Not all behavioral changes are due to learning. Some changes are due to maturation. For instance, infants begin to walk at about 15 months because at that time their neuromuscular system reaches the necessary level of maturity. Other changes come about through temporary conditions such as fatigue or the influence of drugs.

The limits of what we can learn and how we learn it are determined by the nature of our brains, but the substance of what we learn and the methods of learning are culturally determined. For example, our mental capacity for language allows us to speak, but in order to speak a particular language, we have to learn it. Presumably a similar situation prevails in sexual learning.

Human learning is so complex that psychologists have had to study the mechanisms of learning in simpler situations using experimental animals like rats and pigeons. Therefore, our knowledge of how sexuality is learned is based on inferences from general theories of learning. These theories focus on the influence of learning rather than the influence of biological determinants. They focus on conscious, cognitive processes, rather than unconscious motives.

Kinsey, despite being a biologist, viewed most aspects of human sexual behavior as the product of learning. He assumed that exposure to various sexual attitudes and experiences shaped an individual's sexual preferences and behavior. Masters and Johnson also base their therapeutic approaches on behavior modification techniques derived from learning theory (Chapter 15).

Learning theories fall into three categories: classical conditioning, operant conditioning, and observational learning. None of these processes are specific to sexuality, but we shall explain them by using examples of sexual learning.

Classical Conditioning    The original experiments in classical conditioning were conducted by Ivan Petrovich Pavlov in the 1920s. He was exploring a form of learning based on association (Pavlov, 1927). Pavlov noted that dogs reflexively salivated when food was placed in their mouths. By association, dogs became conditioned to salivate in response to a host of other stimuli, such as the sight of food or even the dish in which it was served. If a buzzer was sounded before the food was served, the dog would eventually salivate in response to the sound of the buzzer alone. Pavlov called the dog's reflexive salivation to food in its mouth an *unconditioned reflex* that was based on the connection between an *unconditioned stimulus* (UCS) (food in the mouth) and *unconditioned response* (UCR) (salivation). By contrast, the buzzer represented a *conditioned stimulus* (CS), salivation in response to it a *conditioned response* (CR), and the association constituted a learned or *conditioned reflex*.

Learning expands by *stimulus generalization*. Conditioned stimuli similar to the original one will also elicit the conditioned response. (For instance, a sound similar to the original buzzer works just as well). However, learning is not permanent: the CR may disappear (or become *extinguished*) if food ceases to follow the buzzer. It may reappear (*spontaneous recovery*) after a rest period during which the animal is not exposed to these stimuli.

Classical conditioning supposedly applies to a large array of human experiences, including sexual behavior, but how this works is hard to demonstrate. One of the basic problems is to find an unconditioned erotic stimulus that reflexively elicits the unconditioned response of sexual arousal. Physical stimulation of the genitals would qualify, because sexual arousal in response to it is a proven reflex. Sights, sounds, and smells that are erotic bring on no reflex responses in humans (Chapter 3).

If we stop looking for a reflex, then greater possibilities open up for sexual learning by association. For instance, if sexual arousal happens to coincide with a particular scent (such as a body odor or a perfume), sound (utterances during coitus, a piece of music), or sight (nudity, undergarments), then these sources of stimuli may become conditioned stimuli (or eroticized) and elicit sexual arousal on their own. Such learning must often be taken on faith. Rarely can we trace a learned sexual trigger or preference to its source. For example, a man may find women with long legs sexy and a woman may find men with slim buttocks appealing, but they would be hard pressed to trace back these preferences to when they were learned.

**Operant Conditioning**    Classical conditioning presumes a stimulus-response linkage, called an S-R bond; where there is no stimulus, there is no response. This is a rather passive way of learning, when in reality animals manifest a great deal of spontaneous activity. To differentiate spontaneous behavior from actions elicited by specific external stimuli, the term *operant behavior* is used (the animal "operates" or acts on its environment). The shaping of spontaneous behavior is called *operant conditioning* (Skinner, 1938). Operant conditioning is a much more versatile and comprehensive framework than classical conditioning for understanding sexual behavior.

In operant conditioning, learning occurs because of the consequences of a given behavior. For instance, an animal learns to perform an act to get a reward. When the outcome of an act is rewarding, the behavior is *reinforced*. Reinforcement may be a positive reward (such as food) or the elimination of something bad (like electric shock). Furthermore, the reinforcers need not always be *primary*, that is, they need not satisfy some basic biological need. Stimuli acquire *secondary* reinforcing potential by being paired with primary reinforcers. Thus, a chimpanzee will work for a token once it has learned that the token can be used to get food.

How would operant conditioning work in sexual behavior? When a child presses against the mattress or fondles the genitals, the pleasure is reinforcing; hence the act is repeated until one day it is carried to orgasm. The child has now learned to masturbate. Furthermore, as the person continues to explore ways to enhance sexual pleasure, approaches that prove successful get repeated and learned; others do not. Once sexual arousal and orgasm become sought-after goals, a person will go through considerable trouble to obtain them.

## Social Learning Models

The principles of classical and operant conditioning have been developed under rigorous experimental conditions, but real life is much more complicated. Many behavioral scientists think that these learning models alone are inadequate to explain how children acquire the behaviors characteristic of their society. To allow for these more subtle and complex forms of learning, social learning theory offers additional modalities of learning (Bandura, 1986).

One such modality is *observational learning* or learning by imitation from the behavior of others who act as models (Bandura, 1969; DeLameter and MacCorquodale, 1979; Mischel, 1981). Such learning does not require the repeated pairing of stimulus with reinforcement, eliminating the necessity of direct personal experience. It opens up vast possibilities for learning sexual behaviors by observing people in the act, listening to them describe it, reading about it, seeing it portrayed on TV, and so on. That a great deal of such learning goes on all the time seems self-evident. The question is only by what mechanism such learning takes place.

All learning theorists view socialization as a process of molding. In social learning, the individual is seen as being shaped not by simple learning devices but by the entire force of culture. Moreover, as Biehler (1981) notes, social learning theorists, such as Bandura, treat the child as an active learner who tries to make sense of a wealth of information, not as a passive recipient of such information. Let us see how social learning might apply to sexual development.

The Role of Experience    During the first two years of life, the infant is engaged primarily in comfort-seeking behaviors, such as nursing, thumb-sucking, and rocking. All of these behaviors are soothing and rewarding, and all have human contact, be it with self or others. Some researchers have suggested that these experiences prepare the child for erotic behavior in adulthood (Hingham, 1980).

Differences begin to emerge in the patterns of sexual arousal and sexual play of older children (Kinsey et al., 1948, 1953). By the time children reach puberty, boys appear to engage in sexual activities such as masturbation to orgasm far more frequently than girls, although females steadily increase their mas-

turbatory activities as they get older. One explanation for this early sex difference is derived from social learning theory: girls and boys experience different models of sexual behavior and different reinforcement patterns.

Many studies support this idea. For example, Goldman and Goldman (1982) have demonstrated that girls place greater value on romantic attachments, whereas boys focus on companionship. Williams (1987) has suggested that although puberty, with the emergent secondary sexual characteristics, makes sexual differentiation more visible and heightens libidinal interest, differential sanctions are imposed on boys and girls. Welbourne-Moglia (1984) suggests that girls are learning to be dependent by pleasing others, particularly male others. As a result, girls may learn to focus on falling in love and acquiring a steady boyfriend, whereas boys may learn to develop their independence through physical control of the opposite sex. Two recent studies (Blumstein and Schwartz, 1983; Hendrick et al., 1985) have found very different attitudinal patterns concerning sexual issues for females and males.

Such disparities in social learning are common. Our culture is full of mixed messages about sexual behavior. In an early study of parental attitudes towards childhood sexuality, Bandura and Walters (1959) found that although parents claimed to find nothing wrong with childhood masturbation, they vehemently denied that their own children might engage in such behavior, and said that if they did, they would be taken at once to the family physician. More currently, Williams (1987) has noted that romance novels, aimed at women, are seldom sexually explicit, whereas pornography, aimed at men, is seldom romantic.

Experience seems to be the key to learning many of our sexual responses, such as orgasm (Bardwick, 1971; Kaplan, 1974; Kinsey, 1953; Williams, 1987). Social learning theory accounts for experience better than any other theory. Psychoanalytic theories set basic personality patterns by the age of 5 or 6; traditional learning theories talk about stimulus generalization, but pay little attention to accumulated experiences of a lifetime; developmental stage theories stress cognitive reorganization due to maturation but not to experience. Whatever approach appeals to you, bear in mind that children are active learners. They use their own experience of the world to build a cognitive structure.

Scripts Some behavioral scientists have used the metaphor of "scripts" for the shaping and expression of sexual behavior. Through childhood and adolescence every individual develops a *sexual script* that acts as a record of past sexual activities, a standard for present behavior, and a plan for the future. Laws and Schwartz (1977) define sexual scripts as a "repertoire of acts and statuses that are recognized by a social group, together with the rules, expectations, and sanctions governing these acts and statuses" (p. 2). Like a blueprint your script regulates five key variables: with whom you have sex; what you do sexually; when sex is appropriate (both time of life and specific timing); where is the proper setting for sex; and why you have sex (Libby, 1976; Gagnon, 1977).

Scripting of sexual behavior occurs at several levels (Simon and Gagnon, 1986). The cultural scripts consist of the general social expectations for a given sexual relationship, for instance, that a married couple should engage in sex or that a couple should engage in sex play before having sexual intercourse. These social expectations can be quite specific and closely adhered to. This is why the sexual behavior of many people is quite predictable, as with actors on stage enacting their scripted roles.

In order for the cultural script to be played out by the individual, it should be made part of his or her own personal script. It is in this process that variations and improvisations take place. While scripting theory recognizes this, its main focus is on the predictability rather the spontaneity of sexual behavior.

Scripts provide a couple with a common program of action to follow, provided they share the script. For instance, in a prostitute-client interaction each party knows what to expect. The situation is often more ambiguous with a dating couple where the woman may be following a romantic script and the man a sexual script (or vice versa). Moreover, scripts change. The script of premarital sex for current college students is different than that of their parents and grandparents. A clear understanding of your own sexual script and that of the person you are hoping to interact with helps to avoid misunderstanding.

The theory of sexual scripts challenges other schemes of psychosexual development on several grounds (Gagnon and Simon, 1973; Gagnon, 1977). First, it denies a biologically based sexual drive. Sexual behavior is the expression of a social script, not of some primordial urge. We are born with the capacity to behave sexually, but we are not driven to behave sexually, or to do so in a particular way. It is sexual learning and social contingencies that shape our erotic life.

Second, unlike the stage theories, which trace development along a continuum, it is argued that sexual experiences are far more discontinuous. The infant fondling his penis is not masturbating in an adult sense, but merely engaging in an act that is diffusely pleasurable. Childhood and adolescent sexual behaviors, therefore, do not necessarily have a developmental linkage. We impose continuity because we want to bring the past into harmony with our present identities, roles, and needs.

Finally, the scripting theory rejects sharp distinctions between what is "sexual" and what is "nonsexual." Beyond reproductive functions, what is defined as sexual is culturally determined and socially scripted. In short, sex is what society says it is. Indeed, cultures define a wide diversity of signals, symbols, and behaviors as "sexual." Sexual activity need not be associated with erotic arousal, nor arousal with behavior you call sexual.

The reason that culturally shared themes and symbols tend to be fairly uniform is that they are based on common childhood experiences. Interpersonal scripts tend to be more idiosyncratic, but both are shaped by social learning.

Patterns of sexual behavior are intimately

Figure 8.10    Growing up to be like mother.

linked with gender-role learning (Chapter 10). Of all the experiences of the child, such learning exerts the greatest influence in shaping sexual behavior (Figure 8.10). In other words, after learning to be male or female, the person will grow up to act in certain socially prescribed ways.

Theories of sexual development vary in the emphasis they place on sexual experience in childhood. At one extreme, classical psy-choanalytic theory considers that your sexual orientations and behavioral tendencies were set for life by the time you were six. Scripting theory, at the opposite extreme, sees sexual development as discontinuous; childhood is no more crucial than any other phase of life. Most modern theorists of sexual development agree at least that sexual development is a lifelong process. We therefore turn next to the unfolding of sexuality in adolescence and adult life.

## REVIEW QUESTIONS

1. What is the evidence for the existence of sexuality in childhood?

2. How do boys and girls differ in their sexual play alone and together?

3. What are the main influences in the sexual socialization of children?

4. What theories of sexual development rely heavily on a sexual drive?

5. What are the main theories that link sexual development to learning?

## THOUGHT QUESTIONS

1. What do you consider the ethical limits of studying childhood sexuality?

2. How would you respond to the argument that since children have been kept in the dark about sex for hundreds of years, there must be good reasons for keeping it that way?

3. How would you divide the responsibility for sex education between the family and school?

4. Where do you stand on the nature vs. nurture controversy? What are the bases of your position?

5. How would the ideas of Freud, Erikson, and Skinner change what you do as a parent or a teacher?

6. What sexual scripts do you follow?

## SUGGESTED READINGS

Sheffield, M., (1978). *Where do babies come from?* New York: Knopf. The basic elements of reproduction for young children from conception to birth.

Calderone, M., and Ramey, J. (1982). *Talking with your child about sex.* New York: Random House. A guide for parents communicating with their children about sexual topics.

Goldman, R., and Goldman, J. (1982). *Children's sexual thinking.* London: Routledge. An extensive comparative study of childhood sexual behavior in North America and three other Western countries. Detailed but full of interesting findings and insights.

James, A., Green, R., and Kolodny, R. (1982). *Childhood sexuality.* Boston: Little, Brown. Comprehensive overview of various aspects of sexual behavior in childhood.

# Sexuality in Adolescence and Adulthood

CHAPTER

9

*Confound not the distinctions of thy life which nature hath divided; that is, youth, adolescence, manhood, and old age, nor in these divided periods, wherein thou art in a manner four, conceive thyself but one. Let every division be happy in its proper virtues, nor one vice run through all. Let each distinction have its salutary transition, and critically deliver thee from the imperfections of the former; so ordering the whole, that prudence and virtue may have the largest section.*

SIR THOMAS BROWNE
(1605–1682)

OUTLINE

ADOLESCENT SEXUALITY
Adaptation to Puberty
  The Changing Body Image
  Early and Late Maturers
  Upsurge in Sexual Drive
Sexual Behavior
  Sexual Fantasy
  Erotic Dreams
  Masturbation
  Petting
  Oral Sex
  Sexual Intercourse
  Homosexual Relations
Sexual Values
  The Peer Culture
  Sex and Adult Status
  Sex and Family Characteristics
Consequences of Sexual
  Intercourse
  Positive Consequences
  Negative Consequences

Sex Education for Adolescents
SEXUALITY IN YOUNG
  ADULTHOOD
Sociosexual Aspects
Premarital Sex
  Prevalence
  Reactions
  Interpersonal Context
SEXUALITY IN MIDDLE
  ADULTHOOD
Male Midlife Transition
Female Midlife Transition
  Menopausal Symptoms
  Treatment of Menopausal Symptoms
  Psychosocial Changes
SEXUALITY IN LATE ADULTHOOD
Changes in Sexual Response
  Male Response
  Female Response
Patterns of Sexual Behavior

Traditional concepts of development have focused on childhood and adolescence. Adulthood has represented a plateau until the final changes of old age. Common perceptions of sexuality fitted into a similar model: sexual stirrings in childhood, awakening in adolescence, peak performance in early adulthood, gradual decline in middle age, and extinction of sexual desire and performance in old age. This perception has changed during the past several decades. Adulthood is now seen as a distinct phase of life with its own developmental characteristics (Bee, 1987).

Adolescence spans the second decade of life. Adulthood is roughly divided into three phases: ages 18 to 39 constitute *young adulthood;* 40 to 59, *middle adulthood* (or middle age); 60 and above *late adulthood* (or old age).

Most theorists of lifespan development conceive of the life cycle as a series of stages (Erikson, 1963a; Loevinger, 1976; Levinson, 1978). Others challenge the existence of such predictable patterns of maturation beyond childhood and see adult changes simply as continuing adjustments to external stresses and circumstances (Pearlin, 1980).

Childhood and adulthood are distinctive in their general and sexual characteristics. The transitional period of adolescence is more difficult to characterize, because it blends some of the features of childhood with those of adulthood. For instance, adolescents are biologically capable of bearing children, but most of them are socially unprepared to become parents in modern society. Currently, adolescent sexuality has come to have more in common with adult forms of sexual behavior, and its reproductive consequences clearly set it apart from childhood sexuality. That is why we will discuss adolescent sexual behavior in this chapter as the precursor of adult sexual development.

## ADOLESCENT SEXUALITY

The dramatic transformation of the body from child to adult during *puberty* (Chapter 4) is accompanied by the equally important process of psychosocial development in *adolescence*. The second decade of life, during which these changes occur, is one of the most eventful, exciting, and sometimes turbulent times of life. Sexual behavior and relationships undergo major transformations as adult patterns emerge. From here on, sexuality is no longer a form of play but an activity with far-reaching potential consequences, biological, psychological, and social.

Changes in adolescence follow a fairly predictable schedule, but not all adolescents are alike. Early adolescence is an extension of childhood; late adolescence is the precursor of young adulthood. A 13 and 18 year old are both "teenagers," but their behaviors are very different. Equally important differences may set apart adolescents in the same age range but of different social, economic, and ethnic backgrounds. When we compare adolescents from different cultures or from different historical periods in our own culture, we encounter even greater diversity (Elder, 1980).

Little can be said about adolescent sexuality that would necessarily apply to everyone in this age group. Moreover, the lives of adolescents are constantly changing. It is as if they were marching across a bridge from the shore of childhood to the shore of adulthood. This sense of being in transit, suspended in mid-air, imparts to adolescence its exhilarating, as well as its exasperating character.

### Adaptation to Puberty

The effects of puberty on sexual development are both direct and indirect (Peterson and Taylor, 1980). The growth and maturation of the genital organs make youngsters see themselves as sexual beings. The upsurge of the sexual drive in adolescence may be the result of increased sex hormone production. Other effects are more indirect. For instance, changes in the size and shape of the body enhance sexual attractiveness according to culturally determined standards. Although the effects of biological factors on sexual development cannot be neatly separated from the psychosocial factors, we shall try to discuss them separately.

# Box 9.1

## A YOUNG WOMAN AND HER CHANGING BODY

Every day, just about, something new seems to be happening to this body of mine and I get scared sometimes. I'll wake up in the middle of the night and I can't go back to sleep, and I toss and I turn and I can't stop my mind; it's racing fast, and everything is coming into it, and I think of my two best friends, and how their faces are all broken out, and I worry mine will break out, too, but so far it hasn't, and I think of my sizes, and I can't get it out of my head—the chest size and the stomach size and what I'll be wearing and whether I'll be able to fit into this kind of dress or the latest swimsuit. Well, it goes on and on, and I'm dizzy, even though it's maybe one o'clock in the morning, and there I am, in bed, so how can you be dizzy?

Everything is growing and changing. I can see my mother watching me. I can see everyone watching me. There are times I think I see people watching me when they really couldn't care less! My dad makes a point of not staring, but he catches his look, I guess. I'm going to be "big-chested"; that's how my mother describes herself! I have to figure out how to dress so I feel better—I mean, so I don't feel strange, with my bosom sticking out at everyone! I have to decide if I should shave my legs! I will! Damn! I wish a lot of the time I could go back to being a little girl, without all these problems and these decisions!

My brother isn't doing too good, either! He's got acne, and he can't shave without hurting himself because of those pimples. He doesn't like an electric shaver; he says they don't feel clean to his face. He's a nut about taking showers. Two a day! He's always using deodorant. He's got all that hair under his arms. So do I! We will have our "buddy talks," and a lot of the time we just ask, "When will it end—so we can just have a body that looks the same, from one week to other?"

Paul Burlin, *Young Man Alone with His Face*, 1944.

We're in this together, my brother and me, and my friends. That's what I think about in the night: how we're all sweating it out—including my parents, and my little sister. It used to be my brother and I ran around naked, or almost naked, but now I don't even look at my own bottom; I just get into a state, wondering and realizing how much has happened to me down there, so fast. And my brother—he's always closing his door, and no one's going to catch him dressing or undressing!

(From Coles, R., and Stokes, G. (1985). *Sex and the American Teenager*. New York: Harper & Row, pp. 2–3.)

---

The Changing Body Image  Though we have all been through it, it is easy to forget the disconcerting feeling of seeing yourself change from yesterday's child into tomorrow's adult (Box 9.1). The dramatic transformations of puberty require major adjustments in self-perception of the body, or the *body image*.

There is a great deal of pride and pleasure in growing into manhood and womanhood—a satisfaction shared by parents. There is also the potential for tension and distress. As the parts of the body grow at different rates, teenagers feel curiosity and concern about their ultimate shape and size. Typically boys worry more about being too short; girls worry more about being too tall (Betancourt, 1983a, 1983b). Long hours in front of the mirror are not just to satisfy vanity (though there is some of that) but to monitor the transformations of face and body.

Changes in the genital organs tend to be more emotionally charged than those of the rest of the body. Other changes, such as growth in stature or the appearance of facial hair, are in the open and can be discussed with others; changes in the genitals must be adjusted to in private. The breasts among girls and the genitals among boys are special worries with respect to size and shape.

Menarche used to be a stressful period for girls, but most teenagers are now prepared to welcome it; some parents celebrate by sending their daughter flowers and gifts, or taking her out to dinner. If a girl is not well informed or if her first period is not managed with sensitivity, the experience still can be stressful.

The reactions of others, especially the parents, are important for a healthy redefinition of body image. Parents who are made anxious by the emerging sexuality of their teenage children may communicate their anxiety in various ways, making their children uneasy in turn. These parents may not know enough about early adolescence (Cohen et al., 1986). Often children enter adolescence before parents expect it or are willing to recognize it. When some parents show undue preoccupation with their children's sexual lives or act seductively toward them, youngsters may become guarded or bewildered. We shall return to how parents deal with their adolescents' sexuality shortly.

Adolescents gradually become aware that their developing bodies attract a new form of attention from adults. Girls attract heterosexual men; less often boys attract homosexual men. Adult women may also be attracted to adolescents of either sex, but they are less likely to reveal or act on such interest. Their

expressions of affection (such as hugging or kissing) are socially more acceptable.

Even in the absence of overt sexual interest, adolescents become keenly aware of the value parents, other adults, and peers place on their physical attractiveness. Not only does the youngster have to come to terms with a changing body, but also with every pimple, blemish, and unruly lock of hair that may convey an unattractive image. Girls are especially apt to become preoccupied with their weight (Davies and Furnham, 1986), which may lead to unhealthy diets and food fads. Anorexia with severe weight loss principally affects girls soon after puberty (Russell, 1985).

A certain measure of self-consciousness is almost inevitable for adolescents. It takes time before they feel comfortable in their own skin. The level of self-esteem strongly influences this process. Adolescents who suffer from low self-esteem are more likely to be anxious about and disapproving of their bodies than others with comparable levels of physical attractiveness (Jacobson, 1964; Schonfeld, 1971).

The sense of "sexiness" influences how desirable we think we are as a sexual partner and the "value" others place on us as sexual beings. Should physical characteristics (which are easily influenced by fads) be more important than enduring personality factors? We shall return to this issue in Chapter 16.

Early and Late Maturers   Because adolescents are keenly aware of their peers, differences in their rates of maturation are a significant worry. Even though early and late maturers end up as well developed, some of the psychological effects of being off-schedule persist beyond adolescence.

The basic issue is being different from others. Such difference may be perceived by peers as a sign of status or of deviance. Studies of early-maturing boys generally show them to be more self-confident, relaxed, attractive, and popular with peers (Jones, 1965). Early-maturing girls, despite their enhanced social prestige, may feel conspicuous because of their tallness and bigger breasts. Late-maturing girls are described as having more outgoingness, confidence, and leadership ability. These differences are influenced by social class: they apply to middle-class girls but not those from less advantaged backgrounds (Clausen, 1975). Furthermore, physical maturation affects not only sexual relationships but friendships in general. For instance, girls in the fifth to seventh grades with the most advanced breast development have been reported to have more close friends than those who had not yet begun to develop (Brooks-Gunn et al., 1986).

Upsurge in Sexual Drive    Sexual interest and activity intensify during adolescence. This is ascribed to the hormonal changes of puberty causing an upsurge in sexual drive (Udry et al., 1985). As shown in Figure 9.1, the increase in the level of testosterone appears to correlate directly with a number of typical adolescent behaviors in males. Among girls, hormonal levels have a strong effect on sexual interest but a weak effect on sexual behavior (Udry et al., 1985b).

However, there is no firm evidence that hormones directly cause such behavioral changes. For instance, in precocious puberty, higher hormonal levels are generally not accompanied by early dating, romantic, or sexual experiences, despite an early awakening of sexual fantasies (Money and Ehrhardt, 1972).

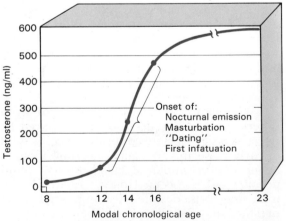

Figure 9.1    Amount of testosterone in the plasma in males at different ages.

Evidence that more black boys than white boys initiate intercourse before puberty suggests a stronger environmental effect on such behavior (Clark et al., 1984).

In general, when a teenager starts dating is influenced more by social factors (such as parental and peer expectations) than by hormone levels (Dornbusch et al., 1981). Once dating becomes the norm in a group, everyone tends to do it, no matter how far they have matured. Particularly during early adolescence, a social gathering like a school dance will bring together boys and girls at different levels of biological maturation, with the girls generally ahead of the boys (Figure 9.2).

Possibly the role of hormones in sexual drive is not specific but part of a more general behavioral influence. It may include the greater aggressivity of teenagers (especially boys) and their increased energy, which is expressed by exuberance and impulsiveness. Sexuality may be just one part of this "enormous internal energy suddenly exerting itself—a gift, a threat, a mystery, a force to be reckoned with" (Coles, 1985).

Sexual Behavior
Sexual behavior in adolescence is in some ways continuous with its childhood antecedents, but the transition is by no means a simple progression from sexual play to the "real thing." The meaning of sexual acts in childhood is different from their meaning later on. Also, adolescence is a time of sexual exploration, and its patterns of sexual behavior are bound to change over time.

Sexual Fantasy    An increase in erotic thoughts and imagery is the harbinger of adolescent sexual interactions. Their frequency and explicitness are based on three main factors.

The first factor is probably hormonal. Boys with precocious puberty have sexual fantasies ahead of their peers, even though they are not typically ahead in sexual behavior. The upsurge in sexual drive is readily expressed in fantasies, which are not subject to the social constraints on sexual behavior.

The second factor is cognitive. To con-

Figure 9.2   Junior high students at a school dance. How teenagers dress and behave at such functions vary greatly. In this rather formal setting, these youngsters look like aspiring yuppies.

struct the elaborate imagery of erotic thoughts requires a certain intellectual competence, which develops after the child grows older. The third contributor is social exposure. As teenagers move into the adult world, they come into contact with sexually explicit materials (movies, magazines, videos) and observe sexual interactions among their peers, all of which adds fuel to their erotic fire.

Erotic fantasies not only provide a source of sexual arousal, they also help adolescents explore and define their emerging sexual orientations and preferences. Erotic fantasies range from fleeting thoughts to elaborate scenarios that may be quite imaginative. One teenage boy had the fantasy of being able to "freeze" people as if stopping a film. He could then approach women who struck his fantasy and undress, fondle, or do with them as he pleased, after which he would "unfreeze" everyone and life would go on as usual (Box 11.1).

Adolescents are sometimes dismayed by what seems to arouse them. Fantasies of homosexual attraction and activity may be disturbing for those who are yet unsettled in their sexual orientation. Scenes of sexual coercion where one is forced into sex or forces someone else into sex may be equally upsetting. Imagining other unusual behaviors may lead them to feel "perverted," "abnormal," and subject to social condemnation. Adolescents are relieved to learn that erotic fantasies of all sorts are common, and that such thoughts neither "define" us nor are likely to lead to socially unacceptable behaviors (Chapter 11).

Erotic Dreams   Dreams are fantasies that occur during sleep. They may lead to *nocturnal orgasm* or *nocturnal emission.* (Nocturnal orgasm may also occur without dreams, or the person may not remember them on waking up.) Soiled pajamas or bedsheets are telltale evidence that may cause embarrassment. It can also be alarming when a boy experiences orgasm for the first time in his sleep (which is the case for one out of eight boys). Girls do not face these problems because they do not ejaculate, but they too experience nocturnal orgasm. Some of them are unaware of it in the morning.

Nocturnal orgasms are not an important sexual outlet, nor do they act as a "safety valve" to release pent-up sexual tension. Nonetheless, they do get less frequent as the person grows older.

Masturbation    Erotic fantasies are closely linked to masturbation; fantasies may lead to masturbation and the wish to masturbate conjures up erotic fantasies (Hass, 1979). Fantasies are used regularly by at least half of adolescents during masturbation, but 11 percent of boys and 7 percent of girls say they never fantasize when stimulating themselves to orgasm (Sorensen, 1973).

Masturbation is the most common source of orgasm in adolescents of both sexes. The first ejaculation among boys results from masturbation in two out of three instances. Among males in the Kinsey sample, the earliest ejaculation remembered was at about 8 years and the latest first ejaculation at 21 years of age. The majority (about 90 percent) of all males had had this experience between the ages of 11 and 15 years (mean age close to 14) (Kinsey et al., 1948).

Masturbation provides an available, safe, and secure sexual outlet. It allows the release of sexual tension and self-exploration. It is an end in itself as well as a rehearsal for sex with others. Its prevalence has changed over the years. As shown in Table 9.1, the prevalence of masturbation among 13 year olds had gone up considerably between the Kinsey and Hunt surveys over two decades. The percentage for

boys rose from 45 percent to 63 percent, and for girls it more than doubled, from 15 percent to 33 percent. On the other hand, the rates seem to have declined between the Sorensen and Coles and Stokes studies, separated by a decade. The older the teenagers, the higher are the rates, as shown by the Haas sample.

The discrepancies between these surveys are partly due to their methods. The consistently higher percentage figures among boys than girls probably reflect a higher prevalence of masturbation among boys, but boys might also be more willing to report it. Many girls may not label the self-stimulation they engage in as "masturbation." If a girl is asked whether she puts her hand between her legs to obtain pleasure, she may say "yes," but to the question "Do you masturbate?" she may say "no." Erection and ejaculation in boys are easier to label as "masturbation."

Masturbation is no longer condemned as in the past; yet some shame and embarrassment continue to be attached to it. These and other aspects of masturbation will be discussed further in Chapter 11.

Petting    By the time they get to high school, most adolescents have crossed the line from autoerotic to sociosexual behaviors. Petting represents a significant advance because it requires the ability to approach, respond, and negotiate a sexual encounter. The activities of petting follow a fairly predictable progression from the less intimate (holding hands) to the more intense interactions up to coitus. Hence at successive ages, the percentage of boys and girls who have engaged in a particularly sexual activity progressively gets higher.

Petting or "making out" involves activities that induce sexual excitement but stop short

**Table 9.1    Adolescents Who Have Masturbated**

|  | KINSEY et al. (1948, 1953) | HUNT (1974) | HAAS (1979) | COLES AND STOKES (1985) |
|---|---|---|---|---|
| *Ages* | *13 Years* | *13 Years* | *17–18 Years* | *13–18 Years* |
| Males | 45% | 63% | 80% | 46% |
| Females | 15% | 33% | 59% | 24% |

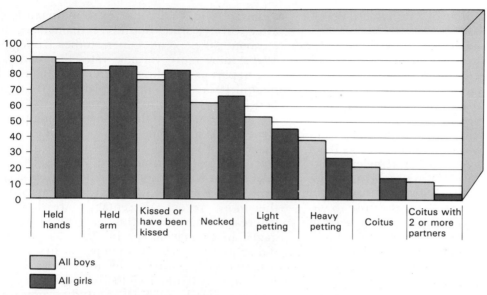

Figure 9.3    Prevalence of heterosexual activities at age 15.

of vaginal, anal, or oral intercourse. They in-clude kissing, hugging, caressing, fondling, and breast and genital stimulation. Distinctions are made among "necking" (prolonged hug-ging and kissing); "light" petting (above the waist) and "heavy" petting (below the waist).

The activities of petting are identical to those of "foreplay," which typically precede coitus. Currently, there is a move away from viewing such interactions as preliminary to coi-tus, or as second-best substitutes for it. Rather, such erotic play is seen as a sexual activity in its own right, which need not lead to coitus or orgasm to be "complete." This issue is of spe-cial interest today because safe sex relies heav-ily on sexual play (Chapter 5).

In the Kinsey sample, 39 percent of girls and 57 percent of boys had engaged in petting by age 15; 80 percent of both sexes had done so by age 18. Less than a quarter of the sample, however, had carried it to the point of orgasm. More recent figures show a higher proportion of petting to orgasm both by high school boys (50 percent) and girls (40 percent) (Kolodny, 1980).

The social relationship in which petting typically occurs is "dating." The terminology

and to some extent the nature of dating prac-tices have changed over the years. The full courtship sequence several decades ago pro-gressed from casual dating to "going steady"; then in early adulthood, it led to engagement, and marriage. Adolescents now have more in-formal associations (Murstein, 1974, 1980)—they "hang out together"—but the basic pat-terns of interaction have not changed. At some point in the friendship or the love relationship, the couple becomes physically intimate and moves through a set of increasingly intensive sexual interactions which may or may not lead to coitus. As shown in Figure 9.3, about 90 percent of 15-year-old boys and girls have held hands, but only 11 percent of boys and 4 per-cent of girls have engaged in coitus with two or more partners. Compared to a few decades ago, teenagers in the United States now engage in more sexual activity, of a greater variety, and start younger.

The importance of dating behavior goes beyond its sexual aspects. Sex is by no means a necessary or central part of it. Developing affectionate bonds, sharing common interests, dealing with another person at an intimate level, and knowing how to behave in public as a couple are key aspects of psychosocial development to adulthood.

Oral Sex    In the Kinsey sample, 8 percent of males and 14 percent of females reported having engaged in cunnilingus during adolescence; more recently 50 percent of males and 41 percent of females report similar activity. The incidence of fellatio has also gone up from 23 percent to 44 percent for males and from 12 percent to 32 percent for females (Newcomer and Udry, 1985). Boys report enjoying both experiences more than girls (Coles and Stokes, 1985). Some adolescents refuse to engage in oral sex even if they have engaged in intercourse because they see it as a more intimate activity with deeper relational requirements. Others use oral sex as a substitute for coitus to avoid pregnancy.

Sexual Intercourse    The most important sexual landmark that heterosexual adolescents cross is sexual intercourse. Not only is coitus considered to be the most intimate of all sexual relationships, but it also has the most significant consequences. Couples who sleep together "cross a line" that unalterably changes the character of their relationship. Pregnancy and sexually transmitted diseases make coitus a high-risk activity if the proper precautions are not taken. For such reasons the prospect of coitus among adolescents, especially at younger ages, raises serious social concerns.

There are few studies of adolescent sexual behavior among high school age populations. Table 9.2 shows the results of four studies beginning with Kinsey. Although the studies differed in method and sampling, the percentage of boys at about age 16 with coital experience appears to have stayed fairly steady at close to 45 percent; the percentage of girls of comparable ages who have coital sex went up ten-fold after Kinsey's study but then remained steady at about 30 percent. Other studies from the 1970s show more variable rates that may be due in part to sampling differences (Miller and Simon, 1974; Vener and Stewart, 1974; Jessor and Jessor, 1975).

Figures showing the same increasing prevalence of coitus come from two studies conducted in 1971 and 1976 on national probability samples (Kantner and Zelnik, 1972b; Zelnik and Kantner, 1977). For women aged between 15 and 19 who had never married, the more recent percentages are higher: whereas 27 percent of this age group had engaged in premarital sex in 1971, 35 percent did so in 1976. The median age at first intercourse declined during this interval by about four months (from 16.5 to 16.2 years).

The Zelnik and Kantner studies show significant differences between blacks and whites. The rate of premarital coitus for black women between 15 and 19 years of age is much higher than for white women: 51.2 percent against 21.4 percent for whites in 1971, and 62.7 percent versus 30.8 percent for whites in 1976. The higher ratio for blacks is true for each age group for both studies, but the relative differences are smaller in 1976, because the rates are rising more steeply for whites. The figures for males from Zelnik and Kantner (1980) show 56 percent of 17 year olds and 78 percent of 19 year olds to have engaged in coitus.

The fact that black adolescents become sexually active on average two years earlier than whites may be due to ethnic or socioeconomic factors. A number of other factors also influence the onset of sexual activity. Those who are religiously devout (of whatever faith) are less likely to engage in early coitus. There is a strong association between low intellectual

**Table 9.2    Adolescents Who Have Engaged in Coitus**

|  | KINSEY et al. (1948, 1953) | SORENSEN (1973) | HAAS (1979) | COLES AND STOKES (1985) |
|---|---|---|---|---|
| *Ages* | *15 Years* | *13–15 Years* | *16 Years* | *16 Years* |
| Males | 39% | 44% | 43% | 44% |
| Females | 3% | 30% | 31% | 30% |

ability, academic grades and achievement, and early sexual experience among blacks and whites. (National Research Council, 1987). Other associations with family and peer group will be discussed below.

The likelihood that the first coital experience will be positive is greater for boys than girls. In the Coles and Stokes (1985) sample, 60 percent of the boys were "glad" about the experience, 34 percent "ambivalent," 1 percent "sorry," and 5 percent reported "no feelings." By contrast, 23 percent of the girls were glad, 61 percent ambivalent, 11 percent sorry, and 4 percent had no feelings about it. Girls valued virginity more than boys: about half said they wanted to be a virgin when they married. Only one-third of the boys wanted to marry a virgin. Fifteen percent of the girls who had intercourse said they would have preferred to have waited until they got married.

Homosexual Relations    Just as children engage in sexplay with members of their own sex, it is not unusual for adolescents to have homosexual contacts with peers, and less often with either adults or children. Typically, such encounters are exploratory and transient; they do not necessarily lead to a homosexual orientation in adulthood. On the other hand, adult homosexuals usually trace their behaviors back to adolescence. A person who does not already have homosexual inclinations by adolescence is unlikely to develop them in adulthood; but most adolescent homosexual experiences give way to a heterosexual orientation.

Despite the recent liberalization of social attitudes, adolescents strongly disapprove of homosexuals and some are quite hostile to them. Lesbians are viewed with more tolerance, and girls are generally more tolerant than boys toward gay people.

Given these facts, self-reported homosexual behaviors tend to be particularly unreliable. Available figures for at least a single adolescent homosexual experience are 17 percent of 16- to 19-year-old boys and 6 percent of girls (Sorenson, 1973); 14 percent of teenage boys and 11 percent of teenage girls (Haas, 1979a).

Very few of the adolescent subjects in the Coles and Stokes (1985) sample admitted to any sexual interest in members of the same sex—only one boy in over 1000 subjects considered himself homosexual; 3 percent said they were bisexual; and 5 percent said they had participated in some sort of homosexual activity. However, one-third of them knew someone who was homosexual, and one in ten said they had a gay friend.

Adolescents who are openly gay face special problems. The revelation or discovery of their homosexuality resulted for one group of gay teenagers in strongly negative reactions from parents (43 percent) and friends (41 percent). They were discriminated against by peers (37 percent), verbally abused (55 percent), and physically assaulted (30 percent). (Remafedi, 1987a). The majority of these subjects also experienced school problems, substance abuse, and emotional problems. Nearly half of them had contracted a sexually transmitted disease, run away from home, or gotten into trouble with the law (Remafedi, 1987b).

Unlike older gay men and women, who obtain support from each other, adolescents feel more isolated and must deal with the implications of their sexual orientation on their own. However, an increasing number of families are now more understanding and supportive of their gay children. Even if parents do not approve, they are willing to accept their children's sexuality rather than blaming themselves or their children.

Sexual Values
The sexual values of adolescents become most sharply defined with respect to premarital sex. The standards among youth in the United States have been characterized by Ira Reiss (1960, 1967, 1980) as falling into four categories: (1) *abstinence*—premarital intercourse is wrong for both men and women, regardless of circumstances; (2) *permissiveness with affection*—premarital intercourse is right for both men and women under certain conditions in a stable relationship with engagement, love, or strong affection; (3) *permissiveness without affection*—premarital intercourse is right for both

men and women regardless of affection or stable relationship, based purely on sexual attraction; and (4) *double standard*—premarital intercourse is acceptable for men, but is unacceptable for women.

What adolescents uphold as their moral standard and how they behave are not always consistent. Adolescents are generally more restrictive in what they believe to be acceptable conduct, but more permissive in how they act and even more permissive in their perception of how others act (Roche, 1986). That perception may help mitigate their sense of guilt in not living up to their own standards. Furthermore, during the early stages of dating (when there is as yet no strong affection), males and females differ widely in their perceptions of what is proper behavior; males are more likely to approve of sexual intimacy and sooner. In the later stages of dating (when the couple is in love) there is virtually no difference in moral attitudes between male and female.

The Peer Culture    Much has been written about how the adolescent *peer culture* and a broader *youth subculture* shape sexual attitudes and behaviors (Coleman, 1980). Adherence to the group values supposedly determines popularity. Moreover, these values are seen as opposing the values of parents and society.

Others question this notion. Instead, adolescents are seen to belong to a diversity of groups, which neither simply repeat nor wholly reject the sexual values and expectations of the adult social system.

Peer pressure can take the form of challenges or dares, the threat of social rejection and ostracism, and more direct forms of coercion. White teenagers are more susceptible to peer pressure than blacks; girls are more readily influenced by their peers than boys. This makes white girls most likely to be swayed in their sexual decision-making by their peers (National Research Council, 1987).

Sex and Adult Status    Adolescents may engage in sex because they feel sufficiently adult, or because they want to win such recognition among adults.

Unlike many preliterate cultures, industrialized societies do not have commonly accepted *rites of passage,* including puberty rites that signal to the individual and to the community that a shift to adult status has taken place (Muuss, 1970). There are, nonetheless, strong social expectations of how adolescents should behave, which vary in different cultures (Box 9.2). As measured against prevailing standards, lack of sexual interest, excessive sexual interest, or the wrong kind of sexual interest alarms parents and other significant adults. Parents concerned over teenage pregnancy and sexually transmitted illness, or those with strong moral convictions, may feel a responsibility to guide and protect their offspring. Other parents may try to enforce behavioral codes on their children that they themselves neither believe in nor follow; they may be more concerned with the family "image" than the intrinsic merits or demerits of their children's sexual behavior. Still other parents simply stay out of their teenagers' lives as long as they do not get into trouble. Adolescents in these situations enjoy their freedom, but they may yearn for guidance and limits, which show that their parents care.

Sexuality is often used by rebellious adolescents to express defiance and independence (Giovacchini, 1986). During adolescent sexual development, what the person wants to do may not be what society expects. The conflict may be between acting or not acting sexually, or choosing one form of sexual behavior over another. The adolescent is forced to come to terms with satisfying sexual needs and peer expectations without getting into trouble with the adult world. If the sexual values of the adult culture are reasonable and clearly defined, there is less potential for conflict; if they are unduly restrictive or chaotically loose, the adolescent has a harder transition to make into adulthood.

Sex and Family Characteristics    Parental influence is manifested in other ways as well. There is a strong relationship between a mother's age at first coitus and that of her daughter in initiating sexual experiences (Newcomer and

# Box 9.2

## PREMARITAL SEX IN OTHER CULTURES

In about half of the preliterate societies surveyed by Ford and Beach (1951), women were allowed to have premarital coitus. If societies that overtly condemn but covertly condone such behavior are included, then the figure rises to 70 percent. Where they have free access to each other, young men and women appear to engage in sex almost daily, but the choice of partners is not indiscriminate.

Marshall has provided a detailed account of a sexually permissive society of Polynesians living on the island of Mangaia (one of the Cook Islands in the South Pacific):

The standard pattern for premarital sex is "sleep crawling" (*motoro*) which proceeds as follows: A youth bent on courting must first slip out of his own home and then avoid village policemen who are out searching for violators of the nine o'clock curfew. He must then get to the girl's house before other suitors. His effort may be made at sometime between ten o'clock in the evening and midnight; if successful, he may remain until three o'clock in the morning. If the girl has invited him to visit her, or if he is a regular visitor, his task is much easier. If not, he is faced with the alternative of "sweet talking" her (with the risk of waking the family) or of smiting her or gagging her mouth with his hand or a towel until he has made his penetration. Mangaian boys believe that most girls will not call the family if the suitor talks to her but that many a girl will call out to her father if the boy tries force. In any event, once penetration is made, most resistance is gone; "She has no voice to call." Less aggressive boys or the darker-skinned and other less sociably desirable youths may take up to a year of "sweet talk" to win the girl they desire; others may speed their suit by serenades. Most of them simply take what they want, when they want it.*

The majority of cultures surveyed by Ford and Beach (1951) were characterized less by differences in sexual codes for juveniles than by the lack of vigor in enforcing existing prohibitions. For example, the Alorese (polygynous agriculturalists of Indonesia), the Andamanese (monogamous seminomadic gatherers, hunters, and fishers), and the Huichol (monogamous Mexican herders and farmers) all formally disapproved of premarital intercourse, but made little effort to check it. As long as the practice was not flaunted and did not result in pregnancy, it was generally tolerated. When pregnancy occurred the couple was pressured into marriage. Contraceptive measures were therefore frequently used by youngsters in these cultures. Methods included coitus interruptus, ejaculation between the girl's legs, placing a pad in the vagina, and washing the vagina after coitus. A pregnant girl might also have resorted to abortion.

In sexually restrictive societies, female virginity at the time of marriage is highly valued and society goes to great pains to enforce prohibitions on preadolescent sexual behavior. Chaperoning and segregation are some preventive measures. Disgrace, punishment, and even death are invoked when prevention fails. Among the Chagga (advanced polygynous agriculturalists of Tanzania), for instance, if a boy who had been initiated was caught in the sex act, he and his partner were placed one on top of the other and staked to the ground.

*Donald Marshall, "Sexual behavior in Mangaia," in Marshall and Suggs (1971), p. 129. Reproduced by permission.

---

Udry, 1983). Adolescent girls are more likely to engage in coitus if their mothers do not combine affection with the setting of clear and firm limits. For boys, having discussion with mothers on several topics is associated with less subsequent sexual activity; but discussions with fathers is associated with more activity (possibly because mothers discourage—while fathers may tacitly encourage— such activity. Other studies have tended to substantiate these findings. Children in intact families or in families with fewer siblings are less likely to engage in coitus during adolescence (National Research Council, 1987).

## Consequences of Sexual Intercourse

During the past two decades, the liberalization of the sexual behavior of youth has been one of the most far-reaching social changes in the United States (Chapter 21). Starting with college students, the shifts in sexual attitudes have rapidly moved down to the high-school and often the junior-high levels. The changes in the sexual behavior of youth have been matched by shifts in parental and social permissiveness—part grudging concession to the ways of the young and part tacit endorsement of a new outlook on sexuality.

At the same time there is deep and widespread concern over exposing the young to pregnancy and sexually transmitted diseases. This concern has become especially acute with the catastrophic prospect of AIDS spreading into the adolescent population.

How we judge the consequences of adolescent sexuality depends in part on what sector of the adolescent population we look at. On the positive side, there are sexually active adolescents whose lives are enriched by the experience with no apparent ill effects. On the negative side are the teenagers whose sexual lives are a joyless concession to peer pressure; pregnant girls whose psychological and social development is seriously hampered; teenage boys and girls whose growing bodies suffer the effects of sexually transmitted diseases. Other concerns are damage to social reputation and to subsequent marital happiness (Miller and Simon, 1980). Adolescent girls are at higher risk for most of these dangers, though boys are by no means immune to their effects.

Positive Consequences     Few adult voices openly celebrate the fact that adolescents now engage in sexual intercourse in greater numbers and at younger ages. Parents are not likely to congratulate their teenage children for crossing the line. Yet there is a definite sense, in some sectors of society, that there is a positive value in the greater sexual freedom of today's youth.

Sex is now openly endorsed as a good thing by almost everyone, even though there may be much disagreement about the forms that sexual experience must take. If sex is beneficial to our lives, why withhold it from the young? Dissatisfied with the inhibitions of the past and the hypocrisy of the double standard, some people see the open, honest, and egalitarian sexual behavior of the young as a refreshing change, provided it is handled responsibly.

Negative Consequences     No reasonable person can dismiss the potential serious consequences of teenage sex today; yet it could be argued that they mainly reflect the failure of our society to provide timely and adequate sexual information, guidance, and protection.

The threat of AIDS (Chapter 5) has not stopped teenagers from becoming sexually active, but many seem to be more cautious and selective in the choice of their sexual partners. Other teenagers continue to deny the threat of AIDS, labor under misconceptions, or feel themselves to be invulnerable.

Another widespread problem is teenage pregnancy (Figure 9.4). Though STDs represent a health threat to both sexes, girls take the health risk in pregnancy. Girls suffer more socially, even though boys are also affected.

In addition to intense professional interest in the topic, the public media have been giving extensive coverage to "children having children" (Time, 1985; Newsweek, 1987). For good reason: the United States has the highest teenage pregnancy rate in the developed world (Jones et al., 1987). It is highest for all ages between 15 and 19 years, but especially for the older teens: the pregnancy rate for 19-year-old women in the United States is three times that in the Netherlands, a country known for its sexual liberality. Each year for the past ten years, over a million teenagers have become pregnant. In 1984, an estimated 1,004,859 girls under age 20 became pregnant, which represents about 11 percent of the female adolescent population. Close to half of the 9 million women aged 15 to 19 were sexually active in 1985. Figure 9.5 shows the various outcomes

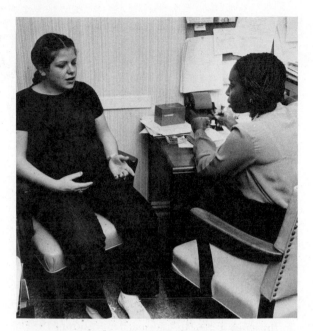

Figure 9.4 Pregnant teenager meeting with counselor.

(Lewin, 1988). An estimated four out of ten women in the United States become pregnant at some point in the course of their adolescent years. Half a million teenagers become mothers each year; about 10,000 babies are born to children under age 15; one-third of all teenage mothers have a second child before age 20. Half of all teenage pregnancies occur within six months of the first act of coitus; girls 15 years and younger are twice as likely to become pregnant within that period as girls who are 18 or 19 (Zelnik, 1980).

There has been a recent leveling-off of pregnancy and birth rates among teenagers, but a higher proportion of teenage parents than ever are unmarried. In 1970, there were 68.3 births for every 1,000 teenage girls; in 1985, that figure was down to 51.3 for every 1,000. The percentage of unmarried teenage parents had gone up from less than 33 percent in 1970 to 58 percent in 1985 (Lewin, 1988). Black teenagers are 2.3 times more likely to give birth outside marriage than are whites, although the fastest rise in the number of births to unwed teenagers has been among whites; it is this rise among whites that explains the overall increase in the birth rate of unmarried teenagers (National Research Council, 1987). If present trends continue, 40 percent of girls now aged 14 will be pregnant at least once before age 20. They are trapped in a cycle

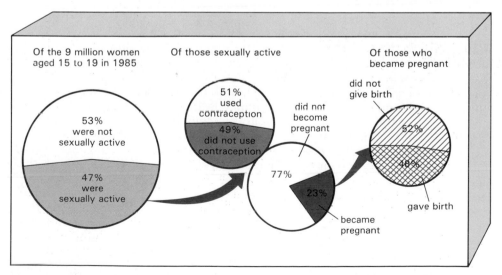

Figure 9.5 Reproductive outcomes of sexual activity among teenage women.

# Box 9.3

## EFFECTS OF ADOLESCENT CHILDBEARING

### COMPLICATIONS OF PREGNANCY AND CHILDBIRTH

Pregnant teenagers have four to five times as many pregnancy complications as older women (Menken, 1972). These complications appear to be associated with lifestyle—teenagers' failure to seek adequate prenatal care, poor nutritional habits—not with physical immaturity.

Proportionately more younger teenagers give birth to infants with low birth weight (under 2500 grams) than do older mothers. For example, among whites, twice as many infants of mothers under 15 have low birth weight than do infants of mothers aged 20 to 24 (National Center for Health Statistics, 1980).

### EDUCATION

Only 50 percent of teenage women who have given birth before age 18 complete high school, compared to 95 percent who have not given birth by age 20.

Seventy percent of teenage men who become parents complete high school, compared to 95 percent who do not become parents. (This study used samples matched for race, socioeconomic status, academic aptitude, achievement, and educational expectations at age 15) (Card and Wise, 1978).

Teenage parents who live with parents or relatives (compared to those who live separately) are:

11 percent more likely to remain in school
14 percent more likely to graduate from high school
19 percent more likely to get a job
22 percent less likely to receive welfare assistance

(Alan Guttmacher Institute, 1981).

### FAMILY INCOME AND EARNINGS

Teenagers who have children when they are 18 or younger earn about two-thirds as much as those who wait until they are 20 or older (Suchindram, 1978).

Families headed by mothers 25 or under are seven times more likely to be poor than all families in this country (Alan Guttmacher Institute, 1981).

About 61 percent of women on AFDC (Aid for Families with Dependent Children) gave birth as teenagers (Moore, 1978).

Every year about $8 billion in social welfare services is spent on first births to teenage parents.

(From Cook et al., *Sexuality education: A guide to developing and implementing programs.* Santa Cruz, CA: Network Publications, 1984, p. 15).

---

that perpetuates itself: 82 percent of teenage mothers aged 15 or younger were themselves daughters of teenage mothers (Pitt, 1986).

Teenage pregnancy also entails significant health risks for both the mother and the child; the younger the mother, the higher the risk (Alan Guttmacher Institute, 1981). About half of teenage women who get pregnant will give birth and keep the child; very few place their babies up for adoption (Zelnik et al., 1981). Thus, in addition to the effects of early childbearing on the health of the mother and infant, the process of raising a child as a young single parent has enormous consequences both for the individuals involved and to society (Box

9.3). In monetary terms alone, the support of unwed mothers with children cost about $16 billion in 1985 (*Carnegie Quarterly,* 1986).

Though the primary burden of adolescent pregnancy falls on the teenage mother, there are serious consequences for teenage fathers as well. In addition to hampering education and career, teenage fatherhood generates considerable stress and conflict. Many of these young men are prevented from contact with their children after the relationship of the couple has ended. They feel frustrated in being unable to provide financial support and suffer from the highly negative stereotypes society holds of them (Heindricks, 1980). Because fathering a child may be one of the few ways of acquiring adult status in inner-city communities, dealing with the plight of disadvantaged young men is one of the important elements in preventing teenage parenthood.

Abortion obviates many of the consequences of adolescent pregnancy, and teenagers increasingly rely on it, but abortion raises serious moral issues for many teenagers and their families. Compared with adults, adolescents have somewhat more negative psychological reactions to abortion, experiencing greater loss and guilt (along with relief). The trauma is reduced if the pregnant teenager participates actively in making the decision, with full information and psychological support (Adler and Dolcini, 1986).

Sex Education for Adolescents   The negative consequences of sexual intercourse in adolescence have led to greater public acceptance of sex education in high school. Many of those who are hesitant on the subject of sex education for younger children see little choice when it comes to teenagers. All told, 85 percent of respondents to a 1985 public opinion poll said sex education should be taught in high school. Among the topics to be included, birth control and sexually transmitted diseases top the list (Harris Poll, 1985).

Yet teaching adolescents about sex remains a divisive issue. Its critics claim that such instruction encourages sexual experimentation, hence compounding the problem instead of solving it. Others would like to see such courses focus only on moral education with the emphasis on abstinence ("say no"). The proponents of sex education would like to see sex education courses go beyond problem areas and aim at enhancing the sexual lives of youngsters through positive attitudes and responsible behavior. There are now several sexuality curricula available for elementary and secondary school students (McCaffree, 1986), but their success depends on the quality of teacher preparation (Manley, 1986).

The charge that sex education acts as an inducement for engaging in sex is unsubstan-

tiated. A large proportion of sexually-active teenagers initiate coitus before they have taken a sex course (Marsiglio and Mott, 1986). Countries like England, Canada, Sweden, and Holland have far more extensive sex education programs than the United States and also much lower teenage pregnancy rates (Dryfoos, 1985; Welbourne-Moglia and Edwards, 1986).

Several studies have now shown promising, positive effects of sex education on reducing the teenage pregnancy rates in the United States as well. Welbourne-Moglia and Edwards (1986) report that researchers from Johns Hopkins evaluated a school pregnancy program and found both a substantial decrease in the number of pregnancies and a longer delay until first intercourse (Alan Guttmacher Institute, 1986). Another extensive and careful evaluation of adolescent sexuality education programs has shown that these programs increase students' factual knowledge both during the course and at a follow-up five months later (Kirby, 1984). Similarly, Zelnik and Kim (1982) found that sexually-active teenage girls were less likely to become pregnant if they had been exposed to sex education. Sex education did not cause a higher level of sexual activity among these young women. The number of sexually active female teenagers remained the same regardless of exposure to these classes.

The effectiveness of sex education programs are greatly enhanced if coupled with school clinics that provide contraceptives (Kirby, 1984). In several high schools in St. Paul, Minnesota, with such clinics, the teenage pregnancy rate fell from 59 to 26 per 1000 between 1977 and 1984 (Wallis, 1985).

The potential benefits of sex education notwithstanding, it is not likely to be sufficient in itself. Particularly among socially-disadvantaged teenagers, it is not just ignorance or the lack of contraceptives that result in pregnancy. As we discussed earlier (Chapter 6) there are both psychological and social reasons which also need to be taken into account. How best to deal with these issues is one of the serious challenges facing American society (National Research Council, 1987).

## SEXUALITY IN YOUNG ADULTHOOD

The shift into adulthood from adolescence takes place through the *early adult transition.* The precise ages for this period depend on what occupational and social paths the person takes. For men, Levinson (1978) assigns ages 17 to 22 to this phase; hence it roughly corresponds to the college years, although not everyone, of course, spends those years in college. If on graduation from high school a person gets a full-time job, forms a stable intimate relationship, or gets married and has a child, he or she effectively becomes a full-fledged young adult.

College students take longer to attain full adult status. Therefore, they have been characterized as belonging to the stage of *youth,* a phase of life that has come about because of the lengthy period of vocational and social maturation in highly industrialized societies like the United States (Erikson, 1963b).

The counterpart of this process, the transition to sexual adulthood, has been called *sexual unfolding* by Lorna and Phillip Sarrel (1979), who divide this process into ten steps:

Adapting to the bodily changes of puberty.
Overcoming guilt, shame, fear, and childhood inhibitions about sex.
Shifting primary emotional attachment from parents to peers.
Answering questions about one's sexual orientation.
Learning and communicating what we like and dislike.
First intercourse.
Coping with sexual dysfunction or compulsion.
Understanding the place and value of sex in our lives.
Becoming responsible about sex.
Intimacy—combining love and sex.

These are issues that the person begins to confront in adolescence and continues to deal with in young adulthood; in some respects, they remain lifelong tasks.

### Sociosexual Aspects

The primary concerns and aspirations of most adults revolve around two areas: work and love (Smelser and Erikson, 1980). The first does not concern us here. The second encompasses the entire gamut of intimate relationships within and outside of the family, some of which are closely related to sexuality.

Young adulthood is the time when many people search for intimate relationships in addition to more casual sexual encounters. They get married and make other long-term commitments. Many have children and undertake the task of raising them. They may engage in a variety of sexual behaviors that supplement or compete with their primary sexual partnerships. All of these are issues we shall deal with in greater detail in subsequent chapters.

Erikson (1963b) characterizes the phase-specific task of young adulthood as *intimacy versus isolation. Intimacy* means getting emotionally close with somebody without losing your sense of yourself. Therefore, true intimacy can only be established after the sense of identity is forged in adolescence. Many young people form relationships in order to find themselves, but Erikson finds this venture to lead nowhere; you cannot define yourself successfully in terms of someone else.

This sequence may not be as true for women, whose identity is often created in a network of relationships. Some authors argue that for women intimacy must precede identity formation (Sangiuliano, 1978). Gilligan (1982) argues further that a woman's identity is from the beginning interdependent rather than independent; women define themselves in terms of relationships; men, by what they do and who they are separate from relationships. If true, this difference has an important bearing on how men and women approach intimate relationships (Chapter 16).

The failure to develop intimacy leads to shallow relationships and loneliness. Those who cannot get close to another have difficulty committing themselves to a relationship or maintaining them over long periods of time. However, the opposite of intimacy, which

Erikson calls isolation or distantiation, is also important. It protects us from getting into and remaining stuck in destructive associations that are not of our choosing or in our best interest. Simply because someone loves you is not enough reason to love that person in return. The mature person thus can say "no" as well as "yes" to emotional and sexual engagements.

## Premarital Sex

For many people, young adulthood is the most sexually active time of their lives. Especially when young men and women leave for college, there is a sense of emancipation from parental influence and greater sexual freedom. Sometimes it takes the form of flamboyant public displays of carefree behavior (Figure 9.6). More typically, college students go through a period of more private sexual exploration and experimentation. Whether through dating, casual sexual contacts, or short-term relationships, they get a sense of what sort of person they want to settle down with, where and how to look for that person, and what sort of compromises to make between what they want and what they can get. Emotional attachment during this period is equally, if not more, important than sexual involvements.

The form of sexual behavior most closely linked to young adult development is "premarital sex." Premarital sex literally means "sex before marriage." Until fairly recently, the term designated the coital experience of young adults, because it typically took place in couples who had some intention of getting married. With the age at first intercourse going down and the age at first marriage going up, the term "premarital" is no longer as appropriate. In the college age population, let alone adolescents, such relations are not usually a prelude to marriage with the sexual partner. The term makes even less sense to describe sexual relations between unmarried adults (single, divorced, widowed) in the older adult years. However, because the term is entrenched in the literature and there is no clearly preferable term ("nonmarital sex" is too

Figure 9.6     College-age men and women may give vent to sexual impulses through "rowdy" behavior and alcohol.

general), we continue to use the term "premarital sex" to designate sexual intercourse in the younger age groups.

Prevalence     Some of the more dramatic effects of the sexual revolution involved changes in the prevalence of premarital sex (Chapter 21). Among the Kinsey subjects, 71 percent of men and 33 percent of women had engaged in premarital coitus by age 25 (Kinsey et al., 1948, 1953); two decades later, these figures had risen to 97 percent of men and 67 percent of women (Hunt, 1974).

Premarital sex among college students in particular became more prevalent during the 1960s and 1970s. This change reflected an increase in the overall prevalence of premarital coitus, an increase in the number of sexual partners, and a decrease in the average age of starting sexual intercourse (Clayton and Bokemeier, 1980; Earle and Perricone, 1986).

Though various studies report different rates, women have registered the sharper increases. Between 1971 and 1976, the proportion of women aged 15 to 19 who were nonvirgins doubled from 17 percent to 35 percent. Reiss (1980) estimates that by the 1980s, 75 percent of all women and 90 percent of men were entering marriage as nonvirgins.

It is especially instructive to look at changes within the same institution. For instance, in a ten-year study at one university, the prevalence of premarital sex for males increased from 41 percent in 1970 to 62 percent in 1975 and remained steady at that level in 1981; the corresponding figures for females climbed from 36 percent to 45 percent and 53 percent (Earle and Perricone, 1986).

Large differences exist from one college to another. For instance, in one institution, 90 percent of the women were still virgins at age 16 (Jackson and Potkay, 1973). In more conservative settings, where such studies would not even be tolerated, the proportion of virgins could be even higher.

Reactions    Premarital sex constitutes a landmark in sexual development for those who experience it, but it is not a normative event for everyone. Although increasing numbers of young men and women voluntarily engage in premarital intercourse, others are rushed and pushed by peers before they are psychologically ready or comfortable. As the proportion of those with sexual experience increases, the pressure is likely to mount on those who would rather wait.

Engaging in sex before feeling ready may be one of the reasons why in the Hunt sample only four out of ten women said their first coital experience had been "very pleasurable." More than one-third of young males and close to two-thirds of young females felt regret and worry afterward. Their concerns were most often emotional and moral conflicts, fear of STD and pregnancy, and worry about adequacy of performance (Hunt, 1974).

A more recent study has similar findings: first coitus was highly pleasurable for one-third of young women; another third reported high levels of anxiety and guilt; the balance had a mixture of pleasure and guilt with anxiety. The most important factor was the quality of the male partner; men who were loving, tender, and considerate elicited the most positive reaction; those who acted in a rough and inconsiderate manner left the women feeling anxious, guilty, and exploited. These reactions prevailed no matter what the relationship (such as being engaged). The experience also tended to be more positive if the woman was in her later teens, had extensive dating and petting experience, and had known her partner for a longer period (Weis, 1983).

Young adults do not engage in coitus thoughtlessly. They seem to give considerable thought to the prospect of first coitus and will usually discuss it at some length; only in some cases do they plunge into it impulsively. In 68 percent of cases first coitus occurs between close friends (closer in the case of girls than boys); only 5 percent do it first with a casual acquaintance. More than half (54 percent) have their first coital experience at their own or the partner's house; 15 percent at a third party's house; 15 percent outdoors; 12 percent in a parked car; and 2 percent in a hotel or motel (Coles and Stokes, 1985).

Interpersonal Context    There seems to be a remarkable constancy in the nature of the relationships within which premarital sexual interactions occur. Kinsey noted that premarital coitus usually occurred between people who intended to marry or were in a committed relationship. In the Hunt sample, even among 18 to 24 year olds, sex outside an affectionate relationship was considered wrong for a man by 53 percent of the women and 29 percent of the men; for a woman in the same situation the corresponding percentages were 71 percent for women and 44 percent for men. Whether this difference reflects the persistence of the sexual double standard or is somehow determined by more intrinsic gender differences is an open question. Even among the sexually liberal respondents of the *Cosmopolitan* survey, 64 percent women listed their first sexual partner as a steady boyfriend, 6 percent as their fiancé, 5 percent as their husband, and only 16 percent as a casual acquaintance (Wolfe, 1981). Although current premarital attitudes among young adults are notably permissive, the dominant norm is permissiveness with affection, rather than indiscriminate sexual associations.

Young adults continue to be influenced by their peer group, but that influence depends on gender and whether the friends' sexual behavior or attitudes are at issue. For college men, the expected degree of approval of male friends does not influence their premarital sexual activity, but the number of friends thought to be sexually active does have an influence. In other words, men are more influenced by what their peers do than what they say. For college women, both factors make a difference (Sack et al., 1984).

Although few young couples are in a position to settle down, the general expectation that they should be in a fairly committed relationship in order to engage in sex continues to prevail. In more recent surveys, women aged 15 to 19 who have had their first coital experience with men aged 17 to 21 say that in 80 percent of cases they were going steady or dating their partners; another 7 percent were friends, and 9 percent were engaged. In only 4 percent the partner was a recent, presumably casual acquaintance. Being in a steady relationship is relatively less common for the men; 52 percent of them had their first coital experience with a woman they were dating; 38 percent had it with more casual friends; 9 percent involved women they had met only recently. Less than 1 percent were engaged to their sexual partner when they had their first coital experience (Zelnik and Shah, 1983).

The tendency to postpone marriage (Chapter 17) and the greater proportion of women pursuing higher education and careers mean that a decade or longer now separate the attainment of biological maturity and the likelihood of establishing a stable sexual partnership in marriage or some other relationship. An active and satisfying sex life during this interval holds the promise of making life more fulfilling. Furthermore, it could be argued, the opportunity to test and learn before making a serious commitment would help people make more intelligent choices and form more compatible sexual partnerships.

Despite a good deal of preoccupation, the question of the impact of premarital sex on subsequent marital happiness remains unanswered. It is hardly surprising in view of the varied reasons for which people engage in premarital sex and the numerous variables that determine marital satisfaction.

Those who value sexual loyalty in marriage argue that premarital sexual experiences lays the groundwork for future extramarital involvements. In fact, those with extensive premarital sexual experience have reported more extensive extramarital activity (Athanasiou and Sarkin, 1974). Various studies have shown that marriage tends to be rated as more successful when premarital chastity has been maintained (the correlation is positive but not a strong one) (Shope and Broderick, 1967). More current research shows that commitment to the spouse after marriage is important (Lauer and Lauer, 1985), but prior chastity is not, for marital satisfaction.

Others find such evidence unpersuasive. Sexually conservative persons who shun premarital sex may also accept their marriages as "happy" because they are supposed to be; some respondents who rate their marriages "very happy" rank below average in their measures of coital frequency and sexual enjoyment (Athanasiou et al., 1970). Despite their correlation, there may not be a *causal* connection between engaging in premarital and extramarital coitus; both may be the result of another variable such as "sexual liberalism" (Reiss, 1967). One could also argue on common-sense grounds that the best way to find out if a couple is sexually compatible would be to test it before marriage.

Cross-cultural evidence offers a third viewpoint: how premarital sex affects marriage depends on whether values match behavior (Box 9.2). Premarital sex will hinder marital happiness if it creates tension between your values and behavior, or between your choice and society's standards. Christensen (1966) applies this argument to her analysis of contemporary shifts in sexual values.

## SEXUALITY IN MIDDLE ADULTHOOD

The two decades between the ages of 40 and 60 are the "middle" segment of adult life, between young and late adulthood. It is a transitional period of life with some similarities to the earlier transitional period of adolescence. Just as the adolescent is no longer a child but not yet fully adult, the middle-aged man or woman is no longer young but not yet old.

Periods of transition tend to be stressful because they entail a reorientation of life goals, intimate relationships, and career aspirations. Some of these shifts are precipitated by biological events (such as the menopause); others are more purely psychosocial in origin.

Middle-aged men and women face many challenges and opportunities in common. The changes in their bodies are harbingers of old age and mortality. As their grown-up children leave home, the marital relationship undergoes important shifts. There are subtle shifts in their sense of masculinity and femininity and other changes in their sexual relationships.

The experience of middle age is, however, unlike in other ways for men and women. They face different biological changes and different psychosocial shifts in occupational and social role. We shall discuss men and women separately, without losing sight of the similarities in their midlife experiences (Katchadourian, 1987).

### Male Midlife Transition

According to Levinson (1978) the critical period of the male midlife transition is between the ages of 40 and 45. The events of this period have become popularly known as the "midlife crisis," with age 40 taking on special symbolic significance (Brandes, 1985).

A broader view would suggest that these changes are more likely to be stretched out over ten or twenty years. The midlife male is likely to undergo some profound personality changes. These changes are due to a variety of causes. They are likely to precipitate a "crisis" in midlife if there are multiple, simultaneous demands for personality change (Brim, 1976).

In Levinson's view, the midlife transition confronts a man with several main tasks. The first is to reappraise his life as a young adult and determine not only how successful he has been but also whether or not he has found what he was looking for. He asks not only "Have I done well enough"? but also, "Is this what I wanted?" Coming to terms with his life as young adult, he is helped by *de-illusionment*— giving up unrealistic expectations. This process entails loss but also liberation.

A second important feature is a shift from the past to the future and an attempt to restructure life. More drastic changes involve divorce, remarriage, career shift, and new lifestyle. Most men do not undergo such external shifts but change their life structure in more internal ways, such as changing their values or reaffirming close relationships.

All your life you work on *individuation*— defining your relationship to yourself and the world. This process becomes more prominent during transitional periods like midlife. The tasks that are especially significant to midlife individuation are relocating yourself across four polarities: young/old, destruction/creation, masculine/feminine, and attachment/separateness.

Everyone occupies a shifting position along these dimensions through life. At midlife, a man feels alternately young, old, and "in between." He becomes more keenly aware of the ways in which people, including his loved ones, have acted toward him in destructive ways and how he, in turn, has harmed others; by the same token he becomes more aware of the creative and altruistic potential within himself. Likewise, a man at midlife comes to terms more fully with the masculine and feminine parts of himself (Chapter 10) and integrates his strong need for attachment to others with his equally important need for separateness (Levinson, 1978).

These developmental events are not specific to sexuality, but it is easy to see how they would profoundly influence a man's self-perception as a sexual being, his confidence in his virility, his gender identity, and his intimate relationships and commitments. Look for all these effects as you read later chapters.

The midlife transition of men has no clear biological basis. Unlike women, men typically do not experience a rapid loss of gonadal function in midlife, but show a gradual, variable decline in testicular function and testosterone production. Rarely, a man may undergo hot flushes, depression, and other signs similar to the female menopause, when testosterone production drops suddenly (Bermant and Davidson, 1974).

The midlife transition may present special sexual problems nonetheless. The fear of declining potency is an important source of anxiety and sometimes the cause of sexual dysfunction. Some middle-aged men slowly and quietly give up sex; others exhibit an adolescent-like urge to sleep around or fall head-over-heels in love "one last time." It is no wonder that marital relationships come under special stress at these times. Most people emerge from the turmoil in midlife with some restructuring and reorientation of their sexual life: some go on to live sexually fulfilling lives; others become casualties, with their sexual relationships disrupted or gone stale.

## Female Midlife Transition

Our perception of midlife women has been dominated by the events of the *menopause* ("stopping of menses"). For unknown reasons, ovarian function declines markedly sometime between the ages of 45 and 55 (average age, 51 years) leading to infertility and a sharp decrease in the production of estrogens and progestins (Wilson, 1983). The alternative term *climacteric* (from Greek for "crisis") more broadly encompasses the many biological and psychological changes of this period. Another common term is "change of life."

In physiological terms, the source of change is the ovary and not the pituitary, which continues producing gonadotropins. For some reason, the ovarian follicles stop responding to gonadotropin stimulation and no longer produce estrogen. Infertility and other manifestations of the menopause are then the direct result of estrogen deprivation.

In Chapter 4 we discussed the effects of the menopause on sexual drive and behavior. To recapitulate, though the drop in ovarian hormones reduces sexual drive for some women, for others it actually enhances interest in sex. Nevertheless, the menopause continues to worry many women. They may feel less attractive, because there is such a strong association between youthfulness and sexual attractiveness in most people's minds (more so with respect to women than men).

Menopausal Symptoms     The most common of the physical symptoms of the menopause are *hot flashes* (or flushes), which are present in the majority of menopausal women. A sensation of warmth rises to the face from the upper body, with or without perspiration and chilliness. These flashes come at about hourly intervals over a period of a few months or several years. Other physical symptoms include dizziness, headaches, palpitations, and joint pains. The bones tend to lose calcium and become more porous (*osteoporosis*) following midlife, making postmenopausal women more liable to suffer fractures (London and Hammond, 1986). To keep her bones strong a woman should remain physically active, eat an adequate diet supplemented with calcium, and avoid excessive use of tobacco, alcohol, and caffeine. Estrogen replacement (discussed below) will also counteract osteoporosis.

Among the psychological symptoms of the menopause, sadness is the most prominent (experienced by about 40 percent). It may range from mild moodiness to severe depression. Other symptoms are tiredness, irritability, and forgetfulness.

For sexual function, the most important

menopausal changes affect the reproductive system. These changes include loss of elasticity of the vaginal wall and thinning of the vaginal lining, with marked decrease of the lubricatory response during sexual excitement; atrophy of the uterine endometrium, with decline in cervical mucous secretion; and shrinkage of the breast. The vaginal changes may lead to painful coitus, but the problem of the "dry" vagina is easily remedied by the use of lubricants (Chapter 15). Women on estrogen replacement therapy do not experience a reduction in vaginal lubrication.

Older women also develop a tendency toward burning during urination following intercourse, because the penis irritates the bladder and urethra through the thinner vaginal wall. Discomfort may persist for several days following coitus. It does not follow orgasm through masturbation. Women who remain sexually active seem less likely to manifest some of these changes.

Following the menopause, all women become infertile, but sterility does not set in abruptly. As with menarche, there is a period of several years of menstrual irregularity and relative infertility. Pregnancies are rare beyond age 47, though some have been medically documented as late as 61 years.

Treatment of Menopausal Symptoms    Much of what we said in Chapter 4 about menstrual distress applies to the menopause. The menopause is also not a disease. Many women experience no significant ill effects. Among those that do, only one out of ten is markedly inconvenienced. The lingering stereotype that the menopause is a very difficult time for all women is not true.

Nonetheless, some women do experience physical distress. Furthermore, cultural and psychological factors can worsen the experience. The fear of losing attractiveness and the idea of being past her prime is likely to have a greater impact on a woman's self-esteem and well-being than the hormonal changes of the menopause.

An effective treatment for some of the symptoms of the menopause is *estrogen replacement therapy* (ERT). When such therapy became available several decades ago it was enthusiastically hailed; then, with the cancer scare in the 1970s, estrogen use fell into disrepute. Present opinion is that estrogen replacement is a legitimate form of therapy when needed, but it should be used in the lowest effective doses, for the shortest possible period of time, and under medical supervision (Mosher and Whelan, 1981; Judd, 1987).

Estrogen helps to lessen the hot flushes, counteract vaginal atrophy and dryness, and prevent osteoporosis. It appears to have no effect on sexual responsiveness (Myers and Morokoff, 1986). The side-effects of estrogen use are the same as those for birth control pills (Chapter 7), but a more serious threat in the case of menopausal use is a five-fold higher risk of endometrial cancer. However, endometrial cancer is rare to begin with; it causes only 1 percent of all female deaths from cancer. Women with relatives who have had cancer of the reproductive system are at higher risk. There are also higher risks if estrogen use is associated with vascular disease and certain pelvic disorders (Judd, 1987).

Psychosocial Changes    There is far more happening in the life of middle-aged women than the menopause. Even though the female life cycle has been less extensively studied than that of the male (Gilligan, 1982), we know some of the important personality and social changes.

As women go through midlife, they become more self-assertive, less sentimental, and more dominant. Simultaneously, as the men become more mellow and less aggressive in midlife, there is a definite shift in a couple's relationship. As men and women become more equal they also become more alike in their gender characteristics.

These changes can bring couples closer and lead to greater intimacy and satisfaction (Chapter 16). Couples may also drift apart during midlife. The departure of children removes one of the key reasons why a man and woman have stayed together. As husbands become more dependent on their wives, while women turn away from providing nurturance toward independence, then the relationship becomes precarious (Lowenthal and Chiriboga, 1973; Lowenthal et al., 1975).

Should a marriage end in midlife due to a divorce or a death, a woman has a progressively smaller chance to remarry (if she wants to) than the divorced man or the widower. Because women live longer, eligible men become more scarce, and men tend to remarry younger women. The sexual relationships of middle-aged and older women are thus shaped in part by demographic realities outside of their control (Chapter 17).

## SEXUALITY IN LATE ADULTHOOD

Sexual activity, like vigorous physical effort, has often been assumed to be the prerogative of youth. Having performed their reproductive functions and obtained whatever satisfaction they could, older individuals have been expected to have no further interest in sex or chance to act on it, because they lose sexual attractiveness and capability.

Such attitudes are by no means common to all cultures, many of which unabashedly accept the sexuality of the elderly. Cross-cultural surveys show sexual activity to be an important part of the lives of older men in 70 percent and of older women in 85 percent of these cultures (Winn and Newton, 1982). In the United States people are also becoming more accepting and encouraging of sexual experiences among the elderly. They realize that older individuals can have active sex lives (Starr and Weiner, 1981).

### Changes in Sexual Response

Aging entails distinctive, albeit not fully understood, physiological changes in the sexual response cycle. Some sexual responses continue uninterrupted, others are modified, and a few cease altogether. Basically, older men and women respond as before and continue to be capable of orgasm (Masters and Johnson, 1966). Physiological changes and shifts in sexual desire typically result in a reduction of sexual behavior and a *decline* in sexual capacity, not sexual *dysfunction*. This change is no different from changes in other physical capacities, such as the ability to run, as one gets older.

Male Response    Several physiological changes influence sexual response in the older man. First, his reaction to erotic stimulation is slower; he needs more time to achieve erection, no matter how exciting the stimulation is. Second, after age 50 or so, psychological stimulation is often not enough; he requires direct physical stimulation to achieve erection. However, the erection can be maintained longer, perhaps because of better control based on experience or because of changes in physiological functioning. Should the older male lose his erection before orgasm, he will encounter greater difficulty in reviving it. During orgasm contractions die out after a few throbs, ejaculation is less vigorous, and the volume of ejaculate is reduced.

During the resolution phase physical changes disappear with greater speed; in fact, some responses disappear before they can be detected. Penile detumescence occurs in a matter of seconds after orgasm, rather than in a lingering two-stage process. Few older men seek multiple orgasms, and even fewer can achieve them; but given a longer stimulation period, some men do go on to have additional orgasms.

Female Response    As we discussed earlier, the postmenopausal woman has progressive and marked anatomical changes. The vaginal walls lose their thick, corrugated texture and elasticity, becoming thin and pale. Vaginal lubrication response takes longer (several minutes) and is less profuse; the tenting effect is limited and delayed; the orgasmic platform develops less fully. In the orgasmic and resolution phases the older vagina is comparable to the older penis: orgasmic contractions are fewer and less intense, and resolution is prompt and swift.

Despite these changes, there is even less physiological cause for women to stop sexual activity than for men during late adulthood.

activity than for men during late adulthood. The use of simple vaginal lubricants can fully compensate for the lack of natural lubrication (Chapter 15). Most important, an active sexual life seems to significantly counteract the effects of aging and maintain the sexual fitness of older men and women. Time takes its toll, but it need not quench sexual desire or cripple its fulfillment.

## Patterns of Sexual Behavior

Romance and sex are alive and well for many older individuals (Figure 9.7). In a sample of over 800 repondents aged over 60, 36 percent

Figure 9.7    Sex and romance continue to be a part of life for many older people.

felt that sex was better than when younger; 39 percent said it was the same; and only 25 percent thought it had gotten worse. These men and women expressed a strong interest in sex; they thought it was good for their health, and the great majority (including the widowed, divorced, and single) were sexually active (Starr and Weiner, 1981).

In a survey of 4246 men and women aged 50 and older (the largest such sample to date), the prevalence and variety of sexual activity is even more impressive (Brecher, 1984). This study involved a self-selected sample of respondents to a questionnaire sponsored by *Consumer Reports* (response rate 0.2 percent). As with other magazine surveys, its findings in all likelihood reflect the behavior of respondents who are sexually more open and active than the population at large.

The *Consumer Reports* sample shows that though there is a decade-by-decade decline in sexual activity, among those aged 70 and older, 81 percent of the married and 50 percent of the unmarried women remain sexually active, as do 81 percent and 75 percent of the corresponding groups of men. Fifty percent of these sexually active women and 58 percent of the men have sex at least once a week; 61 percent of the women and 75 percent of the men report "high enjoyment of sex." Masturbation is reported by 43 percent of the men and 33 percent of the women aged 70 or older. About half of the subjects have oral sex; some have experimented with anal sex and vibrators.

Getting older does not have to mean a decline in sexual activity. Even a fall in coital frequency need not reflect a failure of other forms of sexual satisfaction. Also, the chances of getting sick become higher as one grows older; sexual dysfunction reflects illness rather than aging itself. Moreover, the state of our sexual satisfaction in the older years is a function in part of how we have lived our younger years. Regretting the past leads to despair; making the best of the present sustains vigor (Box 9.4).

The potential causes for the decline of sexual interest and activity in older years are many: physiological changes; medical prob-

# Box 9.4

## POEMS ON AGING AND SEXUALITY

*"An Old Man" by C. P. Cavafy\**
In the inner room of the noisy cafe
an old man sits bent over a table;
a newspaper before him, no companion beside
   him.

And in the scorn of his miserable old age,
he meditates how little he enjoyed the years
when he had strength, the art of the word, and
   good looks.

He knows he has aged much; he is aware of it, he
   sees it,
and yet the time when he was young seems like
yesterday. How short a time, how short a time.

And he ponders how Wisdom had deceived him;
and how he always trusted her—what folly!—
the liar who would say, "Tomorrow. You have
   ample time."

He recalls impulses he curbed; and how much
joy he sacrificed. Every lost chance
now mocks his senseless prudence. . . .

But with so much thinking and remembering
the old man reels. And he dozes off
bent over the table of the cafe.

*"Finding the Fountain" by a 74-year-old woman†*
The slim young man I married
Has slowly gone to pot;
With wrinkled face and graying pate,
Slender he is not!
And when I meet a mirror,
I find a haggard crone;
I can't believe the face I see
Can really be my own!

But when we seek our bed each night,
The wrinkles melt away:
Our flesh is firm, our kisses warm,
Our ardent hearts are gay!
The Fountain of Eternal Youth
Is not so far to find:
Two things you need—a double bed,
A spouse who's true and kind!

\*From *The Complete Poems of Cavafy*. Translated by Rae Dalven. New York: Harcourt, Brace, Jovanovich, 1968, p. 7.

†From Brecher, E. M., *Sex, Love, and Aging*. Boston: Little, Brown, 1984, p. 379.

lems (heart disease, stroke, diabetes, arthritis, anemia, prostatic conditions, gynecological conditions); drugs used to treat these conditions; psychological problems (fear of impotence, expectation of sexual decline, feelings of sexual unattractiveness, interpersonal conflicts, depression, grief, guilt, shame); and practical considerations (constraints in sexual interaction among the elderly, especially in nursing homes and other institutions).

Demographic factors confront women with serious problems because of their relative longevity and hence their larger numbers. In the 40–44 age group, there are 213 single, separated, and divorced women for every 100 men. In addition to the 7 percent of women who never marry, there are 644 widows to 100 widowers. Age is also a serious impediment to remarriage: women divorced in their 20s have a 76 percent chance of remarriage; for those in their 50s or older the chances are less than 12 percent (Blumstein and Schwartz, 1983, p. 32). There are simply not enough eligible older men, and the prospects of finding younger sexual partners are even worse because of cultural and other constraints. As a result of these factors, the sexual options available to older women can be severely limited.

Another impediment to sex in the older years comes from concerns that sexual activity is itself debilitating. There are indeed certain illnesses, including acute heart ailments, during which sexual activity, like other kinds of activity, must be restricted, but by and large sex helps maintain older individuals in better health.

A critical requirement in maintaining good sexual function in the older years is the sustenance of sexual activity throughout adulthood. The aging woman who is sexually inactive experiences greater shrinkage of vaginal tissues; the aging male has greater difficulty in resuming sexual activity after a long period of abstinence. Therefore to retain sexual function in the older years it is important to remain active sexually all along (Comfort, 1976; Kolodny et al., 1979). This purpose is facilitated by keeping fit through exercise, proper nutrition, rest, attention to personal appearance, and keeping up with intellectual interests and community life.

The "use it or lose it" dictum is apt (Masters and Johnson, 1982), but it must be qualified on two counts. First, using it does not mean you may not lose at least some of it; it means you have a better chance of keeping more of it. Second, using it may not be the cause of not losing it; instead, both may be a function of a more basic underlying variable. In a study of 60- to 79-year-old married men, the level of sexual activity—whether high or low—seemed to be fairly consistent through life. These patterns were not correlated with factors like marital adjustment, sexual attractiveness of wives, sexual attitudes, or the demographic features of the marital history. Instead, frequency of sex, erotic responsiveness to visual stimuli, and "time comfortable without sex" were closely interrelated and thus possibly linked to the strength of a person's basic sexual motivation. Furthermore, those with potency problems seemed to be free of performance anxiety, feelings of sexual deprivation, and loss of self-esteem (Martin, 1981).

If you recognize that each phase of life has its particular joys and sorrows, you will find more sexual satisfaction in the older years. The sexuality of youth is urgent and impulsive, aimed at genital pleasure. That of young adulthood is generative, bound by intimacy. As we grow older, sex can serve an increasingly broad range of emotional needs, from showing enduring affection to sharing the pleasures of being touched. Awareness of the approaching end of life can impart a special tenderness to each act of love.

## REVIEW QUESTIONS

1. What are the typical responses of teenagers to their changing body image?
2. What are the consequences of teenage pregnancy for the mother, father, and infant?
3. What are the steps in "sexual unfolding"?
4. What are the symptoms of the menopause?
5. How does aging affect the sexual response cycle?

## THOUGHT QUESTIONS

1. As a future parent, when would you want your daughter or son to start engaging in coitus?
2. What are the arguments for and against requiring parental consent before performing an abortion on a pregnant 13 year old?
3. What stance does your college take on premarital sex? What would you do if you were in charge?
4. How could you determine whether the changes in sexual interest during the menopause are due to biological or psychological factors?
5. What policy would you institute for the sexual interactions of men and women living in a nursing home?

## SUGGESTED READINGS

Coles, R., and Stokes, G. (1985). *Sex and the American teenager*. New York: Harper & Row. The results of an extensive survey on adolescent sexual behavior. Clearly organized tables and interesting excerpts from interviews.

National Research Council (1987). *Risking the Future*. Washington, D.C.: National Academy Press. The views of a panel of experts on adolescent sexuality, pregnancy, and childbearing from health, psychosocial, and policy perspectives. An excellent overview.

Sarrel, L., and Sarrel, P. (1979). *Sexual unfolding*. Boston: Little, Brown. Development of sexuality in adolescence and young adulthood. Especially pertinent for college students.

Butler, R. N. and Lewis, M. I., (1986) *Love and Sex after 40*. New York: Harper & Row. An authoritative and well-written guide to sexuality in the middle years. By the same authors, *Sex after 60* (1977) deals with sexuality in the older years.

Katchadourian, H. (1987). *Fifty: Midlife in perspective*. New York: W. H. Freeman. Overview of biological and psychosocial aspects of sexuality in midlife.

Brecher, E.M. (1984). *Sex, love, and aging*. Boston: Little, Brown. An extensive survey of sexual behavior in late adulthood. Clearly written with interesting quotes.

# Gender and Sexuality

CHAPTER

# 10

*He's fancier on the outside,*
*but I am prettier on the inside.*
Young girl commenting on
her brother's genitals.

OUTLINE

COMPONENTS OF SEXUAL
   IDENTITY
Gender Identity
Gender Role
Gender Stereotyping
Androgyny
   Testing Gender Differences
   Effects of Androgyny
GENDER DIFFERENCES
   THROUGH THE LIFE CYCLE
Infancy
Childhood
Adolescence
Adulthood
HOW GENDER IDENTITY
   DEVELOPS

Interactional Models
Special Cases
Sex-Dimorphic Behavior
GENDER DISORDERS
Gender Identity Disorder
   of Childhood
Later Gender Identity Disorder
Transsexualism
GENDER AND SEXUAL BEHAVIOR
Sexual Drive and Behavior
Response to Erotica
Orgasmic Capacity
Relational Aspects
Explaining the Differences
   Evolutionary Perspective
   Differential Socialization

Next to being human, your most obvious characteristic is being male or female. Not only are the physical differences obvious, but cultures exaggerate them. In our society men and women wear different hairstyles, clothing, and ornamentation. The combination of physical and culturally contrived differences makes it possible to identify you as male or female quickly, even at a distance.

You are equally marked by your behavior. Virtually every society expects men and women to behave differently both in occupational and relational settings—particularly in sexual interactions. Although not every culture has the same ideas of what it means to be masculine or feminine, and what social roles men and women should play, the fact that such expectations are universal has led to the widespread conviction that sex differences are "natural" or biologically determined, a "normal" part of us.

These beliefs have recently come under critical scrutiny. The very notion of what it means to be male and female, masculine or feminine, is changing. In industrialized countries, a great deal has already changed in the relationships of men and women, and greater change is at hand.

As we focus on gender in this chapter, bear in mind that gender and sex roles do not exist in isolation. Gender development is part of the lifelong development of sexuality, which we traced in the last two chapters. It is part of the sexual behaviors that we shall discuss in the following chapters. Sex and gender are thus two sides of the same coin. It is impossible to act sexually without at the same time acting as a man or a woman; and it is nearly as impossible to act as a man or a woman without simultaneously acting sexually at some level.

## COMPONENTS OF SEXUAL IDENTITY

The term *identity* refers to the persistent individuality of a person over time and under different circumstances. Your identity defines who you are no matter where you happen to be or what you do. Your *sexual identity* has sev-

eral components: your basic perception of yourself as male or female; your sexual characteristics ("sexy," "not sexy," "oversexed," "undersexed"); sexual orientation ("heterosexual," "homosexual"); sex values ("permissive," "liberal," "conservative"); and gender identity ("masculine," "feminine").

Your genetic, hormonal, and anatomical characteristics form the biological basis of sexual identity. They are responsible for your maleness or femaleness—your sex. On this biological bedrock we build psychological and cultural meaning. Thus, beyond being male or female, you have a sense of masculinity or femininity—your *gender identity*. Social expectations of gender-linked behavior are, in turn, known as *gender roles*.

Gender roles are also commonly referred to as *sex roles*. Psychologists use the term *sex-typed behavior* for "role behavior appropriate to a child's gender" and *sex-typing* for "the developmental process by which behavioral components of one or another gender role are established" (Sears, 1965). Sex-typed behavior is thus basically synonymous with gender-specific behavior.

We use sex to get to know each other as well as to define ourselves. When we behave sexually, it is not possible to always tell whether we are fulfilling sexual needs or trying to live up to social expectations of what it means to be a man or woman.

Gender identity and sex roles are important in shaping interpersonal relationships. Gender is integral to all social interactions, particularly sexual ones. It will help us understand sexual intimacy and love (Chapter 16), their institutional contexts like marriage and cohabitation (Chapter 17), sexual exploitation (Chapter 18), and aggression (Chapter 18).

Gender Identity
The term "gender identity" is recent, but the concept is ancient. In Chinese philosophy and religion, the masculine principle *Yang* and the female principle *Yin* were attributed not only to men and women, but to everything in ex-

istence, including inanimate objects, spirits, and events (Gulik, 1974).

The concept of the *animus* and *anima* is a more modern, Western expression of the same basic idea. Carl Jung conceived of the anima and the animus as images we share in our "collective unconscious." The anima represents the feminine personality element within the male and the image that the male has of feminine nature in general—in Jung's words, it is the "archetype" of the feminine. Likewise, the animus represents the masculine personality components of the female and her concept of masculine nature. Normally, both masculine and feminine characteristics are present in every individual, but you express outwardly only the set of characteristics that are considered socially appropriate to your sex, and are therefore not disturbing to the ideal self-image (Jung, 1969).

The word "gender" is derived from the Latin *genus* meaning "birth," "origin," or a class of things from a common source. The term "gender identity" was introduced by Stoller (1968) because the use of the word "sexual" in "sexual identity" was confusing. Stoller is also credited with the concept of *core gender identity* (Money, 1973)—the deep-seated conviction that the assignment of a person's sex was anatomically and psychologically correct—that you are what you appear to be (Stoller, 1985). Once gender identity is established, it is impossible to change it without serious psychological disruption. As we shall discuss later, there is some controversy over when core gender identity develops, and at what point in life it can no longer be reversed.

John Money and Anke Ehrhardt (1972) call gender identity and gender role the two sides of the same basic entity. They define gender identity as:

> the sameness, unity, and persistence of one's individuality as male, female, or ambivalent, in greater or lesser degree, especially as it is experienced in self-awareness and behavior; gender identity is the private experience of gender role, and gender role is the public expression of gender identity. (p. 4)

## Gender Role

The term as well as the notion of *role* originated in the theater. The Latin word *rotula* means a small wooden roller. The parchment containing the actor's script was rolled around this rod, so it was referred to as the roll ("rowle"). The actor's role in the play was defined by this script.

The definition of gender role by Money and Ehrhardt (1972) is the obverse of their definition of gender identity. Gender role is:

> Everything that a person says and does to indicate to others or to the self the degree that one is either male, or female, or ambivalent; it includes but is not restricted to sexual arousal and response. Gender role is the public expression of gender identity, and gender identity is the private expression of gender role. (p. 4)

Sex roles or gender roles are defined by society's expectations. Some expectations govern what women and men do vocationally. Others pertain to how they are supposed to behave sexually. Such social expectations are enormously influential. They determine, for instance, who should take the initiative in sexual encounters or establishing intimate relationships: whether the man or the woman (or either one) asks for a date; proposes marriage; makes a pass; or decides when and how to engage in sex. Even the different roles to which the two sexes are relegated in ostensibly nonsexual contexts such as the workplace may significantly affect their sexual interactions.

## Gender Stereotyping

In printing, a *stereotype* is a plate that produces identical copies. In biology, stereotypical behavior is a repeated, predictable pattern of activity, such as the courtship of animals. In human behavior, stereotyping means ascribing preconceived and oversimplified models of behavior to individuals, based on their belonging to a group. *Gender stereotypes* or *sex-role stereotypes* are the ways men and women are supposed to behave by virtue of their gender.

# Box 10.1

## LANGUAGE AND GENDER STEREOTYPES

We learn a great deal about sex roles from what others say, how they say it, and how they communicate nonverbally.

Sex differences have been found both in how men and women talk to and about each other. For example, Zimmerman and West (1975) coded the number of interruptions made by males and females in two-party conversations. In opposite-sex pairs males made 96 percent of the interruptions. In same-sex pairs, however, interruptions were equally distributed between the two people (McMillan et al, 1977). Women also try harder to introduce a topic and keep a conversation going, often by asking questions (Fishman, 1978).

The sexes differ in styles of speech as well. Women's speech uses more modifiers ("I'm so happy to see you"), poses more questions ("It's a nice day, isn't it?"), and frames requests more indirectly, often in question form ("Won't you please come in?"), than men's speech (McMillan et al., 1977). Probably as a result, men's speech is perceived as more dynamic (Mulac et al., 1985). Women's speech has been characterized as more polite, exaggerated, indirect, and expressive than men's (Lakoff, 1975; Haas, 1979b); men's speech as more harsh, and more frequently profane (Selnow, 1985). Other studies have shown similar speech differences between individuals who differ in status, with the higher status person displaying the male pattern (Henley, 1977).

It is conceivable that by listening to these patterns, we learn that, as women, we should not make direct requests about our sexual desires and needs, that the language of sexuality is more direct or "harsh" than we are supposed to be comfortable with, and that we can expect to work harder to make our needs known. As men, we learn to be direct about our needs, to feel comfortable expressing ourselves, and to pay less attention to a partner's attempts to tell us of her needs.

The lexicon of our language also reinforces the sexual roles of women and men. For example, we have a richer vocabulary to describe women in sexually derogatory terms than we have for men. Farmer and Henley (1965) found 500 synonyms for "prostitute" but only 65 for the man who uses a prostitute's services. Similarly, Schulz (1975) found that originally neutral words for women acquire obscene or debased connotations, whereas neutral words for men do not become pejorative.

Similarly, titles that are used for females tend to carry more information regarding their sexual status than titles for males. "Mister" conveys only that the person is a male. "Miss" or "Mrs." tell us not only that the person is female, but her marital status, something about her age ("Misses" are generally younger than "Mrs."s), and therefore her sexual status. The use of masculine pronouns (he, his) to represent unspecified human beings is now generally perceived as sexist, as are words such as "mankind" and "chairman," which presuppose males to be the models or the standard for human behavior.

Nonverbal communication patterns also reinforce stereotypic behavior. Males and high status individuals initiate touching, maintain longer eye contact, take up more space, and keep others waiting more often than do females and low status individuals (Henley and Freeman, 1976; Henley 1977; Mayo and Henley, 1981). Such differences in behavior contribute to mixed sexual messages between men and women.

---

Such expectations are inculcated early in life and are reinforced by language and by nonverbal communication (Box 10.1).

In its original sense, stereotyping involves false generalizations. Current usage has expanded its meaning to include any generalization that has negative connotations or potentially undesirable social consequences. Thus, to say that men are generally taller than women or that women have higher pitched voices may be thought by some to enhance gender stereotypes, although both statements are obviously true. There are, of course, many women who are taller or have lower voices than some men, but such exceptions do not invalidate the statement in general for a random population. Otherwise we could hardly generalize about anything, because there are almost always exceptions.

Generalizations become more problematic when they are poorly defined. For example, if we say that "Men are physically superior to women," what do we mean? Men generally can outperform women in athletic competitions, which seems like a reasonable test of physical prowess (Chapter 4). On the other hand, women outlive men in every decade of life, which is even a more significant index of physical fitness. The term "superior" is meaningless unless properly qualified.

Why do we need to generalize at all? Valid generalizations provide us with a greater opportunity to predict what is likely to happen. Stereotypes are also useful as a way of organizing vast amounts of information and giving us a framework for including new information. Kahneman, Slovic, and Tversky (1982) have shown that people will use information based on stereotypes more readily than base-rate information (such as statistical probability). Thus, knowing stereotypes can help us predict how people think about a person, event, or situation.

Keep two important issues in mind as we proceed. First, no matter how valid a generalization is for a group, it can never apply to every person within the group. Women still do most of the housework, but not every woman you meet is a "housewife."

Second, the destructive influence of sex-role stereotyping has been pointed out repeatedly (Broverman et al., 1970; Maccoby and Jacklin, 1974). Stereotyping is often derogatory. By emphasizing the negative characteristics of any group it only serves prejudice.

## Androgyny

Gender stereotyping exaggerates differences between male and female. By placing people into separate boxes, we make them look consistently different. For those who adhere to traditional images of men and women, gender stereotypes are comforting: a man looks male and acts masculine; a woman looks female and acts feminine. Each has a place in the scheme of things. Even if real men and women do not conform to this ideal, at least there is an ideal to aspire to—a model for the socialization of children and standards of behavior for adults. Victorian society upheld these standards as behaviors that befitted ladies and gentlemen, but men and women of all classes were urged to imitate them. People strove to act "like a lady" or "like a gentleman."

Modern, democratic societies are far less regimented in their codes of gender behavior and allow far more overlap in how men and women should behave. During the past several decades, the gender boundaries in many occupational fields have become largely eliminated; men and women now essentially behave the same way in the workplace. In their social interactions, though, especially where sex is involved, important gender differences still persist.

In the forefront of the shift from the traditional to the modern pattern has been the concept of *androgyny* (from the Greek roots *andros*, "man" and *gyne*, "woman"). Contrary to gender stereotyping, androgyny focuses on gender similarities and aspires to enhance them. The ideal of androgyny has been applied to everything from haircuts to "unisex" clothing but most of the current research pertains to psychological androgyny.

Particularly on college campuses, the differences between distinctively male and female clothing, hairstyle, and ornamentation have been lessening; jeans and sweaters, jewelry, and length of hair now have many common elements. Though we are far from uniformity, the androgynous image of some popular figures (Figure 10.1) reflects at least greater acceptance of that alternative.

Testing Gender Differences    Researchers in the 1920s began to study personality traits that would differentiate between men and women (Terman and Miles, 1936). These studies yielded correlations between gender and various traits (such as assertiveness or passivity)

Figure 10.1    Michael Jackson: the androgynous model?

opposite poles of a continuum; if you scored high in masculinity, you had to score low in femininity, and vice versa.

This approach to the study of gender differences is now considered inadequate (Constantinople, 1973; Spence and Helmreich, 1978; Bem, 1981). Instead of viewing gender traits as mutually exclusive, we think they coexist in various combinations. A man or woman can be assertive or dependent in one context and meek in another without being typecast as less or more masculine or feminine.

Sandra Bem (1974) has extended this line of inquiry by developing a Sex Role Inventory (BSRI) that measures the ratio of masculine, feminine, and neutral traits in men and women. These traits are identified by key terms like "aggressive" and "ambitious" for masculinity, "affectionate" and "yielding" for femininity, and "happy" for the neutral category. In repeated samples of college students, approximately 35–40 percent emerge as *sex-typed*—they highly endorse the masculine or feminine categories consistent with their sex; 35 percent are *androgynous*, showing a fairly equal endorsement of masculine and feminine characteristics; 15 percent are *cross-typed* men who endorse feminine traits and women who endorse masculine traits; and 15 percent are *undifferentiated,* showing low endorsement of either masculine or feminine traits.

but did not explain why and how these sex differences came about. Furthermore, these masculinity-femininity tests revealed no personality characteristics that were exclusively male or female; rather, various traits were unevenly distributed among males and females.

Although these gender tests did not claim that the perceived differences between men and women were innate, immutable, or socially desirable, they nonetheless reinforced common perceptions of "natural" behavior for male and female. They also perpetuated a gender model that was *unidimensional* and *bipolar:* gender was viewed as a single personality dimension with masculinity and femininity at the

Effects of Androgyny    Considerable research has been done on the correlates of being androgynous (Rathus, 1987). They generally point to the greater adaptiveness and flexibility of androgynous over sex-typed individuals. By relying on both "masculine" and "feminine" traits, the androgynous person has a wider repertory of psychological traits and behaviors to call upon in various situations. They can act independently under group pressure (Bem, 1975) yet be nurturant when dealing with a baby (Bem et al., 1978). They are as comfortable with "masculine" activities (nailing boards, oiling hinges, or playing basketball) as they are with "feminine" activities (winding yarn, ironing a tablecloth, or taking a dance class) (Bem and Lenney, 1976; Helmreich et al., 1979; Matteo, 1987). They show greater self-esteem (Flaherty and Dusek, 1980), ability to bounce back from failure, and willingness to share leadership roles in groups (Porter et al., 1985).

Some argue that the benefits of androgyny derive not from the combination of masculine and feminine traits but the contribution of masculine traits, such as assertiveness and independence, to self-esteem (Whitley, 1983). In other words, androgyny benefits women more than it does men. On the other hand, evidence shows that feminine traits in both sexes contribute to marital happiness (Autil, 1983). Men who are married to feminine women are happier, as are women married to androgynous men (who are sympathetic, warm, tender, and love children). The implication is that masculine and feminine behaviors are neither good nor bad—their value depends on the context. For both men and women it seems that "masculine" traits work better in the marketplace, whereas "feminine" traits work better at home. If men and women have equal access to and responsibility in both roles, then gender disparities cease to be a problem.

Androgyny does not mean gender "neutrality" or the lack of distinctive traits. It is not a negative but a positive personality configuration. People who are least differentiated in gender terms or show neither clearly masculine nor feminine traits seem to be at a disadvantage. Such undifferentiated women are viewed less positively by more masculine or feminine women (Baucom and Danker-Brown, 1983), and are less satisfied with their marriages (Baucom and Aiken, 1984). Using Bem's category, undifferentiated individuals seem least attuned to society's sex role norms. They do not seem to identify with either masculine or feminine traits or behaviors. Because much of the work on sex roles has focused on sex-typed versus androgynous people, much less is known about correlates of undifferentiated types.

The concept of androgyny is intriguing but raises some further questions. Some of its terminology is rather confusing. How can we call a personality trait "masculine" or "feminine" if it is not distinctive of men or women? The underlying supposition is that certain traits are basically masculine or feminine, but that they are also widely shared by both sexes; yet this supposition reinforces the very gender stereotypes that it tries to combat (Lott, 1987). Bem's response to this charge would be that "androgyny" means transcending sex roles—no longer equating basketball with masculinity or pink with femininity. Bem's *gender schema theory* sets up androgyny as a description of people who do not use the masculine/feminine categories or dimensions to evaluate behavior. They are *gender-aschematic* individuals—they have no gender-based schema for organizing information; they use other dimensions instead. An androgynous woman who is trying to decide whether to take up karate will not think, "That's masculine and therefore not for me."

## GENDER DIFFERENCES THROUGH THE LIFE CYCLE

Gender identity and roles are not clear-cut. Men and women are not just this or that by virtue of being male or female. A similar consideration applies to gender at various phases of life. Like other aspects of the personality, gender identity evolves over time.

In a review of over 1400 studies (most published betwen 1966 and 1973), Maccoby and Jacklin (1974) found only four definite sex differences: girls show higher verbal ability; boys do better in visual-spatial tests and show higher mathematical performance. These differences usually become apparent during adolescence. Of more direct relevance to sexual behavior is the fact that boys were generally found to be more aggressive than girls, both verbally and physically.

There is some but not convincing evidence that girls are more timid or anxious, whereas boys are more active and competitive; the same is true for boys being more concerned with dominance in their relationships and girls more compliant and nurturant. There is no support for the commonly held views that girls are more social and suggestible or that they have lower self-esteem. Nor are boys better at tasks that are intellectually more complex and endowed with greater achievement motivation. Unfortunately, these reviewers did not deal with gender differences in sexual behavior, although they acknowledge that "sexual behavior per se may of course be the sphere of behavior most affected by the biology of sex." (Maccoby and Jacklin, 1974; also see Astin et al., 1975; Ortner and Whitehead, 1981).

Fewer sex differences are identified when behaviors are assessed objectively; more differences appear when judgments are made from observed behavior, raising the possibility that the results are more likely a function of the observers than the subjects.

A more critical look raises doubts about the validity of the evidence in even the better established findings (Fausto-Sterling, 1985). Therefore, at one extreme researchers claim that there are no behavioral differences that reliably distinguish between male and female; at the other, there are those who believe that there are many more sex differences than the studies show.

## Infancy

Boy or girl—it is the first question we ask about a baby. There are more similarities than differences between female and male newborns, but the announcement of the newborn's sex triggers a host of beliefs and expectations about the disposition, physical appearance, and behavior of the child (Rubin, Provenzano, and Luria, 1974; Hoffman, 1977; Haugh, Hoffman, and Cowan, 1980). From the time the pink bow is attached to the baby girl, parents will see her as smaller, prettier, softer, finer-featured, and more inattentive than her male counterpart (Rubin, et al., 1974), even though objective measurements show the two to be the same.

Similar results are found when researchers ask people to interact with infants presumed to be either a girl or a boy (Bell and Carver, 1980; Culp et al., 1983; Seavey et al.,

1975; Sidovowicz and Lunney, 1980; Smith and Lloyd, 1978). In general, these studies show that babies are given toys thought appropriate for their sex (dolls for girls, hammers for boys), are described in sex-appropriate terms ("boy" babies as strong, "girl" babies as round and soft), and are treated in sex-consistent ways ("girls" receive more verbal attention, "boys" more direct action).

Condry and Condry (1976) showed women and men a videotape of a nine-month-old's reaction to a jack-in-the-box, a doll, a teddy bear, and a buzzer. Half the observers were told the child was a boy; the other half were told it was a girl. All were asked to rate the child's fear, anger, and pleasure with each event. When the child's reactions were clear (smiling at the teddy bear or crying at the buzzer) observers agreed on what emotion the child was feeling. However, interpretations of the child's reaction to the jack-in-the-box—agitation followed by tears—depended upon what sex observers thought they were watching. The "female" child was described as afraid, whereas the "male" child was described as angry.

Reviews of the infancy literature have found few stable sex differences and have pointed, instead, to the wide variability in individual responses (Birns, 1976; Brackbill and Schroder, 1980). The few stable sex differences, found by Phillips et al., (1978), showed boys tended to be awake more, made more facial grimaces, and displayed more low-intensity motor movement than girls.

## Childhood

What do infants' sex differences, real or imagined, mean for the child's later development, especially sexual development? As Lott (1987) has pointed out, children of both sexes have an enormous capacity for learning. Several researchers have shown that children as young as two years can tell you the sex-appropriate behavior for males and females and will choose the sex-appropriate toy to play with (Fein et al., 1975; Smith and Daglish, 1977; Kuhn et al., 1978; Cowan and Hoffman, 1986; Fagot et al., 1986). There is evidence that their

Figure 10.2    Girls and boys playing at traditional gender roles.

thinking shows even greater alignment with adult expectations as the child grows older (Leahy and Shirk, 1984).

What did you play with as a child? Children's toys, books, and television programs are a strong source of information about cultural expectations and stereotypes. Advertisements for toys send strong messages about sex-appropriateness (Schwartz and Markham, 1985) and so do salespeople (Kutner and Levinson, 1978; Ungar, 1982). Lott (1987) has argued that girls' toys encourage approval-seeking and dependence on others, whereas boys' toys encourage problem solving. Currently, children both play at traditional gender roles and experiment with new ones (Figures 10.2 and 10.3).

Similarly, children's books and television programs often depict females as less visible than men; as helpless, passive followers; as servers of others; as indoors most of the time, particularly in the home; as in need of rescue; or as wives or mothers. Males are typically shown doing physical activities (climbing trees) or achieving results; as rescuers; as active leaders; as outdoors most of the time; and in a variety of occupations but less often as husbands or fathers (Charnes et al., 1980; O'Kelly, 1974; Rachlin and Vogt, 1974; Sternglanz and Serbin, 1974).

## Adolescence

There is less research on adolescence than on infancy and childhood. Many researchers characterize this period as a time of self-definition (Lott, 1987). Male and female adolescents share a number of concerns, such as developing a sense of autonomy from the family, spending more time with peers and deriving a value system from them, exploring their sexuality, thinking about their vocational futures, and developing a sense of personal identity. Nevertheless, the paths adolescents set upon to discover themselves are often mapped by the sex role norms of our society.

Especially in sexuality, adolescent males are encouraged to be active rather than passive, to develop ways of "being in control" and to structure situations to meet their needs. It is the male who arranges the date, picks up the female, opens all doors, drives her to their des-

Figure 10.3    Children playing at nontraditional gender roles.

tination, pays for the entertainment, and sees that she gets home again. If there is sexual activity, it is usually the male who sets the pace. On the negative side, the male risks rejection. On the positive side, he is getting experience with how to handle rejection and is learning to take control of his life.

Adolescent females, on the other hand, are encouraged to wait for the male's overtures, meanwhile making themselves as attractive as possible and developing interpersonal skills that will facilitate intimacy. Further, the female is given the primary responsibility for keeping sexual activity in check, which means she must deny her own sexual needs and development. The negative side for the female is that she gets less practice taking control of her life and may become caught between the personal need for independence and the social reward for being dependent (Welbourne-Moglia, 1984). The positive side is that she may develop more finely-tuned interpersonal skills (Lott, 1987).

The sex role stereotypes and norms learned throughout childhood might reinforce a double standard of behavior, particularly sexual behavior, in adolescence and adulthood. If children learn from parents, teachers, and the media that males are expected to be active and take control, whereas females are expected to be passive and wait for things to happen to them, they may readily transfer these patterns to dating and sexual relationships. As Tavris and Wade (1984) have noted, these patterns may also result in dominance and submissiveness in erotic fantasies and behaviors as well.

## Adulthood

By the time men and women reach adulthood, their gender-distinctive behavioral patterns are fairly well set, including their differential sexual ideologies (Kitzinger, 1986). For women, sexual relationships are characterized in terms of romance: finding the one and only "right" man, obtaining an exclusive commitment that will last forever, and solidifying that commitment with marriage (Chapter 16).

Women's magazines publish countless "how-to" articles on the subject, and romance novels are enjoying a resurgence of interest among women of all ages. Self-help books on love abound, most of which are addressed to women; usually they carry the message that it is the woman's responsibility to make relationships work or understand why they do not work.

For men, sexual relationships are more often characterized in terms of physical sex: performance levels are important, number of partners is equated with masculinity, and marriage is to be postponed until after a career has been established. Pornographic magazines are aimed primarily at a male audience and foster the notion of the ideal woman as a purely sexual object. Sexuality is often portrayed as violent, dominant, and unrelated to warmth and caring (Chapter 18).

Men and women get exposed to different messages about sexual relationships. No wonder they have erroneous beliefs about women's and men's interest in sexual behavior (Miller and Fowlkes, 1980; Lott, 1987; Matteo, 1987) or about how they respond to sexual imagery (Byrne and Lamberth, 1971; Heiman, 1975; Fisher and Byrne, 1978; Morokoff, 1985). Sexual ideologies, then, are a function of the time and culture in which we live.

Gender differences continue to affect beliefs about sexual interest and sexual behavior well into the later years of life. As we saw in Chapter 9, starting with the middle years, there is a tendency for men and women to become more alike. However, the double standard of aging (de Beauvoir, 1972; Sontag, 1972; Robinson, 1983) makes it more difficult for women than men to pursue sexual relationships. As Weg (1983) and others have noted, older men are judged primarily by their success; the fact that they are graying or balding, have gained weight or gotten out of shape detracts far less from their image as distinguished and mature than it does for women. Would you react the same to the entrance of an older man with a young woman on his arm, and to an older woman with a young admirer?

## HOW GENDER IDENTITY DEVELOPS

How does gender identity develop? Researchers agree that biological and social variables interact (Katchadourian, 1979), but they disagree about the relative importance of biology and culture. Do societies merely reinforce biologically determined gender traits, or do they invent gender models and then ascribe biological roots to them? In either case, it is clear that children acquire their gender identity at a young age and act out sex roles consistently.

### Interactional Models

Money and Ehrhardt (1972) have proposed an interactional model of psychosexual differentiation. It does not pit "nature versus nurture, the genetic versus the environmental, the innate versus the acquired, the biological versus the psychological, or the instinctive versus the learned."

Figure 10.4 traces this concept. It shows gender differentiation as a continuous process starting at fertilization and culminating in adulthood. The stages of sexual differentiation succeed each other as in a relay race. First the "program" of instructions for sexual differentiation is carried by the chromosomes and handed on to the undifferentiated gonad, which in turn passes it on through its hormones to various tissues. Genes and hormones cause male and female body differences, or *genital dimorphism* (Chapter 2). The perception of ourselves in these physical terms gives us our body image.

Simultaneously social factors are at work. From the moment of birth, boys and girls are treated differently. Such differential treatment persists throughout life, constantly reinforcing culturally defined gender models and stereotypes. With body image it shapes our juvenile gender identity.

At the next stage, changes brought about by pubertal hormones set apart male and female even further in physical form (*pubertal morphology*) and sexual functions (*pubertal ero-*

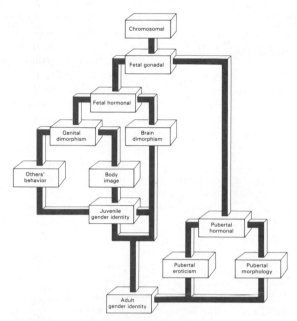

Figure 10.4   A model of gender-identity differentiation from conception to adulthood.

*ticism*). Together all these developments lead to adult gender identity.

In addition to the two main avenues of influence by hormones, a third path shown in Figure 10.4 leads to *brain dimorphism*. Just as the genitals are shaped differently by hormones, so presumably are the male and female brains (Chapter 4). If true, a difference in your brain could contribute to different gender-related behavior. Of course, it would still be modified by social learning.

Robert Stoller (1985) offers a similar multidetermined explanation for the development of core gender identity. He begins with a biological "force," usually genetic, that influences the organization of the fetal brain. Sex assignment at birth or the constant impact of parental attitudes based on sex become an integral part of gender definition. "Biopsychic" phenomena, such as the way an infant is handled, conditioning, imprinting, and other early learning experiences further mod-

ify the infant's brain. Meanwhile various bodily sensations, especially from the genitals, shape the infant's developing *body ego* (a sense of the dimensions, uses, and significance of the body), which also contributes to gender identity. Usually, these factors cooperate; only when something goes wrong do we see their separate effects.

## Special Cases

As children, we become aware of our genitals. Is there any other biological basis for our sense of being male or female? Do we start life with our brains "wired" one way or another? Does social learning merely amplify the difference, or is it the sole basis for it?

Much of the research undertaken to answer these questions has involved individuals born with various hormonally induced abnormalities (see Chapter 4). Consider, for instance, cases of female infants with congenital adrenal hyperplasia (CAH), who are born with masculinized or ambiguous-looking genital organs. Parents have the option of raising these children either as boys or girls. Once the decision is made, hormones and surgery make the appearance of the genitals conform to the gender in which the child is to be raised. At puberty, the appropriate male or female hormones are given to enhance the secondary sexual characteristics of the chosen sex (Money and Ehrhardt, 1972).

If gender were determined by the genes and the dominant prenatal hormones (the organizational effect), we would expect these children to develop a female gender identity, no matter how they are raised. If the process of rearing is the decisive factor, then one child should develop male gender identity, another female gender identity, consistent with the sex of rearing. Most evidence in this area of research supports the latter outcome (Money and Ehrhardt, 1972; Ehrhardt and Meyer-Bahlburg, 1981), even though these girls experience some adjustment problems at adolescence having to do with body image and delays

# Box 10.2

## CRITICAL PERIOD OF GENDER DIFFERENTIATION

The reproductive system becomes male or female before birth on a predictable timetable (Chapter 2). Does gender identity too differentiate on a set schedule? If it does, then there must be a critical period during which the core gender identity is fixed, even though it is later refined.

Money and Ehrhardt (1972) have pinpointed the period of core gender identity formation at around eighteen months. By the age of 3 or 4 years, the sense of gender identity—being a boy or a girl— is normally so set, both in the child's and the parents' minds, that any attempt to change it is said to result in serious psychosexual trouble. This time of gender identity differentiation coincides more or less with the period of language acquisition.

This model of gender identity differentiation in early childhood seems to be contradicted by the experience of individuals with a rare type of enzymatic defect called *5-alpha-reductase deficiency*. Genetic males with this defect cannot convert testosterone to *dihydrotesterone*, which is necessary for the development of the male external genitalia during embryonal life. As a result, they are born with female-looking genitals. But at puberty, the surge in testosterone causes growth of the penis and the appearance of male secondary sexual characteristics.

In the early 1970s a group of investigators located a group of 24 girls in two isolated villages in the Dominican Republic who had "turned into" boys at puberty. They were known locally as *guevodoces* ("penis at twelve") and were actually genetic males suffering from the enzymatic defect referred to above (Imperato-McGinley et al., 1974, 1976). Remarkably enough, these youngsters who were brought up as girls seemed to have no problem in shifting their gender identities at puberty to grow up into men, which would indicate that the core gender identity "gate" is not closed in early childhood.

Further inquiry, however, shows the transformation of guevodoces to be not as abrupt as initially suggested (Baker, 1980). At least some of these children are apparently aware of genital ambiguity, if not abnormality, before puberty, in which case they cannot be said to have developed normally as girls. Because it is advantageous to be a male in their culture, these "girls" may willingly embrace the chance to become male; hence the shift in gender identity may be more apparent than real. Moreover, their adaptation to the adult male role seems to be inconsistent. Methodological concerns raise additional questions about conclusions drawn from the experience of guevodoces.

---

in dating and sexual relations (Hurtig and Rosenthal, 1987).

The preeminence of rearing in gender definition is also attested by an unusual case where one of twin infant boys lost his penis through a surgical mishap during circumcision. Because it was easier to alter his genitals to make them look female than to reconstruct the penis, he was castrated, his genitals were surgically reshaped, and he was treated with estrogen at puberty. Reared as a girl, the child was reported to have successfully developed an essentially female gender identity (Money and Tucker, 1975). But some questions have been raised about how successful that process really has been (Diamond, 1982).

On such evidence it is maintained that gender identity is not shaped by the effect of hormones on the brain but by social learning. Research with hermaphrodites suggests that gender is undifferentiated at birth and that we become masculine or feminine in the course of growing up (Money and Ehrhardt, 1972). There may be limits in the timing of this process (Box 10.2).

This model of *gender neutrality* at birth has not gone unchallenged. The counterargument is that an individual's biological heritage sets limits to the definition of gender identity. Within these limits social forces can exert their influence (Diamond, 1965, 1976, 1979). In this view, it would have made more sense to rear the boy with the lost penis as male, despite the problems he would have had to confront (Diamond, 1982).

At present, the more widely held view is that the sex of rearing, established by parental and early social influences, is the primary determinant of gender identity.

## Sex-Dimorphic Behavior

Like gender identity, gender role is heavily laden with cultural expectations and strongly influenced by social learning. Nonetheless, there is evidence that hormones predispose us before birth to develop certain sex-typed behaviors (Ehrhardt and Meyer-Bahlburg, 1981). These behaviors are not erotic, but they are intimately bound with sexuality by virtue of helping to define the context of relationships.

These behaviors have been studied in children and adolescents (as well as nonhuman primates). They cluster in six areas:

- energy expenditure in active play and athletics
- social aggression (physical and verbal fighting)
- parental rehearsal (doll play, playing "house," play-acting the role of mother or father, participating in infant care, fantasies about having children)
- preference of playmates by sex; gender role labeling (knowing existing norms of masculine and feminine behavior)
- grooming behavior (dress, makeup, hairdo, use of jewelry)

Girls whose behavior is markedly different from traditional feminine patterns are labeled "tomboy"; boys who are "feminine" in their behavior are called "sissy."

Among animals, there is good evidence linking prenatal hormonal influence with sex differences in juvenile sex-dimorphic behaviors like rough-and-tumble play, threat behavior and fighting, parenting, dominance behavior, sex-segregated play, and grooming. Among humans, studies have largely focused again on individuals with unusual prenatal

hormonal histories (MacLusky and Naftolin, 1981). Much of the evidence is based once again on research with girls who were exposed to abnormal levels of androgens before birth. Some of them were cases of adrenogenital syndrome or CAH. Others were born to mothers who had been treated with progestins (to prevent miscarriage), when it was not known that progestins would be converted in the body to testosterone.

These baby girls were born with masculinized genitals (Figure 10.5). Those with adrenogenital syndrome were treated early to suppress the excessive production of androgens. Furthermore, these children had their genital abnormalities corrected by surgery and they were brought up as girls. Nonetheless, the prenatal exposure to high levels of androgen seems to make a significant difference in the sex-dimorphic behavior of these girls: they engage in a great deal of active outdoor play, show increased association with male peers, tend to be identified as "tomboys" by themselves and others, show decreased parental rehearsing behavior such as doll play and baby

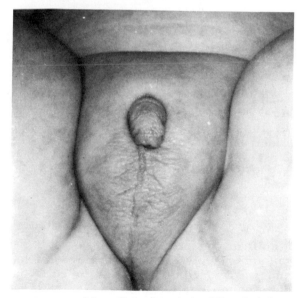

Figure 10.5   Masculinized genitals of female infant due to mother's ingestion of androgenizing hormones (Donerzol) while pregnant.

care, and have a low interest in the roles of wife and mother, as against having career aspirations (Ehrhardt et al., 1968; Ehrhardt and Baker, 1974; Ehrhardt et al., 1981).

Further confirmation comes from the study of females whose mothers were given masculinizing sex steroids during pregnancy (Money and Ehrhardt, 1972; Ehrhardt et al., 1984). These girls had no intrinsic hormonal abnormality, their masculinized genitals were corrected early, and they were reared as girls, yet they showed behavioral patterns similar to CAH girls.

Of course, tomboyish behavior need not always mean hormonal abnormality. Many perfectly normal girls act like tomboys, and such behavior is increasingly acceptable in our culture. Moreover, this line of research has been criticized for the small number of cases involved and methodological pitfalls (Bleier, 1984). Similar objections can be raised to research with CAH girls showing gender identity to be the result of the sex of rearing. It is thus questionable whether research based on abnormal conditions should be used to describe the development of gender among normal children.

## GENDER DISORDERS

Even in the most traditional of societies, there is an acceptable range of variation in the cultural stereotypes of masculinity and femininity. In more liberal societies, this range is even wider, but at some point males and females cross over an arbitrary line beyond which they are perceived as *effeminate* men and *masculine* or *manly* women.

Most individuals in these categories are *normal variants*. They are quite clear about being male or female and generally satisfied with their gender. They simply do not fit the cultural stereotypes of masculinity and femininity. These individuals may be teased as children or made to feel awkward as adults, but they experience no inner conflict over their gender. They are not considered to suffer from a gender identity disorder.

*Homosexuality* is a sexual orientation in which people are attracted to members of their own sex (Chapter 13). There are homosexuals who dress in the clothes of the opposite sex (cross-dressing); other gay men are markedly "effeminate" and some lesbian women look and behave in a "masculine" fashion. However, homosexuals typically have no doubt or conflict about being male or female. They do not suffer from a gender identity disorder.

Similarly, there are some heterosexual men who are sexually aroused by wearing female clothing. They may do it occasionally and in private, or they may wear female clothing in public most of the time. This practice is called *transvestic fetishism*. Transvestite men also have no confusion or conflict with their maleness; they too do not suffer from a gender identity disorder.

To qualify as a gender disorder, there must be a mismatch between the person's anatomical sex and his or her gender identity. In its mild form, such a person is aware of being male or female but feels unhappy with it. At its most extreme, the person feels "trapped" in the wrong body. These individuals fall into three categories: children with identity disorders; adolescents with identity disorder; and transsexuals (American Psychiatric Association, 1987).

### Gender Identity Disorder of Childhood

*Gender identity disorder of childhood* is an uncommon condition characterized by a persistent rejection by a child of his or her anatomic sex, accompanied by the desire to be, or the insistence that one is, a member of the opposite sex. Girls may seek male peer groups, show an avid interest in aggressive sports and rough-and-tumble play, and refuse to play with dolls or play house unless they get to be the "father". Such behavior goes beyond that of an ordinary tomboy. Occasionally a girl will claim that she will not grow into a woman but will become a man, and that she will grow (or already has) a penis. Some of these children have additional disturbances like nightmares and phobias. These tendencies appear early in childhood, but most girls yield to social pressure by adolescence and give up their open attachment to male activities and attire. A minority retain a strong masculine identification, and some develop a homosexual orientation.

Many more boys are brought in for help for gender problems than girls. That fact may reflect the tendency of parents to become more disturbed by atypical gender behavior of sons than of daughters. Boys with this disorder show a preference for dressing in female clothes (three-fourths begin to cross-dress before age four) and a compelling interest in girls as playmates and in girls' games (playing with dolls, being the mommy when playing house). Rough-and-tumble play and other boyish activities are avoided, making these children subject to teasing and rejection by other boys. These boys express disgust at their penis and wish that it would disappear, or they believe they will grow up to become women.

By age seven or eight, these boys may become seriously ostracized by their peers and may refuse to go to school ("sissies" have a harder time at school than "tomboys"). Under social pressure, such behavior may lessen in adolescence, but as many as half develop homosexual orientations in adolescence, and some carry the gender disturbances into adult life (Green et al., 1982; Green, 1986).

## Later Gender Identity Disorder

A counterpart of the childhood gender disorder occurs in later life. Its essential features are a recurrent or persistent discomfort with anatomical or assigned gender and cross-dressing. Unlike the transvestite fetishist, these individuals get no erotic satisfaction from cross-dressing; it merely fits better with their self-perceived gender identity. If prevented from cross-dressing, they feel anxious and depressed. These persons do not seek to have their bodies altered to fit their gender image.

## Transsexualism

The most extreme form of gender disorder is *transsexualism*. In order to be diagnosed as a

transsexual (or suffering from the *gender dysphoria syndrome*) a person must feel persistent discomfort and sense of inappropriateness with assigned gender and genital organs, wish to be rid of them, and want to live as a member of the opposite sex. The person should be free of hermaphroditic abnormalities and must not be psychotic or suffer from a mental illness. The condition must have been continuous over at least two years (Steiner, 1985).

To varying degrees, the behavior, dress, and mannerisms of transsexuals imitate those of the opposite sex (which for the transsexual is his or her true gender). A male transsexual will dress up in female clothing, like a male transvestite. However, the transsexual male does not derive sexual pleasure from dressing up as a female—so far as he is concerned, he is merely putting on the appropriate clothing for his true gender, which he believes to be female. Similarly, the transsexual male, like the homosexual, will be sexually attracted to other men. Unlike the homosexual who is seeking a partner of the same sex, the transsexual male feels the way a woman would toward a man.

The world became widely aware of transsexualism in 1953 when an ex-Marine underwent surgery in Denmark to become Christine Jorgensen. Since then, several thousand transsexual men and women have had sex changes through hormones and transsexual surgery, some of them gaining international prominence. Among the more notable cases was Dr. Richard Raskin, an ophthalmologist and accomplished tennis player who became Dr. Renee Richards and began to compete in women's tennis tournaments with some controversy. John Morris, noted British journalist and writer, became Jan Morris, whose autobiography, *Conundrum*, is a highly insightful and moving account of her experience as a transsexual. The estimated prevalence of transsexualism is 1 per 30,000 males and 1 per 100,000 females. Among those who seek help in clinics dealing with transsexuals the ratio of males to females varies from 8:1 to 1:1 (American Psychiatric Association, 1987).

The sexual orientation of transsexuals varies. Some are asexual, showing little erotic

Figure 10.6     Female to male transsexual change.

interest and deriving no pleasure from their genitals. Others appear homosexual to outsiders or have heterosexual histories, occasionally involving marriage and children.

The cause of transsexualism—biological or psychosocial—is unknown despite a good deal of research (Stoller, 1975; Sorensen and Hertoft, 1982). Transsexuals show no hormonal abnormality (Hoenig, 1985; Goodman et al., 1985). Attempts to find familial or rearing patterns have been inconclusive. Most transsexuals trace their gender problems back to childhood. The intense desire to undergo the full change usually comes in young adulthood but may occur as late as midlife (Roback and Lothstein, 1986).

The extreme dissatisfaction transsexuals experience in their biological gender often results in severe psychological problems leading to alcohol or drug abuse and attempted suicides (Dixen et al., 1984; Verschoor and Poortiuga, 1988). They may be so desperate to undergo sex change that they may fall victim to unscrupulous and poorly qualified surgeons or illicit practioners (Chastre et al., 1987). Responsible programs combine psychological, so-

cial, hormonal, and surgical treatment (Laub and Dubin, 1979). Following careful selection, the candidate receives psychological counseling; practical guidance on matters like grooming, vocational choice, and legal issues; and hormonal therapy to bring about changes in secondary sexual characteristics, especially growth of breasts in males and facial hair in women (Heresova et al., 1986; Meyer et al., 1986). Full breast development requires about two years of estrogen treatment (Meyer et al., 1986). The transformation can be spectacular (Figure 10.6).

Sex change and sex reassignment surgery is the last phase of treatment (which not all transsexuals undergo). It is usually undertaken after two years of living and working successfully as a member of the sex the person wants to become. Some treatment centers have found that sex reassignment surgery does not significantly help in the social rehabilitation of the transsexual and no longer perform such surgery (Abramowitz, 1986).

There are two main stages in the surgical procedure. First, the existing organs (such as the testes, penis, ovaries and breasts) are removed. Second, artificial genitals of the new sex are constructed (Lim, 1986). The artificial vagina created for the male-to-female transsexual may be indistinguishable from a normal vagina, even to a gynecologist (Figure 10.7). Made from a transplanted segment of the rectum, it responds with lubrication during sexual excitement, and some patients are able to reach orgasm during coitus. Lacking internal female organs (the male internal sex organs are removed) they cannot have children.

The creation of male genitals for the female-to-male transsexual is technically more difficult (Figure 10.7). The artificial penis allows the person to urinate like a male; the organ is sensitive but cannot achieve an erection except through inflatable implants (Chapter 15).

The outcome of such programs is usually positive. The problems are related to the genital surgery. In a lengthy follow-up study (average 12 years) only one-third had retained a functional artificial vagina. Though half of the transsexuals experienced orgasm, only one-third had made a successful sexual adjustment after surgery (Lindemalm et al., 1986).

In some cases patients regret the sex change and must be reoperated on to restore their previous genital status. This reversal is only partly possible, because in the original surgery internal sex organs were removed that cannot be restored.

## GENDER AND SEXUAL BEHAVIOR

The influence of gender on sexual behavior is so pervasive that to discuss it fully we would have to anticipate almost everything that is to be said in the rest of this book. Instead we will focus on basic trends that differentiate male and female sexual behaviors. You will learn more when we discuss specific sexual activities (Chapters 11 to 14) and relationships (Chapters 16 to 19).

### Sexual Drive and Behavior

By all apparent indicators, men seem to be sexually more eager, active, and preoccupied than women. In heterosexual relationships men usually take the initiative and press for sexual involvement sooner than women. Most (but not all) studies show they want to engage in sex more frequently than their partner.

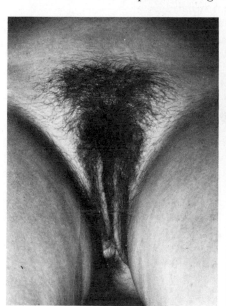
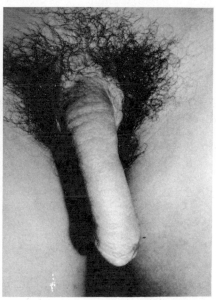

Figure 10.7  Surgically constructed female genitals in male - to - female transsexual (*left*) and male genitals in female-to-male transsexual (*right*) after reassignment of anatomic sex.

The gender differences are far greater in sexual activities other than coitus; men are by far more likely to take part in other sexual behaviors. Men are more likely to masturbate and do so more frequently. Presumably they also have a more active erotic fantasy life (Chapter 11). There are three gay men for every lesbian woman (Chapter 13). The great majority of paraphiliacs who engage in sexual activities with children, commit incest, and are apprehended for exhibitionism, voyeurism, or other sexual offenses are male (Chapter 14).

The purveyors and consumers of pornography are mostly male. Prostitution exists primarily to serve male needs, be it heterosexual or homosexual (Chapter 18). Almost all forms of sexual coercion from sexual pressuring to rape are perpetrated by men (Chapter 19).

Does this mean that men are more interested in sex than women? The question is not rhetorical, nor the answer self-evident. Society has allowed men and women very different freedom of sexual expression. Perhaps women are not as sexually active as men because they have not been permitted to do so. Given half a chance, women have successfully taken on many traditional male career roles; they may do likewise with sexual roles. We see that they have done so in some sexual behaviors when we compare early studies like the Kinsey study with more recent surveys. Women now are sexually more active than before, both in level of involvement and degree of satisfaction.

However, these changes are selective. Women generally still do not behave like men. For instance, there are now large numbers of independent, self-assertive, single women who are not as likely as their male counterparts to engage in casual sex or atypical sexual behaviors (Chapter 14). Is the double standard still making its influence felt? Is that a sufficient explanation? If not, a certain measure of difference seems to characterize male and female behavior that is attributable to free choice rather than social constraints. How do we explain it?

In discussing the relationship of hormones to sexual behavior (Chapter 4), we considered the possibility that sex hormones, in particular, androgens, may induce and sustain the sexual drive in both sexes. Men have higher levels of androgen; would that explain all the gender differences in sexual behavior? It is unlikely, although hormones may play an important role in predisposing men and women towards certain forms of sexual behavior and determining their level of activity. Human sexual behavior is so complex and its gender differences so strongly influenced by social factors that no hormonal explanation is likely to do justice to it. Then what is the explanation?

## Response to Erotica

It is commonly believed that men and women respond differently to *erotica*, literature or art of an erotic nature or materials intended to cause sexual arousal. Do men respond more readily and intensely to erotica than women? Are they "turned on" by different sorts of material? Are all these allegations just stereotypes we attach to men and women? If such differences do exist, are they mainly biological or cultural? Despite widespread interest in such questions, amazingly little research until recently explored what males and females find erotically stimulating.

Kinsey reported that men are generally more readily stimulated than women by viewing sexually explicit materials (such as pictures of nudes, genitals, or sexual scenes) but that women are as responsive as men in reaction to motion pictures and literature with romantic content. This finding seemed to conform to gender expectation at the time, although on reconsideration, it is possible that the perceived gender difference was an artifact of the way the questions were phrased (Gebhard, 1973).

In the 1970s, experimental evidence began to appear (Kinsey used self-reports). In one study, a group of students at Hamburg University were shown sexually explicit pictures under experimental conditions (Schmidt and Sigusch, 1970). In general, men were more responsive than women to nude pictures, but when the scenes had an interpersonal or affectionate component (such as kissing couples) women were equally if not more responsive. Scenes of coitus were somewhat more arousing to men, but not much more so than to women. Sexual arousal in these contexts was reported by the women as vaginal warmth, itching, pulsations, and moistening; the men usually responded with erections.

A larger sample (128 males and 128 females) were shown films featuring male and female masturbation, petting, and coitus (Schmidt, 1975). Among the women, 65 percent experienced genital sensations; among the men 31 percent had full erections and 55 percent had partial erections. About one in five men and women reported some masturbatory activity while viewing the film, and during the following 24 hours there was some increase in sexual activity for both sexes, especially masturbation. These findings tended to confirm the notion that males respond more readily than females to erotic visual material, especially of the more "hard-core" variety, but also showed that the gender differences reported by Kinsey had diminished (Schmidt, 1975; Osborn and Pollack, 1977).

With the development of new technologies, special instruments have provided objective means of studying physiological arousal (Box 3.2 in Chapter 3). They have added a whole new dimension to our understanding of these issues. For example, in one study subjects listened to tape-recorded stories with erotic and romantic themes. Their reactions were self-reported and monitored with instruments. Both sexes reported that the tape with explicit erotic content (with or without a romantic element) was more stimulating than those with only romantic or erotically neutral content. There was, however, an interesting discrepancy between the verbal reports of the women and their physiological reactions: only half of the women who were physiologically aroused reported this fact. The men, on the other hand, never failed to report their physiological arousal (Heiman, 1975). Possibly, women who perceive sexual arousal are not comfortable saying so.

Women's failure to report sexual arousal may also be explained by anatomical differences (it is harder to miss an erection than signs of female arousal) or by psychological mechanisms repressing such reporting. Women have traditionally inhibited expressions of sexual arousal and interest because of their social unacceptability. Although such attitudes are currently changing, they may still have an effect. Current studies continue to report a stronger correspondence between subjective and physiological measures of arousal for males than females (Steinman et al., 1981).

The laboratory study of sexual responsiveness promises more objective data; on the other hand, it may trivialize what it sets out to investigate. For instance, a woman with a highly satisfying sexual life may find exposure to erotica under laboratory conditions uninteresting. Her failure to respond to contrived erotic cues would be of little real-life significance and hardly reflect her true sexual potential (Heiman, 1980). Even more misleading would be to draw conclusions from what can be observed publicly about the differential sexual responses of males and females to erotic themes. Because much of what passes for erotic and pornographic material in our mass culture (films, books, magazines, and so on) is produced by men for men, the fact that women find them unarousing or offensive may say nothing about women's capacity to respond to erotic visual cues in general (Chapter 18).

There is a definite trend in more recent studies for males and females to be more similar in their arousal responses than reported earlier (Rubinsky et al., 1987). Better experimental methods are allowing women to report their sexual reactions more freely. In addition, there may have been an actual increase in female responsiveness over the past few decades because of changes in the sexual socialization of women (Griffith, 1987).

## Orgasmic Capacity

Are there gender differences in how easily men and women reach orgasm? Could they explain differences in sexual drive? Orgasm is the physiological end point of sexual arousal and the peak of sexual pleasure for most people; if men are more certain of reaching it, they might have a greater incentive to engage in sexual behavior.

Among married couples, wives consistently report lower rates of reaching orgasm than their husbands. This pattern was established in the Kinsey studies and has been confirmed in subsequent investigations (Chapter 15). Whereas practically all male subjects who engaged in coitus reached orgasm every time, women in general reached orgasm three out of four times (Kinsey et al., 1953). Evidence from a variety of studies shows that 10 percent of women never reach orgasm during intercourse, and another 10 percent do so only sporadically (Chapter 15). Failure to reach orgasm among men is mostly due to the inability to have an erection, which is far less common. Even in a sample of couples not seeking sex therapy, the prevalence of sexual dysfunction of various forms is considerably higher among women than men (Anderson and Rubinstein, 1978).

This pattern for coitus among spouses may not be a true reflection of sexual responsiveness. Some women who have difficulty reaching orgasm in coitus have no problem when they masturbate. The reliance on a male partner, not infrequently inept, may not allow the free and full expression of female sexuality. Because most women rely on coitus, usually with a spouse, for their sexual satisfaction, we get a false impression of potential female response.

Moreover, the proposal that men are better at orgasms runs smack against the greater ability of women to reach multiple orgasm (Chapter 3). In the aggregate, women chalk up many more orgasms than do men. It would seem that orgasmic capacity gives no better clues to explain sex differences than responses to erotica.

## Relational Aspects

The most consistent difference in sexual behavior is in how men and women approach its relational aspects. Compared with males, females tend to be more cautious in sexual matters. When sex is looked at only as a source of physical pleasure, men clearly seem more interested; when it is part of a broader relationship, it appeals more to women. Of course, women want sexual pleasure and men care about relationships; it is merely a matter of relative emphasis. Men are more willing to forego friendship or love in having sex with a casual partner or a prostitute. Women are far less interested in sex for its own sake. This difference is equally true for heterosexuals and homosexuals. Women are more concerned with the risk of pregnancy and acquiring a "loose" reputation (Griffith, 1987). Men are called "studs" but women are called "sluts" for the same sort of sexual behavior.

Men and women give different reasons for engaging in coitus. When a sample of college students were asked if "emotional involvement" was a prerequisite for engaging in sexual intercourse, 45 percent of the women but only 8 percent of the men said it was "always." Given that 94 percent of the men and 80 percent of the women had engaged in premarital sex, their sexual behavior was fairly similar, but not the basic justification for it. Moreover, the men emphasized physical need and pleasure, whereas the women cited relationships, emotional commitment, and love as their basic motives (Carroll et al., 1985).

From these basic differences (which we shall discuss more fully in Chapters 16 and 17) flow many of the behavioral discrepancies in male and female sexual behaviors. For instance, men are more aroused by female nudity and the sight of female genitals than women by the male body. Coitus is focused on the genitals and orgasm for men; women see it as a total body interaction and a more diffusely sensuous experience. This is why, in the study cited earlier, even when women show higher rates of sexual dysfunction (usually not reaching orgasm) their ratings of sexual satisfaction are almost the same as those of men. A man who does not reach orgasm will view the sexual encounter as a failure; a woman is less likely to. Perhaps women are willing to settle for less; or perhaps there is an important difference in their source of sexual satisfaction.

A second significant factor is the infusion of aggression and dominance into male sexuality. Language itself betrays the tendency of the male to view sexual encounters as a form of conquest ("I scored"), possession ("I had her"), and aggression ("I screwed her"). The lack of a relational element combined with these incentives may explain the male proclivity to seek multiple sexual partners, to indulge in varieties of sexual experiences, and to use force in sexual interactions. When women resort to seduction or other forms of manipulation in their sexual encounters, the aim is usually not to get sexual satisfaction but some other objective.

It looks like relational differences are the key to gender differences in sexual behavior. What is at their root?

## Explaining the Differences
Like gender identity, gender differences in sexual behavior are the result of the interaction of biological and social factors.

Evolutionary Perspective   Dimorphism in sexual behavior—the different ways in which males and females behave sexually—is shared by humans and animals. The basic biological reason is the same. Physical sex differences allow the male and female to identify each other in order to mate, and behavioral patterns enhance the chances that they will.

Just as the major groups of vertebrates have evolved their distinctive reproductive strategies, males and females within each group have evolved special patterns of sexual behavior to maximize reproductive success (Chapter 1) (Raven and Johnson, 1986). The measure of reproductive success is not simply how many offspring an animal produces but the number of its young that survive to produce their own offspring, perpetuating the genetic lineage (and more broadly, the species) to which the animal belongs.

Animals, unlike humans, are unaware of this process; males and females do not come together because of a magnanimous desire to share in the production and care of offspring (Campbell, 1987). Male and female "use" each other as a necessary vehicle to help their genes get into the next generation (or be represented in the "gene pool"). The probability that an animal will survive to produce viable offspring defines its *fitness,* in an evolutionary sense.

Male and female cannot reproduce alone. Also, for mammals, birds, and some reptiles, rearing offspring requires the continued involvement of the mother, and sometimes the father. Thus reproductive success depends on collaboration between the two sexes. However, the interests of male and female do not always coincide. There is also an element of competition between the male and female that form a mating pair, because the behavior by which one sex maximizes fitness may be different, if not antagonistic, to that of the other sex. These differences pertain to sexual or *parental investment* in the offspring.

Among vertebrates, females have in general a greater parental investment than males. Females produce fewer eggs than males produce sperm. Eggs are much bigger and "costly" to produce. Furthermore, in mammals, females invest much more time and energy in carrying the young before birth and then nurturing it until it can fend for itself. Because the number of times they can conceive is limited, and each instance is quite "costly," it is in the interest of the female to be selective in choosing a mate.

By contrast, sperm is "cheap" and little is required of the male after insemination. A more "profitable" male strategy is to inseminate as many females as possible. However, because staying with the female and helping to rear the young maximizes the chances of survival for his progeny as well, there is an incentive for the male to help and protect the mother–infant unit.

Governed by these purposes, male and female animals of each species behave in distinctive and predictable patterns. The courtship patterns and the pairings vary widely (Chapter 16), but the goal is the same. For instance, mating relationships among many birds tend to be monogamous—one male mates for keeps with one female. Mammals are more typically polygamous or promiscuous, with no strong pair bonds or lasting relationships. Often a single male will mate with many females; less often one female will mate with many males (Campbell, 1987).

To what extent do these animal patterns apply to human courtship behavior? Sociobiologists (Chapter 1) have attempted to cast human relationships in an evolutionary mold with highly controversial results. In the evolutionary view, men and women maximize their reproductive fitness, just as animals do, by behaving in ways that produce as many offspring as possible—offspring who survive to reproduce in turn, thereby perpetuating their genes (Symons, 1979).

Applied to modern men and women, this idea appears to make no sense. Although a few people want to have all the children they can, most others limit the number of children through birth control.[1] Still, the "logic" dictated by our evolutionary heritage is not always the same as our conscious reasoning. Even though rationally we may be inclined or persuaded to behave a certain way, the inner "push" of genetic influences could make us behave differently without our being aware.

If this is the case, even when men and women engage in sex, not for reproduction but for pleasure, love, or another reason, they still tend to behave as if they were maximizing their parental investment. Given the greater limitations on the number of offspring females can produce compared to males, the two sexes use different strategies. Females go after quality; men after quantity (Symons, 1979). Wilson sums it up:

> It pays males to be aggressive, hasty, fickle and indiscriminating. In theory, it is more profitable for females to be coy, to hold back until they can identify the males with the best genes. In species that rear young, it is also important for the females to select males who are more likely to stay with them after insemination. (Wilson, 1978, p. 129)

Critics of sociobiology find its conclusions farfetched and unwarranted. Its behavioral descriptions are seen as ethnocentric, its behavioral units lacking in definition, its choice of animal models flawed, and its language inappropriate (Bleier, 1984). Such objections that are aimed at sociobiology, are not necessarily directed at the whole evolutionary approach to behavior (Hrdy, 1981).

There is also a political side to the debate. Those concerned with the oppression of women bristle when they see sociobiology seem to justify men philandering and mistreating women (Fausto-Sterling, 1985). Others worry that even if that is not the intent of sociobiologists, there is the potential for the misapplication of their theories to sexist ends. On the other hand, if these evolutionary influences do motivate our sexual behavior, by identifying and confronting them we stand a better chance of controlling their consequences (Symons, 1979). We shall return to this issue in Chapter 16.

Differential Socialization    Suppose that none of the biological arguments were valid. Could we explain gender differences in sexual behavior purely on the basis of how males and females are socialized? Can we demonstrate that boys and girls are taught to behave differently, and that these differences are maintained and reinforced through adolescence and adulthood? Does it all come down to male and female developing different social "scripts"?

Many behavioral scientists would answer yes. Why then do virtually all societies choose

[1] The *Guiness book of world records* credits the unnamed wife of Feodor Vassiliyev, a Russian peasant, with 69 children born through 27 pregnancies (16 pairs of twins, 7 sets of triplets, and 4 sets of quadruplets) during the 18th century. The paternity record is said to be held by Moulay Ismail, "the Bloodthirsty," former emperor of Morocco (1672–1727), who reputedly fathered 548 sons and 340 daughters (McWhirter, 1987).

to socialize males and females differently (D'Andrade, 1966)? Why the remarkable consistency in certain sexual scripts despite enormous cultural variations? Why are men across various cultures more like each other in their sexual behaviors than like the women in their own cultures, with whom they have so much else in common (Gregersen, 1983)?

One way to explain this consistency is to find a highly significant and universal male or female characteristic that will induce cultures to socialize the two sexes differently. That characteristic is most likely the female capacity to bear children. Although this is a biological feature, it is the social reactions to it that count.

Before the contraceptive revolution a few decades ago, every time a fertile woman engaged in coitus she ran the risk (or had the opportunity) of getting pregnant. Over the millenia the consequences to women of bearing children have been enormous. Until the advent of modern medicine, each time a woman got pregnant, she risked losing her life in childbirth. The children she bore either died or became one more mouth to feed with scarce resources. Sex could hardly have been fun and games under these circumstances. Despite the availability of contraception, the fear of pregnancy is still a significant deterrent to a woman's free expression of sexuality; men are concerned about it, but to a lesser extent.

In making reproduction the key function of female sexuality, and the rearing of children a woman's primary task, human societies have relegated sexual pleasure to a secondary role, at best, or denied it altogether to women. Although many women have managed to live sexually fulfilling lives, and modern women feel fully entitled to their sexual pleasure, attitudes that have survived over thousands of years do not vanish in a few decades.

In recorded history, most cultures are *patriarchal*, ruled by men.[2] In them a woman bears the children of a man and is considered a man's property (first the father, then the husband). She has been jealously guarded both before and after marriage. Premarital chastity and marital fidelity have therefore become an integral part of the moral fabric and legal structure of society (Chapters 22 and 23). Almost universally, a *double standard* has been applied to sexual behavior, with men accorded greater freedom. Why? Because men make the rules, and men do not get pregnant.

The double standard is sustained by both external and internal sanctions. The external sanctions in response to sexual transgressions range from loss of reputation, to compromised standing in the marriage market, to death for adultery; women have been penalized more harshly than men. The internal sanctions take the form of shame and guilt. Once again, women feel more ashamed and more guilty than men. Female sexuality has been what patriarchal societies have said it should be. These influences still hold, albeit less strongly, for modern men and women.

Having children greatly increases the dependency of women on men. Until recently, it was hard enough for a single woman to fend for herself; with children the burden became harder still. Even today, child care is one of the most critical problems for single working mothers.

Given the responsibilities of motherhood and the even broader impact of traditional marriage on a woman's life, the importance of the *relational* component must have become deeply ingrained in the female character. Today, even under radically changed circumstances, a woman still seeks a meaningful relationship within which to engage in sex. Even a woman who is in no danger of getting pregnant, is not looking for a husband, is unconcerned about public opinion, and risks no punishment still chooses to behave in ways that

[2]The belief that women ruled human societies in prehistory has been put forth by various writers over the past century, and has been revived more recently. Yet there is no convincing evidence that *matriarchal* societies were ever a universal stage in human evolution. *Matrilineal* societies do exist whereby children are primarily identified with the mother's family and inherit through her *mother*. Yet even in these cases, male members of the mothers family govern the family's collective affairs (Hrdy, 1981).

were originally intended to guard her against these liabilities. Unaware, she now behaves this way not because she has to but because she wants to.

Other considerations lead men and women to believe sexual activity serves different purposes. Experiences during sexual development are thought to be especially significant (DeLamater, 1987). Up to adolescence, boys are much more likely to masturbate than girls. This act provides direct experience of sexual arousal and gratification and a sense of personal control over their sexual experience (Rook and Hammen, 1977). With the onset of puberty, ejaculation marks the experience of boys, menstruation that of girls. As a result, females are more likely to view their emerging sexuality in a reproductive context and in relation to the roles of wife and mother; sexuality becomes perceived as a means to a social rather than sexual end (Gagnon and Simon, 1973). Finally, the primary source of sexual information for girls is the mother. From mothers girls hear most about the reproductive purpose of sex and about what is right and wrong (Fox and Inazu, 1980).

These differences in preadolescence lead males to focus on their genitals and sexual enjoyment, while females focus on relationships, seeing sexuality as a means of reinforcing emotional intimacy under psychologically secure circumstances. The male thinks, "If it feels good, do it." The female, in comparison, thinks, "If it feels right, do it" (DeLamater, 1987, p. 131).

These differences are reflected in and reinforced by the first coital experience. As we discussed in Chapter 9, women are twice as likely as men to have as their first partner someone they are in love with, engaged to, or married to. Males are far more likely than women to have their first coital experience with a casual relationship.

As a consequence, females and males form different orientations towards heterosexual relationships. Men are likely to perceive most women they find sexually attractive, even strangers, as potential sexual partners; women are likely to perceive as sexual partners mostly men with whom they already have a close relationship. Men generally initiate and press for sexual intimacy earlier than women, and they exercise greater control over the sexual interaction.

Both perspectives—evolution and socialization—have something to teach us. If we also make room for some measure of free will, we can work towards a world where equity and freedom of choice will let men and women determine how they will behave sexually.

## REVIEW QUESTIONS

1. Define gender identity, gender role, gender stereotyping, and androgyny.
2. Diagram the interactional model of gender identity differentiation.
3. What is the evidence that hormones shape gender identity? Sex-dimorphic behavior?
4. How does transsexualism differ from other gender identity disorders?
5. How do experiences in socialization determine gender differences in heterosexual relations?

## THOUGHT QUESTIONS

1. Would you buy your five-year-old son a doll for Christmas? Would you buy his twin sister a toy tractor?
2. Should children be required to dress the same way throughout elementary school to encourage androgyny?

3. Ethical considerations aside, how would you set up an experiment to determine if hormonal factors determine gender identity in both sexes?

4. Should insurance companies pay for transsexual surgery?

5. When women achieve complete social equality with men, will gender differences in sexual behavior disappear?

## SUGGESTED READINGS

Money, J., and Ehrhardt, A. A. (1972). *Man and woman, boy and girl.* Baltimore: Johns Hopkins. Somewhat dated, but still a fine general presentation of gender development research.

Kelley, K. (Ed.) (1987). *Females, males and sexuality.* Albany: State University of New York. Well researched and interesting contributions on the effects of biology and socialization on sexual and gender development.

Reinisch, J. M., Rosenblum, L. A., and Sanders, S. A. (1987). *Masculinity and Femininity.* New York: Oxford University Press. Contributions from leading biological and social scientists in the field of gender studies. Rather technical but informative.

Katchadourian, H. A. (Ed.) (1979). *Human sexuality: A comparative and developmental perspective.* Berkeley: University of California. Contributions to understanding gender and sexual development from a variety of biological and behavioral viewpoints.

Symons, D. (1979). *The evolution of human sexuality.* New York: Oxford University Press. The evolutionary perspective applied to human sexual behavior and gender differences.

Bleier, R. (1984). *Science and gender.* New York: Pergamon. A feminist critique of biological theories on women by a neuroscientist.

# PART 4

# Varieties of Sexual Experience

Hieronymus Bosch. *The garden of earthly delights (detail)*.

# Solitary Sexual Behavior

CHAPTER

# 11

*Michelangelo said to Pope
Julius II, "Self-negation is
noble, self-culture is
beneficent, self-possession is
manly, but to the truly grand
and inspiring soul they are
poor and tame compared to
self-abuse."*

MARK TWAIN

OUTLINE

EROTIC FANTASY
The Nature of Erotic Fantasies
  Patterns
  Purposes
  Problems
Fantasy and Sexual Behavior
  Masturbatory Fantasy
  Coital Fantasy
  Prelude or Substitute?
Gender Differences
Theoretical Perspectives
SEXUAL DREAMS
The Neurophysiology of Dreaming
Nocturnal Orgasms

MASTURBATION
Methods of Masturbation
  Manual Stimulation
  Friction against Objects
  Muscular Tension
  Special Devices
Prevalence of Masturbation
  Frequency
  Social Correlates
Functions of Masturbation
Masturbation, Health, and Society
  Mental Health
  Guilt and Shame

Thoughts and feelings, language and action, are all part of an intricate web linking our private inner self with our observable public behavior. Erotic images are part of this web. They both express and shape our sexual longings and activities.

This chapter is about the most private forms of sexual activity, in which we engage in solitude and which we rarely share with another person. They consist of sexual fantasies, erotic dreams, and masturbation.

At the turn of the century, Havelock Ellis coined the term *autoerotism* for episodes of sexual arousal that were "spontaneous"; that is, they came from within (Ellis, 1942, vol. I, p. 61). It is still useful to distinguish such solitary sexual activities from "sociosexual" behaviors, which involve direct interactions between people.

Autoerotic activities bear the same relationship to sociosexual behaviors as talking to yourself does to talking to others. What you say to yourself is often a rehash, rehearsal, and substitute for what you say to others. Conversely, when you seem to be talking to others, you are sometimes really talking to yourself. So it is with sex; sexual fantasies invoke human interactions and having a sexual partner can merely be a front for a sexual monologue. Autoerotic and sociosexual behaviors thus are two sides of the same coin.

Autoerotic activities are becoming more a part of interactive sex, as lovers share erotic fantasies and stimulate themselves and each other to orgasm without sexual intercourse. Such activity, which may be called *mutual masturbation,* is now an important part of safer sex practices (Chapter 5).

## EROTIC FANTASY

There is a whole world of sexual activity that is confined to the mind. Fleeting erotic images, intricately woven fantasies, fading sexual memories, and fresh hopes are moving in and out of consciousness a good deal of the time. Many men and women fantasize about sex quite often (Crepault et al., 1977; Zimmer et al., 1983).

Figure 11.1 *Young Man Fantasizing* (artist unknown).

Fantasies may be spontaneous or triggered by external stimuli. They may lead to, or accompany, other sexual activity, such as masturbation and sexual intercourse, or they may exist on their own.

Medieval theologians called sexual reveries *delectatio morosa* and thought them worse than simple sexual desire or intent. A medieval penitential (a book of church laws) assigned penances for this offense: for a deacon 25 days, for a monk 30 days, for a priest 40 days, for a bishop 50 days (Ellis, 1942, vol. II, p. 184).

The propensity of adolescents to daydream especially about sexual themes is well known (Figure 11.1). Boys say they think about sex more often than girls do (Cameron, 1970). Sexual fantasies continue through adulthood, as do other forms of autoerotic activity. The frequency of erotic thoughts, however, does decline with age. Whereas those 18 to 22 years old say they think about sex 20 percent of the time, those 28 to 35 years old do so 8 percent, and those 60 years and older, 1 percent of the time (Cameron, 1970; Verwoerdt et al., 1969). Even people with satisfactory sex lives ruminate about past experiences (particularly missed opportunities) and future prospects.

## The Nature of Erotic Fantasies

Like other fruits of the fertile human imagination, there is no end to the variety of erotic images and activities that people invoke in the private recesses of their minds. Fantasies are like plays enacted on stage (just as theater itself is an artistic medium for expressing fantasies). In the private and safe theaters of our minds, we endlessly rehearse our favorite fantasies.

In this self-contained world each of us performs the roles of director, actor, and audience all at once. There is usually a certain core plausibility to the story, but reality is suspended as necessary. The trick is to maintain enough of a balance between the likely and the unlikely so that the fantasy remains believable while being shaped to the person's wishes.

The cast of characters that we bring into our plays vary widely. They may be people dear and near to us, casual acquaintances, public figures (like movie stars), or fictitious characters with vague or changing features. There may be also animals, objects, and whatever else we conjure up. The activities we fantasize are likewise countless and suggested by past experiences, unfulfilled yearnings, curiosity, other sexual motives, and imagination.

Patterns   Despite their variability, sexual fantasies tend to cluster into some common patterns. First is the fantasy with the repetitive plot. The same story is enacted over and over with minor variations. For example, the fantasy may consist of having sexual intercourse with a particular woman or man on a deserted beach. A different person or a different setting may be occasionally introduced for variety.

A second pattern has a thematic consistency. The person primarily interested, for instance, in fantasizing about coercive sex may resort to a great many different plots involving force, dominance, and submission, involving a wide variety of actors. Finally, there are people whose fantasies do not seem to have a predominant theme but range over a wide selection of themes.

Fantasies also vary in complexity. Some are brief images of sexual acts or just of genitals. Others involve elaborate plots and specific details. Still others have a rich emotional texture worthy of a romantic novel. The same person may have all types of fantasy at one time or another, but tend to fantasize a certain way.

Finally, people differ with respect to the degree of control they exercise over their fantasies. At one end are those who can turn their fantasies "on" or "off" at will. More typically, fantasies impose themselves like uninvited guests. In the middle of studying, erotic thoughts may impinge on a student's attention with increasing urgency, inducing the person to masturbate to get relief.

Such intrusiveness can be troublesome if the fantasies are unacceptable or repugnant to the individual. In this case, yielding to the fantasy is no help; it would generate even more anxiety and guilt.

Purposes   The themes of erotic fantasy can be highly individualistic. Self-generated fantasy is generally more arousing than sexually vivid stories produced by others (Campagna, 1985).

Your own fantasies are more responsive to your erotic needs. Boxes 11.1 and 11.2 provide samples of erotic fantasies of college men and women.

Fantasies serve many needs. First is *wish fulfillment*. In their most common and direct form, fantasies enact in the imagination what the person would like to have in reality but cannot have. There is no mystery, conflict, or guilt involved. Your beloved is away, so you imagine making love together under the idyllic moon of a tropical island, or in your own good old bed. To this theme you can add having sex with someone you would like to be your lover but is not. The idea can include virtually any

# Box 11.1

## SOME EROTIC FANTASIES OF COLLEGE MEN*

I am slashing my way through thick underbrush in a remote jungle. I have not seen another person for a week. Suddenly I come upon a clearing. Ahead I see a house on the river terrace. As I reach the river I spot a naked woman of my age running toward me upstream. She stops in front of me and says, "Mother always said gods would give me a man to cure the loneliness of the jungle." I respond, "The jungle is lonely for me too." Taking that as a cue she eagerly takes off my pack and clothes. We have sex on the sand by the river. Afterward we lie in mutual embrace and sleep until the rising river drenches us. During the next month we live in her house, having sex every day. Then we leave the jungle to return to civilization.

I am lying on my back (naked) on a comfortable bed (down-silk comforter) kissing a beautiful woman (of course also naked). She slowly begins to move down my body kissing everything along the way until she reaches my penis. Then she straddles my face with her smooth soft legs and we perform fellatio and cunnilingus on each other. We climax simultaneously.

To be on some small tropical island with my girlfriend, lots of delicious food, good wine, sunshine, starry nights, a down quilt, no clothes, a thatched hut, and no threat of pregnancy. Wow! What a time.

I am with a stranger male; handsome, well built, who is tender and loving. The physical encounter is rarely completed.

I am at a party in a dorm. I meet a woman whom I have never met before. Having had a few beers and having danced (or talked) with her, we find ourselves in a dark corner of a room. I make some kind of opening line, or rub her on the thigh. She does the same to me. Our eyes meet and we go upstairs where we have a long sex session.

When I was about 10 to 12, I had a recurring fantasy in which I had the power to stop time. Everything would stop. People would freeze in their position. Then I would walk around and fondle attractive females, usually teachers or older women. Then I would release the woman, and she would consent to anything I would ask her to do. We would have wild sex, and then I would unfreeze her again, and she would not remember anything that had occurred.

Now I usually fantasize about sex with attractive women I have met. Sometimes the sex occurs in unusual places such as closets, offices, Jacuzzis, etc. The sex involves coital, oral, and anal sex much of the time. Occasionally, I fantasize of having sex with two girls at the same time.

*From a questionnaire survey conducted in the author's sexuality class. Responses edited slightly for length. Unpublished.

---

sexual activity that is conflict-free and has some likelihood of fulfillment—in short, anything you would love to do if given a reasonable chance.

The second motivation to fantasize is *exploration* and *experimentation*. No society allows the unbridled expression of all sexual wishes, and we all have personal inhibitions. We also have a certain fascination with these forbidden and rejected sexual prospects, so we fantasize about them, satisfying our curiosity or longing. There is an element of wish fulfillment here,

but it is ambiguous. We are often uncertain whether or not we would want these "wilder" fantasies to come true, or we want to avoid them coming true under any circumstances.

Sexual fantasies are substitutes for action: temporary satisfactions while awaiting concrete ones (the weekend date, the honeymoon) or compensation for unattainable goals. Through mental exploration they provide partial fulfillment of sexual needs and desires; they provide excitement with safety and allow for the controlled expression of sexually un-

# Box 11.2

## SOME EROTIC FANTASIES OF COLLEGE WOMEN.*

My sexual fantasy is to make love to a man I really care about in a cabin, in the mountains, in front of a raging fire, on a bearskin rug, during a rainstorm, with "Moonlight Sonata" playing in the background. The final touch is that just as I start to reach orgasm the rain starts falling even harder so that it is *pounding* and completes the crescendo.

\*     \*     \*

I am lying on my bed naked feeling extremely sexually aroused and in frustration begin to masturbate. My roommate (female) walks in on me, but instead of being shocked at my behavior takes off her clothes and begins to perform oral sex on me. I'm really excited now, but really desire a man since I want to experience vaginal penetration. At this point of the fantasy one of two things happens: either a man appears from nowhere, or I call a particular man (whomever I'm thinking of at the time). In either case I have sex with the man and my roommate, who devote themselves to totally pleasing me.

\*     \*     \*

I imagine an almost surreal (perhaps in slow motion) situation—we kiss and touch each other all over our bodies, exploring and eliciting much pleasure. When he enters me, we make love with slow and passionate abandon. The movement is slow, rhythmic, and he moves in very deeply. If I am masturbating, it is actually when he first enters that I orgasm—but when I am only fantasizing, I envision making slow, tender, and incredibly pleasurable love, experiencing a slow, throbbing orgasm as opposed to a high-speed one.

\*     \*     \*

I think of making love to someone very close and special to me. There are candles all around, dimly lighting the sparsely furnished bedroom. We sit on the bed and he puts his arms around me. We begin kissing and caressing each other's body. His hand slips under my T-shirt and he begins to massage my breasts. His shirt is already off and he takes mine off. My hand finds its way down to his pants and I undo them as he slips them off. I put my warm wet lips and slowly suck his cock. Speeding up and slowing down, I take him all into my mouth.

All the time he is caressing me. He comes and his warm sperm enters my mouth, but I continue the in-out motion for a little while longer. We kiss and caress and then he goes down on me. His tongue darts in and around my clit, massaging and rubbing. Tension begins to penetrate my lower body and a warm rush passes through me. I feel great. I begin to convulse and my hips lift off the bed. My body aches and my heart is beating faster. The orgasm is so powerful I convulse and pant, but it feels marvelous. I begin to relax and he takes me back up for more orgasmic pleasures.

Exhausted, we cuddle and caress, kissing—just being close to each other after the glorious sharing we finished. We both enjoy a peaceful and exhilarating sleep.

\*     \*     \*

I'm a romantic. I love the classic scene on a cold winter night of a gentle cuddling and loving in front of a fire with hot spiced wine or brandy—just the two of us and the crackling fire.

\*     \*     \*

I have been reading a book related to sex and gotten very horny. I go to the bedroom and begin to touch myself, still reading. I lightly touch my nipples but move quickly to the hot spot—my clitoris. First I touch softly the whole area—tickling myself, and then I begin rubbing steadily. I read as time goes on, getting more and more excited. Just as I begin to feel orgasm approaching, I stop and quit reading. After a moment, I start fingering myself again and reading, and suddenly my husband comes in—I haven't heard him come home. He sees that I'm very excited and throws his books down. He dives for my clitoris and goes down on me, bringing my orgasm shudderingly. But this is only a partial satisfaction and he readily allows me to take his clothes off and suck on the head of his penis—at this point he's begging me to put it inside me and I do so. Violent sex! Orgasm! Orgasm! Exhaustion. Peaceful sleep.

*From a questionnaire survey conducted in the author's course. Responses edited slightly for length. Unpublished.

acceptable or hostile sexual thoughts and feelings. Fantasies cannot yield full gratification, but they ease the frustration of unfulfilled wishes.

Fantasies that revolve around future events can actually be of help in coping with real-life situations. By anticipating problems, planning for contingencies, and mentally rehearsing alternative modes of action, a person develops a better sense of control, reduces anxiety, and masters novel situations. There is an important difference between fantasies that substitute for action and those that prepare for it (Sullivan, 1969; Singer, 1975).

Problems    Sexual fantasizing is part of normal everyday mental life. It is a rich source of erotic pleasure, and it may greatly enhance sexual interactions. However, fantasizing beyond a certain point about sex, or anything else, is wasteful. Particularly during adolescence, if erotic fantasies become too absorbing they interfere with the development of more rewarding interactions.

If we had a commonly accepted set of criteria for separating healthy from unhealthy forms of sexual behavior, then it would also apply to fantasies. We have no such yardstick. Furthermore, subjective reactions are highly variable: some people are disturbed by thoughts of rather innocuous activities, whereas others are unaffected by the most bizarre fantasies. Feelings of guilt interfere with the enjoyment of sexual fantasies and have an inhibiting effect on them. Those who experience high levels of guilt produce more restricted fantasies; this affects women more than men (Follingstead and Kimbrell, 1986).

Fantasies involving unconventional or socially unacceptable behaviors are very common, but they do not "define" us as adults. It bears repeating that most such fantasies are rarely acted upon. What really matters is not what we think or feel but what we do.

Unpleasant or disturbing fantasies become more of a problem when they persist. Conscious attempts to dispel them simply cause us to focus on them more strongly. Yielding to them only generates more guilt and anxiety. It is better to take them lightly for what they are: isolated thoughts that do not usually mean much in practical terms.

Fantasies sometimes do mirror problems. For instance, fearful fantasies about intercourse may interfere with sexual enjoyment. It could be worthwhile to talk over such fears with a counselor.

Fantasies that become clearly pathological are *delusions*. In a delusion a person firmly believes what is patently untrue. For instance, paranoid persons may interpret innocent comments as obscene propositions; they may hear voices accusing them of sexual misconduct. A woman may develop the delusion that she was raped; a man may become convinced that he was anally assaulted. Extreme jealousy may lead to delusions of infidelity and accusations that a lover is unfaithful. In the Middle Ages, mentally disturbed women in convents sometimes formed the belief that they had been impregnated by Jesus (Chapter 20).

## Fantasy and Sexual Behavior

Erotic fantasies can be part of other sexual behaviors. When there is a sexual partner, as in coitus, they raise special issues. There may also be undesirable consequences in acting out one's sexual fantasies.

Masturbatory Fantasy    Unlike pure erotic fantasy, masturbatory fantasies are accompanied by self-stimulation, frequently leading to orgasm. Not everyone does fantasize during masturbation. Some, for instance, focus on the sensations of sexual arousal.

During masturbation, the person usually evokes memories, but especially among better-educated people, erotic photographs or literature may be used as sources of stimulation. In the Hunt (1974) sample, about half of the men and one-third of the women, both married and single, indicated that exposure to erotic pictures or movies increased their desire to masturbate. Reading erotic literature was found to be even more potent than visual material, especially among women.

Kinsey (1948, 1953) reported an interesting sex discrepancy in the role of fantasy in masturbation. Among males, 72 percent almost always fantasized while masturbating, 17 percent did so sometimes, and 11 percent did not fantasize at all. The corresponding percentages for females were 50 percent, 14 percent and 36 percent.

In the Hunt (1974) survey, the masturbatory fantasy most commonly mentioned involved sexual intercourse with a loved one (reported by three-quarters of all men and four-fifths of all women). Nearly half of the males and more than one-fifth of the females also fantasized sex with more casual acquaintances in various forms. A higher percentage of men than women reported fantasies of having intercourse with strangers, engaging in group sex, or forcing someone to have sex.

The patterns of masturbatory fantasy are already established by adolescence. For example, in the Sorensen (1973) sample of 13- to 19-year-olds, 57 percent of boys versus 46 percent of girls reported fantasizing "most of the time" while masturbating; but almost twice as many girls as boys said they combined masturbation with fantasy "some of the time," and 20 percent of boys but only 10 percent of girls rarely or never fantasized while masturbating. Boys reported fantasies involving sex with someone who was forced to submit (including themselves), sex with more than one female, oral sex, anal sex, and group sex. The girls reported fantasies of sex with someone they liked, having to submit to several males, and inflicting mild pain on the sexual partner.

Coital Fantasy    It is easy to understand why people fantasize while masturbating, but why do they fantasize while actually engaged in sexual intercourse? Primarily to facilitate sexual arousal. That was the reason given most often (46 percent of females, 38 percent of males) by a sample of college students (Sue, 1979). The second most common reason was to increase the partner's attractiveness (30 percent of males; 22 percent of females). To imagine activities that the couple do not engage in was the third reason (18 percent of males; 13 per-

cent of females). In other words, coital fantasies are a form of make-believe to generate excitement.

People sometimes substitute a more desirable or merely different partner from the one they are sleeping with. They invoke all sorts of imaginary encounters that are more spicy than going through the same kind of sex with the same person in the same place at the same time. Even with an "ideal" partner, the power of fantasy may be greater than reality. A "groupie" who ardently fantasized having sex with Mick Jagger and worked her way through lesser rock stars finally got her chance. When finally in bed with him, she still found it necessary to resort to her standard fantasy of making love to Mick Jagger when she was actually doing so in person (Singer, 1980).

Fantasies with coitus raise two questions: Is it disloyal to the partner to have them? Should fantasies be shared with the partner? Reactions to the first question vary. Some feel ill at ease or even guilty bringing a "third party" into their lovemaking without the partner's knowledge or consent. Others see it as a welcome device to enhance the sexual experience. There are those who actually need the fantasy to be able to get aroused and reach orgasm. In troubled relationships, sexual fantasies may serve as safety valves for the discharge of sexual frustration and hostility in ways that are not openly disruptive to the relationship (Byrne, 1977).

The question of whether or not the fantasies should be revealed to the partner also draws contradictory answers. Some advocate openness and sharing. At best, partners will find mutually exciting erotic themes that enhance their lovemaking; at least they will know about the private sexual yearnings of their partner, even though they may not share them.

For others, being asked to reveal private thoughts is intrusive and possibly destructive to the relationship. To be intimate does not mean always baring the soul; some things are best kept to oneself, and some sexual fantasies may be among them. Because fantasies have a certain forbidden element to them, one risks ridicule and condemnation by revealing them. Imaginary substitutes may threaten the actual partner. Another concern with revealing fantasies is that something gets lost in the telling. Fantasies in fact fizzle out if repeatedly brought out into the open. Remember that part of the charge that fantasies pack is their secrecy.

A compromise would be for a couple to reveal their fantasies selectively. Even better, they could construct fantasies together, creatively weaving erotic themes that are exciting for both. What is lost in taming some darker erotic thoughts may be more than compensated by inventing shared "secrets," which add an element of playfulness as well as intimacy to a couple's lovemaking.

### Prelude or Substitute?

One of the worries in sharing fantasies is that the expression of a wish may be the prelude to carrying it out. If one knew with certainty that a partner's fantasy would remain just that, there would be less to worry about.

The great majority of fantasies are not enacted in real life. This is partly because considerations of reality would not allow it, and partly because the person has no real wish to see them fulfilled. Consider, for example, the man who fantasizes engaging in sex with two women at the same time. It would not be easy for him to negotiate such an arrangement involving his wife, lover, friends, or acquaintances. It would not be hard, however, to do so with a pair of prostitutes who would be willing to do far more onerous things for a fee. Nevertheless, the majority of men will not cross that line; they go on fantasizing about the delights of the erotic triad. Consider, too, the woman who fantasizes being coerced into sex. Does she actually want to be raped? Hardly. What she is engaging in is a safe form of make-believe. To imagine being coerced into sex is not the same as wanting to be raped. No sane person would ever want to suffer the agony of a true rape experience. Under experimental conditions, although women may be sexually aroused in response to imaginary rape scenes, they react with fear and disgust when confronted with

more realistic rape scenarios (Bond and Mosher, 1986).

The appeal of many fantasies is easy to understand. But why should women want to fantasize about any form of sexual coercion, no matter how "gentle"? One explanation often put forth is that women are socialized to be passive about sex, to resist it, and to feel guilty about it. If a man "coerces" them (without pain or humiliation), then they cannot be blamed for what happens. Of course, even if this explanation were true, it would not justify the real use of pressure and coercion—a point that is apparently difficult for some men to get into their heads. Those who abhor sexual violence and the subjugation of women are particularly appalled by violent erotic fantasies and the interpretations attached to them. Susan Brownmiller, for example, rejects the psychoanalytic view that women may have unconscious wishes that lead to rape fantasies. She accepts the fact that some women have conscious rape fantasies, but she ascribes them to the imposition of male rape fantasies on women. She states, "Fantasies *are* important to the enjoyment of sex, I think, but it is a rare woman who can successfully fight the culture and come up with her own non-exploitation, non-sadomasochistic, non-power-drive imaginative thrust." Instead, "when women do fantasize about sex, the fantasies are usually the product of male conditioning and cannot be otherwise" (Brownmiller, 1975, p. 360).

In some cases, people do fulfill their fantasies. The man on an out-of-town trip will get a pair of prostitutes to his hotel room. Others resort to more organized services, which provide "kinky sex"—often mild versions of sadomasochism. Such acting out of sexual fantasies may provide enough gratification to become an established or occasional practice. On the other hand, the actual performance of the fantasy may prove so disappointing that it ceases to be exciting (Shanor, 1977). Even if it is not a complete letdown, having gone through it, the person may no longer have any need for it. For every person who rejoices in the fulfillment of a sexual fantasy, there are several others who find the experience disappointing (Friday, 1975).

This benign view of fantasies as substitutes for action, or at most leading to innocuous partial fulfillment of the urges they represent, may not tell the whole story. The controversy over pornography is in large part based on the concern that fantasies that involve violence and degradation of women are fueled by pornographic materials, making it more likely that they would be acted out, at least by certain men. There is some evidence that the likelihood of rape is correlated with reports of coercive sexual fantasies (Greendlinger and Byrne, 1987). This is an important issue, which we shall discuss at length in Chapters 18 and 19.

In rare instances people realize that they are losing control over a fantasy and are likely to commit a seriously antisocial act. Such a person must seek help, or should be prevailed upon to do so. In such situations it is better to find professional assistance than to turn to family or friends.

## Gender Differences

Fantasies, at some level, mirror our sexual character. Do they reveal fundamental distinctions between men and women and between heterosexuals and homosexuals?

It has been generally assumed that men have more frequent, more "kinky," and "wilder" fantasies than women. Female fantasies are reported to dwell more on emotional, romantic, relational elements (Box 11.2), whereas male fantasies deal more with "raw," impersonal sex and sound more "pornographic" (Barclay, 1973) (Box 11.1). In one study, when asked to elaborate on sexual fantasy themes, men wrote longer, more explicit, and more varied fantasies than women (Follingstad et al., 1986).

Male and female fantasies show similarities as well as differences. In the survey of college students we referred to earlier (Sue, 1979), the most common fantasy theme during coitus for both genders was having sex with a former lover (43 percent men, 41 percent women). Men were twice as likely to think

about imaginary lovers as women (44 percent against 24 percent). A higher proportion of men (24 percent) than women (16 percent) fantasized about forcing others into sexual relationships or overcoming the resistance of potential partners (37 percent men, 24 percent women); more women (36 percent) fantasized being forced into a sexual relationship than men (21 percent). Women (9 percent) more than men (3 percent) had same-sex fantasies.

Table 11.1 compares the fantasy preference of males and females within heterosexual and homosexual samples. Note that all four groups think about "cross-preference" en-

**Table 11.1   Fantasy Themes and Sexual Orientation (1957–1968)**

| HOMOSEXUAL MALE | HETEROSEXUAL MALE |
|---|---|
| 1. Imagery of sexual anatomy | 1. Replacement of established partner |
| 2. Forced sexual encounters | 2. Forced sexual encounter |
| 3. Cross-preference encounters | 3. Observation of sexual activity |
| 4. Idyllic encounters with unknown men | 4. Cross-preference encounters |
| 5. Group sex | 5. Group sex |
| HOMOSEXUAL FEMALE | HETEROSEXUAL FEMALE |
| 1. Forced sexual encounters | 1. Replacement of established partner |
| 2. Idyllic encounter with established partner | 2. Forced sexual encounter |
| 3. Cross-preference encounters | 3. Observation of sexual activity |
| 4. Recall of past sexual experience | 4. Idyllic encounters with unknown men |
| 5. Sadistic imagery | 5. Cross-preference encounters |

Themes are listed in order of frequency. From W. Masters and V. Johnson, *Homosexuality in perspective.* Boston: Little, Brown, 1979, p. 178. Reproduced with permission.

counters—heterosexuals fantasize about homosexual associations and vice versa. Similarly, "forced sexual encounters" are present in the fantasies of all four groups. Group sex experiences are cited for both male groups but not for females. Sex with someone other than the established partner tops the lists of both male and female heterosexuals (Masters and Johnson, 1979).

## Theoretical Perspectives

By far the most extensive and elaborate examples of sexual fantasy are in literature and art. Depending on the times, such works of the imagination have been called serious literature and fine art, or pornography (Chapter 18). The distinction continues to divide and perplex humanists, social scientists, and legal experts, as well as causing conflict in society (Chapter 22).

The similarities between private sexual fantasies and what most people consider to be pornographic materials are striking. The literary critic Steven Marcus has offered an insightful analysis of the basic characteristics of pornography, which also sheds light on fantasies (Box 18.2).

Surprisingly, the contributions of sex researchers to our understanding of erotic fantasy have been slight. Kinsey, who set the tone of modern efforts in this field, was preoccupied with quantifying concrete behaviors that led to orgasm (Chapter 1). The will-o'-the-wisp world of fantasy did not figure prominently in his work, nor has it in the work of most other survey researchers. This gap has been partly filled by journalists and writers who have gathered sexual fantasies from people willing to express them (Friday 1973, 1975, 1980). They make fascinating reading, but their manner of collection and presentation does not allow scientific analysis.

Because the study of fantasies does not readily fit the research models of cognitive psychologists, it has also been largely left out of their work. Clinical psychologists do cover it, but their studies are mainly descriptive. In the psychoanalytic perspective, fantasies represent the symbolic and half-concealed expressions of repressed sexual wishes and conflicts. Every fantasy therefore means something in addition to what it appears to be, but the person is unaware of its "true" or unconscious meaning.

Aggression in sexual fantasy has been of particular interest to psychoanalysts. Freud claimed that people are driven to debase their sexual partners. This admixture of sex and aggression has since been a salient theme in the psychoanalytic literature. Robert Stoller has further expanded on this association by claiming that *hostility*, the overt or covert desire to harm another, is central to generating sexual excitement, not just for sadomasochists, but for everyone. Through fantasies, adults reenact childhood hurts and fears, and in order to master them, they retaliate by debasing or hurting their imaginary sexual partners. In this process they become sexually aroused: "Triumph, rage, revenge, fear, anxiety, risk are all condensed into one complex buzz called sexual excitement" (Stoller, 1979).

Among sex therapists there is no consensus as to whether sexual fantasies enhance or interfere with intimate relationships. Many consider sex fantasies useful to help combat loneliness or boredom and defuse forbidden urges. Others take a more negative view, seeing fantasy as second-rate, "a pale substitute for the complexities of joy and pain which are requisites for loving a real person" (Offit, 1977, p. 201). If they intrude into and dilute the intimacy of a couple they become a cause of alienation.

## SEXUAL DREAMS

Sexual dreams are a form of erotic fantasy that is fragmentary and difficult to describe. Some sexual dreams have an obvious erotic content (Figure 11.2); others are ambiguous. Moreover, a person may dream of a flagrantly sexual activity without feeling aroused, or feel intense excitement while dreaming of an apparently nonsexual situation like climbing stairs, flying in the air, and so on.

Psychoanalysts explain dreams, like fan-

Figure 11.2    *The Shepherd's Dream*, a Roman frieze.

tasies, in terms of their symbolic meaning. The interpretation of dreams is an important part of their work. Freud (1900) thought that the function of dreams was to protect sleep. During sleep, when the vigilance of the ego relaxes, repressed (often sexual) wishes threaten to break through into consciousness and disrupt sleep. These wishes are permitted partial expression in disguised form as dreams.

In psychoanalytic reckoning a great many dream symbols have sexual significance. For example, objects like sticks, tree trunks, knives, daggers, and nail files (because they rub back and forth) symbolize the penis; they are *phallic symbols*. By the same token, boxes, chests, cupboards, ovens, rooms, ships—any enclosed space or hollow object—are vaginal symbols. Actions involving such objects or places likewise carry sexual significance. The opening of an umbrella may represent erection; going in and out of a room could signify intercourse. (However, you cannot simplistically make such symbolic conversions in do-it-yourself interpretations of your own dreams.)

Sexual dreams, particularly those culminating in orgasms, are intensely pleasurable but sometimes bewildering. It has been suggested that nightmares have a sexual basis, and that the fear, anxiety, and feeling of helpless paralysis that characterize nightmares may reflect the experience of being sexually coerced (Jones, 1949).

Most behavioral scientists doubt these concepts. Instead, over the past several decades, a new approach to the study of dream phenomena has attracted much interest. Rather than dealing with content and symbolism, this approach studies the neurophysiological basis of the dream process.

### The Neurophysiology of Dreaming

Sleep is not the uniform state that it appears to be, nor are dreams erratic events that punctuate it unpredictably. Rather, there is a definite *sleep-dream cycle* that recurs nightly. Brain waves in electroencephalogram (EEG) tracings show four distinct sleep patterns. One of them is characterized by a fast rhythm and bursts of *rapid eye movements (REM)*. A person who is awakened during REM sleep will report vivid dreams. During the other sleep phases dreaming has been found to be erratic and less vivid (Reike, 1985).

*REM periods* are times of intense physiological and sexual activity; in a remarkably high number of instances (85–95 percent) partial or full erections have been observed even among infants and elderly men. These erections are not necessarily accompanied by sexual dreams, and their full significance remains unclear (Gulevich and Zarcone, 1969; Karacan et al., 1976). The presence or absence of erection in sleep is an important diagnostic test to separate organic from psychological cases of impotence (Chapter 15).

Evidence of sexual arousal during REM sleep has been harder to detect among women, but it has now been convincingly demon-

strated. Women manifest cyclic episodes of vascular engorgement during REM periods equivalent to erection in men and at the same high frequency (95 percent) (Fisher et al., 1983).

### Nocturnal Orgasms

"Visitations by the angel of the night" is what the pioneer sexologist Paolo Mantegazza called orgasm during sleep. Babylonians believed in a "maid of the night" who visited men in their sleep and a "little night man" that slept with women. Such imaginary beings became more prominent in medieval times in the form of demons who would lie upon women (*incubus*) and under men (*succubus*). The West African Yoruba believed in a single versatile being who could act either as male or female and visit members of either sex in their sleep (H. Ellis, 1942).

Although *nocturnal emission* (*wet dreams*) or *nocturnal orgasm* are common terms for this experience, it may happen anytime one is asleep, not just at night.

Orgasms during sleep accounted only for 2–3 percent of the total sexual outlet for females and 2–8 percent for males in the Kinsey sample. Nevertheless, substantial numbers of people experience them; by age 45 almost 40 percent of females and more than 90 percent of males have had such experiences at least once (Kinsey et al., 1948, 1953). Among men they occur most frequently in late adolescence and the early twenties; among women between the ages of 30 and 50. Nocturnal emissions were seven times more frequent among the college-educated Kinsey men than in the lower educational groups. The incidence of female nocturnal orgasm among women appears to have gone up since the Kinsey survey. Among a group of college women in 1986, 37 percent reported they had experienced nocturnal orgasm, 30 percent of them in the past year. Nocturnal orgasms were not related to sexual dreams or sexual activity (Wells, 1986).

Nocturnal orgasms are present among paraplegic men with spinal cord injuries, in whom nerve inpulses from the brain (where

Figure 11.3    Masturbating figure on a Greek black-figure cup by the Amasis Painter, 530–520 B.C.

dreams are enacted) cannot reach the spinal cord centers. Similarly, animals like cats, dogs, bulls, and horses have spontaneous emissions in their sleep. It is assumed that in these cases the periodic release of sperm improves its quality (Levin, 1975a). It used to be thought that nocturnal orgasms acted as a safety valve, or natural way of releasing pent-up sexual tension. In effect, they are not an adequate substitute for other forms of sexual activity.

## MASTURBATION

*Masturbation* is any sexual activity that involves physical self-stimulation. The Latin verb *masturbare* may have derived from the words for "hand" (*manus*) and "to defile" (*sturpare*) or the Greek for "virile member" (*mazdo*) and Latin for "disturbance" (*turba*). Pejorative terms like "self-abuse" and "solitary vice" have been replaced by slang expressions like "jerking off," "jacking off," "whacking off," "beating one's meat," "hand job," and so on (Haeberle, 1978). Some sex researchers and therapists now refer to it as *self-pleasuring*.

Like fantasy, masturbation is usually car-

ried on in solitude. It is one of the most common sexual activities in all cultures (Box 11.3), and it is represented in the art of many cultures (Figure 11.3).

Among males of animal species masturbation to the point of orgasm has been well documented. It is less certain for female animals, whose capacity to attain orgasm appears to be less developed (Ford and Beach, 1951). Dogs and cats lick their penises before and

Figure 11.4    Young monkey masturbating.

# Box 11.3

## MASTURBATION IN CROSS-CULTURAL PERSPECTIVE

The anthropologist Paolo Mantegazza (who was prominent in the 1930s) called Europeans a "race of masturbators." He reasoned that Western civilization simultaneously stimulates and represses sexuality and that restrictions on nonmarital coitus compel people to masturbate instead.

Masturbation has been documented for many ancient cultures, including the Babylonian, Egyptian, Hebrew, and Indian. The Egyptians believed that the creation of the universe began with the god Atum ejaculating into his hand (Chapter 1). This myth suggests that masturbation may have been used in some religious rites (Gregersen, 1983). Greeks and Romans believed that Mercury had invented the act to console Pan after he had lost his mistress Echo. Zeus himself was known to indulge occasionally. Aristophanes, Aristotle, Herondas, and Petronius refer to masturbation. Aristophanes finds it unmanly but acceptable for women, children, slaves, and feeble old men. Demosthenes was condemned for the practice, whereas Diogenes was praised for doing it openly in the marketplace (H. Ellis, 1942, vol. I, part I, p. 277).

Masturbation is reported by Ford and Beach (1951) for about forty cultures. It is thought to be less prevalent in societies that are permissive toward nonmarital coitus and rare in many preliterate groups (Gebhard, in Marshall and Suggs, 1971, p. 208). Most groups consider it normal adolescent behavior but disapprove of it for adults (Gregersen, 1983). For instance, Trukese men (monogamous fishermen of the Caroline Islands) were said to mas-turbate in secret while watching women bathe. Men of Tikopia (Pacific island agriculturists) and of Dahomey (West African agriculturists and fishermen) masturbated occasionally, even though both cultures permitted polygamy.

Female masturbation has been reported less often and has been generally disapproved. Vaginal insertions seem more common than clitoral stimulation among some peoples: African Azande women used wooden dildos (and were severely beaten if caught by their husbands); the Chukchee of Siberia used the calf muscles of reindeer; Tikopia women relied on roots and bananas; Crow women used their fingers, and so did the Azanda of Australia.

Among the Lesu (polygamous tribesmen of New Ireland) female masturbation was condoned. Powdermaker has reported:

Masturbation . . . is practiced frequently at Lesu and regarded as normal behavior. A woman will masturbate if she is sexually excited and there is no man to satisfy her. A couple may be having intercourse in the same house, or near enough for her to see them, and she may thus become aroused. She then sits down and bends her right leg so that her heel presses against her genitalia. Even young girls of about six years may do this quite casually as they sit on the ground. The women and men talk about it freely, and there is no shame attached to it. It is a customary position for women to take and they learn it in childhood. They never use their hands for manipulation (Powdermaker, quoted in Ford and Beach, 1951).

---

after coitus; elephants use their trunks; captive dolphins rub their erect penises against the floor of the tank, and one male was observed stimulating himself by holding his penis in the jet of the water intake.

Self-stimulation is common among primates in captivity (Figure 11.4). Male apes and monkeys manipulate their penises by hand or foot and also take them into their mouths or rub them against the floor. Male baboons in one African park have reportedly developed erotic responses to automobiles and are in the habit of jumping on the hoods of cars and ejaculating at the windshield (Bates, 1967).

Female mammals of subprimate species apparently masturbate only rarely. Masturbation is also less frequent among female primates than among males, both in the wild and in captivity. Females can be seen fingering or rubbing their genitals, but often only perfunctorily. Even when such activity is clearly auto-erotic, it does not seem to lead to orgasm.

## Methods of Masturbation

The common forms of masturbation are manual stimulation, genital friction against objects, muscular tension, and the use of special devices. These methods are not mutually exclusive. Just as most people do not use a single coital position, neither do they rely on just one method of masturbation.

Manual Stimulation    Manual techniques are the most common for both sexes. The most frequent form for males involves stroking and rubbing the penis and moving the hand over it firmly to and fro or in a "milking" motion (Figure 11.5). Women also rely primarily on genital manipulation. In the Hite (1976) sample almost 80 percent of the women exclusively relied on manual stimulation of the clitoral/vulva area while lying on their back. The clitoris and the labia minora are the structures most commonly stroked, pressed, and rhythmically stimulated (Figure 11.6). Because they are the most sensitive parts of the femal genitals, the motions are usually gentle and delib-

erate. Women usually avoid the glans of the clitoris; instead, they concentrate on the clitoral shaft, which they can stimulate on either side. If too much pressure is applied or manipulation is prolonged over an area, the site may become less sensitive. Switching hands or moving the fingers about is therefore common.

Men commonly think that women insert their fingers or objects into their vaginas when they masturbate, but only one in five women in the Kinsey et al. (1953) sample reported such practice, and it often consisted of slight penetrations of the vaginal entrance. Among the Hite (1976) subjects only 1.5 percent of women said they used this method exclusively. It was used more often in conjunction with other techniques, such as clitoral stimulation (Hite, 1976). Some women, however, do derive additional pleasure from deep finger penetration, perhaps because it simulates coitus or it yields special sensations.

Particularly among homosexual men, stimulation of the anus with or without putting in a finger may be arousing. As an occasional

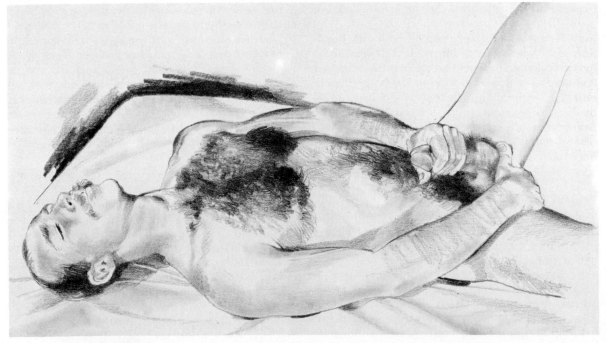

Figure 11.5    Masturbating man.

Figure 11.6  Masturbating woman.

experiment, heterosexual males (and women) also try out anal masturbation. The urethra may be similarly explored with various objects. Sometimes the object inserted in these orifices gets "lost" inside and must be retrieved by special surgical instruments. Everything from hairpins to small bottles have been recovered by doctors from the rectum. Occasionally such practices result in injury. In one case a piece of spaghetti introduced by a woman into the urethra broke up, requiring surgical treatment (Bacci and Porena, 1986).

Friction against Objects  Those who do not wish to touch their genitals may resort to friction against objects. The possibilities are many: a pillow, towel, nightclothes tucked between the legs, the bed cover, or the mattress itself may provide a convenient surface to rub and press against the genitalia. A jet of warm water from a hand-shower directed at the clitoral region can be stimulating. (It is not safe to aim inside the vagina, because germs may spread into the uterus.)

Muscular Tension  Associated with friction against objects is the use of thigh pressure. Muscular tension is necessary whatever the technique used, but some women are able to reach orgasm through this method alone. When a women's legs are crossed or pressed together, steady and rhythmic pressure can be applied to the whole genital area, a method which combines the advantages of direct stimulation and muscular tension. One of the women respondents to the *Cosmopolitan* survey wrote: "I have a beautiful way of masturbating. By rubbing my legs together. *No one* can tell. I used to do it all the time in grade school—at my desk—especially when I was under pressure taking a test. (Now you know where I got my 3.5 to 4.0 average in college.")" (Wolfe, 1981, p. 119).

Special Devices  Most people make do with whatever is around to stimulate themselves, but others go to greater lengths. For example, they may avail themselves of hand lotions, scented oils, special kinds of underwear, or other objects of fetishistic significance. Various objects may also be used for vaginal insertion. Cucumbers, bananas, sausages, candles, brush handles, and similar devices have occasionally been pressed into such service throughout history. A poem in the *Arabian Nights* extolls the erotic virtues of bananas: "O bananas, of soft and smooth skins, which dilate the eyes of young girls . . . you alone among fruits are endowed with a pitying heart, O consolers of widows and divorced women" (quoted in H. Ellis, 1942). It is also not unusual for girls to insert objects like pencils or brush handles into their vagina just to explore, rather than to arouse.

Masturbatory aids can be quite specialized. Artificial penises in many cultures have been fashioned from gold, silver, ivory, ebony, horn, glass, wax, wood, and stuffed leather; they range from crude specimens to products of fine craftsmanship. Currently they are made of plastic (Figure 11.7). Their common name is *dildo* (from the Italian *diletto*, "pleasure"). The Greek dramatist Aristophanes refers to dildos in his plays, and Herondas has a play (*The Private Conversation*) in which two women friends discuss the fine workmanship of a particular cobbler in fashioning such devices. Despite the numerous references to the use of dildos in pornographic novels, their use is not common among women; often it is done to entertain men, who find the spectacle sexually arousing. Dildos are also used by homosexual men for anal penetration.

There are other ingenious devices. One is the Japanese *rin-no-tama* or *ben-wa*, consisting of two metal balls: one is hollow and introduced first into the vagina; the other contains a smaller metal ball, lead pellets, or mercury, which is inserted next. The metal balls are then made to vibrate by movements, especially by swaying in a hammock, in a swing, or rocking chair.

Over the past several decades, hand-held vibrators have become much more popular. Some are mechanized dildos; others have vibrating tips of various shapes or are attached to the back of the hand, through which they transmit their vibrations. They may be sold

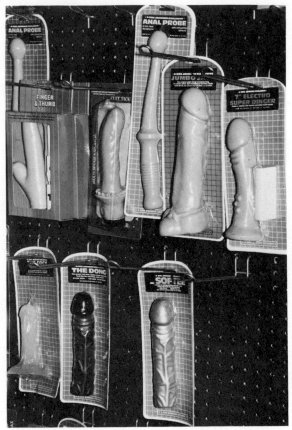

Figure 11.7    Dildos.

openly or advertised coyly for "soothing massage." Vibrators are intensely stimulating and may lead to orgasm even if a woman has difficulty otherwise (Chapter 15).

Among the *Redbook* survey respondents, 21 percent of women reported having used some form of gadget—"vibrators, oils, feathers, and dildos" (Tavris and Sadd, 1977, p. 76). Among the younger women in the Masters and Johnson (1966) sample, half of those who masturbated had tried a vibrator at least once; one-quarter preferred it to other forms of self-stimulation, making it the second most popular method next to manual stimulation of the genitals. Given that all these subjects were self-selected, these figures are probably higher than average.

Those who favor the use of vibrators see them as effective and harmless devices to intensify autoerotic pleasure, a form of "super-masturbation." Those who object to the sexual dependency of women on men see in vibrators a liberating device with which no penis could compete. For women who cannot reach orgasm any other way, it is a necessary path to sexual satisfaction (Dodson, 1987).

Those who object to using vibrators and similar gadgets see them as evidence of the mechanization of our lives, the alienation within human relationships, and the trivialization of our sexuality. These concerns especially bear on the use of "masturbatory dolls"— life-size rubber or vinyl inflatable bags shaped like a woman with open mouth, vagina, and anus for receiving the penis. More sophisticated versions have vibrating and sucking devices. There are also separate artificial "vaginas" and "anuses," which simplify matters even further.

Some therapists are concerned that if women became conditioned to mechanical stimulation, it may interfere with their personal relations. Vibrators may also become sexual crutches, deflecting attention from underlying problems. However, vibrators serve a therapeutic purpose in the treatment of orgasmic problems (Chapter 15). Ultimately, vibrators must be judged like any other erotic stimulant: do they serve the user, or does the user serve them?

Some rare methods of self-stimulation are highly dangerous. For instance, some individuals try to heighten the masturbatory climax through partial asphyxiation, usually by tightening a rope around the neck. Occasionally the person (usually a man) doing this hangs himself inadvertently. In 1978, a woman in Texas found her husband hanging from their bedroom door dressed in her wig, bra, and panties. Through an arrangement of pulleys, the man had intended to control the tightness of the rope around his neck; but he had slipped, placing his full weight on the noose and hanging himself (*San Francisco Chronicle*, October 29, 1981, p. 29). Deaths from such sexual mis-

haps, particularly among young men, often are mistaken for suicides.

## Prevalence of Masturbation

In the Kinsey sample, 92 percent of males and 58 percent of females had masturbated to orgasm at some time in their lives (an additional 4 percent of women had masturbated without reaching orgasm). Figure 11.8 shows the percentages at various ages in the Kinsey samples with such experience. These graphs (known as *accumulative incidence curves*) answer the question: "How many people ever have such experiences by a given age?" A person who masturbates only once and one who does so many times are counted in the same way. Between ages 10 and 15 the male curve climbs dramatically and then levels off as it approaches age 20. Practically every man who is ever going to masturbate has already done so by this time. Nonetheless, the curve does not go beyond 92 percent; 8 out of every 100 males do not ever masturbate. The female curve peaks at 62 percent after a gradual climb. Up to the age of 45 increasing numbers of women were still discovering this outlet (Kinsey et al., 1948, 1953).

The Hunt (1974) survey two decades later found essentially the same: 94 percent of males and 63 percent of women had masturbated. The male figure is so high that it has not reg-

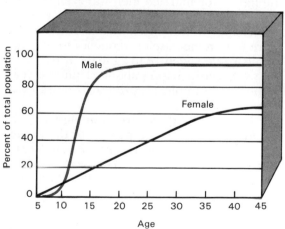

Figure 11.8   Incidence of masturbation by a given age. (Kinsey et al., 1953).

istered any further increases over the past decade, but the female rates have continued to rise. It is likely that the higher female rates in some of these surveys is a matter of which women were asked. Nonetheless, similar patterns are reported from other countries: West German women are reported as masturbating earlier and more often now than a decade or two ago (Clement et al., 1984).

The prevalence of masturbation is highest among the better-educated young male and female adults. Philip and Lorna Sarrel (1987) estimate that by the time they enter college, five out of six males and four out of five women are masturbating. The practice persists at the older end of adulthood as well. About one out of two men and women aged 60 and above say they still masturbate, and 40 percent of those who do so are married and living with a spouse (Starr and Weiner, 1981).

Frequency   How frequently do people masturbate? Various factors, like age and marital status, make a good deal of difference. Among males in the Kinsey sample, this practice was at its peak during adolescence, when the mean frequency of masturbation was twice a week. Frequencies decreased steadily with age: unmarried men 45–60 years old masturbated on the average fewer than once every two weeks; the figure for married men was even smaller.

The Hunt sample did not reveal a significant change in how often men masturbate, but there was an increase in frequency for women. Single women aged 18 to 24 in the Kinsey sample were masturbating about 21 times a year; in the Hunt sample, they did so 37 times a year (Hunt, 1974).

Frequency figures are even higher in the *Cosmopolitan* sample: 35 percent of the women who masturbate do so rarely; 37 percent several times a month; 25 percent several times a week; and 3 percent daily (Wolfe, 1981). The average frequencies for the active female sample stayed the same up to the mid-fifties; they did not show the steady decline with age that was characteristic of males.

The frequency of masturbation among current college students varies widely. For example, 1 percent of freshman males and a smaller proportion of females report masturbating daily; 17 percent of freshman males and 25 percent of freshman females masturbate less than once a month (Gagnon, 1977). In another college sample, daily rates were about 6 percent for the active population of both sexes (some masturbating "several times a day"); 76 percent averaged "a few times a week"; another third or so, "a few times a month" (Arafat and Cotton, 1974).

Social Correlates   The better-educated person in the Kinsey sample was more likely to masturbate: 89 percent of males with only grade-school educations compared to 96 percent of those with college educations. The corresponding figures for females were 34 percent and 60 percent. For college-educated males, masturbation constituted not only the chief source (60 percent of orgasm before marriage but also almost 10 percent of orgasms following marriage (Kinsey et al., 1948).

Why does educational level correlate with masturbation? Masturbation is not something one learns in college. Rather, the better educated person is more likely to come from a middle-class background, with more liberal attitudes toward masturbation.

Does marital status matter? There was an increase in the prevalence of masturbation among both single and married women in the Hunt sample compared to the Kinsey sample. The same was true for married men, but not single men (Hunt, 1974). Women respondents in the *Redbook* survey say that since their marriage, 16 percent have masturbated often, 51 percent occasionally, 7 percent once, and 26 percent never (Tavris and Sadd, 1977).

Kinsey found religion to have a greater effect on females than males. A man may feel guilty about masturbating, but sooner or later more than nine out of ten indulge in the practice. In the Hunt sample, a higher proportion of Jewish men and women than non-Jews reported masturbating. Catholics and Protestants had similar patterns of activity, but Catholics masturbated more often. Hunt reports that devoutness continues to influence masturbation: the nonreligious are more likely to masturbate; they start doing so at a younger age; and they are more likely to continue it into adult life (Hunt, 1974).

## Functions of Masturbation

Masturbation serves the same needs as sexual fantasy. Like fantasy, masturbation is indulged in for its own sake or as a substitute for other sexual activities.

Masturbation plays an important role in psychosexual development (Chapter 8). Starting with self-exploration, the child discovers the pleasurable potential of the genitals, which encourages further learning and sexual maturation. In adolescence, masturbation continues to develop self-knowledge and provides sexual release. Masturbation continues to teach people about themselves throughout adulthood (Marcus and Francis, 1975).

Most professionals in sexuality today see masturbation in childhood and adolescence as a normal part of development—a way of finding out how the body works and rehearsing for interpersonal sex. Those who masturbate in adolescence seem less likely to develop sexual problems as adults. However, masturbation is not for everyone. Those who think it is wrong or sinful can develop perfectly normal lives without it (Kaplan, 1987).

The most common function of masturbation in adulthood is as a substitute or supplement to coitus or other sociosexual outlets. It may be used by people without sexual partners, those who are temporarily separated, or couples with different needs for having sex. Others use masturbation to avoid the risks of pregnancy and sexually transmitted diseases.

The relief of sexual tension is the most frequently mentioned reason adults give for masturbating (four out of five men and two out of three women in the Hunt survey). In the Arafat and Cotton (1974) sample of college students, "feeling horny" was the reason given by 48 percent of the men and 39 percent of the women; an additional 21 percent of men and 24 percent of women cited pleasure as the motivation. In the *Redbook* survey close to 40 percent of married women said they masturbated when their husband was absent; 18 percent did it when coitus had not been satisfying (Tavris and Sadd, 1977).

Some people prefer masturbation to coitus. Masturbatory orgasm can be more intense (truer for women than men). Special devices like vibrators provide a whole range of new sexual sensations. There is a free rein for sexual fantasy and for the use of erotic materials. One may reach orgasm whenever and however one prefers; there is no need to wait for a slow partner or fear being left behind by a fast one.

Masturbation has currently attained particular importance for several reasons. Women generally learn about their own sexuality through male initiative. Masturbation allows them to become free of such dependence (Dodson, 1987). It lets them discover their own eroticism and their own sexual responses without male dominance. The second consideration is safer sex. AIDS is passed by infected bodily fluids. Masturbation—either alone or with a partner—provides a safe sexual outlet as long as partners do not come in direct contact with semen or vaginal secretions. Masturbation also plays an important role in certain forms of sex therapy (Barbach, 1975), as we shall discuss in Chapter 15.

Finally, masturbation, like other sexual behaviors, can serve nonsexual needs. Some 12 percent of college men and 16 percent of women gave "loneliness" as a reason for masturbation; and about 10 percent of each indulged in it to combat psychological frustration and mental strain (Arafat and Cotton, 1974). It is not uncommon to masturbate in order to fall asleep, especially under stress.

Given the high proportion of people who masturbate, it is easy to lose sight of the fact that not everyone does. College students who refrain (11 percent of men, 39 percent of women) mostly cite lack of desire (76 percent of women, 56 percent of men). Others think it is a waste of energy or cite shame ("makes me feel cheap"), guilt, religious prohibition, and other objections (Arafat and Cotton, 1974).

## Masturbation, Health, and Society

"There is really no end to the list of real or

# Box 11.4

## MASTURBATORY INSANITY

From the time of Hippocrates physicians have voiced concern that overindulgence in sex is detrimental to health. Only in the last 250 years, however, has masturbation been singled out as a particularly harmful activity. Early in the eighteenth century, a book entitled *Onania, or the heinous sin of self pollution* appeared in Europe. The probable author was a clergyman turned quack who peddled a remedy along with the book. Although the word became popular throughout Europe (and is referred to in Voltaire's *Dictionnaire philosophique*), the book had no immediate impact upon medical opinion.*

Then in 1758 appeared *Onania, or a treatise upon the disorders produced by masturbation* by the distinguished Swiss physician Tissot. It reiterated and amplified the claims of the former work. Tissot's views, coming from an unimpeachable authority, found ready acceptance. Despite rebuttals and accusations that he was exploiting his medical reputation to further his private moral point of view, the book became a standard reference. By the end of the eighteenth century the *masturbatory hypothesis* of mental disease was well entrenched (Hare, 1962).

By the early 19th century, these ideas had become accepted in England as well. Sir William Ellis, superintendent of a mental asylum, was writing in 1839 that by far the most frequent cause of "debility of the brain is the pernicious habit of masturbation." By mid-century, when this tide reached its high point, "the habit of solitary vice" was found to give rise to hysteria, asthma, epilepsy, melancholia, mania, suicide, dementia, and general paralysis of the insane (Comfort, 1967).

In view of such dire consequences, physicians and parents went to great lengths to prevent children from masturbating. One little girl was made to sleep in sheepskin pants and jacket made into one garment, with her hand tied to a collar about her neck; her feet were tied to the footboard and by a strap about her waist she was fastened to the headboard so she could not slide down in the bed and use her heels; she had been scolded, reasoned with, and whipped, and in spite of it all she managed to keep up the habit (Comfort, 1967, p. 89).

To combat this evil, parents could order a variety of restraints (see figure). Stubborn cases were subjected to medical treatment, including circumcision, removal of the testes, and clitorodectomy.[†]

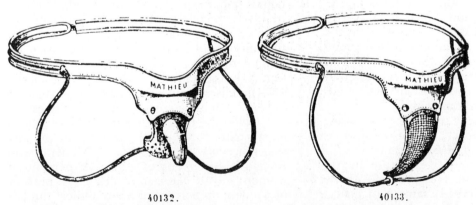

40132.    40133.

Appliances for the prevention of masturbation, illustrated in the Maison Mathieu catalog for 1904.

*The term *onanism* comes from Genesis 8:8–11. Actually the passage describes coitus interruptus, not masturbation.

[†]For further details, see Hare (1962); Comfort (1967); and Schwarz (1973).

supposed symptoms and results of masturbation," wrote Havelock Ellis, earlier in the century. An incredible list of ailments were supposed to have been caused by masturbation at one time or another. They included insanity; epilepsy, headaches, and "strange sensations at the top of the head"; dilated pupils, dark rings around the eyes, and "eyes directed upward and sideways"; intermittent deafness; redness of nose and nosebleeds, hallucinations of smell and hearing, and "morbid changes in the nose"; hypertrophy and tenderness of the breasts; afflictions of the ovaries, uterus, and vagina (including painful menstruation and "acidity of the vagina"); pains of various kinds, specifically "tenderness of the skin in the lower dorsal region"; asthma; heart murmurs ("masturbator's heart"); and skin ailments ranging from acne to wounds, pale and discolred skin, and "an undesirable odor of the skin in women" (Ellis, 1942, vol. 1, part 1, p. 249). Box 11.4 provides the historical background for some of these views.

There is absolutely no evidence to support any such claims. We can flatly say that, in physical terms, whenever sexual intercourse is not harmful, neither is masturbation. Nonetheless, some people still are ambivalent about the practice being carried "to excess," though no one is able to define its "normal" limits.

Mental Health    It is harder to define mental health than physical health. We have to distinguish between masturbation causing psychological maladjustment and masturbation signaling it. This point has been often confused in the past. Physicians would see patients in psychiatric wards openly masturbating and conclude that chronic masturbation had driven them mad. In fact, indulging in such behavior in public was just one more sign of mental disorder. (The same would be true if they urinated or defecated in public.) We must also distinguish between the effects of masturbation itself and the impact of the negative feelings it may engender.

Masturbation can reflect psychological disturbances, but so can coitus, eating, or any other behavior. It is not the behavior that mat-

ters, but its motivation. Masturbation does not cause mental illness. It is necessary to state this fact even in this day and age, because some people still harbor fears it will make them insane (Arafat and Cotton, 1974).

Look at masturbation in the context of the individual's broader life. Is it relied on at the expense of interpersonal encounters? Is it shortchanging deeper sexual gratification? The problem in these cases is more fundamental than masturbation. However, even in pathological conditions, masturbation may provide one of the few forms of sexual release and psychological comfort.

Guilt and Shame    There have been a great many changes since the Victorian era when lives were warped by needless concerns over masturbation (Chapter 20). Nevertheless, for some people it continues to generate guilt, shame, sadness, and loneliness.

Sorenson reports that of his adolescent subjects only 19 percent claimed never to have felt guilty (32 percent did so rarely, 32 percent sometimes, and 17 percent often) (Sorenson, 1973, p. 143). Masturbation implied that they were not mature enough, attractive enough, or sophisticated enough to have a sexual partner, so there was a concurrent feeling of shame. Paradoxically, masturbation was more common among those also engaging in coitus than in those who were not.

Similar attitudes have been reported for college students. In one study, guilt feelings were reported by 42 percent (Greenberg, 1972); in another, 13 percent of men and 10 percent of women reported feelings of guilt, and 11 percent and 25 percent respectively reported feeling depressed after masturbation (Arafat and Cotton, 1974).

Adults are not immune to negative reactions. In the Hunt report, people generally felt ashamed and secretive. "Almost no adults, not even the very liberated, can bring themselves to tell friends, lovers, or mates that they still occasionally masturbate" (Hunt, 1974). One of the *Cosmopolitan* survey respondents, a 39-year-old divorced woman (who had had 25 lovers) wrote, "I have been masturbating since I was

# Box 11.5

## MASTURBATION IN LITERATURE

### PORTNOY'S COMPLAINT*

Then came adolescence—half my waking life spent locked behind the bathroom door, firing my wad down the toilet bowl, or into the soiled clothes in the laundry hamper, or splat up against my medicine-chest mirror, before which I stood in my dropped drawers so I could see how it looked coming out. Or else I was doubled over my flying fist, eyes pressed closed but mouth wide open, to take that sticky sauce of buttermilk and Clorox on my own tongue and teeth—though not infrequently, in my blindness and ecstasy, I got it all in the pompadour, like a blast of Wildroot Cream Oil. Through a world of matted handkerchiefs and crumpled Kleenex and stained pajamas, I moved my raw and swollen penis, perpetually in dread that my loathsomeness would be discovered by someone stealing upon me just as I was in the frenzy of dropping my load. Nevertheless, I was wholly incapable of keeping my paws from my doing it once it started the climb up my belly. In the middle of a class I would raise a hand to be excused, rush down the corridor to the lavatory, and with ten or fifteen savage strokes, beat off standing up into a urinal. At the Saturday afternoon movie I would leave my friends to go off to the candy machine—and wind up in a distant balcony seat, squirting my seed into the empty wrapper from a Mounds bar. On an outing of our family association, I once cored an apple, saw to my astonishment (and with the aid of my obsession) what it looked like, and ran off into the woods to fall upon the orifice of the fruit, pretending that the cool and mealy hole was actually between the legs of that mythical being who always called me Big Boy when she pleaded for what no girl in all recorded history had ever had. "Oh shove it in me, Big Boy," cried the cored apple that I banged silly on that picnic. "Big Boy, Big Boy, oh give me all you've got," begged the empty milk bottle that I kept hidden in our storage in the basement, to drive wild after school with my vaselined

upright. "Come, Big Boy, come," screamed this maddened piece of liver that, in my own insanity, I bought one afternoon at a butcher shop and, believe it or not, violated behind a billboard on the way to a bar mitzvah lesson.

### FEAR OF FLYING†

She is lying beside him very still. She touches herself to prove she's not dead. She thinks of the first two weeks of her broken leg. She used to masturbate constantly then to convince herself that she could feel something besides pain. Pain was a religion then. A total commitment.

She runs her hands down her belly. Her right forefinger touches the clitoris while the left forefinger goes deep inside her, pretending to be a penis. What does a penis feel, surrounded by those soft, collapsing caves of flesh? Her finger is too small. She puts in two and spreads them. But her nails are too long. They scratch.

What if he wakes up?

Maybe she wants him to wake up and see how lonely she is.

Lonely, lonely, lonely. She moves her fingers to that rhythm, feeling the two inside get creamy and the clitoris get hard and red. Can you feel colors in your fingertips? This is what red feels like. The inner cave feels purple. Royal purple. As if the blood down there were blue.

"Who do you think of when you masturbate?" her German analyst asked, "Who do you sink of?" I sink therefore I am. She thinks of no one really, and of everyone. Of her analyst and of her father. No, not her father. She cannot think of her father. Of a man on a train. A man under the bed. A man with no face. His face is blank. His penis has one eye. It weeps.

She feels the convulsions of the orgasm suck violently around her fingers. Her hand falls to her side and then she sinks into a dead sleep.

*From Philip Roth, *Portnoy's complaint*. New York: Random House, 1967, pp. 17–19.

†From Erica Jong, *Fear of flying*. New York: Holt, Rinehart and Winston, 1973, p. 121.

18 years old, but it's something I've never admitted to anyone except my present lover" (Wolfe, 1981).

Though a remarkable percentage of people still feel that masturbation is wrong, there is a clear association between such attitudes and age. In the 55 and older age group, 29 percent of males and 36 percent of females agree that it is wrong. These percentages steadily decrease, so that in the 18- to 24-year-old bracket only 15 percent of males and 14 percent of females still agree with this statement. These figures indicate not only a change in attitude but the disappearance of sex differences in such attitudes.

Though masturbation is still not quite respectable for many people, its acceptability is on the rise. It is explicitly described in popular literary works (Box 11.5). The polite tolerance of earlier marriage manuals has given way to unabashed endorsement by professionals (De Martino, 1979; Sarnoff and Sarnoff, 1979), popular writers ("M," 1971; "J," 1979), and other advocates (Dodson, 1987).

Mark Twain anticipated this turn of events in a satirical address, "Some Remarks on the Science of Onanism," which includes the following memorable lines:

Homer, in the second book of the *Iliad*, says with fine enthusiasm, "Give me masturbation or give me death!" Caesar, in his *Commentaries*, says, "To the lonely it is company; to the forsaken it is a friend; to the aged and to the impotent it is a benefactor; they that are penniless are yet rich, in that they still have this majestic diversion." In another place this experienced observer has said, "There are times when I prefer it to sodomy."

Robinson Crusoe says, "I cannot describe what I owe to this gentle art." Queen Elizabeth said, "It is the bulwark of Virginity." Cetewayo, the Zulu hero, remarked, "A jerk in the hand is worth two in the bush." The immortal Franklin has said, "Masturbation is the mother of invention." He also said, "Masturbation is the best policy." Michelangelo and all the other old masters—Old Masters, I will remark, is an abbreviation, a contraction—have used similar language. Michelangelo said to Pope Julius II, "Self-negation is noble, self-culture is beneficent, self-possession is manly, but to the truly grand and inspiring soul they are poor and tame compared to self-abuse." (Twain, 1876, pp. 23–24)

## REVIEW QUESTIONS

1. What functions are served by erotic fantasies?

2. How do the common fantasy themes for men and women compare among heterosexuals and homosexuals?

3. How does sleep relate to sexual arousal and orgasm?

4. How prevalent is masturbation among males and females?

5. What are the common reasons that lead people to masturbate?

## THOUGHT QUESTIONS

1. How would you deal with an anxiety-provoking erotic fantasy that you have trouble putting out of your mind?

2. If you discount the symbolic meaning of dreams, how do you make sense out of them?

3. What would you say or do if you found your 10-year-old son or daughter masturbating in front of the television?

4. When is a college student masturbating "too frequently"?

5. How would you dissuade a doctor who thinks masturbation is unhealthy for adolescents?

## SUGGESTED READINGS

Friday, N. *My secret garden* (1973); *Forbidden flowers* (1975). New York: Simon and Schuster. Narrative accounts of female erotic fantasies. *Men in love* (1980). New York: Delacorte Press. Male erotic fantasies.

Kiell, N. (1976). *Varieties of sexual experience*. New York: International Universities Press. Excerpts from erotic literature.

Marcus, I. M., and Francis, J. J. (1975). *Masturbation from infancy to senescence*. New York: International Universities Press. DeMartino, M. F. (1979). *Human autoerotic practices*. New York: Human Sciences Press. Essays on various aspects of masturbation.

Webb, P. (1975). *The Erotic Arts*. Boston: New York Graphic Society. A fascinating historical overview of erotic art, with numerous illustrations.

# Sexplay and Coitus

CHAPTER

# 12

*Those who know the art of love are like those who can fix five different flavors in the cooking pot to produce a good meal.*

ANCIENT CHINESE SAYING

## OUTLINE

VARIETIES OF SEXPLAY
Kissing
Touching and Caressing
   Breast Stimulation
   Genital Stimulation
Oral-Genital Stimulation
Other Means of Sexplay
   Anal Stimulation
   Special Practices
   Objects and Devices
Length of Sexplay
COITUS
Intromission
   Physical Considerations
   Psychological Considerations
Coital Postures
   Face to Face
   Rear Entry
Coital Movements
Orgasmic Control
   Prolonging Coitus
   Mutual, Multiple, and Extended
      Orgasms
Variant Forms of Reaching Orgasm
   Coitus Interruptus

Ejaculation Against Body Surfaces
Oral Intercourse
Anal Intercourse
The Aftermath
ENHANCING COITAL PLEASURE
Physical Factors
   Appearance
   Exercise
Time and Place
Erotic Aids and Practices
   Scents
   Sounds and Music
   Clothing
   Lotions
   Bathing
   Motion
   Aphrodisiacs
Psychological Factors
   Gender Considerations
   Reciprocity
   Acceptance
   Freedom from Anxiety
   Affection and Trust
   Communication

Animals *copulate* ("link together") primarily for reproductive purposes; but people *make love* to fulfill other needs as well.

Sexual intercourse that involves penile-vaginal engagement is called *coitus*.[1] Coitus is not the preferred sexual activity for every individual, every time, but for the human species as a whole it is clearly the most important sexual act, because reproduction depends on it. It is no wonder that coitus is the primary sexual behavior in all cultures. The great majority of men and women engage in sexual intercourse at least sometime in life; coitus accounts for most sexual orgasms among adults of both sexes.

In this chapter, we shall describe sexual stimulation through various forms of sexplay, the act of coitus, and how people enhance it. Later chapters deal with the interpersonal and institutional contexts of lovemaking (Chapters 16 and 17).

## VARIETIES OF SEXPLAY

In physical terms, masturbation, petting, and foreplay consist of the same basic activities: in *masturbation,* sexual stimulation is solitary; in *petting,* two individuals arouse each other, sometimes to the point of orgasm; when petting acts as a prelude to coitus, we refer to it as *foreplay.* In sociosexual terms, though, masturbation, petting, and foreplay are not at all the same. Caressing your own thighs and having them caressed by someone else are quite different experiences. Similarly, it matters whether the activity is an end in itself or a way station to coitus.

The term "foreplay" has fallen out of favor among sex researchers and therapists, because it overemphasizes coitus as the "main event." They prefer the terms *noncoital sex play* or *sexual pleasuring* (Masters et al., 1988). The

practical significance of this wording has to do with safer sex. If sexplay sounds like a satisfying activity in its own right, rather than a prelude to coitus, couples may be more content to stop with it, rather than treating it as half-a-loaf.

Another problem with the association of "foreplay" with coitus is that the activities it subsumes, such as kissing and caressing, are the same whether used by heterosexuals or homosexuals, although the latter do not engage in coitus.

We shall be focusing here primarily on various methods of sexual stimulation. Bear in mind that the most important element in all of these interactions is the *emotional* context—what you feel about your partner and the activity in which you are engaged. Without the feelings that accompany them, all "techniques" of sexual arousal become reduced to meaningless mechanical exercises.

Methods of sexual stimulation are based on the process of sexual arousal we discussed earlier (Chapter 3). All forms of stimuli—what we see, hear, smell, or touch—contribute to each of the particular methods involved. Here again, it is the combination of the physical and emotional components that generates the erotic "charge"; it is not just the sound of murmured words but rather their meaning that counts.

### Kissing

In various forms of *social kissing,* touching or caressing with the lips is a sign of affection, respect, comforting, and greeting. When it is used to express and excite sexual passion, it becomes an *erotic kiss* (Perella, 1969). Erotic kissing is a common component of sexplay in our culture (Figure 12.1), but it is by no means a universal practice. Even within our society the more educated individuals are more likely to kiss (Kinsey et al., 1948, 1953).

Erotic kissing may start with simple lip contact. A light, stroking motion may alternate with tentative tongue caresses and gentle nibbling of the more accessible lower lip. Gradually, as the tongue becomes bolder, it ranges

---

[1]Colloquial expressions for coitus include: to have sex, go to bed, sleep together; to ball, bang, hump, fuck, score, screw; to lay, get laid; to get into somebody's pants; to get a piece, a piece of ass, a piece of tail; to make, to make out; to roll in the hay, rub bellies, have the banana peeled, and so on (Haeberle, 1978, p. 492).

Figure 12.1    The erotic kiss.

a higher erotic potential (Chapter 3). The kiss entails far more than stimulating some nerve endings: kissing is a potent symbolic act. Kissing the palm of the hand conveys an intimate and erotic feel. The kissing of finger tips and the sucking of fingers is sexually highly suggestive and may be arousing for both women and men.

Kissing is unknown in some non-Western societies, at least in a form familiar to us (Opler, 1969). It is rejected in other cultures as unhealthy or repulsive (Tiefier, 1978). The Tinquians (monogamous Philippine agriculturists and headhunters) and the Balinese brought their faces together and smelled each other ("rubbing noses") (Figure 12.2). The Thonga of Mozambique (primitive agriculturists) were revolted by the Western kiss, saying, "Look at them—they eat each other's saliva and dirt" (Ford and Beach, 1951).

There are men and women in our society who also feel uneasy about deep kissing in general or with a particular person on a given occasion. Hygiene and aesthetic factors (unbrushed teeth, smell of tobacco, bad breath) as well as psychological considerations (level of intimacy, degree of affection) help determine how they feel about it.

Behavior resembling human kissing can be observed in nonhuman primates and other animals. Chimpanzees occasionally press their lips together as a form of greeting as well as a prelude to further sexual exploration (see Figure 16.5). During coitus a male chimpanzee may occasionally suck vigorously on a female's lower lip. Oral contact during sexual activity also occurs in other animals: for example, male mice lick the female's mouth, sea lions rub mouths, and male elephants insert the tips of their trunks into their partners' mouths (Ford and Beach, 1951). It has been suggested that the origin of deep kissing goes back to the transfer of chewed food from the mother to the infant, a practice that has persisted in some preliterate societies (Wickler, 1972).

## Touching and Caressing

Touching and caressing, like kissing, are means of expressing affection that do not have

freely in the mouth of the partner, who may suck on it. Effective deep kissing entails simultaneous caressing, pressing, and gentle suction of the lips and tongue, it requires a certain artfulness, coordination with the partner, and receptiveness.

The use of the tongue in erotic kissing is sometimes referred to as *deep kissing* (also "French" or "soul" kissing). The merits of such kissing have been widely known in many cultures for a long time. "A humid kiss," says an ancient Arabian proverb, "is better than a hurried coitus."

Kissing need not be restricted to the sexual partner's lips. Any part of the body may be similarly stimulated. However, the *erogenous zones*, such as the breasts, nipples, genitals, inside of the thighs, the neck, and earlobes, have

Figure 12.2    Maori nose-rub.

to be erotic in either intent or effect. Hugging and fondling also can be erotic or not.

The erotic potential of touching also comes out in sensual massage (Inkeles and Todris, 1972). Massage adds many dimensions to lovemaking. It can be used to stimulate the skin, induce deep muscular relaxation, generate a sense of restful contentment, and convey tenderness and caring. (It can also make you rather sleepy.)

Touching for sensual pleasure has attracted much attention (Rueger, 1981; Kennedy and Dean, 1986). To describe the use of touch in conveying sensory and eventually erotic pleasure, sex therapists have introduced the term *sensate focus* (Chapter 15). Another term that has gained currency is *pleasuring*; it subsumes all of the touching and feeling activities that are meant to provide the partner with erotic pleasure and excitement.

Erotic stimulation through touch is part of a much larger pattern of interaction, which relies on touch to convey affection (holding hands, putting an arm over the shoulder), comfort (hugging), greeting (shaking hands, embracing), appeasement (patting), and so on (Montagu, 1986). The animal counterpart of these activities is *grooming*. In a wide variety of species grooming acts as an antidote to aggression (the one groomed is usually the dominant animal); it also shows intimacy between mother and infant and between sexual consorts.

Touching, then, brings together the strands of our evolutionary heritage, memories of the comforting experiences of our childhood, the physical elements of body contact, and the emotional warmth of being liked and loved (Montagu, 1986).

As with kissing, which is a special form of touching, the purely physical component cannot be separated from its symbolic and psychological meaning. Like kissing, touching should range over many gestures and invoke many moods: the light touch, which is tender, tentative, almost tremulous; the more certain caress that confidently moves over the surfaces of the body; the bold and firm fondle; and the all-out embrace when arms and limbs entwine, bodies press together, and two become one.

Touching is a particularly important means of inducing sexual arousal and intimacy. To know how to touch and to enjoy being touched are among the most important attributes of good lovers (Figure 12.3).

Sensitive surfaces respond best to gentle stimulation, whereas larger muscle masses require firmer handling. Once an area has been singled out, it should be attended to long enough to elicit arousal. Frantic shifting from one part of the body to another can be as ineffective as monotonous perseverence. Erotic arousal requires a sense of timing.

Breast Stimulation    The practice of fondling the female breasts is well known in many cultures. In the Kinsey sample 98 percent of respondents reported manual stimulation and 93 percent oral stimulation of female breasts by males. Despite such widespread acceptance not all women find it enjoyable: almost one-third of heterosexual women queried by Masters and Johnson reported that they did not find the stimulation of their breasts to be particularly pleasurable (Masters and Johnson, 1979). Even women who generally do enjoy such stimulation may find the experience uncomfortable during certain phases of the menstrual cycle when the breasts are congested.

Breast stimulation can be enhanced by using both the mouth and the hands. The nipples, though the most responsive parts, need not be the exclusive focus of attention. Women may also enjoy more general fondling, mouthing, and caressing of their breasts. The size

Figure 12.3    Mutual touching is a means of sharing sensual pleasure and excitement.

and shape of the breast has no relation to its sensitivity.

Breast stimulation is an important part of lesbian sex, and women are usually more adept at it than men. Stimulation of the male nipple occurs mainly in homosexual encounters. Masters and Johnson observed nipple stimulation in almost three-quarters of "committed homosexual male couples," whereas no more than three or four among 100 married men were similarly stimulated by their wives.

Genital Stimulation    Tactile stimulation of the genitals is highly exciting for most people. In the Kinsey sample 95 percent of males and 91 percent of females reported manually stimulating the genitals of their sexual partners. Males more often take the initiative to stimulate their female partners. Though women have become more active in this regard, one of the biggest complaints of heterosexual men in the Hite survey was that women did not touch them enough, or if they did, it was not done right—either because women were not interested enough or lacked the expertise (Hite, 1981).

Men and women commonly, and wrongly, assume that what feels good to them must feel good to the partner. Consequently, men may be too forceful in stimulating the female genitals (especially the clitoris); women tend to be too gentle and hence ineffectual in stimulating the penis. Partners can gently communicate their needs.

Men tend to project their own wishes on women, so they assume that the insertion of fingers in the vagina must be pleasurable. Some women find it enjoyable, but others do not. Those who do usually prefer a shallow touch that stimulates the more sensitive vaginal opening and are likely to want the experience late rather than early in sexplay; it may be a good step to take before inserting the penis.

The techniques of genital stimulation during sexplay are similar to those in autoerotic activities; there is, therefore, much that men and women can learn from each other's autoerotic practices. It is also instructive for heterosexuals to know how homosexuals stimulate each other, because they have the gender advantage of knowing about each other's bodies. For instance, in lesbian genital play, the labia, mons pubis, inner thighs, and the vaginal opening are usually approached before the clitoris. Homosexual males dwell on the thighs, lower abdomen, scrotum, and the anal region before turning to the penis.

Oral-Genital Stimulation
A highly effective erotic practice is oral stimulation of the genitals. *Cunnilingus* (Latin, "to lick the vulva") and *fellatio* (Latin, "to suck") are the formal terms for oral stimulation of the female and male genitals respectively. The Dutch gynecologist Van de Velde boldly (for 1926) favored this practice. It was he who coined the term *genital kiss* in preference to the more technical terms cunnilingus and fellatio (Van de Velde, 1965).[2]

The Hunt (1974) survey found 80 percent of single males and females between the ages of 25 and 34 years, and about 90 percent of those married and under 25 years, to have engaged in mouth-genital stimulation during the preceding year. The practice was more prevalent among the better educated and less prevalent among older individuals.

Data from the *Redbook* and Hite surveys show the growing acceptance of these practices, especially among the sexually liberal. They also highlight the reluctance and mixed feelings some people have about them (see Boxes 12.1 and 12.2). Among the *Redbook* wives, about 40 percent had "often" practiced cunnilingus and 40 percent fellatio. Another 48 percent and 45 percent, respectively, had "occasionally" engaged in these activities. Only 7 percent of the women had never had their genitals orally stimulated, and 9 percent had never stimulated a male in similar fashion. Although women engaged in both practices with about equal frequency, they found cunnilingus "very enjoyable" in 62 percent of the cases as

[2]Colloquial terms for oral sex include: frenching, eating, going down, sucking, and blow job (for fellatio)—a curious term because there is no "blowing" involved.

# Box 12.1

## CUNNILINGUS: CURRENT ATTITUDES

### FEMALE VIEWS*

I lie on my back with my partner between my legs, flicking his tongue very gently over the same area, over and over. I like not doing anything else except concentrating on the sensation until I orgasm.

I dislike it when my partner's tongue digs too close to the clitoral nerve inside the hood—it really hurts.

My husband asks me to let him frequently but I shudder at the thought. This is an issue that causes arguments. My husband says that all women do it and like it. I say he's crazy.

Nibbling and nuzzling on the clitoris, like simulated chewing, is good—but gently and tenderly.

I like a slow, steady rhythm, very gentle and circular in motion, right at the front part of my private parts, then moving down to my opening, with a deep penetration of his tongue just before I come.

### MALE VIEWS†

I feel that the genital kiss given by a man to a woman is one of the most intimate expressions of love that there is. I often have dreams involving sex, most of which do not end with my orgasm or ejaculation but do include a protracted period of my kissing the woman's genitals.

I love the way a woman's genitals look when I am close enough to see all of the features. When a woman begins to respond to the act of cunnilingus, her vagina opens like the petals of a flower—her lips fill and enlarge, just as a man's penis does. It tastes like ambrosia that only a woman's body could exude.

I like cunnilingus sometimes, but I think its pleasures are overrated. I think men feel like they have to say they like it, because it's the 'macho' thing to do—like eating raw eggs or raw meat, or drinking a pint of whisky.

It's ghastly. I tried it once and barfed all over my wife.

She has gorgeous legs even at sixty-one. I usually start it. I could wish she would ask, or tell me to eat it, but she is bashful. I massage her with my tongue and she directs me. We have done this for forty-one years, and more frequently the last two years.

*(From S. Hite, *The Hite Report.* New York: Macmillan, 1976, pp. 233 and 245.)

†(From S. Hite, S. *The Hite Report on Male Sexuality.* New York: Ballantine, 1981, p. 702.)

---

against 34 percent for fellatio. Only a small percentage found these activities unpleasant or repulsive (6 percent for cunnilingus, 15 percent for fellatio) (Tavris and Sadd, 1977). The practice has also become more prevalent among adolescents since the time of Kinsey, when only 10 percent reported it; more recently, 53 percent of boys and 42 percent of girls say they have engaged in oral sex. They are slightly more likely to have done so than to have had intercourse, especially among girls (Newcomer and Udry, 1985). Oral sex continues to be more common among the coitally experienced and is usually initiated by males. It has become a common, though not necessarily frequent, component of sexual relations in contemporary marriage as well as in nonmarital relations (Gagnon and Simon, 1987).

Oral-genital contact for both sexes is also reported in other societies (Figure 12.4). Oral stimulation of female genitals is common among primates, and females reportedly respond with obvious pleasure. Stimulation of the male organ is less well documented.

# Box 12.2

## FELLATIO: CURRENT ATTITUDES

**MALE VIEWS***

I believe every man's dream is to have a woman who would, if you'll forgive the vulgarism, suck him off. If I could find the woman who would suck me off in the morning to wake me up, I would lay my life in the mud at her feet, for she would be one woman in a million.

I enjoy very much to have fellatio performed on me. However, I have yet to find a woman who can do it properly. I have orgasmed like this only once, and one other time with the help of masturbation. Many times I feel I could orgasm this way, but something in the way she does it turns me off, either it's getting too repetitive, I hear a sigh, she bites, or I can tell her heart's not in it.

My fear is that I will orgasm in my partner's mouth and choke her, so I retreat from the situation.

I have never had fellatio. I have no desire to have it done, it is repulsive to me.

Coming in a woman's mouth and having her swallow it is something special. I don't associate fellatio with the degrading of woman's aspects that I have heard about it. A man in love loves his woman's cunt and a woman in love loves her man's cock and the oral caresses are just a magnificent way of expressing it.

**FEMALE VIEWS**[†]

Anyone, including so-called doctors, that advocate or engage in oral-genital sex is unsure of whom or what they are. Oral-genital sex is abnormal and immoral. Believe me, everybody doesn't do it! Our mouths are for eating, drinking, speaking, and kissing those we love—not for using on someone's genitals.

I feel that sex is something beautiful and good, but oral sex makes it seem dirty. Animals go around licking each other. Human beings are supposed to be more intelligent.

Women should not object to or feel disgusted by fellatio and cunnilingus. If two people are clean, as they should be for any sexual activity, those practices are as sanitary as sucking one's thumb or french kissing. Orgasms for both parties are usually as intense and pleasurable as coitus, sometimes more so. Of most importance, there is absolutely no fear of unwanted pregnancies; abortion can't exist. Oral procedures, if generally accepted and practiced worldwide, would solve the population explosion in a hurry. With that grave problem under control, hunger, starvation, and low standards of living could largely disappear.

*(From Hite, S. *The Hite report on male sexuality*. New York: Ballantine, 1981, p. 538).

[†](From Tavris, C., and Sadd, S., *The Redbook report on female sexuality*. New York: Dell, 1978).

---

In cunnilingus, the partner gently licks the minor lips, the vaginal entrance, and the clitoris, occasionally sucking and nibbling at them. In fellatio, the glans is the primary focus of excitement: gentle stroking of the frenulum with the tongue and lips, mouthing and sucking the glans while firmly holding the body of the penis and grasping and pulling gently at the scrotal sac are some of the means of stimulation. These activities call for skill, tact, and tenderness. Not many people appreciate a tooth-and-nail assault.[3]

If the penis goes far into the mouth, it will elicit the *gag reflex*, which is a physiological reaction, not a sign of disgust. The woman can

[3]"How-to" books on sex provide explicit instructions for oral-genital stimulation. See, for example, "J" (1969), "M" (1971), Comfort (1972), Franklin and Franklin (1982), Grant and Grant (1983).

Figure 12.4    Mochica pottery, Peru, ca. 500 A.D.

avoid it by controlling how far she takes the penis in. Relaxation and practice also allow the suppression of the reflex.

A couple may engage in mutual oral-genital contact as a prelude to coitus or for its own sake. (Sometimes it is called "sixty-nine" because the bodies are positioned like the numerals: 69.) When oral sex leads to ejaculation into the mouth, it can be thought of as *oral intercourse* (discussed below).

Whether or not one engages in or enjoys oral-genital sex is a matter of personal preference. It is not an activity to be taken for granted or imposed on a partner. For some it requires a greater degree of intimacy with a partner than coitus. Moreover, mouth-genital contact, especially if it involves exposure to semen or vaginal secretions, is not a safe sex practice if there is a likelihood that the partner may be a carrier of the AIDS virus.

## Other Means of Sexplay

Anal Stimulation    Stroking or pressing on the anal orifice and inserting a finger into the rectum are appreciated by some people and rejected by others. The same applies to the oral stimulation of the anus, called *anilingus* (or *rimming*). Apart from the threat of AIDS, oral contact with the anus (even if it is clean) carries the risk of infection with enteric organisms (Chapter 5). Pulling at the buttocks will stretch the anal sphincter, causing mild pleasurable

stimulation without actually touching the anal orifice. Though anal stimulation is more common in gay sexual relationships, heterosexuals do it too (Morin, 1981).

Special Practices    Some couples rely on more unusual practices in sexplay. A good example is the use of *bondage* (such as tying up the partner) or interactions involving *dominance* and *submission*. Although these practices can fall under the category of *sadomasochism* (S-M) (Chapter 14), many people who take pleasure in them are not sadomasochists. They are not interested in harming their sexual partner or in getting hurt themselves. Couples who engage in these practices may also use special clothing (such as black leather garments) and various paraphernalia (such as masks or restraints). Mild pain (such as nibbling or scratching) is sometimes part of these practices or independent of them.

Objects and Devices    Partners can use more than their bodies. Stroking with cotton balls, feathers (peacocks are said to be the best), or any other material of special texture can be stimulating. Everything from ice to living fish (in inverted bowls) has been applied to the genitals to try for novel pitches of excitement.

All of the devices for masturbation (Chapter 11) can also be made part of sexplay. Some men and women find the use of a vibrator together highly arousing, but others reject it as unromantic. Some men feel threatened by it ("How can you compete with a machine?"). It can be a real help if a female partner has difficulty reaching orgasm otherwise.

Numerous other objects and practices may titillate the senses during sexplay—soft lighting, scents, lotions, music, sexy underwear, and so on. They are used all throughout lovemaking, so we shall discuss them later.

## Length of Sexplay

When sexplay is an end in itself, partners stay with it as long as is mutually pleasurable. Mounting excitement may lead to noncoital orgasm, or the couple may forego the climax and "cool down" gradually.

When sexplay is a prelude to coitus, how long should it last? The right timing varies widely among individuals and cultures. Sex manuals have traditionally devoted much attention to the necessity of "preparing" the woman for intercourse. Some even specify various minimum time periods (Kroop and Schneidman, 1977). This perception is a carryover from the old idea that women are the passive and men the active agents in sex: man is the "musician," woman the musical "instrument," and so on. Sex is better viewed as an interaction between equal partners, both of whom need to "prepare" each other.

Among married couples in the Kinsey sample, foreplay took 3 minutes or less in 11 percent, 4 to 10 minutes in 36 percent, 11 to 20 minutes in 31 percent, and beyond 20 minutes in 22 percent. Some couples spent several hours each day in erotic play (Kinsey et al., 1953). In the Hunt sample, single people under 25 typically spent about 15 minutes in foreplay (Hunt, 1974).

It seems best to leave the length of sexplay up to each couple. Aside from personal preferences, different circumstances require different amounts of preparation. Physiologically, full erection and adequate vaginal lubrication indicate readiness. Emotionally, a couple is only ready when both partners feel a mutual urge for sexual union.

A common source of difficulty is the male attitude that sexplay is an obligation to get through. This approach is not likely to be effective, no matter how fervently a man may kiss, caress, lick, suck, twist, and turn. The woman may sense in his utilitarian approach the genital cast of his mind and resent it; as he rushes her, she will drag her feet.

This conflict of interest during sexplay is part of a broader discrepancy in how men and women approach coitus: men are much more genitally oriented and focused on orgasm; women are more attuned to the total experience, of which orgasm is but one part. This difference also explains why in the aftermath of coitus women more often than men want to cuddle up, talk, and extend the experience.

To break this deadlock, each needs to accommodate the other's needs. A man may need to approach sexplay pretending it is just petting, as if that is as far as things are going to go; then he will feel ready to extend the experience.

A woman must realize that her male partner has a problem that she does not: as sexplay stretches out, he might ejaculate too soon if he is young, or lose his erection if he is older. When a woman senses that either will happen, she may have to yield to his tempo. They may then start again, or he may help her reach orgasm by some other means.

*Intromission* (when the penis enters the vagina) marks the start of coitus proper, but it need not end sexplay. In face-to-face coitus, the couple can continue to kiss; in rear entry coitus the breasts and clitoris are easy to fondle. Sexplay is not a separate event but part of the whole experience of making love.

## COITUS

Despite individual variations, a standard script is said to currently guide heterosexual couples in coitus: "Kissing, tongue kissing, manual and oral caressing of the body, particularly the female breasts, manual and oral contacts with both the female and male genitalia, usually in this sequence, followed by intercourse in a number of positions" (Gagnon and Simon, 1987, p. 2). No wonder making love has been compared to a game of chess: the moves are many, but the ending is the same.

Nonetheless, coitus has profound psychological, relational, and moral implications. Most of these issues we shall discuss in subsequent chapters. Our focus here is on coital techniques and the enhancement of coital pleasure.

### Intromission

There is more to intromission than simply inserting the penis into the vagina, or taking the penis into the vagina. Subtle lovers recognize it as an important step in lovemaking both on physical and psychological grounds. Sexplay prepares the couple for coitus; intromission sets the tone for it.

Physical Considerations    To initiate coitus gently, the glans is first placed firmly against the vaginal opening until it relaxes. It is best the man not penetrate even then but keep moving the glans within the entrance as well as in the clitoral region until the woman shows unmistakable signs of wanting deeper penetration.

The woman may gauge even better the best time for intromission and introduce the penis into her vagina. This technique removes doubts about her readiness. If she takes the initiative, she must in turn be mindful of the man's level of arousal. The penis that has not attained a certain firmness may not readily go in, and a sense of failure will cause some men to lose their erection entirely. With some experience, however, a woman may get even a semierect penis into the vagina (*soft entry*), an important consideration when dealing with older men or those with potency problems (Chapter 15).

If the vagina is insufficiently lubricated, intromission must not be attempted. Either further stimulation or an artificial lubricant is called for. Water-soluble lubricants like K-Y jelly or contraceptive jellies, creams, and foams work best. Oily substances are best avoided; Vaseline in particular will damage rubber condoms and diaphragms and make them less effective (Chapter 7). Saliva works reasonably well if there is a lot of it (such as following mouth-genital stimulation); merely moistening the glans with saliva is usually not enough.

Adequate lubrication does not necessarily mean the woman is ready for coitus. The final criterion is her psychological readiness.

Psychological Considerations    Coitus has close associations with feelings of dominance and aggression (Chapter 19). To penetrate and to be penetrated are laden with symbolic meanings. Between affectionate, trusting, and self-confident lovers, all that hardly matters; once the penis and vagina are joined together they become shared organs. However, if a man uses penetration as a form of assertiveness, the woman may resent it. It may take very little to cross the line between the feeling of making love and "getting fucked."

On the other hand, if a woman is oversensitive about who is doing what to whom, then the sexual encounter becomes a confrontation.

Coital Postures

Among nonhuman primates, the male usually mounts the female from behind (Figure 12.5). The cooperation of the female monkey is essential for this process. She must take the appropriate posture and lock her hindlegs to support the male; otherwise he cannot copulate with her. Face-to-face coitus is rare, though it does occur occasionally, for example, among captive gorillas and orangutans. The evolutionary shift of the vagina to a more frontal position, which facilitates face-to-face coitus, may have helped bonding between early men and women.

Pictorial representations of coitus going back to ancient Egypt show all varieties of coital postures. Similar depictions can be found in the art of virtually all cultures (Figure 12.6).

Knowing the mechanics of coitus can im-

Figure 12.5    Basic adult copulatory posture in monkeys.

Figure 12.6  A carved wooden figure from the Luba (or BaLuba) tribe of Central Africa. The sculpture shows the two figures in a coital position.

prove the physical aspects of intercourse, but the benefits are just as much psychological (Wilson, 1984). Through experimenting with various approaches, we become more deliberate, controlled, and purposeful in making love. Such effort implies care and concern for the partner, so that intercourse lives up to the literal meaning of the term: an interaction between two people.

Variety is the second advantage of coital postures. Long-time lovers sooner or later tend to find sex a bit monotonous. As Honoré de Balzac wrote, "Marriage must continually vanquish a monster that devours everything: the monster of habit" (quoted in Van de Velde, 1965). The imaginative use of different positions can prevent boredom.

A simplistic search for body levers and push-buttons leads to mechanical sex; the energy that charges the erotic circuits is emotion. Nonetheless, lovemaking requires some knowledge of sexual technique. As in any other art or skill (which is what "technique" means in Greek), natural aptitude may not always be enough. It cannot substitute for knowledge and practice. There is nothing unromantic about technical expertise, as long as you do not act like a "pro" who does this sort of thing for a living.

There is nothing magical about coital positions, either. Experimentation will show one approach to be more exciting at one time and another more suited to other circumstances. There is no position to end all positions, and the search for mechanical perfection is pointless. The "cookbook" approach to lovemaking robs the act of the spontaneity that ought to be its hallmark.

Despite innumerable variations, the basic coital approaches are few: the couple may stand, sit, or lie down; the partners may face each other, or the woman can turn her back to the man; one can be on top of the other, or they can lie side by side. Figures 12.6 to 12.10 illustrate the common coital postures, so we do not need detailed descriptions. Instead, we shall touch upon their relative advantages.

Face to Face    The primary advantage of face-to-face approaches is the opportunity for direct interaction. The partners can gaze into each other's eyes and communicate their feelings through facial expressions. They can also kiss and caress most easily.

The traditional and probably most common variant (but not necessarily the most enjoyable for everyone), is the *man-above* position, where the woman lies on her back with the man on top of her (Figure 12.7). Western missionaries were observed by natives always to engage in coitus in this manner; so they called it the "missionary position." Among Kinsey subjects, 70 percent had tried no other coital approach. It is also the usual pattern in many societies other than our own (Ford and Beach, 1951).

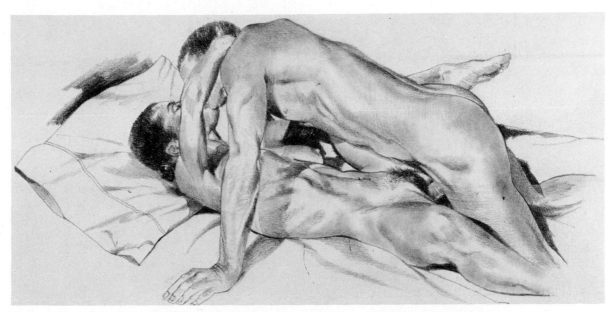

Figure 12.7    Man-above position.

The man-above position is helpful when the erectile capacity of the male is relatively weak. Penetration is shallow unless the woman lifts up her legs. Placing a pillow under her lower back makes this alternative more comfortable. Entwining her legs around the man's provides the woman with good leverage for moving her pelvis to meet his thrusts or for simply sustaining muscular tension.

This position is the most likely to lead to pregnancy (but there are no positions that provide contraceptive protection). To maximize the chance of conception, the woman must maintain this posture for a while after coitus, and the man should not withdraw abruptly.

There are several drawbacks. The man's weight can be a problem: he can support himself on his elbows, but a really heavy man will still be a considerable burden on the woman. Furthermore, in this position the man's hands will not be free to stimulate his partner. A more serious problem is the restriction that this position imposes on the woman's movements. Although she can move her legs, her pelvis remains hard to move. However, this

position can also be used to great advantage. For instance, by spreading her legs widely and pulling them toward her shoulders, a woman can allow for greater depth of penetration; locking her legs around the man's waist provides good leverage for heightening muscular tension in her thighs and buttocks.

An excellent alternative is the *woman-above* position, where the woman sits astride the man or lies on top of him (Figure 12.8). Among the Hunt sample, three-quarters of married couples used this approach at least occasionally (Hunt, 1974). The woman's weight is usually less of a problem for the man, and she has the opportunity to regulate the speed and vigor of her movements, the depth of penetration, and contact of the clitoris with the man's body. Many women find it easier to achieve orgasm in this manner (Chapter 15).

Other choices are *side-by-side* postures (Figure 12.9). Penetration is somewhat more difficult, so partners may begin in some other position, then roll onto their sides. The primary advantage of this approach is the ease and comfort it provides to both partners, elim-

Figure 12.8   Woman-above position.

inating weight-bearing and the issue of "who is on top." Such coitus tends to be prolonged and leisurely. Ovid commended this approach above others, saying: "Of love's thousand ways, a simple way and with least labor, this is: to lie on the right side, and half supine" (quoted in Van de Velde, 1965). It is also recommended by Masters and Johnson for the treatment of certain forms of sexual dysfunction and adopted by three-quarters of the couples they studied who tried it. More than half of Hunt's sample also reported using it.

In *seated* intercourse the man sits in a chair, or on the edge of a bed, or another raised surface. The woman stands in front of him and lowers herself onto his erect penis (Figure 12.10). By keeping her feet on the ground, she can control her pelvic movements; she can also achieve deeper penetration by straddling him and locking her feet behind the chair. The man's pelvic movements are restricted, but his hands are free.

Penetration is difficult when the couple is standing face to face; but if the woman lifts one leg high enough, it can be done. She may then wrap her legs around his waist while he supports her buttocks. This posture works well if she is fairly light and if he has a strong back. Ancient manuals call this position "climbing the tree."

Rear Entry   In the Kinsey sample (1948, 1953) only 15 percent reported having tried the *rear entry* position, but in the Hunt (1974) sample 20 percent in the 18-to-24 age group reported using it. In addition to providing variety, the rear-entry position makes it easy for the man to fondle the woman's breasts and caress her clitoris.

Rear-entry positions somewhat isolate the partners, because they cannot conveniently see each other. On the other hand, close and comfortable body contact is easy to achieve because no other position allows a woman to curl up as snugly in a man's lap. Men, as well as women, enjoy being cuddled in this "spoon position."

Rear entry is possible with the woman lying face down, sitting in the man's lap, leaning over, and on her hands and knees ("doggy style") (Figure 12.11). When the woman is lying flat, penetration is shallow. (Coitus in this manner may be difficult for obese people.) If the two lie on their sides, intromission is easy even with a relatively weak erection. This method is particularly restful. It is good for coitus during pregnancy or ill health, when exertion is to be avoided.

### Coital Movements

Generally *coital thrusts* are slow and deliberate at first, gradually getting deeper. The man may thrust and withdraw; the woman may do the same, or both may thrust and withdraw simultaneously. These movements may be rhythmic, fast or slow, with shallow or deep penetration. They may follow an in-and-out or

Figure 12.9  Side-by-side position.

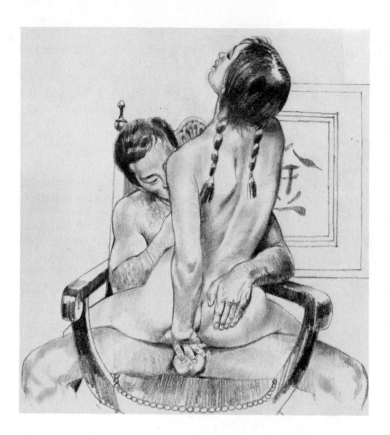

Figure 12.10    Sitting posture.

circular "grinding" motion ("pestle in the mortar"). It is possible for only one person to move while the other is still. Some writers recommend a nine-stroke rhythm: nine shallow thrusts, then one full lunge; or nine full lunges followed by nine shallow thrusts. Variety is exciting, but of course there is no ideal formula.

Ancient erotic manuals describe it in picturesque language: "Deep and shallow, slow and swift, direct and slanting thrusts, are by no means all uniform and each has its own distinctive effect and characteristics. A slow thrust should resemble the jerking movement of a carp toying with the hook; a swift thrust that of the flight of the birds against the wind. Inserting and withdrawing, moving upwards and downwards, from left to right, interspaced intervals or in quick succession—all these should be coordinated. One should apply each at the most suitable time and not always stubbornly cling to only one style alone for reason of one's own laziness or convenience" (quoted in Chang, 1977).

## Orgasmic Control

Because orgasm means loss of erection (although by no means the end of coitus for most men), its control and timing are important. Generally, men are worried about reaching orgasm too soon; women worry about reaching orgasm not soon enough or not at all.

*Prolonging Coitus*    Extending the period of coitus may seem desirable on the grounds that what feels good for 10 minutes should feel twice as good for 20. Sexual intercourse is not an endurance contest, though. The point is for both partners to be as satisfied as possible, whatever time it takes.

Women can keep up coitus for long periods of time; they do not have to worry about maintaining erection. Second, orgasm does not prevent women, as it does men, from continuing with coitus; they can persist with or without later orgasms. The burden is therefore more on the man to sustain his erection and control the timing of orgasm.

Control of orgasm has to be physiological and psychological. Two physiological processes underlie sexual response—vasocongestion and myotonia (Chapter 3). The first is not under voluntary control, but muscular tension can be influenced by various means. The more vigorously a man thrusts, the faster is the build-up to orgasm. Hence, to delay that moment, the man and the woman will need to slow down or stop coital thrusts. Some couples enter and withdraw, engaging in other forms of sexplay between insertions as a way of prolonging intercourse. A balance must be maintained, keeping up erection without pushing on to ejaculation. (Other techniques to achieve this end will be discussed in Chapter 15.)

Equally important is mental control over the level of arousal. During sexual excitement there is constant stimulation through all the senses and through mental imagery. Though there is not much that a man can do to block sensory input, he can distract himself by thinking about a nonerotic topic to reduce arousal. He has to make his shift without losing touch with his partner. All of these measures work best with the partner's cooperation and with practice. The ultimate in ejaculatory control is

Figure 12.11    **Rear-entry position.**

# Box 12.3

## COITUS RESERVATUS

At least as far back as 2,000 years ago, Chinese Taoist physicians claimed that during intercourse, the male absorbed the enriching female essence that prolonged his life; ejaculation, however, depleted the man's own vital fluids (Chapter 20). Hence, the ideal sexual practice was to engage in prolonged coitus without ejaculation, except at carefully regulated intervals. Such caution was especially called for once a man reached middle age (Chang, 1977).

Foregoing the explosive, yet brief pleasure of ejaculation provided a man with a more enduring and healthful form of sexual satisfaction, as well as offering his female partner ample opportunity for gratification. As one Taoist sage put it, "Although the man seems to have denied himself an ejaculatory sensation at times, his love for his woman will greatly increase. It is as if he could never have enough of her (Chang, 1977).

The ancient Chinese clearly understood the distinction between ejaculatory and nonejaculatory orgasm (Chapter 3). Those who mastered the latter avoided the refractory period. They could engage in prolonged coitus with multiple nonejaculatory orgasms.

In the West, the term *coitus reservatus* came to be applied to this technique several centuries ago. The term has been applied to nonejaculatory or-

gasm as well as retrograde ejaculation. Though no semen is ejaculated in either case, the underlying physiology of these two processes is different (Chapter 3). Among others, the practice was adopted by the utopian Oneida community in upstate New York, founded by John Humprey Noyes in the 19th century. The male and female members in this group could freely engage in sex, but every man was not at liberty to have children with every woman. Nonejaculatory coitus became the standard method of birth control and was called *male continence*.

Early in this century, Alice Stockham (1883) advocated this form of coitus in her book *Karezza*, and her views were given a cautious endorsement by Marie Stopes. The practice called for prolonged caressing followed by subdued coitus without ejaculation. Men would conserve their vital energies, women would obtain a sense of union and soothe the nerves, and both participants would be spiritually enriched. The practice did not quite catch on.

Recently, there has been a resurgence of interest in these practices in connection with safe sex. Heterosexual intercourse need not be relentlessly genital and orgasmic in orientation. There is much erotic pleasure to be obtained through tender and affectionate intimacies as an end in themselves.

---

*coitus reservatus*—prolonged coitus without ejaculation (Box 12.3).

Mutual, Multiple, and Extended Orgasms  For a man and woman to reach orgasm simultaneously may increase the shared pleasure. They also may feel proud of being able to synchronize their climaxes. However, *mutual orgasm* is the exception rather than the rule during coitus. It is more common to reach orgasm separately, preferably with the woman coming first. If she wishes to experience orgasm more than once, the last may be made to coincide with the man's ejaculation.

*Multiple orgasm* means having several orgasms in rapid succession (not having more

than one orgasm at once). The ability to reach multiple orgasm is much more common among women than men because of the refractory period in the male (Chapter 3). Men can be trained, however, to have *nonejaculatory orgasms,* which allows them to have multiple orgasms as well (Hartman and Fithian, 1984). The origins of these techniques are ancient (Chang, 1977).

Another approach to orgasmic pleasure is *extended sexual orgasm* (ESO). The idea is to have the vaginal contractions of the single orgasm lead to longer-lasting slow contractions of pelvic muscles. This prolongs the period of sexual pleasure (Brauer and Brauer, 1983).

## Variant Forms of Reaching Orgasm

Defined broadly, heterosexual intercourse includes all the ways a man and woman reach orgasm together, not just coitus. Though some of these activities might just as easily be called mutual masturbation, they are not autoerotic. They are ways of culminating a sexual encounter with something more than petting and less than coitus.

Couples who use vaginal coitus try these behaviors too, because they are unusual, cause novel physical sensations, manifest sexual daring, or provide opportunities to offer something "special" to a sexual partner. For most people, these outlets are occasional variants rather than mainstays.

**Coitus Interruptus**    Coitus that ends by ejaculating outside the vagina is called *coitus interruptus* or *withdrawal*. It is mainly used as a contraceptive method, but it is highly unreliable (Chapter 7). The man may use a towel or whatever else is handy to catch the ejaculate or let it flow against the woman's body.

The interruption of coitus at its climax is likely to be frustrating. Nonetheless, the practice was widespread until modern contraception, and it is still common. (The French call it "watering the bushes.")

**Ejaculation Against Body Surfaces**    Coitus can be simulated by placing the genitals close together without intromission. The genitals of one partner may also be pressed and rubbed against a part of the body of the other. Typically, the thigh of one partner goes between the legs of the other. The male may also ejaculate between the thighs of his partner (*intercrural orgasm*) or between her breasts (*intermammary orgasm*).

**Oral Intercourse**    Fellatio with ejaculation in the mouth is *oral intercourse*. Usually the man remains fairly passive. When he forcefully thrusts his penis into the partner's mouth, it is called *irrumation*. The practice can be uncomfortable to the woman unless she is "constructed to withstand it, excited enough to

enjoy it, or willing to use teeth, if necessary, to stop it" (Offit, 1981).

Ejaculation in the mouth does not present a health hazard, provided the man does not have a sexually transmitted disease. Whether or not a woman should allow semen in her mouth and then either swallow it or dispose of it is a matter of personal preference. However, in the light of the threat of AIDS (Chapter 5) it is unwise for women (and men) to take semen in their mouths unless they are absolutely certain that their partner does not carry the AIDS virus. The use of a condom provides good but not certain protection, and it interferes somewhat with the sensations of direct mouth contact.

Such an orgasm can be highly pleasurable to a man; he may also feel flattered that a woman will allow it or even welcome it (not unlike the reaction of a woman whose lover performs cunnilingus when she is menstruating). A woman may likewise find the experience exciting and novel, or simply tolerate it for the sake of her partner. Others find it unpleasant or offensive.

**Anal Intercourse**    Anal intercourse is often thought of as a male homosexual practice, but a substantial number of heterosexual couples engage in it as well. According to the Hunt (1974) survey, almost half of married men and more than one-quarter of married women between the ages of 18 and 35 had tried anal intercourse at least once. The rates for singles and older married couples were lower (Hunt, 1974; Masters and Johnson, 1979). Anal intercourse for most heterosexual couples is an occasional rather than regular part of their lovemaking.

The anus is highly sensitive, and its stimulation can be highly arousing. Such stimulation may occur in both sexes by the insertion of fingers, objects, or the penis. Among the self-selected male respondents of the Hite (1981) survey, 31 percent of heterosexual men had experienced anal penetration by a finger (either their own or a partner's), and another 12 percent by a penis or similar-sized object.

By contrast 85 percent of homosexual men had had similar experiences.

Anal intercourse is endorsed by some people; others think it vulgar and offensive. Women may allow it as a concession to their partners or because they themselves enjoy it. The attraction of anal sex is based partly on the physical sensations it can yield and partly on its being a novel, unusual activity. It represents for some people the ultimate in receptivity when a woman allows a man to enter the most private and guarded part of her body.

Anal sex may entail some discomfort for the woman even in the best of circumstances; if clumsily done, it can be quite painful. To make it pleasurable (or even feasible) ample lubrication is necessary. The anus must be relaxed and gently stretched first with a finger; then the glans is pushed in carefully and not much beyond the anal sphincter. Movements following penetration must be slow and restrained to avoid injury to the delicate rectal mucosa (Morin, 1981).

Anal sex can safely follow vaginal coitus, but the reverse must be avoided unless the penis (or finger, or vibrator) is carefully washed in between: otherwise bacteria that belong in the rectum will cause vaginal infection. Hemorrhoids, anal fissures, and other local ailments make anal sex particularly uncomfortable; and the prospect of AIDS infection makes unprotected anal intercourse a *very high-risk* activity (Chapter 5).

## The Aftermath

The quality of intercourse is best judged by the mood that follows orgasm. Coitus does not end with orgasm. In its final phase the physiological effects of excitement recede and the participants regather their wits. We looked at these changes in body and behavior in Chapter 3.

Laboratory observation seems to confirm gender differences in postcoital behavior. No matter what their sexual orientation or how they reach orgasm, males tend to rest briefly and then disengage. Women usually desire to remain quiet longer and maintain the embrace. Even before such documentation, marriage manuals dwelled on this phase. Men were warned not to dismount abruptly, turn their backs, and go to sleep; they were to disengage gradually with endearments and tender caresses, and remain attentive to their partner's needs for quiet intimacy (Van de Velde, 1965).

There is a good deal to be said for this advice, but the gender-linked differences should not be exaggerated. A man needs and wants as much tenderness as a woman, unless he is made to feel "unmasculine" for it.

The aftermath of coitus can be a time of quiet reflection. Thoughts meander; earlier experiences, sexual or otherwise, float into consciousness. Though this is a fine time for sharing thoughts and feelings, there must be room as well for parallel solitude. If coitus was not all that it could have been, tenderness restores confidence and makes amends. However, this is no time for clinical postmortems, though there is a strong temptation for "instant replay" and evaluations ("Was it good for you?").

Even if orgasm has been highly pleasurable, the experience may be partially ruined if one partner thinks a victory was scored. Likewise, there may be a sinking feeling if someone was seduced or manipulated. What happens after coitus is said to reveal more about the relationship than the preceding sexual activity (Crain, 1978). Even in the best of circumstances, lovers can feel a sense of wistfulness, perhaps tinged with sadness.

## ENHANCING COITAL PLEASURE

Your body, mind, and your relationship are all important in coitus. It is not enough to be in love to enjoy sex fully, just as all the refinements of erotic technique will be of little avail in an unhappy relationship. All the aspects of sex need attention.

Let us look at the means of making intercourse more satisfying. The purpose of this section is to inform you and get you to think. For "how-to" instruction on sexual enhancement you can turn to specialized sex manuals (Box 12.4). You can read anecdotes about what men and women like about coitus in Hite (1976, 1981). Sexually explicit films and videos

# Box 12.4

## SEX MANUALS

People associate sex manuals with modern liberated times, but in fact, the origins of such books are ancient. They originally came from the East. Chinese handbooks of sex existed 2000 years ago and were widely studied until about the 13th century. These manuals instructed men how to conduct their relations with their women (Gulik, 1974; Chang, 1977). Other illustrated works known as *pillow books* gave specific instructions on coital techniques.

A similar literature in India was brought to the attention of the Western world by Sir Richard Burton and F. F. Arbuthnot, who founded the Kama Shastra Society in London in 1882 to publish translations of Hindu erotic works. Thus came to light the great Indian love manual, the *Kama Sutra,* written about the 3rd century A.D. by Vatsyayana (1966). The summation of existing wisdom on love and sex written in India, it remained the classic treatise in this field for 1000 years (Archer in Comfort, 1965).

Two other works from this same Hindu tradition are the *Koka Shastra,* composed in the 12th century (Comfort, 1965), and the *Ananga Ranga,* written in the 16th century by Kalyana Malla (1964). These books were not merely compilations of erotic techniques, but texts with a broader scope, which influenced art, literature, and popular culture.

Persian and Arabic erotic works of this genre, though not as ancient, are equally extensive. The classic Arabian treatise on physical love (another of Burton's finds) is the *Perfumed Garden,* written in the 16th century by Omar Ibn Muhammed al-Nefzawi (1964).

The West is virtually unique among the great cultures in lacking a tradition of this kind. It was only early in the 20th century that the *marriage manual* appeared on the scene. As exemplified by Van de Velde's *Ideal Marriage* (1965; first published in 1926), these books were written by physicians in the staid language of science, in contrast to the celebratory manner of the ancient love manuals, which were written by poets.

Van de Velde's book remained the standard manual for almost four decades. Though positive in tone and daring for its time, it did not survive the freewheeling 1960s, which saw the emergence of a new style of *sex manual*—explicit, unabashedly enthusiastic, and addressed to all women and men, married or not.

Of the recent sex manuals Alex Comfort's *Joy of Sex* (1972) and *More Joy* (1974) are most valuable. Comfort is a scientist and scholar; the authors of the more typical popular sex manuals have modest credentials. They reiterate commonplace and commonsense information and advice in a light-hearted and titillating style. When Van de Velde wrote of the "genital kiss," he cautioned his readers that from the sublime to the ridiculous is but a step. His modern counterparts are less troubled by such distinctions. For instance, the following "recipe" for fellatio is in *The Sensuous Woman* (which went through over ten printings in 1970).

*The Whipped Cream Wriggle*
If you have a sweet tooth, this is the one for you. Take some freshly whipped cream, to which you have added a dash of vanilla and a couple of teaspoons of powdered sugar and spread the concoction evenly on the penis so that the whole area is covered with a quarter-inch layer of cream. As a finishing touch, sprinkle on a little shredded coconut and/or chocolate. Then lap it all up with your tongue. He'll wriggle with delight and you'll have the fun of an extra dessert. If you have a weight problem, use one of the many artificial whipped creams now on the market (available in boxes, plastic containers, and aerosol cans) and forego the coconut and chocolate ("J," 1969).

These books must fulfill a need: they sell in the millions. Their informational content is meager. What they provide is reassurance and "permission" to act more freely. They also offer erotic titillation, which makes them a form of soft-core pornography. These modern sex manuals are also very much a part of the self-help literature, which tells us how to cook, diet, exercise, play, work, and get ahead in life.

for commercial use have some value, but films made especially for teaching and sex therapy are more useful. They are designed to remove sexual inhibitions and negative attitudes.[4] Finally, trial and error is probably the way most people learn about sex, for better or for worse.

You will not want to try everything you read about. Lovemaking, like eating, offers variety, but it is a matter of personal preference what you choose from the menu. In sex, too, there are gluttons and people with discriminating palates. Eventually, sex must fit in the larger context of our everyday lives. Relatively few of us have the energy, the need, or the means to stage a five-course dinner every night; nor can we mount a comparable production each time we engage in sex. On the other hand, far too many people settle for the sexual equivalent of fast food.

## Physical Factors

Appearance    How we look, sound, smell, and even taste are important to sexual appeal. These sensory modalities have obvious physiological bases (Chapter 3), although their erotic meanings are largely learned and culturally determined.

It is tempting to equate the prospect of sexual satisfaction with *sexiness,* but past the point of arousal the two do not necessarily go together. Nonetheless, there is enormous emphasis placed in our culture (and in many others) on enhancing sex appeal. A good deal of the effort to keep fit, dress up, groom the hair, use makeup, and so on is geared to this aim. Still, the ability to give and take sexual pleasure depends more on who you are and less on how you look.

*Nudity* is a key feature in sexual enhancement, though cultural and personal preferences vary. The degree of body exposure permitted in a culture is a good index of its sexual permissiveness. But nudity does not always enhance eroticism. On the contrary, artful concealment may provoke desire. Sexually permissive cultures go to great lengths to devise clothing and ornaments that make the body more erotically appealing.[5]

Men have been supposed to derive more pleasure from female nudity than vice versa. Even if that assumption were true, it would not apply to every woman. Both sexes tend to want coitus in the nude, to enjoy more skin contact and greater intimacy.

Hygiene also adds a lot to sexual pleasure. The trick here is to combine cleanliness with an earthy reveling in the messiness of sex; you must be prepared to take a fair amount of secretions, noises, and odors in stride. Rumbling sounds in the abdomen can be distracting; belching and passing gas are awkward; the noise made by expelling air sucked into the vagina may be mystifying. People can ignore these noises or laugh at them together. They need not be sources of embarrassment.

Exercise    One need not be an athlete or in brimming good health to enjoy coitus. Getting into good physical condition certainly helps (Lance and Agardy, 1981). In addition, there are books on *sexercise* aimed at strengthening and promoting flexibility in muscles that are purported to be of special significance to sexual activity (Kyon and Benyo, 1982). The classic masters of this art are the practitioners of certain forms of *yoga* (Douglas and Slinger, 1979).

Even more specific to sexual functions are exercises aimed at strengthening the *pubococcygeous muscle,* which makes the vaginal entrance tighter or looser. We shall discuss them in Chapter 15.

## Time and Place

Where and when people make love help determine how pleasurable it will be. The time of day, the level of fatigue, the temperature in the room, the sights, sounds, smells, even the hardness of the bed, affect the sexual experi-

[4]Major outlets for such films include Focus International (333 West 52nd Street, New York) and Multimedia Resource Center (1525 Franklin Street, San Francisco).

[5]For an illustrated historical overview of eroticism in dress, see Glynn (1982). Body ornamentation is discussed in Morris (1977).

ence. Such factors help set the romantic and erotic tone for the participants. People generally do best under circumstances that are restful, safe, and secure on the one hand and exciting, novel, and romantic on the other (a bit like sleeping in a warm bed while a cold wind is howling outside).

There is an almost universal human preference for privacy during coitus. This fact seems to be culturally determined, because animals do not seem to mind copulating in front of one another (although they are vulnerable to attack when so occupied). Coitus occurs in various cultures in or out of doors, depending on which affords more privacy. In our society, the bedroom is where sex usually takes place, but shifting to another room (especially the bathroom) may add novelty and excitement. More adventurous couples seek the great outdoors. (Secluded beaches are great if you can keep the sand out.) Cars are widely used for amorous purposes, and there has been an ongoing romance between sex and the automobile from its rumble-seat days (Lewis, 1980). Novelty, even danger, may endow a location with sexual excitement. New York helicopter police once arrested a teenage couple having coitus on top of a 500-foot tower of the Williamsburg Bridge over the East River (*San Francisco Chronicle*, June 30, 1981a, p. 2).

Bedrooms are usually furnished with some thought to creating a romantic and erotic atmosphere through colors and lighting. Soft lights convey a mellow mood and are kind to physical blemishes; candles are particularly effective as they cast their languorous rays on the intertwined limbs and flushed faces of lovers. Darkness may appeal to those who feel self-conscious; others prefer brighter lights.

There is no end to the refinements that can make the physical setting more erotic. Mirrors may be positioned strategically so that the partners can observe themselves (but rarely is a couple bold enough to fix a mirror on the ceiling, where its exclusively sexual function would be obvious). Such erotic devices work at least for some people some of the time. It is difficult to decide whether these sights, sounds, and smells really awaken the "sexual

animal" within us or are mainly cultural artifacts to whose acquired meanings we are conditioned to respond.

The preferred times for coitus in different cultures are determined by practical as well as psychological considerations. People are more arousable at different times of the day and under different circumstances. So couples need to accommodate each other's sexual "clocks" and erotic moods.

Most couples in our culture make love at night because it fits most conveniently with the routine of everyday life; the lassitude that follows orgasm nicely dovetails with sleep. It is unwise, though, always to relegate coitus to the last waking moments of the day, because stamina and alertness are essential for greatest pleasure. At least an occasional shift to the morning or the middle of the day may freshen up coital routines. Older men can take advantage of their early morning erections.

### Erotic Aids and Practices

Sexual arousal can be further enhanced by devices and practices that titillate the senses. To work, such erotic aids must be novel and exciting, but not so foreign or far out that they induce anxiety.

**Scents**    Pleasant scents are among the most popular erotic enhancers. Men use aftershave lotion, women use perfumes, to excite. Some couples use incense. A great deal of advertising for perfumes is banked on their erotic potential; yet there is no evidence that any scent, natural or artificial, automatically turns people on (see Box 4.4). People learn to associate certain smells with sexual arousal, such as the fragrance used by a lover.

**Sounds and Music**    The most effective erotic sounds are *words* which lovers use to express their feelings and communicate with each other (Chapter 16).

The enormous universal appeal of music is at least partly due to its erotic qualities. Shakespeare called music "the food of love" (*Twelfth Night*, act 1, scene 1). At its most obvious, the pulsating beat and suggestive lyrics of certain forms of rock music leave little to the imagination. More sentimental songs create a romantic mood. In one survey of a popular music station in Connecticut in 1977, about half of the songs pertained to romantic or erotic love (Tennov, 1979, p. 82). An analysis of the lyrics of popular songs in the 1950s revealed that 83 percent concerned love (Horton, 1957). Sex became a prominent theme in such songs later in the decade (Carey, 1979).

It is not only popular music that has erotic potential—virtually any form of classical music can exert a similar effect if it falls on the right ears, under the right circumstances. For some reason, Ravel's *Bolero* has developed a reputation as the ultimate musical turn-on. It has been cited so often in this regard that it probably works as a self-fulfilling prophecy. People can be conditioned, of course, to regard even a funerary dirge as erotic.

Clothing   Sexy female underwear is another widely used turn-on. Even panties and bras for everyday use are often designed with a hint of erotic appeal. Other items range from subtly suggestive bedroom apparel sold at exclusive stores to undergarments peddled through sex catalogs, fit for professional strippers. There is a much more limited market for the sale of such items for men.

Lotions   During recent years, the use of scented oils or lotions has become popular. Tactile stimulation can be greatly enhanced if surfaces are moist. Oils and lotions are often combined with erotic massage (Inkeles and Todris, 1972).

The use of vaginal lubricants and contraceptive jellies and foam was discussed earlier. The application of these substances can be artfully integrated into sexplay so that it enhances the tactile stimulation of the genitals.

Bathing   Combining sex with bathing is an ancient device. Several factors are beneficial: nudity, the relaxing effect of warm water, and the gentle mood induced by soaping and caressing each other. To actually engage in coitus while showering, taking a bath, or swimming may be hard, because erections are difficult to maintain in warm or cold water. Intromission can take place out of the water.

Motion   Motion can add another dimension to lovemaking. The most common form of erotic motion is *dancing*. While dancing may serve other functions as well, it's a powerful stimulant because of its romantic, physical, and rhythmic aspects.

Some people use specially constructed chairs, beds, and the like that vibrate. Waterbeds have a gentle rocking motion. The use of vibrators was discussed earlier.

Speeding trains with their rhythmic noises are much recommended, as are gently rolling ships and boats. Driving and sex cannot be safely combined. Transport animals like horses, camels, and elephants have all been used for the same purpose. Eastern erotic works even show couples balancing upside down on galloping ponies, which is a tribute to their lively imagination.

Aphrodisiacs   Finally, there is the ancient quest for aphrodisiacs (from Aphrodite, Greek goddess of love)—substances that are said to enhance libido, sexual performance, and pleasure. The popular use of aphrodisiacs is discussed in Box 12.5; drugs for sexual dysfunction are described in Chapter 15.

## Psychological Factors

Personality and the quality of a relationship are the most important determinants of sexual enjoyment. What sorts of people make the best lovers? There are no pat answers, but certain aspects of personality and styles of relating work best in sexual relations. Though we will use a heterosexual model, this discussion will apply to homosexual relationships too (Chapter 13).

The quality of sex and other aspects of a relationship do not always match: sexually accomplished lovers do not necessarily make the best friends or spouses (or vice versa). However, it is easier to learn techniques than to learn how to care.

# Box 12.5

## APHRODISIACS

The search for substances to enhance sexual desire and experience is as ancient as the search for the fountain of youth. Over 500 substances have been identified as sexual stimulants (Stark, 1982). None have been shown to be effective in carefully controlled scientific experiments.

Erotic potions are described in medical writings from ancient Egypt (c. 2000 B.C.). Among various societies since that time all the following and many more preparations have been recommended: pine nuts, the blood of bats mixed with donkey's milk, the root of the valerian plant, dried salamander, cyclamen, menstrual fluid, tulip bulbs, fat of camel's hump, parsnips, salted crocodile, pollen of date palm, the powdered tooth of a corpse, wings of bees, jasmine, turtles' eggs, ground crickets, spiders, ants, the genitals of hedgehogs, rhinoceros horn, the blood of executed criminals, artichokes, honey compounded with camel's milk, swallows' hearts, vineyard snails, certain bones of the toad, sulfurous waters, powdered stag's horn, and so on. (For historical overviews on aphrodisiacs, see Licht, 1969; Himes, 1970.)

Presently, people still refer to bananas and oysters, half-jokingly, as sexual enhancers. As with some of the items above, the association is probably due to their shapes. By a primitive logic, a banana is like an erect penis; so if a man eats it his penis will become erect. More typically today, alcohol and other drugs are supposed to be aphrodisiac. Some aphrodisiacs, like *Spanish fly* (derived from a beetle), irritate the urinary system, and cause vasocongestion in response to the irritation. Such substances have unpleasant side effects and are not safe.

*Alcohol* is a central nervous system depressant that actually has a dampening effect on sexual response or performance. In small amounts, it lifts inhibitions and prompts some people to be sexually more open and forward (sometimes to their regret). Alcohol is also touted as a tool for seduction ("Candy is dandy but liquor is quicker"), although it works better on those who are already inclined to be seduced. The use of alcohol can be problematic since it may lead to antisocial behaviors (Chapter 14) and sexual dysfunction (Chapter 15).

The influence of *marijuana*, like that of alcohol, is secondary. It is not a sexual stimulant, but it has an influence on mood. It alters the perception of the sexual experience, which some interpret subjectively as an enhancement of erotic pleasure. Psychedelic drugs, such as LSD, may have similar effects (Grof, 1975).

*Cocaine* and *amphetamines* are claimed by users to increase sexual desire. This effect may be part of the general euphoria they cause or the result of direct brain stimulation (Gay et al., 1975). But the use of drugs may be even more problematic than alcohol. Sexually, they cause dryness and inflammation of the vagina, anxiety, and exhaustion, all of which lessen enjoyment. Apart from their sexual effects, chronic use of these addictive substances ruins your life. *Heroin* depresses sexual desire. Drug addicts may be driven to prostitution to support their habit, not because they enjoy sex more under the influence of drugs.

*Amyl nitrite* causes rapid dilation of blood vessels; hence its use to relieve chest pains in coronary spasm (angina). It comes in vials that are popped open ("poppers") and inhaled. It is claimed that inhaling the substance just before orgasm prolongs and intensifies the experience. A common side effect is severe headache. The sharp drop in blood pressure can also kill you (Hollister, 1974).

The substance with the most promise as a true aphrodisiac is *yohimbine,* a substance derived from the bark of an African tree. It causes sexual arousal in male rats (Clark et al., 1984), and there is some evidence that it may also arouse humans. Its use along with steroid hormones will be discussed in Chapter 15.

---

**Gender Considerations**  Traditionally, sexual attractiveness has been strongly influenced by gender characteristics: the more "masculine" a man or the more "feminine" a woman, the sexier they have been thought to be. Stereotyping provides enough stability to such images to lend them public credibility. Movie stars embody these images in the mass culture. A good lover looks beyond stereotypes, at the whole unique other person.

Sex is also better when partners have an equal chance to take the initiative if they like. When lovemaking becomes a shared and reciprocal pleasure, then sex ceases to be something you do *to* someone and becomes something you do *with* someone.

Reciprocity    Sexual satisfaction has to go both ways. To seek your own sexual gratification at your lover's expense would be selfish; to provide pleasure at your own expense, unfair to yourself. This is not to say that at any given moment each partner must be getting the same share of gratification; attempts at such mindless parity ruin the experience for both. Sexually happy couples compensate for such discrepancies by extending to each other ample "credit." They will go out of their way to please the other, knowing that they will be "paid back" sooner or later. Such confidence eliminates the need for sexual bookkeeping, as the satisfaction of giving pleasure complements the gratification of receiving it.

Acceptance    Those who get high marks as lovers seem to share a number of traits. First and foremost is the ability to be yourself. Sex exposes us psychologically, as it does physically. There is, therefore, a strong temptation to cover up and to pretend to be what you are not. Pretending obtains some immediate gains but robs the experience of its authenticity, reducing it to play-acting.

It is similarly important to accept the other person. What is called for is not stark realism but placing the partner in the best possible light, within the bounds of honesty. Without deluding themselves or lying, partners can emphasize the positive aspects of one another. Lovemaking is not the appropriate occasion to criticize or reform.

Freedom from Anxiety    Anxiety is the enemy of sexual pleasure. If you can be yourself, half the battle is won. Attempts at pretence and

fear of discovery often cause anxiety. Freedom from anxiety also means freedom from guilt and shame. If you believe what you are doing is wrong or unworthy of yourself, you are not likely to get much joy out of it. Similarly, hidden motives like dominance and aggression generate fear and anxiety. Finally, you lose out if you anxiously watch over your own performance, trying to meet some preconceived notion of how you should feel and function.

It is good to have confidence in your *desirability* and *competence* as a lover—not to show off how expert you are, but to show faith in yourself. You do not have to come across as a cool operator. On the contrary, vulnerability is a most endearing quality. People respond both to qualities of a parent (strong, knowledgeable, and trustworthy) and of a child (helpless, innocent, and lovable). It is the ability to handle this paradox that characterizes good lovers.

Affection and Trust    Trust and commitment are basic requirements for a satisfactory sexual relationship. Love is a powerful erotic force, but for many people it is not a precondition to enjoying sex. A more realistic expectation is a level of mutual trust that matches the extent of sexual involvement. The same applies to honesty. You should tell your partner if you are married, if you have herpes—whatever is important to know under the circumstances.

There must be a sense of caring and sharing if intimacy is to develop. This sense of closeness, the coming together of your innermost self with that of another, is the core of a sexually gratifying experience. True intimacy requires the maturing of a relationship over time, but the passage of time alone will not do it. Some couples married for decades may be no more intimate than others who have spent an afternoon in bed together.

Communication    Intimacy and communication feed one another. Nothing could be more appropriate when making love than expressions of affection, and few measures are more effective in arousing a partner. The same is true for the less articulate means of conveying sexual arousal. The sighs and moans, the grunts and groans that we utter on these occasions are in their own way also songs of love.

Communications during lovemaking have their own cryptic style. At its most elementary level, you need to tell the partner what to do and what not to do. Such messages can be conveyed verbally or nonverbally. An especially effective technique is *hand-riding*—guiding the partner's hand to where you want it to be. You need not suffer in frustrated silence, unable or unwilling to speak your feelings and desires because of shyness, fear of ridicule, or hope that your partner will somehow read your mind.

It is not easy to talk about sex; it is even harder to talk during sex. Yet practical necessity as well as emotional need require that we learn to communicate with our sexual partners and make it easier for our partners to communicate with us. All of these considerations are part of the larger context of a good intimate relationship (Chapter 16).

Finally, in our preoccupation with affection and other serious sentiments, we should not neglect the light-heartedness and humor that infuse fun into sex. Wit takes the sting out of awkward situations; a sincere and joyful smile is hard to beat as a source of reassurance. Teasing, bawdy humor, and "dirty talk" also work as sexual stimulants for some. By allowing sex to become a form of adult play we can regain the carefree ability of our childhood to pretend and play-act without losing touch with reality or becoming deceitful. Such play-acting revitalizes sex by allowing our fantasies safe and partial fulfillment. Some people engage in "baby talk." Others pretend to be strangers, romantic characters, or even antagonists in coercive scenes. Whatever the scenario, both partners must find it pleasurable and comfortable; there is no justification for forcing such activity on an unwilling or uninterested partner. Like children's games, it ought to stop when it turns nasty.

All things considered, what contributes most to the enhancement of sexual pleasure is evidence of the partner's enjoyment. If your lover trembles and melts in your arms, you must be doing something right and that makes you feel sexually aroused too. It is such mutual enjoyment that catapults lovers to the heights of sexual ecstasy and makes sexual interaction among the most cherished human experiences, whose memory persists despite the erosion of time. In the twelfth century Héloïse wrote in a letter to her husband, Abélard, after years of enforced separation: "Truly the joys of love, which we experienced together, were so dear to my soul that I can never lose delight in them, nor can they vanish from the mirror of my remembrance. Wheresoe'er I turn they arise before me and old desires awake" (quoted in Van de Velde, 1965, p. 231).

## REVIEW QUESTIONS

1. What are the main techniques of sexual stimulation for couples?
2. Compare cunnilingus and fellatio with respect to prevalence and personal attitudes.
3. How do coital postures enhance sexual pleasure?
4. What other techniques enhance coital pleasure?
5. What are aphrodisiacs?

## THOUGHT QUESTIONS

1. How would you educate adolescents so that coitus does not become the "ultimate" aim of sexual interactions?
2. How would you deal with a sexual partner who dislikes oral sex?
3. Should couples negotiate ahead of time which coital postures they will use?
4. What do you look for in a lover?
5. Your lover urges you to get "high" before sex. What do you do, and why?

## SUGGESTED READINGS

Chang, J. (1977). *The Tao of love and sex.* New York: Dutton. The erotic wisdom of ancient China made accessible to modern readers. Though some of the principles sound strange to Western minds, they make fascinating reading.

Comfort, A. *The joy of sex* (1972) and *More joy* (1974). New York: Crown. The most sophisticated, sensible, and attractively illustrated of modern sex manuals.

Melville, R., *Erotic art of the West* (1973); Dawson, P., *Erotic art of the East* (1968); Dawson, P., *Primitive erotic art* (1973). New York: G. P. Putnam's Sons. Fascinating illustrations of sexual intercourse from a rich variety of cultures, with informative texts. Pictures that speak more eloquently than words.

Montagu, A. (1986). *Touching: The human significance of the skin,* 3rd ed. New York: Harper & Row. Fascinating anthropological and psychological insights into the role of touching in human interactions.

Perella, N. J. (1969). *The kiss sacred and profane: An interpretative history of kiss symbolism and related religious erotic themes.* Berkeley: University of California. The subtitle explains this scholarly book. The approach is literary and historical. Excellent reading for those with a serious interest in the subject.

Sinha, I. (1980). Translation of the *Kama sutra.* New York: Crescent. The classic Indian love manual, with extracts from the *Kaka Shastra, Ananga Ranga,* and other Hindu erotic works, and beautiful color plates of erotic art.

# Homosexuality and Bisexuality

CHAPTER

# 13

*Not all things are black nor all things white. . . . The living world is a continuum in each and every one of its aspects. The sooner we learn this concerning human sexual behavior the sooner we shall reach a sound understanding of all the realities of sex.*

ALFRED C. KINSEY

OUTLINE

THE CONCEPT OF
    HOMOSEXUALITY
The Problem of Definition
    What Criteria?
    A Rating Scale
The Problem of Identification
    Sexual Orientation and Gender
        Identity
    Elective and Obligatory
        Homosexuality
    Bisexuality
The Problem of Bias
    Effects of Homosexual Labeling
    Homophobia
HOMOSEXUAL BEHAVIOR
Prevalence
Sexual Practices
Active and Passive Roles
HOMOSEXUALITY AS A WAY OF
    LIFE
The Homosexual Subculture
Homosexual Relationships
    Covert Homosexuals
    Coming Out

Overt Homosexuals
Homosexual Parents
Meeting Places
    Making Contact
    Gay Bars
    Gay Baths
    Public Sites
THE DEVELOPMENT OF SEXUAL
    ORIENTATION
Biological Determinants
    Genetic Factors
    Hormonal Factors
    Brain Differences
Psychosocial Determinants
    Psychoanalytic Views
    Social Learning Approaches
    Gender Nonconformity
SOCIAL PERSPECTIVES ON
    HOMOSEXUALITY
Social Judgments
Medical Judgments
    Causes
    Treatment

Sexual attraction between members of the same sex is not an issue involving a few people here and there. It concerns millions of men and women. Homosexuals, like heterosexuals, are of all kinds: rich or poor, educated or ignorant, powerful or powerless, happy or unhappy. They are found among all nations, races, social classes, ethnic and religious groups; they live in every city and town across the nation. They are part and parcel of the fabric of society.

In this chapter, we look at three aspects of homosexuality: sexual, interpersonal, and developmental. We shall save some of the social aspects for later: the gay liberation movement will be discussed in Chapter 21, the legal issues in Chapter 22, and moral concerns in Chapter 23.

Even where we focus on heterosexuals, a good deal of this text applies as well to homosexuals. Chapters 16 through 19, for example, have to do with *all* relationships.

A word of caution: the AIDS epidemic among the gay male population has exerted a profound influence on sexual behavior. The effects of these changes have not yet found their way into much of the professional literature; all of the major behavioral studies cited in this chapter are pre-AIDS. Some of their findings may no longer fit the realities of today or the foreseeable future.

## THE CONCEPT OF HOMOSEXUALITY

Homosexuality can be simply defined as sexual attraction and activity between members of the same sex (Chapter 8). Neither this definition nor any other is entirely satisfactory, as you will see.

### The Problem of Definition

The prefix *homo* in "homosexual" is derived from the Greek for "the same" and should not be confused with the Latin *homo*, which means "man." To be "homosexual" means being attracted to someone of the same sex, not having sex with a man. The term "homosexuality" was first used by an obscure Hungarian doctor, Ka-

roly Benkert, in 1869 (Gregersen, 1983). It became popularized in Germany by Magnus Hirschfeld and in the English-speaking world by Havelock Ellis (Ellis, 1942).

Although sexual encounters between same-sex partners have been recorded throughout history, the concept of homosexuality is more recent. When sexual acts between men, such as anal intercourse, were condemned in the past, there was no implication that people who engaged in them were fundamentally different from heterosexuals; the focus was on the act, not the person. As the study of personality development and sexual behavior became better established in the 19th century, homosexuality came to be seen as a distinct psychological entity, and the search began for its causes and treatment (Boswell, 1980). Our legal system actually never adopted this viewpoint; it continued to forbid certain same-sexed behaviors, but not homosexual attraction itself (Chapter 22).

Sexual acts between homosexuals used to be called *sodomy* and *buggery*, which originally referred to anal intercourse. In the 19th century, *sexual inversion* was the common term in medicine and sexology until it was superseded by homosexuality in the 1930s.

Though neutral in meaning, this term became derogatory in common usage. In reaction, homosexuals now prefer to be called *gay*; heterosexuals are referred to as *straight*. Although this usage of "gay" goes back to the 13th century, it is only recently that the term has become popularized. It has now replaced most other colloquial terms, though some continue to be used as insults.[1] However, "gay" has not yet been taken up by the clinical and scholarly literature; hence, the terms *male homosexual* and *female homosexual* (or *lesbian*, derived from the Greek island of Lesbos, home of the female poet Sappho) continue to be used in formal discussions. *Homophile* is the formal term preferred by some gay organizations.

---

[1]Common colloquial expressions include *queer, fag, faggot, fruit, nellie, homo, cocksucker, pansy, queen* for males, and *dyke, lez, lessie,* and *femme* for females (Haeberle, 1978). For a longer list see Rodgers (1972).

What Criteria?  There is no specific homosexual act; fellatio, anal intercourse, or anything else that homosexuals do are also done by heterosexuals. The reverse is also true, except for vaginal intercourse. It is not the nature of a sexual act but the sex of the partners that defines the behavior as homosexual.

What, then, is a homosexual person? If it is someone who engages in homosexual acts, how many such acts are necessary to cross the line—1, 10, 100? Suppose a man or woman is strongly sexually attracted towards members of the same sex but never acts on these wishes: do we nonetheless call that person homosexual? Finally, suppose someone is both attracted to and engages in sexual behavior with same-sexed persons but does not think of himself or herself as being homosexual, in other words, does not have a *homosexual identity*: is that person homosexual? In short, what is it that marks a person as homosexual: behavior, orientation, identity, or all three?

It is common to think of homosexuality as a single entity—a cluster of behavioral and personality characteristics. However, studies of gay men and women show tremendous diversity in how they look, think, feel, and behave sexually or otherwise. There is no one description that characterizes their sexual lives, let alone the rest of it. For this reason the plural term *homosexualities* is sometimes used for this cluster of sexual behaviors (Bell and Weinberg, 1978).

A Rating Scale  When discussing gender, we noted that people tend to see masculinity and femininity as mutually exclusive (Chapter 10). Sexual orientation has been traditionally viewed the same way. Homosexuality and heterosexuality are seen as the opposite poles of a single personality trait. A person is either one or the other; the less of one, the more of the other.

Actually, not all homosexuals are exclusively oriented to members of the same sex; the majority have varying degrees of heterosexual interest and experience. Most of the people with homosexual inclinations are in effect *bisexual* or *ambisexual* (Latin *ambo*, "both";

colloquial names are "AC/DC" and "switch hitter"). Homosexual and heterosexual interests overlap in large numbers of people, if not in behavior, then in fantasies. Just as homosexual thoughts occur to many heterosexuals, 24 percent of homosexual males and 35 percent of lesbians have heterosexual fantasies, and 34 percent of male homosexuals and 54 percent of lesbians have heterosexual dreams (Bell and Weinberg, 1978).

To represent these gradations, Kinsey devised a seven-point heterosexual-homosexual scale (from 0 to 6) based on a person's sexual feelings and experiences (Figure 13.1). Those in category 6 are exclusively homosexual; those in 0 are exclusively heterosexual. Those with equal homosexual and heterosexual activity are in group 3, whereas those in 1 and 5 have predominantly heterosexual or homosexual behaviors, with only incidental experience in the other direction. Categories 2 and 4 include those in whom a clear preference for one sex coexists with a lesser but still active interest in the other.

The Kinsey rating scale depends not only on homosexual behavior but psychological attraction as well. Moreover, this rating scale does not indicate the absolute amount of sexual activity, only the *ratio* between the two sexual orientations. A man with 100 homosexual and 50 heterosexual experiences (2:1) would be placed farther from the homosexual

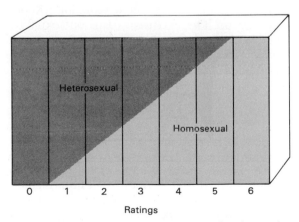

Figure 13.1  Heterosexual-homosexual rating scale.

end of the scale than a man with 20 homosexual and 5 heterosexual experiences (4:1), although the former would have had 5 times as many homosexual experiences as the latter.

People are not evenly distributed across the scale. The figures given by Kinsey vary by age, sex, marital status, and other factors. For example, among the unmarried subjects aged 20 to 35, 3 to 16 percent of males and 1 to 3 percent of females are exclusively homosexual (category 6); 18 to 42 percent of males and 11 to 20 percent of females have had at least some homosexual experience (ranging from category 1 to 6). Exclusively heterosexuals (category 0) account for 53 to 78 percent of males and 61 to 72 percent of females; among married subjects about 90 percent of either sex is exclusively heterosexual (Kinsey et al., 1953). In most intermediate categories the proportion of female homosexuals to male is about one to three.

Kinsey's motivation in devising this scale was to get away from labeling people as homosexual or heterosexual. Instead he focused on their behaviors, which are easier to define. Still, Kinsey's scale has been criticized as promising more than it delivers. What is the real difference between saying that a woman engages only in heterosexual behavior and calling her heterosexual or placing a man in category 6 and calling him homosexual? It is argued that Kinsey's scheme is more cosmetic than substantive and hence adds little to our understanding of sexual orientation (Robinson, 1976). The exclusive focus on sexual behavior also fails to address the crucial issue of sexual identity: what people think of themselves is not only defined by how they behave.

## The Problem of Identification

Can you tell from looks and mannerisms if a person is homosexual? Are homosexual men effeminate and lesbians mannish? Do they dress and act in distinctive ways? There is no single pattern that applies to all homosexuals. Generally speaking, you cannot tell homosexuals from heterosexuals in most settings, such as a college campus (Figure 13.2). However,

Figure 13.2    Gay friends.

some gay men and lesbians do dress and act in ways that signal their homosexual orientation.

Sexual Orientation and Gender Identity    Homosexuality is not a gender disorder, but there appears to be a strong link between gender nonconformity and the development of homosexuality. In other words, adult gay men and women generally think of themselves as male and female, but they may not behave according to culturally defined gender stereotypes; and as children, some of them wished they belonged to the opposite sex.

Just as homosexuals are not transsexuals (Chapter 10) they should not be confused with transvestites or cross-dressers (Chapter 14). Some homosexuals (usually men) like to dress up in the clothes of the opposite sex, but the majority of cross-dressers are heterosexual.

About half of homosexual men and three-quarters of heterosexual men are typically "masculine" in their identity, interests, and appearance; half of homosexual men (and one-quarter of heterosexual men) do not conform to this image. Likewise, one-fifth of lesbians but one-third of heterosexual women are typically "feminine" (Bell et al., 1981). Therefore, gender nonconformity suggests but does not prove sexual orientation.

Gender nonconformity among homosexuals can take exaggerated form in the well-known homosexual stereotypes: the limp-wristed, lisping, bejewelled, and perfumed male *queen* with the mincing gait; the mannish, swaggering, tough-talking female *dyke* (or *butch*); the passive and meek *femme* (or *nelly*); and so on. These characteristics apply to only part of the gay population. Homosexuals may also choose to reveal themselves through distinctive forms of dress, ornamentation, speech, and behavior. Often, though, they are only following the fashion or trying to signal other gays.

One of the outcomes of homosexual stereotyping is the pervasive view that gay men and women are somehow not fully male or female—just as people who have no children are sometimes seen as not fully adult. Underneath both attitudes is the idea that only reproduction counts as the full measure of adult sexuality.

Elective and Obligatory Homosexuality    Another problem in identifying homosexuals is that they do not all have the same degree of choice. Those who prefer homosexual relationships even though they have ample heterosexual opportunities are sometimes called *obligatory* homosexuals. They are free to choose, but they feel a compelling natural inclination to be homosexual. By contrast, other homosexual behaviors are *elective* (or *facultative*), resorted to only under certain circumstances, as substitutes, when heterosexual outlets are unavailable. Prisons, single-sex boarding schools, and other situations that segregate the sexes prompt some people to seek homosexual contact even when they would prefer an opposite-sexed partner. Under some of these conditions, homosexual behavior reflects social dominance. Just as in certain cultures a man of high status may be expected to have a mistress, his counterpart in prison acquires a "girl" (a relatively powerless and sometimes effeminate younger inmate). Some people may also engage in occasional homosexual activities out of curiosity, social defiance, or ideological solidarity.

Bisexuality    Individuals who are attracted to both sexes are even harder to define. They have received far less attention than exclusive homosexuals or heterosexuals (Coleman, 1987). Bisexuals belong to the categories 1 to 5 in the Kinsey scale. But except for those in the middle (3), they tend to be clustered with the more dominant orientation (Kinsey et al., 1953). Either by desire or because of societal expectations, the majority of the gay population ends up having had at least some heterosexual experience. In the Bell and Weinberg (1978) sample, 93 percent of predominantly gay men and women had engaged in coitus at least once.

Researchers find bisexuals more difficult to study, because the features of both orientations are intermingled (Klein, 1978; Wolff, 1979). In one sense, bisexuals may have the best of both worlds; yet they suffer the uncertainties of being neither fully here nor there.

## The Problem of Bias

The condemnation of homosexuality through most of the history of Western culture has led observers to misperceive or deliberately falsify it. Even in ostensibly objective scientific and scholarly debates, the detractors of and apologists for homosexuality have not been above skewing the facts to their purposes.

Effects of Homosexual Labeling    The label of homosexuality has been socially stigmatizing until fairly recently. Because society has for so long regarded such persons as deviants, there has been a tendency for homosexuals to think of themselves as different, marginal, or abnormal. Beyond that, just defining someone on the basis of sexual orientation alone tends to overemphasize the sexual component in that person's character and distorts our perception of who that person really is. If you get to know someone well and then find out that he or she is gay, your impressions of that person may be quite different than if you knew that the person was gay at the outset of your relationship.

Another outcome of the excessive focus on the sexual element in homosexuals is the

# Box 13.1

## SAME-SEX ENCOUNTERS AMONG ANIMALS

Genital exploration and mounting can be observed between same-sexed animals in many mammalian species, but they are often more social then sexual. For instance, mounting serves to define dominance among nonhuman primates. In Japanese macaques, male-male mounting is also part of friendly play and a way of reaffirming social bonds when the group is under stress (Ford and Beach, 1951; Denniston, 1980).

More direct forms of sexual interactions between same-sexed animals have been observed among some monkeys in captivity (Chevalier-Skolnikoff, 1974) that appear to be clearly erotic (see the figure). These interactions usually involve animals that are friendly to each other. It is not clear whether such behavior is a response to captive conditions or is normal (Lancaster, 1979).

Females have also been observed mounting females, but there are no signs of sexual excitement (though such signs would be harder to detect than an erection). Body contact is minimal, and the act is quickly over (Ford and Beach, 1951).

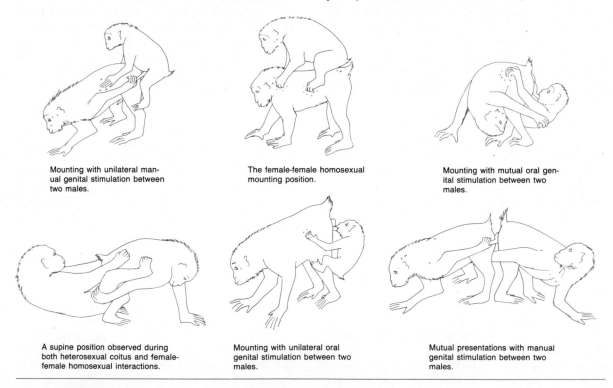

Mounting with unilateral manual genital stimulation between two males.

The female-female homosexual mounting position.

Mounting with mutual oral genital stimulation between two males.

A supine position observed during both heterosexual coitus and female-female homosexual interactions.

Mounting with unilateral oral genital stimulation between two males.

Mutual presentations with manual genital stimulation between two males.

perception that they are "hypersexual," or driven by uncontrollable sexual impulses. In fact, homosexuals are not any more sexually active than their heterosexual counterparts. On the average, homosexual men have sex about two or three times a week; lesbians about one or two times a week (Bell and Weinberg, 1978). There is, of course, considerable variation within the homosexual population (as there is among heterosexuals): 13 percent of men and 21 percent of women have sex once a month or less; about 20 percent of men and women once a week; 17 percent of men and 13 percent of women more than four times a week. Other studies report somewhat higher or lower rates (Westwood, 1960; Saghir and Robins, 1973; Weinberg and Williams, 1974). The impression of hypersexuality may also come from the fact that *some* male homosexuals lead highly prolific sexual lives with numerous sexual partners (much less likely at present because of AIDS).

Many of the old prejudices have given way to greater acceptance of the *new homosexual,* whose homosexual identity is perceived as positive (Altman, 1982). Still, biases persist in various forms.

Homophobia    Irrational fears that have no realistic basis are called *phobias* (the term has more specific meaning to clinicians). Persons with a deep irrational fear of homosexuality could rightly be called *homophobic* (Morin, 1981). Commonly, the term is now also applied to people with irrational, fixed, and intense dislike of homosexual persons and practices. The concept of homophobia (Weinberg, 1973) is important in order to understand the fear and loathing that some people have in response to homosexual feelings both in others and in themselves. It is also a useful device to combat prejudice against homosexuals. But it is not accurate or fair to apply the term indiscriminately to characterize everyone who, for whatever reason, finds one or another aspect of homosexual behavior objectionable.

In some cases, homophobia may reflect a psychological defense mechanism. Long before this concept became popular, Freud described the *neurotic* fear and rejection of homosexuality as an unconscious attempt to repress one's own unacceptable homosexual wishes. Because homosexual affection is not tolerated in our culture, especially for males, a man cannot admit to himself that he loves another man, in a sexual sense. Therefore, he unconsciously changes it to the conviction that he hates men who love other men.

## HOMOSEXUAL BEHAVIOR

It may come as a surprise that some animals engage in sexual activities with members of their own sex (Box 13.1). Similarly, homosexual relationships have been reported from a wide variety of cultures (Box 13.2).

### Prevalence

We do not know with any accuracy how prevalent homosexual behavior is in the general population in our, or any other, society. When the Kinsey statistics first appeared, they seemed astonishingly high: among males, 37 percent had at least one homosexual experience leading to orgasm following puberty; 10 percent had significant levels of such experience over at least three years; 4–6 percent led primarily or exclusively homosexual lives (Kinsey et al., 1948). The corresponding female figures were half to one-third as high, with 13 percent of women having had at least one such experience (Kinsey et al., 1953).

However, the Kinsey study subjects were not randomly chosen. They may not be representative of the general population. There are also problems with the way cases were counted. Do we tally a single episode of mutual masturbation by two young men the same way as a persistent pattern of same-sex activity throughout adulthood? Half of all homosexual experiences reported to Kinsey were single sexual acts in adolescence and young adulthood. However, even by conservative estimates, several million adults in the United States are exclusively homosexual. If persons with bisexual orientations were to be included, these numbers would be much larger.

### Sexual Practices

Homosexuals engage in all of the sexual activities that heterosexuals do, except for vaginal intercourse. Therefore, everything we described about heterosexual relations applies here, other than coitus. Gay men and women kiss, touch, caress, hug, and engage in breast stimulation, genital stimulation, and oral sex, just like heterosexuals do, except that they do it with members of their own sex (Figure 13.3). They may also engage in oral and anal intercourse (Figure 13.4) or attain orgasm through friction against each other's bodies.

# Box 13.2

## HOMOSEXUALITY IN OTHER CULTURES

In their cross-cultural survey, Ford and Beach found data on homosexuality (mostly male) from 76 societies. In one form or another, homosexuality was permissible in 64 percent of them. In the other 36 percent, which did not condone homosexual activity (some punished it severely), homosexual activity went on in secret (Ford and Beach, 1951). In a more recent review of anthropological reports on 294 societies, Gregersen (1983) found clearcut judgments on homosexuality only in 59 cases. Of these cultures, 31 percent condemned it; 69 percent approved it. Range of male homosexual activity varied from almost entirely lacking to virtually total participation. Little is known about female homosexuality cross-culturally.

Homosexual behavior is never the dominant form of sexual activity in any culure. Even groups like the Siwan (who live in the Libyan desert) and the people of the East Bay (several coastal villages in Melanesia), who permit homosexual activity, do not sanction exclusive homosexuality.

In many societies where access to women is rigidly controlled, homosexuality is tacitly accepted as a substitute to coitus. There is no dishonor attached to such activity as long as one takes the "active" role, such as being the inserter in anal intercourse. Effeminate males in these cultures are under some pressure to submit (Carrier, 1980).

A number of societies that have institutionalized male transvestism also permit homosexual activity by these individuals (but the two should not be equated in all cases). They included native American societies in North and South America and island societies in Polynesia. In these contexts, some men (called *Berdache*) put on female dress and took on female functions, including sex with their "husbands"; Devereux's (1937) Mohave informants reported both oral and anal intercourse.

Some societies in the highlands of New Guinea incorporate homosexual acts in their initiation ceremonies. Typically, there is a transfer of semen, anally or orally, from an adult to a teenage boy to ensure proper growth and masculinity. Gilbert Herdt (1981, 1987) has done an extensive study of these practices among the Sambia. These people believe that boys have to swallow semen to develop into men. In secret rituals, the boys are taught the mechanics of fellatio through the use of flutes. The boys then perform fellatio on young men. However, once the Sambia male marries, homosexual practices cease with marital cohabitation and fatherhood (Herdt, 1981).

Little is known about lesbian sexuality in preliterate societies, in part because anthropologists have had limited access to the private lives of women. It is also possible that female homosexuality is, in fact, less common. Lesbian practices were reported in 17 of the 76 societies analyzed by Ford and Beach, but details were limited.

Cross-cultural comparisons of homosexuality usually dwell on their diversity. A recent comparative study of homosexual communities in the United States, Guatemala, Brazil, and the Philippines offers six tentative conclusions: (1) homosexual persons appear in all societies; (2) the percentage of homosexuals in all societies seems to be about the same and remains stable over time; (3) social norms do not change the emergence of homosexual orientation; (4) homosexual subcultures appear in all societies, given enough people; (5) homosexuals in different societies tend to resemble each other in certain behavioral interests and occupational choices; and (6) all societies produce similar continua from overtly masculine to overtly feminine homosexuals (Whitman, 1983).

Not all gay men and women engage in all these activities, any more than heterosexuals do. For instance, some gays object to anal or oral sex on aesthetic, health, or other grounds. The threat of AIDS has made a major impact on the prevalence of unprotected anal and oral intercourse.

The differences in the prevalence of sexual practices between heterosexual and homosexual couples are not that striking. For

Figure 13.3 Gustave Courbet, *Sleep*, 1867 (Petit Palais, Paris. Photo Bulloz).

Figure 13.4 Erotic scenes depicted on a red-figure cup by Nikosthenes. Early 5th century B.C.

instance, 5 percent of heterosexual couples engage in fellatio as against 17 percent of gay men, every time they engage in sex; similarly, 6 percent of heterosexuals use cunnilingus as against 12 percent of lesbians, every time they engage in sex (Blumstein and Schwartz, 1983).

Sexual encounters between gay men and especially gay women tend to be more protracted, with alternating sequences of sexual stimulation, "teasing" withdrawal, and further stimulation (Masters and Johnson, 1979). Same-sexed persons are generally more effective in sexually stimulating their partners; being of the same sex they know from their own body what is likely to be pleasurable rather than dealing with the more mysterious body of a member of the opposite sex. There are sex manuals specifically for sexual encounters among gay men (Silverstein, 1978) and women (Sisley and Harris, 1977).

The danger of AIDS has had a major impact on the pattern of homosexual practices. In one study, sexual activity among gay men was reported to have declined by 78 percent since there has been a greater public awareness of AIDS; exchange of body fluids had declined 70 percent (Martin, 1987). Despite the greater emphasis on safe sex (Chapter 5), AIDS remains a source of serious concern for gay men and their partners (Valdisserri, 1986).

### Active and Passive Roles

In traditional heterosexual relationships, the man has usually taken the active role: it is he who stimulates and then penetrates the female partner. Based on this model (which is changing) and on the assumption that homosexuals imitate heterosexuals, it is often thought that gay couples take on similar active and passive sexual roles. In actual practice, many homosexuals do not sort themselves out along such lines. Preferences are more personal and shared. Gay partners typically take turns, or simultaneously stimulate each other.

Earlier perceptions of the active male partner as more masculine and the passive partner as more feminine are also no longer generally tenable (McWhirter and Mattison, 1984). Lesbian women have become even more egalitarian in their relationships under the influence of the women's movement.

This does not mean that some gay men and women do not cultivate active-passive, masculine-feminine identities and sex roles. Some men believe that they are not even engaging in homosexual behavior unless they take the receptive part in anal intercourse. Especially in cases of power-based homosexual encounters, such as in prison, the dominant male who penetrates other men may be convinced that he is not engaging in a homosexual act, and he will resist the prospect of submitting to anal penetration.

## HOMOSEXUALITY AS A WAY OF LIFE

Over the past several decades professional and public opinion has shifted away from judgments of homosexuality as an illness in favor of homosexuality as a way of life. Large numbers of gay men and women, especially those who are part of the *homosexual subculture*, currently view their sexual orientation as part of an alternative lifestyle.

### The Homosexual Subculture

A *subculture* is a subgroup of society based on some common feature, such as ethnicity, that provides a separate identity and values. When applied to an age group, like the "youth subculture," the concept tends to become diffuse; a group like homosexuals is even more diverse.

Nonetheless, the concept of a *gay subculture* is useful to delineate the common world and lifestyle of an important segment of the gay population. However, simply being homosexual does not amount to membership in the gay subculture. To be a part of it, the person must participate in some active, visible way.

Until the *gay liberation movement* (Chapter 21) in the 1960s, homosexuals in the United States were connected through underground networks and furtive associations. When such a group came to light, it often led to scandal. Most major cities in the United States now have sizable gay communities with distinctive lifestyles. Nonetheless, the majority of gays continue to blend with the general population.

The primary reason for the existence of the gay subculture is the opportunity it provides for sexual interaction, friendships, support networks, political action, recreation, commerce, and all else that constitutes the fabric of urban life (White, 1981).

An important aspect of a gay community that sets it apart from other subcultural enclaves is that those who live there do so by choice; it is not like a ghetto where people are stuck. For this reason, gay communities have a wide representation of socioeconomic levels, but they are almost entirely male.

A striking example of a gay community is in San Francisco, where 40 percent of the single men in the city (close to 70,000 men) are reportedly gay. Most of them are well educated (57 percent are college graduates), they earn on the average over $20,000 a year, and half are in professional and managerial positions (*New York Times*, Nov. 23, 1984b). All but 3 percent say they are completely or mostly open about their homosexuality. The leadership of this group is well represented in the city's power structure and government (Shilts, 1987).

Lesbians do not congregate as much in similar communities; but in a city like San Francisco, prominent gay women share leadership roles with gay men. Unlike males, they attract little attention living as couples within ordinary residential areas (and not all women who live together are lesbians). They also tend to lead more private lives and to depend less on public meeting places.

## Homosexual Relationships

There is no single "homosexual lifestyle" or a standard way in which homosexuals interact with one another. Like heterosexuals, homosexuals' lives are shaped by a host of economic and social factors as well as their sexual orientation. Some homosexual styles are highly visible, but what is most flamboyant must not be equated with what is typical. In addition to general influences like social class, two factors, more than any other, determine the relationships and lifestyles of homosexuals: one is

whether their homosexuality is overt or covert; the other is whether they are male or female.

Covert Homosexuals    *Covert* or *closet* homosexuals are found in all sectors of our society, where they usually pass for heterosexuals in their business and social relationships. They are often married, with or without children, and in most other respects remain indistinguishable from the rest of the population. They may lead double lives, simultaneously engaging in marital (or other heterosexual) and homosexual relations; they restrict their homosexual behavior to periods when they are away from home, suppress their homosexual desires most of the time, or indulge in them at the risk of discovery. A physician in his late fifties, for instance, went to a public toilet every day, save Wednesdays, for fellatio (Humphreys, 1970). Covert homosexuals are resented by their fellow homosexuals and given derogatory names like "canned fruit" or "crushed fruit" (because they are "crushed" by society's mores and afraid to come out) (Rodgers, 1972).

We know relatively little about the nature of the relationships of covert homosexuality, because these persons are hard to identify and resist revealing the details of their lives for understandable reasons. Because we do not know how many covert homosexuals there are, we cannot tell what proportion of the population is gay. Because they keep their sexual lives largely hidden, the public image of homosexual behavior becomes dominated by the activities of overt homosexuals.

Coming Out    When covert homosexuals admit their sexual orientation to outsiders, they are said to have *come out of the closet*. Some cross this line early in life, others late; some do it voluntarily, others are coerced. Whatever the circumstances, it is rarely easy.

Those who come out when still young must often confront the surprise, dismay, and anger of parents. There is often a sense of failure on the part of parents, who search the past for what they did wrong. Even though their gay sons or daughters may seem perfectly content, some parents worry about their leading lonely lives and regret foregoing the pleasure of becoming grandparents. Other parents face this prospect with equanimity and throw their love and support behind their children.

Those who come out later in life have the task of confronting their own spouses and children as well as business associates and friends. The outcomes vary from the break-up of families to a readjustment of relationships; what happens in the workplace often depends on the type of job the person holds.

Coming out does not mean total revelation. A 1982 marketing survey of urban gay males showed that of those who considered themselves "publicly out," only one in five had informed business associates and an equal proportion still hid the truth from their families (*Newsweek*, Aug. 8, 1983, p. 34).

Overt Homosexuals    Overt homosexuals are a far more accessible group. They have given up all pretense and openly rely on the homosexual community for sexual gratification and social support.

In Bell and Weinberg's (1978) study, 71 percent of overt homosexuals could be placed in five general patterns of personal relationships; the remaining 29 percent were too diverse to be categorized. These types of relationships, which we describe below, are not exclusive to homosexuals; they may characterize heterosexual couples as well, although the proportions of people in each and other details may be different.

About 28 percent of lesbians and 10 percent of male homosexuals lived as *close couples,* similar to married heterosexuals. One-third of these lesbian couples had been living together for four or more years, as had 38 percent of these men. The close-couple homosexuals rarely looked for new sexual contacts in gay bars and other public places. They had the fewest sexual, social, or psychological conflicts. They were happy with their partners and enjoyed spending their leisure time at home in warm and caring relationships. In a separate study, close to one-third of male couples had been together for 10 years or longer, up to 30 years. Although most gay couples expected mutual emotional dependability, sexual exclusivity was not necessarily required (McWhirter and Mattison, 1984).

About 17 percent of lesbians and 18 percent of male homosexuals lived as *open couples.* These people were less happy with their partners, less deeply committed to them, and more likely to look for social and sexual gratification outside their relationship. They looked for casual partners ("cruising") more often, and on the whole, they were less happy, less self-accepting, and more lonely than the close-couple homosexuals. Lesbians found the open-couple pattern more unacceptable than male homosexuals did.

Homosexuals who were well adjusted, had few if any sexual problems, did not regularly live with a partner, and followed a "swinging singles" lifestyle were designated as *functionals.* Some 15 percent of the homosexual males and 10 percent of the lesbians were in this group. These people had a high level of sexual activity. They thought of themselves as sexually attractive and were much more interested in having multiple partners than in finding someone with whom to establish a close relationship. Much of their lives centered around sexual activities. They were highly involved in the gay community and cruised a great deal. They had the fewest regrets about being homosexual and were energetic, friendly, and self-reliant; their overall social and psychological adjustment was second only to the close-couple homosexuals.

Homosexuals who had many partners, were not living as couples, and had psychological and sexual problems were designated as *dysfunctionals.* About 12 percent of male homosexuals and 5 percent of lesbians were in this group. These people were prone to worry, found little gratification in life, and showed a poorer overall adjustment than the previous three types. They were most likely to regret being homosexual and worried about their sexual inadequacies, their inability to form an affectionate relationship, and their lack of fulfillment. They came closest to fitting the stereotype of the emotionally disturbed homosexual.

Some homosexuals were found to have a low level of sexual activity, few partners, and no close relationships. These people, designated as *asexuals*, were characterized by their general lack of involvement with others. Some 16 percent of male homosexuals and 11 percent of lesbians followed this solitary lifestyle. They tended to be older than the people in the other categories. Although they described themselves as lonely, their general psychological adjustment was about the same as the homosexual population taken as a whole.

The typical, or perhaps stereotypical, behavior of the overt male homosexual shows a far greater preoccupation with sex than the behavior of lesbians. In Bell and Weinberg's sample, 57 percent of lesbians had had fewer than 10 partners in their lives, whereas 57 percent of the male homosexuals had had more than 250 partners; 45 percent of lesbians were currently living as couples, compared with 28 percent of the male homosexuals; 74 percent of the men said that more than half of their partners were strangers, in contrast to 6 percent for lesbians. Seventy percent of males reported having sex once a week or more, against only 54 percent of females; only 3 percent of lesbians cruised once a week or more for partners, as against 42 percent of males. The tendency of gay men to have a larger number of casual partners has now been lessened considerably in view of AIDS.

In their search for sexual partners, gay men tend to focus more on physical attractiveness and youth than do gay women. The emphasis on youth for sexual contact makes life harder for aging homosexuals. However, though more likely to be living alone and with fewer sexual involvements, older gays do not seem to be psychologically worse off (Weinberg and Williams, 1974). The young are more genitally focused in their sexual interactions than the old.

Homosexual males (like their heterosexual counterparts) are more interested than women in sexual variety, including variant forms of sexual activity (Chapter 14). The interaction of male with male also enhances the potential for violence. Rapes and sadomaso-

chistic practices are much more common in male than female homosexual encounters, just as sexual coercion is mainly carried out by male heterosexuals. Thus, in sexual interactions, *gender overrides sexual orientation*—lesbians behave more like heterosexual women than like homosexual men; and homosexual men act more like heterosexual men than like lesbians (Elise, 1986).

Studies on homosexuality dwell on issues such as sexual behavior, interpersonal relationships, and the gay subculture but say relatively little about homosexual love (Silverstein, 1981). The joys and sorrows of such love, as evident in the lives of gay men and women and in their literature (Box 13.3), are indistinguishable from their heterosexual counterparts (Figures 13.5 and 13.6).

Homosexual Parents    A substantial number of homosexual men and women have children. Strictly speaking, the fact of having a child would label one a bisexual—it would indicate that the person has engaged in coitus at least once. (Of course, lesbians may be artificially inseminated.) Many such persons are in fact bisexual, but there are others whose heterosexual involvements are reluctant. For instance, some gay men use marriage as a cover, and many lesbians have married to meet conventional social expectations and gain economic security.

Though exclusive homosexuals usually forego biological parenthood, being homosexual is not inconsistent with the wish or the competence to be a parent. Gay men and women do not disown their children; on the contrary, in custody cases they fight to keep, or at least keep in touch with, their children. Gay couples who try to adopt children or nurture foster children have to overcome serious social obstacles. Though some people harbor doubts about their fitness to bring up children, so far as lesbians are concerned, research data on children's intelligence, sexual identity, gender role preferences, family and peer group relationships, and adjustment to a single-parent family show no significant differences for boys and few significant differences for girls be-

# Box 13.3

## TWO POEMS BY C. P. CAVAFY*

### DECEMBER, 1903

And if I can't speak about my love—
if I don't talk about your hair, your lips, your eyes,
still your face that I keep within my heart,
the sound of your voice that I keep within my mind,
the days of September rising in my dreams,
give shape and color to my words, my sentences,
whatever theme I touch, whatever thought I utter.

### ON THE STAIRS

As I was going down those ill-famed stairs
you were coming in the door, and for a second
I saw your unfamiliar face and you saw mine.
Then I hid so you wouldn't see me again,
you hurried past me, hiding your face,
and slipped inside the ill-famed house

where you couldn't have found pleasure any more
    than I did.
And yet the love you were looking for, I had to give
    you;
the love I was looking for—so your tired, knowing
    eyes implied—
you had to give me.
Our bodies sensed and sought each other;
our blood and skin understood.

But we both hid ourselves, flustered.

*(From *C. P. Kavafy Collected Poems*, translated by E. Keeley and P. Sherrard. Princeton, N.J.: Princeton University Press, 1975, pp. 178–179).

---

tween the children of lesbian mothers and those of heterosexual, currently unmarried women (Green et al., 1986).

### Meeting Places

The sexual associations of heterosexuals occur in the larger network of their social relation-ships. They meet potential sexual partners during their everyday life, at the places they study, work, and socialize. Every culture, no matter how sexually restrictive, has some means of bringing together its unattached men and women. It is only when dealing with prostitutes that these men move out of their usual circle of social interaction.

Figure 13.5   Gay couple.

Figure 13.6    Lesbian couple.

Homosexuals have been deprived of such socially approved means of finding sexual partners. When a heterosexual man makes a pass at a woman, he may be at most rebuffed; when a homosexual man makes a pass at a man, he may be insulted, disgraced, or even beaten up—unless, of course, the other man is also gay. How does one tell? To resolve this problem, gays rely on two measures: special means of recognizing each other and special meeting places.

Making Contact    Some homosexuals use mannerisms, gestures, ornaments, and dress to signal their sexual orientation. These cues must be distinct enough to be picked up readily, yet not obvious to outsiders. Homosexuals are no different than heterosexuals in their attempts to make sexual contact; what is different are the devices they use, which have had to be covert because of past social ostracism.

Eye signals are the most versatile means of nonverbal communication. Homosexuals use them effectively (as do heterosexuals) in their courtship. Unlike set messages conveyed through appearance, or overt gestures that can be picked up by outsiders, searching looks and meaningful glances can be focused on the potential sex partner and instantly disowned if necessary. These eye signals become more ex-

plicit as they become ritualized; slowly scanning the other person's body, or smiling suggestively, makes the meaning clear.

Another common maneuver is lingering near the other person while ostensibly preoccupied with some other interest, like window shopping (it is not an accident that there are ordinances against loitering). Once the ice is broken, verbal exchanges can be more open.

Homosexuals, like heterosexuals, vary in how subtle or obvious they are when looking for sexual partners. One approach some gay men use is *cruising,* or openly searching for sexual partners. Cruising is most effective in places where gays congregate. These places have usually been gay bars, gay baths, restrooms, and designated (though shifting) parts of streets and parks known as meeting places. The element common to all these sites is that they are most often used by males looking for casual sex (Hoffman, 1968).

The AIDS epidemic has significantly altered these behavior patterns. Gay baths, for instance, have been virtually all shut down under pressure from public health authorities and gay leaders and for lack of clients. With greater social acceptance, gay men and women no longer need to rely on such segregated meeting places and furtive encounters. On college campuses, for instance, gay and lesbian organizations and clubs sponsor the same sort of social functions other students enjoy.

Gay Bars   In cities that allow them (and most major cities now do) the gay bar is the counterpart of the heterosexual singles bar (Chapter 16). It functions as a place for socializing as well as for picking up sex partners, and occasionally for initiating more romantic encounters. Gay bars, however, have more importance than singles bars, because homosexuals have not had as many other institutionalized settings for these purposes as heterosexuals.

Some gay bars cater to special groups, such as those into S-M or fetishism (Chapter 14), or serve as hangouts for male prostitutes; other bars feature drag shows or go-go dancers. The clientele of gay bars is virtually all male. Few women frequent these bars, be they lesbian or straight. Some heterosexual women ("fruit flies") go to gay bars because gay men provide good company without "hassling" them sexually. Gay men, in turn, welcome these women because they do not compete with them for partners and add a certain measure of novelty, interest, and gentility to the group. Lesbians have their own bars (where men are not welcome), but they infrequently go to such bars looking for a pickup; more often they go with a friend to socialize, have a drink, and dance. The patterns of lesbian relationships are generally not as well known and attract less public and professional attention. Partly this obscurity is because lesbians are more private in their intimate relationships, and partly because of the neglect with which women's lives are treated (Vida, 1978).

Gay Baths   Before AIDS, steam baths that catered to gay men (there were none for lesbians, though some establishments had a ladies night) provided the most streamlined settings for fast, multiple, anonymous sexual encounters. These steam baths had a public area ("orgy room") where men engaged in group sex or paired up before heading for private cubicles. A man could simply wait in one of these cubicles with the door ajar; the position he took on the bed would signal the sexual activity desired.

Public Sites   Designated parts of streets and parks are usually only suitable to establish contacts, but not private enough to engage in sex. They are riskier than bars and baths, but they cost nothing; besides, not every city has a bath or bar.

Public toilets (known as "tearooms") have been used by some gay men to make contact or have sex. Under these circumstances, the sexual interaction (usually fellatio) must be particularly fast, furtive, and silent for fear of discovery. This very element of danger, as well as perhaps the excretory functions associated with toilets, appear to impart to the sexual activity an added sense of excitement. In one study, 54 percent of men engaging in sex in a tearoom turned out to be married and living with their wives and children (Humphreys, 1970). Authorities have tried to suppress such encounters by removing toilet doors and employing police decoys; currently, authorities are less likely to use deceptive or heavy-handed methods.

## THE DEVELOPMENT OF SEXUAL ORIENTATION

No one knows for certain why some people develop heterosexual, others homosexual or bisexual, orientations. Some sex researchers since the 19th century have regarded homosexuality as having a "constitutional" origin or some basic biological cause, while most behavioral scientists have attributed homosexual preference to social factors, especially to childhood experiences with parents. The debate is by no means settled.

### Biological Determinants
Those who favor a biological explanation range from those who suspect the presence of predisposing factors to others who think prenatal "programming" of the brain decides the matter primarily.

Apart from scientific evidence, many gay

men (perhaps more than women) feel that the basis of their sexual orientation must be biological. They have never felt that they had much "choice" in the matter (most transsexuals feel the same way). Gay activists also find a biological explanation politically expedient; social judgments are more likely to be favorable if homosexuals are perceived to have had no choice in being who they are (Whitman, 1983).

Genetic Factors    A genetic basis for homosexuality has long been hypothesized, but it was not until the mid-20th century that attempts were made to confirm it. These studies have focused on issues like sex ratios among siblings of homosexuals, their position in the birth order, and the sexual orientation of twins.

Kallmann (1952) reported a much higher *concordance* between identical twins than between fraternal twins or unrelated men. In other words, if one twin was homosexual, there was a far greater likelihood that the brother would be homosexual in identical twins than in fraternal twins.

Identical twins are genetically closer than fraternal twins, so this finding points to a genetic factor. However, Kallmann's identical twins were not reared apart; they shared life experiences as well as genes, and either could explain the outcome. Furthermore, other twin studies have failed to replicate these results (Heston and Sheilds, 1968; Zuger, 1976).

The fact that homosexual men are more likely to have homosexual brothers has been repeatedly confirmed. In one study, 25 percent of the brothers of gay men were also gay (Pillard et al., 1982). Another study showed homosexual men to be four times as likely to have homosexual brothers than heterosexual men, with no difference in the likelihood of having homosexual sisters (Pillard and Weinrich, 1986). Because siblings typically share the same environment as well as some of their genes, such findings do not settle the issue in favor of heredity.

Hormonal Factors    Sex hormones do affect sexual differentiation. The possibility that they influence sexual orientation too has attracted much attention (Money, 1980). According to some studies, homosexual men tend to have lower testosterone levels than heterosexual men; lesbians have higher levels of testosterone than heterosexual women. Inconsistencies in methods and outcomes make these studies inconclusive. For instance, testosterone levels have also been found to be higher among homosexuals, and other studies have failed to find any significant hormonal difference in level at all (Tourney, 1980; Sanders et al., 1985). Other investigators have noted differences in physical structures, blood chemistry, and sleep patterns between homosexual and heterosexual men; likewise, lesbian and heterosexual women have been found to differ in some physical structures.

Clinical evidence is also inconsistent. For example, no homosexual feelings were reported in one sample of girls exposed to excess androgen before birth (Ehrhardt et al., 1968). In another group of women with congenital adrenal hyperplasia who were exposed to excess androgen in prenatal life but reared as females, 37 percent became bisexual, 17 percent lesbian, and only 40 percent exclusively heterosexual, with the balance being noncommittal (Money, 1987).

Dorner (1976) argues that just as androgenization determines male and female mating behavior in lower animals, a similar process operates among humans: the presence of androgens in prenatal life leads to the development of a sexual orientation toward females; a deficiency of prenatal androgens, or insensitivity of tissues to its effect, leads to a sexual orientation toward males, irrespective of genetic sex.

This theory of prenatal influence has been criticized on theoretical and empirical grounds. A major obstacle to such research at the experimental level is that the animal world does not have clear parallels to human sexual orientation, although same-sex sexual interactions occur in many species. Hormones do induce same-sex behavior in animals (Dorner, 1968; Hutchinson, 1978), but does such behavior correspond to human homosexual activity beyond superficial similarities?

Brain Differences   To be truly conclusive, evidence that homosexuality is biological should include brain differences. A few investigators claim to have identified centers in the hypothalamus that govern "male" and "female" sexual response patterns (Chapter 4).

Indirect evidence for brain differences comes from studies in the response pattern of the hypothalamic-pituitary system. As we saw in Chapter 4, the sharp increase in estrogen during the first phase of the menstrual cycle is followed by a surge of LH secretion by the pituitary (Figure 4.8). When heterosexual males are primed with estrogen (to approximate the female condition), then given an extra shot of estrogen, their LH levels do not show this surge. Homosexual men given the same treatment respond at an intermediate level—their LH level rises more than in heterosexual men but not as sharply as in women (Gladue et al., 1985). Other investigators have failed to confirm these findings (Gooren, 1986).

In an adult, giving or taking away hormones does not affect sexual orientation, any more than it influences gender. If there is a biological influence, it must be subtle and early in life (Money, 1987). The case for biology is still open (Ehrhardt and Meyer-Bahlburg, 1981). It has gained indirect support from the failure to demonstrate that psychosocial variables produce homosexuality.

## Psychosocial Determinants

Few would deny the pervasive influence of psychosocial factors upon sexual orientation. Are they enough to explain why some people become heterosexual and others homosexual?

Once again, we have to look at experiences early in life; and again, the evidence is inconclusive. There seems to be no direct connection between childhood experiences and sexual orientation. Homosexual experiences in childhood and adolescence are far more common than the numbers of adult homosexuals: 60 percent of boys and 35 percent of girls have some homosexual interaction before puberty, yet only some of them persist in such activity in adulthood (Elias and Gebhard, 1969).

Cross-cultural evidence from New Guinea is even more intriguing (Box 13.3). Why do Sambia boys who participate in ritual fellatio as part of their normal upbringing go on to become active heterosexual men (Herdt, 1981)? Obviously, same-sex involvement in childhood does not in itself explain a homosexual orientation, even though, as we shall see, most adult homosexuals have had such experiences as children.

Psychoanalytic Views   Freud hypothesized that everyone is born with a *bisexual potential*. During psychosexual development children can develop either a heterosexual or homosexual orientation, depending on the way the Oedipal conflict and related issues are resolved (Chapter 8). Homosexuality is a *fixation* at an early state of development or a *regression* to it. Though Freud clearly considered heterosexuality the norm, he was lenient in his view of homosexuals.[2]

Psychoanalysts explain how an individual becomes homosexual in various ways (Salzman, 1968; Marmor, 1965, 1980). For example, during the Oedipal phase, the fear of retaliation by the father (*castration anxiety*) is said to turn some boys away from the mother as a sexual object and later from all other women. In another version, faced with a harsh and rejecting mother, the boy turns to the father (hence to men) for love and erotic satisfaction. The mechanisms proposed for the development of lesbianism are more complex but basically akin (Deutsch, 1944). The fear and hatred of men, in particular, is commonly cited as why some women turn to other women for sexual love.

To support these claims, Bieber and a group of other psychoanalysts studied 106 male homosexual patients. They concluded that the most significant factors in the families of these men were a detached and hostile

[2]In a letter to the mother of a homosexual requesting therapy for her son Freud wrote, "Homosexuality is assuredly no advantage, but it is nothing to be ashamed of, no vice, no degradation, it cannot be classified as an illness . . ." (Freud, 1951, p. 787)

father and a controlling, seductive, and overly attached mother. This *close-binding-intimate* (CBI) mother dominated her son and depreciated her husband. As a result, the son's masculine behavior was inhibited. The domineering mother discouraged her son's heterosexual impulses except when they were directed at herself, and she was jealous of any interest that her son showed in other females. The boy whose father was aloof or openly hostile lacked a masculine figure with whom to identify. In later life he retained a fear of heterosexual relationships and a frustrated need for the father love that he had failed to receive as a child (Bieber et al., 1962). Such a family did not ensure homosexuality but made it more likely. Seventy percent of homosexuals as against 30 percent of heterosexuals were found to have CBI mothers.

Like all studies based on patients in therapy, Bieber's conclusions may not apply to the broader population. However, a study of nonpatients (Evans, 1969) has turned up similar findings. Bieber's familial role model also seems to apply to some persons in the Bell et al (1981) sample but fails to provide a general explanation for homosexuality.

Social Learning Approaches    Behavioral scientists think other paths lead from social experience to homosexuality. They have focused on *peer relationships* (presumed to be poor among homosexuals); *fortuitous labeling* (people who are called "homosexual" or treated as sexually different begin to act that way); *atypical sexual experiences* (such as lack of opportunity to interact with members of the opposite sex); and *homosexual seduction* in childhood (Bell, Weinberg and Hammersmith, 1981).

An extensive investigation of homosexual development (involving 979 homosexual and 477 heterosexual men and women living in the San Francisco Bay Area in 1969–1970) found these factors of no effect or far weaker effect than had been supposed (Bell et al., 1981). Some of the explanations apply to one homosexual subgroup, but none to homosexuals as a whole.

These investigators followed a path-analytic model—they traced the path of possible influences from childhood, through adolescent peer relationships and sexual experiences, to final adult homosexuality or heterosexuality. Through this model they could see how one factor (such as a boy's lack of identification with the father) could lead to a dislike of traditional male activities and to a chain of homosexual developments; or how that chain could be interrupted at any stage. They reached eight conclusions:

1. By the time boys and girls reach adolescence, their sexual preference is likely to be determined, though they may not yet have become sexually very active.
2. Homosexuality was indicated by falling in love with a person of the same sex two or three years before the first homosexual activity. These romantic feelings, more than any activities, appeared to be crucial in the development of adult homosexuality.
3. The homosexual men and women in the study had heterosexual experiences during their childhood and adolescent years, but they found such experiences ungratifying.
4. Among both the men and the women in the study, there was a powerful link between gender nonconformity and the development of homosexuality; homosexuals were likely to have been "sissies" and "tomboys."
5. Respondents' identification with their opposite-sex parents while they were growing up had no significant impact on whether they turned out to be homosexual or heterosexual.
6. For both male and female respondents, identifications with the parent of the same sex had a weak connection to the development of sexual orientation.
7. For both the men and the women, a poor relationship with the father seemed more important than any relationship with the mother.
8. Gender nonconformity was somewhat more salient for males, and family relationships more salient for females.

Bell and his associates did not set out to look for biological roots of homosexuality, but they were led to the conclusion that their findings were "not inconsistent with what one would expect to find, if indeed, there were a biological basis for sexual preference" (Bell, Weinberg and Hammersmith, 1981, p. 216).

Gender Nonconformity    The association of gender nonconformity with sexual orientation in Bell's study may turn out to be its key finding. It confirms earlier findings. For example, two-thirds of male homosexuals studied by Saghir and Robins (1973) recalled a "girl-like" syndrome during boyhood (including a preference for girls' toys and games, female playmates, and avoidance of rough-and-tumble play). Likewise, two-thirds of female homosexuals, but only 20 percent of heterosexuals, recalled "tomboyish" behavior in their preteens. Such behavior persisted into adolescence among more than half of the homosexual versus none of the heterosexual group. The reliance on recall in such studies is a problem; what people remember cannot be counted on.

Among the subjects studied by Whitman, 47 percent of male homosexuals had been interested in doll play and 47 percent in cross-dressing (none of the heterosexual men had been interested in either); 42 percent of homosexuals and 1.5 percent of heterosexuals preferred female playmates; 29 percent of homosexuals and 1.5 percent of heterosexuals were regarded as "sissies"; 80 percent of homosexuals preferred childhood "sexplay" with other boys; about the same proportion of heterosexuals preferred "sexplay" with girls (Whitman, 1977). Similar findings have been reported by Tripp (1975).

Further confirmation of a link between gender nonconformity and homosexuality among males comes from a 15-year study of "sissy boys" (Green, 1986). Three-fourths of a group of 44 extremely feminine boys who were followed from early childhood to adulthood grew to be homosexual or bisexual males; there was only one bisexual among a control group of more typical boys.

The parents of these boys often encouraged the feminine behavior. Even when they actively discouraged it, the homosexual tendencies of these boys were not reversed, although they were lessened. Professional counseling, likewise, increased conventional masculine behavior and psychological adjustment, but it did not alter the development of homosexual orientation.

Impressive as this study is, we still do not have the whole story. For instance, why is it that one out of four of these feminine boys matured as heterosexuals; and one-third of homosexual men recall quite masculine boyhoods. Still, even if gender nonconformity is not the whole answer, it may be one major pathway for the development of male homosexuality. It has been noted that the absence of masculine behaviors and traits in boys appears to be a more reliable predictor of later homosexual orientation than the presence of feminine traits or cross-sex behaviors (Hockenberry and Billingham, 1987).

The association between gender behavior in childhood and sexual orientation later can be explained in several ways. One is developmental continuity. A boy who acts more like a girl will grow up to choose a sexual partner as a woman would, namely a man; it has been frequently observed that boys whose best friends were girls in childhood are more likely to have male lovers in adulthood, and vice versa. The boy may identify with girls and be socialized by them. Possibly boys who have feminine interests and get attached to a female peer group are socially stigmatized by other boys (and rejected by their fathers); hence they become "starved" for male affection, which they remedy in adulthood by becoming homosexual (Green, 1980).

Gender nonconformity appears to be less of an issue in the development of female homosexuality, but it has been less well studied. Two out of three lesbians report having been tomboys (Tripp, 1975), but unlike sissies, they are not usually ostracized by their peers, so they do not face the same social repercussions. Female homosexuality also appears to develop with less continuity. Many women who eventually become lesbians first get married and have children. This fact may, of course, reflect social limitations on women's choices, and the marriages do usually turn out to be unsatisfactory.

What causes gender nonconformity? Green's study suggests that feminine boys are somehow different from early childhood. Though parental influences are significant, parents do not "create" their feminine boys. Some experts see a biological predisposition—not to homosexuality itself, but to gender-related behavior (Brody, 1986). Perhaps the family factors that have been suggested to explain homosexuality are really results of the prehomosexual son or daughter being, in fact, "different." Perhaps it is not the distant father who "makes" a homosexual out of his son, but the gender-atypical prehomosexual son who "makes" the father distant (Bell et al., 1981).

Gender identity and affectional ties seem to be the basic issues that define sexual orientation. It is these processes that we need to understand if we are to unravel the mystery of sexual choice.

## SOCIAL PERSPECTIVES ON HOMOSEXUALITY

There probably has never existed a society that did not have some homosexual members; yet in no society has homosexuality been the primary form of sexual expression. Most cultures have allowed homosexual interactions at some time during their history (Box 13.3). After long neglect, the historical aspect of homosexuality is now receiving due scholarly attention (Dover, 1978; Boswell, 1980). The story is by no means a tale of relentless condemnation. On balance, though, homosexual behavior has been viewed negatively in Western culture over most of history.

### Social Judgments

Social judgments of homosexuality have taken several main forms. It has been viewed by religious institutions as a sin; by the law, as a crime; by medicine, as an illness; and by public opinion, as a form of social deviance. Opposed to these perceptions is the current view of homosexuality as a lifestyle.

Striking changes have been taking place over the past several decades in public opinion towards homosexuals. Greater acceptance towards homosexuality began in the 1960s. By 1983, 65 percent of people in the United States thought gays should have equal employment opportunities, but close to 60 percent continued to disapprove of homosexuality (*Newsweek*, Aug. 8, 1983, p. 33).

By the mid-1980s, however, public sentiment seemed to be shifting back, possibly as a result of AIDS. In a Gallup poll taken in 1977, 43 percent of respondents favored the legalization of gay relations; in 1986 only 33 percent did so (*San Francisco Chronicle*, Oct. 24, 1986, p. 11). There have also been some setbacks for gays in the legal field (Chapter 22). On the other hand, a complete reversal to former social perspectives appears highly unlikely.

### Medical Judgments

By the 19th century, homosexuality was firmly established as a form of illness within psychiatry. Compared to earlier views of homosexuals as sinners and criminals, the new perception that they were sick was a humane alternative. It called for help and understanding rather than condemnation and punishment. Still, increasing numbers of homosexuals came to view this approach as less than a blessing. To be called sick was in some ways just as stigmatizing as other judgments.

Homosexuality continued to be listed as a disease in the *American Psychiatric Diagnostic Manual* until 1974. When this diagnosis was deleted, homosexuality ceased to be considered officially as a psychiatric disorder (American Psychiatric Association, 1987). This change was brought about by a vote of the membership of the American Psychiatric Association (Bayer, 1981; Spitzer, 1981). It was more a political than a medical action; a subsequent survey of a sample of the APA membership showed that two-thirds of psychiatrists still considered homosexuality a disorder (Lief, 1977a). However, it could be argued that including homosexuality as an illness in the first place was a political act too.

The current official medical stance strikes a compromise. *Ego-dystonic homosexuality* is defined as a psychosexual disorder, but homo-sexuality explicitly is not (American Psychiatric Association, 1987, p. 281). "Ego-dystonic" means that homosexual behavior is unaccept-able to the patient, whose desire to change orientation is a matter of consistent concern. According to this approach, if a homosexual is significantly unhappy with his or her sexual orientation (on intrinsic grounds, not merely because society is making life difficult), then the person has a psychosexual disorder; if not, the person is normal.

There is an extensive literature on psy-chological distress among homosexuals seek-ing therapy.[3] Homosexuals who have sought help may not be representative, of course, of the broader gay population. Studies of those who are not in therapy do also report consid-erable psychological conflict: the rate of suicide attempts among homosexual males is 20 per-cent; among heterosexual men, 5 percent (Bell and Weinberg, 1978). Still, even if homosex-uals are demonstrably less happy, is it their own homosexuality or society's reaction that troubles them?

Other studies show the majority of homo-sexuals to be well-adjusted people.[4] Behavioral scientists are not even able to tell homosexual from heterosexual men in detailed anonymous life histories and psychological tests (Hooker, 1975). Sociologists suggest that when homo-sexuals behave differently, it is because they are living up to the role of deviants to which society assigns them (Weinberg and Williams, 1974).

These contradictory findings present three alternatives: homosexuals are psycholog-ically no worse off than heterosexuals despite social pressures; homosexuals suffer because of the social judgments that condemn them to a state of deviancy; homosexuals have psycho-logical problems quite apart from the prob-lems imposed by society.

[3]See, for instance, Bieber (1962), Ovesey (1969), Hatterer (1970), Stoller (1975), Socarides (1975).

[4]Saghir and Robins (1973). Also see Chang and Block (1960), Freedman (1967), Wilson and Greene (1971), Hooker (1957, 1958, 1975).

There are certainly those to whom homo-sexuality poses no social threat; but to most others, especially people in positions of public life, the threat of disclosure is serious. It is hard to imagine how such circumstances would not affect, to a lesser or greater extent, peo-ples' lives, personalities, and behaviors. As long as these circumstances exist, we can only guess the true effect of being a homosexual.

Causes    Those who accept homosexuality as an illness seek its causes. Those who do not, object to this approach. "Cause" implies that there is something wrong; why not seek the "causes" of heterosexuality? The search for the origins of sexual orientation—homosexual *or* hetero-sexual—is a more legitimate quest.

Treatment    Those who dismiss the notion of homosexuality being an illness deride the treatment of homosexuality as a form of brain-washing or "conversion" into the majority's sexual value system. Asked if they would use a "magic heterosexual pill" to change effort-lessly to heterosexuality, only 5 percent of fe-male and 14 percent of male homosexuals said yes (Bell and Weinberg, 1978). For most who seek help, treatment has been ineffective in changing sexual orientation whether based on psychotherapy, behavior modification, or other methods.

There are several possible reasons for this failure. Many homosexuals have sought ther-apy with no intention of changing their sexual orientations; they are pressured into it by their families or driven to it by anxiety and depres-sion. They play along or seek relief, but few really want to change.

On the other hand, therapy has helped many adjust better to their life circumstances. For instance, workshops help gay adolescents to feel better about being homosexual and to handle informing their families (Schneider and Tremble, 1986).

There are also reports that sexual orien-tation has been shifted by methods ranging from psychoanalysis (Bieber et al., 1962), to behavior modification (Bancroft, 1974), to sex therapy (Masters and Johnson, 1979). The success of these efforts (doubted by some) may largely depend on careful selection of patients.

The bias in the past was to push homosexuals into treatment whether or not they needed or wanted it. There may now be the contrary pressure not to seek treatment, because that would mean admitting that there is something wrong with being homosexual. Homosexuals who are in distress but do not wish to change their sexual orientation seek gay therapists, so that their sexual orientation does not become the focus of treatment; there are also heterosexual therapists who do not impose their own sexual values on patients (Lief and Kaplan, 1986).

The issue of sexual orientation—why some people are homosexual and bisexual when the majority are heterosexual—is likely to remain a puzzle in the foreseeable future. Meanwhile, social attitudes are likely to continue changing toward homosexuals. Whether or not greater tolerance will eventually lead to general acceptance of homosexuality as an equally desirable alternative to heterosexuality remains to be seen—a question we shall reconsider in subsequent chapters.

## REVIEW QUESTIONS

1. What is Kinsey's homosexual-heterosexual scale?

2. How do gender and being an overt or covert homosexual influence patterns of sexual behavior and relationships?

3. How do homosexuals differ from transsexuals and transvestites?

4. What is the evidence for biological factors in the development of sexual orientation?

5. What is the evidence that sexual orientation is determined by childhood experiences?

## THOUGHT QUESTIONS

1. How would you determine if a statement that is critical of the gay subculture is homophobic or not?

2. What prejudice against homosexuals have you seen? Would homosexuals behave more like heterosexuals in their personal relationships if they were no longer discriminated against?

3. How would you help a gay friend who cannot decide whether or not to come out?

4. What sort of research studies would you carry out to find out what determines sexual orientation?

5. A gay person you know has psychological conflicts over being homosexual. What would you recommend?

## SUGGESTED READINGS

Bell, A. P., and Weinberg, M. S. (1978). *Homosexualities*. New York: Simon & Schuster. Descriptions of the sexual and intimate relationships of homosexual men and women in the United States.

Bell, A. P., et al. (1981). *Sexual preference—Its development in men and women*. Bloomington: Indiana University. Exploration of the development of homosexual orientation.

Marmor, J. (Ed.) (1980). *Homosexual behavior*. New York: Basic Books. Contributions from many disciplines representing the current mainstream of professional viewpoints on homosexuality.

Rodgers, B. (1972). *Gay talk*. New York: Putnam. Fascinating insights into the gay subculture through its language.

Silverstein, C. (1978). *The joy of gay sex*. New York: Simon & Schuster. Sisley, E. L., and Harris, B. (1977). *The joy of lesbian sex*. New York: Simon & Schuster. Techniques for the enhancement of gay sexual relationships for men and women.

# Paraphilias

*Homo sum; humani nihil a me alienum puto. (I am human; there is nothing human that is alien to me.)*

TERENCE (185–159 B.C.)

OUTLINE

THE CONCEPT OF PARAPHILIAS
Historical and Current
  Conceptions
Basic Features
PARAPHILIAC BEHAVIORS
Pedophilia
  General Characteristics
  Heterosexual Pedophiles
  Homosexual Pedophiles
  The Impact on the Child
Incest
  The Incest Taboo
  Incestuous Pedophilia
  Dealing with Incest
Zoophilia
Fetishism
  Types of Fetishes
  Psychological Characteristics

Transvestism
Necrophilia
Voyeurism
Exhibitionism
Obscene Calls
Sadomasochism (S-M)
Other Paraphilias
Sexual Addiction
CAUSES AND TREATMENTS
The Development of Paraphilias
  Biological Roots
  The Psychoanalytic Model
  Learning Models
The Treatment of Paraphilias
  Biologically Based Treatments
  Punishment
  Psychotherapy
  Behavior Therapy

Variety in most human interests is encouraged. We prize different tastes in food, music from Bach to rock, art in every medium—why not all the forms of sexual expression?

When we consider fantasies, the human taste for sexual variety becomes apparent (Chapter 11). The obstacle is not lack of inclination but unwillingness to act them out in real life. Psychological inhibitions and social prohibitions hold us back.

Actually, even the ordinary sexual behaviors of most men and women are more varied than you might think. Even though heterosexual intercourse is the preferred and generally permissible mode of sexual expression for most adults, many people try other sexual behavior at various levels of intensity at one time or another; and some do so exclusively.

What makes judgments difficult in this area is that apparently similar behaviors may have different motives and consequences. Consider four men. One enjoys looking at women in bikinis on a public beach; the second pays a fee to see a topless woman dancer perform; the third sneaks a look at a woman's thighs when she is climbing a ladder; the fourth stands at a window at night watching an unsuspecting woman get undressed. All four men have the same objective—to see an exposed female body—yet each situation has different psychological and social implications. A beach is a public place where you look and are looked at by free choice. The topless show is a legal form of sexual commerce—the buying and selling of sexual entertainment. Sneaking a look up the ladder violates a woman's privacy, but the man is not likely to go to jail for it. The fourth man faces serious legal penalties if he is caught.

The term "voyeurism" might be applied to all four behaviors, but we give only the last that formal label. Voyeurism is one of a cluster of atypical and socially problematic behaviors that are loosely grouped together.

The significance of atypical sexual behaviors is as much social as it is psychological. It is where society draws the line between acceptable and unacceptable behavior that is at issue.

## THE CONCEPT OF PARAPHILIAS

The terms that have been used for atypical and sexually problematic sexual behaviors mirror shifting attitudes about them. Originally called "perversions" in the 19th century, these activities came to be known as "deviations" and more recently as "variations" of sexual behavior. The current diagnostic term is *paraphilia* (Greek for "besides" and "love"). This designation reflects a greater tolerance and moral neutrality. It avoids branding people with harsh labels (Tallent, 1977). Those concerned about the rights and freedom of choice of paraphiliacs (provided their behavior is not harmful to others) refer to them as *sexual minorities*; but the courts continue to lump together all paraphiliacs who run afoul of the law as *sex offenders* (Chapter 22).

Other texts refer to these behaviors in general terms (varieties, variations, and so on). In this text, we refer to these behaviors as "paraphilias" because that is their formal name. Euphemisms will not help us understand them better.

### Historical and Current Conceptions

Atypical sexual behaviors have long been known in history. They are represented in the literature, art, and mythologies of many cultures (Chapter 20). It was only in the 19th century that people began to classify them as psychiatric and legal entities.

The first to attempt it was Richard von Krafft-Ebing. In 1886 he provided a comprehensive review of what was known at the time about "aberrant" sexual behavior in his classic *Psychopathia Sexualis* (Chapter 1). Based on concepts of genetic predisposition (since disproven), Krafft-Ebing's work has no current explanatory value, but his case studies continue to be of interest. Krafft-Ebing's work influenced Freud, whose own views were to dominate psychiatric conceptions of atypical behaviors until recently.

Freud assumed that among adults any form of sexual behavior that takes precedence over heterosexual intercourse shows a defect in psychosexual development. Freud labeled the person to whom we are attracted the *sexual object* and what we wish to do with the object the *sexual aim*. In a healthy, mature sexual relationship, he considered an adult of the opposite sex to be the sexual object and coitus to be the sexual aim.[1]

Departures from this pattern can take one of two forms: differences in the choice of sexual object and differences in the choice of sexual aim. In the first instance the alternative object could be an adult of the same sex (as in homosexuality), a child (as in pedophilia), a close relative (as in incest), an animal (as in zoophilia), an inanimate object (as in fetishism), or even a dead body (as in necrophilia). In the second instance, instead of seeking coitus, the individual would prefer to watch unsuspecting others who are naked, undressing or engaging in sexual activity (voyeurism), to expose his own genitals (exhibitionism), to inflict pain (sadism), or to suffer pain (masochism). When deviation involves both choice of object and sexual aim, it is designated by the choice of object.

As we saw in Chapter 13, homosexuality has been deleted from the category of paraphilias. In other respects the classification described here is still widely accepted in psychiatry (American Psychiatric Association, 1987).

Freud did not focus on the social significance of these behaviors. His interest was in how they fitted his theory of infantile sexuality and psychosexual development (Chapter 8). Many behavioral scientists reject Freud's theoretical premises and object to the way paraphiliacs have been dealt with by clinicians.

The alternative approach is to classify the paraphilias by their impact on others. For instance, fetishism and transvestism have no direct negative effect on others. Moreover, fetishists, transvestites, and participants in sadomasochistic practices may show no independent signs of psychological abnormality if

they are not patients or inmates (Gosselin and Wilson, 1980). So some wonder why harmless behaviors engaged in private should be stigmatized by diagnostic labels.

Basic Features

The psychiatric handbook which classifies and defines behavioral disorders is the *Diagnostic and Statistical Manual of Mental Disorders* (DSM III-R). Its current version puts disturbances related to sexuality under the heading of *psychosexual disorders*. This includes three major categories: gender identity disorders, paraphilias, and psychosexual dysfunctions (American Psychiatric Association, 1987). We describe the first in Chapter 10; the second is what we are concerned with here, and the third is dealt with in Chapter 15.

Sexual aggression is not part of this scheme. Coercive sexual behaviors such as rape are not diagnostic entities (just as theft and murder are not). They are considered symptoms of other underlying problems, not disturbances in themselves. We shall discuss coercive sex separately as part of the broader subject of sexual aggression (Chapter 19); but there is a close link between many paraphilias and sexual aggression, as we shall see.

What distinguishes paraphiliacs is how they achieve sexual arousal. Otherwise they reach orgasm in ordinary ways—coitus, its homosexual counterparts, or masturbation.

For arousal, paraphilias rely on unusual and sometimes extreme imagery or acts. Paraphiliac fantasies and acts tend to be insistently and involuntarily *repetitive*. They usually involve either nonhuman objects, the imposition or suffering of pain and humiliation, or nonconsenting partners (American Psychiatric Association, 1987).

Fantasies alone do not count as paraphilias, nor do occasional sexual experiments. To qualify as a paraphilia, the behavior must be the *preferred* or exclusive form of sexual gratification. The person must feel driven to the behavior despite the availability of other, more acceptable outlets and despite the potential social cost.

The sexual imagery of the paraphiliac,

---

[1] "Object" in this context is not intended to imply that people are or should be treated or exploited as inanimate objects. Applied to persons, "object" refers to individuals who fill essential functions in the gratification of others and hence are significant to their lives (Engel, 1962).

however odd, is not uncommon. For instance, many ordinary people have fantasies involving sadomasochism or sex with animals (a common theme in the art and literature of many cultures). Similarly, mild voyeuristic, exhibitionistic, and fetishistic activities are part of our culture; the portrayal of seminudity in advertising, the erotic attraction of female lingerie or high-heeled shoes, and so on are examples. Most men and women who indulge in such fantasies and practices are not paraphiliacs, because their activities are not ends in themselves; they enhance rather than compete with their primary sexual aims. The man who is turned on by frilly black panties is after the woman who wears them, not the panties themselves; and the woman who exhibits herself in them wants to arouse the man, not to shock him. Stoller (1975) calls such behaviors *sexual variants*. These occasional erotic techniques do not entail harming others; they may be engaged in out of curiosity or for adventure. By contrast, he calls *perversion* behaviors in which fantasies are acted out habitually, are necessary for full sexual satisfaction, and are primarily motivated by hostility.

The prevalence and variety of paraphilias are far greater among men than women. Of sexual offenders, over 90 percent (other than rapists and prostitutes) are male (U.S. Department of Justice, 1985). We will address the possible reasons in Chapter 19.

For a paraphiliac, the sexual partner is merely an erotic vehicle: like the mannequin modeling boots and underwear; the arm that wields the whip, the buttocks that receive the blows. The partner's true personality, needs, and preferences are irrelevant; what counts is the role the partner is to play in the enactment of the paraphiliac fantasy.

Given this dehumanizing context and the odd practices that may be entailed, it is hard for paraphiliacs to find ordinary women who would be willing partners; hence, they often rely on prostitutes or S-M "professionals" to stage their fantasies of "kinky sex." Otherwise they must impose these acts on unwilling victims, which is what makes the paraphilias a social problem.

## PARAPHILIAC BEHAVIORS

We do not know enough about praphiliac behaviors. The varieties portrayed in literature and art are fascinating, but it is hard to know how to make systematic sense of this material.

On the other hand, the scientific literature on the paraphilias is too limited. Most studies in this area come from populations who have been either in prison or in treatment. They can hardly be representative of paraphiliacs in the general population.

### Pedophilia

The *pedophile* (Greek, "child lover") is sexually attracted to and engages in sexual activity with children of either sex, as a preferred or exclusive form of erotic gratification (American Psychiatric Association, 1987) (Figure 14.1). To

Figure 14.1  Child pornography movies catering to pedophiles.

differentiate it from sexual activities between children, the diagnosis of pedophilia requires that the person be at least ten years older than the child. Pedophilia is also commonly called *sexual child abuse*, or child molestation.

Pedophilia is by far the most important of the paraphilias. It involves the largest number of individuals. Its victims are the most vulnerable, its effects the most damaging, and it generates the most intense public concerns.

In most cultures, prepubescent children are excluded as sexual partners. After puberty, the age that one is socially recognized as sexually adult varies even within the United States. For instance, the laws of some states define child molesting and statutory rape to include sex with persons as old as 16, 18, or even 21 (Chapter 22). Even greater variance is seen across cultures and through history. Some of the famous lovers in literature may strike us as shockingly young: Romeo and Juliet were teenagers; Dante fell in love with Beatrice when she was 9; Petrarch with Laura when she was 12. Age does not carry the same social significance in all times and places.

Apart from the law, some sex researchers define a child as younger than 12 years old; a minor as between 13 and 15 years old; and an adult as more than 16 years old (Gebhard et al., 1965). Though there are good social reasons why an adult should not engage in sex with those who are legally underage, even if biologically mature, only sexual encounters with children younger than 13 by those 16 or older (and 5 years older than the child) can reasonably be called a paraphilia (American Psychiatric Association, 1987).

General Characteristics    Much of our knowledge of pedophilia comes from studies of convicted offenders. A study of 1500 convicted sex offenders and two control groups, undertaken by the Kinsey Institute for Sex Research in the 1960s, is still one of the main sources of information (Gebhard et al., 1965).

According to one study, heterosexual men are responsible for 95 percent of the cases of the abuse of girls; homosexual men are responsible for the sexual abuse of most boys (Finkelhor and Russell, 1984). We can draw two inferences. First, the great majority of pedophiles are men, but there are also some women (Finkelhor, 1984). Second, heterosexual men are responsible for most cases of child abuse. Two out of three abused children are girls. Many more girls than boys are abused, because there are many more heterosexual than homosexual men. Boys are also less likely to report the experience than girls.

Kinsey found that one woman in four had been sexually approached in childhood by someone five or more years older. Eighty percent had experienced such contacts only once each; 5 percent, nine or more times. More current studies show an even higher prevalence. Rates vary widely depending on what population is sampled, how abuse is defined, and what age is used as a cut-off point, but even by the most conservative estimates, 10 percent of females and 2 percent of males appear to have been sexually abused in their youth. These rates would place the annual number of children abused at 200,000 cases a year, which is ten times the reported rate (Finkelhor, 1984a). The average age of children at the time of the experience was 10 years for girls and 11 years for boys; the average ages of their adult partners were 32 and 27, respectively (Finkelhor, 1979, 1984b).

In addition to sexual orientation and gender, pedophiles vary in age and personality. Pedophilia may be manifested in adolescence, before a boy has had a chance for more mature relationships with his peers. In adulthood, it may occur at any age, but it is more common in the late thirties or over age 50, which may be somehow linked to the developmental stresses of the life cycle.

The image of the pedophiliac as a "dirty old man" is largely a caricature. There are certainly older men who are pedophiles; but some 5 percent of men who engage in such activity are senile, and what appears like a sexual encounter may be their confused and forlorn attempt to be affectionate with a child.

Most pedophiles show an *immature* personality with poorly developed interpersonal skills (Cohen et al., 1969). Unable to cope with adult sexual partners, they befriend children and interact with them sexually. *Regressed* pedophiles manage to establish adult sexual ties but have many marital and sexual problems. During a stressful period of life, they slip back to a more immature level of functioning and seek children as sexual partners. They are also likely to rely on alcohol (Rada, 1976) and to be drunk during their pedophilic encounter (Gebhard et al., 1965). However pedophiles may also use alcohol as an excuse to absolve themselves of responsibility for their actions (MacNamara and Sagarin, 1977). The third and least common is the *aggressive* pedophile. These impulsive men harbor a strong hostility toward women, which spills over into antisocial acts and violence against child victims. Various other explanations have been offered for pedophilia that link it to childhood experiences, obstacles to the normal expression of adult sexual needs, and the failure of inhibitions that ordinarily prevent people from acting on such impulses (Finkelhor and Araji, 1986). Especially significant is the finding that four out of five pedophiles have themselves been sexually abused as children (Groth, 1979). Hence, they may be reenacting a traumatic childhood experience to resolve the residual hurt, to gain mastery over the conflicts it has generated, or to wreak vengeance by treating others the way they were treated themselves.

Characterizations of pedophiles as immature or disturbed should not convey the impression that they are all pathetic emotional wrecks. Actually, some pedophiles are highly accomplished and successful men. Many are married fathers. They may be found in various layers of society and career groups. Such men, however, are more likely to be involved with teenagers than with children. The psychological maturity of pedophiles seems inversely proportional to the age of their sexual partners. Pedophiles are thus a mixed group. They are not restricted to one sexual outlet but respond to adult sexual stimuli and to other paraphiliac stimuli as well (Travin et al., 1986).

**Heterosexual Pedophiles** Though often pictured as a stranger who lurks about the school playground seducing or abducting unsuspecting little girls, in about 85 percent of cases, the pedophile is a relative, family friend, neighbor, or acquaintance. He is a stranger only in about 10 percent of cases; in 15 percent of cases he is a relative (Mohr et al., 1964). He makes advances to the child either in her home, where he is visiting or living (as an uncle, stepfather, grandfather, or boarder), or in his own home, where the child is used to visiting him or is enticed by promises of various treats. Seventy-nine percent of such contacts occur in homes, 13 percent in public places, and 8 percent in cars.

The sexual encounter with the child is often brief, though there may be a series of such episodes; it is unusual for a prolonged or intimate relationship to develop. Actual sexual contact most often consists of the man touching the girl's genitals (38 percent); exposing them (20 percent) and fondling them (17 percent). Coitus is simulated in 10 percent and consumated in 4 percent of cases (Elvik et al., 1986). Physical harm to the molested child occurs in about 2 percent of the instances, although threats of force or some degree of physical restraint is present in about one-third of cases where the person is convicted (Gebhard et al., 1965).

**Homosexual Pedophiles** The homosexual pedophile ("chicken hawk") sexually abuses young and teenage boys. The activities include fondling and masturbation of the boy, mutual masturbation, fellatio, and sometimes anal intercourse. These men are scorned by the majority of homosexuals, who confine their sexual activities to other adults.

Homosexual pedophiles do not usually approach strangers, unless they are boy prostitutes. The children with whom they become involved are most often relatives or the sons of acquaintances. In addition, contacts are sometimes made through youth organizations, which they infiltrate as counselors. They may work in a role that brings them into contact with children, such as driving a school bus. Pedophiles are also known among teachers, child psychiatrists, and psychologists. The sexual abuse of children of either sex by operators of day care centers has attracted much attention recently.

Like their heterosexual counterparts, homosexual offenders against children generally show serious deficiencies in sexual socialization and interpersonal relationships. They often say that they prefer the company of boys because they feel uneasy around adults. Their average age at the time of the first offense is about 30 years. Only 16 percent are married at the time, and their sexual experiences have usually been predominantly, but not exclusively, homosexual (Gebhard et al., 1965).

The Impact on the Child    In Chapter 8, we touched briefly on the impact of child-adult sexual interactions on psychosocial development. Let us consider this issue in more detail.

There has been a dramatic increase in the prevalence of child abuse reports over the past decade to over 20,000 a year. This increase reflects in part changes in public awareness and better reporting of such cases to state authorities; but conceivably, the number of pedophiles has gone up as well, or they are sexually more active.

Despite an enormous increase in public attention and research, there are too few empirical studies with large sample sizes, adequate comparison groups, objective measures, and statistical data analysis to provide a clear picture of the prevalence and consequences of child abuse (Alter-Reid et al., 1986). Investigators cannot even agree on how to define it (Wyatt and Peters, 1986).

Sexual activity between adults and children is generally considered to be detrimental to the child. The immediate reaction of children to these situations is negative in 60 percent of girls and 38 percent of boys (Elvik et al., 1986). The most negative reaction is fear (57 percent of girls; 41 percent of boys). However, some children express interest or even pleasure at the sexual interaction (23 percent of boys; 8 percent of girls). Nevertheless, the child usually recognizes the forbidden aspect of the activity or is instructed to keep quiet about it by the adult. Only 37 percent of girls and 27 percent of boys inform their parents or another adult (Finkelhor, 1979).

Reports on the long-term negative consequences of such childhood experiences are conflicting. Some report harmful consequences, others blame societal reactions for the harmful effects, yet others report few harmful consequences, and some point to benefits to the child (Kilpatrick, 1986; Runyan, 1986).

Studies of former victims in therapy show low self-esteem, guilt, and difficulties with sexual and intimate relationships. Studies of prisoners and prostitutes attribute at least part of their sexually or socially deviant behavior to their being abused as children. Moreover, the experience of being abused as a child appears to predispose the person to abuse other children in turn or to engage in coercive sexual behaviors.

For instance, in a sample of male prisoners convicted of rape, 49 percent reported having had sexual contact when younger than 16 years with a woman at least five years older; the mean age of the boy at the time was 11.5 years, and they had usually engaged in coitus more than once (Petrovich and Templer, 1984). Sexual involvement in childhood with women is also reported to be higher among men who became child molesters as adults. In these cases, too, sexual intercourse is involved in at least half of the encounters (Condy et al., 1987). However, prison inmates convicted of nonsexual crimes also show a higher prevalence of having been abused than samples of college students. Also, prison inmates generally come from lower socioeconomic backgrounds. The pertinent factor may be social background, not sexual experiences in childhood. Overcrowding, chaotic living conditions, broken homes, lack of parental supervision, and low levels of education are among the conditions conducive to such interactions (Renshaw and Renshaw, 1980).

Conclusions drawn from the study of patients and prisoners cannot be generalized, but neither can they be dismissed. The fact that childhood sexual experiences are at least sometimes traumatic is cause enough for concern. On the other hand, it is important to note that childhood sexual contacts with adults may not always lead to negative consequences. For instance, in a sample of middle-class women there were no significant differences between those who had and those who did not have childhood sexual experiences with respect to family relations, marital satisfaction, sexual satisfaction, self-esteem, and depression (Kilpatrick, 1986, 1987).

A few investigators go further, proposing that childhood sex with children and with adults is actually beneficial. One Dutch study with a select number of boys (aged 10–16) involved in a pedophilic relationship with adult males reports predominantly positive reactions to the experience (Sandfort, 1984). It may be that the consequences of childhood sexual experiences with adults are not a function of the sexual activities but of the circumstances under which they take place. For instance, Finkelhor (1979) found that whether or not such experience proved to be traumatic was in direct proportion to the age difference between the adult and the child and the amount of coercion used. Other significant factors are the way parents and other adults respond to the revelation or discovery of these incidents, as we shall discuss shortly in connection with incest.

Such considerations notwithstanding, society remains strongly opposed to sexual interactions between adults and children under any circumstances, as we discussed (Chapter 8) and as we reconsider further in Chapter 22.[2]

## Incest

Incest (Latin, "impure") refers to sexual relations between close relatives. Typically it means sex between parents and children or be-

tween siblings. Beyond the nuclear family, the circle of incest prohibitions varies widely.

The Incest Taboo    Mother-son incest is virtually a universal taboo. Father-daughter and sibling incest has been allowed in some cultures for select groups. For instance, brother-sister marriage was practiced by the royal families of ancient Egypt, Hawaii, and the Incas (Gregersen, 1983). Of the societies surveyed by Ford and Beach (1951), 72 percent had more restrictive incest prohibitions—including the Western cultures. The story of Lot's seduction by his two daughters (Genesis 19:30–37) is related in the Old Testament without comment despite strict laws against incest in Judaism (Figure 14.2); this is an event we shall return to in Chapter 20.

Why is the incest taboo so universal? Mother-son copulations are also avoided among nonhuman primates such as chimpanzees, so the taboo appears to be a cultural elaboration of an underlying biological tendency to avoid inbreeding. Among humans the taboo also encourages *exogamy* (marriage outside of one's own group) to promote kinship ties among communities (Haviland, 1981). The incest taboo also protects the family unit by forbidding sexual competition within the family and sexual exploitation of children.

The very process of growing up together tends to interfere with sexual attraction (but not affection). Edward Westermarck's (1922) contention that intimate sexual association promotes sexual aversion is supported by the experience of children raised together on a kibbutz in Israel (who relate to each other like siblings) and in China. Marriages there uniting close childhood associates are less fertile and more likely to end in divorce (Wolf, 1970).

Incestuous relations among adults are legally forbidden and socially unacceptable.[3] However, such behavior, which does occur oc-

[2]For resources in child sexual abuse education and prevention, see *SIECUS Newsletter*, 15:1, Sept. 1986. *The National Center on Child Abuse and Neglect* provides information to professional and the public. Telephone (301) 251-5157. *The National Child Abuse Hotline* provides information and other assistance. Telephone (800) 422-4453.

[3]A man who had been put up for adoption when he was 3 met and married his mother unknowingly when he was 20 and she 37. Six years later, when their true relationship came to be known, they were indicted for incest and ordered to separate (*New York Times*, Oct. 24, 1984a, p. 11).

Figure 14.2   Incest in the Old Testament. François DeTroy, *Lot and his daughters*.

casionally, does not constitute a paraphilia. It is only when the incestuous interaction is between adults and children that it becomes a paraphilia, which is what we shall be concerned with here.

Incestuous Pedophilia   Prevalence figures on incest with children vary widely from a few cases per million a year, based on men who are convicted of the offense, to 33 percent among one sample of female psychiatric patients (Rosenfeld, 1979a). In the Hunt (1974) sample, 14 percent of males had had sexual contact with a relative before adulthood (13 percent heterosexual; 0.5 percent homosexual). The corresponding figure for females was 9 percent (8 percent heterosexual and 1 percent homosexual). Two-thirds of the male and two-fifths of the female experiences were with cousins; over one-quarter of the males and over half the females went no further than light petting. Sex-

ual contacts within the nuclear family mainly involved siblings: 3.8 percent of the males reported contact with a sister; of the female subjects 3.6 percent reported contact with brothers and 0.7 percent with sisters. Contact with parents was restricted to fathers and daughters (0.5 percent) (Hunt, 1974). In the *Psychology Today* sample, 1 percent of women and 2 percent of men had their first coitus with a relative (Athanasiou et al., 1970).

Among a university student sample, about 1 percent of the women reported having had incestuous relationships with their fathers: applied to the general population, this figure amounts to 16,000 new cases per year among 15- to 17-year-old women in the United States (Finkelhor, 1979). The estimate for the female populations aged 18 and older is 750,000 cases. Daughters are more vulnerable to their stepfathers (and to their friends) than to their own biological fathers (Finkelhor, 1982).

Sex between cousins is more common than among siblings; same-generational or sibling incest is far more common than cross-generational sex between parents and children (which accounts for only 10 percent of cases); father-daughter incest in these cases is far more common than mother-son incest (Finkelhor, 1979). In a study of court cases of incest, 90 percent involved fathers and daughters, stepfathers and stepdaughters, grandfathers and granddaughters; and 5 percent involved fathers and sons (Maisch, 1973; Meiselman, 1978). Only about one in 100 cases of reported incest involve mothers and sons (Weinberg, 1976). Shengold (1980) reports one case of mother-son incest. In rare cases, mothers are known to have sexually abused their infant sons through genital stimulation, fellatio, or masturbation (Chasnoff et al., 1986).

Although incest occurs in a wide variety of family settings, Finkelhor (1984a) has identified factors that increase its likelihood: the presence of a stepfather or a physically unaffectionate father; a mother who has not finished high school, is absent for a period of time, is not close to the child, and is punitive over sexual behavior; family income under $10,000 a year; fewer than two childhood friends. Having a stepfather and a sex-punitive mother are the two strongest predisposing factors to incestuous child abuse.

Incest usually reflects a seriously troubled family (Rosenfeld, 1979b). Typically, the marriage is an unhappy match between a dominating, authoritarian, and impulsive man and a dependent and emotionally distant woman, neither of whom is able to function adequately either as spouse or as parent. The daughter is fearful and submissive to the father's wishes to avoid further family dissension (Selby et al., 1980). Wives in these situations are often physically abused and intimidated by their husbands (Truesdell et al., 1986). Others cannot bring themselves to face the truth. A conspiracy of silence thus allows the incestuous arrangement to persist (Box 14.1). Charges are pressed, usually by the wife, only when some new development disrupts the compromise. Some women do report it as soon as they discover it, or the daughter rebels against the incestuous relationship as she gets older (Finkelhor, 1979).

Other studies have failed to confirm these family descriptions. In particular, they find incest offenders' wives to have normal personalities (Groff, 1987).

Dealing with Incest    Incest has the same effects as other child sexual abuse, but a negative experience is likely to be more traumatic. The child is more dependent on the parent and has a greater sense of betrayal and powerlessness.

Professionals dealing with the incestuous pedophile are sharply divided. Some want the perpetrator criminally prosecuted. This action usually means sending the father to jail. The counter view is that imprisoning the father adds to the victim's burden of self-blame and leads to the impoverishment and sometimes the break-up of the family (Runyan, 1986).

Court action is currently initiated in 30 percent of all child sexual abuse cases. Counseling by social workers occurs in 73 percent of cases, and the child is put in foster care in 17 percent of cases (American Humane Association, 1986).

The way that the child is dealt with is crucial. The child needs to be heard and believed. Fear, shame, and anger must be allowed free expression. The child should be helped not to feel responsible for the interaction or its consequences. The sexual element must be put in perspective and not linked up with guilt or evil. The overreaction of uninvolved family members, friends, and therapists, and insensitive legal procedures have as much potential to harm the child as the incestuous interaction itself.[4]

A line needs to be drawn between neglect and denial on the one hand and overly intrusive and disruptive interventions on the other. This is true for the time when incestuous relations

[4]*Parents United* is a self-help organization for families affected by sexual abuse. Telephone (408) 280-5055. *Parents Anonymous* is a national organization that provides support groups for parents who have abused (or fear they may abuse) their children. Telephone (800) 427-0353.

# Box 14.1

## FATHER-DAUGHTER INCEST*

Marcia's father began genital manipulation and oral-genital relations with her when she was five years old and continued these activities on a regular basis for nearly two years. She thinks that she must have known there was something wrong with the relationship because she was afraid that her mother would find out about it. The father, who was alcoholic and amoral to the point of bringing prostitutes home with him from time to time, once insisted that she go to bed with him while her mother was in the same room. When he asked her to get under the covers with him, her mother laughed and thought it was "very cute" to see them in bed together. While her mother stood by, greatly amused, her father began to fondle her, and she became so disturbed by the situation that she ran from the room in tears. Her mother never did realize that incest was occurring. However, an older sister who had also had an incestuous affair with the father recognized the clues to incest and ordered the father to stop it, threatening him with disclosure to legal authorities.

\* \* \*

DAUGHTER: (raising voice)   You don't see how we could have done it. . . .
MOTHER:   No, un-unh. No.
DAUGHTER: (angrily)   We went to the dump! We went out into the sticks! Right out there in the cow pasture! OK, you went away! Everybody was away from the house! We've had it in your bed! We've had it in my bed! We've had it in the bathroom on the floor!
(Mother utters a loud moan.)
DAUGHTER:   We've had it down in the basement! In my bedroom down there, and also in the furnace room! . . .
MOTHER: (shakily)   I just can't believe it, I just can't, just can't . . .
DAUGHTER:   Mom . . .

MOTHER: (with a trembling voice)   Just can't see how anything like this could possibly happen and how you could treat me this way.
DAUGHTER:   Because . . .
MOTHER: (shouting and weeping)   After all I've done for you! I've tried to be a mother to you, I've tried to be a respectable mother, and you accuse your father of something that's so horrible, that's . . .
DAUGHTER: (shouting)   Mother, it's true! You've got to believe it . . .
MOTHER: (to therapist)   She's my daughter, and I love her, but I cannot believe this!

\* \* \*

Pamela was molested by her stepfather over a period of several months, and although she disliked being touched by him she did not tell her mother immediately because she "didn't want to upset Mom." When she did tell, the mother insisted that her husband leave the home and moved swiftly to get a legal injunction to keep him from harassing them. Since he was unemployed and had been living on her earnings, she was in a position of considerable power in the home. When seen in therapy, the daughter seemed to idolize her mother and spoke of her as if she were a movie star, and the mother was relieved that the marriage had ended.

\* \* \*

Una was ten years old when she was raped by her father while he was acutely psychotic. Her mother arranged for his hospitalization and provided comfort and emotional support to her daughter, carefully explaining to her that her father was not himself when the rape occurred. Una credited her mother with helping her to understand and forgive her father, thus diminishing the traumatic effect of the incident.

*(From Meiselman, K.C., *Incest*. San Francisco: Jossey-Bass, 1978, pp. 169.)

take place as well as when the event is confronted years later. Those who have had such experiences in childhood can still benefit by discussing them in adulthood with a counselor.

## Zoophilia

Sexual contact with animals is called *zoophilia* or *bestiality*. It is a paraphilia only when the act or fantasy of engaging in sexual activity with an animal is a repeatedly preferred or exclusive method of obtaining sexual arousal and gratification.

Fantasies of sex with animals are otherwise common. Recourse to animals when other outlets are not available, or by way of occasional experiment, is more likely than a persistent pattern of such behavior (Tollison and Adams, 1979). These activities would not qualify as paraphilia. Some children may explore the genitals of pets or have them sniff and lick their own genitals. Such exploratory sexual activities in childhood usually are not repeated in adulthood and are not zoophilia either.

Farm animals are most often used by men; women tend to rely on household pets. Animals like donkeys and horses have been used occasionally by both sexes, in the case of women usually for sexual exhibitions. The more common activities are masturbating the animal, inducing it to perform mouth-genital stimulation, and where feasible, vaginal or anal intercourse. Animals may also be drawn into sadomasochism, sometimes leading to their injury or death.

Animal contacts were by far the least prevalent of the six sexual outlets studied by Kinsey. Even though 8 percent of adult males and 3 percent of females reported such contacts with animals, their activities accounted for a fraction of 1 percent of the total sexual outlets. In some groups, however, such behavior was relatively common: among boys reared on farms, as many as 17 percent had had at least one orgasm through animal contact after puberty (Kinsey et al., 1948, 1953).

Humans have a long history of intimate associations with animals (Figure 14.3). This theme has been an important source of inspiration for many works of art. Classical mythology abounds with tales of sexual contacts between the gods disguised as beasts and unsuspecting goddesses and mortals (Chapter 20). Zeus, for instance, approached Europa as a bull, Leda as a swan (Figure 14.4), and Persephone as a serpent.

Historical references to zoophilia are also plentiful. Herodotus mentions the goats of the Egyptian temple at Mendes, which were spe-

Figure 14.3 Ancient petroglyph in a cave in northern Italy.

cially trained for copulating with human beings (Forberg, 1966). More often, we find that references to animals as sexual objects are framed as prohibitions. The Hittite code, the Old Testament, and the Talmud specifically prohibit such contacts for males; and the Talmud extends the prohibition to females. Penalities for such sexual contacts tended to be severe, often mandating death for both human and animal participants (Leviticus 20:15–16). Such sanctions remained in effect in Europe throughout the Middle Ages and, indeed, until fairly recently. In 1944, a United States soldier was convicted at a general court-martial of sodomy with a cow and sentenced to a dishonorable discharge and three years at hard labor.

If one takes a broad view of sexual contacts with animals, the line between psychopathology and culturally sanctioned behavior becomes difficult to draw (Traub-Werner, 1986). Animals, of course, are not inanimate objects and those people concerned with animals' rights would object to their exploitation.

## Fetishism

Anthropologists call *fetishes* those objects that were believed by preliterate cultures to have magical powers. In a more general sense, a fetish is any article that is regarded with exag-

Figure 14.4    *Leda and the swan* (after Michelangelo).

gerated superstitious trust. The term *erotic fetishism* was coined by Alfred Binet, the pioneer of intelligence tests. In fetishism, the preferred or exclusive source of sexual arousal is an inanimate object (*object fetishism*) or a part of the body (*partialism*) (Wise, 1985).

The boundary between attraction to ordinary erotic objects or parts of the body and fetishes is nebulous. Many heterosexual males, for instance, are aroused by the sight of female underwear, and such underwear is often designed for that purpose. Most people are also partial to various parts of the anatomy of the opposite sex besides the genitals. Heterosexual men are typically fascinated by female breasts and legs; many women are partial to slim male buttocks and broad shoulders. Blond female hair and dark male eyes seem to have special erotic attraction for many in our society. Preferences for such features are a normal part of cultural patterns.

Types of Fetishes    Any article or body part can become endowed with fetishistic meaning, but some objects are more commonly chosen than others. The attraction may arise from the shape, texture, color, or smell of the article, or from a combination of features. Most fetishes fall into two categories: *soft fetishes* are "feminine" objects that are soft, furry, lacy, pastel-colored (like panties, stockings, and garters); *hard fetishes* are "masculine" objects that are smooth, harsh, or black (like spike-heeled shoes, black gloves, and other garments and objects made of leather or rubber) (Figure 14.5). Hard fetishes are more often associated with sadomasochistic fantasies and practices.

Fetishes are sexual symbols with both shared and private meanings. For instance, high-heeled women's shoes are regarded as sexy in our culture; but the shoe fetishist will in addition be attracted to particular types of shoes and may collect them in staggering numbers, like a substitute harem (Stekel, 1964). The fetishist uses these objects for sexual arousal, either in conjunction with some other sexual activity or to masturbate with.

Articles of personal clothing are generally preferred if they have been used. Various characteristics thus combine to make an object progressively more arousing. A pair of plain white, new, full-size cotton women's underpants would probably have little arousal value except for the most desperate. Bikini-style black or red panties of a transparent material would be more exciting; even more so if they

Figure 14.5   *The Damned* (1969). Male actor imitating Marlene Dietrich's classic pose in *The Blue Angel*, displaying garter, black stockings, and shoes, which are all fetishistic objects.

have been used, because the stain and odor of vaginal secretions impart a more personal "live" aura. A man does not have to be a fetishist to understand the progression of erotic charge in this example; but to a normal male, the "value" of the panties derives from the woman who wore them, and his excitement would be channeled to her; for the fetishist, the panties are it. He may be so dependent on their arousal value that he cannot sexually engage a woman without the fetish object; a normal man will gladly forgo it for the woman.

Women may have difficulty understanding the fetishist's mental cast. Though traditionally they have used clothing and ornaments to make themselves alluring, male objects seem to pack little erotic value for them: a man's underpants will look like just a piece of clothing to most women; and if it has been used, it will just look dirty. Would women react differently to some other item, or do inanimate objects simply have no sexual appeal

to them? Are lesbians aroused by the same type of female objects as men? We know very little about these issues as they pertain to women.

Fetishes may be symbolic substitutes for the genital organs, but the genitals themselves can be fetishes if they get in the way of perceiving the sexual partner as a whole person. The preoccupation with the penis among some gay men may be a form of fetishism. Hoffman (1968) associates it with the dehumanized sexual interactions that take place in public places, like toilets, where the focus of interest is the penis and little else.

Physical defects, such as a missing limb or crossed eyes, become the object of fetishistic fixation in rare cases. To be sexually attracted to an amputee or someone with a deformity is fine, but to be attracted to such persons *because* of their defects turns it into a fetish.

Psychological Characteristics   What is known about the personality characteristics of fetishists is not particularly instructive. In the Gebhard et al. (1965) sample, these men revealed poorly developed heterosexual relationships since their childhood, except with the mother, to whom they had been strongly attached. Their fetishistic interest could be traced back to their adolescence and earlier years.

Some clinicians view fetishism as yet another substitute form of sexuality for immature men who cannot manage to get into heterosexual adult relationships. Rather than becoming entangled with children and animals, the fetishist presumably resorts to the safe and silent company of inanimate objects.

This view does injustice to the psychological complexity of the fetishist's character, particularly those who are neither distraught enough to be in therapy nor foolish or helpless enough to land in jail for socially harmless behavior.

Transvestism

*Transvestism* (Latin *trans*, "across," and *vestia*, "dress"), or *cross-dressing*, is the recurrent and persistent practice, usually on the part of males, of dressing in the clothing of the op-

Figure 14.6   A transvestite male.

posite sex for purposes of sexual excitement (Figure 14.6). In our society, and most other cultures, male and female clothing is distinctive, although the degree of overlap varies. Women have more latitude in what they wear than men do (pants are worn by many women, but men in the United States do not wear skirts). It is also not uncommon for males to dress up as females in playful situations, dramatic skits, and films (Figure 14.7).

There are other situations where wearing female clothing by men would not qualify as transvestism. Transsexualism is one instance; but in some cases, transsexualism starts as transvestism (Wise and Meyer, 1980). Homosexual men who dress up as women to attract other men (with whom they engage in sexual activities that do not reveal their maleness) or who masquerade in "drag" for reasons other than sexual arousal are not transvestites; nor are female impersonators who act this way to

earn a living. To qualify as transvestism, there must be a compulsion to cross-dress and intense frustration when the practice is interfered with.

Most transvestites are heterosexual males. Their involvement in cross-dressing is *partial* if they are attracted only to certain items of female clothing. They may wear the female garment, such as panties, under their male clothing. The *complete* cross-dresser puts on female garments either as an occasional activity or all the time. Some of these men carry on this practice on their own; others participate actively in the transvestite subculture. In Southern California there is an organization called Chic, which consists exclusively of heterosexual cross-dressers. Its members are mostly professional men who gather for dinner and socializing while elaborately dressed and made up as women, many of them accompanied by their wives.

Cross-dressing typically begins in childhood or early adolescence. The majority of children who play at cross-dressing do not become transvestites; those who do often say that they were punished for it (Stoller, 1977).

Figure 14.7   Flip Wilson as "Geraldine."

Transvestites usually begin to cross-dress in public after they reach adulthood (Croughan et al., 1981; Wise, 1982).

The wives of transvestites may learn to live with their husbands' cross-dressing habits and even help them buy female clothes. Others are distressed by the situation and seek help or break the relationship (Wise et al., 1981).

Female transvestism is rare. For whatever other reasons women may choose to wear men's clothing, apparently few do so for sexual arousal.

## Necrophilia

The most extreme choice of sexual object is the body of a dead person. *Necrophilia* is a very rare entity, usually involving psychotic men. In a highly unusual case, a 23-year-old woman who worked as an apprentice embalmer was convicted in 1982 of sexually molesting the corpse of a 33-year-old man. She admitted to having had sexual contact with up to 40 other bodies. A letter that she left with the corpse after her last episode read, "I've written this with what's left of my broken heart. If you read this, don't hate me. I was once like you. I laughed, I loved, but something went wrong. . . . But please remember me as I was, not as I am now" (*San Francisco Chronicle*, Apr. 25, 1982, p. 2).

According to the Greek historian Herodotus, ancient Egyptians would not give the corpses of noble or beautiful women to embalmers until several days after their death to prevent the cadavers from being sexually violated (Forberg, 1966).

The mixture of horror, death, and eroticism is also discernible in movies and comics that appeal to some teenagers. More gruesome are the "snuff" films of violent pornography which involve mutilation and murder.

## Voyeurism

It is said that Leofric, Lord of Coventry in the eleventh century, agreed to remit an oppressive tax if his wife, Lady Godiva, would ride through the town naked on a white horse. Lady Godiva, a benefactress of monasteries and of the poor, consented. Out of respect and gratitude everyone in town stayed behind shuttered windows during her ride—everyone, except Tom the tailor, who peeped and went blind: hence the name *Peeping Tom*.

The sight of women who are scantily dressed, inadvertently exposed, or in the process of undressing is arousing to many men. Although women have traditionally been assumed not to have similar interests, many more now report that they too like to look at nude or partially clad male bodies. Along with male pastimes like "girl watching," "girlie" magazines, and topless dancing, there are now women's magazines that feature nude male photographs and male strip shows for women. These alternatives as yet seem to appeal to a far smaller proportion of women (Figure 16.4).

Such behavior is loosely called *voyeurism* (French, "to look"), but it is not a paraphilia. True voyeuristic behavior must be repetitive and compulsive; the person being observed must be unaware of it, and would be upset if she were to find out. "It's as bad as being raped. . . . At least when you are raped you know who your attacker is," said a woman whose male coworkers had drilled a hole in the wall of the women's bathroom in a West Virginia coal mine (*San Francisco Chronicle*, July 2, 1981b).

By these strict criteria, virtually all voyeurs are men who secretly watch women undressing, bathing, in the nude, or engaged in sex (Figure 14.8). They typically masturbate during or following the act. As a rule they do not physically molest the victim, although in some cases they do break in to commit rape and burglary.

Part of the excitement of the act comes from the danger and the satisfaction of knowing that the woman would be frightened and angry should she realize her privacy is being violated. For this reason the typical voyeur is not interested in ogling his own wife, female friend, or even strangers in a nudist colony.

Voyeurs tend to be younger men (the average age at first conviction is 23.8 years) (Gebhard et al., 1965; Stoller, 1977). Two-thirds of them are unmarried, one-fourth are married, and the rest are either divorced, wid-

Figure 14.8    Chinese woman bathing, secretly watched by a man (18th century?). Artist unknown.

owed, or separated. Few show evidence of serious mental disorders, and alcohol or drugs are usually not involved in their deviant behavior: only 16 percent of the Gebhard sample were drunk at the time of the offense; none was under the influence of drugs. In intelligence, occupational choice, and family background, "peepers" are a mixed group whose single most common characteristic is a history of deficient heterosexual relationships. Most voyeurs do not have serious criminal records, but many have histories of misdemeanors.

## Exhibitionism

To expose or exhibit (Latin, "to hold out") one's body or genitals for purposes of erotic stimulation is a common part of sexual interaction. The term *exhibitionistic* is also applied to dressing or acting in ways that are sexually provocative. A great deal of exhibitionistic behavior is commercialized—flagrantly in pornographic shows, books, and movies, but also in advertising (Chapter 18).

*Exhibitionism* (also called "indecent exposure") as a paraphilia has a much more restricted meaning. It is in many ways the mirror image of voyeurism. Instead of peeping, the exhibitionist ("flasher," "flagwaver") obtains sexual gratification from exposing the genitals to involuntary observers, usually complete strangers (Figure 14.9). Though most exhibitionists are male, rare cases among females also occur (Hollender et al., 1977). Gittelson and his associates (1978) found 44 percent of women in a British sample to have been subjected to indecent exposure; Zverina et al. (1987), in a Czechoslovakian study, placed the figure at 51 percent for various female patient groups.

In a typical sequence the exhibitionist suddenly confronts a woman with his genitals exposed. He may or may not have an erection as he openly masturbates. He may wear a coat and expose himself periodically while riding on a subway or bus, or he may stand in a park and pretend that he is urinating.

The exhibitionist does not usually molest the victim, although occasional attempts at rape and assault have been reported (MacNamara and Sagarin, 1977). His gratification comes from observing the victim's surprise, fear, or disgust; women who keep calm without entirely disregarding him foil his intent. There is a compulsive quality to the exhibitionist's behavior, which may be triggered by excitement, fear, restlessness, and sexual arousal. Once in this mood, he is driven to find

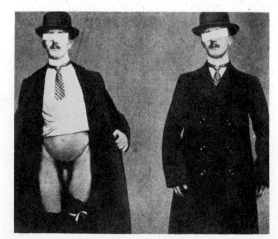

Figure 14.9    Exhibitionist.

relief. The nature of sexually arousing stimuli seems to be different for exhibitionists than for other paraphiliacs and ordinary men. For instance, in laboratory settings, exhibitionists are aroused by images of fully clothed erotically neutral women, which the control groups are not (Fedora et al., 1986).

Exhibitionists tend to be younger men. The average age at conviction is 30 years (Gebhard et al., 1965). About 30 percent of arrested exhibitionists are married; another 30 percent are separated, divorced, or widowed; and 40 percent have never been married. They often have serious sexual problems and are impotent in heterosexual relations. They have also been described as above average in intelligence and without evidence of serious emotional problems (Smukler and Schiebel, 1975). Exhibitionists do not usually show signs of severe mental disorder, and alcohol and drugs are involved only in rare instances (Blair and Langon, 1987).

Exhibitionists seem particularly prone to getting caught. This fact is partly due to the public nature of their act, but there is also evidence that they deliberately court arrest, for instance, by returning to the same spot. It is as if the danger of the situation heightens their arousal (Stoller, 1977). Also, despite previous arrests and convictions, exhibitionists tend to repeat their behavior. One-third of the offenders in this category in the Gebhard study had had four to six previous convictions, and 10 percent had been convicted seven or more times.

## Obscene Calls

The shock value of sex is also used in many other ways. Off-color humor or dirty jokes, sexual innuendo, and like behaviors that are meant to embarrass can be subtle forms of exhibitionism. More flagrant is the practice of *obscene telephone calls*. The caller is usually a sexually inadequate man who tries to have an erotically charged interchange with a woman through this apparently safe method (less safe, as detection mechanisms are improved). His pleasure is derived from eliciting embarrassment as his intent becomes clear to the women.

There are several types of obscene callers. Some will talk about their own sexual experiences; others will seek sexual information by pretending to be conducting surveys for underwear manufacturers or carrying out a sex study (an amazing number of women fall for this ploy). Some men will call telephone counselors and be sexually explicit or abusive to them (Clark et al., 1986). Telephone companies recommend that the recipient of an obscene call remain calm and either hang up immediately or, if possible, alert the operator, by means of another line, to trace the call and notify the police.

The telephone has also been put to the opposite purpose of titillating callers. Like the Dial-It service for time and the weather, one can now listen to women delivering racy recorded "messages." *Phone sex* caters to various interests ranging over anal sex, group sex, and so on. Telephone numbers with sexually explicit invitations are advertised in sexually explicit magazines and newspapers. One such number in New York City attracted 500,000 callers, who earned the producers $10,000 and the telephone company $25,000 a day (*Time*, May 9, 1983, p. 39).

## Sadomasochism (S-M)

Sadism and masochism have been widely explored in art (Figures 14.10 and 14.11) and literature. The terms are derived from the names of two historical figures who wrote on these respective themes. The first is French nobleman Donatien Alphonse François, Marquis de Sade (1740–1814); the second, the Austrian author Leopold von Sacher-Masoch (1836–1895). The works and the biographies of both men are widely known (Ellis, 1942; Thomas, 1976). For a sample of Sade's writing, see Box 14.2.

The infliction of mild pain through biting, scratching, pinching, slapping, and pinning the partner down are part of the sexual repertory of some sexually adventurous couples. Teeth marks and purplish bruises ("hickies") about the neck, caused by passionate kissing, are well-known signs of "wild" lovemaking. In

Figure 14.10    Flagellation scene, around 1770 A.D. Etching from Caylus, *Thérèse Philosophe*.

Figure 14.11    Mauron, *The cully flaug'd*. Eighteenth-century illustration for *Fanny hill*.

the Hunt (1974) sample, about 5 percent of men and 2 percent of women had obtained pleasure by inflicting pain and 2 percent of men and 5 percent of women by receiving pain. In a survey of college students, 2 percent had tried using pain; 4 percent said they would like to try it (*Playboy*, 1986).

As a paraphilia, *sexual sadism* entails the infliction of physical pain or psychological humiliation and degradation on another person; *sexual masochism* is the enjoyment of such suffering for erotic excitement as a preferred form of sexual activity. In this more restricted sense, such behavior is much less common. Sadism and masochism usually have been considered as two sides of the same coin, or *sadomasochism*. Some now consider these tendencies

to be independent of each other (Baumeister, 1988).

Until recently, most of the literature on sadism and masochism was derived from clinical studies on individual behavior. Currently, survey research and sociological approaches have expanded that perspective (Weinberg, 1987). The more accepting view of these practices has led some to view S-M as the "last taboo" waiting to be dismantled (Greene and Greene, 1974).

Sadomasochism demonstrates better than any other paraphilia the intrusion of dominance and aggression into sexual interactions. The role of dominance is most clear in the practices of *bondage and domination* (B-D), where a nonconsenting victim or a willing collaborator is bound, gagged, and immobilized, at the mercy of the *master* or the *mistress* ("dominatrix"). These activities commonly utilize fetishistic trappings like black leather garments and high-heeled shoes, along with the classic chains, shackles, whips, harnesses, and other paraphernalia.

# Box 14.2

## THE LITERATURE OF SADOMASOCHISM*

Upon the spot La Rose opens a closet and draws out a cross made of gnarled, thorny, spiny wood. 'Tis thereon the infamous debauchee wishes to place me, but by means of what episode will he improve his cruel enjoyment? Before attaching me, Cardoville inserts into my behind a silver-colored ball the size of an egg; he lubricates it and drives it home: it disappears. Immediately it is in my body I feel it enlarge and begin to burn; without heeding my complaints, I am lashed securely to this thorn-studded frame; Cardoville penetrates as he fastens himself to me: he presses my back, my flanks, my buttocks on the protuberances upon which they are suspended. Julien fits himself into Cardoville; obliged to bear the weight of these two bodies, and having nothing to support myself upon but these accursed knots and knurs which gouge into my flesh, you may easily conceive what I suffered; the more I thrust up against those who press down upon me, the more I am driven upon the irregularities which stab and lacerate me. Meanwhile the terrible globe has worked its way deep into my bowels and is cramping them, burning them, tearing them; I scream again and again: no words exist which can describe what I am undergoing; all the same and all the while, my murderer frolics joyfully,

his mouth glued to mine, he seems to inhale my pain in order that it may magnify his pleasures: his intoxication is not to be rendered; but, as in his friend's instance, he feels his forces about to desert him, and like Saint-Florent wants to taste everything before they are gone entirely. I am turned over again, am made to eject the ardent sphere, and it is set to producing in the vagina itself, the same conflagration it ignited in the place whence it has just been flushed; the ball enters, sears, scorches the matrix to its depths; I am not spared, they fasten me belly-down upon the perfidious cross, and far more delicate parts of me are exposed to molestation by the thorny excrescences awaiting them. Cardoville penetrates into the forbidden passage; he perforates it while another enjoys him in similar wise: and at last delirium holds my persecutor in its grasp, his appalling shrieks announce the crime's completion; I am inundated, then untied.

*From *Justine* by the Marquis de Sade. New York: Grove Press, 1965, p. 732. Reprinted by permission of Grove Press, Inc. Translated from the French by Austryn Wainhouse & Richard Seaver. Copyright 1966 by Austryn Wainhouse and Richard Seaver.

---

The aggression includes verbal humiliations and whippings. Whippings range from light, symbolic blows to severe ones that raise welts and draw blood. Rarely, sadomasochistic practices cause mutilation and death.

S-M activities primarily involve males. Some women are excited by them, but most do it to please their male partners, consent for money, or are its involuntary victims (Breslow et al., 1985). The practice may be more common and more violent among gay men, because male interacting with male compounds the violence. There are various studies comparing the differences between heterosexuals and homosexuals engaging in S-M practices (Breslow et al., 1986).

Prevalence figures on these practices are

hard to get, and given the wide variety of behaviors, it is hard to know what to count. A great deal of violence pervades our culture, some of which is clearly sexualized. Rock groups, fashion photographers, and other followers of S-M chic are part of the mainstream of society. At a broader level, S-M is a relatively trivial form of sexual violence compared to rape and other forms of sexual coercion (Chapter 19). A more ritualistic, make-believe sort of sexual violence typically characterizes the paraphiliac form of S-M.

Couples who buy S-M paraphernalia at sex shops and stage bondage scenes in their bedroom usually experiment with such activities on an occasional basis (Comfort, 1972). Those who are more earnest (most of whom are male) use prostitutes or go to special S-M establishments to experience bondage, humiliation, and pain, but they are not interested in getting injured (Scott, 1983). A substantial proportion of these men are said to be well-off professionals and executives who seek safe ways of fulfilling their masochistic needs. The Chateau in Los Angeles reportedly offers over 1000 clients the personalized services of 13 women in dominant and submissive roles. These women consider themselves "sex therapists" of sorts, who provide men with "mental trips" of sadomasochistic excitement in a safe and "loving" setting (*Time,* May 4, 1981, p. 73). Other men make contact through newspapers that carry S-M ads.

In such interactions, there is a standard procedure. The couples agree beforehand on a scene to be enacted—who is going to do what to whom—with some leeway for spontaneity. The person playing "bottom," or the submissive part, is given a "safe word," which is a code for the action to stop. This allows the "slave" to plead for mercy or scream bloody murder without interrupting the action, but to have it stopped by using the code word.

The clinical literature has dwelt mainly on sadomasochism as a psychological abnormality. Survey data on nonclinical samples from the *S-M subculture* focuses more on their social and behavioral characteristics. In one study 71 percent of the sample was male and 29 percent was female. Both were predominantly heterosexual, but there was a greater concentration of bisexuals among the females than among the males (32 percent against 14 percent); the proportion of homosexuals was almost the same (about 2 percent). The largest proportion of this sample (about 40 percent) was aged 31 to 40 years; the majority of whom were college educated and over half of them were married. About 80 percent of the men (but only about 40 percent of the women) traced their interest in S-M activities to their adolescence and childhood periods. Table 14.1 lists their preferred sadomasochistic activities. Most of these persons appear socially well adjusted and successful, and 85 percent say no one would guess their S-M involvement. On the other hand, 32

percent have felt close to having a nervous breakdown, some have been hospitalized, and 30 percent worry that their S-M practices may escalate to a dangerous extent. Heterosexuals outnumber homosexuals in this group (Breslow et al., 1985).

**Table 14.1   Preferences of Sadomasochistic Sexual Interests***

| INTEREST | MALE (%) | FEMALE (%) |
|---|---|---|
| Spanking | 79 | 80 |
| Master-slave relationships | 79 | 76 |
| Oral sex | 77 | 90 |
| Masturbation | 70 | 73 |
| Bondage | 67 | 88 |
| Humiliation | 65 | 61 |
| Erotic lingerie | 63 | 88 |
| Restraint | 60 | 83 |
| Anal sex | 58 | 51 |
| Pain | 51 | 34 |
| Whipping | 47 | 39 |
| Rubber/leather | 42 | 42 |
| Boots/shoes | 40 | 49 |
| Verbal abuse | 40 | 51 |
| Stringent bondage | 39 | 54 |
| Enemas | 33 | 22 |
| Torture | 32 | 32 |
| Golden showers | 30 | 37 |
| Transvestism | 28 | 20 |
| Petticoat punishment | 25 | 20 |
| Toilet activities | 19 | 12 |

*From Breslow et al. (1985), p. 315

Specialized S-M magazines that cater to this clientele feature photographs and cartoons of women dressed in black leather with spike-heeled shoes trying to look menacing as they gag, bind, whip, and variously "torture" their "victims." Although there is no evidence that the readers of such material are apt to carry out their violent fantasies on unwilling others, the potential negative effects of violent pornography cannot be dismissed (Chapters 18 and 19).

Sometimes serious injury results from S-M practices from miscalculation, getting carried away, or pure viciousness. Whereas the participants in staged practices are voluntary, the true sadists will inflict pain on involuntary victims who fall into their hands.

The most dangerous practices include putting a "choke hold" (forearm to neck) on the partner, leading to accidental strangulation (Michalodimitrakis et al., 1986). Self-inflicted damage includes burns and accidental hanging (Walsh et al., 1977), which we referred to earlier as a masturbatory practice. Most gruesome are ritualistic sex murders: in one case, a young man reportedly killed his male lover after a sadomasochistic orgy, then tore out the victim's heart and drank his blood out of a wine glass (*San Francisco Chronicle*, Sept. 27, 1985).

## Other Paraphilias

A number of paraphilias are hard to classify. Several of them are closely linked to fetishism. Instead of body parts, the discharges of the body take on erotic significance. These behaviors include erotic fascination with feces (*coprophilia*), enemas (*klismaphilia*), urine (*urophilia* or *urolagnia*), and filth (*mysophilia*) (Money, 1986). These stimuli may be used for excitement in other sexual activities or as erotic ends in themselves.

These paraphilias often serve a sadomasochistic function. For example, during rapes (especially gang rapes), the assailants may urinate and defecate on the victim as an additional means of degradation. Ejaculation itself may become a means of soiling, with semen spurted at the victim's face, hair, and body.

Some paraphiliacs enjoy being urinated on (golden showers). Others sniff dirty socks, lick unwashed feet, drink urine, and taste feces (Krafft-Ebing, 1978).

There are certain behaviors whose sexual intent is more concealed. In *pyromania*, the person setting fires may actually feel aroused and masturbate. In *kleptomania*, where the person steals for the excitement of the act, the stolen objects may have sexual significance in a symbolic sense. In principle, virtually any act may become eroticized and constitute a paraphilia.

In *frotteurism* (French, "to rub") the person, usually a younger male, has an intense urge to fondle and rub against parts of the body of a nonconsenting person (also called *toucherism*) (American Psychiatric Association, 1987). Such urges may not be unusual, but the frotteur acts on them in crowded places such as sidewalks, buses, and subways. The frotteur has fantasies of becoming affectionately involved with the person he has singled out but must make his escape before he is discovered and denounced.

## Sexual Addiction

Men and women with highly active sex lives have been a source of wonder, envy, or condemnation in many cultures. The term *promiscuity* has long been used to describe indiscriminate, casual, and excessive sexual behavior. Similarly, *nymphomania* and *satyriasis* were diagnoses for excessive or insatiable sexual behavior among women and men, respectively.[5]

Kinsey took issue with these concepts, considering high frequency of sexual behaviors as part of the normal variation among individuals; and with the advent of the sexual revolution, these terms and the concepts they represented went out of favor as judgmental and unsound.

In the late 1970s, the term *sexual addiction* began to appear in the literature, followed by *sexual compulsion*. Both referred to inability to control the number of sexual partners and the frequency of sexual activity (Edwards, 1986).

Many sex researchers find these terms, and the behaviors they represent, to be invalid as diagnostic entities, and they are not included among the paraphilias (American Psychiatric Association, 1987). These terms are used with no consistent meaning or opera-

[5]The satyrs (*see* Figure in Box 2.5) of Greek mythology were part-human, part-animal (usually goat) beings and the companions of Dionysus, the god of wine and fertility. Nymphs were young, beautiful, and amorous maidens and the objects of the satyrs' lustful pursuit. These creatures symbolized for the Greeks the uninhibited sexual elements in human nature.

tional definition. They do not fit with established concepts of addiction. Critics say these terms are value-laden, reactionary, and aimed more often at gay men with many partners. In effect, the new ideas are seen as recycled versions of discredited earlier notions (Coleman, 1987).

Other sex researchers and therapists find the concepts of sexual addiction and compulsion useful in dealing with individuals whose uncontrolled sexual behavior has seriously interfered with their health, career, and relationships, and who identify themselves as addicted to sex (Carnes, 1983, 1987; Coleman, 1987).

One way of resolving this issue is to move away from judgments based on frequency of sexual behavior and focus on its meaning to the individual. For instance, Lorna and Philip Sarrel (1979) differentiate *sleeping around,* a phase that increasing numbers of young people are going through, from indiscriminate and compulsive seeking of transient sexual encounters that have no relational or affectionate context. The former, which serves sexual experimentation and discovery, may not involve close relationships with every sexual partner (which makes some women worry about becoming "promiscuous"). In contrast, the compulsively sexual, though they seem to behave no differently, have a driven, uncontrolled, and destructive element to their sexual encounters. Sex for them is a means of reducing anxiety temporarily by providing an illusion of power and intimacy that compensates for feeling worthless (Edwards, 1986).

There is a parallel to the sleeping around of young people in the behavior of the recently separated and divorced. In the aftermath of such traumatic break-ups, it is common for women and men to have a succession of superficial affairs. Here again, we are not dealing with a paraphilia but an attempt at restitution. New sexual partners hold out for these people a means of reaffirming their desirability to counter the rejection they have suffered, to vent their anger and frustration, to distract them from grief, and to make up for lost time (Scarf, 1980). Casual sex under these circumstances is a temporary respite, but it cannot substitute for working through the leftover problems of the old relationship and establishing a better new one.

"Hypersexuality" may also have an aggressive component. The idea of *scoring* or *conquest* of sexual partners carries a dehumanizing connotation. The character of Don Juan, widely represented in literature, art, and music is the male prototype of the sexual "conqueror." Don Juan "loves them and leaves them" with no thought to the consequences for the women who yield to him. His female counterpart is Émile Zola's Nana. A highly coveted courtesan, Nana is seemingly driven by greed; yet the more her lovers lavish money and gifts on her, the more she scorns them. Don Juan and Nana are penis and vagina personified, not as reproductive emblems or as instruments of pleasure, but as weapons of destruction and hatred. It is this element of hatred along with underlying compusion that links these behaviors with the paraphilias.

*Troilism,* in which a third person joins a couple, or other forms of *group sex* raise similar considerations. Why does the image, and sometimes the reality, of a mass of humanity with intertwined limbs and sweating torsos so excite the erotic imagination of many of us? One answer is that it is fun, and as long as all of the participants think so, why is there a need for further explanation? However, beyond novelty and experimentation, such activities may fulfull paraphiliac needs. People are reduced to body parts and genitals (fetishism); one sees (voyeurism) and shows (exhibitionism) the forbidden. As the ultimate erotic fantasy, this behavior is the stuff of pornography at its purest (Chapter 18). Does society disapprove of such behaviors because they are paraphilias, at some level maladaptive; or do we call such behaviors paraphilias because society disapproves of them?

## CAUSES AND TREATMENTS

In the introduction to this chapter, and in connection with specific paraphilias, we have alluded to possible causes. Let us consider the issue more closely.

## The Development of Paraphilias

If you cannot define a behavior with any precision, it is hard to look for its causes. Paraphilias are a case in point. We cannot really agree on what they are, let alone on what causes them. Official definitions are useful and necessary (clinicians need labels to communicate and keep records), but they have no solid conceptual base. They are classifications for convenience that leave people free to call paraphiliacs everything from perverts to sexual minorities.

**Biological Roots**  The 19th-century theories of "hereditary tainting" or "degeneracy" as causes of paraphilias have long been discredited.

Because paraphilias are overwhelmingly more common among men than women, and because there are biological differences between males and females, paraphilias could be at least partly biologically based. Many of the paraphilias are linked with coercive sexual behavior, which is also largely male. We shall return to this issue in Chapter 19.

**The Psychoanalytic Model**  Psychoanalytic theory provides a versatile means of explaining the development of paraphilias, if you accept its basic premises (which most behavioral scientists do not) (Neu, 1987). As we discussed in Chapter 8, the *polymorphously perverse* sexuality of the child is gradually repressed and sublimated into socially adaptive adult forms (Freud, 1905). If not, the persistent themes of these childhood sexual and aggressive impulses come out in one paraphilia or another, each of which can be traced to an infantile form of sexual expression. The paraphilias in this view represent an *arrest* in psychological development (getting stuck) or a *regression* to a childhood stage (sliding back).

Other infantile roots of the paraphilias are said to go back to the Oedipal stage. For instance, voyeurism may reflect leftover unconscious wishes to see the mother's nude body.

The voyeur is not aware of this, nor does he want to see his mother nude as an adult. It is the *infantile* image, which is repressed, that is always the driving force; hence it can never be realistically satisfied.

Robert Stoller (1975) finds hostility to be at the root of paraphilias (and at some level all forms of sexual arousal). The paraphilias in this view are *symbolic reenactments* of childhood traumas. The adult attempts through them to revive and repair old psychological wounds, and to take revenge on substitute people and objects. Paraphilias thus become "the erotic form of hatred." The compulsive, driven element of such behaviors testifies to their deep-seated infantile origins, of which the adult has no conscious knowledge or control. Through such practices, the adult manages to obtain some measure of sexual gratification and triumphs over past deprivations and hurts that continue to haunt.

**Learning Models**  If human behavior is learned, then paraphilias also must somehow be learned. One possible way is through conditioning. When a boy is sexually aroused, even inadvertently, whatever objects he comes in contact with or experiences he has during arousal become eroticized by association (Chapter 8). Once otherwise neutral objects or experiences have become sexually charged, they will cause arousal in the future on their own.

A more sophisticated version of the conditioning model goes beyond chance associations. In this case, linkage of sexual arousal with an object or situation is not enough. The child has to remember the linkage and incorporate it into masturbatory fantasies, which are repeated over and over, for a paraphilia to take root (McGuire et al., 1965). For example, suppose a boy is masturbating in the bathroom and notices his teenage sister's panties on the floor. He is struck by their odor and genital association. If the next time he masturbates, he thinks of the panties and gets a sexual charge out of it, he is more likely to repeat the fantasy. He may then look for women's panties, maybe obtain a pair, and use them as a masturbatory prop. If the prop is elevated to a necessity for sexual arousal, he becomes a fetishist.

Masturbation, in this view, is the key vehicle for the establishment of paraphilias through fantasy. Because males masturbate more commonly than women, this theory seems to explain why most paraphiliacs are male—except that the women who do masturbate are much less likely to become paraphiliacs than the men who do.

John Money (1986) perceives paraphilias as one aspect of *lovemaps*. Lovemaps develop in childhood; they represent areas of relative erotic attraction and arousal. Juvenile sex rehearsal is a prerequisite for healthy development. If the child is deprived of sex rehearsal play because of prohibitions, abusive punishments, or severe discipline, the formation of lovemaps is distorted with one of three outcomes: *hypophilia* (sexual dysfunction), *hyperphilia* (or sexual addiction), and *paraphilia*. In each case, there is a split between love and lust.

## The Treatment of Paraphilias

Investigators and clinicians may find paraphiliacs immature and beset with emotional problems, but paraphiliacs have not been flocking to be treated. Some are unhappy enough to want to change; others want to be left alone to seek sexual fulfillment in ways they know best. The attachment of many paraphiliacs to their atypical sexual behavior is so fixed that giving it up is next to unthinkable (Money, 1986).

Society is fairly united in its rejection of these behaviors once they cross the line of public tolerance—especially pedophilia. The impetus of changing paraphiliac behavior comes mainly from the outside—society in general, or parents and spouses in particular cases.

Biologically Based Treatment    The most intrusive and questionable treatments are surgical procedures and drugs that do not "cure" the paraphiliac but reduce sexual drive. They diminish the compulsive force of paraphiliac fantasies and the likelihood of their being acted out.

The most drastic surgical procedure is *psychosurgery*, which severs the nerve connections between various parts of the brain (such as the hypothalamus) that are thought to control sexual behavior. These procedures are not used in the United States but are experimented with in some European countries (Rieber and Sigush, 1979).

Another drastic procedure is *castration*—removing the testes surgically or, more commonly, suppressing their function through drugs (chemical castration). These drugs are *antiandrogens* that affect the brain and reduce the production of testosterone (Chapter 4) (Neumann and Topert, 1986). Most often used is medroxyprogesterone acetate (MPA), a synthetic hormone (brand name Depo-Provera) that acts like natural progesterone (Wincze et al, 1986).[6] Another drug is cyproterone acetate (CPA), which also reduces sexual arousability and libido (Cooper, 1986; deVries et al., 1986).

Offenders in the United States used to be offered castration as an alternative to long prison sentences, but this practice is no longer condoned. However, the use of antiandrogens on true volunteers is acceptable. It may be a valuable adjunct to psychotherapy or behavior modification. The treatment works best with self-referred, hypersexual individuals without repeated criminal records and with good social supports (Cooper, 1986). Pedophiles are the usual candidates (Berlin and Krout, 1986). Laboratory studies show psychological arousal in response to erotic stimuli is definitely reduced; genital response is decreased only slightly (Wincze et al., 1986).

The use of these chemicals puts the sexual drive "on ice," allowing some breathing room during the slow rehabilitation of the paraphiliac. The person must be maintained on a steady dose, at a high enough level and long enough for progress to take place.

Punishment    The time-honored and standard method used by societies to curb deviant behavior, sexual or otherwise, has been punishment. Although the imprisonment of individuals who represent a danger to society remains a necessity, there is little evidence

---

[6]Depo-Provera is also used as the day-after pill to prevent pregnancy (Chapter 6).

that it changes behavior. We return to this issue in Chapter 22.

Psychotherapy    Psychoanalysis and less intensive therapy have not been notably successful in changing paraphiliacs' behavior. Some psychological counseling is necessary, however, to support them through crises and to help them deal with the consequences of their actions.

Behavior Therapy    Behavior modification techniques are the most actively used methods for treating paraphilias today. They can be carried out over fairly short periods of time, and sometimes they work. Much depends on the willingness of the client to change.

One procedure is *extinction*. This method reverses the process by which an object or behavior was linked with sexual arousal; extinction works by decoupling them. If a voyeur is aroused by certain sights, the therapist contrives situations in safe surroundings that interfere with arousal.

*Aversion therapy* involves reconditioning through various forms of unpleasant effects. A therapist might give painful (but harmless) electric shocks while showing images of paraphiliac stimuli. Extinction takes the wind out of the person's sails; aversion therapy ruins the paraphiliac experience.

Because causing people discomfort is unpleasant for those interested in helping others, and because it raises ethical issues, some therapists use the person's own unpleasant fantasies as "punishment" (Evans, 1980). Instead of getting an electric shock, the person is made to imagine an awful experience, such as being publicly ridiculed and shamed in front of family and friends. This procedure, known as *covert sensitization*, may be combined with other techniques. For instance, in treating an exhibitionist, covert sensitization was used to eliminate deviant fantasies, while private genital exposure to the wife allowed some expression of his paraphilic urge under safe circumstances (Lamontagne and Lesage, 1986).

Once the paraphilic tendencies have subsided, the therapist must strengthen the existing forms of healthy behavior. *Desensitization* procedures are used to counteract the anxiety that may be inhibiting the expression of ordinary behaviors. This is accomplished by gradual exposure in a fantasy to anxiety-provoking situations while the person calms down through relaxation techniques.

Another way of reinforcing the healthier elements of the person's sexual behavior is to teach social skills. Many paraphiliacs have had little experience and lack the social skills necessary in approaching mature adult women and eventually negotiating a sexual relationship with them. These grown men must be taught what most others learn during their adolescence.

Finally, various forms of *group therapy* have been found useful for self-referred or court-referred individuals. Modeled after Alcoholics Anonymous and other therapeutic strategies, groups provide participants the opportunity to confront the nature and consequences of their behavior and to support each other.

The treatment of paraphilia thus requires a multifaceted approach. Various modes of treatment—biological, psychological, social—have to combine in a coherent and practical program, to change a lifetime of maladaptive sexual behavior (Freeman-Longo and Wally, 1986). Most important, it requires a person who genuinely wants to change, and a society with the capability and firmness to impose that change in a humane manner.

## REVIEW QUESTIONS

1. What are historical and current concepts of paraphilia?

2. How do the paraphilias differ from gender disorders?

3. What are the behavioral characteristics of the paraphilias?

4. What are the main theories for how the paraphilias develop?

5. What methods are currently used for treating paraphilias?

## THOUGHT QUESTIONS

1. Your friend wonders if his or her odd sexual fantasies are "normal." What should you tell your friend?

2. A child for whom you babysit tells you her father touches her "down there." What should you do?

3. Should clinics be established where paraphiliacs could indulge their sexual fantasies under safe and supervised conditions with trained volunteers?

4. You find your ten-year-old child reading *Playboy*. How do you deal with it? Why?

5. If a drug or surgical procedure could stop socially unacceptable paraphiliac behavior, would you permit its use on unwilling people?

## SUGGESTED READINGS

Finkelhor, D. (1984). *Child sexual abuse*. New York: Free Press. A thoughtful and thorough consideration of a difficult subject by an expert.

Maltz, W., and Holman, B. (1987). *Incest and Sexuality*. Lexington, Mass., Lexington Books. A guide to understanding and healing for adult incest survivors and their sexual partners.

Stoller, R. J. (1975). *Perversion: The erotic form of hatred*. New York: Deff. Insightful overview of the manifestations and psychodynamics of the paraphilias.

Weinberg, J., and Levi Kamel, G. W. (Eds). (1983). *S and M: Studies in sadomasochism* (1983). Selections with a broad range of viewpoints.

# Sexual Dysfunction and Therapy

*If your life at night is good,
you think you have
Everything; but, if in that
quarter things go wrong,
You will consider your best
and truest interests
Most hateful.*

EURIPIDES, *MEDEA*

OUTLINE

TYPES OF SEXUAL DYSFUNCTION
Definitions
Prevalence
SEXUAL DESIRE DISORDERS
Hypoactive Sexual Desire Disorder
Sexual Aversion
Hyperactive Sexual Drive
SEXUAL AROUSAL DISORDERS
Male Erectile Disorder
Female Sexual Arousal Disorder
ORGASM DISORDERS
Inhibited Female Orgasm
Premature Ejaculation
Inhibited Male Orgasm
SEXUAL PAIN DISORDERS
Dyspareunia
    Female Dyspareunia
    Male Dyspareunia
Vaginismus
CAUSES OF SEXUAL
    DYSFUNCTION
Organic Causes
    Trauma
    Endocrine Disorders
    Neurological Disorders
    Circulatory Disorders
    Alcohol
    Drugs
Organic or Psychogenic?

Psychogenic Causes
    Immediate Causes
    Deeper Causes ·
    Relational Problems
    Cultural Causes
TREATMENTS
Sex Therapy
    The PLISSIT Principle
    The Masters and Johnson Model
    Treatment of Erectile Dysfunction
    Treatment of Anorgasmia
    Treatment of Male Inhibited
        Orgasm
    Treatment of Premature Ejaculation
    Treatment of Vaginismus
Psychotherapy and Behavior
    Therapy
    Psychotherapy
    The Systems Approach
    Behavior Therapy
Group Therapy
Self-Help
Treatment with Drugs
Physical Treatment Methods
    Kegel Exercises
    Masturbation Training
Surgical Methods
Prevention of Sexual Dysfunction

Healthy sexual function and satisfaction are not something to take for granted. It is estimated that 10 million men in the United States have problems with potency (Stipp, 1987); at least as many women may have problems with sexual responsiveness or orgasm.

Despite their prevalence, sexual problems tend to remain hidden. Many people find it easier to tell their friends they have a serious illness than a sexual dysfunction. Many do not feel free to reveal the problem even to their doctor, and some doctors are reluctant to inquire.

No one dies of sexual problems, and fertility may not be impaired. The only loss seems to be in sexual gratification; yet the toll in unhappy marriages and unfulfilled sexual lives is enormous.

## TYPES OF SEXUAL DYSFUNCTION

No human function works flawlessly all of the time, and sex is no exception. It is difficult to define a level of sexual activity as inadequate; there is so much variation in ordinary sexual function, and so much of sexual satisfaction is subjective. The prevalence and frequency of sexual activity also varies with age (Chapter 9), so the same standards cannot be applied across the life cycle.

Nonetheless we can identify some significant failures of sexual function and satisfaction as *sexual dysfunction* (*dys* means faulty or difficult). Such dysfunction is different from diseases of sex organs (such as STDs), reproductive failure (such as sterility), gender disorders (such as transsexualism), and atypical sexual behaviors (paraphilias). The main problems in sexual dysfunction are disturbances of sexual desire (such as lack of interest) or of sexual performance (such as the inability to become sexually aroused or reach orgasm).

### Definitions

Until recently, most male sexual dysfunctions were lumped together as *impotence* and female disorders as *frigidity*. Both terms are now considered inadequate. "Frigidity" has been discarded, but "impotence" continues to be used. Other terms for both male and female dysfunctions have been coined by various sex researchers and therapists (Masters and Johnson, 1970; Kaplan, 1974). Official terms in the Diagnostic Manual of the American Psychiatric Association also keep changing with the refinement of diagnostic categories. As a result, the profusion of terms can be confusing.

The terms that we will use in this chapter are from the 1987 edition of the *Diagnostic Manual (DSM-III-R)* (American Psychiatric Association, 1987). It classifies sexual dysfunctions into four major types: *sexual desire disorders, sexual arousal disorders, orgasm disorders,* and *sexual pain disorders.* Let us clarify what a diagnosis of dysfunction means. There are two approaches. One is to consider all disturbances of sexual function, regardless of cause, as a form of sexual dysfunction. The second is to distinguish between sexual problems that are *symptoms* of some underlying disease (and consider them as part of that disease) and sexual problems that are independent. The Diagnostic Manual follows the latter model, but in practice most sex therapists and clinicians deal with all sexual problems as dysfunctions, whatever their cause.

Many physical illnesses (such as diabetes) can disrupt sexuality. An underlying condition could be affecting a key system, such as the blood vessels or the nerves supplying the genital organs. Similarly, a sexual problem can be the symptom of an underlying psychological illness (such as severe depression). Here too, the sexual disturbance is just one part of a larger disorder.

When the sexual problem is the whole story, it is considered *psychogenic*—caused by psychological or emotional factors. The cause may be intrapsychic (due to inner psychological conflicts), relational (due to conflicts with the partner), or cultural (due to social attitudes towards sex). Whatever the source, sexual dysfunctions today are generally treated as illnesses. Some people object to this model. They would rather deal with the sexual dysfunctions as forms of faulty sexual learning.

To qualify as a dysfunction, the sexual problem must be recurrent or persistent: occasional failure does not count. It is normal to fluctuate in sexual desire. Anyone's performance may occasionally falter. No one is expected to be able to engage in sex at will, with anyone, anywhere, anytime, under any circumstances.

Sexual dysfunctions are disturbances of basic sexual functions. In Kaplan's *triphasic model,* these are desire, arousal, and orgasm (Chapter 3). In physiological terms they reflect problems in the two processes underlying the sexual response cycle: vasocongestion and myotonia, the components of Master's and Johnson's *biphasic model* (Chapter 3). Vasocongestive disturbances account for problems of erection in the male and sexual arousal in the female; disturbances in myotonia are linked to difficulties in orgasm (Kaplan, 1974).

Finally, we need to distinguish between *primary* and *secondary* sexual dysfunctions. In the first case, the condition has always existed. A man has never been able to have an erection, or a woman has never experienced orgasm. In secondary dysfunctions, the person used to be healthy. A man who was once potent can no longer have an erection; a woman who was orgasmic is no longer able to reach orgasm. We discuss the importance of this distinction later.

The study of sexual dysfunctions has focused on problems during coitus, and their treatment is modeled on heterosexual couples. Remember as you read that virtually everything in this chapter applies equally to homosexuals.

## Prevalence

As we noted at the beginning of the chapter, sexual dysfunction is thought to be quite prevalent. How do you find out? Do you ask people, or do you observe them? Is the subjective sensation of sexual pleasure the criterion, or objective measures of performance? How do you measure "sexual desire"? When is coitus "long enough"? What if a woman is able to reach orgasm with one man but not another? What if a man has no problem in getting an

erection when masturbating but cannot do so in coitus?

No wonder accurate statistics on sexual dysfunction are hard to come by. Studies use different diagnostic criteria and call the same entity by different names, so they are hard to compare.

We cannot determine the true prevalence of sexual dysfunction from those who seek sex therapy, because the availability of such help and the willingness of people to use it varies widely. More useful are surveys of more general populations, such as couples seen at a medical clinic. One such study involved 100 couples who were predominantly white, well educated, and middle class. Eighty percent of these couples claimed to have happy marriages; none of the couples were in marital therapy or counseling at the time, although 12 percent had had such help in the past. The prevalence of sexual dysfunction in this group is shown in Table 15.1. Over half the women and over one-third of the men have had some sexual problem (Frank et al., 1978). In a similar study on a general clinic population, lack of sexual desire was reported by 27 percent of women and 13 percent of men; women were also more dissatisfied with the frequency of intercourse (23 percent) than men (18 percent). Premature ejaculation (14 percent) and erection difficulties (12 percent) were the other main male complaints, whereas the women mentioned inability to reach orgasm (25 percent) and pain during coitus (20 percent) (Ende et al., 1984). A review of 22 general sex surveys shows a greater variability in the prevalence of sexual dysfunctions (Nathan, 1986).

## SEXUAL DESIRE DISORDERS

When new methods of sex therapy became established in the late 1960s, those who sought help mainly suffered from disturbances of sexual arousal and orgasm. By the end of the decade, sex therapists began to see a new kind of problem—men and women whose sexual functions were not disturbed but who complained of having lost interest in sex or satisfaction from it. These conditions, known as disorders

**Table 15.1   Prevalence of Sexual Dysfunction in "Normal" Couples**

| | WOMEN (%) | MEN (%) |
|---|---|---|
| *Dysfunctions* | | |
| Difficulty getting excited/getting erection | 48 | 7 |
| Difficulty maintaining excitement/erection | 33 | 9 |
| Reaching orgasm/ejaculation too soon | 11 | 36 |
| Difficulty reaching orgasm/ejaculation | 46 | 4 |
| Inability to have orgasm/ejaculation | 15 | 0 |
| | | |
| *Other Problems* | | |
| Partner chooses inconvenient time | 31 | 16 |
| Inability to relax | 47 | 12 |
| Attraction to person(s) other than mate | 14 | 21 |
| Disinterest | 35 | 16 |
| Attraction to person(s) of same sex | 1 | 0 |
| Different sex practices or habits | 10 | 12 |
| "Turned off" | 28 | 10 |
| Too little foreplay | 38 | 21 |
| Too little tenderness after intercourse | 25 | 17 |
| | | |
| *Sexual Satisfaction* | | |
| "How satisfying are your sexual relations?" | | |
| Very satisfying | 40 | 42 |
| Moderately satisfying | 46 | 43 |
| Not very satisfying | 12 | 13 |
| Not satisfying at all | 2 | 2 |
| "How satisfactory have your sexual relations with your spouse been in comparison to other aspects of your marital life?" | | |
| Better than the rest | 19 | 24 |
| About the same | 63 | 60 |
| Worse than the rest | 18 | 16 |
| "Do you have [sexual dissatisfaction] in your marriage?" | | |
| Yes | 21 | 33 |
| No | 79 | 67 |

Based on Frank, E., Anderson, C., and Rubinstein, D. (1978). Frequency of sexual dysfunction in normal couples. *New England Journal of Medicine*, 299:111–115.

of sexual desire (Kaplan, 1979), have come to occupy center stage in the field of sex therapy, with various theories to explain them. They take two main forms: *hypoactive sexual desire disorder* and *sexual aversion*.

## Hypoactive Sexual Desire Disorder

Hypoactive sexual desire (Latin *hypo,* "under") is still widely called *inhibited sexual desire* (ISD) and other terms, such as *sexual apathy*.

In its mildest form, sexual apathy takes the form of simple indifference. It is like lacking appetite for food. A person just does not feel like having sex, despite favorable circumstances and a willing partner. Sometimes the person is so preoccupied with other activities that sex is almost forgotten for a while.

Judgments of apathy tend to be subjective and relative. Suppose that one-third of the couples in a study had intercourse fewer than two or three times a month. Is that too little, too much, or just right? To answer, people are likely to compare the present against the past ("I am not as interested in sex as I used to be"); the level of interest of one partner as against another ("My spouse is not as interested in sex as I am"); experiences of others ("We think we are not having as much sex as our friends"). In practice, help is usually sought because of discrepancies in sexual desire between steady partners; the unattached are more likely to "solve" the problem by looking for other partners.

To qualify as a disorder of sexual desire, the problem has to be more serious and persistent than normal ups and downs. In *primary* hypoactive desire disorders, a person has never achieved the level of sexual interest typically expected of most healthy adult men and women, although criteria for this level tend to be arbitrary (Schover et al., 1982). Their friendships and intimate relationships are singularly lacking in sexual interest; nor do they resort to masturbation or atypical forms of sexual arousal. This condition seems to be rare. More often, in *secondary* hypoactive desire disorders, a person who used to enjoy sex loses interest. It is these individuals who are more likely to perceive a problem and seek help. Kaplan (1979) further differentiates between *global* inhibition of sexual desire, which involves a total lack of sexual interest in all situations, and *situational* lack of interest with one partner but not another; the causes here are more likely to be relational.

## Sexual Aversion

Sexual aversion goes beyond a passive lack of interest: it involves an active avoidance of all sexual activity. Some people feel distaste. Others feel intense fear and the avoidance takes the form of a *phobia;* confronted with the prospect of sex, the person suffers acute anxiety.

The sexual aversion may be primary or secondary, global or situational. The underlying assumption once again is that there is no compelling or rational reason why a person would want to avoid sex. Sexual apathy or aversion often derives from traumatic sexual experiences (such as rape) or lack of orgasmic response; after all, the less one enjoys an activity, the less the incentive to repeat it. Apathy may also exist in cases where orgasmic ability is not disturbed or is restored through sex therapy, as illustrated in the following example, involving a 32-year-old woman married for six years:

> At the time of evaluation, both husband and wife expressed frustration with the state of their sexual relationship. This frustration led to increasingly strained and infrequent sexual encounters. During the course of her pregnancy, intercourse was discontinued altogether. Although it initially appeared that her diminished interest in sex was related to the primary anorgasmia, her subsequent progress in therapy indicated that this was not the case. Despite the fact that a program of guided self-stimulation exercises was successful in permitting Mrs. O to achieve orgasm, her interest in sex with her husband showed little change and, if anything, declined over the course of treatment. It became painfully clear to both partners that her inability to achieve orgasm at the outset of therapy had little bearing on her more fundamental lack of sexual interest (*Journal of Sex Research*, May 1987, *23*:2).

## Hyperactive Sexual Desire

The concept of hypoactive sexual desire implies that there is a standard for a normal level of sexual desire. In that case, there should also be a *hyperactive* counterpart in sexual desire disorders (Latin *hyper*, "beyond"). Though there is currently no such diagnosis, the Diagnostic Manual does refer to *nonparaphiliac sexual addiction*.

As we discussed in Chapter 14, the concept of sexual addiction goes back to the idea that "too much" sex is maladaptive if it distresses the individual or others. Whether such behavior is a problem or a form of paraphilia or a disorder of sexual desire is a matter of how you choose to define it.

## SEXUAL AROUSAL DISORDERS

Desire normally leads to sexual arousal, and vice versa. Arousal is both psychological (feeling "turned on") and physiological (the excitement phase).

The primary physical sign of sexual arousal in the male is *erection* of the penis; in the female it is *vaginal lubrication* with accompanying changes (Chapter 3). In disorders of sexual arousal a man is unable to attain or maintain erection, and a woman, lubrication. The subjective sensations of sexual arousal usually go together with the physiological changes. But the reverse is not always true; a person may feel psychologically aroused without the physical signs of arousal. Because erection is under the control of spinal reflexes that are part of the autonomic, not the voluntary nervous system, a man cannot "will" an erection, but can only "let it happen"; the same is true for vaginal lubrication. This point is important for understanding arousal disorders.

## Male Erectile Disorder

The inability to attain and maintain erection is the most incapacitating of all male coital dysfunctions. In its *primary form* a man has never been able to have coitus. In its *secondary form* a previously functional person develops the problem; this form is ten times more common.

Occasional inability to have an erection is

exceedingly common, especially as a man gets older; it is not sexual dysfunction. Nor is there any absolute scale against which to evaluate the length or strength of an erection. Obviously, a man must keep his erection long enough to enter the vagina if he is to have coitus. Beyond that, judgments are relative. For clinical purposes a man is considered functionally impotent if his attempts at coitus fail in one out of four instances (Masters and Johnson, 1970).

Erectile dysfunction affected about one of every hundred males under 35 years of age in the Kinsey et al. (1948) sample, but it seriously incapacitated only some of them. At 70 years of age about one in four males was impotent. Most men progressively lose some erectile function with age, but some men retain their potency well into old age (Chapter 9). Therefore getting older is not enough to explain erectile dysfunction. Among the subjects studied by Masters and Johnson, 31 percent had problems of potency, of which 13 percent were primary and 87 percent of the secondary type (Masters and Johnson, 1970).

For many men, it is difficult to imagine a more humiliating problem. "Impotence" means "powerlessness," and its consequences go far beyond the loss of sexual pleasure. Male notions of masculinity and personal worth are so closely linked to potency that serious dysfunction is damaging to a man's self-esteem. In most cultures impotent men have been objects of derision. The classical Arabian love manual, *The Perfumed Garden* has this to say about sexually inadequate men:

> When such a man has a bout with a woman, he does not do his business with vigor and in a manner to give her enjoyment. . . . He gets upon her before she has begun to long for pleasure, and then he introduces with infinite trouble a member soft and nerveless. Scarcely has he commenced when he is already done for; he makes one or two movements, and then sinks upon the woman's breast to spend his sperm; and that is the most he can do. This done he withdraws his affair, and makes all haste to get down again from her. . . . Qualities like these are no recommendation with women (Nefzawi, 1964 ed., p. 110).

More sensible and compassionate views put sexual potency in a less negative light. There is more to sexual satisfaction than erection and ejaculation. A less genital focus fosters a broader perception of sexuality, with an emphasis on pleasure rather than performance (Zilbergild, 1978). There are handicapped men with spinal cord injuries, for instance, who are incapable of coitus yet able to engage in other pleasurable forms of sexual relations without thinking of themselves as being less of a man (Box 15.1).

## Female Sexual Arousal Disorder

Disorders of sexual arousal in women have received little attention until recently (Musaph and Abraham, 1977; Kolodny et al., 1979), and still attract much less attention than those in men (Leiblum and Pervin, 1980). This fact in part is due to the general neglect of female sexuality. Also, problems with female arousal are physically harder to detect; and unlike male erection, they do not interfere with a woman's ability to engage in coitus, although it may be lacking in enjoyment.

For these and related reasons, problems of female sexual arousal have taken second place to orgasmic problems. The term "frigidity," which implies emotional coldness, has been indiscriminately applied to both sets of problems and does justice to neither. Whether women are affectionate, aloof, or "cold" may have no bearing on their sexual arousability or responsiveness.

At the psychological level, female and male consciousness of being aroused basically appears to be the same (although women may be less genitally focused than men). At the level of physiology, vaginal lubrication is less consistently linked to sexual arousal than erection among males, although the underlying vasocongestion is the same. For instance, although erection usually remains fairly steady, lubrication may decrease during the plateau phase (Chapter 3). The level of female arousal cannot always be gauged by the level of vaginal lubrication, especially after the menopause (Chapter 9). Some women become highly aroused and reach orgasm with no perceptible

# Box 15.1

## SEX AND THE HANDICAPPED

Many people think that the physically handicapped are neither capable of nor interested in sex, or that the lack of sex should be the least of their problems. That is not the case (Boyle, 1986). Much can be done to sexually rehabilitate the handicapped and to educate the public (Warren and Kempton, 1981).

Disabilities take many forms, affecting physical, sensory, and mental functions. Those with visual and hearing impairments, for instance, must overcome special challenges to communication. The mentally handicapped may struggle to interact in ways that others take for granted. That does not mean that they do not have the same needs for affection and sex as everyone else.

Especially compelling is the plight of over 100,000 persons in the United States who have sustained spinal cord injuries leading to paralysis of the legs (*paraplegia*) or of the legs and arms (*quadriplegia*). They tend to be young, more often male (85 percent) than female (15 percent) (Higgins, 1979). The most common causes of such injuries are accidents and war injuries.

Paraplegics usually lack all sensation below the level of the injury and lose normal bladder and bowel control. Sexual functions are seriously disrupted but by no means always absent. Two-thirds of men with cord lesions retain some erectile response to physical stimuli (without being able to feel it). Ejaculatory disturbance is more severe; usually fewer than 5 percent can ejaculate, and they are usually infertile (Bors and Comarr, 1960). Paraplegic women likewise lack genital responsiveness and orgasm, but they are more likely to retain fertility. They may attain orgasm instead through stimulation of the nipples, lips, and other erogenous areas. Both males and females can experience erotic dreams with orgasm ("phantom orgasm").

Some seriously handicapped persons give up sex; yet others manage to maintain an active and joyful interest. They learn to use whatever parts of their bodies allow them to give and receive sexual pleasure. Sexuality for them takes on a broader meaning than the mere coupling of genitals. As one man put it, "I can't always be genital, but that gives me more permission to be gentle" (Cole, 1975).

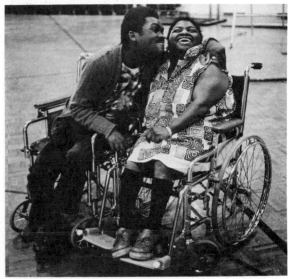

The handicapped have the same need for sex and affection as the non-handicapped.

The following guidelines intended for the physically handicapped hold a larger lesson for all of us:

A stiff penis does not make a solid relationship, nor does a wet vagina.

Absence of sensation does not mean absence of feeling.

Inability to move does not mean inability to learn.

The presence of deformities does not mean the absence of desire.

Inability to perform does not mean inability to enjoy.

Loss of genitals does not mean loss of sexuality. (Anderson and Cole, 1975).[1]

[1]For a list of resources and bibliographic sources on sex and disability see *Siecus Report*, Vol. 14, No 4, March 1986. Various organizations provide information and assistance to the disabled and their families: *Clearinghouse on the Handicapped*, telephone (202) 472–3796; and *Parents Helping Parents*, telephone (408) 272–4774.

vaginal lubrication, for reasons that are unclear.

## ORGASM DISORDERS

Despite the efforts of sex educators and therapists to steer people away from a genital-orgasmic focus to a wider body-pleasure orientation, orgasm appears to be the central sexual experience for many people, both physically and psychologically. Moreoever, male intravaginal orgasm is the primary (although no longer the exclusive) means of impregnation. Disorders of orgasm are therefore a matter of much concern.

### Inhibited Female Orgasm

Persistent or recurrent delay in, or absence of, orgasm in a female following a normal sexual excitement phase during sexual activity constitutes *inhibited female orgasm* (also called *anorgasmia*). Some women are able to experience orgasm during noncoital clitoral stimulation, but are unable to experience it during coitus in the absence of manual clitoral stimulation. Because over half of all women seem to require clitoral stimulation during coitus to reach orgasm (Kaplan, 1974; Hite, 1976), most sex therapists do not consider the need for clitoral stimulation an indication of orgasmic dysfunction. Furthermore, at least some women who are unable to reach orgasm do not suffer from a sexual dysfunction but a sexually inept partner. Other women feel that orgasm is not a necessary condition for sexual satisfaction every time they engage in coitus (Kaplan, 1974). Unlike men, not only are these women able to engage in sex and conceive without orgasm, but at least some say that they enjoy coitus even without it. Whether there are physiological and psychological explanations for this, or women are still simply willing to settle for less, is not clear.

All these qualifications aside, anorgasmia is reported to be by far the most common form of female sexual dysfunction. Most studies put the prevalence of primary coital anorgasmia (no orgasm ever) at 10 percent, with another 10 percent of women having coital orgasm sporadically (Kolodny et al., 1979). There are some indications, however, that the problem is significantly receding. In the Hunt (1974) survey, 53 percent of women who had been married for 15 years reported that they always or nearly always reached orgasm in coitus; the corresponding figure in the Kinsey et al. (1953) survey two decades earlier was only 45 percent. Likewise, the proportion of wives who never reached orgasm had gone down from 28 percent in the Kinsey sample to 15 percent in the Hunt sample. A 1983 *Family Circle* poll shows some 85 percent of wives basically satisfied with their sex lives, but that does not mean that all of these women were orgasmic (*Time,* Jan. 31, 1983, p. 80).

### Premature Ejaculation

*Premature ejaculation* is the most prevalent form of orgasmic disorder in the male. It consists of ejaculation which occurs with minimal sexual stimulation before, upon, or shortly after penetration and before the person wishes it. The condition must be recurrent and persistent to qualify as a dysfunction. It must take into account factors that affect duration of the excitement phase, such as age, novelty of the sexual partner or situation, and frequency of sexual activity (American Psychiatric Association, 1987).

Armed with the finding that three out of four men reach orgasm within two minutes of intromission, and that most male animals do so even sooner, Kinsey made light of premature ejaculation as a form of sexual dysfunction. However, a significant number of men (and their partners) complain of the inability to delay ejaculation until sufficient mutual enjoyment has been obtained; it is small comfort to them to learn that subhuman primates ejaculate even faster. Our evolutionary forbears were vulnerable to attack while engaged in copulation, so there was, maybe, something to say back then for the "survival of the fastest" (Hong, 1984), but not today.

Although premature ejaculation is a less frequent reason than impotence for seeking help, Masters and Johnson believe it to be the most common male sexual dysfunction in the general population: an estimated 15–20 percent of men have significant difficulty controlling ejaculation (although less than 20 percent of this group seek help) (Masters and Johnson, 1970; Kolodny et al., 1979).

Attempts at defining premature ejaculation have run into many problems. The official definition does not really set a time criteria. Early researchers attempted to specify a time (ranging from 30 seconds to 2 minutes) or a number of thrusts. Later, prematurity was redefined in terms of the partner's needs. For instance, Masters and Johnson (1970) have defined it as the inability to control ejaculation long enough to satisfy a normally functional female partner in at least 50 percent of coital encounters. However, just as a woman should not be declared anorgasmic when her partner does not provide enough stimulation, a man's capacity to delay orgasm should not be judged by the partner's responsiveness, which can vary widely. Some sex therapists do not consider this issue to be a problem if a couple agrees that the quality of their sexual relations is satisfactory, whenever the male ejaculates (LoPiccolo, 1977).

## Inhibited Male Orgasm

*Inhibited male orgasm* (also called *retarded ejaculation*) is the opposite of premature ejaculation. It consists of persistent or recurrent delay in, or absence of, orgasm in a male during coitus. The failure to achieve orgasm is usually restricted to an inability to reach orgasm in the vagina, with orgasm possible with other types of stimulation, such as masturbation. It is the least frequent of all male sexual dysfunctions, accounting for 1–2 percent of most clinical samples (Apfelbaum, 1980). Many males occasionally experience a temporary inability to ejaculate during coitus that is overcome by more vigorous thrusting or some other form of heightening arousal. Those with retarded ejaculation overcome it with much more difficulty if at all. Those who are totally unable to reach orgasm in the vagina are said to suffer from *ejaculatory incompetence* (Masters and

Johnson, 1970). The majority of these men can have orgasm through masturbation, but in some 15 percent orgasm does not occur outside the vagina either. In these cases arousal subsides slowly without the climactic release of orgasm. Ejaculatory disorders are sometimes further delineated by timing, level of pleasure, and so on (Vandereycken, 1986).

If a couple wants to prolong coitus, this condition might seem a mutual blessing; yet beyond a certain point, coitus ceases to be enjoyable for either partner. The man experiences a sense of failure and frustration; the woman may feel responsible for not being sufficiently exciting, or irritated at having to go on beyond the point of enjoyment. Inhibited male orgasm must not be confused with *priapism,* which consists of prolonged erections without sexual arousal. This condition is due to a variety of physical ailments; it is not a sexual dysfunction, although it may result in the loss of erectile ability if not treated promptly (Kolodny et al., 1979).

## SEXUAL PAIN DISORDERS

For most people, pain ruins sexual arousal and enjoyment. Discomfort during coitus is a far more frequent complaint among women, but it also occurs in men. Painful intercourse is frequently cited as a female sexual dysfunction (Sandberg and Quevillon, 1987). It is estimated that 15 percent of women experience pain during sex at various times, and 1–2 percent have it as a chronic problem (Brody, 1988).

## Dyspareunia

*Dyspareunia* is recurrent or persistent genital pain in either a male or a female before, during, or after sexual intercourse. (American Psychiatric Association, 1987).

**Female Dyspareunia** Women feel coital pain more often than men for many reasons. Any ailment in the genital organs and the pelvic region can cause pain during coitus. Women are more vulnerable to these conditions because their reproductive system is more exposed to infection (Chapter 5), traumatized during childbirth (Chapter 6), and subject to hormonal influences (Chapter 4).

The most common (and most easily treated) cause of coital pain among women is vaginal dryness, which causes irritation of the vaginal wall during coitus. Though mainly encountered among postmenopausal women (Chapter 9), vaginal dryness may also be present in women who do not naturally lubricate sufficiently during excitement; nursing women; women making love right after a menstrual period, during radiation therapy, or when using antihistamines (such as decongestants); women under undue stress; and sometimes women following a strenuous exercise program.

Infection is another common source of pain. Those with vaginitis or PID may experience a burning sensation or even bleeding during coitus. Douches, deodorant sprays, tampons, and vaginal contraceptives may also cause irritation. Injuries during childbirth that have healed poorly, tender episiotomy scars, tears in the anal region, and similar conditions are other potential sources of pain.

Male Dyspareunia    Men experience pain during coitus usually because of genital or urinary infections, especially prostatitis. Arthritis of the hip and lower back problems may also cause pain during pelvic thrusts. There is also a rare condition called *Peyronie's disease,* in which deposits of fibrous tissue in the penis lead to the curvature of the penis, painful erections, and erectile dysfunction.

## Vaginismus

When a woman feels pain or expects it, she tenses up. As the muscles surrounding the vaginal introitus contract, they cause *vaginismus,* which makes penetration difficult and painful, if not impossible. Vaginismus occurs more often in response to psychological than physical causes. It affects 2–3 percent of adult women (Kolodny et al., 1979). Generally these

women have no difficulty with sexual arousal and can attain orgasm through noncoital means.

Men too may experience genital muscle spasms, which cause pain during ejaculation. It may be intense enough to be disabling and may last for minutes or hours. As with vaginismus, the cause is usually psychogenic.

## CAUSES OF SEXUAL DYSFUNCTION

Sexual function can be disrupted by physical, psychological, or cultural influences. In principle, all three variables interact in every case; in practice, we choose one as the cause. In most cases there is no specific link between cause and effect, especially where causes are psychological. In other words, the same psychological problem may cause sexual apathy in one woman and anorgasmia in another, erectile dysfunction in one man and premature ejaculation in another. For organic causes the connection is more often evident. For example, a drug that disrupts parasympathetic function will cause impotence; one that interferes with sympathetic function will affect orgasm.

### Organic Causes

Most cases of sexual dysfunction have psychogenic causes. However, in a significant number of cases (perhaps as high as one-third), the sexual disorder has a physical basis (Munjack and Oziel, 1980). Some conditions are more apt to have physical causes. For example, erectile dysfunction is more often due to organic causes (perhaps in as high as 40 percent of cases) than premature ejaculation; deep pelvic pain during coitus is much more likely to have a physical basis than sexual apathy (Kolodny et al., 1979). Even when there are physical causes, psychological factors may still be at work. Unless the physical ailment is incapacitating, whether or not it will lead to dysfunction, or how severe the dysfunction will be, may largely depend on psychological factors. Aging is not in itself a sufficient biological reason for dysfunction.

The sexual organs are well designed to fit (Figure 15.1). Disparities in size and shape of

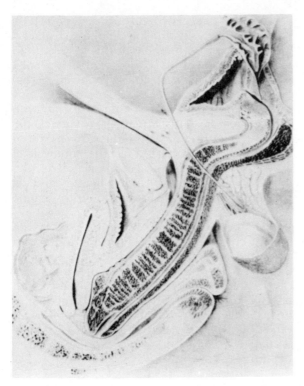

Figure 15.1   Male and female sex organs during coitus.

the penis and vagina are almost never a cause of coital difficulty. Like an elastic structure, the relaxed and lubricated vagina expands to accommodate the erect penis, whatever its size.

Sexual functions can suffer as a result of *acute* (short-term) or *chronic* (long-term) ailments, which may be *local* (affecting only the genital region) or *systemic* (affecting a whole system, especially the circulatory, nervous, or endocrine system). Debilitating illness such as cancer, degenerative diseases, severe infections, or systemic disorders affect sexual function indirectly. Local disturbances, such as pelvic infections, interfere more directly. The common element in a lot of these conditions is that they cause *pain,* which has a dampening effect on sexual interest, arousal, and enjoyment. Two-thirds of patients with chronic pain report a deterioration of their sexual relations

(Maruta and McHardy, 1983). The most common causes of pain were discussed earlier.

Trauma   Injuries from accidents or surgery may interfere with the blood and nerve supply to the pelvis. Among males, certain forms of prostate surgery can damage the nerves in the region. A patient thinking of surgery for an enlarged prostate should ask about risk to sexual function. Newer surgical techniques reduce this risk, especially among men who are younger than 70, even in drastic surgeries for prostate cancer (Sullivan, 1987).

Female surgical procedures that damage the sexual organs (such as poorly repaired episiotomies) often cause pain during coitus. Particularly important are radical hysterectomies (where the ovaries are removed in addition to the uterus) in premenopausal women. The loss of sexual desire that affects some of these women can have a serious effect, especially if they have not been forewarned (Wigfall-Williams, 1987).

A possible consequence of giving birth is the stretching and weakening of the muscles around the vagina. This change interferes with the myotonic response and may inhibit orgasm.

Endocrine Disorders   Radical hysterectomies remove the main sources of female hormones, the ovaries. Other endocrine disorders of significance include low output from the pituitary, the gonads, or the thyroid glands (hypopituitarism, hypogonadism, and hypothyroidism); diabetes; and liver diseases like hepatitis and cirrhosis. Testosterone deficiency is now reported to be a greater cause of sexual dysfunction than previously suspected. In one group of 105 consecutive cases of impotence, 35 percent had abnormalities of the hypothalamic-pituitary-gonadal axis (Sullivan, 1987).

Neurological Disorders   Neurological disorders that may seriously influence sexual functions in both sexes include diseases of the frontal and temporal lobes of the brain, such as tumors or blood clots; nerve injuries; and disturbances in the spinal cord such as birth defects, degenerative conditions, and injury (Box 15.2). Epilepsy usually does not cause sexual problems (Kolodny et al., 1979).

The spinal cord and pelvic nerves may be injured in car accidents or war (Comfort, 1978). They can be injured also by blows to the groin, athletic mishaps (such as landing on another player's knee), or even riding on a stationary bicycle with a seat that is too high (Solomon and Cappa, 1987). In the last case, function returns promptly when the cause is eliminated; but in cases where the spinal cord is damaged, its nerves do not regenerate. Chronic lower back pain, from which many people suffer, usually does not interfere with sexual function except when there is acute pain.

Circulatory Disorders    Any interference with the blood supply to the pelvic region may result in sexual dysfunction. The buildup of cholesterol or high blood pressure will damage the arteries supplying the genital organs. The major causes of cardiovascular disease are also turning out to be associated with impotence, including smoking: 80 percent of the impotent men in one clinic are reported to be smokers (Goldstein, 1987).

The problem may also be in the veins. As we saw in Chapter 3, for the penis to be engorged with blood, the inflow must increase and the outflow must decrease. "Leaky" veins may not stop the outflow enough (Bookstein et al., 1987). (Think of trying to fill a bathtub when the drain is open.) This problem may occur more often in older men, accounting for their softer and briefer erections.

Sexual dysfunction may be the indirect result of some other circulatory ailment. For instance, people who have strokes may suffer a significant decline in sexual desire. The ratio of those who enjoyed sex in an older sample of stroke patients (average age 68 years) went down from 84 percent to 30 percent of the men and from 60 percent to 31 percent of the women. Even so, psychological factors remained important; the most common factor identified as causing decline in sexual activity was the fear that having sex might cause another stroke (Monga et al., 1986).

Similar concerns tend to disrupt the sexual lives of persons who have had heart attacks. Men are more vulnerable in this respect than women. In one study, 76 percent of the men who had had a heart attack reported sexual dysfunction (42 percent was erectile dysfunction) as compared with a control group with similar health status but no heart attack (68 percent). Counseling can reduce anxiety about "coital death" and related fears (Dhabuwala et al., 1986). Under medical guidance many who have had heart attacks can live healthy and active sex lives, just as they are able to resume physical activity and exercise.

Diabetes is another case in point. Though it is an endocrine disorder (having to do with carbohydrate metabolism) it is through the damage caused to arteries and nerves that it causes erectile impairment. It is associated with a high prevalence of sexual dysfunction in men. Some forms of diabetes have little or no effect on women; other types do lessen female sexual desire and orgasmic capacity (Schreiner-Engel et al., 1987).

Alcohol    Alcohol is a common cause of sexual dysfunction: 40 percent of chronic alcoholics have problems with potency and 15 percent with orgasm (Kolodny et al., 1979). Chronic alcohol usage interferes with hormone production, liver function, and nutrition, and causes nerve damage, all of which are detrimental to sexual function. These organic effects are compounded by the psychological and social problems caused by alcoholism.

Alcohol is widely believed to enhance sexual activity, but in fact it puts a physiological damper on sexual arousal and performance (Box 12.5). Even well below levels of intoxication, alcohol has been shown to inhibit erections (Wilson and Lawson, 1978b), female arousal (Wilson and Lawson, 1978a), and orgasm (Malatesta, 1979; Klassen and Wilsnack, 1986).

Although alcohol intoxication retards orgasm, women who do reach orgasm under its influence report a heightened sense of pleasure; men report decreased arousal and less pleasurable orgasm. Alcohol can also be the trigger for psychogenic impotence: a man will fail to have an erection after having too much to drink; then he will feel anxiety and experience failure even when sober (O'Farrell et al., 1983).

Drugs   Drugs are another important source of sexual difficulty—especially *sedatives* (such as barbiturates) and *narcotics* (such as heroin) because of their effects on the central nervous system.

*Marijuana,* like alcohol, has a widespread reputation as an enhancer of sexual experience (Box 12.5), but marijuana use has been linked with erectile problems, lowered testosterone production, and disturbance in sperm production (Kolodny et al., 1979). Men who smoke four or more marijuana cigarettes per week have significant decreases in testosterone production. The decrease in testosterone is related to the amount smoked; the heavier the usage the lower the levels of hormone production. *Nicotine* in cigarettes causes constriction of blood vessels and may thus interfere with genital blood supply.

Another class of drugs that may impair libido and sexual response is the *antiandrogens,* which include estrogen, adrenal steroids such as cortisone, and ACTH (often used to treat allergies and inflammatory reactions). The effect of drugs like Depo-Provera and cyproterone acetate was discussed in connection with the suppression of certain compulsive sexual behaviors (Chapter 14).

Other drugs block nerve impulses to the genitals. Drugs that block the effects of the parasympathetic system interfere with arousal and erection; those which block the effect of the sympathetic system interfere with orgasm (Chapter 3). It is on this basis that drugs for high blood pressure (*antihypertensives*) often impair sexual function in both sexes, but more often cause erectile dysfunction (Smith and Talbert, 1986). This effect may be avoided by shifting from one type of drug to another. Patient and doctor together should weigh the benefits of such drugs against the loss of potency.

Drugs used in the treatment of psychosis (*antipsychotic agents*) are more likely to cause ejaculatory problems, including retrograde ejaculation. Such patients have less choice in using the drug. Antidepressant drugs may also cause impairments of orgasm, which compounds the problem often caused by the depression itself (Harrison et al., 1986). Commonly used *tranquilizers* like Valium and Librium are less likely to cause problems; they may actually help sexual function by allaying anxiety.

Once the use of drugs is discontinued, their effects subside. The main thing to remember is that whenever a person is using a drug—any drug—and develops sexual problems, the drug is the first possible cause of the difficulty.

## Organic or Psychogenic?

Though organic and psychogenic factors usually interact in causing sexual dysfunction, we need to determine the role of each in a given case for effective treatment. It is therefore essential that any significant organic cause be identified or ruled out first in all cases of sexual dysfunction. This procedure speeds treatment of physical conditions that have a remedy; and when that is not possible, it lets the person and the clinician know the limits to which psychological treatment is likely to help and set their therapeutic expectations accordingly.

The attempt to tell organic from psychogenic dysfunction begins with taking the history of the symptoms (Segraves et al., 1987). For example, psychogenic impotence usually has a sudden onset; organic impotence comes on gradually over months or years. The pattern of dysfunction also tends to be different. Organic impotence tends to be more consistent and global, affecting all forms of sexual activity. Psychogenic impotence is more inconsistent; it may occur at one time but not another, during coitus but not masturbation, with one partner but not another. Even the timing of the symptom may be different. A woman who experiences pelvic pain following orgasm is more likely to have a physical ailment than another who complains of coital pain when

424 VARIETIES OF SEXUAL EXPERIENCE

penetration has barely occurred (unless she has an infection right at the vaginal opening).

The circumstances under which the problem starts may also help to decide the issue. If sexual dysfunction follows a significant event like divorce or death of the spouse, it is more likely to be psychogenic. Evidence of conflict between a couple or signs of emotional distress point in the same direction. However, such distress may be the result and not the cause of dysfunction. The partner of a person with an organic problem is apt to feel inadequate, guilty, or angry if the physical basis of the disorder is not suspected.

Ultimately, the decision has to be based on concrete physical evidence. Impotence is a good example. As we discussed in Chapter 11, virtually all healthy males have erections during REM sleep. Absent or seriously deficient nocturnal erections suggest an organic cause. If *nocturnal penile tumescence* (NPT) is normal, psychogenic factors are much more likely to be the underlying problem (Marshal et al., 1981; Bohlen, 1981).

This process can be tested in some simple ways. A ring of stamps is attached at the base of the penis before going to sleep. If the ring is found broken in the morning, the man has had an erection. A more reliable device is the Snap-Gauge, which consists of Velcro straps with three connectors, each of which breaks at a defined penile pressure (Bradley, 1987; Condra et al., 1987). Most reliable is a complete penile tumescence recording carried out in a sleep laboratory, where the pattern of sleep can be followed with an electroencephalographic recording and monitoring of eye movements. Penile erections occurring during sleep are detected by special instruments such as strain gauges at the base of the penis that accurately record the magnitude, duration, and pattern of erection. Portable units now allow such monitoring while the person sleeps at home (see Box 3.2).

More specialized studies investigate the blood flow patterns in the penis. For instance, radio-opaque dyes (which show up on X-rays) are injected. Their flow provides specific data on how well the arteries and veins within the corpora of the penis are working (Bookstein et al., 1987). This procedure is called *cavernosography*. If papaverine (which dilates the arteries) is injected instead, a sonogram can show problems in blood flow (Trapp, 1987).

## Psychogenic Causes

Psychogenic factors are more difficult to identify and classify than organic causes, especially if they are deep-rooted intrapsychic conflicts. In the past, treatment of sexual dysfunction mainly focused on fundamental personality problems. In current forms of the "new sex therapy" the emphasis is on more immediate psychological factors.

**Immediate Causes**  The fear of failure is possibly the most common immediate cause of psychogenic impotence. Other sources of sexual problems are the demand for performance and the excessive need to please the partner. Such attitudes elicit resentment and anger, which interfere with sexual enjoyment and function. Another important cause of difficulty is "spectatoring"—anxiously and obsessively watching your own reactions during sex (Masters and Johnson, 1970). For satisfactory sex people must lose themselves in the interaction. Spectatoring distracts the person and prevents sexual responses from building up to orgasm (Kaplan, 1974).

The failure to communicate forces a couple to guess what is desired and what is ineffective or objectionable in the sexual interaction. Communication that is clear and appropriate to the occasion is necessary to provide both information and reassurance. Even when failure to communicate is not the primary cause of the dysfunction, it helps to perpetuate other problems (Fay, 1977).

The deeper causes of sexual malfunction in both sexes are internal conflicts related to past experiences. When these conflicts dominate a person's sex life to the extent that inadequate performance is the rule, then the causes can be considered to be primarily *in-*

*trapsychic.* On the other hand, when the sexual problem seems to be part of a conflict between two particular people, it is more convenient to label it as *interpersonal.* This distinction, though arbitrary, has practical merit in treatment. Intrapsychic causes must be dealt with. As veterans of successive divorces discover, even though marital partners change, the conflicts remain the same. Interpersonal conflicts often may be worked out without deeper therapy.

Psychological conflicts occur unpredictably at any time in adult life; certain developmental stages have more predictable stresses (Chapter 9). These stresses may predispose the person to sexual dysfunction. The "midlife crisis" is a good example of such a stressful period. There is some value, therefore, in evaluating sexual problems in a broader life cycle perspective (Fagan et al., 1986).

Deeper Causes     Learning theorists have proposed a variety of models to explain the genesis of sexual malfunction which are extensions of the more basic theories of sexual learning (Chapter 8). Central to many models is conditioning, in which the unpleasant feelings associated with an experience determine future reactions to a similar situation—the same process we discussed in connection with socialization (Chapter 8) and the paraphilias (Chapter 14). Sometimes the antecedents of the experience are easy to trace. For instance, if a man suffers a heart attack during coitus, thereafter the very thought of sex makes him anxious and unable to perform. Similarly, after a rape, a woman may find coitus difficult even with a loving partner (Wolpe and Lazarus, 1966).

More often the causes are a complex series of long-forgotten learning experiences. The transmission of certain sexual attitudes and values to children—like sex being dirty or dangerous—is one example (Chapter 8). A person may not remember specific or implied parental warnings and punishments, but their damaging effects persist.

Psychoanalysts explain sexual malfunctioning by infantile conflicts that remain unconscious. For instance, conflicts arising from unresolved oedipal wishes may be major causes of difficulties in both sexes. Castration anxiety is another common explanation for failures of potency, just as it is for paraphilias (Chapter 14). When a man is impotent with his wife but not with a prostitute, he may be unconsciously equating his wife with his mother. Men who distinguish between "respectable" women (to be loved and respected) and "degraded" women (to be enjoyed sexually) are said to have a "madonna-prostitute complex."

The female counterparts to these conflicts involve the father. As certain types of men may be unconsciously identified with the father, coitus with that type of man, or any man, elicits guilt and dysfunction. By failing to enjoy the experience, the woman feels less guilty about her unconscious incestuous wishes.

Another deep psychological factor is the threat of loss of control. As orgasm implies a certain self-abandonment, some men and women are afraid that aggressive impulses will also be triggered. Still another fear is that the erect penis will tear apart the vagina or that the penis will be trapped and choked by the vagina. Such concerns may be experienced consciously but more often are unconscious: the man simply fails to have an erection, or the woman fails to reach orgasm, neither quite realizing why.

Relational Problems     Intrapsychic problems usually spill over into interpersonal conflicts, but sometimes problems arise only in a particular type of relationship. Intense disappointment, muted hostility, or open anger obviously poison sexual interactions. Subtle insults are just as detrimental. Women, for instance, are sensitive about being "used." If a man seems to be interested predominantly in a woman's body and neglects her person, she will feel that she is being reduced to the level of an inanimate object. Some women associate coitus with being exploited, subjugated, and degraded and rebel against it by failing to respond.

The attitudes most detrimental to the male's enjoyment are those that threaten his masculinity. Lack of response on the part of the woman, nagging criticism, and open or covert derision lessen male enjoyment.

Other relational causes include contractual disappointments. When people establish sexual partnerships or get married, their sexual expectations are seldom clearly communicated or negotiated. There is much room for misunderstanding and anger when the partner does not live up to what was expected. Also, as people change, new needs and new preferences alter the original relationship, and the couple may have trouble adjusting.

In power struggles, many forms of sexual sabotage can operate: one partner will pressure the other into sex at inopportune moments; sex is withheld as punishment; people make themselves undesirable or even repulsive by neglecting their bodies, cultivating the wrong physical image, or behaving in ways that are irritating and embarrassing to the other. Sabotage may even interfere with the progress of couples in sex therapy. As one partner begins to improve in sexual performance, the other (often without being aware of it) may attempt to stall or make things difficult; a significant change in the partner would alter the old pattern of the relationship, in which he or she may have a vested interest.

Cultural Causes    Societies influence sexual function by the way children are raised and by the contexts in which they let sexual relations occur (Chapter 21). Feelings of sexual inadequacy commonly stem from ignorance, misconceptions, distorted views of the opposite gender, unwarranted fears, unresolved guilt, and unrealistic expectations of what sex has to offer (Jacobs, 1986). These attitudes all have historical and cultural roots, as we shall see in Part 6.

Cultural patterns also influence intimate relationships. One of the major sources of problems in heterosexual relationships has been the *double standard of morality*—different, often contradictory expectations of how men and women should behave sexually. The general effect of the double standard has been to

inhibit female sexual responsiveness and relegate women to passive and resistive roles in sexual interactions. These attitudes have now been overcome by many men and women. As a result, women are more likely to have more positive attitudes toward sex and be more active and assertive sexual partners (Koblinsky and Palmeter, 1984).

Some people fear that these more liberal and egalitarian attitudes have generated new problems. Disorders of sexual desire have emerged prominently at a time when our society has become much more open about sexual topics, and some of those complaining of sexual apathy may be among the most sexually liberated. The problem may be related to the stress faced by women trying to combine career and family goals, which continues to be much less of an issue for men. In a study of 218 couples who had sought help at the Masters and Johnson Institute, married women who were pursuing careers outside the home were twice as likely to present a primary complaint of inhibited sexual desire (and had a higher ratio of vaginismus) than married women who were working at a job with no particular career prospects, or those who were not employed outside the home (Avery-Clark, 1986b). The husbands of the women who worked outside the home—either at a "career" or at a "job"—presented almost half as often primary complaints of inhibited sexual excitement and desire as the husbands of unemployed women (Avery-Clark, 1986a).

Another concern in the popular media is that the greater assertiveness of women is having a negative effect on male sexual functioning (the "new impotence"); however, there is no proof of such claims (Gilder, 1973).

Since the sexual dark ages, women have pretended (or "faked") orgasm to please their partners. Surely, such deception should no longer be needed or called for; yet the practice of pretending orgasm is reportedly increasing. In a survey of 805 professional nurses nearly two out of three said that they had pretended orgasm at one time or another (Darling and Davidson, 1986). Those who had become sexually active at a younger age and had been sexually more explorative were more likely to have pretended orgasm than others. The explanation given is that because female orgasm is now expected, women feel a greater need to live up to the standard, even if they have to fake it.

The premium we put on competence and success, combined with an overemphasis on sex, can create a formidable hurdle to its enjoyment. Orgasm becomes a challenge, rather than the natural climax of coitus. Inability to achieve it or a certain form of it (multiple, mutual, and so on) becomes not only a signal of sexual incompetence but also a reflection of personal inadequacy. As we become freer about sex, we may be thus generating new problems—excessive demands for performance and wholly unrealistic expectations of what sex can be and do.

## TREATMENTS

Sexual dysfunction may be mild and transient, requiring no therapy, or it may present formidable challenges to treatment. Its remedies range from fairly simple short-term programs to highly specialized, intensive treatments, involving psychological methods, drugs, and surgery.

Until the late 1960s, sexual dysfunctions were treated by physicians, psychologists, and marriage counselors. Following the work of Masters and Johnson (1970) new methods of treating sexual dysfunctions were developed that are more effective and less time-consuming. The applications of these newer methods constitute the *new sex therapy*. Its focus is on the elimination of sexual symptoms, rather than on personality change or on restructuring relationships outside the sexual realm. Although all forms of treating sexual dysfunction could be thought of as "sex therapy," the use of the term is usually restricted to specific approaches focused on the elimination of sexual symptoms.

## Sex Therapy

At present, sex therapy has no distinctive theoretical base of its own. Its practitioners may be physicians or clinical psychologists with many perspectives. The basic methods of sex therapy are derived from behavior modification techniques developed in psychology (Caird and Wincze, 1977; Jehu, 1979). These techniques have been refined and adapted for dealing with sexual dysfunction (LoPiccolo and LoPiccolo, 1978; Leiblum and Pervin, 1980). Physicians combine medical approaches with various aspects of sex therapy. For instance, Helen Kaplan (who is also a psychoanalyst) integrates psychodynamic principles with sex therapy approaches in her work (Kaplan, 1974). Urologists who implant penile prostheses primarily approach these problems from a surgical angle.

Sex therapy has clear merits, but definite shortcomings. It has as yet no solid conceptual base and a young clinical tradition. It is likely to be most effective within a broader program treating psychological problems and interpersonal conflicts (Arentewicz and Schmidt, 1983).

The PLISSIT Principle    Common sense dictates that simpler and briefer methods of therapy be tried first. This principle is embodied in the PLISSIT model for treating sexual dysfunction. The acronym stands for Permission, Limited Information, Specific Suggestions, and Intensive Therapy (Annon, 1976). Therapists take these approaches either sequentially or more or less concurrently. *Permission* takes the form of reassurance, reinforcement of positive values, and encouragement to behave sexually according to the needs and values of the individual. *Limited information* provides facts and self-knowledge about the issues that are specific to a person's sexual problem. *Specific suggestions* are the sort of techniques originally developed by Masters and Johnson (1970) and modified by others. *Intensive therapy* goes beyond the techniques of behavior modification and delves into the person's intrapsychic con-

# Box 15.2

## PSYCHOSEXUAL TREATMENT OF A SEXUALLY DYSFUNCTIONAL COUPLE*

The couple consisted of a handsome and successful 42-year-old real estate broker and his 40-year-old wife, who was a teacher. When they applied for treatment, they had been married for 18 years and had three daughters.

Their chief complaints were the husband's impotence and the wife's inability to attain coital orgasm. Neither spouse had had psychiatric treatment previously. On the surface, both functioned well and neither had ever experienced significant psychiatric symptoms. It became apparent early on, however, that both husband and wife had personality problems. . . .

Basically, their marital relationship was good. Despite their difficulties, they respected, loved, and were committed to one another. At the time of the initial consultation, however, there was a great deal of anger and hostility between them. She would often explode in violent tantrums and he would respond to these outbursts by withdrawing. . . .

The patient's history revealed that he had always had some sexual difficulty. He had been shy with girls in his teens, so that he did not have his first coital experience until he was in his early twenties. In college he had several dates with a girl after she had indicated interest in him, and had become extremely aroused when they petted. However, he experienced erectile difficulties when he attempted coitus and was unable to consummate the act.

Shortly afterward he met his wife, who also took the initiative in their relationship. And again he was very excited by kissing and petting, and had frequent and urgent erections in her presence, although they did not take off their clothes. They had known each other for a year when they decided to get married. No attempt was made to have premarital sexual relations, because both felt that this would not be "proper."

On their honeymoon, when faced with the inevitability of intercourse, the patient was unable to achieve an erection in his wife's presence. However, he stimulated her clitorally and she was very responsive. . . .

Occasionally, with a great deal of stimulation, he was able to have intercourse. She never reached orgasm on these occasions, although she continued to be responsive to clitoral stimulation. Frequency of sexual contact was limited to approximately once every two or three months. On such occasions the husband always took the initiative. . . . Since he was "in charge," he never allowed himself a passive role in sex, and felt guilty about not pleasing his wife. . . .

Treatment began with the prohibition of coitus. As usual the patient and his wife were instructed to take turns gently caressing each other and to tell one another what each found especially pleasing. This experience produced an erection in him, while he reveled in his role as the passive recipient of pleasure, a role he had previously denied himself because it wasn't "manly." He especially enjoyed it when his wife gently played with his penis.

She, on the other hand, was furious and weepy. She enjoyed the experience when it was her turn to receive his caresses, but felt fatigue first, and then rage, when it was her turn to pleasure him and she saw his erectile response. . . . She perceived her "obligation" to him, particularly the fact that she was required to "service" his penis, as a humiliation which evoked feelings of persecution. On the other hand, because she was an extremely intelligent and basically stable person, she was struck by the intensity and irrational quality of her reactions. . . .

The next obstacle to treatment was created by the patient in the form of obsessive self-observation and doubt regarding his sexual competence. He was able to respond to and enjoy their mutual caresses, but when coitus seemed imminent he would begin to "turn himself off" with fears, e.g., "It won't work," "She'll be mad at me . . . ," etc. This difficulty was surmounted by the usual instructions that he consciously avoid such thoughts and focus his attention on sexual sensations. In addition, he was advised to immerse himself in fantasy if he could not control the tendency by conscious effort. . . .

This couple's sexual relationship improved considerably as a result of treatment, but the patient did not achieve complete erectile security. When treatment was terminated, the couple was having intercourse approximately twice a week, and occasionally the husband still lost his erection. However, the couple regarded these experiences as minor "setbacks," and accepted them with equanimity; consequently, they did not have a detrimental effect on their subsequent lovemaking.

*(From Helen Singer Kaplan (1974), *The new sex therapy.*)

flicts with some form of intensive therapy. Kaplan (1974) approaches these issues through *psychosexual therapy*, which helps the patient gain insights into the unconscious conflicts underlying the sexual problem. An account of the treatment of a couple with psychosexual therapy is in Box 15.2.

The Masters and Johnson Model    The Masters and Johnson (1970) sex therapy format, though modified by others, still defines the basic approach in sex therapy. It has a number of general procedures for the treatment of all dysfunctions, supplemented by specific strategies for particular conditions. After organic factors are ruled out, the key task is to have the dysfunctional couple accept sex as a natural function that requires no heroic effort, but only a relaxed, accepting attitude. The focus is on the couple, not the individual. Neither partner is at fault or sick; there are merely inhibitions to overcome. Each must learn to give, as well as to receive, sexual pleasure, to get actively involved rather than be a spectator or a passive participant.

Treatment progresses along two complementary tracks. The first involves discussions between the couple and two cotherapists (one male, one female). Detailed sexual histories are taken from each patient and roundtable sessions explore past experiences, conflicts, feelings, and attitudes on both sexual and nonsexual matters that have a bearing on the dysfunction; successes and failures in the ongoing treatment are analyzed; and so on. Concurrently, the couple goes through a sequence of sexual assignments in private that eventually culminate in mutually satisfactory sexual intercourse, if the treatment is successful. Because of the focus on the couple, Masters and Johnson provided female *partner surrogates* to men without partners early in their work. Legal and ethical considerations have made this practice a problem although some sex therapists continue to rely on surrogate partners in treating select cases. The practice of using a pair of therapists (which is expensive) is not considered essential by others (Kaplan, 1974). The effectiveness of treatment does not seem to de-

pend on the number of therapists (LoPiccolo et al., 1985).

Of importance in the early phase of therapy are *sensate focus* exercises, which prepare the ground for tackling specific problems. These exercises overcome the common immediate causes of sexual dysfunction: anxiety, spectatoring, demand for performance, noncommunication. They start with activities focused on touch awareness and pleasuring rather than sexual arousal. The couple is comfortably positioned so that the helping partner has easy access to the body of the person with the primary problem: when the symptom is female anorgasmia, the man is seated behind the woman (Figure 15.2); in impotence, the position is reversed. What follows next depends on the nature of the problem.

Treatment of Erectile Dysfunction    In cases of erectile dysfunction, the woman takes the initiative to touch, caress, or gently fondle the man's body, initially keeping away from the genitals. The man guides his partner by his verbal or nonverbal responses as well as by leading her hand (*handriding*). In subsequent stages, the couple alternates in pleasuring one another, with more direct communication to guide each other's actions.

After the couple becomes adept at general physical enjoyment, they move on to more explicitly erotic techniques, with the woman now stimulating the man's genitals, along with the rest of his body (Figure 15.3). The interaction continues in a relaxed, nondemanding manner; the man is not expected to have an erection at any particular moment, and neither person is allowed to rush to coitus. When erections do occur in the natural course of events (which is often quite soon in treatment), they are allowed to come and go to instill in the man the conviction that he does not "will" an erection but lets it happen; and should it subside, there need be no sense of failure. Intercourse is forbidden at this stage; it is to be attempted only when erections become frequent and stable during sensate focus exercises.

The transition from sensate focus exercise to coitus is gradual. When the man has gained

Figure 15.2   The training position for the treatment of female sexual dysfunction.

enough confidence, the woman positions herself astride him and inserts his penis into her vagina, relieving him of taking responsibility and risking fumbling and failure (Figure 12.8). Intercourse then proceeds with the primary aim of providing the man with adequate satisfaction: the man is encouraged to be "selfish" during these periods; the sharing of pleasure will follow later. In sum, the basic aim in the treatment of erectile dysfunction is to reduce anxiety so that physiological reflexes can take their natural course.

Treatment of Anorgasmia    The procedure for dealing with female anorgasmia is basically the same. This time the man takes the initiative with early sensate focus exercises; but when it comes to coitus, again the woman assumes the woman-above position. This position lets her be in charge, counteracting her fears of being hurt, used, or put down. It also enables her to gauge the depth of intromission and the force and frequency of coital thrusts, all to suit her needs and help achieve orgasm.

Other strategies focus on more particular issues. For instance, women are more likely than men to have concerns over their physical attractiveness, to be inhibited in allowing themselves sexual pleasure, and to be reticent about exposing their erotic needs. Such issues

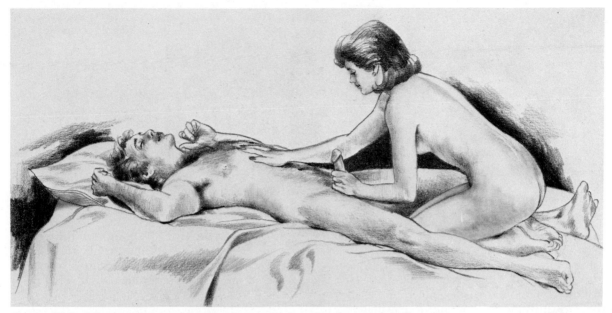

Figure 15.3    The training position for the treatment of male sexual dysfunction.

are dealt with both in discussion and practice. A woman who has never experienced orgasm must be made to have that experience first, however it is attained. She may be encouraged to stimulate her own body and genitals or be brought to orgasm by the partner manually or orally (some also advocate the use of vibrators). Once the inhibiting barrier is broken, the woman will know what it feels like to have an orgasm and can be gradually helped to transfer the experience to coitus. Other "bridging" techniques consist of clitoral stimulation by the man or woman during coitus. The basic aim in treating failures of female sexual arousal and orgasm is to help the woman let go of the inhibitions that block orgasm.

Treatment of Male Inhibited Orgasm    The first goal in the treatment of male ejaculatory incompetence is similarly to cross the orgasmic barrier. The man is helped to reach orgasm first through solitary masturbation; then he does it in the partner's presence, or she masturbates him (having him ejaculate at her genitals). Coitus is attempted last, with her bringing him to a high pitch of excitement and

inserting the penis as he is about to ejaculate. This is the only instance of the man-above position (Figure 12.6). It lets him enter while she continues to stimulate the base of his penis manually.

Treatment of Premature Ejaculation    The basic aim in treating premature ejaculation is to train the man to anticipate orgasm and modulate his level of arousal accordingly. The woman assumes the stimulating position (Figure 15.3) and gently brings him to erection. When the man says that ejaculation is imminent, she uses the *squeeze technique* to avert it—squeezing the glans between thumb and forefinger or putting pressure at the base of the penis (Figure 15.4). She must be gentle yet firm in applying pressure at the front and back of the glans for three to four seconds, being careful not to hurt. Why this maneuver works is not known. It results in partial loss of erection, which is then brought back with further stimulation, and the cycle is repeated. The basic procedure in this approach was reported originally by Semans (1956).

Coitus takes place in the woman-above po-

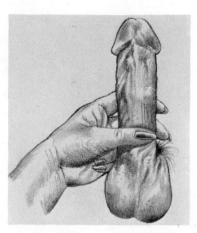

Figure 15.4  Two versions of the "squeeze technique."

sition. During it, the squeeze cycle is repeated a number of times; as he senses the approach of ejaculation she takes out the penis, squeezes the glans, and reinserts it. This maneuver is followed by slow thrusting, and the cycle is repeated until the man wishes to ejaculate.

To avoid coital disengagement, the woman either puts the pressure on the base of the penis or tries a *stop-and-go* technique: as excitement mounts, thrusting stops; after a few moments of rest, when ejaculatory urgency is past, thrusting resumes.

Treatment of Vaginismus    The basic aim in treating vaginismus is the elimination of the vaginal spasm. The treatment utilizes *desensitization*. The patient is taught the nature of the problem and is made aware of the muscular tension at the vaginal opening. Then in a relaxed and safe setting (with the male partner present), a small plastic dilator is gently inserted in her vagina, as she watches in a mirror. The woman then uses these dilators, moving from the smallest to the largest, which is about the size of an erect penis, leaving each in place for short periods of time. When the couple moves on to coitus, she takes charge, inserting the penis herself, controlling the thrusts, and so on.

These treatment strategies sound straightforward, but they only work in a broader therapeutic context. Their success calls for skillful therapists, motivated patients, and resourceful and compassionate sexual partners; these tasks

are not for the squeamish. Sex therapy is still a new field, and its methods are being refined. There are still important questions to be answered about its effectiveness (Box 15.3).

Psychotherapy and Behavior Therapy
Psychotherapeutic methods of treating sexual dysfunction long antedate sex therapy. Their practitioners are a diverse group of specialists with different theoretical orientations: psychoanalysts, psychiatrists, clinical psychologists, psychiatric social workers, and marriage and family therapists. The common element in their approach is the reliance on verbal interchange to resolve personality problems and interpersonal conflicts.

Psychotherapy    Psychotherapists frequently deal with sexual issues, but most of them do not think of themselves as sex therapists; the methods they use to treat sexual problems are the same methods they use to treat any other kind of problem. *Psychoanalysis*, the most intensive form of psychotherapy, involves analyzing erotic fantasies, dreams, events, and past and present sexual relationships. Improvements in the patient's condition depend on insight into the origins of the difficulties. A scaled-down version of psychoanalysis is *insight-oriented therapy*, which pursues more limited goals (DeWald, 1971). It is the basis of Kaplan's psychosexual therapy (Box 15.3).

# Box 15.3

## TREATMENT OUTCOMES OF SEX THERAPY

How well does sex therapy work? The results originally reported by Masters and Johnson were spectacular. Their experience with a total of 1872 cases showed an overall success rate of 82 percent (85 percent for males; 78 percent for females), ranging from 99 percent for vaginismus and 96 percent for premature ejaculation to a relatively more modest 67 percent for primary impotence, 78 percent for secondary impotence, 76 percent for ejaculatory incompetence, 79 percent for primary anorgasmia, and 71 percent for situational anorgasmia (Masters et al., 1982).

Moreover, these results were achieved over periods of treatment lasting a matter of weeks, using methods that seemed so beguilingly simple that almost anyone could master them. Almost everyone tried to do so in a surge of therapeutic optimism that led, during the 1970s, to the emergence of a whole new field with numerous practitioners.

A decade after Masters and Johnson inaugurated sex therapy, questions began to be raised about the effectiveness of their methods and the replicability of their reported results (Zilbergeld and Evans, 1980). In other hands, the same techniques have produced less spectacular results. One factor in this shift is that the more superficial types of sexual dysfunction now get taken care of through educational and self-help methods, leaving the harder cases, with more deep-seated personality problems, in sex therapy.

Despite these concerns, the results of sex therapy continue to be impressive. In a systematic study of sex therapy outcomes, using modifications of the Masters and Johnson techniques, Arentewicz and Schmidt (1983) have reported the following cures, according to the therapists:

| | |
|---|---|
| Orgasmic dysfunction | 19% |
| Vaginismus | 67% |
| Ejaculatory dysfunction | 49% |
| Premature ejaculation | 40% |
| Overall rate | 49% |

Patients and their partners agreed that their sexual problems were much better: the overall rate was 65 percent for patients, 58 percent for partners; but only 8 percent of patients and 11 percent of their partners said the symptoms were fully removed.

Are the improvements in sex therapy sustained over time? Follow-up studies show that after three years some forms of sexual dysfunction tend to return, although the person may feel less distressed about it. Sexual desire dysfunction appears to be particularly resistant to sustained change (DeAmicis et al., 1985).

It may be some time before the treatment of sexual dysfunction occupies its rightful place among respected medical and behavioral specialties; but that day will surely come, since sexual dysfunction deserves to be attended to as much as any other form of human suffering.

The Systems Approach    Rather than focusing on the past, the systems approach focuses on the current relationship of an individual with the sexual partner (LoPiccolo and Stock, 1986). The aim is to learn what function the sexual symptom serves in their relationship. Once the couple can deal with the underlying issue, the sexual dysfunction is next to resolve.

Behavior Therapy    Behavior therapy is another form of psychotherapy, but for historical reasons it is more often referred to as *behavior modification*. Its focus is the problem behavior itself, which it aims to change by techniques derived from learning theory (Chapter 8).

Behavior therapy subsumes a variety of techniques. *Systematic desensitization* is based on the principle of *reciprocal inhibition*—the fact that contrary emotional states are mutually exclusive. For instance, you cannot be simultaneously anxious and calm; if anxiety interferes with a certain function, its effects can be counteracted by relaxation.

Anxiety-producing situations cause distress at various gradations. For example, a woman may find it very difficult to have intercourse with her husband in the nude, although coitus when partially clothed may be more tolerable. The behavior therapist and the patient draw up a detailed list of situations in order from the most unbearable to the comfortably tolerable (for instance, being kissed on the cheek).

The patient is then trained in the techniques of deep-muscle relaxation (which is incompatible with anxiety) and desensitization proceeds. When the woman is fully relaxed, she is asked to fantasize the least fearful of the anxiety-provoking situations on the list; if she gets anxious, she switches back to the relaxation routine; otherwise she tackles the next troublesome scene. This process is repeated until the patient is able to confront in fantasy the anxiety-provoking situation in full (coitus in the nude). The next step is to transfer this mastery of the anxiety-producing stimulus to real-life situations. The same process may be used in connection with other techniques without the use of relaxation.

## Group Therapy

The therapies we have described so far treat individual patients or couples. In *group therapy* a small number of individuals (usually about six to eight) work with one or two therapists. The members of a group may be chosen on the basis of having similar or different problems; they may be unrelated or couples. In addition to the economy in the therapist's time, this approach allows members of the group to share and learn from their problems and lend each other emotional support. On the other hand, this format does not allow for as much individual attention, and especially with a topic like sexual dysfunction, a person may be less open or candid.

Helen Kaplan (1974) has worked effectively with groups of dysfunctional couples, and Lonnie Barbach (1975) has reported good results working with groups of five to seven women with orgasmic problems. These women met with two female therapists for discussions and also carried out daily assignments aimed at "getting in touch" with their own body and

sexual feelings. Orgasm is initially attained through masturbation and eventually through coitus (the sexual partners were not directly involved in the treatment program). After five weeks, 93 percent of these women could reach orgasm through masturbation, and three months later, half were orgasmic during coitus.

## Self-Help

The outpouring of books on various aspects of sexuality, including dysfunction, has reached a mass market. During the 1970s, best-seller lists virtually always included one or more books on sex. Many of these were "how-to" sex manuals with explicit texts and illustrations (Box 12.4). Such books, films, and videos have been helpful to some people with varying degrees of sexual dysfunction. However, some of them contain incorrect information and foster unrealistic goals and expectations.

More specifically aimed at the dysfunctional are instructional books that approach these issues in more thoughtful and systematic ways, including graduated exercises for overcoming inhibitions and gaining sexual satisfaction (Barbach, 1975).

Sexual experience itself probably remains the greatest teacher and therapist of all. With a serious problem, however, practice does not make perfect—it makes matters worse by failure compounding failure. Couples merely trying harder may dig themselves deeper into the problem. On the other hand, the experience of having a caring, compassionate, and competent partner goes a long way in sorting out many sexual problems and imparting confidence. When these approaches prove insufficient, it is time to seek help from a sex therapist. Box 15.4 addresses that choice.

## Treatment with Drugs

Drugs are among the oldest forms of treatment. Their application to sexual dysfunction is one facet of the search for aphrodisiacs (Box 12.5). However, until modern times, the drugs available to physicians to treat sexual disorders

# Box 15.4

## GETTING HELP FOR SEXUAL DYSFUNCTION

We usually seek help when pain or distress becomes more than we can bear, or when we fear that it will get worse. Sexual dysfunction does not hurt in the same way; so it is harder to decide when to seek help, especially if the problem is not sexually incapacitating, such as total impotence or anorgasmia.

If you experience a fairly rapid and consistent change in sexual function, it is important to get a medical checkup. Because symptoms of sexual dysfunction may be the early signs of an underlying illness, there may be more at stake than sex.

On the other hand, the fact that a sexual problem has hung around for many years does not mean that you should simply accept it and learn to live with it. If you wonder whether the dysfunction warrants therapy, you can always seek a consultation. Seeing a physician or sex therapist does not necessarily mean committing yourself beforehand to treatment.

Sex therapy, like other forms of specialized care, is, in principle, best sought not directly but through your doctor or a counselor at a student health center.

Unlike other health care professions, the practice of sex therapy is still unregulated. Anybody entitled to see patients or clients can set up shop as a sex therapist; as a result there are people in practice who simply lack the skills and training to do sex therapy well.

It is generally better to seek help from individuals and clinics affiliated with hospitals, medical schools, and universities. Even if such institutions themselves do not provide such care, they may refer you to reputable therapists. Similar advice may be obtained from medical and psychological societies and the directories of professional organizations in this field, such as the American Association of Sex Educators, Counselors and Therapists (AASECT); 11 Dupont Circle, Suite 220. Washington, D.C. 20036.

Membership requirements in such groups are not stringent, so you must continue to exercise good judgment before making a final choice. Deal with therapists who have a graduate degree from a reputable institution, who show clear evidence of having received serious training in the treatment of sexual dysfunction, and who are willing to discuss openly their qualifications, methods, time schedules, and fees. If there is any hint that sexual intimacies with the therapist are expected, go elsewhere.

The choice of a competent therapist is important, but the success of sex therapy largely depends on the individuals or couples who seek it. Going through the motions of seeking help to placate a spouse, or hoping that things are somehow going to change without serious effort, are futile exercises. Enthusiasm may be too much to expect from those contemplating therapy, but a certain measure of motivation and determination is essential for success.

---

were neither effective nor safe. A well-known example is *Spanish fly,* a powder made from dried cantharis beetles (hence also called *cantharides*). It causes urethral irritation and penile vasocongestion, which may result in erection but also has dangerous side effects.

*Yohimbine* (from the bark of the African yohimbe tree) is a nervous system stimulant (Gilman et al., 1985). Though long claimed to be a sexual stimulant, its "prosexual" effects have only been recently established in experimental animals (Kwong et al., 1986). There is also some evidence that it can be effective in treating impotence.

The great chemical hope for the treatment of sexual dysfunction, especially impotence, has resided in sex hormones—a hope that has been largely unfulfilled. Given their indispensable role in the organization and activation of sexual functions, it was reasonable to expect that hormones would enhance sexual drive and potency. To this end, testicular extracts began to be used way back in the 19th century. Furthermore, since sexual decline and aging are closely associated in people's minds, such treatments also held high hopes for rejuvenation, or regaining youthfulness. Though there has never been any convincing proof that they work, extracts of testicular, placental, and embryonal tissue from animals continue to be used in various parts of the world in futile attempts to fight the effects of aging.

The popularity of testosterone treatment has waxed and waned over the years. There is little question that it can be effective in restoring libido and potency in males if there is androgen deficiency. There is also some evidence that testosterone may enhance sexual function in cases of psychogenic impotence by giving the body a temporary physiological boost (Kaplan, 1974). Testosterone is therefore a legitimate drug for the treatment of select cases, but there is no convincing evidence that it counteracts the effects of aging. Furthermore, the use of testosterone by older persons poses the risk of prostatic hypertrophy and cancer (Chapter 5).

The effect of estrogens on female libido remains unclear (Chapter 4). Estrogen in menopausal women can improve sexual function, counteracting the changes in the vaginal lining and the drying out of the lubricatory response (Chapter 9). The effect of androgens on women's sex drive is ambiguous, and their virilizing side effects so unacceptable that testosterone is not used to treat female sexual dysfunction.

Various drugs have occasionally appeared on the scene with aphrodisiacal side effects, but none of them is reliable and safe for treating sexual dysfunction. Examples are L-dopa, which is widely used in treatment of Parkinson's disease (a neurological disorder); PCPA (p-chlorophenylalanine), an experimental psychiatric drug; and vitamin E (used in some cases of infertility) (Gessa and Tagliamonte, 1974; Hyppa et al., 1975).

During a conference of urologists in Las Vegas in 1983, a British researcher, presenting a paper on the effect of a drug injected into the penis, drove the point home by unzipping his pants to show the audience his own induced erection. The drug in question was a smooth muscle relaxant that causes the penile tissues and arteries to relax, increasing the blood flow into the penis.

A number of substances have since been used with similar effects in causing vasodilation. Most commonly used is a mixture of *papaverine* and *phentolamine,* which must be injected directly into the penis (the pain is said to be minimal). It gives many impotent men a firm erection that lasts more than an hour. The drug will not work on those with severe blood vessel problems. Nonetheless, 14,000 men in the United States are now reportedly using it, many by injecting themselves at home (Stipp, 1987).

In about half of the cases of organic impotence and even a greater proportion of cases with psychogenic impotence, a single injection will be followed by spontaneous erections, in some cases for several weeks (Kiely et al., 1987). In 5 percent of cases the drugs cause sustained erections (priapism) that will permanently damage penile tissues if not relieved. Reducing the dosage often avoids a recurrence.

## Physical Treatment Methods

Kegel Exercises    It is not uncommon for women, following childbirth, to develop *stress incontinence*—involuntary loss of spurts of urine when they cough or strain (raising abdominal pressure on the bladder). The cause is loss of tone of the pubococcygeal (PC) muscle (Chapter 2). To correct this problem, a set of exercises were devised whereby squeezing and relaxing the vaginal orifice gradually strengthened the muscles in the region. In the 1950s, the gynecologist Arnold Kegel discovered that these exercises helped improve his patients' sexual responsiveness and orgasm ability. These *Kegel exercises* have become a part of various sex therapy programs (Kegel, 1952).

One of the merits of Kegel exercises is their simplicity. The woman first learns to control the PC muscle by squeezing on a finger inserted in the vagina, or by alternately interrupting and releasing the stream of urine. She is then instructed to tighten and relax these muscles in a prescribed manner (such as tighten for 3 seconds, relax for 3 seconds, in sets of 10, three times a day) (Kline-Graber and Graber, 1978). The use of a *perineometer* (see Box 3.2) or similar devices allows for more accurate assessments of vaginal muscle tone (McKey and Dougherty, 1986). It also provides an aid to Kegel exercises by allowing the woman to monitor the effect of contracting her PC muscle.

Despite much clinical evidence of the value of strengthening the perineal muscles, data on the correlation of vaginal muscle tone with orgasmic capability have been lacking. One study with normal subjects did not find pubococcygeal strength to be positively correlated to frequency or self-reported intensity of orgasm (Chambless et al., 1982). Another study, though, has shown Kegel exercises to enhance the sexual arousal of a group of normal women (Meese and Geer, 1985).

Masturbation Training    Masturbation, with or without vibrators, is recommended by some therapists, especially in cases that do not yield to more standard approaches. Its main purpose is to allow a woman with primary anorgasmia to experience what it feels like to have an orgasm, which then serves as the goal. As more powerful sources of stimulation, vibrators may bring about orgasm when other means fail.

Various regimens have been devised for such masturbation training, with the purpose of eventually enabling anorgasmic women to attain coital orgasm (LoPiccolo and Lobitz, 1977). These attempts are often successful (LoPiccolo and Stock, 1986). It can be argued that as long as a woman reaches orgasm, by any means, she need not be considered dysfunctional. In this view, the attainment of masturbatory orgasm alone would be a successful outcome.

Surgical Methods

The use of splints to support a limp penis has been known in many cultures. These splints have been in the form of flat rods or hollow dildos housing the flaccid penis.

Advances in surgery have made it possible to implant *penile prostheses*. These devices do not cure impotence; they are mechanical aids that make intercourse possible. Mainly intended for cases of impotence that are due to irreversible organic causes, such as a severed spinal cord, such surgery is currently used for psychologically caused impotence as well. They are also a last resort for cases that do not respond to sex therapy and otherwise would have no hope of coital function. Some 30,000 prostheses are now impanted per year in the United States, mostly with good results. In select cases, the procedure can even be done on an outpatient basis (Small, 1987).

One type of penile prosthesis is a fixed or flexible plastic rod. Implanted in the penis, it provides enough rigidity to allow coitus. A more sophisticated prosthesis is the inflatable variety (Figure 15.5). This device has a reservoir filled with a fluid, which is implanted in the abdomen. It is connected by tubes to a small pump lodged in the scrotal sac, which in turn has tubes leading to the inflatable cylinders implanted in the penis. To attain erection, the man pumps the fluids into the cylinders; to return the penis to a flaccid state, a valve in the pump is released, sending the fluid in the penile cylinders back to the reservoir. The disadvantages of the inflatable device include the greater technical difficulty of installing it. Complications that occasionally arise include infection or leakage of pump fluid (Fishman, 1987); yet in 98 percent of cases, the implanted cylinders remain intact after a year, and in 92 percent of cases after three years (Gregory and Purcell, 1987). If a prosthesis is removed because of infection or malfunction, reimplantation of another device at a later date is not always possible (Gasser et al., 1987), but success rates are now quite high.

A mechanically inflated penis does not feel exactly the same as a naturally erect one, but these surgical methods restore a level of function and mutual satisfaction that would be otherwise unavailable to these men and their partners. Ninety percent of men with penile implants say they would do it over again (Steege et al., 1986).

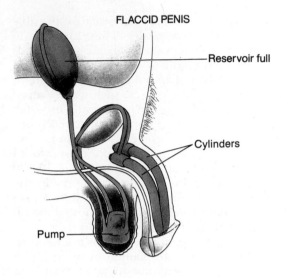

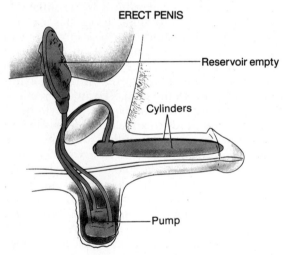

Figure 15.5    An inflatable penile prosthesis.

## Prevention of Sexual Dysfunction

An ounce of prevention is worth a pound of cure—the truism applies to sexual dysfunction as to any other problem. Unfortunately, we do not yet have a clear enough understanding of the causes of sexual dysfunction to speak with confidence about their prevention. Nonetheless, we do have some guidelines (Qualls et al., 1978).

Sex is a physiological function whose full enjoyment requires a healthy and vigorous body. Preventing and treating disease, exercising, eating right, and following proper sexual hygiene all help avoid sexual dysfunction.

Sex is also a psychological function that is highly vulnerable to anxiety, depression, and interpersonal conflict. There is no way to banish these painful emotions forever from your life, but you can face your feelings and your partner's feelings with understanding and sensitivity. A healthy relationship, like a healthy body, increases the chances of a healthy sex life. These are issues we shall deal with in the following chapters. Also, the more you can keep sex free from other conflicts, the better off you will be sexually. Some couples treat sex as a "demilitarized" zone: they can retreat to it as a haven from conflict. At least one important facet of their lives remains satisfying and heartens them to keep working on the rest. But sex is not a balm to be used indiscriminately to smooth over all difficulties.

Sex is also highly influenced by culture. Shame and guilt serve certain legitimate social purposes, but they can also reflect unwarranted antisexual prejudice that will cripple sexual development and enjoyment. You do not have to stick to all the assumptions you grew up with. It is healthy to think them through. At the moment, our culture does not have a clear common understanding of how to raise children who will be sexually healthy and fulfilled adults; you can help develop such understanding.

One of the most important requirements for preventing sexual dysfunction is sexual activity itself. To keep at it, to work and play at its enhancement, to deal with its shortcomings are what it takes to remain sexually alive. Equally important is to place sexual fulfillment in a realistic perspective for each stage of life. The best way to get sexual satisfaction is not to chase it constantly like a rainbow. Sex is one of the greatest joys in life, yet sex alone cannot make life fulfilling. On the other hand, even people with inhibited and faltering sexual lives need to remember that it is not sex that gives up on people, but people who give up on sex.

## REVIEW QUESTIONS

1. What are the main types of sexual dysfunction?

2. What are the main physical and psychological causes of sexual dysfunction?

3. How would you tell if a sexual dysfunction is mainly organic or psychogenic?

4. How does the new sex therapy differ from traditional psychological methods of treating sexual dysfunctions?

5. How are sexual dysfunctions treated medically and surgically?

## THOUGHT QUESTIONS

1. Why was the recognition and treatment of sexual dysfunctions neglected for so long?

2. What are the advantages and disadvantages of using the illness model in approaching sexual dysfunctions?

3. What do you think about using surrogate partners in the treatment of sexual dysfunction?

4. Should sexual interactions between therapist and patient or client be considered a form of sex therapy or a breach of professional ethics?

5. What educational programs would you institute to help prevent sexual dysfunctions?

## SUGGESTED READING

Barbach, L. G. (1982). *For each other: Sharing sexual intimacy*. New York: Doubleday. A well-written book aimed at helping women to fulfill their sexual potential.

Belliveau, F., and Richter, L. (1970). *Understanding human sexual inadequacy*. New York: Bantam. An abbreviated and simpler account of Masters and Johnson's *Human sexual inadequacy* that established the modern field of sex therapy.

Kaplan, H. S. (1974). *The new sex therapy*. New York: Quadrangle. A comprehensive and clearly presented work on sex therapy, with excellent illustrations.

Leiblum, S., and Pervin, L. (Eds.) (1980). *Principles and practice of sex therapy*. London: Tavistock. Valuable contributions on sexual dysfunctions and their treatment.

Zilbergeld, B. (1978). *Male sexuality*. Boston: Little, Brown. An interesting and insightful account of male sexuality, including attitudes that limit male sexual fulfillment.

# PART 5

# Sex and Human Relationships

Auguste Rodin. *The kiss*

# Sexual Intimacy and Love

CHAPTER

# 16

*Love is our true destiny. We do not find the meaning of life by ourselves alone — we find it with another.*

THOMAS MERTON

OUTLINE

SEXUAL ATTRACTION
Physical Aspects
Psychological Determinants
Social Factors
Gender Differences
SEXUAL INTIMACY
Patterns of Sexual Interaction
   Procreational and Relational Sex
   Relational and Recreational Sex
   Sexual Negotiation
   Cooperation
   Seduction
   Coercion
Building and Sustaining Intimacy
   Communication and Self-Disclosure
   Caring and Affection
   Sharing

Honesty and Trust
Commitment
Problems in Intimacy and
  Commitment
  Personality Factors
  Gender Differences
EROTIC LOVE
Varieties of Love
  Components of Love
  Love and Dependency
Falling in Love
  The Chemistry of Love
  Behavioral Aspects
Companionate Love
The Relationship of Sex and Love
  The Effect of Love on Sex
  The Effect of Sex on Love

For some people, sex and love are inseparable, or one a prerequisite for the other. Other people can be in love without ever becoming sexually intimate, or be sexually intimate without love. What determines these patterns? Are they the same for men and women? What happens if you link or separate the elements of intimacy? These are the questions we shall discuss in this chapter.

## SEXUAL ATTRACTION

Think of someone you have been strongly attracted to sexually and another person who leaves you cold. What are their characteristics? You will probably come up with a number of physical features; if you think further, you will identify personality traits and social characteristics that also contribute to how you feel. If you want to share your conclusions with a good friend who has carried out a similar self-assessment, you will find quite a few similarities but also some differences in your ideas of sexual attractiveness. Were you to compare these perceptions with those of strangers from your own society and then to people from different cultures, you will discover an ever-increasing variety of what passes for sexual attractiveness.

Anthropologists cannot agree on any universal patterns of sexual attractiveness, except for some general elements like youthfulness and good health, as manifested by good teeth, clear eyes, and a firm gait (Symons, 1979). Bodily filth, bad odor, and blemished skin are thought unattractive in most cultures.

*Sexiness* (being sexually appealing) and *physical attractiveness* (being beautiful or handsome) share many features, but the two are not the same. Sexiness is as much a reflection of personality (which includes sexual attitudes and values) as it is of looks. Finally, to be sexual, or to seek sexual gratification and fulfillment, is the prerogative of every one of us, no matter how we are judged on someone else's scale of attractiveness or sexiness.

### Physical Aspects

In Chapter 3, we described how the five senses—sight, hearing, taste, smell, and touch—provide the cues for sexual arousal. The most important sources of such erotic signals are other people; so at its most basic physical level, sexiness is determined by how a person looks, sounds, feels, and smells, which makes "body-watching" such a popular pastime (Morris, 1985). Appearance seems to play the primary role in defining sexual attractiveness.

Cultures vary in what parts of the body are considered sexy, but the genital regions and the secondary sexual characteristics of the body have wide erotic appeal. Even at that there are important cultural and gender differences. For example, breasts and buttocks are important components of a woman's sexual allure in the United States (Davenport, 1977). In a number of other cultures, breasts are not considered sexually arousing (which is one reason why they are not concealed).

Some biologists ascribe the evolution of the larger human breasts to the loss of estrus. During estrus, the buttocks and genital region of some female primates become swollen and turn red (because of vasocongestion). These changes act as visual triggers or *sexual releasers* for the male. Because women have no estrus period, an important source of erotic stimulation is presumably lost. To compensate, larger breasts have been selected through human evolution; they are more visible and accessible releasers, which replicate and reinforce the erotic attraction provided by the buttocks (Morris, 1969).

The function of the male genitals as erotic releasers for women appears far less important. The erect penis often displayed in phallic symbols has more to do with expressions of dominance and aggression than with eroticism (Chapter 19). This fact may explain why heterosexual women find the sight of the male genitals less arousing than heterosexual men find the female genitals. It may be one facet of a more basic gender difference in how men and women regard physical features of attractiveness.

Because physical features are genetically determined (as well as influenced by the environment), cultural preferences must operate within certain biological limits. It would make no sense for pygmies to prefer people six feet tall. Up to a point, culturally valued features (such as long legs or broad shoulders) that are somewhat exaggerated may become a prized feature, but marked departures from the norm are usually not considered sexy. As Darwin observed, people usually admire and tend to exaggerate the typical characteristics of their group. Where men have sparse facial hair, they tend to remove what hair there is altogether; in hairier groups they tend to admire beards. Such practices also vary through history: beards were popular in the United States before World War I, then went out of fashion, only to come back in the sixties and go out of favor again.

Cultures also modify the physical appearance of the face and the body, including the genitals, for aesthetic, erotic, and social reasons. Typically, these alterations are readily reversible. The most prevalent example in our culture is the use of cosmetics and various hairstyles, in addition to shaving facial hair, plucking eyebrows, removing hair from armpits and legs, and so on.

More permanent changes are brought about in various cultures through tatooing; scarification (cutting or burning to make scars); the insertion of rings and other objects into the ears, nose, and lips; and the alteration of various body parts (head, neck, feet, teeth, and so on) by stretching, enlarging, compressing, cutting, or knocking off (Virel et al., 1979; Brain, 1979; Gregersen, 1983). As a result, what is considered attractive in one culture may look exotic or strange to outsiders (Figure 16.1). Body markings not only decorate but also signify marital status (like a wedding ring), making public the pattern of sexual behavior expected of that person (Thevoz, 1984).

In our culture, the piercing of earlobes is widely used by women and sometimes men.

Figure 16.1   Standards of attractiveness vary from culture to culture.

Plastic surgery makes more marked changes, including the reshaping of noses, facelifts, breast augmentation (less often reduction), liposuction (to suck out localized fat deposits), and other procedures that do not improve physiological function but restructure a healthy body part in order to enhance its aesthetic and sexual appeal. Whether or not people should spend substantial sums of money and subject themselves to the risks of such surgery for relatively trivial "defects" is a matter of personal choice.

There has been a longstanding preoccupation with the nude body in the art of many cultures (Lucie-Smith, 1981). Nudity is considered sexually provocative in many (but not all) cultures, so clothing has been typically used to conceal the body. Modesty may be achieved by as little as the loincloth of aboriginal people or as much as the head-to-toe coverings of women in traditional Islamic countries. The use of clothing and ornamentation to enhance sexual attractiveness is equally common. Advertising for such goods unabashedly plays up their erotic potential (Chapter 18). This market has been mostly geared to women but is now extending to men. Evidence of cultural shifts in what is considered a sexy body come from changes in clothing fashions (Glynn, 1982).

Another fluctuating feature is girth. At the turn of the century men of means in the United States were corpulent, and women had ample hips and bosoms. Now slimness is equated with higher class status and sexiness (according to the Duchess of Windsor, one can never be "too thin or too rich.") The slender look may have also become popularized as young women became more athletic (runners are thin) and moved away from the big-breasted sex-symbol type of the 1950s, in favor of a more androgynous, boyish figure. Figure 16.2 shows the fluctuating body measurements of Miss America contestants since 1940, reflecting some of the shifts in one version of the feminine "ideal" body.

Until a few generations ago, Western women of privileged classes prided themselves on the whiteness of their skin and guarded it from the sun with parasols. Now it is consid-

ered chic and sexy to sport a tan for both men and women. To have tanned skin in the past meant you were a laborer working outdoors; to have a tan now means you can vacation where the sun is, whatever the season.

Some of these dictates of fashion are harmless, if frivolous. Others represent serious health hazards. Suntans, for example, markedly increase the risk of skin cancer. Women stand to be harmed by more of these cultural expectations and practices than men. Women used to deform their rib cages by wearing tight corsets. Now unhealthy eating habits and dietary abuse among young white women are leading to *anorexia* and *bulimia*.[1] The preoccupation with body weight is not only rampant among high school students but also appears to start even earlier. Although there are no universal standards of beauty, as judgments of sexual attractiveness change over time, there is considerable agreement on what is appealing within a culture (or its subcultures) at a given time (Hatfield and Sprecher, 1986).

Socialization into a culture's norms of physical and sexual attractiveness is an adaptive process. When it becomes exaggerated into an "overadaptation" (Mazur, 1986), a person can suffer ill-effects.

### Psychological Determinants

We tend to overemphasize physical attractiveness, forgetting that personality factors also make a man or woman sexually attractive. Not only is the choice of a spouse or long-term sexual partner heavily influenced by such factors, but even in casual sexual encounters, personality can count more than looks.

Among the psychological determinants of sexiness, nonsexual personality factors provide the basic framework. Just as physical attrac-

[1]Anorexia is a serious and persistent loss of appetite leading to emaciation and metabolic disturbances. It is caused by an extreme fear of becoming overweight. Bulimia involves repeated eating binges, followed by self-induced vomiting or laxative use to avoid gaining weight. Both are serious health hazards.

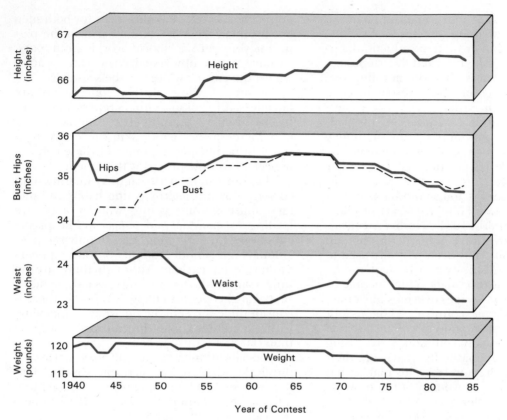

Figure 16.2  Body measurements of Miss America contestants by year of contest.

tiveness is built on a reasonable level of bodily health, psychologial attraction also presupposes a certain soundness of the mind and personality. In other words, the person who you want to go to bed with is no different at that level from someone with whom you want to have dinner, study, or play tennis.

Personality traits of sexiness that are more specific are less obvious than their physical counterparts. Furthermore, the psychological variables we respond to are probably more numerous and complex than physical ones; so individual differences are likely to be greater. There are also gender differences in how sexual attractiveness is perceived.

Personality features that are sexy may seem contradictory, because we need both excitement and security. We find exciting those who convey a sense of dash, daring, and ad-

venture, those who are unconventional, individualistic, and "different"—provided they are not too wild, weird, or social outcasts. We also find those with solid and stable characters, who have the seal of social approval and are comfortingly familiar, to be sexually interesting—provided they are not dull, stolid, and undistinguishable from a dozen others.

*Romance* triggers many erotic associations. Sometimes it is a synonym for sexy; sometimes it conveys feelings of emotional closeness that transcend the purely sexual. People who are fun to be with, easy to talk to, are usually thought sexier than others. Those who intimidate, threaten, deprecate, dehumanize, and degrade you are definitely not sexy.

One of the most important considerations in eliciting sexual interest is the sexual interest the other person shows in you. To be considered sexy is very sexy. Of course, the expression of such interest must occur at the right time, in the right place, and in the right manner. Otherwise it becomes sexual harrassment, which is far from sexy.

Intellectual attributes (intelligence, wit, artistic talent), physical prowess or athletic ability, and other gifts and talents also are part of sexiness. So are shared spiritual and ideological values. The characteristics that help establish and sustain sexual intimacy are inseparable from these contributions to sex appeal—the ability to care and share, empathy and tenderness, trust, commitment, and above all love.

Other features—far less socially desirable—may also contribute to sexiness. The forbidden has a potent power to excite. Hostility fuels sexual arousal, perhaps far more than we wish to acknowledge (Stoller, 1979). Such considerations not only stir paraphiliacs but to a lesser degree all of us.

## Social Factors
The social factors that influence sexual attraction demonstrate even more graphically how far sexiness can stray from sex. The social aspects of a person, such as social class, ethnicity, and religious affiliation, affect us both as individuals and as a group.

The attitudes, beliefs, values, and prejudices of the group we belong to strongly influence our sexual likes and dislikes. They also affect the level of our own sexual appeal for others. For example, people of higher social status generally look sexier. There are several reasons, some of them physical. The better-off do not engage in hard, back-breaking labor that wears the body out; they can afford to take better care of themselves and are generally healthier; they have the means to dress well, and obtain the services of cosmeticians and plastic surgeons. Money and status allow people a greater choice of sexual mates, so they tend to choose the sexually more attractive ones (as would anyone else, given the chance). Beyond such benefits, social status confers an aura of power and exclusiveness that many people find sexy. For people ambitious to

marry upward, higher-status "catches" tend to appear more attractive then they actually are.

Status derived from power and authority is equally sexy in our society. Typically, such status has conferred more sex appeal on men. As more women gain power, it will be interesting to see if they also gain greater sexual attractiveness to men.

At least part of the power struggle between men is in the service of enhancing their sexual potential. An important reason why older men are still able to attract younger women is that they have power and status. The effect of dominant status goes beyond sex appeal; it has a profound influence on sexual relationships as a whole. It influences who initiates sex, what form it takes, even the positions of coital partners and many other related factors (Blumstein and Schwartz, 1983).

Sexual associations in turn influence status. The more attractive a man's wife, mistress, or date, the more it reflects his worth. The same is true for women: the more attractive and socially desirable her man, the greater her status. With the political and social emancipation of women, profound changes are taking place. Many women are not willing anymore to be ornaments and testimonials to the social status of men. Still, the use of social dominance to obtain sexual aims and the use of sex to enhance social standing continue to be very much part of our relationships.

Sexual attractiveness continues to be a highly desired characteristic because it confers benefits beyond the realm of sexuality. The sexually attractive are seen as better people and are rated by college students of both sexes as happier in their work and socially, as well as obviously more marriageable (Dion et al., 1972). The tendency to equate beauty with goodness goes back to the ancient Greeks and remains a common myth (Hatfield and Sprecher, 1986).

## Gender Differences
Among heterosexual men and women, physical attractiveness should be, in principle, complementary: men should be sexually aroused

by the female body and women by the male body. By the same token, homosexuals should find sexually attractive the bodies of members of their own sex.

Instead it is a truism in our culture (supported by what studies there are) that heterosexual men respond more to female physical attractiveness, whereas women respond more to male personality characteristics (such as sensitivity) and social assets (such as status and wealth). This is not to say that women do not care for male looks nor that men are oblivious to anything but female looks; it is only a matter of relative emphasis (Berscheid and Walster, 1974; Huston and Levinger, 1978).

Whether this gender difference is based on biological factors shaped through evolution (Symons, 1979) or the result of a persistent bias in socialization, women are under more pressure than men to conform to whatever ideal of beauty prevails. They learn early that their social opportunities are affected by their physical attractiveness. A sense of beauty (or lack of it) becomes important for a woman's body image and self-concept (Mazur, 1986).

Will changes in the social status and economic independence of modern women change this picture? There is a general tendency among professional and college women to shun or reduce makeup and to emphasize comfort and utility in clothing. On the other hand, practices like the refusal to shave the legs, which made a "political statement" a decade or so ago, has now all but vanished even among women with strong feminist convictions.

It would be a mistake to assume that whatever women do to their appearance is to please and attract men. Actually women are as interested in the impact of their appearance on other women, and some decidedly do not care what men think about it. The same applies to men, though in their case dress codes are more power-oriented (Von Furstenberg, 1978). Moreover, both men and women adjust their physical appearance to their own body image.

Traditionally, people have associated physical attractiveness and sex appeal with culturally defined gender types. In other words,

all else being equal, the more feminine a woman and the more masculine a man, the more attractive and sexier they are thought to be. This idea too is changing as more androgynous images become prevalent (Chapter 10).

"Sex symbols"—public figures like movie stars and rock stars with wide sex appeal—often shape the public images of sexual attractiveness and reinforce gender stereotypes. Traditionally, famous stars have been strikingly "feminine" (Marilyn Monroe, Rita Hayworth) or "masculine" (Clark Gable, Marlon Brando). Though times have changed, the images of these stars continue to convey a sense of raw sex appeal (Figure 16.3). The recent trend toward androgyny (Figure 10.1) is more evident among male stars (David Bowie, Michael Jackson) than female (Madonna).

Comparisons between men and women sometimes get reduced to their preferences for body parts. Men seem easier to categorize in this respect than women (for instance, "leg men" or "breast men"), although such simple-minded clichés reduce them to caricatures. Contrary to the stereotype of the muscular, broad-shouldered male ideal, women seem to prefer flat stomachs and small buttocks. Generally, the rule of averages seems to prevail. Contrary to report, most men prefer women with medium-sized breasts, buttocks, and legs to the more exotic body shapes of models. Women in turn like men with medium-sized shoulders, medium-thick waist and hips, and thin legs based on choices of body silhouettes (Hatfield and Sprecher, 1986).

Both men and women value highly an attractive face, particularly the eyes, which are its most expressive part. But because the face reflects a person's "character" more than the body, women are perhaps more attentive to its details than are men. The face offers even more variations than the body and hence many more ways of looking attractive. In one study, although there was general agreement on what faces were most appealing, even the least popular face was chosen by some as the best within its category (Cross and Cross, 1971).

Traditionally, men have looked at women with less disguised sexual interest ("ogling,"

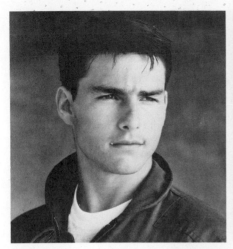

Figure 16.3   **Sex symbols in the entertainment world: Tom Cruise** (*left*) **and Madonna** (*right*).

"undressing with the eyes") while women have been more discreet. An interesting example of how gender differences may be changing in this regard is the recent emergence of male "strippers." Typically, it is women who exhibit themselves to male audiences through various forms of dancing while scantily clad (belly dancing, go-go dancing) or undressing (burlesque, striptease). Male strippers now do the same for female audiences (Figure 16.4).

Such performances exemplify *sexual objectifying*, whereby a person is reduced to a body as an *erotic object*. While some have taken advantage of the willingness of men to pay for such performances, other women have seen this practice as another instance of the exploitation and degradation of women. It is unclear as yet if male strippers will prove to be a passing fad or a more established form of sexual entertainment. Do women get erotic pleasure comparable to that claimed by men when watching these spectacles? Or is female interest in male strippers a political counterstatement to the long-established practice of using the exposed female body for male entertainment? Does the parity achieved by having male strippers make this practice more acceptable? These questions relate closely to other issues we shall discuss in connection with sexual exploitation (Chapter 18).

The most significant gender difference is not whether women prefer some parts and men others but the tendency for men to think in terms of body parts, whereas women view the body in its totality. This tendency may be part of sexual objectifying, to which men are more inclined. Through this process, the person of the sexual partner is seen as a body, which in turn is reduced to its erotic parts. Beyond that stage preferred body parts become a fetish through partialism, or an actual object comes to symbolize the part (Chapter 14). This tendency affects not only sexual attractiveness but also the broader issue of sexual intimacy.

## SEXUAL INTIMACY

Sexual attractiveness, valued and overvalued as it is, means little if it leads nowhere. To obtain sexual satisfaction, one must be able to establish sexual intimacy with another person. Sexiness helps initiate and sustain that process but does not guarantee its success by any means; it may even sometimes get in the way of getting close to someone in a deeper sense.

To be intimate with someone means to have a close personal relationship. Many forms of intimacy, such as that between friends and relatives, have no sexual side. By the same token, to have engaged in a sexual act with someone cannot be equated with having been emotionally intimate. *Sexual intimacy* has to be both psychological and sexual.

Figure 16.4  Female and male "strippers" exhibiting themselves to audiences.

## Patterns of Sexual Interaction

There are three main purposes for establishing and sustaining sexual partnerships: *procreational*—to have babies; *relational*—to share sexual satisfactions within an affectionate and trusting relationship; and *recreational*—to have fun (Comfort, 1972).

### Procreational and Relational Sex

For most people, the procreative and relational aspects of sex are closely tied. Children need a lot of care, and it is best to share the task. There are, of course, single parents who fulfill the role of parenting better than some couples; but generally, single parenthood is not a matter of preference but the result of divorce, separation, or death.

Most women and men still view marriage as the best relationship within which to have children. Although it is true that "illegitimacy" has lost much of its social stigma, and there are nonmarital relationships that are just as stable as any marriage, society still makes it much easier for married people to function as parents (Chapter 17).

The teachings of the Catholic church completely link the procreative and relational ("unitive") aspects of sex. They are seen as inseparable in every sexual act, and as legitimately fulfilled only within marriage (Chapter 23). Other churches allow the separation of the procreative from the unitive aspects of sex (as do most Catholics in practice) by condoning contraception.

Less traditional people may believe in greater freedom of sexual associations outside of marriage. In radical departures from convention, some people now question the necessity of marriage and cohabit instead; others would like to extend marriage to incude gay couples. The traditional childbearing role of women as mothers and their roles as wives are being reevaluated in economic and political terms for their effect on women's personal freedom, equality, and self-fulfillment.

### Relational and Recreational Sex

Most people find sex safer and more satisfying within a stable and meaningful relationship. It may be marriage, romantic love, more sedate forms of affection, friendship, or at a minimum, some measure of mutual respect and liking. Sex in such safe and loving relationships can be deeply satisfying. These couples know each others' likes and dislikes, which eliminates fumbling and false starts; they can be counted upon to be trustworthy and forgiving when there are failings and problems.

*Casual sex,* exemplified by the "one-night stand," is a sexual encounter with no emotional involvement. The sexual partner may be a friend, an acquaintance, or a stranger met at a bar or a party. In relational terms it is a "low-cost" relationship. The objective is sexual pleasure with no strings attached and no expectations beyond having a good time together. Casual sex makes it easier to have a variety of sexual partners while staying free of emotional entanglements or commitments.

Apart from the health hazards in casual sex with multiple partners, especially the risk of AIDS (Chapter 5), many women (more than men) find casual sex unsatisfactory. They see it as shallow, trivializing the sexual experience; it may lower their self-esteem, making them feel compromised or used. In a sample of college students both males and females who approved of premarital sexual intercourse in a serious relationship stressed the importance of feeling loved and needed. However, the men found it easier to engage in coitus without an emotional commitment (and with more partners). The women were unlikely to want intercourse for physical pleasure without emotional involvements (Carroll et al., 1985).

Those who defend recreational sex do not deny that there may be unhappy reactions to it, but they blame social attitudes, the double standard, and irresponsibility. The failures, they say, do not represent recreational sex at its best. After all, a great deal of misery results from relational and marital sex as well. They also concede that the inability to have stable sexual attachments or the exclusive reliance on casual sex often betrays a social or psychological deficiency. What is the harm, though, they ask, if two adults who are social equals and mean well engage in sex purely for the fun of it without expecting (or precluding) that personal commitments will precede or follow? Furthermore, why not have the whole range of relationships: a spouse or a steady mate,

good friends to go to bed with occasionally, and purely sexual encounters as the opportunities present themselves?

Why would people want casual sex when they already have satisfying, stable relationships? The common explanation is to find variety or to compensate for inadequacies in the sexual aspects of the stable relationship. Approval of this reasoning varies with gender and sexual orientation (Table 16.1, page 464). Men are more likely to approve of casual sex than women; gay men and married women are at the opposite ends of the spectrum.

Some explain these gender differences on evolutionary grounds, as will be discussed later. Other possible explanations are psychological. Sex serves to express dominance: we speak of sexual "conquest," "scoring," and other metaphors that clearly imply the subjugation of the sexual object. People may seek new partners to validate their sexual worth and competence; being sexually desired by an established partner is taken for granted. A good deal of sexual provocation and flirtation that are not meant to lead to sexual activity also fulfills these self-validating functions in milder form. The line is thin between being seen as a sexually exciting and vibrant person who stays within bounds and being a tease who goes too far in offering sexual enticement but not far enough in providing sexual satisfaction.

If the forces of sexual variety are so potent and the climate of our society is so permissive, why has recreational sex not taken the country by storm? Why are its exponents mainly, although not exclusively, among the young (who are experimenting), those in transition between more stable relationships (such as the recently divorced), those who occasionally stumble into it with varying degrees of misgiving, and those unwilling or incapable of forming stable ties?

One answer is that we are still hopelessly bound up in traditional conventions and concerns. The day will come when unwanted pregnancy and sexually transmitted diseases will cease to be a threat; the double standard of sexual morality will have been demolished, allowing women as free a rein with their sexuality as men; and love and marriage will be devoid of sexual jealousy and possessiveness. This is the utopia of *free love.*

The counterargument is that this vision of total *sexual liberation* is illusory. What stops people from playing at sex the way they would play at some sport is not just external constraints. There is something deeper, which prompts them to regard sex as not another game but as much more serious. Even when given a free choice, people recognize that they cannot have it both ways in sexual relations; that the relational and recreational aspects at some level become mutually exclusive; what you gain in breadth of experience you lose in depth. Freedom becomes, in the words of a popular song "just another word for nothin' left to lose."

Sexual Negotiation    Give and take underlies all human relationships. It is most evident in commercial interactions—you pay and the service or object you buy is yours. In sexual interactions, sex-for-pay follows this model closely; but prostitution is not the only instance where the rule operates. Reciprocity characterizes all types of sexual interactions, without reducing them all to the same cold, cash-and-carry model or forcing all forms of human affection and caring into an impersonal bottom-line mentality.

Like any valued "commodity," sex cannot be had for the asking; it is not free, no matter what the context of the relationship. Every sexual interaction entails *negotiation*; you and your partner reach an agreement or compromise. Sexual negotiations may be free and easy between compatible lovers; more indirect and guarded, when potential lovers are testing each other; or open and direct, when one is bargaining for a casual sexual encounter.

Although sexual negotiation may be more complex when a couple is considering crossing the line the first time, it is not a once-and-for-all agreement. Even couples in committed relationships say their sexual interactions have to be negotiated time and again to remain viable and to allow for growth and change in sexual needs and expectations.

Typically, sexual negotiations are con-cealed within the broader fabric of social interactions, and are carried out silently. The wife who is angry at her husband may not sexually reject him out loud, but she may pretend to be asleep, or go to bed early, or somehow convey her unavailability ("I have a headache"). The husband in a similar situation may develop an intense interest in a late television program or seek some other phony diversion. (There are, of course, times when a person is not in the mood for sex for reasons that have nothing to do with the partner.)

In either case, the partner who is being denied sexual access may simply or reluctantly forego it on that occasion. Other choices are to try to overcome the apparent problem by acting in ways that excite the partner, by escalating the demand ("I really want you"), or by retreating into a sulk and planning to retaliate. The best choice is to find out what is realy wrong and work it out.

Occasional mismatch in sexual interest is common even in happily compatible couples. They disagree not only on whether or not to engage in sex but on what kind of sexual activity to engage in. The frequency with which such differences come up, and how effectively they are resolved, shows the strength of an intimate relationship.

Successful negotiations call for a number of essential qualities—communication, trust, caring, sharing, and commitment, among others. Their net effect is to generate emotional good will or credit. To pursue the metaphor, the more of an investment you have in the sexual partner—the more you like, love, or need the person—the more generous you will be in extending "credit." You will give more and ask for less, with the assurance that eventually the balance will even out, and if necessary you will be willing to cheerfully forget the debt. How long a relationship can operate with a negative balance depends on many other factors.

Finally, there is the matter of negotiating style. Do you stay up all night talking, write letters, or storm out of the house? The manner in which you negotiate issues may drive your partner to distraction or lead to a happy outcome.

All of these features form part of *negotiating strategies*, or what some sociologists call *influence tactics*. They include manipulation, supplication, bullying, autocracy, disengagement, and bargaining (Howard et al., 1986). Supplication (begging) and manipulation are "weak" strategies used by the less dominant member of a couple; bullying and autocratic tactics are "strong" strategies (but not desirable). Bargaining and disengagement are more complex and cross power relationships.

Traditionally our culture, like many others, has expected men and women to take different negotiating postures. These differences apply both to long-term strategy and to immediate tactics. Supposedly, in sexual negotiations, men press for immediate sexual gratification, while women seek long-term advantages. These strategies make men more eager to initiate sexual encounters than women; but once women engage in a sexual relationship, they are more eager to prolong it.

This difference applies both to a single sexual encounter (Figure 16.5) and to a sexually intimate relationship.

The fact that men typically initiate sexual overtures and tend to entice or coerce women into sexual activity does not necessarily mean that males are more interested in sex than females. The difference may not be in sexual interest but in cultural prescriptions for sexual behavior. For example, women perceived as sexually experienced were evaluated more negatively by their peers than less experienced women (Garcia, 1982). Combined with sex role expectations that males should push for sexual activity whereas females should avoid it (McCormick, 1979; McCormick and Jessor, 1983), it is no surprise that women report being less comfortable initiating sex.

Differences in styles of sexual initiative are already fairly well established by the time of adolescence and come out during dating. Among adolescent subjects in one study boys

Figure 16.5   William Hogarth (1697–1764). *Before* and *After.*

relied on the following strategies: direct approach ("Do you want to?"); declaration of affection ("I love you"); get what you can ("hump and dump"); contrived behavior ("I shouldn't ask you to do this"); persistence ("please, oh please"); and seeking girls who are known to engage in sex ("easy lays") (Martinson, 1976).

Adolescent girls may use some of the same direct methods, suggesting, propositioning, or physically initiating sexual activity (one teenage boy reports, "Then to my amazement, she sat astride me, grasped my overheated penis as if it were a doorhandle, and in a rather business-like fashion, lowered herself onto it"). More typically, girls will initiate sexual activity by leading on the male partner in subtle ways (touching his thigh, playing with his hair, looking at him invitingly, and so on).

Cooperation    To "co-operate" means to operate or work together toward a common goal. It presupposes two interested partners who feel free to engage in sex. The basic issue is not whether or not to have sex but when, where, and how often. Cooperation does not mean that each side is equally eager (that rarely happens in human affairs) but that they are heading in the same direction.

Cooperation includes a large measure of bargaining in good faith. There may be some elements of other tactics like supplication and manipulation, but if they become prominent, they will interfere in the cooperative process.

However willing the partners may be, no sexual interaction occurs unless someone takes the initiative. The way in which this may be done is culturally defined. The signaling of sexual interest is often nonverbal, by facial expression, gestures, and other cues. When the sexual invitation is more explicit, it takes the form of *propositioning* (making a pass).

Even under the best of circumstances, many people find it hard to negotiate about sex. There is the possibility of rejection, which is humiliating. There is concern over putting the other person in an embarrassing position. Where atypical sexual wishes are present, there is the fear of being thought "weird." There is just not knowing what to say without

seeming to be crude, vulgar, calculating, and "only" interested in sex.

Seduction    When there is an element of enticement, we call it *seduction* ("leading away"). In a benign sense, seduction involves the playful elicitation of sexual interest in a partner. More typically, it involves exploiting the other person's psychological weaknesses. There may be supplication ("just this once") and flattery ("I have never wanted anyone so desperately"), shaming ("Don't act like a freaked-out child"), or other forms of bullying. Money, gifts, and other favors may be offered to break down resistance. Deception through false declarations of love and promises of marriage have been standard tactics of unscrupulous individuals. In addition to these various manipulative techniques, the seducer may also rely on fake disengagement ("I give up") or threat ("I'll kill myself").

Coercion    The element of imposing one person's sexual desires on another becomes clearest in various forms of coercion. Psychological coercion is *pressuring;* the threat or use of physical force is *rape*. The use of coercion is a serious problem at many levels of intimacy and sexual interactions. We shall deal with its various manifestations in detail in Chapter 19.

## Building and Sustaining Intimacy

The elements of successful negotiation and the ingredients of a fulfilling intimate relationship overlap and reinforce each other. The basic reason is that sexual intimacy does not just happen but is the outcome of a process that entails a good deal of negotiation. After intimacy is attained, it can be sustained only through further negotiation.

Lovers are not like a pair of lawyers representing labor and management. Negotiation in intimate relationships is more subtle, informal, and often nonverbal, but occasionally more direct and sometimes confrontational.

Moreover, intimacy itself facilitates sexual negotiation, and often makes it superfluous. Unlike first-time lovers, there is less need for testing and fencing. Each one already knows the other's basic likes and dislikes (but there is always a need to ascertain the mood of the moment). An inviting smile is all it may take to send the couple to the bedroom.

This shortcut is possible because the psychological and social ground is already firmly laid between intimate lovers. Contraception and health concerns have been sorted out. Such factors stabilize a relationship and make it safer and more predictable; but by the same token, they may routinize it and diminish its excitement.

Communication and Self-Disclosure The importance of communication goes beyond negotiating or conveying sexual directives in coitus (Chapter 12). Communication is essential for the building and sustaining of intimacy. Lovers need to express their affection and appreciation—through words or through a touch, hug, or kiss. It is not enough to know that you are liked and loved; you need to hear about it over and over. As with any other form of sustenance, love needs to be replenished and nourished. Expressions of affection need not be flowery (though it is fine if they are); they can be subtle and subdued. You do not need to shout how you feel from rooftops. It can be heard just as well whispered into an ear; but your feelings must come across crystal clear without hemming and hawing.

Communication is equally important for the anticipation and resolution of conflict. There is some friction in all intimate relationships, which causes trouble if allowed to build up. Communication is the grease that cuts down such friction.

Women generally are more eager and able to express their feelings in intimate relationships and need such communication to achieve sexual satisfaction. Among the subjects of the *Redbook* survey, the more often wives could discuss their sexual feelings and wishes with their husbands, the more likely they were to describe the sexual aspect of their marriage as "good/very good" (Levin, 1975b). Men are no less in need of expressing their feelings, but they are socialized to shy away from it. A boy

learns early that crying is not manly, even if it is for a good reason. Attitudes may be slowly changing in this regard.

Those who are fortunate enough to have compatible partners and have a natural way of dealing with issues as they arise do not need to pay special attention to communication. A lot of other couples need to work at it, and therapists provide useful advice to help them along.

An aspect of communication that is particularly important for establishing intimacy is *self-disclosure,* revealing your private thoughts and feelings as well as providing personal information about yourself and your background. Even in the most impersonal sexual encounters there is a need to know something about the other person. Such knowledge makes the interaction a bit more personal (although what one tells another is highly selected). It also makes it safer; for example, knowing about the partner's past sexual contacts helps assess the risk of AIDS infection.

In intimate relationships, self-disclosure becomes even more essential, and it works both ways: sexual partners and lovers become more intimate as they tell each other about their private lives; and as they become more intimate, they will reveal more of themselves to each other. Self-disclosure that is reciprocated and does not backfire generates confidence and self-esteem, so it leads to greater revelations (Taylor et al., 1981). The sharing of secrets creates a sense of exclusivity ("the two of us only") and trust.

Self-disclosure is a form of psychological and emotional undressing, sometimes more difficult than taking your clothes off. By expressing your innermost thoughts and feelings and relating your past experiences that are not generally known, you make yourself more vulnerable psychologically (to ridicule, rejection, and disapproval) as well as socially (to gossip, blackmail, and difficulties with the law). Information is a form of power. By giving it to another you hand over a certain measure of control over yourself, which is perhaps why men in the United States find self-disclosure more difficult than women (Cozby, 1972). It may also be perceived by males as unmanly because it entails the expression of intimate feelings.

Perhaps because women are socially more vulnerable in sexual interactions and more focused on the relational aspects of a sexual relationship, they show both a greater need for and a greater capacity for self-revelation (Markel et al., 1976). This gender difference is already established before adolescence: girls tend to have closer friends in whom they confide, whereas boys tend to run in packs with fewer close personal interactions. Heterosexual males retain their reluctance to "open up" to other men, even more than to women: college men in intimate relationships with women will disclose more of themselves to their girlfriends than to their male peers; the closer and more comfortable their relationship to the woman, the greater is the tendency to self-disclosure (Komarovsky, 1974).

Other studies reveal no significant gender differences. Both men and women risk self-disclosure in gradual degrees and in about equal measure (Davis, 1976). Close to 60 percent of college dating couples in one study had made a full disclosure of their past sexual experiences to their current partner (Rubin et al., 1980).

Communication is essential, but there is nothing magical about it: it does not resolve all sexual conflicts. Many couples who complain of poor communication actually communicate well. The problem stems from the fact that what is coming across loud and clear is the other's dissatisfaction, anger, and hatred, which the person does not want to hear (Baucom and Hoffman, 1983).

Caring and Affection    Sexual intimacy entails varying levels of affection, all the way to being in love. Intimacy requires that you care and be cared for. Couples who feel compelled to stay together even though they hate each other's guts are hostages to a forced type of intimacy.

To care for someone is more than an abstraction. It cannot be simply declared—it has to be practiced. One key indicator is whether or not you take pleasure in another's company

and want to spend time with that person. You do not have to live together, let alone be inseparable. Everyone needs private space and time, no matter how fond of one another. Maintaining a sense of personal identity (to be just you, apart from being someone else's spouse, lover, or friend) does not compete with an intimate relationship but supports it (Laurence, 1982). A sense of intimacy can be maintained over great distances and long periods of time under conditions of enforced separations; but it can fade if opportunities to be together dwindle down below a critical point.

Sharing    The sharing of experiences is a corollary of spending time together. Simply being together does not always make for shared experience. There is such a thing as "parallel solitude"—being with someone physically while your mind is far away in a world of fantasy.

Moreover, it is not the sharing of just any experience that maintains intimacy. Couples who are fond of each other take pleasure in carrying out mundane and even tedious chores, such as doing the laundry or weeding the garden. Cooking together and caring for a child can be especially rewarding. Still, a couple also needs to share intellectual and artistic interests, physical activities and sports, social and political efforts, particularly if the intimate relationship is intended to last over the long run and evolve into a life partnership.

Whatever we do becomes more enjoyable if it is done with someone we are intimate with and care for. (Partners need not be equally good—just equally willing.) Conversely, an experience we like will make the person we do it with seem more likable (Hatfield, 1982). Even in a casual encounter we will find someone more attractive in a comfortable rather than overheated room (Griffitt, 1970). A glorious day outdoors, a riveting lecture or play, a breathtaking musical performance, a fabulous meal, an uplifting spiritual experience—or more modest experiences—generate waves of contentment that will wash over your companion.

The willingness to share cannot be restricted to good times. Intimacy requires that we stand by each other during times of distress, illness, and unhappiness. The phrase "for better or for worse" in the traditional marital vow must also apply, to some measure, to all intimate relationships. At a minimum you need *empathy*—understanding another's feelings, and being able to put yourself in that person's place. You do not have to agree with how the other feels, although so much the better if you can.

Honesty and Trust   In an ideal relationship, two people are totally open with each other and can absolutely trust one another. In reality few couples attain such a state, and it is questionable if everyone should even try.

Honesty becomes a problem if it requires total self-disclosure. To do so means revealing the innermost recesses of your self, where even you yourself may not trespass lightly. Such total self-exposure may interfere with basic individual privacy. The truth makes us free, but it can also be destructive. There may be fleeting thoughts and passing moods unrelated to your partner that are best kept to yourself, as well as experiences from the past whose airing will not help anyone.

Always telling another how you feel—exposing every flash of anger, voicing every bit of criticism—creates endless and needless irritation; it makes no sense to always "let it all hang out." The ability to keep certain feelings and thoughts to yourself is a mark of maturity.

Short of total and needless self-disclosure, honesty is essential for maintaining intimacy. Tactfully airing even unpleasant thoughts at the right time will help keep you close.

Trust comes from confidence in each other's honesty. Deceitfulness or lying destroys it. Trust also means being able to reveal to the partner things that reflect poorly on yourself. It is based on the confidence that the partner may reject some of your behaviors or attitudes but will not reject you as a person.

Trust is often tested in connection with sexual fidelity—every couple has an agreement, spoken or unspoken, on whether to engage in sex with others. We discuss this issue further in Chapter 17.

Commitment   To commit yourself means, in its widest sense, to place yourself in the care of another. It is a way of saying "I am yours," and "We belong to each other." There are, however, degrees of commitment; and contrary to some romantic ideals, the sense of belonging to another must be reconciled with the equal need to preserve your own identity. A commitment may be formal or informal, broad or limited, but ultimately it entails a pledge to live up to a certain set of agreements and responsibilities. To commit to an intimate relationship or the partner in it is to pledge yourself to it, to promise a measure of predictability, stability, and permanence.

In commitment, all the strands of the relationship—caring, affection, sharing, trust, and communication—come together and lead to *communion*, a sense of basic unity (Merton, 1979).

The most common formal and binding commitment to an intimate relationship has been *marriage* (Chapter 17). Other forms of sexual commitment are more privately negotiated and may involve *cohabitation*, or living together.

In the past, commitments to marriage were expected to be for life. That model now persists more as an ideal than as practical reality. Even couples who have stayed together for years in fairly happy relationships may grow apart or find other partners more compatible with their changing needs. The principle of personal growth and self-actualization (Maslow, 1968), which gained prominence in the 1960s, comes into conflict with commitment to a relationship that no longer satisfies one or both parties. Modern attitudes tend to view commitment in provisional terms—it should last only as long as it makes sense. Shifting gender roles and changing family values have also changed commitments (Chapter 17).

### Problems in Intimacy and Commitment
Sexual intimacy is not easy, but it seems particularly difficult for some people. They never get far enough in becoming intimate with someone, or they fail to sustain relationships

long enough. One measure of this problem is inability to find and hold a mate in marriage or a comparable long-term relationship. Marriage is a complex institution, though, involving factors in addition to intimacy, and whether it breaks up in divorce or not may not be a fair test of the capacity to be intimate. A better measure would be loneliness, which is different than being alone or having few close friendships and family ties. *Affiliative needs,* or the desire for human company and interaction, vary greatly. Some people cannot stand being alone; others cannot stand company. The United States is a gregarious society, which values openness and informality. To want to be alone is often seen as a sign of social maladjustment or churlishness. As a result the need for extended periods of solitude—time with and for yourself—is often denied (Merton, 1979). The life of doing overwhelms the life of being. There is much satisfaction in being alone, and those who choose such a course do not suffer from failures of intimacy; they make a free choice and are happy with it.

*Loneliness* is different. It entails emotional deprivation and emptiness. Although usually alone, the lonely can also be married, ostensibly involved in an intimate relationship but in effect cut off from meaningful ties, starved for affection, and bored with life.

Loneliness is not unusual during certain periods of life—in adolescence, for psychological reasons, and among the elderly poor, for economic reasons. It is most common among those alienated from their families or those who have severe handicaps.

Personality Factors    Problems of sexual intimacy cannot be readily separated from those of intimacy in general. Sexual intimacy presupposes the capacity to get close to people, although that in itself may not be enough. A host of economic, social, and health reasons may isolate people, although some are resourceful enough to overcome such barriers. Similarly, a variety of psychological factors interferes with establishing and maintaining close ties: the shy are too inhibited to make contact; the overly aggressive scare people

away; the self-centered alienate them. In short, the whole range of maladaptive personal behavioral traits interferes with close ties (Gunderson, 1988). Such behaviors are in turn explained by immature ego defense mechanisms (Vaillant, 1977), poor patterns of social learning, and other theoretical perspectives.

Psychotherapists have long maintained that the patterns of intimacy and love in adulthood reflect a person's childhood experiences with parents. The reason why an individual whose life appears to be otherwise so well ordered and successful can be so immature (easily hurt, jealous, anxious, demanding) in love relationships must be sought in that person's childhood as well as adult life circumstances. Empirical research lends some support to these clinical observations. Romantic love in adulthood and love of the parents in infancy emerge as the same response at different points in life (Coleman, 1985).

For example, Ainsworth et al. (1978) classified infants according to the bonds they form with their parents (particularly the mother) in the first year or two of their lives. Infants who are secure can rely on the mother being available and responsive to them. Infants who are insecure either become anxious and clinging, or withdraw. About two-thirds of infants are secure, the rest equally divided between the anxious and the withdrawn. Shaver (1985), finds roughly the same proportions for adults (aged 15 to 82) in their romantic relationships: over half fit a secure style of romantic love; they are happy and secure in their relationships. The rest are anxious—obsessed with their lovers, intensely jealous, and swinging between emotional highs and lows; or they withdraw, shying away from all romantic ties. These styles of adult relationships seem to match the recollected experience of childhood. For instance, anxious lovers reported having had emotionally intrusive mothers and distant fathers who were unhappy in their own marriage. Such linkage is not objective evidence, though. Anxious adults may reconstruct their childhood as being anxious as well.

Hindy (1985) avoids this objection by studying men and women whose early family histories were known in detail from a previous investigation. Hindy borrows the concept of "anxious attachment" from Bowlby's well-known work with infants (1969, 1973). Adults who show this behavior in their love relationships feel extreme depression when a relationship ends and jealousy when it is threatened. They cling to the partner, try to extort signs of affection, and do not seem to get enough of love and attention. Lacking a stable sense of love and affection in childhood, they carry their anxieties and doubts into their adult relationships, which as a result fail to mature and satisfy them. Others with a similar childhood background remain calm and detached even when the relationship is threatened or breaks up; men are more likely than women to show this alternative pattern.

Finally, there are people who have no apparent trouble getting close and are willing to make commitments but cannot broach the sexual barrier. A shy bachelor will begin to date a woman. Because he makes no sexual overtures, she will take the initiative; instead of responding, he will stop seeing her. These roles may be reversed. Underlying such behavior may be fears of intimacy or sexuality or both. The fears of intimacy are derived from the risks we discussed earlier. The sexual fears may be based on anxiety over sexual performance, the threat of rejection, or paralyzing guilt. Orgasm entails loss of control, and that scares some people. In short, many of the psychological causes of sexual dysfunction may be at work (Chapter 15), even though the person may not be actually dysfunctional.

The ability to give and take in an intimate relationship finally comes down to a generosity of the spirit and the ability to hold your ground. For whatever reasons, some people are more spontaneously giving. Those who deal with them never leave empty-handed. However, the capacity to give cannot be sustained without looking out for yourself as well. People in healthy intimate relationships can joyously say "yes," but they can also firmly say "no" or "not now" without rejecting the other.

Similar considerations apply when people seek intimacy but are unable or unwilling to make commitments. Some recognize the difficulty, but others profess not to know what the problem is. Why can't they be intimate yet also free? Intimacy cannot survive over time without commitment; it cannot even begin.

Not everyone is willing to promise the same degree of *exclusivity* and *permanence*. Exclusivity includes emotional factors ("I will love only you" or "you more than others"), sexual relations ("you will be my only lover" or "the main one"), and institutions ("I will marry you" or "live with you"). Permanence ranges from an agreed upon period (such as while in college), to the foreseeable future, to life. People who cannot offer enough exclusivity and permanence are not ready for sexual intimacy. People who demand too much of them have their own problems (Box 16.1).

Often each person in a couple wants a different commitment. There may be good reasons. One may not be in a position to settle down yet, may not be sure the partner is the right person, or simply may not be ready to take the step for a host of emotional or other reasons. At the same time, the person does not want to give up the relationship. This person is capable of commitments in general but not in this case.

Other people repeatedly face this problem. The perceived obstacle is not always the same, but there is always something that stops them. As time passes, excuses begin to lose credibility. Sooner or later they run out of time. At the root of such procrastination there may be unrealistic expectations, an inflated sense of one's own worth, the neurotic search for an infantile wish, an obsessive search for "perfection," and a variety of other psychological factors. (We are supposing, of course, that there are reasonably good and willing candidates out there.)

Gender Differences    Generally, men seem to have more difficulty forming and sustaining intimacy than women; this appears true for both heterosexuals and homosexuals. Some of the evidence is circumstantial and subject to different interpretation. For instance, having numerous sexual partners, as a consistent pat-

# Box 16.1

## SEXUAL JEALOUSY

Sexual jealousy is the negative emotional response triggered by the real or imagined sexual attraction or involvement of a romantic partner with a third person (Buunk and Hupka, 1987). Feelings of jealousy are present in childhood or even earlier, usually in sibling rivalry based on the unwillingness to share the love of the mother or primary caregiver. Adult jealousy replays this fear of being displaced in the affections of the beloved.

Jealousy can be seen among animals, and it is among the universal human emotions, although its intensity varies in different cultures. The subject of jealousy, like love, has been explored widely in literature and art (Friday, 1985). Shakespeare's *Othello* is among the great classics in the literature of jealousy. It has also been the subject of much clinical inquiry (Pao, 1982).

There are many gradations of jealousy. At one end of the spectrum, there is the ordinary self-interest in preserving your stake in a valuable relationship by seeing that others do not intrude into it; the more intense and valued the association, the greater is the justification for being protective. In that sense, "normal" jealousy is a stress reaction that increases people's alertness and fuels their ability to act (Brody, 1987).

At the next level, jealousy is motivated by an excessive sense of "ownership" in a partner. Jealousy in these cases may have little to do with love. For instance, a husband may not care for his wife sexually but would still not want anyone else to touch her because she "belongs" to him. A wife's possessiveness has traditionally been enhanced by the threat of losing her source of economic support, should the husband be lured away. Even when such considerations are absent, many women are still

acutely sensitive to the threat of rivals (Kaufman, 1988).

At the extreme, there is pathologic jealousy. Intense suspiciousness without good reason makes the person highly intolerant of any friendly interaction or attention involving the partner.

Jealousy is not only a painful but also a potentially dangerous emotion. It causes emotional devastation, provokes violence, and sometimes leads to murder; jealousy is a primary factor in wife abuse.

Persons who are unreasonably jealous tend to suffer from a sense of inadequacy and low self-esteem. They view what is of value to be in limited supply; if someone else has it, then they will be deprived of it. They may interpret the behavior of their partner as a reflection on their own adequacy and a blow to their self-esteem (White, 1981); or they may project onto the partner their own unconscious wishes to betray.

To provoke jealousy in order to invite greater affection and interest is an ancient device, but a double-edged sword. It is a manipulative tactic that may obtain short-term gain at the expense of longer-term trust. There is no room for bluffing between true lovers.

Freedom from all feelings of jealousy is hard to separate from not caring, but jealousy is not a barometer of love. Particularly in its more possessive and pathological forms, it is but another form of sexual coercion.

It is difficult to deal with a jealous lover. Counterhostility, withdrawal, or giving in to keep the peace are usually unproductive. Calm and firm handling of the situation works better. Psychological counseling may also be necessary to resolve the problem.

---

tern, instead of maintaining one or a few close relationships, is taken as evidence for lack of intimacy (or the unwillingness to make lasting commitments). Could a number of "little intimacies" add up to one "big intimacy"? Most people do not think so. Intimacy takes time and effort; spreading yourself thin will not al-

low that; you cannot have it both ways, if for no other reasons than time, resources, and energy.

Men clearly show a pattern of multiple sexual partnerships, more so than women. In the Blumstein and Schwartz (1983) sample, 7 percent of husbands had had more than

20 sexual partners, as against 3 percent of wives; 4 percent of male and 1 percent of female cohabitors; and 43 percent of gay men but only 1 percent of lesbians. The very high rate of gay men could mean male tendencies are compounding each other.

One problem for men has to do with emotional expressiveness and self-disclosure. As we discussed earlier, women are generally more open than men, which helps them form intimate relationships with men as well as other women. By the same token, if intimacy means vulnerability or dependency, then men who are socialized to be more autonomous are more likely to be threatened by it. There is experimental evidence among mammals that the introduction of a new sexual partner revives sexual interest (Dewsbury, 1981). This phenomenon, known as the *Coolidge effect,* is more widely and clearly observed among males than females (Wilson, 1982). For instance, a bull or ram may have stopped copulating with a receptive female, but when a new female animal is made available, the male will resume his sexual activity with the new female with renewed vigor.[2]

Whether a similar mechanism operates among humans has not been demonstrated under comparable laboratory conditions (such research would raise many eyebrows), but is noted in connection with group sex. Moreover, the yearning for many sexual partners, successive or simultaneous, is a common fantasy. As we discussed earlier (Chapter 11), it is an erotic theme that seems to appeal more to men than to women. The issue may also be

seen more broadly as the different investments men and women have in intimate relationships. As was discussed in Chapter 10, sociobiologists who see men and women having different "parental investments"—men going for quantity, women for quality—apply the same principle to other relationships, even where reproduction is not the purpose (Symons, 1979). If men want to avoid being tied down (while getting their sexual needs fulfilled), then intimacy is a trap to avoid.

Sociologists look at the "economics" of intimate relationships, the incentives for making commitments. As we shall discuss in the next chapter, apart from true love or romance, potential mates wonder, "What's in it for me?" "How can I get the best deal?" From that perspective, marriage has served men better than women in most traditional relationships, but the situation has changed. The sexual revolution has made it possible for single men to have sex with women who are their social peers—the sort of women they could marry, but may or may not. Simultaneously, the women's movement has changed the role expectations of wives "at the expense" of men, at least as some men see it. The "price" of marriage is now higher, and the "rewards" not as exclusive as before. Hence it is argued that there is no point in criticizing men for dodging commitments or refusing to grow up while we praise women for wanting to be independent (Farrell, 1986).

## EROTIC LOVE

*Love* is intense emotional attachment to another person. It is the most basic of all human emotions, and its antecedents can be traced back to our evolutionary origins (Buss, 1988) and observed in the interactions of nonhuman primates (Rosenblum, 1985). In the evolutionary perspective, the key consequences of love center around reproduction. There are important differences, however, between such emotions among animals and humans, and among different cultures.

Sex is part of only some love relationships, just as only some sexual interactions involve

[2]The derivation of the term "Coolidge Effect" is related to the following story: One day the President and Mrs. Coolidge were visiting a government farm. Soon after their arrival, they were taken off on separate tours. When Mrs. Coolidge passed the chicken pens, she paused to ask the man in charge if the rooster copulates more than once each day. "Dozens of times" was the reply. "Please tell that to the President," Mrs. Coolidge requested. When the President passed the pens and was told about the rooster, he asked "Same hen every time?" "Oh no, Mr. President, a different one each time." The President nodded slowly, then said, "Tell that to Mrs. Coolidge." (Bermant, 1976. Quoted in Symons, 1979.)

love. Hence, we need to set erotic love in its proper context.

## Varieties of Love

The theme of love has been explored by writers and artists throughout history. There is an immense literature on love (de Rougemont, 1956; Singer, 1984), and a profusion of popular books (Buscaglia, 1984), films, television programs, magazines, and other materials. It is now also being studied more systematically by psychologists (Pope et al., 1980; Sternberg and Barnes, 1988).

Love carries many meanings, ranging from the casual ("I love ice cream") to the personal ("I love you") and the spiritual ("I love God").[3] Love arises from the recognition of attractive qualities in another person, from natural relationships (such as between parent and child), or from sympathy (as in friendship). Its signs are concern and caring for the well-being of the loved person, delight in his or her presence, and desire for approval and reciprocal affection.

Though loving entails a good deal of liking, the two do not always go together (think of a relative you love but do not particularly like). The traits we want in a friend are not always the traits we seek in a lover, even though lovers who are good friends will have a far more enduring relationship.

By comparing the reactions of college couples to their dates and their best friends of the same sex, Rubin (1973) found that men and women liked their dating partners and friends about equally but loved the partners more. Women loved their friends more than men did. Men discriminated less than women between their feelings of liking and loving their dating partners.

There are many ways to classify love (Murstein, 1988). C. S. Lewis (1960) distinguished four kinds. Others have come up with more elaborate schemes based on the same fundamental types (Lee, 1988). *Affection* (Greek *storge*) is a feeling of warmth and attachment that typically binds together parents and children, siblings, and other relatives. There is a "built-in" or unmerited character to these bonds; many family members would have no interest in each other if they were not related. *Friendship* (Greek *philia*) is a tranquil form of personal attachment based on "appreciative love" or fondness between kindred spirits who share personal, intellectual, aesthetic, and other values. *Sexual love* (Greek *eros*) is typified by sexual attraction ("lust") and the experience of "being in love." *Selfless love* (Greek *agape*) is exemplified in St. Paul's sublime passage:

> Love is patient, love is kind and envies no one. Love is never boastful, nor conceited, nor rude; never selfish, nor quick to take offense. Love keeps no score of wrongs; does not gloat over other men's sins, but delights in the truth. There is nothing love cannot face; there is no limit to its faith, its life, and its endurance (1 Cor. 13:4–7).

Components of Love    Love is hard to define because it is not a simple behavioral entity; it has many components (Berscheid, 1988). Robert Sternberg (1986, 1988) has proposed a *triangular theory of love* with three main elements. Intimacy (feelings of caring, support, and closeness) is the *emotional* component of love. Passion (erotic and romantic feeings) is the *motivational* component of love. Decision (to love a person) and commitment (to continue to love that person) are the *cognitive* components of love.

These three components, which can be pictured as a triangle, are present in different degrees in each form of love (Figure 16.6). Infatuation is mainly passionate attachment with little intimacy or commitment, perhaps best exemplified by the "puppy love" of adolescence. Romantic love is closer to the falling-in-love experience we will discuss shortly; it combines intimacy with passion but has no lasting commitment. Fatuous love, like infatuation, is mainly based on passion. Though it has a

---

[3]The word "love" has ancient roots. It is derived from the Indo-European root *leubh* (as is the German *liebe*). Also from the same source are the Latin *libere* (to be dear) and *libido* (desire). The Latin word for love, *amor*, gives rise to the Spanish *amor* and French *amour*, as well as related words in English like *amorous*. The Greek for one form of love, *eros*, is the root for *erotic*.

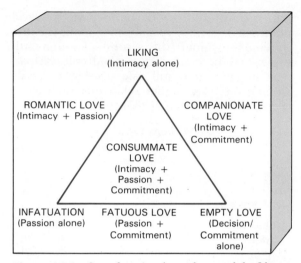

Figure 16.6   Sternberg's triangular model of love.

greater measure of commitment, as in hasty marriages, it lacks true intimacy and has little lasting value. Empty love is the opposite. Couples remain committed to a stagnant relationship that has lost its passion and intimacy. Companionate love has intimacy and commitment but little passion, characteristic of many conventional "satisfactory" marriages. Consummate love combines all three components—intimacy, passion, commitment—and represents the ideal love relationship. Not many couples attain it, and fewer still maintain it (Chapter 17).

These components of love constantly change over the life of a relationship (Figure 16.7). Each of these ingredients blossoms at its own pace, and the courses they follow are not the same. Ordinarily, passion is the first to rise and the quickest to fade. Intimacy takes more time to develop, and commitment is slower still. Because the basic three ingredients change all the time, no love relationship is fully stable: to love is to be in a dynamic, not a static, state. Moreover, these patterns do not apply rigidly to every single relationship; passion could bloom late between friends, commitment may be threatened and then reaffirmed, and so on.

Though the relative intensity of the three basic ingredients changes, they all remain essential. Passion declines to a plateau after it

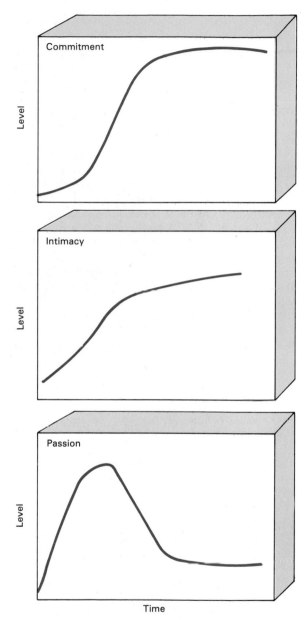

Figure 16.7   Changing ingredients of love over time.

peaks, yet it continues to matter a good deal. Love is not "blind." It continues to be fueled by physical attractiveness. Spouses make a mistake in thinking their looks do not matter because they have the security of being loved. By neglecting their appearances, they convey the message that they do not care enough to make an effort to please.

Similarly, although intimacy will seem to fade even in a strong relationship (as a couple becomes more familiar with each other, there is less to reveal) it remains crucial to continue to know about each other's feelings, wants, and needs, and to share common values.

Because commitment is central for holding a couple together, it may be overemphasized at the expense of the other two factors. Commitment is not enough, though; without passion and intimacy, it becomes hollow, more an obligation than a free choice. Rather than take each other for granted, couples need to work constantly at rejuvenating their relationship, investing the kind of energy into it that they put into new relationships, children, and career.

Love and Dependency    Love is a form of *attachment* modeled on our early experiences in childhood (Shaver et al., 1988). Closely related to love are feelings of *dependency* (literally "to hang from"). Dependency in adulthood entails reliance on those who love us; the phrase that most often follows "I love you" is "I need you." Affectional bonds provide the best insurance for the satisfaction of our physical and emotional needs. The ultimate proof is our sometimes romanticized willingness to suffer and even die for the person we love.

To isolate the factor of dependency, Lewis (1960) differentiates between need-love and gift-love. *Need-love* is part of being human: we are born helpless and remain in need of each other physically, emotionally, and intellectually. Need-love crosses over into selfishness when it makes excessive, self-serving demands that disregard the needs of the other and fails to reciprocate the favors received; by contrast, *gift-love* is selfless. Maslow (1968) makes a similar distinction between *deficiency-love*, which is selfish, and *being-love*, which is not.

In the sexual sphere, the love object may also be the sex object. For some, the two are inseparable; for others they can even be opposites. "If you love me, you will sleep with me" is countered by "If you love me, you will not insist on sex." Typically, men make the first statement, women the second. Though attitudes may be changing, the old cultural pattern lingers: men still rate sex higher while women rate love higher relative to each other (Peplau and Gordon, 1985).

Table 16.1    Sex Without Love

|  | % APPROVING |
|---|---|
| Married |  |
|    Men | 52 |
|    Women | 37 |
| Cohabitants |  |
|    Men | 72 |
|    Women | 67 |
| Gay Couples |  |
|    Men | 79 |
|    Women | 57 |
| (From Blumstein and Schwartz, 1983.) | |

The notion of dependency offends some people, because it smacks of immaturity, weakness, and helplessness. It could be argued that love is more compatible with independence or interdependence than it is with dependence. A popular concept now is *supportiveness*: the proof of affection is to be helpful, not critical, sustaining those we love in what they want to do, assisting them to become who they want to be.

We take it for granted that we will take care of those whom we love; we also resent it if they take advantage of us. This is a special problem for older adults who make a late-in-life commitment to a person who is more apt to become ill or disabled, hence heavily dependent. The threat of isolation and loneliness is countered by the threat of subjugation to another person's will and whim. The challenge is to love in such a way that, in the words of John Donne, "Our affections kill us not, nor die."

Falling in Love
The experience of being in love is distin-

guished from other states of loving (Hatfield, 1988). Unlike parental love, which is supposedly "given," and other forms of affection into which we "grow," we "fall" in love in a precipitous and involuntary manner. We call this experience *romantic*, or *passionate,* love ("having a crush," "lovesickness," and so on). Metaphors involve being smitten and struck—by a thunderbolt ("coup de foudre"), say the French; by the arrows of Eros, said the Greeks. The element of suddenness ("love at first sight") is compounded by a sense of inevitability and helplessness. Being in love is also distinguished by its exclusivity: we can love many but usually claim to be truly in love with only one person at a time.

The Chemistry of Love   King Kong fell in love with a woman, but that was a hopeless situation. In more natural conditions, animals can become strongly attached to each other, forming lifetime *pair bonds*. A similar "biosocial case" presumably underlies the human desire to bond intimately with another person (Perper, 1985). Still, falling in love appears to be a uniquely human experience. It presumably evolved because sexual partners who were bound with such intense emotions created more stable attachments, which enhanced the care of offspring (Rizley, 1980).

We loosely talk of the "chemistry" between people who fall in love, but does a biochemical process actually underlie it? Liebowitz (1983) thinks there actually is such a "love chemistry," involving neurotransmitters that mediate impulses at nerve endings in the brain. Two of them, *norepinephrine* and *dopamine*, are supposedly activated by visual cues from the potential love object and generate feelings of intense pleasure; then we are raised to even greater heights of ecstasy by another chemical, *serotonin.*

Far less speculative are the well-known associations between emotions like fear and norephinephrine and epinephrine (which act as hormones as well as neurotransmitters). These chemicals mimic the effects of the sympathetic nervous sytem, stimulating the heart rate and raising the blood pressure when you are scared. Steroid hormones from the adrenal glands are also activated in response to stress and may help regulate your mood as well. There has been a long-standing debate among psychologists as to which comes first, the emotion or the sensation. Do you feel afraid first, and then feel your heart start to pound; or do you feel afraid because your heart is pounding? It can work both ways.

Although no hormone has been specifically linked to love on solid evidence, an intriguing theory put forth by Stanley Schachter explains how emotions get hold of people (Schacter and Singer, 1962; Schacter, 1964). In this model the same physiological mechanism applies to all forms of intense feelings. When Schacter injected male college student volunteers with epinephrine, they all had the same predictable physiological response—increased heart rate, sweaty palms, flushed faces, and so on. How they felt about it—whether the experience was perceived as positive or negative—was determined by the experimenter, who manipulated the social context and cues through confederates in the laboratory.

By this reasoning the identification of an emotion is a function of *cognitive labeling*—an emotion is what we call it, and what we call it depends on the context. We must attach a label to how we feel, because not to do so is anxiety-provoking. So when your heart pounds as you kiss your sweetheart, you say it's "love"; if there is a dog at your heels, you call it "fear."

Berscheid and Walster (1974) have elaborated on the Schacter model by proposing a two-stage love theory. Physiological arousal (which may be based on sexual excitement, fear, joy, or even physical exertion) is followed by cognitive labeling that identifies the arousal as love.

Is labeling the whole story in defining emotion? Many people insist they know how they feel, and say they can tell how others feel through independent cues, including facial expression. However, facial expressions are not easy to read out of context. If you look at photographs of faces alone, you may have trouble identifying the emotions they express. How people look during orgasm is particularly misleading if you expect to see "happiness" written all over their faces. At any rate, this interesting view leaves much unexplained about the complex emotion of love. There is even some evidence that the physiological correlates of emotions may have more specific autonomic nervous system components than was thought to be the case (Elkman et al., 1983).

Behavioral Aspects     It is popularly believed that women are more romantic than men, and that image is portrayed in much literature. However, Rubin and his associates (1981) found that college men were more likely than their female counterparts to "fall in love" quickly. The women placed more emphasis on enhancing their attractiveness, and only after the relationship had taken hold did they report the same degree of being "in love." However, women are more likely to report emotional and euphoric feelings upon falling in love than men (Dion and Dion, 1973).

Dorothy Tennov (1979) has coined the term *limerence* for the condition of being in love, the behavioral manifestations of which she has studied in a sample of several hundred people. The trigger for falling in love is often a simple act like a gesture, a glance, or some other expression that suggests interest, or hints at the possibility of reciprocal interest. The eyes communicate this message most eloquently: "Love's tongue is in the eyes," wrote the Jacobean dramatist Phileas Fletcher (quoted in Tennov, 1979, p. 282). Of course, people stare at each other all the time without falling in love; for love to follow there must be a constellation of factors that impart a certain "wholeness" to the experience; everything must be right for the "chemistry" to work.

In full bloom, being in love has certain basic components. There is constant thinking about the loved person ("can't get him/her off my mind"), to the point of pushing all other concerns to the background. An acute longing to be loved in return makes the lover detect even the slightest evidence in the actions of the beloved, or imagine it where none exists. The person in love shows an extraordinary ability for dwelling on what is admirable, and denying what is not, in the loved person. Faults are recognized at a factual level but then dismissed. "I abhor the sight of toothmarks on a pencil, they disgust me," says one man. "But not her toothmarks. Hers were sacred; her wonderful mouth had been there" (Tenner, 1979, p. 31). There is at once a process of *idealization* (which makes a crooked nose appear straight) (Figure 16.8) and one of *crystallization* (which makes the crooked nose look cute).[4]

Being loved in return induces a state of exhilaration ("walking on air"). By contrast, the fear of rejection induces uncertainty, awkwardness, confusion, and shyness. Frustration and adversity may also intensify the limerent person's longings, while vivid fantasies of reciprocal love provide fleeting relief from the pangs of unrequited passion. "Heartache," palpitations or tremors, flushing or pallor, and weakness accompany moments of doubt. Those in love are vulnerable to pangs of jealousy and other negative feelings (Box 16.1).

The average length of an episode of being in love is two years, but it may range from a few weeks to a lifetime (Box 16.2). The end may be friendly, but more often it is painful and followed by lingering unhappiness. The breakup may be sudden and highly emotional (occasionally leading to suicide or murder). Or, the affair winds down less dramatically as one "lover's quarrel" after another chips away at the relationship. As the capacity to see the other person more realistically returns, shortcomings become more visible and then magnified. Those who settled down together may end up disillusioned, finding it hard to understand how they could have been so crazy about someone they can now barely stand. Those who go throught repeated unhappy love experiences are thought by some to suffer from *addictive love* (Box 16.3).

Love experiences that are not wrecked by failure evolve into stable relationships with

[4]The term "crystallization" is a metaphor: a branch cast into a salt mine is transformed by salt crystals into an object of shimmering beauty, while underneath it remains a tree branch (Stendhal, 1983).

Figure 16.8    An idealized image of love. François Gerard (1770–1837), *Cupid and psyche*.

more sedate forms of love. They may become *companionate love,* with its deep and enduring affectionate bonds of intimacy and commitment.

## Companionate Love

Companionate love is "the affection we feel for those with whom our lives are deeply entwined" (Hatfield and Walster, 1978, p. 9). People tend to think of it as the live coals that remain when the flames of passion die down. However, companionate love must be understood in its own right rather than as the residue of passionate love (Hatfield, 1988).

These two forms of love are both blessings. Each has its own merits and shortcomings. If passionate love is like the 100-yard dash, companionate love is like running a marathon. The first is exciting and exhilarating, but it leaves you winded; the latter is enduring, but less dramatic. Companionate love is not the dilution of passionate love but its transformation. It is a necessary adjustment to the demands of adult life—rearing children, running households, establishing careers, doing the work of the world, serving the community. Total absorption of lovers in each other would not allow any of that: instead it would stunt adult development.

Because it takes maturity, companionate love is more common among adults past the stage of youth and in long-lasting marriages or partnerships; yet it can grace any age or relationship.

If passionate love is to graduate into companionate love, the couple needs to go through a gradual change. Instead of interpreting the change as "falling out" of love, they can see themselves moving into a new phase of abiding affection. There are couples who remain deeply in love for many years despite the frictions of everyday living. These couples tend to exhibit characteristic behaviors (Box 16.4). Their behaviors could be thought of as the manifestations of enduring love, but in turn, they keep love alive.

## The Relationship of Sex and Love

Love and sex interact at many levels—physiological, psychological, and social. We know little about the first, and the last we will deal with later.

Should you engage in sex outside of love? The usual rule among college age and younger adults is "permissiveness with affection," which translates into "It's O.K. if you are in love." ("Love" is defined in variable terms.)

There is more tolerance and endorsement of sex without love among well-educated adults. That too is the predominant feeling among professionals in the field of human sexuality who see nothing inherently wrong about impersonal sex, if it is clearly consented to by all parties. Such views do not devalue love; they simply do not insist on it in all sexual

# Box 16.2

## A LOVE AFFAIR*

I remember the way the light touched her hair. She turned her head, and I saw her face. She turned still more, and our eyes met and held. We saw each other, a momentary awareness, in that raucous fifth-grade schoolroom to which I'd just been assigned. I felt as though I'd been struck a blow under the heart. Thus began my first love affair, a surge of adrenaline, a rush of blood, a thing of innocence and pain that has lasted all my life.

Her name was Rachel. I suppose our story, rooted in romance now out of favor, is one of absurdity today, and—who knows?—the innocence may really have been ignorance, in view of all that has happened since. Whatever it was, I mooned my way through grade and high school, stricken at the mere sight of her, tongue-tied in her presence. Does anyone, any more, linger in the shadows of evening, drawn by the pale light of a window—*her* window—like some hapless summer insect? That delirious swooning sickness, asexual but urgent and obsessive, that made me awkward and my voice crack, is like some impossible dream now. I know I was so afflicted, but I cannot actually believe what memory insists I did. Which was to suffer. Exquisitely.

I would catch sight of her, walking down an aisle of trees to or from school, and I'd become paralyzed. She always seemed so poised, self-possessed, slightly amused. At home, in bed, I'd relive each encounter, writhing at the thought of my inadequacies, feeling less than worthless. Even so, as time passed and we entered our teens, I sensed her affectionate tolerance for me.

"Going steady" implied a maturity we still lacked. Her orthodox Jewish unbringing and my own Catholic scruples imposed a kind of idealism, a celibate grace that made even kissing a distant prospect, however fervently desired. As for the rest of it, we were babes in arms. I managed to hold her, at a dance, and at a party—chaperoned, of course—we experienced a furtive embrace that made her giggle, a sound so childish and trusting that I hated myself for what I'd been thinking.

At any rate, my love for Rachel remained unrequited. We graduated from high school, she went on to college, and I joined the Army. World War II was about to engulf us, and when it did I left for overseas in the first task force after Pearl Harbor. For a time we corresponded, and to receive one of her letters at mail call was the highlight of those grinding, endless months that became years. Once she sent me a snapshot of herself, a guileless pose in a bathing suit, which drove me to the wildest of fantasies. I mentioned the possibility of marriage in my next letter to her, and almost immediately her replies became less frequent and personal.

I returned to the States for reassignment during the final throes of the war. The first thing I did on reaching home was to call Rachel, whose recent mail I had failed to keep up with on my travels. Her mother answered the door. Rachel no longer lived there. She had married a medical student she'd met in college. "I thought she wrote you," her mother said.

Her "Dear John" letter finally caught up with me while I was awaiting discharge. She gently, compassionately explained the impossibility of marriage between us, even had she not found someone else. Looking back on it, I think I must have recovered rather quickly, although for the first few months of having learned of her marriage, I think I didn't want to live very much. Like Rachel, I found someone else, whom I learned to love with a deep and permanent commitment that has lasted to this day.

Then, fairly recently, I heard from Rachel again—after an interval of more than 40 years. Her husband had died. She would be passing through the city on her way to live with a daughter in California, and had learned of my whereabouts through a mutual friend. We made a date to meet during her brief layover.

I felt both curious and excited at the prospect. In recent years, I hadn't thought about her, and her sudden call, one morning, had taken me aback. The actual sight of her can only be described as shock. Was this white-haired matron the Rachel of my dreams and desires, the supple mermaid of that snapshot I'd subsequently lost?

Yet time had given us a common reference and respect. We met and talked as old friends, and quickly discovered we were both grandparents.

"Do you remember this?" she said. We were sitting in a restaurant, and she reached into her purse and took out an envelope from which she extracted a slip of worn paper. It was a poem I'd written her while still in school. I examined the crude meter and pallid rhymes: "will" and "thrill," and "strove" and "love." Watching my face, she snatched the poem from me and returned it to her purse, as though fearful I was going to destroy it.

I told her about the fate of the snapshot, how I'd carried it all through the war.

"It wouldn't have worked out, you know," she said.

"How can you be sure?" I countered. "Ah, Colleen, it might have been grand indeed, my Irish conscience and your Jewish guilt!"

Our laughter startled people at a nearby table. During the time left to us, our glances were furtive, oblique. I think that what we saw in each other repudiated what we'd once been to ourselves, we immortals.

Before I put her into a taxi, she turned to me and, with a resolute expression, said, "I just wanted to see you once more. To tell you something." Her eyes pleaded with me, "I wanted to thank you for having loved me as you did." We kissed, and she got into the taxi and drove off.

My reflection stared back at me from a store window on Fifth Avenue, an aging man with gray hair stirred by an evening breeze. I decided to walk home, and entered Central Park. Her withered kiss still burned on my lips. Something strange was happening. I was feeling lighter with each step. All around me the grass and trees were shining in the surreal glow of sunset. Then I felt faint, and sat on a bench. Something was being lifted out of me. I was becoming someone else. Something had been completed, was ended, and the scene before me was so beautiful that I wanted to shout and dance and sing for joy—like Blake, like Whitman.

But that soon passed, as everything must, and presently I was able to stand and start for home.

*John Walters, "A love affair." *The New York Times Magazine*, November 22, 1987, p. 74).

---

encounters. But there is also a moral dimension to this issue which must be faced as well (Chapter 23).

The Effect of Love on Sex   Whether sex is the better or the worse for love depends on psychological and social attitudes. Much has been made of the Victorian conflict between love and sex (Chapter 20): a woman who thinks sex is dirty or vulgar will find her love sullied and soiled by it; a man who thinks likewise may enjoy sex with a woman he does not love but not with one he does.

Such attitudes have been largely abandoned. Love and sex are now seen not only as compatible but as enhancing each other. In principle, sex now should be more enjoyable with someone you are in love with. In practice, though, we fall short of this ideal. Among Tennov's subjects, 73 percent of the women but only 51 percent of the men agreed that "I enjoy sex best when I am in love with my partner." Fourteen percent of the sample found sex disappointing when "very much in love."

A number of factors may account for this finding. One is that women, in particular, have been more thoroughly socialized than men to equate sexual enjoyment with a relationship. Men may have learned that good sex can happen regardless of whether they love their partner, whereas women may believe good sex is more likely to occur between couples in love.

Another possibility is that the intense emotional state of being in love, with its hypersensitivity and anxiety to please the other, to appear in the best possible light, to perform superlatively, may interfere with down-to-earth sexual responses.

The Effect of Sex on Love   Sexual attraction is a common ingredient of being in love. The erotic element may dominate the experience, coexist with it, or be shunned. Over 90 percent of Tennov's subjects rejected the statement that "the best thing about love is sex." The dominant yearning of someone in love is not sex but a "return of feelings"—the wish to be loved in return. In this context the sexual

# Box 16.3

## ADDICTIVE LOVE

The power of passionate love has long been held in awe. The irresistibility of love and its demonic forces are expressed in the chorus in Sophocles' *Antigone:* "Love, invincible love, you swoop down on our flocks and watch, ever alert, over the fresh faces of our maidens; you float above the waves and across the countryside where the wild beasts crouch. And among the gods themselves, or mortal men, there is no one who can escape you. Whoever touches you is at once thrown into delirium."

The notion that passion constitutes a form of illness, *lovesickness,* has been present in many cultures. An eighth-century Arabian physician referred to insanity caused by love as *Ishik,* after a creeper that twines round a tree causing its death. Marriage was recommended as the best treatment (Balfour, 1876).

There are innumerable examples in literature of lovers wasting away as they pine for each other; of despair of unrequited love leading to suicide; of the rage of the spurned lover leading to murder. In these instances, and in countless clinical case reports, love takes on a pathological, destructive form. The latest twist is to view certain forms of love as addiction:

> When a person goes to another with the aim of filling a void in himself, the relationship quickly becomes the center of his or her life. It offers him a solace that contrasts sharply with what he finds everywhere else, so he returns to it more and more, until he needs it to get through each day of his otherwise stressful and unpleasant existence. When a constant exposure to something is necessary in order to make life bearable, an addiction has been brought about, however romantic the trappings. The ever-present danger of withdrawal creates an ever-present craving (Peele and Brodsky, 1975, p. 70).

Peele (1988), Carnes (1983), and others have further elaborated on this idea, and a spate of popular books on the topic has reached a wide audience (Cowan and Kinder, 1985; Norwood 1985). Love addiction has certain similarities to sex addiction (Chapter 13) but with one important difference: men are more prone to be addicted to sex, women to love. As the titles of popular books make clear (*Women Who Love too Much; Smart Women/Foolish Choices*), it is women who seem to be more susceptible to getting stuck in unfulfilling and destructive relationships and become "fools for love" (Peele, 1988).

The application of the addiction model to love is intriguing, but it raises a number of problems similar to those we described in connection with sexual addiction (Chapter 14). There is ample evidence that some love relationships are unhealthy. By their very nature and impact, such relationships are antithetical to the very essence of what it means to love. But as with other facets of behavior, such forms of "love" could be explained on the basis of neurotic or other unhealthy needs. Whether or not invoking the concept of addiction helps to explain these needs better remains to be seen.

---

union may epitomize such reciprocity ("giving yourself" to your lover). Whatever the motivations and constraints, a couple engaging in coitus crosses a threshold that forever changes the relationship.

Common sense suggests that because sex is highly pleasurable, sharing it would lead to or intensify affection. This positive reinforcement model seems to work only in a limited sense. A satisfying sexual experience certainly invites repetition and evokes appreciation; but purely at the level of physical satisfaction, sex does not seem to generate love, any more than fondness for a particular dish leads you to fall in love with the cook.

Men and women in love go to great lengths to initiate and sustain sexual relationships; yet sex may be as much a source of

# Box 16.4

## KEEPING LOVE ALIVE*

Couples who remain happily in love over long periods of time more consistently exhibit these behaviors:

1. *They tend to express love verbally.* This simply means saying "I love you" or some equivalent (in contrast to that attitude best summarized by "What do you mean, do I love you? I married you, didn't I?").

"Saying the words," one married woman remarked, "is a way of touching. Words can nurture feelings, keep love strong and in the forefront of the relationship." Her husband commented, "Saying 'I love you' is a form of self-expression. It's putting a bit of myself out there. So my feelings are in reality, not just inside of me."

2. *They tend to be physically affectionate.* This includes hand-holding, hugging, kissing, cuddling, and comforting—with a cup of tea, a pillow, or a woolly blanket.

3. *They tend to express their love sexually.* People who are happily in love are inclined to experience sexual intimacy as an important vehicle of contact and expression. Sex remains vital for them long after the excitement of novelty has passed.

This does not mean that they regard sex as the most significant aspect of their relationship. They are far more likely to regard their connection at the level of soul (for want of a better word) as the core of their relationship.

4. *They express their appreciation and admiration.* Happy couples talk about what they like, enjoy, and admire in each other. As a result, they feel visible, appreciated, valued. "My husband has always been my best audience," a woman said to me.

5. *They participate in mutual self-disclosure.* This is a willingness to share more of themselves and more of their inner lives with each other than with any other person. They share thoughts, feelings, hopes, dreams, aspirations; hurt, anger, longing, memories of painful or embarrassing experiences. Such couples are far more comfortable with self-disclosure than the average and, as a corollary, more interested in each other's inner life.

6. *They offer each other an emotional support system.* They are there for each other in times of illness, difficulty, hardship, and crisis. They are best friends to each other. They are generally helpful, nurturing, devoted to each other's interests and well-being.

7. *They express love materially.* They express love with gifts (big or small, but given on more than just routine occasions) or tasks performed to lighten the burden of the partner's life, such as sharing work or doing more than agreed-upon chores.

8. *They accept demands or put up with shortcomings* that would be far less acceptable in any other person. Demands and shortcomings are part of every happy relationship. So are the benevolence and grace with which we respond to them.

Another way of thinking about this point is to say that couples who know how to live together happily do not torment themselves or each other over "imperfections." Each knows he or she is not perfect and does not demand perfection of the other. They are clear that, for them, the partner's virtues outweigh the shortcomings—and they choose to enjoy the positives rather than drown the relationship in a preoccupation with the negatives. This does not mean they do not ask for—and sometimes get—changes in behavior they find undesirable.

9. *They create time to be alone together.* This time is exclusively devoted to themselves. Enjoying and nurturing their relationship rank very high among their priorities: they understand that love requires attention and leisure.

Such couples tend to regard their relationship as more interesting, more exciting, more fulfilling than any other aspect of social existence. Often they are reluctant to engage in social, political, community, or other activities that would cause them to be separated unless they are convinced there are very good reasons for doing so; they are clearly not looking for excuses to escape from each other, as is evidently the case with many more socially active couples.

*Excerpts from Nathaniel Branden, "A vision of romantic love," in *The Psychology of Love.* Sternberg, R. J. and Barnes, M. L. (Eds). pp. 225-228. New Haven: York University Press.

agony as it is of ecstasy. As Franz Kafka put it, "Coitus is the punishment for the happiness of being together."

Sexual associations, like delicate flowers, wilt with neglect; but they can also, like hardy weeds, invade and choke out other worthwhile feelings. One reason is that sexuality is often as much intertwined with aggression and hostility as it is with affection (Chapter 19). Another reason is that sexual relationships are imbedded in a social context that can nurture or stifle them. It is to those social contexts that we turn in the next chapter.

## REVIEW QUESTIONS

1. What are the main physical, psychological, and social determinants of sexual attraction?

2. What are the basic characteristics of procreational, relational, and recreational sex?

3. What are the components of sexual intimacy and the gender differences in managing intimate relationships?

4. How does the triangular model of love fit with other characterizations of the love experience?

5. Describe the psychological process of falling in love.

## THOUGHT QUESTIONS

1. How can you make yourself physically attractive without being perceived as seductive?

2. Is beauty always in the eye of the beholder, or do evolution and society determine what attracts you?

3. Should intimacy precede sex, or should sex be used to promote intimacy?

4. What would happen if it turned out that neurochemical reactions generate love?

5. Should you marry someone while you are in love?

## SUGGESTED READINGS

Buscaglia, L. (1984). *Loving each other*. Thorofare, N.J.: Slack. A good example of contemporary popular writing on love in human relationships.

Pope, K. S. (Ed.). (1980) *On love and loving*. San Francisco: Jossey-Bass. Psychological perspectives on the nature of romantic love through the life cycle.

Singer, I. (1984). *The nature of love*. Chicago: Chicago University Press. A highly scholarly three-volume examination of ideas about love from Plato to the present time. An enormously rich source for the serious student.

Sternberg, R. J., and Barnes, M. L. (Eds.). (1988) *The Psychology of love*. New Haven: Yale University Press. Research and theoretical perspectives on various aspects of love. An excellent current source.

Tennov D. (1979). *Love and limerence*. New York: Stein & Day. The experiences of falling in love studied from a psychological perspective. A good descriptive account.

# Marriage and Its Alternatives

CHAPTER

# 17

*To have and to hold from this day forward, for better for worse, for richer for poorer, in sickness and in health, to love and to cherish, till death us do part.*

*BOOK OF COMMON PRAYER:*
*SOLEMNIZATION OF*
*MATRIMONY (1549)*

OUTLINE

MARRIAGE
Demographic Changes
  Rate of Marriage
  Age Differentials
Changes in Family Patterns
Mate Selection
ALTERNATIVE COMMITMENTS
Cohabitation
  Prevalence
  Pros and Cons
Gay Couples
Other Alternatives
BEING SINGLE
The Never Married
The Divorced
  Divorce Statistics
  Causes of Divorce
The Widowed

SEXUAL ACTIVITY AND
  SATISFACTION
Marital Sex
  Sexual Activity in Marriage
  Sexual Satisfaction in Marriage
Extramarital Sex
  Patterns of Extramarital Sex
  Patterns of Comarital Sex
  Motivations
  Prevalence
  Effects
Cohabiting Couples
Nonmarital Sex
  The Never Married
  The Divorced
  The Widowed
Celibacy

Not even the most private sexual encounter is carried on in isolation. It fits into a social context. The most important of these contexts are *institutional*. We usually think of institutions as organizations dedicated to public service, such as schools. Sociologists define institutions more broadly as a "set of social processes and activities, including the norms or values they express or embody, focused on some major societal goal" (Goode, 1982). The family is an excellent example.

Marriage is the institution that has had the most direct bearing on sexual relationships; most heterosexual activity occurs within it, and even sexual behaviors that fall outside it are defined in relation to it, such as premarital or extramarital sex. Therefore, to understand the institutional context of sexual behavior, we need to begin with marriage.

## MARRIAGE

The institution of *marriage* ("to take a bride") is difficult to define in a way that would do justice to all of its various forms across cultures (Reiss, 1980; Goode, 1982). Basically it is a heterosexual union between a man and a woman (sometimes more than one of each) whereby the children that may be born to the woman are recognized as the legitimate offspring of the couple.

*Legitimacy* is central to any formal concept of marriage—not only for the children that are born into it but also for the economic, social, and sexual aspects of the couple's relationship itself. Society does not permit marriage to be just a private arrangement between two people; it must be a publicly acknowledged act, formalized by a religious or social agency and bound by the law. The public marriage ceremony (Figure 17.1) is one of the most common and important rituals in the United States and in many other societies.

Marriages exist in several major forms in different cultures, and multiple marital arrangements may also coexist in a single culture. In West Africa, the Dahomey permit 13 different kinds of marriages, based on different economic arrangements. In ancient Rome, a "free marriage" allowed the wife to keep her own property; in its alternate form, the woman and her property were incorporated into the man's family, so legally she became his child (Gregersen, 1983).

In an extensive review of 250 cultures, George P. Murdock (1949) found that *polygyny* (one man having several wives) accounted for 75 percent of marriages, *monogamy* (having a single spouse) for 24 percent, and *polyandry* (one woman having several husbands) for 1 percent.

We are so used to the model of monogomous marriage that alternative forms strike us as odd and lead to many misconceptions. For example, most people tend to view the taking of multiple wives as mainly motivated by the wish for sexual variety. The idea of a harem (forbidden place) filled with wives and concubines of a caliph is the sort of image that inflames the erotic imagination of many men. But this fairy tale image has little to do with reality.

The practice of taking multiple wives and concubines goes back to Old Testament times (King Soloman, for instance). Chinese emperors, Turkish sultans, and, more recently, some Arab royalty, among others, have also had multiple wives. But even though Islam continues to allow having up to four wives, very few men have the means and motivation to avail themselves of this possibility, and less and less women are willing to submit to it.

The motivations underlying polygyny are mainly political and economic. Marriages cement alliances, acquire property, and produce heirs. Although they also provide sexual variety, there are simpler ways for men to attain that than by contracting multiple marriages.

Wives are not passive acquisitions in these marriages. For instance, in Madagascar, the first marriage is a love match. Other wives are added as needed to help take care of the family lands. These women are acquired at the suggestion of the first wife, who remains preeminent (Linton, 1936). In polygomous marriages,

Figure 17.1    Traditional wedding ceremony.

each wife usually has her own separate house (or quarters). The husband is expected to spend each night with a separate wife in strict rotation. Such devices are meant to avoid jealousy and conflict.

Western societies recognize as legal only the traditional monogamous marriage, the union between a single adult man and a single adult woman formalized by a religious ceremony or civil procedure (often both). People are permitted to remarry after divorce or widowhood, and many do, so in effect we have *serial monogamy* as a legal alternative.[1] Society also recognizes certain rights and obligations in *common-law marriages* and *cohabitation,* in both of which a man and a woman live together in an intimate relationship without being married. Same-sex cohabitation is not legally recognized, although some refer to it as *gay marriage* and would like to have it legally validated. More experimental alternatives are *group marriage, family network systems* (several families living together), and *communes* (larger groupings) that may or may not involve sexual

sharing of partners.

The concept of the family is closely tied to marriage, but the two are not the same. The word "family" is derived from "dwelling place" and has both residential and kinship connotations. Every intact marriage, with or without children, constitutes a family; yet other associations, such as several college students living in the same house, sharing meals (or having sex together), do not. The census bureau defines the family as two or more people related by blood, marriage, or adoption, living together.

Murdock (1949) found the *nuclear family* (father, mother, and their dependent children) to be the working unit in all family systems (Figure 17.2). Even when the members of an *extended family* (with members of several generations) live together, grandparents and their married children function as separate nuclear family units.

Murdock ascribed four universal functions to the nuclear family: sexual relations, reproduction, socialization of children, and economic cooperation. This concept of the nuclear family generally holds true for Western societies, but some other cultures do not fit this

[1] One man has been married 27 times, setting the record for serial monogamy (*Guinness book of world records,* 1987).

Figure 17.2    A nuclear family.

model. For example, among the Nayars of India, fathers have little to do with socializing their children or with supporting their wives; the women continue to live with their kin and may have more than one husband who visit them periodically (Reiss, 1980).

Sex, marriage, and the family are intimately bound together, but each can be separate: there is nonmarital sex as well as sexless marriages; children are born to unmarried couples, while some marriages are childless. For most people, though, the family is the main setting for sexual interaction and parenthood.

For this reason, all societies have had to devise means for men and women to form families, facilitating some types of behavior and inhibiting others to that end. *Courtship* provides the means of finding future mates.[2] Its forms are highly varied, but it follows two basic patterns: either parents select the mates for their children, or the young people do it themselves. Courtship, marriage, and the family form an integrated unit that Reiss (1980) calls the *family system,* through which new generations succeed existing ones.

Most adults in American society are expected to marry. In the 1950s, when the United States had entered the most family-oriented period of the century, 96 percent of people in the childbearing years married (Blumstein and Schwartz, 1983). Now over 90 percent still do. Nevertheless marriage evokes many strong and varied feelings. Traditionalists see it as the only legitimate outlet for sexual relationships and raising a family. Pragmatists see it as a practical arrangement for a comfortable life of companionship and sex.[3] Feminist critics of marriage see it as a primary vehicle for the subjugation and exploitation of women. The roles of wife and mother isolate

---

[2] The term comes from the traditions of courtly love in medieval Europe (Chapter 20). "Courtship" is now used for all forms of mate selection, including among animals.

[3] When Darwin was considering marriage, he wrote in his diary, "Only picture to yourself a nice, soft wife on a sofa with a good fire, and books, and music perhaps—compare this with the dingy reality of Gt. Marlbor's Street [where he had lodgings]. Marry—Marry—Marry" (quoted in Moorehead, 1979, p. 249).

women in the private domain ("cult of domesticity") and limit their contributions to the public domain (Barrett and McIntosh, 1982; Pleck, 1985). Even within dual career couples, women usually carry more of the domestic responsibilities (Steil, 1982), although many more men are now willing to share in these tasks as well as in childcaring responsibilities.

The reason there are so many views on marriage is because it fulfills different purposes for different people. There are also some basic functions that are important to most marriages: the practical benefits of joint living arrangements; the pooling of economic resources; the division and sharing of labor; the expansion of social ties; the fulfillment of parental and societal expectations; and—most important for our purposes—affection, intimacy, sexual satisfaction, and parenthood. All of these aims can also be fulfilled in other arrangements, like cohabitation. Why, then do most people still insist on getting married?

The basic benefits and costs of marital relationships, though fairly stable, are not fixed. They have changed since your grandparents' time, and are rapidly changing now in response to different economic and social circumstances and shifts in gender roles.

## Demographic Changes

The American family has changed more in the last 30 years than in the previous 250 (Blumstein and Schwartz, 1983). In the late 1960s and early 1970s, the rate of fertility began to decline. This trend had set in two centuries ago, but with the Pill and access to abortion, it became more marked. The decline in the rate of fertility could be due to a higher rate of infertility and additional factors: fewer people marry or stay married; they marry later; they have fewer children. All three factors have recently been operative.

Rate of Marriage    During the 1960s the marriage rate began to decline steadily, particularly for younger women in the prime childbearing ages. Out of 1000 unmarried women

aged 14 to 44, 199 got married in 1946; in 1987, this figure had fallen to fewer than 100 (Exner, 1987). Part of this difference is a shift toward later first marriages for both women and men.

Since the turn of the century, the ages at first marriage have gradually dropped, reaching their lowest point in 1956 when the median age of marriage reached 20.1 years for women and 22.5 years for men. The rates then began to rise. Between 1960 and 1970, the proportion of women who remained single until the ages of 20 to 24 increased by one-third. In 1960, 28 percent of women between the ages of 20 and 24 had not yet married. By 1979, this figure had gone up to 49 percent; by 1981, 52 percent of women in this age group were single (Blumstein and Schwartz, 1983). The median age for first-time brides has now reached 23.3 years; for bridegrooms, 25.5 years.

As the age at first marriage goes up, so does the ratio of people who have never been married. Figure 17.3 shows the percentages of never-married men and women in three age groups at three time periods. In both sexes, the 1986 figures show the highest percentages for all three age groups.

Because women outlive men and men tend to marry younger women, for women who want to be married (not all women do) there is a distinct lessening of marital prospects as they get older. The probability of marrying in a given year increases from almost zero at age 15 to over 1 in 10 between ages 20 and 24 (that is, 1 in 10 women will marry before she turns 25). After 24, the chances of marrying drop each year (Exner, 1987). What is not clear is the rate of this drop. A study by a Harvard-Yale team came up with the startling prediction that only 20 percent of never-married 30-year-old college graduates were likely to ever marry; by age 45 their chances had dropped to almost zero (Bennett et al., 1986). These projections were contradicted by Moorman (1987) of the Census Bureau, who claimed that even at age 45, never-married college graduate women had a 10 percent chance of marrying by age 65. Table 17.1 shows the probabilities of marriage at various ages according to the

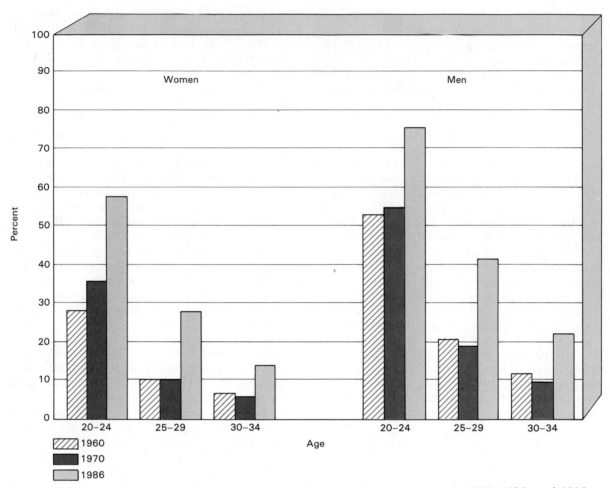

Figure 17.3    Percentage of never married women and men in three age groups in 1960, 1970, and 1986.

two studies. The Harvard-Yale study assumes that women who have not married early have foregone it altogether by design or default; the Census Bureau study assumes that many college women who have postponed marriage will eventually marry.

Age Differentials    Husbands are usually older than their wives, usually by a few years, but sometimes as much as a decade or more (especially in the older generations). Society generally accepts "December-May" matches unless the age differential is extreme. Even at that some highly esteemed figures (Charlie Chap-

lin, Pablo Casals) have had much younger wives in their older years. The reverse situation, when an older woman marries a younger man, has been less common. Recently this trend has been shifting, with more women marrying or establishing committed relationships with younger men (Derenski and Landsburg, 1981). When it occurs with celebrities it makes news.[4] There were also over 150,000

[4] Mary Tyler Moore at age 50 married Robert Levine, 34; Joan Collins at 54 married Peter Holm, 39; Miriam Makeba at 55 married Stokely Carmichael, 45; and 400 years ago, William Shakespeare married Anne Hathaway when she was 26 and he 18 (Gavzer, 1987).

marriages in 1983 in which the bride was five years older or more than the groom: this is still only 6 percent of all marriages, but a 67 percent increase since 1970 (Gavzer, 1987).

The greatest likelihood of such marriages is for women aged 35 to 44 (who account for 40 percent of these cases). Typically they are successful career women who are divorced with children, who meet their future husband in a business context. Like older men, they offer the younger partner not only social status and financial assets but also greater life experience, sexual sophistication, mature affection, and other personal ingredients that are independent of age. These younger men typically have had a working mother and sisters who also have careers (Houston, 1987).

Generally such couples do not want children of their own, although the woman may already have children from a previous marriage. If the man wants children, the issue is likely to be divisive. Other sources of conflict have to do with differences in health and vigor and stage of adult development (Chapter 9).

## Changes in Family Patterns

Apart from demographic shifts, everyone agrees that marriages and families are changing in the United States, to the delight of some and the dismay of others. Some of these changes are illusory. For instance, despite its nostalgic image, the extended family of the past, where members of several generations lived together, was not as common as people think (Reiss, 1980). The nuclear family is not just a modern phenomenon.

One generational change of significance is greater freedom in making marital decisions. Whereas in the past parents asserted authority over whom their children married, now they are more likely to use persuasion or indirect tactics. Because the young have more social and geographic mobility, families also have less opportunity for matchmaking.

Important changes in marital dynamics have come about because of the women's movement and shifts in gender roles. Female power in the marital relationship has in-

**Table 17.1  Probabilities of College Women Getting Married**

| AGE | CENSUS BUREAU STUDY (FOUR YEARS COLLEGE) | HARVARD-YALE STUDY (FOUR YEARS COLLEGE OR MORE) |
|---|---|---|
| 25 | 85% | 52% |
| 30 | 58 | 20 |
| 35 | 32 | 5 |
| 40 | 17 | 1 |
| 45 | 9 | 0 |

(Based on Exner, 1987.)

creased; greater equality between husband and wife now characterizes middle-class marriages. These changes are embraced by many, but they have disquieting aspects for others.

Another shift, which has been both beneficial and disruptive, has been the rise of emphasis on personal happiness. The marital values of the past extolled forbearance and self-sacrifice to keep the family intact. Unhappy families tended to stick together and make the best of a bad situation. Now we expect people to put their personal happiness ahead of others. Furthermore, the expectation of lifelong happiness has extended the battlefield of love from youth to the rest of adulthood. The gains in life expectancy have in turn increased, by many decades, the time couples will live together if they stay married. A 50-year-old woman now can expect to live for another 30 years; a man, several years less.

The upshot has been to make people more cautious and selective about commitments. Commitments themselves have become more provisional; it is no longer "until death do us part" but "as long as we are happy," which translates to "as long as I am happy." Marriage and other intimate associations have therefore become more "costly." Career women, in particular, now may see having a husband as more a burden than an asset; men, on their part, see having a wife to be less of an advantage than was the case in earlier times.

All these changes have led some people to conclude that marriage is "dying" or at least is a severely ailing institution. The disenchantment voiced by the women in the Hite (1987) sample is echoed in other studies. In a 1986 survey of 60,000 women conducted by *Woman's Day* magazine, 38 percent of the women said they would not choose the same spouse if they had to do it again; 39 percent felt like their husband's housekeeper, 27 percent like his mother, and only 28 percent like his lover; a 1986 survey of 34,000 women conducted by *New Woman* magazine showed 41 percent of unattached women were not looking for a relationship or were undecided. Thus the increasing ratio of single women in the 25 to 34 age group may mean women are not just postponing marriage but avoiding it altogether (Wallis, 1987).

Other sources contradict these contentions. A 1986 Gallup poll found 45 percent of respondents to be "very satisfied" and 93 percent to be at least "mostly satisfied" with their family life; both figures are somewhat higher than the results of a similar poll taken in 1980. Furthermore, 53 percent say that as a general rule, the family life of the people they know has gotten better in the last 15 years or so; 33 percent say it has gotten worse (Gallup, 1986). All told, 95 percent of women in a 1987 Harris poll say they would remarry their present spouses (Wallis, 1987).

There is no doubt about the changing roles of women. The combined results from dozens of marital polls show that 63 percent of women surveyed want to combine marriage and children with careers (up from 52 percent a decade ago); the ratio of women who want families but no careers has dropped from 38 percent to 26 percent over the past decade; more than 50 percent of the women and the men say taking care of the home and children should be a shared responsibility although in only 15 percent of cases the women say the chores are in fact divided (in 41 percent the women do them; 41 percent get some help; in only 2 percent the husbands do more). Teenagers, as a group, believe most in equality.

Reports of marital happiness depend on whom you ask. People who respond to magazine surveys and questionnaire studies with very low response rates are likely to be more unhappy than people in more random national samples (Reinisch, 1987).

Moreover, not only is "happiness" a relative term, but it is not an all-or-nothing issue. Most marriages are happy at some time but not another. In fact, as shown in Figure 17.4, marital satisfaction follows a fairly predictable pattern. The percentage of people who say they are very happy rises with marriage, declines with the arrival of children, and goes through further shifts. Also note that the two female patterns 19 years apart show greater differences than the corresponding male patterns.

## Mate Selection

The people we choose to have sex with or fall in love with are not always the ones we pick for a mate. There are practical considerations, and the issue is not only a matter of choosing but also of being chosen.

There are two opposite perspectives on choosing. The first is the romantic approach: you trust your heart to make the right choice and hope all else will fall in place. The second is practical or the pragmatic approach: you trust your head to get the best deal and hope you will come to love it.

Most people realize that a purely romantic tack is unrealistic (although the inexperienced young often fall for it) and the purely practical alternative is too heartless and manipulative (although some hardened adults do not mind it). So they combine the judgments of their hearts and heads and hope for the best.

We assume we are free to choose our mates. You may be, nonetheless, far less independent than you think. Setting aside the actual or anticipated influence of parents, siblings, friends, and others, whom we choose to marry is also governed by practical and social considerations we are often unaware of.

One obvious factor is *propinquity*, which means being near someone or moving in the same social circles. You are not likely to marry an Eskimo unless you are an Eskimo.

People are now geographically and socially much more mobile than in the past. Yet

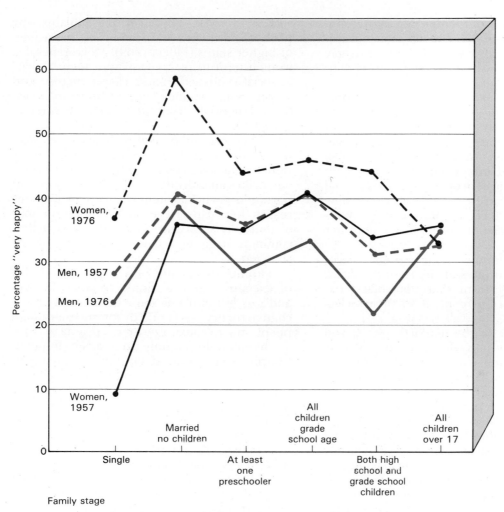

Figure 17.4  Family stage and marital happiness.

more often than not the person you marry will be either from the town you grew up in, the college you attended, or the city where you work. Because of the large numbers of women who now work, offices have become the new "mating zone" (Ingrassia, 1986). Institutions like churches, and cultural, social, or leisure organizations provide further opportunities to meet eligible mates. Purely chance meetings that lead to marriage are exceptional. Apart from the fact that you cannot get to what is not within reach, nearness in itself engenders attraction. Students who live in the same dor-

mitory rate one another as more attractive than their peers living elsewhere on campus (Nahemow and Lawton, 1975).

A related factor is *homogamy,* the principle of "like marries like." With respect to demographic characteristics like age, race, socioeconomic status, and religion, people choose mates who are like them (Murstein, 1976). To some extent this is also true for personality characteristics (Autill, 1983). Because similarity between partners is thought to facilitate communication, understanding, and shared values, partner homogamy has been described as a good predictor of relationship satisfaction. This idea appears to be true not only for married couples but also for cohabitors and gay and lesbian relationships (Kurdek and Schmitt, 1986).

Propinquity and homogamy reinforce each other, because people from similar backgrounds tend to segregate themselves. Both rules are sometimes broken in exceptional matches; but even there, if you look closely, you will still find important underlying similarities. For instance, people who cross national or ethnic boundaries are still likely to come from similar social classes. Rarely does a purely personal attraction overwhelm all other considerations.

Further limitations in our personal choices come from the dictates of the *marriage market,* a crass-sounding term that nonetheless describes an important context for mate selection.

If you think of the married couples you know (or even couples who only date) you may notice certain similarities between the partners, quite apart from homogamy. For instance, they are likely to have roughly "equivalent" degrees of physical attractiveness, or comparable levels of education and intelligence. If you combine these factors with social ones like class background, what you typically get is not a perfect symmetrical match but *parity.* In other words, despite discrepancies in this or that valued characteristic, on balance the couple comes out fairly even. In the absence of parity, the couple will look mismatched to others and they will wonder what holds them together. Parity does not just happen. It is a function both of what attracts two people to each other and of the "market forces" that generally see to it that what you get is about what you can offer.

In more formal terms, matches are explained by theories that emphasize *exchange* or *equity.* Exchange involves trade-offs of resources, some of which are always valued alike (such as health), others more unevenly; for instance, women have traditionally counted on their looks, men on their actual or potential success at work. This principle explains why physically attractive women tend to marry men of higher status (Elder, 1969). More generally, women tend to marry "up" and men "down" in social status, education, career success, and so on. Some studies support these observations, but others contradict them (Walster et al., 1978).

The concept of equity helps to explain how trade-offs balance each other. Each of us values some assets highly, but ultimately everyone makes an individual assessment of how important a particular item is for them. For this reason there can be a virtually limitless number of mutually satisfying combinations as well as common nagging feelings of getting short-changed.

Equity theory not only expands the idea of exchange from a simple equation of gain and loss but explains some behaviors that exchange theory does not. For instance, although people try to maximize their advantage, they are happy doing so only up to a certain point. Couples who are most satisfied in a relationship are those who find it equitable. Those who value themselves significantly lower than their partner are less content because they feel guilty, or their self-esteem suffers from feeling second best (Berscheid et al., 1973).

This whole notion of "assets" and "trade-offs" in a cost-benefit analysis of the people we are supposed to love and cherish runs against the grain of our finer sentiments. Women may be particularly bothered by this approach because they have been bartered and exchanged throughout much of history and still have less control over their marital choices than men in general. Therefore, although exchange and equity do affect us, we can work to make the marriage market more free and fair. We can try to look less at aspects of our bodies and social status over which we have had no control, and more at personality aspects that define us as individuals. We can choose personal qualities like gentleness and decency over greed and aggressiveness, even if the latter mean having more money. We can have the courage to make our choices reflect our values.

# Box 17.1

## I AM NOT A "SIGNIFICANT OTHER"*

I feel demoted, dispossessed, deprived. A friendly invitation arrived the other day. Intending no offense but rather to offer inclusion, it urged guests to "bring your significant other and any associated children."

From an isolated occurrence, the use of the phrase "significant other" can now be found everywhere: magazines, newspapers, school documents, public-opinion surveys, advertisements, and so on and on.

When my wife and I went to the obstetrics section of our rather staid hospital, an officious sign notified us that "every woman in labor may have one significant other accompany her in the laboring room."

I am a husband. I know what the role of husband is, or at least I know the vows I accepted in adopting the role. I'm familiar with a husband's social relations, attendant expectations, and some ideal role models, including those found in our literary heritage.

Furthermore, to my wife I am not merely an "other," even a "significant other." Indeed, I expect, or hope, that I am less other and more an elemental part of her being, as she is of mine. I hope that we, like the very concepts of husband and wife, must be known together. But through no choice of my own, and without my consent, I have been reduced to a mere "significant other." Without my approval, I have found myself joined to this amorphous being of otherness.

Does my new role have any special obligations? Any defined social relations? Any ideal types? Any necessary characteristics? If we don't consent to it, don't swear any vows, how does it come to be part of our identity? Through the choice of another?

My distinctive, nay, unique role as a husband has been taken away as I have become assimilated into the entirety of humanity. I have become distinguished only by my "significance," which is also no doubt shared with many other "others"—brothers, mothers, boyfriends, lovers, mentors, friends, roommates, business partners, scientific collaborators, etc.

Don't misunderstand, I am no conservative antiquarian hoping to recover an idyllic yesteryear. I am as liberated and liberal as the next guy. I am the primary "caretaker" for my daughter. I cook the dinners, wash the dishes, clean the house more frequently than my wife. I find such changes both progressive and positive. But I object to being robbed of my identity, the roles I accept, the relationships I affirm.

Maybe I am asking too much of this small linguistic modification. After all, we do live in the 20th century, and all sorts of traditional relationships have been transformed, redefined, or simply eliminated by evolving social practices. So the traditional marriage, whatever that is, is being preempted and replaced by a whole diversity of cohabitation arrangements, and our language must evolve to incorporate these changes.

If we all are "significant others," no one is a wife, a husband or anything else. We have lost one of our chosen roles. Dispossessed of part of our identifying characteristics, we become more alike.

Soon, no doubt, the power of our language will have done what social transformations have not. Only a few people, maybe some historians, students of literature, and etymologists will recall what it means to be a husband or wife. The dictionary will list "husband" and "wife" as obsolete or archaic. And having lost the specific words to refer to husbands and wives, we speakers will forget what was so unique about the marital relationship.

So, just as there are no longer any ladies and gentlemen, except in 19th-century novels, there will no longer be husbands and wives, except as historical curiosities. We will all, willingly or not, be caught in the Cuisinart of American English and mixed into "significant others."

*(Ezekiel J. Emanuel, *New York Times*, Nov. 15, 1986.)

## ALTERNATIVE COMMITMENTS

Monogamous marriage based on romantic love and companionship is an ideal that evades many couples. In practice, there are many different forms of marital relationships: some that are not sexually monogamous, others based not on romantic love but on practical advantages, and yet others with varying forms and intensities of companionship and intimacy.

In the past, when divorce was frowned upon, these departures from the ideal were concealed, while marriages were maintained, seemingly intact, for the sake of appearances. That is generally no longer the case, although there are still plenty of marriages around that are an empty shell.

The traditional form of marriage has come under sharp criticism during the past several decades from feminists and others in the younger generation. As a result, the institution of marriage is not dying but changing. The most common alternatives to the traditional model are marriages based on greater equality, shared responsibilities, and overlap (or reversal) of traditional gender roles.

More radical departures from the pattern reject some aspect—social, legal, or interpersonal—of marriage. They range from cohabitation, which now involves a significant segment of the younger adult population, to group marriage, which is rare.

### Cohabitation

Living with a sexual partner of the opposite sex without being married is called *cohabitation*. Couples who got serious about each other used to go steady. With or without sex, this relationship implied a commitment that could lead to engagement and marriage. Today, living together may be a temporary arrangement like going steady, a period of trial or preparation for marriage like engagement, or a permanent alternative to marriage itself. In urban areas it is also not uncommon for members of the opposite sex just to be roommates.

The U.S. Census Bureau blandly defines cohabitants as "persons of opposite sex sharing living quarters" (POSSLLQ). Some are doing just that, but the majority are couples engaged in an intimate and sexual relationship. So far no good term has been found for those who live together; "the man/woman I live with" is most commonly used (Box 17.1).

Prevalence    An estimated 2.2 million unmarried couples are now living together in the United States—four times the number in 1960 (U.S. Bureau of the Census, 1986). Cohabitation in the United States is still nowhere as common as in Sweden, where 90 percent of the adult population has had such experience (Reiss, 1980). Figure 17.5 shows the distribution of cohabitants by marital status and age.

Cohabitation is quite prevalent among college students, a quarter of whom have reportedly tried it. Twice as many more say they would like to (Bower and Christopherson, 1977). The majority of students do not see cohabitation as a long-term commitment (Macklin, 1978), but almost all who have had the experience say they eventually want to be married. In their daily living arrangements, cohabitants are basically like any married couple usually without children (Figure 17.6).

Cohabitation is not restricted to college students or to young adults. Although the majority are below age 30, the practice extends all the way into the ranks of the elderly, some of whom resort to this practice because marriage would curtail their tax and financial benefits.

Pros and Cons    Cohabitation became popular in the 1970s. Over a decade the numbers of unmarried men and women living together tripled to 1.6 million (Spanier, 1983). Several factors contributed to its emergence. In the 1960s sexual attitudes became liberalized, especially among the young, who became independent of parents and college administrators by setting up their own living arrangements. Wider use of contraceptives and abortion prevented many of the pregnancies which in the past

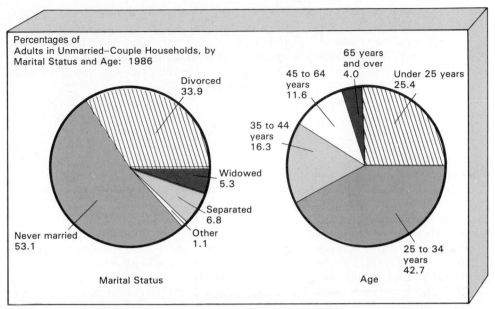

Figure 17.5    Adults in unmarried-couple households by marital status and age, 1986.

would have forced couples into marriage. Ideological shifts led political radicals to reject the "bourgeois" institution of marriage and some feminists to denounce its sexist, heterosexist, and exploitative nature. The large numbers of

divorced people found in cohabitation a means of avoiding another hasty marital commitment (about half of cohabiting persons have been married).

Some choose this alternative because of

Figure 17.6    Cohabitation is no longer a rarity. However, the fact that two people have different last names does not necessarily mean they are not married to each other.

disenchantment with the more traditional form of marriage. It allows a woman the advantages of a stable and affectionate relationship without compromising her professional aspirations, sense of independence, and identity. Men like it because it provides many of the advantages of a marital relationship without its legal and economic ties and obligations. It gives both sexes an extended chance to test the relationship: if it works, they can enter marriage with more confidence; if it does not, they can part company without a divorce. Others are simply not interested in marriage on ideological or personal grounds. For them cohabitation stands or falls on its own merits without reference to the prospect of marriage.

Living together is no panacea, though. As a permanent alternative to marriage, it makes the tasks of parenthood far more complicated in a society whose customs and laws favor marriage. Cohabitation now works mainly as a childless lifestyle: most of these couples have no children living with them. Even though some have custody of children from previous marriages who do live with them, most couples are reluctant to bring new children into the relationship without getting married.

Cohabitation may lead to procrastination in making definite commitments and keep the future in suspense. Meanwhile, cohabitation does not spare the couple from facing many of the same joys and sorrows as married people. If the relationship breaks up it leaves women in their 30s or older at a disadvantage should they be interested in getting married in the future. Although marriage is no guarantee of permanence, it is likely to have a more binding effect. For this reason, although the likelihood of marrying is fairly strong among cohabiting men (38 percent) and women (35 percent), a higher proportion of women is eager to marry, more so if they have never been married before (68 percent) than if they have (61 percent) (Blumstein and Schwartz, 1983).

Preliminary reports from a Swedish study show that couples who lived together before marrying have an almost 80 percent higher divorce rate than those who did not. This finding does not mean that cohabiting dooms a relationship but that cohabitants are less committed to the institution of marriage. It may reflect special social conditions that prevail in Sweden but not in the United States. In the Blumstein and Schwartz (1983) study the divorce rate of cohabitants was no higher than the rate of those who did not cohabit. Cohabiting seemed neither to predict the breakup of a marriage nor to increase its stability. Newcomb and Bentler (1980) also found that cohabitants who marry are as likely to divorce or to be satisfied with their marriage as those without such experience. Meanwhile, as long as marriage retains its image as the highest form of commitment, cohabitating couples will feel under pressure to get married or else appear lacking in their love for each other (Blumstein and Schwartz, 1983).

Cohabitation is perceived as a positive experience by most who have tried it (Macklin, 1978) and as a precondition to marrying someone. Though it is possible that cohabitation will become a more integral part of courtship before marriage (Cherlin, 1981), it seems unlikely to replace marriage. Nonetheless, there is now wider recognition of cohabitation as an acceptable alternative to marriage. Through *palimony* settlements (which compensate the financially disadvantaged member of a cohabitating couple who separate) the courts have tacitly recognized cohabitation as a legitimate partnership. Similar recognition has been given in the past to common-law marriage, a union entered into by common agreement without benefit of a formal marriage.

## Gay Couples

As we discussed in Chapter 13, gay men and lesbians form committed associations of various types. The freedom for gay couples to openly live together is quite recent, and there are still numerous social obstacles to overcome; most importantly, the law still does not permit the legalizing of such partnerships by marriage with all its social prerogatives and obligations. Therefore, as a group, gay couples are closest to cohabiting heterosexual couples.

## Other Alternatives

Other alternatives to monogamy have been tried at various times, with no general or lasting success. As in other societies, *group marriages* have been sporadically set up, and *communes* have been part of the United States for centuries. A good example was a utopian religious group called the Oneida Community founded in 1841 in Vermont by the radical clergyman John Humphrey Noyes and his wife (Talese, 1980). All the men and the women in the group behaved as husbands and wives toward each other, with full sexual privileges. Such experiments had a short-lived revival in the late 1960s in the form of counterculture communes that ranged from the idealistic to the exploitative and bizarre (Chapter 21). More current examples of such groups commonly emerge as cults where members live together and are encouraged to sleep with each other (Lewin, 1988).

The basis for a commune is not sexual, although sex can be an important incentive. The broader purposes may be economic, ideological, or religious; sex may not always be shared. Members of group marriages have access to each other sexually, but they do not necessarily engage in group sex.

A *multilateral marriage* is a voluntary family association of three or more individuals based on affectionate bonds and sexual intimacy. Typically these arrangements involve two couples who may have been married to other people earlier and may have children; members of the group are not married to each other in the legal sense of the term.

To accommodate these changed marital patterns, Reiss proposes a new definition of family: a "small kinship-structured unit" whose key function is the "nurturant socialization of the newborn" (Reiss, 1980). In this context, "kinship" does not imply connection by blood or by marriage, nor does it specify that they belong to opposite sexes.

## BEING SINGLE

To be single means to be unattached, not one of a pair. It includes the never married (with which it is often equated), the divorced, and the widowed. The separated are legally not single, though they generally behave like singles. By contrast, cohabitants are legally single, but in effect they are not. That is why "unmarried" is not an adequate synonym for "single."

Important demographic changes have occurred in the unmarried population in the United States from 1960 to 1986. The proportion of unmarried men and women who have never married has doubled; the number of divorced persons has gone up from 35 to 131 per 1000 persons in an intact marriage; the proportion of children under 18 who live with one parent has gone up from 9 to 24 percent (U.S. Bureau of the Census, 1986).

Among the never married, it is important to distinguish between younger adults in their twenties and those in older groups. The younger segment is a "premarital group," because the majority will get married. They usually are in college or getting established at work, and they may still be attached to their families, even if no longer living at home. They are thus in a transitional phase. Those older are more likely to be heading toward a life of being single. It is this latter group that we will describe here. We dealt with younger adults in Chapter 9.

The lives of men and women who are not married share a number of characteristics and misconceptions. First, to be single does not mean to live alone. A large proportion of single people live with a member of their family, most often a child. Others live with a same-sex friend, with or without sexual attachments. Although about one in ten adults in the United States does live alone (triple the number since 1960), they are not necessarily lonely. Single people may have close and rewarding friendships, in which they enjoy greater intimacy than many a married couple. Nor is singlehood to be equated with sexual deprivation. Though the public perception of "swinging singles" tends to be exaggerated, many single men and women have rewarding sexual lives.

One of the major recent changes in the family has been the increase in single-parent households. In 1985, 23 percent of all children under the age of 18 lived with only one parent (90 percent with the mother). In 1960, such children accounted for only 9 percent and in 1970 for 12 percent of their age group. Some 10 million children now live with a single parent, either because of divorce or because the parents were unmarried (U.S. Bureau of the Census, 1986).

Although many single parents face financial hardships, being single does not have to mean being poor. There are many unmarried professional men and women whose high incomes and low family obligations allow them a good deal of financial leeway. Even those who have more modest resources exercise greater control over them, because they are not accountable to a spouse.

Finally, a substantial proportion of the unmarried are single by choice. Many single persons could get married if they lowered their standards and expectations. Others do not want to trade in their independence or hamper their career interests by getting tied down.

However, for other men and women, to be single does mean to be alone, lonely, sexually deprived, and poor; it represents a way of life that they would dearly love to get out of. The point is that there are many ways of being single, just as there are many ways of being married: the elderly man living in a run-down hotel room on a dwindling income, the teenage mother of two on welfare, the professional men and women in their thirties living in fancy apartments are all single—but a world of difference separates their intimate relationships and sexual lives.

In the best of circumstances, does being single imply coping with a void in life (however full it may otherwise be)? Does it reflect some failure in the ability to connect or stay connected with someone (no matter how gregarious the single may be)? These questions draw impassioned responses from the single, both positive and negative. Though there have always been "bachelors" and "spinsters" (terms that have gone out of fashion), recent public attention has mostly focused on the life circumstances of high-achieving single career women who either shun marriage by choice or are unable to find men to their liking. The conflict between independence and intimacy, confronting the social stigma and practical consequences of being single, and foregoing motherhood until it may be too late are some of the issues that single women and men now struggle with (Gross, 1987). Moreover, these are not only problems for individuals but for society as well (Onorato, 1987).

## The Never Married

One out of twenty Americans has never married by age 50 (U.S. Bureau of the Census, 1984) and is likely to remain single. A substantial proportion of this population is gay, and more of them are men because there are more gay men than women. Of course, not to have married should not be equated with homosexuality; this group includes many heterosexuals as well. Gay couples who live together are single only in a technical sense; they live like heterosexual cohabitants. Many of them consider themselves to be married, although the law does not recognize such unions as legally valid.

Never-married women are more likely than married women to have been successful at full-time careers. These women may not have married because being financially independent let them be more selective or made them more threatening to men as potential spouses. Alternately, women who are not interested in getting married may pursue their careers more diligently and freely, and so be more successful (Bee, 1987).

By contrast, the never-married middle-aged man is more likely to be socially and occupationally less competent, a poor provider or unfit in some other manner. The gender discrepancy also holds at the educational level: men with less than five years of schooling and women with more than four years of college are most likely to have never married in the 35- to 54-year-old population (which has the highest proportion of married couples) (Troll, 1985). Lack of education often reflects a mental, physical, or social handicap and in turn leads to poor earning capacity. Nonetheless, there is also no lack of educated, successful, and highly eligible bachelors among unmarried men.

Other exceptions to the above patterns are those who have committed themselves to religious celibacy, such as Catholic priests, monks, and nuns, who are not permitted to marry.

## The Divorced

The most serious charge against marriage is the rate at which it breaks up in separation and divorce. Although the dissolution of a marriage clearly suggests that it was not working well, it does not always follow that it must have been a mistake to begin with; some happy marriages do go sour as spouses drift apart, just as some unhappy marriages get better in time.

Divorce Statistics    We rightly associate high divorce rates with modern times, but the trend goes back over a century. The divorce rate climbed sharply during World War II, declined during the 1950s, and rose higher than ever before in the 1960s and 1970s; it has declined slightly in the 1980s. The number of divorces tripled each year between 1962 and 1981, when they peaked at a high of 1.2 million; the rates then began dropping slowly and had gone down to 1,187,000 in 1985.

For white women, marriages ending in divorce went up from 14 percent between 1940 and 1945 to 45 percent between 1975 and 1980; for black women the rates were even higher, making them the most likely group in the United States to be divorced. In 1986, there were 131 divorced people for each 1000 who were living with a spouse. The ratio for men was 106 as against 157 for women, because men are more likely to remarry after their marriage ends and do so sooner than women (U.S. Bureau of the Census, 1986).

Divorce statistics are confusing. They are easy to misinterpret, and rates computed by different methods yield different figures. For instance, it is commonly stated that one out of every two marriages ends in divorce. This ratio is arrived at by comparing the number of marriages and divorces in a given year: for instance, at their highest rate in 1981, there were 1.2 million divorces and 2.4 million marriages. That does not mean that anyone who gets married has a 50 percent chance of getting divorced. The rates are pushed up by people who divorce repeatedly. Furthermore, such comparisons do not take into account older marriages that remained intact during the year in question. In other words, the married group in 1981 were not just the 2.4 million who got married that year but all the rest of the couples married earlier whose marriages remained intact. Pollster Louis Harris, taking account of that fact, concludes that one in eight marriages, not one in two, ends in divorce (*Time*, July 13, 1987).

Causes of Divorce    Divorce is most common among younger people: for both sexes the highest numbers are in the 25 to 29 age group and decline markedly with the approach of middle age; the divorce rate for couples below age 30 is more than double the national average, accounting for 40 percent of all divorces (Yarrow, 1987). Men who marry before 21 and women before 20 are most likely to divorce, all else being equal.

Age itself is not necessarily a cause of divorce; many people have married young and stayed married. The effect of age has to do with its associated patterns of mate selection and the social and psychological characteristics of the young in the modern world. The young are much more likely to be carried away by romantic than realistic considerations in choosing a mate. They will overvalue the more visible physical and personality assets of a potential mate, ignoring characteristics that provide more staying power in a relationship.

The young have an idealized image of marriage; they are taken aback by its problems and lack the skills and the patience to solve them (for instance, they will lash out at each other or withdraw rather than resolve issues through compromise). Their unrealistically high expectations make even perfectly workable marriages seem inadequate. They also know that they can try again and count on doing better the next time.

The marital problems of the young can be

readily understood in terms of the tasks and conflicts at their phase of adult development (Chapter 9). With their identities not fully defined, they do not quite know yet who they are (or are going to become); hence they cannot make the most compatible choices. The challenges in developing their careers likewise compete with the demands of marriage. Many teenagers who marry drop out of school or must settle for whatever job they can get. The very lack of financial resources strains the marriage.

It may be easy to understand why teenage marriages easily break down, or why there was a rash of divorces during the enforced separation and the hardships of World War II. It is harder to explain why marriages without such handicaps do not last (or why some other marriages with similar handicaps do).

In addition to age, other variables correlate with the likelihood of divorce. Marriages are at higher risk during their first two to three years. If a couple has been acquainted for less than two years or engaged less than six months, the likelihood of divorce is higher. Marriages are more vulnerable if people come from urban backgrounds, different religious faiths (or faiths they do not practice), dissimilar backgrounds, and low social status. Parents with unhappy marriages have children who are more likely to divorce. People with divorced parents tend to marry others who also have divorced parents, and are more likely to divorce themselves. When family and kin disapprove of the marriage, the risks are higher. Disagreements over roles add obvious stresses (Goode, 1982). Many psychological factors also have been proposed as possible causes of divorce.

Not all these correlations are causes. Furthermore, there are plenty of couples with such "loaded" backgrounds who nonetheless have happy and lasting marriages. Such correlations apply at the group level, but not to everyone in the group.

Ultimately, there are as many reasons for getting divorced as there are for getting married (although there is also some truth to Tolstoy's statement that "All happy families resemble one another, but each unhappy family is unhappy in its own way"). Some variables operate at the level of mate selection; others follow it. Like a game of cards, whether you win or lose depends both on the hand you are dealt and how you play it. It also depends on the social climate and the rules of the game. Liberal divorce laws, lack of social stigma, and the fact that so many others are doing it will encourage divorce if there is marital discontent. The growing economic independence of wives and the fact that working women interact with potential mates increase their choices of opting out of an unhappy marriage. The key factor here is not the amount of money but guaranteed income. A woman on welfare may not get much, but she can count on it, and that makes her less dependent on her husband.

Divorce is a painful experience for the couple, their children, and all concerned; but the extent of the psychological trauma and social damage varies widely. Rarely is divorce entirely friendly, but some breakups are far better than others. The first two years after divorce are the most stressful period, both for the couple and the children; but the period of separation that precedes divorce may be the toughest to handle. Within two years most are able to pull their lives together; the speed and success of recovery depend on inner resources, social support, and finances.

Divorce affects men and women differently, as does marriage. Divorce actions are more often initiated by women (though men may precipitate them); but the consequences of divorce are generally harder on the woman, especially in economic terms. Recent changes in divorce laws that were part of the reform in marital law have worsened the plight of divorced women. The alimony payments and settlements of the past have been replaced with the division of community property in "no-fault" divorce (Chapter 22). Because women often do not end up with their fair share and have limited job skills and opportunities, their standard of living generally falls by 73 percent, while that of men rises by 42 percent following divorce (Weitzman, 1986).

A divorced woman is less likely to remarry

than a divorced man, and this discrepancy increases as they get older. A woman divorced in her 20s has a 76 percent chance of remarriage; that figure goes down to 56 percent in her 30s, 32 percent in her 40s, and 12 percent in her 50s and beyond (Blumstein and Schwartz, 1983). Though men fare better financially and on the remarriage market, divorce disrupts their lives more in the domestic area. They have more problems in maintaining a household.

Children aged 3 to 5 have the hardest time after divorce. Those younger are less aware of the problems, and those older have greater resources to deal with them. Though children of divorce usually live with the mother, in 15 percent of cases the father now gets custody of the child (Bee, 1987).

It has been common for divorced men and women to experience loss of self-esteem and to perceive themselves as failures in love and parenting (Spanier and Thompson, 1984). There is a greater tendency now to view divorce in less harsh terms. They can either come to terms with past errors or focus on the good in the marriage that has ended. Most relationships that end in divorce have had some happiness to remember. Instead of accusations, the divorced can focus on the incompatibility of the partners. Some people are not good for each other without being bad in themselves. Growth means change, and change will draw some couples apart.

The fact that five out of six men and three out of four women decide to remarry is a tribute to the strength of the institution of marriage (Cherlin, 1981). On the other hand, some people evidently do not learn through experience: the divorce rate among the remarried is even higher than among those married for the first time. Even though the remarried do not generally report feeling better than during the time they were divorced, the psychological and social pull of the institution continues to draw people into it.

The breakup of nonmarital relationships, such as between cohabiting or gay couples, attracts far less public attention than divorce. There are usually no legal entanglements to sort out or children to worry about, but the personal anguish and the disruption of lives are as painful as in divorce.

## The Widowed

Prior to 1900, only 40 percent of women in the United States got married, brought up their children to adulthood, and survived their husbands. The other 60 percent died before adulthood, died unmarried, died before having children, or were widowed while their children were young. Widowhood used to be a common experience in midlife: now only 1 in 20 women aged 45 to 50 becomes widowed. Because a 50-year-old woman on the average expects to live another 30 years, there is a high probability of her being a widow part of that time. The likelihood of a middle-aged man being a widower is far smaller (1 in 1000). Widowhood is more common among women than among men, because women outlive men, tend to marry men who are older, and are less likely to remarry than widowed men.

The widowed share some of the life circumstances of the divorced. On the other hand, a widowed woman is less likely to suffer the economic setback of divorced women, because inheritance and death benefits offset the loss of the husband's income. Psychologically, grief rather than conflict, shame, and anger is the dominant feeling. Socially, death of a spouse rallies friends and relatives around; divorce generates mixed reactions or avoidance. A widowed man suffers the consequences of having lost his primary caretaker, sexual partner, and main link to friends; but if he has not retired, his work helps to sustain him (as is the case with working wives). He finds himself in high demand if he chooses to remarry, which most widowers do.

The loss of a spouse is a major source of stress. One-fifth of the widowed still show signs of depression after a year and a higher death rate for five years than the comparable age population; beyond that there is no difference in life expectancy (Parkes, 1964). Eventually, most widowed women and men resolve their grief and feel whole again.

## SEXUAL ACTIVITY AND SATISFACTION

Patterns of sexual activity are very much a part of the interpersonal relationships and the larger life circumstances of various marital states. Sex and reproduction have always been among the main reasons why people get married. Now that women are economically and socially more independent and psychologically more self-reliant, they are far more reluctant to barter their bodies for a roof over their heads. Similarly, men can now have sex with respectable women without having to marry them. Thus, the formula that marriage is the price men pay to get sex and sex is the price women pay to get married is no longer true.

However, the importance of sex in marriage and other stable relationships is not less but more important. Sexual satisfaction has become as much the woman's expectation as the man's. Moreover, marital status has a greater influence on the frequency and nature of sexual activity than any other social factor, especially for women.

### Marital Sex

People who get married are expected to make themselves sexually available to each other. A marriage that is not sexually consummated because either spouse is unable or unwilling to engage in coitus can be legally annulled. Similarly, a spouse's failure to be reasonably accommodating as a sexual partner is legal ground for divorce.

**Sexual Activity in Marriage**    Coitus is the predominant but not the only sexual outlet for married people; marital coitus accounted for 85 percent of orgasms of married males in the Kinsey sample. The remaining 15 percent was extramarital coitus, homosexual contacts, masturbation, nocturnal emissions, and other outlets (Kinsey et al., 1948, 1953). Individuals, of course, varied in this regard: some had only marital coitus; others had one or more additional outlets. For women younger than the middle thirties, the proportion of orgasms from conjugal sex was similar to those of mar-

ried men. For older women, other outlets became more prominent; by their late forties only slightly more than 70 percent of female orgasms were from marital coitus.

The frequency of marital coitus is usually taken by researchers not only as an index of the level of sexual activity (which is fair enough) but also as a reflection of the couple's sexual compatibility or sexual satisfaction. This use is questionable: it is not just the "quantity" of activity (which is easier to count) but the quality of the experience that counts. When we cite statistics, keep this consideration in mind.

The prominence of sex in marriage varies widely, as reflected in the frequency of coitus. The median frequency of marital coitus in the younger couples Kinsey surveyed was about three times a week and steadily declined with age. This pattern of decline in the frequency of marital coitus persists in subsequent studies, especially for the early years of marriage. For instance, in one survey the mean frequency of marital coitus was about 15 times a month during the first year of marriage. In the next two years it had gone down to about 12 times a month, and by the sixth year to slightly over 6 times a month (Greenblatt, 1983).

Marital sexual relations often follow a predictable pattern. After the first few years, the novelty, romance, and excitement wears off, with a sharp drop in sexual activity as spouses take each other for granted. The arrival of children and career pressures make competing demands on time and energy and put further pressures on the relationship. Conflicts and disenchantment with other aspects of the relationship also chip away at the sexual bond. The transitional period of midlife then leads either to further devitalization or a rekindling of the relationship in old age. Such changes can also be monitored in terms of the ages of the couples and sexual activity: average couples in their twenties and thirties engage in coitus two to three times a week; by middle age, once a week or less.

This pattern is not fixed by any means, and there is much individual variation among couples of all ages and in marriages of varying duration. Some couples rarely engage in coitus even when young; others do it often even in their older years.

A trend that also goes against the decline pattern is the greater likelihood of women experiencing orgasm in successive years of marriage. Among the Kinsey subjects, one in four women married for a year was inorgasmic during marital coitus; after 20 years only one woman in ten still had not experienced orgasm (Kinsey et al., 1953). Just as passionate love matures to companionate love, the quality of marital sex can also improve as it mellows.

Over the past two decades not only are couples generally engaging in sex more often, but their repertory of sexual activity has also expanded (Trussel and Westoff, 1980). For instance, there is greater use of oral sex in foreplay and varied coital postures. Among college-educated married men, the percentage engaging in cunnilingus went up from 45 percent among the Kinsey subjects to 66 percent in the Hunt report; in the high-school-educated group the increase was even more dramatic (15 percent to 56 percent). Similarly, whereas 52 percent of married college-educated women had engaged in fellatio, 72 percent did so in the later report, with less educated women showing a more modest increase from 46 percent to 52 percent (Kinsey et al., 1948, 1953; Hunt, 1974). Younger groups were more likely to show the effects of liberalization. These changes indicate a willingness on the part of couples to be more experimental and on the part of wives to be more active in marital sex.

Sexual Satisfaction in Marriage    Sexual satisfaction is harder to assess than sexual activity. The importance of sex in marriage varies: for some couples sex is the icing on the cake, for others its pivotal point, and for still others the sore spot in an otherwise compatible relationship. People who enjoy a harmonious relationship are more likely to share sexual pleasures, and a happy sex life endears people to each other. In other words, good sex makes a good marriage better, but poor sex makes a bad one worse. There is thus some truth to both contentions that sex between longtime partners

goes stale and that old knots get stronger with time (Box 17.2).

In the Hunt survey there was a close correlation between people rating their marriage "very close" and marital sex as "very pleasurable," as well as between the level of satisfaction with marital sex and the frequency of intercourse. Among women in the *Redbook* survey who were having marital sex 16 or more times a month, over 90 percent described their sex life as "good" or "very good"; when marital coitus was absent, 83 percent said their sex life was "poor" or "very poor." Still, an active sex life is no guarantee of sexual happiness: some 9 percent of those in the sexually active group were unhappy in their sex life; paradoxically, a similar percentage of women in the sexually inactive group expressed satisfaction with theirs (Levin and Levin, 1975b).

The study by Blumstein and Schwartz (1983) reconfirms this pattern. Almost 90 percent of husbands and wives who engage in coitus three times a week or more are satisfied with the quality of their sex life; just 32 percent of those who have sex once a week or less express equal satisfaction (Blumstein and Schwartz, 1983). It may work both ways: those who enjoy sex do it more; those who do it more get greater enjoyment. Because people's sexual needs vary, sexual satisfaction in marriage is more a matter of equal levels of sexual interest in husband and wife than of frequency.

There is a similar association between orgasm and sexual satisfaction: in the Levin and Levin (1975b) survey, 81 percent of the women who were regularly orgasmic considered sex in their marriage to be good as against 52 percent of those who were only occasionally orgasmic and 29 percent who never were orgasmic (or were uncertain about it).

Evidently, orgasm is not a perfect index of satisfaction, either. Some people scoff at reports that women enjoy sexual intercourse even when they do not reach orgasm, or prefer it that way. However, when Ann Landers (1985) asked her readers, "Would you be content to be held close and treated tenderly, and forget about the 'act'?" 72 percent of the 90,000 female respondents said they would;

# Box 17.2

## OLD KNOTS JUST GET STRONGER*

There is something perfect and easy about the embrace of a longtime lover. The arms slip easily through; left up, right down, whatever; the decisions have been made although not announced.

Noses and chins and foreheads and optical appliances sort themselves out without struggle or strain; planning is not required. You mesh like well-designed gears, you fold into each other like melted butter and sweet cream; you slide like otters through calm waters.

You kiss before you know that you are kissing. The impulse; the act; nothing between.

It is said that people who have been together for a long time begin to resemble one another. It is equally possible to believe that familiarity has bred natural bumps and hollows in the body. A concave spot in the shoulder, a certain crook of the elbow, a knee automatically bent to preserve equilibrium.

Made for each other.

Literally.

This is a song about Valentine's Day, but it is not a song about young love. The confusion about young love is immediate and complete; the confusion of old love is complete and eternal. The first mystery has been solved; it is the mystery beyond (more complex, more amusing, more satisfying) that rivets the attention now.

These are embarrassing matters. New love is not embarrassing, at least not to the new lovers. So heavily involved are they in private embarrassment—I didn't mean, I never thought, of course you, certainly you, a thousand times you—that public embarrassment fades into the wallpaper.

But eventually we swim up to consciousness again, and we become more circumspect. Compared to the volumes written about the first flush of passion, the words composed about longtime love would fill no more than a slim book.

A slim book with wide margins.

A slim book that soon finds its way to the bargain bins.

Affection informed by tolerance and patience is not a commercial emotion. Old friends and old lovers are valued privately, which is probably as it should be.

We get along; we go along; the ecstasy is implicit. Implicit ecstasy would seem to be paradox; the continuing experience, however, denies the apparent contradiction.

Then there is this moment in the longtime love affair: the moment of intellectual joy.

You have seen this person in every conceivable context. You have seen her (or him; you may freely substitute "or him") at her absolute worst. Also at her best. Also during the boring moments in between.

You have seen her sleeping, unaware, innocent, slack-mouthed. You have seen her awake, interested, bolt-upright, unself-conscious, eyes glittering, gathering information. You have seen her awkward and graceful; you have seen her reaping and sowing.

And just when you think you have discovered all the somethings about her, there is something else. Valentine's Day would be a stupid holiday, were it not for that.

Were it not for the unknown at the center of the known.

Were it not for the pulse of the blood under your hands.

Were it not for the embrace of the longtime lover.

*(Jon Carroll, *San Francisco Chronicle*, Feb. 14, 1986.)

---

and 40 percent who said so were younger than 40.

Do these women care less about sex than affection? Are they just settling for less? Or does sexual satisfaction mean different things to men and women?

## Extramarital Sex

Sex outside marriage may be *pre*marital, *extra*marital, *co*marital, or *post*marital. *Extramarital sex* is the neutral term behavioral scientists use for sexual relations between a married person and someone other than the spouse. *Adultery* ("to pollute"), the traditional term, is still used widely (including in the law); it implies wrongdoing. *Infidelity* ("being unfaithful") implies a breach of faith; *comarital sex* implies permission. Colloquial terms include "cheating," "double-timing," "having an affair," and so on.

Basically going outside an established relationship for sex is no different for married couples, cohabitants, or gay couples. Some researchers use the term *non-monogamous sex* to cover all these groups (Blumstein and Schwartz, 1983). Because the literature is based mainly on studies of married couples, we shall stick to the term "extramarital."

Patterns of Extramarital Sex  Cultures and individuals within them vary widely in the sexual freedom they allow to spouses. Conservative Moslem husbands do not allow men other than close relatives to look at their wives, whereas in some Eskimo groups, a man would include his wife in the hospitality extended to a visiting friend. Though most traditional moral codes prohibit adultery (Chapter 22) and laws of various strictness have tried to inhibit it, extramarital sex has gone on since marriage began. Cross-cultural attitudes towards extramarital sex strongly reflect the double standard. In a survey of world cultures (some long vanished), 63 percent of societies approved of it for the husband and 13 percent for the wife; and 23 percent disapproved for both (Broude, 1980).

In the United States, flirtation and limited physical contact with erotic overtones (such as dancing) are common, often public, and fairly well tolerated by spouses, especially among better educated groups. Such behavior does not amount to extramarital sex, as the term is commonly understood. Most people draw the line at sexual intercourse or at activities that typically lead to it.

Despite the liberalization of sexual attitudes, the majority of people in the United States continue to uphold fidelity as the sexual standard for married couples. Surveys typically show three out of four consider extramarital sex always wrong, others qualifying their judgment, and a small percent maintaining it is never wrong (Tavris and Sadd, 1978). Sexual jealousy in marriage continues to be a serious source of conflict (Reiss, 1986).

Extramarital coitus is usually a sporadic fling. One episode does not mean that a person has embarked on a pattern of extramarital relations (Blumstein and Schwartz, 1983). Of course, it can also be a regular behavioral pattern. It may be a primarily sexual encounter, like a "one-night stand," or an intensely emotional love affair. The sexual partners may be casual acquaintances, friends, friends of the spouse, business associates, or others (including prostitutes).

Relationships with extramarital partners are typically short-lived; but they can also be enduring and sometimes institutionalized. The *concubine* in ancient times had a formal status (Chapter 20). Later, the *mistress* fulfilled a similar role in an exclusive sexual relationship with a married man who supported her. Far less common today is the *kept man* retained by an older woman (or a homosexual lover). When the lover of either spouse lives with the couple it is called *ménage à trois* (French for "household of three"). These terms all have been replaced by more neutral terms like "lover" or "sexual partner."

Recently, a new pattern has emerged. Independent, professional, unmarried women have affairs with married men. Called the *new other woman* by sociologist Laurel Richardson (1986), such associations are one reaction to new social circumstances: an increasing number of women pursuing promising careers who do not want to get married (at least at the moment), nor to be entangled in a heavy romantic relationship, but do want intimate association with a man. Others are women trying to recover from divorce without getting reattached.

Sex is not the primary incentive for most of these women, but it usually becomes part of the relationship. Some, however, want to experiment sexually with safe and disposable lovers. The more important elements are relational—the companionship, the chance to share secrets, the mutual vulnerability and excitement.

Women who are satisfied with such relationships are able to keep them compartmentalized and retain control of their own role. With 233 single women for every 100 single men (not all of them interested in women) in the 40–44 age bracket, to have an intimate male friend who is attractive, successful, and fun to be with offers distinct advantages with none of the costs of a more conventional relationship. However, these relationships work to the woman's disadvantage if she falls in love with the man. As she becomes emotionally dependent on the relationship, her life comes to center more and more on his schedule for their meetings, and she yearns for the rewards of a stable and open relationship, which she cannot get (unless the man gets a divorce and marries her, which is rare). The "overwhelming majority" of 700 subjects told Richardson they would not advise any woman to get involved with a married man, even though some were veterans of a succession of such affairs.

We have no firsthand information about the married men who are involved with these "new other women" in Richardson's study: Who are they, why do they get involved, and what is the impact on their lives? There may be an underlying assumption that married men have affairs because they want to have the best of two worlds; the reality may be more complicated.

Patterns of Comarital Sex     Usually extramarital sex goes on without the prior knowledge or approval of the spouse. It can also be part of an understanding between spouses or even involve them both. To highlight the fact of mutual consent, these relations are called *comarital* since they do not exclude the spouse, or *consensual* since the spouse approves.

Traditionally wives, less often husbands, have tolerated extramarital relations by looking the other way. Even though persistent or repeated affairs are hard to conceal over time, a remarkable number of people still manage not to be aware of them. Other couples openly agree to allow each other the freedom to go outside the marital relationship for sex. They may or may not want to hear about it.

Such arrangements are usually conces-

sions or compromises. A man with serious potency problems may not want his wife to be deprived, or a man with low sexual interest married to a sexually charged woman may want to shift or share the "burden." More commonly, a wife will tolerate her husband's need for sexual variety because in other respects she is happy with him, or she cannot afford to disrupt the marriage.

In a more recent pattern, people who neither lack marital sex nor profess to be dissatisfied with their marital partners see monogamy as restricting their full development as individuals and as a couple. They establish an *open marriage* that by mutual consent does not exclude other intimate relations. These spouses feel loyal to their primary relationship; secondary relationships are permissible and desirable if they are not disruptive (Libby and Whitehurst, 1977; Knapp and Whitehurst, 1978).

The term "open marriage" as against the traditionally restrictive or "closed" variety was the title of a popular book by Nina and George O'Neill (1972). Though they focused on expanding nonsexual association to bring new sources of social and emotional enrichment to the couple, it was the possibility of extramarital sexual freedom that captured the popular imagination. In relationships where such freedom is granted, the term *sexually open marriage* makes it more explicit.

Some people see sexually open marriage as a travesty of the marital bond. If one is not going to be faithful to a spouse, why marry in the first place? Other people see it as a new phase in the evolution of marriage.

Do sexually open relationships work? Problems include jealousy, conflicts about ground rules, the role of the "secondary" partner, relationships with children, and so on (Watson and Whitlock, 1982). Yet no appreciable differences have been found in marital adjustment between open and sexually exclusive marriages (Rubin, 1982).

Extramarital sex can also occur as *spousal exchange*. Some cultures have practiced wife-lending either as a temporary accommodation for a visitor or as a longer-term exchange of

# Box 17.3

## SWINGING

Swinging typically involves two married couples exchanging partners to engage in sex. In some cases, a married couple swings by adding one other person of either sex or getting together with more people to engage in group sex. Typically, it is the husband who draws his wife into swinging with people they do not otherwise know or plan to become intimate with. A basic rule of swinging is not to become emotionally involved, and people usually conceal their true identities. Swinging also requires that participants have a low level of jealousy and not feel anxious or hurt by the partner's sexual involvement with another person (Harmatz and Navak, 1983).

Swingers are predominantly middle-class, white, married couples who otherwise lead fairly conventional lives. Hunt (1974) estimated that about 2 percent of married couples have tried swinging on at least one occasion. Many never repeat the experience; only a minority of these couples continues to swing occasionally. The *Redbook* survey found that about 4 percent had tried swinging, but half of them only once (Tavris and Sadd, 1977). Figures in these self-selected samples are probably higher than in the general population. The likelihood of couples experimenting with swinging may have further declined since the 1970s.

Couples get involved in swinging by stages. To begin with, they have a highly active interest in sex and the personal attitudes (low jealousy, liberal values) that are conducive to swinging. Couples then go through a passive phase of learning and talking about swinging, an active phase of making contact with other swingers, and a committed phase of participating in it.

Swingers locate prospective couples at swingers' clubs, through personal referral, and by advertising in underground papers and swinger magazines. After an exchange of pictures and preliminaries, the sexual encounter occurs at a motel or the home of one of the couples. The couples may switch partners and go to separate rooms (*closed swinging*) or engage in sexual encounters in the same room (*open swinging*). On these occasions or during group sex, homosexual contact is rare among males but common among females, who are often pressed into it by the men (Bartell, 1971; Gilmartin, 1977).

The primary justification offered for swinging is that it provides sexual variety for both partners in an open and safe form, free of deception. It is said to expand the sexual horizon of a marriage without threatening the primary relationship ("the family that swings together clings together") (Denfield and Gordon, 1970).

Yet swinging seems riddled with problems for many of its participants (Bartell, 1971; Talese, 1980). The requirement that it entail no emotional involvement, so as to make it safe for the primary relationship, makes these sexual encounters shallow and impersonal. They can also be anxiety-provoking. Women are likely to worry about the attractiveness of their bodies; men about their potency. Not to be wanted by anyone in a sexual free-for-all can be devastating. Then there are the practical problems of catching a sexually transmitted disease, fear of discovery, blackmail, and so on. Yet swinging continues to fuel a lot of fantasies even though they are fulfilled only some of the time.

---

spouses. For example, the Chukchee of Siberia, with the consent of their wives, made such reciprocal arrangements to allow themselves the comforts of home during their extended travels (Ford and Beach, 1951). A modern counterpart in our culture, though by no means a socially approved one, is *wife-swapping* or *swinging*, in which husband and wife participate together (Box 17.3).

Motivations    Unlike those who divorce, people who engage in extramarital sex are not giving up their marriage but trying to modify it sexually and emotionally. Extramarital sex is not just for sex, and sex is not necessarily its most rewarding part.

Though the desire for sexual variety or better sex has been a classic justification for extramarital sex, its physical satisfactions often seem to fall short. In the Hunt sample, 53 percent of women regularly reached orgasm with their husbands, but only 39 percent did so in extramarital coitus; only 7 percent of women never reached orgasm with their husbands, against 35 percent in extramarital affairs. Two-thirds of married males rated coitus with their wives as "very pleasurable," but fewer than half rated the extramarital experience as highly.

People seek experiences outside their marriage for a host of reasons. Some are compensatory: lengthy separations, chronic illness, lack of interest on the part of the spouse, or any other reason that makes sex no longer available within marriage prompts some to seek it elsewhere.

Under a second set of conditions, marital sex is available but unsatisfactory. Reasons include the effects of aging, the monotony of habit, mismatches in intensity of desire or in liking a particular form of sex, and the need for variety. Among the reasons women give, emotional dissatisfaction with the husband ranks highest at 72 percent; sexual dissatisfaction comes next at 46 percent (Grosskopf, 1983).

Extramarital sex can be retaliatory if it is motivated by anger and smoldering resentment. Close to 60 percent of the women in the study just cited say they did it to take revenge on the husband—35 percent after they found out the husband had an affair, 23 percent because of some other grievance. Men may also do it to settle similar scores.

The motivation may have developmental associations. Certain life phases seem to predispose people to turn to extramarital outlets. For instance, there may be an increased tendency for extramarital sex during the transition into middle age ("midlife crisis"), when the person tries to fulfill unresolved yearnings of youth "before it is too late," or hopes to magically avert the onslaught of age by clinging or regressing to youthful activities epitomized by sexual adventures. The birth of a child turns a woman into a mother, which sexually inhibits some men. If having an affair becomes the "in" thing to do among a group

of friends, peer pressure and the need to belong will impel some to go ahead who might not have otherwise.

Extramarital sex can be used to bolster self-esteem. To be sexually desired by the spouse is always good for the ego, but like being loved by parents, it comes to be expected. There is a temptation to test oneself in the sexual marketplace to see if the old magic still works. Each new sexual partner thus revalidates sexual worth. The sexually insecure are apt to go on obsessively seeking an endless string of lovers. The motivation for extramarital sex is like the more general wish to have multiple partners (Chapter 11). It may also include the use of extramarital sex as a source of income (many part-time prostitutes are married), or as a means of career advancement.

Often as not, those who engage in extramarital sex have no profound reasons to offer. They say they felt like doing it, were "seduced," or simply did not know why they did it. Thus, what motivates people in this regard is far from fully known (Thompson, 1983). Although some people are more prone than others to yield to temptation, opportunity also determines who will engage in extramarital sex. So far, men have had more chances than women. With career women having similar latitude in their travels and contacts, they too are taking more advantage of such opportunities: in the *Redbook* sample, 27 percent of full-time housewives have had extramarital sex, as against 47 percent of married women working outside the home (Levin, 1975c). These figures may reflect other differences between these two groups as well.

Prevalence    In the Kinsey sample, about half of married men and a quarter of women admitted that by age 40 they had had at least one extramarital affair. Like premarital coitus, it was generally irregular, occurring once every one to three months, and accounting for less than 10 percent of all orgasms.

More current findings show no change in the acceptability of extramarital sex, except for possibly higher rates for younger women. In the Hunt sample, half of married men and 20 percent of married women have had affairs by the time they reached 45 years. Female rates approach male rates in younger groups. The *Redbook* survey found that 38 percent of wives 35 to 39 years old had extramarital experience. The *Cosmopolitan* survey figures were even higher: half of wives 18 to 34 years old and over two-thirds of those 35 or older reported such experience. It would be necessary, however, to have more reliable evidence than magazine surveys to confirm this trend; such surveys reflect little more than the views of their readership. For example, a 1983 *Playboy* survey of its readership reports that by age 50 nearly 65 percent of wives have had affairs; a similar poll by the *Ladies Home Journal* reports only 21 percent. As a public pollster put it, "If *Reader's Digest* surveyed its readers, it would probably find that *nobody* had any extramarital affairs" (quoted in *Time,* Jan. 31, 1983, p. 80). The true prevalence is probably closer to the figures reported by Blumstein and Schwartz (1983), which show 26 percent of married men and 21 percent of married women to have engaged in extramarital sex.

Table 17.2 compares the percentage of men and women who have engaged in extramarital sex or its equivalent in other committed relationships during the first two years. The percentage for males is higher in every group, ranging from negligible sex differences among the married and cohabitors to a striking sex difference among homosexuals. Gay and cohabiting men are most likely and cohabiting women and lesbians are least likely to engage in coitus with someone other than their partner.

Effects    The effect of extramarital sex on marriage is even more difficult to assess than its prevalence, because it involves such varied motivations, forms, and ethical judgments. For example, a couple that allows each other sexual freedom is different from a couple whose dealings are veiled in deception or based on one spouse coercing the other into grudging tolerance. The effects of quietly supplementing marital sex with due regard to the sensibilities of the spouse are not the same as aggressively

**Table 17.2  Prevalence of Sex Outside a Committed Relationship (During the First Two Years)\***

| RELATIONSHIP | % SEEKING SEX WITH OTHERS |
|---|---|
| Married couples | |
|   Husbands | 15 |
|   Wives | 13 |
| Cohabitants | |
|   Men | 21 |
|   Women | 20 |
| Homosexual couples | |
|   Gay men | 66 |
|   Lesbians | 15 |
| Dating college couples | |
|   Men | 35 |
|   Women | 12 |

\*(Data for married, cohabiting, and homosexual couples from Blumstein and Schwartz (1983, p. 274). Data on college couples from Hansen (1987, p. 386). No information given for the period of dating; assumed to be less than two years for comparison.)

flaunting extramarital affairs to offend and humiliate. A person who gets involved after due thought differs from the uncontrollably driven individual who gets embroiled in one senseless liaison after another (Ellis, 1969; Neubeck, 1969).

Such contrasts are innumerable. To carry on an affair takes time, energy, and money. The impact of taking away resources from the spouse depends on how much reserve there is. To have an affair with a single person simplifies the logistics, such as finding a private place to meet, but can put more pressure on the marriage since the relationship is asymmetrical. Affairs between two married lovers double the scheduling difficulties and the chances of confronting an outraged mate. AIDS has added a potential threat to such relationships. At risk are not only one's own health and life but that of the spouse, and possibly of the children to be born into the family.

One of the classic justifications for extramarital sex is that it sustains marriages by tiding couples over difficult times. For instance, if one of the spouses feels shortchanged in the marriage, the opportunity to go outside may rectify the "balance" in that person's mind. Extramarital liaisons supposedly keep the marital relationship afloat as the couple sort out their problems.

Nevertheless, extramarital sex is a problematic and guilt-ridden activity for many of its participants. It takes time and energy away from the marital relationship. Its concealment causes anxiety and its discovery frequently endangers the marriage.

The discovery of a spouse's extramarital affair usually results in a marital crisis. The first reaction of the spouse is typically a sense of betrayal ("How could you do this to me?"). It may be followed by denial (looking the other way) or explaining away the betrayal through rationalization ("He/she didn't mean to hurt me"). Fear of abandonment may be counterbalanced by depression and anger. The actions that follow may lead to resignation, reconciliation, and rebuilding of the relationship, or to its breakup (Dolesh and Lehman, 1985). An occasional indiscretion may leave a scar but not compromise the marriage; repeated transgressions are harder to tolerate, unless the couple redefine their expectations of each other or the injured party takes action (such as having an affair too).

It could be argued that these liabilities need not exist: if there is no deception, there need be no guilt. Husbands need not feel cuckolded, nor wives deceived, if extramarital relations cease to reflect on the spouse's desirability as a lover. Perhaps if society changed its rules, there would be no penalties to pay.

What if we are not dealing here with arbitrary rules? What if there are irreconcilable conflicts between primary affectionate bonds and their dissipation in secondary sexual relationships? How would a change in societal values then allow a compromise between these competing tendencies? Should we opt for truly open marriages, or listen to Francine du Plessix Gray (1977): "I believe that both the discipline of fidelity and a measured use of the untruth offer more alternatives for the future than the brutal sincerity of open marriage."

There are important social considerations with respect to extramarital sex (Chapter 22). Adultery as a breach of marital trust is a common ground for divorce in most cultures, but such violations are not defined uniformly. For instance, the Old Testament definition of adultery is having sex with someone else's wife, not with just any woman. The general condemnation of extramarital sex no doubt stops some people who would engage in it otherwise: 80 to 90 percent of couples found infidelity objectionable, and most of these couples refrained from extramarital sex because it was "sinful," "wrong," and "dishonest" (as well as out of fear of disease and pregnancy). On the other hand, the fact that people regularly attend church or synagogue does not seem to make it less likely that they will have extramarital sex (Blumstein and Schwartz, 1983).

Punishments for adultery in various cultures have tended to be quite severe, especially for the woman. The biblical practice of stoning the woman to death has its counterparts in other cultures (Box 22.3). Although penalties for adultery are often cast in moral terms, the offense is basically perceived as a violation of the husband's property rights, a challenge to his manhood and social standing ("honor"). Although penalties for adultery still exist in American law, they are rarely invoked nowadays (Chapter 22).

## Cohabiting Couples

In some respects, the sexual behavior of cohabiting couples is similar to that of married couples. However, cohabiting couples tend to be more liberal in their sexual attitudes and less conventional than married people. They usually do not have children, and other considerations may set them apart.

Cohabitants have had greater and earlier sexual experience than others. In general, they are no more or less monogamous in their relationships than married couples, according to some studies (Newcomb, 1986).

In the Blumstein and Schwartz (1983) study, cohabitants engaged in sex somewhat more frequently than married couples: among those who had been together for less than two years, 61 percent of cohabitants and 45 percent of spouses engaged in coitus one to three times a week. Cohabitants were also somewhat more likely than spouses to have sex with people outside the relationship (Table 17.2).

## Nonmarital Sex

How is sex different for people outside committed relationships? The main difference is the absence of a steady sexual partner with whom to share other aspects of life.

Although they do not live with someone, some men and women may maintain a stable sexual relationship with a sexual partner, either exclusive or supplemented by other occasional sexual contacts. Many people now confine themselves to a small group of friends, with whom they have sex on a random or rotating basis. This arrangement provides greater protection against sexually transmitted diseases and AIDS, provided all the participants are healthy to begin with and restrict their sexual contacts to the group.

Those without steady sexual partners are confronted with finding one. Potential partners may be found in the workplace, through mutual interests, or through mutual friends. Other people look for them in singles clubs, bars, and other locations where unattached men and women meet.

The participants in the social activities of singles clubs sponsored by religious institutions, alumni clubs, and other social organizations tend to be middle-aged divorced men and women. The emphasis in these settings is more on companionship and the chance to meet potential mates than on sexual contact. Cruises and other travel activities involve the more affluent; ski resorts and organizations like Club Med appeal to younger crowds. For some people, the prospect of meeting others is incidental to the activity; others use them primarily to meet people.

Single men and women also try to make contacts through dating services and "personal ads" in various and specialized magazines. Here are some examples:

*Bright, Beautiful, 52!* Working in financial product sales. M.A. Degree, former stewardess. 5'7", brown hair, blue eyes, good figure. Looking for man 50 +, who is volitional, vocal, virile, versatile, virtuous, vivacious, vulnerable.

*Best of Both Worlds.* Are you healthy, wealthy, and wise, married to your work, but missing something special? This bright, attractive, medium-build, sensual, 28, brunette, student and struggling writer seeks a special generous gentleman for weekly meetings of warmth and friendship.

*Tall, Attractive Male* professional, 33, sincere, friendly, sense of humor, part-time parent to an eight-year-old daughter. Variable interests that include "The Far Side," aerobic dance, BMWs. Interested in meeting someone with similar qualities.

The singles bar is frequented more by those pursuing a "swinging singles" lifestyle and exemplifies the "sexual marketplace" in one of its starker forms. Although a good deal of socializing takes place at these bars and not everyone is there with sex in mind, their primary purpose is to bring together potential sexual partners (Figure 17.7). The young and the not so young (the elderly do not have much of a chance), the unmarried and those pretending to be unmarried, those searching for sex and those for love come together in singles bars to check and sort each other out.

Singles bars are an efficient way for persons with similar sexual interests to meet each other; but the promise they hold often falls short of expectations. Sooner or later, women (sooner) and men (later) get tired of being on view (the "meat rack"). The risk of AIDS has now added real danger to the sexual encounters offered in these impersonal settings.

**The Never Married**    Younger adults in their twenties who are in the "premarital" phase of their lives are open to sexual experience and for potential mates. Their assets as sexual partners are their youthful looks, energy, liberal attitudes, and their claim on the future; their

Figure 17.7    Singles bar.

liabilities are lack of sexual experience, limited resources, and sometimes immaturity.

If still single by middle age, these men and women may have withdrawn from active sexual involvements (assuming they ever developed them) or settled into a more stable pattern of sexual intimacy with one or more friends. A few others keep up their youthful pace, or pretend to. Older singles are more cautious in their sexual engagements, and some opt for celibacy.

The Divorced    The majority of men and women in the Hunt (1974) sample had resumed sexual relations within a year after their divorce. It is not unusual for some men and women to plunge into an active sex life right after divorce. The incentive is not just sexual pleasure (though they may be making up for past deprivations) but to obtain psychological release of pent-up tensions and to reaffirm their freedom and their sexual desirability. The divorced as a group tend to be sexually more active than other singles. They have had the predisposition to marry, the ability to attract a mate, and the experience of a steady and active sex life. All of these factors lead to a sustained interest in sex and remarriage.

Divorce, however, can also lead to a decline in sexual activity. In the study just cited, 36 percent of the women and 27 percent of the men reported less active sex lives after the breakup of their marriage. Some of the reasons are practical. Unlike the never married, the divorced are not free; there are often children to attend to, limited financial resources, and a lack of desirable partners—problems that more often affect women than men. The psychological effects of the divorce are no less binding. Anger, shame, guilt, and regret may all interfere with the desire to resume sexual relations.

Divorced women are under greater pressure to engage in sex, even with casual acquaintances or on first dates. They may not yield to it and resent the "easy lay" image; but given the relative scarcity of eligible men, some may feel obliged to compromise.

Another common problem for both divorced men and women who are somewhat older is to be able to reenter the dating game. After being married for 10 or 20 years, not only are they out of practice making contacts and negotiating sex, but the rules of the game may have also changed.

The Widowed    The widowed share many of the assets and liabilities of the divorced in reestablishing sexual relationships and finding another mate, if they so desire. Mourning and lingering loyalty to the dead spouse may inhibit some widowed men and women from resuming their sex lives. Some never do, but the majority of widowers and almost half of widows eventually engage in postmarital coitus (Gebhard, 1968) even though far fewer are likely to find another spouse.

## Celibacy

*Celibate* originally meant "unmarried," but in modern usage it refers to anyone who refrains from sexual relations, or more strictly defined, from all forms of sexual experience. An old-fashioned synonym, *chaste,* implies moral considerations.

There are two broad categories of celibacy: *religious celibacy* ("sacerdotal celibacy"), exemplified by the vows of chastity of Catholic priests, monks, and nuns; and *secular celibacy,* refraining from sex temporarily or permanently for personal reasons. It is with the latter category that we are concerned here.

Most celibate people refrain from sex because they do not have acceptable partners. Many other women lead sexually inactive lives because of the scarcity of eligible men. Men are more often held back by illness and problems of sexual potency. With young adults, absti-

nence is more often elective. Some men and women prefer to wait until they are married or fall in love, or until the right person and the right circumstances come together. It is not unusual for some people to feel not yet ready to engage in a sexual relationship, without knowing why. Others decide that sexual relationships are too distracting, risky, and troublesome. They may have more absorbing interests, or wish to lead quiet lives. Casual sex may seem distasteful or dangerous, more intense attachments too burdensome. They believe they can get more out of their relationships by keeping sex out of them.

Celibacy can also reflect more negative reasons for rejecting sex. Those who feel sexually unattractive may want to avoid the humiliation of not being wanted. Others, who have been hurt in love affairs, want to avoid repetition of the experience. It is not unusual for rape victims to shun sex until they feel whole again. Those who suffer from sexual dysfunction may decide to give up the struggle. The inability to initiate or sustain sexual relations may be a facet of more basic failures in the capacity for intimacy.

Modern perceptions of sex as a good thing have tended to cast all forms of celibacy in a negative light. "The Victorian nice man or woman was guilty if he or she did experience sex," says Rollo May. "Now we feel guilty if we don't" (May, 1969). There is a growing perception that we have inflated the importance of sex in human relations, that overemphasis is detrimental to broader human ties and eventually to the full enjoyment of sex itself. A new form of celibacy is said to be emerging—people do not basically reject sex but forgo it for a while to regain perspective, to deepen their personal relationships, to attend to other neglected aspects of their lives, or even to become rejuvenated sexually (Brown, 1980).

The rapid changes in the status and self-perception of women have also generated some hesitancy. Now that the "old rules" of sexual interaction have become suspect, some people want to "wait and see." Once again, the universals in human sexuality are meeting cultural realities and finding new expression.

## REVIEW QUESTIONS

1. What changes have occurred since the 1960s in age at first marriage, the rate of marriage, and the respective ages of couples getting married?

2. What considerations enter into the selection of mates?

3. How does cohabitation compare to marriage in the advantages and disadvantages to the man, the woman, and the relationship?

4. What do the life circumstances of the never married, divorced, and widowed have in common, and how do they differ?

5. Compare the sexual activity and levels of satisfaction in people of different marital status.

## THOUGHT QUESTIONS

1. Despite the shortcomings and unpredictable outcome, why do people continue to get married in such large numbers? Why has cohabitation not replaced marriage?

2. Should a college student become the lover of an older married man or woman?

3. Should unhappy couples stay together because of the children?

4. How should a college woman plan to combine career and family and negotiate her expectations with a potential mate?

5. How could sexual interest and satisfaction in committed relationships be kept active over time?

## SUGGESTED READINGS

Blumstein, P., and Schwartz, P. (1983). *American couples.* New York: Morrow. An extensive investigation of the relationships of married, cohabiting, and gay couples, including their sexual interactions. A clear writing style, excellent charts, and excerpts from interviews make this massive volume highly readable.

Reiss, I. L. (1980). *Family systems in America,* 3rd ed. New York: Holt, Rinehart and Winston. A detailed but informative and interesting text on family systems by a sociologist with a special interest in sexuality.

Scarf, M. (1987). *Intimate partners.* New York: Ballantine. An insightful and interesting look at marriages and how to make them work.

Schickel, R. (1981). *Singled out: A civilized guide to sex and sensibility for a suddenly single man or woman.* New York: Viking. A slim volume, witty and urbane, to guide the recently divorced.

# Sexual Exploitation

CHAPTER

# 18

*Pornography manifests itself in some form in every society . . .*
        *MARGARET MEAD*

OUTLINE

THE VALUATION OF SEX
The Sexual Value of the Person
The Value of Emotional
    Commitment
Fair Exchange
    Informed Consent
    Symmetry of Status
Gender Considerations
PROSTITUTION
Types of Prostitutes
    Female Prostitutes
    Homosexual Prostitutes
Prevalence
Psychosexual Aspects
    Why Women Become Prostitutes
Consequences
    Risks for the Client
    Risks for the Prostitute
    Effects on Society
PORNOGRAPHY
The Problem of Definition
    The Criterion of Explicitness
    Literary and Artistic Criteria

Political Criteria
The Nature of Pornographic
    Materials
The Economics of Pornography
The Problem of Consequences
    Potential Harm
    Potential Benefits
    Pornography as Socially Insignificant
The Problem of Censorship
SEX AND ADVERTISING
Advertising to Sell Sex
    Selling Sexual Products
    Selling Sexual Services
Sex to Sell Advertising
    Attention-Getting
    Sexual Innuendo
    Sexual Symbolism
    Sexual Modeling
Effects of Sex in Advertising
    Potential Benefits
    Potential Harm

One of the most common terms of condemnation nowadays is *exploitation*. The accusation may be aimed at remote nations, at amorphous social groups, or at individuals who are dear and near. It is an accusation rarely acknowledged by the accused as valid, especially where sexual transactions are concerned.

The term "to exploit" has several distinct meanings. The ones that concern us have both a positive and negative cast. In its positive sense, to exploit is to take maximum advantage of a situation, especially by performing a brilliant or heroic deed. In its negative sense, it means to use another person selfishly or unethically. In other words, exploitation has connotations of both fair use and abuse. Because sex can be thought of as a personal asset, we need to examine first how it is valued; then we can determine its fair use and abuse.

## THE VALUATION OF SEX

Assessing a person's sexual worth sounds like putting a price tag on people, which is demeaning. However, not all values are measured in monetary terms. Even if that were the case, it would not be such an outlandish idea. Like so many other services, sexual favors are in fact often assessed in monetary terms—most directly in prostitution.

Appearances can be misleading in this regard. For instance, in a variety of cultures the bride's family requires payment of a *bride price* by the groom or his family upon marriage. Such payment is not to "buy" the bride but part of a series of exchanges between families at marriage. It may compensate the bride's family for the economic loss of the productive labor of a member of the family. Conversely, where the bride brings a *dowry* to the husband in the form of money or property, it does not mean that the man is being bribed into marrying her (although money may sometimes be used to "sweeten" the deal).

Although such practices are not common in the United States, the prospect of economic advantage remains a significant motivation in whom we associate with intimately. A person's financial "worth" and earning capacity are for many people an important aspect of his or her eligibility as a mate. They look for the "best deal" or at least a fair exchange.

Such considerations play an important part in our sexual interactions and intimate relationships as well. As we discussed in Chapter 16, by a process of sorting out, couples become matched more or less evenly, or have their different assets and liabilities compensate for each other. The extent to which such considerations enter sexual choices varies from cynical calculation to romantic abandon.

## The Sexual Value of the Person

At the most basic level what each of us brings to a sexual interaction is our body and personality. Judgments of a potential sexual partner's desirability are two-fold: physical attractiveness and psychological qualities. The net effect, the person's *sex appeal* (Chapter 16), includes how sexy we look, how effective we are as sexual partners, and how motivated we are to interact sexually with a given partner. As we discussed earlier (Chapter 16) sexual attraction is not synonymous with physical attractiveness. You do not have to be good-looking, young, and athletic to be sexually desirable. At some level or other, everyone is sexually attractive to someone.

A second value consideration is the uses to which the body is put. There is no "charge" for just looking; but to earn the right to gaze into someone's eyes (without being offensive) you must be quite intimate with that person. To see the body in various degrees of undress requires further gradations of intimacy. A similar range exists with respect to touching: handshakes, casual hugs and kisses, erotic kisses, necking, petting, oral sex, and sexual intercourse have quite different relational requirements. In this progression, there is a switch from being passive, letting someone do things to you, to being active, reciprocating in kind. The latter carries a higher value for most people.

When dealing with a prostitute who is clearly in the business of selling sex, there is an explicit price schedule for all activities, which is determined by the "class" of the prostitute and the particular sexual services offered. In less blatantly commercial sexual interactions, the compensation to the person whose sexual favors are being sought may take many forms, such as expensive gifts, favors in the workplace, or some other tangible benefit.

When friendship and love characterize a sexual relationship, sex and affection become inseparable. However, the relationship may become the "price" paid for the sexual favor (Chapter 16). This reasoning is carried by some to the point where even a traditional marital relationship is seen as a form of barter. As Betty Dodson puts it,

> Saving sex for my lover/husband was my gift to him in exchange for economic security—called meaningful relationship or marriage.... With that romanticized image of sex, in a society that does not have economic equality between the sexes, I was forced to bargain with my cunt for any life of financial security. Marriage under these circumstances is a form of prostitution (Talese, 1980, pp. 577–578).

Biologically, the primary value of the body is its reproductive use. To have a child with someone has traditionally required the most intense emotional and formal commitment. Many of our moral and legal codes have been based on confining this prerogative to committed and socially approved relationships like marriage (Chapters 22 and 23).

Much has changed in this regard. A great many divorced men and women participate in the raising of the spouse's children from a previous marriage. An even more dramatic development is the complete decoupling of the reproductive function of the body from its sexual and relational associations. The man who sells his sperm for the artificial insemination of a woman is basically selling part of his reproductive capital. The surrogate mother who, for a fee, carries the child of a man whose wife cannot conceive and then gives the baby to the couple is also selling part of her reproductive capital as well as "renting" her uterus for the duration of the pregnancy (Chapter 6). Such services may or may not be legitimate, ethical, or altruistic; but because they involve money, they raise the question of reproductive value in a most direct way.

## The Value of Emotional Commitment

The value of sex is at least as much a function of its emotional components as it is of its bodily component. Who you are as an individual is often more critical than the shape of your body.

It is far more difficult to place a price tag on emotional value. Love, respect, and affection cannot be broken down into units like sexual services. As a result, the interaction of lovers on the emotional plane is more difficult to assess, and it is harder to determine whether or not it is exploitative.

## Fair Exchange

Paying and getting paid for goods and services is the basis of modern economic life. Simply because there are economic advantages to a sexual association does not make it exploitative. Setting aside for the moment the issue of monetary payment for sexual services, what would determine whether or not sex is exploitative? What are the ingredients of fair dealing and fair exchange in sexual interactions?

Informed Consent  You are responsible for your own actions; but if your consent is going to be meaningful, it must be given freely and on the basis of adequate information. You must know fully what you are getting into. To coerce someone into sexual intercourse is exploitative because it lacks the freely given consent of the partner. Not to tell a sexual partner that you have a genital infection or the AIDS virus or are married is exploitative because the partner's consent is not informed.

All dealings with children are generally considered sexual exploitation, because they are not mature enough to give informed consent. The same may be true for sexual interactions with the mentally handicapped or mentally ill (although special considerations may prevail in those cases). People whose judgments are temporarily clouded by alcohol or drugs are also unable to give informed consent.

Symmetry of Status   Exploitation is largely a function of who has power. Not everyone who has power uses it exploitatively, but you can hardly exploit another without having an advantage over that person or something to offer that the person wants. It follows that the more equal two people are, the less the danger of exploitation.

Discrepancy in status may be determined by many factors. One is age: the young are dependent on and vulnerable to adults, which is another reason why they are not appropriate sexual partners. Another is gender. When women are considered to be socially inferior to men, they cannot be full-fledged sexual partners without being vulnerable to exploitation. A third factor is role. Physicians and patients, lawyers and clients, teachers and adult students, and similar associations often entail close relationships. In each case there is a special purpose to the association. To introduce a sexual element is unprofessional, because it interferes with the primary purpose of the interaction. There is a difference between a doctor's examining a woman's breast and fondling it, or performing a rectal examination on a man and anal stimulation.

The clients of lawyers may be vulnerable in other ways. If your chances of staying out of jail or getting a fair settlement depend on how effectively you will be represented in court, you are clearly in an unequal position. Similarly, a professor exercises considerable power over the student by determining the grade in a course and by writing recommendations. With graduate students, the professor has even more power over careers.

Asymmetry of status sets the stage for sexual harrassment, which we shall discuss in the next chapter. But simply because a sexual interaction occurs between two persons with different power does not in itself prove the relationship exploitative. You are certainly entitled to be attracted to and love someone with more or less power, as long as the power differential is not used exploitatively. If so, it is best to pursue the personal relationship after the professional association has ended. Under these circumstances, happy unions between bosses, doctors, lawyers, professors, and their former employees, patients, clients, or students are certainly possible.

## Gender Considerations

So far we have maintained a fairly gender-neutral stance in examining these issues. The realities are far from gender-neutral. There are significant differences in what men and women confront in these areas. They are important in the rest of this chapter.

First, traditionally and still to a considerable extent, the female body is the erotic object and women are the "sellers" and men the "buyers" of sexual services when they are offered outside of intimate relationships. On the other hand, in situations like prostitution, pornography, or advertising women rarely "sell" independently. It is men who organize, run, and primarily benefit from such commerce.

Second, traditionally and still to a considerable extent men control society by making and enforcing its rules. Even though an individual woman may exercise great influence on an individual man and may use her power exploitatively, when we speak of exploitation in the aggregate, it is primarily men who are in a position to exploit women.

Third, men and women have somewhat different needs and expectations of sexual interaction. As we discussed earlier (Chapter 16), women generally place a higher value on the relational aspects of sexual relationships and a lesser value on its physical components than men do. Therefore in effecting a fair exchange, the "currency" used by the two sexes is not always the same. Unless there is an equitable way to convert these "currencies" to a common unit of shared goals, men and women are likely to find their interests sometimes at odds. Whoever prevails in these conflicts is likely to be seen by the other as being exploitative.

Let us turn to three areas where the issue

of fair use and abuse of sexual assets calls for significant personal and social choices.

## PROSTITUTION

Roman law defined *prostitution* (Latin, "to expose publicly") as the offering of one's body for sale, indiscriminately and without pleasure (*passim et sine dilectu*). This definition has by and large stood the test of time. More simply stated, prostitution is engaging in sex for money.

Prostitution is a complex institution with ancient roots ("the world's oldest profession") that has taken many forms in various cultures. We discuss the historical, social, and legal aspects in Chapters 20–23. Our concern at this point is with its common forms and interpersonal aspects.

Sex with prostitutes represents, in principle, nonrelational sex in its starkest form. The prostitute provides sex with no questions asked; the client pays for it with no further obligations. Typically, the encounter takes place once only. In practice, those who go to prostitutes often have other, more personal

needs, and a relational component can develop. Occasionally, long-term relationships are established with prostitutes, some leading to marriage (Young, 1970).

### Types of Prostitutes

A prostitute (*hooker, whore*) is usually a woman who sells her sexual services to men. Male prostitutes usually cater to homosexual men (Chapter 13). Very few women buy the sexual favors of men or of other women. The *gigolo* (French, "dance-hall pick-up") is a young man who lives with older women, providing companionship and sometimes sex in exchange for financial support.

**Female Prostitutes**   Female prostitutes operate in several modes, but the services they provide and the nature of the relationship with the customer (called the "John") are basically the same. The *streetwalker* solicits men in public places such as streets, and B-girls do the same in bars (Figure 18.1); sex takes place in a hotel room, house, car, or some other secluded spot. A streetwalker's fee is usually in the $10 to $50 range, but she may settle for what she can get.

Figure 18.1   Streetwalkers in New York City with potential customers.

Figure 18.2  The "presentation" in a legal Nevada brothel.

Most of her earnings are taken over by her pimp.

A *housegirl* works in a *brothel* ("whorehouse," "cathouse," "bordello," "house of pleasure") along with other prostitutes. They are supervised by a *madam* (usually an older woman) who runs the operation. (The madam of one of Nevada's brothels reportedly was the former manager of graduate housing at a major university.) In their heyday, the top-flight brothels were luxuriously furnished and elaborately run establishments catering to many tastes (Murphy, 1983).

At present, the only legal brothels in the United States are a cluster of houses and trailers in sparsely populated areas of Nevada (Chapter 22). Typically, a dozen or so licensed women work in each of these establishments. The method of operation has long been standardized. As a customer walks in, the available women line up; the man makes his choice and the couple retreats to a room to engage in sex (Figure 18.2). The women split their earnings with the brothel owner. Even then, a successful prostitute may earn as much as $100,000 a year. Until recently, some three

dozen of these brothels housed over 300 prostitutes, generating a $15 million a year business. With the AIDS scare, their clientele has declined sharply, even though the women get monthly checkups and insist on their clients wearing condoms (Swan, 1986).

Depending on the level of public tolerance, prostitutes also use a variety of guises and institutional fronts. For instance, *massage parlors, escort services, sex clubs,* and so on offer various sexual services (legitimate massage establishments now advertise their services as "nonerotic massage"). Massage parlors may provide a variety of sexual services, the simplest of which is masturbation (called a "local"). Women who provide such services are called *hand whores* (Talese, 1980). Prostitutes may also provide a wide range of specialized sexual activities that cater to the needs of paraphiliacs such as sadomasochists (Chapter 14).

*Call girls* are the elite of the profession. These women are usually attractive, stylishly dressed, and socially sophisticated. They live in fashionable apartments but usually conduct their business in hotels. They may operate on their own or through a referral, or call-girl service (Barrows and Novak, 1987). They charge hundreds of dollars for their services.

The personal and professional relationship of prostitutes with their employers varies. Streetwalkers usually work for a *pimp,* who runs a "stable" of women (Figure 18.3). The *panderer* (or procurer) works as a broker who tries to match prostitutes and clients. The pimp sometimes but not always acts as the panderer. The pimp offers his women protection, procures customers, provides a measure of sexual and social companionship, and gives a sense of belonging. In exchange, he takes most of their earnings. The relationship may be voluntary, but typically it is highly coercive, with the pimp using psychological enticement, intimidation, drugs, and physical violence to control the women.

The pimp may keep as much as 95 percent of a woman's earnings after expenses (Young, 1970). He typically dresses in extravagant clothes and drives fancy cars. Though women typically have little choice in turning over their earnings to the pimp, some lavish all they have on him because they are emotionally attached to him and take pride in keeping their "man" in high style.

Prostitutes who work in brothels can do better, sharing about half their earnings with the brothel owner or manager. However, at least in the past, women have been virtual prisoners in these houses. The call girl, who

relies on referral agencies for customers, comes closest to being self-employed (Esselstyn, 1968).

The definition of prostitution is sometimes expanded to encompass other sexual relationships for financial gain. Expensive gifts that men give their girlfriends in indirect exchange for sexual favors are thought by some to represent more subtle forms of prostitution. When a woman has an exclusive sexual relationship with a man (who may be married) and is supported by him, she is known as his *mistress* (or *kept woman*). Such associations may also be based on love, with the economic support the man provides incidental to the relationship. Where to draw the line is hard to know.

Homosexual Prostitutes     Homosexual prostitutes are virtually all male and are called *hustlers* (or "trade") (Figure 18.4). Lesbians rarely sell or buy sex. Generally quite young, gay prostitutes fall into four categories: full-time street and bar hustlers, full-time call boys or kept boys, part-time hustlers, and juvenile delinquents who use prostitution as an extension of other illegal acts like robbery or selling drugs (Drew and Drake, 1969; Allen, 1980).

Street hustlers often deny being gay and pretend to be in the business for the money only. To reinforce their claim of being straight, they may have girls tagging along. They may also consent only to certain forms of sex, such as being the inserter in anal intercourse. Typically, they perform fellatio on the client.

Hustlers work in known locations and often are picked up by men in cars; or they may make contact in bars and other public locations. Rechy (1963, 1977) provides insightful portrayals of the life of hustlers (Box 18.1).

*Male models* or *call boys* more readily admit being gay. Like the street hustlers, they bank on their youth and good looks. Masculine appearance and large ("well-hung") genitals are important selling points.

Call boys may work through matchmaking agencies, which may simply transmit phone messages or provide more elaborate services, such as rooms or entire male brothels with specialized sexual services.

Figure 18.3   A pimp and prostitutes who work for him.

Figure 18.4   Gay hustlers in New York's Times Square area.

## Prevalence

Prostitution is illegal in the United States except for the state of Nevada (subject to provisions discussed in Chapter 22). Because it is hidden and takes many forms it is difficult to know how many prostitutes there are in the country and how many clients they service.

Arrest records suggest that at least 100,000 women work as prostitutes on a more or less full-time basis (Sheehy, 1973). Only the most visible and vulnerable streetwalkers are likely to get arrested, so the true figure may be five times as large.

Estimating the number of part-time prostitutes is virtually impossible. A housewife, unemployed single woman, or student may work at it for a short period to tide over a financial crisis. Others see a few regular clients over longer periods. Still others avail themselves of opportunities that come their way without seeking them out. A prostitute's earnings may provide a means of survival, support for a luxurious lifestyle, or pocket money.

A particularly disturbing aspect of prostitution is the sexual exploitation of teenagers and children of both sexes. Of the estimated 20,000 runaways aged 16 in New York City, many end up working for some 800 pimps who use persuasion, drugs, coercion, and violence to keep them under their control. In Los Angeles alone there may be as many as 3,000 girls and boys under the age of 14 who are engaged in prostitution. Even small towns have their young prostitutes, some of whom live at home and "turn tricks" for pocket money.

A successful prostitute will have sexual encounters with thousands of men over the years. Assuming that a full-time prostitute averages 10 to 20 clients a week, the men using the services of prostitutes during a week would number several millions. Some 70 percent of males in the Kinsey sample reported having

# Box 18.1

## THE HUSTLER*

There is a terrific, terrible excitement in getting paid by another man for sex. A great psychological release, a feeling that this is where real sexual power lies—not only to be desired by one's own sex but to be paid for being desired, and if one chooses that strict role, not to reciprocate in those encounters, a feeling of emotional detachment as freedom—these are some of the lures; lures implicitly acknowledged as desirable by the very special place the male hustler occupies in the gay world, entirely different from that of the female prostitute in the straight. Even when he is disdained by those who would never pay for sex, he is still an object of admiration to most, at times an object of jealousy. To "look like a hustler" in gay jargon is to look very, very good.

\* \* \*

Outside of a busy coffee shop where hustlers gather in clusters throughout the night, an older man in a bright new car parked and waited during a recent buyers' night. Young men solicited anxiously in turns, stepping into the car, being rejected grandly by him, stepping out, replaced by another eager or desperate young man. Smiling meanly, the older man—one of that breed of corrupted, corrupt, corrupting old men—turned down one after the other,

finally driving off contemptuously alone, leaving behind raised middle fingers and a squad of deliberately rejected hustlers—some skinny, desolate little teenagers among the more experienced, cocky, older others; skinny boys, yes, sadly, progressively younger, lining the hustling streets; prostitutes before their boyhood has been played out, some still exhibiting the vestiges of innocence, some already corrupted, corrupt, corrupting—an increasing breed of the young, with no options but the streets—which is when it is all mean and ugly, when it is not a matter of choice; wanted for no other reason than their youth, their boyhood . . . And yet, later that very night, I met a man as old as the contemptuous other one—but, this one, sweet, sweet, eager to be "liked," just liked, desperate for whatever warmth he might squeeze out, if only in his imagination, in a paid encounter, eager to "pay more"—to elicit it—simply for being allowed to suck a cock. . . . Hustling is all too often involved in mutual exploitation and slaughter, of the young and the old, the beautiful and the unattractive.

*From Rechy, J., *The sexual outlaw*. New York: Grove Press, 1977, pp. 153—154.

---

had at least one contact with a prostitute (the rates being inversely proportional to level of education). The Hunt (1974) survey showed a marked decrease in the proportion of males who were sexually initiated by prostitutes or had sex with them, and the average frequency with which they did so. Thus the estimated use of prostitutes by single males in the 1970s appears to be no more than half as widespread as it was in the 1940s. Whereas in the past, many men were sexually initiated by prostitutes, they are now more likely to have their first sexual experience with a peer. This change is ascribed to the greater sexual freedom in recent years.

## Psychosexual Aspects

The phrase *turning a trick* succinctly summarizes the bare-bones minimum that sex with prostitutes is supposed to be: a man pays the fee, ejaculates, goes on his way. The men who seek prostitutes are often reduced to a few basic stereotypes: men who are away from home (sailor on shore leave, traveling salesman) or men who cannot find desirable partners because they are sexually unattractive, shy, sexually incompetent, dysfunctional, or "kinky."

The women also are stereotyped. In literature there is the "whore with the golden heart," a delightful woman as kind as she is voluptuous. Despite the hardships of her life, love remains paramount for her. John Cleland's *Memoirs of a Woman of Pleasure* (1749), popularly known as *Fanny Hill*, is a good example of this genre (Box 18.2). By contrast, the whore of demonic power dominates and

# Box 18.2

## PORNOTOPIA

From his study of the Victorian pornographic novel, Steven Marcus characterizes the sexual fantasies expressed in pornographic novels as utopian. He calls them *pornotopia*—a vision that regards all human experience as a series of exclusively sexual events or considerations. Pornotopia has no historical or other reality; it occurs at no particular place or time. The participants have no identity or self outside of their narrowly defined sexual roles; people are reduced to their sexual organs and orifices.

The principal object in the world of pornotopia has been the female body, or whatever parts of it are considered erotic. As for man, "he is an enormous erect penis, to which there happens to be attached a human figure" (Marcus, 1966, p. 275). The penis in pornography becomes a magical instrument, a source of wonder, an object of worship, which works its effects on women who are helpless, suffering, but eventually ever so grateful for the untold delights it bestows upon them. It is the celebration of the erect penis without conscience or consciousness. The following excerpt illustrates this attitude:

I stole my hand upon his thighs, down one of which I could both see and feel a stiff hard body, confined by his breeches, that my fingers could discover no end to. Curious then, and eager to unfold so alarming a mystery, playing, as it were, with his buttons, which were bursting ripe from the active force within, those of his waistband and fore-flap flew open at a touch, when it started; and now, disengaged from the shirt, I saw, with wonder and surprise, what? not the plaything of a boy, not the weapon of a man, but a maypole of so enormous a standard that, had proportions been observed, it must have belonged to a young giant: yet I could not, without pleasure, behold, and even venture to feel such a length, such a breadth of animated ivory! perfectly well-turned and fashioned, the proud stiffness of which distended its skin, whose smooth polish and velvet softness might vie with that of the most delicate of our sex, and whose exquisite whiteness was not a little set off by a sprout of black curling hair round the root, through the jetty sprigs of which the fair skin showed as in a fine evening you may have remarked the clear light ether through the branchwork of distant trees overtopping the summit of a hill: then the broad and bluish-casted incarnate of the head, and blue serpentines of its veins, altogether composed and most striking assemblage of figure and colors in nature. In short, it stood an object of terror and delight.*

The *Romance of Lust,* published in the 1870s, in four volumes, is characterized by Steven Marcus as coming "as close as anything is known to being a pure pornotopia in the sense that almost every human consideration apart from sexuality is excluded from it" (Marcus, 1966, p. 279). Here is a sample:

I then took my aunt's arse while the lecherous Dale was underneath gamahuching [cunnilingus] and dildoing her, and by putting the Dale close to the edge of the bed, the Count stood between her legs, which were thrown over his shoulders, and thus he fucked her, having taken a lech to fuck her cunt, which was an exquisite one for fucking; her power of nip being nearly equal to the Frankland, and only beaten by aunt's extraordinary power in this way. We thus formed a group of four enchanted in love's wildest sports together.

The Frankland was gamahuched by uncle while having Harry's prick in her arse, Ellen acting postilion to Harry's arse while frigging herself with a dildo.

The closing bout of the night was the Count into aunt's arse, my prick into the Frankland's arse, Harry enjoying an old-fashioned fuck with his mother, and Ellen under aunt to dildo and be gamahuched and dildoed by aunt. We drew this bout out to an interminable length, and lay for nearly half-an-hour in the annihilation of the delicious afterjoys. At last we rose, purified, and then restoring our exhausted frames with champagne, embraced and sought well earned sleep in our separate chambers.

This work also well illustrates Vladimir Nabokov's analysis of the pornographic novel:

> Thus, in pornographic novels, action has to be limited to the copulation of clichés. Styles, structure, imagery should never distract the reader from his tepid lust. The novel must consist of an alternation of sexual scenes. The passages in between must be reduced to sutures of sense, logical bridges of the simplest design, brief expositions and explanations, which the reader will probably skip but must know they exist in order not to feel cheated (a mentality stemming from the routine of "true" fairy tales in childhood). Moreover, the sexual scenes in the book must follow a crescendo line, with new variations, new combinations, new sexes, and a steady increase in the number of participants (in a Sade play they call the gardener in), and therefore the end of the book must be more replete with lewd lore than the first chapters (Nabokov, 1955, p. 315).

*Cleland, J. *Memoirs of a woman of pleasure.* New York: Putnam, 1963 (first published in 1749), pp. 94–95.

---

destroys the men who fall for her charms. As exemplified by Émile Zola's *Nana* (1880), she is the devourer of men and all that they possess (Purdy, 1975a).

The real picture is more complex. Prostitutes fulfill as many emotional needs as they do sexual ones.

Why Women Become Prostitutes    Much has been written about why women become prostitutes (Bess and Janus, 1976). There are two basic factors: susceptibility and exposure. *Susceptibility* refers to feelings of worthlessness, alienation, and self-abasement. In personal crises or traumatic events (such as incest or rape) these feelings make women vulnerable to prostitution. Whether or not they do become prostitutes depends on *exposure:* people who are part of the subculture of prostitution must induce them by various means into "the life" (Potterat et al., 1985). The traffic in women ("white slavery") is no longer a significant factor in forcing women into prostitution; so on the face of it, women who become prostitutes seem to do so by their own choice. However, there are powerful forces pushing them into the practice over which they may have little control. For instance, a drug habit or starvation limits free will considerably.

The most obvious reason why women become prostitutes is because it pays and there is a demand for their services (Cohen, 1980). The majority of prostitutes come from lower-class backgrounds and broken homes. Poverty and the prospect of making a better living (or just staying alive) for women with little education and no special skills are clearly major motivating factors.

The necessity of supporting a drug habit is another compelling reason that drives many individuals to prostitution. A common ploy used by pimps is to get a woman "friend" hooked on drugs first and then force her into prostitution in exchange for supplying her with the drug.

The hope of romance, glamor, sexual excitement, enticement, and the coercion by pimps are additional incentives. At the more personal level, adolescent rebellion, family conflicts, the inability to establish mature emotional ties, hostility toward men, and masochistic needs may be among the factors that decide why some women gravitate to prostitution. A history of sexual abuse in childhood and adolescence is common among prostitutes (Satterfield and Listiak, 1982). It may lead youngsters to run away from home and become prostitutes to support themselves; or the sexual experience may itself predispose them for psychological reasons to follow this path. Keep in mind the wide diversity among prostitutes. The sophisticated call girl financing her education, the street-wise hooker making a living, and the pathetic teenage drug addict supporting her habit have different motives and present different challenges to society.

There are two general classes of prostitutes to contend with. The first readily fit the image of exploited women: they are mostly young, poorly educated, lacking in vocational skills, addicted to drugs and alcohol, emotionally dependent on pimps, and preyed on by a criminal subculture. The second group may share some of these liabilities (such as drug abuse), but women in this group are far more independent, educated (including some college graduates), and affluent. They say they are in this business because they want to be. The more militant among them are organized to press for legal reforms and argue for safer and better working conditions. Two such groups in the United States are the National Task Force on Prostitution and COYOTE ("Call Off Your Old Tired Ethics"), founded by Margo St. James, an avowed former prostitute and an advocate of the rights of prostitutes.

## Consequences

If cast in the best possible light, prostitutes provide a useful service to men who seek out their services. In turn, they benefit financially and sometimes personally.

This pattern may well apply to some cases. Generally, though, there are serious potential consequences both to the prostitute and to the client.

### Risks for the Client

The typical client of a prostitute is a white, middle-aged, and middle-class married man (James, 1977). Consider the risks in the context of these men's lives.

Foremost is the danger of contracting a sexually transmitted disease. With the AIDS epidemic, this prospect has become especially serious. Prostitutes engage in some of the highest risk behaviors: they have numerous sexual partners (who in turn may have many sexual contacts); they are likely to engage in a variety of sexual practices (including anal sex); and a substantial portion may be intravenous drug abusers or have sexual partners who are. However, although the risk of infection is real, some sophisticated prostitutes protect themselves and their clients somewhat by insisting on condoms. For instance, women working in the legal brothels in Nevada have generally been reported to test negative for AIDS antibodies. Nonetheless, sex with prostitutes in general is considered an unsafe practice so far as AIDS is concerned.

In rougher neighborhoods, the client is subject to being robbed by the prostitute or mugged ("rolled") by her accomplice. In principle, there is danger of the client being arrested by the police, who sometimes use female officers as "decoys." Should that become public knowledge, a man's reputation will be damaged.

Other considerations are psychological or relational. No matter what form it takes, anything other than the purely physical sexual act is a charade. No matter how enthusiastically they may apply themselves to the task, female prostitutes rarely have orgasm. In fact, they make a clear distinction between what they will do with a client and with a husband or boyfriend. They are not involved with the client in any real sense. In effect, the client cheats himself of the chance for sex with meaning.

To have to pay for sex reflects poorly on a man's ability to attract and interact with women. Therefore sex with prostitutes can lower a man's self-esteem and his sexual potential.

The final risk is guilt. A man who patronizes a prostitute helps maintain a system in which many women get exploited and hurt. A street-hardened 20-year-old woman may come across as so eager and solicitous that a man feels like he is doing her a favor by engaging her. Underneath the façade, though, there may be a pathetic youngster who never had a chance to grow up.

### Risks for the Prostitute

All of the problems faced by the client affect the prostitute much more seriously. The risk of contracting STDs and now AIDS in particular is compounded because of her multiple contacts. The likelihood of arrest is far greater. It is true that prostitutes spend little time in jail, but they are subject to harassment by the police and other officials whenever they are under pressure to clean up the street.

Prostitutes run a serious risk of being physically abused by their clients, their pimps, and the police. Mass murderers like Jack the Ripper have typically chosen their victims from the ranks of prostitutes. In many ways they are the most vulnerable members of the criminal subculture to which they belong. Alcohol and drug addiction are common among them, both because addiction drives women into prostitution and because it provides relief from misery.

As social outcasts, prostitutes are alienated from society and suffer from poor self-esteem. One of the dangers of part-time prostitution is that once stigmatized, a woman may find it hard to break out of the system. Because the working life of a prostitute is relatively short, unless a woman can save and invest, the prospects for her future are bleak. Though some women stay in the business into their middle years, their "value" declines sharply. When old, they become "fleabags," catering to derelicts and the utter rejects of society.

It could be argued that many of the above problems are a function of poverty and social inequity rather than prostitution. Middle-class call girls who effectively manage their lives do not suffer similar consequences. In male prostitution, there are no pimps, no comparable exploitation except for teenage boys. As adult men, hustlers are better able to take care of themselves. Hence, the argument goes, it is not prostitution but how society manages it that determines its consequences.

Effects on Society    Prostitution touches not only clients and prostitutes, but society as a whole. It takes a toll today in crime, in public health, and in wasted young lives. No one knows how much money it channels into a vicious subculture. There are hidden consequences for the family and for women's position in society.

Prostitution raises many questions: are women entitled to use their bodies any way they wish, or does society have a say about that? Is prostitution a threat to the family, or does it provide a safeguard for "respectable" women? Should prostitution be decriminalized and legalized? Should it be taxed and controlled by the state? We shall return to these questions in Chapter 22.

## PORNOGRAPHY

Pornography, like prostitution, involves the exploitation of sex—both using sex to make money and putting sex to potentially selfish and harmful uses. The issue of pornography is just as intimately linked to sexual aggression. It is the element of violence in its depictions of sexual interactions that provokes the most serious objections.

Why is pornography currently such a controversial issue? Two national commissions, one appointed by the President, the other by the Attorney General, of the United States, have tried to come to terms with it (Chapter 22). The Supreme Court has ruled on it and continues to be confronted with it. Catholics, evangelical Christians, civil libertarians, feminists, artists, writers, and a host of others are deeply enmeshed in the debate over it. The issues that are at stake include the freedom of expression and the right to privacy, the safety and integrity of women and children, preserving the moral fabric of society and public decency, and a multibillion dollar industry.

The issue of pornography revolves around three basic problems: what is pornography? What are its effects? Should the state control it?

In this chapter we shall address these issues from a behavioral perspective. Later we will consider the social aspects and the legal perspective (Chapter 22).

### The Problem of Definition

The term *pornography* in Greek means "writing about prostitutes." In common usage it refers to art or writing that is sexually explicit or titillating: a similar sense is conveyed by "lewd," "indecent," "raunchy," "smutty," "bawdy," "ribald," and so on. More recently the elements of degradation and sexual violence have come to determine what is considered pornographic. In the law, the word *obscene* is the term used for the same basic concept. It is derived from the Latin for "repulsive" and can be used to designate anything offensive to accepted standards of decency, though it is usually understood in a sexual sense.

Attempts to define pornography more precisely have generally turned out to be exercises in futility. Justice Potter Stewart, in a famous statement, said he could not define pornography, "but I know it when I see it" (*Jacobellis* v. *Ohio*, 378 U.S. 197, 1964). In fact what people see as pornographic varies a great deal, because they use different criteria.

The Criterion of Explicitness    Traditionally, whether a text or a picture is judged decent or pornographic has depended on how open, candid, or *explicit* it is. The degree of nudity portrayed is a case in point. In the 1950s, nudist magazines got away with showing photographs of naked men and women sunbathing but their pubic hair had to be airbrushed because otherwise they would have looked too erotic. Magazines like *Playboy* and *Playgirl* now show untampered photographs of nude men and women in rather neutral poses; magazines like *Hustler* have more explicit close-ups of genitals ("beaver shots"), while other publications show even more blatant sexual activities of all sorts.

People vary widely in their tolerance for explicitness. For many people, portrayals of nudity seem commonplace. Some draw the line at an arbitrary point (for instance, some bookstores sell *Playboy* but not *Hustler*). There are others for whom any public sexual expression is obscene, including fine art.

Literary and Artistic Criteria    Even at the height of the Victorian period, when respectable women could not bare their ankles, paintings of female nudes graced museum walls because they were art (Figure 20.15). A similar tolerance was extended to works of literature. Although artists and writers did not get complete license, they got away with work of intellectual or aesthetic merit. Quality remains an important consideration today in legal determination of obscenity (Peckham, 1971).

The criterion of artistic merit does not impress everyone. As the chairman of the Georgia State Literature Commission put it, "I don't discriminate between nude women, whether or not they are art. It's all lustful to me" (quoted in Peckham, 1971, p. 12). No wonder that 13 percent of subjects in one study found Leonard Da Vinci's *Christ* to be pornographic (Brown et al., 1978).

Another criterion might be the intent of the work. The erotic impulse underlies a good deal of artistic creativity. Some of the earliest representations of the human form in prehistoric art have a sexually explicit character, but such images have served diverse functions, magical (Figure 20.1) religious (Figure 20.5), erotic, and pornographic. Does the purpose help us to draw the line (Webb, 1975)?

Political Criteria    Some of the most hotly contested issues in pornography have to do with its political significance—how it reflects and influences the power relationships between men and women. This is the main concern of most feminist critics of pornography, who are not disturbed about sexual explicitness and who are unwilling to let the issue rest on artistic merit. For example, Gloria Steinem (1978) characterizes as pornographic any depiction of sex where "there is clear force, or an unequal power that spells coercion." The criterion for her is not one of sexual explicitness, but the lack of *equal choice* or *equal power* between sexual partners. Catharine MacKinnon (1987) views pornography as a *civil rights violation,* a perspective we shall return to in Chapter 22.

The same consideration underlies Russell's (1980) more formal distinction between pornography and erotica, which is based on whether or not the depiction of sexual behavior, verbal or pictorial, represents a "degrading or demeaning portrayal of human beings, especially women" (p. 218).

Such a definition goes a long way in sorting the diverse components that get lumped together as "pornography." It also raises a number of questions: who determines what is

Figure 18.5    Violent pornographic movie theater (*left*). Soft-core scene from *Behind the Green Door*, 1972 (*right*).

"degrading or demeaning"? The extreme forms of such depictions may not be hard to identify, but where do we draw the line? Is an advertisement showing a woman wearing scanty underwear or a man sporting a jock-strap demeaning? The terms "degrading or demeaning" are more judgmental than descriptive, so the definition does not allow us to determine what is pornographic.

The Nature of Pornographic Materials    One problem in defining pornography is that it includes so many materials and behaviors. Virtually any medium used to depict sexual themes could qualify. Most commonly involved are printed matter (books, magazines), visual materials (paintings, drawings, sculpture, photographs), moving pictures (films, videotapes), live performances (theater, burlesque, strip shows, topless/bottomless dancing, sex acts on stage), aural sex (obscene phone calls, "dial-a-porn"), and other more unusual means of public sexual expression. Such materials are readily available in at least some sections of most large cities in the United States. When these displays are public, it is hard for people not to be exposed to them at least in passing (Figure 18.5).

The distinction between erotica and pornography also tends to be arbitrary. *Erotica* are materials that are primarily intended to arouse sexual desire. They do not aspire to be fine art or literature, but neither are they degrading or violent (Russell, 1980). Most people currently distinguish between the erotic and pornographic, although their criteria vary. Box 18.3 presents some examples of how a random group of college seniors views this issue. In the sample as a whole, the primary factor which defined pornography for women was violence; men used a more diverse set of variables.

Erotica merge into *soft-core* pornography, which depicts nudity or highly suggestive sexual interactions. *Hard-core* pornography portrays genitals in close focus and shows scenes of genital penetration and other explicit sexual encounters that leave little to the imagination. The lines are obviously hard to draw, but generally X-rated films would be hard-core, R-rated films would be soft-core. Two famous

# Box 18.3

## PORNOGRAPHY OR EROTICA: STUDENT VIEWS*

### HOW WOMEN DISTINGUISH BETWEEN EROTICA AND PORNOGRAPHY

Erotic material is sexual in nature, directly or indirectly. I feel erotic materials celebrate sex or sexual feelings in a realistic and non-threatening way.

"Erotic" is anything that arouses a sexual response. Pornography can be erotic but not all erotica is pornographic.

Erotic acts are those in which both partners are giving sensual pleasure to the other. Each person is sensitive to the desires of the other, and the goal is mutual satisfaction.

I do not know the distinction between pornographic and erotic.... My only guess would be that pornographic is more along the lines of nude bodies (for example, "Playboy" or "Playgirl") whereas erotic (materials) show the example pictures of two people having sexual intercourse.

Anything that is dehumanizing to men or women. Film or photographs that show men and women acting aggressively toward each other or one person being the aggressor in a sexual context. Objectifying individuals.

Pornographic material is, in my mind, sexual acts performed for the purpose of violence against women. Sexual organs are used in assault, not in affection, and are used to degrade women, to make them "pieces of meat," and for men to acquire a sense of dominance.

Pornography elicits uncontrollable sexual desires or urges which can lead to violent or harmful acts.

### HOW MEN DISTINGUISH BETWEEN EROTICA AND PORNOGRAPHY

Erotica is something which is sensual, and sexually exciting.

Pornography is any picture in which a person's sexual organs are visible or only scantily covered.

Pornographic to me means material that depicts sexual images which do not depict love, but rather portray women as sexual objects, or depict violent sex, etc.

To me something is pornographic if material (magazine, film, literature) depicts relations between male, female or anything else with the explicit attempt at obtaining arousal.

Erotica are materials which appeal to one's sexual being or emotion. These materials need not be pornographic. Eroticism is more sexually appealing because it is more subtle and less denigrating to the subject.

The erotic and the pornographic are not mutually exclusive. The line which separates them is vague as evidenced by the controversy that surrounds this subject, both constitutionally and definitionally. Subordination, if reciprocal, can, I think, be part of a normal and healthy sexual relationship. Consequently, the addition of power relationships to sexually explicit material can be legitimately arousing and, therefore, erotic. The problem lies in the *over-emphasis* on human beings as sex objects and the fixation with the subjugation of *women* by men.

*From Lieske, C., *Pornography—defining the limits*. Honors Thesis, Program in Human Biology, Stanford University, Unpublished, 1988.

---

films that have served as landmarks of sorts are *I Am Curious Yellow* (1970) and *Deep Throat* (1973), which played to wide audiences and established the norms of "soft" and "hard" pornography, respectively. Others consider

hard-core any pornography that is degrading or violent irrespective of how explicit it is.

*Kiddie porn* features stories, pictures, and films showing children who are either nude or engaging in sexual acts, often with adults (Figure 14.1). Kiddie porn is inseparable from child abuse; because children cannot give informed consent, their very involvement in such activities represents a form of sexual abuse. In addition, such involvement may expose them to further sexual exploitation by those who produce such materials (Burgess, 1984).

There has been an enormous expansion in sexually explicit mass-produced materials. The Attorney General's Commission (1987) identified 2325 separate magazines alone. They cater to every conceivable sexual interest. A content analysis of 430 sexually explicit magazines shows women to be the predominant objects, shown in various degrees of nudity (18 percent) or engaged in heterosexual activity (24 percent) (Winick, 1985).

The Economics of Pornography    The problem of definition also involves the economics of pornography: whose profits are we going to count? Advertising, as we shall discuss, is suffused with erotic images, sexual innuendos, and highly suggestive phrases. Art, entertainment, books, films, public television, the fashion industry, sometimes gingerly, sometimes boldly, step over the line into the sexually explicit. A substantial segment of the national economy is more or less directly involved in the exploitation of sexual themes for profit.

Even in a more circumscribed view, pornography is a multibillion dollar business (Serrin, 1981). An estimated $4 to $6 billion a year are spent on all forms of pornography and erotica. Some 20,000 stores in the United States sell hard-core magazines generating several hundred million dollars in income. There are hundreds of sexually explicit magazines, ranging from *Playboy* to *Penthouse* to *Hustler* and down the line. The ten best-selling softcore magazines had a circulation of 16 million copies and made over $500 million in 1981. *Deep Throat* cost less than $25,000 to produce and had netted $25 million within a decade ("Video Turns Big Profit," 1982). The imaginative folks who thought up the idea of placing an erotic recording on the public telephone system ("Oh yes, yes, do it, do it"), which came

to be known as *Dial-a-porn,* were making $10,000 a day for a while.

A substantial segment of this industry deals in kiddie porn magazines, pictures, and films. An estimated 1.2 million children are involved each year in pornography, prostitution, or both. The yield is $1 billion (Ditkoff, 1978). The people who produce child pornography are men with an average age of 43 years, who are usually known to the child before engaging them in the activity. Typically, they are family friends, relatives, neighbors, teachers, or counselors (Burgess, 1984). Child pornography is not only a cottage industry. Like other illegal activities that are highly profitable, it attracts unscrupulous operators and may become controlled by crime syndicates.

The pornography industry offers something for every pocket. Collectors can spend thousands of dollars on films and videocassettes. Twenty-five cents will buy a few minutes viewing time of a silent videotape in a "peep show" in the back of an "adult bookstore."

The point is that underneath lenient definitions and arguments in favor of pornography, there may also be some crass motives. From parents who push their children into kiddie porn for a few hundred dollars, to professional pornographers who make their living at it and the businesses that dispense it, a substantial number of people have a considerable stake in it.

Finally, the customers also have a stake. By all indications, the consumers of pornography are primarily men in the mainstream of society rather than social outcasts or sex offenders who have run afoul of the law. Typically, they are middle-class, fairly well-educated men aged 22 to 34 (Mahoney, 1983). Nor are women absent from its clientele, although they are less numerous. In a college sample, 59 percent of white men and 35 percent of women had gone to X-rated movies or read pornographic books; 9 percent of men and 5 percent of women did so regularly (Houston, 1981).

The Problem of Consequences
The second problem of pornography is its con-

sequences: are they harmful, useful, or inconsequential? One reason there are no definitive answers is because the problem of definition has not been solved. Anyone who makes a claim about the effects of "pornography" immediately faces the question: what kind of pornography?

Researchers currently try to distinguish among the effects of three general types of sexually explicit materials: *erotica,* which depict sexual interactions between adults characterized by voluntary participation, mutuality, equality, and a sharing of pleasure; *degrading and dehumanizing* pornography, which objectifies and denigrates the participants; and *violent* pornography, which depicts aggression and brutality in the form of rape, sadomasochism, mutilation, and murder. By and large, women and children are victimized by these practices most directly.

These distinctions have not always been made. For example, the report on pornography issued by the Attorney General's Commission on Pornography (1987) lumped all pornography together as "material which is predominently sexually explicit and intended primarily for the purpose of sexual arousal" (pp. 228–229).

Until after World War II, sexually explicit materials were considered obscene and prohibited by law. Their potential harmfulness was taken for granted. Over the decade of the 1960s, as sexual attitudes became liberalized, sexual materials became more acceptable, leading to the redefinition of the laws on obscenity by the Supreme Court of the United States (Chapter 22). In the 1980s attitudes toward pornography have become more restrictive again.

These shifts are reflected in the views of two national commissions. In 1967 Congress created a commission to investigate the effects of pornography and to analyze the obscenity laws. After extensive investigations and special studies this Commission on Obscenity and Pornography issued a report (1970). The general thrust of its findings was that there was no correlation, let alone a causal relationship, between exposure to pornography and immedi-

ate or delayed antisocial behavior among adults. Pornography was deemed a nuisance rather than an evil; hence the recommendation of the commission (by a vote of 12 out of 18) was that laws "prohibiting the sale, exhibition, and distribution of sexual materials to consenting adults should be repealed" (Commission on Obscenity and Pornography, 1970).

The report caused a lot of controversy. Some dissenting members of the commission called its report a "Magna Carta for the pornographer"; others wanted to go even further than the commission's recommendation in removing statutory restrictions on obscenity and pornography. Subsequently, the Senate adopted a resolution rejecting the commission's findings and recommendations (Reimer, 1986).

Though it was not enacted into law, the work of the commission helped perpetuate the view that pornography, though a nuisance and morally repugnant to some, was essentially harmless and did not warrant the abridgement of the freedom of expression through censorship.

Some 15 years later, a second national commission, this time appointed by Edwin Meese, the Attorney General of the United States, came out with a report differing sharply from the previous one (Attorney General's Commission on Pornography, 1987). Its central thesis is that exposure to pornographic materials causes harm in a number of ways. Some of its key conclusions and recommendations are presented in Box 18.4.

The 1970 Commission Report was criticized as too tolerant of pornography. The 1986 report is criticized as too intolerant not only of pornography but of freedom of sexual expression as a whole. Six of its members have been singled out for having shown their clear antipornography bias, even before the work of the commission began (Lynn, 1986). Two commission members (including the only psychologist on the panel) dissented from one of the key conclusions of the report, that sexually violent and degrading pornography leads to sexually aggressive behavior towards women. They objected that the materials presented to

# Box 18.4

## ATTORNEY GENERAL'S COMMISSION ON PORNOGRAPHY (1986): SOME CONCLUSIONS*

It is clear that the conclusion of "no negative effects" advanced by the 1970 Commission is no longer tenable. It is also clear that catharsis, as an explanatory model for the impact of pornography, is simply unwarranted by evidence in this area, nor has catharsis fared well in the general area of mass media effects and antisocial behavior.

This is not to say, however, that the evidence as a whole is comprehensive enough or definitive enough. While we have learned much more since 1970, even more areas remain to be explored.

What do we know at this point?

• It is clear that many sexually explicit materials, particularly of the commercial variety, that are obviously designed to be arousing, *are,* in fact, arousing, both to offenders and nonoffenders.

• Rapists appear to be aroused by both forced as well as consenting sex depictions, while nonoffenders (our college males) are less aroused by depictions of sexual aggression. On the other hand, when these portrayals show the victim as "enjoying" the rape, these portrayals similarly elicit high arousal levels.

• Arousal to rape depictions appears to correlate with attitudes of acceptance of rape myths and sexual violence and both these measures likewise correlate with laboratory-observed aggressive behaviors.

• Depictions of sexual violence also increase the likelihood that rape myths are accepted and sexual violence toward women condoned. Such attitudes have further been found to be correlated with laboratory aggression toward women. Finally, there is also some evidence that laboratory aggression toward women correlates with self-reported sexually aggressive behaviors.

What we know about the effects of nonviolent sexually explicit materials is less clear. There are tentative indications that negative effects in the area of attitudes might also occur, particularly from massive exposure. The mechanics of such effects need to be elaborated more fully, however, particularly in light of more recent findings that suggest that degrading themes might have effects that differ from nonviolent, nondegrading sexually explicit materials. This is clearly an area that deserves further investigation.

• There are suggestions that the availability of pornography may be one of a nexus of sociocultural factors that has some bearing on rape rates in this country. Other cross-cultural data, however, offer mixed results as well, so these findings have to be viewed as tentative at best.

• We still know very little about the cause of deviancy, and it is important to examine the developmental patterns of offenders, particularly patterns of early exposure. We do have some convergence on the data from some rapists and males in the general population in the areas of arousal and attitudes, but again, this remains to be examined more closely.

Clearly, the need for more research remains as compelling as ever. The need for more research to also examine the efficacy of strategies for dealing with various effects is as compelling. If learning—both prosocial and antisocial—occurs from various depictions, and there certainly is clear evidence of both, the need for strategies that implicate the same learning principles must be evaluated.

*Final Report of the Attorney General's Commission on Pornography,* pp. 1031–1033. Washington, D.C.: U.S. Justice Department.

---

the commission were not representative and that the conclusions drawn from them were simplistic and not supported by social science.

Both commissions had the benefit of extensive consultations with experts and analyses of the existing literature; yet their conclusions went in opposite directions. One explanation is that, in each case, the majority on each commission found what they were looking for. The findings of such commissions are therefore said to reflect the mood of the times rather than the facts (Stengle, 1986). The majority of professionals in the field of sexuality appear to be opposed to the work of the Meese Commission, seeing it as a patent effort to impose conservative sexual values on society. The issue has split feminists. Determined opponents of pornography like Catharine MacKinnon and Andrea Dworkin have welcomed the Commission's tough line. Others have demurred, not because they approve pornography but because they believe the infringement of freedom of sexual expression represents a greater threat in the long run (Leo, 1986).

A second explanation, not mutually exclusive with the first, is that the nature of pornography has changed since the 1970s. The conclusions of both commissions may be valid for the materials they were dealing with. Common observation seems to support this, although we would need exhaustive content analyses of materials from both periods to firmly establish if there is more violence in pornography today (Donnerstein et al., 1987).

Potential Harm    The negative effects of sexually explicit materials have to be examined at two levels. First is the short-term effect. Suppose a photograph showing a sexual act circulates in your class. Some students immediately feel offended or disturbed. There is no need to demonstrate any further damage.

More compelling arguments are based on possible long-term harm. These broader dangers are usually supposed to affect several groups. Most vulnerable are children. Early exposure to even healthy forms of sexual expression, such as nudity or sexual intercourse, might prematurely stimulate and confuse children. Then there is the further danger that exposure to unhealthy forms of sex, such as sexual violence, might warp the child's sexual development.

As a result of these concerns some people want to ban all exposure of children to sexually explicit materials, including sex education programs in schools. Others draw the line at materials that are unconventional or pathological.

When children themselves are used as pornographic subjects (Figure 14.1) in kiddie porn, we have child abuse. The issue here is not the exposure of children to such materials but the effects on the child who is induced or coerced into producing such material by modeling or engaging in sexual acts with adults that are photographed and filmed (Burgess, 1984).

The impact of sexually explicit materials on children is difficult to research. The same obstacles that stand in the way of studying childhood sexuality (Chapter 8) prevail here even more strongly. Social and ethical considerations simply do not allow the exposure of children to sexually explicit materials under controlled experimental conditions. Therefore research must depend on ascertaining the harmful effects of such exposure after the fact and in the presence of numerous confounding variables.

Another population that has been considered especially vulnerable to the effects of pornography is potential sex offenders. The concern here is that pornography prompts some men to commit sex crimes. When a child molester is arrested with "kiddie porn" in his possession, the association between the stimulus and behavior seems self-evident; but when this association was tested systematically in a study comparing imprisoned sex offenders with other prisoners and ordinary people, no significant differences were found among the three groups in the possession, use, or exposure to pornography. Rather, the differences were factors such as age, education, and socioeconomic class (Goldstein, 1974). Furthermore, child molesters are often aroused by materials that are generally not thought of as pornographic, such as photographs of children modeling underwear in ordinary mail-order catalogs found in millions of homes.

Although pornography might have some indirect influence on men who commit sexual aggression against women, the general opinion among investigators is that "pornography, whether violent or nonviolent, is not the causal link for sexual crimes" (Donnerstein et al., 1987, p. 71). Although a rapist may be sexually aroused by pornography like anyone else, "pornography does not cause rape; banning it will not stop rape . . ." (Groth, 1979, p. 9); it is anger, not sexual arousal, that leads to rape. Pornography is thus not an excuse for rape and does not reduce a rapist's accountability for his crime (Chapter 19).

Other research has shown that sex offenders tend to have less exposure than nonoffenders to pornography during both adolescence and adulthood (Cook et al., 1971). Sex offenders usually come from sexually conservative and repressive backgrounds with a low tolerance for sexually explicit materials. This very fact is interpreted by other investigators to point to a greater vulnerability of sex offenders to pornography: not being exposed to it, they are less able to deal with it appropriately (Check and Malamuth, 1984). Some researchers think sex offenders may be selectively influenced by some forms of pornography, such as images that depict violence. Whatever the mechanism, there are persistent claims that pornography leads to an increased prevalence of rape (Court, 1985).

What about the effects of pornography on ordinary people? The exposure of laboratory subjects to sexually explicit erotica has at most a slight and transient effect. It may make it more likely that the person will subsequently masturbate or engage in some other form of sexual activity typical for that person. This is true not only for one-time exposure but even for subjects who are exposed to erotica for 90 minutes a day, five days a week, for three weeks (Howard et al., 1973). The intense exposure is even likely to have a depressing effect on sexual interest (a little bit of this stuff goes a long way).

The effect of violent pornography under laboratory conditions appears similar; it too does not significantly alter sexual behavior in ordinary people. This is true even if they are shown five full-length pornographic movies a day for several weeks (Malamuth, 1984).

The only significant impact of violent pornography appears to be on aggressive behavior. Experiments that try to demonstrate this link have two components: the subject must be exposed to pornography in a controlled manner; the subject must be provoked to anger by

an independent means to see if the exposure to pornography affects the level of aggression provoked. The exposure to pornography in one study involved reading an illustrated story of a pirate raping a woman (aggressive pornography), reading a story and looking at pictures of nonaggressive sexual interaction, and reading an erotically neutral source (Malamuth, 1984). In another study, subjects were shown films: one group saw a sexually explicit and aggressive film; the second, a sexually explicit but nonaggressive film; the third, a neutral film on both counts (Donnerstein, 1980). The subjects in both experiments were angered by a confederate of the researcher and then were led to believe through an elaborate ruse that they were in a position to administer electric shocks to the confederate stationed elsewhere (there actually were no shocks involved). The test was to see whether the exposure to the three varieties of stimuli would make a difference in how punitive or aggressive the subjects would be toward the person who had angered them. In the first experiment, those exposed to violent pornography showed significantly higher levels of aggression than the others. In the second experiment, the films—sexually explicit but nonaggressive—led subjects to aim equally intense shocks at male confederates, but exposure to the aggression film led to more punitive behavior towards the female confederate (Donnerstein, 1980). It appears therefore that it is the fusion of erotic images with aggressive images or even aggressive images alone that lead to an increased propensity to violence, particularly towards women (Donnerstein et al., 1987).

These experimental situations are obviously contrived and do not establish a clear linkage between pornography and sexual violence toward women in real life. This fact does not mean pornography is innocuous or should be encouraged. Its potential harm must be evaluated not only from a clinical or experimental point of view but also from a social perspective. What does pornography reveal about our cultural attitudes towards women? What sorts of attitudes does it teach about the relationship of men and women? Research on pornography is fraught with many uncertainties, but several conclusions are beginning to get established: sexually explicit material, erotica, does not as such foster negative attitudes or behavior unless it is combined with images of violence. Such images are not restricted to what commonly passes for pornography. The most common scenes of sex and aggression in public media—mainstream fiction and film—often surpass the levels of violence portrayed in even the most graphic pornography (Donnerstein et al., 1987).

There is a growing consensus that degrading and violent pornography is, at the least, an insult to women. By making women seemingly legitimate targets of abuse and humiliation, it confers inferior status. Even when it does not lead a man to attack women, it makes him more tolerant of those who do. This desensitization to sexual violence may be one of the most damaging effects of aggressive pornography. The common theme in pornography is that deep down, women enjoy being abused. This lie makes a mockery of the suffering of those who are victims of sexual violence.

Potential Benefits     Sexually explicit but nonviolent materials have a number of potentially good effects. The first is in sex education. If we are going to move beyond the birds and the bees in the teaching of sexuality, we will need to rely on varying degrees of sexually explicit materials. In the younger grades there is clearly a need to be selective and careful, but by the time young men and women reach college a spade will have to be called a spade. Consider some of the explicit illustrations in this textbook and slides and films your professor has shown in class. You may not find them pornographic, but plenty of others are likely to, even though they serve a serious and useful purpose.

No responsible person would expose children to hard-core pornography; but pornography may be instructive for adults who have had limited exposure to sexuality. A hard-core film showing a copulating couple may teach nothing about sexual affection, but it will certainly provide a graphic depiction of the "mechanics" of sexual intercourse, which are an integral part of the act.

Sexually explicit material can contribute to the enhancement of sexual fantasy (Chapter 11). There are a lot of lonely people in this world who may get a measure of pleasure from looking at sexually explicit pictures (Figure 18.6). Should they be denied that pleasure? Why not allow anyone to plaster his or her walls with naked pictures if they so choose? Some people argue that pictures of naked women on the walls enhance the male tendency to objectify women (Chapter 16). Others take a more tolerant view. Whether employed as a masturbatory aid or to stir up the erotic imagination of couples, explicit books and pictures have long been used to enhance sexual excitement; films and videotapes have now expanded this resource by bringing it into people's homes. Similar materials are used in sex therapy to help couples with sexual dysfunction (Chapter 15).

All of the benefits so far pertain to erotica, the "good" kind of pornography or material that many people no longer even consider to

Figure 18.6   A man looking at a "girlie" magazine.

be pornographic. What about degrading and violent pornography? What possible good could it do?

St. Thomas Aquinas likened prostitution to the open sewers of a medieval city, necessary to accommodate the refuse produced by society. A similar argument could be put forth for pornography. Given that some men are going to have degrading and aggressive thoughts about women, why not deflect them into fantasies, lessening the chances of their being acted out? In this sense pornography might serve a *cathartic* function, providing a safety valve for socially unacceptable sexual impulses. Does it really work that way?

The most compelling evidence that it may comes from Denmark. In 1967, Denmark legalized the publication and sale of all erotic printed matter, no matter how explicit or pornographic; in 1969, it extended the law to include the sale of pictures to anyone over age 16.

The immediate reaction was an increase in the sale of sexually explicit materials, a trend that subsided in a few years (the pornographic trade from then on has catered mainly to tourists). There also followed a reduction in the incidence of reported sex crimes. This change is partly because of the liberalization of community attitudes and police practices. In other words, the Danes no longer considered certain sexual behaviors as illegal, just as they had ceased to consider the sale of pornographic materials as unacceptable. Thus, the fact that exhibitionism against women in Copenhagen dropped by 58 percent may be due to the fact that the Danes had learned to look the other way. The 80 percent drop in voyeurism cannot be explained the same way, because the Danes found it no less offensive; the 69 percent drop in the molesting of girls was even more certainly not due to greater legal tolerance, because Danes continued to object to it as strongly as before. The 16 percent drop in rapes between 1959 and 1969 was not as dramatic as the other changes and may be further evidence for the weak link between pornography and rape (Kutchinsky, 1973). Additional support in this connection comes from studies that suggest that exposure to nonviolent erotica decreases aggression under some circumstances (Donnerstein et al., 1987).

Pornography as Socially Insignificant    Amid the controversy, perhaps we are losing sight of the possibility that exposure to pornography does not significantly affect behavior one way or the other. In Denmark, social changes may have brought about both the drop in sexually aberrant behavior and the rise in pornographic material, without one being the cause of the other. Similarly, the increased rates of child molestation and rape on the one hand and the flood of pornographic materials in the United States on the other may both reflect certain underlying social changes; pornography need not be the cause.

The problems of showing concrete negative effects under experimental conditions may be due to the fact that there are no negative effects to show. The few findings that investigators have wrung out of contrived laboratory experiments may be more a confirmation of social expectations than objective proof of harm. Could it be that pornography is after all more like a bad odor than a deadly social pollutant? Given the level of violence of some of the pornographic material on the market, it is hard to imagine it as harmless. The basic question perhaps comes down to this: is it the sex or is it the violence that represents the danger? Society is waiting for the definitive answer to this question.

## The Problem of Censorship

Society deals with harmful and unethical practices by prohibiting them. The prohibition of pornography takes the form of *censorship*—the law defines what sort of sexually explicit materials are not permissible to produce, distribute, and use. How should society draw the line in the light of divergent views about what pornography is and conflicting evidence of its effects? These questions make pornography a major social issue. We will examine its legal aspects in Chapter 22.

## SEX AND ADVERTISING

The most pervasive use of sex for commercial purposes is in advertising. The basic intention of advertising is to proclaim the availability, qualities, and advantages of a product or service. As such, it is an integral part of business and of life everywhere in the Western world, especially in the United States.

In ancient times, town criers circulated through the streets, calling attention to the sales of such items as slaves and cattle. With the invention of printing in the 15th century, mass communication began, eventually ushering in the modern era of advertising. Newspapers are now the largest advertising medium, followed by television. Along with other media, they now pervade virtually every aspect of modern life.

The significance of advertising to sexuality is two-fold. First, its messages and images portray (with varying faithfulness) popular perceptions of such notions as sexual attractiveness or gender stereotypes. Thereby, advertising serves as a mirror of the sexual attitudes and values of society. Second, by publicly displaying certain appearances and behaviors as desirable, advertising helps to teach them as standards. As soon as children are old enough to be concerned with their appearance, advertising plays an important role in socializing them into what the mass culture thinks is physically attractive, sexy, masculine, feminine, and so on.

Both of these linkages of advertising to sexuality are inadvertent. Advertisers are interested in one thing—selling. They are not concerned with mirroring, maintaining, or modifying social attitudes and behavior, except when it is likely to enhance sales (which is where advertising differs from political propaganda). Honest advertisers refrain from unethical practices (such as misleading consumers or pushing harmful products) but even at best their primary loyalty is to the businesses who buy their services. Although further restrictions are imposed by the media, which may refuse to accept an ad, a substantial part of their income comes from advertising; the profit motive, and sheer economic survival, tends to overshadow all other considerations.

### Advertising to Sell Sex

Advertising can be used to sell sexual products and services; but it is not always easy to define what is a "sexual" product or service, any more than it is to determine what is "pornographic."

Selling Sexual Products   In principle, any item that is intended to enhance sexual attractiveness, lead to sexual stimulation, or serve in sexual interactions can be thought of as a sexual product. Advertisements for sexually explicit magazines, books, films, videos, and similar erotica make no bones about the sexual nature of the products they present—if anything, they exaggerate how explicit or erotic these materials are. The practice in porno shops of wrapping magazines in cellophane is largely due to the fact that the contents rarely deliver what the cover promises, as you find out after you buy it.

Sexually explicit magazines and mail order catalogs advertise an array of "erotic" materials ranging from sexy underwear to dildos, vibrators, and other "marital aids." They also offer false promises in the form of creams, exercises, and equipment for penis "enlargement" and breast "enhancement," as well as various aphrodisiacs (*Adam and Eve,* 1978).

Mainstream media refrain from showing ads for explicitly sexual materials. In fact, until recently, they steadfastly refused to advertise condoms. It was the outbreak of AIDS that broke the barrier. The immense potential of using advertising to convey information about "safe sex" is only now beginning to be explored.

Advertising for sexual products, like pornography, has its own "hard" and "soft" variants. What we see in general circulation publications and on public television is usually of the "soft" variety. Advertisements for a musical like *Oh Calcutta* (which has been running in New York for years) show nude actors in views that do not show their genitals. Books with erotic themes are touted openly but in somewhat restrained language.

Innuendo and sexually suggestive images and text also characterize the enormous amount of advertising involving cosmetics, underwear, clothing, and other items that are more or less explicitly touted to enhance the user's sex appeal (*Victoria's Secret*, 1987).

### Selling Sexual Services

An enterprising prostitute in ancient Greece had the soles of her shoes studded with large nails that left an imprint on the ground that read "Follow me." Roman brothels advertised their services with carved marble panels. In such pure forms of sexual commerce, advertising has always played an integral part.

At the turn of the century brothels in New Orleans relied on special "guidebooks" to attract customers (Murphy, 1983). For some years prostitutes in London have been permitted to post discrete notices giving their telephone numbers and "specialties" on bulletin boards in select areas (Gosling and Warner, 1967). In a more open display, prostitutes in the red light districts of cities like Hamburg and Amsterdam sit in front of windows to attract customers. The line-up of prostitutes in front of brothel customers accomplishes the same purpose.

Only those seeking sexual services are usually exposed to its advertising. More public are thinly veiled advertisements for "escort services," "erotic massage," and other fronts for sexual services. Noncommercial forms of self-advertising are engaged in by men and women looking for a sexual partner in singles magazines and "personal" columns (Chapter 17).

### Sex to Sell Advertising

"Sex sells" seemingly anything and everything, judging from the way advertisers use sexual themes and images. As a result, it is not always easy to tell whether the product being advertised is meant to be a "sexual" item, or sex is simply the bait. Consider, for instance, an ad for lipstick. Why do women use lipstick? To appear more attractive, would be the general answer. To what extent does "attractiveness" mean erotic appeal? The same question would apply to after-shave lotions for men, and clothing ads for both sexes. Similarly, the erotic elements in advertisements for alcoholic beverages and cigarettes are deliberately ambiguous.

There are also a wide variety of products, such as automobile tires or construction materials, where the use of erotic imagery is entirely gratuitous. Sexual themes are used in such ads for several reasons.

### Attention-Getting

An attractive blond woman in shorts in a calendar ad for truck tires or tractors merely serves as "bait," attracting a potential buyer's attention to the ad. The use of the female body for such purposes is common. Aimed at men, it makes them stop and look. Many look no farther than the woman, but the hope is that others will. Moreover, the favorable impression the woman makes is expected to extend to the product, far-fetched as the connection may be.

### Sexual Innuendo

Another device to get attention is to "eroticize" the product. One ad for construction materials shows a rear view of a reclining, voluptuous nude woman with the caption "She's built like all our products, heavy where she has to take the strain." An airline ran a series of ads that showed a female flight attendant with a plane in the background. The caption would be something like "I am Barbara, fly me to Miami." The "Barbara" in question was supposed to be the plane, but the more likely association was to the woman, and "fly me" could mean many things. Liquor ads often rely on innuendo; one ad for a liquor says, "May all your screwdrivers be Harvey Wallbangers."

### Sexual Symbolism

The ad just referred to shows a couple standing face-to-face with the long-necked bottle of the product superimposed on the figure of the woman. In the context of the ad, the phallic symbolism is hard to miss. A lipstick cylinder aimed at a half-open mouth with tantalizing red lips also leaves little to the imagination. An ad for a man's cologne showing a cylindrical bottle with a round top is no less obvious.

Sexual Modeling    Models who appear in ads with erotic connotations are usually attractive young women and men. The ads imply that should you use the product advertised, you will look like the models themselves, or engage in the same sort of activity that they are shown in. The scene may range from a couple amorously gazing at each other to a tangle of nude bodies suggesting an orgy.

## Effects of Sex in Advertising

As we did with pornography, let us look at the potential benefit and harm of using sexual themes and images in advertising. We will not be concerned here with whether or not advertising itself is a good or a bad thing, even though that is an important issue in its own right.

Potential Benefits    In a "sex-positive" society (Chapter 21) we would expect to have a joyful acceptance of the human body, free of prudery and false modesty. It would be natural, therefore, to tap its power to attract attention to worthwhile products and services through advertising.

At its best, advertising is a form of art. Applied to erotic themes it can generate attractive images of sexuality that enrich our perceptual world. The truthful and tasteful sexual themes and images in advertising can also fulfill an important educational role. Ads can teach us how to improve our appearance, in effect how to look and act more sexual. They may also perform an important public health function, such as promoting the use of condoms.

Looked at broadly, eroticism in advertising is no different than in literature, art, and pornography. The issue is what sort of sexual themes should be used, and to what purpose.

Potential Harm    Objections to the use of sex in advertising can be raised on the same grounds as the arguments against pornography.

One set of objections focuses on the public display of nudity in ads and their use of sexual themes either directly or by innuendo. Because advertising reaches into every corner of society, those who prefer to keep sex private find its ubiquitous use objectionable. Because children cannot be sheltered from ads, the argument gains additional force.

A second set of objections derives from the nature of the sexual messages conveyed by ads. Like pornography, ads make use of women and invite us to see them as sexual objects. The sexual messages conveyed by ads are often false promises. Despite its claims, the garment or scent that is advertised will not turn you into a replica of the model shown. Alcohol will not lead to romance. Cigarettes will not make you sexy.

There is even deeper distortion in the way that the human body, especially the female body, is portrayed in ads. The average ratio of legs to trunk among women is about 8:4; in advertising figures it is more often 10:4. The long-legged look that is presented as attractive or sexy is therefore illusory. As models grow taller and thinner each year, they create an increasing gap between what is valued (the ideal) and what is normally attainable (the reality).

Ordinary women are rarely shown in fashion magazines unless they are targeted for makeovers. Similarly, there is strong emphasis on youthfulness. Rather than promoting the realistic ideal that there are different ways of looking attractive at different ages, advertising fosters the notion that only the young can be sexy; hence the endless quest to retain youthfulness through means from cosmetics to surgery.

Some of these advertising practices merely promote false hopes; others are more worrisome. For instance, given the growing incidence of eating disorders among women (such as anorexia and bulimia), the relentless push to sell laxatives, diuretics, fiber pills, and other means to control weight is a significant health hazard. The exploitation of the image of the "liberated woman" to sell cigarettes is equally alarming.

Even when it sets up more realistic

models, advertising overly emphasizes the physical aspects of people (especially women) over personal qualities (Figure 18.7). The effect is superficiality and shallowness. Women are often portrayed in ads as mindless, coquettish, and frivolous. They are often shown in silly poses, such as standing on one leg, jumping in the air, or contorting their bodies. Ads tend to reduce women to body parts by showing only the portions of the body that suit the needs of the ad.

Just as in pornography, subtle and not so subtle displays of coercion have seeped into advertising. Jean Kilpatrick has explored such ads in great detail in the Cambridge Documentary film *Killing Us Softly*. Though most of the ads depicted in that film are no longer used, they have been replaced by similar ads that carry the same message. The use of sex, violence, or the implied threat of violence has become the new wave of sexy advertising. Perfume ads play on images of women being pursued, engaging in sexual orgies, or being "taken" by men no longer able to control themselves after exposure to these heady scents. Perfumes are often named to convey these images.

The combination of sex and violence is still a popular technique. During the 1960s, several ads emerged that depicted chained, beaten, or otherwise captive women in provocative poses to sell popular albums. Some of these ad campaigns were so offensive that they were taken off the market. (The Rolling Stones' ad for one of their albums showed a chained, badly beaten and bruised woman sitting in a chair with her hands tied above her head, saying, "I'm black and blue all over from the Rolling Stones and I love it.") You can find examples of such album covers in record stores today.

In attempting to persuade women to buy their products, ads put forth a competitive, almost predatory model of intimate relationships. They encourage women to compete with other women, even rejoice in the envy and hatred they may experience if they are successful in their quest for younger-looking hair, skin, and bodies. One ad for a skin product crowed, "They're gonna hate you a whole lot

Figure 18.7   The use of the body in advertising.

longer back home" and showed several older women looking enviously at their radiant friend. A similar campaign was mounted by a stockings manufacturer. Each of these ads shows an elegantly dressed couple out for the evening. The woman is always wearing a floor-length gown or pants. The man's attention is caught by a second woman, seductively posed to expose most of her legs from under a much shorter dress. The obvious message to women is to do whatever you can to take away another woman's date.

A more recent ad for jeans portrayed a young, tough-looking teenaged girl with a boy she had just stolen from another girl. The girl's monologue accompanying the ad berated the "loser" on a number of items, the most "important" of which was that the poor girl had not had the sense to wear the right clothes. Therefore she did not deserve the spoils.

Finally, there has been a consistent trend toward using young children, primarily girls, dressed and made up to appear sexual and much older than they actually are to sell merchandise. One ad for kneesocks presents a young girl wearing an older woman's high heels, attempting to hold down the skirt of her dress, which is being blown above her waist. Like child pornography, such imagery might encourage child abuse.

Advertisers counter these criticisms by saying that they merely reflect existing social values and give to people what they want. The negative stereotypes of women they represent are not their doing but a social problem they did not create. This same argument is applied to pornography.

In the exploitation of sex, it is fruitless to look for villains. Although some are more responsible than others for exploiting sex to their own selfish ends, ultimately all of us have a share, individually and collectively, in generating and sustaining the sexual culture in which we live.

## REVIEW QUESTIONS

1. What are the principles of fair exchange in sexual tradeoffs? What are the gender differences in these interactions?

2. What forms does prostitution currently take in the United States?

3. Why do women become prostitutes, and what are the consequences to their lives?

4. What are the potentially harmful effects of pornography?

5. What are the uses of sex in advertising?

## THOUGHT QUESTIONS

1. How could you educate people to focus more on emotional commitment than on the body in the valuation of sex? Why would you?

2. How can you determine if a woman is making a free choice in becoming a prostitute?

3. Should prostitution be recognized as a legitimate business?

4. An artist and an advertising agency each offer you $500 to pose nude. What do you do, and why?

5. Would you ban the use of sex in advertising of nonsexual products? Explain.

## SUGGESTED READINGS

Bullough, V., and Bullough, B. (1978). *Prostitution: An illustrated social history.* New York: Crown. A historical overview of prostitution from ancient to modern times with considerations of its current status. Well illustrated and good references.

Donnerstein, E., Linz, D., and Penrod, S. (1987). *The question of pornography.* New York: Free Press. Comprehensive overview of research findings on pornography and their implications for public policy.

Rechy, J. *City of night* (1963) and *The sexual outlaw* (1977). New York: Grove. The world of the hustler evoked in a literary vein.

Webb, P. (1976). *The erotic arts.* Boston: New York Graphic Society. Fascinating and profusely illustrated survey of erotic art from ancient to modern times and its tenuous distinction from pornography.

# Sexual Aggression

CHAPTER

# 19

*Man's discovery that his genitalia could serve as a weapon to generate fear must rank as one of the most important discoveries of prehistoric times...*

SUSAN BROWNMILLER

OUTLINE

AGGRESSIVE ELEMENTS IN SEX
Dominance
Hostility
Coercion
SEXUAL HARASSMENT
Determinants
   The Sexual Component
   Unwanted Imposition
   Unequal Power
Contexts
   Courtship
   Social Settings
   The Workplace
   College
   Professional Services
Handling Sexual Harassment
RAPE
The Nature of Rape
The Setting

Prevalence
Varieties of Rape
   Stranger Rape
   Acquaintance and Date Rape
   Marital Rape
   Statutory Rape
   Group Rape
   Rape of Males
The Rape Victim
   The Role of the Victim
   The Consequences of Rape
   Helping the Rape Victim
The Rapist
   Psychosocial Characteristics
   Typologies of Rapists
   Background Characteristics
   Facilitating Factors
   Dealing with Rapists

Our everyday language is an eloquent reflection of how intimately sex and aggression may get intermingled. Sex is a vehicle for the sharing of pleasure, for the expression of affection and love; yet the common vernacular terms for sexual intercourse ("fuck," "screw") also mean to cheat, trick, take advantage of, and treat unfairly. Their derivatives ("fucked-up," "screwed-up") stand for inferior, unpleasant, difficult, confusing, blundering, wasteful, disorganized, and neurotic. The same words that express the desire to make love also express dismay, annoyance, or anger. Our language thus betrays mixed feelings. It reflects the fact that sexual encounters involve far more than the gratification of our erotic and reproductive needs.

We have already touched upon various aspects of this issue: the possible hormonal roots of aggression (Chapter 4) and gender differences in its manifestations (Chapter 10); child sexual abuse and the erotization of pain and humiliation in sadomasochism (Chapter 14); the role of hostility in disrupting sexual functions (Chapter 15) and intimate relationships (Chapter 16); and finally, the undercurrent of aggression in sexual exploitation, particularly violent pornography (Chapter 18).

In this chapter we will consider first the general way aggression motivates and contaminates sexual relationships and then turn to two specific manifestations: sexual harassment and rape.

The coercion of women into sexual activities against their will and the sexual exploitation of children are currently among the most serious problems in the United States. In the face of such abhorrent behavior, it is tempting for socially aware women and men to focus right away on the means of stopping it. Attempts to look at the broader cultural, let alone evolutionary, contexts of such behaviors meet with impatience and irritation: never mind why many men behave this way, just concentrate on doing something about it.

There is indeed an urgency to protect women and children, and less often men, from being sexually victimized. As a society and individually, we need to act with all the means at our disposal to that end. One of the best means is understanding. We can learn the nature and causes of sexual aggression only by looking at all possible factors without preconceived notions.

To answer why so many individuals in our society are bent on sexual aggression we need to examine both the personal and the social factors. In other words, we need to understand what it is in our culture that is conducive to sexual violence and then determine why some persons but not others act it out, either using violence to attain sexual aims or using sex to attain aggressive aims.

## AGGRESSIVE ELEMENTS IN SEX

*Aggression* (Latin, "to step forward") denotes vigor and initiative in one sense; in another, it represents violence and hostility. Both meanings of aggression are applicable to sexuality, and the boundary between the two is not always clear. *Dominance*, or mastery of some individuals over others, generates social hierarchies. Dominance is usually achieved through the threat of aggression and less often through actual fighting. Like aggression, it is linked to sexual interactions.

### Dominance

In vertebrates (animals with a backbone) that live in social groups, it is common for some individuals to dominate the group and control the opportunity for mating with the opposite sex (Raven and Johnson, 1986). Because males are generally larger and more aggressive than females, they are usually, but not always, socially dominant over females. In many species, individuals within each sex rank themselves as well in *dominance hierarchies* (called the "pecking order" among chickens). An animal's position in such hierarchies is fairly stable but not fixed; it must be maintained through competition, threats, and continuous self-assertion. The primary significance of dominance for sexual behavior is with respect to opportunities to mate. As a rule, dominant males have a greater choice and easier access to females; but among wolves, for instance, a dominant female will determine who will mate with the males, restricting the choice to herself when food is scarce (Campbell, 1987).

Animals maintain dominance and settle disputes mainly through *threat gestures*. This practice limits fighting and maintains a stable group with a minimum of violence (Raven and Johnson, 1986). Different species have their characteristic threat gestures as well as special physical features that enhance such displays. Primates have no antlers, claws, or other elaborate fighting tools, so they convey threat by frontal displays and facial expressions. For instance, a *stare*, which often precedes attack, is intimidating, whereas shifting the eyes indicates fear and submissiveness. It is hypothesized that the erect penis fulfills a similar function (Wickler, 1972). Monkeys and apes guarding territory may display erections to look more fierce. When primates use mounting for nonsexual purposes, it is usually to convey dominance (Chapter 8). In fact, it is through such behavior that copulatory patterns are learned in childhood (see Figure 8.7).

Do humans follow this pattern? Men are generally more dominant than women, which may be linked to men's greater propensity for sexual violence and exploitation (Malamuth et al., 1986); whether this gender difference is due to biological or cultural reasons raises intriguing and controversial issues. In physical terms, many masculine features have been commonly correlated with dominant status. Facial hair reflects male maturity with overtones of sexual potency, whereas the flowing white beards of patriarchs command respect. The square chin (Dick Tracy style), broad shoulders, piercing stare, and bushy eyebrows are all part of the stereotypical image of the man who is dominant and virile, even though in reality none of these features have any necessary bearing on either.

The male preoccupation with penis size may be a residue of its earlier threat potential. The human penis is larger than those of other primates and may have been selected during

Figure 19.1   Codpiece.

evolution because of its role in male-to-male competition. Various cultures have developed further means of enhancing its appearance. The *codpiece,* a pouch at the crotch of tight-fitting breeches, worn by men in the 15th and 16th centuries, made the genitals look prominent (Figure 19.1). Gourds have been used as *penis sheaths* and as artificial extensions of the penis by men in New Guinea as well as in early African and American cultures (Heider, 1973). The penis as a symbol of dominance has been used openly in some cultures, as in the headdress of certain Ethiopian village chiefs (Figure 19.2). More examples of *phallic symbolism* are discussed in Chapter 20.

The association of social status with sexual power and erotic appeal is clear. At least part of the power struggle between men is, at some level, in the service of enhancing their sexual

Figure 19.2    Phallic bow ornament made of metal worn by a southern Ethiopian as an insignia of rank.

potential.[1] An important reason why older men are still able to attract younger women is that they have power and status. In short, dominance status has a profound influence on sexual relationships. It influences who initiates sex, what form it takes, even the positions of coital partners, and many other related factors (Blumstein and Schwartz, 1983).

Sexual associations in turn influence status. The more attractive a man's wife, mistress, or date, the more it reflects his worth. The same is true for women: the more attractive and socially desirable her man, the greater her status.

With the political and social emancipation of women, profound changes are redefining the association of sex and dominance. Many women are not willing any more to be ornaments and testimonials to the social status of men; and as women gain greater financial and

[1]Secretary of State Henry Kissinger was quoted as saying, "Without an office, you have no power, and I love power because it attracts women" (*Washington Post,* Jan. 7, 1977).

political power, male social status may become less of a determinant of sexual attraction. Yet the use of social dominance to obtain sexual aims and the use of sex to enhance social standing are likely to continue.

## Hostility

We use sex to insult one another not only in language but in gestures (Morris, 1977). Though typically used by men, gestures like "giving the finger" (Figure 19.3) may be used by women as well (to mean "fuck you!").

There are countless ways in which men and women hurt each other by using sex as the vehicle of their hostility. Usually, such interactions involve not physical violence but psychological devices like sexual indifference, deprecation, ridicule, and other means of injuring the partner's self-esteem. Such factors often characterize conflicted intimate relationships (Chapter 16) and underlie various forms of sexual dysfunction (Chapter 15).

The relationship of sex and hostility operates both ways: sexual frustration, dissatisfaction, and jealousy provoke anger, whereas hostility breeds sexual unresponsiveness, sabotage, and violence. The closer we feel to someone, the more vulnerable we are to that person. Lack of reciprocation in love or sexual interest by the object of our affections is deeply frustrating. Real or imagined fickleness or in-

Figure 19.3    Phallic gesture with the middle finger.

fidelity generates intense jealousy and anger. It is no wonder that the most extreme form of violence—murder—is often an extension of male-female relationships: 87 percent of all female victims are murdered by men and 84 percent of all female murderers kill men. In 42 percent of cases the murderer and victim know each other; in 16 percent they are relatives (*Uniform Crime Reports,* 1986). One out of three murder victims are spouses, mistresses, lovers, or sexual rivals of the murderer. Seven percent of homicides follow a "lover's quarrel" (Tennov, 1979).

Other forms of physical violence (such as hitting, shoving, arm twisting, hair pulling) occur often in some intimate relationships. More serious harm in the form of broken bones and internal injuries is also not uncommon. The *battered wife* has become a focus of attention in recent years. Their plight is especially compelling since many of them have nowhere to turn. Social agencies and voluntary organizations are beginning to address their needs more actively. Such violence is by no means restricted to marriage or to males battering females (although women remain by far the more frequent victims). On some college campuses 60 percent of single respondents report having been subjected to abusive or aggressive behavior or having inflicted it during courtship (Athanasiou et al., 1970).

Such violence is more common in relationships that have a high level of emotional involvement than in those that are casual. Ironically, such quarrels between some lovers are twisted signs of caring; it is not unusual to precipitate an argument just to get a response out of the other person. Any show of emotion, even anger and abuse, may seem preferable to indifference.

The pervasive presence of hostility in eroticism prompted Freud to argue that most men are driven to debase their partner (he called it "the most prevalent form of degradation in erotic life"). Robert Stoller (1975), whose views on the relation of hostility to the paraphilias we discussed in Chapter 14, proposes that hostility is the basis of all sexual excitement. In this view, the keys to our sexual inner life are our fantasies. By these coded scripts we silently seek to work out lingering problems from childhood and choose our sexual partners and behaviors. We carry much hurt and frustration from our childhood. We desire to hurt the sexual partner to retaliate for that early hurt and to obtain mastery over the experience by reliving it. During this process, says Stoller, "Triumph, rage, revenge, fear, anxiety, risk are all condensed with a complex buzz called 'sexual excitement.'" It should be clear that Stoller is explaining people's fantasy life; these urges need not be, and often are not, carried out, and people can overcome their hostility in affectionate and caring relationships.

## Coercion

Some people try to fulfill their sexual goals and emotional needs through coercion. Coercion can be psychological intimidation by threats or physical force. It also includes engaging individuals (such as children) in sexual activities to which they are not able to give informed consent. Coercive sexual activities inevitably have a victimizer and a victim, who stands to suffer varying degrees of psychological, social, or physical harm. Some people prefer the term *survivor*, because it is an "empowering" word.

Coercive sex is a serious problem. Its most extreme manifestation is rape, but it takes many other forms. Any activity that forces sex on another person, in any shape or form, is sexual coercion. To broaden the definition, to interfere with another person's freedom to act or not to act sexually (except to prevent harm) may be a form of sexual coercion.

Coercion is dependent on social and physical power. Adults usually victimize children, and men usually victimize women. Occasionally, a minor coerces a younger child or adult. Men are sometimes sexually coerced by other men, and less often by women.

## SEXUAL HARASSMENT

*Sexual harassment* has attracted public attention only recently. There has been a male tendency to view women as passive sexual objects—fair game to be had, if you can get away with it. In addition, respectable women have been expected to be defensive about sex, saying "no" even when they mean "yes." This attitude has meant that if couples are to get anywhere sexually, men should push, women should resist, but eventually yield. As a result, sexual pressuring has earned a certain social legitimacy, even when women have clearly felt annoyed, exploited, and humiliated by it.

In one study, college students were asked what behaviors were potentially offensive or constituted sexual harassment (Padgitt and Padgitt, 1986). They included sexist comments; unwanted flirting and other verbal sexual advances, body language (standing too close), thinly veiled insinuations, and unwelcome physical contact (kissing, hugging); explicit propositions (without threats); and sexual bribery. Some of these behaviors are part of the regular repertory of men and women who wish to interact with each other sexually, or are just being friendly. How do you determine when such behavior constitutes sexual harassment?

## Determinants

Catherine MacKinnon (1979) defines sexual harassment as "the unwanted imposition of sexual requirements in the context of a relationship of unequal power" (p. 1). Condensed in this statement are three key components, which we will discuss separately. To qualify as harassment, the behavior must be persistent.

The Sexual Component   In order to qualify as sexual harassment (rather than just annoying behavior), a clearly erotic element must be present.

In principle, a great many people could be potential sexual partners; in practice, most are excluded from such partnership. In the marketplace, the classroom, other institutional settings, and various social occasions not intended for sexual interactions, countless men and women interact in ways that are not supposed to be sexual. Often, though, a covert and sometimes overt erotic element is injected into these relationships.

Such erotic elements vary both in kind and intensity. Both factors are important in determining when the line is crossed from sexual interest to harassment. For example, one common activity is *sexual appraisal*. People often size up how attractive or sexy a person is. This activity may go no farther than aesthetic enjoyment, or it may lead beyond. Men are generally more open in their sexual appraisal of women and more apt to focus on physical characteristics. Women may sexually appraise men just as avidly, but they tend to be subtle about it and to look at a broader range of features; hence they appear less overtly sexual in their attentions.

When sexual appraisal takes the form of persistent ogling, when the person being looked at becomes aware of it, or when people around cannot help but notice it, then the first requirement of harassment may be fulfilled. When you look at someone from a distance appreciatively or look into one another's eyes, the expression of sexual interest remains private; but if a man gets close to leer at a woman's breasts or a woman comes up to a man to stare amorously at his face, the interaction becomes public. The object of attention is drawn into an open engagement, or a "sexual requirement" has been imposed. Even if you look or walk away, you have become drawn, or in a sense coerced, into an erotic interaction.

The sexual appraisal becomes potentially more offensive if it moves beyond looking into touching. Some forms of touching are obviously sexual. Pinching, squeezing the breasts and buttocks, and rubbing the genitals against the body (*frottage*) leave little doubt about sexual intent. When ostensibly friendly hugs, pats, caresses, and kisses become eroticized, the recipient who does not want the sexual attention is in an awkward situation. Casual acquaintances are easily rebuffed, but friends, colleagues, and other valued (and feared) persons are harder to deal with.

Not all sexual overtures could be called harassment. Two other conditions are necessary to cross the line.

Unwanted Imposition   To constitute harassment, the sexual interest or activity must be unwanted by the recipient. It must be imposed either by deception (such as pretending to give a "friendly" hug), by psychological pressure (such as putting the person in a position where making a fuss would be embarrassing), or by physical force (such as forcing a kiss on someone).

How do you know that the expression of erotic interest or a sexual pass will be unwelcome? There is much room for misunderstanding as men and women send out and receive ambiguous signals of interest. One can make an honest mistake or act inadvertently. To avoid doing so talk before you touch. However, attentions that persist after a clear refusal are not mistakes.

A blatant pass may drag the person into an unwelcome engagement the first time around. More often, persistent sexual approaches, even if subtle, despite clear signals of rejection, entrap the victim in an unwanted relationship over time. It is difficult to lay down hard and fast rules about when the line is crossed (how many passes, how insistent). As a general rule, after it has been made plain that the sexual overtures are not welcome, should the person persist, then the behavior is unacceptable.

Unequal Power   The potential for coercion, like exploitation (Chapter 18), is greater when two persons occupy positions of unequal power. Power relationships are complex. Relative to another person you may have an advantage in one area and a disadvantage in another. The key issue is not power in the abstract but vulnerability in a particular situation.

There are several broad categories of interactions in which a person is more vulnerable. One is employer-employee relationships. Another is teacher-student associations. A third is interactions between professionals and the people they serve, such as lawyers and clients or doctors and patients.

People on the "receiving" end of these interactions are not helpless, but they are at a disadvantage. Generally the young are vulnerable to the more mature, and women more susceptible to harassment from men, though reversals certainly occur.

## Contexts

In principle, sexual harassment may occur under any circumstances where potential sexual partners interact. In practice, it is more likely in interactions between people of different power status (Chapter 18). Let us focus on the most likely contexts.

Courtship   Couples in committed and affectionate relationships who are sexually attracted to each other seldom require persuasion to engage in sex. Sometimes, though, even in the most loving couples, the sexual inclinations of the partners do not coincide. One person may try to stimulate sexual interest in the other through gentle requests, declarations of love, seduction, or psychological pressure. The use of physical force is not uncommon even in close couples and spouses to attain sexual aims. When people request, cajole, plead, and demand sex, the lines between negotiation, persuasion, and coercion are hard to draw, but important.

Social Settings   Couples in early stages of courtship or in more casual relationships are more apt to exploit each other for selfish ends. Two gender differences, which we have already discussed, complicate such interactions. First is the greater emphasis placed by women on the relational aspects of sexual partnerships and the greater willingness of men to engage in sex without a relational component. Second is the traditional allocation of the role of "buyer" to men and that of "seller" to women with respect to sexual services and favors. Moreover, women have been expected to "save" themselves for the most advantageous match, give of themselves grudgingly, and act hard to get. This setup confronts men with the choice of being supplicants or predators.

Our culture places men and women at odds. Ideally, there is an honest and caring concern for each other's needs, the ability to say "yes" and "no," and the willingness to negotiate and compromise. In practice, there is the temptation to take advantage of the other and to take more than you give.

Because men usually have a greater share of power than women, sexual harassment offers them a way of getting more than they want to give. What a man does not give under these circumstances is the recognition of a woman's autonomy and her worth as a person. He also bypasses the relational requirements by going directly for the sexual "reward"; he reaches out and grabs what he can before earning the right to it.

Women, in turn, seek their advantage by promising more than they intend to deliver. By acting in a coquettish or seductive manner when she has no intention of pursuing a sexual relationship, or when the circumstances would not permit such association even if she wanted to, a woman may mislead a man into granting her attention and favors. Such behavior may take the form of playful teasing or serious deception.

It could be argued that because women have been powerless, they have been forced to use any means of influence available to protect their interests. It could be said that they behave flirtatiously because men want them to. Both these arguments make women sound like puppets, not autonomous beings.

Men often misinterpret how women behave. When a young man goes about in shorts or bare-chested, people do not pay much attention to it. A young woman who wears equally revealing clothing may be seen as a seductive "tease." When women wear shorts because it is hot or short skirts because it is fashionable, men think it is for their benefit; sometimes it is, but just as often it is not.

Similarly, women have been socialized to be pleasant, cordial, and friendly. Because they value relationships, they are more keen on initiating and sustaining them. When they relate to men in this manner, it is not always to entice them into romantic or sexual relationships. Some women also enjoy being courted even under circumstances that hold little prospect

for the establishment of an erotic relationship, because it makes them feel valued.

Men often have trouble reading these signals correctly. Some men interpret every gesture of friendship as a form of sexual interest. They do not understand that even if a woman is candidly interested in sex, she may still be uninterested in them personally as sexual partners. That is a hard pill to swallow, so they doggedly persevere, insensitive to the fact that women do not want uninvited attention, let alone being pawed, clawed, and slobbered over. Nor are some women above pestering men with their attentions, even when they are clearly unreciprocated and unwelcome.

The Workplace    Sexual harassment in social settings is a nuisance, but you can usually tell off a pest at a party or part company with an overly persistent admirer. However, because of the power inequality between employer and employee, sexual harassment is especially serious at work.

With increasing numbers of women in positions of responsibility, the potential of a female boss harassing a man under her is now present. It is also possible to have sexual harassment between same-sex individuals. By and large, though, the more common problem involves male bosses sexually harassing female employees. Because women employees are likely to be particularly dependent on their jobs (for instance, as single mothers) and more subject to discrimination (for instance, in advancement), they are in a specially vulnerable position. We shall focus on their experience.

Sexual harassment is now recognized as a violation of civil rights. Employers are held legally responsible for acts of harassment to which their workers have been subjected. Nevertheless, 90 percent of women respondents to a magazine survey on sexual harassment have reported such experience (Safran, 1976). In a more representative, larger sample, 42 percent of the women and 15 percent of the men report having had a similar experience at work during the preceding two years. Despite the sizable proportion of male victims, the harassers were male in 78 percent of cases (Tangri et al., 1982).

It is difficult to get an accurate picture of how prevalent the practice is, because the forms that sexual harassment takes vary and because people have different ways of interpreting such behavior. In its most flagrant form, an employer demands of an employee sexual favors as a condition for being hired or for keeping a job. Others hold out raises and promotions as inducements for sex. Some employees respond freely to such offers or even initate them in an attempt to "sleep their way" to the top. More often, they feel humiliated, degraded, taken advantage of, and helpless.

The majority of cases of sexual harassment take less direct forms. The boss may go no farther than "playfully" tickling or patting his female secretary, stand uncomfortably close when there is no need, or interact with her physically in the guise of being friendly or patronizingly "encouraging." Sexual harassment can also be purely verbal. Off-color jokes, sexual innuendos, even compliments with erotic overtones ("You have great legs") are apt to be unwelcome. Although men have no problem recognizing overt forms of harassment, women are more sensitive to its less flagrant forms (Gutek et al., 1985).

Many men in these situations deny erotic intent or ascribe their acts to "innocent fun." They may even believe their own protestations; yet the effect on the victim of sexual harassment is no less disturbing.

College   A survey of women undergraduates at the University of California, Berkeley, revealed that about one in three had been subjected to unwelcome sexual interest by a male instructor (Benson and Thomson, 1982). In its most blatant form, the student was directly propositioned or offered a higher grade in exchange for sex. More often, the sexual advances took less obvious forms—"friendly" hugs and kisses, suggestive body language, romantic overtones, or too solicitous behavior.

The effect on students of unwanted sexual attention is generally negative. Women students are apt to experience self-doubt about their academic ability and their capacity to produce quality work. Assuming that the faculty member's interest in them is purely sexual (which may not be the case) they lose both self-esteem and respect for the instructor. The experience is particularly devastating if the man in question is someone highly respected by the student and a person with whom she has an ongoing relationship (such as a graduate student and thesis supervisor). Nor is the negative effect purely psychological; a woman's educational opportunities may be compromised by such experience and her career development jeopardized.

Although we could make a case against all sexual interaction between students and their teachers, what we are concerned with here is unwanted sexual pressure imposed on the more vulnerable person. There are other cases of romantic and sexual engagements that are entered into voluntarily without harassment.

Professional Services   The potential for sexual harassment exists in all situations where a professional is in a position of influence, such as a lawyer and a client. The prospects are greater, however, when the interaction involves physical contact (such as with doctors and dentists) or dealing with the intimate details of one's life (such as with psychotherapists). The ancient Greeks recognized the special vulnerability of patients to their physicians. They codified specific prohibitions in the Hippocratic Oath to which all physcians swear never to take sexual advantage of patients. ("Whatsoever house I enter, there will I go for the benefit of the sick, refraining from all wrongdoing or corruption, and especially from any act of seduction, of male or female, of bond or free.")

Though most doctors and other health professionals adhere to these standards (and are severely punished if they do not) sexual interactions between caregivers and their patients and clients continue to occur occasionally.

The effects are usually bad for the person

receiving care and for the treatment. The asymmetry of the relationship, the special dynamics of the doctor or therapist relationship, the problem of consent, and related considerations combine to make such interactions a form of sexual harassment.

## Handling Sexual Harassment

Dealing with sexual harassment is a difficult and delicate issue. Blanket rules forbidding sexual interactions in the workplace or within institutions are likely to be resented and unenforceable, though they may serve a useful function by sensitizing people to the problem. The workplace is one of the most promising locations to meet potential mates or sexual partners. Though people recognize the problem of confusing work roles and personal relationships, they are unwilling to restrict their interactions to one sphere.

Patients, clients, and students are not entirely helpless in these interactions. They can protect themselves by reporting, exposing, or suing the offending professional. Consensual participation on the part of the person with less power may make the actions of the person with greater power more difficult to condemn as exploitative. You can refuse to be part of an exploitative relationship.

Beyond passive acquiescence, some persons with less power actively use the promise of sexual favors to gain an advantage, be it a promotion or a better grade. This reversal too is exploitative (even though it entails no coercion), because it is a misuse of sex for crass purposes and unfair to peers. Those in greater power have the responsibility to decline such advances, not to profit by them.

The practical way to deal with sexual harassment is not to dwell on the right of people to pair off but to focus on harassment itself. First the person being harassed should send a clear message (such as through a private letter) that the sexual attentions of the other person are not welcome and must stop; if that does not work, then the person should decide whether or not to take more formal steps to be free of the harassment. You can change your doctor, lawyer, or therapist and consider reporting them to their professional organizations. To file a complaint in a work setting is more risky, depending on the circumstances. Many businesses have safeguards to protect the employee from further harassment as well as retaliation but these measures may not always work. Colleges and universities have now established grievance procedures and special officers to counsel victims of sexual harassment, resolve conflicts arising from it, and discipline offending staff and faculty members. In all such settings, pressing charges requires courage, time, and energy. It is not a step to be taken lightly. The gravity of the offense must be weighed against the consequences of taking formal action for all concerned.

Because of these complications, the problem of sexual harassment is better prevented than dealt with after the fact. A few pointers may keep you from becoming embroiled in such unhappy encounters. First and foremost, use your common sense. Women should not let the fear of appearing unfriendly make them go along with unwelcome attention. Do not "set yourself up" by being alone with those who have made, or are likely to make, unwanted advances. Men must realize the enormous impact of their unwanted sexual attentions on women. Those in positions of responsibility must recognize the extent of the damage they may cause, even inadvertently. Men must also be aware of the serious damage they risk to their reputation, career, and relationships by such behavior. Increasingly, women are now fighting back and they are by no means helpless.

Men must be careful not to misconstrue women's behavior. What you find seductive in how a woman looks or acts may not be intended to be erotic; even if it is, it may not be aimed at you. You are entitled to convey your sexual interest to a woman, but be tactful. Start with steps that can be readily retracted without putting her or yourself in an embarrassing position. Wait for the right time and right place, and respect her reaction. Talk before you touch, and do not touch without asking.

Women in turn must try not to confuse men. Perfume and a plunging neckline in the workplace convey different signals than a woman's business suit. The traditional and modern ways of being a woman are compatible in some ways but not others; you cannot have it both ways.

As soon as you recognize that the man you are dealing with has a sexual interest in you, be clear in your own mind what you want. Especially when dealing with someone who has power over you, decide if your sexual assets will in any way, directly or indirectly, be part of the relationship. Then act accordingly. As an autonomous and self-respecting woman, be sure that you are giving as much as you are getting in terms of the primary goals of the association. If you accept favors not accorded to your peers, or find yourself offered privileges you have not earned, ask yourself why. By using up such credit, you may be mortgaging your independence and integrity.

You may still be sexually harassed, but you will be in greater control of yourself and of the situation. If there is room for doubt, be charitable, while standing firm. Humiliating a person in power is not the only way to keep him in check; the clear threat of consequences is often more effective.

What we have said so far assumes that men take the initiative in sexual encounters. Increasing numbers of women now make the first move. When that happens, all of this advice holds in reverse.

## RAPE

When sexual coercion relies on the actual use or threat of physical force, it becomes *sexual assault*, the flagrant example of which is *rape* (Latin, "to seize"). Rape is a topic of great psychological and social significance, which has been highlighted recently through our greater awareness of the exploitation of women.

Nevertheless, rape is an ancient behavior. There are references to it in the Old Testament and in historical records of many other ancient cultures (Chapter 20). In one form or another, it has probably existed in all societies at all times. This is not to suggest that rape is a "natural" form of behavior, which cannot be

Figure 19.4 Jacopo Tintoretto (1518–1594), *Tarquin and Lucretia*, ca. 1560.

avoided. Rather it is a reflection of the tendency for sex and aggression to become intermingled.

Rape is a common theme in literature and art. Its expressions have ranged from romantic representations in Renaissance art (Figure 19.4) to realistic explorations of its brutality in the modern cinema (Figure 19.5). This chapter covers the descriptive and psychological aspects of rape. We will return to its historical (Chapter 20), social, and legal significance (Chapter 22).

### The Nature of Rape

Rape is the most extreme form of sexual coercion. Its basic psychological dynamics have a great deal in common with sexual harassment. Rape itself takes different forms, both in behavior and in degree of violence. For instance,

Figure 19.5 Kurosawa's *Rashomon* (1950) presents three conflicting versions of the rape of a woman, from the perspectives of the rapist, the husband, and an uninvolved witness.

rape may involve no overt physical violence, as when a man prevails by threatening an unwilling woman to engage in coitus or extreme violence when a rapist murders the victim.

In formal terms, rape is a legal rather than a clinical term. There is no diagnosis for rapists, just as there is no such designation for murderers. This is not because rape and murder are normal behaviors but because there is no one psychological syndrome that underlies such behavior. Therefore, rapists and murderers are legally accountable for their behaviors unless there is some other evidence for the existence of a mental disorder.

The law has traditionally defined rape as an act of sexual intercourse with a woman other than one's wife, against her will, by using

threat or force or by taking advantage of circumstances that render her uncapable of giving consent (Chapter 22). The precise legal definition of rape varies from one state to another, and in many cases some of the basic requirements are changing. For example, the fact that the victim is the wife may no longer exempt the case from constituting rape. The victim is now defined in gender-neutral terms. Sexual acts other than coitus (such as oral sex or insertion of foreign objects into the body orifices) may also be sufficient sexual violation to constitute rape.

Some people define rape in still broader terms. For example, Susan Brownmiller (1975), whose writings focused a great deal of public attention on these issues, defines it this way: "A sexual invasion of the body by force, an incursion into the private, personal inner space without consent—in short, an internal assault from one of several avenues by one of several methods—constitutes a deliberate violation of emotional, physical, and rational integrity and is a hostile act of violence that deserves the name of rape" (p. 422). Even more broadly, any act that sexually debases women or robs them of their sexual autonomy is sometimes referred to as rape, such as voyeurism ("visual rape") and "compulsory pregnancy" (meaning lack of choice for abortion) (Figure 22.1).

The political purpose of extending the meaning of rape is to stress that all sexual exploitation is traumatic; but if we apply the term to situations that do not even entail physical contact with the victim, it could lose its specificity and its force. Should the power of this word be used to make other undesirable behaviors equally repugnant? If looking at degrading pornography is called "visual rape," is it likely to inhibit men from indulging in it? Most such men do not think of themselves as rapists; could it lead them to think that if that is what rape is all about, then it could not be so bad? The situation is not different from the considerations that enter the use of the term "pornography" (Chapter 18). In both cases, a definitional problem is complicated by the social effects of language usage.

Another critical issue is whether rape is sex or violence. It was assumed in the past that rape was perpetrated by lusty men who had no other sexual outlets. Hence, prostitution was justified on the grounds that it safeguarded the virtue of decent women by accommodating male lust.[2] In this perspective, rape is like mugging; if a man cannot get sex for the asking, he will take it by force.

Others hold that rape is not a sexual act at all, but a form of violence. Moreover, they say it is a reflection of the domination of women by men as a whole. As Brownmiller (1975) puts it, rape is "a conscious process of intimidation by which all men keep all women in a state of fear."

Blaming aggression makes the experience no less horrifying for the victim; but it does support a "sex-positive" outlook. If rape is bad and sex is good, then rape cannot be sex. There are three problems with this view. First, to claim that coitus can be a nonsexual act undermines the concept of sexual behavior as objectively definable. Second, it has us pretend that everything about sex is wonderful, when in reality, sex can also be awful, and rape is a good example of it. Third, it does not allow a context for experiences like date rape or acquaintance rape, which may or may not be violent, but are certainly centered around the issue of sexuality.

There is now a growing recognition of the inseparability of the sexual and hostile elements in rape. The question is not whether rape is sex or aggression, but which factor predominates in a given case.

## The Setting

The setting in which rape occurs depends on the relationship between the victim and rapist. One woman may be raped by a stranger in an isolated spot where she is driven by her assailant; another woman may be raped by her husband in their own bed. Nevertheless, there are some locations that are more likely than others as the setting for rape. In a 13-city survey, about one-fifth of all rapes occurred in the victim's residence; an additional 14 percent were nearby (such as in the yard, driveway, or sidewalk). About half of all rapes took place in an isolated area (street, park, playground, parking lot) where the victim was either accosted or taken. All in all, some 65 percent of rapes occurred outdoors (Hindelang and Davis, 1977). These surveys were based mainly on stranger rape. Date rapes are much more likely to occur indoors. Monthly totals show the greatest number of forcible rapes to be reported during the summer, peaking in August (*Uniform Crime Reports*, 1987).

[2]After the Australian government closed down brothels in Queensland, there was an increase of almost 150 percent in rapes and attempted rapes (Barber, 1969). Increases in rape in the United States appear unrelated to the extent of prostitution (Geis, 1977).

Victim and assailant must be present together at a time and place that permit the assault to take place. Many factors must fit: the motivation to commit rape, factors that reduce internal and external inhibitions, and those that provide the opportunity for the act to occur (Malamuth, 1986). Apart from all of the sociological and psychological factors that contribute to the making of potential rapists and their victims, purely circumstantial factors may play an important part. This fact is important in preventing rape. We need to worry about mundane factors such as adequately lit streets or campus escort services in addition to the deeper social and psychological issues.

Some rapes are completely unpremeditated and unpredictable. A female Internal Revenue Service agent came to audit a man's taxes at his home. He handcuffed her, raped her, and let her go; then he shot himself (*San Francisco Chronicle*, March 20, 1987). Other rapes are premeditated: when a rapist furnishes a room for a ritualistic enactment of a sadistic assault it is merely a matter of time until he settles on a victim.

A whole set of factors determines the statistical likelihood of the key elements—rapist, victim, and circumstances—coming together. This is why, although we can usefully discuss the prevalence rates of rape nationally, the likelihoods of being raped for given groups of women, and for a specific woman, are uneven. No woman is entirely safe, but some women are far more likely to be raped than others.

## Prevalence

In 1986, over 90,000 rapes were reported in the United States, one forcible rape every 6 minutes (compared to one murder every 25 minutes) (*Uniform Crime Reports*, 1987). Despite greater public awareness of rape, we have only an incomplete picture of its prevalence. The sexual assaults that gain the most notoriety through the media are by no means representative of the majority of rapes that occur.

Rape is among the most underreported crimes: estimates of its true incidence range from 5 to 20 times the reported figures (Amir,

1971). A national survey administered by the Census Bureau showed that half of all rapes in 1979 were unreported (U.S. Department of Justice, 1981). The actual proportion may be much higher (Ageton, 1983; Koss et al., 1987).

Even when rapes are reported, only half of the offenders are caught; of those, only three out of four are prosecuted; and of those, only half are found guilty. Because the national rape statistics put out by the FBI and most studies of rapists are based on convicted rapists, conclusions from such data cannot be extended to rapists at large.

Nonetheless, rape (including attempts to commit rape) is the most rapidly increasing violent crime in the United States. Reported cases increased from 17,190 in 1960 to 63,020 in 1977, to 82,088 in 1980, and to over 90,434 in 1986—a 42 percent increase over a decade (*Uniform Crime Reports*, 1987). One in four adolescent females is expected to be sexually assaulted sometime in her life if current rates persist. Regionally, the highest female rape rate is in the western states (86 victims per 100,000 females); the lowest rate (55/100,000) is in northeastern states. The prevalence of rape has also been correlated with urbanization, poverty, and a high percentage of divorced men (Jaffee and Strauss, 1987).

Although the rates of all major violent crimes (murder, assault, and robbery) have been on the rise, that of rape began going up faster in the 1970s than those of other crimes combined (Hindelang and Davis, 1977), and has continued to do so.

These increased rates may be partly the result of the greater willingness of women to report rapes, because of changed social attitudes. According to some sources, up to 50 percent of sexual assaults are now reported to the police or other agencies (Feldman-Summers and Norris, 1984). Women who are married, seriously injured, assaulted by a stranger, or sure they have a strong legal case are more likely to report the rape (Lizotte, 1985). The higher rates may also reflect an actual increase in the incidence of rape, which some ascribe to the effects of violent pornography (Chapter 18).

Estimates of sexual assault based on general population surveys (albeit nonrepresentative samples) show even higher figures. Nine percent of the males responding to a 1977 *Redbook* questionnaire reported that they had used force, or the threat of force, to make a woman engage in sex. In addition, 8 percent of the males reported using less direct forms of force, such as threatening a woman with loss of a job or monetary assistance (Tavris, 1978). One out of every four of the women in the *Cosmopolitan* survey had had at least one experience of rape or sexual molestation (Wolfe, 1980).

The greater recognition of acquaintance and marital rape has added yet another dimension to the prevalence of this problem. In a national survey of 32 educational institutions, 28 percent of women (average age 21; 85 percent single; 86 percent white) reported that they had been subjected to sexual coercion since age 14, including incidents in which alcohol or drugs were used to overcome their resistance against their will: 15.4 percent of the women had experienced sexual intercourse, oral and anal intercourse, or penetration of objects; another 12.1 percent had experienced attempts. Among the men, only 4.4 percent admitted performing, and 3.3 percent attempting, such acts (Koss et al., 1987).

When the investigators applied the more restrictive definition of rape used by the federal government (based on attempted or actual vaginal intercourse) 38 women per 1000 reported having been raped during the previous six months. This figure is much higher than the 2.5 rapes per 1000 reported in the federal National Crime Survey for the 20–24 year old age group. The federal sample is not restricted to college students, so the two populations are not comparable; but because the prevalence is higher in disadvantaged groups, the discrepancy between the actual rates may be even higher than shown above.

Other surveys from institutional settings (such as colleges and the military) show similarly high rates. In one study, 59 percent of the women had been subjected to a coercive sexual experience, ranging from unwanted sexual intercourse (25 percent) to genital fondling (21 percent). Most of the offenders were friends, dates, or lovers (Mims and Chang, 1984). Figures on marital rape are harder to come by. Some investigators have found that one in ten wives in their study sample has been sexually assaulted at least once by her husband (Finkelhor, 1987).

Reports about the existence of rape vary widely. Among some Pacific islanders, like the Yapese and the Trukese, rape is unknown, whereas on Tonga, it is the most frequent criminal offense (Gregersen, 1983). In cross-cultural comparisons of the prevalence of rape, the United States emerges in an intermediate position (Sanday, 1981). However, comparisons between widely divergent cultures may be misleading. For instance, among the Gusii in Africa, the abduction of young women became highly prevalent because the burden of paying the bride price to get a wife was increasingly difficult for young men to meet (Levine, 1959). By sexually taking possession of a woman a man got himself a wife. This practice is "rape" in some sense, but it clearly entails a different set of psychosocial dynamics (whether good or bad) than in our culture. Therefore, in compiling rape statistics, the use of purely behavioral criteria with no reference to cultural context may be misleading.

## Varieties of Rape

Heterosexual rape has several important types, depending on the relationship between the rapist and victim.

Stranger Rape   A man wearing a ski mask enters the house of a single woman in the middle of the night, holds a knife to her throat, and rapes her. A college student returning to her dorm on an unlit path is dragged behind the bushes by an assailant; she fights him off and runs away. These and similar episodes of completed and attempted sexual assaults are the most commonly reported examples of rape.

The extent to which rape is committed by strangers rather than by persons known to the victim differs in various studies. The *Uniform*

*Crime Reports* (1987) indicate that in one-third to one-half of *reported* rapes, the victim knew the assailant at least casually. Because stranger rapes are more likely to be reported and taken seriously by the police, the proportion of assailants known to the victim in all rapes would be actually higher. In the *Cosmopolitan* survey, 33 percent respondents who had been "sexually assaulted" (which is a broader category than rape) had been victimized by strangers, as against 46 percent by friends and acquaintances, and 7 percent by husbands (Wolfe, 1980).

One important reason that the prevalence of rape by strangers appears higher is that women have no problem recognizing such acts of sexual coercion for what they are; and women are far more likely to report the rape than when the assailant is a friend or a spouse. If the full story of rape in all its forms were to be known, those perpetrated by strangers would probably account for a lesser share. Meanwhile, rape by men who are either strangers or casual acquaintances of the women have come to represent the primary model, and most studies of rape have so far relied on it. The profiles of the "typical" rapist or victims based on this model may by no means be representative.

Sometimes the rapist and victim are true strangers to each other. A man who surprises a woman during a burglary and rapes her on the spur of the moment would be one example. More often, the victim is known to the rapist, at least from a distance, and not infrequently, she may be slightly acquainted with him. The key issue is that in "stranger" rapes, the man and his victim have no past or present sexual association, nor are they in a relationship (such as dating) that has the potential of developing into a sexual partnership. Hence, a sexual element is imposed by the man on a nonsexual relationship or where no relationship of any kind exists. This fact makes the coercive aspect of the act plain to see.

Acquaintance and Date Rape    Awareness has dawned over recent years that rape is not only a problem of being assaulted by nameless and faceless strangers but also by acquaintances, friends, and even lovers and husbands. Moreover, such experiences are likely to occur in ordinary settings, such as houses, dormitories, and cars, rather than in dark alleys and strange locations. Their occurrence on college campuses has attracted special attention (Box 19.1).

The term *acquaintance rape* refers to the fact that the rapist and victim know each other but are not involved in a relationship. The fact that the woman knows the rapist more or less casually facilitates the contact, such as being at the same party. Acquaintance rape lacks the more personal issues involved when a date or close friend is the assailant. Box 19.1 provides an example of a woman taken advantage of by an acquaintance and his friends.

Sexual coercion in a dating situation, or *date rape*, may involve couples in varying degress of intimacy. The common element is that the woman has willingly gone out with the person and has said "yes" to several of his requests (to go to a movie, have a pizza and a beer, give a goodnight kiss) but has refused to yield to his consequent demands for sex. Having been voluntarily involved in some aspect of the relationship, having consented to some sexual activities, many women in these situations blame themselves and excuse the assailant, or at least minimize his offensive behavior. This reaction is reinforced when other people call her guilty or at best careless ("She led him on").

The coercive sexual act may follow even greater degrees of sexual intimacy. For instance, a couple engaged in petting reach a point where she wants to go no further but he wishes to engage in oral sex or sexual intercourse. Though she verbally and then physically resists his attempts, he overpowers her and consummates the act. In another instance, the couple may have engaged in coitus in the past but she refuses to do so on this occasion; he persists and ends up forcing her into coitus.

Often a good deal of ambiguity remains in the minds of both parties. The woman recognizes that she was subjected to a sexual experience against her will, but was it rape? If

# Box 19.1

## SEXUAL COERCION IN COLLEGE

Although sexual violence is opposite to every principle that institutions of higher learning stand for, it has become more prevalent on college campuses. There may be many reasons. The factors that account for the escalation of sexual violence in the country as a whole may also be at work; after all, college students are part of the same culture. In addition, the concentration of men and women in an age group that is more susceptible to sexual coerciveness, who live largely outside of parental or institutional supervision, and who have access to alcohol and drugs compound the problem.

This problem is not new. Over 30 years ago, Kirkpatrick and Kanin (1957) reported that 62 percent of college women had experienced at least one episode of sexual coercion in their last year of high school, and 56 percent had a similar experience during any given year in college. That women were not imagining these happenings was confirmed by the admission of 22 percent of college men that they had used force in attempts to coerce coitus (Kanin, 1969). More recent studies have reported even higher rates (Amick and Calhoun, 1987).

In an extensive survey of students at 35 colleges and universities, Koss and her associates (1987) found one woman in eight had been raped in the year previous to the survey; of the women raped, 90 percent knew their assailants, and almost half were dating them; one of every 12 men had participated in rape or an attempted rape. Fewer than 20 percent of the assaulted women told the police about the rape; more than one-third did not discuss their experience with anyone.

Many a college campus is shocked once in a while by reports that a woman has been raped by a stranger. Far more common are cases of acquaintance and date sexual assaults, whether or not they are full-fledged rapes. These encounters are not likely to involve weapons or serious physical injury. More typically, women are held down against their will, shoved about as the man tries to kiss, fondle, undress, or maneuver them into position. Slapping, choking, and more brutal beatings do also occur; but most common are persistent attempts at verbal persuasion, pleading, shaming, threats of breaking off the relationship, and other forms of psychological pressuring.

The women typically react by resisting, arguing, pleading, crying, fighting back, or trying to get away; 69 percent of women in these situations resist the most severe attempts (Amick and Calhoun, 1987). In the aftermath of these experiences, women often feel anger, guilt, and disgust. Women who are more self-assertive are less likely to suffer these reactions.

Often alcohol figures prominently in women being taken advantage of sexually either during a date or at a party. The following account relates the experience of one college woman under such circumstances, as reported in a student newspaper (Metcalfe, 1988).

> Although "Susan," a university student, had originally planned to spend the evening with her boyfriend, a call from another friend changed her mind. According to Susan, "Jeff" said he really needed to talk to her in person. It was too important to discuss on the phone. Susan was dropped off at the campus fraternity house where her friend was a member, not expecting to stay long.
>
> No one seemed to know where Jeff was, but Susan was invited to play drinking games while she waited. The alcohol flowed, and soon she was drunk. The men began to make overt sexual advances, first alone and then as a crowd.
>
> It was at this point that Susan knew she was in trouble.
>
> "I didn't know what was going on," she says today. "I felt really out of control. All of a sudden the situation was out of my hands."
>
> Finally, Susan remembers, Jeff entered the crowded room wearing only a rubber raincoat and told Susan about a sexual fantasy he wanted to act out. She protested but was ignored.
>
> "He forced himself on me, and that started a lot of guys. There was always at least one guy,

sometimes two. There were guys I didn't know coming in and doing stuff to me, and I didn't know what was going on.... They would hold me ... I would try to leave, but they would pull me back down...."

"I didn't have any control, (and) it didn't matter if I agreed at that point.... I passed out after that."

The next day Susan called Jeff to confront him with what had happened the previous night.

"He said, 'You were drunk. You've been here before, and its your own problem. I think you really need help if you think something was wrong,'" she recalls.

Susan didn't report the rape. When she returned home the next day, her boyfriend was waiting for her. She told him what had happened but didn't go to the police.

"I thought it was my own fault," she says. "I didn't know what to do."

---

there was no vaginal penetration (or no ejaculation), she may conclude that it was not. People who are less sure that date rape is a form of rape tend to be relatively more accepting of it (Fisher, 1986).

The fact that a woman was freely involved in some sort of sexual interaction, or was sexually aroused, or cared about him, or would rather not face up to the fact that she was raped, may lead her to leave the matter unresolved in her mind or deny it. If the couple had been drinking or high on drugs, the memory of the experience may be even more hazy. This is why date rape is less likely to be reported, and there are many difficulties in preventing it. Rape education programs on campus inform women about these issues and help prevent their occurrences.

Marital Rape    A man breaks into a house occupied by his wife, from whom he is separated, and rapes her. The circumstances of such an act are very much like stranger rape, and courts have generally treated such cases as rape. A man beats his wife into submitting to him sexually; he is liable to prosecution for assault and battery, but the courts have been, until recently, unwilling to charge him with rape. Especially if there is no evidence for the overt use of force, courts have felt bound by the consideration of *spousal exclusion*, in effect saying that a husband cannot be accused of raping his wife.

This situation has now changed dramatically. As we will discuss in Chapter 22, it is now a crime in half of the states for a husband to rape his wife while the two are living together. The fact that sexual access to a spouse is one of the basic expectations of marriage does not entitle one of the partners to coerce the other into sex on any particular occasion. Failure to provide sexual satisfaction may constitute grounds to terminate the marriage, but the use of coercion is not an acceptable way of "solving" the problem.

Sex is usually not the aim in marital rape. The man engages in the sexual brutality out of anger, with the intention of humiliating and degrading the wife. Marital rape is thus part of the plight of the physically abused wife. Countless women are trapped in this predicament. Some leave; others cannot or do not want to. They stay because of economic necessity or fear; because they have nowhere to go; or because they feel attached to the man, have invested years into the marriage, and hope that he will change (Finkelhor, 1987).

Statutory Rape    The central issue in rape is the principle of free choice. In the cases so far, the victim is deprived of the freedom of choice by being threatened or forced into unwanted sexual activity. In statutory rape, the victim is considered to be deprived of the freedom to choose by being younger than the age of consent, hence incapable of making such a choice. The determination of *statutory rape* is therefore based on the age limit set by the law, not on whether the younger person was a willing participant or whether coercion of any kind was used. Most states prosecute coercive acts with minors under sexual assault statutes, invoking the statutory element only in the absence of coercion.

There is good reason for protecting children from being sexually abused; but when dealing with older teenagers, statutory law is clearly an arbitrary way of determining rape. Does a young woman magically become competent to exercise judgment between one day and the next when she turns 18? The problem is no different than allowing people to vote or drink at 18. Any legal age limit must be more or less arbitrary.

Group Rape    There is a common perception that rape is typically commited by a solitary male. Yet in Amir's study, 43 percent of the victims had been subjected to *group rape* where two ("pair rape") or more men ("gang rape" or "gang bang") had raped a woman. Altogether 71 percent of these offenders had been involved in multiple rapes (55 percent in group rape, 16 percent in pair rape). Men who participated in group rape tended to be younger and to have arrest records. These rapes were usually planned (even if the victim was not always preselected) and perpetrated on a woman who lived in the neighborhood.

Gang rapes tend to be particularly vicious because the victim is totally defenseless and her assailants try to outdo each other in violating and degrading her. Male rape victims are usually overpowered by a group of assailants, as in homosexual rapes in prison. In the rare instances when women rape men, there is nearly always more than one woman involved.

Rape of Males    Most male victims of sexual coercion are children. The only significant risk of adult males being raped is in prison. Though one man forcing another to perform oral sex or to submit to anal intercourse could be termed *homosexual rape*, the perpetrators in these cases usually do not consider themselves to be gay and do not engage in homosexual relationships outside of prison. Occasionally, men may be raped by women (Box 19.2).

The Rape Victim

The profiles based on the statistics of reported rapes portray the typical rape victim as a young unmarried woman who lives in an urban, lower-class neighborhood. She generally shares the demographic characteristics of her assailant, who is a poorly educated young man with few vocational skills and low socioeconomic status. This characterization still adequately describes a significant proportion of rape victims, but the prospect of rape is not restricted to any particular socioeconomic or ethnic group. Rape victims have ranged in age from infants to women in their eighties, including members of every ethnic group, social class, marital status, and vocational category. In particular, middle-class women working and living in urban settings and on college campuses have recently become more frequent targets of rape. Women who are highly mobile (working women, students, and younger women in general) are at higher risk (Ploughman and Stensrud, 1986). On the other hand, the inclusion of marital rape makes the victim population even more heterogenous.

The Role of the Victim    Are there behavioral patterns that correlate with the likelihood of a woman being raped? Such a question would ordinarily not be asked of victims of some other crime. It is sometimes assumed, though, that rape is a more interactive process, that women are not passive victims who are randomly assaulted but people who invite being victimized.

Women who live under high-risk circumstances have little choice in being exposed to sexual assault. The same would more or less hold true for most victims of stranger rape. What about rapes that occur in relationships where the woman has willingly associated herself with her assailant? Could she somehow be involved in determining the outcome?

The misconceptions that surround the behavior of women in these conditions often amount to *blaming the victim*. It has been assumed that most women who get sexually assaulted somehow bring it on themselves through incaution ("She should have known

# Box 19.2

## MEN AS RAPE VICTIMS

Men are almost always raped by other men, and most such cases of rape occur in prisons (Weiss, 1974). Younger inmates who are physically timid and unable to defend themselves become common targets, but they are by no means the only victims. To avoid repeated assaults, some young inmates attach themselves to one of the more dominant men, becoming his "girl" (Braen, 1980). Sexual deprivation in prison is self-evident, but power and dominance are also major motivations in such attacks, especially the most violent. The victim is often overpowered and gang-raped by a group of inmates. The presence of guards does not entirely deter such assaults, which may even occur when inmates are being transported in police vans (Davis, 1968). The fear of retaliation often inhibits victims from "snitching" to the authorities. Men who end up in jail for minor offenses or for upholding a principle (such as protestors) thus face a potential nightmare. Prison authorities have not found an effective way of dealing with this problem (Lockwood, 1980).

Outside of prison, adult male rapes are rare, accounting for very few of the cases reported to the police or seen in rape crisis centers. These victims are often hitchhikers who are overpowered by force or the threat of weapons. The rapists are usually strangers, but there have also been cases when an employer, even a brother or father, has been the assailant. The most common acts in male rape are sodomizing the victim and forcing him to perform fellatio.

It has been long assumed that women are incapable of raping men and that their involvement in rape is usually in the role of an accomplice who restrains or subdues another woman, who is then raped by the man. In gang rapes, female partners may actively participate in the sexual degradation of the victim. Legally, a woman may be charged with rape if she aids and abets the crime. Lesbian sexual assaults are rare and confined to prison settings.

Recent evidence shows that women can and do occasionally rape men. These rapes usually involve one or several armed women, who force a man to perform cunnilingus and to have sexual intercourse. These victims can also be abused by being urinated on and injured (in one case, castrated). There are only a few cases of heterosexual male rape on record, because such cases are rare and also because men may be even more reluctant to report it than are women rape victims. As a consequence of being raped, men develop a "post-assault syndrome" characterized by depression, sexual aversion, and dysfunction—reactions that are quite similar to the experience of women following rape (Groth, 1979; Sarrel and Masters, 1982).

Women are much less likely than men to be the assailants in rape cases for much the same reasons that women commit far fewer violent crimes. The typical way for a woman to use sex to express her anger has been to withhold sex, rather than force it on a man. Whether or not changing sex roles and greater willingness of women to take the sexual initiative will be reflected in more of them acting like rapists remains to be seen. It seems highly unlikely that being raped by women will ever present a comparable threat to the safety and sexual integrity of men, as it does for women.

better") or provocation ("She was asking for it"). Furthermore, it has been thought that rapists succeed only when a woman deep down wants to be raped ("No woman can be raped against her will"), that women want to be raped ("They fantasize about it all the time"), or that they even enjoy it (some rapists actually ask the victim if they did). Women themselves may share these misconceptions, which is why they often blame themselves for being raped. They may also derive false comfort from a sense of invulnerability ("It could never happen to me"), because some personal characteristic does not make them fit the "type" of women who presumably get raped.

These ideas are all wrong. The fact that we fail to exercise caution does not mean that we want to court disaster (do drivers speed because they want to get into accidents?). A few women (and men) may provoke attacks on their person, but most are hapless victims. Fantasies of rape are different than actual wishes to be raped (Chapter 11). The fact that a woman's vagina lubricates in response to sexual stimulation (just as a man gets an erection) despite the humiliation and terror of being raped does not mean the victims "enjoy" the experience.[3] Finally, women can certainly be raped against their will (just as men can) either through being overpowered or threatened with serious harm.

To bandy about such allegations adds insult to the grievous injury experienced by rape victims. In no way would such considerations excuse the actions of the rapist, anyhow.

Rape victims have been dealt with for so long with suspicion and callousness by the public, police, courts, and even physicians that there is now a strong resistance to examining their behavior for fear that such inquiry might once again shift the blame onto the victim. Nonetheless, *victim precipitation* is a useful concept in criminology. It focuses on contributory behavior on the part of the victim (Wolfgang, 1958), seeking whether the crime might have been avoided if the victim had behaved differently. It does not blame the victim for the crime, nor does it ever justify the crime. Its potential usefulness is to find ways of modifying behavior to reduce risk (Box 19.3).

Victim precipitation is obvious in other crimes. For example, if the victim of an assault was the first to use physical force, or insulted the assailant, that behavior was provocative. If a woman has prominent breasts that incite the rapist's lust, is she "precipitating" the assault? If a woman dresses and behaves in a sexually provocative manner because she enjoys doing so or wants to attract the attention of men she finds congenial, does that mean that any man should feel free to force his attention on her? If a college student hitches a ride, or a house-

wife lets a delivery man into her house, are they inviting sexual assault?

Amir (1971) considered one in five rapes to have been victim-precipitated on the basis of a variety of criteria, such as the victim going to the offender's house to drink and getting into other "risky situations marred by sexuality." When stronger criteria are used (such as the victim making sexual advances or agreeing to sexual relations but then changing her mind), victim precipitation is a factor in only 4 percent of cases. Victim precipitation turns out to be a factor less frequently in rape than in other violent crimes, such as homicides (22 percent) and nonsexual assaults (14 percent) (Mulvihill et al., 1969).

Nonetheless, many adolescents hold the victim responsible. In a survey in Los Angeles, most teenage boys considered forcing a girl to have sex to be acceptable behavior under certain circumstances, and 42 percent of the girls agreed. The circumstances that justified the use of force involved sexual encouragement by the girl ("to get him sexually excited," "to lead him on," "to say yes") followed by her refusal to have sex. Force was especially acceptable if the girl was known to have slept with other boys or showed up at a party where she knew there would be drinking and drugs. In other situations, girls who meant to be stylish by going braless or wearing tight jeans were misunderstood by boys, who interpreted such behavior as a sexual invitation. (There was general agreement that spending money on a girl did not give a boy a right to her body.) Race, age, sexual experience, and socioeconomic status made little or no difference in the attitudes of these youths (*Los Angeles Times*, Sept. 30, 1982).

A common problem is the failure of men to understand that a woman who engages in sexual play may not wish to go on to have coitus; that the fact that she has slept with others does not mean that she must have sex with him as well; and that even if a woman begins a sexual encounter with the intention of going all the way, she is entitled to change her mind. In a situation like that, a man is entitled to feel frustrated and annoyed, but not to use force.

[3]The possibility of sexual arousal on the part of the victim raises special problems. It is known to occur, but none of the 50 women investigated by Becker (cited in Geis, 1977) or the 90 cases seen by Burgess and Holmstrom (1976) had experienced orgasm during rape. Should a woman feel aroused, she is likely to experience additional guilt.

# Box 19.3

## PREVENTING RAPE

The disadvantaged and grim circumstances under which high-risk victims live do not allow them much choice in being exposed to sexual assault. Once an assault takes place, most victims usually have limited choices. This is not to say that women in these situations should feel helpless and meekly yield to their assailants. On the contrary, one out of four cases of rape is not completed, due to the woman's reactions during the assault. Nonetheless, when a woman has to contend with a group of men, a rapist who is armed, or bent on hurting her, her willingness to undergo the degradation of rape, rather than get seriously injured or killed, is by no means reflective of a desire to be a willing participant.

A number of measures that a woman can take will substantially reduce the risks of being sexually assaulted. We shall focus here primarily on precautions against stranger rapists.

Because many rapes occur in the victim's home, there should be locks on doors and secure windows. Doors to the outside should be equipped with a dead-bolt lock and a chain lock and always kept locked when a woman is alone. To prevent strangers from getting into the house, doors should not be opened to unknown people. Requesting identification from service people may deter a potential rapist.

When away from home, it is best to avoid deserted, enclosed stairwells. Car keys should be out and ready before arriving at the car to minimize the time needed to open the door. The back seat should be checked to make sure no one is there. It is important to keep the car doors locked while driving. Picking up strangers is very dangerous, as is hitchhiking. At her job, a woman should refuse to work alone in a deserted building. Outside, it is wise to avoid walking alone at night, especially in dark, deserted streets or open areas. If a woman has to walk outside at night, she should scan ahead for possible trouble, stay close to the curb on well-lighted streets, walk quickly, wear shoes that are easy to run in, and carry something in her hand that could be used to disable an attacker temporarily. A handbag, umbrella, books, keys, and other suitable objects can be used effectively for this purpose. A freon horn that creates a loud noise can be especially useful. Taking a course on self-defense may prove valuable, pro-

vided the woman becomes proficient and knows when and how to resort to physical force. The use of weapons of any sort is risky, because they can be seized and turned against the victim. Their use is also illegal, and a woman may be liable for harming her assailant, even in self-defense.

It is much harder to advise women what to do in an actual rape encounter. It depends on what sort of rapist she is dealing with—not easy to figure out fast.

The basic strategy will depend on whether the potential rapist is primarily after sex or expressing anger by degrading and humiliating her. The amoral and sexually inadequate rapist form the majority and fall in the first group; the hostile and sadistic types, the latter group.

A woman has a much better chance of dissuading, intimidating, and fighting off the rapists in the first category. What they want is sexual exploitation or compensation for their sexual inadequacy, and they will back off if the woman makes the satisfaction of their aim costly. With a hostile or especially a sadistic rapist, the struggle of the woman will further enrage and arouse him; for him sex and violence have become fused. A rapist out to enact a compulsive, ritualized fantasy is most difficult to stop.

Women are confronted with many recommendations for dealing with these situations, some of them contradictory. The following ideas from Prentky and Burgess (1985) come from a study of the behavior of convicted rapists.

The first and best choice is to escape if possible. Failing that, a woman should start talking to the rapist, keeping the conversation "real" and "in the here-and-now." Women should "gently but persuasively convey the message that you are a stranger." "The victim should never say anything that might justify a rapist's anger, such as claiming she has a venereal disease."

If the rapist listens or responds, the woman is probably dealing with a "compensatory" rapist, and the best idea is to continue talking to him, confronting him with the reality of her feelings. Such rapists are most likely to be stopped by active resistance, such as yelling for help, and least likely to inflict physical injury (however, a woman should never use force against any rapist who has a lethal weapon).

If the rapist pays no attention to what the victim says but does not seem to be using gratuitous violence, he is likely to be the "exploitative" type. The recommendation is to keep talking, trying to "engage the rapist, making yourself a person to him," and diverting him with questions about himself. Breaking the initial tension of the confrontation may "derail" the rapist.

If the rapist responds to talk by increasing his aggression and seems to want to humiliate and demean his victim, he is likely to be the kind of rapist motivated by displaced anger about what he perceives as abuse by women. The best strategy here is to show empathy; "try to demonstrate some sense of interest, concern, or caring if you can muster it," the report advises.

If the rapist makes bizarre sexual demands, he is likely to be a sadist, perhaps the most dangerous, though rarest, type of all. Here the advice is to sense the potential danger early in the encounter, and to end it. Once the assault starts, however, the advice is to struggle and do anything possible to escape.

"That may mean feigning participation, and at a critical moment making maximum use of surprise, attacking the genital or facial areas as viciously as you can. This requires converting your fear into rage and your sense of helplessness into nothing less than a struggle to live" (Goleman, 1985).

---

Another approach to the role of the victim is cultural rather than individual. It focuses on the socialization patterns that make women likely rape victims. Our traditional model of femininity emphasizes passivity and dependency. Women are expected to be nurturant, warm, and altruistic. When confronted with hostility and aggression, they turn to men for protection. Women are not expected to fight, nor are they trained to do so. Against this background, when a woman confronts a determined and aggressive rapist she has little choice but to be a helpless victim. To avoid this outcome, it is argued that radical changes will need to be made in how we teach women to perceive themselves and to handle confrontation (Russell, 1984).

The Consequences of Rape    The most direct impact of rape is on the victim. In addition, those who are close to the victim, especially the sexual partner, are significantly affected by the experience. It would also be interesting to know about the aftereffects on the rapist himself.

Beyond the immediate participants in the rape experience, the prospect of sexual violence has an important and pervasive bearing on the lives of all women, particularly women who live and work in high-risk environments. The possibility of rape extends a constant restriction, for example, on their freedom to move about at night. The burden of rape therefore goes beyond its statistics to affect the lives of millions of others.

The major potential consequences of rape for the female victim include physical trauma, unwanted pregnancy, sexually transmitted diseases, and the emotional disturbances on which we shall focus here.

The psychological consequences of rape are called the *rape trauma syndrome* (Burgess and Holmstrom, 1974). An *acute disorganization phase* immediately follows the rape and lasts from a matter of hours to several weeks (Figure 19.6). Typically a woman responds by being upset, tearful, disbelieving, anxious, and fearful. She may express anger at the rapist or blame herself, feeling guilty and depressed.

In other cases, the victim suppresses her painful emotions and appears unusually calm and collected. Victims with these "silent" reactions to rape may first be stunned and then give way to the more typical outpouring of emotion. Sometimes the suppression of feelings persists until the victim can be gently encouraged in counseling to come to terms with them.

In most cases, the woman is able to overcome the initial acute phase and move on to the longer-term *reorganization phase*. Over a period of several months, but sometimes much longer, the rape victim is able to work through the emotional trauma, come to terms with the experience, and take practical steps to protect herself. She may change her telephone number, or residence, or move altogether to an-

Figure 19.6   A victim receiving counseling in a rape crisis center.

other city. The problems at this stage are mainly in repairing the damage to her sexual life and her intimate relationships (Sales et al., 1984).

Masters and Johnson (1976) identified several sexual problems in women after they have been raped. The most common sexual problem after rape was the development of an aversion for sexual activity and a diminishing interest in sex. In one sample, 40 percent refrained from sex for six months to a year. In about 75 percent, the level of sexual activity remained lower than before the rape for four to six years (Burgess and Holmstrom, 1979). In a more recent study, 59 percent of sexual assault victims reported experiencing sexual dysfunction, as against 17 percent in a control group. Table 19.1 shows the distribution of the types of sexual dysfunction (Becker et al., 1986). Many women report multiple problems. Men who have been raped by women also develop sexual problems. In cases treated by Masters (1986), though these men had been able to function sexually during the rape, they were unable to do so with their own partners for over two years.

Some women experienced severe rela-tional problems. The most common one in-volved a married woman's relationship with her husband. Some husbands were unable to deal with the rape, especially if the rape was public knowledge; they felt that everyone now knew that their wife had been "dirtied." Some husbands wanted to seek revenge on the rapist. Such male reactions added greatly to the wife's distress and increased the likelihood that she would develop sexual problems. In some cases the husbands of rape victims developed sexual dysfunctions themselves. However, most hus-bands were understanding and helpful to their wives.

Helping the Rape Victim   Dealing with the rape victim is in some ways like dealing with an ac-cident victim: medical, legal, and psychological needs must be attended to simultaneously. It is not easy to do, and one need may be met at the expense of the others.

A woman who is raped should contact the police and receive medical attention immedi-ately before doing anything else, such as wash-ing, changing clothes, or tidying the rape scene. Contacting a Rape Crisis Center can be helpful; such centers have personnel who

**Table 19.1    Sexual Dysfunction in Sexual Assault Survivors and Nonassaulted Women***

| DYSFUNCTION | SEXUAL ASSAULT SURVIVORS† (n = 152) | NONASSAULTED WOMEN (n = 17) |
|---|---|---|
| Problems in early response | | |
| Fear of sex | 53.9% | 23.5% |
| Arousal dysfunction | 50.7% | 23.5% |
| Desire dysfunction | 55.9% | 5.9% |
| Orgasmic problems | | |
| Situational secondary nonorgasmia | 11.3% | 11.9% |
| Primary nonorgasmia | 7.2% | 11.8% |
| Secondary nonorgasmia | 6.6% | 0.0% |
| Intromission problems | | |
| Dyspareunia | 10.7% | 0.0% |
| Vaginismus | 2.0% | 0.0% |

*From Becker, J., Skinner, L., Abel, G., and Cichon, J. (1986). Sexual functioning of rape victims. *Archives of Sexual Behavior*, vol. 15, no. 1.

†These women reported that their sexual problems were assault-related.

provide emotional support, transportation, clothes, information, and numerous other services. Close friends and relatives can also be a source of comfort. Rape is not the sort of experience to handle alone.

Unlike the accident victim, the person subjected to rape carries an extra burden of shame and sometimes guilt. It is not easy for a woman to be questioned, examined, and exposed to official scrutiny over matters that are so intensely personal. It is no easier for a male victim to withstand the shattering blow to self-esteem that being sexually violated represents. The problems in running the legal gauntlet to prosecute the rapist will be dealt with in Chapter 22.

Although a rape victim may require psychological counseling and therapy (Rose, 1986), persons close to her can also help a great deal. Though women are most likely to turn to female friends, they find male friends the most helpful in the post-rape period (Mims and Chang, 1984). The role of the friend is to provide psychological support. The best and safest way of doing so is to listen to the victim. She should be allowed to express herself at her own pace and in her own manner, covering the

same ground over and over again if necessary. The listener's role is neither to help her avoid the unpleasant nor to probe; nor is this the time to point out inconsistencies in her statements and behavior, let alone question or criticize her judgment. The aim is eventually to help the woman regain control of her feelings, reestablish her mastery of herself, and get on with her life (Castleman, 1980).

### The Rapist

Investigators, if not the public, have been long aware that men who rape women do not fall into a single, simple pattern. There are several types of rapists and a variety of motivations that may underlie the actions of even a single rapist.

Psychosocial Characteristics    Sociological studies based on crime statistics and surveys provide broad sketches of the men who rape. More intimate psychological profiles have come from clinical studies of individual rapists.

Of those arrested for rape in 1986, 45 percent were men under age 25; 30 percent were in the 18- to 24-year-old age group. Fifty-two percent were white (12 percent hispanics), 47 percent black; other races accounted for 1 percent (*Uniform Crime Reports*, 1987).

Police records and sociological samples of convicted rapists place the majority of these men within a subculture of violence. Most of these men are poor, with minimal education, simple vocational skills, and low social status; they are angry at the dominant culture and prone to violence to obtain what they cannot otherwise get.

One of the best-known sociological studies of rape was conducted by Menachem Amir (1971) during 1958–1960, in Philadelphia. Based on police records, his salient findings were as follows: the majority of rapists and their victims were 15 to 19 years old, and mostly unmarried.[4] Ninety percent belonged to the "lower part of the occupational scale" (from skilled workers down to the unemployed). Blacks were overrepresented both among offenders and victims.[5] In 82 percent of cases, offender and victim lived within the same area. Fifty-seven percent of offenders had a previous police record (as did 20 percent of the victims).

This characterization continues to apply to a subset of the men who rape, but clearly not to a great many rapists—perhaps the majority—who are not socially deprived. In fact, the "average" rapist may not be much different than the "average" person in most demographic characteristics.

A closer scrutiny of the social attitudes of college men who admit to forcing their dates into coitus, compared to a control group who have not, shows a similar proclivity towards violence. In their case, the violence is not di-

rected at society, as with convicted rapists, but at women.

The date rapists are generally more exploitative than their peers in achieving their sexual aims: 80 percent admit relying on alcohol and 86 percent false expressions of love to prevail on their girlfriends to engage in sex; nonrapists engage in similar behavior in 23 percent and 25 percent of cases respectively. Date rapists belong to peer groups that glamorize sexual coercion and view certain types of women as appropriate targets for it. These men thought their peer group reputation would be enhanced if they raped a woman picked up at a bar (54 percent, against 16 percent of controls), a woman who was a "teaser" (81 percent, against 40 percent of controls), and a woman who exploited men for money (73 percent, against 39 percent of controls) (Kanin, 1985). Date rapists were also under greater peer pressure to achieve sexual exploits.

It would seem that the convicted men who raped women indiscriminately, the date rapists who did it more selectively, and the control group who did not rape (though some of them thought about it) fall along a continuum. They see women as sexual objects to be taken advantage of, especially if they appear to be easily available or to use sexual lures to manipulate men.

Coercion under these circumstances is considered justified by date rapists in 86 percent of cases and 19 percent of controls. Conversely, one out of five considers coercion unjustified even though that does not stop him from using it; and one out of five men in the control group consider sexual coercion justified yet do not act out that conviction.

In discussing the factors that contribute to the likelihood of women becoming rape victims, we considered a number of cultural expectations of how women should behave in their interactions with men. Similarly, it could be argued, men are socialized in ways that help them justify sexually coercing of women. Boys are taught to be clear in their objectives and full of initiative in achieving them. Aggressively refusing to take "no" for an answer and

---

[4]This finding is true for violent crimes in general. In California, nearly 90 percent of those arrested for homicide in 1981 were men, half of them younger than 25 years.

[5]Amir's finding that about 80 percent of rapists and victims were black reflects, in part, the large proportion of blacks in Philadelphia; national statistics show about half of arrested rapists to be black. Historically, black men themselves have been the most frequent victims of false accusations of rape in racist white communities.

using muscle when persuasion fails are among the core masculine values of a pioneering society. Once women are converted to desirable sexual objects, then their conquest follows the same rules.

Comparisons of "rape-prone" and "rape-free" cultures show distinct differences in the status of women and the relationship of the two sexes (Sanday, 1981). In rape-prone societies, males are socialized to be competitive and aggressive. Physical prowess is glorified and force is perceived as a legitimate way of winning. By contrast, in "rape-free" societies, men and women share power more equally and children of both sexes are socialized to avoid aggression in their dealings with each other. We shall return to these social perspectives on sexual violence.

The cultural setting is clearly significant in determining whether or not men will rely on sexual coercion. Men are not merely passive agents of their society. Why is it that only some men and not others from the same social segment become rapists? Here the typology of individual rapists comes in.

Typologies of Rapists    There have been a number of attempts to classify rapists by their primary motivations in committing rape. For example, Burgess and Holmstrom (1974) have categorized rapists into amoral, sexually inadequate, hostile, and sadistic types. Groth and Hobson (1983) divide them by the type of rape they commit: sexual gratification rape, anger rape, power rape, and sadistic rape. There is a fair degree of overlap in these typologies. Moreover, rapists typically combine features from the various types in different proportions. Nonetheless, it is instructive to examine these categories separately.

The *amoral rapist* is typically a predatory, aggressive young man who seeks whatever sexual gratification he can find, regardless of the consequences to others. These men violate women in the same way that they help themselves to other people's property, and use whatever force is necessary to achieve their aim. They tend to be the most opportunistic; if they encounter a woman in a vulnerable situation (such as a woman who is alone in a house during a burglary or a woman who is drunk at a bar or at a party), they often take advantage of her.

Amoral rapists are probably responsible for the majority of rapes for sexual gratification, and they may be the most common type among date rapists. A woman who forcefully fights back is often likely to dissuade them from going through with the rape attempt.

Second is the *sexually inadequate rapist*. His primary aim is also to obtain sexual gratification, but he seems unable to achieve it through nonviolent means. Shy and inept in his dealings with women, he compensates for his inadequacies through paraphilias and fantasies of being a great lover. These rapists are most likely to select their victims carefully and strike at an opportune moment. Alcohol is often used to boost their self-confidence and to reduce inhibitions (Ladouceur and Temple, 1985). If the victim fights back vigorously, they are likely to give up and flee. If they do proceed with the rape they are likely to prove impotent, fail to ejaculate, or ejaculate prematurely. Groth and Burgess (1977) found 34 percent of rapists to have suffered such dysfunction during the assault.

The issue of sexual deprivation as a motive for rape has several facets. In rational terms, it makes no sense for a man to resort to rape to gain access to a woman. Even if a man fails to attract a sexual partner on his own merits, there are prostitutes willing to accommodate him. Date rapists in particular show a greater level of sexual activity and experience than their peers who do not rape, but a higher proportion of date rapists (79 percent) than their peers (32 percent) express dissatisfaction with their sexual lives (Kanin, 1985). Dissatisfaction may be construed as a form of sexual deprivation, but rape is not a reasonable way of dealing with it. Moreover, it is likely that the very attitudes towards women that lead them to sexual coercion are responsible for their dissatisfying sexual lives.

Even though the motivation of the amoral rapist and the sexually inadequate rapist is mainly sexual gratification, a certain measure of hostility is also at play. However, unlike the first two types, the *hostile rapist* has a primary interest in hurting his victim. His hostility may be aimed at a particular woman or at women in general, whom he sees as sexually frustrating, untrustworthy, and hostile. Though the roots of his rejection of women and all things feminine may not be apparent to him, his pursuit of exaggerated "masculine" activities and behavior is already evident in adolescence. These men are more likely to rape older women. Their acts of rape are typically triggered by an upsetting experience with a woman who is important to them, but the victim is usually a stranger, on whom the rapist seems to displace his rage. The hostile rapist is out to settle a personal score and the woman he rapes is an innocent and unknowing victim of his private rage.

Hostile rapists are largely responsible for stranger rapes. Their attacks are premeditated and savage. Their victims are depersonalized and degraded with little reference to who they really are as individuals. The hostile rapist is likely to resort to a variety of means both sexual and otherwise to achieve these crimes. The victim may be forced into oral and anal sex and foreign objects may be used to penetrate her. These means may be resorted to because of their symbolic meaning and also because the man is often unable to attain or maintain an erection. Even when he succeeds in raping the woman, he attains little sexual gratification from it.

The "power rape" is primarily perpetrated to assert the rapist's deficient sense of masculinity and worth. Beyond shoring up his sense of inadequacy, the rapist may have no desire to hurt the victim. In "anger rape," the man is motivated by more uncontrollable feelings of hatred and rage; the use of violence becomes an end in itself. In either case, the behavior of the hostile rapist clearly shows a shift of the sexual element from an end to a means for the perpetration of violence.

The fourth type is the *sadistic rapist,* whose sexual satisfaction comes primarily from tormenting his victim. Such a man relishes the struggles and suffering of the woman and may

be further aroused by her anger and resistance. In the sadistic rape the sexual and aggressive elements become most completely fused. Like the hostile rapist, the sadist has a primary interest in hurting the victim, but the hostility and power become critical—the rapist obtains sexual satisfaction from the helplessness and suffering of the victim. Such assaults are usually preplanned and are carried out in a ritualistic manner with sadomasochistic paraphernalia and symbols.

Violent pornography is most likely to appeal to this type of rapist. He may also use other sources of fantasy materials that are not typically thought of as pornographic, such as "detective magazines" with lurid descriptions of murder, rape, and torture (Dietz et al., 1986).

This group is psychologically the most disturbed, with long histories of cruel behavior toward children and animals. Beyond inflicting the trauma of rape, they are the most likely to torture and seriously injure their victim (1 in 500 rapes ends in death) (Figure 19.7). Some will also mutilate the corpse and have further sexual contact with it. Every decade or two a Jack the Ripper type murderer terrorizes entire cities.[6] Though these criminals attain the most public notoriety, they represent the smallest proportion of rapists (Groth et al., 1977; Groth and Birnbaum, 1979).

Background Characteristics    Typologies of rapists are useful descriptive devices but they do not have much explanatory value. To say that one rapist is amoral and another sadistic does not help us understand why they are that way. What is it in their family background, developmental history, and current life circumstances that leads them to become rapists?

To answer such questions, we need deeper knowledge of rapists of all varieties. However,

---

[6]Jack the Ripper was an unidentified person who murdered and mutilated prostitutes in London in 1886. A modern counterpart is the Boston Strangler, who during the early 1960s strangled, stabbed, and sexually mutilated 11 women, ranging in age from their 20s to their 70s (Frank, 1966).

Figure 19.7    Franz Masareel, *Sex murder*.

the typical convicted rapist sitting in jail is not a good candidate for psychological study; nor is the date rapist likely to submit to probing personality investigations. As a result, we only have fragmentary assessments of the background and personality forces that motivate men to commit rape.

What information we do have shows rapists to have had behavioral problems in childhood and to have grown up in chaotic family environments marked by deprivation, neglect, and extreme sibling jealousy. Of special interest are reports that rapists have been sexually abused as children (Delin, 1978). In one study of convicted male rapists, 59 percent had been sexually abused in childhood, usually by a female family member, friend, or neighbor (Petrovich and Templer, 1984). Just as child molesters have often been sexually victimized as children (Chapter 14), rapists too may be reenacting their earlier traumatic experience, this time as victimizer rather than victim.

Otherwise, rapists appear to have had sexually more restrictive childhoods and to have had conservative views on issues like nudity and masturbation (Alford and Brown, 1985). Their proclivity to sexual violence is already evident, though, in teenage fantasies. These fantasies may spill over into atypical sexual behaviors such as voyeurism and exhibitionism or be acted out in molestation of children. Ultimately, rape becomes the end point of the rapist's displaced anger towards women (Abel, 1981).

Other evidence points to more general personality defects of rapists. These men often come across as immature characters who act younger than their age. They seem lacking in self-esteem, uncertain of their masculinity, and intent on reassuring themselves on both counts. Rapists are often sexually less competent (Stermac and Quinsey, 1986) and especially deficient in heterosexual skills (Overholster and Beck, 1986). As we saw, their attitudes towards women tend to be exploitative and demeaning.

Facilitating Factors    A number of other factors may encourage men to commit rape, if they are prone to it. First is the use of alcohol. In Amir's (1971) sample, alcohol was used in one-third of cases (in 63 percent of these cases, both offender and victim had been drinking). Periods when people are more likely to drink are reflected in higher rates: 53 percent of rapes occurred on weekends (the highest number occurred on Fridays between 8 P.M. and midnight). The significance of drinking both among rapists and victims has also been pointed out in date rape. Alcohol affects behavior in these encounters at several levels. By interfering with higher cerebral functions, it "releases" certain behaviors that the person would otherwise suppress. This fact being common knowledge, it provides the perpetrator with an excuse of sorts ("I was drunk; I didn't know what I was doing"). Finally, by drinking, the victim makes herself less able to resist. The potential rapist can misinterpret drunkenness as consent, removing the last vestiges of his self-restraint.

Finding himself in a group situation where peer pressure proves compelling may turn a man into a rapist who would not act this way on his own. Being in uniform under the stress of war and other special external circumstances may likewise be decisive.

The role of pornography in facilitating, if not causing, rape was raised earlier (Chapter 18). The developing consensus is that violent pornography, even when sexually not explicit (such as in "slasher" films), leads to more accepting attitudes toward rape. It gives credence to myths that portray women as instigators and willing participants; it makes light of the suffering and degradation of the victim; and thus it increases the willingness of men to think of raping a woman if they could get away with it (Donnerstein and Linz, 1984). In short, it contributes to the eroticization of violence and the legitimization of violence in achieving erotic aims.

Dealing with Rapists    Rape is among the most difficult and frustrating forms of antisocial behavior to deal with. Public indignation often prompts punishment, yet imprisonment seems to have little effect on subsequent behavior; rapists tend to be repeat offenders (Grunfeld and Noreik, 1986). Prison does keep the rapist out of circulation for the duration of the sentence, but even at best, the arm of the law reaches only a fraction of the men who perpetrate this crime.

Attempts at behavior modification through conditioning, psychotherapy, and antiandrogens, which we discussed in connection with convicted pedophiliacs (Chapter 14), have also been used with rapists, with limited success.

One of the serious problems with the punishment and treatment of the rapist is the diversity of the men who commit this offense. The college student who occasionally coerces his date into coitus and the sadistic murderer are not likely to respond to the same measures; yet a rape is a rape. In fact, there is currently considerable impatience in some quarters with drawing distinctions among rapists and scrutinizing their pasts and motivations; the fear is that by finding some biological or psychosocial "cause," we will open the way for rapists to be exonerated on the grounds that they could not help it (Fausto-Sterling, 1985). On the other hand, how can we deal with these issues without understanding them?

Even more disconcerting is the underlying social problem. Where do we start bringing about the massive social changes required to prevent the rape-prone mentality of our culture? This and numerous other considerations we have raised earlier necessitate that we finally turn next to the historical and societal perspective of human sexuality.

## REVIEW QUESTIONS

1. What is the association of sex, dominance, and aggression?

2. What makes a behavior qualify as sexual harassment?

3. What are the different forms of rape?

4. How does date rape differ from stranger rape?

5. What is known about the rapist and the rape survivor?

## THOUGHT QUESTIONS

1. Does the existence of dominance hierarchies among animals explain and justify them among humans?

2. How can women express their interest in men without being hassled and harassed?

3. How would you deal with a teaching assistant who expressed a persistent sexual interest in you? First assume you reciprocate the interest; second assume you do not.

4. How would you deal with sexual coercion on campus if you were a college administrator?

5. What type of programs would you institute at various school levels to prevent rape?

## SUGGESTED READINGS

Brownmiller, S. (1975). *Against our will*. New York: Simon & Schuster. Detailed historical perspective on rape serves as the background for a powerful polemical analysis of the problem of rape in the modern United States.

Grossman, R., and Sutherland, J. (Eds.) (1982). *Surviving sexual assault*. New York: Congdon and Weed. Sensitive and helpful perspectives on dealing with the aftermath of rape.

Groth, A. N. (1979). *Men who rape*. New York: Plenum. An in-depth study of the behavior and psychology of rapists.

MacKinnon, C. (1979). *Sexual harassment of working women*. New Haven: Yale University. A comprehensive and eloquent discussion of a difficult problem and what to do about it from a legal perspective.

Russell, D. (1982). *Rape in marriage*. New York: Macmillan. Informative and valuable insights into a controversial form of sexual coercion.

# PART 6

# Sex and Society

# Sexuality in Historical Perspective

CHAPTER

# 20

*Civilized people cannot fully
satisfy their sexual instinct
without love.*

BERTRAND RUSSELL

OUTLINE

SEXUALITY AND THE ORIGINS
  OF CULTURE
THE JUDAIC TRADITION
Sexuality in Biblical Times
Judaic Attitudes to Sexuality
  Sex and Marriage
  Proscribed Sexual Behavior
  The Judaic Moral Heritage
GREECE AND ROME
Eros in Greece
  Greek Homosexuality
  Prostitution
  Erotic Art and Literature
Sexuality in Rome
  Phallic Symbolism
  Prostitution
  Erotic Art and Literature
THE RISE OF CHRISTIANITY
The Influence of Judaism
The Influence of Stoicism
The Apocalyptic Expectation
The Patristic Age

The Challenge of Gnosticism
The Challenge of the Manichees
THE MIDDLE AGES
The Early Middle Ages
The Late Middle Ages
THE RENAISSANCE AND THE
  REFORMATION
Renaissance Sexuality
The Reformation
THE ENLIGHTENMENT
Manners and Morals
Erotic Art and Literature
Life in the American Colonies
THE NINETEENTH CENTURY
Victorian Sexual Ideology
  The Repressive Model
  Control of Male Sexuality
Erotic Art and Literature
Sexual Behavior
  Marital Sex
  Socially Problematic Behaviors
THE MODERNIZATION OF SEX

To understand who we are as adults, we need to learn about our childhood. Likewise, to understand the place of sexuality in our culture, we need to learn about its historical origins. Such learning does not come easily. We tend to be pressed by the present, preoccupied with the future, and blind to the past.

With sexuality, there is now the temptation to dismiss the past as irrelevant at best and oppressive at worst. Even though there is much that is objectionable about the sexual values and attitudes of the past, it will take time to know how to make the future better. Each generation and cultural era is entitled to fashion its own solutions to the basic sexual needs, which are more or less constant, yet we must not lose sight of the past so as to preserve what was worthwhile and to avoid repeating its mistakes.

## SEXUALITY AND THE ORIGINS OF CULTURE

Sexual representations are among the earliest surviving artifacts of human culture. The people who produced the statues and cave paintings of the Paleolithic era (30,000 to 10,000 B.C.) were not erotic artists in the conventional sense of the term. It is conjectured that such art was produced for magical-religious purposes. *Fertility symbols* promoted fecundity both within the human group and in the herds of wild animals on which hunters depended.

As in preliterate cultures of more recent times, we assume that sexuality permeated the beliefs and rituals of our earliest forbears and that they used *sexual magic* to promote their welfare and to protect themselves from the forces of evil. Such magic was believed to work by endowing the created object with a life of its own, which then influenced events in the natural world: by painting figures of bison on a cave wall, they hoped to increase the size of the herd; by showing a bison being pierced with a spear, they sought to promote the success of the hunt.

Modern interpretations of Paleolithic art attribute sexual meaning to a wide variety of images, ranging from the obviously sexual (such as representations of the vulva) to the

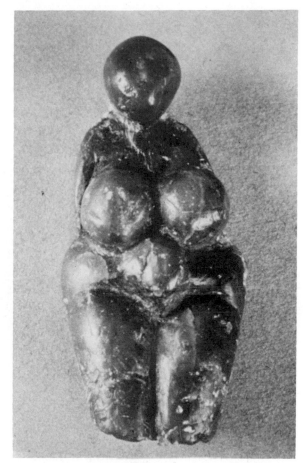

Figure 20.1    Paleolithic "Venus," an early stone age carving from Liguria, Italy.

ambiguously abstract. For instance, in the case of the wounded bison, it is conjectured that spear and wound represented phallic and female emblems whose union symbolized the renewal of life through coitus.

Of special interest are Paleolithic *Venus statuettes,* with distinctly exaggerated breasts, buttocks, and midsections (Figure 20.1). They are thought to be fertility goddesses, emblems of veneration of female fecundity and nurture. Their male counterparts are *ithyphallic figures* (males with erect penises), which are sometimes shown carrying a club or a spear (Figure 20.2). *Phallic symbols,* which may have started as fertility emblems, gradually had become en-

Figure 20.2 Bronze Age rock carvings in Sweden.

dowed with added significance of power and authority by the time of the ancient Egyptian civilization. By 3000 B.C. the great civilizations of Egypt and Mesopotamia had emerged, and their written texts express more directly the pervasive importance of sexuality in their religious life and culture (Manniche, 1987). Mythology and sexuality are often intermingled in the origins of culture (Thompson, 1981).

These early cultures are the source of all subsequent civilizations; but the roots of Western culture are traced more directly to Judaism and the classical cultures of Greece and Rome (Kagan et al., 1979).

## THE JUDAIC TRADITION

Judaism is not a monolithic faith with a single established creed or code of sexual behavior but a religious culture spanning over 4000 years. It is a way of life whose precepts, embodied in the law (*Halakhah*), shape the daily

routine into a pattern of religious observance and sanctity. During its long history, various trends and moods have characterized the sexual outlook of Judaism; but its overall tone has been frank acceptance of sex, coupled with a self-imposed sexual restraint. (Epstein, 1967)

### Sexuality in Biblical Times

The early Israelites were a nomadic people. Abraham is regarded as the father of the Israelite nation, but Moses is its central figure. At about 1200 B.C., he led the Israelites out of Egypt (the Exodus) and received the law that bound his people in a covenant with God (*Yahweh;* mistranslated as "Jehovah"). Circumcision is the sign of the covenant. Jewish male infants are circumcised and named on the eighth day following birth. Female infants are not circumsised; they are usually named on the sabbath following birth. Moses is thus the first rabbi ("master") or teacher and the model of the ideal Jew (Neusner, 1970).

Sex does not seem to have been much of an issue for the nomadic Jews. Sexual intercourse in lawful settings was highly regarded and most forms of nonreproductive sex were frowned upon; but there was no preachment and preoccupation with sexual guilt and sin, and sexual misbehavior was treated no differently from other forms of misconduct. Personal relations had passion and tenderness: Jacob was so smitten with Rachel that he served his prospective father-in-law for seven years "and they seemed to him but a few days, so much did he love her" (Gen. 29:30).

The deportation of Jews to Babylon (by Nebuchadnezar, in 597 B.C.) exposed Jews to a worldly culture. Sexual behavior after this exile became more lax; in consequence, moral teachings turned more legalistic and ascetic. The innocence and joy of earlier times were now tinged by a pervasive pessimism. People were seen as driven by sexual lust; no one was free of sin; living lost its purpose. "All is vanity," says Ecclesiastes (1:2–3). Concurrently, there was a decline in the status of women. They were veiled and confined to the home. Unlike earlier times, when the sexuality of women was accepted, now women were held accountable for leading men astray: "I consider more bitter than death the woman whose heart snares and nets, and whose hands are fetters," wrote the author of Ecclesiastes (7:26). These changes, however, were not as dramatic as it may sound. The *Song of Songs,* with its joyous celebration of erotic love dates from the postexilic period (about the third century B.C., although its material is much more ancient).

Some of the more pessimistic sexual attitudes persisted into the Hellenistic period and greatly influenced early Christian perceptions of sex. To a lesser extent they also lingered within the rabbinic Judaism (2nd to 18th centuries) that produced the detailed behavioral codes embodied in the Talmud.

## Judaic Attitudes to Sexuality

The dominant perspective in Judaism views sex as God's gift. It does not advocate world renunciation and has little taste for asceticism. Orthodox Jews observe the law to its most minute detail, but even at their most strict, they renounce neither the body nor its physical pleasures as evil. Sex becomes unethical when it violates the integrity of human relationships as envisaged by the law, not some abstract moral principle.

**Sex and Marriage**    In Judaism, all forms of sexual behavior are evaluated as to their morality and desirability with respect to the institution of marriage. This centrality of marriage and procreative sex within it are among the key legacies from Judaism that have profoundly influenced sexual attitudes in Western culture (Box 20.1). The early Israelites permitted polygamy and were discouraged from marrying non-Jews (Larue, 1983).

As expressed in the story of creation in Genesis, God intended man and woman to complement each other. It is to this end that a man "leaves his father and mother and cleaves to his wife, and they become one flesh" (Gen. 2:24). Building on this tradition, Judaism came to view marriage as a religious duty. Husband and wife represented the model of integrated

humanity, and a person was not fully adult unless married.

Sex and procreation, the key elements in traditional Jewish marriage, imposed reciprocal obligations. Wives were expected to submit to the sexual desires of their husbands; likewise, each man was obliged to perform his marital duty. (For donkey drivers this duty meant coitus once a week; for camel drivers, once in 30 days; for scholars and gentlemen of leisure, every night.)

Sex is not just a procreative duty in Judaism but was meant to be enjoyed by both sexes, a meritorious act. In the world-to-come, says the Talmud, every man will be called to account for all the legitimate pleasures which he failed to enjoy (Bokser, 1962). Nevertheless, there were some who tried to impose restraints on sexual enjoyment, or accepted it grudgingly for reproductive purposes only. For example, couples were warned that children conceived while using unorthodox coital postures would be born lame, genital kissing would make the child mute, conversation during coitus would cause deafness, and gazing at each other's nakedness would cause blindness in the offspring. The more authentic voices of Judaism spoke for the freedom of husband and wife to do as they pleased, to have intercourse at any time and in any manner that they wished. These same sentiments are manifest in the *Song of Songs,* which celebrates the passion of love in lyric poems sung at ancient wedding feasts. However, the reason it was included in the Bible is because it was considered to be an allegory of the relationship of God with Israel; and in the Christian tradition, that of Christ and the church.

**Proscribed Sexual Behavior**    Judaism has treated harshly those who transgress laws of proper sexual conduct. Judaic judgments in this regard are based on pragmatic grounds and not on any notions of sex being inherently evil. The core concern is to protect the integrity of marriage; all other considerations emanate from that aim.

Strict laws of consanguinity guarded Jews against incest. It was forbidden to commit in-

# Box 20.1

## JEWISH MARRIAGE

The term for the Jewish marriage ceremony is *kiddushin* ("sanctification"). It is said that at the "wedding" of Adam and Eve God acted as the "best man" and plaited Eve's hair to adorn her for her husband (Parrinder, 1980). Given that marriage was the preferred state, parents tried to arrange marriages for their children (especially daughters) as soon as possible. For girls, engagement (*betrothal*) became desirable on entering puberty at about age 12; marriage followed a year later.* If a girl remained single into adulthood, her father lost the power to contract marriage for her (and to collect the bride-price). She was also liable for her own sexual conduct. Under these circumstances, it is no wonder that daughters were a source of lifelong distress for fathers (Cohen, 1949).

Fathers also arranged the marriage of their sons (usually in their late teens) and negotiated the dowry. To help a new couple settle down, the law stipulated that "when a man is newly married, he shall not go out with the army or be charged with any business; he shall be free at home one year, to be happy with his wife whom he has taken" (Deut. 24:5).

Monogamy has been the norm in Judaism, but considerable latitude existed for some men of special status. Multiple wives and concubines were maintained by tribal chiefs like Abraham and Jacob, and later on by the nobility (Solomon had several hundred women in his household) to cement political allegiances, to increase progeny, and to provide sexual variety. Polygamy was abolished in Judaism in the 11th century by Rabbi Gershon, followed by the right to keep concubines (*pilegesh*) which was

particularly opposed by Maimonides, the 12th-century codifier of the Talmud (Borowitz, 1969, pp. 43–49).

The "good wife" commanded much respect in Judaism. ("A good wife who can find? She is far more precious than jewels," says Proverbs 31:10.) She is not noted for her beauty (which is "fleeting") nor charm (a "delusion"), but is praised for her God-fearing nature, dedication to her husband and family, and the expert management of her home. "Extoll her for the fruit of all her toil," says Proverbs, "and let her labors bring her honor in the city gate" (Prov. 31:31). For Jews and Christians alike this feminine ideal proved to be a durable model until modern times.

The grounds for divorce were quite liberal for the man. If the wife did not "win his favor" because he found "something shameful in her," he could dismiss her (Deut. 24:5). "Something shameful" was interpreted by the school of Shammai to mean sexual infidelity; the school of Hillel understood it as virtually anything displeasing to the husband (including bad cooking) (Parrinder, 1980).

Women had some protection against capricious dismissal because the husband was obliged to repay the bride-price, often a substantial sum, on divorce. However, if it could be shown that the wife had been guilty of scandalous behavior, then she could be dismissed without compensation.

---

*Puberty was determined by degree of breast development. In comparison to figs, girls were considered "unripe," "ripening," and "ripe."

---

cest even when threatened by death. The seeming lack of disapproval with which the Old Testament reports Lot's seduction by his two daughters (Gen. 19:31, 36) is puzzling, but this event took place under extraordinary circumstances. Sodom had been destroyed, Lot's wife was dead, he was stranded with his daughters in the hills, and they had gotten him drunk. Most important, the motivation behind the act was to ensure the perpetuation of the

family line. Similarly, if the story of creation in Genesis is taken literally, we would have to assume the occurrence of at least brother-sister incest for the propagation of the progeny of Adam and Eve.

The Judaic concept of adultery was based on the violation of the husband's exclusive rights to the sexual and reproductive assets of his wife. A wife committed adultery if she had sex with anyone other than her husband. A husband committed adultery only when he had sex with another man's wife, not when he had sex with anyone other than his wife. This is the original meaning of the Seventh Commandment: "You shall not commit adultery" (Exod. 20:14). The concern over violation of property rights is reiterated in the Tenth Commandment, which says, "You shall not covet your neighbor's wife, nor his horse, ox, ass, or any other belonging" (Exod. 20:17). The wife owed faithfulness to her own marriage, the husband to the marriages of his kinsmen ("neighbor") (Epstein, 1967).

Seduction of a virgin required compensation to the father and marrying the maiden if she so desired. Rape was an ever-present danger. Ravishing the women of the enemy was taken for granted; but even in peacetime, young women were not always safe.

The Old Testament does not explicitly forbid premarital intercourse. Practically all women got engaged on reaching puberty; so there were not many unattached young women to have sex with. When sex took place between an engaged couple, community reaction tended to be only mildly disapproving; loss of virginity under these circumstances was not stigmatizing.

Because marriage for men came later and not everyone could afford to take a wife, some resorted to prostitutes. Married men who sought sexual variety could do the same without committing adultery. The attitude of Judaism toward prostitution was highly ambivalent, not because of some abstract moral principle but because of the nature of prostitution at the time.

Judaism expressly forbade fathers to give their daughters to whoredom; so sex with prostitutes meant consorting with foreign women. Furthermore, there were two kinds of prostitutes. The *zonah* was the ordinary prostitute; the *kadesha* (and her male counterpart, the *kadesh*), was the religious or cult prostitute. These priestesses were "married" to the god in whose temple they served, and their duties included ritual coitus with worshippers and others willing to pay their fee. This practice existed for short periods even within Judaism.

For instance, during the reign of Rehoboam, son of Solomon, there were cult prostitutes attached to the Temple of Jerusalem. The real offense in consorting with cult prostitutes was not sex but sacrilege; it meant worshipping a god other than the Lord—the one absolute, unforgivable sin in Judaism.

Given the centrality of reproductive sex, we would expect Judaism to frown upon all forms of nonreproductive sexual activity. In general, that has been the case, but Judaism has not been as strict in this regard as, for example, the Catholic church with respect to contraception, sterilization, and abortion.

The Old Testament has no explicit prohibitions of these practices. The sin of Onan (Gen. 38:9) involved coitus interruptus to avoid conception; but the Lord's wrath was aroused at Onan because he was shirking his responsibility to provide heirs to his deceased brother (as required by the *Levirate law* in Deut. 25:5–6) while enjoying sex with his widow. The Old Testament does not forbid abortion and considers the embryo to be part of the mother. Later authorities differed widely about the legitimacy of these practices. Contraception was forbidden only in the Middle Ages (when Jewish populations were being decimated through persecution). Although some orthodox Jewish authorities still oppose it, Judaism as a whole does not.

The Old Testament repeatedly condemns bestiality as a capital offense. The Talmud even prohibits the keeping of pet dogs by widows to avoid suspicion of sexual contact. The case against masturbation is far more ambiguous. Clearly the act of Onan had nothing to do with masturbation as such.

Nocturnal emissions rendered a man "unclean" and required a ritual bath of purification, but the same requirement extended to coitus as well (Lev. 15:16–18). The Israelites were awed by vital bodily fluids like semen, menstrual blood, and discharges accompanying childbirth, since they were associated with the generation of life, and built rituals and taboos around them, as have other cultures.

There are only two passages in the Old Testament that explicitly condemn homosexual acts, both of them in Leviticus: "You shall not lie with a male as with a woman; it is an abomination" (Lev. 18:22); "If a man lies with a male as with a woman, both of them have committed an abomination; they shall be put to death" (Lev. 20:13). Whether these prohibitions were based on ritualistic concerns (as in the case of sex with cult prostitutes) or intended as moral condemnation of the sexual act itself is a matter of dispute.

Even more problematic is the curious story of the destruction of Sodom (Gen. 18–19). Traditionally it has been assumed that the Lord destroyed Sodom because its people tried to rape the two angels of the Lord whom Lot was sheltering in his home (hence *sodomy*). More recent scholarship has questioned the sexual interpretation of these texts and hence the validity of their representing biblical condemnations of homosexuality (Bailey, 1959; Boswell, 1980, pp. 92–99), as we shall discuss in Chapter 23.

The Judaic Moral Heritage    The concept of specific moral rules regulating sexual behavior, so deeply embedded in Western culture, is directly traceable to Judaism. When a society sets out to regulate the behavior of its members in concrete and precise ways, as traditional Judaism does, regulations to deal with all conceivable contingencies must abound. Furthermore, to protect the core ethical values, additional rules are made as warnings in more peripheral areas on the principle of "building fences," resulting at times in a sterile and oppressive legalism. Judaism has struggled to free itself from this predicament by formulating broadly applicable ethical principles to guide human conduct. Thus, on the one hand, there are the hundreds of commandments given to Moses, and on the other, the all-encompassing principle of Leviticus 19:18: "You shall love your neighbor as yourself", repeated by Jesus (Mark 12:31), and rephrased by Rabbi Hillel in the first century as, "What is hateful to yourself, do not do to your fellow man. That is the whole Torah" (Neusner, 1970, p. 87).

The legal code, even at its most demanding, only sets a minimum standard. Beyond behavioral considerations, a Jew must be concerned about "purity of mind" (motivation and intent) as well as action. Christianity expanded some of these expectations—for example, the principle of "sinning in one's heart" means being guilty of impure thoughts even though they are not acted upon.

Judaism has had a profound influence on Christian sexual morality, but this influence has been selective. Christianity owes to it the centrality accorded to marital sex and the condemnation of all other sexual behaviors. The shared belief in the Old Testament has continued to link the two religious traditions in important ways; yet with sexuality, some important differences have emerged. Jews understand the scriptures as a legal system, albeit divine in origin. They understand that all laws must change to fit changing times. Rabbis have always acted with the authority to teach the law for their own day and age to make possible the continuing faithfulness of the people of Israel (Borowitz, 1969). By contrast, the Christian approach to morality has been more abstract; legal precepts from the past have been elevated to absolute and immutable standards that retain their validity independent of changed historical circumstances. This attitude has generally made the Christian interpretation of the Old Testament sexual morality far more restrictive than it has been for Jews.

## GREECE AND ROME

Beginning with its archaic origins in the 8th century B.C., Greek civilization extended to the Hellenistic period, culminating in the establishment of the Roman Empire in the 1st century B.C.

### Eros in Greece

Unlike the nomadic Jews, whose character was forged in the desert, the early Greeks were farmers. Agricultural concerns shaped their values. Sex for Jews was primarily a means of reproduction and cementing family bonds. The family was also central to Greek culture, but the Greeks allowed sex far more freedom in its varied expressions. The proper role for women of the citizenry was the sheltered life of wife and mother. (The Greek word for woman, *gyne*, means "bearer of children"). Greek men went outside of the family for supplemental sexual pleasures.

The Athenian attitude to sex was uninhibited, much like that of contemporary Western societies. That does not mean that people behaved as they pleased; conservative elements coexisted with more liberal and radical factions, as they do today. The Greeks differed from us in their conception of romantic love. Instead of making it the basis of marriage and the justification for sex, the Greeks viewed romantic love and erotic passion as troublesome emotions that, like anger, upset reason (see Box 16.3). They were best avoided as the basis of serious decisions like marriage. Sexual pleasure nonetheless was to be had freely as an end in itself or else sublimated to attain higher philosophical ideals.

Outside of literary and a few historical sources, we have no information about the actual behavior of the ancient Greeks; the ancient world offers no counterparts to our clinical case studies and sex surveys. Therefore, whatever inferences are drawn about Greek sexual behavior must be drawn cautiously.

As in other cultures, most Greek men and women married, had sex, begat children, and kept up the cycle of life. However, two aspects of Greek society imparted a special quality to their sexuality: the close association of men with each other, which led to homosexual attachments; and the presence of a slave population that engendered sexual exploitation on a large scale.

Greek Homosexuality    Greece was very much a man's world. Men spent most of their time with other men, especially in time of war (which was a good deal of the time). Their friendships and associations were with other men, including, for some, erotic attachments.

Greek homosexuality has been a source of much confusion. This has been partly the doing of scholars. Licht (1969), Dover (1980), and Boswell (1980) point out how some classical scholars denied and distorted the evidence; Karlen (1971) says other scholars used their research to justify their own disguised homosexuality. Another reason for confusion is how different the practice was from today.

The Greek male was essentially bisexual, equally attracted to young males and females without necessarily engaging in sex with both. The Greeks found physical beauty sexually arousing, irrespective of gender (Dover, 1988). They did not categorize people into heterosexuals and homosexuals (as character types or lifestyles); they assumed that some men by preference and others by force of circumstance would seek sexual gratification from other males. Such practice was socially approved, tolerated, or disapproved depending on a number of factors.

Of special interest is the institution of *pederasty*, or "boy love." The term "boy" is confusing in this regard. The Greek *pais* (or *paidika*) had a number of meanings: child, girl, slave, youth, and the "passive" partner in homosexual relationships (Dover, 1978). In the pederastic context the younger person was an adolescent or youth, never a child (Figure 20.3).

When a boy reached puberty, it was customary for him to be attached to an older mentor who helped to guide his development to adulthood. The relationship could be based on

Figure 20.3    A man courts a boy. Attic black-figure vase, 6th century B.C.

respect and affection but without any romantic passion or sex. When the mentor qualified as an *erastes* ("lover") because of his ardent interest in the youth, the youth became the *eromenos* ("beloved"). These same words were used when a man had a "crush" on a woman, but "lover" could also simply mean being an admirer of a youth's beauty, which the Greeks glorified.

The sexual component of the erastes-eromenos relationship was usually left unclear (just as we do not always know if dating couples are having sex). It was assumed that the erastes would seek sexual contact and the eromenos would resist it or yield to it reluctantly and with certain qualifications. For example, it would not be proper for the eromenos to be used like a prostitute by permitting anal intercourse; he would merely allow ejaculation between his thighs (without himself reaching orgasm). It is questionable, of course, to what extent these niceties were observed in actual practice. At any rate, whatever the nature of the relationship, it ended with the young man attaining adulthood and going on to get married and perhaps becoming an erastes himself. Men also engaged in anal intercourse with women, but whether they did this only with prostitutes or with their wives as well is unclear.

Plato describes episodes and ascribes statements to Socrates which show him as greatly preoccupied with youthful beauty and love. "I can't think of a time when I wasn't in love," says Socrates (clearly not referring to his wife), and love was the only subject he claimed to know anything about (Dover, 1978).

The Greeks sometimes exploited homosexual attachments for military purposes by having pairs of lovers fight side by side. Most famous was the Theban "Sacred Band" whose 150 pairs of lovers fought to the death against Philip of Macedon. Moved to tears by their heroism, their conqueror declared, "Woe to them who think evil of such men" (Licht, 1969, p. 391). Another celebrated couple was Harmodios and Aristogiton, who died trying to overthrow the tyrant Hippias and his brother Hipparkhus, who had tried to seduce Harmodios (Boswell, 1980).

Philip's statement implies that some people did think evil of such men. The Greeks did not indiscriminately approve of all forms of homosexuality, and a common insult was to call someone "wide-assed."[1] In passing such judgment, the Greeks were not preoccupied with abstract principles but with how an act reflected on manhood and social status. A citizen who prostituted himself was barred from holding public office, because a man capable of selling his body was thought likely to compromise the interests of the community as well (Dover, 1980). Similarly, a man who was penetrated in anal intercourse placed himself in the submissive position of a woman; hence, he could not be trusted on the battlefield (the example of the Theban band to the contrary). Not "homosexuality," but Athenian concepts of manhood and dominance determined social perception of these sexual practices.

We know relatively little about female homosexuality or the attitudes of Greek women to male homosexuality. In Sparta women formed the counterpart of the male eromenos-erastes relationship, but to what extent this bond had a sexual component is unclear. No more certain is the nature of Sappho's relationship with the girls she tutored, to some of whom she seemed ardently attached. (Sappho lived in the 7th century B.C., but the few biographical details of her life come from Hellenistic times.)

Prostitution    Only a minority of the people in the Greek city-states were citizens. The rest were foreigners and slaves. It was from this sector of the population, rather than the citizenry, that the large number of prostitutes was drawn.

The common prostitute, called *porne*, sold her sexual favors on her own or in a brothel. The fees were set by the state, which taxed their revenues. Other prostitutes worked the

---

[1]Referring to the Trojan war, Eubolos says, "No one ever set eyes on a single hetaira. . . . It was a poor sort of campaign; for the capture of one city they went home with arses much wider than [the gates of] the city that they took" (quoted in Dover, 1978, p. 35).

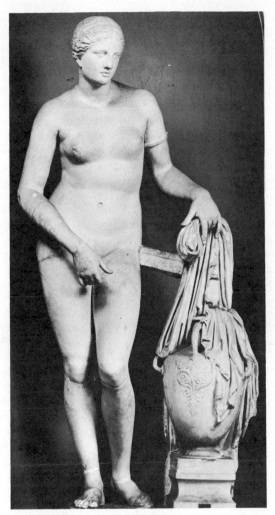

Figure 20.4 *Aphrodite*. Roman copy after the *Aphrodite of Cnidos* by Praxiteles, the original dating from c. 349 B.C.

streets; one enterprising street-walker had the sole of her shoe fitted with large nails, which left an imprint that read, "Follow me."

More privileged were the *hetairae* ("companions"). These sophisticated and ambitious women were at times the mistresses of some of the most influential personalities. The inspiration and models of artists, the more famous hetairae had their statues set up in temples and public buildings side by side with those of em-inent generals and statesmen; the breathtaking beauty of Phryne was immortalized in the statue of *Aphrodite of Cnidus* by Praxiteles (Figure 20.4).

Hetairae could also be attached to temples as sacred prostitutes, the *hierodoules*, whose earnings went to the temple treasury. People sometimes donated slaves to temples for this purpose. The Corinthians in particular believed that the prayers of sacred prostitutes to Aphrodite protected them in times of danger. It is likely that large numbers of men availed themselves of the services of prostitutes, but extramarital license by men was by no means lightly tolerated by Greek women. Hence, the motto "Courtesans for pleasure, concubines for daily needs, and wives to conceive children and be loyal housekeepers" was probably more male fantasy than a reflection of the realities of Greek life (quoted in Marcade, 1962, p. 132).

Erotic Art and Literature Greek literature abounds in sexual themes and references, including its treatment of the gods (Box 20.2); but the fact that the Greek gods were portrayed as fully sexual in literature must not be equated with their being so in Greek religion. The lurid tales of Zeus pursuing divine and mortal, male and female notwithstanding, the Greeks were respectful of their divinities and serious about their religion.

The Greeks treated female nudity in art and daily life with the same acceptance as we do; but they were far more open with the public display of male genitals. This prominence of phallic symbolism is a striking feature of Greek eroticism. The erect penis was as much a part of the consciousness of the Greeks as the circumcised penis was for the Jews. Giant phalluses made of wood were carried in Dionysiac processions; others hewn out of stone stood on pedestals. *Herms* (representing the god Hermes), pillars with human head and penis (Figure 20.5), were common sights, as were various other phallic monuments guarding the fields and phallic amulets hanging from people's necks.

The use of these phallic symbols was not

# Box 20.2

## EROTIC THEMES IN GREEK MYTHOLOGY

In Hesiod's account, Eros is the god of love who at the dawn of creation emerges from Darkness and brings all other things to life. Similarly, he places the birth of Aphrodite, the goddess of love, in the misty origins of the world when Earth was embraced by Heaven, and Time (Kronos) was born. Kronos turned against his father and castrated him; the amputated genitals swollen with sperm fell into the sea, and from their white foam arose the lovely Aphrodite. As the goddess of love, Aphrodite was the central figure in Greek eroticism (Grigson, 1976; Friedrich, 1978).

In Homeric legends, 12 Olympic gods (a third of them female) conducted their divine business, like a royal family, under Zeus (Graves, 1959; Holme, 1979; Grimal, 1981). Zeus was married to his sister Hera, but he also pursued other women: he carried off Europa by disguising himself as a snow-white bull, seduced Leda by taking the form of a swan (Figure 14.4), and impregnated Danae by descending on her in the guise of a shower of gold. Through such unions were born the great heroes like Heracles (who, true to his father, deflowered all 50 daughters of King Theseus in a single night). Nor was Zeus partial only to women. One of his most celebrated loves was Ganymede, a handsome Trojan youth whom he snatched up while disguised as an eagle and carried off to Olympus to supplant Hebe (the goddess of youth) as the cup-bearer to the gods.

Aphrodite, the goddess of love, was married to her lame and ugly half-brother Hephaestos, the god of fire and the celestial blacksmith; but she was enamored of another half-brother, Ares, the splendid god of war. Helios, the all-seeing sun god, leaked the news of the affair to Hephaestos, who forged a fine net ensnaring Aphrodite and Ares in bed. Their predicament, however, created more merriment than outrage, when Hermes volunteered to change places with Ares. He must have had his chance some other time, since from their union was born Hermaphrodite, whom the Hellenistic Greeks glorified for representing the complementarity of male and female beauty. Another of Zeus' daughters, Athena, was delivered from Zeus' head and became patroness of virgins (and Athens).

The character of Eros, the god of love, changed over time. From creator of the world in Hesiod, he was later cast as the son of Aphrodite who would smite people with passion at her bidding. Shown as a handsome youth, Eros represented the ideal of male beauty and pursued his own loves, as in the haunting story of Psyche ("soul"). By the Hellenistic period Eros had taken on his more familiar cherub's form, in which he persisted into Roman times as Amor and Cupid.

Aphrodite's patronage of love and fertility was shared by Dionysus (another issue of Zeus's illicit loves), who discovered the vine and became the god of wine.* The association of flowers with Aphrodite and the vine with Dionysus points to the close connections among religion, sex, and agriculture in ancient Greece. The great Dionysian festivals celebrated the passing of seasons and invoked the blessing of deities to insure good harvests (Licht, 1932; Marcade, 1962; Webb, 1975). Sexual activity in these contexts was bound with the broader cycles of life and fecundity in nature.

The companions of Dionysus included *satyrs,* or the *sileni* (named after Silenus, their "father," who had tutored Dionysus). Greek satyrs were men with horse ears, tail, and hoofs. In the Hellenistic period, they got mixed up with *Pan* (the protector of flocks and nature) and took on their more familiar image as goat-men (Figure 20.12). These creatures represented unbridled, earthy sensuality. They endlessly pursued the forest nymphs (*maenads*), whose songs and dances enchanted them. Crude and lewd as the satyrs could be, they were of a benign nature. Not so the centaurs, who were brutish (with some exceptions like Chiron, the tutor of Achilles). Where the satyrs seduced, the centaurs raped; the escapades of satyrs led to sexual pleasure, the frenzy of centaurs to tragedy and death.† Centaurs thus represented the lawless and violent aspects of male sexuality, whereas satyrs stood for its pleasurable side.

---

*The philosopher Friedrich Nietzsche distinguished between "Dionysian," which is ecstatic, sensual, irrational, and suffused with creative energy, as contrasted with "Apollonian," which stands for the rational, well ordered, serene, and dignified.

†A famous instance is the battle of the centaurs with the Lapiths, which ensued when the centaurs tried to rape the bride and guests at a wedding. The scene is depicted on the frieze of the Parthenon and the Temple of Zeus at Olympia.

Figure 20.5    Herm.

meant to be obscene, frivolous, or even erotic. The Greeks seriously associated phallic symbols with protection, fertility, and immortality. In phallic worship, sexual emblems were part of Greek religious life, just as other religions rely on other symbols for devotional purposes (Vanggaard, 1972).

Erotic elements in Greek drama are present both in the tragedies and comedies. A major theme in tragedy is incest. The legend of King Oedipus (which provided the name for Freud's Oedipus complex) was first related by Homer and retold by the great dramatists. The most renowned versions are the plays by Sophocles: *King Oedipus* (about 427 B.C.) and *Oedipus at Colonus* (about 408 B.C.)

Greek tragedies were presented in sets of three accompanied by a fourth *satyr play* for comic relief. The revolt of women is a common theme in the comedies of Aristophanes (c. 488–380 B.C.). In *Women in Parliament,* they establish a communistic society where property and sex are shared (a parody of Plato's *Repub-*

*lic*); in *Lysistrata* the women seize the Acropolis and declare a sex strike until the men of Greece come to their senses and stop fighting.

The ribaldry in Greek comedy is traceable to its ancient roots in the rituals of *phallic cults.* In the early comedies, actors customarily wore leather phalluses, as was the custom in Dionysian festivals. Comedies openly dealt not only with sexual relations between men and women but also with other forms of sexual behavior, such as homosexuality, masturbation, and bestiality.

The treatment of love and sex was more subtle in the hands of the lyric poets, prominent among whom was Sappho of Lesbos. We think of her predominantly in connection with lesbianism, but the Greeks regarded her as one of their greatest poets and called her the "Tenth Muse." Only fragments of her work have survived.

Love of beauty suffused Greek culture, and its genius could combine the unabashedly sensual with the highest aesthetic and ethical ideals. It makes no sense to speak of erotic art in Greece as a thing apart; no meaningful distinction can be made between artists (or writers) who dealt with erotic themes and others who did not. Sex was part of art as it was part of life.

### Sexuality in Rome

Rome was the first heir to Greek culture. From its humble beginnings as an agrarian society in the 8th century B.C., it grew to be master of the Mediterranean world well into the 5th century A.D., encompassing a vast conglomerate of diverse societies, which had their own sexual customs.

**Phallic Symbolism**    Phallic worship was an important part of Roman religious observance since Etruscan times. Phallic emblems were placed in tombs, whose walls were decorated with erotic scenes (as in the famous *Tomb of the Bulls* in Tarquinia). Sex, associated with the renewal of life, was thought to be an antidote to the ravages of death.

Phallic symbols were endowed with magical powers. Statues of the ithyphallic god Priapus stood in Roman gardens to warn potential thieves that the god would rape them if they tried to steal (Richlin, 1983). Widespread in the Roman world were representations of the penis in fantastic forms. Some were hung around the neck as amulets (Figure 20.6). Others cast their protective spell from above the doors of homes, shops, and city gates. The reasoning behind these practices was that when the gaze of someone with the "evil eye" turned to a person, the phallic amulet deflected the evil force and spared its wearer. A legacy of this belief is the word "fascinate," which is derived from *fascinum,* a Latin term for penis that first meant "bewitchment."

The Greek agricultural festivals had a parallel in the Roman *Bacchanalia* and *Liberalia,*

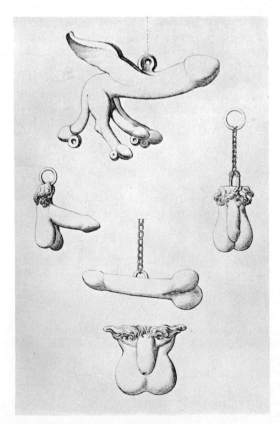

Figure 20.6    Roman phallic amulets.

during which wine, sex, and phallic rituals ensured the fertility of the fields, beasts, and people for another year (Webb, 1975).

Prostitution    Prostitution was rife in Rome. With their typical administrative flair, the Romans established brothels along major thoroughfares at set intervals so that a man could have his sexual needs serviced while his horse was being tended. Prostitution lost all its religious associations and became purely a form of commerce, prostitutes now being called *meretrices* ("sellers"; the source of our term "meretricious").

Erotic Art and Literature    In the excavations at Pompeii (which include a high-class brothel) are frescoes portraying various forms of coital activity (Grant and Mulas, 1975). Roman statuary art was largely imitations of earlier Hellenistic models (Figure 20.7). The Romans completed the shift from the male to the female nude as the ideal human form, a trend already in evidence in the later phase of Greek civilization.

Roman erotic literature shows more originality than art. Ovid's *Art of Love* is a manual of seduction for predatory men and women. The works of Ovid, Catullus, Horace, and other Roman poets (which greatly influenced later writers like Shakespeare), viewed love with a lighthearted and cynical eye and women as wayward, mercenary, tormenting, but nevertheless delightful creatures (Webb, 1975). The rich Latin sexual vocabulary has been extensively studied (Adams, 1982).

With the disintegration of traditional Roman values, life became increasingly brutal and sex sadistic. The combination of boundless power with unbridled license came to be epitomized in decadent emperors like Nero and Caligula. (Nero committed incest with his mother, and eventually killed her by cutting open her abdomen to see the uterus that had contained him. Caligula did the same to his sister.) These odd characters were by no means representative of Romans generally, though, and the accounts of this period in the writings of Petronius (*Satyricon*), Martial (*Epigrams*), Ju-

Figure 20.7    Roman marble relief of Hercules and nymph.

venal (*Satires*), and Suetonius (*Lives of the Caesars*) are often exaggerated and sensationalized.

## THE RISE OF CHRISTIANITY

A momentous development for Western culture during the Roman era was the rise of Christianity. From an insignificant sect in the 1st century, Christianity became the dominant spiritual, intellectual, and political force in the West over the next 20 centuries.

Jesus lived in one of the distant provinces of the Roman Empire and was executed by the Roman authorities in about A.D. 33. Information regarding his preaching and actions comes from his immediate followers (the apostles) and their disciples. At first circulated orally, this information was eventually incorporated into the four Gospels of the *New Testament*. There is relatively little in the deeds and words of Jesus that explicitly relates to sex-

ual behavior, as we shall discuss in Chapter 23. Following Jesus, the central figure in Christianity is Paul, a Hellenistic Jew and a Roman citizen. It was Paul (who never met Jesus during his earthly ministry) who played the dominant role in the shaping of early Christianity. His letters or *epistles* to the early churches, which dealt with key doctrinal and organizational matters, also refer to a number of sexual issues.

### The Influence of Judaism

The Bible of the earliest Christians was the Old Testament. The remembered words and deeds of Jesus, which were to become the Gospels, and letters of the apostles to various churches were increasingly important sources of guidance; but the New Testament in its present form did not appear until the 4th century.

Because all of the early Christians were Jews, they assumed that converts to Christianity had to observe the Judaic laws. Paul opposed this view, arguing that the new covenant of Jesus superseded the old; non-Jews could become Christians directly, without conversion to Judaism. This fact greatly facilitated the extension of Christianity to the Gentiles and made possible its transformation from a small Jewish sect to a world religion.

Early Christians were nonetheless much affected by the prevailing sexual attitudes in Judaism, which had become more restrictive since early Old Testament times. Philo, the foremost philosopher of the Jewish diaspora ("scattering") in the 1st century, condemned "the passion of love" and physical attraction as the source of wickedness. Also influential may have been the Essenes, a small Jewish sect that adhered to celibacy and the use of sex for procreation only. Their rejection of sexual pleasure as sinful may have been particularly influential in shaping a similar view in early Christianity.

## The Influence of Stoicism

Hellenistic Jews and Gentiles who were converted to Christianity brought their own intellectual perspectives to their chosen religion, helping shape Christian moral doctrines and sexual attitudes. Especially important were the tenets of Stoicism. Founded by Zeno in about 315 B.C., Stoicism held virtue to be the highest good, best attained by repression of emotion, indifference to pleasure and pain, and patient endurance (Russell, 1945; Noonan, 1967). Sexual emotions were particularly suspect, whatever the context for their expression. Seneca, a first-century Stoic philosopher wrote:

> All love of another's wife is shameful; so too, too much love of your own. A wise man ought to love his wife with judgment, not affection. Let him control his impulses and not be borne headlong into copulation. Nothing is fouler than to love a wife like an adulteress. . . . Let them show themselves to their wives not as lovers, but as husbands (quoted in Noonan, 1967, p. 67).

As Noonan puts it, "Stoicism was in the air the intellectual converts to Christianity breathed. Half consciously, half unconsciously, they accommodated some Christian beliefs to a Stoic sense" (Noonan, 1967, p. 66). Paul himself was influenced by Stoic ideals, as were some of the most influential Church figures who followed him. Thus, the notion that there is something shameful and objectionable about sex even in lawful relationships, which came to dominate Christian thinking over the centuries, owed its origins not to Judaic roots, not to the teachings of Jesus, but to prevailing currents in Greek secular thought.

## The Apocalyptic Expectation

The Jews believed that at a preordained time, God would bring the world to an end by establishing His kingdom on earth and abolishing injustice, suffering, and death. Jesus shared this *apocalyptic* ("revelation") vision, and certain statements he made were interpreted by his followers to mean that these cataclysmic events would occur during their own lifetime; so the early Christians lived with an acute sense of impermanence, anxiously awaiting the return of the Lord.

This same expectation had a major influence on Paul's views. He wrote about the "imminent distress" (1 Cor. 7:26) that the early Christians faced. Whether he meant the persecutions that were to befall Christians, or the second coming of Christ that would "end the world," his letters to the churches were written in the anticipation of extraordinary times. The advice he gave on whether or not to get married was formulated in that context rather than in the abstract, for all times (1 Cor. 7:25–28).

All the views of Paul and other early teachers of Christian sexual morality must be understood in their social context. Paul had to contend with the unbounded sexual license of the Hellenistic society within which Christians lived, as well as with the special challenges of particular churches. For example, in the church in Galatia devout and conservative moralists wanted to uphold the letter of the

Mosaic law; in the Corinthian church, radical elements claimed that as Christians they were above all laws, free to behave as they wished, even if that meant committing incest and having sex with cult prostitutes.

## The Patristic Age

The period from the martyrdom of Paul in Rome under Nero (probably in A.D. 66) to the fall of the Roman Empire in the 5th century is referred to as the Patristic Age, because the development of Christian doctrine was dominated during this time by a select group of men. These *Fathers of the Church* lived in Hellenistic Alexandria, a great center of learning. Included in this group were Ambrose, Origen, Jerome, Clement, Gregory, and most important, Augustine, whose views strongly influenced Catholic doctrine on sexuality over the next thousand years and Protestant attitudes beyond that.

Stoicism continued to exert a powerful influence on Christian sexual morality in the Patristic Age, leading to ascetic beliefs and practices. The most extreme forms of self-denial were practiced by the *anchorites* ("those who have fled"), who lived alone in the desert. As exemplified by the temptations of Father Anthony, these hermits continued to be tormented by sexual visions. St. Jerome castrated himself in a fit of sexual self-denial, an act he regretted subsequently. The tradition of asceticism (self-denial) in early Christianity contributed further to the perception of sexual feeling and activity as a sign of sinfulness and degeneracy (Sherrard, 1976).

Many of the teachings of Jerome and Origen were based on the writings of the Roman philosopher Seneca. Abstinence and virginity were glorified. "A virgin," declared Saint Ambrose, "marries God." Saint Jerome considered as adulterers all who were "shameless" with their wives (presumably by enjoying sex). Stoicism also contributed to the Christian doctrine of "natural law," which proved highly influential in condemning nonreproductive sexual behaviors and the use of contraception.

## The Challenge of Gnosticism

While suppressing lust, the Church had to simultaneously fight those who condemned all sexual experience, including marital intercourse for procreation. The main challenge in this respect was posed by the *Gnostics*. Members of this heretical Christian group claimed superior knowledge ("gnosis") of spiritual truths. Based on a mixture of Iranian myths, Jewish mysticism, Greek philosophy, and Christian doctrines, Gnosticism was a serious threat to the early Church (as far back as the time of Paul) because it capitalized on the same values of moral virtue and chastity endorsed by early Christians.

Paradoxically, the sexual beliefs and practices of the Gnostics placed them at two polar opposites (which they referred to as "left" and "right"). On the extreme right were the Gnostic ascetics who rejected all sex and considered marriage a form of fornication. In support, they cited the celibacy of Jesus and certain statements by Paul ("It is well for a man not to touch a woman," 1 Cor. 7:1). At the extreme left were those who claimed freedom from all moral laws. It is against these *antinomian* elements that Paul may have been warning that Christian liberty not be used as an excuse for sensuality and sexual misbehavior. Still these practices persisted, and certain factions in the Alexandrian church believed that women should be shared. They considered sexual intercourse a form of communion that led to salvation, and according to their detractors, they would engage in indiscriminate and perverse sexual practices.

The net effect of the Gnostic doctrines was to negate the concept of marriage as an orderly way of procreation and a lawful sexual experience. Hence the Church was pressed to uphold the legitimacy of marriage and procreative sex. Condemning both kinds of Gnostics, the Catholic church steered a middle course, which it had to defend over and over again from attacks from both the "right" and the "left".

This characterization of the Gnostics has been based mainly on Catholic accounts and judgments, because the Church systematically destroyed the writings of heretics. Recent archeological finds have led to a more positive evaluation of Gnostic beliefs, revealing their insistence on the primacy of personal experience, pursuit of a solitary path to self-discovery, and distrust of institutional guidance and control. Their rejection or subordination of sex was part of a broader attempt to set aside worldly distractions, which stood in the way of their search for inner truth (Pagels, 1979).

The Challenge of the Manichees    *Manicheanism* was founded by Mani (A.D. 216–277) in Babylon. Largely derived from Gnosticism, Iranian folk religion, and Christianity (Mani referred to himself as "an apostle" of Jesus Christ), it envisioned a world dominated by the struggle between the forces of *light* and *darkness*. All living things, including people, were largely generated by the demons of darkness, but imprisoned within their bodies was some light; the Manichean purpose in life was to set this light free (Noonan, 1967).

Because procreation perpetrated the work of Evil, it was evil. Hence, sexual desire, which led to procreation, was impure and had to be suppressed; if it was allowed expression, its procreative consequences had to be avoided. To achieve this end, the Manichees relied on the infertile period during the menstrual cycle—ironically, the only method to be subsequently accepted by the Catholic Church. Again the Church was confronted with the task of reaffirming the legitimacy of conjugal sex for procreation, while still upholding the virtues of sexual abstinence. The Church therefore accused the Manichees both of denigrating marriage and procreation and of sexual perversity. (It was said, for instance, that Manichees spilled semen on grain, which then they ate as a eucharist, the Christian sacrament of the Lord's supper.)

The Manichean challenge was met head on by St. Augustine, one of the monumental figures of the Christian Church. The association between *original sin* and sexuality had been made by Clement, but it was through Augus-

tine that it became entrenched in Catholic theology. The concept of *concupiscence* was central to Augustine's concept of sexuality. The term, which literally means "strong desire," referred to the "heat" and "confusion of lust" that accompanies copulation, in short, the libidinal, erotic, pleasurable component in sexual arousal and orgasm. By damning concupiscence, Augustine struck at the heart of the sexual impulse. He condemned all sexual experience as serving lust and hence shameful. Sexual activities that served no procreative purpose (including coitus with contraception) were especially evil, because they were aimed purely at the gratification of lust. Conjugal sex was legitimate in serving procreative ends, but tainted with evil to the extent that it was contaminated by concupiscence (Bullough and Brundage, 1982).

This doctrine was by no means a universal belief within the Church. For example, Ambrose thought Adam's original sin was not sex but pride. Saint Chrysostom also made no connection between original sin and sexuality; nor did he consider concupiscence a sin. Only when immoderate sexual desire failed to keep within the bonds of marriage and led to adultery, did sin occur. It was therefore not sex but its abuse that was condemned. If the view of Chrysostom, instead of Augustine, had governed theological developments in the West, a different moral tone, and a different way of looking at sex in marriage, might have prevailed through the centuries (Noonan, 1967).

## THE MIDDLE AGES

In western Europe, the civilization that became heir to the classical tradition was largely a peasant society, and its dominant social institution was the Church. It was in the context of this medieval society that Western sexual attitudes and behaviors were forged further.

### The Early Middle Ages
The early Middle Ages were a chaotic and sorry time for Europe. Vast movements of

people reshaped the demographic face of the continent, then bereft of any central authority. Whatever survived of the learning and culture of antiquity was preserved in monasteries, which did not exist for the glorification of sex.

Erotic art and literature had begun to decline during the eclipse of the Roman Empire. The Church, which had established itself firmly in the 4th century, suppressed anything that smacked of licentiousness. The fear of obscenity and paganism pervaded all art; when religious themes required the showing of nude bodies (such as with figures of Adam and Eve before the Fall) they were represented without any hint of eroticism. A comparison of the medieval Eve (Figure 20.8) with the classical Aphrodite (Figure 20.4) illustrates this change in sexual values (Eitner, 1975).

Building on the ascetic values of the Church Fathers and the concept of unquestioned law (*nomos*), the Church had formulated, by the 8th century, a rigid code of sexual morality regulated by *Canon Law* (Brundage, 1982). *Penitentials* gave detailed lists of sins to be examined during confession and their corresponding penances—various acts of self-mortification (such as abstaining from sex or meat) and of devotion. Sins included fornication with a virgin, various forms of incest, bestiality, homosexual relations, erotic fantasy, and so on.

Underlying this medieval code was the belief that sexual pleasure was innately sinful. A grudging acceptance of sex as a necessity for reproduction was coupled with prohibitions against all other forms of erotic feeling and expression. Based on these suppositions, sexual restraints could be carried to absurd lengths; some pious couples, for instance, would have coitus wearing heavy nightshirts (*chemise cagoule*) with a hole in front, which allowed penetration while preventing other bodily contact. Intercourse could be performed properly in the man-above position only (the "dog" posture called for seven years of penance) (Taylor, 1970). Husband and wife were urged to abstain from sex on Thursdays (in memory of the arrest of the Lord), on Fridays

Figure 20.8 *Eve* c. 1240. Portal sculpture from the Cathedral of Trau, Dalmatia, by Magister Rodovan.

(in commemoration of his death), on Saturdays (in honor of the Blessed Virgin), on Sundays (in honor of the Resurrection), and on Mondays (in honor of the faithful who had died). Continence was necessary for 40 days before Easter, three months before the birth of a child, and two months thereafter. Some couples abstained altogether from sex through *chaste marriage* (McNamara, 1983).

Even involuntary nocturnal emissions were not exempt from judgment. The offender had to rise at once to say 7 penitential psalms followed by 30 in the morning. If the sin was committed while asleep in church, the whole psalter had to be sung in penance.

This bleak erotic landscape of the early medieval Church reflected the monastic ideal, but it hardly mirrored the real sexual behavior of the times. Church law no doubt imparted to the pious feelings of guilt, and a sense of gloom suffused all sexual themes in moral theology, but large segments of the population were untouched. In the 8th century, Boniface despaired of the licentiousness of the English, who "utterly despise matrimony" and "live in lechery and adultery after the manner of neighing horses and braying asses. . . . " A century later, Alcuin found the land "absolutely submerged under a flood of fornication, adultery, and incest, so that the very semblance of modesty is entirely absent" (Taylor, 1970, p. 20).

Eroticism persisted even within the bosom of the Church. Driven underground, erotic art manifested itself in the most unlikely places, such as in the margins of illuminated devotional books, carvings on choir stalls, and decorations on churches. Ostensibly religious sculptures from the period show provocative female nudes; men with erections; and couples fondling each other, engaging in coitus, and having oral sex (in the "sixty-nine" position, no less) (Webb, 1975). Moreover, representations of women with exposed genitals, called *Shelah-na-Gig*, were carved on the façades of some medieval Irish churches, suggesting a persistence of the belief that genital symbols protected against evil forces (Figure 20.9) (Andersson, 1977). Ancient agricultural festivals with

Figure 20.9    *Shelah-na-Gig.*

their phallic symbols can also be detected in celebrations of spring, which took place in May; people danced around a decorated wooden *maypole,* a practice that has persisted until recent times. Among the Franks in the 10th century, unmarried women danced naked on these occasions in front of the men. Though in time these practices were tamed, they never quite lost their ancient erotic roots.

The image of sexuality that emerges from the early Middle Ages is mixed. There is the sexually repressive posture of the Church with its ascetic ideals, and then the residues of sexual hedonism from the Roman world, the rough ways of the nominally Christian Germanic tribes, and the lapses in clerical discipline. In this context, too, the Catholic Church had to fight a dual battle. To impose some semblance of order on the chaotic world around it required repressing sexuality. At the same time the Church fought fiercely against the tendency towards extremes of asceticism, which denigrated all forms of sexual expression.

## The Late Middle Ages

By the time Europe entered the second millenium of the Christian era, expanding populations had settled new lands, commerce had revitalized urban life, government had become more effective, and the Church had begun a significant reform movement, with the finest minds and artistic talents of the period at her service. Centers of monastic learning began to evolve into universities of scholastic distinction.

We still know little about the sex life of the common people; but the abundant vernacular literature of the period reveals much about the amorous life of the more privileged classes. Especially pertinent here is the lyric poetry of the *troubadours,* celebrating women and love, which emerged in southern France and entered its age of greatness in the 12th century. As expressed in the tradition of *courtly love,* the troubadours worshiped from afar the idealized and often unattainable noble ladies who managed the family estates during the frequent absences of their men. From the poetic explorations of love by troubadours (such as *The Art of Courtly Love* by Andreas Cappelanus) evolved many of our *romantic* traditions. By separating love from marriage, and by extension, sex from reproduction, the troubadours also helped establish a secular alternative to the exclusively generative purposes of sex as taught by the Church.

During the 14th century, the "dirty" story (fabliau) was raised to an art form. The men and women portrayed in the stories by Chaucer (*Canterbury Tales*) and Boccaccio (*The Decameron*) are witty, worldly, wily, and cynical in their views of sex and marriage. A recurring character is the cuckolded husband, who is sometimes cast as a clod who deserves his fate, at other times as the innocent victim of a faithless wife. If these figures are representative, they provide interesting glimpses into the sexual relationships of medieval men and women (Atkins, 1978). Similar insights are obtained from medieval art (Figure 20.10).

Prostitution never died out in the Middle Ages, and it became more prevalent with urbanization (Bullough and Brundage, 1982). Even Saint Thomas Aquinas grudgingly acknowledged that prostitutes served a useful function by helping to preserve the chastity of decent women. The Crusaders reintroduced public baths to Europe, some of which also served as brothels.

Hostility toward homosexuals had been considerable in the declining years of the Roman Empire, and during the early Middle Ages homosexuals do not seem to be much in evidence. With the urban revival in the 11th century, a substantial homosexual community developed, with representatives among prominent and respected figures of European society. However, in the second half of the 12th century public sentiment once again turned hostile, as part of intolerance towards minorities in general, including heretics and Jews. These attitudes became incorporated into the theological, moral, and legal documents of the later Middle Ages and continued to influence Western attitudes toward homosexuality for centuries.

Despite greater secularization, the Church remained the dominant social institution in the later Middle Ages, legislating sexual morality and behavior. The chief influence in moral theology in the 13th century was the towering figure of Saint Thomas Aquinas (1225?–1274), the quintessential scholastic theologian whose aim was a grand synthesis of the faith of Augustine with the reason of Aristotle. Aquinas addressed himself to virtually all forms of sexual behavior, including touching, kissing, fondling, seduction, virginity, marital sex, fornication, adultery, rape, incest, prostitition, homosexuality, and bestiality.

Medieval eroticism manifested itself in curious ways. Individual fantasies and delusions were interpreted sometimes as divine inspiration and sometimes as the work of the devil. In either instance, women (especially nuns) were likely to be involved. Bear in mind that although many medieval women who took religious vows were seeking a life of devotion and service, medieval convents also served as catchalls for social rejects, the morally delinquent, and the mentally disturbed (Saint Bernardine called them "the scum and vomit of the world" Chambers et al., 1979, p. 370). It is no wonder

Figure 20.10    *Amorous feast,* engraving by the Master of 1465.

that in this mixed company, erotic fantasy and mystical piety sometimes got intermingled: Christine Ebner believed herself to be pregnant by Jesus; and Veronica Giuliani took a real suckling lamb to her breast in memory of the lamb of God (Taylor, 1970). Other women felt themselves assaulted by devils in the form of *incubi* (as *succubi* tormented males). Jeanne Pothière swore that a demon had forced her to copulate 444 times (Clugh, 1963).

This period also had extraordinary manifestations of sadomasochism. Asceticism has had a long association with self-inflicted suffering, but in the Middle Ages, *flagellation* (whipping) was inflicted on penitents; during the calamitous 14th century, when war, famine, and plague ravaged Europe, hordes of self-flagellants took to the roads in an effort to expiate their sins. Despite these aberrations, most medieval men and women just went about their sexual business, like others before and since, as amply evident in the boisterous scenes painted by Pieter Brueghel, Hieronymus Bosch and other great artists of later periods.

## THE RENAISSANCE AND THE REFORMATION

Over the 14th and 15th centuries, as the civilization of the Middle Ages declined, a period of renewal—the *Renaissance* ("rebirth")—began to reshape European culture, marking the beginning of modern Western civilization. The men and women of the Renaissance generated a sexually richer culture in two centuries than did their medieval forebears in ten (Box 20.3).

The secularization of Renaissance society and the greater worldliness of the Church diversified the sexual options. An emphasis on individual will, the hallmark of Renaissance mentality, was largely responsible for the bewildering mixture of the glorious and the awful within its culture.

### Renaissance Sexuality

The exuberant sexuality of the classical world, long dormant during the Middle Ages, re-emerged in Renaissance society. Immense wealth combined with a passion for elegance and luxury led the ruling class to indulge its sexual appetites on a grand scale. The extreme individualism of the young and impetuous men who dominated Renaissance society added a violent aspect to it. It was not unheard of for a band of armed youths to invade a convent and rape the nuns. Every woman was fair game to the man who could seduce her; he, in turn, became fair game to her husband's or father's dagger if caught in the act. The sexual behavior of some of the pillars of Renaissance society rivaled that of the most decadent Roman emperors: a prominent Florentine, Sig-

ismondo Malatesta, was convicted of murder, rape, adultery, incest, sacrilege, perjury, and treason (his son Roberto had to defend himself with a dagger against his father's sexual assaults) (Johnson, 1981). Although many churchmen led exemplary lives, other Renaissance cardinals and popes shared some of the more outrageous ways of their culture. Numbered among them were great humanists and patrons of art, but also men who were fond of pleasure and luxury. On one occasion, Rodrigo Borgia (Pope Alexander VI) had 50 naked women picking chestnuts off the floor for his dinner guests, who then competed with each other to see who could copulate with the largest number of them (Taylor, 1970).

The Renaissance also saw the revival of the *courtesans,* while ordinary prostitutes flourished as well. Like their classical predecessors, the Renaissance courtesan could be a woman of intelligence, refined manner, and charm. The women of the aristocracy were also often cultured, worldly, and sometimes as vicious as the men. The sexual lives of ordinary men and women became more free as well without the flamboyance of the ruling classes.

### The Reformation

The excesses of Renaissance society evoked a strong reaction both among the clergy and laity. The threat of censure from here on hung over the heads of artists of even Michelangelo's eminence; in 1559 Pope Paul IV ordered the nudity of some of the figures in the *Last judgment* to be painted over.

Less dramatic but more lasting was the influence of other reformers who were dismayed at the moral laxity and secularization of the Renaissance Church. As Italian humanists had revived the love of classical learning, Christian humanists, like Thomas More in England and Desiderius Erasmus in Holland, attempted a similar return to the teachings and traditions of the early Christian Church. These early reformers paved the way for Martin Luther's (1483–1546) *Protestant revolution,* which irrevocably split the Christian church in the West. The views of Luther and John Calvin exerted a profound influence on sexual morality that persists to this day, particularly in the United States, as the *Protestant sexual ethic*.

Though less systematic than Aquinas in his consideration of sexual issues, Luther had an earthier perception of sex and expressed himself with remarkable candor. For a summary of Luther's views on sex and marriage, see Feucht (1961). Among Luther's own works that bear on this area is his *Treatise on Married Life*. Luther rejected the Catholic belief that marriage was a sacrament, because he could find no biblical support for it. Instead he considered marriage a divinely ordained duty and privilege, harking back to the Judaic tradition of marital relationships. Particularly in his earlier writings, Luther laid much emphasis on the erotic component in marriage. The sexual urge was part of God's creation, and there was no point or possibility in resisting it; instead it had to be harnessed and put to good use. Luther compared marriage to a hospital that cured people of lust and fornication. Where a marriage failed to fulfill sexual needs, it lost a main purpose for its existence; hence impotence on the part of the husband and repeated refusal to have sex by the wife constituted grounds for divorce.

Luther initially respected voluntary celibacy, while opposing its imposition on the clergy. Eventually he came to regard celibacy and virginity as unnatural, impractical, and false forms of piety. He himself broke his earlier monastic vow of chastity by marrying at age 42 Katharine von Bora ("Katie"), a 29-year-old former nun, and fathered three children.

Protestantism reaffirmed the Catholic emphasis on the reproductive function of marriage, but it also made much more of affection and companionship ("love and honor") between spouses. Even the Catholic Church, which vigorously opposed almost everything that Luther stood for, came to adopt (in the Council of Trent in 1563) the reformer's view in this regard, and it has stood for the Western ideal of marriage since then. Luther cannot be held responsible for our romantic notions of conjugal bliss, though. He thought husband and wife had to make concessions to the

Figure 20.11    Agostino Carracci (1557–1602), *Satyr and nymph*, c. 1590, engraving.

drudgery of daily marital life and the burdens of rearing children; marriage taught couples how to be humble and patient.

Luther and the Protestant reformers, having blessed sex in marriage, categorically disapproved of all other forms of sexual expression. Because everyone, including the clergy, could be married, there was no excuse any more for the existence of other sexual alternatives. That also applied to prostitution; Luther would have none of it (but as a practical politician, he cautioned against abruptly closing down brothels). As Jeremy Taylor summed up this point of view at a later time, "There is no necessity that men must either debauch matrons or be fornicators; let them marry, for that is the remedy which God hath appointed" (quoted in Tannahill, 1980, p. 328).

John Calvin (1509–1564) left his own imprint on Protestant sexual morality. Where Lu-

# Box 20.3

## EROTIC ART AND LITERATURE IN THE RENAISSANCE*

Revival of interest in the sensuous art of the classical world and the growth of sophisticated secular patronage stimulated an extraordinary flowering of erotic art in the 15th and 16th centuries which profoundly influenced the subsequent development of erotic art in the West. Medieval art, as a vehicle of the teachings of the Church, was meant for everyone. The select patronage of Renaissance art, by contrast, preserved it for the more privileged, and its secular patrons were attracted to the very erotic elements which had been absent from medieval art. Nudity and sensuality could now be freely portrayed through the representation of mythological characters and events, with the figure of Venus holding the place of honor (among the more celebrated being the Venuses by Botticelli, Giorgione, and Titian). Even religious art in the Renaissance has its own sexual motifs (Steinberg, 1983).

Michelangelo's sculptures are not explicitly sexual, but a special sensuality endows works like the *Dying slave* and the *Pietà*. There are also a few works of Michelangelo's with overtly erotic content, such as the drawing of a man wearing a penis on his bonnet, and other phallic themes (possibly linked to Michelangelo's homosexual interests) (Wilson, 1973, p. 17).

Renaissance artists relied heavily on classical themes such as the amatory escapades of Zeus, the interactions of other Olympian gods, and the erotic antics of satyrs and nymphs (Figure 20.11). The erotic portrait as a new form of painting also now makes its appearance with Raphael's *La fornarina*, portraying his mistress with bared breasts.

The secular interest in the erotic notwithstanding, the Church remained the primary patron of the arts, much of which remained of a religious nature. But even here erotic themes found their way through the portrayal of Old Testament episodes, such as the temptation of Joseph by Potiphar's wife (Tintoretto, Titian, Veronese), Lot's incest with his daughters (Raphael and Carracci), and Susanna being spied upon at her bath by the elders (Tintoretto). Raphael also painted erotic frescoes for the bathroom of Cardinal Bibbiena in the Vatican (not open to public view).

The Renaissance preoccupation with the human figure was further pursued in the 16th century by certain followers of Michelangelo and Raphael in a distinctive style known as *Mannerism.*[†] Relying on complex metaphorical themes, Mannerist painters portrayed the human body in convoluted and contorted forms, often in more explicitly erotic ways than did their Renaissance mentors. A central figure of Italian mannerism was Giulio Romano, one of Raphael's most gifted pupils and an erotic artist of unblushing explicitness. His set of drawings of coital postures became the prototype of "sex-manual" art in the West. Romano's drawings, engraved by Marcantonio Raimondi and embellished with erotic sonnets by Pietro Aretino, were known as the *Sedici modi* (Figure 20.12). Published in 1527, they caused quite a stir and were much copied (only parts of the original prints have survived). Agostino Carracci painted another famous series of the same type. Developments in mass reproduction (through woodcuts, engravings, and etchings) allowed lesser artists to turn such art into commercial pornography.

Two of the greatest writers of the 16th century, François Rabelais and William Shakespeare, were not self-consciously erotic writers, but their works are noted for their bawdy humor. Though "Rabelaisian" has come to characterize all that is lustily humorous, the incisive wit of Rabelais (who was both monk and physician) was meant to satirize the lapses of the clergy and the morality of his time. Similarly, though Shakespeare's plays abound with sexual references, sex for him was but one facet of the far more complex emotions of love and hatred with their often tragic consequences. Such pessimism pervades the most famous tragedies of Shakespeare, as exemplified by *Romeo and Juliet* (whose plot comes from Boccaccio).

*This section is based mostly on Eitner (1975) and Webb (1975).

†"Mannerism" is descriptive of the excessive adherence to the distinctive style or manner characteristic of this art; there is also a pejorative connotation to the term in the same sense that we call people with affectations manneristic.

Figure 20.12   *Pair of lovers.* Late copy after an engraving by Marcantonio Raimondi, based on designs by Giulio Romano.

ther saw marriage as the remedy for sexual desire, *Calvinism* viewed marriage as a veil that covered sin. To avoid the excessive enjoyment of sex, he urged that a husband approach his wife "with delicacy and propriety" and that she in turn be circumspect, so as to avoid touching or looking at his genitals. This mentality extended to disapproving everything that was sensuous, exuberant, or frivolous. The Puritans in England elaborated these attitudes into a distinctively dour form of Protestant sexual morality. Transplanted to New England, these views in turn proved highly influential in shaping the moral ideals of the fledgling American nation.

## THE ENLIGHTENMENT

During the 18th century, the conviction began to spread in Europe that change and reform were possible and desirable. This period came to be known as the Enlightenment (Kagan et al., 1987). As scientific evidence increasingly became the basis for reality, skepticism began to undermine the religious faith and moral assumptions of the past. In the absence of divine guidance, a secular morality had to be found to regulate human conduct. This was to have profound repercussions on attitudes towards sexuality.

Montaigne proposed to make human welfare and self-determination the bases of morality. The purpose of life shifted from the aspiration to eternal life in heaven to attaining happiness on earth. The Declaration of Independence of the United States codified this view by including "the Pursuit of Happiness" among the inalienable rights given by the Creator.

### Manners and Morals

At the turn of the 18th century, the rate of

illegitimacy in France was less than 5 percent; but in England and in New England it may have been as high as 50 percent. Almost everyone got married (the men at around age 27, women at 25). We do not have further details of the sexual practices and attitudes of the common people other than what can be surmised from such demographic facts and literary references.

In Europe, the strictest sexual morals were to be found among the middle classes, they being the most vulnerable as well as the most desirous of improving their social standing. The upper classes felt secure and the poor had little to lose. The law forbade homosexuality on pain of death, but that did not apply to royalty. Romantic love was accepted as a relief from marriage, but not as a reason for it. Almost everyone who could afford a mistress had one. Married women felt neglected if no one but their own husbands desired them. The principle of live and let live kept the peace.

The 18th century also saw the birth of the condom. It was the age of Casanova, of the Marquis de Sade, and of the literary character Don Juan. These personifications of *libertinism* marked a new phase in the ageless game of seduction that now was played out on the stage of the fashionable world. It was a game of calculated viciousness where men selected, seduced, and abandoned a succession of naive and trusting women. In the fevered fantasies of de Sade, sex took on an explicitly sadistic character (see Box 14.2).

## Erotic Art and Literature

By the start of the 17th century the sexual exuberance of late Renaissance art ("mannerism") had given way to the highly ornate *baroque* style. If eroticism is considered outside of the simplistic equation with explicitness, then the 17th century produced two of the great masters of erotic art in the West: Peter Paul Rubens and Rembrandt van Rijn. The powerful eroticism of Rubens is evident in his fleshy and sensuous nudes. Rembrandt, the greatest artist of the age, is more subtle in his sexual expression: his nudes in erotic mythology or biblical scenes are convincing representations of real women and more compelling erotically. His etching known as the *Ledikant* (or *The four-poster bed*) is extraordinary in its frank and tender vision of a couple making love (Figure 20–13).

Figure 20.13   Rembrandt, *The four-poster bed,* 1646.

The 18th century witnessed the triumph of more explicit eroticism in art. Sexual tolerance allowed artists of high quality to devote themselves to erotic subjects without fear or embarrassment. Of these artists, Jean Antoine Watteau was the most gifted. His *fête galante* paintings portrayed contemporary men and women in elaborate costumes celebrating love in a wistful, dreamlike world filled with the trappings of antiquity. Jean Honoré Fragonard used classical motifs playfully, and his erotic subjects are full of movement, wit, and surprise. The work of François Boucher is the most sexually explicit of the three, and his use of mythological figures was clearly calculated to exploit their full erotic potential. By the close of the century there was such a surfeit of licentious pictures that Diderot was moved to write, "I think I have seen enough tits and behinds." (Eitner, 1975)

The great French dramatists of the 17th century—Corneille, Molière, and Racine—explored various aspects of love, often using classical themes. There was hardly a serious writer, in fact, who did not touch in one fashion or another upon issues of love and erotic relationships. The 18th century is also well represented in literary forms that deal with sexual themes (Purdy, 1975a). Of the literature on prostitution, outstanding examples are Daniel Defoe's *The Fortunes and Misfortunes of the Amorous Moll Flanders* (1722) and John Cleland's *Memoirs of a Woman of Pleasure* (1749) (commonly known as *Fanny Hill*). Both works provide moral lessons about the folly of vice while giving explicit examples of its pleasures.

Another 18th-century literary form is erotic autobiography. The prototypical work here is *The History of My Life* (or *The Memoirs*) of Giovanni Casanova de Seingalt (1725–1978). Casanova was a Venetian adventurer, who after a lifetime of travel and intrigue retired to the castle of a prominent friend to write and study. His memoirs are regarded as an important historical document (Casanova, 1958).

## Life in the American Colonies

The men and women who migrated to the English colonies in America brought with them several beliefs shaped by the Protestant Reformation. These beliefs were in sharp contrast to the more liberal sexual practices of Native American tribes (D'Emilio and Freedman, 1988). Sexual life in America during the 17th-century period was quite different as well from Europe (Schlesinger, 1970). We may think of the Puritan founders of this nation as prudes; yet the Puritans in the 17th century were quite open about sex and viewed it as a natural and joyous part of marriage. One James Mattock was expelled from the First Church of Boston for refusing to sleep with his wife. Puritan maidens with child were married by understanding ministers, as is indicated in the town records of the time. The Puritans were stern and God-fearing people, who could be harsh with adulterers; yet their wrath was aroused only because such behavior threatened the sanctity and stability of marriage. A general sexual openness was even apparent to outsiders. A visitor from Maryland who was in Boston in 1744 reported: "This place abounds with pretty women who appear rather more abroad than they do at New York and dress elegantly. They are for the most part, free and affable as well as pretty. I saw not one prude while I was there."

With the coming of national independence in the 18th century, there was a reaction against romantic notions that were associated with Old World feudalism and aristocracy. The republic was pledged to liberty, equality, and rationality. Marriage became more and more a service institution to populate the nation and strengthen the labor force. Native as well as visiting observers were quick to comment on this victory of rationality over romantic love. "No author, without a trial," complained Hawthorne, "can conceive of the difficulty of writing a romance about a country where there is no shadow, no antiquity, no mystery, no picturesque and gloomy wrong, nor anything but a commonplace prosperity, in broad and simple daylight, as is happily the case with my dear native land." The French writer Stendhal observed that Americans had such a "habit of reason" that abandonment to love became all but impossible. In Europe, he wrote, "desire is sharpened by restraint; in America it is blunted by liberty."

## THE NINETEENTH CENTURY

Victorian manners and morals were already well established when the young Queen Victoria ascended the British throne in 1837, and they outlived her death in 1901 (Quinlan, 1941). Until recently, Victorian sexual morality was seen as rigid, pretentious, oppressive, and hypocritical. Historians have now shown that picture to be not entirely correct (Gay, 1984, 1986). One of the main reasons for the conflicting images from this period is that life of the middle classes was highly varied—open and secretive, ordered and chaotic at the same time. Attitudes towards the show of affection, the supervision of girls, the use of contraceptives, and other significant ingredients of sexuality "differed drastically from decade to decade, from country to country, from stratum to stratum" (Gay, 1984, p. 5). Another source of confusion has been the failure to differentiate between sexual behavior and sexual ideology, or as Carl Degler (1974) has phrased it, "What Ought to Be and What Was." Far from suppressing sexual discussion, Victorian society reveled in it (Foucault, 1978).

### Victorian Sexual Ideology

Sexual repressiveness, especially the suppression and denial of female sexuality, while by no means characteristic of all of Victorian society, was a significant element within it (Marcus, 1966).

The Repressive Model    The laxity prevalent in 18th-century England awoke concern in religious and social reformers like John Wesley (1703–1791), the founder of the Methodist Church, and the prototype of the evangelical preacher (what we now call "born again" Christianity). Likewise, the French Revolution, coming on the heels of the loss of the American colonies, posed a profound threat to the ruling classes in England. It was therefore of paramount importance for Church and state to find ways of stabilizing society, and moral reform appeared to hold the best prospects. In this climate of urgency the evangelical successors of John Wesley and the reform societies came into their own.

These reform measures were successful in stabilizing English society, but at the cost of making Victorian morality rigid and oppressive, its manners smug and pretentious. The effect of this killjoy mentality was to drive sexual enjoyment underground. Respectable women, placed on a pedestal of purity, were asexualized; women relegated to whoredom were dehumanized. Influential physicians like William Acton fostered the notion that respectable women had no sexual desires or should suppress them if they did. Marital sex became a conjugal duty for procreation, which women were supposed to suffer with resignation. By contrast, prostitutes were assumed to be sexually insatiable.

Men had to contend with a similar split; a man could neither enjoy sex freely with his wife whom he was free to love and respect, nor could he love and respect the prostitute with whom he could freely enjoy sex. A burden of guilt or frustration became inextricably attached to sex whichever way people turned.

Victorian physicians turned on sex itself because of its presumed health hazards. The venereal diseases, which were widespread, were rightly to be feared, but there was no basis for the imagined sexual and bodily "wasting" presumed to result from the involuntary loss of semen (*spermatorrhea*) and masturbation (Box 11.4). In the name of health, physicians now became the arbiters of sexual morality through the "medicalization of sin."

Control of Male Sexuality    Some historians have recently modified the repressive image of Victorian sexuality in two important ways. First, they point out that the ideology of the period was by no means inexorably repressive, and that people did not always pay heed to the sexual pessimists; second, that the underlying motivation in the control of sexuality was not the suppression of female sexuality or the oppression of women—but the control of male sexuality and the liberation of women (Degler, 1980).

In the sexual advice literature of the early 19th century, coital relations for married couples were placed at four to five times a week, with expectations of mutual orgasm. Female sexual interest was taken for granted; if anything, it was thought to be stronger and more enduring than that of the male.

It was only during the 1840s and 1850s that the more repressive ideology made its appearance. It coexisted with more positive views of sex, which saw it as necessary for health, and which recognized and validated the sexual need and capacity of women. Even when these authors referred to the sexual unresponsiveness of women, they put the blame on negative sexual attitudes and the insensitivity and clumsiness of husbands. It was nevertheless the more repressive viewpoint that came to prevail as representative of the age, and its prescriptive statements of how people should behave were accepted as descriptive of how they did behave.

In the United States, this pessimistic image was reinforced by the highly vocal activities of a number of social reform organizations, which came into being after the Civil War. Known as the *Social Purity* movement, its efforts were aimed at combatting liquor and prostitution, raising the age of consent for girls, and establishing a single standard of sexual behavior for both sexes.

The earnestness and rhetoric of crusaders for social purity made them sound antisexual. However, their basic purpose was not to suppress sex but to protect women against the abuse of prostitution and to promote the sexual autonomy of women within marriage. Women played an active and prominent part in these social movements. They recognized that repeated and unwanted pregnancies threatened the health of women, and the burden of a large family precluded their taking on professional and social responsibilities outside the home.

Given the relative unavailability and unreliability of contraceptives, the only certain assurance against indiscriminate pregnancies was sexual restraint. To this end, a variety of arguments and exhortations was marshaled by physicians, social reformers, and feminists. Dr. Alice Stockham's (1883) objection to a wife's submitting meekly to her husband's sexual demands has a curiously modern ring: "She gives up all *ownership* of herself to her husband, and what is the difference between her life and the life of the public woman? She is sold to one man, and is not half so well paid" (p. 154). Even the "passionlessness" of women may have been useful for them, giving them moral parity with men and a measure of control over their reproductive functions (Gordon, 1976). The delicacy and fragility of Victorian women may have been similarly fostered to keep men at bay. The justification of the campaign against prostitution and the condemnation of men who seduced and abandoned women make sense in this light.

These efforts were largely successful. The marital fertility rate declined from 7.04 births in 1800 to 3.56 births in 1900. The attempts to legalize prostitution were successfully resisted. Perhaps most significantly, the separation of sex from reproduction began to be established at this time. With better contraceptives available, abstinence and restraint became less important for the control of fertility. The acceptance of nonreproductive sex was to have enormous repercussions in attitudes towards a variety of sexual behaviors, including sex outside of marriage and homosexuality (Freedman, 1982).

All of these changes were important for the sexual liberalization of subsequent periods, but at the time, social purity took its toll. By supporting men like Anthony Comstock (Chapter 22), purists got the expression of all sexual themes severely censored; by combatting unrestrained sex, they ended up checking healthy sexual experiences as well.

## Erotic Art and Literature

Despite the presumed prudishness of the 19th century, a great deal of sexually explicit art was produced. Among established artists in the romantic tradition, erotic themes are discernible in the works of Theodore Gericault, Eugene Delacroix, Jean Antoine Ingres, and Francisco Goya. Among the realists, erotic elements are notable in the work of Gustave Courbet, who was able to get away with a painting like *Sleeping women* (Figure 13.3), which the artist called *Laziness and sensuality.* Henri de Toulouse-Lautrec documented life in the brothels and places of entertainment patronized by the demimonde. Such forthright treatment of erotic subjects infuriated the respectable classes, who much preferred the more teasingly exposed nudes portrayed in classical guise in the work of Cabanel, Bouguereau, and Alma-Tadema (Figure 20.14). In addition, a vast outpouring of frankly pornographic art flooded the market from the Victorian underground, purveyed largely by artists of meager talent (Eitner, 1975).

In the second half of the 19th century, as artists became increasingly alienated from society, they developed a decadent art aimed at shocking respectable sensibilities. Aubrey Beardsley and Marquis von Bayros (1968) were part of this new realist tradition, as was

Felicien Rops, whose work is unparalleled in its brutal assault on some of the most hallowed images in Western culture (Webb, 1975). For example, in a painting by Rops called *Mary Magdalene,* a voluptuous and darkly sinister woman is shown masturbating next to a cross to which is tied a giant phallus (Rops, 1975).

In 19th-century literature the same excessive sense of propriety coexists with the crudest eroticism of mass pornography. It was during this century that pornographic writing became an industry (Marcus, 1966). It was also during this period that translations of the erotic literature of the East were introduced into the English-speaking world. The dominant figure here was Sir Richard Burton, whose numerous accounts of his explorations and his translations of Eastern erotica confronted Victorian society with the freer sexual mores and attitudes of the high cultures of the East. Among Burton's major works were the translations of *The Arabian Nights* and other well-known erotic classics like *The Perfumed Garden* (Purdy, 1975a).

## Sexual Behavior

Given these cross-currents of sexual ideology,

Figure 20.14 Lawrence Alma-Tadema (1836–1912). *In the tepidarium.* The object in the right hand is an instrument for cleaning the skin.

what was actual behavior like? Some Victorian men and women must have been overwhelmed by the guilt and shame engendered by the expectations of abstinence, repression, and self-restraint. Others paid no heed to the prophets of sexual doom. As Alex Comfort (1967) has put it, "The astounding resilience of human common sense against the anxiety makers is one of the really cheering aspects of history."

We get a more realistic picture of Victorian sexual behavior from historical accounts, autobiographical materials, the art and literature of the period, and at least one sex survey conducted by a woman physician in the United States, Dr. Clelia Mosher (Chapter 1). One reason that evidence in this area is not more plentiful is because of the Victorian reticence to discuss sex publicly. Though we could take that as evidence of sexual repressiveness, the reluctance to talk about sex cannot be equated with the reluctance to enjoy it.

Marital Sex    The legitimacy of marital sex was not questioned even by those who voiced concerns over sexual excess. A good deal of evidence attests to the passionate and joyful relationship of many Victorian couples. The Mosher survey shows that at least for its sample of well-educated, married women, the capacity to reach orgasm was not much different from the rates reported during the 1970s. These women also practiced birth control methods beyond abstinence and withdrawal, even though the inadequacy of the means at their disposal was a source of anxiety.

Even more compelling are the biographical vignettes and amorous correspondence of some couples, which reveal an unabashed celebration of sexual desire and a romantic intensity compared with today's uninhibited language of love sounds insipid. "Oh joy! Oh! Bliss unutterable" wrote Mable Todd of her wedding night (Gay, 1984).

*Engagement* was a period of intense emotional and erotic involvement for Victorian middle-class couples, although it probably did not entail coitus. Given the dependence of women on men, the uncertainties of available contraception, and sexual convention, premar-

ital sex would have been a problem, hence the premium on premarital virginity. Premarital pregnancies were nonetheless fairly prevalent in the United States. Their rates declined from close to 30 percent of all births in the late 18th century, to less than 10 percent in the middle of the 19th century, then went up to 20 percent by the end of the 19th century (Smith and Hindus, 1975). These shifts are ascribed to young people adhering more faithfully to the ethic of continence in the first half of the 19th century, then moving away from that ideal, asserting their independence from family control.

Socially Problematic Behaviors    Prostitution was very much a part of Victorian society. Typically, the "fallen woman" was a working girl, employed at pitiful wages, who supplemented her income by selling her sexual services. An appalling proportion were teenagers, some barely out of childhood. The Victorian craze for virginity prompted the keepers of bawdy houses to have these pathetic youngsters stitched up over and over so they could be deflowered by wealthy patrons willing to pay premium fees for the pleasure. Doctors attached to these houses provided certificates of virginity after performing the surgery. Some Victorian courtesans lived in great luxury, but they did not quite attain the refinement of their earlier counterparts. The best that women like Cora Pearl could do was dance nude on a carpet of orchids and bathe in a silver tank full of champagne in front of dinner guests. Pearl could earn 5,000 francs a night when the daily wage of a skilled craftsman was 2 to 4 francs (Tannahill, 1980).

Prostitution was also part of the 19th-century scene in the United States (D'Emilio and Freedman, 1988). The estimate that there were 20,000 prostitutes in New York City in the 1830s led a social reformer to compute that if each woman received three clients a day, then half of the adult males in the city visited them three times a week. A visiting English journalist in 1867 wrote, "Paris may be subtler, London may be grosser in its vices; but for largeness of depravity, for domineering insolence of sin, for rowdy callousness to censure, they tell me Atlantic City finds no rival on earth" (quoted in Tannahill, 1980, p. 357). As the population of San Francisco swelled from less than 1,000 in 1848 to over 25,000 a few years later, some 3,000 prostitutes converged on it from all over the country and from as far away as China and Chile. Other women of pleasure temporarily resided in Washington when Congress was in session.

The ambivalent sexual attitudes of the age also extended to homosexuality. It was declared criminal, immoral, and indecent, yet not only did male prostitution flourish in London, but a homosexual undercurrent characterized life in elite English all-male educational institutions. Though the privileged classes usually dismissed the matter with tactful disinterest, it was possible to get caught in the grip of public indignation, as Oscar Wilde discovered when he was sent to jail. Shortly before his death, Wilde said, "I never came across anyone in whom the moral sense was dominant who was not heartless, cruel, vindictive, log-stupid, and entirely lacking in the smallest sense of humanity. Moral people, as they are termed, are simply beasts. I would sooner have fifty unnatural vices than one unnatural virtue" (Karlen, 1971, p. 255).

The use of the cane for punishing children has been blamed for the "English vice" of flagellation. Sadomasochistic themes are common in Victorian pornography as well as some of its serious literature. Brothels specialized in offering the joys of being whipped by a woman, whipping her, or simply watching others go through the experience. A small fortune was made by a Mrs. Berkley, who invented a contraption that looked like a padded ladder to which the customer would be tied; as the "governess" whipped his bare buttocks, another woman fondled his genitals.

Within the United States, prevailing sexual mores were challenged by *utopian communities*. The Shakers rejected coitus even for reproductive ends. The Oneida community used "coitus reservatus" (Chapter 3) to enjoy sex while avoiding conception. The Mormons allowed polygamy while limiting sex to repro-

ductive purposes. The Free Lovers, whose ideas gained currency toward the end of the century, were more radical. They opposed all forms of social control, advocating the rights of single women to bear children as well as enjoy sexual pleasure.

## THE MODERNIZATION OF SEX

The turn of the 20th century witnessed major changes. They laid the foundations of the modern way of thinking about sex, or what Paul Robinson (1976) has called the "modernization of sex."

Sexual modernism was a reaction to the repressive side of Victorianism, or the victory of its liberal side. It saw sex as a valuable human asset to be managed properly, rather than a drain on health or a threat to morality.

The most important early exponent of this point of view in the English-speaking world was Henry Havelock Ellis (Chapter 1). A "sexual enthusiast," Ellis saw sex in highly positive terms. Basing his views on cross-species and cross-cultural comparisons, he substituted for the prevailing concepts of sexual normality the notion of a continuum of sexual behaviors. In this idea Ellis anticipated Kinsey and the permissive views of modern sexologists; but on other issues, such as the role of women, he remained rooted in the 19th century.

Early 20th-century society did not become liberalized overnight, but now there was open talk about subjects that had been shunned. The issues addressed went beyond the standard topics to questions like how to combine the requirements of marriage with the need for sexual variety. Homosexuality and other behaviors formerly considered deviant were now considered to be in the realm of general human experience. Under the impact of Freud's work, the theme of sexuality came out of the closet and began to pervade all aspects of learning and culture.

The upheaval of World War I accelerated the changes that were already in ferment. The increased knowledge of contraception and the larger proportion of people living in the greater anonymity of urban life further contributed to the shifts in sexual behavior. The most striking change in this respect was the increase in premarital sex among women between 1916 and 1930: among the women in the Kinsey sample who were born before 1900, less than half as many had had premarital coitus as among the females born in any subsequent decade (14 percent as against 36 percent among women still unmarried by age 25). A similar increase was noted for premarital petting. The most significant change for males was the frequency with which they had sex with prostitutes; it was reduced to half of what it had been in the previous generation (Kinsey et al., 1953, p. 298).

The "roaring twenties" saw a sexual revolution among the younger generation. There was both alarm and exhilaration:

> The younger generation is behaving like a crazy man who for one lucid moment has suddenly realized that the physicians in charge are all demented, too. The elders who have for so long been the sacred guardians of civilization have bungled their task so abominably as to have lost irrevocably their influence for sobriety and sanity with the youth of the world. The failure of the church to treat sex and natural impulse with dignity and candor is the largest single fact in that disintegration of personal codes which confronts us in these hectic times: the inevitable swing of the pendulum from concealment to exhibitionism, from repression to expression, from reticence to publicity, from modesty to vulgarity. This revolutionary transition is inevitable and essentially wholesome, for all its crudity and grotesquerie (Calverton and Schmalhausen, 1929, p. 11).

The "younger generation" to which this paragraph refers were the grandparents of the youths who went through the sexual revolution of the 1960s.

Developments in art and literature followed the same trends. The main shift was to bring erotic themes into the cultural mainstream. The autobiographical works of Henry Miller (starting with *Tropic of Cancer* in 1934)

were not more explicit than the Victorian *My Secret Life*, but whereas the latter was written anonymously and read furtively, Miller's books were taken as serious literature. *Ulysses* (1922) by James Joyce, one of the greatest 20th-century novels, is suffused with eroticism.

Erotic art went through a dramatic transformation. Major artists like Gustav Klimt and Auguste Rodin, whose work straddled the turn of the century, produced highly sensuous works. Shortly thereafter, erotic themes became submerged in the gloomy and contorted visions of artists like Edvard Munch, Egon Schiele, and Jules Pascin.

Modern art tends to be abstract. Though rife with erotic symbolism (Figure 20-15), its

Figure 20.15    Constantin Brancusi, *Princess X*.

nonfigurative imagery does not lend itself to erotic interest, even when a work has a sexual theme. For this reason, even though a compulsive eroticism characterizes 20th-century art, it has ceased to be an effective form of commercial pornography—a function that has been taken over by film and photography (Eitner, 1975).

The sexual legitimization of erotic themes in art and literature did not come easily, and not until very recently; but after centuries of struggle, eroticism now appears firmly entrenched in Western culture. But history is an evolving process and its pendulum will continue to swing as sexual actions generate their own reactions. The past is always part of the present, and it is to the present that we now turn in the next chapter.

## REVIEW QUESTIONS

1. Compare the sexual attitudes and practices of the two main sources of Western sexual values—Judaism and the classical world of Greece and Rome.

2. What were the changes in sexuality between the early and late Middle Ages?

3. What were the main features of Renaissance sexuality?

4. Compare the repressive and permissive sexual components in Victorian culture.

5. What was the modernization of sex?

## THOUGHT QUESTIONS

1. Roman culture was sexually permissive, so how do you explain the restrictive sexual morality of St. Paul, a Roman citizen?

2. Why did the Greek acceptance of homosexuality not persist in subsequent ages?

3. What aspects of modern sexual culture can you trace back to the Renaissance? To the Protestant sexual ethic?

4. How do you account for the "split" sexuality of the Victorian period? Do you see a similar split today?

5. What sexual features in modern society cannot be traced back to an earlier period?

## SUGGESTED READINGS

Boardman, J., and LaRocca, E. (1975). *Eros in Greece*. New York: Erotic Art Book Society. Informative text with splendid illustrations.

D'Emilio J., and Freedman, E. B. (1988). *Intimate matters*. New York: Harper & Row. A history of sexuality in America from its early days to the present.

Dover, K. J. (1978). *Greek homosexuality*. New York: Vintage. A scholarly and clear account of Greek attitudes and practices with regard to homosexuality.

Epstein, L. M. (1967). *Sex laws and customs in Judaism*. New York: Ktar Publishing. A comprehensive and interesting presentation of the perspective of Judaism on sexuality.

Tannahill, R. (1980). *Sex in history*. New York: Stein & Day. Informative and entertaining overview of sexuality from prehistoric to recent times.

Webb, P. (1976). *The erotic arts*. Boston: New York Graphic Society. Comprehensive, profusely illustrated history of erotic art from ancient times to the present. Highly informative.

# Sexuality in Cultural Perspective

CHAPTER

# 21

*Society is like the air, necessary to breathe, but insufficient to live on.*

GEORGE SANTAYANA

OUTLINE

THE SEXUAL REVOLUTION
CAUSES OF THE SEXUAL
  REVOLUTION
Political Events
Economic Factors
The Separation of Sex and
  Reproduction
The Resurgence of Feminism
MANIFESTATIONS OF THE
  SEXUAL REVOLUTION
The Rise of the Counterculture
The Liberation of Female Sexuality
Gay Liberation
Public Sexual Expression
Sex and Marriage
  Reproductive Control
  The Family
  Premarital Sex
Is the Sexual Revolution Over?
The Conservative Reaction
The Balance Sheet

SOCIAL REGULATION OF
  SEXUALITY
Socialization
Social Norms and Sanctions
  External Control
  Internal Control
Sources of Social Control
Social Judgments
Justifications for Social Control
  Reproductive Consequences
  Ownership Rights
  Sexual Exploitation
  Social Stability
Sex and Social Status
CROSS-CULTURAL PATTERNS OF
  SOCIAL CONTROL
Sexual Diversity and Unity
Repressiveness and Permissiveness
  Sexually Repressive Cultures
  Sexually Permissive Cultures

The historical account of the last chapter brought us to the doorstep of modern times. We are now ready for a closer look at sex in our own society today. Then we can explore how all societies manage sexuality.

No matter where you live in the world, sexuality, and its spinoffs like gender roles, are everywhere around you: the family, religious institutions, the legal system, networks of personal relationships, and countless other human associations have a sexual element. Gender, marital status, social class, ethnic background, and other variables, in turn, shape and regulate your sexual behavior. Similarly, art, literature, and popular culture (such as movies, television, and advertising) are suffused with sexual themes that both reflect and influence your sexual attitudes.

*Society* (Latin, "fellowship") is the network of human relationships and institutions that binds together a group of people with a common culture. *Culture* (Latin, "cultivate") is the characteristic behavior patterns of members of a society, including their language; their customs; and their intellectual, artistic, and material accomplishments. These terms are often used interchangeably and sometimes combined in the broader term *sociocultural*.

Societies are constantly changing and evolving, but the rate of change is not uniform. Not much new seems to be happening over some periods, while at other times change appears to be bewilderingly rapid. World War II was a major watershed for our society. No other epoch experienced as many major changes as the period following it (Bailey and Kennedy, 1979; Degler, 1974). The sexual culture that exists today was shaped mainly during the 40 years since the war.

## THE SEXUAL REVOLUTION

The decade between 1965 and 1975 was a period of such rapid change in sexual attitudes and behaviors that many people call it a *sexual revolution*. Or, given the simultaneous streams of change—feminism, gay liberation, political activism—they refer to it in the plural as "sexual revolutions" (D'Emilio and Freedman,

1988). Others see these events as but another ripple in the constantly shifting social tides, unworthy of such a dramatic name. We need more time to judge the significance of these recent events. Meanwhile, we shall use the term, at least for the sake of convenience.

The revolution in sexual attitudes and behaviors became visible in the mid-1960s, but it did not start then. In the mid-1950s, sociologist Pitirim Sorokin (1956) wrote an indictment of the "American sex revolution" that had been in progress for "the last few decades." He saw millions of men and women yielding to "sexual freedom" and United States society becoming "sexualized." Without knowing the date of Sorokin's book, we would be certain he was reacting to the changes of the 1960s and 1970s, rather than writing a decade earlier.

The history of sexuality is part of the larger flow of events. The sexual component of a culture is influenced by economic, social, and political changes and, in turn, influences them. For example, the technological breakthroughs that led to the birth control pill and the establishment of the contraceptive industry became possible because there was a popular demand for such a device, and the social climate favored its development in the postwar period. The availability of the Pill, in turn, exerted a profound influence on our sexual attitudes and behaviors. As this example makes clear, the causes of the sexual revolution cannot always be neatly separated from its manifestations.

## CAUSES OF THE SEXUAL REVOLUTION

The roots of the sexual revolution must be sought first in the political and economic conditions that prevailed at the end of World War II, just as the previous upheaval in sexual behavior followed World War I.

### Political Events
The United States emerged from World War II a changed nation. The social upheavals of wars exert their influence on sexuality in several ways. At the practical level, spouses be-

come separated, and circumstances make it difficult for singles to get married, creating pressure to have sex outside of marriage. The enormous stress of wartime and the uncertainty of the future propel people to seek whatever emotional comforts and sexual satisfaction they can get. The armed forces bring together men and women of diverse social class, backgrounds, and sexual values and experiences; even more striking is the exposure to other cultural norms when men and women are sent overseas. New situations, the duress of war, and the anonymity of being away from home and in uniform—these factors prompt people to behave sexually in ways that they would ordinarily refrain from. Having crossed these lines, their sexual attitudes are often changed irrevocably.

World War II had a number of other long-range influences. The large numbers of women who joined the labor force had a dramatic impact on sex roles. The postwar role of the United States as a superpower ultimately led to its involvement in the Vietnam War, which caused widespread disenchantment among youth, as we shall see.

The civil rights movement also contributed to the questioning of conventional values and prejudices. Following the 1954 ruling of the Supreme Court that declared segregation in public schools unconstitutional, this movement gathered enormous momentum. Although aimed only at removing racial discrimination, the widespread concerns it raised for the rights of minorities and the tactics of political protest that it spawned first galvanized the antiwar movement and then encouraged women and homosexuals to pursue their own civil rights and liberties.

The civil rights activists served as models, but they did not cause a chain reaction. The fact that various liberation movements bunched together just shows that society was ripe for cultural upheaval. Besides, this upheaval was selective: not every attempt at rebellion attracted a following, and not every underdog rebelled. Workers did not take over factories, nor were churches overwhelmed by atheists (Harris, 1981).

## Economic Factors

It has been argued that periods of economic hardship lead to the curtailment of sex, whereas times of plenty encourage it. In the face of scarcity, thoughts and energies must turn to the tasks of economic survival and reconstruction. Sex, especially nonreproductive sex, like other pleasures and frivolities, is deemed incompatible with times of austerity (Schmidt, 1982).

The early phase of industrialization in Western societies presented such an economic challenge; hence the sexual restrictiveness of the Victorian era. In the post-World War II United States, however, different conditions prevailed. After a shaky start, the economy experienced a dramatic upsurge in the 1950s, boosting millions of people into middle-class affluence. The United States became a society of consumers living in a land of plenty. Not only was there no need for self-denial, but thrift was now downright detrimental to an economy that relied on consumers to keep it booming. The satisfaction of the desire for goods and services, and the creation of more and newer needs, became the norm. In this atmosphere, the satisfaction of sexual needs received tacit approval as well.

As society became more permissive and advertisers more aggressive in their use of erotic themes and images (Chapter 18), sex became an ally of business. Not only did sex sell in the form of erotic movies, books, and other entertainment, but entire industries became dedicated to its enhancement and used it to peddle their wares. Manufacturers of cosmetics, clothing, alcohol, cigarettes, cars, and even more unlikely products based their appeals on the promise of making people sexy and sought after. As sex became commercialized, commerce became sexualized. The net effect was to make sex seem freer, more open, more available, and more acceptable for a broad spectrum of middle-class, respectable, mainstream society. "The business of America is business," President Calvin Coolidge had declared in the 1920s. Now that sex became part of that business, people took it to their bosom as never before. The commercial exploitation of sex, in turn, facilitated its entry into the mass culture (D'Emilio and Freedman, 1988).

## The Separation of Sex and Reproduction

Sex has long been used for purposes other than reproduction, but the control of its reproductive consequences was, until recently, unreliable. When the contraceptive pill became commercially available in the 1960s, it ushered in an unprecedented era. For the first time there was widespread use of a highly reliable and relatively safe contraceptive. Montagu ranks the social significance of the Pill with that of the discovery of fire, learning how to make tools, the development of urbanism, the growth of scientific medicine, and the harnessing of nuclear energy (Montagu, 1969).

Widespread use of contraceptives had a major influence on sexual attitudes and behavior, which spurred the development of still newer contraceptives. Because moral and legal codes of sexual behavior probably originated to prevent illegitimate offspring, decoupling sex from reproduction puts them in a new light. Without important breakthroughs in contraceptive technology, it is doubtful if many of the subsequent changes in sexual behaviors would have taken place. It would have been difficult, for instance, to allow greater premarital permissiveness without at least some assurance that it would not generally lead to pregnancy. Similarly, extramarital sex would have been far more problematic if the risk of pregnancy had remained substantial.

Most important, effective contraception enabled women, especially unmarried women, to exercise a far greater choice over one of the key elements in their lives. The ability to delay or altogether avoid motherhood without relinquishing sex opened up a far greater range of vocational prospects for women. It was an important factor in the resurgence of the womens' movement, with its own attendant impact on sexual attitudes and behavior.

## The Resurgence of Feminism

Some of the most important recent influences on our sexual attitudes and behaviors have come from changes in the gender identity and the sex roles of women, and to a lesser extent, those of men.

World War II played a crucial part in this transformation. As men were drafted into the armed forces, more than 5 million women took their places in traditionally male occupations, including heavy industry. A great many of these women stayed in their jobs following the war, and many more joined them subsequently: the percentage of women in the work force went up from less than 20 percent early in the century to 60 percent in the 1970s. This fact is a matter of importance. Contrary to the belief that women's liberation created the working woman, it was working women—especially the working housewife—who created the women's liberation movement (Harris, 1981). Working women must not be confused with "working-class women." The women's movement has been, and remains, primarily a middle-class phenomenon. Once the movement was under way, it prompted other women to seek careers outside the home.

The inequities in job opportunities and pay for women became more evident and less tolerable with the massive influx of women into the labor force. Working outside the home further burdened many women with guilt for deviating from the traditional roles of wife and mother—what Betty Friedan called the "feminine mystique" (1964).

Women's revolt against sex discrimination was spearheaded by the feminist movement. If feminism is defined as the advocacy of the political, economic, and social equality of women and men, then it can be found throughout history. As a focused political effort, though, the roots of modern feminism go back to the mid-19th and early 20th centuries.

American feminism, popularly known as the women's liberation movement, has followed two main paths during the past two decades. In 1961, President John Kennedy appointed a Commission on the Status of Women. It advised broad reforms for sexual equality. The National Organization for Women (NOW), founded by Betty Friedan in 1963, sustained this thrust, working primarily within the established political order. The other wing of the women's movement emerged from activist groups within the New Left and took a more radical stance. Whereas mainstream feminists generally worked toward sexual equality within heterosexual and marital relationships, the more radical women's liberationists more often opted for *separatism* (Freeman, 1973).

A number of writers proved highly influential in bringing the feminist message to large audiences. Simone de Beauvoir's *The Second Sex* (published in French in 1949) set the stage for the rise of a new feminist consciousness by examing the effects of patriarchal societies on women's lives, the ways in which men "act" while women are "acted upon," and how women came to be the "second sex" (de Beauvoir, 1952).

In the 1960s, Betty Friedan addressed the predicament of women who were in the "housewife trap," having relinquished opportunities for higher education, careers, and political power in order to live up to the "feminine mystique"—being a "truly feminine" and "sexually successful wife and mother" (Friedan, 1964; for her more current views see Friedan, 1981). In the next decade, Kate Millett focused on sex and aggression in contemporary literature in *Sexual Politics* (Millet, 1970); and Germaine Greer, in *The Female Eunuch,* dealt with women who are socially "castrated" to become "feminine" instead of "female" (Greer, 1971; for her subsequent views see Greer, 1984).

The feminist revolt was primarily a gender revolution, not a sexual revolution, focusing on gender identity and sex roles. Although the quest for sexual freedom and opposition to sexual exploitation have always been important themes in feminist ideology, its more basic concerns are social, and its efforts are directed at the elimination of *sexism* (a term patterned after "racism"). In the feminist perspective, women are victims of institutional discrimination, as in educational and vocational settings, and of cultural discrimination, as in sexist language, personality stereotyping, social and behavioral theories, and characterizations in the public media (Kando, 1978). The key terms in

feminism became "choice," "autonomy," and "authenticity"; its central aim, "full equality for women, in truly equal partnership with men"—the goal of NOW, the National Organization for Women (*Signs,* 1980).

## MANIFESTATIONS OF THE SEXUAL REVOLUTION

The changes in sexual attitudes and behaviors that swept through society during the 1960s and 1970s took many forms. The dominant sexual ideology of the period was sexual liberation. "Liberation" is a value-laden term: it means freedom from undesirable constraints. The most visible manifestations of the sexual revolution were in the public expression of sexual themes and images. Its most significant institutional impact was probably the greater acceptance of sex outside of marriage.

### The Rise of the Counterculture

Youth was at the vanguard of the sexual revolution and the group most affected by it. Their sexual stance, however, was part of a broader new ideology and way of life, which, because it rejected the values of the established culture, came to be known as the *counterculture* (Roszak, 1969).

The prominence of youth on the social scene in the 1960s was in part due to sheer numbers. The *baby boom* that followed World War II generated over 11 million people aged 15 to 24 by 1970 (the birthrate leveled off in the 1960s). This generation was brought up by relaxed and permissive childrearing and educational precepts ("the gospel according to Dr. Spock"). Its members were also more highly educated and affluent than ever before: in the 1970s one in four persons aged 18 to 24 was enrolled in an institution of higher learning; adolescents in the 1960s were spending $20 billion a year, much of it on clothes, rock music, and other entertainment. These factors made United States youth idealistic, outspoken, and self-indulgent, likely recruits for the social causes and political turmoils facing the nation (Keniston, 1965).

In the 1950s, "beat" writers like Alan

Ginsberg and Jack Kerouac expressed disenchantment with the materialism and conformity of their times. Like their bohemian predecessors earlier in the century, the *beat generation* of intellectuals and their followers ("beatniks") adopted manners and mores, in sexual and other terms, different from those approved by the majority of society.

The rise of the counterculture in the 1960s was in part an outgrowth of these earlier themes of alienation. The social liberation movements for civil rights and women's rights, along with antiwar protests, challenged the legitimacy and values of the established order (Keniston, 1968, 1971).

The antiwar movement led people into acts of civil disobedience and some to violence. College youth became its most vocal component. This fact contributed to the development of a *generation gap*. Substantial segments of the nation's youth rejected the sexual values and norms of those in authority (the "Establishment") and adults in general ("never trust anyone over thirty").

Some of these political dissenters were social activists who wanted to change the world. Others wanted to withdraw from conventional society ("turn on, tune in, drop out") and evolve alternative lifestyles based on peace, love, harmony with nature, self-knowledge, and spiritual values. Seemingly overnight, a whole new subculture, the counterculture, emerged with its own dress, language, music, and philosophy of life. The quickest way to attain its goals seemed to be through drugs and sexual activity.

The converts to this *psychedelic culture* came to be known as "hippies" and "flower children" (Figure 21.1). They shared a sexual outlook that rejected conventional morality for individual freedom ("Do your own thing"). Their sexual ethic went beyond tolerance and championed sex as an antidote to violence ("Make love not war").

The momentum and the more florid manifestations of the counterculture had fizzled by

Figure 21.1   Counterculture gathering.

the late 1970s. Though the flower generation wilted away, the decade left its unmistakable mark (and casualties)—premarital sexual permissiveness, tolerance of unconventional sexual behaviors, greater acceptance of sex generally, and the liberalization of public sexual expression were among its legacies.

## The Liberation of Female Sexuality

The sexual revolution influenced women more than men. It is in the sexual behavior of women, within and outside of marriage, that the more dramatic shifts have occurred. The behavior of men has not changed much, and it has changed mostly in reaction to women's new sexuality.

The liberation of female sexuality led women to be sexually more candid, interested, tolerant, active, and fulfilled than probably at any earlier period of the nation's history. No institution, however conservative, is opposed any more to the right of women for sexual satisfaction. For instance, the Catholic church and fundamentalist evangelicals are in favor of female sexual fulfillment, at least in monogamous heterosexual relationships. Of course, not everyone agrees on the proper context for fulfillment.

At its inception, the women's movement appeared to convey conflicting sexual messages. On the one hand, there was the image of the liberated woman who was now ready to meet and beat men at their own game. On the other, radical feminists seemed to repudiate all traditional precepts of femininity and sexiness: they refused to alter or to adorn their bodies (unshaven legs, no makeup), or to dress, act, and talk in ways that would be expected to please and entice men. In 1969 a group of feminists publicly burned their bras, false eyelashes, steno pads, and copies of *Playboy* while crowning a live sheep "Miss America" ("Ain't she sweet/making profit off her meat") to protest the national beauty pageant being held in Atlantic City. A fashion show for brides was disrupted by the Women's International Terrorist Conspiracy from Hell who sang to the tune of the wedding march, "Here come the slaves/Off to their graves." Thousands of women marched with placards that warned "male chauvinist pigs" that their world was coming to an end and advised women, "Don't Cook Dinner Tonight—Starve a Rat" (Harris, 1981, p. 76).

As the women's movement progressed, its focus on sexuality tended to vary. Betty Friedan downplayed it, maintaining that when women have gained social parity with men, sex will take care of itself; Germaine Greer urged liberated women not to marry (though she is not opposed to heterosexual sex); while Shulamith Firestone called for "a revolution in every bedroom" (Firestone, 1970). Lesbian feminists have tended to place heavier stress on sexual liberation, because they are engaged in a two-pronged struggle: one for gender equality, another for freedom of sexual choice. For some of them, the fundamental drive of feminism is sexual liberation, which is only possible through total sexual independence from men. The contention that a true commitment to feminism is compatible only with lesbianism, has proven divisive within the broader feminist movement (Hole and Levine 1971).

Feminists see traditional marital and heterosexual relationships as oppressive and exploitative of women, and the double standard of sexual morality for men and women as discriminatory and unfair. However, no specific sexual norms would fairly characterize all feminists, who are mainly women but include many men as well. As for marriage, feminists range from those who accept marital relationships along companionate rather than traditional lines, to others who reject marriage but approve of cohabitation, to some who would shun all sexual dealings with men (Johnston, 1973; Koedt, 1976).

The liberation of female sexuality was not confined to the ranks of feminists. Women in general, including those in traditional marriages, came to view sex in more liberal terms. Even ideological opponents of feminism who decried the erosion of traditional gender roles and marital relationships became ardently in favor of active and exciting conjugal sex. For example, Maribel Morgan (1973), in her book *The Total Woman*, advocates that a wife cater to her husband's special quirks, "whether it be in salads, sex, or sports." Morgan's gender ideals may be traditional, but her unabashed endorsement of female sexual initiative is not. Wives are instructed to call their husbands at work an hour before quitting time and say, "I want you to know that I just crave your body!" She also advises that "A frilly new nighty and heels will probably do the trick as a starter"; "Be prepared mentally and physically for intercourse every night this week. Be sure your attitude matches your costume. Be the seducer, rather than the seducee."

Phyllis Schlafly (1977) endorses the "positive woman," whose satisfactions and influence come through the traditional wife-mother role. By contrast, she says, the new morality of the sexual revolution "robs the woman of her virtue, her youth, her beauty, and her love—for nothing, just nothing. It has produced a generation of young women searching for their identity, bored with sexual freedom, and despondent from the loneliness of living without commitment."

Feminist attitudes to sexuality have evolved considerably over the past decade. There is a recognition that permissiveness can make sex into "an almost chaotically limitless and therefore unmanageable realm in the life of women." The sexual revolution has robbed women of their traditional right of refusal; therefore, a "new chastity" must now restore the right of women to say no (Decter, 1973, p. 80).

Even some of the staunchest feminists accept that while many women remain determined to struggle for their rights, they do not necessarily wish to reject men or forego the trappings of femininity (Brownmiller, 1984). Similarly, there is a move back to marriage or cohabitation as the basis of a stable relationship (Quinn, 1981).

The sexual issues that most preoccupy feminists at present are reproductive control, pornography, and rape. The feminist victories won over contraceptive control and a woman's right to get an abortion are law but remain vulnerable. Pornography has mushroomed to unprecedented levels and rape has attained appalling proportions. Betty Friedan thinks the current "second stage" of the women's movement will break this vicious cycle of sexual violence and usher in a new mode of sexual interaction between men and women.

> The second stage of the women's movement is not unisex. It is human sex, for women as for men—active or passive, responsive, responsible, playful or profound, no longer an acting out of eroticized rage, or manipulation of covert power, joyless dues for economic support, or brutal revenge of love denied (Friedan, 1981).

Large numbers of modern working women now aspire to combine the rewards of having a family with those of an independent career. Like men, they want sexual freedom over a period of being unattached followed by a stable and committed relationship. These women share many of the goals of feminism, although they may not want to be identified with its more radical image. In that respect they are more like traditional women, concerned with physical attractiveness, clothes, having a good time, and finding the right man at the right time. Equality for women is a widely shared goal. But when it comes to a concrete proposal like the Equal Rights Amendment (ERA) there is a great deal of uncertainty and opposition by both men and women. Since the 1920s, attempts had been made to amend the Constitution so that "equality of right under the law shall not be denied or abridged by the United States or by any state on account of sex." The ERA was ratified by 30 states by 1972, but it failed to make further headway in the others and went down in defeat in 1982 (Bullach, 1988). Its fate is a telling reflection on continuing disagreement over what sexual equality should mean in American society.

## Gay Liberation

Through the centuries of oppression inflicted on homosexuals (Figure 21.2) there have been many voices raised in protest (Boswell, 1980).

Figure 21.2     Burning at the stake of homosexual monks in the 16th century in Ghent. Etching by F. Hogenbergh, 1578.

The modern movement for gay rights is a post-World War II phenomenon with two phases. The first was the homophile movement of the 1950s; the second, the gay liberation movement began in the late 1960s and 1970s (Katz, 1976).

The ground for the rise of the *homophile movement* was laid down during World War II. The circumstances of wartime were conducive to it. At its peak, the armed services of the United States held 12 million men. Though there was an attempt to screen out homosexuals during induction exams, patriotism and the fear of ostracism inspired the majority of homosexuals to pass the cursory tests. Living in close quarters, the stress of combat, and separation from families generated close emotional ties between men. Even though in most cases these ties did not include a sexual element, those with homosexual orientations and inclinations had an enhanced opportunity to

establish such ties as well. Though the numbers of women in the armed forces were fewer than 150,000, the selection procedures and policies of the Women's Army Corps inadvertently favored the congregation of a large number of lesbians, under circumstances they would not have encountered in civilian life.

The publication in 1948 of the Kinsey report on male sexuality had a major impact in bringing homosexuality into public consciousness. Not only were the statistics astounding, but Kinsey took a clearly sympathetic stand in favor of homosexuality as an acceptable and normal sexual alternative.

For many years, a "conspiracy of silence" had made the majority of homosexuals invisible; they lay low, "passing" for heterosexuals, while the public treated the issue as if it did not exist. The minority of homosexuals who came to public attention were those who sought therapy, ran afoul of the law, or lived on the fringes of respectable society: this fact reinforced the views that homosexuals were sick, criminal, and socially deviant.

Under the changed circumstances of the 1950s, homosexuals began to make efforts to get organized. In 1951 the Mattachine Society was established in Los Angeles as the first homophile organization in the United States. The name is derived from a medieval French society of masked dancers, whose members may have been homosexual. The man most responsible for its establishment was Henry Hay, an actor, whose experiences during the Depression years had led him to become a committed member of the American Communist party. Hay's gay collaborators shared his political views, so the Mattachine Society at its conception adopted a Marxist ideology and was modeled after the Communist party, with secret membership, a tight hierarchy, and centralized leadership. Its purpose was "to unify isolated homosexuals, educate homosexuals to see themselves as an oppressed minority, and lead them in a struggle for their own emancipation".

The McCarthy era went into full swing in the early 1950s, with the State Department purges of real or presumed communist sympathizers. Homosexuals were especially suspect on the grounds that they were a security risk, being subject to blackmail. As a congressional scrutiny of the Mattachine Society became likely, it was clear that Hay and the other founders could not survive the double jeopardy of their political past and homosexuality. Furthermore, the expanded new membership, consisting now mainly of middle-class men, was oriented toward legal reforms and social acceptability; it also included staunch anticommunists. The leadership of the Mattachine Society, therefore, yielded to a much more cautious and conservative group of men seeking an accommodation with society.

This group showed little interest in the issues that concerned lesbians. Hence, a small group of women, led by Del Martin and Phyllis Lyon, established a separate gay organization for women in 1955, called the Daughters of Bilitis (named after an erotic poem by Pierre Louys that purported to be the translation of a poem of Sappho). A 1920s lesbian novel, *The Well of Loneliness* by Radclyffe Hall, shaped the lesbian consciousness.

The *gay liberation movement* was born in a riot when police raided the Stonewall Inn in New York's Greenwich Village, on the night of Saturday, June 29, 1969, and the gay customers fought back. These events acted as a dramatic catalyst, but the shift within the homosexual consciousness had already occurred. After the quiet advocacy of the homophile movement, a new militancy had begun to assert itself in the sixties under the leadership of men like Franklin Kameny. It culminated in the much more activist and publicly visible gay liberation movement (Figure 21.3). The younger men who became the mainstay of the more activist orientation had not been cowed by living through the McCarthy era. On the contrary, they were participants in broader social upheavals, such as the civil rights movement and the rise of the counterculture, among whose prominent representatives were gay poets like Alan Ginsberg. Within the feminist movement, radical lesbians played an important role in shaping the goals and tactics of the women's liberation movement. In short, homosexuals were no more the isolated and beleaguered minority shunned even by other activist groups. They were now allied with and broadly represented within the wider spectrum of the social protests of the time (Harris, 1981).

The gay liberationists differed from their predecessors in the homophile movement (whom they openly disdained for being timid and ineffectual) not only in their assertive tactics but in their goals. Instead of seeking accommodation and compromise, they demanded the full rights of citizenship; rather than dwelling on self-help and education, they put their efforts into political action; instead of trying to become like everyone else, they celebrated their differences. As a result, within a decade of the Stonewall riots, the United States had the largest, best organized, and most visible homosexual minority in the world.

Figure 21.3   Gay parade in New York City.

## Public Sexual Expression

In the past, a small group of individuals had determined what was fit or unfit for the public to see and read. They often passed negative judgment on some of the greatest works of contemporary literature as well as a great deal of trash. None of this censorship was generally viewed as in conflict with First Amendment rights of free speech until the postwar era. During the sexual revolution, the Supreme Court upheld the public expression of sexual themes. Virtually any form of sexual description and depiction became permissible, subject to a few qualifications (Chapter 22).

This change had several effects. First, it allowed serious writers and artists to explore and express sexual themes without fear of reprisals. Sex researchers and educators likewise became far more free to study and teach sex-

uality (Chapter 1). Even more broadly, there was a greater candor and willingness on the part of ordinary people to communicate sexual feelings and thoughts. Sex as a legitimate subject for public discourse took its rightful place in our society.

On another plane, sex became a major vehicle for entertainment and commerce. This change was striking in television and advertising—the two media that reach the largest sectors of the population (Chapter 18).

Equally important was the influence of popular culture in portraying the interpersonal aspects of sexual and love relationships. Best-selling books and popular movies typically presented sexual partners as young and single, physically attractive and healthy. Relationships were short-term; "playing it cool" the way to go. Contraception, sexually transmitted diseases, and sexual dysfunction were rarely mentioned, let alone explored. Sexual passion between ordinary couples in monogamous relationships, sexual interest of the elderly, and the sexual adaptation of the physically disabled were left out with rare exceptions (such as Jon Voight's portrayal of a disabled veteran in the film *Coming Home*). As a result, "sex in the media served as a fallacious model of human sexual behavior by creating unrealistic and infeasible sexual expectations" (Zilbergeld, 1978).

There has always been an intimate association between music and sexuality (Chapter 12); but never before was music so flagrantly eroticized in our culture as during the sexual revolution. Rock and roll and other distinctive musical styles of the period were both an outcome of the sexual revolution and a force in its popularization among youth. (For a history of rock and roll, see Miller, 1980.)

These concerns become more serious with regard to pornography. Produced mostly by people of modest talents and even less social responsibility, pornography (hard as it is to define precisely) callously exploited the sexual freedoms that had become available. Its consequences continue to be a source of social concern (Chapter 18).

### Sex and Marriage

One of the key consequences of the sexual revolution was a greater separation between sex and marriage. Particularly among the young, marriage became less of a precondition for engaging in sexual intercourse. The institution of marriage itself went through significant changes, particularly among younger and better educated people.

Reproductive Control   Society regulates several aspects of reproductive control: contraception, sterilization, and abortion. Over the past two decades, sweeping changes widened individual choice in all these matters. There has never been a time in our history when women have been given as complete control of their reproductive options as now. (The landmark deci-

sions concerning these issues are discussed in Chapter 22.)

Progress in reproductive technology has continued to create unprecedented new opportunities through means like in-vitro fertilization, embryo freezing, and surrogate motherhood (Chapter 6); their development have in turn created equally novel sexual, ethical and legal problems (Chapter 22). Looming on the more distant horizon, perhaps by the next decade or two, are even more startling possibilities: the use of an animal surrogate mother (such as a cow) to carry a transplanted human pregnancy; an abdominal pregnancy in a male achieved by embryonal implantation (like an ectopic pregnancy in a female) and delivered by C-section; cross-fertilization of a human with a nonhuman primate. Such prospects raise the specter of an Orwellian Brave New World to some and the dawn of a bright new era to others (Francoeur, 1985).

The dramatic rise in teenage pregnancies and abortions (Chapter 9) has been one of the most serious consequences of the changes in sexual behavior patterns following the sexual revolution. Contraceptive use by adults is no longer a serious social concern, except for those affected by the continuing opposition of the Catholic Church. The provision of contraceptive services to adolescents remains a conflicted issue. Those who favor it point to the urgent necessity of preventing teenage pregnancies. Those who oppose it perceive in it tacit approval of adolescent sexual activity. Others oppose the provision of contraception to teenagers without parental knowledge, arguing that such practice usurps parents' right to know what their children are doing, especially because contraceptives carry certain health risks. The counterargument is that if parents have to be notified, many teenagers will not seek help.

A source of even greater contention is abortion. Opinions range in this regard from those who would provide pregnant women with full freedom to abort at will to others who would prohibit abortion on virtually all grounds. Pro-life and pro-choice groups are locked in an uncompromising battle over this issue, from marching in the streets to maneuvering in Congress (Chapter 22).

The Family   The family has changed more in the United States in the last 30 years than in the previous 250 (Blumstein and Schwartz, 1983). In the late 1960s and early 1970s, the rate of fertility began to decline. This trend had set in two centuries ago, but with the Pill and legal abortion, it became more marked. As we discussed earlier (Chapter 17), the marriage rate similarly began to decline to levels that had existed at the end of the Depression. Between 1960 and 1970, the proportion of women who remained single until the ages of 20 to 24 increased by one-third. The divorce rate soared to a level where one out of three marriages of women 30 years or younger was ending in divorce (excluding desertions). These changes are persisting in the 1980s, but their rates are slowing down. In 1987, the United States had the lowest marriage rate (9.9 weddings per 1,000 people) and the lowest divorce rate (4.8 per 1,000 people) since 1977.

   Monogamy and serial monogamy (a succession of marriages) persisted as the predominant family institutions. They were associated in as many as half of the cases with extramarital relationships, usually covert but occasionally in an "open" marital relationship. Newer alternatives emerged: cohabitation, group marriage, family network systems, and communes (larger groupings) that may or may not involve sexual sharing of partners (Chapter 17).

Premarital Sex   A dramatic aspect of the sexual revolution was the change in attitudes towards premarital sex. Figure 21.4 places these changes in historical perspective by graphing the remarkable increase in premarital sexual permissiveness over the century between 1880 to 1980. The steady gradient of the curve supports the contention that change has been steady; the sharp upsurge from 1915 to 1925 and 1965 to 1975 in premarital permissiveness points to the more "revolutionary" character of these periods.

   In an opinion survey of a representative

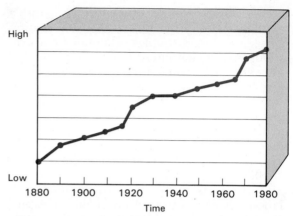

Figure 21.4   Estimate of changes in premarital sexual permissiveness, 1880–1980 (Reiss, 1980).

sample of adults in the United States, conducted in 1963, about 80 percent stated that premarital intercourse was always wrong: this figure had gone down to 30 percent in 1975 (Reiss, 1980, Chapter 7). The more dramatic shifts in premarital behavior are among women, and the attenuation of the double standard is one of the most striking outcomes of the sexual revolution.

   Between 1971 and 1976, the proportion of women aged 15 to 19 who were nonvirgins went up from 27 percent to 35 percent, an increase of 30 percent over a period of just five years. Reiss estimates that in the 1980s, 75 percent of all women and 90 percent of men were entering marriage as nonvirgins. Though premarital attitudes among young adults became more permissive, the dominant norm within the group was permissiveness with affection, not indiscriminate sexual activity (Chapter 9).

Is the Sexual Revolution Over?
It was clear by the late 1970s that the sexual revolution had lost its momentum. The revolutionary expectations of sexual liberationists, gay activists, and radical feminists were clearly not going to be realized.

   In the 1980s a wider chorus of voices began to declare the end of the sexual revolution—or as some put it, the "end of sex" (Leonard, 1982). John Leo (1984) expressed these sentiments in a *Time* magazine cover story:

> From cities, suburbs, and small towns alike, there is growing evidence that the national obsession with sex is subsiding. Five-speed vibrators, masturbation workshops, freshly discovered erogenous zones, and even the one-night stand all seem to be losing their allure. Veterans of the revolution, some wounded, some merely bored, are reinventing courtship and romance. . . . Many individuals are even rediscovering the traditional values of fidelity, obligation, and marriage (p. 74).

The herpes scare and the AIDS epidemic in the late 1980s have further dampened the residual glow of the more freewheeling ways of the sexual revolution. The impact has been particularly marked on male gay sexual relationships.

On the other hand, others have claimed that the true sexual revolution is just beginning. As evidence, Lester Kirkendall (1984) cites new reproductive techniques, alterations in male and female life patterns, the breakdown of limitations of acceptable sexual expressions, and the reappraisal of the sources of moral-ethical judgments.

Whether the sexual revolution is ending or continuing is in fact a function of what aspect of sexual life we look at. Meanwhile, a strong conservative counter current has become established in American society which needs to be looked at in its own right.

## The Conservative Reaction

Most people seemed to welcome the greater sexual honesty, openness, acceptance, and equality of the sexual revolution. Others felt disquiet over some of its consequences, and feared that things had gone too far.

Among a substantial sector this disenchantment was strong. They made a commitment to contain and to reverse the changes. These conservative sentiments were given their most vocal expression by organizations like the Moral Majority, a loose coalition

founded by the Reverend Jerry Falwell in 1979. It is hard to know how many people belong to the organization. Estimates have ranged from fewer than half a million to many times that number (Yankelovich, 1981). Whatever the hard-core membership, its influence has varied widely with the issues at hand.

The sexual conservatives represent a broad coalition of Christian fundamentalists and political conservatives. As part of the New Right, they are allied with the Republican party. Their aim is to restore traditional sexual values. They attribute to sex the power to corrupt and weaken the American family and society (D'Emilio and Freedman, 1988). They are opposed to abortion, premarital sex, sex education in schools, homosexuality, pornography, the Equal Rights Amendment, and the ideology of "secular humanism" with its emphasis on individual freedom, a pluralistic value system, and a questioning attitude toward institutional authority. They are in favor of sexual restraint in youth, marital fidelity, and a strong and traditional family with parental authority over children. They endorse censorship of school texts and television programs. To achieve these aims, they are prepared to use the political process and the legal system, as well as to rouse public opinion.

Sexual conservatism shares some of the ideology of earlier purity movements in American history (Chapter 20). But it has been thoroughly modern in its use of computerized mailing lists, direct-mail fundraising, and political campaigns to mobilize its constituencies.

Some of the efforts of this movement have attracted national attention (such as the anti-gay campaign spearheaded by singer Anita Bryant in Florida). But most of its efforts have been at the grass-roots level. In the late 1970s, SIECUS counted over three hundred organizations opposing sex education in public schools.

Sexual conservatism has contributed significantly to the broader shift toward conservatism in the 1980s. But just as the sexual revolution did not sweep everyone off their feet, the conservative reaction has failed to roll back its major changes. The recent shift to conservatism may signal a time of consolidation and readjustment rather than the wholesale shift to traditional sexual values and behaviors (Francoeur, 1987).

## The Balance Sheet

It is too early to make a reasoned assessment of the net gains and losses that we have incurred through the sexual revolution. Sexual pessimists are likely to decry any liberalization of sexuality, turning a blind eye to its benefits. Sexual optimists can be counted on to be enthusiastic about everything and anything that sexual liberalization has brought about.

It is also difficult to evaluate how much change has occurred in attitudes versus behavior. Neither sexual radicalism nor sexual conservatism has captured the loyalty of the majority of men and women. Despite lurching first to the left and then to the right, the massive center of American society appears to have stayed in a holding pattern.

On the other hand, American society has also become considerably more "sexualized." John D'Emilio and Estelle Freedman (1988) conclude their history of sexuality in America with the following summary:

> Whatever the outcome of the current crisis over sexuality, Americans will have to account of the legacy of three centuries of sexual change. Birth control is so embedded in social life that a purely reproductive matrix for sex is no longer even remotely possible. Women's role in the family and the public realm has altered so profoundly that a gender-based system resting on female purity is not likely to be resurrected. The capitalist seizure of sexuality has destroyed the division between public reticence and private actions that the nineteenth-century middle class sought to maintain. Perhaps what the study of America's history allows us to say with assurance is that sexuality has become central to our economy, our psyches, and our politics. For this reason, it is likely to stay vulnerable to manipulation as a symbol of social problems and the subject of efforts to maintain social

hierarchies. As in the past, sex will remain a source of both deep personal meaning and heated political controversy (p. 360).

As Americans struggle to define a place for sex in their personal lives and in society, the specter of AIDS is likely to loom in our reflections and deliberations. But there are also other questions to confront.

How do we maintain our hard-won sexual freedoms? What is the price of all this freedom? In overcoming needless guilt, are we losing our capacity for shame? By taking the mystery out of sex, are we robbing it of its meaning (Tyrmand, 1970)? Has the availability of casual sex eroded our capacity for commitment? Is the price of freedom of sexual expression the exploitation and brutalization of women and children? These issues concern us all (Schmidt, 1982). We have so far taken a descriptive approach to these issues. Now we need to turn to the mechanisms that societies use to regulate sexual behavior. We shall first look at our culture and then to other cultures to see how this is accomplished.

## SOCIAL REGULATION OF SEXUALITY

So far you may have the impression that society, like some ponderous, passive elephant, lumbers on through time, occasionally hurrying over a short stretch of history, driven by many forces. True—but society is also an active agent. All societies purposefully regulate the sexual behavior of their members (Ford and Beach, 1951). How do they do this?

First, all societies encourage and facilitate sexual interactions for some groups, such as adult men and women. However sexually restrictive a society may be, there is usually some provision for men and women to meet and to mate. Sexually more liberal societies also allow sexual interactions between youngsters, members of the same sex, and various other alternatives.

Second, all societies establish norms of sexual behavior for those who are permitted to interact sexually. For instance, having approved of heterosexual coitus, social norms determine who can sleep with whom under what circumstances, and even how often.

Third, all societies inhibit some sexual behaviors. They may be generally repressive, making grudging allowance even for reproductive sex (sometimes not even that) and no more; or they will allow some behaviors but not others, being selectively repressive.

## Socialization

The only way that a society can preserve itself is by insuring that its ranks are replenished by successive generations. To this end, society must insure that its members mate, look after their children, and bring each new generation into its social structure through *socialization*—the process by which individuals acquire the knowledge and the skills that enable them to function as members of society (Brim, 1966).

Sexual socialization is an important component of this process. Through it we learn the sexual values and behavioral patterns of our culture. We find out how to express sexual interest and obtain satisfaction of our needs. It is through sexual socialization that we learn how to make a pass, declare love, propose marriage, or establish other sexual associations in sexually approved forms. Equally important, we acquire the sexual inhibitions and taboos of our society that check the expression of sexual impulses considered socially unacceptable. In short, sexual socialization imparts cultural substance and form to our sexual drive, or writes our sexual scripts during psychosexual development (Chapter 8) and throughout adult life (Chapter 9).

If socialization is successful, it is the most effective form of social control. The person will behave sexually in ways expected by society because he or she *wants* to and does not need to be compelled to do so. Because socialization is rarely that successful, societies must establish and enforce social norms and sanctions to keep sexual behavior in line.

## Social Norms and Sanctions

The rules by which interactions among individuals are defined and patterned are known as *social norms.* In the sexual realm, many of these behavioral expectations are understood informally. We learn from family members and peers what forms of sexual behavior are socially acceptable or unacceptable. The social norms also may be formally expressed in legal statutes and moral codes that specifically state what we ought or, more often, ought not to do.

**External Control**   Social norms are enforced by *sanctions,* which are socially prescribed rewards (positive sanctions) or punishments (negative sanctions). Sanctions, like norms, may be informally or formally enforced. The anticipated reactions of people whose opinions matter to us, or in a more general sense, public opinion, is a powerful informal force that keeps many of us in line. We fear stigma (being branded as disgraceful, unworthy of respect) and ostracism (being shut out of the group, shunned). Penalties imposed by the law are examples of formal negative sanctions.

Behaviors like sex are socially regulated through clusters of norms, which are called *institutions.* Marriage is an excellent example (Chapter 17). Through such institutions societies attempt to provide ready-made solutions for succeeding generations, satisfying individual needs in ways that society considers best for its broader purpose (Goode, 1982).

Sex is among the most highly institutionalized forms of behavior. Not only does society take an active interest in how we behave sexually in public, but it tries to pervade the private recesses of our lives. In addition to determining who can have sex with whom and under what circumstances, society has passed judgment on solitary activities like masturbation or the private sexual interactions of married couples. Until recently, if all the sex laws on the books had been enforced, 95 percent of the male population would have ended up in jail (Kinsey et al., 1948).

**Internal Control**   Society controls us best by teaching us *values,* the key to self-control. Most of us refrain from engaging in sexual acts that are socially unacceptable not because we are afraid of going to jail or ending up in hell but because we would feel ashamed, guilty, and ignoble.

Sexual values expressed in moral tradition, the law, or public opinion perform two functions: guidance and social control. Guidance can be helpful. As with travel guidebooks, if the information provided is sensible, you get the benefit of the experience and expertise of others who have been there before. You also run the risk of prejudging matters in the light of someone else's preferences and biases.

More direct forms of control tell you what to do and what not to do. Various mechanisms help insure that you respond accordingly. One psychological mechanism that we develop in childhood is *guilt*. To a variable degree, we all develop a capacity to feel guilty when we violate what we consider to be legitimate moral precepts. Guilt is a painful emotion, because it calls into question our sense of integrity and worth. It ranges in intensity from a mild prick of the conscience to such overwhelming anguish that it drives some to suicide.

A related feeling is *shame*. Shame is experienced as embarrassment, or loss of face in the eyes of significant others or broader public opinion. Shame over sexual matters takes one of two forms. One has to do with bodily manifestations such as nudity. In our culture, genital exposure or activity engenders the same sort of shame associated with other private functions like urination, menstruation, and defecation. Either we carry over shame from eliminatory functions to nearby sexual ones, or shame over sex extends to neighboring functions. The second form of shame is over sexual behaviors we consider wrong.

Feelings of guilt and shame usually follow wrongdoing. They also can squelch the desire for a prohibited act. This nipping in the bud of forbidden desires before they arise is the most effective means of inhibiting socially unacceptable sexual activity. Of course, sometimes the prohibition of an act makes it exciting, a form of rebellion.

## Sources of Social Control

In childhood we do not want to upset the people who are important to us and on whom we are dependent. Individuals in key institutional roles, such as parents and educators, have power to teach us social norms through informal and formal sanctioning systems (DeLamater, 1981).

Later, especially for adolescents and young adults, the *peer group* is an important source of social control. Even though most of us eventually do accept the sexual norms prevalent in adult society, adolescence is typically a time for experimentation and deviation from adult norms (Chapter 9). The adolescent subculture acts as a bridge between the world of childhood and adult society. Children absorb the sexual values of their parents on faith, but for adolescents such uncritical conformity will not do. Though they are in need, teenagers are rarely given consistent and workable sexual guidelines, and they become acutely aware of the inconsistencies between adult sexual values and behaviors.

Adolescents begin to balance two sets of social norms: that of their own youth subculture and those of the adult world. These two sets of behavioral expectations are often contradictory, so there is turmoil. A young man or woman who uncritically embraces all of the normative expectations of the peer culture is in danger of becoming labeled a delinquent. This outcome is more likely on sexual than other grounds, because sexual misbehavior, especially for girls, has been one of the main traditional causes of social disgrace. If, on the other hand, the youngster entirely disregards the sexual norms of the peer culture, then he or she is likely to suffer social isolation. In either case, the transition to adulthood is made more difficult.

Most adolescents negotiate this transition successfully by going along with the expectations of the peer culture in the short run, while bearing in mind the requirements of the adult world in the long run. Parents and other adults can help if they uphold traditional sexual values but allow youngsters considerable autonomy. Parents, in fact, are just as likely to be upset by a lack of sexual interest in their children as they are by sexually irresponsible behavior. Typically, parents have worried that teenage boys who are not interested in girls will be homosexuals, and that girls who are indifferent to boys will never find husbands.

Adulthood does not free us from social controls. On the contrary, what may have been tolerated during youth ("sowing your wild oats," "raising hell," "playing around") becomes unacceptable for responsible and settled adults. Though we become emancipated from the control of parents and teachers, powerful social forces continue to keep us in line. When our employers, friends, and neighbors disapprove of our sexual behavior, we may not get promoted, may lose our jobs, fail to receive social invitations, and become unwelcome in the neighborhood; such sexual ostracism may even extend to our children, who may get shunned by their friends under pressure from their parents.

The United States makes a strict constitutional separation between church and state; yet the *Judeo-Christian tradition* has always been an important source of social influence on our sexual behavior. In recent years, large numbers of people from different religious backgrounds, such as Buddhists and Moslems, have immigrated into the United States, enriching further the religious diversity of the country. Even if you have no formal affiliation with a religious institution, your sexual morality probably is influenced by these traditions. Whether you adhere to traditional sexual morality or react against it, many sexual norms are still defined in that context (Chapter 23).

For the majority of people, the social norms of sexual behavior are based less on formal theological arguments than on *folk theory* (Davenport, 1977). Such popular assumptions about sexual behavior blend traditional beliefs, popular versions of the opinions of social scientists, personal beliefs, and prejudices. For example, many people adhere to the notion that in sexual partnerships it is proper for the man to be older, but not the woman.

Given all these sources of social control, how much autonomy do you really have? Does your sexual behavior reflect real choice, or is it merely the outcome of various biological and social forces that shape you in childhood and buffet and steer you through adulthood? There is no clearcut answer. It is easy enough to see ourselves as puppets, manipulated by biological and social strings. Think, though, of the enormous variety of sexual behavior within your age group or social class. Think how you differ even from your friends. Does individual variance merely reflect special combinations of determinants, or are we endowed with a free will which allows for independent choice? This fascinating issue is worth some thought.

## Social Judgments

Society makes a variety of judgments about what constitutes desirable and undesirable sexual behavior. Such judgments are generally made on the basis of four criteria: *statistical* (How common is the behavior?), *medical* (Is the behavior healthy?), *moral* (Is the behavior ethical?), and *legal* (Is the behavior legitimate?).

Sometimes these four criteria are mutually reinforcing. For example, incest is a statistically infrequent form of sexual behavior that is considered psychologically unhealthy, morally inadmissible, and illegal in almost all societies. It would be difficult, however, to find many other examples that are so clearcut. In principle, we must judge sexual behaviors according to one criterion at a time; yet there is a strong tendency to seek corroboration from the rest. In fact, one set of judgments is often predicated on another: an act may be considered immoral or illegal because it is unhealthy or offends the majority, or vice versa; an activity that we consider immoral may seem even worse if we assume it to be rare, unhealthy, and illegal.

In our pluralistic society such judgments have resulted in confusion. The meaning of the statistical norm has been distorted, in ignorance or deliberately: the prevalence of homosexuality, for instance, tends to be underestimated by its opponents and overestimated by its proponents. Medical judgments on sex have often lacked scientific support; the presumed harmfulness of masturbation in the past is a case in point. Morality has been confused with tradition and the preferences of those in power. Statutes and ordinances have frozen into law many dubious health claims and moral conclusions. Not infrequently, the original determination that an act, such as oral sex, is unhealthy or uncommon turns out to be incorrect or outdated, but the moral and legal judgments based on it persist.

Societies set up norms and assert various judgments on sexual behavior because it is widely assumed that the untrammeled expression of all sexual impulses would prove socially disruptive by causing conflict. It is easy to argue that incest would wreak havoc in families. It is harder to understand why society has made so much fuss over the details of lovemaking between married partners in the privacy of their bedroom. Some of our sex laws and the social attitudes they reflect would be laughable if as a result of them people had not been harrassed, ostracized, jailed, and condemned to death—all for participating in sexual activities that claimed no victims, displeased no participants, and would not even have come to light unless authorities and self-appointed guardians of public morality had not relentlessly unearthed them.

Several principles help explain, if not justify, some of these seeming absurdities that have characterized the treatment of sex in our society and many others. First is the ancient Talmudic precept of "building fences." In order to defend a fundamental moral principle or to insure that a key commandment is not violated, we enact subsidiary rules, like building concentric fences, around the core principles to be defended. In this way people can learn the error of their ways at the lesser cost of minor transgressions committed at the "periphery," and they are saved from committing the graver central sins.

To apply this principle to sexual behavior, let us assume that the central social concern is to protect the integrity of the family. Behaviors like incest or extramarital relations can be said to pose direct threats; so they are clearly forbidden. Premarital relations represent a less direct danger, presumably jeopardizing marital happiness in the future. A wider circle of prohibitions extends to drinking, provocative clothing, and acting in ways that could sexually arouse people, leading them into those sexual behaviors that are threats to the marital unit.

This principle is logical but easy to abuse. Moral fences can be extended in ever-widening circles to the point where they cease to bear any evident relationship to the core virtues that they are supposed to defend. The preoccupation with externals and secondary concerns becomes so ritualized that upholding them becomes a substitute for the original purposes of moral behavior.

Another principle in the setting of sexual norms is to protect the most vulnerable or the least sensible people. For example, there are many individuals who are able to engage in premarital or extramarital sex without harming anyone. On the other hand, what about the countless others under similar circumstances who would be seriously hurt? How can we say that engaging in a given behavior is socially acceptable for some and not for others? What choice do we have but to declare as unacceptable all sexual behaviors in which some individuals are likely to get harmed?

This position does sound socially responsible. Still, thoughtful and responsible men and women cannot help feeling that the sexual norms of our society seem to have little bearing on their own lives and that they are being held to some lowest common denominator of responsibility. Furthermore, if thoughtless and irresponsible people are not likely to pay attention to social norms anyway, why encumber everyone else with rules of behavior designed for them? But then, as we shall see, the more sophisticated may need the blanket rules more than they think they do.

## Justifications for Social Control

Why should society exert so much effort, and often so unsuccessfully, to regulate the sexual behavior of its members, even when it is engaged in by mutual consent and in private? Why the countless and convoluted moral prohibitions and legal strictures to regulate a normal physiological process?

Justifications for such control have generally rested on four considerations: reproductive consequences, ownership rights, sexual exploitation, and social stability.

Reproductive Consequences   At the most fundamental level, society's interest in sex is connected to its reproductive consequences. Even when social judgments about a particular sexual behavior appear unrelated to reproduction, looking deeper reveals the linkage. Given the unpredictable association of sex and reproduction, coitus has had to be regulated so children are not brought into situations where they cannot be cared for. This consideration has been central to attempts to control premarital sex.

Other behaviors may be checked because of the fear that they would compete with reproductive sex. That is perhaps one of the reasons that homosexual relationships have been prohibited. It is only recently that we have been able to decouple sex from reproduction through voluntary, large-scale use of reliable contraceptives.

Ownership Rights   Whatever they state in principle, the practical impact of social regulations has been mainly to restrict the sexual behavior of women. Whether in her father's house before marriage, or in her husband's house following marriage, the central male figure in a woman's life has had a proprietary interest in guarding sexual access to her. The need to keep women in check has been further reinforced by the notion that they are emotional, easily deceived, and perhaps as suggested by Sherfey (1973), sexually insatiable. The belief that women are sexually more volatile, combined with the fact that they are the ones who give birth, has reinforced the need for greater control of female sexuality.

Children inherit their father's property and name. Because men could never be absolutely sure of the paternity of their children, sexual access to their wives has had to be carefully guarded. Men own their reputations, too. They have interpreted the seduction of their wives by other men as a loss of honor.

At the relational level, women fully reciprocate these sentiments. Whether in marriage or some other committed relationship, most women are strongly intolerant of any incursion by other women into their primary relationship (Chapter 17). Because sexual associations rouse such strong possessiveness, societies have seen fit to impose external controls, reducing the chances of conflict and disruption of stable relationships. This reasoning is the basis of the social sanctions against extramarital sex.

Sexual Exploitation   For as far back as we could go in history or to the farthest corner of the world, there is no lack of evidence for sexual exploitation, usually perpetrated by men on women and children (Chapters 18 and 19). It is a key function of society to protect its vulnerable members from harm; hence, the setting up of social controls.

Social Stability   Finally, extra sexual restrictions are often imposed on the supposition that with unbridled sexuality, society would collapse.

This social tendency to keep sex tightly in check appears to be based on two assumptions. The first is that sexual permissiveness will lead to sexual license that can disrupt the family, erode the social fabric, sap the strength of the nation, and lead to social disintegration. The decline and fall of the Roman Empire is often held up as an example (Figure 21.5). Though we can just as plausibly argue that unbridled sexual license is a symptom and not a cause of social disintegration, so ingrained is the belief in the licentiousness-decline-fall sequence that sexual permissiveness, particularly among youth, is interpreted in downright conspiratorial terms. Some people suspected a Communist plot behind the sexual revolution of the 1960s. These suspicions were fueled by the fact that many sexually adventurous youth were also political radicals who openly preached revolution. Soviet youth who imitate the lifestyle and sexual ways of their Western counterparts are similarly denounced by their political elders for succumbing to bourgeois decadence and playing into the hands of the

**Figure 21.5**    Thomas Couture, *Romans of decadence* (1847). A 19th-century Frenchman's view of Roman sexual excess.

capitalist enemies of their society. Thus, whatever the dominant ideology, those who are disenchanted with it also seem to favor permissive sexual attitudes. Is this because political dissidents wish to violate the established sexual norms of the Establishment as part of their revolt, or do those who feel sexually oppressd become political dissidents?

The second social concern is that uncontrolled sexual behavior dissipates energy that would otherwise be put to constructive and creative uses: sex is so much fun that were we to have free access to it, none of us would want to work or strain ourselves to do anything useful. These dual presumptions treat sexuality like a rushing stream: if unchecked it will sweep everything away; if unharnessed it goes to waste. Repression of sexuality thus becomes the price we need to pay for civilization (Box 21.1).

## Sex and Social Status

Sexual behavior and social status are interdependent at a number of levels. What is considered proper sexual behavior and what you can get away with have always been linked to social class.

Early in the 19th century, Hawaiian aristocrats, but not the common people, enjoyed sexual freedom as a matter of hereditary privilege. In other cases, people (usually men) acquire such rights by rising to positions of power and prominence. Among Solomon Islanders, adultery and rape are severely disapproved and punished; but men of renown may engage in both with relative impunity. These examples from other cultures illustrate in exaggerated form what is also commonplace in our society. The rich and famous often act as if they are not bound by the social norms of their society. Movie stars flaunt their amorous

# Box 21.1

## CIVILIZATION AND ITS DISCONTENTS

The relationship of sex and society greatly interested Freud, particularly toward the end of his life, when he turned his attention from narrower clinical concerns to wider cultural issues.* Freud's central thesis was that there is an irreconcilable antagonism between instinctual demands (erotic and aggressive) and the restrictions of civilization. Free gratification of instinctual needs was incompatible with society, so those needs had to be repressed and subordinated to the disciplines of work and reproduction.

Freud saw this process of sexual repression operating simultaneously at the individual and social level. He traced the roots of sexual repression both to the development of the individual (*onto-genesis*) and to the history of the human race (*phylo-genesis*). The social pattern was set in our dim prehistoric past; as individuals, each of us must go through the process during our own life cycle.

Freud theorized that the id, the seat of the sexual instinct, operates on the basis of the *pleasure principle*. The harnessing of this libidinal force is the task of the ego and the superego (representing reason and conscience), which are governed by the *reality principle*. Whereas the pleasure principle seeks immediate gratification, the reality principle requires restraint and delayed satisfaction. The desire for play, pleasure, and freedom on the one hand is balanced by the requirements of work, productivity, and security on the other. Although these internal forces may appear to be at odds, they work for a common purpose in the long run. As we give up the unrestrained, fleeting pleasures of the moment, more reliable and lasting pleasures accrue to us in due time. In this way the reality principle safeguards rather than nullifies the pleasure principle. Meanwhile, through the process of *sublimation* our libidinal energies are channeled into intellectual and artistic creativity, which enriches our lives and increases culture and civilization.

*Freud's ideas about the relationship of sex and society pervade many of his writings. See, in particular, *Civilization and Its Discontents*, Vol. 21 of his collected works. For an introduction to Freud's sociological views see Marcuse (1955); Jones (1957, Vol. 3). For a broader overview see Gay (1988).

To sustain this process, society incorporates the reality principle in its institutions. Individuals growing up within a social system learn the reality principle in the form of norms and other requirements of law and order and then, in turn, transmit them to the next generation. Members of society must diligently sustain their culture, because the tendency to go back to a "state of nature" is never vanquished.

"The price of progress in civilization," wrote Freud, "is paid by forfeiting happiness through the heightening of the sense of guilt" (quoted in E. Jones, 1957, Vol. 3, p. 342). Though he thought the repression of our primitive erotic and aggressive behavior was necessary for the exercise of our higher interests and capacities, Freud was also keenly concerned with the price. Because libidinal repression, especially when harsh and excessive, resulted in neurotic disorders and sexual dysfunction, Freud expressed the fear that the restrictions on sexual behavior, which had channeled so much energy into civilization, now posed the danger of throttling the instinctual sources of life and happiness. Freud wrote:

A certain portion of the repressed libidinal impulses has a claim to direct satisfaction and ought to find it in life. Our civilized standards make life too difficult for the majority of human organizations. Those standards consequently encourage the retreat from reality and the generating of neuroses, without achieving any surplus of cultural gain by this excess of sexual repression. We ought not to exalt ourselves so high as completely to neglect what was originally animal in our nature. Nor should we forget that the satisfaction of the individual's happiness cannot be erased from among the aims of our civilization. The plasticity of the components of sexuality, shown by their capacity for sublimation, may indeed offer a great temptation to strive for still greater cultural achievements by still further sublimation. But, just as we do not count on our machines converting more than a certain fraction of the heat consumed into useful mechanical work, we ought not to seek to alienate the whole amount of the energy of the sexual instinct from its proper ends. We cannot succeed in doing so; and if the restriction upon sexuality were to be carried too far it would inevitably bring with it all the evils of soil-exhaustion (*Five Lectures on Psychoanalysis*, p. 52).

---

escapades, people in positions of authority take advantage of their power, and so on.

Privileged social status may, however, also place special constraints on sexual freedom and choice. Edward VIII was forced to abdicate the throne of England in 1936 before he could marry Wallis Simpson, because she was a divorcee. Adlai Stevenson's campaign for the presidency of the United States suffered from his being a divorced man. Gary Hart had to give up his chance to run for president because of a presumed extramarital affair. Yet President Kennedy's political fortunes or personal popularity did not suffer from his sexual indiscretions (which were largely unknown by the public at the time). It would be most unlikely, currently, for an avowed homosexual to be elected or appointed to national high office.

A great deal depends, of course, on the particular area within which a person is prominent. The reputation of an Einstein or Picasso is not likely to be jeopardized by his sexual behavior; stars in some entertainment fields even have their reputation enhanced by being sexually adventurous. On the other hand, public figures such as judges, executives, and elected officials who are thought to sexually misbehave are likely to face a loss of public confidence in their integrity and judgment. Those in sensitive positions with access to classified information are furthermore considered to be subject to blackmail if they have a "secret vice." There are many examples of people in high positions whose careers ended because of sexual scandals.

## CROSS-CULTURAL PATTERNS OF SOCIAL CONTROL

All societies institutionalize sex in ways that are common in some respects and different in others. For instance, procreative sex is considered a legitimate and desirable aim in virtually all societies. However, societies differ widely in the norms and sanctions concerning other forms of sexual behavior. The important distinction between societies is not how strict their rules are but how rigorously they enforce them (Ford and Beach, 1951).

### Sexual Diversity and Unity

Diversity marks all human experience, but in sex it is particularly striking. People may have one, two, or three major meals a day, but everyone eats every day and no one eats ten times a day. Not so with sex: some have daily orgasms; others go without it for years. The greater uniformity of other physiologically driven behaviors like eating is clearly because of their greater biological imperative. Sex is an activity that is not essential for life or health at the individual level.

Cultures define what is sexual and what is not above and beyond genital interactions. For example, our culture does not imbue eating with any direct sexual significance. We eat freely in public with strangers and at home with members of our family. But in some tribal societies the sharing of food is characteristic of the marital relationship—hence, brothers and sisters may not eat together without appearing to indulge in a sexual act.

Embedded within the bewildering array of intercultural differences in sexual attitudes and behaviors, there are a number of elements common to all cultures (Gregersen, 1983). The most fundamental constant in sexuality is its universality. Sex is present in all societies; it does not have to be discovered or invented. Equally constant is the role that every society takes on to shape and regulate the sexual behavior of all its members through socialization in childhood and rewards and punishments throughout adult life. All peoples are convinced that sexual activity is necessary, although reasons for this conviction vary. It is also widely believed that a man's sexual interests exceed those of a woman, and this opinion persists even in cultures that grant equal sexual privileges to both sexes.

In every society, the culture of sex is anchored in two directions: "In one direction, it is moored to the potentialities and limitations of biological inheritance. In the other direction, it is tied to the internal logic and consistency of the total culture" (Davenport, 1977, p. 161). In order for a society to maintain a coherent structure, its sexual attitudes and regulations must be integrated with all the other rules and regulations governing other forms of behavior; sexual rules are not meaningful in isolation.

Intercultural similarities are manifested in the common sexual beliefs and behavioral patterns of individuals in various societies; similarities are also present in the relationship of sexuality to the structure and function of society as a whole. Those aspects of sexual behavior that are tied closely to biological foundations show relatively less variance. For instance, of all sexual behaviors only coitus can lead to pregnancy (except for artificial forms of insemination that hardly qualify as sexual behavior). Hence, behaviors centered around reproduction may take numerous forms in the choice of partners, patterns of courtship, coital behaviors, and so on, but by necessity the endpoint is the same whatever the culture.

At the other end, the symbolic and intellectual aspects of sex are highly variable; it is these aspects that are more closely tied to the "internal logic" of the culture as a whole. For instance, ideals of sexual attractiveness, moral judgments, and definitions of gender are in large measure manifestations of the way a given culture is oriented.

Lying behind all the rules, regulations, sanctions, and taboos are the implicitly or explicitly shared value systems upon which a society must be founded, and which it must preserve or perish. These value systems and the cultural mechanisms related to them constitute what Davenport (1977) defines as a society's "internal logic and consistency." It is the rela-

tion of sexuality to this more general aspect of any society that we must seek to understand.

Universal rules are harder to apply to specific sexual activities without qualification except for a few basic behaviors. Sexual fantasy and self-stimulation are part of the sexual repertoire of every group, if not of every individual within it. Heterosexuality is the dominant sexual orientation and coitus the primary sociosexual behavior in all cultures but never the only one. Marriage is the primary setting for coitus, but not all societies attempt to confine coitus to married partners; those that do, vary in their effectiveness in preventing sex outside marriage. Despite these similarities at the level of principle, cultures vary widely with respect to specifics and the manner in which these principles are applied.

## Repressiveness and Permissiveness

Another important source of dissimilarity between societies is the level of control they exercise over sexual behavior. In Chapters 8 and 9, we discussed cross-cultural variations in levels of repressiveness and permissiveness with respect to childhood and adolescent sexuality. Similar contrasts can be based on criteria other than socialization patterns, although there is likely to be a close correlation between the manner in which a society rears its children and the eventual behaviors expected of its members.

Cultures also vary in the emotional tone with which people engage in sex. Thus, the sexual joyfulness and the exuberance of the Mangaians contrasts with the intense hostility that imbues sexual intercourse for the Gusii of southwestern Kenya (Levine, 1959). For these people, even marital coitus is an act in which the man must overcome the woman's resistance and cause her pain and humiliation; women retaliate by taunting and frustrating the men. This pattern of interaction is inculcated during youth. When adolescent males are in seclusion following circumcision, girls are brought to the area to dance in the nude while making disparaging remarks about the boys' freshly mutilated genitals, arousing painful erections.

Sexually Repressive Cultures   Inis Beag (pseudonym) is a small Irish island community that shows a pattern of extreme denial and suppression of sexuality. As described by John Messenger, the people of Inis Beag shroud in mystery all manifestations of sex as well as other natural functions like menstruation and urination (Messenger, 1971). Nudity is abhorred to the point where a man is embarrassed even to bare his feet in public and reluctant to see a nurse when ill to avoid exposing his body. Marital coitus is the only acceptable sexual outlet, a "duty" which women "endure" and men hazard despite its presumed debilitating effects. Sex is always initiated by the husband, foreplay is restricted to touching and fondling the buttocks, coitus occurs only in the man-above position, underclothes are not removed, and it is doubtful if women ever reach orgasm.

The only other discernible sexual activity in Inis Beag is male masturbation and occasional petting encounters involving a few of the island girls or occasional visitors. The men who engage in these acts are so ashamed that they even shun the confessional. The village curate, who was hospitalized in a mental institution, was assumed to have been driven mad by the frustration of living in the same house with his pretty housekeeper. If any but the most conventional form of sex is ever practiced in Inis Beag, its existence is effectively kept secret from the community, which lives in fear of clerical disgrace, public censure, and ridicule.

It may be tempting to ascribe the prudishness of Inis Beag to Irish Catholicism, but similar attitudes can also be found in cultures that are neither Irish nor Catholic. For example, in the tribal tradition of the Manus of Papua-New Guinea, coitus between husband and wife was regarded as sinful and degrading, to be undertaken only in the strictest secrecy. Women in particular were averse to sex, which they endured occasionally to produce offspring. Intercourse outside of marriage was an even worse offense, which brought on supernaturally ordained punishments. So secretive were Manu women about menstruation that Manu men denied that their women experienced monthly cycles (Davenport, 1977).

For the people on Yap Island in the Pacific the repression of sexuality came not from moral scruples but concerns over health. Yappese men believed coitus caused weakness and susceptibility to illness. Women were similarly vulnerable, particularly for the period of several years following the birth of a child.

Sexually Permissive Cultures   The best-known examples of sexually permissive cultures come from the Polynesian islands of the central Pacific. Observations of the Tahitians' free-wheeling sexuality go back to Captain Cook, the 18th-century British explorer who discovered these islands. Before the impact of the West, Tahitian children and youth of both sexes were encouraged to masturbate and engage in premarital intercourse with few restrictions. Marital and extramarital coitus was freely engaged in and openly discussed. The life of the community, its modes of aesthetic expression, song and dance, were suffused with eroticism.

Some of this sexual tradition of old Polynesia has persisted on the island of Mangaia described by D. S. Marshall (1971). As we discussed in connection with childhood and adolescent sexual development (Chapters 8 and 9), Mangaian boys and girls start masturbation between the ages of seven and ten, and coitus at about 14. Virtually everyone has had substantial sexual experience prior to marriage and keeps up an active sex life following it. Sex is as regular a part of the life of these people as dinner.

Sex for Mangaian men and women means coitus, pure and simple. To that end, foreplay (including mouth-genital stimulation) is freely practiced; "dirty talk," music, scents, and nudity further heighten arousal. Women are active sexual partners in both psychological and physical terms. Female orgasm, often multiple, is considered a necessary outcome of successful coitus; its absence is feared to be injurious to the woman's health. Pregnancy does not inhibit Mangaians, who continue to engage in sex up to the onset of labor pains. Parenthood strengthens further the sexual ties of a couple.

The Mangaian experience also demonstrates the constraints and contradictions that exist even in a society known for its unabashed and unrestrained celebration of sex throughout life. Much of premarital sexual activity, for instance, goes on covertly for the sake of appearances, and there is a certain ambivalence coloring the relationship of sexual partners. Unlike our culture, where sex is expected to follow love, the Mangaians start with sex and hope that it will lead to affection. This fact tends to cast their sexual relations in a more physical and mechanistic mold.

Ultimately, all societies rely on two sets of restraints to regulate the sexual behaviors of their members: externally imposed laws, and internalized moral codes of behavior. In the next two chapters, we turn to their more detailed consideration.

## REVIEW QUESTIONS

1. What were the main causes of the sexual revolution in the 1960s?

2. What were the main manifestations of the sexual revolution in female sexuality?

3. Trace the development of the gay liberation movement.

4. What are the main justifications offered for the social control of sexual behavior?

5. How are sexual diversity and unity manifested in cross-cultural settings?

## THOUGHT QUESTIONS

1. Do you think the sexual revolution was a good thing? Did it go too far or not far enough? Explain.

2. What evidence do you see around you that a sexual revolution is still in progress?

3. Is a conservative backlash inevitable after a period of sexual liberalization? If so, why? How can it be avoided, and should it be?

4. How far is your sexual behavior up to you? Explain.

5. How would you go about studying the sexual behavior of another culture in ways that would allow comparisons with your own?

## SUGGESTED READINGS

D'Emilio, J. (1983). *Sexual politics, sexual communities.* Chicago: University of Chicago Press. A well-researched, coherent, and sympathetic account of the gay liberation movement in the United States from 1940 to 1970.

Francoeur, R. T. (Ed.). (1987). *Taking sides.* Clashing views on controversial issues in human sexuality.

Gregersen, E. (1983). *Sexual practices.* New York: Franklin Watts. Wide-ranging, fascinating, and well-illustrated overview of cross-cultural sexual attitudes, customs, and behaviors.

Ford, C. S., and Beach, F. A. (1951) *Patterns of sexual behavior.* New York: Harper & Row. A comprehensive and well-organized compilation of cross-cultural information on sexual behavior and human relationships. A classic source.

Sorokin, P. (1956). *The American sex revolution.* A highly critical view of the sexual revolution, even before it had fully emerged. Many of the arguments made by this conservative sociologist against sexual liberality are presently repeated by others.

# Sex and the Law

*The welfare of the people is the chief law.*

CICERO (106–43 B.C.)

OUTLINE

LAWS ON MARRIAGE AND
  PROCREATION
Marriage Law
  Divorce Law
  Child Custody
Laws on Reproduction
  Contraception
  Sterilization
  Abortion
  Surrogate Motherhood
AIDS AND THE LAW
Mandatory Testing
Quarantine
Legal Liability
LAWS ON ADULT CONSENSUAL
  BEHAVIOR
Heterosexual Behaviors
Homosexual Behaviors

Decriminalization of Sodomy
Discrimination and Prejudice
SEXUAL OFFENSES AGAINST
  PERSONS
Rape
Marital Rape
Sexual Offenses Against the Young
  Statutory Rape
  Child Molestation
Public Nuisance Offenses
LAWS ON COMMERCIAL
  EXPLOITATION OF SEX
Prostitution
  Arguments Against Legalization
  Arguments in Favor of Legalization
Pornography
  The Dangers of Pornography
  The Problem of Censorship

How free ought we to be? In all human interactions, there is a potential for conflict between the individual's freedom of action and harm to others. All societies have had to enact rules both to minimize harm and to protect freedom. Sexuality has been traditionally considered an area that especially needs regulation (Chapter 21), but what kinds of sex the law should cover is a matter of disagreement (Box 22.1). In principle, there is a clear separation between church and state in American society. Yet our social institutions, including the law, are heavily influenced by moral principles, often based on traditional religious beliefs (Chapter 23). Whether or not any kind of behavior should, by itself, be sufficient justification for making that behavior illegal remains one of the central problems of our times (Wasserstrom, 1971).

## LAWS ON MARRIAGE AND PROCREATION

Societies are keen on upholding the integrity of the family, even though its form and functions may vary (Chapter 17). We will look only at laws that deal specifically with sexual conduct, although other laws in the vast body of *family law* have great impact on the operation of the marital unit. A similar consideration applies to issues of *sex discrimination*, which has become a prominent legal concern and which also has important implications for sexual behavior (Dolgin and Dolgin, 1980).

### Marriage Law

In the United States, monogamy is the only legal form of marriage. Bigamy or polygamy have been criminal offenses in the United States since the formation of the union. These laws go back to the statutes of James I in 1603. The Mormons challenged this position, but in 1878 the Supreme Court rejected the claim that antipolygamy legislation violated the religious liberty embodied in the First Amendment (*Reynolds v. United States*, 98 U.S. 145, 1878).

Given the significance attached to marriage, it is surprising that the law makes it easier to obtain a marriage license than a driver's license (Slovenko, 1965). Most states prohibit marriages of minors under the age of 16 or 17, and parental consent is required for marriages of minors under the age of 18 in most states. If younger individuals marry by falsifying their ages, the marriage is usually considered valid.

### Divorce Law

During the past decade the legal dissolution of marriage through divorce has become remarkably easy. In 1970, California was the first state to adopt *no-fault divorce,* in which either party asserts "irreconcilable difficulties that have caused irremediable breakdown of the marriage" (California Civil Code, Section 4506). Thus, either spouse may obtain a divorce, regardless of the objections of the other party. It is no longer necessary to show that the other party was guilty of one of the traditional "fault" grounds for divorce, such as adultery. Specific conduct is in fact no longer admissible as evidence, except where child custody is at issue (California Civil Code, Section 4509). All other states have followed California's lead, no longer limiting divorce to traditional "fault" grounds.

In addition, unless agreed otherwise, shared ("community") property must be divided evenly (California Civil Code, Section 4800). The financially dependent former spouse (usually the wife) may be awarded *alimony,* an allowance for support for a limited period of time, if there are sufficient funds. Cohabiting couples do not have comparable legal obligations and can break up the relationship without legal proceedings. But an interesting side-note to property settlements is the claim for *palimony,* which has recently allowed for compensation even when a couple living together were not married to each other.

The law views sexual intercourse as a fundamental part of marriage. If a union is not sexually consummated (that is, intercourse does not take place even once), it is grounds for *annulment* of the marriage. Should either spouse refuse sex after consummation, the aggrieved party could assert a case of "irreconcilable difference."

# Box 22.1

## THE NATURE AND USE OF SEX LAWS

The laws of the United States, which started in the colonies, come from two main sources: state legislatures enact *statute law;* courts build on *common law,* based on precedent. Because legislators are elected and judges are appointed by elected governmental executives, at least in theory, the citizenry is the keeper of the nations's laws.

Those who support the use of the law to regulate sexual behavior avow a strong commitment to the protection of public morals and the integrity of the family. They view sex as potentially highly disruptive to both and consider the law an appropriate tool to uphold the majority's moral values. The law should assert itself so that deviant sexual values and practices do not contaminate private and public life and weaken the moral fiber of the nation.

Objections to this view are based on several grounds, some procedural, others substantive (Packer, 1968). Sex laws are often vague. Rather than defining behaviors, they forbid "crimes against nature," begging the question. The difficulty of detecting private behavior between consenting adults may lead to undesirable police practices, while the capricious enforcement of these laws raises questions about arbitrary prosecutions.

The discrepancy between what the law says and what people do in their sexual lives is also striking: if these laws were seriously applied and sexual behavior effectively monitored, the majority of the citizenry would be liable to prosecution. The fact that sex laws are by and large "dead" on the books does not make them wholly innocuous. Widespread violation with impunity of any law, dead or alive, generates disrespect for the law generally; and these laws still retain a power for abuse when selectively applied to harass individuals or groups.

The discrepancy between the law and common behavior reflects the law's failure to represent contemporary moral sentiments. This failure is due, in part, to the law's reliance on precedent. Precedent

in sexual matters tends to be conservative and often is based on outdated claims. It also reflects the fact that few politicians are willing to challenge inactive and antiquated sexual laws because of risk to reputations and careers. For instance, Pennsylvania revised its criminal code in 1972 and in the process deleted its laws against fornication and adultery. The press reported this act as a decision "to legalize premarital and extramarital sex"; the laws were reinstated within months. Idaho went through a similar experience at about the same time.

It has also been argued that sex laws reflect a particular religious perspective and therefore are unconstitutional. These "separation of church and state" arguments have not found much favor with the Supreme Court. No one denies that our sexual morality derives from the Judeo-Christian tradition; but over time, these values have become secularized. Are they the contemporary values of the majority, or merely of persons and groups with the means, the access to the media, and the political connection to push them—the "people who count"? These are complex matters, which are particularly vexing with regard to sexual behavior, where our knowledge is uncertain, values disparate, and emotions high.

During the past two decades a remarkable change has taken place in laws against consensual behaviors, such as homosexual acts in private, as opposed to laws that prohibit sexual offenses against individuals, such as rape. In 1962 the American Law Institute, a private organization composed of prominent judges, lawyers, and law professors, published the *Model Penal Code,* which proposed eliminating criminal penalties for sexual activities between consenting adults (with the exception of prostitution) (American Law Institute, 1962). Based on the recommendations of the Model Code, 22 states have so far removed criminal sanctions on sexual activities between consenting adults.

---

**Child Custody**  Traditionally, mothers have been given custody in divorce cases. Recently more fathers have won joint custody or taken on the full responsibility of bringing up their children. Bisexual men encounter even more difficult hurdles in this area. Courts have been reluctant to award custody to a parent involved in a homosexual relationship. However, in custody conflicts between lesbians and their heterosexual former spouses, the women win almost half the cases (Sheppard, 1985). Even in states that proscribe homosexual behavior no woman has been deemed unfit simply because of her sexual orientation.

The trend in settling marital and family disputes is increasingly moving toward settling differences through bargaining and negotiation ("private ordering") rather than litigation. The law still sets the limits, but matters are settled more often in lawyers' offices than get to court.

## Laws on Reproduction

Society's interest in regulating reproduction is among the primary reasons for legal preoccupation with the family. No society can trifle with the welfare of its young and hope to exist for long. We shall consider reproductive laws in four areas: contraception, sterilization, abortion, and surrogate motherhood.

Contraception   Over most of its history, Western morality has opposed the limitation of offspring; it is only since the 19th century that arguments controlling family size have gained popularity (Noonan, 1967). Contraceptive practice in the United States became restricted from 1873, when Congress made it illegal to disseminate contraceptive information, until 1965, when the Supreme Court declared unconstitutional laws restricting the use or discussion of methods of contraception for *married* couples. The Court reached this landmark decision in *Griswold v. Connecticut* (381 U.S. 479, 1965) on the grounds that the statute invaded the constitutionally protected "right to privacy." Connecticut was the only state at the time to prohibit the dissemination of contraceptives to married couples, so the importance of the Court's decision seemed academic; but it proved to have far-reaching consequences in connection with abortion.

States were allowed to prevent *unmarried* persons from obtaining contraceptives until 1972, when the Supreme Court extended the "zone of marital privacy" to them as well (*Eisenstadt v. Baird*, 405 U.S. 438, 1972). The reasoning was the same: contraception is a matter of individual privacy and it is unconstitutional for the state to invade it.

Sterilization   Voluntary sterilization, like other forms of contraception, has no legal restrictions and is now the most popular method of birth control for people over 30 (Chapter 7). Legal concerns with sterilization persist where the procedure is involuntary or undertaken in circumstances that restrict the person's choice, such as in cases involving the mentally handicapped and sex offenders.

Justification for the sterilization of select cases of mental retardation has been based on preventing transmission of genetic disability and on grounds that people who are severely handicapped could not be expected to function adequately as parents. In 1927 the Supreme Court upheld a statute under which an institutionalized mentally retarded patient could be sterilized on the order of the superintendent of the state mental hospital (*Buck v. Bell*, 274 U.S. 200, 1927). However, there was an outcry when two teenage girls, aged 12 and 14, were sterilized through a federally funded family planning program in Montgomery, Alabama, allegedly without either their or their parents' consent (*Relf v. Weinberger*, 372 F. Supp. 1196, D.D.C., 1974). The federal government has now issued regulations calling for standards of *informed consent*, including a 30-day waiting period between the giving of such consent and the date of the procedure. The use of federal funds is prohibited for sterilizing persons younger than 21, those who are institutionalized or mentally incompetent, and women whose consent is obtained while in labor or undergoing abortion (42 C.F.R. Section 50.2101, 1986). The regulations are applicable only if federal funds are used.

Currently ten states authorize compulsory sterilization for the mentally retarded.[1] Despite considerable variance in policy (for in-

[1] Delaware, Georgia, Maine, Mississippi, North Carolina, Oklahoma, Oregon, South Carolina, Utah, and Virginia.

stance, some courts but not others recognize the right of parents to have their retarded child sterilized), the trend is to allow sterilization only after a retarded person has been accorded due process through a judicial hearing. California forbids outright the sterilization of minors. Only when the retarded person reaches adulthood may the parents (or other guardians of the retarded person) petition a court for sterilization.

Abortion    Abortion is a subject as complex as it is emotionally charged. As Callahan puts it, "Abortion is a nasty problem, a source of social and legal discord, moral uncertainty, medical and psychiatric confusion, and personal anguish. If many individuals have worked through a position they find satisfactory, the world as a whole, and most societies, have not" (Callahan, 1970, p. 1).

Up to 1970 various states allowed abortions where pregnancy had resulted from incest or rape, or where it constituted a risk to the physical or mental health of the mother. The breadth and vagueness of the mental health provision made it possible for many women to obtain legal abortions, whatever their real reasons.

The Supreme Court decisions, starting with *Griswold v. Connecticut,* which we cited earlier with regard to contraception, eventually extended the right of privacy "to encompass a woman's decision whether or not to terminate her pregnancy." Thus, on January 22, 1973, the United States Supreme Court, in *Roe v. Wade,* by a 5-to-2 decision, declared unconstitutional all laws that prohibited or restricted abortions during the first trimester of pregnancy (*Roe v. Wade,* 410 U.S. 113, 1973). The Court limited state intervention in the second trimester but left the option of prohibiting third-trimester abortions to the separate states. In 1976 the Court further ruled that a woman's decision to terminate her pregnancy could not be made subject to the consent of her spouse or parents. If a minor, she had to be old enough or "mature" enough to give effective consent (*Planned Parenthood v. Danforth,* 428 U.S. 52, 1976).

The legal freedom to have an abortion is not the same as being able to get one. If a woman is poor, she is dependent on inexpensive clinics or financial assistance, as well as on the availability of physicians and nurses who are willing to perform the operation (the law does not compel them to perform abortions if it violates their moral principles). This problem for the poor could become more difficult because the states were left free to close their public health facilities to abortions (*Poelker v. Doe,* 432 U.S. 519, 1977), and free to deny public funding of abortions (*Maher v. Roe,* 432 U.S. 464, 1977; *Harris v. McRae,* 488 U.S. 197, 1980). They were also left free to require parental notice (but not consent) for a dependent minor's abortion (*H.L. v. Matheson,* 450 U.S. 398, 1981).

Publicly funded programs always remain vulnerable to cutbacks in federal or state support, which deprives part of the population of such services. For example, the Reagan Administration was going to forbid (as of March 3, 1988) all federally funded family planning clinics even to mention abortion to their 4.3 million clients in 4000 clinics; but a judge found the restriction to violate the dictates of the First Amendment (*Time,* March 14, 1988, p. 31).

The impact of the law on behavior is dramatically demonstrated by the statistics on abortion. Following the 1973 legislation, the number of legal abortions went up from 744,600 to a million and a half by 1979; teenage abortions almost doubled to 400,000 a year; the proportion of all pregnancies (excluding miscarriages and stillbirths) that end in abortions went up from 19 percent to 30 percent during the same period (*Time,* April 6, 1981, p. 22).

The curtailment of federal funding is one way that those who oppose abortion have tried to fight it. Another is to persuade Congress to pass a bill that would extend 14th Amendment protection to *persons unborn,* defining "person" in this context to include "unborn offspring at every stage of their biological development" since conception. This law would presumably allow states to pass laws defining abortion as

Figure 22.1    March in support of the right of women to obtain abortions.

murder. As of 1987, efforts to achieve this legislation had failed. Abortion foes in Congress had tried two tactics. First, a constitutional amendment, sponsored by Senator Orrin Hatch of Utah, would have given the states and the federal government authority to outlaw abortion. Second, Senator Jesse Helms of North Carolina proposed a law that would declare that "life" began at conception; it would have made abortion a form of murder and forced the Supreme Court to review its past decisions. A more ambitious alternative is to call a constitutional convention to develop an amendment to the Constitution to make abortion illegal. If 18 states, in addition to the present 16, make a request to Congress, a constitutional convention must be called to develop such an amendment to the Constitution, an unlikely prospect at the moment. A similar change could come about through a reversal

in the majority view of the Supreme Court, another unlikely prospect.

Meanwhile the issue has engaged the passions and committed efforts of various parties to the dispute. Considerations range from thoughtful discussion to impassioned assertions by *pro-choice* (Figure 22.1) and *pro-life* partisans (Figure 22.2). Box 22.2 shows some of the reasoning. Some pro-life zealots have gone beyond reasoning and resorted to violence, such as bombing abortion clinics.

Surrogate Motherhood    In Chapter 6, we saw that an infertile couple can ask a *surrogate mother* to be artificially inseminated by the man and then to give the child to the natural father and his wife upon birth.

Over 500 children have been born to surrogate mothers and turned over to parents who paid for them. There is now a National

Association of Surrogate Mothers, and lawyers specializing in matching potential surrogates with couples are doing a brisk business (Fleming, 1987); yet the legal ramifications of the practice are far from resolved.

As of 1987, no states had enacted statutes to regulate surrogate motherhood, although about a dozen states were considering such legislation (Capron, p. 695, 1987). Some of these proposed laws would legalize the procedure; others would ban it. Under present law in about half the states, an obstacle to surrogate motherhood contracts is the illegality of paying someone to give up her child for adoption. The Michigan Supreme Court has already interpreted such Michigan law as forbidding surrogate mother arrangements, and the ruling of the New Jersey Supreme Court in the highly publicized Baby M case has set a national precedent invalidating such contracts. This land-mark case illustrates the dilemmas of surrogate motherhood.

Mary Beth Whitehead, a 29-year-old married woman with two children, had entered into a contractual agreement with William Stern and his wife, Elizabeth, to be a surrogate mother for them. Elizabeth Stern, a 41-year-old pediatrician, was not sterile but feared that a pregnancy might aggravate her multiple sclerosis.

For a fee of $10,000, Mrs. Whitehead agreed to be artificially inseminated with Mr. Stern's sperm, and give the baby to the couple at birth. However, when the baby girl was born on March 27, 1986, Mrs. Whitehead was emotionally overwhelmed. She gave up the baby but refused the money and then wanted her baby back. When the Sterns refused, she threatened suicide. The Sterns relented and agreed to let the baby stay with her for a week;

Figure 22.2   Demonstration in support of making abortion illegal.

# Box 22.2

## ISSUES IN ABORTION

When does life begin? The question may appear deceptively simple, but it is impossible to answer to everyone's satisfaction. The Supreme Court, in ruling on the issue, admitted its inability to resolve this question, as have numerous experts in biology, medicine, and philosophy. As geneticist Joshua Lederberg explains, "Modern man knows too much to pretend that life is merely the beating of the heart or the tide of breathing. Nevertheless he would like to ask biology to draw an absolute line that might relieve his confusion. The plea is in vain. There is no single, simple answer to 'when does life begin?' " (quoted in the *San Francisco Chronicle*, May 23, 1981, p. 34).

One point of demarcation might be the time when the fetus becomes *viable* outside the uterus. To interrupt the life of the fetus before it could survive outside of the uterus would be allowed; to do so at a point when it could be kept alive outside the mother would not. However, our ability to sustain extrauterine life is likely to continue to improve. Should the morality or legality of abortion be based on the existing level of medical competence? What do we do with the more fundamental objection that if we just let the nonviable fetus alone, it would become viable in due time?

Another basic point of contention is who *owns* the developing organism before birth. The obvious answer is that the mother owns it; after all, it is an integral part of her own body. Then does the father of the unborn infant have no claim on it? If not, could it not be argued that women should be solely responsible for contraception as well as the consequences of their pregnancy?

Even if we were to concede that the mother alone "owns" the fetus, it would not necessarily follow that she could do with it as she pleased. We do not allow physicians to remove healthy organs simply because the owner wants to be rid of them; every such procedure requires some additional medical justification. If the fetus is a healthy part of the mother's body, should a similar justification be required?

Perhaps nobody owns the fetus. It can be thought of as an independent life. Unlike any other part of the mother's body, the fetus will eventually become a person with individual rights. If society has the right to intrude in cases of child abuse and forbid infanticide, why not extend such protection to prenatal life as well?

The counterargument to all these points comes back to a woman's right to control her own body. However we look at it, the fetus is part of the mother's flesh and blood; and after the baby is born, the child is usually her primary responsibility. How can anyone decide the matter for her?

Almost everyone agrees that abortion must be allowed if the mother's life is jeopardized by the pregnancy; but people part company over less compelling indications: health problems that are not life-threatening, psychological considerations, concerns with the impact of the child on the mother's or father's career, the financial burden on the family or society, and some of the other reasons we discussed earlier (Chapter 7) that prompt women to seek abortions.

There are also compelling practical issues. If abortions become illegal, women will not stop obtaining them. They will resort to illegal means, and poorer women will likely receive substandard medical care.

---

but the Whiteheads took the baby (called Melissa Elizabeth by the Sterns and Sara Elizabeth by Mrs. Whitehead) and fled to Florida, where they were ultimately tracked down.

After a protracted court battle, the judge ruled in favor of the Sterns, upholding the validity of the contract between the surrogate mother and the adoptive couple, also taking into consideration the "best interests of the child"—the fuzzy but well-established principle guiding the resolution of custody cases (Barron, 1986). On appeal, the New Jersey Supreme Court reversed the decision on the grounds that contracts that pay a woman to bear a child amount to the selling of babies. The ruling upheld custody of the baby for William Stern, the donor, and his wife but rejected Mrs. Stern's adoption of the baby and restored parental rights to the mother, Mary Beth Whitehead (Hanley, 1987). The case has created an enormous stir among legal scholars, legislators, ethicists, social activists, and everyone else concerned with this issue (Fleming, 1987).

Surrogate motherhood generates a number of irreconcilable conflicts. There is a woman's right to freely and voluntarily use her body—"rent" her uterus or "sell" her ova; yet in our society we place limits on what can be traded in the marketplace: babies for one are not for sale. A natural mother should be entitled to keep her child if she so wishes; but what about the natural father—does he have no stake, is he only "Mr. Sperm" (as Mrs. Whitehead came to call Mr. Stern)? What about the adoptive mother, if she is formally promised that she will have a child? The baby's own interests are even more difficult to fathom. As one critic of surrogate motherhood wrote, "And what about Baby M's ruined life?" (Gould, 1987).

When relatives, like sisters, have carried children for each other, the family dynamics become even more tangled. A 48-year-old grandmother in South Africa was impregnated with the sperm of her son-in-law and ended up carrying triplets for her daughter (Battersby, 1987). The mother of these children will be in fact their sister. The unforeseen consequences of their arrangements make many people uneasy. The Catholic church, among other institutions, has expressed grave reservations about new reproductive technologies and practices (Chapter 23).

## AIDS AND THE LAW

The law is deeply involved in safeguarding the health of the public. The Food and Drug Administration, for instance, must approve all drugs before they can be marketed. Other regulatory agencies deal with the licensing of health professionals and many other aspects of public safety. Most of us are either unaware of or take for granted the activities of the state in these areas. At times of crisis, such as an epidemic illness, the intervention of the state becomes much more visible and intrusive, thus creating a potential conflict between individual privacy and freedom on the one hand and the safety of the public on the other.

We may be on the threshold of a legal confrontation with issues related to AIDS. This may occur on several fronts: laws to make testing for the AIDS virus mandatory, quarantine for infected populations, and prosecuting individuals for knowingly transmitting the virus.

### Mandatory Testing

Apart from considerations of practicality and cost (Chapter 5), there are serious concerns that involuntary, or mandatory, blood testing for the AIDS virus would violate individual privacy and constitutional restraints on unreasonable search (Hunter, 1987). Civil liberties can be legitimately breached for good causes. For instance, the police can stop and check drivers who may be drunk. Couples to be married are required to be tested for syphilis. In these instances, there is a concrete remedy if the problem is identified: the drunk driver is gotten off the road; the person infected with syphilis is treated. What do we do with people who test positive for the AIDS virus? The most tangible benefit is that persons who test positive could avoid endangering others by abstaining from sex, by taking precautions, or at least by alerting their sexual partners. On the other hand, since carrying the virus entails an even chance of getting AIDS, which is fatal, do we have the right to impose that truth on someone who does not want to know it? Furthermore, people who are known to carry the AIDS virus are likely to be ostracized and discriminated against. Do we have the right to expose people to such jeopardy? Given that with present tests, a third of the people who test positive in low-risk populations are false positives, do we have the right to impose such an awesome burden on those who do not even have the virus? Another fear is that mandatory testing will scare away people from seeking help and drive many carriers of the virus underground. It will provide others with a false sense of security. A person who is infected may test negative for as long as a year.

Despite these problems, there is widespread sentiment among the public in favor of mandatory testing. In one poll, 52 percent of respondents favored testing everyone, and even more people supported screening special groups; for instance, 90 percent wanted immigrants to be tested. Less educated groups were more in favor of testing than better educated ones: 64 percent of high school graduates and 39 percent of college graduates approved all inclusive testing (*San Francisco Chronicle*, June 6, 1987). Because most of these respondents believe themselves to be free of the virus, they see testing as a way of identifying the "others" who carry it. This perspective is shared by parts of the federal government that favor widespread testing. However, neither the public nor the government has a clear or reasonable idea of what to do with the results.

By contrast, when the National Centers for Disease Control convened a conference to consider wider uses of the AIDS blood test, the majority of health officials opposed mandatory testing (Shilts, 1987). Instead, they encouraged the voluntary testing of select groups: people seeking treatment at venereal disease clinics or drug treatment centers, pregnant women seeking prenatal care (especially intravenous drug users), and women at family planning centers. The point of testing pregnant women is that those who test positive may elect to have an abortion rather than give birth to an infected baby. Furthermore, health officials stressed the need for strict confidentiality and the provision of psychological counseling for those who test positive and are likely to be emotionally affected by the finding. Anonymous testing would provide greater safeguards than confidentiality, but it would be harder to follow up on the tested individuals.

Other groups have come forth with similar recommendations. The American Medical Association has endorsed the mandatory testing of blood donors, sperm and egg donors for artificial insemination, organ donors, military personnel, and prisoners. The State Department has approved a plan to test its foreign service employees, the Immigration Service to screen applicants for immigration. Other proposals aim at testing applicants for marriage licenses, all admissions to hospitals, and so on. It is not clear at present to what extent all this ferment will lead to the actual imposition of testing on large groups.

## Quarantine

The segregation of persons with an infectious disease has been one way in which societies have sought to protect themselves. Leper colonies, tuberculosis sanatoria, and special hospital wards for infectious diseases are some of the examples. Should AIDS patients and carriers of the virus also be quarantined?

Like the prospect of mass testing, the notion of enforced isolation for AIDS virus carriers has a certain simple-minded appeal to people who feel certain they will not be personally affected; but it is a solution that is no better than the problem.

The first and most obvious obstacle to such a measure is its impracticality. Some 1.5 million people in the United States now carry the virus; that is three times the number of all inmates of all state and federal prisons. In a matter of a few years, that number may be doubled or tripled. Where will all these people be stashed away? Practical considerations aside, can you imagine what such an act would do to the character of a free society?

The second problem is that AIDS is not like other infectious diseases where quarantine works. It is not transmitted by casual contact—you do not get it by living with other people. Moreover, once acquired, it is lifelong—there is no limited period to wait out the course of illness.

There have been few formal attempts so far in this direction. In California, the followers of Lyndon LaRouche succeeded in placing Proposition 64 on the 1986 ballot; if passed, it would have made AIDS carriers subject to quarantine and isolation regulations (Eu and Vickerman, 1986). The referendum failed by more than 2 to 1; but the fact that it was even considered and supported by substantial numbers of people is noteworthy. Even more significant is when a powerful political figure like Senator Jesse Helms declares that "I think somewhere along the line we are going to quarantine, if we are really going to contain this disease" (*New York Times,* June 17, 1987).

The issue is both explosive and exploitable. In the event of a catastrophic epidemic, it is hard to say how the population would react. In a 1986 Gallup poll, 54 percent of respondents were willing to see active cases of AIDS be quarantined; it might not take much to extend that willingness to carriers of the virus as well (*Newsweek,* Nov. 24, 1986).

## Legal Liability

If quarantine is impractical and inhumane, what do we do with infectious individuals who knowingly and recklessly endanger the lives of others by engaging in unprotected sex with unsuspecting partners? One way is to prosecute people on a case-by-case basis.

It is a well-established principle of American law that one is exposed to civil liability (subject to laws dealing with the rights of private citizens) for willfully or negligently exposing others to disease (Baruch, 1987). For example, courts have awarded monetary damages to wives who had contracted syphilis from their husbands (despite the general doctrine that spouses cannot sue one another); in another case, a man with syphilis was held criminally liable for assault and battery for having sex with his wife without informing her of his condition (Baruch, 1987).

AIDS victims unknowingly infected by a partner who knew, or should have known, his or her condition will probably have legitimate causes for legal action. Some 30 criminal and civil cases had been filed by 1987 accusing people of trying to transmit the virus by sexual acts, biting, or spitting (Boorstin, 1987). The U.S. Army court martialed a soldier for allegedly having had sex with one man and one woman, although he knew he was an AIDS virus carrier. A Los Angeles man was charged with attempted murder for selling his blood and engaging in prostitution even though he allegedly knew he had AIDS (Lacayo, 1987). Some of these charges are of dubious merit (there is no evidence, for example, that AIDS can be transmitted by bites); but in other instances the threat can be real. Legal experts doubt that many such cases could be successfully prosecuted at present. More than half the statutes deal with the willful transmission of AIDS, but most have so far hesitated to classify AIDS as a venereal disease (Boorstin, 1987). Nonetheless they foresee an explosion of lawsuits over AIDS-related issues: people suing their lovers, AIDS victims claiming discrimination and seeking protection under laws intended for the physically handicapped, and so on. The law will undoubtedly become further enmeshed in this problem. Whether it will add a measure of appropriate protection or become part of a witch-hunt remains to be seen (Bullough, 1986).

## LAWS ON ADULT CONSENSUAL BEHAVIOR

Why would the law regulate the private sexual behavior of a married couple? Why should society care if they engage in anal intercourse? All states had sodomy statutes forbidding such behavior until 1967 (*Bowers v. Hardwick,* 1065 Ct. 2841, 2845, 1986). The current trend is to eliminate laws regulating private sexual acts between consenting adults, but 24 states and the District of Columbia still had sodomy statutes as of 1986.

## Heterosexual Behaviors

It is easier to understand why the law has been concerned with behaviors like sex outside marriage, where there is the likelihood of an aggrieved third party or a perceived threat to the institution of marriage. The law distinguishes here between *fornication,* which is intercourse between consenting unmarried adults, and *adultery*, where at least one of the participants is married to someone else. As of 1985, 25 states considered adultery a criminal offense.[2]

A handful of states have felony penalties with the possibility of lengthy prison sentences; however, as a practical matter, fines are the usual alternative. Massachusetts, for example, provides a maximum three-year sentence or a fine of not more than $500 (Massachusetts Ann. Laws, Ch. 272, Section 14). Although it is now generally recognized that behaviors like adultery should be beyond the reach of the criminal law, legislatures are reluctant to eliminate these proscriptions.

Our laws on fornication go back to the Puritans of New England. The tendency over the last several decades has been to decriminalize acts of intercourse between unmarried adults; but as of 1985, 12 states still considered it a criminal offense.[3] Usually it is a misdemeanor punishable by a fine ($10 in Maryland, $500 in Mississippi). There are further variations in state laws: some, for instance, punish the offense only when the parties are "living in a state of open and notorious cohabitation."[4] This requirement stems from common law, where an illicit sexual relation was considered a secular offense when it became a public nuisance (*Model Penal Code,* Article 213, Comment, revised 1980).

An interesting component of fornication laws deals with *seduction.* For example, the California statute reads:

> 268. *Seduction*—Every person who, under promise of marriage, seduces and has sexual intercourse with an unmarried female of pre-

vious chaste character, is punishable by imprisonment in the State prison, or by a fine of not more than five thousand dollars ($5000), or by both such fine and imprisonment (California Penal Code, Section 268).

If pressed, a man could escape prosecution from this charge by marrying the woman (but if she were underage, he could still be prosecuted for statutory rape). Such attempts to protect women now sound quaint, but once served a useful function when women were more socially vulnerable.

## Homosexual Behaviors

Homosexuality, that is, the admission of having a homosexual preference or orientation, has never been a criminal offense. It is the commission of certain acts, considered to be a "crime against nature," that has been unlawful. A typical statute states: "Every person who shall be convicted of the abominable and detestable crime against nature, either with mankind or with a beast, shall be imprisoned not exceeding twenty (20) years nor less than seven (7) years" (Rhode Island, Section 11-10-1).

The unspecified criminal behavior is generally understood to be sodomy, which usually means anal intercourse but may also mean oral sex. Strictly speaking, the legal prohibition is not aimed specifically at homosexuals; but since heterosexual anal intercourse is not likely to be prosecuted, and bestiality is rare and difficult to document, sodomy laws for all practical purposes have primarily dealt with homosexual acts.

Long-standing moral concerns over homosexuality were gradually translated into secular statutes carrying harsh punishments. In England, punishment by death for sodomy was decreed by Henry VIII in 1533, repealed by his daughter Mary in 1553, and revived by his other daughter, Elizabeth, in 1562. The American colonies perpetuated this tradition. For example, North Carolina retained the death penalty for sodomy until 1869 (North Carolina, Chapter 34, Section 6, 1854). Then a 60-year maximum prison sentence was permissible until 1965, when imprisonment was

---

[2]Alabama, California, Colorado, Connecticut, Florida, Georgia, Idaho, Illinois, Kansas, Maryland, Massachusetts, Michigan, Mississippi, Nebraska, New Hampshire, New York, North Carolina, North Dakota, Oklahoma, Rhode Island, South Carolina, Utah, Virginia, West Virginia, and Wisconsin (Shepperd, 1985).

[3]Florida, Georgia, Idaho, Illinois, Massachusetts, North Carolina, Rhode Island, South Carolina, Vermont, Virginia, West Virginia, and Wisconsin (Shepperd, 1985).

[4]As in Alaska, Arizona, Illinois, Michigan, New Mexico, and North Carolina.

# Box 22.3

## PUNISHMENTS FOR SEXUAL MISCONDUCT*

Laws are upheld by voluntary compliance and enforced by penalties. When a society truly disapproves of a behavior, it puts teeth into its prohibition. Actually the main difference between sexually repressive and permissive societies is not so much in how different their ethical and legal codes are but in how rigorously they enforce their rules.

Across cultures, the most severely punished sexual acts are incest, adultery, and rape. Sexual relations between parents and offspring are universally forbidden (with very rare historical exceptions). Sibling incest is also generally prohibited. But beyond the nuclear family, there is a bewildering variety of roles in determining who may mate with whom on the basis of consanguinity. However defined, the punishment for incest has usually been death. The Ganda of East Africa drowned the offenders; the Aztecs and Vietnamese executed them by strangulation; the Cayapa of Ecuador reportedly roasted them slowly to death by suspending them over lighted candles.

Adultery and rape are much more common offenses and their punishments are far more varied. Prohibitions against rape have generally applied to the women in a man's own group—the women of the enemy have always been fair game. Where the women of one's own group is concerned, rape is regarded in most societies as a serious offense, calling for severe penalties, including death. Sometimes the offender is merely ridiculed or given a token punishment. The rape of a married woman is generally more serious than if the woman does not have a husband.

Tolerance for extramarital relationships varies considerably from one culture to another. But once the boundaries are defined as to who a married person can and cannot have sex with, the violations of the rules are taken seriously. Thus adultery is widely

disapproved of, but it needs to be specified what constitutes adultery. The Bible expressly forbids adultery by the seventh commandment (Exodus 20:14) and defines it as sexual relations with another person's spouse—not just any man or woman other than the spouse, which is how we currently interpret it.

Nonconsensual adultery typically has led to disgrace, scandal, and divorce. It constitutes a breach of the marital vow and offends the pride and honor of the spouse. Since traditionally men have had a greater sense of "ownership" and power in the marital relationship, wives have generally been punished more severely for adultery than husbands.

The biblical penalty for adultery was death by stoning, a tradition carried into Islam. The offended husband has typically been permitted to kill or mutilate both the wife and her lover (for example, by cutting off their noses or castrating the man).

The Vietnamese had specially-trained elephants trample the guilty woman to death. Among the Cheyenne, the woman would be gang raped by a dozen men in the husband's military unit (except her relatives). Elsewhere, torture would precede death. The Romans would insert a spiny fishhead into the man's anus; the Zulu thrust a cactus into the woman's vagina. The Igbo (West Africa) punished a chief's wife for adultery by forcing her to copulate in public with her lover while a stake would be hammered through his back until it came out through her body.

All laws are defended by lofty moral principles and are meant to deter crime. But as these practices would seem to suggest, they may also become the vehicles for the expression of sadistic impulses.

*(Based on Gregersen, E., *Sexual Practices* (1983) and Ford, C. S. and Beach, F. A., *Patterns of Sexual Behavior*, 1951.)

---

left to the discretion of the court (North Carolina, Section 14-177).

The law has been used capriciously in prosecuting homosexuals. Even though only a few homosexuals were ever prosecuted, the existence of these laws was part of the broader

pattern of social harassment to which homosexuals were subjected. Public attitudes toward homosexuality began to shift in the 1960s. An important contribution to this change were the enlightened findings and recommendations of *The Wolfenden Report* (1963) issued in 1957 in

Great Britain after a ten-year study concluded that homosexual behavior between consenting adults in private should no longer be a criminal offense.

Decriminalization of Sodomy    The dramatic change in social attitudes toward homosexuals is now reflected in the law. As of 1986, 36 states had decriminalized sodomy between consenting adults in private (Figure 22.3). In 24 states where homosexual acts are still outlawed, the penalties ranged from misdemeanor fines to felonies; but in practice, few homosexuals are ever arrested. So it appeared that by and large, adult homosexual consensual behavior was no longer regulated by the law.

In 1982, Michael Hardwick was arrested in Atlanta for engaging in oral sex with another man, an act forbidden in Georgia. The state declined to prosecute but Hardwick filed suit anyway challenging the constitutionality of the state law. When the case reached the Supreme Court in 1986, the Court ruled five to four to uphold the constitutionality of sodomy laws, at least as applied to unmarried people (*Bowers v. Hardwick* 106 S. Ct. 2841, 1986). Justice White argued for the majority that the constitutionally protected right to privacy was not meant to cover any and all sexual behavior, including homosexual interactions. He said that whether or not they are "wise or desirable," prohibitions against homosexual conduct was "forbidden by the laws of the original 13 states when they ratified the Bill of Rights." In his dissenting opinion, Justice Blackmun countered, "Depriving individuals of the right to choose for themselves how to conduct their intimate relationships poses a far greater threat to the values most deeply rooted in our nation's history than tolerance of nonconformity could ever do . . ." (Church, 1986, p. 23). A Gallup poll (1986) shows 51 percent (54 per-

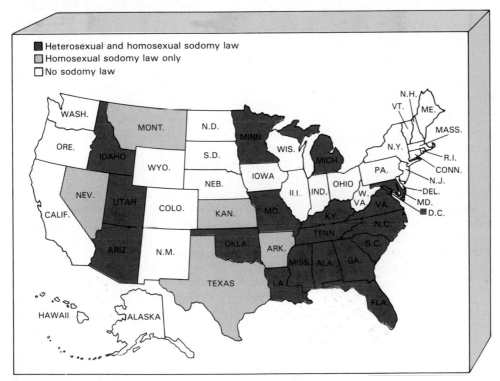

Figure 22.3    Sodomy laws in the United States.

cent of men; 47 percent of women) approving the Supreme Court decision.

Although the Court was careful to express no opinion about sodomy among heterosexuals, the implication of the ruling is that consenting adults are not free to engage in private in whatever sexual acts they wish should the state choose to prohibit such behavior. The decision was a severe setback for gay rights. Whether or not it also threatens to reverse the protection of privacy in heterosexual relations (which is the basis of the liberalization of laws in contraception and abortion) remains to be seen.

Independent of there considerations, the law still prohibits *solicitation* and *loitering* in public places. Most arrests of homosexuals are for such behavior: according to one study in the late 1960s, they accounted for 90–95 percent of homosexual arrests in the Los Angeles area (Hoffman, 1968, p. 84). The pertinent California statute reads:

> 647. *Disorderly Conduct Defined Misdemeanor.*— Every person who commits any of the following acts shall be guilty of disorderly conduct, a misdemeanor:
> (a) Who solicits anyone to engage in or who engages in lewd or dissolute conduct in any public place or in any place open to the public or exposed to public view.
> (b) Who loiters in or about any toilet open to the public for the purpose of engaging in or soliciting any lewd or lascivious or any unlawful act (California Penal Code, Section 647).

As is clear from their wording, none of the laws aimed at homosexuals discriminate between men and women; but in effect, lesbians have been practically exempt from legal persecution. For example, between 1930 and 1939, there was a single case of a woman being convicted of a homosexual offense in New York City, as against 700 convictions of males on homosexual charges and several thousand cases of males prosecuted for public indecency, solicitation, or other homosexual activity (quoted in Kinsey et al., 1953, p. 485). Kinsey ascribed this discrepancy to a number of factors: homosexual acts are more common among men and more likely to involve behaviors like public solicitation; society is more tolerant toward female homosexuals because it knows less about their activities and is less offended by their homosexual behavior. Female, unlike male homosexuals, are not perceived as dangerous with regard to seducing or sexually molesting youngsters. Studies such as Gebhard's have failed to substantiate these fears for male homosexuals as well; they are not more likely to molest youngsters than are heterosexuals (Gebhard et al., 1965).

Discrimination and Prejudice   The lives of gays are affected not only by the decisions of the Supreme Court but by the everyday interactions they have with other people and social institutions.

On many fronts, the advances in gay rights achieved over the past several decades have been quite impressive. Sexual orientation has now taken its place with race and gender to protect gays against discrimination in housing, jobs, and other areas. The armed forces can still discharge those convicted of homosexual conduct, but they can no longer dismiss or refuse to hire those who merely admit having a homosexual orientation, after a federal appeals court ruled such discrimination to be a violation of civil rights (Henry, 1988).

Gays have made less headway in having their partnerships legalized as marriages. Unlike in Sweden, where gay couples now have the same rights as common-law marriages, there is no provision in American law to recognize such associations. Nonetheless, gay men and women have begun to win some battles in custody and adoption cases. A San Diego judge awarded custody of a 16-year-old youth to his late father's homosexual lover—consistent with the boy's wishes and over his mother's objections (*New York Times*, Nov. 6, 1987). A lesbian couple in San Francisco were permitted to be the adoptive parents of two young girls (Dullea, 1988). But such cases are still rare.

What the law ordains is likely to reflect mainstream public opinion. Public opinion about legalizing gay sex has shifted considerably over the past decade. Gallup polls show that the percentage of people saying it should be legalized has gone down from 43 percent in 1977 to 33 percent in 1986; the ratio of those who say gay sex between consenting adults should not be legalized has gone up from 43 to 54 percent (Gallup, 1986). These findings reflect a growing public antipathy towards gays. This is also reflected by the greater prevalence of assaults against homosexuals ("gay bashing"), who have become probably the most frequent victims of hate-motivated violence (Zuckerman, 1988).

The greater antipathy toward gays is ascribed mainly to the AIDS epidemic. The way that the AIDS problem evolves is likely to have further impact on the legal status of gays in the foreseeable future.

## SEXUAL OFFENSES AGAINST PERSONS

It is clear that we need laws on sexual offenses against persons. What sorts of laws would be best, both to deter such behavior and to protect the rights of the offenders?

### Rape

Common law defines rape as unlawful sexual intercourse by a man with a woman other than his wife and without her consent. "By force and against her will' is the common phrase used in statutory definitions, but rape need not, and does not always, involve physical violence. Sexual intercourse under the threat of violence or under circumstances when the woman is incapable of giving consent (such as when drunk or unconscious) can also constitute rape. If the victim is below the "age of consent," the act is called *statutory rape,* irrespective of the issue of consent (Chapter 19).

Social attitudes toward rape have ranged from fairly mild to severe condemnation. Rape was punishable by death under Saxon laws and under English common law. This English tradition was carried to the colonies, where the earliest statutory prohibition of rape appeared in 1649 in the laws of Massachusetts: "If any man shall ravish any maid, or single woman,

committing carnal copulation with her by force, against her will . . . he shall be punished either with death or some other grievous punishment according to the circumstances" (quoted in *Commonwealth v. Chretien,* 1981). Other cultures have also punished rape with severity (Box 22.3).

At present rape is punishable only by imprisonment. For example, in California it carries a sentence of three, six, or eight years, depending on circumstances (California Penal Code, Section 264). The sentence, however, can be longer if multiple crimes were committed, if a weapon was used, or if great bodily injury was inflicted. One study, based on 1976–77 sentencing data, showed that nationally the average time served for rape was 52 months (*National Law Journal,* 1981).

One of the primary legal problems in rape cases is the determination of *consent.* Because it has been linked to the character and sexual motivations of the woman, rape cases in the courtroom have been tellingly called "man's trial, woman's tribulation." The wish to be spared this tribulation is one of the reasons so many women have let rapes go unreported. Legal practices and attitudes have been changing, but consent continues to be a problem.[5]

Under traditional rape statutes, courts usually demanded proof of utmost resistance by the victim to show that the act was against her will: "A mere tactical surrender in the face of assumed superior physical force is not enough . . . resistance must be to the utmost" (*King v. State,* 357 S.W.2d 42, 45) (Tennessee, 1962). In this regard, rape laws have been unique. If you are being robbed, for example, the law does not require that you put up any resistance; yet a woman who was sexually assaulted had to demonstrate her lack of consent by resisting in every possible way until overcome by force, exhaustion, fear of death, or great bodily harm. There is an interesting presumption underlying this discrepancy:

[5]For a description of the legal procedure in a trial for rape, see Lasater (1980). The hardships imposed on rape victims by the legal system are discussed in detail by Brownmiller (1975).

whereas no one willingly parts with wallet or purse, the abuse of a woman's body may conceal a hidden wish on her part to give herself to the molester (see the discussion of "victim precipitation" in Chapter 19).

There have been recent major revisions in rape laws. It is much less likely that a victim will now undergo the sort of humiliating experience that formerly characterized rape trials. The police are more sensitive in dealing with victims, and states like New York have established special investigation units, staffed by women who combine counseling with obtaining evidence. The woman's sexual history may still be admissible in some states, but the majority now have restrictions in this regard. Similarly, the tendency is to minimize or eliminate altogether resistance requirements with the recognition that fear can have a paralyzing effect on a woman's behavior and that a woman should not be expected to risk bodily injury in addition to suffering the agony of rape. In Michigan, for instance, the rape statute flatly states that the woman "need not resist" (Michigan, Section 750.520). California removed the resistance requirement in 1980 (California Penal Code, Section 261-2). In addition, the majority of states have ruled out testimony about the victim's past sexual relations with third parties.

The severity of punishment for rape may contribute to the difficulty of getting convictions. It is sometimes argued that if penalties for rape were milder, many more offenders would be convicted; thus the law might be a better deterrent. On the other hand, making the penalty more severe might also deter more rapes.

Courts are also concerned with the rights of the accused. A man could be falsely accused of rape, and where there is no sign of struggle or injury, it would be a case of her word against his as to what really happened. Gary Dotson was convicted for a rape and sentenced for a 25- to 50-year prison term. Six years later his accuser recanted her testimony and said she had lied at the time because she thought she was pregnant by her boyfriend and wanted to conceal the fact. The description she made up

of the "rapist" somehow fit Dotson. Though Dotson was subsequently released on probation, doubts of his innocence have continued to linger (Starr and King, 1985). The case has proven troublesome, because it can be used to cast doubt on the testimony of rape victims. Fear of unjustly punishing the innocent may allow the guilty to go unpunished.

Another controversial issue is whether and to what extent an offender should be allowed to use the defense that the victim precipitated the attack. In a 1977 case in Madison, Wisconsin, involving the rape of a teenage girl by another student in the school stairwell, the judge let the offender off with a probation sentence because he considered the victim to have acted provocatively: "Whether women like it or not, they are sex objects. Are we supposed to take an impressionable person, 15 or 16 years of age, and punish that person severely because they react to it normally?" (*New York Times*, May 17, 1977). The judge in this case was voted out of office, and such considerations are now increasingly viewed as inappropriate.

### Marital Rape

Another recent debate has been on the issue of the *spousal exclusion* from rape laws. According to the Anglo-American Common Law, a husband could not be charged with the rape of his wife; the classic statement of the doctrine is Lord Matthew Hale's declaration that "the husband cannot be guilty of rape committed by himself upon his lawful wife, for by their mutual matrimonial consent and contract the wife hath given up herself in this kind unto her husband, which she cannot retract" ("To Have and to Hold," 1986, pp. 1255–56). It has been assumed that "marriage constitutes a blanket consent to sexual intimacy which the woman may revoke only by dissolving the marital relationship" (*Model Penal Code*, Article 213(1), Comment, revised 1980). As of June 1980, 37 states do not recognize a woman's right to charge her husband with rape while they are living together. (She can charge him with assault if he physically molests her.)

Currently, ten states expressly allow the prosecution of a man for raping his wife. Eight state legislatures have rejected the marital rape exemption (Florida, Kansas, Massachusetts, Nebraska, New Jersey, Oregon, Vermont, and Wisconsin), and in two states (New York and Georgia) the courts have invalidated the doctrine. ("To Have and to Hold," 1986, p. 1259).

In states that still have the marital rape exemption, its coverage depends on the stability of the marriage. Some states suspend the exemption only if the husband and wife are living apart at the time of the incident; some states only if the two are separated by court order; some states only if one party has filed for annulment, separation, divorce, or separate maintenance; and some only if the final divorce decree has come down ("To Have and to Hold," pp. 1259–60).

Massachusetts was the first to convict a husband for raping his wife (*Commonwealth v. Chretien,* Massachusetts, 1981). The couple were in the process of getting divorced when the man broke into his wife's home and raped her. The matter is more complex when a woman is raped when living with her husband. The *Stave v. Rideout* case (Oregon Cir. Ct., 1978) was the first prosecution of this type and brought national attention to the issue. The husband was charged with rape by his wife, but he was acquitted; shortly after the verdict the couple was reconciled; then they separated again (*New York Times,* March 10, 1979).

The law presumes women to be incapable of forcing sex on men against their will; hence there are no laws protecting men against heterosexual rape (though some laws use the gender-neutral term "spouse" instead of "husband" or "wife"). As we saw in Chapter 19, some men are in fact raped by women. Similarly, rape laws do not extend to homosexual assaults; the law deals with them through sodomy statutes. Currently many states, including California, have adopted statutes that define rape in sex-neutral terms. These laws would apply to homosexual rapes as well.

## Sexual Offenses Against the Young

Our society considers unacceptable all sexual interactions between adults and children (Chapters 8 and 14). The behaviors proscribed by law in this area fall in two categories: sexual interactions with *postpubescent* but legally underage youth and sexual exploitation of *prepubescent* children.

Statutory Rape    The law prohibits sexual intercourse with persons below the age of consent, which in most states is set between the ages of 16 and 18. The age of consent for statutory rape may be as low as 12 years (as in North Carolina), but a man would still be guilty of the lesser offense of "taking indecent liberties with a child" by having sex with a girl younger than 16. Well over half the states (but not California and New York) have adopted a sex-neutral definition of victim and offender, although the overwhelming majority of adult offenders are male (Chapter 19).

Rarely a woman is prosecuted for having had sex with a male under the age of consent. In 1978 the New Mexico Supreme Court reversed a court of appeals ruling that had found sexual intercourse permissible between a 23-year-old woman and a 15-year-old boy (*San Francisco Chronicle,* February 26, 1978, p. 3). In a challenge to the California statutory rape law, the Supreme Court upheld its constitutionality even though the statute clearly discriminates against men in that the male offender himself need not be an adult. In another Supreme Court case, a 16-year-old female and a 17-year-old male had intercourse; the girl's parents filed charges against the young man, and he was arrested. In a 5-to-4 opinion the Court held that such discrimination was justified on the grounds that males, unlike females, were not subject to the consequences of teenage pregnancy (*Michael, M. v. Superior Court,* 450 U.S. 464, 1981).

The law in this area reflects society's concerns over the sexual abuse and exploitation of youngsters by adults; but it also reflects an assumption that sex ought not to be part of preadult behavior, however unrealistic that assumption may be. How these age limits are set and why they are changed is itself not always clear. For example, the age of consent in California was raised from 10 to 14 in 1889, to 16 in 1897, and to 18 years in 1913, where it now stands. Meanwhile, the age of puberty has gone down and teenagers have come to enjoy a far greater range of sexual freedom. The legal assumption that 16- or 17-year-old women are incapable of consent seems inconsistent with other freedoms being accorded to them, which also have considerable social consequences (such as the license to drive cars).

The dissociation of biological maturity from arbitrary legal limits also raises the possibility of men being deceived by girls who look older and lie about their age. Such considerations could not be used as a defense against a charge of statutory rape in the past, but today a majority of states do not consider as criminal sexual interactions engaged in by men under a reasonable belief that the girl is above the age of consent. Evidence of the girl's promiscuity or being a prostitute is also considered relevant in some states.

Child Molestation    Sexual offenses involving younger children are severely punished in all states. The California statute is typical:

> 288. *Crime Against Children: Lewd or Lascivious Acts.* (a) Any person who shall willfully and lewdly commit any lewd or lascivious act, including any of the acts constituting other crimes provided for in Part I of the Code, upon or with the body, or with any part or member thereof, of a child under the age of fourteen (14) years, with the intent of arousing, appealing to, or gratifying the lust or passions or sexual desires of such persons, or of such child, shall be guilty of a felony and shall be imprisoned in the State prison for a term of three, five, or seven years (California Penal Code, Section 288).

Incest with minors constitutes another form of child molestation. All states have criminal prohibition against incest, usually in the form of *consanguinity laws,* which restrict marriage and sexual relationships between close relatives (about half the states also forbid marriages between first cousins).

Consanguinity laws go back to Leviticus 18:6–18 and 20:11–12. Although incest was not a crime under English common law, it attained criminal status in English statutory law in 1908. Laws governing incest vary a good deal from one state to another. They also tend to be confusing, because incest statutes simultaneously try to accomplish two separate aims: the prevention of consanguinious marriage between relatives and the prevention of the sexual abuse of children. For instance, a typical statute reads:

> *Incest.* Any person who knowingly marries or has sexual relations with an ancestor or descendant, a brother or sister of whole or half blood, or an uncle or aunt, nephew, or niece of whole blood commits incest, which is a Class 5 felony.

> *Aggravated Incest.* (1) Any person who has sexual intercourse with his or her natural child, stepchild, or child by adoption, unless legally married to the stepchild or child by adoption, commits aggravated incest [which is] a Class 4 felony (Colorado Rev. Stat., Section 18-60-302).

The most common penalty for incest in the United States is ten years in prison, though some states (Georgia and Nebraska) have maximum sentences of up to 20 years. The more specific problem of parent-child incest is further dealt with through the statutory rape laws.

## Public Nuisance Offenses

Unwarranted exposure of the body or furtive attempts to view someone else's exposed body intrude upon people's privacy and are considered offensive; therefore, laws prohibit such conduct. The legal definitions of *voyeurism* and *exhibitionism* are not identical with the broader meaning in which these terms are used in the sexual literature (Chapter 14). As legally defined, virtually all exhibitionists and voyeurs are male. The law's concern with female nudity is from the perspective of obscenity, rather than exhibitionism.

Laws are currently highly liberal with regard to *nudity.* People sunbathing in nudist camps or in the privacy of their own backyards are left alone; the concern of the law is with people who offend public sensibilities by making a spectacle of themselves.

The majority of sexual nuisance offenses are committed by male exhibitionists ("flashers"), who constitute almost one-third of all reported sex offenders. Exhibitionists do offend and frighten women and children, but they do not generally molest them physically. Therefore in California the offense is now classified as a misdemeanor, but it becomes a felony on repetition (California Penal Code, Section 314). Some people question the appropriateness of imprisonment for these offenders.

## LAWS ON COMMERCIAL EXPLOITATION OF SEX

### Prostitution

As we discussed earlier (Chapter 18), Roman law defined prostitution as the offering of one's body for sale, indiscriminately and without pleasure. The term encompasses a wide range of sexual interactions with varying meanings at the personal and societal levels.

Prostitution is illegal in the United States with the exception of the state of Nevada, which permits prostitution by local option in counties with populations of less than 250,000 (Nevada Rev. Stat., Section 244.345 1979). This provision makes prostitution illegal in Nevada's two major cities: Las Vegas and Reno. Although numerous prostitutes operate in these cities, legalization would reinforce their reputation as "sin cities" and possibly scare away tourism and conventions.

Prostitution is a misdemeanor in most states with maximum jail sentences of 90 to 180 days, but the usual penalty is a fine or a few days in jail. In a "revolving door" pattern, prostitutes who get arrested are back on the streets before the ink has dried on the police blotter and consider the fines part of the expense of running their business.

Current statutes are gender-neutral and define acts of prostitution in terms broader than coitus. The California statute, for instance, prohibits anyone from soliciting or engaging in "any lewd act between persons for money or other consideration" (California Penal Code, Section 647). The offense most frequently prosecuted is not prostitution but *solicitation,* which is a misdemeanor. A typical ordinance makes it illegal to loiter in or near a public place:

> Any person who remains or wanders about in a public place and repeatedly beckons to, or repeatedly stops, or repeatedly attempts to stop, or repeatedly attempts to engage passers-by in conversation, or repeatedly stops or attempts to stop motor vehicles, or repeatedly interferes with the free passage of other persons, for the purpose of prostitution, or of patronizing a prostitute shall be guilty of a misdemeanor (New York Penal Law, Section 240.37).

There are more severe penalties in all states for *pimping* (living off the earnings of a prostitute) and *pandering* (recruiting prostitutes). They are usually felonies with maximum sentences ranging from four to ten years. Inducting a child into prostitution is an even more serious offense.

The person least threatened by the law is the customer (or the "John," as prostitutes call him). In some jurisdictions it is not an offense to use the services of a prostitute; even where there are laws against the practice, the customer is much less likely to be arrested. The justification is that the customer may be a married and respectable man; prosecuting him would constitute a disproportionately serious penalty, whereas the reputation of the prostitute is not an issue. Apart from the matter of equity, experience has shown that cracking down on customers is a more effective deterrent; yet police crackdowns are opposed by those with commercial interests on the grounds that it would be bad for the tourist and convention business (Kaplan, 1977).

If the success of prostitution laws is to be judged by their efficacy in eliminating it, then clearly they have failed: an estimated 100,000 prostitutes operate full time and an undetermined number of others do so on an occasional basis. Whether we would be better off without these laws has been debated endlessly.

Those who support the legal status quo are aware of its shortcomings, but they regard present laws as preferable to the alternatives: *decriminalization,* which would remove criminal sanctions for prostitution itself but would retain some legal penalties for related offenses such as pimping or procurement; full-scale *legalization,* which would free the whole area of all legal constraints; and *regulation,* which would impose licensing and other regulatory requirements (including taxation) by the state.

Arguments Against Legalization    Some of the arguments for keeping prostitution illegal are based on moral considerations. Given the general assumption that prostitution at best is a necessary evil, a state's formal declaration of its legality would reflect poorly on society's ethical standards. Others compare prostitution to slavery (*white slavery*) in which women are exploited, degraded, and held captive by circumstances beyond their control; hence, prostitution could not be legitimized in good conscience. If the legal restraints were lifted, it is feared that prostitution would become even more prevalent, with attendant increases in venereal disease and criminal behaviors, like muggings and drug abuse, which often go with it. (This increase did not happen in several European countries such as Holland when prostitution was legalized.)

Other concerns have to do with the potential impact of legalizing prostitution on women who are on welfare. Given the general expectation that people should not be dependent upon the state whenever possible, social agencies may pressure poor women into such gainful activity once it is legal. The Welfare Mothers of Nevada has already lodged complaints to this effect (Kaplan, 1977).

Any attempt to regulate prostitution will inevitably involve some form of registration of prostitutes for certification, health, and tax purposes. Given the value placed on exclusivity in sex and the onus placed on "selling" oneself, prostitution is likely to remain a socially despised activity even if legalized. Hence, registration will *stigmatize* these women for the rest of their lives. Large numbers of women work as prostitutes for limited periods of time and then go on to marry or get a respectable line of work; in either case, getting out of prostitution may well be complicated by their being formally branded with this label.

Arguments in Favor of Legalization    Arguments in favor of legalizing prostitution seek a frank and realistic appraisal of where matters stand. *The Wolfenden Report,* which we cited with regard to homosexuality, also dealt with prostitution. It made the following assessment:

> Prostitution is a social fact deplorable in the eyes of moralists, sociologists and, we believe, the great majority of ordinary people. But it has persisted in many civilizations throughout many centuries, and the failure of attempts to stamp it out by repressive legislation shows that it cannot be eradicated through the agency of the criminal law. It remains true that without a demand for her services the prostitute could not exist, and that there are enough men who avail themselves of prostitutes to keep the trade alive. It also remains true that there are women who, even when there is no economic need to do so, choose this form of livelihood. For so long as these propositions continue to be true there will be prostitution, and no amount of legislation directed towards its abolition will abolish it (*The Wolfenden Report,* 1963).

The fact that the law does not prohibit a given behavior does not mean that society condones it. That the quality of interpersonal relationships in sex with prostitutes leaves something to be desired, does not mean that it should be the responsibility of the law to improve it. Besides, prostitution does not really compete for the affections of those who are fortunate enough to have warm and loving relationships, but acts as a temporary or permanent substitute for persons lacking such ties. For at least some of their clients, prostitutes may represent the only available sexual outlets.

The money-making potential of prostitution, particularly for those with limited education and skills, gives rise to concern that the market would be flooded with new recruits if the practice were legalized. However, it does not seem to have happened in countries where prostitution is legal (such as in Sweden, Holland, and parts of Germany). As long as the moral, social, and psychological constraints against the practice remain as strong as they are now, it is not a likely prospect in this country either.

The danger of STDs is real, and it has gained a new urgency with AIDS. However, if prostitutes are going to be out there (as they have always been), there is much to be gained by lessening the risk of infection through safer sex practices, regular medical checks, and treatment if necessary, which the law could enforce and monitor, as in Nevada brothels (Chapter 18).

Regulation, rather than blanket prohibition, makes it possible to deal more appropriately with different types of prostitution (Chapter 18). Streetwalkers, for instance, pose the greatest hazards to themselves and to their clients. Such activity could be more realistically suppressed if a preferred form of prostitution (such as licensed brothels) could be allowed to meet the need.

Critics of the present law argue that it not only fails to eradicate prostitution but creates other problems. For instance, having been declared a criminal, the prostitute has little to lose if she robs her client as well. Because the enterprise needs to be run by someone, criminal elements (including organized crime) inevitably take charge; the prostitute is caught between the law, which prosecutes her, and the pimps who exploit and keep her in bondage. It is therefore conceivable that if prostitution were legalized and properly regulated, many of its unsavory characteristics could disappear.

We get a glimpse of this possibility from the experience of surrogate partners used by some sex therapists (Chapter 15). The detractors of this practice may think of these women as prostitutes, but the women themselves and their therapeutic sponsors do not, which allows them to maintain self-esteem and prompts them to deal with their clients in ways different from the way most prostitutes do.

The debate over prostitution may be cast in abstract terms, but the main practical concern is getting the streetwalkers off the streets. The approach in Britain has been to legalize prostitution but not solicitation; sexual services are made known through discreet cards affixed to doors in select areas. In this country, call girls operate with similar discretion. Another alternative would be to legalize houses of prostitution. This approach would permit the state to protect the prostitute and the client (and tax the earnings of the house). It would significantly free the prostitute from exploitation and at least some of her dependence on the pimp. In short, prostitution would become one more service industry.

Finally, some feminists argue that a woman owns her own body, and how she uses it is her own business, including the selling of sexual services (Millett, 1973). To prevent the exploitation of prostitutes by pimps without shifting control to the state, it is proposed that prostitution be decriminalized, but not regulated by the state—a solution with its own problems.

## Pornography

In Chapter 18 we discussed attempts to define pornography. The main burden of that task eventually falls on the law; if pornography is to be controlled by laws against it, they must first clearly state what pornography is.

The law has avoided extreme views that hold as obscene either all or no form of public sexual expression. The law thus reflects the commonsense feeling that some sexual expression is healthy but that at some point such expression crosses over to the pornographic. The problem is in drawing the line.

Over the past decade, an unprecedented degree of explicitness has become permissible in public media, including films. The courts have faced two basic problems: first is the *threat of pornography* to public morality and safety; second is the *threat of censorship* to our constitutionally guaranteed freedom of expression.

The Dangers of Pornography    As we discussed in Chapter 18, the potential harm of pornography is both immediate and long-term. Long-term damaging effects are thought to include a greater likelihood of violence against women and discrimination against them. But there is still no general agreement about the effects of pornography on sexual behavior as such. Meanwhile, other critics call pornography a form of sexual discrimination.

A model antipornography law has been drafted by feminist legal activists Catherine MacKinnon and Andrea Dworkin which makes it a civil rights violation to coerce someone into the production of pornography, trafficking in pornography, forcing pornography on a person, and to cause assault or physical attack due to pornography. Pornography is defined as "a systematic practice of exploitation and subordination based on sex that differentially harms women" (Blakely, 1985, p. 46).

This model antipornography law has been tested in several locations, and as we shall discuss farther on, it has been turned down by voters or in court, usually on the grounds that it is too vague and would limit free speech (Blakely, 1985). For example, the MacKinnon-Dworkin ordinance was offered in Minneapolis to legally limit the production and distribution of pornography. The ordinance would have allowed private parties to sue the makers, distributors, and exhibitors of pornography for injuries directly caused by specific pornography. The most controversial provision of the act would have allowed any women to sue any trafficker of pornography. The proposed justification was that pornography is exploitative of women; it harms women's opportunity for employment and education and promotes "degradation such as rape, battery, and prostitution" (Brest and Vandenberg, 1987, p. 616). The proposal never became law in Minneapolis, but a similar ordinance was passed in Indianapolis. That ordinance was struck down by the U.S. Court of Appeals for the Seventh Circuit as a violation of the First Amendment. More specifically, the ordinance could operate against works which have serious literary, ar-

tistic, political, or scientific value and are therefore protected by the First Amendment according to *Miller v. California.* The Supreme Court summarily affirmed the decision in 1986 (Brest and Vandenberg, 1987).

Other feminists (Duggan et al., 1985) and a wide array of civil libertarians oppose such legislation—not because they are in favor of pornography but because they fear such laws will compromise hard-won sexual freedoms and threaten fundamental civil liberties. The threat is censorship.

The Problem of Censorship    Free speech is one of the key safeguards of democratic freedom, and attempts to interfere with it raise the specter of suppression of political dissent. Arguments over the freedom of artistic expression, which constitute the bulk of the debate in this area, are thus but one manifestation of a more fundamental political concern.

Social perceptions of what is obscene and attempts at its control have varied in Western culture, but prevailing attitudes have generally been restrictive. Heightened public preoccupation with censorship in the 19th century was not merely a reflection of the greater prudishness of the times, but a reaction to technological developments that made it possible for sexually explicit materials to come into the hands of the masses (Chapter 18).

In the United States, the most significant response to this threat was the passage of Section 1461, Title 18, of the U.S. Code in 1873, which made it a felony to knowingly transmit through the United States mail any "obscene, lewd, lascivious, indecently filthy, or vile article. . . ." Popularly known as the *Comstock Act,* it was in part the fruit of the efforts of Anthony Comstock (1844–1915), founder of the New York Society for the Suppression of Vice. As a special agent of the United States Post Office and through the efforts of his organization, Comstock was responsible, over a period of eight years, for the confiscation of 203,238 pictures and photographs and the destruction of 27,548 pounds of books and 1,376,939 circulars, catalogs, songs, and poems that were considered obscene (Kilpatrick, 1960).

Over the past several decades decisions by the Supreme Court have reversed this trend and placed pornography in a new legal perspective. The first landmark case in recent times involved a New York publisher and bookseller, Samuel Roth, who was convicted of mailing a book and other sexually explicit materials in violation of federal obscenity statutes. In ruling against Roth, the Court held obscenity to be outside of the area of the freedom of speech protected by the First Amendment (*Roth v. U.S.*, 354 U.S. 476, 1956); but the Court also made a distinction between what is pornographic and what is merely sexually explicit, using the criteria of prurience and absence of redeeming social importance. These considerations were refined in *Miller v. California* in 1973 to set the standards that currently govern decisions in this area. They define obscenity based on

> (a) whether the average person, applying contemporary community standards, would find that the work, taken as a whole, appeals to the prurient interest; (b) whether the work depicts or describes, in a patently offensive way, sexual conduct specifically defined by the applicable state law; and (c) whether the work, taken as a whole, lacks serious literary, artistic, political, or scientific value (*Miller v. California*, 413 U.S. 15, 1973).

The condition of *prurience* means evident erotic intent (thus a protester carrying a sign that says "fuck the draft" is not guilty of obscenity) (*Cohen v. California*, 403 U.S. 15, 1971). The object of concern is the *average person* and not those who are overly sensitive or insensitive to these matters; the standards are those of a particular *community*, making it possible for something to be obscene in one place but not another.

The second condition requires that the item in question be *patently offensive* to violate the law. State rules in this regard cannot be vague, but must clearly specify what it is they are proscribing. The third and last condition is broader than its historical antecedents, which required that the offensive item be shown as being "utterly without redeeming so-

cial importance." The burden has now shifted to the character of the work "taken as a whole." Thus, "a quotation from Voltaire in the flyleaf of a book will not constitutionally redeem an otherwise obscene publication" (*Miller v. California*, supra.). By the same token, the presence of isolated obscene segments in a work will not necessarily condemn it. Under earlier law some of the world's greatest art and literature (even the Bible) could be declared pornographic, because isolated segments could conceivably be called obscene.

Within these constitutional bounds set by the Supreme Court, individual states are free to adopt their own definitions of obscenity. It is also constitutionally permissible for states to restrict a minor's access to sex materials that may not be considered obscene by adult standards. For example, in California, "every person who, with knowledge that a person is a minor, or who fails to exercise reasonable care in ascertaining the true age of a minor, knowingly distributes . . . or exhibits any harmful matter to the minor is guilty of a misdemeanor" (California Penal Code, Section 313.1a).

To counter "kiddie porn," California has made its distribution a felony punishable by imprisonment for two, three, or four years, or a fine not exceeding $50,000 (California Penal Code, Section 311.2). Nebraska has passed an ordinance that proscribes possession of child pornography, and several other states have initiated similar statutes.

Generally, however, the law's concern is not with the private but with the public aspects of pornography. The possession of obscene matter or its use in private has not been a crime (*Stanley v. Georgia*, 394 U.S. 557, 1969), but this right of privacy does not extend beyond the home. The government has the right to regulate commerce in such materials, including the prohibition of their distribution through the mails (*U.S. v. Reidel*, 402 U.S. 351, 1971).

The Supreme Court has not spoken with one voice on the issue of obscenity; in the 33 obscenity cases in which the Court has written opinions, the justices have articulated 121 separate opinions. The Court's seeming vacillation frustrates many people. Some object on principle to the law's impinging on any and all freedom of sexual expression; or if they concede the need for such restraint, they have problems with the particular criteria used. Others are frustrated at the inability of the law to curtail what seems to them so obviously offensive.

Neither the judiciary nor the public is, by and large, concerned any more with what hangs on museum walls. Rather, their problem is with the exploitation of every freedom granted by the courts to the purveyors of pornography. No less distressing is the sort of material that has found its way to television, the most widely shared experience in the country.

Almost everyone agrees that there is a problem at one level or another. The disagreement is over what the law should do about

it. The twin specters of pornography and censorship have split feminists into antipornography and anticensorship camps. Sex educators, researchers, and clinicians are equally ambivalent. They fret about the pervasive negative effects of pornography and they fear that antipornography legislation will "slouch toward censorship" (Lynn, 1986), be used as an elitist weapon (Udow, 1985), and reverse the hard-won freedoms of the sexual revolution.

The dilemma is not new and reflects our broader attitude towards government. Americans have always wanted it both ways: individual freedom and social control. As Gunnar Myrdal, the Swedish economist, once pointed out, Americans will say, "No one can tell me what to do" and add in the same breath, 'There ought to be a law against that" (Stengel, 1986).

## REVIEW QUESTIONS

1. What is the current status of laws regulating contraception and abortion?

2. How do laws governing heterosexual and homosexual behavior differ?

3. What are the laws that pertain to different types of rape?

4. What are the arguments for and against legalizing prostitution?

5. What are the legal grounds on which a book or painting can now be declared obscene?

## THOUGHT QUESTIONS

1. Argue in favor of or against having laws concerning sexual behavior other than offenses against persons.

2. How would you reconcile a woman's right to control her body and society's need to safeguard the welfare of generations "yet unborn"?

3. If prostitution were legalized, how would you react to the prospect of college students supporting their education through part-time prostitution? Would it be more acceptable if unskilled and unemployed high school dropouts were to do it?

4. Argue for and against the idea that convicted rapists should be imprisoned for life.

5. How would you devise an antipornography law that would simultaneously prohibit the exploitation of women and safeguard the freedom of sexual expression?

## SUGGESTED READINGS

Estrich, S. (1987). *Real rape.* Cambridge, MA.: Harvard University Press. An overview of rape laws and ways of reforming the present legal approaches to rape.

MacNamara, D. E. J., and Sagarin, E. (1977). *Sex, crime, and the law.* New York: Free Press. An overview of the behavioral and legal aspects of socially problematic sexual behaviors and offenses.

Reimer, R. A. (1986). *Legal analysis of the Attorney General's Commission on Pornography's final report.* Washington, D.C.: Library of Congress. Summary and critique of the Meese Commission report.

Wasserstrom, R. A. (Ed.) (1971). *Morality and the law.* Belmont, Ca.: Wadsworth. A collection of readings on the question of whether the immorality of a behavior can ever, by itself, be sufficient justification for making that kind of behavior illegal.

*The Wolfenden Report* (1963). New York: Stein and Day. Despite the passage of more than 20 years, this thoughtful treatise on the laws pertaining to homosexuality and prostitution (in the United Kingdom) remains a good model of clear thinking and common sense.

# Sex and Morality

*The experience of sin in sexual relations does not wither away even for those who are emancipated from restrictive rules of conduct.*

JAMES M. GUSTAFSON

OUTLINE

THE BASES OF SEXUAL ETHICS
Secular Bases
Religious Bases
THE CONSERVATIVE MORAL
  PERSPECTIVE
The Case for Conservative Morality
  Biblical Grounds
  The Teaching of the Church
  Natural Law
The Case Against Conservative
  Morality
  The Biblical Record
  The Teaching of the Church
  Natural Law

THE LIBERAL MORAL
  PERSPECTIVE
The Case for Liberal Morality
  The Perspective of Judaism
  New Directions in Catholic Morality
  Experiential Bases of Moral
    Judgment
  Situation Ethics
  Secular Morality
The Case Against Liberal Morality
  The Conceptual Critique
  The Consequences

The topic of morality may sound dull to you, but nothing could be farther from the truth. You probably have had strong reactions to something in every chapter of this book—considered it good or bad, right or wrong. You probably have weighed your own choices, experiences, and hopes against all the human possibilities we have explored. If so, your moral sense has been at work.

People tend to think of sexual morality as a set of "thou shalt nots." True, some moral principles have been abused to suppress sexuality, but they also can keep sexual relationships fair, honest, and strong. Rules of conduct protect our freedom and independence as individuals and as a society. If some moral laws are regularly broken, it may mean that they have outlived their usefulness—or it may mean we need a stronger sense of responsibility.

The words *morality* and *ethics* are derived from the Latin *mores* and Greek *ethos,* terms for habit or custom. They represent society's judgment as to what is right or wrong, virtuous or evil, in the actions and characters of human beings. Morality is that aspect of our human nature and experience that "expresses in personal conduct, in society, and in culture ways to order our natural impulses and to guide and govern our actions and relations for the sake of individual and collective well-being" (Gustafson 1981, p. 484).

The issue of responsibility is central to all moral judgments and is in turn based on the concept of *free will.* You can only be held morally responsible for acts over which you have some control, where your actions are voluntary. Concepts like free will become especially perplexing if we take into account social and biological determinants of behavior. These influences seem to leave us little autonomy; yet we still need to make responsible choices. Moral considerations are, for better or worse, part of the fabric of our society and our laws.

## THE BASES OF SEXUAL ETHICS

Individuals and societies make their moral judgments either on religious or secular grounds. In the Western world the first is based on faith in the will of God; the second, on human principles. Secular and religious morality start with different assumptions, but they have a great deal in common, because all ethical considerations ultimately revolve around human welfare. Though the modern world appears to be largely secular, four out of five persons in the United States continue to profess some form of religious belief. Nevertheless, secular thought now exerts a powerful moral influence, even when it coexists with religious belief.

### Secular Bases
*Moral philosophy* is the field of knowledge that deals with ethical issues. Typically, the thoughts of individual philosophers have been based on certain assumptions about human nature and the common good, which are expanded through abstract arguments. For example, for Aristotle, the guide to ethical action was the avoidance of extremes and adherence to the "mean" or middle ground. Emmanual Kant's "categorical imperative" restated the principle of the "Golden Rule": "Do not do unto others what you do not want others to do unto you."

In modern secular societies, moral precepts are based on political ideology. For instance, in the Western democracies, individual freedom and personal responsibility are guiding principles; in Communist countries, morality is based on Marxist-Leninist principles of the responsibility of individuals to the community.

When sociologists and psychologists deal with attitudes and values, they address some of the very problems that have preoccupied moral philosophers. Their work on the causes and effects of sexual behavior has a clear bearing on ethics. For example, if it could be reliably determined what impact premarital sex has on marital happiness, it would help us decide whether sex before marriage is right. Similarly anthropologists and historians who show us morality across cultures and times give us insight into our own moral views on sex today.

The most recent contributions to this field have come from ethologists and sociobiologists who have examined the evolutionary development of *altruism*. There are numerous examples in the animal world where members of a group come to each other's aid, sometimes endangering themselves in the process. For example, porpoises will circle around females giving birth, protecting them from sharks; if one is wounded, others will carry it to the surface where it can breathe (Wilson, 1975). When soldiers die for their country and parents go hungry to feed their children, to what extent are they behaving like altruistic animals?

## Religious Bases

There are two fundamental differences between the religious and secular derivation of moral precepts. The secular approach relies on *reason;* the religious approach, on *revelation.* The basis for the former is thinking and observation; for the latter, it is faith. In the secular perspective, human happiness is the final goal. Happiness may be understood in different ways; the emphasis may be on the individual or on the collective good; yet in all circumstances, human beings are the measure. In the Judeo-Christian perspective, God is the measure and all other considerations, including human happiness, are secondary. The religious perspective does not disregard reason nor human welfare and happiness, but it considers them subservient to doing God's will.

Although moral judgments sound absolute, more often right and wrong lie on a continuum. Still, to highlight the issue of ethical choices, we will discuss the issue of sexual morality from two contrasting perspectives: *conservative* and *liberal.* We shall first describe the main premises of each and then present arguments for and against them. Centuries of debate over these issues have yet to exhaust these arguments and counterarguments. Our purpose here is neither to tell it all nor to take sides, but to challenge your thinking. Then you can figure out where you stand, and why.

## THE CONSERVATIVE MORAL PERSPECTIVE

Those who adhere to the conservative moral view usually uphold traditional morality; they "conserve" the ethical outlook that has been tried and found true in the past. Within Christianity, the conservative view is exemplified by the teachings of the Catholic church and Evangelical Protestants. However, sexual conservatism need not be religious or traditional. For instance, Chinese communism, whose sexual values are highly conservative, is purely secular and vehemently antitraditional.

The conservative perspective is absolutist. Its behavioral codes are predetermined for you. Certain sexual behaviors are deemed right, others wrong; individuals do not have a say about it. Specific rules are to guide your conduct; hence the conservative approach tends to be legalistic. Moral precepts in this view are systematically argued and their application to sexual behaviors is explicitly spelled out.

The conservative moral view generally restricts the range of sexual behaviors. Typically, it accepts heterosexual coitus in marriage as the only morally acceptable form of sex. To illustrate the applications of the conservative moral perspective to sexual behaviors, we will focus on the Catholic church, which has addressed these issues over many centuries (Chapter 20), and claims to have maintained a clear and constant perspective on these issues.

The authoritative current statement of the Catholic church on sexuality is the 1968 Encyclical Letter of Pope Paul VI, *Humanae Vitae* (Box 23.1). An *encyclical* is a papal "letter" on a specific subject addressed to the hierarchy and the faithful of the church. Encyclicals are pastoral devices, not formally argued, comprehensive theological documents. Nevertheless they carry enormous weight in the official teaching of the church.

Though primarily addressed to the issue of contraception, *Humanae Vitae* ("human life") expounds a fundamental moral standard for all sexual behaviors. Sexuality is a source of "great joy," but marriage is the only legitimate context for sexual experience that is "honor-

# Box 23.1

In the light of these facts the characteristic features and exigencies of married love are clearly indicated, and it is of the highest importance to evaluate them exactly.

This love is above all fully *human,* a compound of sense and spirit. It is not, then, merely a question of natural instinct or emotional drive. It is also, and above all, an act of the free will, whose dynamism ensures that not only does it endure through the joys and sorrows of daily life, but also that it grows, so that husband and wife become in a way one heart and one soul, and together attain their human fulfillment.

Then it is love which is *total*—that very special form of personal friendship in which husband and wife generously share everything, allowing no unreasonable exceptions or thinking just of their own interests. Whoever really loves his partner loves not only for what he receives, but loves that partner for her own sake, content to be able to enrich the other with the gift of himself.

Again, married love is *faithful* and *exclusive* of all other, and this until death. This is how husband and wife understood it on the day on which, fully aware of what they were doing, they freely vowed themselves to one another in marriage. Though this fidelity of husband and wife sometimes presents difficulties, no one can assert that it is impossible, for it is always honorable and worthy of the highest esteem. The example of so many married persons down through the centuries shows not only that fidelity is connatural to marriage, but also that it is the source of profound and enduring happiness.

And finally this love is *creative of life,* for it is not exhausted by the loving interchange of husband and wife, but also contrives to go beyond this to bring new life into being. "Marriage and married love are by their character ordained to the procreation and bringing up of children. Children are the outstanding gift of marriage, and contribute in the highest degree to the parents' welfare."

This particular doctrine, often expounded by the Magisterium of the Church, is based on the inseparable connection, established by God, which man on his own initiative may not break, between the unitive significance and the procreative significance which are both inherent to the marriage act.

The reason is that the marriage act, because of its fundamental structure, while uniting husband and wife in the closest intimacy, actualizes their capacity to generate new life—and this as a result of laws written into the actual nature of man and woman. And if each of these essential qualities, the unitive and the procreative, is preserved, the use of marriage fully retains its sense of true mutual love and its ordination to the supreme responsibility of parenthood to which man is called. We believe that our contemporaries are particularly capable of seeing that this teaching is in harmony with human reason.

We take this opportunity to address those who are engaged in education and all those whose right and duty it is to provide for the common good of human society. We would call their attention to the need to create an atmosphere favorable to the growth of chastity in such a way that true liberty may prevail over license and the norms of the moral law be fully safeguarded.

Everything therefore in the modern means of social communication which arouses men's baser passions and encourages low moral standards, likewise every obscenity in the written word and every form of indecency on the stage and screen, should be condemned publicly and unanimously by all those who have at heart the advance of civilization and the safeguarding of the outstanding values of the human spirit. It is quite absurd to defend this kind of depravity in the name of art or of culture or by pleading the liberty which may be allowed in this field by the public authorities.

\*(From Horgan, J. (Ed.). *Humanae vitae and the bishops* (1972, p. 33 ff.). Footnotes omitted.)

able and good." Marital sex fulfills two key functions: *procreative* and *unitive*. The procreative aspect is the conception and rearing of children. The unitive function is the bond between husband and wife, based on "true mutual love" and the voluntary sharing of the supreme responsibility of parenthood. There is an "inseparable connection, established by God, which man on his own initiative may not break, between the unitive significance and the procreative significance which are both inherent to the marriage act." The tie between these two aspects of sex is to be maintained not only in general but with regard to each and every act of coitus, which "must retain its natural potential to procreate human life" (*Humanae Vitae* 1972).

In this view of morality, all attempts at contraception and all forms of nonreproductive sexual behaviors are unacceptable because they fail to meet the procreative purpose of sex. Within marital relations, though, not all coital activity that lacks reproductive potential is excluded. It is perfectly lawful, for instance, for men and women who are sterile (from causes not of their making) to engage in coitus. The same would apply to women who are pregnant, or in the "safe" period of their menstrual cycle. The moral prohibition is not against every act of coitus that has no reproductive potential, but against interfering with the reproductive process through the deliberate use of "artificial" means of birth control, which would include all contraceptive devices other than "natural" means like the rhythm method (Chapter 7).

In subsequent statements, Pope John Paul II has reaffirmed the church's teachings on birth control. Moreover, in a recent doctrinal statement, the Vatican extended the ban on artificial methods of contraception to some of the new reproductive technologies, such as in vitro fertilization and surrogate motherhood (Ratzinger and Bovone, 1987).[1]

The use of the unitive criterion in turn eliminates all forms of heterosexual intercourse outside of marriage, because only marriage is considered the proper context for sex and parenthood. All forms of premarital and extramarital sex are morally unacceptable, as are masturbation, homosexual activities, and other sexual behaviors. In a 1986 document sent to the bishops of the Catholic church, the Vatican restated its view that homosexual practices are a sin and that homosexuality is an "objective disorder" (Suro, 1986). Its guidelines suggest that pastors encourage homosexual Catholics to practice the sacraments and to remain celibate as long as they feel homosexual urges.

Except for the prohibition against contraception, and other reproductive concerns, the conservative sexual ethic is by no means exclusively Catholic. Evangelical and other conservative Protestant churches basically adhere to it, as do orthodox elements in other religions such as Judaism and Islam and the secular culture of China. For instance, at the 1988 national convention of the Southern Baptist church, 35,600 delegates (representing 14.7 million members) declared that "[While] God loves the homosexual and offers salvation, homosexuality is not a normal lifestyle and is an abomination in the eyes of God" (*San Francisco Chronicle,* June 17, 1988, p. A6).

The adherents of the conservative moral perspective do not agree on all specific issues. Thus, abortion is fiercely opposed by Catholics and Evangelical Christians, permitted in Judaism, and encouraged by the Chinese state as a means of population control.

## The Case for Conservative Morality

The case for the conservative moral view as

---

[1]The Catholic church appealed to governments to curb birth technology and to outlaw surrogates. The document attracted mixed support from theologians and was largely rejected by specialists in the field of reproduction. Legal experts doubt if its recommendations could pass into law in the United States, given the right to privacy in decisions controlling a person's body and the doctrine of the separation of church and state under the First Amendment of the Constitution (Chambers, 1987). Even where Catholics are concerned, the Vatican document does not carry the full weight of moral law. Hence unlike abortion, which would be clearly sinful, the use of artificial insemination could be determined ultimately by the individual's conscience (Johnson, 1987).

expounded by the Catholic church rests on *biblical* grounds, the traditional *teachings* of the church, and its understanding of *natural law* (Bouyer, 1961; Doherty, 1979; Dennehy, 1981).

Biblical Grounds    Because Jesus and his disciples were Jews, they shared the Judaic sexual traditions of their time. The Old Testament, therefore, is one basis of Christian sexual morality. Even if we set aside its ritualistic concerns which do not apply to Christians, the Old Testament can be taken to stand for a conservative morality (Jensen and Stuhlmueller, 1979).

The New Testament says little about the views of Jesus on sexual matters (Chapter 20). Jesus is generally believed to have been chaste and celibate. There has been speculation that Jesus may have been married (as were most men at the time), but there is no biblical evidence of this whatsoever. Sex was not even among the temptations that Jesus confronted in the wilderness. On the other hand, he did not shun the company of women, including prostitutes, and because of the special circumstances of his life, we cannot assume that he intended his own celibacy to serve as a general model. The fact that Jesus took part in the wedding of Cana (where he miraculously turned water into wine) is taken as evidence that he approved of marriage. He reiterated the scriptural statement that "a man shall leave his father and mother and be joined to his wife, and the two shall become one flesh" (Mt. 19:5). The love Jesus showed children is also clearly attested to in numerous passages.

The few explicit statements Jesus made with respect to sexual behavior dealt with adultery (Figure 23.1). Jesus restated the command, "You shall not commit adultery" (Matt. 19:18). When confronted with a woman caught in adultery, Jesus was quite forgiving; he shamed her accusers ("Let him who is without sin among you be the first to throw a stone at her") and then told the woman, "Neither do I condemn you; go and do not sin again" (Matt. 8:3–11). Then in the Sermon on the Mount, Jesus went beyond the morality of acts to that of unchaste thoughts: "You have heard that it was said, 'You shall not commit adul-

Figure 23.1    Gustave Doré (1833–1883), *Jesus and the woman taken in adultery.*

tery.' But I say to you that everyone who looks at a woman lustfully has already committed adultery with her in his heart" (Matt. 5:27–28).

Jesus similarly condemned divorce except on the grounds of "unchastity" (Matt. 19:9); otherwise, every man who divorces his wife, "makes her an adulteress; and whoever marries a divorced woman commits adultery" (Matt. 5:31–32).

These statements convey a highly demanding sense of sexual morality, which was further elaborated by Saint Paul, the first major Christian figure to write explicitly on sexual behavior. By his personal example and various statements, Paul advocated chastity and celibacy; his acceptance of marital relations was a concession to human frailty and a safeguard against fornication:

If anyone thinks that he is not behaving properly toward his betrothed, if his passions are strong, and it has to be, let him do as he wishes: let them marry—it is no sin (1 Cor. 7:36).

To the unmarried and the widows I say that it is well for them to remain single as I do. But if they cannot exercise self-control, they should marry. For it is better to marry than to be aflame with passion (1 Cor. 7:8–9).

It is well for a man not to touch a woman. But because of the temptation to immorality, each man should have his own wife and each woman her own husband (1 Cor. 7:1–3).

Paul counseled those who were married to remain together and to "Be subject to one another out of reverence for Christ" (Eph. 5:21). "The husband should give to his wife her conjugal rights, and likewise the wife to her husband. For the wife does not rule over her own body, but the husband does; likewise the husband does not rule over his own body but the wife does" (1 Cor. 7:3–5). Given his qualified endorsement of even marital sex, St. Paul was predictably opposed to all other forms of sexual activity.

Taking the texts of the New Testament that form its doctrine on sexuality, Noonan (1967) subsumes them under the following themes:

> the superiority of virginity; the institutional goodness of marriage; the sacral character of sexual intercourse; the value of procreation; the significance of desire as well as act; the evil of extramarital intercourse and the unnaturalness of homosexuality; the connection of Adam's sin and the rebelliousness of the body; the evil of "medicine."[2]

Taken literally and at face value, the New Testament passages dealing with sex constitute a strong base of support for conservative morality.

[2]"Medicine" refers to various herbs and drugs associated with sorcery, conceivably including contraceptives and potions to induce abortion.

**The Teaching of the Church**    Traditional Christian teachers, Catholic or Protestant, have generally espoused a conservative sexual morality. The starting point for Catholic moral theology is the doctrine of *original sin* derived from the fall of Adam and Eve (Figure 23.2). The Augustinian doctrine of concupiscence (Chapter 20) has been particularly influential in shaping the sexual doctrines of the Church. Even the most restrictive views now present would be quite liberal compared to those of the Church Fathers (Chapter 20). It is only recently that Christian voices of any official credibility have advocated a more liberal perspective in sexual morality. Church tradition over 20 centuries is squarely behind sexual conservatism.

**Natural Law**    Arguments from "natural law" have been an integral part of Catholic moral teaching. The Christian conception of the *law of nature* goes back to St. Paul (Rom. 2:14). Elaborated by the Stoics and Church Fathers, and systematized by Saint Thomas Aquinas, this concept has been used as a way of integrating theological doctrines and naturalistic observations. Its underlying assumption is that living patterns uncontaminated by human sin and error are natural. Thus, the sexual processes evident in plant and animal life represent natural models by which to judge human behavior. Similarly, the organs of the human body have their self-evident natural functions: eyes are for vision, genitals for reproduction. Based on these models, procreation is seen to be the only natural sexual function.

In sum, the Church would claim that its moral doctrines represent God's will for human sexuality, whatever the historical circumstances. Its doctrines are not against sex but against its sinful uses. Furthermore, the Church recognizes human frailty and approaches sexual transgressions with compassion and forgiveness as long as people are willing to recognize the error of their ways.

**The Case Against Conservative Morality**
Many people object to the conservative moral

Figure 23.2   Adrien Isen-
brandt (active 1510–51),
*Adam and Eve.*

perspective because they neither accept the authority of the Bible nor of the Church. However, opposition to traditional sexual ethics is
not always based on wholesale rejection of
Christian values. There are many Christians,
including some within the Catholic church,
who do not accept the conservative stance as
the authentic Christian message for today's
world.

**The Biblical Record**   There are many competent theologians, some of them Catholics, who
disagree with the way moral conservatives interpret biblical passages dealing with sexuality.
Homosexuality provides a good example of
such conflicting interpretations of the same
biblical texts.

A frequently cited passage in condemnation of homosexuality is the story of the de-

struction of Sodom in Genesis 19. This story is where the term *sodomy* comes from. The term *homosexuality* does not exist in the Bible, nor in any of the languages in which the original biblical texts were written (Boswell, 1980).

The key phrase on which rests the sexual interpretation of the story is the demand that Lot bring out the two men he is sheltering so that the Sodomites may "know them." If to "know" is interpreted in sexual terms, then there is obviously a homosexual theme to the story. Lot's desperate offer of his two daughters to the mob to protect his guests adds a further sexual aura to the episode. We may surmise, then, that the "sin of Sodom" that so angered the Lord must have been homosexuality, and the Sodomites' attempt to rape the angels the final iniquity, which brought down on them the wrath of the Lord.

Other biblical scholars reject the sexual connotation to the story of Sodom (except for the offer of Lot's daughters). D. S. Bailey (1955) points out that the Hebrew verb "to know" occurs 943 times in the Bible; only in 10 cases is it used in a sexual sense, and in none of them (except for the presumed case of Sodom) with respect to homosexual sex. He interprets "to know" in this case in the literal sense of "becoming familiar with." The people of Sodom were angry at Lot because he was harboring strangers in his house after sunset when the gates of the town had closed down. The security consideration was especially important because Lot himself was a stranger who had settled in town. For Lot to turn over his guests would have violated the crucial rule of hospitality; so Bailey suggests that the wickedness of Sodom was inhospitality, not homosexuality. Inhospitality may not sound like a grave offense to our ears, but within the nomadic tradition of the Middle East, it was one of the most crucial norms of behavior. Unless travelers could seek shelter and protection in alien territory, no one would be able to travel far.

There are two places in the Old Testament that clearly refer to homosexual acts between men. These are Leviticus 18:22 and 20:13, which respectively state, "You shall not lie with a male as with a woman; it is an abomination," and "If a man lies with a male as with a woman, both of them have committed an abomination; they shall be put to death, their blood is upon them."

These condemnations are explicit enough, but was the problem homosexuality, or some special aspect of it? In the verses preceding Leviticus 18:22, there is an equally firm prohibition against approaching "a woman to uncover her nakedness while she is in her menstrual uncleanliness" (Leviticus 18:19). The people of Israel shared with the ancient world a certain awe with regard to sexual discharges, particularly blood and semen, the elements out of which came life. Thus just as the demand for cultic purity was manifested in prohibitions against having sexual intercourse with a woman in her menstrual period, similar considerations may have been applied to contact with semen in the context of homosexual activity between men (Kosnik et al., 1977). The fact that no reference is made to homosexual behavior between women further reinforces this view.

So far as we know, Jesus said nothing explicit about homosexuality (even though he does refer to Sodom); but there are several statements in the writings of Paul that have a clear bearing on this issue: 1 Corinthians 6:9 states that "neither the immoral nor idolators, nor adulterers, nor sexual perverts, nor thieves, nor the greedy, nor drunkards, nor revilers, nor robbers will inherit the Kingdom of God"; 1 Timothy 1:10 similarly cites "Sodomites"; and Romans 1:26–27 states, "For this reason God gave them up to dishonorable passions. Their women exchanged natural relations for unnatural, and the men likewise gave up natural relations with women and were consumed with passion for one another. Men committing shameless acts with men and receiving in their own persons the due penalty for their error."

For some scholars, these passages clearly indict homosexual acts as immoral. Others question the precise meaning of key terms in each. For example, the term translated as "sexual pervert" in 1 Corinthians 6:9 is a Greek word that means "soft." According to Boswell (1980), it is a common term, which occurs elsewhere in the New Testament meaning "sick"; in patristic writings it was used for "cowardly," "refined," "weak-willed," "delicate," "gentle," and "debauched." In more specifically moral contexts it frequently meant "licentious," "loose," or "wanting in self-control." The term may also be broadly translated either as "unrestrained" or "wanton." Boswell concludes that "to assume that either of these concepts necessarily applies to gay people is wholly gratuitous. The word is never used in Greek to designate gay people as a group or even in reference to homosexuals generally and it often occurs in writings contemporary with the Pauline episodes in reference to heterosexual persons or activity" (p. 107).

The Teaching of the Church    Critics of the conservative interpretation of church doctrine reject the idea of its having expressed a clear and constant perspective on all sexual matters throughout its history (Maguire, 1987). It was not until the church synod at Elvira in Spain, early in the 4th century, that the church hardened its sexual teaching, mainly for political reasons (Laeuchli, 1972). Ever since, there has been considerable diversity of church opinion over issues such as abortion. Until the 13th century, theologians could not agree when the fetus was endowed with a soul ("ensouled"). Until that happened, the fetus would not be considered human and abortion would not be an issue. It was not until the 19th century that the church consolidated its conservative stance on abortion, which it has since maintained.[3]

Thus this is an issue of historical relevance. Those who reject the moral wisdom of men like Jerome and Augustine may accept its relevance for the past but no longer for the

modern world; others wish that their advice had been disregarded altogether. Here are two men, we could say, who led (what they considered) dissolute lives in their youth and then as a reaction to their own internal conflicts perpetrated an oppressive sexual morality with crippling effects on the lives of others. Or, we could argue, even if Augustine and Aquinas did wonders for their time, are their moral views any more relevant to the modern world than the pre-Copernican conception of the universe to modern astronomy?

Modern teachers of conservative sexual morality are likewise criticized for refusing to adapt moral doctrines to current realities and for failing to take into account the opinions and experiences of Christian men and women whose sexual lives are being regulated. For instance, so far as is known, not a single woman has ever had any significant role in shaping Catholic doctrine on contraception.

Catholic opposition to contraception has been a particularly sore point both within the church and outside it, given the lack of clear biblical authority in support of it (hence the approval of contraception by Evangelical Protestants), and the enormous burden the ban places on individuals and society. In allowing "natural" forms of birth control, the Church appears to some to be compassionate, and to others to be inconsistent. It allows Catholics to avoid pregnancy while remaining faithful to the teaching of the Church; but when a couple uses the rhythm method to avoid pregnancy, does that not constitute a deliberate and conscious effort to separate the reproductive from the unitive aspects of sex? What is the moral difference between shielding yourself from a ball coming at you and ducking it?

It is no wonder that over 90 percent of Catholic women aged 15 to 44 who engage in coitus rely on artificial methods of birth control (Chapter 7). What is the point of a moral rule, we may ask, when the overwhelming majority of those who are supposed to observe it cannot do so?

Natural Law    Biologists and investigators of animal behavior would not quarrel with the as-

---

[3]The issue of when the fetus becomes human is central to all debates on abortion. In Judaism, the fetus is not considered to be fully human until birth; hence abortion is permissible but to be practiced only for compelling reasons, not "on demand" (Brickner, 1987). Currently, the abortion debate revolves on the issue of "when life begins" (Box 22-2), which is the secular counterpart of the ensoulment issue.

sumption that what prevails in the animal world has relevance to human behavior. However, naturalistic observation of animal behavior shows that they engage in all sorts of sexual activities that have no reproductive potential, including masturbation and sexual contacts between members of the same sex. If by "natural" we mean what takes place in nature, then these activities must be considered natural for humans as well.

Even within the more limited knowledge of biology of earlier times, the moral position of the church could not be supported by the empirical evidence. Likewise, it was deemed acceptable to tamper with nature, as by damming up rivers, so why not "block" conception? It seems, therefore, that the church uses the natural law argument to bolster its theological position by using spurious examples from nature.

## THE LIBERAL MORAL PERSPECTIVE

The liberal approach to sexual morality is the perspective of mainstream Protestants and Jews, liberal Catholics, and the majority of secular middle-class people in the United States (Box 23.2).

The liberal perspective is more difficult to characterize than the conservative view, because it has no common voice to speak for it. Moreover, it encompasses a far broader spectrum of moral views. At its conservative end, the liberal perspective also relies on traditional sources of authority like the Bible and church tradition, but it interprets these sources more liberally; that is, behavior continues to be judged by predetermined rules, but the rules are less strict. At its liberal end, individual choice determines the morality of a particular sexual act. Because individual choice depends on the situation or context, this perspective has come to be known as *situation ethics*.

As the conservative stand is traditional, the liberal alternative is said to be modern; hence the *new morality* is a synonym for situation ethics. This term does not mean that liberals reject all of the past, any more than conservatives cling to everything old.

The sexual revolution of the 1960s added a more radical dimension to the liberal moral perspective. Like others who rejected the traditional values of society in other areas, they adopted the word *humanistic* to indicate the primacy of human beings in their choice of alternative lifestyles and moral orientations.

The humanistic sexual perspective has its own religious and secular components. Radical Protestant and Catholic clergy (many of whom have left the church) have been among the vanguard of sexual liberation movements. Box 23.3, which represents the view of one Unitarian minister and sexologist, conveys the general sense of this viewpoint. Nonetheless, the humanistic approach is primarily secular in thrust and its proponents are concentrated among the younger generation and among groups whose sexual preferences run counter to traditional morality, such as gays.

This perspective is also the dominant moral orientation among professionals in the field of human sexuality. Within this ethos of tolerance, though, we find considerable variation in the level of permissiveness with which they approach moral issues in their work and personal lives.

Marital sex reemerges in the more conservative end of mainstream liberal Christian views as the ideal sexual experience, but this time with no strings attached. Procreation continues to be highly valued, but there is no objection to the use of contraception. Sex remains linked with love, but sexual pleasure is also accepted as good in itself, and a couple is free to use whatever reasonable means they choose to attain it.

Masturbation is acceptable for youth, but viewed more ambivalently for adults unless it is used as an unavoidable substitute for coitus. Premarital sex is viewed with cautious tolerance; extramarital relations are suspect. In short, nonmarital relationships are seen as possibly moral, but the cards are generally stacked against them.

Attitudes toward homosexuality are generally one of tolerance. Some mainstream Protestant churches accept homosexuality on the grounds that it is determined by factors

# Box 23.2

## WHAT'S WRONG, WHAT'S RIGHT—THE POPULAR VIEW

What we know about sexual ethics from the past is what people were expected to do; we know very little about what ordinary people believed was right or wrong, let alone if they behaved accordingly. Now the public media focus much more on moral attitudes—what people believe, rather than what they ought to believe. Just as what theologians deem right may be far apart from popular ethical views, what people think right may not really be moral. Who is to decide?

The table below represents the results of a newspaper poll of views of a sample of residents in the San Francisco Bay Area, a cluster of several dozen small towns and the cities of San Francisco and San Jose, with a combined population of about 6 million. It is a liberal, affluent, and cosmopolitan area, with a free-wheeling element since the Gold Rush days. San Francisco is one of the most important enclaves for the gay community in the United States. On the other hand, 38 percent of the population has a middle-of-the-road ideology, with a somewhat larger segment of the strongly liberal (12 percent, versus 10 percent statewide) and smaller segment of the strongly conservative (11 percent, versus 15 percent statewide).

**Adult Activities from the Most Wrong to the Least Wrong***

|  | ALWAYS OR ALMOST ALWAYS WRONG | SOMETIMES OR NEVER WRONG |
|---|---|---|
| 1. Getting high or drunk on job | 97% | 3% |
| 2. Using cocaine | 82 | 15 |
| 3. Extramarital sex | 80 | 18 |
| 4. Paying for hooker services | 54 | 42 |
| 5. Sex with same gender | 47 | 48 |
| 6. More than 4–5 drinks at one sitting | 45 | 52 |
| 7. Having child outside wedlock | 34 | 63 |
| 8. Attending X-rated nightclub act | 27 | 69 |
| 9. Having an abortion | 23 | 74 |
| 10. Watching an X-rated TV movie | 23 | 75 |
| 11. Unmarried sex | 21 | 77 |
| 12. Cohabitation | 16 | 81 |
| 13. Marrying someone of another race | 8 | 90 |
| 14. Marrying someone of another religion | 4 | 95 |

*From *San Francisco Chronicle*, Sept. 29, 1986, p. 1.

outside the person's control. The Episcopal bishop of New York, Paul Moore, who ordained Ellen Barrett, an acknowledged lesbian, as a priest in 1977 has said, "Homosexuality is a condition which one does not choose; it is not a question of morality" (Berger, 1987). Various Christian organizations ("Dignity" for Roman Catholics, "Integrity" for Episcopal-

ians") provide support groups for their gay members (Tivan, 1987).

The more radical humanistic wing of the liberal perspective is more unabashedly accepting of all varieties of sexual behavior, as long as it inflicts no demonstrable harm on another. Masturbation is not only condoned but encouraged. Premarital sex is taken for

# Box 23.3

## THE HUMANISTIC PERSPECTIVE ON MARITAL FIDELITY*

We consider traditional monogamy, with its rigid requirement for exclusive devotion and affection, even though hallowed by the theological concept of fidelity, to be a culturally approved mass neurosis. It should be clearly understood that we do not deny anyone the freedom to enter conventional marriage—an absolute covenant between two persons of the opposite sex. Each person has the freedom to make decisions for life affirmation according to his/her deepest convictions and highest priorities, and sometimes what may outwardly appear to be merely a conventional form of marriage may be for the two people involved the epitome of love, joy, and hope. It is possible for a man and a woman to be content and happy only with each other and family members. Indeed, we support all the efforts of various human relations disciplines to strengthen and make more rewarding conventional monogamy. What we do emphatically reject, however, is our society's sanction of this marital model as normative and supreme. We believe all civic and constitutional rights should be extended to personal lifestyles. We prefer a model of monogamy which celebrates comarital intimacy and does not equate fidelity with sexual exclusiveness. For too long, traditional moralists have been passively allowed to preempt other conscientious lifestyles by propagating the unproven assumptions that we cannot love more than one person (of the opposite sex) concurrently; that comarital or extramarital sex always destroys a marriage; that "good" marriages are totally self-contained and self-restrictive and sufficient; that only emotionally unstable people seek and need intimate relationships outside the husband-wife bond. We repudiate these assumptions and consider them half-truths at best. When these assumptions are dogmatically upheld by society as eternal truths we consider the phenomenon to be a cultural neurosis in the sense that the issue is predetermined, all nonconformists are castigated, and there is no openness to new experience in new contexts.

The semantics of conformity are intimidating. Relational innovators are constantly accosted with negative terms such as promiscuity, adultery, and infidelity. The word "promiscuous," for example,

refers to people who lack standards of selection, who are indiscriminate in sexual relations. It should be obvious that it's possible for a person to be sexually intimate with any number of persons chosen according to conscientious standards. The word is commonly used, however, as a judgment against anyone who has more than one socially approved sexual relationship, and especially in a double-standard way against women. This shows a mistaken emphasis on the quantity rather than the quality of interpersonal relationships. It also insists that people cannot have casual sexual experiences. Not all intimate relationships must have the same intensity. Millions of men and women are able to make rapid appraisals of others with whom they can exchange warmth without subsequent emotional strings attached.

Even the term "extramarital" is misleading in the context of open-ended marriage. For it is precisely *within* marriage rather than outside it that open-ended marriage incorporates the freedom for two spouses to enjoy multilateral sexual and friendship relations. "Extramarital" is an all-encompassing term referring to all forms of relationship, usually sexual, with partners other than the spouse. "Comarital" is a more appropriate term for open-ended marriages because it at least carries the connotations of togetherness and cooperation within the structure of marriage. . . . Within such marriages the possibility of adultery is totally absent because such exclusion, possessiveness, and jealousy have no place in the relationship. "Adultery" is a theological judgment which can apply only to the restrictive type of covenant. When one partner breaks the vow of "to thee only do I promise to keep myself," a relationship of trust is broken and he or she is unfaithful. But it's also possible to create a model of marriage—a covenant—monogamous in the sense that it's based upon an intended lifetime commitment between two, but which nevertheless is open-ended because it does not exclude the freedom to have any number of intimate relationshps with others.

*From Mazur, R. (1973). *The new intimacy* (Boston: Beacon, pp. 12–14).

granted. Extramarital sex is accepted subject to a number of qualifications. Homosexuality is given full parity with heterosexuality. Noncoercive paraphilias are tolerated. Sexual coercion and exploitation are condemned. Differences in sexual desire are acknowledged and respected, but there is a clear preference for the sexually more active over the less active; virginity is no virtue; continence is no occasion for moral celebration.

The differences between the conservative and liberal religious perspectives are sharper at the doctrinal level than at the behavioral level: conservative clergy are more flexible in dealing with their parishioners than we would surmise from the teachings of their theological mentors, whereas liberals behave more conservatively than they talk. The conservative absolutists bend their rules, while liberal relativists make up rules, improving the less workable aspects of each system.

### The Case for Liberal Morality

The justification for the liberal perspective starts with the contention that the conservative approach does not work, or that it exacts an inordinate price in human freedom and happiness. The conservative moral perspective is too legalistic. It does not reflect the lucidity and compassion of the original and authentic Christian message. Biblical passages are used to score points rather than to get to the truth; there is too much reliance on theological abstractions and not enough trust in the sincerity and competence of the individual conscience to sort right from wrong. As a consequence, the Western moral tradition has been burdened with the gloom and doom of sexual guilt and shame, as exemplified in images of Dante's *Inferno* (Figures 23.3 and 23.4).

To remedy these shortcomings, the liberal perspective focuses on human sexual needs and their realistic management and satisfaction. Laws are made to serve people instead of people serving laws. In defense of this approach, we will first examine perspectives of Judaism, then turn to the views of liberal

Figure 23.3 Gustave Doré, *The lustful.* (Illustration for Dante's *Divine Comedy.*)

Catholic theologians, Protestant ethicists, and sexual liberationists.

*The Perspective of Judaism* As we discussed in our earlier historical overview (Chapter 20), Judaism has generally taken a positive view of sex. It has also allowed for steady change and adjustment of sexual values and practices to fit the needs of the times.

The Judaic perspective is highly compatible with the more conservative end of liberal sexual morality. Human sexuality, in this view, is not a grudging concession to reproductive purposes or uncontrollable lust, but rather a worthy and meritorious activity in the eyes of God (Brickner, 1987).

In Judaism, sex and love are linked—there is no distinction between eros and agape

Figure 23.4    Gustave Doré, *Devils and seducers*. (Illustration for Dante's *Divine Comedy*.)

(Chapter 16), between physical and spiritual union. Love between God and a person, among people in general, and between a man and a woman are all expressed by the same word for love—*ahavah*.

There is, however, no freewheeling sexual license in Judaism; that is, not everything goes. There are high expectations of moral behavior within the broader context of Judaic law, which at one extreme regulates every facet of life.

Judaism makes allowances for human frailty and accommodates change. Divorce is allowed, but is a tragedy. Homosexuality is condemned in rabbinic texts, but modern rabbis are willing to reconsider its nature. If sexual orientation is not a matter of voluntary choice but biologically determined, then one cannot be morally "faulted" over its outcome (Gordis, 1978). If homosexuality is unethical, people should be subject to divine, not human, judgment—it is not a crime to be punished by human agencies like the law.

Liberal Christian moralists sympathize with this view. They would like to recapture the lost biblical wisdom which created the *Song of Songs* and exulted in erotic marital love: "Let her affection fill you at all times with delight,

be infatuated always with her love" (Proverbs 5:19).

New Directions in Catholic Morality    We see the ferment within Catholicism for a more liberal approach to sexual morality in the conclusions of a study commissioned by the Catholic Theological Society of America. In a marked departure from the traditional Catholic approach, the authors of the report took a far less absolutist view: "Morality must never allow itself to be reduced to a simple external conformity to prejudged and prespecified patterns of behavior. For this reason, we find it woefully inadequate to return to a method of evaluating human sexual behavior based on an abstract absolute predetermination of any sexual expressions as intrinsically evil and always immoral" (Kosnik et al., 1977, p. 89).

This "new direction" in Catholic thought stops short of trusting individual judgment with no further prescriptive rules, because that would place morality at the mercy of individual preferences, dispositions, and moods. To avoid the pitfalls of a purely objective absolutism or a purely subjective relativism, the proponents of this view start with three presuppositions, from which they derive criteria to assist a person in making moral judgments. First, we must consider both the "objective and subjective" aspects of the sexual behavior—what the person thinks and what others think about it. Second, the "complexity and unity" of the person's sexual nature must be acknowledged, without establishing hierarchies among its components. The procreative aspects of sex must not be set in competition with its "creative and integrative" components. Third, we must have a constant awareness of the "interpersonal dimension" of behavior, the effects on the other person or persons. In sum, we have to care about both motivations and actions.

To apply this approach, instead of asking the question, "Is this act moral or immoral?" we ought to ask if it is "conducive to creative growth and integration of the human person." Proper values are "self-liberating, other-enriching, honest, faithful, socially responsible, life-serving, and joyous" (Kosnik et al., 1977).

There are sharp divisions within the Catholic church over these issues. The Vatican has been generally intolerant of dissent. For instance, in 1986, it revoked the teaching license of Charles Curran, a priest and professor of theology at the Catholic University of America, because of his teachings on homosexuality, abortion, contraception, and other moral issues. Yet Father Curran is hardly a sexual radical. For instance, he considers homosexual relations and masturbation to fall "short of the full meaning of human sexuality" (Curran, 1986). What he has been unwilling to do is to condemn any and all sexual behaviors other than marital coitus without qualification.

As with contraceptive practice, many American Catholics appear to disagree with the official views of the church on sexuality. In a 1986 Gallup poll, 57 percent of all Catholics said the church's stance on moral issues should change; 36 percent said it should not (Gallup, 1986). In an earlier poll, 79 percent thought it is possible to disagree with the Pope on birth control, abortion, or divorce and still be a good Catholic (*New York Times*, Nov. 25, 1985).

**Experiential Bases of Moral Judgment**    Protestant moral theologians often apply the essential teachings of Christianity to contemporary realities by drawing on the natural and behavioral sciences. A good representative of this approach is James Gustafson, who argues that "there are fundamental bases in human nature and experience which necessarily must be taken into account" in sexual morality (Gustafson, 1981, p. 490). Traditional Christian ethics of sex and marriage had an experiential foundation; modern ethics ought to be considered in the same light.

Gustafson proposes that three aspects of our experience as sexual beings must be taken into account in moral judgments. First is the fact that sex is part of our *biological and personal nature*. The biological aspect of sexuality is self-evident, but sex is just as importantly a vehicle for expression of psychological needs as well. A key ethical issue then is the relationship between the biological and personal components in human sexuality. Moral codes that shortchange either are not likely to be successful guides.

The second basis for sexual ethics is the *reality of sin*—the human propensity to cause harm to others. In modern times we may have sought to banish the notions of sin and guilt, but the reality of human relations continues to attest to their presence, even though we may now refer to them by other terms like "sexual exploitation." Such terms approximate "one of the most profound traditional meanings of immorality—to use another person for purely selfish ends, to fail to recognize that respect is due to another person as a human agent with capacities to determine his or her own sense of purpose and well-being. It is to make another instrumental to one's own end, and to manipulate others to consent to fulfilling that end. The other becomes an object rather than a person. Sexuality, like other aspects of human relations, is deeply subject to exploitation and exploitation of others is immoral" (Gustafson, 1981).

The third basis for any system of sexual ethics is *covenant*: the "commitments which persons make to one another, implicit ones that are subject to deception and self-deception and exploitation, and explicit ones such as marriage vows." Such commitments entail the willingness to accept accountability for one another and for the consequences of sexual relations. Rather than simply being externally imposed rituals or contracts, covenants are based on a profound human need, to be related to one another over time in a way that allows the well-being of each and the well-being of both together to be sustained (Gustafson, 1981).

Traditional marriage services, like the very old service from the Church of England, formalize the covenant between bride and groom in the presence of the congregation. The first step is public announcement ("publication of banns") of the impending marriage, to inquire if anyone has serious objection to the proposed union. During the service, the minister's address to the congregation states the basic purposes of marriage: the procreation and nurture of children; the satisfaction of sexual needs; the help, comfort, and companionship to be provided by husband and wife to each other, both in prosperity and adversity. The couple and the bride and groom individually make a public acknowledgment of their voluntary commitment to fulfill the agreed-upon conditions: to love, comfort, honor, and be faithful to each other. The "giving of the bride" signifies the break with the family of origin (a consideration that now applies to the groom as well) and the establishment of an independent family. The vows undertaken by the couple finalize their marital commitment, which is symbolized by the exchange of rings.

This ceremony is cast within the beliefs and symbols of Christianity and reflects the historical and social contexts within which it was formed; but, Gustafson argues, the ends it serves are not arbitrary. Even if we update the ceremony, its fundamental purposes remain valid, with or without its religious justification.

Such commitments provide a setting of reliable trust and confidence as well as an understanding of the duties and obligations that are essential to our well-being. Even though they also do check and control sexual behavior, they are meant to facilitate and not hinder human sexual relations. Like the other two bases for sexual ethics, covenants are based upon human experience and biological, social, and personal needs that remain constant, even though the social conventions and institutions through which we obtain our sexual satisfactions change.

Situation Ethics   In the late 1960s, the most widely read Christian exponent of the liberal approach to sexuality was Joseph Fletcher, an Episcopal clergyman. The title of his first book, *Situation Ethic: The New Morality* provided the labels; and its message, oversimplified by others, lent a moral voice to what youth were already practicing at the time (Fletcher, 1966).[4]

Fletcher places the main burden of moral choice on the individual. The morality of choices is relative to their contexts; hence, situation ethics is also known as *contextual ethics*. In other words, whether a given sexual behavior is right or wrong cannot be determined in the abstract; it all depends on the circumstances.[5] In principle, situation ethics is liberal only in the sense of allowing freedom of choice. In practice, it also turns out to be liberal in the sense of being sexually permissive, since the freer people are to choose, the more they choose to behave sexually freely. Sexual rules, like rules in general, are prohibitive—they tell us what not to do; so the more rules there are in an ethical system, the more sexually restrictive that system is likely to be. However, the fact that Fletcher sets no predetermined norms as to whether a given sexual behavior is good or bad does not mean that he expects people to do as they please. To help steer sexual conduct in the right direction, he provides certain guidelines within which to exercise moral judgment.

[4]For other Protestant views see Thielicke (1964), Feucht (1961), and the bibliography in *Siecus Report*, vol. 15., no. 5, 1987.

[5]This core concept of the "new" morality is hardly new. Thomas Aquinas, one of the pillars of the medieval church, wrote, "human actions are good or bad according to their circumstances" (*Summa Theologica*, 111, q. 18, a.3. Quoted in Maguire, 1987, p. 3).

Fletcher builds his defense of situation ethics on four general principles. The first is *pragmatism:* what is considered to be lawful must be expedient, constructive, and workable; not some lofty principle that cannot be reasonably put to practice in everyday life by most people. Second, a moral code should be *relativistic:* meaningful only in a specific context, subject to given circumstances. The third principle is *positivism:* moral decisions are "posited" or affirmed by faith; we start with faith in God and a commitment to love others; reason then determines the application of this commitment to sexual behavior. The fourth principle is *personalism:* people, not abstract values, are the center of concern. Laws are obeyed when they serve a good purpose, broken when they do not.

The cardinal principle of the situational ethical approach is love. This love is defined as *agape,* the selfless Christian love of "neighbor," not erotic love, not even the *philia* of friendship (Fletcher, 1966, 1967). Selfless love that seeks nothing in return is intrinsically good. Nothing else has any value, any ethical quality. If love is the only good, then only love and nothing else can be the norm ruling behavior.

Secular Morality    Secular moralists within the liberal perspective similarly invoke love as the basis for moral action, but they use the term in the sense of commitment and loyalty, not agape. Respect for the rights of others, "no one getting hurt," and similar considerations underlie their moral decisions. In essence, what they advocate is sexual freedom within the context of responsible behavior where people show concern for the physical and emotional well-being of themselves and their partner.

Less stringent in its demands and less formal in articulating its principles, the secular sex code operates as a do-it-yourself sort of morality, where personal interests are tempered by altruism, decency, and fear of social disapproval. Additional constraints on sexual behavior come from secular ideologies (democratic respect for individual freedom, Marxist responsibility to the community, feminist op-

position to the exploitation of women), from class-based behavioral codes (acting like a "lady" or "gentleman"), from loyalty to national ethnic and family tradition ("It's un-American. It's not done in our family"), and folk wisdom ("Don't look for your honey where you make your money").

The humanistic perspective is, first and foremost, *libertarian* in outlook. "Libertarian" in this sense should not be confused with "libertine," which signifies irresponsible and hedonistic pursuit of sexual pleasure without moral restraints. A libertarian extends the right of freedom of individual action far beyond the mainstream liberal position. The primary responsibility is to be true to your own needs and desires ("do your thing"), and society has no right to impinge on that privilege except for preventing palpable harm to others.

The humanistic perspective is *pluralistic.* It does not assume that the traditional sexual values of Western society are superior to those of other cultures. On the contrary, it points to the rich admixture of sacred and sexual themes in Hinduism (Box 23.4) and other world religions (Parrinder, 1980).

Within our own society, the liberal perspective rejects the imposition of white, middle-class moral values on other ethnic or socioeconomic subgroups. Similarly, it does not accept heterosexuality as the only normative sexual orientation but considers homosexuality an equally moral form of sexual behavior. It believes homosexual publications and representations in art belong within the mainstream of society (Figure 23.5).

The opposition to social control of sexual behavior by rules and regulations gives the humanistic perspective an *antinomian* ("against the law") flavor. There is a refusal to morally condemn behaviors that are merely unconventional. Diagnostic terms and distinctions between "normal" and "abnormal" are rejected in favor of terms like "sexual minorities" to characterize people with atypical sexual preferences (Chapter 14).

The humanistic perspective prides itself in being *sex-positive.* Sex is valued as a good thing in all its manifestations. The primary purposes

# Box 23.4

## EROTICISM IN EASTERN RELIGIONS

Comparisons of attitudes towards sex in various religions can be both illuminating and misleading. Religious traditions have much in common in their basic human concerns and cannot be simplistically labeled "sex-positive" or "sex-negative." In a single tradition one belief system may be permissive with respect to one issue and restrictive with respect to another: Confucianism accepts sex as a natural function untainted by any innate sense of guilt; yet traditional Chinese society has been extraordinarily reticent in its public expressions of sexuality (Thompson, 1969; Parrinder, 1980). Islam shelters its women but does not deny female sexuality (Parrinder, 1980). Japanese Buddhism has strict rules governing the interactions of men and women (Earhart, 1969); yet Japan has produced fine erotic art (*Shunga*).

Particularly instructive is Hinduism, with its extremes of asceticism and religiously inspired voluptuousness. Compared to the far more neutral sexual images of Christian iconography, Indian goddesses (see figure) and the erotic statuary of medieval temples are startling. "Nowhere," says Parrinder, "have the close relationship of religion and sex been displayed more clearly than in India and, with divine and human models of sexual activity, sacramental views of sex more abundantly illustrated" (Parrinder, 1980, p. 5). The sexual experience has been so exalted that Indian eroticism begins at every point with God (Rawson, 1969, p. 29).

Shiva is one of the principal and most complex gods of India (Hopkins, 1971). Of particular interest are those episodes of his life that deal with his relationship with his wife, Parvati. It was Parvati who approached Shiva when he was meditating in the Himalayas, wanting to marry him. Kama, the god of love, tried to kindle Shiva's desire for Parvati, but Shiva churlishly reduced him to ashes with the fire from his third eye in the forehead (but then revived him). Shiva then appeared before Parvati as an ascetic and, to test her resolve, described in most unpleasant terms the austere circumstances of his home in the cremation grounds. Parvati was undaunted and Shiva married her.

The passionate sexual encounters with Parvati

Indian Goddess. Yakshi figure from Stupa at Sanchi.

weakened Shiva's powers, so he retreated to the forest to revive himself. As he danced around naked in full erection, the wives of the forest sages fell in love with him. Their husbands cursed Shiva's penis, which fell to the ground, generating a terrible fire. Peace was finally restored when all agreed to worship Shiva's penis symbolized by the *lingam;* this widespread Indian practice has persisted to modern times.

Like Shiva, there are many aspects to Parvati. She is the benevolent Mother Goddess whose genital symbol, the *yoni,* joined with Shiva's lingam, is worshipped as the source of life. Simultaneously, there is a terrible aspect to Parvati when she appears as Durga or Kali, the goddess of death, shown as a naked figure with a garland of skulls, trampling demons, standing on the prostrate body of Shiva in the cremation grounds, or copulating with his erect penis.

Vishnu is another great deity whose life manifests many episodes involving love and sex. From his early Vedic origins, Vishnu became prominent after his reincarnation as the popular god Krishna.

Some of the most popular episodes of Krishna's life were his amorous adventures with the Gopis (women who herded cows), among whom he lived for a while. As a divinely handsome youth, Krishna captured the hearts of these lowly women and played erotic pranks on them. Once, while the Gopis were bathing in the nude, Krishna gathered their clothes and climbed a tree: they had to approach him with their hands raised, uncovering their full nudity, in order to get back their garments. When Krishna played his flute, the Gopis flocked to him in bewitched fascination. He led them in a round dance and then made love to each and every one of them; yet he made each woman feel that she was dancing and making love with him alone. As legend embroidered variations on this theme, the number

of women grew into the hundreds and thousands, as Krishna continued to blissfully satisfy all of them.

Though many of Krishna's amorous adventures, such as his seduction of married women, contradicted moral precepts, they were justified by the primacy of divine love over all other forms of human attachments. For instance, the story of the Gopis baring their bodies was interpreted as symbolic of the nakedness of the soul in the divine presence. In more human terms, Krishna's multiple loves and simultaneous devotion to Radha, his favorite among the Gopis, seemed to provide men with the best of both worlds. Most importantly, the unabashed celebration of sex by the loftiest of divinities vindicated it to Krishna's countless followers (Rawson, 1969).

of sex are erotic pleasure and the enhancement of personal intimacy ("the pleasure bond"). Reproduction is valued but no more than contraceptive responsibility. The guiding ethical principle is *permissiveness with affection.* The key terms in its ethical vocabulary are *pleasure, acceptance, sharing, communication, negotiation, personal enhancement, nonsexist, nonexploitative, honest, affectionate,* and *commitment.*

The humanistic perspective draws support from scientific arguments. Given the interplay of biology and culture in shaping sexual behavior, there is not much room for blame. Can you "decide" on your sexual orientation? If not, how can people be held morally responsible for behaviors over which they have no control? Besides, given the variety of moral codes across cultures, all of them set up with the best of intentions, who is to determine by which code to judge someone else's behavior?

The humanistic argument from nature, unlike that of "natural law," is based on empirical evidence. Naturalistic observation shows many sexual activities proscribed for human beings manifested by animals. That makes "unnatural," as Kinsey puts it, only those sex acts "that can't be performed."

An important impetus to the growth of the humanistic perspective has come from feminism. Traditional sexual morality has

been especially oppressive of female sexuality and has perpetrated a double standard. It has presumed women to be sexual objects whose purity must be defended in virginity and whose fecundity must be cultivated in marriage. They are also said to have tempted men, inflamed their lust, and led to their downfall since Eve got Adam into trouble. Venerated or vilified, women have been molded in every conceivable sexual image but given scarce chance to express how they themselves feel and what they want—all in the name of sexual morality. Nonetheless, feminists do not subscribe to a sexual ethic where anything goes. While tolerant of sexual diversity, they are as harsh as any sexual conservative in their condemnation of activities that debase and hurt women, such as pornography and rape.

### The Case Against Liberal Morality
No one quarrels with the ideals of the liberal view. No one is against the joy to be derived from sexual intimacy; everyone is in favor of sharing, honesty, and personal enhancement, and opposed to exploitation in sexual relationships. However, the critics of the liberal perspective find fault with its conceptual underpinnings and its behavioral consequences.

The Conceptual Critique    Religious conservatives claim that secular methods of analysis

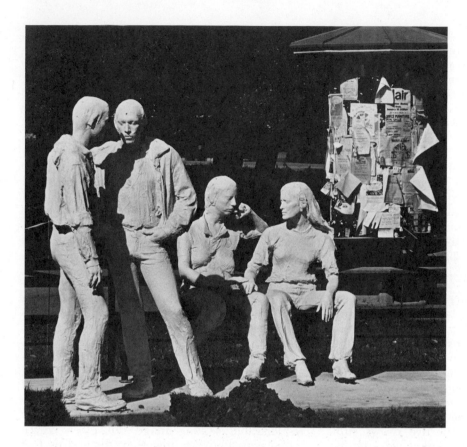

Figure 23.5 George Segal, *Gay liberation*, 1980.

cannot be indiscriminately applied to the Bible without compromising its religious integrity. What the Bible says about sexual morality must be taken at face value as representing eternal truths, which are just as valid today as when they were enunciated. Otherwise, why bother with it? Why not let each generation figure out its own rules? If there is going to be a Christian sexual ethic, it must have a consistent core of moral teaching, rather than be a collection of shifting cultural views. Given the repeated attempts over 20 centuries to dilute and distort the fundamentals of the Christian message, the church could hardly be blamed for keeping matters as unambiguous as possible to guard the integrity of its moral teaching.

The liberal contention that we must judge motivation and not acts makes no practical sense: acts are the only concrete entities we have; motivation is at best nebulous. It is what people do, not why they do it, that matters. How else can moral judgments function except by declaring some behaviors good and others not? Moral laws exist for God's purposes to avoid human suffering; how can they be faulted for not being person-oriented?

Love is indeed the ultimate basis of all moral choice, and individual conscience is the most reliable guardian we have to save us from error—but only if there is a mature personal conscience to begin with (or a well-developed ethical sense, in secular terms). How many people have these attributes? Do teenagers necking in a parked car care about what *agape* is? When sexual passion confuses reason, can we seriously expect people to judge their motivations and circumstances reliably? Without clear and concrete ethical guidance to bring to these situations, will people not improvise as they go along? Is not equivocation on the part of moral teachers particularly damaging to the young, whose sexual drives are strong, whose self-control is in need of all the help it can get, and whose experiences are likely to affect them for the rest of their lives?

In sum, conservative moralists charge that the liberal viewpoint reduces morality into a set of personal preferences. All the talk about *agape* notwithstanding, it simply makes it moral for people to behave as they please.

The Consequences    The conservative moral perspective is faulted for engendering sexually oppressive values, which have stymied the expression of sexual feelings and tainted harmless sexual practices with guilt. What about the consequences of the liberal moral perspective?

One criticism leveled at the more conservative end of the liberal spectrum is that its proponents have eroded the authority of religion and other traditional sources of guidance without achieving any clear gains. For instance, if the conservative Catholic position makes the enjoyment of sex morally impossible, its liberal alternative makes it nearly as difficult. Consider, for instance, the moral criteria proposed as the liberal Catholic yardstick. Pious affirmations aside, who can in all honesty measure up to them in actual practice? What other human endeavor sets the moral threshold that high? As a thoughtful (and by no means radical) Catholic couple has put it, "There are few human acts of any kind that can be at a given moment self-liberating, other-enriching, honest, faithful, socially responsible, life-serving, and joyous" (Mohs and Mohs, 1979, p. 160). Applied to business, such expectations would bring it to bankruptcy. If this is the "new direction" for sexual morality, can it point to anything other than failure and guilt, with an added measure of shame at not measuring up to even the "liberal" standard?

The liberal perspective rejects the making of rules, then substitutes more subtle and ambiguous forms of rule-making, replacing "You shall not" with "You probably should not." All it does is confuse people and make it more difficult for them to behave morally.

Even worse are the consequences of the values at the humanistic end of the liberal perspective. The lessons of the sexual revolution of a decade or two ago, during which freedom was rampant, are still fresh. Love was celebrated in song and dance, but there was little evidence of it in the lives of forlorn youth, drugged out of their minds, wandering the streets like the walking wounded. There was plenty of sex, of any kind, for free. There were no rules to obey, no shame or guilt to stop anyone. It was a freedom in which the vicious preyed on the lost.

The liberation of female sexuality was to have been one of the benefits of the sexual revolution, and sexual equality that of radical politics. However, women in these movements soon found themselves mimeographing flyers during the day and servicing the sexual needs of their comrades during the night. Women continued to be sexually used as they had always been, but now they had lost the right even to say no. Some male radicals used sex to build solidarity by sharing time "balling a chick" together before going on a demonstration (D'Emilio and Freedman, 1988, p. 310).

The flamboyance and the excesses of the sexual revolution have largely subsided, but its consequences are very much with us: the spawning of the modern pornography industry; the alarming rate of teenage pregnancy; the outbreak of epidemics of sexually transmitted diseases.

Libertarian principles sound fine, conservatives say, but they do not work. We cannot keep up freedom of individual action and still defend the rights of others; we soon run into trouble over defining where one person's untrammeled freedom impinges on another's inalienable rights. Clearly we have to draw a line sooner or later and devise moral codes to define it and laws to defend it.

## ENVOI

We close this book with the consideration of

sexual morality; we could just as easily have begun with it. The ethical dimension is as crucial as any other dimension to sexuality. It is bound to have the greatest impact on our lives, individually and collectively.

Moral decisions require reflection, but morality is not an intellectual exercise. It is a commitment to seek out what is right and to act on it. It is neither necessary nor feasible for each of us to develop our own unique ethical system. However, unless we make them our own, the moral precepts we choose will be of little help to us in avoiding doing the wrong deed, as well as, in the words of T. S. Elliot, "the right deed for the wrong reason."

What moral stance will you take on the vital issues related to sex that face us today and in the future? How will you order your life so that, as Sir Thomas Brown put it three centuries ago, "prudence and virtue may have the largest section"?

## REVIEW QUESTIONS

1. Compare the secular and religious bases of sexual morality.

2. What are the arguments for and against the conservative moral perspective?

3. What are the arguments for and against the liberal moral perspective?

4. What current sexual issues have ethical implications?

5. How do moral assessments of sexual behavior differ from legal judgments?

## THOUGHT QUESTIONS

1. If sex no longer had any unwanted reproductive or health consequences, would we need sexual ethics?

2. Why are some college students sexually less liberal than others although they belong to the same youth subculture?

3. Is being gay incompatible with sexual conservatism?

4. What are your thoughts about how to deal with the moral issue raised by some with regard to AIDS?

5. What will you tell your children about the morality of premarital sex?

## SUGGESTED READINGS

Durkin, M. G. (1983). *Feast of love: Pope John Paul II on human intimacy.* Chicago: Loyola University Press. Summaries and commentary on talks given by the Pope on various aspects of sexuality. An authentic expression of conservative sexual morality by the man who speaks for the Roman Catholic church.

Fletcher, J. (1966). *Situation ethics;* (1967). *Moral responsibility: Situation ethics at work.* Philadelphia: Westminster. The original, and still best, statements of situation ethics.

Hallingby, L., and Richie, D. (1987). Bibliography of religious publications on sex education and sexuality. *Siecus Report,* vol. 15, No 5, pp. 14–16. An extensive list of sources on sexuality published by various Christian denominations.

Kosnik et al. (1977). *Human sexuality: New directions in American Catholic thought.* New York: Paulist Press. A liberal reconsideration of traditional Catholic thinking on sexuality.

Larue, G. (1983). *Sex and the Bible.* New York: Prometheus. Biblical passages with brief explanations concerning a wide variety of sexual behavior.

Parrinder, G. (1980). *Sex in the world's religions.* New York: Oxford University Press. Scholarly yet nontechnical and interesting overview of sexuality in Judaism, Christianity, Islam, and Asian and African religions.

# Glossary

**abortion** The ending of a pregnancy before the fetus is mature enough to survive outside the uterus; may be induced (done intentionally) or spontaneous (see **spontaneous abortion**).

**abstinence** Voluntarily not engaging in sexual acts, such as intercourse.

**Acquired Immune Deficiency Syndrome (AIDS)** Primarily a sexually transmitted disease that destroys the immune system's ability to fight infections; however, can also be passed by needle sharing among intravenous drug users or contaminated blood products.

**adolescence** The term used to describe the psychosocial development of a child into an adult.

**adrenal glands** A pair of endocrine glands, located above the kidneys, that produce and secrete (among other things) androgens.

**adultery** The traditional Western term for a married person having sexual intercourse with someone other than his or her spouse.

**afterbirth** The placenta and amniotic sac that are expelled from the mother's body right after giving birth.

**ambisexual** See **bisexual.**

**amenorrhea** (ah meh NOR ee auh) The absence of menstruation; see **menstruation.**

**amniocentesis** (AM nee oh sen TEE sis) A procedure in which amniotic fluid is removed from a mother's uterus and tested to see if the fetus has genetic disorders or other abnormalities.

**amniotic fluid** (AM nee ot ik) The fluid within the amniotic sac that surrounds the fetus and cushions it from shock until birth.

**anal intercourse** Sexual behavior in which one person's penis is inserted into another's anus.

**anal stage** According to psychoanalytic theory, the stage of psychosexual development in which the child receives sexual gratification from the anal region.

**androgen** (ANN dro gin) A generic term used to describe a class of hormones (such as testosterone) that are primarily responsible for the development and functioning of the male reproductive system.

**androgen insensitivity** A condition in which a genetic male develops female genitals and breasts because of his body's failure to respond to testosterone; sometimes called testicular feminization syndrome.

**androgyny** (ann DRODGE ih nee) The blending of stereotypically masculine and feminine characteristics in the same person.

**anilingus** (AA nul LING gus) The oral stimulation of the anus; sometimes referred to as rimming.

**annulment** (auh NULL ment) The legal abolution of a marriage—treating it as if it never occurred—usually because sexual intercourse between the husband and wife never took place.

**anorgasmia** (ann ore GAZ mee ah) A female sexual dysfunction characterized by a persistent inability to reach orgasm; also called inhibited female orgasm.

**aphrodisiac** (AF ruh DIZ ee ak) A substance thought to increase a person's sexual desire, sexual performance, and/or sexual pleasure.

**areola** (AIR ee oh lah) The dark, circular area of skin that surrounds the nipple.

**artificial insemination** The placement of semen into a woman's vagina or uterus by means other than sexual intercourse so as to induce pregnancy.

**autoeroticism** A general term used to describe all forms of sexual self-stimulation or arousal, such as masturbation.

**autonomic nervous system** (AW toe NAWM ik) The part of the nervous system that regu-

675

lates the glands and organs of the body, including sexual reflexes.

**aversion therapy**    A form of behavior modification therapy that attempts to modify or eliminate certain behaviors by associating them with unpleasant stimuli, such as electric shock; sometimes used to treat paraphiliacs.

**Bartholin's glands** (bahr TOE linz)    Two small glands located on either side of the vaginal opening which are thought to secrete fluid to lubricate the vagina during sexual arousal.

**basal body temperature method** (BAY sul)    A method of birth control in which the changes in a woman's temperature are recorded in order to determine when she ovulates.

**bestiality** (BEE stee ah lih tee)    Engaging in sexual activity with an animal; also called zoophilia.

**Billings method**    A method of birth control in which a woman monitors the changes in the amount and consistency of her cervical mucus, thus identifying when she ovulates.

**birth control**    See **contraception.**

**bisexual**    A person who feels sexually attracted to or has had sexual contact with both males and females.

**blastocyst** (BLAS toe sist)    A small mass of cells, formed from the morula, that attaches itself to the uterine wall during the first week of pregnancy.

**bonding**    The process by which a parent and child become emotionally attached to each other.

**brothel**    A house where prostitutes work.

**call boy**    A high-priced male prostitute who works through match-making agencies; high-priced female prostitutes are called call girls.

**candidiasis** (KAN dih DYE ah sis)    A vaginal infection that is caused by the excessive growth of a yeastlike fungus that occurs normally in the body.

**castration** (kas TRAY shun)    The surgical removal of the testes.

**castration anxiety**    According to psychoanalytic theory, the unconscious fear in boys of losing their genitals as a form of punishment for feeling sexual desire toward their mother.

**celibacy** (SEL uh buh see)    Historically, the state of remaining unmarried as members of some religious orders do; currently, voluntarily abstaining from sexual activity.

**cervical cap** (SIR vih kull)    A contraceptive device, made of plastic or rubber, that fits over the mouth of the cervix and acts as a barrier to sperm.

**cervix** (SIR vix)    The lower portion of the uterus that opens into the vagina.

**Cesarean section** (see SAIR ee uhn)    A surgical procedure whereby the infant is delivered through an incision in the uterus and abdominal wall.

**chancre** (SHAN ker)    A hard, raised sore (usually painless) that characterizes the first stage of syphilis.

**chancroid** (SHAN kroid)    A bacterial sexually transmitted disease that causes soft, painful ulcers to appear on the genitals.

**chlamydia** (clah MID ee uh)    A bacterial sexually transmitted disease that in men causes painful urination, itching, and discharge, but in women may only cause a slight vaginal discharge.

**chorionic villi sampling (CVS)**    A procedure in which a sample of tissue is taken from the membrane that surrounds the fetus to test for possible birth defects.

**chromosome** (KROW moe sohm)    The genetic material found in the nucleus of every human cell; each cell has 46 chromosomes, except those in sperm and eggs which carry 23.

**cilia** (SIL eh uh)    The numerous hairlike structures that line the fallopian tubes and propel the egg to the uterus.

**circumcision** (SIR come SIH zhun)    The surgical removal of the foreskin **(prepuce)** of the penis.

**climacteric** (KLI mack tur ik)    A midlife period for both men and women during which many physiological changes take place due to the transition from fertility to infertility; also see **menopause.**

**clitoris** (KLI tore iss)    In females, a small highly sensitive genital organ; its function is to provide erotic pleasure when stimulated.

**cohabitation**    A situation in which a man and woman, romantically involved with each other, live together without being married (same-sex cohabitation is not legally recognized); also referred to as common-law marriage.

**coitus** (COY tus)   The technical term for the insertion of the penis into the vagina; commonly referred to as sexual intercourse.

**coitus interruptus** (COY tus in tur RUP tus) A birth control method in which the male removes his penis from a woman's vagina before ejaculation; also called withdrawal.

**coitus reservatus** (COY tus reh zur VAH tus) Sexual intercourse in which a man intentionally refrains from ejaculating.

**colostrum** (cuh LAW strum)   A watery substance, rich in protein and antibodies, secreted from the mother's breasts immediately following delivery; precursor to breast milk.

**common-law marriage**   see **cohabitation.**

**conception**   The beginning of a new life, marked by fertilization.

**condom** (KON dum)   A male contraceptive device—usually a thin, latex sheath—that fits over the penis; also used to prevent sexually transmitted diseases.

**congenital adrenal hyperplasia**   A condition in which the adrenal glands of the female fetus produce an excess amount of androgen, resulting in masculinized genitals upon birth; also referred to as adrenogenital syndrome.

**contextual ethics**   See **situational ethics.**

**contraception**   Techniques, devices, or drugs used to prevent pregnancy; also called birth control.

**copulation** (cop you LAY shun)   Sexual intercourse as a means of reproducing; applies to animals (and humans).

**corona** (cor OH nah)   The sensitive rim of the glans.

**corpora cavernosa** (CORE pour ah kah ver NOH sa)   Two parallel masses of erectile tissue, located in the shaft of the penis and the clitoris, that become engorged with blood during sexual arousal.

**corpus luteum** (CORE pus LOO tee um)   The part of the ovarian follicle that is left in the ovary after the egg has been released; its primary function is to secrete progesterone.

**corpus spongiosum** (CORE pus spun gee OH sum)   Within the penis, a column of spongy, erectile tissue that contains the urethra and becomes engorged with blood during sexual arousal; also called spongy body.

**couvade** (koo VAHD)   The male experience of symptoms that mimic pregnancy and/or childbirth.

**Cowper's glands** (KOW perz)   Two small structures, attached to the urethra in the male, that secrete a few drops of clear, sticky fluid during sexual arousal.

**cremasteric muscle** (KRE mah ster ik)   A muscle, located under the scrotum, that involuntarily elevates the testes in response to cold, sexual excitement, and other stimuli.

**cremasteric reflex**   The reflexive contractions of the cremasteric muscle when the inner thigh is stroked.

**critical period**   A point during development when key events must take place or development is forever altered.

**cross-dressing**   See **transvestism.**

**cryptorchidism** (krip tor KID ism)   A condition in which the testes fail to descend from the abdominal cavity into the scrotal sac.

**culture**   A society's characteristic behavior patterns, such as language, customs, beliefs, and artistic accomplishments.

**cunnilingus** (KUN ih LING gus)   The oral stimulation of the female genitals.

**cystitis** (sis TIE tiss)   An inflammation of the urinary bladder causing painful and frequent urinations.

**date rape**   A violent crime in which a woman is forced by her date or a close friend to have sexual relations with him.

**desensitizaton**   A form of behavior modification therapy in which the patient, while relaxed and in a safe environment, is gradually exposed to the anxiety-provoking situation until his anxiety extinguishes.

**diaphragm** (DYE uh fram)   A dome-shaped rubber contraceptive device that is inserted into the vagina to block the cervical opening.

**dihydrotestosterone** (die HIE dro tes TOSS tur ohn)   A hormone, similar to testosterone, that is responsible for the embryonic development of the male's external genitals.

**dilation and curettage (D & C)** (CURE eh taj) A process in which the cervix is dilated and then an instrument scrapes the uterine lining, used to treat uterine disorders or abort fetuses.

**dilation and evacuation (D & E)**   A method of abortion in which the cervix is dilated and the fetus is removed from the uterus with forceps, curettage, and suction; it is generally used in the second trimester.

**dildo**   An artificial penis, usually made of plastic, that is used for vaginal or anal stimulation.

**divorce**   The legal termination of a marriage.

**douch** (DOOSH)   To rinse out the inside of the vagina with water or chemical solutions.

**Down's syndrome**   A chromosomal disorder causing mental retardation and defects of the internal organs.

**dysmenorrhea** (diS men OR ee uh)   Pain experienced before or during menstruation—typically backaches, abdominal cramps, and aches in the thighs.

**dyspareunia** (DIS par OO nee ah)   Persistent pain during or after sexual intercourse.

**ectopic pregnancy** (EK top ik)   A pregnancy in which the fertilized egg implants itself in a site other than the uterus, most often a fallopian tube.

**ejaculation** (ee JACK you LAY shun)   The expulsion of semen from the penis, usually during orgasm.

**ejaculatory ducts** (ee JACK you la TORE ee) Two tubelike structures that serve as a pathway for sperm and seminal fluid to move from the prostate gland to the urethra.

**ejaculatory incompetence**   A male sexual dysfunction characterized by an inability to ejaculate during intercourse.

**embryo** (EM bree oh)   The term used to refer to the unborn child during the first eight weeks of pregnancy.

**endocrine glands** (EN doe krin)   Ductless glands that produce and secrete hormones into the bloodstream.

**endometrium** (en doe MEE tree um)   The inner lining of the uterus, which is partially shed during menstruation.

**epididymis** (ep ih DID ih mus)   A tightly coiled tube, located at the upper back of each testis, in which sperm mature.

**episiotomy** (eh PIZ ee ot uh me)   An incision made, during delivery, between the vagina and anus to give the baby's head more room to emerge and to avoid injury to vaginal tissues.

**erectile dysfunction**   See **impotence.**

**erogenous zones** (eh RAW jeh nus)   Areas of the body particularly responsive to sexual stimulation.

**Eros**   According to psychoanalytic theory, erotic love or libidinal instinct.

**erotica** (e ROT ih ka)   Sexually oriented materials that the reader or viewer finds sexually arousing and non-offensive.

**estrogen replacement therapy**   A treatment before and during menopause in which a woman takes supplemental estrogen.

**estrogens** (ES tro ginz)   A group of "female" hormones—produced primarily by the ovaries—responsible for sexual maturation, regulation of the menstrual cycle, and maintenance of the uterine lining.

**estrus** (ES truss)   The period in which many nonhuman female mammals are ovulating or sexually active; also referred to as "being in heat."

**eunuch** (YOU nik)   A castrated male.

**excitement phase**   The first phase of the human sexual response cycle, in which the person begins to feel physically and/or psychologically aroused: heart rate quickens, muscles tense, and genitals become engorged with blood.

**exhibitionism**   The act of exposing one's genitals to unwilling strangers to feel sexually aroused.

**Fallopian tubes** (fah LOW pee un)   The two narrow tubes that serve as a pathway for the eggs (ova) to move from the ovaries to the uterus; the place where fertilization usually takes place.

**fellatio** (feh LAY shee oh)   The oral stimulation of the male genitals.

**feminism**   A theory that supports political, economic, and social equality for men and women.

**fertility symbols**   Primitive art, used for magical-religious purposes, that was thought to promote human and animal fertility; art objects included spears, clubs, erect penises, and exaggerated breasts, buttocks, and stomachs.

**fertilization**   The moment when the sperm and ovum unite.

**fetal alcohol syndrome**  A birth disorder due to the mother's heavy drinking while pregnant; abnormalities may be as serious as mental retardation.

**fetishism** (FET ish iz um)  Obtaining sexual arousal primarily from an inanimate object or a particular part of the body.

**fetus** (FEE tus)  The term used to refer to the unborn child from the ninth week of pregnancy to birth.

**follicle** (FALL ih kul)  The group of cells in the ovary that contain an egg.

**follicle-stimulating hormone (FSH)** (FALL ih kul)  A pituitary hormone that stimulates the maturation of ovarian follicles in the female and sperm production in the male.

**foreplay**  Kissing, touching, genital stimulation, and other forms of physical contact between two people that leads to sexual intercourse; see **petting.**

**foreskin**  See **prepuce.**

**fornication** (for nuh KAY shun)  Legal term for sexual intercourse between two consenting, unmarried individuals.

**frigidity** (fri JID ih tee)  An outdated term once used to describe most sexual dysfunctions common to females.

**gametes**  See **germ cells.**

**gay liberation movement**  The organized demand of America's homosexual community for political, economic, and social equality.

**gender identity**  The view of one's self as being either male or female.

**gender roles**  The behaviors and traits that a given culture deems appropriate for males and females.

**gene**  The DNA molecules, found on chromosomes, responsible for hereditary transmission from parent to child.

**genitals** (JEN ih tulz)  The sex organs of males and females, typically the penis, testes, and scrotum in males and the vulva in females.

**genital tubercle** (TOO ber kul)  A small bud of fetal tissue that develops into either a penis or a clitoris.

**genital warts**  Warts on the genitals, caused by a sexually transmitted virus.

**germ cells**  Sperm or egg cells.

**gigolo**  A man who provides companionship as well as sexual services to women for money.

**glans**  The tip of the penis or clitoris, rich with nerve endings.

**gonadotropin releasing hormone (GnRH)**  A hormone, produced by the hypothalamus, that controls the output of LH and FSH by the pituitary.

**gonadotropins** (goe NAD o TROE pinz)  Pituitary hormones that stimulate the gonads (testes and ovaries) to secrete their own hormones.

**gonads** (GOE nads)  The testes or ovaries—reproductive glands.

**gonorrhea** (GONE or REE ah)  A venereal disease caused by bacteria, causing urethral and vaginal discharge.

**Graafian follicle**  The mature follicle; it houses the egg that is released during ovulation.

**Grafenberg spot** (GRAY fen berg)  An erotically sensitive area presumably located in the anterior wall of the vagina; sometimes called the G-spot.

**granulosa cells** (gran oo LOW suh)  The cells that line the ovarian follicle, and later become the corpus luteum.

**group marriage**  A situation in which several couples or families live together; it may or may not involve sexual sharing of partners.

**group rape**  A violent crime in which a person (usually a woman) is forced to have sexual relations with two or more men.

**hepatitis** (HEP ah TIE tis)  An inflammation of the liver caused by a virus, which may be transmitted through sexual contact.

**hermaphrodite** (her MAF roe dite)  A person who has both ovarian and testicular tissue, and thus has genital features of both sexes.

**herpes** (HER peez)  Painful blisters of the genitals or mouth that are caused by a virus, transmitted through sexual contact.

**heterosexuality**  A sexual orientation in which a person is sexually, emotionally, and socially attracted towards members of the opposite sex.

**homogamy**  The principle that "like marries like," with respect to characteristics like age, race, socioeconomic status, and religion.

**homophobia** (home oh FOBE ee uh)   An irrational fear of or hostility toward homosexuals.

**homosexual rape**   A violent crime in which a man is forced by another man to have oral sex or anal intercourse.

**homosexuality**   A sexual orientation in which a person is sexually, emotionally, and socially attracted toward members of the same sex.

**hormones** (HOR mohnz)   Chemical substances, secreted by the endocrine glands into the bloodstream, that have an effect on physiological functioning and psychological behavior.

**hot flashes**   A common symptom of menopause in which the woman experiences sudden sensations of warmth, sweating, or chilliness.

**human chorionic gonadotropin** (KORE ee ON ik goe NAD o TROE pin)   A hormone produced by the placenta and similar to pituitary gonadotropin. Normally found only in the urine of pregnant women.

**human immunodeficiency virus (HIV)** (ih MEW no dee FIH chun see)   The retrovirus that causes AIDS.

**hustlers**   Male prostitutes who have other males as their clients.

**hymen** (HI men)   The delicate tissue partially covering the vaginal opening, usually until a female first has intercourse.

**hypoactive sexual desire disorder**   A sexual dysfunction characterized by a persistent absence of both sexual fantasies and desire for sex.

**hypothalamus** (hie poe THAL uh mus)   The part of the brain that regulates (among other things) sexual functions by controlling the production and release of gonadotropic hormones.

**hysterectomy** (HISS tur EK tuh me)   A surgical procedure in which a woman's uterus is removed.

**impotence** (im PUH tence)   The inability to have or maintain a firm erection despite stimulation; also called erectile dysfunction.

**incest**   Sexual activity between close relatives, for example, between fathers and daughters.

**infertility** (in fur TILL ah tee)   The inability of a man, woman, or couple to conceive a child, usually after one year of trying.

**inhibited female orgasm**   See **anorgasmia.**

**inhibited male orgasm**   See **retarded ejaculation.**

**interstitial cells** (in tur STISH ee ul)   The cells, located between seminiferous tubules in the testes, that produce most of the androgens in the male; also called Leydig's cells.

**intrauterine device (IUD)** (IN tra YOU ter in)   A small plastic device inserted into the uterus for birth control.

**in vitro fertilization (IVF)** (in VEE trow)   A procedure in which a woman's mature eggs are extracted from her body, fertilized with sperm in a laboratory, and then implanted in her uterus.

**Kegal exercises**   A series of exercises aimed at strengthening the muscles surrounding the vagina and urethra.

**kiddie porn**   Pornographic printed or visual materials that show children engaging in sexual acts, usually with adults.

**Klinefelter's syndrome**   A sex chromosome disorder in which a male is born with an extra X chromosome, resulting in an XXY pattern; these men have small testes and penises and are infertile.

**labia majora** (LAY bee uh MUH jor ah)   The two, outer elongated folds of skin surrounding the labia minora, the clitoris, and the urethral and vaginal openings.

**labia minora** (LAY bee uh mi NOR uh)   The two, small inner folds of skin surrounding the urethral and vaginal openings.

**labioscrotal swelling**   The fetal tissue that develops into the scrotum in the male or the labia majora in the female.

**labor**   The process involved in giving birth: rhythmic uterine contractions, cervical dilation, the baby's birth, and expulsion of the placenta.

**lactation** (lak TAY shun)   The production of breast milk in the female that begins about two to three days after giving birth.

**Lamaze method** (lah MAHZ)   A method of prepared childbirth emphasizing muscle relaxation and controlled breathing.

**lesbian** (LEZ bee un)   A female homosexual.

**leukorrhea** (LOO kor REE ah)   Whitish or puslike vaginal discharge caused by various infections or irritating chemicals.

**Leydig's cells** (LEE digz)    See **interstitial cells.**

**libido** (lih BEE doe)    The psychoanalytic term for sexual drive or energy.

**limbic system** (LIM bik)    A set of brain structures that regulate our sexual and emotional behavior.

**limerance** (LIH mer ence)    The term coined by Dorothy Tennov to describe being in love.

**lochia** (LOH key ah)    A reddish-brown uterine discharge lasting several weeks following childbirth.

**luteinizing hormone (LH)** (LOO tuh nye zing)    A pituitary hormone that stimulates the corpus luteum in the ovaries to produce progesterone, and the Leydig cells in the testes to produce androgens.

**madam**    A woman who runs a brothel.

**mammory glands** (MAM ah ree)    Milk-producing organs in the female breast.

**marital rape**    A violent crime in which a woman is forced by her husband to have sexual relations with him.

**mastectomy** (mass TEK toe me)    The surgical removal of a breast.

**meiosis** (my OH sis)    Germ cell division in which the number of chromosomes is reduced by half.

**menarche** (MEN ark)    A pubescent girl's first menstrual period.

**menopause** (MEN oh pause)    The gradual ending of a woman's menstrual cycles, usually beginning in her late forties.

**menorrhagia** (men or HAG ee ah)    An increase in the amount or duration of menstrual bleeding.

**menstruation** (MEN stroo a shun)    A bloody vaginal discharge caused by the sloughing off of the uterine lining, occurring at about monthly intervals. Also called **menses** or **period**.

**midwife**    A woman who assists in another's childbirth.

**mitosis** (my TOE sis)    A type of cell division in which the cell splits into two identical cells.

**monogamy** (mah NAW guh mee)    A type of marriage in which a person has only one spouse at a time.

**mons pubis** (monz PEW bis)    The soft, fatty tissue over the female pubic bone that becomes covered with pubic hair during puberty; also called mons veneris or mound of Venus.

**morning sickness**    The nausea upon awakening, followed by an aversion to food, commonly experienced by women during their first eight weeks of pregnancy.

**morula** (MOHR oo lah)    A round mass of cells developing from the zygote within a few days of fertilization.

**Mullerian ducts** (mew LAIR ee un)    The parts of the female fetus that develop into the Fallopian tubes, uterus, and upper portion of the vagina.

**myotonia** (MY oh TONE ee ah)    Increased muscle tension that occurs during the sexual response cycle.

**nature versus nurture**    The theoretical controversy over whether nature (biology) or nurture (environment) is primarily responsible for behavior—including sexuality.

**necrophilia** (NEK roe FILL ee ah)    Engaging in sexual activity with a dead person.

**nipple**    The prominent tip of the breast, made of smooth muscle and nerve fibers, that in females is the outlet of the milk ducts.

**nocturnal emission**    Ejaculation while asleep; also called a wet dream.

**no-fault divorce**    A type of divorce in which either spouse may claim irreconcilable differences to break up the marriage; neither party is considered at "fault."

**nursing**    The infant's sucking of milk from a woman's breast; also called breastfeeding.

**nymphomania** (NIM foe MAY nee uh)    Hyperactive sexual desire in women.

**Oedipus complex** (ED ih pus)    According to psychoanalytic theory, a child's sexual attraction toward the parent of the opposite sex and hostility toward the parent of the same sex.

**open marriage**    A type of marriage in which the couple mutually consent to have emotional (and sometimes sexual) ties to other people as well as to each other.

**oral stage**    According to psychoanalytic theory, the stage of psychosexual development in which the infant's sexual gratification is derived from the mouth.

**orgasm** (or GAZ um)    An intensely pleasurable subjective sensation marking the sudden discharge of accumulated sexual tension.

**orgasmic platform**   As part of the female sexual response, the expansion of the outer vaginal walls and narrowing of the vaginal opening due to vasocongestion.

**osteoporosis** (ah stee oh poh RO sis)   A condition, common in postmenopausal women, in which the bones become thin and brittle due to calcium loss.

**ovaries** (OH vah reez)   The pair of female reproductive glands, located on each side of the uterus, which produce eggs and sex hormones; also called the female gonads.

**ovulation** (ohv you LAY shun)   The process by which a mature egg is released from the ovary.

**ovum** (OH vum)   A mature egg cell.

**oxytocin** (ahk see TOK sin)   A pituitary hormone that stimulates the release of breast milk as well as uterine contractions.

**pair bonds**   The strong, lifelong attachments that naturally take place between two animals; it includes "love" when speaking of humans.

**palimony** (PAH lih mow nee)   A legal term for the property settlement of a couple who lived together, but were not married to each other.

**panderer**   A person who procures prostitutes for clients; also see **pimp.**

**pap smear**   A routine test for cervical cancer; a small sampling of cervical cells are lightly scraped from the cervix for examination.

**paraphilias** (pare uh FILL ee ahz)   Variations in sexual behavior that society deems unusual or atypical.

**parasympathetic nervous system**   One of two subdivisions of the autonomic nervous system associated primarily with the vasocongestive response in sexual arousal (among other effects on the body). See **sympathetic nervous system.**

**pedarasty** (PEH dur AS tee)   An ancient Greek custom in which an older man (usually a mentor) has a sexual relationship with a young man.

**pediculosis pubis** (peh DIK you LOW sis PYOU bis)   Lice infesting pubic hair, usually acquired through sexual contact but sometimes through infected clothing or bedding; commonly called crabs.

**pedophilia** (PEH doe FILL ee ah)   Engaging in sexual activity with children as the preferred form of erotic gratification.

**pelvic inflammatory disease**   An inflammation of the Fallopian tubes, the lining of the uterus, and/or the lower abdominal cavity as a result of various bacterial infections—gonorrhea or chlamydia for example.

**penis** (PEE nis)   The male sexual organ of copulation that also expels urine from the body.

**petting**   Kissing, touching, genital stimulation, and other forms of physical contact between two people that does not include sexual intercourse; see **foreplay.**

**Peyronie's disease** (pay ROH neez)   A rare condition, caused by abnormal fibrous tissue in the penis, resulting in painful erections.

**phallic stage** (FAHL ik)   According to psychoanalytic theory, the psychosexual stage of development in which the child's sexual energies are focused on its genitals.

**phallic symbols**   Objects that symbolize the penis, such as sticks, knives, and cylindrical monuments.

**phallus**   The penis.

**pheromones** (FARE oh mohnz)   Chemical substances that send out messages, including sexual ones, through the sense of smell.

**pimp**   A prostitute's agent; he lives off her earnings in exchange for protection, social companionship, and emotional support.

**pituitary gland** (pih TEW ih tare e)   A small endocrine gland at the base of the brain, that secretes several hormones important to sexual development and functioning—like FSH and LH.

**placenta** (pluh SEN tah)   The organ attached to the uterine wall through which the fetus receives nutrients and oxygen from the mother and expels waste products.

**plateau phase**   Following excitement, the phase of human sexual response in which sustained sexual tension precedes orgasm.

**pleasure principle**   According to psychoanalytic theory, the concept that libido is motivated to seek immediate gratification, regardless of realistic constraints; also see **reality principle.**

**polyandry** (PAW lee ANN dree)   A type of marriage in which one woman has several husbands.

**polygyny** (paw LIH jih nee)   A type of marriage in which one man has several wives.

**pornography**   Printed or visual materials aimed at arousing sexual feelings that (unlike erotica) may be offensive to the viewer. **Hard-core pornography** is explicit sexual material that focuses on coitus, cunnilingus, fellatio, and atypical sexual behavior, including violence. **Soft-core pornography** resembles erotica in that it focuses on nudity and suggestive sexual interactions.

**postpartum depression**   The mild to moderate depression that women may experience after giving birth; also called "the baby blues."

**postpartum period** (post PAR tum)   The six-to-eight-week period following childbirth in which a woman is adjusting to many physiological and psychological changes.

**premature ejaculation**   A common male sexual dysfunction in which ejaculation uncontrollably occurs before or shortly after intercourse begins.

**premenstrual syndrome (PMS)**   A combination of physical and psychological symptoms (fatigue, depression, irritability) that some women experience prior to menstruation.

**prepuce**   The fold of skin over the clitoris (also called the clitoral hood) or the loose, movable skin that covers the penis (also called the foreskin).

**priapism** (PRY ah PIZ um)   Prolonged erection independent of sexual arousal.

**primary sexual characteristics**   The internal sex organs and the external genitalia.

**primary sexual dysfunction**   A sexual dysfunction which has always existed; for example, a man has never been able to have an erection or a woman has never experienced an orgasm; see **secondary sexual dysfunction.**

**progesterone** (pro JES tur own)   Primarily a "female" hormone—produced by the corpus luteum—that maintains the uterine lining during pregnancy.

**prolactin** (pro LACK tin)   A pituitary hormone that stimulates milk production in lactating women.

**prostaglandins** (pro stah GLAN dinz)   Hormones, produced by the prostate glands and other tissues, that cause uterine contractions, especially during labor; sometimes used to induce abortion.

**prostate gland** (PROS tate)   A gland, located at the base of the bladder, that produces most of the seminal fluid in a male.

**prostatitis** (PRO state I tis)   An inflammation of the prostate gland that causes frequent and painful urination in men.

**prostitution**   Engaging in sexual activity for money.

**pseudocyesis** (sue doe CYE ah sis)   A false pregnancy; whereby the female experiences symptoms—morning sickness, tender breasts, abdominal sensations—but she is not pregnant.

**pseudohermaphrodite** (sue doe her MAF roe dite)   A person with the sex chromosomes and gonad of one sex but the external genitals of the other sex.

**psychoanalytic theory**   A psychological theory, originated by Sigmund Freud, in which unconscious processes and infantile sexuality receive a particularly strong emphasis.

**puberty** (PEW burr tee)   The stage of life between childhood and adulthood during which the reproductive system matures and secondary sexual characteristics develop.

**pubococcygeus muscle** (pew bow cock SEE gee us)   The muscle that surrounds the vaginal opening.

**rape**   A violent crime in which a person is forced to have sexual relations with another.

**rape trauma syndrome**   The emotional and psychological turmoil—guilt, fear, anger, depression—that a victim (typically a woman) experiences after being raped; see **rape.**

**reality principle**   According to psychoanalytic theory, the concept that the rational, conscious self operates in harmony with the real world; see also **pleasure principle.**

**refractory period**   In males only, the period of time immediately following an orgasm in which it is physiologically impossible to experience another orgasm.

**resolution phase**   The final phase of the human sexual response in which the body returns to its initially unaroused state—muscles relax, breathing slows down, and sex organs return to their usual color and size.

**retarded ejaculation**   A male sexual dysfunction in which ejaculation occurs (if at all) only after lengthy intercourse and effort; sometimes called inhibited male orgasm.

**retrograde ejaculation**   A condition in which semen is expelled into the urinary bladder during orgasm instead of out of the penis.

**Rh incompatibility**   A condition in which the mother's antibodies destroy the red blood cells of the fetus, leading to anemia, jaundice, and even death.

**sadomasochism** (say doe MASS ah kiz um)   A combination of two paraphilias—sadism: obtaining sexual gratification from inflicting physical or psychological pain on another person, and masochism: obtaining sexual gratification from receiving such pain.

**saline abortion**   A method of abortion, used in the second trimester, in which a strong salt solution is injected into the uterus to induce labor.

**satyriasis** (SAH ter RYE uh sis)   Insatiable sexual desire in men.

**scabies** (SKAY beez)   A highly contagious infection, caused by tiny parasitic mites, that may be sexually transmitted.

**scrotum** (SKRO tum)   The loose sac of skin that lies behind the penis and contains the testes.

**secondary sexual characteristics**   The physical characteristics, other than genitals, that indicate sexual maturity in a female or male, such as breasts, pubic hair, facial hair, and a deepened voice.

**secondary sexual dysfunction**   A sexual dysfunction caused by a physiological and/or psychological problem that has not always existed; see **primary sexual dysfunction.**

**semen** (SEE men)   The milky white fluid, containing sperm, that is ejaculated from the penis during orgasm.

**seminal vesicles** (SEM in nul VES ih kulz)   Two saclike organs that continue secretions to seminal fluid.

**seminiferous tubules** (sem ih NIF er us)   Thin coiled tubes, located in the testes, that produce and store billions of sperm.

**sensate focus**   A sex therapy exercise in which people touch each other with the goal of giving pleasure and not with the expectation of subsequent intercourse; the purpose is to reduce anxiety and thereby reduce sexual dysfunctions.

**sex chromosomes**   A single pair of chromosomes that determine the sex and related characteristics of each individual.

**sex flush**   A rashlike redness of the skin that appears on the chest and/or breasts during sexual arousal; more common in women.

**sexism**   The institutionalized and/or culturally based discrimination against women; for example, sexist language or the exaggeration by the media of stereotypic masculine or feminine behaviors.

**sex skin**   The pink or red coloration of the labia minora (minor lips) when a woman is sexually aroused to the point of orgasm.

**sex therapy**   A variety of general procedures (such as couple-counseling) and specific strategies (such as sensate focus) used to treat sexual dysfunctions.

**sexology**   A general term encompassing sex research, education, and therapy.

**sexual addiction**   Engaging in sexual activity in a compulsive, sometimes uncontrollable and destructive manner, to reduce anxiety temporarily or create an illusion of intimacy.

**sexual assault**   Sexual coercion that relies on physical force.

**sexual aversion**   A persistent and extreme fear of or distaste for sexual activity.

**sexual coercion**   Psychologically and physically intimidating someone to have sexual relations; the extreme form is rape.

**sexual dimorphism** (die MORE fih zum)   The differences between male and female anatomical and physiological differences and sexual behavior.

**sexual dysfunction**   A disturbance with sexual desire (such as lack of interest) or sexual performance (such as inability to reach orgasm) for physical, psychological, interpersonal, and/or cultural reasons.

**sexual harassment**   Unwanted sexual comments and advances most often linked to the workplace; may also include sexual bribery.

**sexual identity**   The view of one's own sexual

characteristics (degree of sexiness), sexual orientation (heterosexual, homosexual, bisexual), sex values, and gender identity.

**sexual intercourse** See **coitus.**

**sexually transmitted disease** A contagious infection (caused by a bacteria, virus, or protozoa) that is transmitted primarily through sexual contact; also called venereal disease.

**sexual revolution** Period in the late 1960s and early 1970s in which American society developed a more liberal view of sexuality.

**situational ethics** A way of making ethical decisions based on the considerations of the particular people involved and the specific context in which behavior takes place; also referred to as contextual ethics.

**smegma** (SMEG muh) A yellowish substance that is secreted under the foreskin of the penis or the hood of the clitoris.

**society** A network of human relationships organized in such a way to bind a group of people together; also see **culture.**

**sodomy** (SAH doe me) Anal intercourse usually between two men, but sometimes refers to bestiality (sex with animals) or mouth-genital sex.

**Spanish fly** An alleged aphrodisiac derived from the dried powder of beetles. See **aphrodisiac.**

**spectatoring** Anxiously watching or judging one's own sexual performance.

**sperm** The male reproductive cell which contains half of the chromosomes necessary for fertilizing an egg.

**spermatogenesis** (SPUR mat oh GEH neh sus) Sperm production.

**spermicides** (SPUR mih sidez) Contraceptive chemicals that kill sperm.

**spontaneous abortion** An abortion due to medical problems with the fetus or mother; sometimes called a miscarriage; also see **abortion.**

**squeeze technique** A technique used to reduce the tendency for rapid ejaculation; it consists of squeezing the glans or the base of the penis.

**statutory rape** Sexual intercourse with a person under the legal age of consent.

**sterilization** A surgical procedure performed to make a person incapable of reproducing.

**steroids** (STARE oidz) A group of chemical substances, including the sex hormones—estrogen, progesterone, and testosterone.

**sublimation** (sub lih MAY shun) According to psychoanalytic theory, the process by which libido is channeled into socially acceptable activities, like art or athletics.

**surrogate mother** A woman who carries a baby for a couple because the wife is sterile; she contractually agrees to relinquish the child to them following birth.

**surrogate partner** A member of a sex therapy team who engages in sexual activity with a client as part of the therapy process.

**swinging** The two-couple practice of exchanging marital partners for sex; sometimes referred to as wife-swapping.

**sympathetic nervous system** One of two subdivisions of the autonomic nervous system associated primarily with the orgasmic response (among other effects on the body). See **parasympathetic systems**.

**syphilis** (SIH fil lis) A venereal disease caused by a microorganism; if left untreated, it progresses through three stages—primary, secondary, and tertiary—with serious consequences.

**teratogen** (teh RAT oh jinz) A substance, such as a chemical or drug, that causes birth defects.

**testes** (TESS teze) The pair of male reproductive glands, located in the scrotum, which produce sperm and sex hormones; also called the male gonads.

**testosterone** (tess TOSS tur ohn) Primarily a "male" hormone, secreted by the testes in the male and the adrenal cortex in both sexes.

**thanatos** (THAN ah tose) According to psychoanalytic theory, aggression or death instinct; the opposite of **Eros.**

**toxemia** An abnormal condition that occurs in pregnant women; symptoms include high blood pressure, protein in the urine, and fluid retention.

**toxic shock syndrome** An illness associated with bacteria present in highly absorbent menstrual tampons.

**transsexualism** A condition in which a person feels persistently uncomfortable about his (or her) assigned sex, and desires to change his (or her) anatomy so as to live as a member of the opposite sex.

**transvestism** (trans VESS tizm)    Obtaining sexual gratification when dressed in the clothes of the opposite sex; also called cross-dressing.

**trichomoniasis** (TRIH ko mon I ah sis)    A common vaginal infection, characterized by a smelly, yellowish discharge and vaginal itching; caused by a parasite.

**tubal ligation** (lie GAY shun)    A surgical procedure in which a woman is sterilized by cutting or tying her fallopian tubes.

**Turner's syndrome**    A sex chromosome disorder in which a female is missing a chromosome, resulting in an XO pattern; these women are infertile, may have webbing between the fingers and toes or neck and shoulders, and usually have organ defects.

**ultrasonography**    A procedure in which sound waves are converted into a photographic image of the fetus to detect possible fetal abnormalities or to forecast complications in delivery.

**umbilical cord**    The cord that connects the fetus to the placenta.

**urethra** (ur REE thrah)    A tube through which urine passes from the bladder to outside the body; in men, it is also the passage way for semen.

**urethral meatus** (you REE thral ME a tus)    The opening of the urethra to the outside.

**urogenital folds**    The fetal tissue that develops into the penis and urethra in the male and the labia minora in the female.

**uterus** (YOU ter us)    A hollow, muscular organ in which a woman nourishes a fetus until birth; the womb.

**vacuum aspiration**    The preferred method of abortion during the first trimester in which the cervix is dilated and the contents of the uterus are extracted through a suction tube.

**vagina** (vah JYE nah)    The female organ of copulation through which menstrual blood is passed and babies are born.

**vaginal sponge**    A circular, highly absorbent sponge, treated with spermicide, that is placed in front of the cervical opening to block sperm.

**vaginismus** (VAH jih NIS mus)    A female sexual disorder marked by involuntary spasms of the muscles surrounding the vagina; it makes intercourse painful if not impossible.

**vaginitis** (VAH jih NIT is)    An inflammation of the vagina caused by any of a number of vaginal infections; symptoms include itching, pain, discharge, and discomfort during intercourse.

**vas deferens** (vas DEH fur renz)    Ducts that carry sperm from the testes to the base of the urethra.

**vasectomy** (vah SEK tuh mee)    A surgical procedure in which a man is sterilized by cutting or tying the vas deferens.

**vasocongestion** (VAH so con JES chun)    In response to sexual arousal, the accumulation of blood in the vessels and tissues of various body parts, especially the genitals.

**vasovasectomy** (VAH so vah SEK tuh mee)    A surgical procedure in which the vas deferens are reattached after a vasectomy; see **vasectomy.**

**venereal disease** (vah NEAR ee ul)    See **sexually transmitted disease.**

**voyerism** (VOY yer ism)    Obtaining sexual gratification from spying on people while they are undressing, nude, or engaging in sexual activity.

**vulva** (VUL va)    A collective term for the external genitals of the female—the mons pubis, the labia majora and minora, the clitoris, and the urethral and vaginal openings.

**wet dream**    See **nocturanal emission.**

**Wolffian ducts** (WOOL fee un)    The tissue in the male fetus that develops into the epididymus, vas deferens, and seminal vesicles.

**womb**    See **uterus.**

**women's liberation movement**    American feminism; see **feminism.**

**Yohimbine**    An alleged aprodisiac derived from the bark of the African Yohimbe tree. See **aphrodisiac.**

**zoophilia**    See **bestiality.**

**zygote** (ZY goat)    A single cell created by the union of an egg and sperm.

# References

Abel, G. (1981). The evaluation and treatment of sexual offenders and their victims. Paper presented at St. Vincent Hospital and Medical Center, Portland, OR, October 15. Cited in Crooks, R. & Baur, K. *Our Sexuality,* 3d ed. Menlo Park, CA: Benjamin/Cummings.

Abplanalp, J. M., Haskett, R. F., & Rose, R. M. (1980). The Premenstrual Syndrome. *Advances in Psychoneuroendocrinology, 3,* 327–347.

Abplanalp, J. M., Rose, R. M., Donnelly, A. F., & Livingston-Vaughan, L. (1979). Psychoendocrinology of the menstrual cycle: II. The relationship between enjoyment of activities, moods, and reproductive hormones. *Psychosomatic Medicine, 41,* 605.

Abramowitz, S. (1986). Psychosocial outcomes of sex reassignment surgery. *Journal of Consulting and Clinical Psychology,* April, *54*(2), 183–189.

Ackman, C. F. D., MacIsaac, S. G., & Schual, R. (1979). Vasectomy: Benefits and risks. *International Journal of Gynecology and Obstetrics 16,* 493–496.

*Adam and Eve.* (1978). Catalogue. Carrboro, NC: No publisher listed.

Adams, J. N. (1982). *The Latin sexual vocabulary.* London: Duckworth.

Addiego, F., Belzer, E. G., Comolli, J., Moger, W., Perry, J. D., & Whipple, B. (1981). Female ejaculation: A case study. *The Journal of Sex Research, 17*(1), 13–21.

Adler, N. E., & Dolcini, P. (1986). Psychological issues in abortion for adolescents. In G. B. Milton (ed.), *Adolescent Abortion,* pp. 74–95. Lincoln: University of Nebraska Press.

Ageton, S. (1983). *Sexual assault among adolescents.* Lexington, MA: Lexington Books.

AIDS: A public health crisis (1986). *Population Reports: Issues in World Health,* July–August, *14*(3), 193–228.

Ainsworth, M. D. S., Blehar, M., Waters, E., & Wall, S. (1978). *Patterns of attachment: Observations in the strange situation and at home.* Hillsdale, NJ: Erlbaum.

Alan Guttmacher Institute (1986, July 9). School based health program helps inner-city teens delay sex and prevent pregnancy. News Release.

Alan Guttmacher Institute (1981). *Teenage pregnancy: The problem that hasn't gone away.* Alan Guttmacher Institute.

Alford, J., & Brown, G. (1985). Virgins, whores, and bitches: Attitudes of rapists toward women and sex. *Corrective and Social Psychiatry, 31,* 58–61.

Allen, D. M. (1980). Young male prostitutes: A psychosocial study. *Archives of Sexual Behavior, 9*(5), 399–426.

Allgeier, A. R., & Allgeier, E. R. (1988). *Sexual interactions,* 2d ed. Lexington, MA: D.C. Heath.

Alter-Reid, K. et al. (1986). Sexual abuse of children: A review of the empirical findings. *Clinical Psychology Review, 6*(4), 249–266.

Altman, D. (1982). *The homosexualization of America.* Boston: Beacon Press.

Altman, L. D. (1982, July 22). Measuring the benefits of the pill. *San Francisco Chronicle,* p. 23.

Altman, L. K. (1987, June 30). AIDS mystery: Why do some infected men stay healthy? *New York Times.*

Altman, L. K. (1986, November 20). Global program aims to combat AIDS "disaster." *New York Times,* p. 4.

Alzate, H., & Hoch, Z. (1986). The "G spot" and "female ejaculation": A current appraisal. *Journal of Sex and Marital Therapy,* Fall, *12*(3), 211–220.

Amann-Gainotti-Merete (1986). Sexual socialization during early adolescence: the menarche. *Adolescence, 21*(83), 703–710.

American Humane Association. (1986). Referred to in Runyan, D. K. (1986). Incest: The trauma of intervention. *SIECUS Report, 15*(1), 2.

American Law Institute, Model penal code: Revised. (1980). Philadelphia.

American Psychiatric Association. (1987). *Diagnostic and statistical manual* (DSM III-R). Washington, DC: American Psychiatric Association.

American Social Health Association. (1982). Gays and STDs. Pamphlet.

Amick, A. E., & Calhoun, K. S. (1987). Resistance to sexual aggression: Personality, attitudinal, and situational factors. *Archives of Sexual Behavior,* *16*(2), 153–163.

Amir, M. (1971). *Patterns of forcible rape.* Chicago: University of Chicago Press.

Andersch, B., Wendestam, C., Hahn, L., Ohman, R., & Goteborgs, U. Premenstrual complaints: I. Prevalence of premenstrual symptoms in a Swedish urban population (1986). *Journal of Psychosomatic Obstetrics and Gynecology,* March, *5*(1), 39–49.

Anderson, C. L. (1975). What are psychology departments doing about sex education. *Teaching of Psychology, 2*(1), 24–27.

Anderson, F. C., & Rubinstein, D. (1978). Prevalence of sexual dysfunction in "normal" couples. *New England Journal of Medicine, 299,* 111–115.

Anderson, J. (1977). *The witch on the wall: Medieval erotic sculpture in the British Isles.* London: Allen & Unwin.

Anderson, T. P., & Cole, T. M. (1975). Sexual counseling of the physically disabled. *Postgraduate Medicine, 58,* 117–123.

Annon, J. S. (1976). *The behavioral treatment of sexual problems: Brief therapy.* New York: Harper & Row.

Ansbacher, R. (1978). Artificial insemination with frozen spermatozoa. *Fertility and Sterility, 29,* 375–379.

Apfelbaum, B. (ed.). (1980). *Expanding the boundaries of sex therapy.* Berkeley, CA: Berkeley Sex Therapy Group.

Arafat, I. S., & Cotton, W. (1979). Masturbatory practices of college males and females. In M. F. DeMartino (ed.), *Human autoerotic practices.* New York: Human Sciences Press.

Arafat, I. S., & Cotton, W. L. (1974). Masturbation practices of males and females. *Journal of Sex Research, 10,* 293–307.

Aral, S., Mosher, W., & Cates, W., Jr., (1985). Self-reported pelvic inflammatory disease in U.S. women of reproductive age, 1982: A common occurrence. *American Journal of Public Health, 75,* 1216–1218.

Arentewicz, G., & Schmidt, G. (eds.). (1983). *The treatment of sexual disorders.* New York: Basic.

Arey, L. B. (1974). *Developmental anatomy,* 7th ed. Philadelphia: Saunders.

Aries, P. (1962). *Centuries of childhood.* New York: Knopf.

Arms, K., & Camp, P. S. (1987). *Biology,* 3d ed. Philadelphia: W. B. Saunders.

Arms, S. (1975). *Immaculate deception.* Boston: Houghton Mifflin.

Arsdalen, V. K. N., Mallow, T. R., & Wein, A. J. (1983). Erectile physiology, dysfunction and evaluation. *Monographs in Urology,* 136–156.

Athanasiou, R., & Sarkin, R. (1974). Premarital sexual behavior and postmarital adjustment. *Archives of Sexual Behavior, 3*(3), 207–225.

Athanasiou, R., Shaver, P., & Travis, C. (1970). Sex (A report to *Psychology Today* readers). *Psychology Today, 4,* 37–52.

Atkins, J. (1973, 1978). *Sex in literature.* Vol. II, Vol. III. London: Calder.

Attorney General's Commission on Pornography. (1987). *Final Report.* Washington, DC: U.S. Government Printing Office.

Augustine, St. (1955). *Treatises on marriage and other subjects.* Wilcox, C. et al.: translators. New York: Fathers of the Church.

Augustine, St. (1934). *The city of God, book XIV.* J. Healey, translator. New York: Dutton.

Austin, C. R., & Short, R. V. (eds.). (1972). *Reproduction in mammals* (5 volumes). London: Cambridge University Press.

Autill, J. K. (1983). Sex role complementarity versus similarity in married couples. *Journal of Personality and Social Psychology, 45,* 145–155.

Avery-Clark, C. (1986a). Sexual dysfunction and disorder patterns of husbands of working and nonworking women. *Journal of Sex-Marital Therapy,* Winter, *12*(4), 282–296.

Avery-Clark, C. (1986b). Sexual dysfunction and disorder patterns of working and nonworking wives. *Journal of Sex-Marital Therapy,* Summer, *12*(2), 93–107.

Bacci, M., & Porena, M. (1986). Masturbation injury resulting from intraurethral introduction of spaghetti. *American Journal of Forensic Medical Pathology,* September, *7*(3), 254–255.

Bailey, D. S. (1963). *Sexual ethics: A Christian view.* New York: Macmillan.

Bailey, D. S. (1959). *Sexual relations in Christian thought.* New York: Harper & Row.

Bailey, D. S. (1955). *Homosexuality and the western Christian tradition.* London: Shoestring.

Bailey, T., & Kennedy, D. (1979). *The American pageant,* 6th ed. Lexington, MA: Heath.

Baird, D., & Wilcox, A. (1985). Cigarette smoking associated with delayed conception. *Journal of the American Medical Association, 253,* 2979–2983.

Baker, S. W. (1980). Biological influences on human sex and gender. *Signs, 6,* 80–96.

Bakwin, H. (1974). Erotic feelings in infants and young children. *Medical Aspects of Human Sexuality, 8*(10), 200–215.

Balfour, J. G. (1876). An Arab physician on insanity. *The Journal of Mental Science, 98,* 241–249.

Bancroft, J. (1986a). Reproductive hormones and sexual function. Abstracts: Conference on the scientific basis of sexual dysfunction. Bethesda, MD: National Institutes of Health.

Bancroft, J. (1986b). The role of hormones in female sexuality. *Proceedings of the 8th International Congress of Psychosomatic Obstetrics and Gynecology.* Amsterdam: Excerpita Medica.

Bancroft, J. (1983). *Human sexuality and its problems.* Edinburgh: Churchill-Livingstone.

Bancroft, J. (1980). Endocrinology of sexual function. *Clinics in Obstetrics and Gynecology, 7*(2), 253–281.

Bancroft, J. (1974). *Deviant sexual behavior.* Oxford: Clarendon Press.

Bancroft, J., & Wu, F. C. W. (1983). Changes in erectile responsiveness during androgen therapy. *Archives of Sexual Behavior, 12,* 59–66.

Bandura, A. (1986). *Social foundations of thought and action—A social cognitive theory.* Englewood Cliffs, NJ: Prentice-Hall.

Bandura, A. (1969). *Principles of behavior modification.* New York: Holt, Rinehart and Winston.

Bandura, A., & Walters, R. H. (1959). *Adolescent aggression. A study of the influence of child-training practices and family interrelationships.* New York: Ronald Press.

Barbach, L. G. (1975). *For yourself: The fulfillment of female sexuality.* New York: Doubleday.

Barber, R. N. (1969). Prostitution and the increasing number of convictions for rape in Queensland. *Australian and New Zealand Journal of Criminology, 2,* 169–174.

Barclay, A. M. (1973). Sexual fantasies in men and women. *Medical Aspects of Human Sexuality, 7*(5), 105–216.

Barclay, D. (1987). Benign disorders of the vulva and vagina. In M. Pernoll & R. Benson (eds.), *Current obstetric and gynecologic diagnosis and treatment 1987.* Los Altos, CA: Appleton & Lange.

Bardwick, J. (1971). *Psychology of women.* New York: Harper & Row.

Barker, R. L. (1987). *The Green-eyed marriage: Surviving jealous relationships.* New York: Macmillan.

Barron, J. (1987, November 8). Learning the facts of life. *New York Times,* pp. 16–18.

Barron, J. (1986, March 30). Views of surrogacy harden after baby M ruling. *New York Times.*

Barrows, S. B., & Novak, N. (1987). *Mayflower madam: The secret life of Sydney Biddle Barrows.* New York: Ballantine.

Bartell, G. D. (1971). *Group sex.* New York: Wyden.

Baruch, D. W. (1987). AIDS in the courts: Tort liability for the sexual transmissions of acquired immune deficiency syndrome. *Tort and Insurance Law Journal,* Winter, 165–193.

Basmajian, J. V. (1980). *Grant's method of anatomy.* Baltimore, MD: Williams & Wilkins.

Bates, M. (1967). *Gluttons and libertines.* New York: Vintage.

Battersby, J. D. (1987, April 9). Woman pregnant with daughter's triplets. *New York Times.*

Baucom, D., & Hoffman, J. (1983). Common mistakes spouses make in communicating. *Medical Aspects of Human Sexuality, 17*(11).

Bauman, K. D., & Wilson, R. R. (1974). Sexual behavior of unmarried university students in 1968 and 1972. *Journal of Sex Research, 10,* 327–333.

Baumeister, R. F. (1988). Masochism as escape from self. *The Journal of Sex Research, 25,*(2), 28–59.

Bayer, R. (1981). *Homosexuality and American psychiatry: The politics of diagnosis.* New York: Basic.

Bayros, M. V. (1968). *The amorous drawings of the Marquis Von Bayros.* New York: Cythera Press.

Beach, F. A. (1977). *Human sexuality in four perspectives.* Baltimore, MD: Johns Hopkins University Press.

Beach, F. A. (1976). Cross-species comparisons and the human heritage. *Archives of Sexual Behavior, 5*(5), 469–485.

Beach, F. A. (1971). Hormonal factors controlling the differentiation, development, and display of copulatory behavior in the ramstergig and related species. In E. Tobach, L. R. Aronson, & E. Shaw (eds.), *The biopsychology of development,* pp. 249–295. New York: Academic.

Beach, F. A. (ed.). (1965). *Sex and behavior.* New York: Wiley.

Beach, F. A. (1947). A review of physiological and psychological studies of sexual behavior in mammals. *Physiological Review, 27*(2), 15.

Beauvoir, S. D. (1972). *The coming of age.*

New York: Putnam.

Becker, J., Skinner, L., Abel, G., & Cichon, J. (1986). Level of postassault sexual functioning in rape and incest victims. *Archives of Sexual Behavior*, February, *15*(1), 37–49.

Bee, H. L. (1987). *The journey of adulthood*. New York: Macmillan.

Behrman, R. E., & Vaughan, V. C. (1983). *Nelson Textbook of Pediatrics*, 12th ed. Philadelphia: W. B. Saunders.

Bell, A. P. (1982). Sexual preference: A postscript. *SIECUS Report, 11*(2).

Bell, A. P., Weinberg, M. S., & Hammersmith, S. K. (1981). *Sexual preference: Its development in men and women*. Bloomington: Indiana University Press.

Bell, A. P. (1974). Homosexualities: Their range and character. In J. K. Cole & R. Dienstbier (eds.), *Nebraska symposium on motivation*. Lincoln: University of Nebraska Press.

Bell, A. P., & Weinberg, M. S. (1978). *Homosexualities*. New York: Simon & Schuster.

Bell, N., & Carver, W. (1980). A re-evaluation of gender label effects: Expectant mother's responses to infants. *Child Development, 51*, 925–927.

Bell, R., & Bell, P. (1972). Sexual satisfaction among married women. *Medical Aspects of Human Sexuality, 6* (12), 136–74.

Bell, R. R., & Gordon, M. (eds.). (1972). *The social dimension of human sexuality*. Boston: Little, Brown.

Belliveau, F., & Richter, L. (1970). *Understanding human sexual inadequacy*. New York: Bantam.

Belzer, E. J., Jr. (1981). Orgasmic expulsions of women: A review and heuristic inquiry. *The Journal of Sex Research, 17*, 1–12.

Bem, S. L., & Lenney, E. (1976). Sex-typing and the avoidance of cross-sex behavior. *Journal of Personality and Social Psychology, 33*, 48–54.

Bem, S. L., Martyna, W., & Watson, C. (1978). Sex typing and androgyny: Further explorations of the expressive domain. *Journal of Personality and Social Psychology, 34*, 1016–1023.

Bem, S. L. (1981). Gender schema theory: A cognitive account of sex typing. *Psychological Review, 88*, 845–864.

Bem, S. L. (1975). Sex role adaptability: One consequence of psychological androgyny. *Journal of Personality and Social Psychology, 31*(4), 634–643.

Bem, S. L. (1974). The measurement of psychological androgyny. *Journal of Consulting and Clinical Psychology, 42*, 155–162.

Bem, S. L. (1952). *Psychosexual functions*

Benderly, B. (1984, October). Rape free or rape prone. *Science Magazine*, pp. 40–43.

Bennett, N. G., Bloom, D. E., & Criag, H. (1986). Black and white marriage patterns: Why so different? Unpublished paper, cited in Exner, T. (1987).

Benson, D. J., & Thomson, G. E. (1982). Sexual harassment on a university campus: The confluence of authority relations, sexual interest and gender stratification. *Social Problems, 29*, 236–251.

Benson, G. S., McConnell, J. A., & Schmidt, W. A. (1981). Penile polsters: Functional structures or atherosclerotic changes? *Journal of Urology, 125*(6), 800–803.

Benton, D., & Wastell, V. (1986). Effects of androstenol on human sexual arousal. *Biology of Psychology*, April, *22*(2), 141–147.

Berkeley, S. F., Hightower, A. W., Broome, C. V., & Reingold, A. (1987). The relationship of tampon characteristics to menstrual toxic shock syndrome. *Journal of the American Medical Association*, August 21, *258*(77), 917–920.

Berlin, F., & Krout, E. (1986). Pedophilia: Diagnostic concepts, treatment, and ethical considerations. *American Journal of Forensic Psychiatry, 7*(1), 13–30.

Bermant, G., & Davidson, J. M. (1974). *Biological bases of sexual behavior*. New York: Harper & Row.

Bernstein, A. C., & Cowan, P. A. (1975). Children's concepts of how people get babies. *Child Development, 46*, 77–92.

Bernstein, R. (1981). The Y chromosome and primary sexual differentiation. *Journal of the American Medical Association, 245*(19); 1953–1956.

Berscheid, E., & Walster, E. (1974). A little bit about love. In T. L. Huston (ed.), *Foundations of interpersonal attraction*. New York: Academic Press.

Berscheid, E., Walster, E., & Bohrnstedt, G. (1973). The body image report. *Psychology Today, 7*, 119–131.

Bess, B. E., & Janus, S. S. (1976). Prostitution. In B. Sadock et al. (eds.), *The sexual experience*. Baltimore, MD: Williams & Wilkins.

Betancourt, J. (1983a). *Am I normal? An illustrated guide to your changing body*. New York: Avon.

Betancourt, J. (1983b). *Dear diary: An illustrated guide to your changing body*. New York: Avon.

Bettelheim, B. (1962). *Symbolic wounds*. New York: Collier.

Bieber, I., et al. (1962). *Homosexuality: A*

*psychoanalytic study*. New York: Basic.

Biehler, R. F. (1981). *Child development: An introduction*, 2d ed. Boston: Houghton Mifflin.

Billings, E. L., & Billings, J. J. (1974). *Atlas of the ovulation method*. Collegeville, MN: The Liturgical Press.

Billstein, S. Human lice. (1984). In K. Holmes, P. Mardh, P. Sparling, & P. Wiesner (eds.), *Sexually transmitted diseases*. New York: McGraw-Hill.

Birns, B. (1976). The emergence and socialization of sex differences in the earliest years. *Merrill-Palmer Quarterly, 22*, 229–254.

Blair, C. D., & Langon, R. I. (1971). Exhibitionism: Etiology and treatment. *Psychological Bulletin, 89*(3), 439–463.

Blakely, M. K. (1985, April). Is one woman's sexuality another woman's pornography? *Ms.*, pp. 37–47.

Bleier, R. (1984). *Science and gender*. New York: Pergamon Press.

Blos, P. (1980). Modifications in the traditional psychoanalytic theory of female adolescent development. *Adolescent Psychiatry, 8*, 8–24.

Blos, P. (1962). *On adolescence*. New York: Free Press.

Blumstein, P., & Schwartz, P. (1983). *American couples*. New York: Morrow.

Boardman, J., & LaRocca, E. (1975). *Eros in Greece*. New York: Erotic Art Book Society.

Boffey, P. M. (1988, March 6). Masters and Johnson say AIDS spread is rampant. *New York Times*, p. 14.

Bohlen, J. G. (1981). Sleep erection monitoring in the evaluation of male erectile failure. *Urological Clinics of North America, 8*(1), 119–134.

Bohlen, J. G., Held, J. P., & Sanderson, M. O. (1982a). Response of the circumvaginal musculature during masturbation. In B. Garber (ed.), *Circumvaginal musculature in sexual functions*. New York: Krager.

Bohlen, J. G., Held, J. P., & Sanderson, M. O. (1980). The male orgasm: Pelvic contractions, measured by anal probe. *Archives of Sexual Behavior, 9*, 403–521.

Bohlen, J. G., Held, J., Sanderson, M., & Ahlgren, A. (1982b). The female orgasm: Pelvic contractions. *Archives of Sexual Behavior, 2*(5).

Bokser, B. Z. (1962). *Wisdom of the Talmud*. New York: Citadel.

Bonaparte, M. (1953). *Female sexuality*. London: Imago, 1953.

Bond, S. B., & Mosher, D. L. (1986). Guided imagery of rape: Fantasy, reality and willing victim myth. *Journal of Sex Research, 22*, 162–183.

Bonsall, R. W., & Michael, R. P. (1978). Volatile odoriferous acids in vaginal fluid. In E. S. E. Hafez & T. N. Evans (eds.), *The human vagina*, pp. 167–177. New York: Elsevier.

*Book of Common Prayer*. (n.d.). London: Oxford University Press.

Bookstein, J., Valji, K., Parsons, L., & Kessler, W. (1987). Penile pharmaco-cavernosography and cavernosometry in the evaluation of impotence. *Journal of Urology*, April, *137*(4), 772–776.

Boorstin, R. O. (1987, June 19). AIDS spread brings action in the courts. *New York Times*, p. 1.

Borneman, E. (1983). Progress in empirical research on children's sexuality. *SIECUS Report, 12*(2).

Borowitz, E. B. (1969). *Choosing a sex ethic: A Jewish inquiry*. New York: Schocken.

Bors, E., & Comarr, A. E. Neurological disturbances of sexual function with special reference to 529 patients with spinal cord injury. *Urological Survey, 10*, 191–222.

Boston Women's Health Book Collective. (1976). *Our bodies, ourselves*, 2d ed. New York: Simon & Schuster.

Boswell, J. (1980). *Christianity, social tolerance, and homosexuality*. Chicago: University of Chicago Press.

Botwin, C. (1986). *Is there sex after marriage?* New York: Pocket Books.

Bouyer, L. (1961). *Introduction to spirituality*. Collegeville, MN: Liturgical Press.

Bowen, S. (1988). *Sexually transmitted diseases and society*. Stanford, CA: Stanford University Press.

Bower, D. W., & Christopherson, V. A. (1977). University student cohabitation: A regional comparison of selected attitudes and behavior. *Journal of Marriage and the Family, 39*, 447–452.

Bowlby, J. (1973). *Separation: Attachment and loss*, Vol. II. New York: Basic.

Bowlby, J. (1969). *Attachment: Attachment and loss*, Vol. I. New York: Basic.

Boyle, P. S. (1986). Sexuality and disability. *SIECUS Report, 14*, 1–3.

Brackbill, Y., & Schroder, K. (1980). Circumcision, gender differences, and neonatal behavior: An update. *Developmental Psychology, 13*, 607–614.

Bradford, J. M. (1986). The use of a bioimpedance analyzer in the measurement of sexual arousal in male sexual deviants. *Canadian Journal of Psychiatry*, February, *31*(1), 44–47.

Bradley, W. E. (1987). New techniques in evaluation of impotence. *Urology*, April, *29*(4), 383–388.

Braen, G. (1980). Examination of the accused: The heterosexual and homosexual rapist. In C. Warner (ed.), *Rape and sexual assault*. Germantown, MD: Aspens System Corp.

Brain, R. (1979). *The decorated body*. New York: Harper & Row.

Brandes, S. (1985). *Forty: The age and the symbol*. Knoxville, TN: University of Tennessee Press.

Brandt, A. M. (1987). *No magic bullet*. New York: Oxford University Press.

Brauer, A., & Brauer, D. (1983). *ESO; How you and your lover can give each other hours of extended sexual orgasm*. New York: Warner Books.

Breasted, M. (1970). *Oh! Sex education!* New York: New American Library.

Brecher, E. M. (1984). *Sex, love and aging*. Boston: Little, Brown.

Brecher, E. M. (1969). *The sex researchers*. Boston: Little, Brown.

Brecher, E., & Brecher, J. (1986). Extracting valid sexological findings from severely flawed and biased population samples. *The Journal of Sex Research, 22*(1), 6–20.

Breslow, N., Evans, L., & Langley, J. (1986). Comparisons among heterosexual, bisexual, and homosexual male sadomasochists. *Journal of Homosexuality*, Fall, *13*(1), 83–107.

Breslow, N., Evans, L., & Langley, J. (1985). On the prevalence and roles of females in the sadomasochistic subculture. *Archives of Sexual Behavior, 14*, 303–317.

Brest, P., & Vandenberg, A. (1987). Policies, feminism, and the Constitution: The anti-pornography movement in Minneapolis. *Stanford Law Review, 39*, 607–661.

Brickner, B. (1987). Judaism and contemporary sexuality. *SIECUS Report, 15*(5), 5–8.

Brim, O. G. (1976). Theories of the male mid-life crisis. *Counseling Psychologist, 6*, 2–9.

Brim, O. G. (1966). Socialization through the life cycle. In O. G. Brim & S. Wheeler (eds.), *Socialization after childhood*. New York: Wiley.

Brim, O. G., & Kagan, J. (eds.). (1980). *Constancy and change in human development*. Cambridge: Harvard University Press.

Brody, J. E. (1988, March 10). Personal health. *New York Times*, p. 16.

Brody, J. E. (1987, December 3). Jealousy. *New York Times*, p. 16.

Brody, J. E. (1986, December 16). Effeminacy and Homosexuality. *New York Times*, p. 17.

Brookhouser, P. E., Sullivan, P. Scanlan, J. M., & Garbarino, J. (1986). Identifying the sexually abused deaf child: The otolaryngologist's role. *Laryngoscope*, February, *96*(2), 152–158.

Brooks-Gunn, J., Warren, M., Samelson, M., & Fox, R. (1986). Physical similarity of and disclosure of menarcheal status to friends: Effects of grade and pubertal status. *Journal of Early Adolescence*, Spring, *6*(10), 3–14.

Broude, G. J. (1980). Extramarital sex norms in cross-cultural perspective. *Behavior Science Research, 5*(3), 181–218.

Broude, G. J., & Greene, S. J. (1976). Cross-cultural codes on twenty sexual attitudes and practices. *Ethnology*, October, *15*, 409–429.

Broverman, I. K., Broverman, D. M., Clarkson, F. T., Rosenkrantz, P. S., & Vogel, S. (1970). Sex role stereotypes and clinical judgments of mental health. *Journal of Consulting Clinical Psychology, 34*, 1–7.

Brown, C. et al. (1978). Community standards, conservatism, and judgments of pornography. *Journal of Sex Research, 14*, 81–95.

Brown, G. (1980). *The new celibacy*. New York: McGraw-Hill.

Brown, L. (1981). *Sex education in the eighties*. New York: Plenum.

Brown, L., & Holder, W. (1979). The nature and extent of sexual abuse in contemporary American society. In N. H. Greenberg (ed.), *Incest: In search of understanding*. Washington, DC: National Center on Child Abuse and Neglect.

Browne, A., & Finkelhor, D. (1986). Impact of child sexual abuse: A review of the research. *Psychological Bulletin*, January, *99*(1), 66–77.

Brownmiller, S. (1984). *Femininity*. New York: Simon & Schuster.

Brownmiller, S. (1975). *Against our will: Men, women and rape*. New York: Simon & Schuster.

Brozan, N. (1987). "How effective is breast self-examination?" *New York Times*, May 4.

Brozan, N. (1985, March 9). Fetal health: New early diagnosis studied. *New York Times*.

Brundage, J. A. (1982). Sex and Canon law. In V. L. Bullough & J. Brundage (eds.), *Sexual practices and the medieval church*. Buffalo, NY: Prometheus.

Budoff, P. (1980). *No more menstrual cramps and other good news*. New York: Putnam.

Bullough, V. L. (1986). AIDS: Avoiding witch hunts. *SIECUS Report*, January, *14*, 1–3.

Bullough, V. L. (1982). The Christian Inheritance. In V. L. Bullough & J. Brundage (eds.), *Sexual practices and the medieval church*. Buffalo, NY: Prometheus.

Bullough, V. L., & Brundage, J. (1982). *Sexual practices in the medieval church*.

Buffalo, NY: Prometheus.

Bullough, V. L., et al. (1977). *A bibliography of prostitution.* New York: Garland.

Bureau of the Census. (1986). Marital status and living arrangements, March 1986. *Current Population Reports* series P-20, No. 418. Washington, DC: U.S. Government Printing Office.

Bureau of the Census. (1985–1986). *Child support and alimony.* Washington, DC: U.S. Government Printing Office.

Bureau of the Census. (1985). Marital status and living arrangements. *Current Population Reports,* series P-20. Washington, DC: U.S. Government Printing Office.

Bureau of the Census. (1984). *Current Population Reports.* No. 389, p. 20. Washington, DC: U.S. Government Printing Office.

Bureau of the Census. (1983). *Child support and alimony.* Washington, DC: U.S. Government Printing Office.

Burgess, A. W. (1984). *Child pornography and sex rings.* Lexington, MA: Lexington Books (D.C. Heath).

Burgess, A. W., & Holmstrom, L. L. (1979). *Rape: Crisis and recovery.* Bowie, MD.: Brady.

Burgess, A. W., & Holmstrom, L. L. (1976). Coping behavior of the rape victim. *American Journal of Psychiatry, 133*(4), 413–418.

Burgess, A. W., & Holmstrom, L. L. (1974a). Rape trauma syndrome. *American Journal of Psychiatry, 131,* 981–986.

Burgess, A. W., & Holmstrom, L. L. (1974b). *Rape: Victims of crisis.* Bowie, MD.: Brady.

Burnham, J. C. (1972). American historians and the subject of sex. *Societas, 2,* 307–316.

Burton, R. F., (translator). (n.d.). *The thousand and one nights.* Printed by the Burton Club for subscribers only.

Buscaglia, L. (1984). *Loving each other: The challenge of human relationships.* Thorofare, NJ: Slack.

Buss, D. M. (1988). Love acts: The evolutionary biology of love. In R. J. Sternberg & M. L. Barnes, (eds.), *The psychology of love,* pp. 100–118. New Haven: Yale University Press.

Buunk, B., & Hupka, R. B. (1987). Cross-cultural differences in the elicitation of sexual jealousy. *Journal of Sex Research, 23*(1), 12–22.

Byrne, D. (1977). The imagery of sex. In J. Money & H. Musaph (eds.), *Handbook of sexology,* pp. 327–350. New York: Elsevier/North-Holland.

Byrne, D., & Lamberth, J. (1971). The effect of erotic stimuli on sex arousal, evaluative responses, and subsequent behavior. In *Technical Report of the Commission on Obscenity and Pornography,* vol. 8. Washington, DC: U.S. Government Printing Office.

Caird, W., & Wincze, J. P. (1977). *Sex therapy: A behavioral approach.* Hagerstown, MD.: Harper & Row.

Calder-Marshall, A. (1959). *The sage of sex.* New York: Putnam.

Calhoun, L. et al. (1981). The influence of pregnancy on sexuality: A review of current evidence. *Journal of Sex Research, 17*(2), 139–151.

Callahan, D. (1970). *Abortion: Law, choice and morality.* New York: Macmillan.

Calverton, V. F., & Schmalhausen, S. D. (1929). *Sex in civilization.* New York: Citadel.

Cameron, P., (1970). Note on time spent thinking about sex. *Psychological Reports, 20,* 741–742.

Camp, S. L., & Speidel, J. (1987). *The international human suffering index* (pamphlet). Washington, DC: Population Crisis Committee.

Campagna, A. F. (1985–1986). Fantasy and sexual arousal in college men: Normative and functional aspects. *Imagination, Cognition and Personality, 5*(1), 3–20.

Campbell, N. A. (1987). *Biology.* Menlo Park, CA: Benjamin/Cummings.

Capraro, V., Ridgers, D., & Rodgers, B. (1983). Abnormal vaginal discharge. *Medical Aspects of Human Sexuality, 17*(8).

Capron, A. M. (1987). Alternative birth technologies: Legal challenges. *U.C. Davis Law Review,* Summer, *20,* 679–704.

Card, J., & Wise, L. (1978). Teenage mothers and teenage fathers: The impact of early childbearing on the parents' personal and professional lives. *Family Planning Perspectives, 10*(4), 199–205.

Carey, J. T. (1979). Changing courtship patterns in the popular song. *American Journal of Sociology, 74,* 720–731.

Carmichael, M. S., Humbert, R., Dixen, J., Palmisano, G., Greenleaf, W., & Davidson, J. M. (1987). Oxytocin increase in human sexual response. *Journal of Clinical Endocrinology and Metabolism.*

*Carnegie Quarterly.* (1986). Adolescent pregnancy: Testing prevention strategies. *31*(3, 4), 1–7.

Carnes, P. J. (1987). Progress in sexual addiction: An addiction perspective. *SIECUS Report, 14*(6), 4–6.

Carnes, P. J. (1983). *Out of the shadows: Understanding sexual addiction.* Minneapolis: Compeare Publishers.

Carnes, P. J. (1983). *The sexual addiction.* Minneapolis: CompCase.

Carrier, J. M. (1980). Homosexual behavior in cross-cultural perspective. In J. Marmor (ed.), *Homosexual behavior.* New York: Basic.

Carroll, J., Volk, K., & Hyde, J. (1985). Differences between males and females in motives for engaging in sexual intercourse. *Archives of Sexual Behavior, 14,* 131–139.

Casanova de Seingalt, G. G. (1958–1960). *Memoires.* Paris: Gallimard.

Castleman, M. (1980). *Sexual solutions.* New York: Simon & Schuster.

Catania, J., McDermott, L., & Pollack, L. (1986). Questionnaire response bias and face-to-face interview sample bias in sexuality research. *The Journal of Sex Research, 22*(1), 52–72.

Cates, W. Jr., & Holmes, K. (1986). Sexually transmitted diseases. In W. Cates, Jr. & K. Holmes (eds.), *Public Health and Preventive Medicine,* 12th ed., pp. 257–295. Atlanta: U.S. Public Health Service.

Centers for Disease Control Task Force on Kaposi's Sarcoma and Opportunistic Infections. (1982). Epidemiologic aspects of the current outbreak of Kaposi's sarcoma and opportunistic infections. *New England Journal of Medicine, 306,* 248–252.

Chambers, M. (1987, March 18). Legal doubts raised by call for ban on birth technology. *New York Times.*

Chambers, M. et al. (1979). *The Western experience,* 2d ed. New York: Knopf.

Chambless, D., et al. (1982). The pubococcygeus and female orgasm: A correlational study with normal subjects. *Archives of Sexual Behavior, 11*(6).

Chang, J. (1977). *The Tao of love and sex.* New York: Dutton.

Chang, J., & Block, J. (1960). A study of identification in male homosexuals. *Journal of Consulting Psychology, 24*(4), 307–310.

Chappel, D., Geis, R., & Geis, G. (eds.) (1977). *Forcible rape: The crime, the victim, and the offender.* New York: Columbia University Press.

Charnes, R., Hoffman, K. E., Hoffman, L., & Meyers, R. S. (1980). The Sesame Street library—Bad books bring big bucks. *Young Children, 35*(2), 10–12.

Chasnoff, I. et al. (1986). Maternal-neonatal incest. *American Journal of Orthopsychiatry,* October, *56*(4), 577–580.

Chastre, J., Brun, P., Soler, P., Basset, F., Trouillet, J. L., Fagon, J. Y., Gibert, C., & Hance, A. J. (1987). Acute and latent pneumonitis after subcutaneous injections of silicone in transsexual men. *American Review of Respiratory Disorders*, January, *135*(1), 236–240.

Chayen, B., Tejani, N., Verman, U. L., & Gordon, G. (1986). Fetal heart rate changes and uterine activity during coitus. *Acta-Obstet-Gynecol-Scand.*, *65*(8), 853–855.

Check, J. V. P., & Malamuth, N. M. (1984). Can there be positive effects of participation in pornography experiments? *Journal of Sex Research, 20*, 14–31.

Cherlin, A. J. (1981). *Marriage, divorce, remarriage.* Cambridge, MA: Harvard University Press.

Chevalier-Skolnikoff, S. (1974). Male-female, female-female, and male-male sexual behavior in the stumptail monkey, with special attention to female orgasm. *Archives of Sexual Behavior, 3,* 95–116.

Christensen, H. (1966). Scandanavian and American sex norms: Some comparisons with sociological implications. *Journal of Social Issues, 22,* 60–75.

Christenson, C. V. (1971). *Kinsey: A biography.* Bloomington: Indiana University Press.

Church, G. J. (1986, July 14). Knocking on the bedroom door. *Time*, pp. 13–14.

Clark, J. T., Smith, E. R., & Davidson, J. M. (1984). Enhancement of sexual motivation in male rats. *Science, 224,* 847–849.

Clark, S., Borders, D., & Knudson, M. (1986). Survey of telephone counselors' responses to sexual and sexually abusive callers. *American Mental Health Counselors Association Journal*, April, *8*(2), 73–79.

Clarke, A. M., & Clarke, A. D. B. (1977). *Early experience: Myth and evidence.* New York: Free Press.

Clarkson, T. B., & Alexander, N. J. (1980). Long-term vasectomy: Effects on the occurrence and extent of atherosclerosis in rhesus monkeys. *Journal of Clinical Investigation, 65*(1), 15–25.

Clausen, J. A. (1975). The social meaning of differential physical and sexual maturation. In S. E. Dragastin & G. H. Elder (eds.), *Adolescence in the life cycle.* New York: Halsted.

Clayton, R. R., & Bokemeier, J. L. (1980). Premarital sex in the seventies. *Journal of Marriage and the Family, 42,* 759–775.

Clayton, R. R., & Voss, H. L. (1977). Shacking up: Cohabitation in the 1970's. *Journal of Marriage and Family, 39,* 273–283.

Cleland, J. (1963). *Memoirs of a woman of pleasure.* New York: Putnam.

Clement, U., Schmidt, G., & Kruse, M. (1984). Changes in sex differences in sexual behavior: A replication of a study on West German students (1966–1981). *Archives of Sexual Behavior, 9,* 235–244.

Clifford, R. (1978). Subjective sexual experience in college women. *Archives of Sexual Behavior, 7,* 559–573.

Clugh, J. (1963). *Love locked out.* London: Spring Books.

Cohen, A. (1949). *Everyman's Talmud.* New York: Dutton.

Cohen, B. (1980). *Deviant street networks.* Lexington, MA: Lexington Books.

Cohen, H. D., Rosen, R. C. & Goldstein, L. (1976). Electroencephalographic laterality changes during human sexual orgasm. *Archives of Sexual Behavior, 5*(3), 189–199.

Cohen, M., Adler, N., Beck, A., & Irwin, C. (1986). Parental reactions to the onset of adolescence. *Journal of Adolescent Health Care*, March, 7(2), 101–106.

Cohen, M. L., Seghorn, T., & Calmas, W. (1969). Sociometric study of the sex offender. *Journal of Abnormal Psychology, 74,* 249–255.

Cole, T. M. (1975). Sexuality and physical disabilities. *Archives of Sexual Behavior, 4,* 389–401.

Coleman, D. (1985, September 10). Patterns of love charted in studies. *New York Times*, pp. 13–18.

Coleman, E. (1987). Sexual compulsion vs. sexual addiction: The debate continues. *SIECUS Report, 14*(6), 7–10.

Coleman, J. C. (1980). Friendship and the peer group in adolescence. In J. Adelson (ed.), *Handbook of adolescent psychology*, pp. 432–447. New York: Wiley.

Coles, R. (1985). A psychological perspective. In R. Coles & G. Stokes (eds.), *Sex and the American teenager*, p. 2. New York: Harper & Row.

Coles, R. & Stokes, G. (1985). *Sex and the American teenager.* New York: Harper & Row.

Collins, J., & Lewandowski, B. (1987). Experience with intracorporeal injection of papaverine and duplex ultrasound scanning for assessment of arteriogenic impotence. *British Journal of Urology*, January, *59*(1), 84–88.

Collis, J. S. (1959). *Havelock Ellis: Artist of life.* New York: Sloane.

Comfort, A. (1978). *Sexual consequences of disability.* Philadelphia: George F. Shickley.

Comfort, A. (1976). *A good age.* New York: Simon & Schuster.

Comfort, A. (1974). *More joy.* New York: Crown.

Comfort, A. (1972). *The joy of sex.* New York: Crown.

Comfort, A. (1967). *The anxiety makers.* New York: Delta.

Comfort, A. (1965). *The Kokashastra.* New York: Stein & Day.

Commission on Obscenity and Pornography. (1970). *The report of the commission on obscenity and pornography.* Washington, DC: U.S. Government Printing Office.

Condra, M., Fenemore, J., Reid, K., Phillips, P., Morales, A., Owen, J., & Surridge, D. (1987). Screening assessment of penile tumescence and rigidity. Clinical test of Snap-Gauge. *Urology*, March, *29*(3), 254–257.

Condry, J., & Condry, S. (1976). Sex differences: A study of the eye of the beholder. *Child Development, 47,* 812–819.

Condy, S., Templer, D., Brown, R., & Veaco, L. (1987). Parameters of sexual contact of boys with women. *Archives of Sexual Behavior, 16*(5).

Conn, J., & Kanner, L. (1940). Spontaneous erections in childhood. *Journal of Pediatrics, 16,* 337–240.

Connell, E. B. (1979). Barrier methods of contraception: A reappraisal. *International Journal of Gynecology and Obstetrics, 16,* 479–481.

Constantinople, A. (1973). Masculinity-femininity: An exception to a famous dictum? *Psychological Bulletin, 80,* 389–407.

Cook, R. F., Fosen, R. H., & Pacht, A. (1971). Pornography and the sex offender: Patterns of previous exposure and arousal effects of pornographic stimuli. *Journal of Applied Psychology, 55,* 503–511.

Cooper, A. J. (1986). Progestogens in the treatment of male sex offenders: A Review. *Canadian Journal of Psychiatry*, February, *31*(1), 73–79.

Cooper, J. F. (1928). *Technique of contraception.* New York: Day-Nichols.

Cooper, P. T., Cumber, B., & Hartner, R. (1978). Decision-making patterns and post-decision adjustment of child-free husbands and wives. *Alternative Lifestyles, 1*(1), 71–94.

Corey, L. (1984). Genital herpes. In K. Holmes, P. Mardh, P. F. Sparling, & P. Wiesner (eds.), *Sexually transmitted diseases.* New York: McGraw-Hill.

Court, J. H. (1985). Contemporary pornography as a contributor to sexual offenses against women. In M. Safer, M. Mednick, D. Izraeli, & J. Bernard (eds.), *Women's worlds: The new scholarship.* New York: Praeger.

Couzinet, B. (1986). Termination of early pregnancy by the progesterone antagonist Ru486 (mifepristone). *New England Journal of Medicine*, December

18, *315*(25), 1565–1569.

Cowan, C., & Kinder, M. (1985). *Smart women/foolish choices*. New York: Carkson N. Porter.

Cowan, G., & Hoffman, C. (1986). Gender stereotyping in young children: Evidence to support a concept-learning approach. *Sex Roles, 14,* 211–224.

Cozby, D. C. (1972). Self-disclosure, reciprocity and liking. *Sociometry, 35,* 151–160.

Craig, G. J. (1987). *Human development,* 4th ed. Englewood Cliffs, NJ: Prentice-Hall.

Crain, I. J. (1978). Afterplay. *Medical Aspects of Human Sexuality, 12,* 72–85.

Crapo, L. (1985). *Hormones*. New York: W.H. Freeman.

Crepault, C., & Couture, M. (1980). Men's erotic fantasies. *Archives of Sexual Behavior, 9,* 565–581.

Crepault, C. et al. (1977). Erotic imagery in women. In R. Gemme & C. C. Wheeler (eds.), *Progress in sexology,* pp. 267–283. New York: Plenum Press.

Cross, J. F. & Cross, J. (1971). Age, sex, race, and the perception of facial beauty. *Developmental Psychology, 5:* 453–459.

Croughan, J., Saghir, M., Cohen, R., & Robins, E. (1981). A comparison of treated and untreated male crossdressers. *Archives of Sexual Behavior, 10*(6).

Culp, R., Cook, A., & Housley, P. (1983). A comparison of observed and reported adult-infant interactions: Effects of perceived sex. *Sex Roles, 9,* 475–479.

Curran, C. (1986, August 20). Quoted in *New York Times,* p. 9.

Cutler, W. B., Preti, G., Huggins, G. R., Erikson, E., & Garcia. C. R. (1985). Sexual behavior frequency and biphasic ovulatory type menstrual cycles. *Physiological Review, 34,* 805–810.

Dalton, K. (1979). *Once a month*. New York: Hunter.

Dalton, K. (1972). *The premenstrual syndrome*. London: William Heineman Medical Books.

Dalton, K. (1969). *The menstrual cycle*. New York: Pantheon.

Daly, M., & Wilson, M. (1978). *Sex evolution and behavior*. Belmont, CA: Wadsworth.

Damon, L., Todd, J., & MacFarlane, K. (1987). Treatment issues with sexually abused children. *Child Welfare,* March–April, *66*(2), 125–137.

D'Andrade, R. G. (1966). Sex differences and cultural institutions. In E. E. Maccoby (ed.), *The development of sex differences*. Stanford, CA: Stanford University Press.

Darling, C. A., & Davidson, J. K. Sr., (1986). Enhancing relationships: Understanding the feminine mystique of pretending orgasm. *Journal of Sex and Marital Therapy,* Fall, *12*(3), 182–196.

Davenport, W. H. (1977). Sex in cross-cultural perspective. In F. A. Beach (ed.), *Human sexuality in four perspectives,* pp. 115–163. Baltimore, MD: Johns Hopkins University Press.

Davidson, J. M. (1981). The orgasmic connection. *Psychology Today, 15,* July.

Davidson, J. M. (1980). The psychology of sexual experience. In J. M. Davidson & R. J. Davidson (eds.), *The psychobiology of consciousness*. New York: Plenum.

Davidson, J. M. (1977). Neurohormonal bases of male sexual behavior. In R. O. Greek (ed.), *Reproductive Physiology II,* 13. Baltimore University Park Press.

Davidson, J. M., Kwan, M., & Greenleaf, W. J. (1982). Hormonal replacement and sexuality in men. *Clinics in Endocrinology and Metabolism, 11*(3), 599–623.

Davidson, J. M. et al. (1979). Effects of androgen on sexual behavior in hypogonadal men. *Journal of Clinical Endocrinology and Metabolism, 48*(6).

Davies, E., & Furnham, A. (1986). Body satisfaction in adolescent girls. *British Journal of Medical Psychology,* September, *59*(pt. 3), 279–287.

Davis, A. J. (1968). Sexual assault in the Philadelphia prisons and sheriff's vans. *Trans-action, 6,* 8–17.

Davis, H. P. (1978). Abortion: A continuing debate. *Family Planning Perspectives, 10,* 313–316.

Davis, J. D. (1976). Self-disclosure in an acquaintance exercise: Responsibility for level of intimacy. *Journal of Personality and Social Psychology, 33,* 87–92.

Dawood, M. Y. (1986). Current concepts in the etiology and treatment of primary dysmenorrhea *Acta Obstet-Gynecologi-Scand.* (Suppl.), *138,* 7–10.

Dawson, D. A., Meny, D. J., & Ridley, J. C. (1980). Fertility control in the United States before the contraceptive revolution. *Family Planning Perspectives, 12*(2), 76–86.

DeAmicis, L., Goldberg, D., LoPicollo, J., Friedman, J., & Davies, L. (1985). Clinical follow-up of couples treated for sexual dysfunction. *Archives of Sexual Behavior, 14,* 467–489.

de Beauvoir, S. (1952). *The second sex*. New York: Knopf.

Debrovner, C. H. (1983). Premenstrual syndrome. *Medical Aspects of Human Sexuality,* 215–216.

Decter, M. (1973). *The new chastity and other arguments against women's libera-*

*tion*. London: Wildwood.

DeGroat, W. C. (1986). Organization of the reflex pathways mediating penile erection. In *Abstracts: Conference on the scientific basis of sexual dysfunction*. Bethesda, MD: National Institutes of Health.

DeGroat, W. C., & Booth, A. M. (1980). Physiology of male sexual function. *Annals of Internal Medicine, 92*(2), 329–331.

Degler, C. (1980). *At odds: Women and the family in America from the Revolution to the present*. New York: Oxford University Press, p. 264.

Degler, C. (1974). What ought to be and what was: Women's sexuality in the nineteenth century. *American Historical Review, 79*(5).

DeJong, F. H., & Sharpe, R. M. (1976). Evidence for inhibin-like activity in bovine follicular fluid. *Nature, 263,* 71–72.

DeLacoste-Utamsing, C., & Halloway, R. L. (1982). Sexual dimorphism in the human corpus callosum. *Science, 216,* 215–216.

DeLamater, J. D. (1987). Gender differences in sexual scenarios. In K. Kelley (ed.), *Females, males and sexuality,* pp. 127–139. Albany: State University of New York Press.

DeLamater, J. D. (1981). The social control of sexuality. *Annual Reviews of Sociology, 7,* 263–290.

DeLamater, J. D., & MacCorquodale, P. (1979). *Premarital sexuality: Attitudes, relationships, behavior*. Madison, WI: University of Wisconsin Press.

Delaney, J. et al. (1988). *The curse*. New York: Dutton.

Delin, B. (1978). *The sex offender*. Boston: Beacon.

D'Emilio, J., & Freedman, E. B. (1988). *Intimate matteris: A history of sexuality in America*. New York: Harper & Row.

DeMartino, M. F. (ed.). (1979). *Human autoerotic practices*. New York: Human Sciences Press.

Denfield, D., & Gordon, M. (1970). The sociology of mate swapping: Or the family that swings together clings together. *Journal of Sex Research, 6,* 85–100.

Dennehy, R. (ed.). (1981). *Christian married love*. San Francisco: Ignatius Press.

Dennerstein, L. et al. (1980). Hormones and sexuality: Effect of estrogen and progestogen. *Obstetrics and Gynecology, 56*(3), 316–322.

Denniston, R. H. (1980). Ambisexuality in animals. In J. Marmor (ed.), *Homosexual behavior*. New York: Basic.

DePalma, R., Emsellem, H., Edwards, C., Druy, E., Schultz, S., Miller, H., & Bergsrud, D. (1987). A screening sequence for vasculogenic impotence. *Journal of Vasculogenic Surgery*, February, 5(2), 228–236.

Derenski, A., & Landsburg, S. (1981). *The age taboo: Older women-younger men relationships*. Boston: Little, Brown.

DeRougemont, D. (1956). *Love in the western world*. New York: Pantheon.

DeSade, D.-A.-F. (1965). *Justine, in The Marquis de Sade: Three Complete Novels*. New York: Grove.

DesJarlais, D. C. (1987, June 4). Quoted in *New York Times*, p. 1.

Deutsch, H. (1944). *The psychology of women*. New York: Grune & Stratton.

Devereux, G. (1937). Institutionalized homosexuality of the Mohave Indians. In *Human Biology, 9*, 498–527. Detroit: Wayne State University Press.

deVries, C., Gooren, L., & van der Veen, E. (1986). The effect of cyproterone acetate alone and in combination with ethinylestradiol on the hypothalamic pituitary adrenal axis, prolactin and growth hormone release in male-to-female transsexuals. *Hormone-Metabolic-Research,*March, 18(3), 203–205.

DeWald, P. A. (1971). *Psychotherapy: A dynamic approach*, 2d ed. New York: Basic.

Dewsbury, D. (1981). Effect of novelty on copulatory behavior: The Coolidge effect and related phenomena. *Psychological Bulletin, 89*, 464–482.

deYoung, M. (1982). *The sexual victimization of children*. Jefferson, NC: McFarland & Co.

Dhabuwala, C. B., Kumar, A., & Pierce, J. M. (1986). Myocardial infarction and its influences in male sexual function. *Archives of Sexual Behavior, 15*(6), 499–505.

Diamond, M. (1982). Sexual identity: Monozygotic twins reared in discordant sex roles and a BBC follow-up. *Archives of Sexual Behavior, 11*(2).

Diamond, M. (1979). Sexual identity and sex roles. In V. Bullough (ed.), *The frontiers of sex research*. Buffalo, NY: Prometheus.

Diamond, M. (1976). Human sexual development: Biological foundations for sexual development. In F. Beach (ed.), *Human sexuality in four perspectives*. Baltimore, MD: Johns Hopkins University Press.

Diamond, M. (1965). A critical evaluation of the ontogeny of human sexual behavior. *Quarterly Review of Biology, 40*, 147–175.

Dickinson, R. L. (1949). *Atlas of human sex anatomy*, 2d ed. Baltimore, MD: Williams & Wilkins.

Dick-Read, G. (1932). *Childbirth without fear*. New York: Harper & Row.

Dienhart, C. M. (1967). *Basic ·human anatomy and physiology*. Philadelphia: Saunders.

Dietz, P., Harry, B., & Hazelwood, R. (1986). Detective magazines: Pornography for the sexual sadist? *Journal of Forensic Science*, January, 31(1), 197–211.

Dion, K. L. (1981). Physical attractiveness, sex roles and heterosexual attraction. In M. Cook (ed.), *The bases of human sexual attraction*. New York: Academic Press.

Dion, K. L., Berscheid, E., & Walster, E. (1972). What is beautiful is good. *Journal of Personality and Social Psychology, 24*, 285–290.

Dion, K. L., & Dion, K. K. (1973). Correlates of romantic love. *Journal of Consulting and Clinical Psychology, 41*, 51–56.

Ditkoff, M. (1978). Child pornography. *American Humane Society Magazine, 16*(4), 30.

Dixen, J. M., Maddever, H., Van Maasdam, J., & Edwards, P. W. (1984). Psychosocial characteristics of applicants evaluated for surgical gender reassignment. *Archives of Sexual Behavior, 13*, 269–276.

Djerassi, C. (1981). *The politics of contraception*. New York: Norton.

Dodson, B. (1987). *Sex for one*. New York: Harmony Books.

Doherty, D. (ed). (1979). *Dimensions of human sexuality*. Garden City, NY: Doubleday.

Dolesh, D., & Lehman, S. (1985). *Love me, love me not: How to survive infidelity*. New York: McGraw-Hill.

Dolgin, J. L., & Dolgin, B. L. (1980). Sex and the law. In B. B. Wolman & J. Money (eds.), *Handbook of human sexuality*. Englewood Cliffs, NJ: Prentice-Hall.

Donnerstein, E. (1980). Aggressive-erotica and violence against women. *Journal of Personality and Social Psychology, 3*, 269–277.

Donnerstein, E., & Linz, D. (1984). Sexual violence in the media: A warning. *Psychology Today, 18*(1), 14–15.

Donnerstein, E., Linz, D., & Penrod, S. (1987). *The question of pornography*. New York: Free Press.

Dornbusch, S. M. et al. (1981). Sex development, age, and dating: A comparison of biological and social influences upon one set of behaviors. *Child Development, 52*(1), 179–185.

Dorner, G. (1976). *Hormones and brain differentiation*. Amsterdam: Elsevier.

Dorner, G. (1968). Hormonal induction and prevention of female homosexuality. *Journal of Endocrinology, 42*, 163–164.

Doty, R. L. et al. (1975). Changes in the intensity and pleasantness of human vaginal odors during the menstrual cycle. *Science, 190*, 1316–1318.

Douglas, N., & Slinger, P. (1979). *Sexual secrets*. New York: Destiny Books.

Dover, K. (1988, February 5). Quoted by T. Johnston in the *Stanford Observer*, p. 5.

Dover, K. J. (1978). *Greek homosexuality*. New York: Vintage.

Dowdle, W. R. (1987, October 16). Quoted in *New York Times*, p. 11.

Draper, N. E. E. (1976). Birth control. In *Encyclopaedia Britannica, 2*, 1065–1073. Chicago: Benton.

Drew, D., & Drake, J. (1969). *Boys for sale: A sociological study of boy prostitution*. New York: Brown Book.

Droegemueller, W., & Bressler, R. (1980). Effectiveness and risks of contraception. *Annual Review of Medicine, 31*, 329–343.

Dryfoos, J. (1985). What the United States can learn about prevention of teenage pregnancy from other developed countries. *SIECUS Report*, November, 14(2), 1–7.

Duggan, L., Hunter, N., & Vance, C. (1985). False promises: New antipornography legislation in the United States. *SIECUS Report*, May, 13, 1–5.

Dunn, H. G. et al. (1977). Maternal cigarette smoking during pregnancy and the child's subsequent development: II. Neurological and intellectual maturation to the age of 6½ years. *Canadian Journal of Public Health, 68*, 43–50.

Durfee, R. B. (1987). Obstetric complications of pregnancy. In M. Pernoll, & R. Benson (eds.), *Current obstetric and gynecologic Diagnosis and Treatment 1987*, 6th ed. Los Altos, CA: Appleton & Lange.

Dworkin, A. (1981). *Pornography: Men possessing women*. New York: Putnam.

Earhart, H. B. (1969). *Japanese religion: United and diversity*. Belmont, CA.

Earle, J. R., & Perricone, P. J. (1986). Premarital sexuality: A ten-year study of attitudes and behavior on a small university campus. *The Journal of Sex Research, 22*(3), 304–310.

Easterling, W. E., & Herbert, W. N. P. (1982). The puerperium. In D. N. Danforth (ed.), *Obstetrics and gynecology*, 4th ed. pp. 787–799. Philadelphia: Harper & Row.

Eckholm, E. (1988, March 8). Sex researchers defind AIDS book. *New York Times*, p. 12.

Eckholm, E. (1986, October 28). Heterosexuals and AIDS: The concern is growing. *New York Times*, p. 25.

Edman, I. (ed.). (1956). *The works of Plato*. (The Jowett Translation). New York: Modern Library.

Edwards, S. R. (1986). A sex addict

speaks. *SIECUS Report, 14*(6), 1–3.

Ehrhardt, A. A., & Baker, S. W. (1974). Fetal androgens, human central nervous system differentiation, and behavioral sex differences. In R. Friedman, R. Richart, & R. Van de Wiele (eds.), *Sex differences in behavior.* New York: Wiley.

Ehrhardt, A. A., Epstein, R., & Money, J. (1968). Fetal androgens and female gender identity in the early treated adrenogenital syndrome. *Johns Hopkins Medical Journal, 122,* 160–167.

Ehrhardt, A. A., Ince, S. E., & Meyer-Bahlburg, H. F. L. (1981). Career aspiration and gender role development in young girls. *Archives of Sexual Behavior, 10,* 279–297.

Ehrhardt, A. A., & Meyer-Bahlburg, H. (1981). Effects of prenatal sex hormones on gender-related behavior. *Science, 211*(4488), 1312–1318.

Ehrhardt, A. A., Meyer-Bahlburg, H., Feldman, J., & Ince, S. (1984). Sex-dimorphic behavior in childhood subsequent to prenatal exposure to exogenous progestogens and estrogens. *Archives of Sexual Behavior, 13,* 457–477.

Ehrlich, P., & Ehrlich, A. (1968). *Population resources, environment,* 2d ed. San Francisco: Freeman.

Eitner, L. (1975). The erotic in art. In H. Katchadourian & D. Lunde (eds.), *Fundamentals of human sexuality,* 2d ed. New York: Holt, Rinehart and Winston.

Ekman, P., Levonson, R., & Friesen, W. (1983). Autonomic nervous system activity distinguishes among emotions. *Science, 221,* 1208–1210.

Elder, G. (1969). Appearance and education in marriage mobility. *American Sociological Review, 34,* 519–533.

Elder, G. H. (1980). Adolescence in historical perspective. In J. Adelson (ed.), *Handbook of Adolescent Psychology.* New York: Wiley.

Elias, J., & Gebhard, P. (1969). Sexuality and sexual learning in childhood. *Phi Delta Kappa,* March, 401–405.

Elise, D. (1986). Lesbian couples: The implications of sex differences in separation-individuation. Special Issue: Gender issues in psychotherapy. *Psychotherapy,* Summer, *23*(2), 305–310.

Ellis, A. (1979). Foreword. In M.F. De Martino (ed.), *Human autoerotic practices.* New York: Human Sciences Press.

Ellis, A. (1969). Healthy and disturbed reasons for having extramarital relations. In G. Neubeck (ed.), *Extramarital relations,* pp. 153–161. Englewood Cliffs, N.J.: Prentice-Hall.

Ellis, A. & Abarbanel, A. (eds.). (1967). *The encyclopedia of sexual behavior.* New York: Hawthorn.

Ellis, G., & Sexton, D. (1982). Sex on TV. *Medical Aspects of Human Sexuality, 16*(6).

Ellis, H. (1942). *Studies in the psychology of sex.* New York: Random.

Ellis, H. (1939). *My life.* Boston: Houghton Mifflin.

Elvik, S., Berkowitz, D., & Greenberg (1986). Child sexual abuse: The role of the NP. *Nurse Practitioner,* January, *11*(1), 15–16, 19–20, 22.

Ende, J., Rockwell, S., & Glasgow, M. (1984). The sexual history in general medicine practice. *Archives of Internal Medicine, 144,* 558–561.

Engel, G. L. (1962). *Psychological development in health and disease.* Philadelphia: Saunders.

Engelmann, G. (1883). *Labor among primitive peoples.* St. Louis, MO: Chambers.

Epstein, B. (1981). *The politics of domesticity: Women, evangelism and temperance in nineteenth century America.* Middletown, CT: Wesleyan University Press.

Epstein, L. M. (1967). *Sex laws and customs in Judaism,* Rev. ed. New York: Ktav Publishing.

Erikson, E. H. (ed.). (1978). *Adulthood.* New York: Norton.

Erikson, E. H. (1968). *Identity: Youth and crisis.* New York: Norton.

Erikson, E. H. (1963a). *Childhood and society,* 2d ed. New York: Norton.

Erikson, E. H. (ed.). (1963b). *Youth: Change and challenge.* New York: Basic.

Erikson, E. H. (ed.). (1959). Identity and the life cycle. *Psychological Issues, 1*(1). New York: International Universities.

Eschenbach, D. (1986). Pelvic infections. In D. Danforth & J. Scott (eds.), *Obstetrics and gynecology,* 5th ed. Philadelphia: J.B. Lippincott.

Esselstyn, T. C. (1968). Prostitution in the United States. *Annals of the American Academy of Political and Social Science, 376,* 123–135.

Essex, M. (1985, August 12). Cited in *Time,* p. 44.

Eu, M. F., & Vickerman, J. L. (1986). California Ballot Pamphlet, November 4. Sacramento: California Office of State Printing.

Evans, D. R. (1980). Electrical aversion therapy. In D. Cox & R. Daitzman (eds.), *Exhibitionism: Description, assessment and treatment,* pp. 85–122. New York: Garland.

Evans, J. R. et al. (1976). Teenagers: Fertility control behavior and attitudes before and after abortion, childbearing or negative pregnancy test. *Family Planning Perspectives, 8,* 192–200.

Evans, R. B. (1969). Childhood parental relationships of homosexual men. *Journal of Counseling and Clinical Psychology, 33,* 129–135.

Evans, R. I. (1969). *Dialogue with Erik Erikson.* New York: E.P. Dutton.

Exner, T. (1987). How to figure your chances of getting married. *American Demographics,* June, 50–52.

Fagan, P., Meyer, J., & Schmidt, C., Jr. (1986). Sexual dysfunction within an adult developmental perspective. *Journal of Sexual and Marital Therapy,* Winter, *12*(4), 243–257.

Fagot, B. (1974). Sex differences in toddlers' behavior and parental reaction. *Developmental Psychology, 10,* 554–558.

Fagot, B., Leinbach, M., & Hagan, R. (1986). Gender labeling and the adoption of sex-typed behaviors. *Developmental Psychology,* July, *22*(4), 440–443.

Fairbanks, B., & Scharfman, B. (1980). The cervical cap: Past and current experience. *Women vs. Health, 5*(3), 61–80.

Farmer, J. S., & Henley, N. M. (1965). *Slang and its analogues.* Reprint of 7 vols published 1890–1904. New York: Kraus Reprint Corp.

Farrell, W. (1986). *Why men are the way they are.* New York: McGraw-Hill.

Fausto-Sterling, A. (1985). *Myths of gender.* New York: Basic Books.

Fawcett, J. T. (1970). *Psychology and population. Behavioral research issues in fertility and family planning.* New York: Population Council.

Federal Bureau of Investigation (1987). *Uniform Crime Reports, 1986.* Washington, DC: U.S. Government Printing Press.

Federman, D. D. (1968). *Abnormal sexual development.* Philadelphia: W.B. Saunders.

Fedora, O., Reddon, J., & Yeudall, L. (1986). Stimuli eliciting sexual arousal in genital exhibitionists: A possible clinical application. *Archives of Sexual Behavior,* October, *15*(5), 417–427.

Fein, G., Johnson, D., Kesson, N., Stark, L., & Wasserman, L. (1975). Sex stereotypes and preferences in the toy choices of 20-month-old boys and girls. *Developmental Psychology, 11,* 527–528.

Feldman, D. M. (1974). *Marital relations, birth control and abortion in Jewish law.* New York: Shocken Books.

Feldman-Summers, S., & Norris, J. (1984). Differences between rape victims who report and those who do not report to a public agency. *Journal of Applied Psychology, 52,* 1054–1061.

Fenwick, P., Mercer, S., Grant, R., Wheeler, M., Nanjee, N., Toone, B.,

& Brown, D. (1986). Nocturnal penile tumescence and serum testosterone levels. *Archives of Sexual Behavior*, February, *15*(1), 13–21.

Feucht, O. E. (ed.). (1961). *Sex and the church*. St. Louis, MO: Concordia.

Field, J. H. (1975). Sexual themes in ancient and primitive art. In P. Webb, (ed.), *The erotic arts*. Boston: New York Graphic Society.

Finch, S. (1982). Sexual disturbances in children. *Medical Aspects of Human Sexuality, 16*(5).

Finkel, M., & Finkel, D. (1975). Sexual and contraceptive knowledge, attitudes and behavior of male adolescents. *Family Planning Perspectives, 7*, 256–260.

Finkelhor, D. (1987, May 13). Cited in the *New York Times*, p. 10.

Finkelhor, D. (1984a). *Child sexual abuse*. New York: Free Press.

Finkelhor, D. (1984b, May 14). Quoted in *Newsweek*, p. 13.

Finkelhor, D. (1982). Child abuse in a sample of Boston families. Paper presented to the Symposium on Family and Sexuality. Minneapolis, April.

Finkelhor, D. (1980). Sex among siblings: A survey on prevalence, variety, and effects. *Archives of Sexual Behavior, 9*(3), pp. 171–194.

Finkelhor, D. (1979). *Sexually victimized children*. New York: Free Press.

Finkelhor, D., & Araji, S. (1986). Explanations of pedophilia: A four-factor model. *The Journal of Sex Research, 22*, 145–161.

Finkelhor, D., & Russell, D. (1984). The gender gap among perpetrators of child sexual abuse. In D. Russell (ed.), *Sexual exploitation: Rape, child sexual abuse, and workplace harassment*, pp. 215–231. Beverly Hills, CA: Sage.

Finkle, A. L. (1959). Potency among a sample of men aged between fifty-six and eighty-six. *Journal of the American Medical Association, 170*, 1391–1393.

Firestone, S. (1970). *The dialectic of sex: The case of a feminist revolution*. New York: Morrow.

Fischer, J. L., & Narus, L. R., Jr. (1981). Sex roles and intimacy in same sex and other sex relationships. *Psychology of Women Quarterly, 5*, 444–455.

Fisher, C. et al. (1983). Patterns of female sexual arousal during sleep and waking: Vaginal thermo-conductance studies. *Archives of Sexual Behavior, 12*(2).

Fisher, G. J. (1986). College student attitudes toward forcible date rape: I. Cognitive predictors. *Archives of Sexual Behavior, 15*, 457–466.

Fisher, S. (1973). *The female orgasm*. New York: Basic.

Fisher, W. A., & Byrne, D. (1978). Sex differences in response to erotica: Love versus lust. *Journal of Personality and Social Psychology, 36*, 117–125.

Fishman, I. J. (1987). Complicated implantations of inflatable penile prostheses. *Urology Clinic of North America*, February, *14*(1), 217–239.

Fishman, P. M. (1978). Interaction: The work women do. *Social Problems, 25*, 397–406.

Flaherty, J., & Dusek, J. (1980). An investigation of the relationship between psychological androgyny and components of self-concept. *Journal of Personality and Social Psychology, 38*, 984–992.

Fleming, A. T. (1987, March 26). Our fascination with Baby M. *New York Times Magazine*, Sec. 6, pp. 33–38, 87.

Fletcher, J. (1967). *Moral responsibility: Situation ethics at work*. Philadelphia: Westminster.

Fletcher, J. (1966). *Situation ethics: The new morality*. Philadelphia: Westminster.

Follingstead, D. R., & Kimbrell, C. D. (1986). Sex fantasies revisited: An expansion and further clarification of variables affecting sex fantasy production. *Archives of Sexual Behavior*, December, *15*(6), 475–486.

Forberg, F. C. (1966). *Classical Erotology*. New York: Grove. (First published in 1884).

Ford, C. S., & Beach, F. A. (1951). *Patterns of sexual behavior*. New York: Harper & Row.

Ford, K. (1978). Contraceptive use in the United States, 1973–1976. *Family Planning Perspectives, 10*(5), 264–269.

Ford, K., Zelnik, M., & Kanter, J. F. (1981). Sexual behavior and contraceptive use among socioeconomic groups of young women in the United States. *Journal of Biosocial Science, 13*(1), 31–45.

Forrest, J., & Henshaw, S. (1983). Contraception in America. *Family Planning Perspectives, 15*, 154–156.

Foucault, M. (1978). *The history of sexuality*, Vol. 1. New York: Pantheon.

Fox, C. A., & Fox, B. (1969). Blood pressure and respiratory patterns during human coitus. *Journal of Reproduction and Fertility, 19*(3), 405–415.

Fox, G. L., & Inazu, J. K. (1980). Patterns of mother-daughter communication about sexuality. *Journal of Social Issues, 36*(1), 7–29.

Francoeur, R. T. (1985). Reproductive technologies: New alternatives and new ethics. *SIECUS Report, 14*(1), 1–5.

Frank, E., Anderson, C., & Rubinstein, D. (1978). Frequency of sexual dysfunction in "normal" couples. *New England Journal of Medicine, 299*, 111–

115.

Frank, G. (1966). *The Boston strangler*. New York: New American Library.

Franklin, J., & Franklin, S. (1982). *The ultimate kiss: A guide to oral sex*. Los Angeles: Media Publications.

Freedman, E. B. (1988). *Intimate matters: A history of sexuality in America*. New York: Harper & Row.

Freedman, E. B. (1982). Sexuality in nineteenth-century America: Behavior, ideology, and politics. *Review of American History, 10*(4).

Freeman, D. (1983). *Margaret Mead and Samoa*. Cambridge, MA: Harvard University Press.

Freeman, E. D. (1978). Abortion: Subjective attitudes and feelings. *Family Planning Perspectives, 10*, 150–155.

Freeman, E. W. (1985). PMS treatment approaches and progesterone therapy. *Psychosomatics*, October, 811–815.

Freeman, J. (1973). The origins of the Women's Liberation Movement. *American Journal of Sociology, 78*, 792–811.

Freeman-Longo, R., & Wally, R. (1986). Changing a lifetime of sexual crime. *Anthropology and Education Quarterly*, March, *20*(3), 58–64.

Freud, S. (1957–1964). *The standard edition of the complete psychological works of Sigmund Freud*. J. Strachey, ed. London: Hogarth Press and Institute of Psychoanalysis.

Freud, S. (1951). Letter to an American mother. *American Journal of Psychiatry, 107*, 787.

Freud, S. (1905). Three essays on the theory of sexuality. In, *Standard Edition of the Psychological Works of Sigmund Freud*, vol. 7. London: Hogarth Press.

Freund, K. (1980). Therapeutic sex drive reduction. *Acta Psychiatr. Scand, 62*, 5–38.

Friday, N. (1985). *Jealousy*. New York: William Morrow.

Friday, N. (1980). *Men in love*. New York: Delacorte.

Friday, N. (1975). *Forbidden flowers*. New York: Pocket Books.

Friday, N. (1973). *My secret garden*. New York: Pocket Books.

Friedan, B. (1981). *The second stage*. New York: Summit.

Friedan, B. (1964). *The feminine mystique*. New York: Dell.

Friedland, G. H., & Klein, R. S. (1987). Transmission of human immunodeficiency virus. *New England Journal of Medicine, 317*(18), 1125–1135.

Friedrich, P. (1978). *The meaning of Aphrodite*. Chicago: University of Chicago Press.

Frisch, R. E. (1974). Critical weight at menarche, initiation of the adolescent growth spurt, and control of puberty. In M. M. Grumbach et al. (eds.), *Control of the onset of puberty*. New York: Wiley.

Fromuth, M. E. (1986). The relationship of childhood sexual abuse with later psychological and sexual adjustment in a sample of college women. *Child Abuse and Neglect, 10*(1), 5–15.

Gadpaille, W. J. (1975). *The cycles of sex.* New York: Scribner.

Gagnon, J. H. (1965). Sexuality and sexual learning in the child. *Psychiatry, 28*, 212–228.

Gagnon, J. H. (1977). *Human sexualities.* Glenview, IL.: Scott, Foresman.

Gagnon, J. H. (ed.). (1977). *Human sexuality in today's world.* Boston: Little, Brown.

Gagnon, J. H. (1974). Scripts and coordination of sexual conduct. In J. K. Cole & R. Deinstbrier (eds.), *Nebraska symposium on motivation 21.* Lincoln: University of Nebraska Press.

Gagnon, J. H., & Simon, N. (1987). The sexual scripting of oral genital contacts. *Archives of Sexual Behavior, 16*(1), 1–25.

Gagnon, J., & Simon, W. (1973). *Sexual conduct: The social sources of human sexuality.* Chicago: Aldine.

Gagnon, J. H., & Simon, W. (eds.). (1970). *The sexual scene.* Chicago: Aldine.

Gal, A., Meyer, P., & Taylor, C. (1987). Papillomavirus antigens in anorectal condyloma and carcinoma in homosexual men. *Journal of the American Medical Association*, January 16, 257(3), 337–340.

Galenson, E., & Rolphe, H. (1976). Some suggested revisions concerning early female development. *Journal of the American Psychoanalytic Association, 24*(5), 29–57.

Galenson, H. (1975). Early sexual differences and development discussion. In E. Adelson (ed.), *Sexuality and psychoanalysis.* New York: Brunner-Mazel.

Gallo, R. (1987). Henry S. Kaplan Memorial Lecture, October 13, Stanford Medical School, Stanford, CA.

Gallup, G. (1987, November 26). Public learns AIDS lessons. *San Francisco Chronicle.*

Gallup, G. (1986, December 25). Almost all Americans find family life satisfying. *San Francisco Chronicle.*

Gallup, G., Jr. (1986, November 3). Many Catholics back easing of sexual dogma. *San Francisco Chronicle*, p. 8.

Gallup, G., Jr. (1986, October 24). Drop in support for legalizing gay sex. *San Francisco Chronicle*, p. 11.

Garcia, L. T. (1982). Sex-role orientation and stereotypes about male-female sexuality. *Sex Roles, 8*, 863–876.

Gasser, T., Larsen, E., & Bruskewitz, R. (1987). Penile prosthesis reimplantation. *Journal of Urology*, January, 137(1), 47–47.

Gavzer, B. (1987, May 24). Why more older women are marrying younger men. *Parade Magazine.*

Gay, P. (1988). *The bourgeois experience: The tender passion*, Vol. II. New York: Oxford University Press.

Gay, P. (1984). *The bourgeois experience: Education of the senses.* New York: Oxford.

Gaylord, J. J. (1981). Indecent exposure: A review of the literature. *Medical Science Law, 21*(4), pp. 233–242.

Gebhard, P. H. (1973). Human sexual behavior: A summary statement. In D. S. Marshall & R. C. Suggs (eds.), *Human sexual behavior*, pp. 206–217. Englewood Cliffs, NJ: Prentice-Hall.

Gebhard, P. H. (1973). Sex differences in sexual response. *Archives of Sexual Behavior, 2*, 201–203.

Gebhard, P. H. (1968). Postmarital coitus among widows and divorcees. In P. Bohannan (ed.), *Divorce and after.* Garden City, NJ: Doubleday.

Gebhard, P. H., & Elias, J. (1969). Sexuality and sexual learning in childhood. *Phi Delta Kappa, 50*, 401–405.

Gebhard, P. H., Gagnon, J. H., Pomeroy, W. B., & Christenson, C. V. (1965). *Sex offenders.* New York: Harper & Row.

Gebhard, P. H., & Johnson, A. B. (1979). *The Kinsey data: Marginal tabulation of the 1938–1963 interviews conducted by the Institute for Sex Research.* Philadelphia: W. B. Saunders.

Geer, J. H., Morokoff, P., & Greenwood, P. (1974). Sexual arousal in women: The development of a measuring device for vaginal blood flow. *Archives of Sexual Behavior, 3*, 559–564.

Geis, G. (1977). Forcible rape: An introduction. In D. Chappell, R. Geis, & G. Geis (eds.), *Forcible rape: The crime, the victim, and the offender.* New York: Columbia University Press.

Gesell, A. (1940). *The first view years of life: The preschool years.* New York: Harper and Brothers.

Gesell, A., & Ilg, F. L. (1946). *The child from five to ten.* New York: Harper and Brothers.

Gesell, A., Ilg, F. L., & Ames, L. B. (1956). *Youth: The years from ten to sixteen.* New York: Harper & Row.

Gessa, G. L., & Tagliamonte, A. (1974). Role of brain monoamines in male sexual behavior. *Life Science, 14*(3), 425–436.

Ghadirian, A. M., & Kamaraju, L. S. (1987). *Premenstrual mood changes in affective disorders.*

Gilbert, D., Hagen, R., & D'Agostino, J. (1986). The effects of cigarette smoking on human sexual potency. *Addictive Behavior 11*(4), 431–434.

Gilbert, F. S., & Bailis, K. L. (1980). Sex education in the home: An empirical task analysis. *Journal of Sex Research, 16*, 148–161.

Gilder, G. F. (1973). *Sexual suicide.* New York: Quadrangle.

Gillan, P., & Brindley, G. S. (1979). Vaginal and pelvic floor responses to sexual stimulation. *Psychophysiology, 16*, 471–481.

Gilligan, C. (1982). *In a different voice: Psychological theory and women's development.* Cambridge, MA: Harvard University Press.

Gilman, A. G., Goodman, L. S., Rall, T. W., & Murad, F. (eds.). (1985). *Goodman and Gilman's pharmacological basis of therapeutics*, 7th ed. New York: Macmillan.

Gilmartin, B. G. (1977). Swinging: Who gets involved and how? In R. W. Libby & R. N. Whitehurst (eds.), *Marriage and alternatives: Exploring intimate relationships*, pp. 161–185. Glenview, IL: Scott, Foresman.

Ginsburg, G. L. et al. (1972). The new impotence. *Archives of General Psychology, 28*, 218.

Giovacchini, P. L. (1986). Promiscuity in adolescents and young adults. *Medical Aspects of Human Sexuality*, May, 20(5), 24–31.

Gittelson, N. L., Eacott, S. E., & Melita, B. (1978). Victims of indecent exposure. *British Journal of Psychiatry, 132*, 61–66.

Giuliano, A. (1987). The breast. In M. Pernoll & R. Benson (eds.), *Current obstetric and Gynecologic Diagnosis and Treatment 1987.* Los Altos, CA: Appleton & Lange.

Gladue, B., Green, R., & Hellman, R. (1984). Neuroendocrine response to estrogen and sexual orientation. *Science, 225*, 1496–1499.

Gleitman, H. (1983). *Basic psychology.* New York: Norton.

Glynn, P. (1982). *Skin to skin.* New York: Oxford University Press.

Goedert, J., Biggar, R., Melbye, M., Mann, D., Wilson, S., Gail, M., Grossman, R., Digioia, R., Sanchez, W., Weiss, S. et al. (1987). Effect of T4 count and cofactors on the incidence of AIDS in homosexual men infected with human immunodeficiency virus. *Journal of the American Medical Association*, January 16, 257(3), 331–334.

Gold, A. R., & Adams, D. B. (1978). Measuring the cycles of female sexuality. *Contemporary Obstetrics and Gynecology, 12*, 147–156.

Gold, E. (1986). Long-term effects of sexual victimization in childhood: An attributional approach. *Journal of Consulting and Clinical Psychology*, August, 54(4), 471–475.

Goldberg, D., Whipple, B., Fishkin, R., Waxman, H., Fink, P., & Weisberg, M. (1983). The Grafenberg spot and female ejaculation: A review of initial hypotheses. *Journal of Sex and Marital Therapy*, 9, 27–37.

Goldberg, M. (1983). Importance of little messages in marriage. *Medical Aspects of Human Sexuality*, 17(12).

Goldberg, S. (1979). Premature birth: Consequences for the parent-infant relationship. *American Scientist*, 67, 214–220.

Goldfoot, D. A. et al. (1976). Lack of effect of vaginal lavages and aliphatic acids on ejaculatory responses in rhesus monkeys: Behavioral and chemical analyses. *Hormones and Behavior*, 7, 1–27.

Goldman, R., & Goldman, J. (1982). *Children's sexual thinking*. Boston, MA: Routledge & Kegan Paul.

Goldstein, I. (1987, April 14). Quoted in the *Wall Street Journal*, p. 1.

Goldstein, I. (1986). Impact of drugs on penile smooth muscle. *Abstracts: Conference on the scientific basis of sexual dysfunction*. Bethesda, MD: National Institutes of Health.

Goldstein, M. (1974). *Pornography and sexual deviance*. Berkeley: University of California Press.

Goldstein, S., Halbreich, U., Endicott, J., & Hill, E. (1983). Premenstrual hostility, impulsivity and impaired social functioning. *Journal of Psychosomatic Obstetrics and Gynecology*, March, 5(1), 33–38.

Goleman, D. (1985, May 5). Study tests ways to deter rapists. *New York Times*, p. 15.

Gong, V. (1987). Signs and symptoms of AIDS. In V. Gong & N. Rudwick (eds.), *AIDS*. New Brunswick, NJ: Rutgers University Press.

Gonzalez, E. R. (1980). Contraceptive vaccine research: Still an art news. *Journal of the American Medical Association*, 244(13), 1414–1415, 1419.

Goode, W. J. (1982). *The family*, 2d ed. Englewood Cliffs, NJ: Prentice-Hall.

Goodman, G. S. (1987). Children's report of sexual behavior. In S. J. Ceci, M. P. Toglia, & D. F. Ross (eds.), *Children's eyewitness memory*. New York: Springer-Verlag.

Goodman, R. E., Anderson, D. C., Bulock, D. E., Sheffield, B., Lynch, S. S., & Butt, W. R. (1985). Study of the effects of estradiol on gonadotropin levels in untreated male-to-female transsexuals. *Archives of Sexual Behav-*

*ior*, 14, 141–147.

Gooren, L. (1986). The neuroendocrine response of luteinizing hormone to estrogen administration in heterosexual, homosexual, and transsexual subjects. *Journal of Clinical Endocrinology and Metabolism*, September, 63(3), 583–588.

Gordis, R. (1978). *Love and sex: A modern Jewish perspective*. New York: Farrar, Strauss & Giroux.

Gordon, J. W., & Ruddle, F. H. (1981). Mammalian gonadal determination and gametogenesis. *Science*, 211, 1265.

Gordon, L. (1976). *Woman's body, women's right: A social theory of birth control in America*. New York: Grossman.

Gordon, S. (1986). What kids need to know. *Psychology Today*, October, 20(10), 22–26.

Gorski, R., Gordon, J., Shryne, J., & Southam, A. (1978). Evidence for a morphological sex difference within the medial preoptic area of the rat brain. *Brain Research*, 148, 333–346.

Goslin, D. A. (ed.). (1969). *Handbook of socialization theory and research*. Chicago: Rand McNally.

Gosling, J., & Warner, D. (1967). London today. In *Fille de Joie*, pp. 373–380. New York: Grove Press.

Gosselin, C., & Wilson, G. (1980). *Sexual variations: Fetishism, sadomasochism and transvestism*. New York: Simon & Schuster.

Gottlieb, M. S., Schroff, R., Schanker, H. M. et al. (1981). Pneumocystis curinii pneumonia and mucosal candidiasis in previously healthy homosexual men: Evidence of a new acquired cellular immunodeficiency. *New England Journal of Medicine*, 305, 1425–1431.

Gould, R. E. (1987, March 26). And what about Baby M's ruined life? *New York Times*.

Gould, R. L. (1978). *Transformations*. New York: Simon & Schuster.

Goy, R. W., & McEwen, B. S. (1980). *Sexual differentiation in the brain*. Cambridge, MA: MIT Press.

Grafenberg, E. (1950). The role of urethra in female orgasm. *International Journal of Sexology*, 3(3).

Grant, M., & Mulas, U. (1975). *Eros in Pompeii*. New York: Morrow.

Grant, S., & Grant, D. (1983). *Joys of oral love*. New York: Carlyle Communications.

Graves, R. (1959). *The Greek myths*. New York: Braziller.

Gray, D. S., & Gorzalka, B. B. (1980). Adrenal steroid interactions in female sexual behavior: A review. *Psychoneuroendocrinology*, 5(2), 157–175.

Green, R. (1986). *The sissy-boy syndrome*

*and the development of homosexuality: A 15-year prospective study*. New Haven: Yale University Press.

Green, R. (1980). *Sexual identity conflict in children and adults*. New York: Basic.

Green, R., Mandel, J., Hotvedt, M., Gray, J., & Smith, L. (1986). Lesbian mothers and their children: A comparison with solo parent heterosexual mothers and their children. *Archives of Sexual Behavior*, April, 15(2), 167–184.

Green, R., Williams, K., & Goodman, M. (1982). Ninety-nine tomboys and non-tomboys: Behavioral contrasts and demographic similarities. *Archives of Sexual Behavior*, 11(3).

Greenberg, J. S. (1972). The masturbatory behavior of college students. *Psychology in the Schools*, 9(4), 427–432.

Greenblatt, C. S. (1983). The salience of sexuality in the early years of marriage. *Journal of Marriage and the Family*, 45, 289–299.

Greendlinger, V., & Byrne, D. (1987). Coercive sexual fantasies of college men as predictors of self-reported likelihood of rape and overt sexual aggression. *Journal of Sex Research*, 23, 1–11.

Greene, G., & Greene, C. (1974). *The last taboo*. New York: Grove Press.

Greenspan, F. S., & Forsham, P. H. (1986). *Basic and clinical endocrinology*, 2d ed. Los Altos, CA: Lange Medical Publications.

Greer, D. M. et al. (1982). A technique for foreskin reconstruction and some preliminary results. *Journal of Sex Research*, 18, 324–330.

Greer, G. (1984). *Sex and destiny*. New York: Harper & Row.

Greer, G. (1971). *The female eunuch*. New York: McGraw-Hill.

Gregersen, E. (1982) *Sexual practices*. New York: Watts.

Gregory, J., & Purcell, M. (1987). Scott's inflatable penile prosthesis: Evaluation of mechanical survival in the series 700 model. *Journal of Urology*, April, 137(4), 676–677.

Griffith, W. (1987). Females, males, and sexual responses. In K. Kelley (ed.), *Females, males, and sexuality*. Albany: State University of New York Press.

Griffitt, W. (1970). Environmental effects on interpersonal affective behavior: Ambient effective temperature and attraction. *Journal of Personality and Social Psychology*, 15, 240–244.

Grigson, G. (1976). *The goddess of love*. New York: Stein & Day.

Grimal, P. (ed.). (1981). *Larousse world mythology*. New York: Excalibur.

Groff, M. G. (1987). Characteristics of incest offenders' wives. *Journal of Sex Research*, 23(1), 91–96.

Groopman, J. E. (1988). The acquired immunodeficiency syndrome. In J. B. Wyngaarden & L. H. Smith (eds.), *Cecil textbook of medicine*, pp. 1799–1805. Philadelphia: W. B. Saunders.

Gross, J. (1987, October 12). The deadly specter of AIDS brings added turmoil for gay teenagers. *New York Times*, p 12.

Grosskopf, D. (1983). *Sex and the married woman*. New York: Simon & Schuster.

Grosskurth, P. (1980). *Havelock Ellis*. New York: Knopf.

Groth, A. N. (1979). *Men who rape*. New York: Plenum.

Groth, A. N., with Birnbaum, H. J. (1979). *Men who rape: The psychology of the offender*. New York: Plenum.

Groth, A. N., & Burgess, A. W. (1980). Male rape: Offenders and victims. *American Journal of Psychiatry, 137*(7), 806–810.

Groth, A. N., & Burgess, A. W. (1977). Sexual dysfunction during rape. *The New England Journal of Medicine, 297*, 764–766.

Groth, A. N., Burgess, A. W., & Holmstrom, L. (1977). Rape: Power, anger and sexuality. *American Journal of Psychiatry, 134*, 1239–1243.

Groth, A. N., & Hobson, W. (1983). The dynamics of sexual assault. In L. Schlesinger & Revitch (eds.). *Sexual dynamics of anti-social behavior*. Springfield, IL: Thomas.

Grumbach, M. M. (1980). The neuroendocrinology of puberty. *Hospital Practice, 15*(3), 51–60.

Grumbach, M. M., & Conte, F. A. (1985). Disorders of sexual differentiation. In J. D. Wilson & D. W. Foster (eds.), *Williams Textbook of Endocrinology*, 7th ed., pp. 313–401. Philadelphia: W. B. Saunders.

Grumbach, M. M. et al. (1974). Hypothalamic-pituitary regulation of puberty: Evidence and concepts derived from clinical research. In M. M. Grumbach, G. D. Grave, & F. E. Mayer, (eds.), *Control of the onset of puberty*, Chapter 6. New York: Wiley.

Grunfeld, B., & Noreik, K. (1986). Recidivism among sex offenders: A follow-up study of 541 Norwegian sex offenders. *International Journal of Law and Psychiatry, 9*(1), 95–102.

Gulik, R. H. V. (1974). *Sexual life in ancient China*. Leiden: Brill.

Gunderson, J. G. (1988). Personality disorders. In A. M. Nicholi (ed.), *Harvard guide to psychiatry*, pp. 337–357. Cambridge, MA: Belknap.

Gustafson, J. M. (1981). Nature, sin, and covenant: Three bases for sexual ethics. *Perspectives in Biology and Medicine*, Spring, 483–497.

Gutek, B. A. (1985). *Sex and the workplace*. San Francisco, CA: Jossey-Bass.

Gutek, B. A., & Nakamura, C. G. (1983). Gender roles and sexuality in the world of word. In E. Allgeier & M. McCormick (eds.), *Changing boundaries: Gender roles and sexual behavior*. Palo Alto, CA: Mayfield.

Guyton, A C. (1986). *Textbook of medical physiology*, 7th ed. Philadelphia: W. B. Saunders.

Haas, A. (1979a). *Teenage Sexuality*. New York: Macmillan.

Haas, A. (1979b). Male and female spoken language differences: Stereotypes and evidence. *Psychological Bulletin, 86*, 616–626.

Haeberle, E. J. (1984). Sexology: Conception, birth, and growth of a science. In R. T. Seagraves & E. J. Haeberle (eds.), *Emerging Dimensions of sexology*, pp. 9–28. New York: Praeger Scientific.

Haeberle, E. J. (1983a). The future of sexology—A radical view. In C. M. Davis (ed.), *Challenges in sexual science*.

Haeberle, E. J. (ed.), (1983b). *The birth of sexology*. 6th World Congress of Sexology Proceedings, Washington, DC.

Haeberle, E. J. (1982). The Jewish contribution to the development of sexology. *The Journal of Sex Research, 18*(4), 305–323.

Haeberle, E. J. (1981). Swastika, pink triangle, and yellow star: The destruction of sexology and the persecution of homosexuals in Nazi Germany. *The Journal of Sex Research, 17*(3), 270–287.

Haeberle, E. J. (1978). *The sex atlas*. New York: Seabury.

Hafez, E. S. E. (1980). *Human reproduction*, 2d ed. New York: Harper & Row.

Hagen, I. M., & Beach, R. K. (1980). The diaphragm: Its effective use among college women. *Journal of the American College Health Association, 28*(5), 263–266.

Hahn, S. R., & Paige, K. E. (1980). American birth practices: A critical review. In J. E. Parsons (ed.), *The psychology of sex differences and sex roles*. New York: McGraw-Hill, Hemisphere.

Hall, R., Kassees, J., & Hoffman, C. (1986). Treatment for survivors of incest. Special issue: Support groups. *Journal for Specialists in Group Work*, May, 11(2), 85–92.

Hällstrom, T. (1973). *Mental disorder and sexuality in the climacteric*. Stockholm: Scandinavian University Books.

Halverson, H. M. (1940). Genital and sphincter behavior of the male infant. *The Journal of Genetic Psychology, 56*, 95–136.

Hamerton, J. L. (1988). Chromosomes and their disorders. In J. B. Wyngaarden & L. H. Smith (eds.), *Cecil textbook of medicine*, pp. 161–171. Philadelphia: W.B. Saunders.

Hampson, J. L. (1965). Determinants of psychosexual orientation. In F. A. Beach (ed.), *Sex and behavior*, pp. 108–132. New York: Wiley.

Hanley, R. (1987, February 5). Parents of Baby M in a recorded call. *New York Times*.

Hansen, G. L. (1987). Extradyadic relations during courtship. *Journal of Sex Research, 23*(3), 382–290.

Hansfield, H. H. (1984). Gonorrhea and uncomplicated gonococcal infection. In K. Holmes, P. Mardh, P. F. Sparling & P. Wiesner (eds.), *Sexually transmitted diseases*. New York: McGraw-Hill.

Harbison, R. D., & Mantilla-Plata, B. (1972). Prenatal toxicity, maternal distribution and placental transfer of tetrahydrocannabinol. *Journal of Pharmacology and Experimental Therapeutics, 180*, 446–453.

Hare, E. H. (1962). Masturbatory insanity: The history of an idea. *Journal of Mental Science, 452*, 2–25.

Hariton, E. B., & Singer, J. L. (1974). Women's fantasies during sexual intercourse: Normative and theoretical implications. *Journal of Counseling and Clinical Psychology, 42*, 312–322.

Harlow, H. F. (1958). The nature of love. *American Psychologist, 13*, 673.

Harlow, H. F., McGaugh, J. L., & Thompson, R. F. (1971). *Psychology*. San Francisco: Albion.

Harmatz, M. G., & Novak, M. A. (1983). *Human sexuality*. New York: Harper & Row.

Harris, C. et al. (1983). Immunodeficiency in female sexual partners of men with the acquired immunodeficiency syndrome. *The New England Journal of Medicine, 308*, 1181–1184.

Harris, L. (1987). *Inside America*. New York: Vintage Books.

Harris, M. (1981). Why it's not the same old America. *Psychology Today, 15*.

Harrison, W. M., Rabkin, J. G., Ehrhardt, A. A., Stewart, J. W., McGrath, P. J., Ross, D., & Quitkin, F. M. (1986). Effects of antidepressant medication on sexual function: A controlled study. *Journal of Clinical Psychopharmacology*, June, 6(3), 144–149.

Harris Poll (1985, November 25). In *New York Times*, p. 11.

Harry, J. (1986). Sampling gay men. *The Journal of Sex Research, 22*(1), 21–34.

Hart, B. L., & Leedy, M. G. (1985). Neurological bases of male sexual behavior. In N. Adler, D. Pfaff, & R.

Gay (eds.), *Handbook of behavioral neurobiology*, Vol. 7 *Reproduction*. New York: Plenum Press.

Hartman, W., & Fithian, M. (1984). *Any man can: The multiple orgasmic technique for every loving man.* New York: St. Martin's Press.

Harvey, S. M. (1987). Female sexual behavior: Fluctuations during the menstrual cycle. *Journal of Psychosomatic Research, 31*(1), 101–110.

Harvey, S. M. (1980). Trends in contraceptive use at one university: 1974–1978. *Family Planning Perspectives, 12*(6), 301–304.

Haseltine, F. P., & Ohno, S. (1981). Mechanisms of gonadal differentiation. *Science, 211,* 1272.

Hatcher, R. A. (1982). *It's your choice.* New York: Irvington.

Hatcher, R. A., Guest, F. A., Stewart, F. H., Stewart, G. K., Trussel, J., Bowen, S. C., & Cates, W. (1988). *Contraceptive Technology 1988–1989: AIDS a special section.* New York: Irvington.

Hatfield, E. (1988). Passionate and companionate love. In R. J. Sternberg & M. L. Barnes (eds.), *The psychology of love*, pp. 191–217. New Haven: Yale University Press.

Hatfield, E. (1982). Passionate love, companionate love, and intimacy. In M. Fisher & G. Stricker (eds.), *Intimacy*, pp. 267–292. New York: Plenum Press.

Hatfield, E. & Strecher, S. (1986). *Mirror, Mirror.* New York: New York University Press.

Hatfield, E., & Walster, G. W. (1978). *A new look at love.* Latham, MA: University Press of America.

Hatterer, L. J. (1970). *Changing homosexuality in the male.* New York: McGraw-Hill.

Haugh, S., Hoffman, C., & Cowan, G. (1980). The eye of the very young beholder: Sextyping of infants by young children. *Child Development, 51,* 598–600.

Hausfater, G., & Skoblick, B. (1985, January 4). Premenstrual problems may best baboons. Reported by E. Eckholm in *New York Times*, p. 19.

Haviland, W. A. (1981). *Cultural anthropology.* New York: Holt, Rinehart and Winston.

Hawton, K., & Catalan, J. (1986). Prognostic factors in sex therapy. *Behavior Research and Therapy, 24*(4), 377–385.

Hayden, M. (1986). Psychoanalytic resources for the activist feminist therapist. In D. Howard (ed.), *The dynamics of feminist therapy.* New York: Haworth Press.

Hayes, R. W. (1975). Female genital mutilation, fertility control, and the patrilineage in modern Sudan: A functional analysis. *American Ethnologist, 2,* 617–633.

Haynes, D. M. (1982). Course and conduct of normal pregnancy. In D. N. Danforth (ed.), *Obstetrics and Gynecology*, 4th ed. Philadelphia: Harper & Row.

Hearst, N., & Hulley, S. B. (1988). Preventing the heterosexual spread of AIDS. *Journal of the American Medical Association*, April 22, *259*(16), 2428–2432.

Heath, R. G. (1972). Pleasure and brain activity in males. *Journal of Nervous and Mental Disease, 154,* 3–18.

Heider, C. B. (1973). The penis gourd of New Guinea. *Annals of the Association of American Geographers, 63*(3), 312–318.

Heim, N. (1981). Sexual behavior of castrated sex offenders. *Archives of Sexual Behavior, 10,* 11–19.

Heim, N., & Hursch, C. J. (1979). Castration for sex offenders: Treatment or punishment? A review and critique of recent European literature. *Archives of Sexual Behavior, 8,* 281–305.

Heiman, J. A. (1980). Female sexual response patterns. *Archives of General Psychiatry, 37,* 1311–1316.

Heiman, J. P. (1975a). The physiology of erotica: Women's sexual arousal. *Psychology Today, 8*(11), 90–94.

Heiman, J. R. (1975b). Women's sexual arousal: The physiology of erotica. *Psychology Today*, April, 91–94.

Heindricks, L. E. (1980). Unwed adolescent fathers. *Adolescence, 15,* 861–869.

Helmreich, R. L., Spence, J. T., & Holahan, C. K. (1979). Psychological androgyny and sex-role flexibility: A test of two hypotheses. *Journal of Personality and Social Psychology, 37,* 1631–1644.

Helms, J. M. (1987). Acupuncture for the management of primary dysmenorrhea. *Obstetrics and Gynecology*, January, *69*(1), 51–56.

Hendrick, S., Hendrick, C., Slapion-Foote, M. J., & Foote, F. H. (1985). Gender differences in sexual attitudes. *Journal of Personality and Social Psychology, 48,* 1630–1642.

Henley, N. M. (1977). *Body politics: Power, sex and nonverbal communication.* Englewood Cliffs, NJ: Prentice-Hall.

Henley, N. M., & Freeman, J. (1976). The sexual politics of interpersonal behavior. In S. Cox (ed.), *Female psychology: The emerging self.* Chicago: Science Research Associates.

Henriques, F. (1962–1968). *Prostitution and society: A survey.* Vol 1: *Primitive, classical, oriental.* Vol 2: *Prostitution in Europe and the New World.* Vol. 3: *Modern sexuality.* London: MacGibbon & Kee.

Henry, W. A. (1988, February 22). Uniform treatment of gays. *Time*, p. 55.

Henslin, J. M., & Sagarin, E. (eds.). (1978). *The sociology of sex.* New York: Schocken.

Herbst, A. L. (1981). Clear cell adenocarcinoma and the current status of DES-exposed females. *Cancer, 48* Suppl (2), 484–488.

Herdt, G. H. (1987). *The Sambia.* New York: Holt, Rinehart and Winston.

Herdt, G. H. (1981). *Guardians of the flute.* New York: McGraw-Hill.

Heresova, J., Pobisova, Z., Hampl, R., & Starka, L. (1986). Androgen administration to transsexual women. II. Hormonal changes. *Exploring Clinical Endocrinology*, December, *88*(2), 219–223.

Herman, J., & Hirschman, L. (1981). Families at risk for father-daughter incest. *American Journal of Psychiatry, 138*(7), 967–970.

Herman, J., Russel, D., & Trocki, K. (1986). Long-term effects of incestuous abuse in childhood. *American Journal of Psychiatry, 143*(1), 1293–1296.

Heston, L., & Shields, J. (1968). Homosexuality in twins. *Archives of General Psychiatry, 18,* 149–169.

Hiernaux, J. (1968). Ethnic differences in growth and development. *Eugenics quarterly, 15,* 12–21.

Higgins, G. E. (1979). Sexual response in spinal cord injuries: A review. *Archives of Sexual Behavior, 8,* 173–196.

Higham, E. (1980). Sexuality in the infant and neonate: Birth to two years. In B. B. Wolman & J. Money (eds.), *Handbook of human sexuality.* Englewood Cliffs, NJ: Prentice-Hall.

Hill, E. (1987). Premalignant and malignant disorders of the uterine cervix. In M. Pernoll & R. Benson (eds.), *Current obstetric and gynecologic diagnosis and treatment 1987*, 6th ed. Los Altos, CA: Appleton & Lange.

Himes, N. (1970). *Medical history of contraception.* New York: Gambut.

Himmelweit, H.T., & Bell, N. (1980). Television as a sphere of influence of the child's learning about sexuality. In L. Brown (ed.), *Childhood sexual learning: The unwritten curriculum.* Cambridge, MA: Ballinger.

Hinde, R. A. (1974). *Animal behavior: A synthesis of ethology and comparative psychology.* New York: McGraw-Hill.

Hindelang, M. J., & Davis, B. J. (1977). Forcible rape in the United States: A statistical profile. In D. Chappell et al.

(eds.), *Forcible rape*, pp. 87–114. New York: Columbia University Press.

Hindy, C. (1985, September 10). Cited in Coleman, D. *New York Times*, p. 18.

Hingham, E. (1980). Sexuality in the infant and neonate: Birth to two years. In B. J. Wolman & J. Money (eds.), *Handbook of human sexuality*. Englewood Cliffs, NJ: Prentice-Hall.

Hite, S. (1987). *Women and love, a cultural revolution in progress*. New York: Knopf.

Hite, S. (1981). *The Hite report on male sexuality*. New York: Ballantine.

Hite, S. (1976). *The Hite report*. New York: Macmillan.

Hoch, Z. (1986). Vaginal erotic sensitivity by sexological examination. *Acta-Obstet-Gynecol-Scand, 65*(7), 767–773.

Hockenberry, S. L., & Billingham, R. (1987). Sexual orientation and boyhood gender conformity. *Archives of Sexual Behavior, 16*(6), 475–493.

Hoenig, J. (1985). Etiology of transsexualism. In B. W. Steiner, (ed.), *Gender dysphoria: Development, research, and management*. New York: Plenum.

Hoenig, J. (1977). The development of sexology during the second half of the 19th century. In J. Money & J. Musaph (eds.), *Handbook of Sexology*. Amsterdam: Excerpta Medica.

Hoffman, C. H. (1981). Sexually transmitted diseases. *Journal of the American Medical Association, 246*(15), 1709.

Hoffman, L. (1977). Changes in family roles, socialization and sex differences. *American Psychologist, 32*, 644–657.

Hoffman, M. (1968). *The gay world: Male homosexuality and the social creation of evil*. New York: Basic.

Hole, J. & Levine, E. (1971). *Rebirth of feminism*. New York: Quadrangle.

Hollender, M., Brown, C., & Roback, H. (1977). Genital exhibitionism in women. *American Journal of Psychiatry, 134*, 436–438.

Hollingshead, W. H., & C. Rosse (1985). *Textbook of anatomy*, 4th ed. New York: Harper & Row.

Hollister, L. (1974). Popularity of amyl nitrite as sexual stimulant. *Medical Aspects of Human Sexuality, 8*(4), 112.

Holme, B. (1979) *Bulfinch's mythology*. New York: Viking.

Holmes, K., March, P. A., Sparling, P. F., & Weisner, P. J. (1984). *Sexually transmitted diseases*. New York: McGraw-Hill.

Holmstrom, N., Hutchinson, J. H., Fraser, D., Kooh, S. W., & Farquahar, J. W. (1985). Disorders of the endocrine glands. In J. O. Forfar & G. C. Arneil (eds.), *Textbook of pediatrics*, 3d ed., Vol. 2, pp. 1106–1195. Edinburgh: Churchill Livingston.

Holt, L. H., & Weber, M. (1982). *Woman care*. New York: Random House.

Hong, L. K. (1984). Survival of the fastest. *Journal of Sex Research, 20*, 109–122.

Hooker, E. (1975). The adjustment of the male overt homosexual. *Journal of Projective Techniques, 21*(1), 18–31.

Hooker, E. (1969). Parental relations and male homosexuality in patient and non-patient samples. *Journal of Counseling and Clinical Psychology, 33*, 140–142.

Hooker, E. (1958). Male homosexuality in the Rorschach. *Journal of Projective Techniques, 25*, 22–54.

Hopkins, J. R. (1977). Sexual behavior in adolescence. *Journal of Social Issues, 33*(2), 67–85.

Hopkins, T. J. (1971). *The Hindu religious tradition*. North Scituate, MA: Duxbury.

Hopson, J. S. (1979). *Scent signals: The silent language of sex*. New York: Morrow.

Horney, K. (1973). *Feminine psychology*. New York: Norton.

Horton, D. (1957). The dialogue of courtship in popular songs. *American Journal of Sociology, 62*, 569–578.

Hotvedt, M. (1983). The cross-cultural and historical context. In R. B. Weg (ed.), *Sexuality in the later years*. New York: Academic Press.

Houseknecht, S. (1978). Voluntary childlessness. *Alternative Lifestyles, 1*(3), 379–402.

Houston, L. N. (1981). Romanticism and eroticism among black and white college students. *Adolescence, 16*, 263–272.

Houston, V. (1987). *Loving a younger man*. New York: Contemporary Books.

Howard, J., Blumstein, P., & Schwartz, P. (1986). Sex, power, and influence tactics in intimate relationships. *Journal of Personality and Social Psychology*, July, *51*(1), 102–109.

Howard, J. L., Lipzin, M. B., & Reifler, C. B. (1973). Is pornography a problem? *Journal of Social Issues, 29*, 133–245.

Hrdy, S. B. (1981). *The woman that never evolved*. Boston: Harvard University Press.

Huelsman, B. R. (1976). An anthropological view of clitoral and other female genital mutilations. In T. P. Lowry and T. S. Lowry (eds.), *The clitoris*. St. Louis, MO: Warren H. Green.

Hull, C. L. (1943). *Principles of behavior*. New York: Appelton-Century-Crofts.

Humanae Vitae: Encyclical letter of Pope Paul VI. (1972). In J. Horgan (ed.), *Humanae Vitae and the bishops: The encyclical and the statements of the national hierarchies*. Blackrock, Ireland: Irish University Press.

Humphreys, L. (1970). *Tearoom trade: Impersonal sex in public restrooms*. Chicago: Aldine.

Humphreys, L., & Miller, B. (1980). Identities in the emerging gay culture. In J. Marmor (ed.), *Homosexual behavior*. New York: Basic.

Hunt, M. (1976). Special, today's man: *Redbook's* exclusive Gallup survey on the emerging male. *Redbook, 147*(6), 112ff.

Hunt, M. (1974). *Sexual behavior in the 1970's*. Chicago: Playboy Press.

Hunter, N. (1987). AIDS prevention and civil liberties: The false security and mandatory testing. *SIECUS Report, 16*(1), 1–2.

Hurtig, A., & Rosenthal, I. (1987). Psychological findings in early treated cases of female pseudohermaphroditism caused by virilizing congenital adrenal hyperplasia. *Archives of Sexual Behavior, 16*(3), 209–223.

Hussey, H. H. (1981). Vasectomy—A note of concern: Reprise editorial. *Journal of the American Medical Association, 245*(22), 2333.

Huston, T. L., & Levinger, G. (1978). Interpersonal attraction and relationships. *Annual Review of Psychology, 29*, 115–156.

Hutchinson, J. B. (ed.). (1978). *Biological determinants of sexual behavior*. New York: Wiley.

Hyppa, M. T., Falck, S. C., & Rinne, V. K. (1975). Is L-dopa an aphrodisiac in patients with Parkinson's disease? In M. Sandler and G. L. Gessa (eds.), *Sexual behavior: Pharmacology and biochemistry*, New York: Raven.

Imperato-McGinley, J. (1985). Disorders of sexual differentiation. In J. B. Wyngaarden & L. H. Smith, Jr. (eds.), *Cecil Textbook of Medicine*, 17th ed. Philadelphia: W.B. Saunders.

Imperato-McGinley, J., Guerrero, L., Gautier, T., & Peterson, R. (1974). Steroid 5-alphareductase deficiency in man: An inherited form of male pseudohermaphroditism. *Science, 186*, 1213–1215.

Ingrassia, M. (1986, October 29). Love among the labor force. *San Francisco Chronicle*.

Inkeles, G. & Todris, M. (1972). *The art of sensual massage*. San Francisco, CA: Straight Arrow.

J. (1969). *The sensuous woman*. New York: Lyle Stuart.

Jackson, E., & Potkay, C. (1973). Precollege influences on sexual experiences of coeds. *Journal of Sex Research*, *4*, 150–161.

Jacobs, L. (1986). Chief complaint: Sexual inadequacy. *Medical Aspects of Human Sexuality*, May, *20*(5), 44–50.

Jacobs, P. A., Brunton, M., Melville, M. M., Britain, R. P., & McClemont, W. F. (1965). Aggressive behavior, mental subnormality, and the XYY male. *Nature, 208*, 1351–1352.

James, B. (1983). The "silent treatment" in marriage. *Medical Aspects of Human Sexuality, 17*(2).

James, J. (1977). Prostitutes and prostitution. In E. Sagrin & F. Montanino (eds.), *Deviants*. Morristown, NJ: General Learning Press.

James, J., & Meyerding, J. (1977). Early sexual experience and prostitution. *American Journal of Psychiatry, 134*, 1381–1385.

James, W. H. (1971). The distribution of coitus within the human intermenstruum. *Journal of Biosocial Science, 3*, 159–171.

Jayne, C. (1986). Methodology in sex research in 1986: An editor's commentary. *The Journal of Sex Research, 22*(1), 1–5.

Jehu, D. (1979). *Sexual dysfunction*. New York: Wiley.

Jenks, R. (1985). Swinging: A test of two theories and proposed new model. *Archives of Sexual Behavior, 14*(6), 517–527.

Jensen, J., & Stuhlmueller, C. (1979). The relevance of the Old Testament. In D. Doherty (ed.), *Dimensions of human sexuality*. Garden City, NY: Doubleday.

Jessor, S., & Jessor, R. (1975). Transition from virginity to nonvirginity among youth: A social-psychological study over time. *Developmental Psychology, 11*, 473–484.

Jick, H. et al. (1981). Vaginal spermicides and congenital disorders. *Journal of the American Medical Association, 245*(13), 1329–1332.

Johns, D. R. (1986). Benign sexual headache within a family. *Archives of Neurology*, November, *43*, 1158–1159.

Johnson, D. (1987, May 4). Infertile Catholics must make own decisions, Cardinal says. *New York Times*.

Johnson, M. (1981). *The Borgias*. New York: Holt, Rinehart and Winston.

Johnson, S., Jr., & Joseph, S. C. (1987, December 20). Pro and con: Free needles for addicts to help curb AIDS? Interview in the *New York Times*.

Johnson, W. (1985, January 16). Landers' survey does not surprise experts. *Times Tribune*, p. B-1.

Johnston, J., & Ettema, J. S. (1982). *Positive images: Breaking stereotypes with children's television*. Beverly Hills, CA: Sage.

Jones, C. (1982). *Sex or symbol: Erotic images of Greece and Rome*. Austin: University of Texas Press.

Jones, E. (1957). *The life and work of Sigmund Freud*. 3 vols. New York: Basic.

Jones, E. (1949). *On the nightmare*. London: Hogarth.

Jones, E. et al. (1987). *Teenage pregnancies in industrialized countries*. Alan Guttmacher Institute, New Haven: Yale University Press.

Jones, M. C. (1965). Psychological correlates of somatic development. *Child Development, 36*, 899–911.

Jost, A. (1953). Problems of fetal endocrinology: The gonadal and hypophyseal hormones. *Recent progress in hormone research, 8*, 379–418.

Judd, H. L. (1987). Menopause and postmenopause. In M. L. Pernoll & R. C. Benson (eds.), *Current obstetric and gynecologic diagnosis and treatment*. Norwalk, CT: Appleton & Lange.

Judson, F. (1983). What practical advice can physicians give patients on avoiding genital herpes. *Medical Aspects of Human Sexuality, 17*(8).

Jung, C. G. (1969). *Animus and anima*. New York: Springer.

Jung, C. G. (1968). *Archetypes of the collective unconscious*. Princeton, NJ: Princeton University Press.

Jung, C. G. (1960). General aspects of dream analysis. In R. F. C. Hull, (translator), *Structure and dynamics of the psyche*, Vol. 8. New York: Pantheon.

Kagan, D., Ozment, S., & Turner, F. M. (1987). *The western heritage*, 3d ed. New York: Macmillan.

Kahn, J., & Kline, D. (1980). Toward an understanding of sexual learning and communication: An examination of social learning theory and nonschool learning environments. In E. Roberts (ed.), *Childhood sexual learning: The unwritten curriculum*. Cambridge, MA: Ballinger.

Kahneman, D., Slovic, P., & Tversky, A. (1982). *Judgment under uncertainty: Heuristics and biases*. New York: Cambridge University Press.

Kaiser, I. (1986). Fertilization and the physiology and development of fetus and placenta. In D. Danforth & J. Scott (eds.), *Obstetrics and Gynecology*, 5th ed. Philadelphia: J.B. Lippincott.

Kallman, F. J. (1952). A comparative twin study on the genetic aspects of male homosexuality. *Journal of Nervous and Mental Disease, 115*, 283–298.

Kando, T. M. (1978). *Sexual behavior and family life in transition*. New York: Elsevier/North Holland.

Kanin, E. (1985). Date rapists: Differential sexual socialization and relative deprivation. *Archives of Sexual Behavior, 14*, 219–231.

Kanin, E. (1969). Selected dyadic aspects of male aggression. *Journal of Sex Research, 5*, 12–28.

Kanter, J. F., & Zelnick, M. (1972b). Sexual experience of young unmarried women in the United States. *Family Planning Perspectives, 4*(4), 9–18.

Kantor, T. G. (1986). Use of diclofenac in analgesia. *American Journal of Medicine*, April 28, *80*(4b), 64–69.

Kaplan, H. S. (1987, November 5). Cited in Brody J., Changing attitudes on masturbation. *New York Times*.

Kaplan, H. S. (1979). *Disorders of sexual desire*. New York: Brunner/Mazel.

Kaplan, H. S. (1974). *The new sex therapy*. New York: Brunner/Mazel.

Kaplan, J. (1977). The Edward G. Donley memorial lecture: Non-victim crime and the regulation of prostitution. *West Virginia Law Review, 79*, 593–606.

Kaplan, J., Spira, T., Fishbein, D., Pinsky, P., & Schonberger, L. (1987). Lymphadenopathy syndrome in homosexual men. Evidence for continuing risk of developing the acquired immunodeficiency syndrome. *Journal of the American Medical Association*, January 16, *257*(3), 335–337.

Karacan, I. (1978). Advances in the psychophysiological evaluation of male erectile incompetence. In J. LoPiccolo & L. LoPiccolo (eds.), *Handbook of sex therapy*. New York: Plenum.

Karacan, I., Marans, A., Barnet, A., & Lodge, A. (1968). Ontogeny of penile erection during sleep in infants. *Psychophysiology, 4*, 363–364.

Karacan, I., Salis, P. J., Thernby, J. I., & Williams, R. L. (1976). The ontogeny of nocturnal penile tumescence. *Waking and Sleeping, 1*, 27–44.

Karlen, A. (1971). *Sexuality and homosexuality*. New York: Norton.

Kassel, V. (1983). Long-term care institutions. In R. B. Weg (ed.), *Sexuality in the later years*. New York: Academic Press.

Katchadourian, H. (1987). *Fifty: Midlife in perspective*. New York: W.H. Freeman.

Katchadourian, H. (1981). Sex education in college: The Stanford experience. In L. Brown (ed.), *Sex education in the eighties*. New York: Plenum.

Katchadourian, H. (ed.). (1979). *Human sexuality: A comparative and developmental perspective*. Berkeley: University of California Press.

Katchadourian, H., & Martin, J. A. (1979). Analysis of human sexual behavior. In H. Katchadourian (ed.), *Human sexuality: A comparative and developmental perspective*, Berkeley: University of California Press.

Katz, J. (1976). *Gay American history*. New York: Crowell.

Kaufman, A. et al. (1981). Recent developments in family planning in China. *Journal of Family Practice, 12*(3), 581–582.

Kaufman, M. (1988, February 11). Hers. *New York Times*, p. 18.

Kegel, A. (1952). Sexual functioning of the pubococcygeus muscle. *Western Journal of Surgery, Obstetrics and Gynecology, 60*, 521–524.

Kelley, K. (ed.). (1987). *Females, males, and sexuality*. Albany: State University of New York Press.

Kelly, G. F. (1981). Parents as sex educators. In L. Brown (ed.), *Sex education in the eighties*. New York: Plenum.

Keniston, K. (1971). *Youth and dissent.* New York: Dial.

Keniston, K. (1968). *Young radicals.* New York: Dial.

Keniston, K. (1965). *The uncommitted.* New York: Dial.

Kennedy, A., & Dean, S. (1986). *Touching for pleasure: A guide to sensual enhancement.* Chatsworth, CA: Chatsworth Press.

Kessel, R. G., & Kardon, R. H. (1979). *Tissues and organs.* San Francisco: W.H. Freeman.

Keusch, G. T. (1984). Enteric bacterial pathogens: Shigella, Campylobacter, Salmonella. In K. Holmes, P. Mardh, P. F. Sparling, & P. Wiesner (eds.), *Sexually transmitted diseases.* New York: McGraw-Hill.

Kiely, E., Williams, G., & Goldie, L. (1987). Assessment of the immediate and long-term effects of pharmacologically induced penile erections in the treatment of psychogenic and organic impotence. *British Journal of Urology*, February, *59*(2), 164–169.

Kilmann, P. et al. (1982). The treatment of sexual paraphilias: A review of the outcome research. *The Journal of Sex Research, 18*(3), 193–252.

Kilmann, P. et al. (1981). Sex education: A review of its effects. *Archives of Sexual Behavior, 10*(2).

Kilpatrick, A. C. (1987). Childhood sexual experiences: Problems and issue in studying long-range effects. *The Journal of Sex Research, 23*, 173–196.

Kilpatrick. A. C. (1986). Some correlates of women's childhood sexual experiences: A retrospective study. *The Journal of Sex Research, 22*, 221–242.

Kilpatrick, J. J. (1960). *The smut peddlers.*

Garden City, NY: Doubleday.

Kimmons, L., & Gaston, J. (1986). Single parenting: A fimography. Special issue: The single parent family. *Family Relations: Journal of Applied Family and Child Studies,* January, *35*(1), 205–211.

Kinch, R. A. H. (1979). Help for patients with premenstrual tension. *Consultant.* April, 187–191.

Kingsley, L., Detels, R., Kaslow, R., Polk, B., Rinaldo, C., Jr., Chmiel, J., Detre, K., Kelsey, S., Odaka, N., Ostrow, D. et al. (1987). Risk factors for seroconversion to human immunodeficiency virus among male homosexuals. Results from the Multicenter AIDS cohort study. *Lancet*, February 14, *1*(8529), 345–349.

Kinsey, A. C., Pomeroy, W. B., & Martin, C. E. (1948). *Sexual behavior in the human male.* Philadelphia: Saunders.

Kinsey, A. C., Pomeroy, W. B., Martin, C. E., & Gebhard, P. H. (1953). *Sexual behavior in the human female.* Philadelphia: Saunders.

Kirby, D. (1984). *Sexuality education: An evaluation of programs and their effects.* Santa Cruz, CA: Network Publications.

Kirby, D. (1983). The mathtech research on adolescent sexuality education programs. *SIECUS Report, 12*(1).

Kirkendall, L. A. (1984). The sexual revolution is only beginning. *The Humanist*, November/December.

Kirkendall, L. A. (1981). Sex education in the United States: A historical perspective. In L. Brown (ed.), *Sex education in the eighties.* New York: Plenum.

Kirkpatrick, C., & Kanin, E. (1957). Male sex aggression on a university campus. *American Sociological Review, 22*, 52–58.

Kitzinger, S. (1986). *Woman's experience of sex.* New York: Penguin Books.

Klassen, A. D., & Wilsnack, S. C. (1986). Sexual experience and drinking among women in a U.S. national survey. *Archives of Sexual Behavior*, October, *15*(5), 363–392.

Klaus, M. H., & Kennell, J. H. (1976). *Maternal-infant bonding.* St. Louis, MO: Mosby.

Kleeman, J. A. (1975). Genital self-stimulation in infant and toddler girls. In I. M. Marcus & J. J. Francis (eds.), *Masturbation: From infancy to senescence.* New York: International Universities.

Klein, F. (1978). *The bisexual option: A concept of one-hundred percent intimacy.* New York: Arbor House.

Klein, H. G., & Altar, H. J. (1987). Blood transfusions and AIDS. In

*AIDS,* Vol. 11, pp. 7–10. Chicago, IL: American Medical Association.

Kline-Graber, G., & Graber, B. (1978). Diagnosis and treatment procedures of pubococcygeal deficiencies in women. In J. LoPiccolo & L. LoPiccolo (eds.), *Handbook of sex therapy.* New York: Plenum.

Knapp, J. J., & Whitehurst, R. W. (1978). Sexually open marriage and relationships: Issues and prospects. In B. I. Murstein (ed.), *Exploring intimate life styles*, pp. 35–51. New York: Springer.

Knuppel, R., & Godlin (1987). Maternal-placental-fetal unit; fetal and early neonatal physiology. In M. Pernoll & R. Benson (eds.), *Current obstetric and gynecologic diagnosis and treatment 1987.* Los Altos, CA: Appleton & Lange.

Knussmann, R., Christiansen, K., & Couwenbergs, C. (1986). Relations between sex hormones levels and sexual behavior in men. *Archives of Sexual Behavior*, October, *15*(5), 429–445.

Koblinsky, S., & Palmeter, J. (1984). Sex-role orientation, mother's expression of affection toward spouse, and college women's attitudes toward sexual behaviors. *Journal of Sex Research, 20*, 32–43.

Koedt, A. (1976). The myth of the vaginal orgasm. In S. Cox (ed.), *Female psychology: The emerging self.* Palo Alto, CA: Science Research Associates.

Kohlberg, L. (1969a). *Stages in the development of moral thought and action.* New York: Holt, Rinehart and Winston.

Kohlberg, L. (1969b). The cognitive developmental approach to socialization. In D. A. Goslin (ed.), *Handbook of socialization theory and research.* Chicago: Rand McNally.

Kolata, G. B. (1988, March 29). Fetuses treated through umbilical cords. *New York Times*, p. 20.

Kolata, G. B. (1988, June 7). The evolving biology of AIDS: Scavenger cell looms large. *New York Times*, p. B5.

Kolata, G. B. (1988, January 25). Multiple fetuses raise new issues tied to abortion. *New York Times.*

Kolata, G. B. (1987, October 28). Earlier U.S. AIDS incursions hinted. *New York Times.*

Kolodny, R. C. (1980). Adolescent sexuality. Presented at the Michigan Personnel and Guidance Association Annual Convention. Detroit, November.

Kolodny, R. C., Masters, W. H., & Johnson, V. E. (1979). *Textbook of sexual medicine.* Boston: Little, Brown.

Kolodny, R. C. et al. (1979). *Textbook of human sexuality for nurses.* Boston: Little, Brown.

Komarovsky, M. (1974). Patterns of self-disclosure of male undergraduates. *Journal of Marriage and the Family, 36,* 677–686.

Koop, E. (1986). Acquired immune deficiency syndrome. *Journal of Medical Association,* November 28.

Korner, A. F. (1969). Neonatal startles, smiles, erections and reflex sucks as related to state, sex, and individuality. *Child Development, 40,* 1039–1053.

Kosnik, A. et al. (1977). *Human sexuality: New directions in American Catholic thought: A study commissioned by the Catholic Theological Society of America.* New York: Paulist Press.

Koss, M. P. (1986, February 17). Cited in Gang rape: A rising campus concern by N. Brozan. *New York Times.*

Koss, M. P. (1985). The hidden rape victim: Personality, attitudinal, and situational characteristics. *Psychology of Women Quarterly, 9,* 192–212.

Koss, M. P., Gidycz, C. A., & Wisniewski, N. (1987). The scope of rape: Incidence and prevalence of sexual aggression and victimization in a national sample of higher education students. *Journal of Counseling and Clinical Psychology, 55,* 162–170.

Krafft-Ebing, R. V. (1978). *Psychopathia sexualis.* New York: Stein & Day.

Krane, R. J., & Siroky, M. B. (1981). Neurophysiology of erection. *Urologic Clinics of North America, 8*(1).

Kuhn, D., Nash, S., & Brucken, L. (1978). Sex role concepts of two- and three-year-olds. *Child Development, 49,* 445–451.

Kurdek, L. A., & Schmitt, J. P. (1987a). Partner homogamy in married, heterosexual cohabiting, gay and lesbian couples. *Journal of Sex Research, 23,* 212–232.

Kurdek, L. A., & Schmitt, J. P. (1987b). Relationship quality of partners in heterosexual married, heterosexual cohabiting, and gay and lesbian relationships. *Journal of Personality and Social Psychology,* October, *51*(4), 711–720.

Kurdek, L. A., & Schmitt, J. P. (1986). Early development of relationship quality in heterosexual married, heterosexual cohabiting, gay, and lesbian couples. *Developmental Psychology,* May, *22*(3), 305–309.

Kutchinsky, B. (1973). The effect of easy availability of pornography on the incidence of sex crimes: The Danish experience. *Journal of Social Issues, 29,* 163–182.

Kutner, N. G., & Levinson, R. M. (1978). The toy salesperson: A voice for change in sex role stereotypes? *Sex Roles, 4,* 1–8.

Kwan, M., Greenleaf, W. J., Mann, J.,

Crapo, L., & Davidson, J. M. (1983). The nature of androgen action on male sexuality: A combined laboratory and self-report study in hypogonadal men. *Journal of Clinical Endocrinology and Metabolism, 57,* 557–562.

Kwan, M., Van Massdam, J., & Davidson, J. M. (1985). Effects of estrogen treatment on sexual behavior in male-to-female transsexuals: Experimental and clinical observations. *Archives of Sexual Behavior, 14*(1), 29–40.

Kwong, L., Smith, E., Davidson, J., & Peroutka, S. (1986). Differential interactions of prosexual drugs with 5-hydroxytryptamine-sub(1A) and alpha-sub-2-adrenergic receptors. *Behavioral Neuroscience,* October, *100*(5), 644–668.

LaBarbera, J. D., & Dozier, J. E. (1981). Psychologic responses of incestuous daughters: Emerging patterns. *Southern Medical Journal, 74*(12), 1478–1480.

Lacayo, R. (1987, July 20). Assault with a deadly virus. *Time,* p. 63.

Lacey, C. (1987). Premalignant and malignant disorders of the uterine corpus. In M. Pernoll & R. Benson (eds.), *Current obstetric and gynecologic diagnosis and treatment 1987.* Los Altos, CA: Appleton & Lange.

Lacoste-Utamsing, C., & Holloway, R. L. (1982). Sexual dimorphism in the human corpus callosum. *Science,* 216.

Ladas, A. K., Whipple, B., & Perry, J. D. (1982). *The G spot.* New York: Holt, Rinehart and Winston.

Ladd, F. (1980). Human sexuality: Messages in public environments. In E. Roberts (ed.), *Childhood sexual learning: The unwritten curriculum.* Cambridge, MA: Ballinger.

Ladouceur, P., & Temple, M. (1985). Substance abuse among rapists: A comparison with other serious felons. *Crime and Delinquency, 31,* 269–294.

Laeuchli, S. (1972). *Power and sexuality: The emergence of Canon law at the Synod of Elvira.* Philadelphia: Temple University Press.

Lakoff, R. (1975). *Language and woman's place.* New York: Harper & Row.

Lamaze, F. (1970). *Painless childbirth.* Chicago: Regnery.

Lamb, S. (1986). Treating sexually abused children: Issues of blame and responsibility. *American Journal of Orthopsychiatry,* April, *56*(2), 303–307.

Lamontagne, Y., & Lesage, A. (1986). Private exposure and covert sensitization in the treatment of exhibitionism. *Journal of Behavior-Therapy-Exp-Psychiatry,* September, *17*(3), 197–201.

Lancaster, J. B. (1979). Sex and gender

in evolutionary perspective. In II. A. Katchadourian (ed.), *Human sexuality: A comparative and developmental perspective,* pp. 51–80. Berkeley: University of California Press.

Lance, K., & Agardy, M. (1981). *Total sexual fitness for women.* New York: Rawson, Wade.

Landers, A. (1985, January 16). Cited in *Peninsula Times Tribune,* p. B-1, Palo Alto, CA.

Langfeldt, T. (1981). Sexual development in children. In M. Cook & K. Howells (eds.), *Adult sexual interest in children.* London: Academic Press.

Larue, G. (1983). *Sex in the Bible.* Buffalo, NY: Prometheus.

Lasater, M. (1980). Sexual assault: The legal framework. In C. Warner (ed.), *Rape and sexual assault,* pp. 231–264. Germantown, MD: Aspen Systems.

Laub, D., & Dubin, B. (1979). Gender dysphoria. In W. C. Grabb & J. W. Smith (eds.), *Plastic surgery,* 3d ed. Boston: Little, Brown.

Lauer, J., & Lauer, R. (1985). Marriages made to last. *Psychology Today,* June, 22–26.

Laurence, L. T. (1982). *Couple constancy: Conversations with today's happily married people.* Ann Arbor, MI: UMI Research Press.

Lauritsen, J. (1982). Research review: The cytogenetics of spontaneous abortion. *Research in Reproduction, 14,* 3ff.

Laws, J. L., & Schwartz, P. (1977). *Sexual scripts.* Hinsdale, IL: Dryden.

Laws, S. (1983). The sexual politics of pre-menstrual tension. *Women's Studies International Forum, 6,* 20.

Lazarus, A. (1977). Overcoming sexual inadequacy. In J. LoPiccolo & L. LoPiccolo (eds.), *Handbook of sex therapy.* New York: Plenum.

Leahy, R., & Shirk, S. (1984). The development of classificatory skills and sex-trait stereotypes in children. *Sex Roles, 10,* 281–292.

Leary, W. E. (1988, July 17). Sharp rise in rare sex-related diseases. *New York Times,* p. B9.

LeBoeuf, B. J. (1978). Sex and evolution. In T. McGill, D. Dewsbury & B. Sachs (eds.), *Sex and behavior: Status and prospectus.* New York: Plenum.

Leboyer, F. (1975). *Birth without violence.* New York: Knopf.

Lederer, W. (1968). *The fear of women.* New York: Harcourt Brace Jovanovich.

Ledger, W. A. (1987). AIDS and the obstetrician/gynecologist: Commentary. In *AIDS,* Vol. 2, pp. 5–6. Chicago: American Medical Association.

Lee, J. A. (1988). Love styles. In R. J. Sternberg & M. L. Barnes (eds.), *The psychology of love*, pp. 38–67. New Haven: Yale University Press.

Legman, G. (1963). *Love and death: A study in censorship.* New York: Hacker Art Books.

Lehrman, D. S. (1970). Semantic and conceptual issues in the nature-nurture problem. In L. R. Aronson & E. Tobach (eds.), *Development and evolution of behavior.* New York: Freeman.

Leiblum, S. R., & Pervin, L. A. (1980). *Principles and practice of sex therapy.* London: Tavistock.

Leibovici, L., Alpert, G., Laor, A., Kalter-Leibovici, O., & Danon, Y. (1987). Urinary tract infections and sexual activity in young women. *Archives of Internal Medicine*, February *147*(2), 345–347.

Lein, A. (1979). *The cycling female.* San Francisco: Freeman.

Lemon, S. M. (1984). Viral hepatitis. In K. Holmes, P. Mardh, P. F. Sparling & P. J. Wiesner (eds.), *Sexually transmitted diseases.* New York: McGraw-Hill.

Leo, J. (1986a, July 21). Pornography: The feminist dilemma. *Time*, p. 18.

Leo, J. (1986b, November 24). Sex education. *Time*, pp. 54–63.

Leo, J. (1986c, November 24). Men have rights too. *Time*, pp. 87–88.

Leo, J. (1984, April 9). The revolution is over. *Time.*

Leonard, G. (1982, December). The end of sex. *Esquire*, pp. 70–80.

Lertola, J. (1986, November 3). Illustration in *Time*, p. 69.

Lesnick-Oberstein, M., & Cohen, L. (1984). Cognitive style, sensation seeking, and assortative mating. *Journal of Personality and Social Psychology*, *46*, 112–117.

Lesser, H. (1967). The Hirschfeld Institute for Sexology. In A. Ellis & A. Abarban (eds.), *Encyclopedia of sexual behavior.* New York: Hawthorn.

Lessing, D. (1962). *The golden notebook.* London: Michael Joseph.

Levin, R. J. (1981). The female orgasm: A current appraisal. *Journal of Psychosomatic Research*, *25*(2), 119–133.

Levin, R. J. (1980). The physiology of sexual function in women. *Clinics in Obstetrics and Gynecology*, *7*(2), 213–252.

Levin, R. J. (1975a). Masturbation and nocturnal emissions: Possible mechanisms for minimizing teratozoospermia and hyperspermia in man. *Medical Hypothesis*, *1*, 130.

Levin, R. J., & Levin, A. (1975b, September). Sexual pleasure: The surprising preferences of 100,000 women. *Redbook*, pp. 51–58.

Levin, R. J. (1975c, October). The *Redbook* report on premarital and extra-marital sex: The end of the double standard? *Redbook*, pp. 38–44, 190–192.

LeVine, R. (1959). Gusii sex offenses: A study in social control. *American Anthropologist*, *61*(6), 965–990.

Levinson, D. J. (1978). *The seasons of a man's life.* New York: Knopf.

Lewin, T. (1988). Custody suit lifts veil of "Psychotherapy cult." *New York Times*, p. 10.

Lewin, T. (1988, March 20). Fewer teen mothers, but more are unmarried. *New York Times*, p. E6.

Lewis, C. S. (1960). *The four loves.* New York: Harcourt.

Lewis, D. L. (1980, Fall). Sex and the automobile: From rumble seats to rockin' vans. *Michigan Quarterly Review*, pp. 518–528.

Lewis, R. A., & Burr, W. R. (1975). Premarital coitus and commitment among college students. *Archives of Sexual Behavior*, *4*, 73–79.

Libby, R. W. (1976). Social scripts for sexual relationships. In S. Gordon & R. W. Libby (eds.), *Sexuality today and tomorrow.* N. Sciuate, MA: Duxbury Press.

Libby, R. W., & Whitehurst, R. N. (1977). *Marriage and alternatives: Exploring intimate relationships.* Glenview, IL: Scott, Foresman.

Licht, H. (1969). *Sexual life in ancient Greece.* London: Panther (first published in 1932).

Liebowitz, M. R. (1983). *The chemistry of love.* Boston: Little, Brown.

Lief, H. I. (1977). Inhibited sexual desire. *Medical Aspects of Human Sexuality*, *11*(7), 94–95.

Lief, H. I., & Kaplan, H. (1986). Ego-dystonic homosexuality. *Journal of Sex and Marital Therapy.* Winter, *12*(4), 259–266.

Lim, S. M. (1986). Surgery in transsexuals. *Annual Academy of medicine—Singapore*, January, *15*(1), 122–126.

Lindemalm, G., Korlin, D., & Uddenberg, N. (1986). Long-term follow-up of "sex change" in 13 male-to-female transsexuals. *Archives of Sexual Behavior*, June, *15*(3), 187–210.

Linton, R. (1936). *The study of man.* New York: Appleton.

Lipkin, M., Jr., & Lamb, G. S. (1982). The Couvade syndrome: An epidemiologic study. *Annals of Internal Medicine*, *96*, 509–511.

Lipson, J., & Engleman, E. (1985). Special Report on AIDS. *Stanford Medicine*, Spring, pp. 24–25.

Lisk, R. D. (1967). In L. Martinini & W. F. Ganong (eds.), *Neuroendocrinology*, Vol. 2. New York: Academic, p. 197.

Lizotte, A. (1985). The uniqueness of rape: Reporting assaultive violence to the police. *Crime and Delinquency*, *31*, 169–190.

Lockwood, D. (1980). *Prison sexual violence.* New York: Elsevier.

Loevinger, J. (1976). *Ego Development.* San Francisco: Jossey-Bass.

Logue, C. M., & Moos, R. (1986). Perimenstrual symptoms: Prevalence and risk factors. *Psychosomatic Medicine*, July–August, *48*(6), 388–414.

London, S. N., & Hammond, C. B. (1986). The climacteric. In D. N. Danforth & J. R. Scott (eds.), *Obstetrics and Gynecology*, 5th ed. Philadelphia: J. B Lippincott.

LoPiccolo, J. (1977). Direct treatment of sexual dysfunction in the couple. In J. Money & H. Musaph (eds.), *Handbook of sexology.* New York: Elsevier.

LoPiccolo, J., & Heiman, J. (1978). The role of cultural values in the prevention and treatment of sexual problems. In C. B. Qualls, J. P. Wincze & D. H. Barlow (eds.), *The prevention of sexual disorders*, pp. 43–71. New York: Plenum.

LoPiccolo, J., Heiman, J., Hogan, D., & Roberts, C. (1985). Effectiveness of single therapists versus cotherapy teams in sex therapy. *Journal of Consulting and Clinical Psychology*, *53*, 287–294.

LoPiccolo, J., & Lobitz, W. C. (1977). The role of masturbation in the treatment of orgasmic dysfunction. In J. LoPiccolo & L. LoPiccolo (eds.), *Handbook of sex therapy.* New York: Plenum.

LoPiccolo, J., & LoPiccolo, L. (1978). *Handbook of sex therapy.* New York: Plenum.

LoPiccolo, J., & Stock, W. (1986). Treatment of sexual dysfunction. *Journal of Consulting and Clinical Psychology*, April, *54*(2), 158–167.

Lott, B. (1987). *Women's lives: Themes and variations in gender learning.* Monterey, CA: Brook/Cole.

Lowenthal, J. F., & Chiriboga, D. (1973). Social stress and adaptations: Toward a life-course perspective. In C. Eisdorfer & M. P. Lawton (eds.), *Psychology of adult development and aging*, pp. 281–310. Washington, DC: American Psychological Association.

Lowenthal, M. F., Thurber, M., Chiriboga, D. and Associates (1975). *Four stages of life.* San Francisco: Jossey Bass.

Lowry, T. P. (ed.). (1978). *The classic clitoris.* Chicago: Nelson-Hall.

Lowry, T. P., & Lowry, T. S. (1976). *The clitoris.* St. Louis, MO: Warren H. Green.

Lucie-Smith, E. (1981). *The body.* New York: Thames and Hudson.

Ludeman, K. (1981). The sexuality of the older person: Review of the literature. *Gerontologist, 21*(2), 203–208.

Luria, Z., & Meade, R. G. (1984). Sexuality and the middle-aged woman. In G. Baruch & J. Brooks-Gunn (eds.), *The middle-aged woman.* New York: Plenum.

Lynn, B. W. (1986). The new pornography commission: Slouching toward censorship. *SIECUS Report,* May, *5,* 1–6.

M. (1971). *The sensuous man.* New York: Lyle Stuart.

Mabie, B. and Sibai (1987). Hypertensive states of pregnancy. In M. Pernoll & R. Benson (eds.), *Current obstetric and gynecologic diagnosis and treatment 1987.* Los Altos, CA: Appleton & Lange.

Maccoby, E., & Jacklin, C. N. (1974). *The psychology of sex differences.* Stanford, CA.: Stanford University Press.

MacKinnon, C. A. (1987). *Feminism unmodified.* Cambridge, MA: Harvard University Press.

MacKinnon, C. A. (1979). *Sexual harassment of working women.* New Haven: Yale University Press.

Macklin, E. D. (1978). Nonmarital heterosexual cohabitation. *Marriage and Family Review, 1,* 1–12.

MacLean, P. D. (1976). Brain mechanisms of elemental sexual functions. In B. J. Sadock, H. I. Kaplan, & A. M. Freedman (eds.), *The sexual experience.* Baltimore, MD: Williams & Wilkins.

MacLusky, N. J., & Naftolin, F. (1981). Sexual differentiation of the central nervous system. *Science, 211*(4488), 1294–1302.

MacNamara, D., & Sagarin, E. (1977). *Sex, crime, and the law.* New York: Free Press.

Maguire, D. C. (1987). Catholic sexual and reproductive ethics: A historical perspective. *SIECUS Report, 15*(5), 1–3.

Mahler, H. (1986, December 1). Quoted in *Time,* p. 45.

Mahood, J., & Wenburg, K. (1980). *The Mosher survey.* New York: Arno.

Maisch, H. (1973). *Incest.* London: Andre Deutsch.

Makepeace, J. M. (1981). Courtship violence among college students. *Family Relations, 30*(1), 97–102.

Malamuth, N. M. (1986). Predictors of naturalistic sexual aggression. *Journal of Personality Social Psychology,* May, *50*(5), 953–962.

Malamuth, N. M. (1984). Aggression against women: Cultural and individual causes. In N. Malamuth & E. Donnerstein (eds.), *Pornography and sexual aggression.* New York: Academic Press.

Malatesta, V. J. (1979). Alcohol effects on the orgasmic ejaculatory response in human males. *The Journal of Sex Research, 15,* 101–107.

Malla, K. (1964). *The anaga ranga.* R. F. Burton & F. F. Arbuthnot, translators. New York: Putnam.

Manley, J. (1986). Teacher selection for sex education. *SIECUS Report,* November/December, *15*(2), 10–11.

Mannarino, A., & Cohen, J. (1986). A clinical-demographic study of sexually abused children. *Child Abuse and Neglect, 10*(1), 17–23.

Manniche, L. (1987). *Sexual life in ancient Egypt.* London: KPI.

Marcade, J. (1962). *Eros Kalos: Essay on erotic elements in Greek Art.* New York: Nagel.

Marcus, G. E. (1983, March 27). One man's Mead? *The New York Times Book Review.* pp. 3, 22.

Marcus, I. M., & Francis, J. J. (eds.). (1975). *Masturbation from infancy to senescence.* New York: International Universities.

Marcus, S. (1966). *The other Victorians.* New York: Basic.

Marcuse, H. (1955). *Eros and civilization.* New York: Vintage.

Marmor, J. (1980a). Epilogue: Homosexuality and the issue of mental illness. In J. Marmor (ed.), *Homosexual behavior.* New York: Basic.

Marmor, J. (ed.). (1980b). *Homosexual behavior.* New York: Basic.

Marmor, J. (ed.). (1965). *Sexual inversion: The multiple roots of homosexuality.* New York: Basic.

Marshall, D. S. (1971). Sexual behavior in Mangaia. In D. S. Marshall & R. C. Suggs (eds.), *Human sexual behavior.* Englewood Cliffs, NJ: Prentice-Hall.

Marshall, D. S., & Suggs, R. C. (eds.). (1971). *Human sexual behavior.* Englewood Cliffs, NJ: Prentice-Hall.

Marshall, J. (1987). Infertility. In M. Pernoll & R. Benson (eds.), *Current obstetric and gynecologic diagnosis and treatment 1987.* Los Altos, CA: Appleton & Lange.

Marshall, P., Surridge, D., & Delva, N. (1987). The role of nocturnal penile tumescence in differentiating between organic and psychogenic impotence: The first stage of validation. *Archives of Sexual Behavior, 10*(1).

Marshall, W. A., & Tanner J. M. (1974). Puberty. In J. A. Douvis & J. Dobbing (eds.), *Scientific foundations of pediatrics.* London: William Heinemaun Medical Books.

Marsiglio, W., & Mott, F. L. (1986). The impact of sex education on sexual activity, contraceptive use and premarital pregnancy among American teenagers. *Family Planning Perspectives,* July–August, *18*(4), 151–162.

Martinson, F. M. (1981). Eroticism in infancy and childhood. In L. Constantine & F. Martinson (eds.), *Children and sex: New findings, new perspectives,* pp. 23–35. Boston: Little, Brown.

Martinson, F. M. (1980). Childhood Sexuality. In B. B. Wolman & J. Money (eds.), *Handbook of human sexuality.* Englewood Cliffs, NJ: Prentice-Hall.

Martinson, F. M. (1976). Eroticism in infancy and childhood. *Journal of Sex Research, 12,* 251–262.

Martin, C. (1981). Factors affecting sexual functioning in 60-79-year-old married males. *Archives of Sexual Behavior, 10*(5).

Martin, J. L. (1987). The impact of AIDS on gay male sexual behavior patterns in New York City. *American Journal of Public Health,* May, *77*(5), 578–581.

Maruta, T., & McHardy, M. (1983). Sexual problems in patients with chronic pain. *Medical Aspects of Human Sexuality, 17*(2).

Maslow, A. H. (1968). *Toward a psychology of being.* New York: Van Nostrand.

Masson, J. (1984). *The assault on truth: Freud's suppression of the seduction theory.* New York: Farrar, Straus & Giroux.

Masters, W. J. (1986). Sexual dysfunction as an aftermath of sexual assault of men by women. *Journal of Sex and Marital Therapy,* Spring, *12*(1), 35–45.

Masters, W. H. (1980). Update on sexual physiology. Paper presented at the Masters and Johnson Institute's Postgraduate Workshop on Human Sexual Function and Dysfunction. St. Louis, MO: October 20, cited in Masters, W. H., Johnson, V. E., & Kolodny, R. C. (1988). *Human sexuality.* 3d ed. Boston: Little, Brown.

Masters, W., & Johnson, V. (1982). Sex and the aging process. *Medical Aspects of Human Sexuality, 16*(6).

Masters, W. H., & Johnson, V. E. (1979). *Homosexuality in perspective.* Boston: Little, Brown.

Masters, W. H., & Johnson, V. E. (1976). The aftermath of rape. *Redbook, 147*(2), 74ff.

Masters, W. H., & Johnson, V. E. (1970). *Human sexual inadequacy.* Boston: Little, Brown.

Masters, W. H., & Johnson,V. E. (1966). *Human sexual response.* Boston: Little, Brown.

Masters, W. H., Johnson, V. E., & Kolodny, R. C. (1988a). *Crisis: Heterosex-*

*ual behavior in the age of AIDS*. New York: Grove Press.

Masters, W. H., Johnson, V., & Levin, R. (1976). *The pleasure bond*. New York: Ballantine.

Matsumoto, A. M. (1988). The testis. In J. B Wyngaarden & L. H. Smith (eds.), *Cecil textbook of medicine*, 18th ed. Philadelphia: W. B Saunders.

Matteo, S. (1987). *Female sexuality, experimental psychology and feminism: Presenting a unified picture*. Unpublished manuscript, Stanford University.

Matteo, S., & Rissman, E. F. (1984). Increased sexual behavior during the midcycle portion of the human menstrual cycle. *Hormones and Behavior, 18*, 249–255.

Mattox, J. (1987). Abortion. In J. R. Wilson & E. Carrington (eds.), *Obstetrics and Gynecology*, 8th ed. St. Louis, MO: C. V. Mosby.

May, R. (1969). *Love and will*. New York: Norton.

Mayer, E. L. (1985). Everybody must be just like me: Observations on female castration anxiety. *International Journal of psychoanalysis, 66*, 331–347.

Mayo, C., & Henley, N. M. (eds.). (1981). *Gender and nonverbal behavior*. New York: Springer-Verlag.

Mazur, A. (1986). U.S. trends in feminine beauty, and overadaptation. *Journal of Sex Research, 22*(3), 281–303.

Mazur, R. (1973). *The new intimacy*. Boston: Beacon.

McCafree, K. (1986). Sex education curricula: Selection for elementary and secondary school students. *SIECUS Report*, November/December, *15*(2), 4–6.

McCance, A. A., Luff, M. C., & Widdowson, E. C. (1952). Distribution of coitus during the menstrual cycle. *Journal of Hygiene, 37*, 571–611.

McCance, D. J. (1986). Human papillomavirus type 16 and 18 in carcinomas of the penis from Brazil. *International Journal of Cancer, 37*, 55–59.

McCary, J. L. (1975). Teaching the topic of human sexuality. *Teaching of Psychology, 2*(1), 16–21.

McCauley, E., & Ehrhardt, A. A. (1976). Female sexual response: Hormonal and behavioral interactions. *Primary Care, 3*, 455.

McClintock, M. K. (1983). Pheromonal regulation of the ovarian cycle. In J. G. Vandenbergh (ed.), *Pheromones and reproduction in mammals*, pp. 113–149. New York: Academic Press.

McClintock, M. K. (1971). Menstrual synchrony and suppression. *Nature, 299*, 244–245.

McCormack, A., Janus, M., & Burgess, A. (1986). Runaway youths and sexual victimization: Gender differences in an adolescent runaway population. *Child Abuse and Neglect, 10*(3), 387–395.

McCormick, N. B. (1979). Come-ons and put-offs: Unmarried students' strategies for having and avoiding sexual intercourse. *Psychology of Women Quarterly, 4*, 194–211.

McCormick, N. B., & Jessor, C. J. (1983). The courtship game: Power in the sexual encounter. In E. Allgeier & N. McCormick (eds.), *Changing boundaries: Gender role and sexual behavior*. Palo Alto, CA: Mayfield.

McDougall, W. (1908). *An introduction to social psychology*. London: Methuen.

McGee, A. (1984). Gonococcal pelvic inflammatory disease. In K. Holmes, P. Mardh, P. F. Sparling, & P. Wiesner (eds.), *Sexually transmitted diseases*. New York: McGraw-Hill.

McGee, E. A. (1982). *Too little, too late: Services for teenage parents*. New York: Ford Foundation.

McGuire, R. J., Carlisle, J. M., & Young, B. G. (1965). Sexual deviation as conditioned behavior: A hypothesis. *Behavior Research and Therapy, 2*, 185–190.

McKey, P. L., & Dougherty, M. C. (1986). The circumvaginal musculature: Correlation between pressure and physical assessment. *Nursing Resource*, September–October, *35*(5), 307–309.

McMillan, J. R., Clifton, A. K., McGrath, D., & Gale, W. (1977). Women's language: Uncertainty or interpersonal sensitivity and emotionality? *Sex Roles, 3*, 545–559.

McNamara, J. A. (1983). Chaste marriage and clerical celibacy. In V. L. Bullough & J. Brundage (eds.), *Sexual practices and the medieval church*. Buffalo, NY: Prometheus.

McQuarrie, H. G., & Flanagan, A. D. (1978). Accuracy of early pregnancy testing at home. Paper presented at the annual meeting of the Association of Planned Parenthood Physicians, San Diego, October 24–27.

McWhirter, D. P., & Mattison, A. M. (1984). *The male couple: How relationships develop*. Englewood Cliffs, NJ: Prentice-Hall.

McWhirter, R. (ed.). (1987). *Guinness book of world records*. New York: Bantam.

Meiselman, K. D. (1978). *Incest*. San Francisco: Jossey-Bass.

Meissner, W. W., Mack, J. E., & Semrad, E. V. (1975). Classical psychoanalysis. In A. M. Freedman, H. I. Kaplan, & B. J. Sadock (eds.), *Comprehensive textbook of psychiatry*, Vol. 1, 2d ed., pp. 482–566. Baltimore, MD: Williams & Wilkins.

Melody, G. F. (1977). A case of penis captivus. *Medical Aspects of Human Sexuality, 11*, December.

Menning, B. (1977). *Infertility: A guide for childless couples*. Englewood Cliffs, NJ: Prentice-Hall.

Merton, T. (1979). *Love and living*. New York: Harcourt Brace Jovanovich.

Mertz, G. J. (1984). Double blind placebo-controlled trial of oral Acyclovir in first episode genital herpes simplex virus infection. *Journal of American Medical Association, 254*, 1147–1151.

Messe, M. R., & Geer, J. H. (1985). Voluntary vaginal musculature contractions as an enhancer of sexual arousal. *Archives of Sexual Behavior, 4*(1), 13–38.

Messenger, J. C. (1971). Sex and repression in an Irish folk community. In D. S. Marshall & R. C. Suggs (eds.), *Human sexual behavior*, pp. 3–37. Englewood Cliffs, NJ: Prentice-Hall.

Metcalfe, J. (1988, January 25). The hidden threat: Date rape is all too common. *The Stanford Daily*, p. 1.

Meyer, C. B., & Taylor, S. E. (1986). Adjustment to rape. *Journal of Personality and Social Psychology*, June, *50*(6), 1226–1234.

Meyer, W. J. 3d., Webb, A., Stuart, C. A., Finkelstein, J. W., Lawrence, B., & Walker, P. A. (1986). Physical and hormonal evaluation of transsexual patients: A longitudinal study. *Archives of Sexual Behavior*, April, *15*(2), 121–138.

Michael, R. P., Bonsall, R. W., & Zumpe, D. (1976). The evidence for chemical communication in primates. *Vitamins and Hormones, 34*, 137–186.

Michael, R. P., Bonsall, R. W., & Warner, P. (1974). Human vaginal secretions: Volatile fatty acid content. *Science, 186*, 1217–1219.

Michael, R. P., & Keverne, E. B. (1968). Pheromones in the communication of sexual status in primates. *Nature, 218*, 746–749.

Michael, R. P., & Zumpe, D. (1978). Potency in male rhesus monkeys: Effects of continuously receptive females. *Science, 200*, 451–453.

Michalodimitrakis, M., Frangoulis, M., & Koutselinis, A. (1986). Accidental sexual strangulation. *American Journal of Forensic Medical Pathology*, March, *7*(1), 74–75.

Miller, D., Rich, L., & Steinberg, C. (1987). STD talk: Students coping with sexually transmitted diseases. Brown University Health Services, Providence, RI.

Miller, J. (ed.). (1980). *The Rolling Stone illustrated history of rock and roll*. New York: Random House.

Miller, J. B. (1976). *Toward a new psychology of women*. Boston: Beacon.

Miller, P. Y., & Fowlkes, M. R. (1980). Social and behavioral constructions of female sexuality. *Signs, 5,* 783–800.

Miller, P. Y., & Simon, W. (1980). The development of sexuality in adolescence. In J. Adelson (ed.), *Handbook of adolescent psychology*. New York: Wiley.

Miller, P. Y., & Simon, W. (1974). Adolescent sexual behavior: Context and change. *Social Problems, 22,* 58–76.

Miller, W. B. (1973a). Psychological vulnerability to unwanted pregnancy. *Family Planning Perspectives, 5*(4).

Miller, W. B. (1973b). Sexuality, contraception and pregnancy in a high-school population. *California Medicine, 119,* 14–21.

Miller, W. (1976). Sexual and contraceptive behavior in young unmarried women. *Primary Care, 3*(3), 427–453.

Miller, W. R., & Lief, H. I. (1976). Masturbatory attitudes, knowledge and experience: Data from the sex knowledge and attitude test (SKAT). *Archives of Sexual Behavior, 5,* 447–467.

Millett, K. (1973). *The prostitution papers*. New York: Ballantine.

Millett, K. (1970). *Sexual politics*. Garden City, N.Y.: Doubleday.

Mims, F., & Chang, A. (1984). Unwanted sexual experiences of young women. *Psychosocial Nursing, 22,* 7–14.

Mischel, W. (1981). *Introduction to personality*, 3d ed. New York: Holt, Rinehart and Winston.

Mishell, D. R. (1982). Control of human reproduction. In D. N. Danforth (ed.), *Obstetrics and gynecology*, 4th ed., pp. 252–280. Philadelphia: Harper & Row.

Mishell, D. R. (1979). Intrauterine devices: Medicated and nonmedicated. *International Journal of Gynecology and Obstetrics, 16,* 482–487.

Mitamura, T. (1970). *Chinese eunuchs*. Tokyo: C. Tuttle.

Mitchell, J. (1974). *Psychoanalysis and feminism*. New York: Penguin.

Moghissi, K. S. (1982). Nutrition in obstetrics and gynecology. In D. N. Danforth (ed.), *Obstetrics and gynecology*, 4th ed, pp. 203–215. Philadelphia: Harper & Row.

Mohl, P. C. et al. (1981). Prepuce restoration seekers: Psychiatric aspects. *Archives of Sexual Behavior, 10*(4), 383–393.

Mohr, J., Turner, R. E., & Jerry, M. B. (1964). *Pedophilia and exhibitionism*. Toronto: University of Toronto

Press.

Mohs, M., & Mohs, P. T. (1979). A word from the home front: Conscience—With compassion. In D. Doherty (ed.), *Dimensions of human sexuality*. Garden City, NY: Doubleday.

Moll, A. (1912). *The sexual life of the child*. New York: Macmillan.

Money, J. (1987). Human sexology and psychoneuroendocrinology. In D. Crews (ed.), *Psychobiology of reproductive behavior: An evolutionary perspective*, pp. 323–344. Englewood Cliffs, NJ: Prentice-Hall.

Money, J. (1986). *Lovemaps: Clinical concepts of sexual/erotic health and pathology, paraphilia, and gender transposition in childhood, adolescence, and maturity*. New York: Irvington.

Money, J. (1980). Genetic and chromosomal aspects of homosexual etiology. In J. Marmor (ed.), *Homosexual behavior*. New York: Basic.

Money, J. (1980). *Love and Lovesickness*. Baltimore, MD: Johns Hopkins University Press.

Money, J. (1975). Ablatio penis: Normal male infant sex-reassigned as a girl. *Archives of Sexual Behavior, 4*(1), 65–77.

Money, J. (1973). Gender role, gender identity, core gender identity: Usage and definitions and terms. *Journal of American Academy of Psychoanalysis, 1,* 397–403.

Money, J., & Erhardt, A. A. (1972). *Man and woman, boy and girl*. Baltimore, MD: Johns Hopkins University Press.

Money, J., & Musaph, H. (eds.). (1977). *Handbook of sexology*. New York: Elsevier.

Money, J., & Tucker, P. (1975). *Sexual signatures*. Boston: Little, Brown.

Monga, T., Lawson, J., & Inglis, J. (1986). Sexual dysfunction in stroke patients. *Archives of Physical and Medical Rehabilitation*, January, 67(1), 19–22.

Montagu, A. (1986). *Touching—The human significance of the skin*, 3d ed. New York: Harper & Row.

Montagu, A. (1969). *Sex, man and society*. New York: Tower.

Mooney, T., Cole, T., & Chilgren, R. (1975). *Sexual options for paraplegics and quadriplegics*. Boston: Little, Brown.

Moore, J. E., & Kendall, D. G. (1971). Children's concepts of reproduction. *Journal of Sex Research, 7,* 42–61.

Moore, K. (1978). Teenage childbearing and welfare dependency. *Family Planning Perspectives, 10*(4), 233–235.

Moore, K. L. (1985). *The developing human*, 3d ed. Philadelphia: Saunders.

Moorehead, A. (1979). *Darwin and the beagle*. New York: Penguin.

Moorman, J. E. (1987). The history and future of the relationship between education and marriage. Cited in Exner, T. (1987).

Moos, R. (1969). Fluctuations in symptoms and moods during the menstrual cycle. *Journal of Psychosomatic Research, 13,* 37–44.

Morbidity and Mortality Weekly Report. (1988). *Journal of the American Medical Association, 259,* 2657–2661.

Morbidity and Mortality Weekly Report. 1982. Genital herpes infection—United States, 1966–1979. *31*(11).

Morgan, M. (1973). *The total woman*. New York: Basic.

Morganthau, T., & Hager, M. (1987, November 10). AIDS: Grim prospects. *Newsweek*, pp. 20–21.

Morin, J. (1981). *Anal pleasure and health*. Burlingame, CA: Down There Press.

Morokoff, P. J. (1986). Volunteer bias in the psychophysiological study of female sexuality. *The Journal of Sex Research, 22*(1), 35–51.

Morokoff, P. J. (1985). Effects of sex guilt, repression, sexual "arousability," and sexual experience on female sexual arousal during erotica and fantasy. *Journal of Personality and Social Psychology, 49,* 177–187.

Morrell, M., Dixen, J., Carter, C. S., & Davidson, J. M. (1967). The influence of age and cycling status on sexual arousability in women.

Morris, D. (1985). *Body Watching*. New York: Crown.

Morris, D. (1977). *Manwatching: A field guide to human behavior*. New York: Abrams.

Morris, D. (1969). *The naked ape*. New York: Dell.

Morris, W. (1981). *The American heritage dictionary of the English language*. Boston: Houghton Mifflin.

Moser, C. (1983). A response to Reiss' "Trouble in paradise." *Journal of Sex Research, 19*(2), 192–195.

Mosher, B. A., & Whelan, E. M. (1981). Postmenopausal estrogen therapy: A review. *Obstetric and Gynecology Survey, 9,* 467–475.

Mulac, A., Incontro, C. R., & James, M. R. (1985). Comparison of the gender-linked language effect and sex role stereotypes. *Journal of Personality and Social Psychology, 49,* 1098–1109.

Mulvihill, D. J. et al. (1969). *Crimes of violence, a staff report to the National Commission on the Causes and Prevention of Violence*. Washington, DC: U.S. Government Printing Office, Vol. II, p. 217.

Munjack, D. J., & Oziel, L. J. (1980). *Sexual medicine and counseling in office practice*. Boston: Little, Brown.

Murad, F., & Haynes, R. C., Jr. (1985a).

Androgens. In A. F. Gilman, L. S. Goodman, T. W. Rall, & F. Murad (eds.), *Goodman and Gilman's, the pharmacological basis of therapeutics*, 7th ed. New York: Macmillan.

Murad, F., & Haynes, R. C., Jr. (1985b). Estrogens and Progestins. In A. F. Gilman, L. S. Goodman, T. W. Rall, & F. Murad (eds.), *Goodman and Gilman's, the pharmacological basis of therapeutics*, 7th ed. New York: Macmillan.

Murdock, G. P. (1949b). The social regulation of sexual behavior. In P. H. Hoch & J. Zubin (eds.), *Psychosexual development in health and disease*, pp. 256–266. New York: Grune & Stratton.

Murdock, G. P. (1949a). *Social structure.* New York: Macmillan.

Murphy, E. (1983). *Great bordellos of the world.* London: Quartet Books.

Murphy, F. K., & Patamasucon, P. (1984). Congenital syphilis. In K. Holmes, P. Mardh, P. F. Sparling, & P. Wiesner (eds.), *Sexually transmitted diseases.* New York: McGraw-Hill.

Murphy, J. (1986, December 29). The month-after pill. *Time.*

Murstein, B. I. (1988). A taxonomy of love. In R. J. Sternberg & M. L. Barnes (eds.), *The psychology of love*, pp. 13–27. New Haven: Yale University Press.

Murstein, B. I. (1980). Mate selection in the 1970s. *Journal of Marriage and the Family, 42*, 777–792.

Murstein, B. I. (1976). *Who will marry whom?* New York: Springer.

Murstein, B. I. (1974). *Love, sex and marriage through the ages.* New York: Springer.

Musaph, H., & Abraham, G. (1977). Frigidity or hypogyneisms. In J. Money & H. Musaph, (eds.), *Handbook of sexology.* New York: Elsevier.

Mussen, P. H. (1970). *Carmichael's manual of child psychology.* New York: Wiley.

Muuss, R. E. (1970). Puberty rites in primitive and modern societies. *Adolescence 5, 17*, 109–128.

Myers, L. S., & Morokoff, P. J. (1986). Physiological and subjective sexual arousal in pre- and postmenopausal women and postmenopausal women taking replacement therapy. *Psychophysiology*, May, *23*(3), 283–292.

*My secret life.* (1966). New York: Grove.

Nabokov, V. (1955). *Lolita.* New York: Putnam.

Nadelson, C. C. (1978). The emotional impact of abortion. In M. T. Notman & C. C. Nadelson (eds.), *The woman patient*, Vol. 1, pp. 173–179. New York: Plenum.

Nadler, R. D. (1977). Sexual behavior of captive orangutans. *Archives of Sexual Behavior, 6*, 457–476.

Nahemow, L., & Lawton, M. (1975). Similarity and propinquity in friendship formation. *Journal of Personality and Social Psychology, 32*, 205–213.

Nakashima, I., & Zakus, G. (1979). Incestuous families. *Pediatric Annual, 8*, 29.

Nathan, S. (1986). The epidemiology of the DSM-III psychosexual dysfunctions. *Journal of Sex and Marital Therapy*, Winter, *12*(4), 267–281.

National Institute of Mental Health (1983). Workshop on PMS. Rockville, MD: National Institutes of Health.

National Research Council (1987). *Risking the Future. Adolescent sexuality, pregnancy, and childbearing* (Washington, DC: National Academy Press)

Nefzawi, S. (1964 ed.). *The perfumed garden.* R. F. Burton, translator. New York: Putnam.

Neiberg, P., Marks, J. S., McLaren, N., & Remington, P. (1985). The fetal tobacco syndrome. *Journal of the American Medical Association, 253*, 2998–2999.

Nelson, N. M. et al. (1980). A randomized clinical trial of the Leboyer approach to childbirth. *New England Journal of Medicine, 302*, 655–660.

Netter, F. H. (1965a). *Reproductive system.* The Ciba Collection of Medical Illustrations, Vol. 2. Summit, NJ: Ciba.

Netter, F. H. (1965b). *Endocrine system.* The Ciba Collection of Medical Illustrations, Vol. 4. Summitt, NJ: Ciba.

Neu, J. (1987). Freud and perversion. In Shelp, E. E. (ed.), *Sexuality and Medicine*, Vol. 1, pp. 153–184. Boston: Academic Publishing Group.

Neubeck, G. (ed.). (1969). *Extramarital relations.* Englewood Cliffs, NJ: Prentice-Hall.

Neugarten, B. I. (ed.). (1968). *Middle age and aging.* Chicago: University of Chicago Press.

Neumann, F., & Topert, M. (1986). Pharmacology of antiandrogens. *Journal of Steroid Biochemistry*, November, *25*(5B), 885–895.

Neusner, J. (1970). *The way of Torah: An introduction to Judaism.* Belmont, CA: Dickinson.

Newcomb, M. D. (1986). Sexual behavior of cohabitors: A comparison of three independent samples. *Journal of Sex Research, 22*(4), 492–513.

Newcomb, M. D., & Bentler, P. M. (1980). Cohabitation before marriage. *Alternative Lifestyles, 3*, 65–85.

Newcomer, S. F., & Udry, J. R. (1985). Oral sex in an adolescent population. *Archives of Sexual Behavior, 14*, 41–46.

Newman, H. F., & Northup, J. D. (1981). Mechanism of human penile erection: An overview. *Urology, 17*(5), 399–408.

Newson, J., & Newson, E. (1968). *Four years old in an urban community.* London: Allen & Unwin.

*Newsweek* (1987, February 16). Kids and Contraception. pp. 54–65.

*New York Times* (1984a, October 24). Man who wed mother is indicted for incest.

Nilsson, L. (1977). *A child is born.* New York: Delacorte.

Nilsson, L. (1973). *Behold man.* Boston: Little, Brown.

Noonan, J. T., Jr. (ed.). (1970). *The morality of abortion: Legal and historical perspectives.* Cambridge, MA: Harvard University Press.

Noonan, J. T., Jr. (1967). *Contraception: A history of its treatment by the Catholic theologians and canonists.* New York: New American Library.

Norwood, R. (1985). *Women who love too much.* Los Angeles: Tarcher/St. Martin's.

Nory, M. J. (1987). The normal puerperium. In M. Pernoll & R. Benson (eds.), *Current obstetric and gynecologic diagnosis and treatment 1987.* Los Altos, CA: Appleton & Lange.

Oakley, G. (1978). Natural selection, selection bias and the prevalence of Down's syndrome. *New England Journal of Medicine, 299*(19), 1068–1069.

O'Farrell, T., Weyand, C., & Logan, D. (1983). *Alcohol and sexuality: An annotated bibliography on alcohol use, alcoholism, and human sexual behavior.* Phoenix, AZ: Oryx.

Offer, D., & Offer, J. (1975). *From teenage to manhood: A psychological study.* New York: Basic.

Offit, A. K. (1981). *Night thoughts.* New York: Congdon and Lattes.

Offit, A. K. (1977). *The sexual self.* New York: Ballantine.

O'Kelly, C. G. (1974). Sexism in children's television. *Journalism Quarterly, 51*, 722–724.

Olds, J. (1956). Pleasure centers in the brain. *Scientific American, 193*, 105–116.

O'Neill, N., & O'Neill, G. (1972). *Open marriage.* New York: Evans.

Onorato, I. M. (1987, April 28). Letter to the editor. *New York Times.*

Opler, M. K. (1969). Cross-cultural aspects of kissing. *Medical Aspects of Human Sexuality, 3*(2), 11–21.

Oriel, J. D. (1984). Genital warts. In K. Holmes, P. Mardh, P. F. Sparling & P. Wiesner (eds.), *Sexually transmitted diseases.* New York: McGraw-Hill.

Orkin, M., & Maibach, H. (1984). Scabies. In K. Holmes, P. Mardh, P. F. Sparling & P. Wiesner (eds.), *Sexually transmitted diseases.* New York: Mc-Graw-Hill.

Ortner, A., Glatzl, J., & Karpellus, E. (1987). Clinical and endocrinologic study of precocious puberty in girls. *Archives of Gynecology, 240*(2), 81–93.

Ortner, S., & Whitehead, H. (eds.). (1981). *Sexual meanings: The cultural construction of gender and sexuality.* Cambridge, MA: Cambridge University Press.

Ory, H. W., Forrest, J. D., & Lincoln, R. (1983). *Making choices.* New York: Alan Guttmacher Institute.

Ory, H. W., Rosenfield, A., & Laudman, L. C. (1980). The pill at 20: An assessment. *Family Planning Perspectives, 12*(6), 278–283.

Osborn, C. A., & Pollack, R. H. (1977). The effect of two types of erotic literature on physiological and verbal measures of female sexual arousal. *Journal of Sex Research, 13*(4), 250–256.

Osser, S., Liedholm, P., & Oberg, S. J. (1980). Risk of pelvic inflammatory disease among users of intrauterine devices, irrespective of previous pregnancy. *American Journal of Obstetrics and Gynecology, 138*(7 pt 2), 864–867.

Ostline, R. N. (1984, December 3). A bold stand on birth control. *Time,* p. 66.

Ostrow, D. G., Sandholzer, T. A., & Feldman, Y. M. (eds.) (1983). *Sexually transmitted diseases in homosexual men.* New York: Plenum.

Overholster, J., & Beck, S. (1986). Multimethod assessment of rapists, child molesters, and three control groups on behavioral and psychological measures. *Journal of Consulting and Clinical Psychology,* October, *54*(5), 682–687.

Ovesey, L. (1969). *Homosexuality and pseudohomosexuality.* New York: Science House.

Packer, H. L. (1968). *The limits of the criminal sanction.* Stanford, CA: Stanford University Press.

Padgitt, S., & Padgitt, J. (1986). Cognitive structure of sexual harassment: Implications for university policy. *Journal of College Student Personnel.* January, *27*(1), 34–39.

Page, D. C. et al. (1987). The sex-determining region of the human Y chromosome encodes a finger protein. December 24, *51*(6), 1091–1104.

Pagels, E. (1979). *The Gnostic Gospels.* New York: Vintage.

Paige, K. E. (1978a). The declining taboo against menstrual sex. *Psychology Today, 12*(7), 50–51.

Paige, K. E. (1978b). The ritual of circumcision. *Human Nature, 1,* 40–48.

Paige, K. E. (1973, April). Women learn to sing the menstrual blues. *Psychology Today,* 41–46.

Pao, P. (1982). Pathologic jealousy. *Medical Aspects of Human Sexuality, 16*(5).

Parkes, C. M. (1964). Effects of bereavement on physical and mental health. *British Medical Journal, 2,* 274–279.

Parrinder, G. (1980). *Sex in the world's religions.* New York: Oxford University Press.

Pavlov, I. P. (1927). *Conditioned reflexes: An investigation of the physiological activity of the cerebral cortex.* London: Oxford University Press.

Pear, R. (1987, May 20). Three health workers found infected by blood of patients with AIDS. *New York Times.*

Pearlin, L. I. (1980). Life strains and psychological distress among adults. In N. J. Smelser & E. H. Erikson (eds.), *Themes of work and love in adulthood.* Cambridge, MA: Harvard University Press.

Peckham, M. (1971). *Art and pornography.* New York: Harper & Row.

Peele, S. (1988). Fools for love. In R. J. Sternberg & M. L. Barnes, (eds.), *The psychology of love,* pp. 159–188. New Haven: Yale University Press.

Peele, S., & Brodsky, A. (1975). *Love and addiction.* New York: Signet.

Pepe, F., Iachello, R., Panella, M., Pepe, G., Panella, P., Pennisi, F., Pepe, P., Salemi, F., Priviteria, D., Sanfilippo, A. et al. (1987). Parity and sexual behavior in pregnancy. *Clinical Exp-Obstet-Gynecol, 14*(1), 60–65.

Peplau, L. A., & Gordon, S. L. (1982). The intimate relationships of lesbians and gay men. In E. Allgeier & N. McCormick (eds.), *Gender roles and sexual behavior.* Palo Alto, CA: Mayfield.

Peralla, N. (1969). *The kiss sacred and profane: An interpretative history of kiss symbolism and related religio-erotic themes.* Berkeley, CA: University of California Press.

Perkins, R. P. (1979). Sexual behavior and response in relation to complications in pregnancy. *American Journal of Obstetrics and Gynecology, 134,* 498–505.

Perlman, D. (1983, November). Puzzling ailments that may be AIDS. *San Francisco Chronicle.*

Pernoll, M., & Benson, R. (eds.), (1987). *Current obstetrical and gynecologic diagnosis and treatment,* 6th ed. Los Altos, CA: Appleton & Lange.

Perry, J. D., & Whipple, B. (1981). Pelvic muscle strength of female ejaculators: Evidence in support of a new theory of orgasm. *The Journal of Sex Research, 17*(1), 22–39.

Perry, J. D., & Whipple, B. (1980). Female ejaculation by Grafenburg spot stimulation. Paper presented at the annual meeting of the Society for the Scientific Study of Sex. Dallas, November 15.

Persky, H. (1983). Psychosexual effects of hormones. *Medical Aspects of Human Sexuality, 17*(9).

Peterman, T. A., & Curran, J. W. (1986). Sexual transmission of human immunodeficiency virus. *Journal of the American Medical Association, 256,* p. 2222–2226.

Petersen, A. C., & Taylor, B. (1980). The biological approach to adolescence. In Adelson J. (ed.), *Handbook of adolescent psychology.* New York: Wiley.

Petersen, I., & Stener, I. (1970). An electromyographical study of the striated urethral sphincter, the striated anal sphincter, and the levator ani muscle during ejaculation. *Electromyography, 10,* 23–44.

Peterson, H. (1928). *Havelock Ellis, philosopher of love.* Boston: Houghton Mifflin.

Peterson, J. R. et al. (1983, January, March). Playboy readers sex survey. *Playboy, 30*(1).

Petrovich, M., & Templer, D. (1984). Heterosexual molestation of children who later become rapists. *Psychological Reports, 54,* 810.

Pfeiffer, E., & Davis, G. S. (1972). Determinants of sexual behavior in middle and old age. *Journal of the American Geriatrics Society, 20,* 151–158.

Pfeiffer, E., Verwoerdt, A., & Davis, G. C. (1972). Sexual behavior in middle life. *American Journal of Psychiatry, 128,* 1262–1267.

Phillips, S., King, S., & DuBois, L. (1978). Spontaneous activities of female versus male newborns. *Child Development, 49,* 590–597.

Piaget, J. (1972). *The child's conception of the world.* Totowa, NJ: Littlefield, Adams.

Piaget, J. (1954). *The construction of reality in the child.* Translated by M. Cook. New York: Basic Books.

Piaget, J. (1952). *The origins of intelligence in children.* New York: International Universities.

Pillard, R., Poumadere, J., & Carretta, R. (1982). A family study of sexual orientation. *Archives of Sexual Behavior, 11*(6).

Pillard, R., Weinrich, J. (1986). Evidence of familial nature of male homosexuality. *Archives of General Psychiatry, 43*(8), 808–812.

Pincus, G. (1965). *The control of fertility.* New York: Academic.

Pitt, E. (1986). Quoted in *Carnegie Quarterly, 31,*(4).

Plessix Gray, F. du (1977). Manners of deceit and the case for lying. *Esquire,*

88(6), 134, 194.

Ploughman, P., & Stensrud, J. (1986). The ecology of rape victimization: A case study of Buffalo, New York. *Genet-Soc-Genetic, Social and General Psychology Monographs*, August, 112(3), 303–324.

Pogrebin, L. C. (1972, September). Down with sexist upbringing. *Ms.*, pp. 18, 32.

Pohlman, E. G. (1969). *Psychology of birth planning*. Cambridge, MA: Shenkman.

Polyson, J., Lash, S., & Evans, K. (1986). Human sexuality courses: Where and how many. *Teaching of Psychology*, December, 15(4), 221–222.

Pomeroy, W. B. (1976). *Your child and sex: A guide for parents*. New York: Delacorte.

Pomeroy, W. B. (1972). *Dr. Kinsey and the Institute for Sex Research*. New York: Harper & Row.

Pope, K. S. et al. (1980). *On love and loving*. San Francisco: Jossey-Bass.

*Population Reports*. (1982). Baltimore, MD: Population Information Program, Johns Hopkins University.

Porter, T. (1985). *Sex signals*. Philadelphia: Isi Press.

Potterat, J., Philipps, L., Rothenberg, R., & Darrow, W. (1985). On becoming a prostitute: An exploratory case comparison study. *Journal of Sex Research*, 21(3), 329–335.

Prentky, R., & Burgess, A. (1985, May 5). Cited in Goleman, D., *New York Times*, p. 15.

Price, W., & Forejt, J. (1986). Neuropsychiatric aspects of AIDS: A case report. *General Hospital Psychiatry*, January, 8(1), 7–10.

Pritchard, J. A., MacDonald, P. C., & Gant, N. (1985). *Williams obstetrics*, 17th ed. Norwalk, CT: Appleton-Century-Crofts.

Purdy, S. (1975a). The erotic in literature. In H. Katchadourian & D. Lunde, *Fundamentals of human sexuality*, 2d ed. New York: Holt, Rinehart and Winston.

Purdy, S. (1975b). The erotic in film. In H. Katchadourian & D. Lunde, *Fundamentals of human sexuality*, 2d ed. New York: Holt, Rinehart and Winston.

Qualls, C. B., Wincze, J. P., & Barlow, D. H. (eds.). (1978). *The prevention of sexual disorders*. New York: Plenum.

Quinlan, M. J. (1941). *Victorian prelude: A history of English manners 1700–1830*. New York: Columbia University Press.

Quinn, S. (1981, February 9). Why I, too, finally had to get married. *San Francisco Chronicle*, p. 16.

Quinn, T. C., Glasser, D., Cannon, R. O. et al. (1988). Human immunodeficiency virus infection among patients attending clinics for sexually transmitted diseases. *New England Journal of Medicine*, January 28, 318(4), 197–203.

Quinn, T. C., Mann, J. M., Curran, J. W., & Piot, P. (1986). AIDS in Africa: An epidiologic paradigm. *Science*, November 21, 955–986.

Rabkin, C., Thomas, P., Jaffe, H., & Schultz, S. (1987). Prevalence of antibody to HTLV-III/LAV in a population attending a sexually transmitted diseases clinic. *Sexually Transmitted Diseases*, January–March 14(1), 48–51.

Rachlin, S. K., & Vogt, G. L. (1974). Sex roles as presented to children by coloring books. *Journal of Popular Culture*, 8, 549–556.

Rada, R. T. (1976). Alcoholism and the child molester. *Annals of the New York Academy of Sciences*, 273, 492–496.

Raisman, G., & Field, P. (1971). Sexual dimorphism in the preoptic area of the rat. *Science*, 173, 731–733.

Ramasharma, K., & Sairam, M. R. (1982). Isolation and characterization of inhibin from human seminal plasma. *Annals of New York Academy of Sciences*, 383, 307–328.

Rathus, S. A. (1987). *Psychology*, 3d ed. New York: Holt, Rinehart and Winston.

Ratzinger, J., & Bovone, A. (1987). Instruction on respect for human life in its origin and on the dignity of procreation: Replies to certain questions of the day. Reprinted in the *New York Times*, March 11, pp. 10–13.

Raven, P. H., & Johnson, G. B. (1986). *Biology*. St. Louis, MO: C.V. Mosby.

Rawson, P. (ed.). (1969). *Erotic art of the East*. New York: Putnam.

Rechy, J. (1963). *City of night*. New York: Grove.

Rechy, J. (1977). *The sexual outlaw*. New York: Grove.

Reich, W. (1969). *The sexual revolution*. New York: Farrar, Straus and Giroux.

Reich, W. (1942). *The function of the orgasm*. New York: Noonday.

Reichlin, S. (1963). Neuroendocrinology. *New England Journal of Medicine*, 269, 1182, 1246, 1296.

Reid, R. L. (1986). Premenstrual syndrome: A time for introspection. *American Journal of Obstetrics and Gynecology*, November, 155(5), 921–926.

Reimer, R. A. (1986). *Legal analysis of the Attorney General's Commission on Pornography's final report (July 1986)*. Report no. 86-148a. Washington, DC: Library of Congress.

Rein, M. F. (1977). Epidemiology of gonococcal infections. In R. B. Roberts (ed.), *The gonococcus*, pp. 1–31. New York: Wiley.

Rein, M. F., & Chapel, T. A. (1975). Trichomoniasis, candidiasis, and the minor venereal diseases. *Clinical Obstetrics and Gynecology*, 18, 73–78.

Reinhold, R. (1987, October 31). AIDS book brings power to a gay San Franciscan. *New York Times*.

Reinisch, J. (1987, October 12). Cited in *Time*, p. 69.

Reiss, I. L. (1986). *Journey into sexuality*. Englewood Cliffs, NJ: Prentice-Hall.

Reiss, I. L. (1982). Trouble in Paradise: The current status of sex research. *Journal of Sex Research*, 18, 97–113.

Reiss, I. L. (1980). *Family systems in America*, 3d ed. New York: Holt, Rinehart and Winston.

Reiss, I. L. (1967). *The social context of premarital sexual permissiveness*. New York: Holt, Rinehart and Winston.

Reiss, I. L. (1960). *Premarital sexual standards in America*. Glencoe, IL: Free Press.

Reite, M. (1985). Sleep and sleep disorders. In R. C. Simons (ed.), *Understanding human behavior in health and illness*, pp. 569–585. Baltimore, MD: Williams & Wilkins.

Remafedi, G. (1987a). Adolescent sexuality: Psychosocial and medical implications. *Pediatrics*, March, 79(3), 331–337.

Remafedi, G. (1987b). Male homosexuality: The adolescent's perspective. *Pediatrics*, March, 79(3), 326–330.

Remy, J. (1979). Mutilations sexuelles: En France aussi. *L'Express* No. 1447, 58–60.

Renshaw, D. C., & Renshaw, R. H. (1980). Incest. In G. William & J. Money (eds.), *Traumatic abuse and neglect of children at home*. Baltimore, MD: Johns Hopkins University Press.

Ricci, L. (1986). Child sexual abuse: The emergency department response. *Annals of Emergency Medicine*, June, 15(6), 711–716.

Richardson, L. (1986). *The new other woman*. New York: Free Press.

Richart, R. (1983). Condyloma viruses that progress to invasive cancer can be identified. *Contraceptive Technology Update*, 4, 143–144.

Richlin, A. (1983). *The garden of Priapus*. New Haven: Yale University Press.

Rieber, I., & Sigusch, V. (1979). Psychosurgery on sex offenders and sexual deviants in West Germany. *Archives of Sexual Behavior*, 8, 523–527.

Rizley, R. (1980). Psychobiological bases of romantic love. In K. Pope et al. (eds.), *On love and loving*, pp. 104–113. San Francisco: Jossey-Bass.

Roback, H., & Lothstein, L. (1986). The female mid-life sex change applicant:

A comparison with younger female transsexuals and older male sex change applicants. *Archives of Sexual Behavior,* October, *15*(5), 401–415.

Robbins, M. B., & Jensen, G. D. (1976). Multiple orgasms in the male. In R. Gemme & C. C. Wheeler (eds.), *Progress of sexology,* pp. 323–338. New York: Plenum.

Roberts, E. J. (1980). *Childhood sexual learning: The unwritten curriculum.* Cambridge, MA: Ballinger.

Roberts, E. J., Kline, D., & Gagnon, J. (1978). *Family life and sexual learning,* Vol. 1. Cambridge, MA: Population Education.

Robinson, I. E., & Jedlicka, D. (1982). Change in sexual attitudes and behavior of college students from 1965 to 1980. *Journal of Marriage and the Family, 44,* 237–240.

Robinson, P. (1976). *The modernization of sex.* New York: Harper & Row.

Robinson, P. K. (1983). The sociological perspective. In R. B. Weg (ed.), *Sexuality in the later years.* New York: Academic Press.

Roche, John P. (1986). Premarital sex: Attitudes and behavior by dating stage. *Adolescence,* Spring, *21*(81), 107–121.

Rodgers, B. (1972). *Gay talk.* New York: Putnam.

Rook, K. S., & Hammer, C. L. (1977). A cognitive perspective on the experience of sexual arousal. *Journal of Social Issues, 33*(2), 7–29.

Root, A. W. (1973). Endocrinology of puberty: Normal sexual maturation. *Journal of Pediatrics, 83,* 1–19.

Rops, F. (1975). *Graphic work of Felicien Rops.* New York: Leon Amiel.

Rose, D. (1986). Worse than death: Psychodynamics of rape victims and the need for psychotherapy. *American Journal of Psychiatry,* July, *143*(7), 817–824.

Roseburg, T. (1973). *Microbes and morals: The strange story of venereal disease.* New York: Ballantine.

Rosenblum, L. (1985). Passion and the nonhuman primate. Cited in Hatfield, E. (1988). Passionate and companionate love. In R. J. Sternberg & M. L. Barnes (eds.), *The psychology of love,* p. 191. New Haven: Yale University Press.

Rosenfeld, A. (1979a). Incest among female psychiatric patients. *American Journal of Psychiatry, 136,* 791–795 June.

Rosenfeld, A. (1979b). Endogamic incest and the victim perpetrator model. *American Journal of Diseases of Children, 133,* 406.

Rosenfeld, A., Nadelson, C., & Krieger, M. (1979). Fantasy and reality in pa-

tients' reports of incest. *Journal of Clinical Psychiatry, 40*(4).

Rosenfeld, A., Nadelson, C., Krieger, M., & Backman, J. (1977). Incest and sexual abuse of children. *The American Journal of Child Psychiatry, 16*(2).

Rosenfeld, A., Smith, D., Wenegrat, A., Brewster, W., & Haavik, D. (1980). The primal scene: A study of prevalence. *American Journal of Psychiatry, 137,* 11.

Rosenfeld, A., Wenegrat, A., Haavik, D., & Wenegrat, B. (1982). Parents' fears of their children's developing sexuality. *Medical Aspects of Human Sexuality, 16*(10).

Ross, C., & Piotrow, P. T. (1974). Birth control without contraceptives. *Population Reports,* Series I (1), June.

Rossi, A. S. (ed.). *The feminist papers: From Adams to Simone de Beauvoir.* New York: Columbia University Press.

Roszak, T. (1969). *The making of a counter-culture.* New York: Doubleday.

Roth, P. (1967). *Portnoy's complaint.* New York: Random House.

Rothenberg, F. (1984, January 25). *San Francisco Chronicle,* p. 1.

Rousso, H. (1986). Confronting the myth of asexuality: The network project for disabled women and girls. *SIECUS Report, 14,* 4–6.

Rowan, R. L., & Gillette, P. J. (1978). *The gay health guide.* Boston: Little, Brown.

Rowell, T. E. (1972). Female reproduction cycles and social behavior in primates. *Advances in the Study of Behavior, 4,* 69–105.

Rowell, T. E. (1972). *The social behavior of monkeys.* Baltimore: Penguin.

Rowse, A. L. (1977). *Homosexuals in history.* New York: Macmillan.

Rubin, A. M. (1982). Sexually open versus sexually exclusive marriage. *Alternative Lifestyles, 5,* 101–108.

Rubin, J., Provenzano, F., & Luria, Z. (1974). The eye of the beholder: Parents' view on sex of newborns. *American Journal of Orthopsychiatry, 44,* 512–519.

Rubin, P. (ed.). (1987). *Clinical oncology: A multidisciplinary approach,* 6th ed. American Cancer Society.

Rubin, R. T., Reinisch, J. M., & Haskett, R. F. (1981). Postnatal gonadal steroid effects on human behavior. *Science, 211* (4488), 1318–1324.

Rubin, Z. (1973). *Liking and loving: An invitation to social psychology.* New York: Holt, Rinehart and Winston.

Rubin, Z. (1970). Measurement of romantic love. *Journal of Personality and Social Psychology, 35,* 767–782.

Rubin, Z., Peplau, L. A., & Hill, C. T. (1981). Loving and leaving: Sex differences in romantic attachment. *Sex*

*Roles, 7,* 821–836.

Rubin, Z. et al., (1980). Self-disclosure in dating couples: Sex roles and the ethic of openness. *Journal of Marriage and the Family, 42,* 305–317.

Rubinow, D. R. (1984). Premenstrual syndrome: Overview from a methodological perspective. *American Journal of Psychiatry,* February, 163–170.

Rubinow, D. R., Roy-Byrne, P., Hoban, M. D., Grover, G. N., Stambler, N., & Post, R. M. (1986). Premenstrual mood changes: Characteristic patterns in women with and without premenstrual syndrome. *Journal of Affective Disorders,* March–April, *10*(2), 85–90.

Rubinsky, H. J., Eckerman, D. A., Rubinsky, E. W., & Hoover, C. R. (1987). Early phase physiological response patterns to psychosexual stimuli: Comparisons of male and female patterns. *Archives of Sex Research, 16*(1), 45–56.

Rubinstein, E., & Brown, J. (1986). *The media, social science, and social policy for children.* NJ: Ablex Corp.

Ruble, D. N., Brooks-Gunn, J., & Clarke, A. (1980). Research on menstrual-related psychological changes: Alternative perspectives. In J. E. Parsons (eds.), *The psychobiology of sex differences and sex roles.* New York: McGraw-Hill.

Ruble, D. N. (1977). Premenstrual symptoms: A reinterpretation. *Science, 197,* 291–292.

Rueger, R. (1981). *The joy of touch.* New York: Simon & Schuster.

Runyan, D. K. (1986). Incest: The trauma of intervention. *SIECUS Report, 15*(1), 1–14.

Russell, B. (1945). *A history of Western philosophy.* New York: Simon & Schuster.

Russell, D. E. H. (1984). *Sexual exploitation: Rape, child sexual abuse, and workplace harrassment.* Beverly Hills, CA: Sage.

Russell, D. E. H. (1980a). Pornography and violence: What does the new research say? In L. Lederer (ed.), *Take back the night: Women and pornography.* New York: William Morrow.

Russell, D. E. H. (1980b). Pornography and the women's liberation movement. In L. Lederer (ed.). *Take back the night: Women on pornography.* New York: William Morrow.

Russell, G. F. M. (1985). Anorexia nervosa. In J. B. Wyngaarden & L. H. Smith (eds.), *Cecil textbook of medicine,* 17th ed., pp. 118–1191. Philadelphia: W. B. Saunders.

Russell, K. P. (1987). The course and conduct of normal labor and delivery. In M. Pernoll & R. Benson (eds.), *Current obstetric and gynecologic diagnosis and treatment 1987.* Los Altos, CA: Appleton & Lange.

Russell, M. J., Switz, G. M., & Thompson, K. (1977). Olfactory influences on the human menstrual cycle. Delivered at the American Association for the Advancement of Science, San Francisco.

Rutledge, F. (1986). Gynecologic malignancy: General considerations. In D. Danforth & J. Scott et al. (eds.), *Obstetrics and gynecology,* 5th ed. Philadelphia: J. B. Lippincott.

Saah, A. J. (1987). Serologic tests for human immunodeficiency virus (HIV). *AIDS, 2,* 11–14.

Sack, A. R., Keller, J. F., & Hinkle, D. E. (1984). Premarital sexual intercourse: A test of the effects of peer group, religiosity, and sexual guilt. *The Journal of Sex Research.*

Sadler, T. W. (1985). *Langman's medical embryology,* 5th ed. Baltimore, MD: Williams & Wilkins.

Sadock, B. J., & Sadock, V. A. (1976). Techniques of coitus. In B. J. Sadock et al. (eds.), *The sexual experience.* Baltimore, MD: Williams & Wilkins.

*Safe sex* guidelines for women at risk for AIDS transmission. (1986). A brochure: Project AWARE, the Women's AIDS Network, COYOTE, and the Lesbian Insemination Project, San Francisco.

Safran, C. (1976, November). What men do to women on the job: A shocking look at sexual harassment. *Redbook,* p. 148.

Saghir, M. T., & Robins, E. (1980). Clinical aspects of female homosexuality. In J. Marmor (ed.), *Homosexual behavior.* New York: Basic.

Saghir, M. T., & Robins, E. (1973). *Male and female homosexuality: A comprehensive investigation.* Baltimore, MD: Williams & Wilkins.

Sales, E., Baum, M., & Shore, B. (1984). Victim readjustment following assault. *Journal of Social Issues, 40,* 117–136.

Salzman, L. (1980). Latent homosexuality. In J. Marmor (ed.), *Homosexual behavior.* New York: Basic.

Salzman, L. (1968). Sexuality in psychoanalytic theory. In J. Marmor (ed.), *Modern psychoanalysis,* pp. 123–145. New York, Basic.

Samuel, T., & Rose, N. R. (1980). The lessons of vasectomy: A review. *Journal of Clinical Laboratory Immunology, 3*(2), 77–83.

Sanday, P. R. (1981). The sociocultural context of rape: A cross-cultural study. *Journal of Social Issues, 37*(4), 5–27.

Sandberg, G., & Quevillon, R. (1987). Dyspareunia: An integrated approach to assessment and diagnosis. *Journal of Family Practice,* January, *24*(1), 66–70.

Sanders, R. M., Bain, J., & Langerin, R. (1985). Peripheral sex hormones, homosexuality, and gender identity. In R. Langerin (ed.), *Erotic preferences, gender identity and aggression in men: New research studies.* Hillsdale, NJ: Ehrbaum.

Sandfort, T. (1984). Sex in pedophiliac relationships: An empirical investigation among a non-representative group of boys. *Journal of Sex Research, 20,* 123–142.

Sanford, J. (1975). *Prostitutes: Portraits of people in the sexploitation business.* London: Secker & Warburg.

Sangiuliano, I. (1978). *In her time.* New York: William Morrow.

Sarnoff, S., & Sarnoff, I. (1979). *Masturbation and adult sexuality.* New York: Evans.

Sarrel, P. M., & Sarrel, L. J. (1987, November 5). Cited in Brody, J. E. Changing attitudes in masturbation. *New York Times.*

Sarrel, P. J., & Coplin, H. R. (1971). A course in human sexuality for the college student. *American Journal of Public Health, 61,* 1030–1037.

Sarrel, P. J., & Masters, W. (1982). Sexual molestation of men by women. *Archives of Sexual Behavior, 11*(2).

Sarrel, P. J., & Sarrel, P. M. (1979). *Sexual unfolding: Sexual development and sex therapies in late adolescence.* Boston: Little, Brown.

Saslawsky, D. A., & Wurtele, S. K. (1986). Educating children about sexual abuse: Implications for pediatric intervention and possible prevention. *Journal of Pediatric Psychology,* June, *11*(2), 235–245.

Satterfield, S., & Listiak, A. (1982). Juvenile prostitution: A sequel to incest. Paper presented at the 135th meeting of the American Psychiatric Association, Toronto, May 15–21.

Savage, D. C. L., & Evans, J. (1984). Puberty and adolescence. In J. O. Forfar & G. C Arneil (eds.), *Textbook of pediatrics,* 3d ed., Vol 1, pp. 366–388. Edinburgh: Churchill Livingston.

Scanzoni, L. D., (1982). *Sex is a parent affair: Guide for teaching your children about sex.* New York: Bantam.

Scanzoni, L. D., & Scanzoni, J. (1976). *Men, women and change: A sociology of marriage and the family.* New York: McGraw-Hill.

Scarf, M. (1980). *Unfinished business.* New York: Doubleday.

Scarpinato, L., & Calabrese, L. H. (1987). Prospects for AIDS therapy and vaccine. In V. Gong & N. Rudnick (eds.), *AIDS.* New Brunswick, NJ: Rutgers University Press.

Schacter, S. (1964). The interaction of cognitive and physiological determinants of emotional state. In Berkowitz (ed.), *Advances in experimental social psychology,* Vol. 1. New York: Academic Press.

Schacter, S., & Singer, J. E. (1962). Cognitive, social and physiological determinants of emotional state. *Psychological Review, 69,* 379–399.

Schally, A. V. (1978). Aspects of hypothalamic regulation of the pituitary gland: Its implications for the control of reproductive processes. *Science, 202,* 18–28.

Scharfman, M. A. (1977). Birth and the neonate. In R. C. Simons & H. Pardes (eds.), *Understanding human behavior in health and illness.* Baltimore, MD: Williams & Wilkins.

Schlafly, P. (1986). School-based clinics vs. sex respect. *The Phyllis Schlafly Report,* June, *19*(11), 1–3.

Schlafly, P. (1977). *The power of the positive woman.* New York: Arlington.

Schlesinger, A., Jr. (1970). An informal history of love U.S.A. *Medical Aspects of Human Sexuality, 4*(6), 64–82.

Schmeck, H. M., Jr. (1987, October 20). Venereal virus strongly implicated in several cancers. *New York Times,* p. 17.

Schmidt, G. (1982). Sex and society in the eighties. *Archives of Sexual Behavior, 11*(2).

Schmidt, G. (1975). Male-female differences in sexual arousal and behavior during and after exposure to sexually explicit stimuli. *Archives of Sexual Behavior, 4,* 353–364.

Schmidt, G., & Sigusch, V. (1970). Sex differences in responses to psychosexual stimulation by films and slides. *Journal of Sex Research, 6*(4), 268–283.

Schneider, M., & Tremble, B. (1986). Training service providers to work with gay or lesbian adolescents: A workshop. *Journal of Counseling and Development,* October, *65*(2), 98–99.

Schonfeld, W. (1971). Adolescent development: Biological, psychological, and sociological determinants. In F. Feinstein, P. Giovacchini, & A. Miller (eds.), *Adolescent psychiatry.* New York: Basic Books.

Schover, L., Friedman, J., Weiler, S., Heiman, J., & LoPiccolo, J. (1982). Multiaxial problem-oriented system for sexual dysfunctions. *Archives of General Psychiatry, 39,* 614–619.

Schreiner-Engel, P. (1987). Developmental psychology. *Infertility.*

Schreiner-Engel, P., & Schiavi, R. (1986). Lifetime psychopathology in individuals with low sexual desire. *Journal of Nervous and Mental Disease,* November, *174*(11), 646–651.

Schreiner-Engel, P., Schiavi, R., Vieto-risa, D., & Smith, H. (1987). The differential impact of diabetes type on female sexuality. *Journal of Psychosomatic Research, 31*(1), 23–33.

Schultz, T. (1980, June). Does marriage give today's women what they really want? *Ladies Home Journal*, pp. 89–91, 146–155.

Schulz, E. D., & Williams, S. R. (1968). *Family life and sex education.* New York: Harcourt Brace and World.

Schulz, M. R. (1975). The semantic derogation of woman. In B. Thorne & N. Henley (eds.), *Language of sex: Differences and dominance.* Rowley, MA: Newbury House.

Schwab, D. F. S. & Fliers, E. (1985). A sexually dimorphic nucleus in the human brain. *Science, 228*, 1112–1114.

Schwartz, L., & Markham, W. (1985). Sex stereotyping in children's toy advertisements. *Sex Roles, 12*, 157–170.

Schwarz, G. S. (1973). Devices to prevent masturbation. *Medical Aspects of Human Sexuality, 7*(5), 141–153.

Scott, J. R. (1986). Spontaneous abortion. In D. Danforth & J. R. Scott (eds.), *Obstetrics and Gynecology,* 5th ed. Philadelphia: J. B. Lippincott.

Sears, R. R. (1965). Development of gender role. In F. A. Beach (ed.), *Sex and behavior.* New York: Wesley.

Sears, R. R., Maccoby, E. E., & Levin, H. (1957). *Patterns of childrearing.* Evanston, IL: Row, Peterson.

Seaver, R., & Wainhouse, A. (eds.). (1965). *The Marquis de Sade.* New York: Grove.

Seavey, C., Katz, P., & Zalk, S. (1975). Baby X: The effect of gender label on adult responses to infants. *Sex Roles, 1*, 103–109.

Seecof, R., & Tennant, F. S., Jr. (1986). Subjective perceptions to the intravenous "rush" of heroin and cocaine in opioid addicts. *American Journal of Drug and Alcohol Abuse, 12*(1–2), 79–87.

Segraves, K. A., Segraves, R. T., & Schoenberg, H. (1987). Use of sexual history to differentiate organic from psychogenic impotence. *Archives of Sexual Behavior, 16*(2), 125–137.

Selby, J. W., Calhoun, L. G., Jones, J. M., & Matthews, L. (1980). Families of incest: A collation of clinical impressions. *International Journal of Social Psychiatry, 26*(1), 7–16.

Selnow, G. W. (1985). Sex differences in uses and perceptions of profanity. *Sex Roles, 12*, 303–312.

Semans, J. H. (1956). Premature ejaculation: A new approach. *Southern Medical Journal, 49*, 353–357.

Serrin, W. (1981). Sex is a growing multimillion dollar business. *New York Times*, pp. B1–B6.

Sesan, R., Freeark, K., & Murphy, S. (1986). The support network: Crisis intervention for extrafamilial child sexual abuse. *Professional psychology: Research and practice,* April, 17(2), 138–146.

Sevely, J. L., & Bennett, J. W. (1978). Concerning female ejaculation and the female prostate. *Journal of Sex Research, 14*, 1–20.

Sex Education and Information Council of the United States. (1970). *Sexuality and man.* New York: Scribners.

Shabecoff, P. (1987, November 3). Panel says Caesareans are used too often. *New York Times.*

Shacknai, J., & Squadron, W. (1987, January 29). Why can't TV advertise condoms? *New York Times.*

Shah, F., Zelnik, M., & Kantner, J. F. (1975). Unprotected intercourse among teenagers. *Family Planning Perspectives, 7*, 39–44.

Shahani, S. K., & Hattikudur, N. S. (1981). Immunological consequences of vasectomy. *Archives of Andrology, 7*(2), 193–199.

Shainess, N., & Greenwald, H. (1971). Debate: Are fantasies during sexual relations a sign of difficulty? *Sexual Behavior, 1*, 38–54.

Shane, J. M., Schff, I., & Wilson, E. A. (1976). The infertile couple: Evaluation and treatment. *Clinical Symposia, 28*(5).

Shanor, K. (1977). *Fantasy file.* New York: Dial.

Shapiro, H. I. (1977). *The birth control book.* New York: St. Martin's.

Shaver, P. (1985, September 10). Cited in Coleman, D., *New York Times*, p. 18.

Shaver, P., Hazan, C., & Bradshaw, D. (1988). Love as attachment: The integration of three behavioral systems. In R. J. Sternberg & M. L. Barnes (eds.), *The psychology of love.* New Haven: Yale University Press.

Sheehy, G. (1973). *Prostitution: Hustling in our wide-open society.* New York: Delacorte.

Shengold, L. (1980). Some reflections on a case of mother/adolescent son incest. *International Journal of Psychoanalysis, 61* (pt 4), 461–476.

Sheppard, A. T. (1985). Lesbian mothers: Long night's journey into day. *Women's Rights Law Reporter,* Fall, 225, 218–246.

Sheppard, S. (1974). A survey of college-based courses in human sexuality. *Journal of the American College Health Association, 23*, 14–18.

Sherfey, M. J. (1973). *The nature and evolution of female sexuality.* New York: Vintage.

Sherrard, P. (1976). *Christianity and eros.* London: SPCK.

Sherwin, B., Gelfand, M., & Brender, W. (1985). Androgen enhances sexual motivation in females: A prospective crossover study in steroid administration in surgical menopause. *Psychosomatic Medicine, 47*(4), 339–351.

Sherwin, R., & Corbett, S. (1985). Campus sexual norms and dating relationships. *The Journal of Sex Research, 21*, 258–274.

Shettles, L. B. (1972). Predetermining children's sex. *Medical Aspects of Human Sexuality, 6*, 172ff.

Shilts, R. (1988). Promising treatment for AIDS. *San Francisco Chronicle,* p. A1–A4.

Shilts, R. (1987). *And the Band Played On.* New York: St. Martin's Press.

Shilts, R. (1983, May 2). How AIDS is changing gay lifestyles. *San Francisco Chronicle.*

Shirai, M., & Ishii, N. (1981). Hemodynamics of erection in man. *Archives of Andrology, 1*, 27–32.

Shope, D. F., & Broderick, C. B. (1967). Level of sexual experience and predicted adjustment in marriage. *Journal of Marriage and the Family, 29*, 424–427.

Short, R V. (1980). The origins of human sexuality. In C. R. Austin & R. V. Short (eds.), *Human sexuality.* Cambridge, MA: Cambridge University Press.

Short, R. V. (1979). The development of human reproduction. Regulation de la fecondité, INSERM, *83*, 355–366.

Sidovowicz, L., & Lunney, G. (1980). Baby X revisited. *Sex Roles, 6*, 67–73.

*Signs.* (1980). Women, sex, and sexuality, *6*(1).

Silber, S. J. (1981). *The male.* New York: Scribner's.

Silber, S. J. (1980). *How to get pregnant.* New York: Scribner's.

Silverstein, C. (1981). *Man to man: Gay couples in America.* New York: Morrow.

Silverstein. C. (1978). *The joy of gay sex.* New York: Simon & Schuster.

Simon, W., & Gagnon, J. H. (1986). Sexual scripts: Permanence and change. *Archives of Sexual Behavior, 15*(2), 97–120.

Simons, G. L. (1975). *A place for pleasure. The history of the brothel.* London: Harwood-Smart.

Simons, R. C., & Pardes, H. (ed.). (1977). *Understanding human behavior in health and illness.* Baltimore, MD: Williams & Wilkins.

Simpson, M., & Schill, T. (1977). Patrons of massage parlors: Some facts and figures. *Archives of Sexual Behavior, 6*(6), 521–525.

Singer, I., & Singer, J. (1972). Types of female orgasm. *Journal of Sex Research,* 8(11), 255–267.

Singer, J. L. (1984). Romantic fantasy in personality development. In K. Pope (ed.), *On love and loving,* pp. 172–194. San Francisco: Jossey-Bass.

Singer, J. L. (1975). *The inner world of daydreaming.* New York: Harper & Row.

Singer, P., & Wells, D. (1985). *Making babies: The new science and ethics of conception.* New York: Charles Scribner's.

Sisley, E. L., & Harris, B. (1977). *The joy of lesbian sex.* New York: Simon & Schuster.

Skaakeback, N. E., Bancroft, J., Davidson, D. W., & Androgen, W. P. (1981). Replacement with oral testosterone undecaonate in hypogonadal men. *Clinical Endocrinology, 14,* 49–67.

Skinner, B. F. (1938). *The behavior of organisms: An experimental analysis.* New York: Appleton-Century-Crofts.

Skolnick, A. (1980). Early attachment and personal relations across the life course. In D. Featherman & R. Lerner, (eds.), *Life span development and behavior,* Vol. 7. Hillsdale, NJ: Erlbaum.

Slayton, W. R. (1984). Lifestyle spectrum. *Siecus Report, 12*(3), 1–5.

Slovenko, R. (1965). *Sexual behavior and the law.* Springfield, IL: Thomas.

Small, C. B., Klein, R. S., Friedland, G. H., Moll, B., Emeson, E. E., & Spigland, I. (1983). Community-acquired opportunistic infections and defective cellular immunity in heterosexual drug abusers and homosexual men. *American Journal of Medicine, 74,* 433–441.

Small, M. (1987). Semirigid and malleable penile implants. *Urological Clinical of North America,* February, *14*(1), 187–201.

Smelser, N. J., & Erikson, E. H. (eds.). (1980). *Themes of work and love in adulthood.* Cambridge, MA: Harvard University Press.

Smelser, N. J. (1973). *Sociology: An introduction.* New York: Wiley.

Smilgis, M. (1987, September 4). Snip, suction, stretch, and truss. *Time,* p. 70.

Smith, C., & Lloyd, B. (1978). Maternal behavior and perceived sex of infant: Revisited. *Child Development, 49,* 1263–1265.

Smith, D. S., & Hindus, M. S. (1975). Premarital pregnancy in America, 1940–1971: An overview and interpretation. *Journal of Interdisciplinary History, 5,* 537–570.

Smith, G. G. (1980). The use of cervical caps at the University of California, Berkeley. *Journal of American College Health Association, 29*(2), 93–94.

Smith, H., & Israel, E. (1987). Sibling incest: A study of the dynamics of 25 cases. *Child Abuse and Neglect, 11*(1), 101–108.

Smith, M. A., & Youngkin, E. Q. (1986). Managing the premenstrual syndrome. *Clinical Pharmacy,* October, 5(10), 788–797.

Smith, P., & Daglish, L. (1977). Sex differences in parent and infant behavior in the home. *Child Development, 48,* 1250–1254.

Smith, P. J., & Talbert, R. L. (1986) Sexual dysfunction with antihypertensive and antipsychotic agents. *Clinical Pharmacy,* May, 5(5), 373–384.

Smukler, A. J., & Schiebel, D. (1975). Personality characteristics of exhibitionists. *Diseases of the Nervous System, 36,* 600–603.

Snell, R. S. (1986). *Clinical anatomy for medical students.* Boston: Little, Brown.

Snyder, S., & Gordon, S. (1981). *Parents as sexuality educators: An annotated print and audiovisual bibliography for professionals and parents.* New York: Oryx.

Socarides, C. W. (1975). *Beyond sexual freedom.* New York: Quadrangle.

Socarides, C. W. (1970). Homosexuality and medicine. *Journal of the American Medical Association, 212,* 1199–1202.

Solomon, S., & Cappa, K. (1987). Impotence and bicycling. A seldom-reported association. *Postgrad-Med,* January, *81*(1), 99–100.

Solomon, S., & Saxe, L. (1977). What is intelligent, as well as attractive, is good. *Personality and Social Psychology Bulletin, 3,* 670–673.

Sondheimer, S. J. (1985). Hormonal changes in premenstrual syndrome. *Psychosomatics,* October, 803–809.

Sontag, S. (1972, September 23). *Saturday Review.*

Sorensen, R. C. (1973). *Adolescent sexuality in contemporary America.* New York: World.

Sorensen, T., & Hertoft, P. (1982). Male and female transsexualism: The Danish experience with 37 patients. *Archives of Sexual Behavior, 11*(2).

Spanier, G. B. (1983). Married and unmarried cohabitation in the United States 1980. *Journal of Marriage and the Family, 45*(2), 277–288.

Spanier, G. B., & Furstenberg, F., Jr. (1982). Remarriage after divorce: A longitudinal analysis of well-being. *Journal of Marriage and the Family, 44,* 709–720.

Spanier, G. B., & Thompson, L. (1984). *Parting: The aftermath of separation and divorce.* Beverly Hills, CA: Sage.

Spark, R. (1983). A new approach to impotence. *Medical Aspects of Human Sexuality, 17*(6).

Spark, R., White, R., & Connolly, P. (1980). Impotence is not always psychogenic: Newer insights into hypothalamic-pituitary-gonadal dysfunction. *Journal of the American Medical Association, 243*(8), 750–755.

Sparks, R. A., Purrier, B. G., Watt, P. J., & Elstein, M. (1981). Bacteriological colonisation of uterine cavity: Role of tailed intrauterine contraceptive device. *British Medical Journal of Clinical Research, 282*(6271), 1189–1891.

Sparling, P. F. (1988). Sexually transmitted diseases. In J. B. Wyngaarden & L. H. Smith (eds.), *Cecil textbook of medicine,* 18th ed., pp. 1701–1706. Philadelphia: W.B. Saunders.

Spence, J. T., & Helmreich, R. L. (1978). *Masculinity and femininity: Their psychological dimensions, correlates and antecedents.* Austin: University of Texas Press.

Spencer, M. J., & Dunklee, P. (1986). Sexual abuse of boys. *Pediatrics,* July, *78*(1), 133–138.

Spiro, R. (1956). *Children of the kibbutz.* New York: Shocken.

Spitz, R. A. (1949). Autoeroticism: Some empirical findings and hypotheses on three of its manifestations in the first year of life. *The Psychoanalytic Study of the Child, 3-4,* 85–119.

Spitz, R. A., & Wolf, K. D. (1947). Anaclitic depression. An inquiry into the genesis of psychiatric conditions in early childhood, II. *The Psychoanalytic Study of the Child, II.*

Spitzer, R. L. (1981). The diagnostic status of homosexuality in DSM. III: A reformulation of the issues. *American Journal of Psychiatry, 138*(2), 210–215.

Stamm, W. E., & Holmes, K. (1984). Chlamydia trachomatis infections of the adult. In K. Holmes, P. Mardh, P. F. Sparling, & P. Wiesner, *Sexually transmitted diseases.* New York: McGraw-Hill.

Stark, E. (1984). The unspeakable family secret. *Psychology Today,* May, 42–46.

Stark, R. (1982). *The book of aphrodisiacs.* New York: Stein & Day.

Starr, B. D., & Weiner, M. B. (1981). *The Starr-Weiner report on sex and sexuality in the mature years.* New York: McGraw-Hill.

Starr & King. (1985, May 20). Rape and the law. *Newsweek,* pp. 60–73.

Stayton, W. (1984). Lifestyle spectrum 1984. *SIECUS Report, 12*(3).

Steege, J., Stout, A., & Carson, C. (1986). Patient satisfaction in Scott and Small-Carrion penile implant recipients: A study of 52 patients. *Archives of Sexual Behavior,* October, *15*(5), 393–399.

Stein, M. L. (1977). Prostitution. In J. Money & H. Musaph (eds.), *Handbook of sexology*. Amsterdam: Excerpta Medica.

Steinberg, L. (1983). *The sexuality of Christ in Renaissance art and in modern oblivion*. New York: Pantheon.

Steinberg, L. (1981). *The life cycle*. New York: Columbia University Press.

Steinberger, A., & Steinberger, E. (1976). Secretion of FSH-inhibiting factor by cultured sertoli cells. *Endocrinology, 99*, 918–921.

Steinem, G. (1978). Erotica and pornography: A clear and present danger. *Ms., 7*, 53–54.

Steinman, D. L. et al. (1981). A comparison of male and female patterns of sexual arousal. *Archives of Sexual Behavior, 10*(6).

Stekel, W. (1964). *Sexual aberrations*. S. Parker, translator. New York: Grove.

Stendahl, M. H. B. (1983). *On love*. New York: Da Capo.

Stengle, R. (1986, July 2). Sex busters. *Time*, pp. 12–21.

Stephens, W. N. (1963). *The Family in cross-cultural perspective*. New York: Holt, Rinehart and Winston.

Stermac, L., & Quinsey, V. (1986). Social competence among rapists. *Behavioral Assessment*, Spring, *8*(2), 171–185.

Sternberg, R. J. (1988). Triangulating love. In R. J. Sternberg & M. L. Barnes (eds.), *The psychology of love*, pp. 119–138. New Haven: Yale University Press.

Sternberg, R. J. (1986). A triangular theory of love. *Psychological Review, 9*, 119–135.

Sternberg, R. J. (1985, September 10). Cited in Goleman, D. Patterns of love charted in studies. *New York Times*, p. 18.

Sternberg, R. J., & Barnes, M. L. (1988). *The psychology of love*. New Haven: Yale University Press.

Sternglanz, S. H., & Serbin, L. A. (1974). Sex role stereotyping in children's television programs. *Developmental Psychology, 10*, 710–715.

Stipp, D. (1987, April 4). Research on impotence upsets idea that it is usually psychological. *Wall Street Journal*, p. 1.

Stockham, A. (1883). *Tokology: A book for every woman*. Chicago: Sanitary Publishing.

Stoller, R. J. (1985). *Presentations of gender*. New Haven: Yale University Press.

Stoller, R. J. (1982). Transvestism in women. *Archives of Sexual Behavior, 2*, 99–115.

Stoller, R. J. (1979). *Sexual excitement*. New York: Pantheon.

Stoller, R. J. (1977). Sexual deviations.

In F. Beach (ed.), *Human sexuality in four perspectives*. pp. 190–214. Baltimore, MD: Johns Hopkins University Press.

Stoller, R. J. (1976). Gender Identity. In B. J. Saddock, H. I. Kaplan, & A. M. Freedman (eds.), *The sexual experience*. Baltimore, MD: Wilkins & Wilkins.

Stoller, R. J. (1975). Gender identity. In A. M. Freedman, H. I. Kaplan, & B. J. Saddock (eds.), *Comprehensive textbook of psychiatry/ II*, pp. 1400–1408. Baltimore, MD: Williams &

Stoller, R. J. (1968). *Sex and gender: On the development of masculinity and femininity*. New York: Science House.

Stoltenberg, J. (1981). Sexual objectification and male supremacy. *M, 5*:5ff.

Stone, K. M., Grimes, D. A., & Magder, L. S. (1986). Primary prevention of sexually transmitted diseases: A primer for clinicians. *Journal of the American Medical Association, 255*, 1763–1766.

Student Committee on Human Sexuality. (1970). *Sex and the Yale student*. New Haven: Yale University Press.

Sturup, G. K. (1979). Castration: The total treatment. In H. L. P. Resnick & M. E. Wolfgang (eds.), *Sexual behavior: Social and legal aspects*, pp. 361–382. Boston: Little, Brown.

Suchindram, C. M. (1978). Consequences of adolescent pregnancy and childbirth. *National Institute of Child Health and Development*.

Sue, D. (1979). Erotic fantasies of college students during coitus. *Journal of Sex Research, 15*, 299–305.

Suitters, B. (1967). *The history of contraceptives*. London: International Planned Parenthood Federation.

Sullivan, P. R. (1969). What is the role of fantasy in sex? *Medical Aspects of Human Sexuality, 3*(4), 79–89.

Sullivan, W. (1987, December 29). Sexual potency saved after surgery to remove prostate. *New York Times*, p. 16.

Sullivan, W. (1986, October 31). Scientists developing a new drug that blocks and terminates pregnancy. *New York Times*, p. 13.

Sulloway, F. J. (1979). *Freud, biologist of the mind*. New York: Basic.

Suomi, S. J., Harlow, H. F., & McKinney, W. T. (1972). Monkey psychiatrist. *American Journal of Psychiatry, 128*, 41–46.

Swan, G. (1986, December 1). Nevada's brothels imperiled. *San Francisco Chronicle*, p. 1.

Symons, D. (1979). *The evolution of human sexuality*. Oxford: Oxford University Press.

Szasz, T. (1980). *Sex by prescription*. New York: Anchor Press.

Taba, A. H. (1979). Female circumci-

sion. *World Health*. Geneva, Switzerland: World Health Organization.

Talese, G. (1980). *Thy neighbor's wife*. New York: Doubleday.

Tallent, N. (1977). Sexual deviation as a diagnostic entity: A confused and sinister concept. *Bulletin of the Menninger Clinic, 41*, 40–60.

Tangri, S., Burt, M., & Johnson, L. (1982). Sexual harassment at work: Three explanatory models. *Journal of Social Issues, 38*(4), 33–54.

Tannahill, R. (1980). *Sex in history*. New York: Stein & Day.

Tanner, J. M. (1984). Physical growth and development. In J. O. Forfar & G. C. Arneil (eds.), *Textbook of pediatrics*, 3d ed., Vol. 1, pp. 278–330. Edinburgh: Churchill Livingstone.

Tanner, J. M. (1978). *Fetus to man*. Cambridge, MA: Harvard University Press.

Tarabulcy, E. (1972). Sexual function in the normal and in paraplegia. *Paraplegia, 10*, 202–204.

Tatum, H. J. (1987). Contraception and family planning. In M. Pernoll & R. Benson (eds.), *Current obstetric and gynecologic diagnosis and treatment 1987*. Los Altos, CA: Appleton & Lange.

Taubman, S. (1986). Beyond the bravado: Sex roles and the exploitative male. *Social Work*, January–February, *31*(1), 12–18.

Tavris, C. (1978). The sex lives of happy men. *Redbook, 150*(5), 109ff.

Tavris, C., & Sadd, D. (1978). *The Redbook report on female sexuality*. New York: Delacorte.

Tavris, C., & Wade, C. (1984). *The longest war. Sex differences in perspective*, 2d ed. San Diego, CA: Harcourt Brace Jovanovich.

Taylor, C., & Pernoll, M. (1987). Normal pregnancy and prenatal care. In M. Pernoll & R. Benson (eds.), *Current Obstetric and Gynecologic Diagnosis and Treatment 1987*. Los Altos, CA: Appleton & Lange.

Taylor, D. A., Gould, R., & Brounstein, P. (1981). Effects of personalistic self-disclosure. *Personality and Social Psychology Bulletin, 7*, 487–492.

Taylor, G. R. (1970). *Sex in history*. New York: Harper & Row.

Tennov, D. (1979). *Love and limerence*. New York: Stein & Day.

Tennov, D. (1975). *Psychotherapy: The hazardous cure*. New York: Abelard-Schuman.

Terman, L. M., & Miles, C. (1936). *Sex and personality: Studies in masculinity and femininity*. (1936). New York: McGraw-Hill.

Terzian, H., & Dale-Ore, G. (1955). Syndrome of Kluver and Bucy reproduced in man by bilateral removal of temporal lobes. *Neurology, 5*,

373–380.

Thase, M., Reynolds, C., Glanz, L., Jennings, R. et al. (1987). Nocturnal penile tumescence in depressed men. *American Journal of Psychiatry*, January, *144*(1), 89–92.

Thevoz, M. (1984). *The painted body.* New York: Skira/Rizzoli.

Thielicke, H. (1964). *The ethics of sex.* J. W. Doberstein (ed.). New York: Harper & Row.

Thomas, D. (1976). *The Marquis de Sade.* Boston: Little, Brown.

Thompson, A. P. (1983). Extramarital sex: A review of the research literature. *Journal of Sex Research*, 19, 1–22.

Thompson, C. (1942). Cultural pressures in the psychology of women. In M. R. Green (ed.), *Interpersonal psychoanalysis: The selected papers of Clara Thompson.* New York: Basic Books, 1964.

Thompson, J. F. (1982). The vital statistics of reproduction. In D. N. Danforth (ed.), *Obstetrics and gynecology*, 4th ed. pp. 281–291. Philadelphia: Harper & Row.

Thompson, L. G. (1969). *Chinese religion: An introduction.* Belmont, CA: Dickenson.

Thompson, R. F. (1985). *The brain.* New York: W.H. Freeman.

Thompson, W. I. (1981). *The time falling take to light.* New York: St. Martin's.

Tiefier, L. (1978). The kiss. *Human Nature, 1*, 30–37.

Tietze, C. (1983). *Induced abortion: A world review*, 5th ed. New York: Population Council.

Tinbergen, N. (1951). *The study of instinct.* Oxford: Clarendon.

Tivan, E. (1987, October 11). Homosexuals and the churches. *New York Times Magazine*, pp. 84–91.

Tollison, C. D., & Adams, H. E. (1979). *Sexual disorders: Treatment, theory, research.* New York: Gardner Press.

Tolor, A., & DiGrazia, P. V. (1976). Sexual attitudes and behavior patterns during and following pregnancy. *Archives of Sexual Behavior, 5*, 539–551.

Tourney, G. (1980). Hormones and homosexuality. In J. Marmor (ed.), *Homosexual behavior*, pp. 41–50. New York: Basic.

*Towards a Quaker view of sex; An essay by a group of friends*, rev. ed. (1964). London: Friends Home Service Committee.

Trapp, J. D. (1987). Pharmacologic erection program for the treatment of male impotence. *Southern Medical Journal*, April, *80*(4), 426–427.

Traub-Werner, D. (1986). The place and value of bestophilia in perversions. *Journal of American Psychoanalysis Association, 34*(4), 975–992.

Travin, S., Bluestone, H., Coleman, E., Cullen, K., & Melella, J. (1986). Pedophile types and treatment perspectives. *Journal of Forensic Science*, April, *31*(2), 614–620.

Tripp, C. A. (1975). *The homosexual matrix.* New York: McGraw-Hill.

Troll, L. E. (1985). *Early and middle adulthood*, 2d ed. Monterey, CA: Brooks/Cole.

Truesdell, D., McNeil, J., & Deschner, J. (1986). Incidence of wife abuse in incestuous families. *Social Work*, March-April, *31*(2), 138–140.

Trussel, J., & Kost, K. (1987). Contraceptive failure in the United States: A critical review of the literature. *Studies in Family Planning, 18*(5), 237–283.

Trussel, J., & Westoff, C. F. (1980). Contraceptive practice and trends in coital frequency. *Family Planning Perspectives, 12*(5), 246–249.

Truxal, B. (1983). Nocturnal emissions. *Medical Aspects of Human Sexuality, 17*(7).

Tsung, S. H. et al. (1979). A Review: Adverse Effects of Oral Contraceptives. *Journal of the Indiana State Medical Association, 72*(8), 578–580.

Tutin, C. E. G. (1980). Reproductive behavior of wild chimpanzees in the Gombe National Park, Tanzania. In R. V. Short & B. J. Weir (eds.), *The great apes of Africa.* Reproduction and Fertility Suppl. *28*, pp. 43–57.

Twain, M. (1976). The stomach club: Some remarks on the science of onanism. In *The Mammoth Cod.* Milwaukee, WI: Maledicta.

Tyrmand, L. (1970). Permissiveness and rectitude. *The New Yorker, 46*, 85–86.

Udow, R. (1985). Censorship: An elitist weapon. *SIECUS Report*, July, *13*, 1–3.

Udry, J. R., Billy, J. O. G., Morris, N. M., Groff, T. R., & Raj, M. H. (1985a). Serum androgenic hormones motivate sexual behavior in adolescent boys. *Fertility and Sterility, 43*, 90–94.

Udry, J. R., & Morris, N. M. (1968). Distribution of coitus in the menstrual cycle. *Nature, 220*, 593–596.

Udry, J. R., Talbert, L., & Morris, N. M. (1985b). Biosocial foundations for adolescent female sexuality. Cited in National Research Council (1987), p. 96.

Ungar, S. B. (1982). The sex-typing of adult and child behavior in toy sales. *Sex Roles, 8*, 251–260.

Uniform Crime Reports. (1987). *Crime in the United States.* Washington, DC: U.S. Government Printing Office.

*Uniform Crime Reports.* (1987). Federal Bureau of Investigation, U.S. Department of Justice, Washington, DC.

*Uniform Crime Reports.* (1985). Federal Bureau of Investigation. Washington, DC: U.S. Government Printing Office.

U.S. Department of Justice. (1981). *National crime survey.* Washington, DC: U.S. Government Printing Office.

Vaillant, G. E. (1977). *Adaptation to life.* Boston: Little, Brown.

Valdiserri, E. V. (1986). Fear of AIDS: Implications for mental health practice with reference to ego-dystonic homosexuality. *American Journal of Orthopsychiatry*, October, *56*(4), 634–638.

Vance, C. (1985). Is it really a novel law? *Psychology Today*, April, 40.

Vance, E. B., & Wagner, N. N. (1976). Written descriptions of orgasms: A study of sex differences. *Archives of Sexual Behavior, 5*, 87–98.

Vandereycken, W. (1986). Towards a better delineation of ejaculatory disorders. *Acta Psychiatrica Belgica*, January-February, *86*(1), 57–63.

Van de Velde, T. E. (1965). *Ideal marriage.* New York: Random House.

Vanggaard, T. (1972). *Phallos.* New York: International Universities Press.

Vatsyayana. (1966). *The Kama Sutra.* R. F. Burton & F. F. Arbuthnot, translators. New York: Putnam.

Veevers, J. E. (1974). The life style of voluntarily childless couples. In L. Larson (ed.), *The Canadian family in comparative perspective.* Toronto: Prentice-Hall.

Veith. I. (1965). *Hysteria: The history of a disease.* Chicago: University of Chicago Press.

Vener, A. M., & Stewart, C. S. (1974). Adolescent sexual behavior in middle America revisited: 1970–1973. *Journal of Marriage and the Family, 36*, 728–735.

Verschoor, A. M., & Poortinga, J. (1988). Psychosocial differences between Dutch male and female transsexuals. *Archives of Sexual Behavior, 17*, 173–178.

Verwoerdt, A., Pfeiffer, E., & Wang, H. S. (1969). Sexual behavior in senescence, II: Patterns of change in sexual activity and interest. *Geriatrics, 24*, 137–154.

*Victoria's secret.* (1987). Catalogue. Columbus, OH.

Vida, G. (ed.). (1978). *Our right to love: A lesbian resource book.* Englewood Cliffs, NJ: Prentice-Hall.

Video turns big profit for porn products. (1982, March 10), *Variety, 306*, 35.

Virel, A., Lenars, C., & Lenars, J. (1979). *Decorated man.* New York: Harry N. Abrams.

Von Furstenberg, E. (1978). *The power look*. New York: Holt, Rinehart and Winston.

Wahl, P. et al. (1983). Effect of estrogen/progestin potency on lipid/lipoprotein cholesterol. *The New England Journal of Medicine, 308*(15), 862–867.

Waller, W. (1937). The rating and dating complex. *American Sociological Review, 2,* 727–734.

Wallis, C. (1987a, January 4). AIDS. *Time*.

Wallis, C. (1987b, October 12). Back off, buddy. *Time*, pp. 68–73.

Wallis, C. (1984, December 9). Children having children. *Time*, pp. 78–87.

Walsh, F. M. et al. (1977). Autoerotic asphyxial deaths: A medicolegal analysis of forty-three cases. In C. H. Wecht (ed.), *Legal Medicine Annual 1977*, pp. 157–182. New York: Appleton-Century-Crofts.

Walsh, P. (1985). Diseases of the prostate. In J. B. Wyngaarden & L. H. Smith (eds.), *Cecil textbook of medicine*, 17th ed., pp. 1375–1379. Philadelphia: W. B. Saunders.

Walster, E., & Walster, G. W. (1978). *A new look at love*. Reading, MA: Addison-Wesley.

Walster, P., Walster, G., & Berscheid, E. (1978). *Equity: theory and research*. Boston: Allyn & Bacon.

Washington, A. E., Cates, W., Jr., & Zaidi, A. A. (1984). Hospitalizations for pelvic inflammatory disease: Epidemiology and trends in the United States, 1975–1981. *Journal of the American Medical Association, 251,* 2529–2533.

Wasserstrom, R. A. (1971). *Morality and the law*. Belmont, CA: Wadsworth.

Watson, M. A., & Whitlock, F. (1982). *Breaking the bonds: The realities of sexually open relationships*. Denver, CO: Tudor House Press.

Watters, W. (1986). Supra-biological factors in the assessment of males seeking penile prostheses. *Canadian Journal of Psychiatry*, February, *31*(1), 25–31.

Waxenburg, S. E., Drellich, M. G., & Sutherland, A. M. (1959). The role of hormones in human behavior, I: Changes in female sexuality after adrenalectomy. *Journal of Clinical Endocrinology, 19,* 193–202.

Webb, P. (1975). *The erotic arts*. Boston: New York Graphic Society.

Webster, G. (1983). Sexual dysfunction in the paraplegic patient. *Medical Aspects of Human Sexuality, 17*(1).

Weg, R. B. (1983). The physiological perspective. In R. B. Weg (ed.), *Sexuality in the later years*. New York: Academic Press.

Wein, A. J., Fishkin, R., Carpiniello, V. L., & Malloy, T. R. (1981). Expansion without significant rigidity during noctural penile tumescence testing: A potential source of misinterpretation. *The Journal of Urology, 126,* 343–344.

Weinberg, G. (1973). *Society and the healthy homosexual*. New York: Anchor.

Weinberg, M. S., & Bell, A. (1972). *Homosexuality: An annotated bibliography*. New York: Harper & Row.

Weinberg, M. S., & Williams, C. J. (1974). *Male homosexuals: Their problems and adaptations*. New York: Penguin.

Weinberg, S. K. (1976). *Incest behavior*, rev. ed. Secaucus, NJ: Citadel.

Weinberg, T. S. (1987). Sadomasochism in the United States: A review of the recent sociological literature. *The Journal of Sex Research, 25*(1), 50–69.

Weis, D. L. (1983). Affective reactions of women and their initial experience of coitus. *Journal of Sex Research, 19,* 209–237.

Weis, D. L. (1983). Reactions of college women to their first coitus. *Medical Aspects of Human Sexuality, 17*(2).

Weisberg, M. (1981). A note on female ejaculation. *The Journal of Sex Research, 17,* 90.

Weiss, D. (1974). *Terror in the prisons: Homosexual rape and why society condones it*. New York: Bobbs-Merrill.

Weitzman, L. (1986). *The divorce revolution*. New York: Free Press.

Weitzman, L. J., Eifler, D., Hokada, E. & Ross, C. (1972). Sex-role socialization in picture books for pre-school children. *American Journal of Sociology, 77,* 1125–1150.

Welbourne-Moglia, A. (1984). Female sexual health. *SIECUS Report*, November, *13*(2).

Welbourne-Moglia, A., & Edwards, S. R. (1986). Sex education must be stopped. *SIECUS Report*, November/December, *15*(2), 1–3.

Wells, B. L. (1988). Predictors of female nocturnal orgasm: A multivariate analysis. *Journal of Sex Research, 22*(4), 421–438.

Wells, B. L. (1986). Predictors of female nocturnal orgasms. *Journal of Sex Research, 22,* 421–437.

Werner, L. M. (1987, January 24). Bennett and Surgeon General disagree on AIDS education. *New York Times*.

Wertz, R. W., & Wertz, D. C. (1979). *Lying-in: A history of childbirth in America*. New York: Free Press.

West, J. B. (ed.) (1985). *Best and Taylor's physiological basis of medical practice*, 11th ed. Baltimore, MD: Williams & Wilkins.

Westermarck, E. (1922). *The history of human marriage*. New York: Allerton.

Westoff, C. F. & Jones, E. F. (1977). The secularization of U.S. Catholic birth control practices. *Family Planning Perspectives, 9,* 203–207.

Westoff, C. F., & Rindfuss, R. R. (1974). Sex preselection in the United States: Some implications. *Science, 184,* 633–636.

Westwood, G. (1960). *A minority: A report on the life of the male homosexual in Great Britain*. London: Longman, Green.

White, E. (1981). *States of desire*. New York: Bantam.

White, G. L. (1981). Relative involvement, inadequacy, and jealousy: A test of a casual model. *Alternative Lifestyles, 4,* 291–309.

White, S., & Reamy, K. (1982). Sexuality and pregnancy: A review. *Archives of Sexual Behavior, 11*(5).

Whitley, B. E. (1983). Sex role orientation and self-esteem: A critical meta-analytic review. *Journal of Personality and Social Psychology, 44,* 765–778.

Whitman, F. (1983). Culturally invariable properties of male homosexuality: Tentative conclusions from cross-cultural research. *Archives of Sexual Behavior, 12*(3).

Whitman, F. (1977). Childhood indicators of male homosexuality. *Archives of Sexual Behavior, 6,* 89–96.

Whyte, L. L. (1960). *The unconscious before Freud*. New York: Basic.

Wickett, W. H., Jr. (1982). *Herpes: Cause and control*. New York: Pinnacle.

Wickler, W. (1972). *The sexual code*. Garden City, NY: Doubleday.

Wiesner, P. J. (1975). Gonococcal pharyngeal infection. *Clinical Obstetrics and Gynecology, 18,* 121–129.

Wigfall-Williams, W. (1987). *Hysterectomy: Learning the facts, coping with feelings, facing the future*. City: Michael Kesend.

Wild, N., & Wynne, J. (1986). Child sex rings. *British Medical Journal*, July 19, *293*(6540), 183–185.

Wilkins, L., Blizzard, R., & Migeon, C. (1965). *The diagnosis and treatment of endocrine disorders in childhood and adolescence*. Springfield, IL: Charles C Thomas.

Will, G. F. (1987, February 16). America gets condomized. *Newsweek*, p. 82.

Williams, J. H. (1987). *Psychology of women. Behavior in a biosocial context*. New York: W. W. Norton.

Williams, P. L., & Warwick, R. (1980). *Gray's anatomy*, 36th ed. Philadelphia: Saunders.

Wilmore, J. H. (1977). *Athletic training and physical fitness*. Boston: Allyn & Bacon.

Wilmore, J. H. (1975). Inferiority of female athletes: Myth or reality. *Journal of Sports Medicine, 3*(1), 1–6.

Wilson, E. O. (1978). *On human nature.* New York: Bantam.

Wilson, E. O. (1975a). *Sociobiology: The new synthesis.* Cambridge, MA: The Belknap Press of Harvard University Press.

Wilson, E. O. (1975b). *On human nature.* Cambridge, MA: Harvard University Press.

Wilson, G. (1983). *Sexual positions: A photographic guide to pleasure and love.* New York: Arlington.

Wilson, G. (1982). *The Coolidge effect.* New York: William Morrow.

Wilson, G. T., & Lawson, D. M. (1978a). Effects of alcohol on sexual arousal in women. *Journal of Abnormal Psychology, 87,* 609–616.

Wilson, G. T., & Lawson, D. M. (1978b). Effects of alcohol on sexual arousal in male alcoholics. *Journal of Abnormal Psychology, 87,* 609–616.

Wilson, J. D., Griffin, J. E., Leshin, M., & George, F. W. (1981). Role of gonadal hormones in development of the sexual phenotypes. *Human Genetics, 58*(1), 78–84.

Wilson, M. L., & Greene, R. L. (1971). Personality characteristics of female homosexuals. *Psychological Reports, 28,* 407–412.

Wilson, S. (1973). In R. Melville (ed.), *Erotic art of the West.* New York: Putnam.

Wincze, J., Bansal, S., & Malamud, M. (1986). Effects of medroxyprogesterone acetate on subjective arousal, arousal to erotic stimulation, and nocturnal penile tumescence in male sex offenders. *Archives of Sexual Behavior, August, 15*(4), 293–305.

Winick, C. (1985). A context analysis of sexually explicit magazines sold in adult bookstores. *Journal of Sex Research, 21*(2), 100–110.

Winkelstein, W., Jr., Lyman, D., Padian, N., Grant, R., Samuel, M., Wiley, J., Anderson, R., Lang, W., Riggs, J., & Levy, J. (1987). Sexual practices and risk of infection by the human immunodeficiency virus. The San Francisco Men's Health Study. *Journal of the American Medical Association,* January 16, *257*(3), 321–325.

Winn, R., & Newton, N. (1982). Sexuality in aging: A study of 106 cultures. *Archives of Sexual Behavior, 11,* 283–298.

Wise, T. (1985). Fetishism—Etiology and treatment: A review from multiple perspectives. *Comprehensive Psychiatry, 26,* 249–257.

Wise, T. (1982). Heterosexual men who cross-dress. *Medical Aspects of Human Sexuality, 16*(11).

Wise, T., Dupkin, C., & Meyer, J. K. (1981). Partners of distressed transvestites. *American Journal of Psychiatry, 138*(9), 1221–1224.

Wise, T., & Meyer, J. (1980). The border area between transvestism and gender dysphoria: Transvestitic applicants for sex reassignment. *Archives of Sexual Behavior, 9*(4), 327–342.

Witkin, H. A. et al. (1976). Criminality in XYY and XXY men. *Science, 193,* 547–555.

Wolf, A. (1970). Childhood association and sexual attraction: A further list of the Westermarck hypothesis. *American Anthropologist, 72,* 503–515.

Wolfe, L. (1981). *The Cosmo report.* Toronto: Bantam.

Wolfe, L. (1980, September). The sexual profile of that *Cosmopolitan* girl. *Cosmopolitan,* pp. 254–265.

Wolff, C. (1979). *Bisexuality: A study.* London: Quartet Books.

Wolfgang, M. E. (1958). *Patterns in criminal homicide.* Philadelphia: University of Pennsylvania Press.

*The Wolfenden report.* (1963). New York: Stein & Day.

Wolpe, J., & Lazarus, A. A. (1966). *Behavior therapy techniques.* New York: Pergamon.

Wong, E. (1983). Nongonococcal urethritis. *Medical Aspects of Human Sexuality, 17*(8).

Wyatt, G., & Peters, S. (1986). Issues in the definition of child sexual abuse in prevalence research. *Child Abuse and Neglect, 10*(2), 231–240.

Wyngaarden, J. B., & Smith, L. H. (eds.). (1988). *Cecil textbook of medicine.* Philadelphia: Saunders.

Yalom, I. D. et al. (1968). Postpartum blues syndrome. *Archives of General Psychiatry, 18,* 16–27.

Yalom, I. D. (1960). Aggression and forbiddenness in voyeurism. *Archives of General Psychiatry, 3,* 305–319.

Yankelovich, D. (1981, November). Stepchildren of the moral majority. *Psychology Today, 15.*

Yankelovich, D. (1976–1977). *Raising children in a changing society.* The General Mills American Family Report.

Yarrow, A. L. (1987, January 12). Divorce at a young age: The troubled 20s. *New York Times.*

Yen, S. (1986). Endocrine physiology of pregnancy. In D. Danforth & J. Scott (eds.), *Obstetrics and gynecology,* 5th ed. Philadelphia: J.B. Lippincott.

Yilo, K., & Straus, M. A. (1981). Interpersonal violence among married and cohabiting couples. *Family Relations, 30*(3), 339–347.

Ying, S., Becker, A., Ling, N., Ueno, N., & Guillemin, R. (1986). Inhibin and Beta type transforming growth factor have opposite modulating effects on the follicle stimulating hormone-induced aromatase activity of cultured rat granulosa cells. *Biochemical and Biophysical Research Communications, 136*(3), 969–975.

Young, W. (1970). Prostitution. In J. D. Douglas (ed.), *Observations of deviance.* New York: Random House.

Yupze, A. (1982). Postcoital contraception. *International Journal of Gynecology and Obstetrics, 16,* 497–501.

Zacharias, L., Rand, W. M., & Wurtman, R. J. (1976). A prospective study of sexual development and growth in American girls: The statistics of menarche. *Obstetrics, gynecological survey* (suppl.), *31,* 325–337.

Zelnik, M. (1980). Sexual activity, contraceptive use, and pregnancy among metropolitan-area teenagers: 1971–1979. *Family Planning Perspectives, 12,* 230–237.

Zelnik, M. (1979). Sex education and knowledge of pregnancy risk among United States teenage women. *Family Planning Perspectives, 11,* 335.

Zelnik, M., Kanter, J. F., & Ford, K. (1981). *Sex and pregnancy in adolescence.* Beverly Hills, CA: Sage.

Zelnik, M., & Kantner, J. F. (1980). Sexual activity, contraceptive use and pregnancy among metropolitan area teenagers: 1971–1979. *Family Planning Perspectives, 12*(5), 230–231, 233–237.

Zelnik, M., & Kantner, J. F. (1977). Sexual and contraceptive experience of young unmarried women in the U.S. 1976 and 1971. *Family Planning Perspectives, 9,* 55–71.

Zelnik, M. & Kantner, J. F. (1972). Sexuality, contraception and pregnancy among young unwed females in the United States. In C. F. Westoff & R. Parke, Jr. (eds.), *Commission on population growth and the American future: Research Reports, Vol 2: Demographic and social aspects of population growth.* Washington, DC: Government Printing Office.

Zelnik, M., & Kim, Y. J. (1982). Sex education and its association with teenage sexual activity, pregnancy and contraceptive use. *Family Planning Perspectives, 14*(3).

Zelnik, M., Kim, Y. J., & Kantner, J. F. (1979). Probabilities of intercourse and conception among U.S. teenage women, 1971 and 1976. *Family Planning Perspectives, 11,* 177–183.

Zelnik, M., & Shah, F. K. (1983). First intercourse among young Americans. *Family Planning Perspectives, 15,* 64–70.

Zelnik, M., & Shah, Y. (1983). Sex education and its association with teenage sexual activity, pregnancy and contraceptive use. *Family Planning Perspectives, 14,* 117–126.

Zilbergeld, B. (1978). *Male sexuality: A guide to sexual fulfillment*. Boston: Little, Brown.

Zilbergeld, B., & Evans, M. (1980). The inadequacy of Masters and Johnson. *Psychology Today, 14*.

Zimmer, D., Borchardt, E., & Fischle, C. (1983). Sexual fantasies of sexually distressed and nondistressed men and women: An empirical comparison. *Journal of Sex and Marital Therapy, 9*, 38–50.

Zimmerman, D. H., & West, C. (1975). Sex roles, interruptions, and silences in conversation. In B. Thorne & N. Henley (eds.), *Language and sex: Difference and dominance*. Rowley, MA: Newbury House.

Zuckerman, L. (1988, March 7). Open season on gays. *Time*, p. 24.

Zuger, B. (1976). Monozygotic twins discordant for homosexuality: Report of a pair and significance of the phenomenon. *Comprehensive Psychiatry, 17*, 661–669.

Zverina, S., Lachman, M., Pondelickova, J., & Vanek, J. (1987). The occurrence of a typical sexual experience among various female patient groups. *Archives of Sexual Behavior, 16*(4).

# Subject Index

Abortion, 211–216
  alternatives to, 215
  availability of, 630
  and the beginning of life, 633, 661
  changing church views of, 661
  contention over, 611–612
  elective, 211
  emotional reactions to, 215–216
  federal funding of, 630–631
  illegal, 211–212
  issues in, 633
  laws affecting, 211, 630–631
  live births resulting from, 213
  methods of, 212–215
  psychological aspects of, 214–216
  reactions to, 215–216
  and reactions to unwanted pregnancy, 214–215
  risks of, 211–212, 213, 214
  spontaneous, 177, 211
  and teenage pregnancy, 267
  therapeutic, 211
  women choosing, 211
Abstinence, 192, 261
Acceptance and sexual satisfaction, 358
Acetylcholine, 78
Acne, 89
Acquaintance rape, 547, 548–550
Acquired immunodeficiency syndrome (AIDS), 132–145
  antibodies to, 138
  antibody test for, 139, 140
  casual conduct not transmitting, 137
  causative agent of, 134
  and choice of sex partner, 142–143
  counseling for, 139
  course of infection, 138
  effect of virus on immune system, 134
  estimating partner's risk for, 144
  legal issues, 634–636
  mandatory testing for, 634–635
  number of cases, 133
  origin of, 133
  as precursor of other diseases, 137–138
  prevention of, 141–145
  quarantine for, 635–636
  reactions to, 132–133
  and risk-taking behaviors, 143–145
  safe sex to avoid, 142–143
  symptoms of, 137–138
  testing for, 139, 140
  transmission of, 134–137

Acquired immunodeficiency syndrome (AIDS) (cont.)
  treatment of, 139–141
  unreliability of tests for, 634–635
  vaccination for, 141–142
Acrosome reaction, 156
Acyclovir, 130–131
Addictive love, 466, 470
Adolescence, 86
  balancing social norms during, 616–617
  gender differences in, 288–289
Adolescent sexuality, 253–267
  adapting to puberty, 253–256
  changing body image, 254–255
  consequences of sexual intercourse, 264–266. See also Teenage pregnancy
  early and late maturers, 255–256
  effect of gender stereotyping on, 289
  erotic dreams, 257–258
  homosexual relations, 261
  masturbation, 258
  oral sex, 260
  peer culture, 262
  petting, 258–260
  reactions to, 262
  sex and adult status, 262
  sex education for adolescents, 267
  sexual drive, 256
  sexual fantasies, 256–257
  sexual intercourse, 260–261
  sexual values, 261–262
Adoption, as an alternative to abortion, 215
Adrenal cortex, 82
Adrenal glands, 82
Adrenogenital syndrome, 101
Adultery, 494–495
  laws concerning, 637
  punishments for, 500, 638
  See also Extramarital sex
Adulthood, gender differences in, 289–290
Adult sexual interactions with children, 238–239
  See also Child sexual abuse
Affection, 462
  See also Love
Affection and trust, and sexual satisfaction, 358
Afferent nerves, 76
Affiliative needs, 458

Afterbirth, 168
Agape, 462
Age
  and childbearing, 181–182
  and fertility, 179, 181–182
Aggressive elements in sex, 534–537
  coercion, 537
  dominance, 534–536
  hostility, 536–537
Aggressive pedophiles, 389
AIDS. See Acquired immunodeficiency syndrome
AIDS-related complex, 138
Alcohol
  and rape, 549–550, 561
  and sexual dysfunction, 422–423
  and sexual response, 357
  use of during pregnancy, 177
Aldosterone, role in premenstrual syndrome, 98
Alimony, 627
Alpha-androstenol, 103
Altruism, 654
Ambisexual, 363
  See also Bisexual
Amenorrhea, 94
Amniocentesis, 161, 162
Amniotic fluid, 157
Amoral rapists, 559
Amphetamines and sexual response, 257
Amyl nitrate and sexual response, 357
Anabolic agents, 83
Analgesics, 96, 170
Anal intercourse, 351–352
  AIDS transmission by, 135
  and risk of AIDS, 352
  See also Sodomy
Anal stage, 243–244
Anal stimulation, 341
Androgen insensitivity, 101–102
Androgens, 82–83
  effect on genital differentiation, 52
  and female sex drive, 110
  functions of, 83
  See also Antiandrogenic drugs
Androgyny, 284–286
  benefits of, 286
  effects of, 285–286
  and gender schema theory, 286
  increased acceptance of, 284
  Sex Role Inventory (BSRI), 285

Anger rape, 560
Anilingus, 341
Animal behavior, relevance to human behavior, 5
Animal instincts, 240–241
Animus and anima, 282
Anorexia, 445
Anorgasmia, 418
  treatment for, 430–431
Anovulatory cycles, 92
Anthropology, contributing to study of sex, 6–7
Antiandrogenic drugs, 107, 408
  and sexual dysfunction, 423
  to treat sex offenders, 408
Antibody tests for AIDS, 139, 140
Antihypertensives and sexual dysfunction, 423
Antipregnancy vaccine, 211
Antiprostaglandins, 96
Antipsychotic agents and sexual dysfunction, 423
Antiviral drugs, 139–141
Anxiety and sexual satisfaction, 358
Aphrodisiacs and sexual enhancement, 356, 357
Appearance and sexual enhancement, 354
Areola, 40
Arousal in response to erotica, 298–299
Art
  contribution to study of sex, 8
  See also Erotic art and literature
Artificial insemination, 181–182
Asexual homosexuals, 273
Asexual reproduction, 31–32
Attachment and love, 464
Attorney General's Commission on Pornography, 522–524
  anti-pornography bias of members, 522
  conclusions not supported by evidence, 523
  reactions to, 524
  See also Pornography
Atypical sexual development, 98–102
  chromosome disorders, 100–101
  delayed puberty, 98
  hermaphroditism, 100
  hormone disorders, 101
  precocious puberty, 98, 99
  sexual infantilism, 98
  tissue disorders, 101–102
Autoeroticism, 309–331
Autoerotic play, 224–225
Autoimmune reactions, 208
Autonomic nervous system, 76
Autonomous ego, 243
Averages, 22
Aversion therapy to treat paraphilias, 409
Azidothymidine (AZT), 140

Baby boom, 604
Barrier methods of birth control, 198–202
  cervical cap, 199
  condom, 200–201
  contraceptive sponge, 199–200
  diaphragm, 198–199
  freedom from side effects, 198
  spermicides, 201–202
Bartholin's glands, 40
Basal body temperature method of fertility control, 203–204
Battered wives, 537
  marital rape suffered by, 550
Beat generation, 605
Behavior therapy for sexual dysfunction, 433–434
Behavior therapy to treat paraphilias, 409
Being-love, 464
Being single, 487–491
  attitudes toward, 488
  by choice, 488
  at different ages, 487
  the divorced, 489–491. See also Divorce
  the never married, 488–489
  sexual activity among the never married, 501–502
  single-parent households, 487–488
  the widowed, 491, 503
Bestiality, 394–395
Bias in sex research, 19
Bioimpedance analyzer, 60–61
Biological determinants of sexual orientation, 376–378
  brain differences, 378
  genetic factors, 377
  hormonal factors, 377–378
Biologically based treatment for paraphilias, 408
Biological perspectives on study of sexuality, 3–5
Biological roots of paraphilias, 407
Biphasic model of sexual function, 413
Biphasic pill, 196
Bipolar hypothesis of orgasm, 74–75
Birth control. See Contraception
Birth control methods. See Contraceptive techniques
Birth control pills, 95, 193–195
  biphasic, 194
  combination, 193–194
  development of, 193
  diaphasic, 194
  effect on female sex drive, 110
  failure rate of, 196
  forms of, 193–194
  male, 210
  minipill, 194
  positive side effects of, 195
  postcoital pill, 195–196, 214
  risks posed by, 194–195
  sequential, 194

Birth control pills (cont.)
  side effects of, 194–195
  triphasic, 194
Birth defects, 178–179
  causes of, 178–179
  risks posed by birth control pills, 195
Birthing centers, 168, 170
Bisexuality, 363, 365
Bisexual potential, 378
Blastocyst, 156
Blindness
  caused by chlamydia, 123
  caused by gonorrhea, 122
Blood transfusions, AIDS transmission by, 137
Bloody show, 168
Body ego, 291
Body image, 448
  changes in adolescence, 254–255
  influenced by reactions of others, 255
Bondage, 341
Bonding, 173, 231–233
  effects of, in maturity, 232–233
  optimal time for, 232
  role of infant in, 232
  role of mother in, 232
Bony pelvis, 32
Brain
  influence of testosterone on, 104
  medial preoptic area of, 104
  sex differences in, 104
  sexual dimorphism in, 106–107, 291
Brain differences and sexual orientation, 378
Brain mechanisms controlling sexual function, 78–80
Breast cancer, 116–117
  risk factors, 116
  self-examination, 117
  treatment of, 116
Breasts, 40–41
  development of, 87
  effect of sexual arousal on, 68–69
  enlargement of, 40–41
  stimulation of, 337–338
Brothel, 510
Buggery, 362
Bulbourethral glands, 40, 45, 46
Bulimia, 445

Calendar awareness method of fertility control, 203
Call boys, 511
Call girls, 510–511
Cancer, 116–120
  of the breast, 116–117
  of the cervix, 118
  of the endometrium, 118
  of the penis, 120
  of the prostate, 118–119
  risks posed by birth control pills, 197
  of the testes, 119–120
Candidiasis, 115
Capacitation, 156

722

Caressing and touching, 335–337
Caring and affection in sexual intimacy, 456
Carpopedal spasm, 69
Case history, 11
Case study, 22
Castration, 83
  anxiety, 378
  effects of, 104–105, 108, 107
  to treat paraphilias, 408
Casual sex, 451
Caudal block, 170
Causes of sexual dysfunction, 420–427
  alcohol, 422–423
  circulatory disorders, 422
  cultural, 426–427
  disease, 412
  distinguishing organic from psychogenic, 423–424
  drugs, 423
  endocrine disorders, 421
  illness, 421
  interpersonal, 425–426
  intrapsychic, 424
  neurological disorders, 421–422
  organic causes, 420–424
  power struggles, 426
  psychogenic, 424–427
  trauma, 421
Celibacy, 489, 503
Central arousal, 56
Cervical canal, 39
Cervical cancer, 118
Cervical cap, 199
Cervical mucus method of fertility control, 204
Cervicitis
  caused by chlamydia, 123
  caused by gonorrhea, 122
Cervix, 38
Cesarean section, 171
Chadwick's sign, 160
Chancres, syphilitic, 125–126
Chancroid, 126, 127
Childbearing, AIDS transmission in, 137
Childbirth, 167–173
  analgesics used, 170
  anesthesia used, 170
  by cesarean section, 171
  false labor, 168
  home delivery, 170
  hospital delivery, 171
  induction of labor, 171
  Lamaze method, 172
  Leboyer method, 172–173
  midwives assisting, 167–168
  natural, 171–173
  premature, 177–178
  prepared, 171–173
  stages of labor, 168
  See also Postpartum period
Child custody, 628
  awarded to homosexuals, 640

Child-free lifestyle, 185
Childhood, gender differences in, 287–288
Childhood sexuality
  inborn responsive capacity, 222–224
  study of, 221–222
  See also Sexual behavior in childhood
Childlessness, choice of, 185–187
Child pornography, 520–521, 524
  See also Pornography
Children, desire to have, 149
Child sexual abuse, 238–239, 388
  impact on child, 390–391
  laws against, 644
  and rape, 561
  See also Pedophilia
Chlamydia, 123
Chorionic gonadotrophin, 157
Chorionic villi sampling, 161, 162
Christianity, rise of, 579–582
Christianity and sexuality
  and apocalyptic expectation, 580–581
  Calvinism, influence on, 588, 590
  Catholic morality, new directions in, 666–667
  Catholic statement on sexuality, 664–666
  Gnosticism, and concept of marriage, 581–582
  Judaic sexual attitudes, influence of, 579–580
  Luther's opinions, 588
  Manicheanism, challenge of, 582
  in the Middle Ages, 582–587
  New Testament teachings, 657–658, 659–661
  original sin associated with sexuality, 582
  in the Patristic Age, 581
  Protestant sexual ethic, 587–588, 589
    reactions to Renaissance church, 587
  St. Augustine, influence of on Catholic doctrine, 581, 582
  St. Paul, influence of, 580–581, 657–658
  sexual conservatives, 613–614
  stoicism, influence of, 580, 581
Chromosomes, 47
  disorders, 100–101
Cilia, 38
Circumcision, 43
  female, 34
Classical conditioning, 246–247
  and sexual response, 247
Climacteric, 273. See also Menopause
Clinical research, 22–23
  problems with, 23
Clitoral hood, 33
Clitoral orgasm, 70–71
Clitoridectomy, 34
Clitoris, 33
  glans of, 34
Clomiphene, 181

Close couples, 372
Closed swinging, 497
Clothing and sexual enhancement, 356
Cocaine and sexual response, 357
Codpiece, 535
Coercion, 454, 537
Coercive sex, 537. See also Rape
Cognitive development models, 245–246
Cognitive labeling, 465
Cohabitation, 457, 474, 483–486
  prevalence of, 483
  pros and cons of, 483, 485–486
  reasons for choosing, 485–486
  and subsequent marriage, 486
Cohabiting couples, sexual activity of, 500–501
Coital fantasy, 314–315
Coital postures, 343–348
  advantage of variety, 344
  among animals, 343
  face-to-face, 344–347
  man-above, 344–345
  rear-entry, 347
  seated, 346
  side-by-side, 345–346
  standing, 346–347
Coital thrusts, 348
Coitus, 334, 342–359
  acceptance important to, 358
  affection and trust important to, 358
  anal intercourse, 351–352
  and aphrodisiacs, 356, 357
  coital movements, 348
  communication important to, 358–359
  enhancing, 352–359
  erotic aids and practices for, 355–356
  freedom from anxiety important to, 358
  gender considerations, 357–358
  intromission, 342–343
  male and female reactions to, 300–301
  orgasmic control during, 348–350
  physical factors enhancing, 354
  postures for, 343–347. See also Coital postures
  reciprocity important to, 358
  scents enhancing, 355
  sensations following, 352
  setting enhancing, 354–355
  simulating, 351–352
  sounds and music enhancing, 355–356
Coitus interruptus, 205–206, 351
Coitus reservatus, 71, 73–74, 350
Colostrum, 174
Comarital sex, 495
  patterns of, 496–497
  See also Extramarital sex
Combination pill, 195–196
Commission on Pornography (1970), 522

Commitment, 667–668
  in sexual intimacy, 457
Common-law marriages, 474
Communes, 474, 487
Communication
  in sexual intimacy, 455–456
  and sexual satisfaction, 358–359
Communion, 457
Companionate love, 467
Conception, 149–156
  fertilization, 155–156
  implantation, 156
  route of egg, 150
  route of sperm, 150
Concubine, 495
Conditioned reflex, 247
Conditioned response (CR), 247
Conditioned stimulus (CS), 247
Conditioning, 246–247
Condoms, 200–201
  failure rate of, 200
  to protect against AIDS, 136, 142,
    200
  to protect against sexually transmit-
    ted diseases, 201
Condylomata acuminata, 131
Confidentiality in sex research, 20
Congenital adrenal hyperplasia (CAH),
    101, 291, 294
Congenital malformations, 178–179
Conjunctivitis caused by chlamydia,
    123
Consanguity laws, 644
  in Judaic tradition, 569–570
Conservative sexual morality,
    654–662
  arguments based on natural law to
    refute, 661–662
  arguments based on natural law to
    support, 658
  biblical arguments against, 659–661
  biblical grounds for, 657–658
  case against, 658–662
  case for, 656–658
  and changing church doctrine, 661
  current Catholic standards, 654–656
  prohibiting masturbation and homo-
    sexuality, 656
  prohibiting premarital and extra-
    marital sex, 656
  and sex and reproduction, 654–656
  traditional Christian teaching sup-
    porting, 658
Contextual ethics, 668–669
Contraception
  access to, 187–188
  Catholic opposition to, 661
  Catholic teaching on, 654–656
  conservative moral attitude toward,
    654–656
  factors correlating with use of, 189
  laws affecting, 629
  and need for population control,
    187

Contraception (cont.)
  need to take responsibility for,
    191–192
  prevalence of use of, 187–189
  primitive methods, 186
  provided by high school clinics, 267
  reasons for not using, 189–191
  reasons for using, 185–187
  risks of, 191
  and the sexual revolution, 603
  for teenagers, 611
  women considered responsible for,
    189
Contraceptive methods, 192–206
  abstinence, 192
  antipregnancy vaccine, 211
  barrier methods, 198–201
  birth control pills, 193–195, 210
  cervical cap, 199
  choice of, 188
  condoms, 200–201
  contraceptive sponge, 199–200
  contraceptive vaginal rings, 210
  diaphragm, 198–199
  failure rates of, 192, 194, 196–197,
    198, 199, 200, 202, 203, 205, 207
  fertility awareness techniques,
    203–205
  future prospects for, 209–211
  hormonal implants, 210
  hormonal methods, 192–196, 210
  intrauterine devices, 196–198,
    210–211
  male pills, 209–210
  postcoital pill, 195–196, 214
  primitive, 186
  prolonged nursing, 205
  spermicides, 201–202
  sponges, 199–200
  sterilization, 206–209
  vaginal rings, 210
  withdrawal, 205–206
Contragestion, 195–196
Coolidge effect, 461
Cooperation and sexual intimacy, 454
Coprophilia, 405
Copulation, 32. See also Coitus
Core gender identity, 282
  interactional models for develop-
    ment, 290–291
Corona of penis, 41
Corona radiata of ovum, 50
Corpora cavernosa, 34, 41
Corpus luteum, 49
Corpus spongiosum, 41
Counseling for AIDS victims, 139
Counterculture, 604–606
  effect of, 606
  elements of, 604–605
Courtship, 476. See also Mate selection
Courtship behavior
  among animals, 301–302
  among humans, 302
Couvade, 166

Cowper's glands, 46
Creation myths, 10
Cremasteric muscle, 44
Cremasteric reflex, 44
Cryptorchidism, 51–52
Crystallization, 466
Cue stimuli, 240
Culdoscopy, 208
Culture, 601
Cunnilingus, 338, 339, 340
Curette, 213
Cybernetic system, 84
Cyproterone, 107
Cystitis, 115
Cytoplasm of ovum, 50

Danazol, 210
Date rape, 548–550
Dating, 259–260
Deception in sex research, 20–21
Defense mechanisms, 243
Deficiency-love, 464
Defloration, 35
Deillusionment, 272
Delectatio morosa, 309
Delivery room, 170
Delusions, 313
Dependency and love, 464
Detumescence, 60
Developmental theories, 239
Diaphragm, 198–199
  disposable, 198
Diethylstilbestrol (DES), 195
Dihydrotestosterone, 292
  effect on differentiation of genitals,
    52
Dilation and curettage (D and C), 213
Dilation and evacuation (D and E), 213
Direct observation and experimenta-
    tion, 25–26
Divorce, 489–491
  age as a cause, 489–490
  and chance of remarriage, 490–491
  consequences of, 490–491
  effects of, on children, 491
  factors increasing likelihood of, 490
  grounds for, 627
  increase in rate of, 612
  racial and sex differences, 489
  sexual activity following, 502–503
  trends in, 489
Divorce law, 627
  and child custody, 628
Dizygotic twins, 156
Dominance, 341, 534–536
  in animals, 534
  link with power and status, 535–536
  penis as a symbol of, 535
  significance for sexual behavior,
    534–535
Dopamine, 465
Double standard for aging, 277, 290
Double standard for sexual behavior,
    262, 303, 426

724

Down's syndrome, 178
Dreaming, 319
  neurophysiology of, 319
  *See also* Sexual dreams
Drive, 241
Drive reduction theory, 241
Drugs
  during pregnancy, 177
  and sexual dysfunction, 423
Drug treatment for sexual dysfunction,
  435–436
Dysfunctional homosexuals, 372
Dysmenorrhea, 95–96
  remedies for, 96
Dyspareunia, 419–420

Eclampsia, 177
Ectoderm, 157
Ectopic pregnancy, 156, 177
Edema, 96
Effeminate men, 294
Efferent nerves, 76
Ego, 243
Ejaculation, 71–72
  control of, 73–74
  expulsion phase of, 71
  premature, 418–419, 431–432
  retarded, 419
  seminal emission phase of, 71
  spinal control of, 76–77
Ejaculatory centers, 76–77
Ejaculatory duct, 45
Ejaculatory incompetence, 419
Elective homosexuality, 365
Electronic perineometer, 61
Embryo, 156
Embryonal development
  during first trimester, 156–158
  theories of, 159
Embryonic disk, 157
Embryo transfer, 182
Empathy in sexual intimacy, 457
Endocrine disorders causing sexual
  dysfunction, 421
Endocrine glands, 82
Endoderm, 157
Endometrial cancer, 118
Endometrium, 39
Endorphins, role in premenstrual syn-
  drome, 98
Enteric organisms, causing sexually
  transmitted diseases, 127–128
Enzyme-linked immunosorbent assay
  (ELISA), 140
Epididymis, 45
Epigenesis, 159, 245
Episiotomy, 170
Erectile dysfunction, 415–416
  treatment for, 429–430
Erection, spinal control of, 76–78
Erection centers, 76
Erogenous zones, 57, 335
Eros, 462
Erotica, 298

Erotica (*cont.*)
  male and female responses com-
    pared, 298–299
Erotic art and literature, 8–9
  in ancient Greece, 575–577
  in ancient Rome, 578–579
  during the Enlightenment, 591–592
  libertinism, 591
  in the Renaissance, 589
  in the twentieth century, 598–599
  in the Victorian period, 594–595
  *See also* Pornography
Erotic dreams in adolescence, 257–258
Erotic fantasy, 309–317
  aggression in, 317
  coital fantasies, 314–315
  delusions, 313
  examples of, 311, 312
  as exploration and experimentation,
    311, 313
  frequency of, 309–310
  fulfilling, 315–316
  gender differences in, 316–317
  hostility in, 317
  masturbatory fantasies, 313–314
  mirroring problems, 313
  nature of, 310–313
  patterns of, 310
  and pornography, 316, 317
  as prelude to or substitute for sex,
    315–316
  problems with, 313
  purposes of, 310–312
  and rape, 315
  revealing to partner, 314–315
  and sexual behavior, 313–317
  themes for, 310, 316
  theoretical perspectives on, 317
  as wish fulfillment, 310–311
Erotic fetishism, 396
Eroticism, in Eastern religions,
  670–671
Erotic kissing, 334
Erotic love. *See* Love
Erotic themes in Greek mythology, 576
Erotic themes in religious traditions, 10
Escort services, 510
Estradiol, 83
Estrogen, 36, 49
  functions of, 83
Estrogen replacement therapy (ERT),
  274
Estrus, 102, 105–106
Estrus cycle, 91
Ethical considerations in sex research,
  20–21
Ethical dimension of sexual behavior,
  10
Ethinyl estradiol, 195
Evolution, 5
Excitement and plateau phases of sex-
  ual arousal, 63–69
  effect on female sex organs, 64–68
  effect on male sex organs, 64

Exclusivity, 459
Exhibitionism, 400–401
  laws against, 644–645
Exploitation, 506
  and power, 508
  in sexual relationships, 508
  *See also* Sexual exploitation
Exploration and experimentation, 311,
  313
Expulsion phase, 71
Extended family, 475
External fertilization, 32
External sex organs, 32
  differentiation of, 52–54
  female, 32–36, 37
  male, 41–45
External sphincter, 45–46
Extramarital sex, 494–500
  and AIDS risk, 499
  comarital, 495, 496–497
  consensual, 496–497
  conservative position against, 656
  disappointment with, 497–498
  effects of, 499–500
  emotional dependency in, 496
  gender differences in, 498–499
  institutionalized, 495
  justifications for, 499–500
  and life phases, 498
  moral considerations, 500
  motivations for, 497–498
  and open marriage, 496
  patterns of, 495–497
  prevalence of, 498–499
  reactions to, 500
  retaliatory, 498
  and spousal exchange, 496–497
  swinging, 497

Facultative homosexuality, 365
Fallopian tubes, 38
False labor, 168
Family, 474–476
  changes in patterns of, 479
  demographic changes affecting,
    477–479
  extended, 475
  impact of sexual revolution on, 612
  nuclear, 474–476
  single-parent, 487–488
Family law, 627
Family network systems, 474
Family planning, 185
Family role in sexual socialization,
  234–236
  sex education at home, 234–235
  sexual communication at home,
    235–236
Fathers' experience during pregnancy,
  165–167
Feedback, 84–85
Fellatio, 338, 340
Female circumcision, 34
Female ejaculation, 67–68

Female midlife transition, 273–275
    demographic realities affecting, 275
    menopausal symptoms and treatment, 273–274
    psychosocial changes, 274–275
Female prostitutes, 509–511
    See also Prostitution
Female reproductive maturation, 87–88
Female sex drive
    androgens responsible for, 110
    effect of oral contraceptives on, 110
Female sex organs
    effect of orgasm on, 72, 74
    effect of sexual arousal on, 64–69
    external, 32–36, 37
    internal, 36–40
Female sexual-arousal disorder, 416, 418
Female sexual drive, 109–110
Female sexuality
    current attitudes toward, 606–607
    liberation of, 606–607
Female sterilization, 208–209
    risks of, 209
Feminine mystique, 603
Feminism, 603–604
    See also Women's liberation movement
Fertility awareness techniques, 203–205
    basal body temperature method, 203–204
    calendar method, 203
    cervical mucus method, 204
    failure rate of, 203, 204–205
Fertility control, 185
Fertility symbols, 567
Fertilization, 155–156
Fetal alcohol syndrome, 177
Fetal development
    during second trimester, 161
    during third trimester, 163
Fetal position, 163
Fetal pulse detector, 161
Fetishism, 395–397
    erotic, 396
    hard, 396
    object, 396
    partialism, 396
    psychological characteristics of fetishists, 397
    soft, 396
    transvestite, 294
    types of, 396–397
Fetus, 156
    determining sex of, 155
    viability of, 178
Film, contribution to study of sex, 9
Fimbriae, 38
5-alpha-reductase deficiency, 292
Follicle-stimulating hormone (FSH), 84
Follicular phase, 92–94

Foreplay, 334
    See also Sexual stimulation
Fornication laws, 637
Fortuitous labeling, and homosexuality, 379
Freudian theories, 241, 243–244
    criticisms of, 244–245
Friendship, 462
Frigidity, 412
Frotteurism, 405
Functional homosexuals, 372
Fundus of the uterus, 39

Gamete development, 46–50
Gametogenesis, 47
Gay bars, 376
Gay baths, 376
Gay communities, 371
Gay couples, 486
Gay liberation, 607–609
Gay liberation movement, 370, 609
Gay marriage, 474
Gays, 362
    See also Homosexuality
Gender and sexual behavior, 297–304
    differences explained, 301–305
    relational aspects of, 300–301
Gender-aschematic individuals, 286
Gender differences
    in adolescence, 288–289
    in adulthood, 289–290
    affecting behavior, 290
    assessing, 286–287
    and casual sex, 451
    in childhood, 287–288
    in erotic fantasy, 316–317
    expectations of, 287
    in extramarital sex, 498–499
    in homosexual relationships, 373
    in infancy, 287
    influences on, 288
    among never married, 488–489
    in orgasmic capacity, 299–300
    in perception of sexual harassment, 539–540
    in physical ability, 87
    in response to erotica, 298–299
    and self-disclosure, 455–456
    and sexual attraction, 447–449
    in sexual drive and behavior, 297–298
    and sexual exploitation, 508–509
    and sexual intimacy, 459–461
    in sexual negotiation, 453–454
    in sexual socialization, 302–304
    in social interactions, 281
    tests, 284–285
Gender disorders, 294–297
    gender-dysphoria syndrome, 295–297
    gender-identity disorder of childhood, 294–295
    later gender-identity disorder, 295
    transsexualism, 295–297
    transvestite fetishism, 294

Gender identity, 281–282
    defined, 282
    disorders of, 294–295
    importance of rearing to, 291–294
    of pseudohermaphrodites, 102
    and sexual orientation, 364–365
Gender-identity development, 290–294
    critical period of, 292
    effect of prenatal hormones on, 293–294
    interactional models of, 290–291
    preeminence of rearing in, 291–293
    sexual dimorphic behavior, 293–294
    special cases, 291–293
Gender model, 285
Gender neutrality, 292
Gender nonconformity, 364–365, 380–381
    causes of, 381
    and sexual orientation, 380–381
Gender role, 281, 282
Gender-role learning, 250
Gender schema theory, 286
Gender stereotyping, 282–286
    and androgyny, 284–286
    effect on adolescent behavior, 289
    and language, 282
    and nonverbal communication, 283
    problems of generalization, 283–284
    testing gender differences, 284–285
Generation gap, 605
Genes, 47
Genetic factors and sexual orientation, 377
Genital dimorphism, 290
Genital discharge, 114–115
Genital ducts, 51–52
Genital herpes, 128–131
    chances of infection by, 129
    fetal infection by, 130
    recurrence of, 130
    symptoms of, 129–130
    transmission of, 129
    treatment of, 130–131
Genital kiss, 338
Genital maturity, 244
Genital responses, 56
Genitals, 32
    See also Female sex organs; Male sex organs
Genital stimulation, 338
Genital tubercle, 52
Genital warts, 131–132
Genitourinary infections, 114–116
    candidiasis, 115
    cystitis, 115
    genital discharges, 114–115
    prostatitis, 115–116
    vaginitis, 115
Genotype, 47
Germ cells, 32
    development of, 46–50
Gift-love, 464
Gigolo, 509

Gonadal hormones, 82–84
  *See also* Sex hormones
Gonadotropins, 84
Gonadotropin-releasing hormone
    (GnRH), 84
Gonads, 36, 82
Gonococcal conjunctivitis, 122
Gonorrhea, 121–123
  blindness caused by, 122
  diagnosis of, 122–123
  incidence of, 121
  symptoms of, 121–123
  transmission of, 121
  treatment of, 123
Gonorrheal arthritis, 122
Gonorrheal cervicitis, 122
Gonorrheal urethritis, 121
Gossypol, 210
Graafian follicle, 49
Grafenberg spot, 40, 67–68
Granuloma inguinale, 127
Granulosa cells, 49
Grooming, 336
Group marriage, 474, 487
Group rape, 551
Group sex, 406
Group therapy
  for sexual dysfunction, 434
  to treat paraphilias, 409
Growth spurt during puberty, 86–87
Guevodoces, 292
Guilt, 616

Heart attacks, risks posed by birth con-
    trol pills, 194–195
Heart rate and breathing
  effect of orgasm on, 74
  effect of sexual arousal on, 69
Helper T cells, 134
Hemophiliacs, at risk for AIDS, 137
Hepatitis virus, causing sexually trans-
    mitted diseases, 127
Hermaphrodites, 100
Heroin, and sexual response, 357
Herpes. *See* Genital herpes
Herpes keratitis, 130
Heterosexual-homosexual rating scale,
    363–364
Heterosexual intercourse, AIDS trans-
    mission by, 135–136
Heterosexual love
  hormonal subsystem of, 231
  mechanical subsystem of, 230–231
  in primates, 230–231
Heterosexual pedophiles, 389
Heterosexuals, AIDS among, 135–136
Hip bones, 32
Historical research, sex bias in, 9
History, contributing to study of sex, 9
Hite Report, 24–25
Home delivery, 170
Home pregnancy tests, 160
Homologues in reproductive system,
    52

Homophile, 362
  *See also* Homosexuality
Homophobia, 367
Homosexual behavior, 367–370
  active and passive roles in, 370
  affected by risk of AIDS, 370
  among animals, 366, 367
  in other cultures, 368
  sexual practices, 367–368, 370
Homosexual identity, 363
Homosexuality, 294
  *See also* Homosexual behavior;
      Sexual orientation
  in adolescence, 261
  in ancient Greece, 573–574
  among animals, 366
  bias a problem, 365–367
  Biblical references to, 659–661
  and bisexuality, 365
  causes of, 382
  and child custody, 640
  conservative position against, 656
  criteria for homosexual identity, 363
  definition, problem with, 362–364
  discrimination against, 640–641
  effects of labeling, 365–367
  elective, 365
  facultative, 365
  and gay liberation, 607–609
  and gender nonconformity,
      364–365, 380–381
  heterosexual-homosexual rating
      scale, 363–364
  homophile movement, 608
  and homophobia, 367
  identification a problem with,
      364–365
  influence of Mattachine Society,
      609
  laws affecting, 637–640
  and masculine and feminine iden-
      tity, 364
  medical judgments on, 381–382
  obligatory, 365
  in other cultures, 368
  psychoanalytic views of, 278–279
  shifting attitudes toward, 638–639,
      641
  social judgments on, 381
  social learning approaches to,
      379–380
  social perspectives on, 381–383
  and stereotyping, 365
  tolerated by liberal sexual morality,
      662–663
  treatment of, 382–383
  in the Victorian period, 597
  as way of life, 370–376
Homosexual labeling, 365–367
Homosexual meeting places, 374–376
  and AIDS epidemic, 375–376
  cruising, 375
  gay bars, 376
  gay baths, 376

Homosexual meeting places (*cont.*)
  making contact, 375–376
  public sites, 376
Homosexual parents, 372–374
Homosexual pedophiles, 389–390
Homosexual rape, 551
Homosexual relationships, 371–376
  in adolescence, 261
  asexuals, 373
  close couples, 372
  closet homosexuals, 371
  coming out, 371–372
  covert homosexuals, 371
  dysfunctional, 372
  functional, 372
  gender differences in, 373
  open couples, 372
  overt homosexuals, 372–373
Homosexual seduction, 379
Homosexual subculture, 370–371
Homunculists, 159
Honesty and trust
  in sexual intimacy, 457
Hooker, 509. *See also* Prostitution
Hormonal methods of birth control,
    192–196
  birth control pills, 193–194
  implants, 210
  postcoital pill, 195–196
  side effects of, 194–195
Hormonal subsystem of heterosexual
    love, 231
Hormone disorders, 101
Hormone implants, 210
Hormones, 82
  *See also* Hormones and sexual behav-
      ior; Sex hormones
Hormones and sexual behavior,
    102–110
  activational influences, 104
  animal studies, 102, 104–105
  female sexual drive, 109–110
  in humans, 106–110
  male sexual drive, 107, 109
  in nonhuman primates, 105–106
  organizational influences, 102, 104
  pheromones, 102, 103
  and sex differences in the brain, 104
Hospital delivery, 170–171
Hostile rapists, 560
Hostility and sex, 536–537
  battered wives, 537
  origins of, 537
Hostility in erotic fantasy, 317
Hot flashes, 273
Housegirl, 510
Human chorionic gonadotrophin
    (HGC), 84, 160
Human immunodeficiency virus, 134
  *See also* Acquired immunodeficiency
      syndrome (AIDS)
  in blood transfusions, 137
  body fluids containing, 134–135
  effect on immune system, 134

Human immunodeficiency virus (*cont.*)
  infecting children, 137
  risk of infection by, 136
  stages of infection by, 138
  testing for antibodies to, 139, 140
Humanism, 8
Humanistic perspectives on study of
    sexuality, 7–10
  *See also* Liberal sexual morality
Human menopausal gonadotrophin
    (HMG), 181
Human papilloma virus, 131, 132
Human sexual drive, 241
Hustlers, 511, 513
Hymen, 35, 36
Hyperemesis gravidarum, 160
Hypernatremia, 213
Hyperphilia, 408
  *See also* Sexual addiction
Hypersexual, 366
Hypoactive sexual-desire disorder,
    414–415
Hypogonadal men, 107
Hypophilia, 408
  *See also* Sexual dysfunction
Hypothalamus, 79, 82
  hormones produced by, 84
Hystera, 38
Hysterectomy, 208

Id, 243
Idealization, 466
Identity formation, 245
Immune system, 134
  *See also* Acquired immunodeficiency
    syndrome
Imperforate hymen, 35
Implantation, 156
Impotence, 412, 415–416
Incentive theory, 241
Incest, 391–394
  avoided among primates, 391
  dealing with, 393
  factors increasing likelihood of, 393
  incestuous pedophilia, 392–393
  laws against, 644
  prevalence of, 392–393
  punishments for, 638
  reflecting seriously troubled family,
    393
  taboo against, 391–392
Individuation, 272
Induction of labor, 172
Infancy, gender differences in,
    286–287
Infanticide, 185
Infant mortality rate, 178
Infant-mother love in primates, 230
Infertility, 179, 181–182
  age as a cause of, 179, 181–182
  artificial insemination to treat,
    181–182
  caused by IUDs, 196
  causes of, 179

Infertility (*cont.*)
  drug treatment of, 181
  embryo transfer to treat, 182
  psychological impact of, 179, 181
  and surrogate motherhood, 182
  treatment of, 181–182
  in vitro fertilization to treat, 182
Infibulation, 34
Infidelity, 495
  *See also* Extramarital sex
Informed consent, 20
  in sexual exchanges, 506–507
Infundibulum, 38
Inhibin, 45, 83–84, 94
Inhibited female orgasm, 418
  treatment for, 430–431
Inhibited male orgasm, 419
  treatment for, 431
Inhibited sexual desire (ISD), 414–415
Innate releasing mechanisms (IRM),
    240
Instincts and drives, 239–241
  animal instincts, 240–241
  human sexual drive, 242
Interactional models of gender-identity
    development, 290–291
Intercourse. *See* Sexual intercourse
Interferon, 141
Interleukin, 141
Internal fertilization, 32
Internal sex organs, 32
  female, 36–40
  male, 45–46
Internal sphincter, 45–46
Interstitial cells, 45
Interviews, for research, 23
Intimacy vs. isolation, 268–269
Intrauterine device (IUD), 196–198
  causing infertility, 196
  causing pelvic inflammatory disease,
    196, 197
  complications of, 197
  early forms of, 196
  failure rate of, 196–197
  future prospects for, 210–211
  side effects of, 197
Intravenous drug users, AIDS trans-
    mission among, 135
Intromission, 342–343
Inverted nipples, 40
In vitro fertilization, 182
Irrumation, 351
Ithyphallic figures, 567

Judaic tradition, 568–572
  attitude toward homosexuality,
    571–572
  attitude toward prostitution, 571
  attitudes toward sexuality, 569–572
  circumcision, 568
  concept of adultery, 570–571
  influence on Christian sexual moral-
    ity, 572

Judaic tradition (*cont.*)
  integrity of marriage protected by,
    569–571
  laws of consanguinity, 569–570
  and liberal sexual morality, 665–666
  man and woman as complementary,
    569
  and marriage and divorce, 570
  moral heritage of, 572
  proscribed sexual behavior, 569–572
  sex and marriage within, 569
  sexuality in biblical times, 568–569

Kaposi's sarcoma, 132, 138
Karezza, 71
Kegel exercises, 436–437
Kiddie-porn, 520–521, 524
  *See also* Pornography
Kissing, 334–335
  deep, 335
  of erogenous zones, 335
  erotic, 334
  social, 334
Kleptomania, 405
Klinefelter's syndrome, 101
Kluver-Bucy syndrome, 79
Koilocytes, 132

Labia majora, 33
Labia minora, 33–34
Labor, 168
Labor room, 170
Lactation, 174
Lamaze method of childbirth, 172
Laminaria sticks, 213
Lanugo, 161
Laparoscopy, 208
Late adulthood, 253
  *See also* Sexuality in late adulthood
Latency, 244
Latency period, 227
Learning models of paraphilias,
    407–408
Leboyer method of childbirth,
    172–173
Lesbian, 362
  *See also* Homosexuality
Leukorrhea, 114
Leydig's cells, 45
Liberal sexual morality, 662–674
  affected by sexual revolution, 662
  case against, 672–673
  case for, 665–669, 672
  and changes in Catholic morality,
    666–667
  conceptual critique of, 672–673
  consequences of, 673
  and experiential bases of moral
    judgement, 667–668
  focusing on human sexual needs,
    665
  and Judaic perspective, 665–666
  pluralistic nature of, 669

Liberal sexual morality (*cont.*)
  range of positions covered by, 662–665
  and secular moralism, 669, 672
  sex-positive nature of, 669, 672
  and situation ethics, 668–669
  and tolerance of homosexuality,
    662–663
  traditional Catholic reaction to, 667
Libido, 241, 243
Limbic system, 79
Limerance, 466
Loneliness, 458
Love, 461
  addictive, 466, 470
  behavioral aspects of, 466–467
  chemistry of, 465–466
  cognitive component of, 462–464
  commitment as component of,
    462–464
  companionate, 467
  and dependency, 464
  effect of sex on, 469–470, 472
  emotional component of, 462–464
  falling in love, 464–465
  intimacy as component of, 462–464
  maintaining, 471
  motivational component of, 462–464
  passion as component of, 462–464
  relationship to sex, 467, 469–470, 472
  and supportiveness, 464
  triangular theory of, 462–464
  varieties of, 462–464
Lovemaps, 408
Lovesickness, 470
Low birth-weight babies, 178
Luteal phase, 94
Luteinizing hormone (LH), 84
Lymphadenopathy syndrome (LAS),
  138
Lymphadenopathy virus (LAV). *See*
  Human immunodeficiency virus
*Lymphogranuloma venereum (LGV)*, 127

Macrophages, 134
Male erectile disorder, 415–416, 417
  treatment of, 429–430
Male midlife transition, 272–273
  disillusionment in, 272
  effect on sexuality, 273
  individuation in, 272
Male prostitution, 511, 513
  in the Victorian period, 597
Male reproductive maturation, 88–89
Male sex organs
  effect of orgasm on, 70–72, 73
  effect of sexual arousal on, 64
Male sexual drive, influence of hormones on, 107, 109
Male sterilization, 206–208
Mammary glands, 40
Mammogram, 117
Marijuana
  and sexual dysfunction, 423
  and sexual response, 357

Marital fidelity
  attitude of liberal sexual morality
    toward, 664
Marital rape, 547, 550
  laws affecting, 642–643
  and spousal exclusion from rape
    laws, 642–643
Marriage, 457, 474–482
  age differentials in, 478–479
  age of, 477
  alternative commitments, 483–487.
    *See also* Cohabitation
  annulment of, 627
  attitudes toward, 479–480
  basic functions of, 477
  and changes in family patterns,
    479–480
  and changing roles of women, 479,
    480
  and concept of family, 474–476
  decline in rate of, 612
  demographic changes affecting,
    477–479
  and emphasis on personal happiness
    479–480
  factors affecting mate selection,
    480–482
  formalizing covenant, 668
  forms of, 474
  importance of sex in, 492, 493
  Jewish, 570
  legitimacy central to, 474
  open, 496
  probability of, 477–478
  and Protestant Reformation, atti-
    tudes toward, 587–588, 590
  rate of, 477–478
  separation of sex from, 611–612
  sexual activity in, 492–493, 596
  sexual satisfaction in, 493–494
  *See also* Being single
Marriage law, 627–629
  and child custody, 628–629
  conditions for divorce, 627
  establishing monogamy, 627
Marriage market, 480
Masculine and feminine traits,
  284–286
Masculine women, 294
Massage parlors, 510
Mastectomy, 116
Masters and Johnson model for sex
  therapy, 429
Masturbation, 320–331, 334
  in adolescence, 258
  among animals, 320–321
  in childhood, 224, 225
  frequency of, 326
  functions of, 327
  guilt and shame associated with, 329,
    331
  health and social aspects, 327–329,
    331
  in infancy, 224–225

Masturbation (*cont.*)
  and insanity, 328, 329
  in literature, 330
  and mental health, 329
  methods of, 322–325
  mutual, 309
  in other cultures, 321
  prevalence of, 325–327
  role in psychosexual development,
    327
  social correlates of, 326–327
  special devices for, 323–325
  as vehicle for establishment of para-
    philias, 407–408
Masturbation training, 437
Masturbatory fantasy, 313–314
Maternal death rate, 177
Maternal feelings
  during first trimester, 159–160
  during second trimester, 161, 163
  during third trimester, 163–164
Maternal love in primates, 230
Mate selection, 480–482
  and equity theory, 480
  and homogamy, 481–482
  and marriage market, 482
  and parity, 480
  role of propinquity, 480–481
Matriarchal societies, 303n
Maturation and sexual learning,
  233–234
Mature oocyte, 49
Meatus, 34
Media role in sexual socialization, 238
Medicine, contributing to study of sex,
  3–4
Medroxyprogesterone, 107, 210
Menage à trois, 495
Menarche, 91–92
  age of onset, 92
  reaction to, 255
Menopause, 91, 273–274
  anatomical changes following, 274,
    275
  estrogen replacement therapy, 274
  hormone reduction in, 273
  physical symptoms of, 273–274
  psychological symptoms of, 273–274
  response to, 109
  sexually negative effects of, 110
  structural changes during, 109–110
  treatment of symptoms, 274
Menorrhagia, 95
Menstrual calendar, 203
Menstrual cycle, 91–98
  anovulatory cycles, 92
  disturbances of, 95–96
  follicular phase, 92–94
  length of, 92
  luteal phase, 94
  menarche, 91–92
  menstrual phase, 94–95
  ovulation, 84
  phases of, 92–95

Menstrual cycle (*cont.*)
  postovulatory phase, 94
  and premenstrual syndrome, 96–98
  preovulatory phase, 92–94
  proliferative phase, 92–94
  secretory phase, 94
Menstrual discomfort, 95
Menstrual extraction, 96, 213
Menstrual taboos, 91
Menstruation, 91, 94–95
  health risks from intercourse during, 114
  while nursing, 175
Mesoderm, 157
Mesonephric ducts, 51
Middle adulthood, 253
  *See also* Sexuality in middle adulthood
Midlife crisis, 272
  *See also* Female midlife transition; Male midlife transition
Midwife, 167–168
Minipill, 196
Miscarriage, 177–178
Mistress, 495, 511
Mitosis, 47
Moniliasis, 115
Monogamy, 474
Monozygotic twins, 156
Mons pubis, 32–33
Mons veneris, 32–33
Moral philosophy and sexual ethics, 653–654
Morning-after pill. *See* Postcoital pill
Morning sickness, 160
Morula, 156
Mosher survey, 16
Motion and sexual enhancement, 356
Motivational theories, 239
Mullerian ducts, 51
Mullerian regression hormone, 51
Multilateral marriage, 487
Multiple orgasm, 62, 350
Mutual masturbation, 309
Mutual orgasm, 350
Myometrium, 39
Myotonia, 63
Mysophilia, 405

Narcotics and sexual dysfunction, 423
Natural childbirth, 168, 171–173
  Lamaze method, 172
  Leboyer method, 172–173
Natural law, and conservative sexual morality, 658, 661–662
Nature vs. nurture, 241, 242
Necrophilia, 399
Need-love, 464
Neonatal mortality rate, 178
Neuroendocrine control of puberty, 89–90
Neurological disorders causing sexual dysfunction, 421–422

Neurosecretory cells, 82
Neurotransmitters, role in sexual functions, 78
Nicotine and sexual dysfunction, 422
Nipple, 40
Nocturnal emissions, 257–258, 319–320
Nocturnal orgasms, 257–258, 319–320
Nocturnal penile tumescence, 424
No-fault divorce, 627
Noncoital sex play, 334
  *See also* Sexual stimulation
Nonejaculatory orgasm, 71, 350
Non-gonococcal urethritis, 123
Nonmarital sex, 501–503
  and AIDS risk, 501
  for the divorced, 502–503
  finding partners, 501
  among never married, 501–502
  and the widowed, 503
Non-monogamous sex, 495
  *See also* Extramarital sex
Norepinephrine, 465
Norethrindrone, 193
Norgestrel, 195
Normal variants, 294
Nuclear family, 474–476
Nucleus of ovum, 50
Nudity, 644–645
  and sexual enhancement, 354
Nursing, 174–175
  advantages of, 175
  inhibiting ovulation, 205
Nutrition and exercise during pregnancy, 176
Nymphomania, 405

Object fetishism, 396
Obligatory homosexuality, 365
Obscene telephone calls, 401
Obscenity. *See* Pornography
Observational learning, 248
Oedipus complex, 244
Onanism, 328
Oogenesis, 47
Open couples, 372
Open-ended interview, 23
Open marriage, 496, 500
Open swinging, 497
Operant behavior, 247
Operant conditioning, 247
  and sexual response, 247
Oral contraceptives. *See* Birth control pills
Oral-genital stimulation, 338–341
  acceptance of, 338–339
  cunnilingus, 338, 339, 340
  fellatio, 338, 340
  frequency of, 338
Oral sex, 341, 351
  in adolescence, 260
  and risk of AIDS, 351
Oral stage, 243–244

Orgasm, 69–75
  bipolar hypothesis of, 74–75
  blended, 70
  clitoral, 70–71
  control of, 348–350
  disorders, 418–419
  effect on female sex organs, 72, 74
  effect on heart rate and breathing, 74
  effect on male sex organs, 70–72, 73
  extended, 350
  female, 70–71
  first-stage, 71
  in infancy, 223
  intercrural, 351
  intermammary, 351
  male and female capacity for, 299–300
  mental control of, 349–350
  multiple, 62, 350
  mutual, 350
  nocturnal, 257–258, 319–320
  nonejaculatory, 71, 350
  physiological control of, 349
  during pregnancy, 165
  prolonging coitus to control, 348–349
  second-stage, 71
  sensations of, 69–70
  uterine, 70
  vaginal, 70–71
  variant forms of reaching, 351–352
  vulval, 70
Orgasmic platform, 67
Original sin, 582, 658
Osteoporosis, 273
Ovariectomy, 208
Ovaries, 36–37
Ovists, 159
Ovulation, 84
  while nursing, 85
Ovum, 32, 36
  development of, 47, 49–50
  migration of, 150
  nucleus of, 50
  size of, 49
Ownership rights, as justification for social control of sex, 619
Oxytocin, 84
  stimulating labor, 168
  stimulating milk flow, 174

Pair bonds, 465
Palimony, 486, 627
Pandering, 511
  penalties for, 645
  *See also* Prostitution
Pap smear test, 118
Paramenstruum, 97
Paramesonephric ducts, 51
Paraphiliac behaviors, 387–406
  bestiality, 394–395
  coprophilia, 405
  exhibitionism, 400–401

Paraphiliac behaviors (*cont.*)
  fetishism, 395–397. *See also*
    Fetishism
  frotteurism, 405
  incest, 391–394. *See also* Incest
  kleptomania, 405
  klismaphilia, 405
  mysophilia, 405
  necrophilia, 399
  obscene calls, 401
  pedophilia, 387–391. *See also* Pedophilia
  pyromania, 405
  sadomasochism, 401–405. *See also*
    Sadomasochism
  sexual addiction, 405–406
  toucherism, 405
  transvestism, 397–399. *See also*
    Transvestism
  urolagnia, 405
  urophilia, 405
  voyeurism, 399–400
  zoophilia, 394–395
Paraphilias
  as an aspect of lovemaps, 408
  basic features of, 386–387
  behavior therapy for, 409
  biologically based treatment for, 408
  biological roots of, 407
  causes of, 406–408
  concept of, 385–386
  dehumanizing nature of, 387
  development of, 406–408
  gender differences in, 407
  historical conceptions of, 385–386
  learning model for, 407–408
  masturbation as vehicle for establishment of, 407–408
  prevalence and variety of, 387
  psychoanalytic model for, 407
  psychotherapy for, 409
  punishment to treat, 408
  treatment of, 408–409
Parasympathetic nervous system, 76
Parental investment, 301
Parent-child interactions
  early attachment and bonding, 231–233
  following birth, 173
  sexual arousal in, 233
  *See also* Bonding
Parenting by homosexuals, 373–374
Partialism, 396
Partner surrogates, 429
Passionate love, 465
Paternal love in primates, 230
Patriarchal cultures, 303
Peak symptom, 204
Pederasty in ancient Greece, 573–574
*Pediculosis pubis*, 128
Pedophilia, 387–391
  and alcohol, 389
  characteristics of, 388–389

Pedophilia (*cont.*)
  consequences depending on circumstances, 391
  following sexual abuse as a child, 389
  heterosexual pedophiles, 389
  homosexual pedophiles, 389–390
  impact on child, 390–391
  incestuous, 392–393
  prevalence of, 388
  *See also* Child sexual abuse
Peer culture, 262
Peer group, as a source of social control, 616
Peer love in primates, 230
Peer pressure, and rape, 558, 562
Peer relationships, and homosexuality, 379
Pelvic inflammatory disease (PID), 114, 122, 123–124
  caused by IUDs, 196, 197
  causing infertility, 123
  causing sterility, 124
  and ectopic pregnancy, 124
  risk of contracting, 124
  symptoms of, 124
  treatment of, 124
Penile strain gauge, 60
Penis, 41–44
  cancer of, 120
  erection of, 63, 64
  glans of, 41
  size of, 44
  spinal control of erection of, 76–78
  as a symbol of dominance, 535
Penis sheaths, 535
Perimetrium, 39
Perioneometer, 61
Peripheral arousal, 56
Permissiveness with affection, 261, 271, 612
Permissiveness without affection, 261–262
Permissive societies, 229
Personality factors and sexual intimacy, 458–459
Perversions, 387
Petting, 334
  in adolescence, 258–260
Phallic cults, 577
Phallic stage, 244
Phallic symbolism, 318, 567–568
  in ancient Greece, 575, 577
  in ancient Rome, 577–578
Pharyngeal gonorrhea, 122
Pheromones, 58, 102, 103
  human, 103
Philia, 462
Philosophy and religion, contributing to study of sex, 9–10
Phimosis, 43
Phone sex, 401
Physical ability, men and women compared, 87

Physical attractiveness, 443
Physical stimulation and sexual arousal, 56–58
Pillow books, 353
Pimping, 511
  penalties for, 645
  *See also* Prostitution
Pituitary gland, 82, 84
Pituitary hormones, 84
Placebos, 98
Placenta, 83
  delivery of, 168
  functions of, 158
Pleasure centers, 79
Pleasuring, 336
PLISSIT principle in sex therapy, 427–428
Pneumocystis carinii pneumonia, 132, 138, 140
Polar body, 49
Polyandry, 474
Polygyny, 474
Polymorphously perverse, 244, 407
Population control, 187
Pornographic films, 9
Pornography, 517–527, 607
  aggressive behavior affected by, 525
  attitudes toward, 518, 522
  and attitudes toward women, 525–526
  cathartic function of, 527
  as a civil rights violation, 518
  commission reports on, 522–524
  customers for, 521
  dangers of, 648
  degrading and dehumanizing effects of, 522
  degrading to women, 518, 525–526
  desensitizing effect of, 526
  distinguished from erotica, 519–520, 522
  economics of, 521
  and erotic fantasy, 316, 317
  explicitness as a criterion, 518
  exploiting sexual freedom, 611
  feminist criticism of, 518–519
  hard-core, 519–520
  impact on children, 524
  impact on potential sex offenders, 524–525
  involving children, 524, 529–521
  laws affecting, 647–650
  literary and artistic criteria for, 518
  model antipornography law, 648
  nature of pornographic materials, 519–521
  ordinances restricting, 648
  patent offensiveness as a criterion for, 649
  political criteria for, 518–519
  potential benefits of, 526–527
  potential harm from, 524–526
  problem of censorship, 527, 648–650. *See also* Censorship

Pornography (*cont.*)
  problem of consequences of, 521–527
  problem of definition, 517–521
  prurience as a criterion for, 649
  and rape, 560, 562
  relationship to violence, 525–526
  as socially insignificant, 527
  soft-core, 519–520
  Victorian, 595
  violent, 522
Pornotopia, 514–515
Postcoital pill, 195–196, 214
  effectiveness of, 196
Postovulatory phase, 94
Postpartum depression, 174
Postpartum period, 173–176
  emotional reactions, 174
  nursing, 174–175
  ovulation and menstruation, 175
  physiological changes, 173
  sex during, 175–176
Power and exploitation, 508
Power rape, 560
Precocious puberty, 99, 101
Preformationists, 159
Pregenital phase, 244
Pregnancy, 156–167
  alcohol hazardous to, 177
  and birth defects, 178–179
  calculating expected date of delivery, 161
  complications of, 177–179
  difficulties in carrying to term, 177–178
  drugs hazardous to, 177
  ectopic, 124, 156, 177
  embryo development in first trimester, 156–158
  false, 160
  father's experience during, 165–167
  fetal development in second trimester, 161
  fetal development in third trimester, 163
  first trimester, 156–161
  maternal changes in second trimester, 161, 163
  maternal changes in third trimester, 163–164
  nutrition and exercise during, 176
  physical signs of, 159–160
  placental development, 158
  prenatal care, 176–177
  psychological aspects of, 164
  reductions, 214
  sexual interest and activity during, 164–165
  signs and symptoms of, 159–160
  smoking hazardous to, 176–177
  teenage. *See* Teenage pregnancy
  tests for, 160–161
  unplanned, 189
  unwanted, 214–215
  *See also* Childbirth; Infertility

Premarital sex, 269–272
  changing attitudes, toward, 612
  consequences of, 264–267
  conservative position against, 656
  defined, 269
  and expectation of marriage, 271
  impact of AIDS on, 264
  impact on subsequent marriage, 271–272
  increase in, 598
  interpersonal context of, 270–272
  negative consequences of, 264–267
  in other cultures, 263
  peer-group influence on, 271
  positive consequences of, 264
  prevalence in young adulthood, 269–270
  reactions of participants, 270
  in the Victorian period, 596
Premature birth, 177–178
Premature ejaculation, 418–419
  treatment for, 431–432
Premenstrual syndrome (PMS), 96–98
  and behavior changes, 97
  and discrimination, 97
  physiological causes of, 98
  placebos helping, 98
  psychological factors in, 96
  remedies for, 96
  studies of, 97
  symptoms of, 96
Premenstrual tension syndrome, 95
Prenatal care, 176–177
  nutrition and exercise, 176
  smoking, alcohol, and drugs, 177
Prenatal hormones and sexual orientation, 377
Preovulatory phase, 92–94
Prepuce of the clitoris, 33
Prepuce of the penis, 43
Pressuring, 454
Priapism, 419
Primary follicle, 47
Primary oocytes, 47
Primary sexual characteristics, 87
Primary sexual dysfunctions, 413
Primary spermatocyte, 47
Primate development, 228, 230–231
  love systems, 230–231
Primate sexual behavior, 105–106
Privacy and sexual enhancement, 355
Procreational sex, 450
Progesterone, 83
  role in premenstrual syndrome, 98
Progestins, 37, 83
  functions of, 83
Prolactin, 84, 174
Proliferative phase, 92–94
Promiscuity, 405–406
Pronatalist society, 186
Prostaglandin abortions, 213
Prostaglandins, 46
  role in dysmenorrhea, 95–96
  stimulating labor, 168, 213

Prostate cancer, 118–119
Prostate gland, 45, 46
Prostatis, 115–116
Prostitution, 509–517
  and AIDS risk, 516
  in ancient Greece, 574–575
  in ancient Rome, 578
  arguments against legalization, 646
  arguments for legalization, 646–647
  consequences of, 516–517
  cult prostitutes, 571
  customers not affected by laws, 645
  and danger of STDs, 647
  decriminalization of, 646
  effects on society, 517
  female prostitutes, 510–512
  fronts for, 510
  hand whores, 510
  homosexual prostitutes, 511, 513
  hustling, 511, 513
  incentives for engaging in, 515–516
  in Judaic tradition, 571
  laws affecting, 645–647
  and madams, 509
  and male models, 511
  prevalence of, 512
  psychosexual aspects of, 513, 514–516
  reasons for women becoming prostitutes, 515–516
  regulation of, 646, 647
  relationship to poverty, 515, 517
  religious prostitutes, 571, 575
  risks for clients, 516
  risks for prostitutes, 516–517
  stigma attached to, 517, 646
  teenagers and children involved in, 512
  types of prostitutes, 509–513
  Victorian attitudes to, 593, 594, 596
Protestant revolution, 587–588, 590
Protestant sexual ethic, 587–588, 590
Protozoa causing STDs, 127
Pseudocyesis, 160
Pseudohermaphroditism, 100, 101–102
  treatment of, 102
Psychedelic culture, 605
Psychoanalytic model of paraphilias, 407
Psychoanalytic theories, 241, 243–245
Psychoanalytic views of homosexuality, 378–379
Psychological stimulation and sexual arousal, 58
Psychology, contributing to study of sex, 6
Psychopathia sexualis, 385
  *See also* Paraphilias
Psychosexual development, role of masturbation in, 327
Psychosexual development stages, 243–244
Psychosocial determinants of sexual orientation, 378–381

Psychosocial determinants of sexual
 orientation (cont.)
  gender nonconformity, 380–381
  psychoanalytic views, 378–379
  social learning approaches, 379–380
Psychosocial perspectives, and study of
 sexuality, 5–7
Psychosurgery, 408
Psychotherapy
  to treat paraphilias, 409
  to treat sexual dysfunction, 432–433
Pubertal eroticism, 290–291
Pubertal morphology, 290
Puberty, 86–90
  adapting to, 253
  delayed, 98
  female reproductive maturation,
   87–88
  male reproductive maturation,
   88–89
  neuroendocrine control of, 89–90
  precocious, 99, 101
  somatic changes during, 86–87
Pubic hair, 88
Pubic lice, 128
Pubococcygeus, 35
Pudendal cleft, 33
Puerperal fever, 177
Puerperium. See Postpartum period
Pyromania, 405

Questionnaires, 23, 25
  poor response rates of, 25
  for sex surveys, 24–25
  strengths of, 25

Radioimmunoassay, 160
Random sampling, 21
Rape, 454, 543–562, 607
  acquaintance and date rape,
   548–550
  and alcohol, 549–550, 561
  anger rape, 560
  blaming the victim, 551–552, 553
  consequences to society, 555
  consequences to victim, 555–557
  cultural setting of, 558–559
  definitions of, 544–545
  facilitating factors for, 561–562
  group rape, 551
  homosexual rape, 551
  laws against, 641–644
  legal definitions of, 544
  of males, 551
  marital rape, 550, 642–643
  men as victims of, 552, 643
  nature of, 543–545
  and pornography, 562
  power rape, 560
  prevalence of, 546–547
  preventing, 554–555
  problem of consent in laws, 641–642
  punishments for, 638, 641

Rape (cont.)
  rape-prone and rape-free cultures,
   559
  reporting of, 546, 548
  and rights of the accused, 642
  settings for, 545–546
  as sex or violence, 545
  sexual deprivation as motive for, 559
  spousal exclusion from rape laws,
   642–643
  statutory rape, 550–551, 643–644
  stranger rape, 547–548
  varieties of, 547–551
  victim-precipitated, 553, 642
  See also Rape victims; Rapists
Rape victims
  blaming, 551–552, 553
  consequences of rape to, 555–556
  cultural approach to, 555
  helping, 556–557
  men as, 552, 643
  precipitating rape, 553, 642
  rape trauma syndrome experienced
   by, 555–556
  relational problems of, 556
  sexual problems following rape, 556
  treatment of, 553
Rapid eye movement (REM sleep), 319
Rapists, 557–562
  age and race of, 557–558
  amoral rapists, 559
  background characteristics of,
   560–561
  childhood sexual experiences of, 561
  dealing with, 562
  hostile rapists, 559–560
  justifying coercion, 558–559
  peer pressure encouraging, 558, 562
  sadistic rapists, 560
  sexually inadequate rapists, 559
  sociological perspectives, 557–559
  typologies of, 559–560
  violence characteristic of, 558
Reciprocity and sexual satisfaction,
 358
Recreational sex, 450–452
Rectal gonorrhea, 122
Reflex, 57
Reflexive responses in infants,
 223–224
Regressed pedophiles, 389
Reinforcement, 247
Relational differences in sexual behav-
 ior, 300–301
Relational sex, 450–452
Releasing factors (RF), 84
Releasing hormones (RH), 84
Religious traditions, erotic themes in,
 10
Representative sample, 24
Repressive and permissive cultures,
 623–625
Repressive societies, 229
Reproduction, control of, 611–612

Reproductive consequences, as justifi-
 cation for social control of sex,
 619
Reproductive maturation, 87–89
Reproductive system, 31–46
  development of, 50–54
  See also Female sex organs; Male sex
   organs
Reproductive technology, 611
Research interviews, 23
Resolution phase of sexual arousal, 75
Response, 56
Retarded ejaculation, 419
Retroviruses, 134
Rh incompatibility, causing birth
 defects, 178
Ribavirin, 141
Rigiscan monitor, 60
Rimming, 341
Rites of passage, 262
Romance, 446
Romantic love, 465
Romantic subsystem of heterosexual
 love, 231
RU 486, 196
Rubella, causing birth defects,
 178–179
Rugae, 39

Sacrum, 32
Sadomasochism (S-M), 341, 401–405
  bondage and domination, 402–403
  death resulting from, 405
  and gender differences, 403
  injury resulting from, 404–405
  literature of, 403
  magazines catering to, 404
  prevalence of, 403
  prostitutes offering, 404
  as a psychological abnormality, 404
  and sexual masochism, 402
  and sexual sadism, 402
  S-M subculture, 404
Safe sex, 142–143
Saline abortion, 213
Salmonella, 127
Sample, 21
Sampling bias, 21
Sampling in sex research, 21
Sarcoptes scabei, 128
Satyriasis, 405
Scabies, 128
Scents and sexual enhancement, 355
School role in sexual socialization,
 236–238
  children's felt needs, 237
  content of sex education, 237
  socialization at school, 237–238
Scripts, 249–250
Scrotum, 44–45
Secondary oocyte, 49
Secondary sexual characteristics, 87
Secondary sexual dysfunctions, 413

Secondary spermatocyte, 47
Second polar body, 49
Second-stage orgasm, 71
Secretory phase, 94
Secular moralism, 669, 672
Sedatives and sexual dysfunction, 423
Seduction, 454, 637
Self-disclosure in sexual intimacy,
  455–456
Self-help for sexual dysfunction, 432
Selfless love, 462
  *See also* Love
Self-selected sample, 21
Self-selection, 23
Semen, 150
Seminal emission, 71
Seminal vesicles, 45
Seminiferous tubules, 45
Sensate focus, 336
Sequential pill, 196
Serial monogamy, 474
Serotonin, 465
Sertoli cells, 45
Setting and sexual enhancement,
  354–355
Sex
  direct and indirect roles of, 3
  effect on love, 469–470, 472
  institutionalization of, 615
  modern attitudes toward, 597–599
  procreative purpose of, 654–656
  relationship to love, 467, 469–470,
    472
  separated from reproduction, 603
  separation from marriage, 611–612
  and social status, 620, 622
  and society, 621–622
  valuation of. *See* Valuation of sex
Sex and advertising, 528–532, 602, 610
  attention-getting function, 529
  combining sex and violence, 531
  effects of, 530–532
  encouraging sexual competition,
    531–532
  encouraging negative stereotypes of
    women, 531–532
  mirroring sexual attitudes, 528
  overemphasizing the physical,
    530–531
  potential benefits of, 530
  potential harm of, 530–532
  selling sexual products, 528–529
  selling sexual services, 529
  sex to sell advertising, 529–530
  standards taught by, 528
  trend to use children, 532
  using sexual innuendo, 529
  using sexual modeling, 530
  using sexual symbolism, 529–530
  using women as sexual objects, 530
Sex appeal, 506
Sex between siblings, 227
Sex chromosomes, 47
  disorders of, 100–101

Sex clubs, 510
Sex dimorphic behavior, 293–294
Sex discrimination, 627
Sex drive, 241
Sex education, 18
  arguments against, 18
  children's need for, 237
  conflict over, 18
  content of, 237
  in different countries, 234
  effectiveness of, 267
  effect on teenage pregnancy, 267
  fears about, 267
  mislabeling, 235
  motivation for, 18
  need for, 236
  nonlabeling, 235
  opposed by sexual conservatives, 613
  parental role, 234, 236
  in school, 236–237
  in Sweden, 234
  unambiguous labeling, 235
Sex flush, 69
Sex history, 23
Sex hormones, 32
  androgens, 82–83
  controlling female reproductive
    cycle, 83
  controlling male sexual maturity, 83
  disorders of, 101
  effect on genital differentiation, 52
  effects on fetus, 101
  estrogens, 36, 49, 83
  functioning as control systems,
    84–85
  hypothalamic hormones, 84
  inducing sexual abnormalities,
    293–294
  inhibin, 83–84, 94
  and neuroendocrine control of pu-
    berty, 89–90
  pituitary hormones, 84
  progestins, 37, 83
  prostaglandins, 46, 95–96, 168, 213
  role in maturation of reproductive
    system, 51
  and sexual orientation, 377–378
  steroids, 82
  synthetic, 83, 95, 193, 210
  testosterone. *See* Testosterone
  used to treat sexual dysfunction,
    435–436
  *See also* Hormones and sexual behav-
    ior
Sexiness, 443
  *See also* Sexual attraction
Sex information for children, 235
Sex Information and Education Council of the United States (SIECUS),
  18
Sex laws
  and abortion, 630–631, 633
  affecting adult consensual behavior,
    636–641

Sex laws (*cont.*)
  against public nuisance offences,
    644–645
  on child molestation, 644–645
  on commercial exploitation of sex,
    645–650
  and contraception, 629
  cultural variations, 638
  decriminalizing sodomy, 639–640
  discrepancy between laws and ac-
    tions, 628
  on discrimination and prejudice, 640
  distinguishing between fornication
    and adultery, 636–637
  and heterosexual behavior, 636–637
  and homosexual behavior, 637–640
  and marriage law, 627–629
  model penal code changing, 628
  nature and use of, 628
  on pornography, 647–650
  on prostitution, 645–647
  punishment for misconduct, 638
  on rape, 641–643
  regulating reproduction, 629–634
  on sexual offenses against the
    young, 643
  on statutory rape, 643–644
  and sterilization, 629–630
  and surrogate motherhood, 631–634
  vagueness a problem, 628
Sex manuals, 353
Sex offenders, 385
  *See also* Paraphilias
Sexology, 11–19
  current status of, 17–19
  foundations of, 11–12
  history of, 11–17
  important figures in, 11–17
  influence of Sigmund Freud, 12–13
  origins of, 11
  sex education, 18
  sex therapy, 19
  *See also* Sex research; Sex research
    methods
Sex partners
  choice of, 142–143
  estimating risk of AIDS from, 144
Sex play, 334
  *See also* Sexual stimulation
Sex research, 11–19
  technology used in, 60–61
  *See also* Sexology
Sex research methods, 19–26
  basic considerations in, 29
  choice of variables for, 19–20
  clinical research, 22–23
  direct observation and experimenta-
    tion, 25–26
  ethical considerations for, 20–21
  problems of bias in, 19
  purpose and perspectives of, 19
  questionnaires, 23, 25
  research interviews, 23
  sampling, 21

Sex research methods (*cont.*)
surveys, 24–25
use of statistics, 21–22
Sex role, 281, 282
Sex role inventory, 285
Sex skin, 68
Sex stereotyping. *See* Gender stereo-
typing
Sex surveys, 23, 24–25
Hite report, 24–25
Hunt survey, 24
Kinsey study, 15, 16, 24
Mosher survey, 16
Playboy Foundation survey, 24
Sex therapy, 17, 19, 427–432, 433
for anorgasmia, 430–431
for erectile dysfunction, 429–430
illustrated, 426
for male inhibited orgasm, 431
Masters and Johnson model for,
429
outcomes of, 433
PLISSIT principles for, 427, 429
for premature ejaculation, 431–432
for vaginismus, 432
Sex-typed behavior, 281
Sex-typing, 281
Sexual activity and satisfaction,
492–503
celibacy, 503
for cohabiting couples, 500–501
extramarital sex, 494–500. *See also*
Extramarital sex
nonmarital sex, 501–503
sexual activity in marriage, 492–493
sexual satisfaction in marriage,
493–494
Sexual addiction, 405–406
aggressive component of, 406
meaning of, 406
Sexual apathy, 414–415
Sexual arousal, 56–58
affected by touch, 57
components of, 56
effect on female sex organs, 64–69
effect on heart rate and breathing,
69
effect on male sex organs, 64
in infants, 222
inhibition of, 58
non-sexual effects of, 64
physical stimulation causing, 56–58
psychological stimulation causing, 58
sights, sounds, and smells influencing, 57–58
sources of, in childhood, 224
Sexual arousal disorders, 415–416,
418
female, 416, 418
male erectile disorder, 415–416
special problems of the handicapped, 417
Sexual assault, 543
*See also* Rape

Sexual attraction, 443–449
and body weight, 445
and clothing, 445
cultural differences in, 444–445
gender differences, 447–449
physical aspects of, 443–445
and power, 447
psychological determinants of,
445–447
sexual releasers, 443
and social factors, 447
Sexual aversion, 415
Sexual behavior
in adolescence, 256
diversity and unit in, 622–623
double standard of, 303, 426
and erotic fantasy, 313–316
ethical dimension of, 10
and gender, 297–304
hormones influencing, 102–110. *See
also* Hormones and sexual behavior
influence of Judeo-Christian tradition on, 617
male/female differences explained,
301–304
male/female differences in orgasmic
capacity, 299–300
male/female differences in relational
aspects, 300–301
male/female differences in response
to erotica, 298–299
men and women compared,
297–298
mixed messages about, 248
relational aspects of, 300–301
role of biology in, 5–6
scripting of, 249–250
social judgments about, 617–618
Victorian, 595–597
Sexual behavior in childhood,
224–229
autoerotic play, 224–225
impact of parental response, 228
in other cultures, 229
parental reaction to, 227–228
in permissive societies, 229
in restrictive societies, 229
sex between siblings, 227
sociosexual play, 225–227
*See also* Sexual socialization
Sexual bias in historical research, 9
Sexual coercion, 534, 537
*See also* Rape
Sexual communication at home,
235–236
Sexual compulsion, 405–406
Sexual concepts, influence of Greek
philosophers on, 9–10
Sexual conservatism, 613–614
opposing sex education, 613
Sexual decline, 275
Sexual deprivation as a motive for
rape, 559

Sexual desire disorders, 413–415
hyperactive, 415
hypoactive, 414–415
sexual aversion, 415
Sexual development theories,
239–250
animal instincts, 240–241, 242
cognitive development models,
245–246
conditioning theories, 246–247
developmental theories, 239
Erikson's approach, 245
human sexual drive, 241
instincts and drives, 239–241
motivational theories, 239
psychoanalytic theories, 241,
243–245
social learning models, 247–250
stages of psychosexual development,
243–244
Sexual dimorphism of the brain, 104
Sexual dreams, 317–320
explanations of, 317–319
and neurophysiology of dreaming,
319
nocturnal orgasms, 319–320
phallic symbols in, 318
Sexual drive, 56
in adolescence, 256
men and women compared,
297–298
Sexual dysfunction, 275
causes of, 412, 420–427. *See also*
Causes of sexual dysfunction
circulatory disorders causing, 422
cultural, 412
definitions used, 412–413
getting help for, 435
models of, 413
orgasm disorders, 418–419
prevalence of, 413
preventing, 438–439
primary and secondary, 413
psychogenic, 412
reflecting illness, 276
sexual arousal disorders, 415–418
sexual desire disorders, 413–415
sexual pain disorders, 419–420
treatments for, 427–438. *See also*
Treatment of sexual dysfunction
Sexual ethics
religious bases for, 654
secular bases for, 653–654
Sexual exploitation
controlled by men, 508
gender considerations, 508
as justification for social control,
619
of runaways, 512
Sexual expression, 610–611
exploited by pornography, 611
in the media, 610–611
Sexual fantasies in adolescence,
256–257

Sexual functions
    biphasic model of, 413
    brain mechanisms controlling, 78–80
    control of, 75–80
    role of neurotransmitters in, 78
    spinal control of, 76–78
    triphasic model of, 413
Sexual harassment, 537–543
    and asymmetry of status, 508
    at college, 541
    as condition of work, 541
    contexts for, 539–542
    during courtship, 539
    decision to press charges, 542
    determinants of, 538–539
    frequency of, at work, 540–541
    gender differences in perception of, 539–540
    handling, 542–543
    preventing, 542–543
    in professional settings, 541–542
    sexual appraisal as, 538
    sexual component of, 538
    in social settings, 539–540
    teasing as, 540
    touching as, 538
    unequal power as component, 539
    unwanted imposition as component, 539
    as violation of civil rights, 540
    in the workplace, 540–541
Sexual health
    avoiding intercourse during menstruation, 114
    avoiding toxic shock syndrome, 113–114
    cancer, 116–117
    genitourinary infections, 114–116
    maintaining thorough hygiene, 113
    See also Sexually transmitted diseases
Sexual identity, 281–286
    androgyny, 284–286
    benefits of androgyny, 285–286
    gender identity, 281–282
    gender role, 281, 282
    gender stereotyping, 282–284
Sexual interaction patterns, 449–461
    casual sex, 451
    coercion, 454
    cooperation, 454
    procreational and relational sex, 450
    reactions to recreational sex, 451–452
    relational and recreational sex, 450–452
    seduction, 454
    sexual negotiation, 452–454
Sexual intercourse
    in adolescence, 260–261
    AIDS transmission by, 135–136
    avoiding during menstruation, 114
    during postpartum period, 175–176
    during pregnancy, 164–165

Sexual intimacy, 449–461
    building and sustaining, 454–457
    commitment to, 457
    gender differences, 459–461
    importance of childhood experiences, 458–459
    and patterns of sexual interaction, 449–454. See also Sexual interaction patterns
    problems in, 457–461
    role of caring and affection, 456
    role of communication and self-disclosure, 455–456
    role of honesty and trust, 457
    role of sharing, 456–457
Sexual inversion, 362
    See also Homosexuality
Sexuality
    Christian views of. See Christianity and sexuality
    male/female perceptions of, 304
    New Testament teachings on, 657–658, 659–661
    and the origins of culture, 567–568
    social regulation of. See Social regulation of sexuality
    study of, 3–11. See also Study of sexuality
    Victorian repression of, 593–594
Sexuality, study of, 3–11
    biological perspectives, 3–5
    contributions of biology to, 5
    humanistic perspectives, 7–10
    psychosocial perspectives, 5–7
Sexuality in ancient Greece, 572–577
    attitude toward physical beauty, 573
    eros in Greece, 572–573
    erotic art and literature, 575–577
    erotic themes in Greek mythology, 576
    Greek homosexuality, 573–574
    pederasty, 573–574
    phallic symbolism, 575, 577
    prostitution, 574–575
    sacred prostitutes, 575
Sexuality in ancient Rome, 577–579
    erotic art and literature, 578–579
    phallic symbolism, 577–578
    prostitution, 578
Sexuality in history
    in the American colonies, 592–593
    in early Middle Ages, 583–584
    erotic art and literature in the Enlightenment, 591–592
    in Greece and Rome, 572–579. See also Sexuality in ancient Greece; Sexuality in ancient Rome
    influence of John Wesley, 593
    influence of Reformation, 587–588, 590
    in Judaic tradition, 568–572. See also Judaic tradition
    in late Middle Ages, 585–587
    manners and morals in the Enlightenment, 590–591

Sexuality in history (cont.)
    medieval attitudes toward sexuality, 585–587
    medieval code of sexual morality, 583–584
    medieval erotic art and literature, 584, 585
    modernization of sex, 597–599
    in the nineteenth century, 593–597
    Protestant sexual ethic, 587–588, 590
    Renaissance erotic art and literature, 589
    Renaissance sexuality, 587–590
    social purity movement, 594
    tradition of courtly love, 585
    utopian communities, 597
    Victorian erotic art and literature, 594–595
    Victorian sexual behavior, 595–597
    Victorian sexual ideology, 593–594
    See also Christianity and sexuality
Sexuality in late adulthood, 275–278
    attitudes toward, 275
    changes in sexual response, 275–276
    female sexual response, 275–276
    male sexual response, 275
    patterns of sexual behavior, 276–278
Sexuality in middle adulthood, 272–275
    and female midlife transition, 273–275
    and male midlife transition, 272–273
Sexuality in young adulthood, 268–272
    intimacy vs. isolation, 268–269
    premarital sex, 269–272. See also Premarital sex
    sexual unfolding, 268
    sociosexual aspects of, 268–269
Sexual jealousy, 460, 495
Sexual learning, 233–234
Sexual liberation, 451
Sexual love, 462
    See also Love
Sexually inadequate rapists, 559
Sexually open marriage, 496
Sexually transmitted diseases (STDs), 120–145
    acquired immune deficiency syndrome. See Acquired immune deficiency syndrome
    bacterial, 121–126
    caused by enteric organisms, 127–128
    causing birth defects, 178
    chancroid, 126, 127
    chlamydia, 123
    genital herpes, 128–131
    genital warts, 131–132
    gonorrhea, 121–123
    granuloma inguinale, 127
    hepatitis, 132
    lymphogranuloma venereum (LGV), 127

Sexually transmitted diseases (*cont.*)
  parasitic infections, 128
  pelvic inflammatory disease,
    123–124
  prevalence of, 120
  pubic lice, 128
  scabies, 128
  syphilis, 124–127
  types of, 120–121
  viral, 128–132
Sexual magic, 567
Sexual masochism, 402
Sexual maturity, problems with timing
  of, 255–256
Sexual morality
  bases for sexual ethics, 654–662
  and commitment, 667–668
  and components of human sexuality,
    667
  conservative perspective on,
    654–662. *See also* Conservative
    sexual morality
  liberal perspective on, 662–673. *See
    also* Liberal sexual morality
  Protestant sexual ethic, 587–588,
    590
  and reality of sin, 667
  Victorian, 593–594
Sexual negotiation, 452–454
  forms of, 452
  gender differences, 453–454
  negotiating strategies used, 453
  styles of, 452
Sexual objectifying, 449
Sexual offenders, drug treatment of,
  107
Sexual orientation
  associated with gender nonconform-
    ity, 380–381
  biological determinants of, 376–377
  development of, 376–381
  and gender identity, 364–365
  genetic factors affecting, 377
  hormonal factors affecting, 377–378
  psychoanalytic views of, 378–379
  psychosocial determinants of,
    378–381
  social learning approaches to,
    379–380
Sexual pain disorders, 419–420
  dysparcunia, 419–420
  vaginismus, 420
Sexual pleasuring, 334
  *See also* Sexual stimulation
Sexual reproduction, 31–32
  evolution of, 32
Sexual response, 58–75
  of the breasts, 74
  and conditioned responses, 247
  excitement and plateau phases,
    63–69
  learned by experience, 248–249
  male and female patterns compared,
    61–62

Sexual response (*cont.*)
  and operant conditioning, 247
  orgasm, 69–74. *See also* Orgasm
  patterns of, 61–62
  physiological mechanism involved,
    63
  resolution phase, 75
Sexual revolution, 601
  and abortion, 611–612
  causes of, 601–604
  civil rights movement affecting,
    602
  and commercialization of sex,
    602–603
  conservative reaction to, 613–614
  and the counterculture, 604–606
  economic factors causing, 602–603
  effective contraception contributing
    to, 603
  evaluating, 614
  exploited by pornography, 611
  feminist movement influencing,
    603–604
  gay liberation a manifestation of,
    607–609
  impact on the family, 612
  liberating female sexuality, 606–607
  manifestations of, 604–614
  in music, 611
  in the 1980s, 612–613
  political events causing, 601–602
  and premarital sex, 612
  and progress in reproductive tech-
    nology, 611
  public sexual expression a part of,
    610–611
  separating sex and marriage,
    611–612
  separation of sex and reproduction,
    encouraging, 603
  and teenage pregnancy, 611
Sexual sadism, 402
  *See also* Sadomasochism
Sexual satisfaction in marriage,
  493–494
Sexual scripts, 249–250
Sexual socialization, 228, 230–239, 615
  early attachment and bonding,
    231–233
  male/female differences in, 302–304
  maturation and sexual learning,
    233–234
  role of family in, 234–236
  role of media in, 238
  role of school in, 236–238
  sexual interactions with adults,
    238–239. *See also* Child sexual
    abuse
  sources of information, 235
  studies of primate development,
    228, 230–231
Sexual stimulation, 334–342
  anal stimulation, 341
  breast stimulation, 337–338

Sexual stimulation (*cont.*)
  emotional content important to, 334
  genital stimulation, 338
  kissing, 334–335
  length of, 341–342
  objects and devices used, 341
  oral-genital stimulation, 338–341
  special practices, 341
  touching and caressing, 335–336
Sexual symbolism, 8
Sexual unfolding, 268
Sexual values, 615–616
  in adolescence, 261–262
  influence of peer culture, 262
Sexual variants, 387
Shame, 616
Shared needles, AIDS transmitted by,
  135
Sharing in sexual intimacy, 456–457
*Shigella*, 127
Siblings, sex between, 227
Sight, role of in sexual arousal, 57–58
Single-parent families, 487–488
Single parenthood, as an alternative to
  abortion, 215
Singles bars, 501
Situation ethics, 668–669
  defenses of, 669
Skene's glands, 68
Sleep-dream cycle, 319
Smegma, 43–44
Smells, role in sexual arousal, 57–58
Smiling response, 173
Smoking, and pregnancy, 176–177
Social factors, and sexual attraction,
  447
Social kissing, 334
Social learning, sexual disparities in,
  248
Social learning approaches to homo-
  sexuality, 379–381
Social learning models, 247–250
  observational learning, 248
  role of experience, 248–249
  scripting theory, 249–250
Social norms, 615–616
Social regulation of sexuality, 614–622
  cross-cultural patterns of, 622–625
  external control enforcing sanctions,
    615
  influence of Judeo-Christian tradi-
    tion, 617
  internal control enforcing values,
    615–616
  justifications for, 618–620
  ownership rights as justification, 619
  repressive and permissive patterns
    of, 623–625
  reproductive consequences as justifi-
    cation, 619
  restricting sexual behavior of
    women, 619
  sexual behavior and social status,
    620, 622

Social regulation of sexuality (*cont.*)
   sexual exploitation as justification, 619
   and sexual socialization, 615
   social judgments, 617–618
   and social norms and sanctions, 615–616
   social stability as justification, 619–620
   sources of social control, 616–617
Social releasers, 240
Social sanctions, 615–616
Social stability, as justification for social control of sex, 619–620
Society, 601
Sociobiology, 302
Sociology, contributing to study of sex, 6
Sociosexual play, 225–227
   age of experiencing, 226
Sodomy, 362
   Biblical references to, 660–661
   decriminalization of, 639–640
   *See also* Homosexuality
Soft-core pornography, 519–520
   *See also* Pornography
Soft fetishes, 396
Solicitation, 645, 647
Sound, role in sexual arousal, 57–58
Sounds and music, and sexual enhancement, 355–356
Spanish fly, 357, 435
Spectatoring, 424
Sperm, 32, 45
   development of, 47
   movement of, 150
   route after ejaculation, 150
Spermatic cord, 44–45
Spermatic fluid, 150
Spermatids, 47
Spermatogenesis, 47
Spermatogonium, 37
Sperm banks, 181–182
Spermicides, 201–202
   failure rate of, 202
   side effects of, 202
Sphincters, 36
Spinal block, 170
Spinal control of sexual functions
   erection and ejaculation, 76–77
   of female sexual function, 78
Spinal reflexes, 76
Spontaneous abortion, 177–178
Spontaneous recovery, 247
Spousal exchange, 496
Spousal exemption, 642–643
*Staphylococcus aureus,* 114
Statistics in sex research, 21–22
*Status orgasmus,* 62
Statutory rape, 550–551
   age limits for, 643–644
   and evidence of promiscuity, 644
   laws prohibiting, 643–644
Sterility, 179

Sterilization, 206–209
   female, 208–209
   informed consent required for, 629
   laws affecting, 629–630
   male, 206–208
   for mentally retarded, 629–630
Steroids, 82
   synthetic, 193
Stimulus, 56
Stimulus generalization, 247
Storge, 462
Straight, 362
   *See also* Homosexuality
Stranger rape, 547–548
Stratified sample, 21, 24
Streetwalker, 509, 511
   *See also* Prostitution
Structured interview, 23
Submission, 341
Suckling, 174
Suction curette, 212
Superego, 243
Surgical treatments for sexual dysfunction, 437–438
Surrogate motherhood, 182, 631–634
   conflicts generated by, 634
Swinging, 497
Symbolical reenactments, 407
Sympathetic nervous system, 76
Symphysis pubis, 32
Synthetic hormones, 95, 195
   in male contraceptive pills, 210
   *See also* Birth control pills
Synthetic steroids, 193
Syphilis, 124–127
   chancres caused by, 125–126
   congenital, 127
   incidence of, 124–125
   latency phase in, 126
   primary stage, 125–126
   screening tests for, 126
   secondary stage, 126
   tertiary stage, 126–127
   transmission of, 124
   treatment of, 126, 127

Target organs, 82
Teenage pregnancy, 189, 190, 264–267, 611
   and abortion, 267
   age of, 264–265
   effect of sex education on, 267
   health risks of, 266
   impact on education, 266
   impact on family income and earnings, 266
   impact on fathers, 266–267
   outside marriage, 265
   rates of, 264
Testes, 44–45
   undescended, 51–52
Testes-determining factor, 51
Testicular cancer, 119–120
   self-examination, 119

Testicular feminization, 101–102
Testicular hormones, role in maturation of reproductive system, 51
Testis cords, 51
Testosterone, 82–83
   deficiency of, and sexual dysfunction, 421
   effect on male sexual drive, 107, 109
   essential for development of male genitalia, 292
   and female sex drive, 110
   functions of, 83
   and maturation of seminiferous tubules, 51
   role in adult sexual behavior, 102, 104–105, 107–109
   used to treat sexual dysfunction, 436
Tissue disorders, 101–102
Touch, role in sexual arousal, 57
Toucherism, 405
Touching and caressing, 335–337
Toxemia, 177
Toxic shock syndrome (TSS), 113–114
Tranquilizers and sexual dysfunction, 423
Transsexualism, 295–297, 398
   cause of, 296
   sex-change surgery for, 296–297
   sexual orientation of transsexuals, 295–296
   treatment for, 296
Transvestic fetishism, 294
Transvestism, 397–399
   complete, 398
   partial, 398
   reactions to, 399
Trauma, causing sexual dysfunction, 421
Treatment of sexual dysfunction, 427–438
   behavior therapy, 433–434
   drugs, 434–436
   group therapy, 434
   Kegel exercises, 436–437
   masturbation training, 437
   physical methods, 436–437
   psychotherapy, 432–433
   self-help, 434
   sex therapy, 427–432, 433
   surgical methods, 437–438
*Treponema pallidum,* 124
Triangular theory of love, 462–464
Trichomonas, 115
Triphasic model of sexual function, 413
Triphasic pill, 196
Troilism, 406
Trophoblast cells, 157
Trust in sexual intimacy, 457
Tubal ligation, 208–209
Tumescence, 60
Turner's syndrome, 101
Twins, 156

Ultrasound, 161
Unconditioned reflex, 246–247
Unconditioned response (UCR), 247
Unconditioned stimulus (UCS), 247
Unconscious, 243
Unidimensional, bipolar gender
    model, 285
Urethra, 34, 41, 45–46
Urethral meatus, 34, 41
Urethral sphincters, 45–46
Urogenital folds, 52
Urogenital sinus, 51
Urolagnia, 405
Urophilia, 405
Uterine orgasm, 70
Uterus, 38–39
    orgasmic contractions in, 74
Utopian communities, 597

Vaccines, 141–142
Vacuum aspiration, 212–213
Vagina, 39–40
    effect of sexual arousal on, 64–67
    lengthening of, 66
    lubrication of, 64–66
    muscular layer of wall of, 40
    size of, 37
    tenting effect in, 66–67, 68
Vaginal introitus, 34–36, 37
Vaginal mucosa, 39
Vaginal opening, 34–36
    muscles in, 37
Vaginal orgasm, 70–71
Vaginal photoplethysmograph, 60
Vaginismus, 420
    treatment for, 432

Vaginitis, 115
Valuation of sex, 506–509
    bride price, 506
    and compensation for sexual favors,
        506–507
    dowry, 506
    and fair exchange, 507
    gender considerations, 508–509
    and informed consent, 507–508
    sexual value of the person, 506–507
    symmetry of status, 508
    value of emotional commitment, 507
Variables in sex research, 19–20
Variance, 22
Vas deferens, 45
Vasectomy, 206–208
    autoimmune reactions to, 208
    failure rate of, 206
    psychological effects of, 208
    reversing, 207
    side effects of, 208
Vasoactive intestinal polypeptide
    (VIP), 78
Vasocongestion, 63
Vasovasostomy, 207
VDRL test, 126
Venereal diseases. See Sexually trans-
    mitted diseases
Venus statuettes, 567
Vestibular bulbs, 36
Violence, linked with aggressive por-
    nography, 525
Viral encephalitis, caused by genital
    herpes, 130
Viral hepatitis, causing sexually trans-
    mitted disease, 127

Vitamin B-complex deficiencies, role in
    premenstrual syndrome, 98
Voluntary nervous system, 76
Voyeurism, 399–400, 644
Vulval orgasm, 70

Western blot test for AIDS, 140
Wet dreams, 319–320
Whore, 509
    See also Prostitution
Widows and widowers, 491
    sexual activity of, 503
Wife-swapping, 497
Wish fulfillment, 310–311
Withdrawal, 205–206, 351
Wolffian ducts, 51
Womb. See Uterus
Women's liberation movement,
    603–604
    current issues for, 607
    and female sexuality, 606
    social concerns of, 604

Yohimbine, 435
    and sexual response, 357
Young adulthood, 253
    See also Sexuality in young adult-
        hood
Youth subculture, 262

Zero population growth (ZPG), 187
Zona pellucida of ovum, 50
Zoophilia, 394–395
Zovirax, 131
Zygote, 156

# Name Index

Abel, G., 557n, 561n
Abplanalp, J.M., 98n
Abramowitz, S., 296n
Ackman, C.F.D., 206n
Adams, J.N., 578n
Addiego, F., 68n
Adler, A., 13
Adler, N.E., 266n
Ageton, S., 546n
Ainsworth, M.D.S., 458n
Alford, J., 561n
Allen, D.M., 511n
Alter-Reid, K., 390n
Altman, D., 195n
Altman, L.D., 367n
Altman, L.K., 133n, 138n
Alzate, H., 68n
Amick, A.E., 549n
Amir, M., 553n, 558n, 561n
Andersch, B., 97n
Anderson, C., 414n
Anderson, C.L., 18n
Anderson, F.C., 300n
Anderson, J., 548n
Annon, J.S., 427n
Ansbacher, R., 208n
Apfelbaum, B., 419n
Arafat, I.S., 326n, 327n, 329n
Arbithnot, F.F., 353
Archer, W.G., 353n
Arentewicz, G., 422n, 427n, 433n
Arey, L.B., 159n
Aries, P., 221n
Arms, K., 241n
Arms, S., 168n
Arsdalen, V.K.N., 78n
Ashford, J., 183n
Athanasiou, R., 25n, 271n, 392n, 537n
Atkins, J., 9n, 585n
Autill, J.K., 286n
Avery-Clark, C., 426n

Bacci, M., 323n
Bailey, D.S., 660n
Bailey, S., 572n
Bailey, T., 601n
Baird, D., 176n
Baker, S.W., 292n
Bakwin, H., 223n, 224n, 225n
Balfour, J.G., 470n
Bancroft, J., 56n, 77n, 79n, 84n, 106n, 107n, 110n, 382n
Bandura, A., 248n
Barbach, L.G., 327n, 434, 439n

Barber, R.N., 545n
Barclay, A.M., 316n
Bardwick, J., 248n
Barre-Sinoussi, 134n
Barron, J., 237n
Barrows, S.B., 511n
Bartell, G.D., 497n
Baruch, D.W., 636n
Battersby, J.D., 634n
Baucom, D., 456n
Baumeister, R.F., 402n
Bayer, R., 381n
Beach, F.A., 56n, 102n, 106n, 241n, 638n
Becker, J., 556n, 557n
Bee, H.L., 253n, 488n, 491n
Behrman, R.E., 101n
Bell, A.P., 363n, 364n, 366n, 372n, 373n, 379n, 380n, 381n, 382n, 383n
Bell, N., 287n
Belliveau, F., 439n
Belzer, E.J. Jr., 68n
Bem, S.L., 284n, 286n
Bennett, N.G., 477n
Benson, D.J., 541n
Benson, G.S., 63n
Benton, D., 103n
Berkely, S.F., 114n
Berlin, F., 408n
Bermant, G., 62n, 102n, 273n
Bernstein, A.C., 233n
Bernstein, R., 51n
Berscheid, E., 448n, 462n, 465n, 482n
Bess, B.E., 515n
Betancourt, J., 255n
Bettelheim, B., 244n
Bieber, I., 378n, 379n, 382n
Biehler, R.F., 248n
Billings, E.L., 204n
Billstein, S., 128n
Birns, B., 287n
Blair, C.D., 401n
Blakely, M.K., 648n
Bleier, R., 104n, 294n, 302n, 305n
Bloch, I., 13
Blumstein, P., 248n, 370n, 447n, 460n, 476n, 477n, 486n, 491n, 493n, 495n, 499n, 500n, 504n, 536n, 612n
Boardman, J., 599n
Boas, F., 242
Boffey, P.M., 136n
Bohlen, J.G., 60n, 71n, 74n, 424n

Bokser, B.Z., 569n
Bonsall, R.W., 103n
Bookstein, J., 422n, 424n
Boorstin, R.O., 636n
Borneman, E., 238n
Borowtiz, E.B., 570n, 572n
Bors, E., 417n
Boswell, J., 9n, 362n, 381n, 572n, 573n, 574n, 585n, 607n, 660n, 661n
Bouyer, L., 657n
Bowen, S.C., 130n, 145n
Bower, D.W., 483n
Bowlby, J., 233n, 459n
Boyle, P.S., 417n
Brackbill, Y., 287n
Bradford, J.M., 61n
Bradley, W.E., 424n
Braen, G., 552n
Brain, R., 444n
Brande, N., 471n
Brandes, S., 272n
Brandt, A.M., 133n
Breasted, M., 236n
Brecher, E., 21n
Brecher, E.M., 15n, 17n, 276n, 277n, 279n
Brecher, R., 80n
Breslow, N., 403n, 404n
Brest, P., 648n
Brickner, B., 661n, 665n
Brim, O.G., 272n, 615n
Brobeck, J.R., 85n
Brody, J.E., 381n, 419n, 460n
Brooks-Gunn, J., 256n
Broude, G.J., 495n
Broverman, I.K., 284n
Brown, G., 503n
Brown, L., 18n
Brownmiller, S., 315, 544n, 545n, 563n, 607n, 641n
Brozan, N., 117n, 162n
Brundage, J.A., 573n
Budoff, P., 98n
Bullough, V., 27n, 532n
Bullough, V.L., 582n, 585n, 636n
Burgess, A.W., 521n, 524n, 553n, 555n, 559n
Burnham, J.C., 9n
Burton, R.F., 353
Buscaglia, L., 462n, 472n
Buss, D.M., 461n
Buunk, B., 460n
Byrne, D., 290n, 314n

Caird, W., 427n
Calderone, M.S., 18, 251n
Calhoun, L., 165n
Callahan, D., 630n
Calverton, V.F., 598n
Cameron, P., 309n, 310n
Camp, S.L., 185n, 187n
Campagna, A.F., 310n
Campbell, N.A., 32n, 240n, 301n, 302n, 535n
Capraro, V., 115n
Capron, A.M., 632n
Card, J., 266n
Carey, J.T., 356n
Carmichael, M.S., 84n
Carnes, P.J., 406n, 470n
Carrier, J.M., 368n
Carroll, J., 300n, 451n
Carroll, Jon, 494n
Castleman, M., 557n
Catania, J., 21n
Cates, W. Jr., 120n, 124n
Cavafy, C.P., 277, 374
Chambers, M, 586n, 656n
Chambless, D., 437n
Chang, J., 37n, 73n, 348n, 350n, 353n, 360n, 382n
Charnes R., 288n
Chastre, J., 296n
Chayen, B., 165n
Check, J.V.P., 525n
Cherlin, A.J., 486n, 491n
Chevalier-Skolnikoff, S., 366n
Christensen, H., 272n
Christenson, C.V., 15n
Church, G.J., 639n
Cichon, J., 557n
Clark, J.T., 357n
Clark, S., 401n
Clarkson, T.B., 208n
Clausen, J.A., 256n
Clayton, R.R., 270n
Clelland, J., 513n, 515n
Clement, U., 326n
Clugh, J., 586n
Cohen, A., 570n
Cohen, B., 515n
Cohen, H.D., 79n
Cohen, L., 481n
Cohen, M., 255n
Cole, T.M., 417n
Coleman, D., 458n
Coleman, E., 405n, 406n
Coleman, J.C., 262n
Coles, R., 254n, 256n, 258n, 260n, 261n, 270n, 279n
Comfort, A., 278n, 328n, 340n, 353n, 360n, 403n, 422n, 450n, 596n
Condry, J., 287n
Conn, J., 222n
Connell, E.B., 198n
Conrad, M., 424n
Constantinople, A., 285n
Cook, R.F., 525n

Cooper, A.J., 408n
Cooper, J.F., 186n
Cooper, P.T., 185n
Corey, L., 128n
Court, J.H., 525n
Couzinet, B., 196n
Cowan, C., 470n
Cowan, G., 287n
Cozby, D.C., 455n
Craig, G.J., 221n, 231n
Crain, I.J., 352n
Crapo, L., 62n, 111n
Crepault, C., 309n
Croughan, J., 399n
Culp, R., 289n
Curran, C., 667n
Cutler, W.B., 103n

Dalton, K., 97n
Daly, M., 105n, 168n
Darling, C.A., 426n
Darwin, C.R., 5
Davenport, C., 242
Davenport, W.H., 6n, 166n, 443n, 623n
Davidson, J.M., 6n, 69n, 74n, 80n, 102n, 107n, 110n
Davies, E., 255n
Davis, A.J., 552n
Davis, J.D., 456n
Dawson, D.A., 186n
Dawson, P., 360n
D'Andrade, R.G., 303n
DeAmicis, L., 433n
de Beauvoir, S., 290n, 604n
Debrovner, C.H., 98n
Decter, M., 607n
Degler, C., 9n, 15, 16, 593n, 594n
de Groat, W.C., 63n, 76n
DeJong, F.H., 84n
DeLamater, J.D., 248n, 304n, 616n
Delaney, J., 91n
Delin, B., 560n
Del Rosario, 129n
Denfield, D., 497n
Dennehy, R., 657n
Dennerstein, L., 110n
Denney, M., 217n
Denniston, R.H., 366n
Derenski, A., 179n
de Rougemont, 462n
Des Jarlais, D.C., 135n
Deutsch, H., 378n
Devereaux, G., 368n
DeWald, P.A., 432n
Dewsbury, D., 461n
Dhabuwala, C.B., 422n
Diamond, M., 292n, 293n
Dickinson, R.L., 44n, 54n
Dick-Read, G., 172
Dietz, P., 560n
D'Emilio, J., 592n, 596n, 599n, 601n, 603n, 609n, 613n, 614n, 673n

Dion, K.L., 447n, 466n
Ditkoff, M., 521n
Dixen, J.M., 296n
Djerassi, C., 185n, 189n, 192n, 193n, 196n, 200n, 210n, 211n, 217n
Dodson, B., 327n, 331n
Doherty, D., 657n
Dolesh, D., 500n
Dolgin, J.L., 627n
Donnerstein, E., 516n, 522n, 523n, 527n, 532n, 562n
Dornbusch, S.M., 256n
Dorner, G., 377n
Doty, R.L., 103n
Douglas, N., 354n
Dover, K.J., 381n, 573n, 574n, 599n
Dowdle, W.R., 135n
Draper, N.E.E., 186n
Drew, D., 511n
Droegemueller, W., 177n, 195n, 197n, 206n
Dryfoos, J., 267n
Duggan, L., 648n
Dunn, H.G., 176n
Durfee, R.B., 179n
Durkheim, E., 242
Durkin, M.G., 674n
Dworkin, A., 648

Earhart, H.B., 670n
Earle, J.R., 270n
Easterling, W.E., 175n
Eckholm, E., 136n, 137n
Edman, I., 10n
Edwards, R., 182
Edwards, S.R., 405n, 406n
Ehrhardt, A.A., 102n, 105n, 291n, 293n, 294n, 294n, 377n, 378n
Ehrlich, A., 187n
Ehrlich, P., 187n
Eitner, L., 8n, 583n, 589n, 595n, 599n
Elder, G., 482n
Elder, G.H., 253n
Elias, J., 378n
Elise, D., 373n
Ellis, A., 46n, 60n, 401n, 499n
Ellis, H.H., 14–15, 309n, 319n, 321n, 324n, 329n, 362n, 597
Elvik, S., 390n
Emanuel, E.J., 484n
Ende, J., 413n
Engel, G.L., 386n
Epstein, L.M., 571n, 568n, 599n
Erikson, E.H., 245n, 253n, 268n
Eschenbach, D., 115n, 124n
Esselstyn, T.C., 511n
Essex, M., 133n
Estrich, S., 651n
Eu, M.F., 636n
Evans, D.R., 409n
Evans, J.R., 190n
Evans, R.B., 379n
Exter, T., 477n, 478n

Fagan, P., 425n
Fagot, B., 287n
Fairbanks, B., 199n
Farmer, J.S., 283n
Farrell, W., 461n
Fausto-Sterling, A., 97n, 104n, 287n, 302n, 562n
Fawcett, J.Y., 149n
Fay, A., 424n
Federman, D.D., 101n
Fedora, O., 401n
Fein, G., 287n
Feldman-Summers, S., 546n
Feucht, O.E., 588n
Field, J.H., 8n, 10n
Finch, s., 236n
Finkelhor, D., 227n, 387n, 388n, 389n, 390n, 391n, 392n, 393n, 410n, 547n, 550n
Firestone, S., 606n
Fisher, C., 319n
Fisher, G.J., 550n
Fisher, S., 70n, 71n
Fisher, W.A., 290n
Fishman, I.J., 437n
Fishman, P.M., 283n
Flaherty, J., 286n
Fleming, A.T., 632n, 634n
Fletcher, J., 668–669, 674n
Follingstead, D.R., 316n
Ford, C.S., 6n, 91n, 165n, 227n, 229n, 263n, 321n, 335n, 344n, 366n, 368n, 391n, 497n, 614n, 622n, 638n
Forel, A., 14
Forrest, J., 189n, 193n, 198n, 200n, 203n, 206n, 209n, 211n
Foucault, M., 9n, 593n
Fox, C.A., 74n
Fox, G.L., 304n
Francoeur, R.T., 611n, 614n, 625n
Frank, E., 413n, 414n
Frank, G., 560n
Franklin, J., 340n
Frayser, S.G., 27n
Freedman, E.B., 9n
Freedman, M.J., 382n
Freeman, D., 242n
Freeman, E.D., 216n
Freeman, E.W., 98n
Freeman, J., 604n
Freud, S., 12–13, 221, 241, 243–245, 318n, 385–386
Friday, N., 316n, 317n, 332n, 460n
Friedan, B., 603n, 604n, 607n
Friedland, G.H., 135n
Friedrich, P., 576n
Frisch, R.E., 89n

Gadpaille, W.J., 226n
Gagnon, J.H., 238n, 249n, 304n, 326n, 339n, 342n
Gal, A., 131n
Galenson, E., 224n

Gallo, R., 134n
Gallup, G., 480n, 641n, 667n
Galton, F., 242n
Garcia, L.T., 453n
Gasser, T., 437n
Gavser, B., 479n
Gay, G.R., 357n
Gay, P., 12n, 621n
Gebhard, P.H., 15, 223n, 225n, 298n, 389n, 390n, 397n, 399n, 401n, 410n, 503n, 640n
Geis, G., 545n, 553n
Geodert, J., 143n
Gesell, A., 221, 221n
Gessa, G.L., 436n
Ghadarian, A.M., 97n
Gilbert, F.S., 236n
Gilder, G.F., 426n
Gilligan, C., 274n
Gilman, A.G., 82n, 83n, 111n, 193n, 210n, 435n
Gilmartin, B.G., 497n
Giovacchini, P.L., 262n
Gittelson, N.L., 400n
Giuliano, A., 116n
Gladue, B., 68n, 103n
Gleitman, H., 246n
Glynn, P., 354n, 445n
Goldberg, D., 68n
Goldfoot, D.A., 103n
Goldman, 1985, 555n
Goldman, J., 217n, 233n, 234n, 235n, 237n, 248n
Goldman, R., 217n, 233n, 234n, 235n, 237n, 248n, 251n
Goldstein, B., 57n
Goldstein, I., 78n, 422n
Goldstein, M., 524n
Goldstein, S., 97n
Gong, V., 142n
Goode, W.J., 474n, 490n, 615n
Goodman, R.E., 296n
Gooren, L., 378n
Gordis, R., 666n
Gordon, J.W., 50n, 51n
Gordon, L., 594n
Gordon, S., 237n
Gorski, R., 104n
Gosling, J., 529n
Gosselin, C., 386n
Gottlieb, M., 132n
Gould, R.E., 634n
Goy, R.W., 102n
Grafenberg, E., 67
Grant, M., 578n
Grant, S., 340n
Graves, R., 576n
Gray, D.S., 110n
Gray, F.duP., 500n
Green, R., 295n, 374n, 380n
Greenberg, J.S., 329n
Greenblatt, C.S., 492n
Greene, G., 402n
Greenspan, F.S., 82n

Greer, G., 604n
Gregersen, E., 7n, 34n, 35n, 37n, 43n, 58n, 73n, 91n, 106n, 321n, 362n, 368n, 391n, 474n, 500n, 547n, 625n, 638n
Gregory, J., 437n
Griffith, W., 299n, 300n
Griffitt, W., 456n
Grigson, G., 576n
Grimal, P., 576n
Grof, S., 357n
Groff, M.G., 393n
Groopman, J.E., 138n
Grosskopf, D., 498n
Grosskurth, P., 15n
Grossmann, R., 563n
Groth, A.N., 119n, 389n, 525n, 552n, 559n, 560n, 563n
Grumbach, M.M., 101n, 560n
Grunfeld, B., 562n
Guerrero, 155n
Gulevich, G., 319n
Gulik, R.H.V., 282n, 353n
Gunderson, J.G., 458n
Gustafson, J.M., 653n, 667n, 668n
Gutek, B.A., 541n
Guyton, A.C., 76n, 82n, 84n, 89n

Haas, A., 258n, 260n, 261n, 283n
Haeberle, E.J., 11n, 14n, 41n, 334n, 362n
Hafez, E.S.E., 84n
Hagen, I.M., 198n
Hallingby, L., 674n
Halstrom, T., 109n
Halverson, H.M., 222n
Hamerton, J.L., 101n
Hanley, R., 634n
Hansen, G.L., 499n
Hansfield, H.H., 121n
Harbison, R.D., 177n
Hare, E.H., 328n
Harlow, H.F., 228, 230n, 231n
Harmatz, M.G., 497n
Harris, M., 602n, 603n, 606n, 609n
Harrison, W.M., 423n
Harry, J., 21n
Hart, B.L., 77n
Hartman, W., 350n
Harvey, S.M., 189n
Haseltine, F.P., 51n
Hatcher, R.A., 114n, 115n, 120n, 130n, 137n, 149n, 150n, 188n, 189n, 191n, 193n, 194n, 195n, 196n, 197n, 198n, 202n, 203n, 204n, 205n, 206n, 209n, 210n, 211n, 212n, 217n
Hatfield, E., 456n, 465n, 467n
Hatterer, L.J., 382n
Haugh, S., 287n
Hausfater, G., 98n
Haviland, W.A., 391n
Hayden, M., 244n
Hayes, R.W., 34n

Haynes, D.M., 156n, 177n
Hearst, N., 136n
Heath, R.G., 79n
Heim, N., 107n
Heiman, J.P., 290n, 299n
Helmreich, R.L., 286n
Hendrick, S., 248n
Hendricks, L.E., 266n
Henley, N.M., 283n
Henry, W.A., 640n
Henslin, J.M., 6n
Herbst, A.L., 195n
Herdt, G., 368n, 378n
Heresova, J., 296n
Heston, L., 377n.
Hiernaux, J., 92n
Higgins, G.E., 417n
Higham, E., 248n
Hill, E., 118n
Himes, N., 186n, 200n, 357n
Himmelweit, H.T., 238n
Hinde, R.A., 5n
Hindelang, M.J., 545n, 546n
Hindy, C., 458n
Hirschfeld, M., 13–14, 362n
Hite, S., 24–25, 69n, 322n, 338n, 339n,
    340n, 351n, 352n, 418n, 480n
Hoch, Z., 68n
Hockenberry, S.L., 380n
Hoenig, J., 11n, 14n
Hoffman, C.H., 120n
Hoffman, M., 375n, 397n
Hole, J., 606n
Hollender, M., 400n
Hollister, L., 357n
Holme, B., 576n
Holmes, K., 116n
Holt, L.H., 98n, 145n
Hong, L.K., 418n
Hooker, E., 382n
Hopkins, T.J., 670n
Hopson, J.S., 58n, 103n
Horney, K., 244n
Horton, D., 356n
Houseknecht, S., 186n
Houston, L.N., 521n
Houston, V., 479n
Howard, J., 453n
Howard, J.L., 525n
Howell, N., 180
Huelsman, B.R., 34n
Hull, C.L., 241n
Humphries, L., 371n, 376n
Hunt, M., 24, 269n, 270n, 313n, 314n,
    315n, 326n, 327n, 329n, 338n,
    342n, 345n, 347n, 351n, 392n,
    402n, 418n, 493n, 497n, 502n,
    513n
Hunter, N., 634n
Hurtig, A., 292n
Hussey, H.H., 208n
Huston, T.L., 448n
Hutchinson, J.B., 377n
Huxley, A., 193n

Huxley, T.H., 242
Hyppa, M.T., 436n

Imperato-McGinley, J., 100n, 292n
Ingrassia, M., 481n
Inkeles, G., 336n
Isung, 194n

Jackson, E., 270n
Jacobs, L., 426n
Jacobson, E., 255n
Jaffee, D., 546n
James, A., 251n
James, J., 516n
Jayne, C., 19n
Jensen, D., 45n, 63n, 77n
Jensen, J., 657n
Jessor, S., 260n
Jick, H., 202n
Johns, D.R., 75n
Johnson, D., 656n
Johnson, M.L., 89n
Johnston, J., 606n
Jones, E., 243n, 264n, 296n, 319n
Jones, M.C., 255n
Jong, E., 330n
Jost, A., 50n
Judd, H.L., 274n
Judson, F., 129n
Jung, C.G., 12, 241, 282

Kagan, D., 8n, 590n
Kahn, J., 236n
Kahneman, D., 284n
Kaiser, I., 150n
Kallmann, F.J., 377n
Kando, T.M., 6n, 604n
Kanin, E., 549n, 558n, 559n
Kaplan, H.S., 142n, 248n, 327n, 412n,
    413n, 414n, 415n, 418n, 424n,
    427n, 428n, 429n, 434n, 436n,
    439n, 646n
Kaplan, J., 138n
Karacan, I., 222n, 319n
Karlen, A., 573n, 597n
Katchadourian, H., 18n, 111n, 272n,
    279n, 290n, 305n
Katz, J., 608n
Kaufman, A., 210n
Kaufman, M., 460n
Kegel, A., 436n
Kelley, J., 111n
Kelley, K., 305n
Kelly, G.F., 236n
Kennedy, A., 336n
Kenniston, K., 605n
Kessel, R.G., 47n, 54n
Keusch, G.T., 127n
Kiell, N., 332n
Kiely, E., 436n
Kilbourne, E.D., 128n
Kilpatrick, A.C., 390n, 391n
Kilpatrick, J.J., 648n
Kinch, R.A.H., 98n

Kingsley, L., 135n
Kinsey, A.C., 6n, 15, 17, 24, 39n, 57n,
    62n, 70n, 107n, 223n, 224n, 246,
    248n, 258n, 260n, 269n, 300n,
    314n, 317, 319n, 322n, 325n,
    334n, 342n, 363–364, 364n, 365n,
    367n, 395n, 418n, 492n, 493n,
    598n, 615n, 640n
Kirby, D., 267n
Kirkendall, L.A., 613n
Kirkpatrick, C., 549n
Kitzinger, S., 289n
Klassen, A.D., 422n
Klaus, M.H., 173n, 232n
Kleeman, J.A., 224n, 225n
Klein, F., 365n
Klein, H.G., 137n
Kline-Graber, G., 437n
Knapp, J.J., 496n
Knuppel, R., 158n
Koblinsky, S., 426n
Koedt, A., 606n
Kohlberg, 245n, 246n
Kohn, B., 24
Kolata, G.B., 133n, 134n, 214n
Kolodny, R.C., 62n, 78n, 259n, 278n,
    416n, 418n, 419n, 420n, 421n,
    422n, 423n
Komarovsky, M., 456n
Konner, M., 181n
Koop, C.E., 137n, 236–237
Korner, A.F., 222n
Kosnik, A., 660n, 666n, 667n, 674n
Koss, M.P., 546n, 547n, 549n
Kost, K., 207n
Krafft-Ebing, R.von, 11–12, 385, 405n
Krane, R.J., 63n
Kroop, M.S., 342n
Kuhn, D., 287n
Kurdek, L.A., 482n
Kutchinsky, B., 527n
Kutner, N.G., 288n
Kwan, M., 107n
Kwong, L., 435n
Kyon & Benyo, 354n, 354n

Lacayo, R., 636n
Lacey, C., 118n
Ladas, A.K., 61n, 68n, 70n
Ladouceur, P., 559n
Lacuchli, S., 661n
Lakoff, R., 283n
Lamaze, B., 172
Lamontagne, Y., 409n
Lancaster, J.B., 366n
Lance, K., 354n
Landers, A., 493n
Langfeldt, T., 222n
Langman, 50n
Larsen, U., 180
Larue, G., 10n, 569n, 674n
Lasater, M., 641n
Laub, D., 296n
Laurence, L.T., 456n

Lauritsen, J., 211n
Laws, J.L., 249n
Leahy, R., 288n
LeBoef, B.J., 5n
Leboyer, F., 172–173
Lederer, W., 244n
Ledger, W.A., 137n
Lee, J.A., 462n
Legman, G., 9n
Lehrman, D.S., 241n
Leiblum, S.R., 416n, 427n, 439n
Leibovici, L., 115n
Lemon, S.M., 132n
Leo, J., 236n, 237n, 522n, 613n
Leonard, G., 612n
Lertola, J., 134n
Lesnick-Oberstein, M., 481n
Lesser, H., 14n
Lessing, D., 71n
Levin, R.J., 63n, 70n, 74n, 320n, 455n, 493n, 498n
Levine, R., 547n, 623n
Levinson, D.J., 268n, 272n, 273n
Lewin, T., 265n, 487n
Lewis, C.S., 462n, 464n
Lewis, D.L., 355n
Libby, R.W., 249n, 496n
Licht, H., 357n, 573n, 574n, 576n
Liebowitz, M.R., 465n
Lief, H.I., 381n, 383n
Lieske, C., 520n
Lim, S.M., 297n
Lindemalm, G., 297n
Lipkin, J., Jr., 166n
Lipsett, 119n
Lipson, J., 137n
Lisk, R.D., 104n
Lizotte, A., 546n
Locke, J., 242
Lockwood, D., 552n
Loevinger, J., 253n
London, S.N., 273n
LoPiccolo, J., 419n, 427n, 429n, 433n, 437n
Lott, B., 286n, 287n, 288n, 289n, 290n
Lowenthal, J.F., 275n
Lowenthal, M.F., 275n
Lucie-Smith, E., 445n
Lynn, B.W., 522n, 650n

Mabie, B., 177n
Maccoby, E., 6n, 222n, 284n, 286n, 287n
MacKinnon, C.A., 518n, 538n, 563n, 648n
Macklin, E.D., 483n, 486n
Maclean, P.D., 79n
MacLusky, N.J., 105n, 293n
MacNamara, D., 389n, 400n
MacNamara, D.E.J., 651n
Maguire, D.C., 661n
Mahler, H., 133n
Mahoney, E.R., 521n
Mahood, J., 15n, 16n

Maisch, H., 393n
Malamuth, N.M., 535n, 546n
Malatesta, V.J., 422n
Malla, K., 57n, 353n
Malthus, T.R., 187
Manley, J., 267n
Manniche, L., 10n, 43n, 568n
Marcade, J., 575n, 576n
Marcus, I.M., 327n, 332n
Marcus, S., 9n, 317n, 514n, 593n, 595n
Marcuse, H., 243n, 621n
Marmor, J., 378n, 383n
Marshall, D.S., 263n, 321n, 624n
Marshall, J., 179n
Marshall, P., 424n
Marshall, W.A., 86n
Marsiglio, W., 267n
Martin, C.E., 15
Martin, E.C., 223n
Martin, J.L., 370n
Martinson, F.M., 223n, 226n, 454n
Maruta, T., 421n
Maslow, A.H., 457n, 464n
Masters, W.H., 17n, 25n, 43n, 44n, 59n, 60n, 61n, 62n, 63n, 65n, 70n, 71n, 80n, 109n, 136n, 165n, 222n, 246n, 275n, 278n, 316n, 317n, 324n, 334n, 337n, 351n, 370n, 382n, 412n, 416n, 419n, 424n, 427n, 429n, 433n, 556n
Matteo, S., 290n
May, R., 503n
Mayer, E.L., 244n
Mayo, C., 283n
Mazur, A., 445n, 448n
Mazur, R., 664n
McCaffree, K., 267n
McCary, J.L., 18n
McClintock, M.K., 193n
McCormick, N.B., 453n
McDougall, W., 239n
McGee, E.A., 123n
McGuire, R.J., 407n
McKey, P.L., 437n
McMillan, J.R., 283n
McNamara, J.A., 584n
McQuarrie, H.G., 160n
McWhirter, D.P., 370n, 372n
Meiselman, K.C., 394n
Meissner, W.W., 243n
Melody, G.F., 37n
Melville, R., 360n
Menken, J., 180, 266n
Menning, B., 179n
Merton, T., 457n, 458n
Messe, M.R., 437n
Messenger, J.C., 229n, 624n
Metcalfe, J., 549n
Meyer, A.W., 159n
Meyer, W.J., 3d., 296n
Michael, R.P., 62n, 103n
Michalodimitrakis, M., 405n
Miller, J., 611n
Miller, P.Y., 260n, 264n, 279n, 209n

Millet, K., 647n
Mims, F., 547n, 557n
Mischel, W., 248n
Mishell, D.R., 197n, 206n
Mitamura, T., 108n
Moghissi, 176n, 279n
Mohr, J., 389n
Mohs, M., 673n
Moll, A., 13, 221
Money, J., 78n, 82n, 99n, 107n, 256n, 282n, 290n, 291n, 292n, 294n, 305n, 377n, 378n, 408n
Monga, T., 422n
Montagu, A., 336n, 360n, 603n
Moore, K.L., 47n, 50n, 52n, 54n, 149n, 156n
Moorehead, A., 476n
Moorman, J.E., 477n
Moos, R., 95n
Morgan, M., 607n
Morgenthau, T., 133n
Morin, J., 341n, 352n, 367n
Morokoff, P.J., 21n, 290n
Morris, D., 57n, 354n, 443n, 536n
Morris, J., 295
Morron, P.A., 18
Moser, C., 11n
Mosher, B.A., 274n
Mosher, C.D., 15, 16
Mulac, A., 283n
Mulvihill, D.J., 553n
Munjack, D.J., 420n
Murad, F., 83n, 195n
Murdock, G.P. 474n
Murphy, E., 510n, 529n
Murphy, F.K., 127n
Murphy, J., 195n
Murstein, B.I., 259n, 462n, 481n
Musaph, H., 416n
Mussen, P.H., 6n
Muuss, R.E., 262n
Myers, L.S., 274n

Nabokov, V., 515n
Nadler, R.D., 105n
Nahemow, L., 481n
Nathan, S., 413n
Nefzawi, S., 41n, 416n
Neiberg, P., 176n
Netter, F.H., 54n
Neubeck, G., 499n
Neumann, F., 408n
Neusner, J., 572n
Newcomb, M., 500n
Newcomb, M.D., 486n
Newcomer, S.F., 260n, 339n
Newman, H.F., 63n
Newson, J., 224n
Nietsche, F., 576n
Nilsson, L., 54n, 183n
Noonan, J.T.,Jr., 185n, 580n, 582n, 629n, 658n
Norwood, R., 470n
Nory, M.J., 173n

Novak, E.R., 118n
Noyes, J.H., 487

Oakley, G., 178n
O'Farrell, T., 423n
Offit, A.K., 317n, 351n
O'Kelly, C.G., 288n
Olds, J., 79n
O'Neill, G., 496n
O'Neill, N., 496n
Onorato, I.M., 488n
Opler, M.K., 335n
Oriel, J.D., 132n
Orkin, M., 128n
Ortner, A., 98n
Ortner, S., 287n
Ory, H.W., 185n, 189n, 211n
Osser, S., 197n
Overholster, J., 561n
Ovesey, L., 382n

Packer, H.L., 628n
Padgitt, S., 538n
Page, D.C., 51n
Pagels, E., 582n
Paige, K.E., 34n, 43n, 98n, 114n
Pao, P., 460n
Parkes, C.M., 491n
Parrinder, G., 10n, 570n, 669n, 670n, 674n
Pavlov, I.P., 246–247
Pear, R., 137n
Pearlin, L.I., 253n
Peckham, M., 518n
Peele, D., 470n
Peele, S., 470n
Pepe, F., 165n
Perella, N.J., 334n, 360n
Perkins, R.P., 165n
Pernoll, M., 156n, 177n
Perry, J.D., 68n
Persky, H., 107n, 109n
Peterman, T.A., 133n
Petersen, A.C., 253n
Peterson, J.R., 25n
Petrovich, M., 390n, 561n
Pfeiffer, E., 109n
Phillips, S., 287n
Piaget, J., 233n, 245–246
Pillard, R., 377n
Pincus, G., 193n
Pitt, E., 266n
Ploughman, P., 551n
Pogrebin, L.C., 288n
Pohlman, E.G., 149n
Polyson, J., 6n, 18n
Pomeroy, W.B., 15, 223n
Pope, K.S., 472n
Porter, T., 286n
Potterat, J., 515n
Price, W., 138n
Pritchard, J.A., 211n
Pritchard, J.A., 183n
Purdy, S., 8n, 9n, 592n, 595n

Qualls, C.B., 438n
Quinlan, M.J., 593n
Quinn, S., 607n
Quinn, T.C., 133n, 136n, 143n

Rabkin, C., 143n
Rachlin, S.K., 288n
Rada, R.Y., 389n
Raisman, G., 104n
Ramasharma, K., 85n
Rathus, S.A., 285n
Ratzinger, J., 656n
Raven, P.H., 32n, 134n, 301n, 534n, 535n
Rawson, P., 670n, 671n
Rechy, J., 511n, 513n, 532n
Reich, W., 13, 243n
Reichlin, S., 99n
Reid, R.L., 97n
Reimer, R.A., 522n, 651n
Reinhold, R., 132n
Reinisch, J., 480n
Reinisch, J.M., 305n
Reiss, I.L., 11n, 261n, 270n, 271n, 474n, 476n, 483n, 487n, 495n, 504n, 612n
Reite, M., 319n
Remafedi, G., 261n
Remy, J., 34n
Renshaw, D.C., 390n
Richardson, L., 495n
Richart, R., 118n
Richlin, A., 578n
Rioux, J., 208n
Rizley, R., 465n
Roback, H., 296n
Robbins, M.B., 62n
Roberts, E.J., 234n
Robinson, P., 9n, 13n, 15n, 17n, 27n, 243n, 364n, 597n, 625n
Robinson, P.K., 290n
Roche, J.P., 262n
Rodgers, B., 34n, 41n, 362n, 371n, 383n, 511n
Rook, K.S., 304n
Rops, F., 595n
Rose, D., 557n
Rosenblum, L., 461n
Rosenfeld, A., 236n, 392n, 393n
Ross, C., 203n
Roszak, T., 604n
Roth, P., 330n
Rousseau, J.J., 11
Rowan, R., 128n, 145n
Rowell, T.E., 105n
Rubin, A., 496n
Rubin, J., 287n
Rubin, P., 116n
Rubin, Z., 98n, 233n, 456n, 462n, 466n
Rubinow, D.R., 96n, 97n
Rubinsky, H.J., 299n
Ruble, D., 98n
Rueger, R., 336n
Runyan, D.K., 390n, 393n

Russell, B., 242n, 580n
Russell, D., 563n
Russell, D.E.H., 518n, 519n
Russell, G.F.M., 255n
Russell, K.P., 168n
Russell, M.J., 103n

Saah, A.J., 140n
Sack, A.R., 271n
Sadler, T.W.L., 47n, 54n, 149n
Sadock, B.J., 165n
Safran, C., 540n
Saghir, M.T., 367n, 380n, 382n
Sales, E., 556n
Salzman, L., 70n, 378n
Samuel, T., 206n
Sanday, P.R., 547n, 559n
Sandberg, G., 419n
Sanders, R.M., 377n
Sandfort, T., 391n
Sanger, M., 15, 185
Sanguiliano, I., 268n
Sarnoff, S., 331n
Sarrel, L.M., 268n, 279n, 326n, 406n
Sarrel, P.J., 18n, 268n, 279n, 326n, 406n, 552n
Saslawsky, D.A., 237n
Satterfield, S., 515n
Savage, D.C.L., 87n
Scanzoni, L.D., 236n
Scarf, M., 406n, 504n
Scarpinato, L., 142n
Schacter, S., 465n
Scharfman, M.A., 173n
Schickel, R., 504n
Schlafly, P., 607n
Schlesinger, A.,Jr., 592n
Schmeck, H.M.,Jr., 131n
Schmidt, G., 298n, 299n, 602n, 614n
Schneider, M., 382n
Schonfeld, W., 255n
Schover, L., 414n
Schreiner-Engel, P., 181n, 422n
Schultz, T., 25n
Schulz, E.D., 237n
Schulz, M.R., 283n
Schwartz, G.S., 328n
Schwartz, L., 288n
Scott, J.R., 177n, 211n
Sears, R.R., 6n, 222n, 235n
Seavey, C., 287n
Segraves, K.A., 423n
Selby, J.W., 393n
Selnom, G.W., 283n
Semans, J.H., 431n
Serrin, W., 521n
Sevely, J.L., 68n
Shahani, S.K., 208n
Shanor, K., 315n
Shaver, P., 458n, 464n
Sheehy, G., 512n
Sheffield, M., 251n
Shengold, L., 393n
Sheppard, A.T., 629n

Sheppard, S., 18n
Sherfey, M.J., 70n, 619n
Sherrard, P., 580n
Sherwin, B., 110n
Shettles, L.B., 155n
Shilts, R., 132n, 135n, 371n
Shope, D.F., 271n
Short, R.V., 105n, 205n
Sidowicz, L., 287n
Silber, S.S., 116n, 120n, 145n
Silverstein, C., 370n, 373n, 383n
Simon, W., 279n
Singer, I., 70n, 472n
Singer, J., 314n
Singer, J.L., 462n
Singer, P., 183n
Sinha, I., 360n
Sisley, E.L., 370n, 383n
Skaakeback, N.E., 107n
Skinner, B.F., 247n
Skolnick, A., 232n
Slovenko, R., 627n
Small, M., 437n
Smelser, N.J., 268n
Smith, C., 287n
Smith, D.S., 596n
Smith, G.G., 199n
Smith, H., 228n
Smith, P., 288n
Smith, P.J., 423n
Smukler, A.J., 401n
Snyder, S., 236n
Socarides, C.W., 382n
Solomon, S., 422n
Sondheimer, S.J., 98n
Sontag, S., 290n
Sorensen, R.C., 258n, 260n, 314n, 329n
Sorensen, T., 296n
Sorokin, P., 601n, 625n
Spanier, G.B., 483n, 491n
Sparks, R.A., 197n
Sparling, P.F., 121n, 123n, 125n, 127n
Speert, H., 167n, 171n
Spence, J.T., 285n
Spiro, R., 225n
Spitz, R.A., 57n, 224n, 225n, 233n
Spitzer, R.L., 381n
Stamm, W.E., 123n
Stark, R., 357n
Starr, B.D., 275n, 276n
Starr & King, 642n
Steege, J., 437n
Steinberg, L., 589n
Steinberger, A., 84n
Steinem, G., 518n
Steinman, D.L., 299n
Stekel, W., 396n
Stendahl, M.H.B., 466n
Stengle, R., 524n
Steptoe, P., 182
Stermac, L., 561n
Stern, C., 50n
Sternberg, R.J., 462n, 471n, 472n

Sternglanz, S.H., 288n
Stipp, D., 412n, 436n
Stockham, A., 350, 594n
Stokes, M., 15
Stoller, R.J., 282n, 291n, 296n, 317n, 382n, 387n, 398n, 399n, 401n, 407n, 410n
Stone, K.M., 121n, 129n
Sturup, G.K., 107n
Sue, D., 314n, 316n
Suitters, B., 186n
Sullivan, P.R., 313n
Sullivan, W., 196n, 421n
Sulloway, F.J., 12n, 244n
Suomi, S.J., 231n
Swan, G., 510n
Symons, D., 5n, 58n, 62n, 302n, 305n, 443n, 448n, 461n

Taba, A.H., 34n
Talese, G., 487n, 497n, 507n, 510n
Tallent, N., 385n
Tangri, S., 541n
Tannahill, R., 9n, 588n, 596n, 597n, 599n
Tanner, J.M., 86n, 92n
Tarabulcy, E., 77n
Tatum, H.J., 185n
Tavris, C., 25n, 324n, 326n, 327n, 339n, 495n, 497n, 547n
Taylor, C., 159n, 176n
Taylor, D.A., 455n
Taylor, G.R., 583n, 584n, 586n, 587n
Tennov, D., 356n, 466n, 472n, 537n
Terman, L.M., 284n
Terzian, H., 79n
Thevoz, M., 444n
Thomas, D., 401n
Thompson, A.P., 498n
Thompson, L.G., 670n
Thompson, R.F., 78n, 80n, 104n
Thompson, W.I., 568n
Tiefer, L., 335n
Tietze, C., 178n, 211n, 212n
Tinbergen, N., 240n
Tivnan, E., 663n
Tollison, C.D., 395n
Tourney, G., 377n
Trapp, J.D., 424n
Traub-Werner, D., 395n
Travin, S., 389n
Tripp, C.A., 380n
Troll, L.E., 488n
Truesdell, D., 393n
Trussell, J., 180, 207n, 493n, 192n, 150n
Tutin, C.E.G., 106n
Twain, M., 331n
Tyler, E.B., 242
Tyrmand, L., 614n

Udow, R., 650n
Ulene, A., 142n, 143n, 144n, 145n

Ungar, S.B., 288n
Urdy, S.B., 302n, 303n

Vaillant, G.E., 458n
Valdisserri, E.V., 370n
Vance, E.B., 70n
Vandereycken, W., 419n
Van de Velde, T.E., 338n, 344n, 346n, 352n, 353, 359n
Vanggard, T., 577n
Vatsyayana, 57n, 1
Veevers, J.E., 186n
Veith, I., 38n
Vener, A.M., 260n
Verschoor, A.M., 296n
Verwoerdt, A., 310n
Vida, G., 376n
Virel, A., 444n
Von Furstenberg, E., 448n

Wahl, P., 194n
Wallis, C., 25n, 155n, 179n, 267n, 480n
Walsh, P., 118n, 119n
Walster, P., 482n
Walters, J., 469n
Washington, A.E., 123n, 124n
Wasserstrom, R.A., 627n, 651n
Watson, J.B., 242
Watson, M.A., 496n
Waxenburg, S.E., 110n
Webb, P., 8n, 332n, 518n, 532n, 576n, 578n, 584n, 589n, 595n, 599n
Weg, R.B., 290n
Weinberg, G., 367n
Weinberg, J., 410n
Weinberg, M.S., 367n, 373n, 382n, 383n
Weinberg, S.K., 393n
Weinberg, T.S., 1987, 402n
Weis, D.L., 270n
Weiss, D., 552n
Weitzman, L., 490n
Weitzman, L.J., 288n
Welbourne-Moglia, A., 248n, 267n, 289n
Wells, B.L., 319n
West, J.B., 82n
Westermarck, E., 391n
Westoff, C.F., 155n, 190n
Westwood, G., 367n
White, E., 371n
White, G.L., 460n
Whitley, B.E., 286n
Whitman, F., 368n, 377n, 380n
Whyte, L.L., 12n
Wickler, W., 335n, 535n
Wigfall-Williams, W., 421n
Wilkins, L., 99n
Williams, J.H., 248n
Wilmore, J.H., 87n
Wilson, E.O., 5n, 104n, 302n, 654n
Wilson, G., 62n, 273n, 344n, 461n
Wilson, G.T., 422n
Wilson, J.D., 50n

Wilson, M.L., 382$n$
Wilson, S., 589$n$
Wincze, J., 408$n$
Winick, C., 521$n$
Winkelstein, W.,Jr., 143$n$
Winn, R., 275$n$
Wise, T., 396$n$, 398$n$, 399$n$
Witkin, H.A., 101$n$
Wolf, A., 391$n$
Wolfe, L., 271$n$, 323$n$, 326$n$, 331$n$, 547$n$, 548$n$

Wolff, C., 365$n$
Wolfgang, M.E., 553$n$
Wolpe, J., 425$n$
Wyatt, G., 390$n$

Yalom, I.D., 174$n$
Yankelovich, D., 613$n$
Yarrow, A.L., 489$n$
Yen, S., 157$n$
Ying, S., 84$n$
Young, W., 509$n$, 511$n$

Yupze, A., 196$n$, 197$n$

Zacharias, L., 92$n$
Zelnik, M., 189$n$, 190$n$, 260$n$, 265$n$, 266$n$, 267$n$, 271$n$
Zilbergeld, B., 416$n$, 439$n$, 611$n$
Zimmer, D., 309$n$
Zimmerman, D.H., 283$n$
Zuckerman, L., 641$n$
Zugar, B., 377$n$
Zverina, S., 400$n$